OKU

4

Orthopaedic Knowledge Update

Spine

Editor

Raj D. Rao, MD
Professor of Orthopaedic Surgery
  and Neurosurgery
Department of Orthopaedic Surgery
Medical College of Wisconsin
Milwaukee, Wisconsin

Coeditor

Matthew Smuck, MD
Associate Professor
Chief of Physical Medicine and Rehabilitation
Department of Orthopaedic Surgery
Stanford University
Redwood City, California

Developed by the
North American Spine Society

NASS
NORTH AMERICAN SPINE SOCIETY

AAOS
AMERICAN ACADEMY OF
ORTHOPAEDIC SURGEONS

AAOS

AMERICAN ACADEMY OF ORTHOPAEDIC SURGEONS

The material presented in *Orthopaedic Knowledge Update: Spine 4* has been made available by the American Academy of Orthopaedic Surgeons for educational purposes only. This material is not intended to present the only, or necessarily best, methods or procedures for the medical situations discussed, but rather is intended to represent an approach, view, statement, or opinion of the author(s) or producer(s), which may be helpful to others who face similar situations. Some drugs or medical devices demonstrated in Academy courses or described in Academy print or electronic publications have not been cleared by the Food and Drug Administration (FDA) or have been cleared for specific uses only. The FDA has stated that it is the responsibility of the physician to determine the FDA clearance status of each drug or device he or she wishes to use in clinical practice.

Furthermore, any statements about commercial products are solely the opinion(s) of the author(s) and do not represent an Academy endorsement or evaluation of these products. These statements may not be used in advertising or for any commercial purpose.

Published 2012 by the
American Academy of Orthopaedic Surgeons
6300 North River Road
Rosemont, IL 60018

Fourth Edition
Copyright 2012 by the
American Academy of Orthopaedic Surgeons

ISBN 978-0-89203-737-7
Printed in Canada

Bone *and* Joint
DECADE
2002 - USA - 2011

Acknowledgments

Editorial Board
Orthopaedic Knowledge Update: Spine 4

Raj D. Rao, MD
Professor of Orthopaedic Surgery and
* Neurosurgery*
Department of Orthopaedic Surgery
Medical College of Wisconsin
Milwaukee, Wisconsin

Matthew Smuck, MD
Associate Professor
Chief of Physical Medicine and Rehabilitation
Department of Orthopaedic Surgery
Stanford University
Redwood City, California

Paul A. Anderson, MD
Professor of Orthopedic Surgery
University of Wisconsin
Madison, Wisconsin

Christopher M. Bono, MD
Chief of Orthopaedic Spine Service
Brigham and Women's Hospital
Assistant Professor of Orthopaedic Surgery
Harvard Medical School
Boston, Massachusetts

John B. Emans, MD
Professor and Director
Division of Spine Surgery
Children's Hospital
Harvard Medical School
Boston, Massachusetts

Eeric Truumees, MD
Director of Spinal Research
Attending Spine Surgeon
Seton Spine and Scoliosis Center
Brackenridge University Hospital
Austin, Texas

North American Spine Society
Board of Directors, 2010-2011

Gregory Przybylski, MD
President

Michael Heggeness, MD, PhD
First Vice President

Charles Mick, MD
Second Vice President

Heidi Prather, DO
Secretary

William Watters III, MD
Treasurer

Ray M. Baker, MD
Past President

Daniel Resnick, MD
Research Council Director

Venu Akuthota, MD
Education Council Director

Alexander Ghanayem, MD
Administration and Development Council
* Director*

William Mitchell, MD
Health Policy Co–Council Director

Christopher Standaert, MD
Health Policy Co–Council Director

Charles Reitman, MD
Evidence Compilation and Analysis Chair

Zoher Ghogawala, MD
Clinical Research Development Chair

Jeffrey Wang, MD
Continuing Medical Education Chair

Eeric Truumees, MD
Education Publishing Chair

Christopher Bono, MD
Professional, Economic and Regulatory Chair

Raj D. Rao, MD
Advocacy–NASS 6 Chair

Jerome Schofferman, MD
Section Development Chair

F. Todd Wetzel, MD
Governance Committee Chair

Marjorie Eskay-Auerbach, MD, JD
Ethics Committee Chair

David Rothman, PhD
Ethicist

Eric Muehlbauer, MJ, CAE
Executive Director

Contributors

Venu Akuthota, MD
Vice Chair and Associate Professor
Department of Physical Medicine and
*   Rehabilitation*
University of Colorado, Denver
Aurora, Colorado

R. Todd Allen, MD, PhD
Assistant Professor of Spine and Orthopaedic
*   Surgery*
Department of Orthopaedic Surgery
University of California, San Diego
San Diego, California

Howard An, MD
Morton International Endowed Chair and
*   Professor of Orthopaedic Surgery*
Department of Orthopaedic Surgery
Rush University Medical Center
Chicago, Illinois

Edward Radcliffe Anderson III, MD
Department of Orthopaedic Surgery
William Beaumont Hospital
Royal Oak, Michigan

Paul A. Anderson, MD
Professor of Orthopedic Surgery
University of Wisconsin
Madison, Wisconsin

Carlo Bellabarba, MD
Associate Professor
Department of Orthopaedics and Sports
*   Medicine*
Harborview Medical Center
University of Washington
Seattle, Washington

Christopher M. Bono, MD
Chief of Orthopaedic Spine Service
Brigham and Women's Hospital
Assistant Professor of Orthopaedic Surgery
Harvard Medical School
Boston, Massachusetts

Helena Brisby, MD, PhD
Associate Professor
Department of Orthopaedics
University of Gothenburg
Sahlgrenska University Hospital
Gothenburg, Sweden

Barbara Buch, MD
Deputy Division Director
Division of Surgical, Orthopedic and
*   Restorative Devices*
Office of Device Evaluation, Center for Devices
*   and Radiological Health*
Food and Drug Administration
Silver Spring, Maryland

Ralph Buschbacher, MD
Professor
Department of Physical Medicine and
*   Rehabilitation*
Indiana University School of Medicine
Indianapolis, Indiana

Eugene Carragee, MD
Professor
Department of Orthopaedic Surgery
Stanford University
Palo Alto, California

Garrick W. Cason, MD
Department of Orthopaedic Surgery
William Beaumont Hospital
Royal Oak, Michigan

Jens R. Chapman, MD
Professor and Acting Chair
Director of Spine Service
Hansjöerg Wyss Endowed Chair
Department of Orthopaedics and Sports
*   Medicine*
Joint Professor of Neurological Surgery
University of Washington
Seattle, Washington

Daniel Clauw, MD
Professor of Anesthesiology
University of Michigan
Ann Arbor, Michigan

Kenny S. David, MS (Orth)
Professor
Spinal Disorders Unit
Department of Orthopaedic Surgery
Christian Medical College and Hospital
Vellore, India

Benjamin J. Davis, MD
Northwestern Memorial Hospital
Chicago, Illinois

Sergio M. de del Castillo, BS
Biomedical Engineer
Division of Surgical, Orthopedic and
  Restorative Devices
Food and Drug Administration
Silver Spring, Maryland

Michael DePalma, MD
Director of Research
Virginia Spine Research Institute
Richmond, Virginia

John P. Dormans, MD
Chief of Orthopaedic Surgery
Children's Hospital of Philadelphia
Professor of Orthopaedic Surgery
University of Pennsylvania School of Medicine
Philadelphia, Pennsylvania

Nabil A. Ebraheim, MD
Chair and Professor
Department of Orthopaedic Surgery
University of Toledo Medical Center
Toledo, Ohio

Frank J. Eismont, MD
Chair
Department of Orthopaedic Surgery
University of Miami Miller School of Medicine
Miami, Florida

Hossein Elgafy, MD, MCh, FRCSEd, FRCSC
Assistant Professor
Department of Orthopaedics
University of Toledo Medical Center
Toledo, Ohio

John B. Emans, MD
Professor and Director
Division of Spine Surgery
Children's Hospital Boston
Harvard Medical School
Boston, Massachusetts

Tom Faciszewski, MD
Chair
Department of Orthopaedic Spine Surgery
Marshfield Clinic
Marshfield, Wisconsin

Reginald S. Fayssoux, MD
Department of Orthopaedic Surgery
Emory University
Atlanta, Georgia

Richard G. Fessler, MD, PhD
Professor
Department of Neurological Surgery
Northwestern University
Chicago, Illinois

Jeff Fischgrund, MD
Spine Fellowship Director
Department of Orthopaedics
William Beaumont Hospital
Royal Oak, Michigan

William M. Foley, DO, MSc
Department of Neuromusculoskeletal and
  Osteopathic Manipulative Medicine
Boston Osteopathic Health
Newton, Massachusetts

Robert J. Gatchel, PhD, ABPP
Nancy P. and John G. Penson Endowed
  Professor of Clinical Health Psychology
Chair
Department of Psychology
University of Texas, Arlington
Arlington, Texas

Gregory Gebauer, MD, MS
Rothman Institute
Thomas Jefferson University
Philadelphia, Pennsylvania

Michael P. Glotzbecker, MD
Pediatric Orthopaedic Surgery
Children's Hospital Boston
Boston, Massachusetts

S. Raymond Golish, MD, PhD
Clinical Instructor
Department of Orthopaedic Surgery
Stanford University
Palo Alto, California

Jonathan N. Grauer, MD
Codirector
Orthopaedic Spine Service
Associate Professor
Department of Orthopaedics and Rehabilitation
Yale University School of Medicine
New Haven, Connecticut

James D. Guest, MD, PhD
Associate Professor
Department of Neurological Surgery
University of Miami
Miami, Florida

Daniel Hedequist, MD
Associate Professor
Department of Orthopaedics
Children's Hospital Boston
Harvard Medical School
Boston, Massachusetts

Michael H. Heggeness, MD, PhD
Professor and Chair
Department of Orthopaedic Surgery
Baylor College of Medicine
Houston, Texas

Harry N. Herkowitz, MD
Chair
Department of Orthopaedic Surgery
William Beaumont Hospital
Royal Oak, Michigan

Martin J. Herman, MD
Associate Professor of Orthopaedic Surgery
   and Pediatrics
Drexel University College of Medicine
St. Christopher's Hospital for Children
Philadelphia, Pennsylvania

Shawn Hermenau, MD
Department of Orthopaedic Surgery
Yale University School of Medicine
New Haven, Connecticut

Alan S. Hilibrand, MD
Professor of Orthopaedic Surgery
Professor of Neurosurgery
Rothman Institute
Thomas Jefferson University
Philadelphia, Pennsylvania

John A. Hipp, PhD
Director of Spine Research
Department of Orthopaedic Surgery
Baylor College of Medicine
Houston, Texas

Brian Hood, MD
Department of Neurosurgery
University of Miami
Miami, Florida

Michael C. Hsu, MD
Staff Physician
Department of Physiatry
Kaiser Permanente, Northwest
Clackamas, Oregon

Christopher Hydorn, MD
Division of Orthopaedics
Children's Hospital of Philadelphia
Philadelphia, Pennsylvania

Ronald P. Jean, PhD
Chief of Orthopedic Spine Devices Branch
Division of Surgical, Orthopedic and
   Restorative Devices
Office of Device Evaluation, Center for Devices
   and Radiological Health
Food and Drug Administration
Silver Spring, Maryland

Louis G. Jenis, MD
Clinical Associate Professor
Department of Orthopaedic Surgery
Tufts University School of Medicine
Boston Spine Group
Newton, Massachusetts

S. Babak Kalantar, MD
Instructor
Department of Orthopaedic Surgery
Emory University
Atlanta, Georgia

James D. Kang, MD
Professor and Vice Chair
Director of Ferguson Laboratory
Department of Orthopaedic Surgery
University of Pittsburgh Medical Center
Pittsburgh, Pennsylvania

Christopher K. Kepler, MD
Department of Orthopaedics
Rothman Institute
Thomas Jefferson University
Philadelphia, Pennsylvania

A. Jay Khanna, MD, MBA
Associate Professor
Departments of Orthopaedic Surgery and
* Biomedical Engineering*
Johns Hopkins University School of Medicine
Baltimore, Maryland

Nancy D. Kishino, OTR/L, CVE
Director and Owner
West Coast Spine Restoration Center
Riverside, California

Mark A. Konodi, MS
Research Analyst
Harborview Injury Prevention and
* Research Center*
University of Washington
Seattle, Washington

Brian K. Kwon, MD, PhD, FRCSC
Assistant Professor
Department of Orthopaedics
University of British Columbia
Vancouver, British Columbia

Ben L. Laplante, DO
Virginia Spine Physicians
Virginia Spine Research Institute
Richmond, Virginia

Lawrence G. Lenke, MD
Jerome J. Gilden Endowed Professor of
* Orthopaedic Surgery*
Cochief of Adult and Pediatric Scoliosis
* and Reconstructive Surgery*
Professor of Neurological Surgery
Department of Orthopaedic Surgery
Washington University School of Medicine
St. Louis, Missouri

Alan M. Levine, MD
Deceased

Ying Li, MD
Department of Orthopaedic Surgery
Children's Hospital Boston
Boston, Massachusetts

Kamran Majid, MD
Orthopaedic Spine Surgeon
Orthopaedic and Spine Specialists
York, Pennsylvania

Gerard A. Malanga, MD
Director of Overlook Pain Center
Clinical Professor of Physical Medicine and
* Rehabilitation*
University of Medicine and Dentistry of New
* Jersey*
New Jersey Medical School
Summit, New Jersey

Geoffrey S. Marecek, MD
Department of Orthopaedic Surgery
Northwestern University
Chicago, Illinois

Brook I. Martin, PhD, MPH
Instructor of Orthopaedic Surgery
Department of Orthopaedics
Dartmouth Medical College
Lebanon, New Hampshire

Eric A.K. Mayer, MD
Staff Physician
Center for Spine Health
Cleveland Clinic
Cleveland, Ohio

Tom G. Mayer, MD
Medical Director
Productive Rehabilitation Institute of Dallas
* for Ergonomics*
Clinical Professor
* Department of Orthopaedic Surgery*
University of Texas Southwestern Medical
* Center*
Dallas, Texas

Fergus E. McKiernan, MD
Director
Center for Bone Disease
Marshfield Clinic
Marshfield, Wisconsin

Sohail K. Mirza, MD, MPH
Professor
Department of Orthopaedics
Dartmouth Medical College
Hanover, New Hampshire

Robert R. Myers, PhD
Professor of Anesthesiology and Pathology
University of California, San Diego
La Jolla, California

Joshua M. Pahys, MD
Department of Orthopaedic Surgery
Washington University School of Medicine
St. Louis, Missouri

George Pasquarello, DO, FAAO
East Greenwich Spine and Sport
East Greenwich, Rhode Island

Amrish D. Patel, MD, PT
Department of Physical Medicine and
*   Rehabilitation*
University of Medicine and Dentistry of New
*   Jersey*
Kessler Institute for Rehabilitation
West Orange, New Jersey

Chetan K. Patel, MD
Medical Director, Spine Center at Altamonte
Global Faculty Member, Nicholson Center
*   for Surgical Advancement*
Department of Orthopaedic Surgery
Florida Hospital Altamonte
Altamonte Springs, Florida

Peter D. Pizzutillo, MD
Director of Pediatric Orthopaedic Surgery
St. Christopher's Hospital for Children
Philadelphia, Pennsylvania

Nathan D. Prahlow, MD
Assistant Professor of Clinical Physical
*   Medicine and Rehabilitation*
Department of Physical Medicine and
*   Rehabilitation*
Indiana University School of Medicine
Indianapolis, Indiana

Joel M. Press, MD
Reva and Daniel Logan Distinguished Chair
*   of Musculoskeletal Rehabilitation*
Professor of Physical Medicine and
*   Rehabilitation*
Feinberg School of Medicine
Northwestern University
Medical Director
Spine and Sports Rehabilitation Centers
Rehabilitation Institute of Chicago
Chicago, Illinois

Kris Radcliff, MD
Assistant Professor
Department of Orthopaedic Surgery
Rothman Institute
Thomas Jefferson University
Philadelphia, Pennsylvania

Raj D. Rao, MD
Professor of Orthopaedic Surgery and
*   Neurosurgery*
Department of Orthopaedic Surgery
Medical College of Wisconsin
Milwaukee, Wisconsin

John M. Rhee, MD
Assistant Professor
Department of Orthopaedic Surgery
Emory University
Atlanta, Georgia

Darren C. Rosenberg, DO
Instructor
Department of Physical Medicine and
*   Rehabilitation*
Harvard Medical School
Medical Director
Spaulding Framingham Rehabilitation Center
Framingham, Massachusetts

Kasra Rowshan, MD
Department of Orthopaedics
University of Miami
Miami, Florida

Björn Rydevik, MD, PhD
Professor
Department of Orthopaedics
University of Gothenburg
Sahlgrenska University Hospital
Gothenburg, Sweden

John F. Sarwark, MD
Professor
Department of Orthopaedic Surgery
Northwestern University
Children's Memorial Hospital
Chicago, Illinois

Thomas A. Schildhauer, MD
Professor and Chair
Department of General Surgery and Trauma
  Surgery
BG-University Hospital Bergmannsheil
Ruhr-University Bochum
Bochum, Germany

Dilip Kumar Sengupta, MD
Department of Orthopaedics
Dartmouth-Hitchcock Medical Center
Lebanon, New Hampshire

Alok D. Sharan, MD
Chief of Orthopaedic Spine Service
Assistant Professor
Department of Orthopaedic Surgery
Albert Einstein College of Medicine
Montefiore Medical Center
Bronx, New York

Patrick Shih, MD
Department of Neurological Surgery
Northwestern University
Chicago, Illinois

Eric Shoemaker, DO
Department of Physical Medicine and
  Rehabilitation
University of Colorado
Aurora, Colorado

Krzysztof B. Siemionow, MD
Assistant Professor
Department of Orthopaedic Surgery
University of Illinois
Chicago, Illinois

Vladimir Sinkov, MD
Towson Orthopaedic Associates
Towson, Maryland

Harvey E. Smith, MD
Department of Orthopaedic Surgery
Methodist Hospital
Houston, Texas

Jeremy S. Smith, MD
Rothman Institute
Thomas Jefferson University
Philadelphia, Pennsylvania

Gwendolyn Sowa, MD, PhD
Codirector, Ferguson Laboratory
Assistant Professor
Department of Physical Medicine and
  Rehabilitation
University of Pittsburgh Medical Center
Pittsburgh, Pennsylvania

Kevin F. Spratt, PhD
Methodologist and Statistician
Department of Orthopaedics
Dartmouth Medical Center
Hanover, New Hampshire

John Thometz, MD
Professor
Medical Director of Pediatric Orthopaedics
Department of Orthopaedics
Medical College of Wisconsin
Milwaukee, Wisconsin

P. Justin Tortolani, MD
Assistant Professor
Codirector, Maryland Spinal Reconstructive
  Fellowship
Towson Orthopaedic Associates
Johns Hopkins Medical Institutions
Baltimore, Maryland

Eeric Truumees, MD
Director of Spinal Research
Attending Spine Surgeon
Seton Spine and Scoliosis Center
Brackenridge University Hospital
Austin, Texas

Vidyadhar V. Upasani, MD
Department of Orthopaedic Surgery
University of California, San Diego
San Diego, California

Alexander Vaccaro, MD, PhD
Vice Chair and Professor of Orthopedic Surgery
Professor of Neurosurgery
Rothman Institute
Thomas Jefferson University
Philadelphia, Pennsylvania

Michael J. Vives, MD
Associate Professor
Department of Orthopaedics
University of Medicine and Dentistry
  of New Jersey
New Jersey Medical School
Newark, New Jersey

Mei Wang, PhD
Associate Professor
Department of Orthopaedic Surgery
Medical College of Wisconsin
Milwaukee, Wisconsin

William P. Waring III, MD, MS
Associate Professor
Department of Physical Medicine and
  Rehabilitation
Medical College of Wisconsin
Milwaukee, Wisconsin

Barrett I. Woods, MD
Ferguson Laboratory
Department of Orthopaedic Surgery
University of Pittsburgh Medical Center
Pittsburgh, Pennsylvania

Praveen Yalamanchili, MD
Department of Orthopaedics
University of Medicine and Dentistry
  of New Jersey
New Jersey Medical School
Newark, New Jersey

Moshe Yanko, MD
Sinai Hospital of Baltimore
Baltimore, Maryland

S. Tim Yoon, MD, PhD
Assistant Professor
Department of Orthopaedic Surgery
Emory University
Atlanta, Georgia

Preface

The fourth edition of *Orthopaedic Knowledge Update: Spine* continues a tradition of excellence in a textbook that serves as a primary source of knowledge in the ever-changing world of spine care. This textbook brings together more than 100 experts in the field of spine disorders, from surgical and nonsurgical perspectives, from clinical and policy viewpoints, and from different parts of the globe, to produce a truly comprehensive understanding of spine disorders.

It has been almost 6 years since the third edition of *OKU: Spine* was published. There has been an explosion of information in the field of spine care over this period of time. *OKU: Spine 4* evaluates the latest technology used in the management of spine disorders and injuries, including the use of fusion and nonfusion devices in both adult and pediatric spine surgery and the use of bone substitutes and biologic agents to promote fusion. To facilitate readers' understanding and put these developments into context, we have organized each chapter to allow an initial review of the established knowledge base followed by the advances in care. A separate section on the nonsurgical management of spine disorders thoroughly reviews the latest advances in pharmacologic options, manipulative therapy, general nonsurgical care, and interventional treatment options for our patients. An updated section on the basic science of spine disorders includes topics not covered in prior editions of *OKU: Spine*. Most notably, given the increasingly complex interactions of national health care policy and the delivery of health care, this edition includes a unique section on spine care and US health policy, which covers basic Medicare policy, workers' compensation issues, factors involved in the design of appropriate research studies and the ascertainment of clinical outcomes, and the role of the US Food and Drug Administration in the field of spine surgery. Overall, we believe that this edition of *OKU: Spine* provides a comprehensive overview of the entire spectrum of knowledge required by an individual taking care of patients with spine disorders.

The widespread use of this textbook by surgeons and nonsurgeons involved in the management of spine disorders, as well as by fellows, residents, and students, mandated our utmost diligence in the development of the project. We were assisted in this process by an outstanding group of authors who are all recognized authorities in the field. Coeditor Matthew Smuck, section editors Paul Anderson, Eeric Truumees, John Emans, and Chris Bono, and our project manager from the American Academy of Orthopaedic Surgeons, Deborah Williams, worked tirelessly to ensure that the chapters were accurate, current, and immaculately organized. The time and effort the authors have put into their chapters, their expertise in their respective areas, and the diligence of the entire editorial team have contributed to making this perhaps the most comprehensive, elegant, and relevant *OKU: Spine* yet. I am confident that readers will benefit from the format of the chapters, the knowledge within, and the overall selection of topics. It is my hope that the knowledge found in this textbook will allow readers to provide even better care for their patients and will stimulate the next generation to greater curiosity on the workings of the spinal column.

All of us involved in this project owe a tremendous debt of gratitude to our families, who bear the brunt of the impact of our academic volunteerism. From a personal viewpoint, I would like to thank my wife Nikita and our children for permitting me to pursue these academic efforts and for the time these efforts took away from them. I would also like to thank two individuals for helping shape my life–my older brother Santi Rao, a spine surgeon and a mentor to me from an early age, and my younger sister Nina Rao.

Raj D. Rao, MD
Editor

Table of Contents

Section 6: Spine Disorders

Section Editor:
Christopher M. Bono, MD

Section 7: Spine Care and US Health Policy

Section Editor:
Raj D. Rao, MD

Section 1

Basic Science of the Spine

SECTION EDITOR
RAJ D. RAO, MD

Chapter 1

Applied Spine Anatomy
Hossein Elgafy, MD, MCh, FRCSEd, FRCSC   Nabil A. Ebraheim, MD

Introduction

A thorough knowledge of the anatomy of the normal spine is central to understanding, diagnosing, and managing any spine pathology. The spine is made up of four zones: the craniocervical spine, the subaxial spine, the cervicothoracic junction, and the thoracolumbar spine. Familiarity with several anatomic spine landmarks can help the surgeon perform safe, appropriate spine decompression and instrumentation.

The Craniocervical Spine

The Occipital Bone, Venous Sinus, and Application of Occipital Screws

Screw fixation into the occipital bone requires a regional thickness of the occipital bone adequate for screw purchase and avoidance of injury to the transverse sinus. A cadaver study found that the maximum thickness of the occipital bone is at the level of the external occipital protuberance and that it ranges from 11.5 to 15.1 mm in men and from 9.7 to 12.0 mm in women.[1] The bone is more than 8 mm thick in an area extending 23 mm laterally from the external occipital protuberance. The occipital bone consists of dense cortical bone, with little or no cancellous bone (Figure 1).

An examination of the relationship between the venous sinuses and occipital screws placed at different sites clearly revealed that sinus injury is most likely to occur when screws are inserted at or 1 cm below the level of the external occipital protuberance.[2] To enhance the safety of an occipitocervical fusion, the external occipital protuberance should be avoided, and occipital screws should be placed at least 2 cm below the superior nuchal line. Screw placement should be bicortical to ensure adequate purchase. Dural laceration with cerebrospinal fluid leakage sometimes occurs and is dealt with by screw insertion into the predrilled screw hole. A 2.5-mm drill bit is used, with an adjust-

able drill guide initially set at 4 mm and increased in 2-mm increments until the far cortex is penetrated. The average length of a screw inserted 1 cm from the midline is 8 mm, and the average length of a screw inserted at the midline is 10 mm.[1]

The Occipitocervical Ligaments

The occiput articulates with the atlas through paired synovial joints. The paired occipital condyles project inferiorly from the occiput at the anterolateral margin of the foramen magnum. The concave atlantolateral masses accept the occipital condyles to form the articulation. These joints are shallower and less well developed in children than in adults, and this factor contributes to the relatively high incidence of atlanto-occipital injuries in children. The atlantolateral masses are connected by an anterior and a posterior arch. The anterior tubercle, located in the midline on the anterior arch, serves as the attachment site for the anterior longitudinal ligament and longus colli muscles. The posterior tubercle serves as the attachment site for the nuchal ligament. The odontoid process, or dens, extends rostrally from the body of the axis to articulate with the posterior aspect of the anterior arch of the atlas. This joint is synovial, as are the laterally placed paired facet joints through which the atlas and axis articulate.

The craniocervical ligamentous anatomy includes intrinsic and extrinsic ligaments (Figure 2). The extrinsic nuchal ligament extends from the external occipital protuberance to the posterior aspect of the atlas and cervical spinous processes. Fibroelastic membranes replace the anterior longitudinal ligament, intervertebral disks, and flaval ligament between the occiput and atlas and between the atlas and axis. The atlanto-occipital and atlantoaxial joint capsules also contribute to extrinsic stability.

The intrinsic ligaments, located within the spinal canal, provide most of the ligamentous stability. These ligaments form three layers anterior to the dura; from dorsal to ventral, they are the tectorial membrane, the cruciate ligament, and the odontoid ligaments. The tectorial membrane connects the posterior body of the axis to the anterior foramen magnum and is the cephalad continuation of the posterior longitudinal ligament. The cruciate ligament lies anterior to the tectorial membrane, behind the odontoid process. The transverse atlantal ligament is the strongest component, connecting the posterior odontoid process to the anterior atlas

Dr. Elgafy or an immediate family member has received research or institutional support from Synthes. Neither Dr. Ebraheim nor any immediate family member has received anything of value from or owns stock in a commercial company or institution related directly or indirectly to the subject of this chapter.

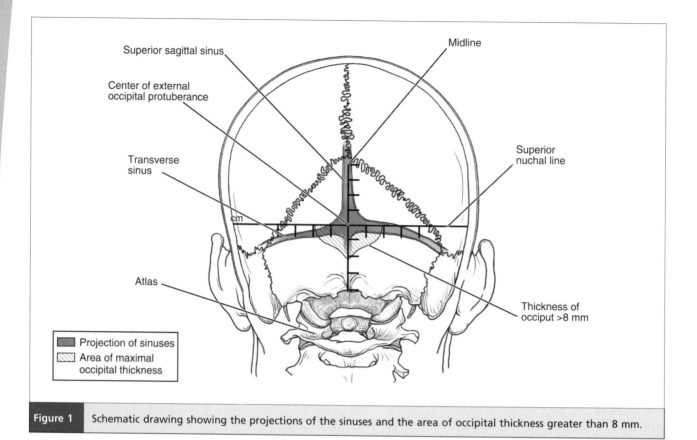

Superior sagittal sinus

Center of external
occipital protuberance

Transverse
sinus

Atlas

Midline

Superior
nuchal line

Thickness of
occiput >8 mm

cm

Projection of sinuses
Area of maximal
occipital thickness

Figure 1 Schematic drawing showing the projections of the sinuses and the area of occipital thickness greater than 8 mm.

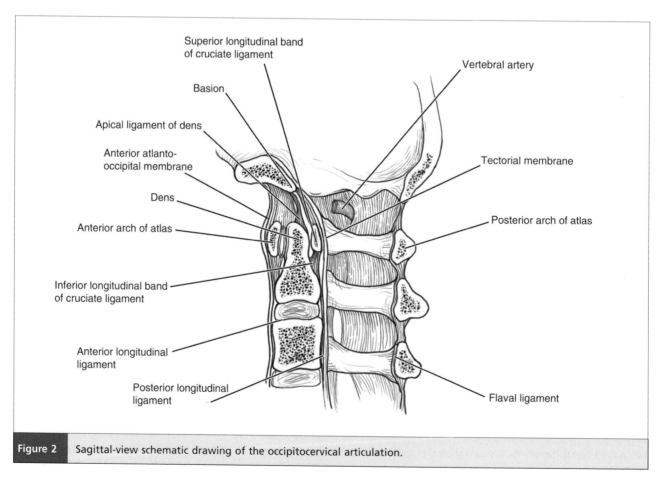

Superior longitudinal band
of cruciate ligament

Basion

Apical ligament of dens

Anterior atlanto-
occipital membrane

Dens

Anterior arch of atlas

Inferior longitudinal band
of cruciate ligament

Anterior longitudinal
ligament

Posterior longitudinal
ligament

Vertebral artery

Tectorial membrane

Posterior arch of atlas

Flaval ligament

Figure 2 Sagittal-view schematic drawing of the occipitocervical articulation.

arch and inserting laterally on bony tubercles. Vertical bands extend from the transverse ligament to the foramen magnum and body of the axis. The odontoid ligaments (the alar and apical ligaments) are the most ventral ligamentous structures. The paired alar ligaments connect the odontoid process to the occipital condyles. These ligaments are 5 to 6 mm in diameter and are stronger than the small apical ligament that runs vertically between the odontoid process and foramen magnum.

The range of motion between the occiput and atlas is 25° in flexion-extension, 5° to each side in lateral bending, and 5° to each side in rotation. The range of motion between the atlas and axis is 20° in flexion-extension, 5° in lateral bending, and 40° in rotation. The major stabilizing structures between the occiput and upper cervical spine are the tectorial membrane and alar ligaments. Flexion is limited by the bony anatomy, and extension is limited by the tectorial membrane. Rotation and lateral bending are restricted by the contralateral alar ligaments. Distraction of more than 2 mm is prevented by the tectorial membrane and alar ligaments. Translation does not normally exceed 1 mm and is limited by the facet joints, provided the tectorial membrane and alar ligaments are intact. Anterior translation of the atlas on the axis can be assessed by using the atlantodens interval, which is measured as the distance between the posterior border of the anterior arch of the atlas and the anterior border of the odontoid process. In adults, a normal atlantodens interval is 3 mm; in children, it is 4 mm. The longest normal atlantodens interval is 5 mm. A measurement of 7 mm represents injury to the transverse ligament, and a measurement of 10 mm represents injury to the transverse and alar ligaments.[3]

Occipitocervical Dissociation (the Harris Rule of 12 mm)

Several methods are used to describe the relationship of the occiput, atlas, and axis. The most popular in the setting of trauma are the basion–posterior axial line interval and the basion-dental interval, which are known as the Harris measurements or the rule of 12 (Figure 3). On lateral radiographs of 400 normal adults, the basion–posterior axial line interval and basion-dental interval were found not to exceed 12 mm in 98% and 95% of adults, respectively.[4,5] The basion–posterior axial line interval extends from the basion (the anterior margin of the foramen magnum) to a vertical extension of the posterior cortex of the axis (the posterior axial line). This measurement should be less than 12 mm. A measurement of more than 12 mm suggests anterior displacement, and a negative value (that is, the basion is located posterior to the posterior cortex of the axis) raises the possibility of posterior displacement. The basion-dental interval is measured from the tip of the dens to the basion. This measurement also should be less than 12 mm; a measurement of more than 12 mm suggests vertical displacement.

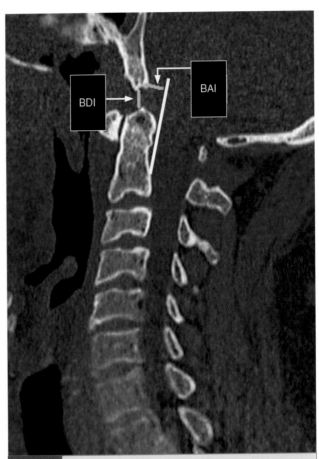

Figure 3 | CT sagittal reformate showing the Harris method of determining relationships at the atlanto-occipital junction, using the basion-dental interval (BDI) and basion–posterior axial line interval (BAI).

The Spence Rule of 6.9 mm

The three common types of atlas fractures are the posterior arch fracture, in which the atlantolateral masses do not spread; the burst, or Jefferson, fracture, in which the atlantolateral masses spread and displace laterally; and the lateral mass fracture, in which lateral displacement of the atlantolateral mass occurs only on the fracture side (Figure 4). The treatment of a burst or lateral mass fracture of the atlas is based on the amount of lateral mass displacement or instability. This measurement is determined using an open-mouth radiograph and CT. The severity of displacement corresponds to the integrity of the transverse ligament; a combined displacement of more than 6.9 mm occurs only with disruption of the transverse ligament[6] (Figure 5). Nondisplaced and minimally displaced fractures (less than 6.9 mm of displacement) can be treated with immobilization in a collar. A displaced fracture requires more definitive treatment.

The Steele Rule of Thirds

The anteroposterior diameter of the ring of the atlas is approximately 3 cm. The spinal cord and the odontoid

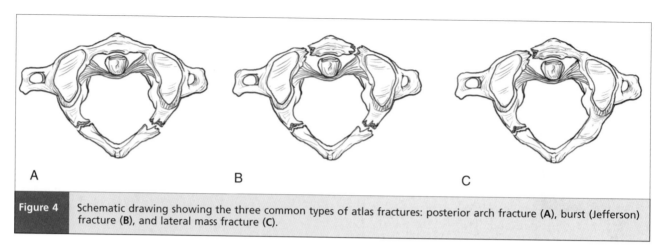

Figure 4 Schematic drawing showing the three common types of atlas fractures: posterior arch fracture (**A**), burst (Jefferson) fracture (**B**), and lateral mass fracture (**C**).

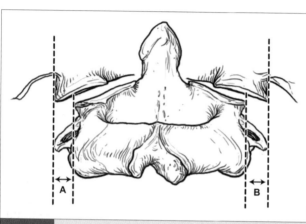

Figure 5 Schematic drawing showing the assessment for transverse atlantal ligament injury on an open-mouth radiograph or CT of C1-C2. The total lateral displacement is measured as the sum of A and B. If the total displacement is greater than 6.9 mm, rupture of the transverse ligament is certain.

process each are approximately 1 cm in diameter (approximately two thirds of the diameter of the ring). According to the Steele rule of thirds, the 1 cm of free space allows some pathologic displacement and explains the lower incidence of neurologic injury in displaced odontoid fractures.[7,8]

Anatomic Considerations in C1-C2 Transarticular Screw Insertion

Posterior transarticular screw fixation of the C1-C2 complex provides rigid internal fixation for patients requiring C1-C2 fusion. The principal limitation of this procedure is the risk of injury to the vertebral artery, internal carotid artery, and hypoglossal nerve. Screw placement too far lateral, combined with a divergent trajectory and perforation of the lateral cortex, may violate the vertebral artery in the transverse foramen of C1 or C2. The vertebral artery also is at risk of injury with too-caudal screw insertion. To minimize this risk, the screw should be placed cephalad to the C2 verte-

bral artery foramen (foramen transversarium), as identified intraoperatively on a lateral image intensifier view. In a survey of 2,492 C1-C2 transarticular screws inserted in 1,318 patients, the risk of vertebral artery injury was found to be 2.2% per screw inserted and 4.1% per patient.[9] The risk of neurologic deficit from vertebral artery injury was 0.1% per screw and 0.2% per patient, and the mortality rate was 0.1%. Directing the screw too far cephalad may injure the occiput-C1 joint.

The hypoglossal nerve lies vertically and is approximately 2 to 3 mm lateral to the middle of the anterior aspect of the C1 lateral mass. The anatomic relation of the internal carotid artery to the anterior aspect of C1 was assessed using CT with contrast medium; the mean distance from the internal carotid artery to C1 was found to be 2.88 mm on the left and 2.89 mm on the right. On at least one side, the proximity of the internal carotid artery to C21 posed a moderate risk in 46% of patients and a high risk in 12% of patients.[10] A screw that penetrates the anterior cortex of the lateral mass of C1 may put the internal carotid artery at risk if the screw is directed laterally, or may put the hypoglossal nerve at risk if it is directed medially. In an anatomic study that involved 20 cervical spine specimens, the mean optimal transarticular C1-C2 screw length was 38 mm (range, 34 to 43 mm).[11] Determination of the optimal C1-C2 screw length should be made on an individual basis using preoperative CT and intraoperative fluoroscopy.

Transarticular screw placement should be avoided, and another method of instrumentation should be used if a safe trajectory cannot be confirmed on preoperative CT (Figure 6). In one study, 20% of patients had an anomalous position of the vertebral artery, with a high-riding transverse foramen that eroded the pedicle and the lateral mass of C2 and thus prevented safe passage of the screw.[12] A low trajectory, with screw placement below the atlas tubercle, was associated with vertebral artery laceration. An intraoperative true lateral fluoroscopic view of the C2 pedicle should be evaluated for screw trajectory during C1-C2 transarticular screw insertion to minimize the risk of this complication.[13]

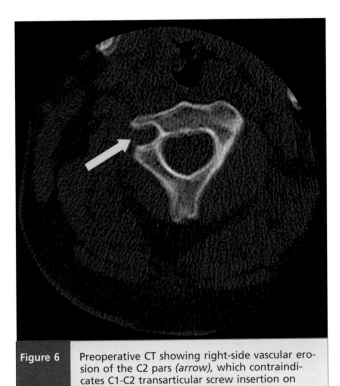

Figure 6 Preoperative CT showing right-side vascular erosion of the C2 pars *(arrow)*, which contraindicates C1-C2 transarticular screw insertion on that side.

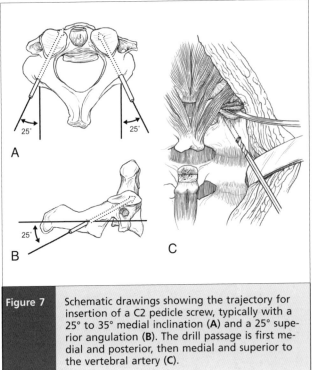

Figure 7 Schematic drawings showing the trajectory for insertion of a C2 pedicle screw, typically with a 25° to 35° medial inclination (**A**) and a 25° superior angulation (**B**). The drill passage is first medial and posterior, then medial and superior to the vertebral artery (**C**).

The Anatomic Basis of C2 Pedicle Screw Insertion

Before any procedure requiring a pedicle screw into C2, CT or a vertebral angiogram with coronal and sagittal reformatting should be done to analyze the relationship of the pedicle to the vertebral artery. The C2 pedicle is 2 to 5 mm wide and angled medially with respect to the sagittal plane. The best way to identify the C2 pedicle is to detach the atlantoaxial membrane and palpate the medial border of the isthmus with a Penfield retractor. The screw must be placed as close as possible to the medial border of the isthmus. The transverse foramen lies immediately lateral to the pedicle. At this level, the vertebral artery forms a mediolateral loop below the superior articular process halfway between its lateral and medial borders. If the pedicle is very narrow, violation of the foramen carries a high risk of vertebral artery laceration. The axial line of the pedicle projects posteriorly halfway between the upper and lower articular surfaces, on the vertical line bisecting the articular mass. From this point, the drill should be oriented 25° cranially and 25° to 35° medially[14] (Figure 7).

The Safe Zone for Halo Pin Insertion

The optimal position for placing anterior halo fixator pins is 1 cm cephalad to the lateral two thirds of the eyebrow and below the level of greatest skull circumference (Figure 8). Placing the pin above the supraorbital rim prevents displacement or penetration of the orbit. Placement of the pin below the level of the greatest

skull diameter minimizes the tendency toward cephalad pin migration, which is especially important if traction is to be applied. The temporalis muscle lies on the lateral aspect of the safe zone. It is preferable to avoid the temporal area because the bone in this region is thin, and the risk of skull penetration or pin loosening is therefore greater. Penetration of the temporalis muscle by the halo pin is painful and impedes mandibular motion. The supraorbital and supratrochlear nerves and the underlying frontal sinus lie on the medial aspect of the anterior safe zone. During anterior pin advancement, the patient is asked to gently close the eyes and relax the forehead; the purpose is to minimize skin or eyebrow tenting or tethering, which hinders eyelid closing after pin insertion. The insertion sites of the posterior pins are less critical because neuromuscular structures are lacking, and the skull is thicker and more uniform in this area. The optimal insertion of the posterior pins is approximately 1 cm cephalad to the ear. This site is inferior to the widest portion of the skull but is sufficiently superior to prevent ring impingement on the ear.

A study of cyclic loading of pins inserted at different angles found that perpendicular insertion is superior to placement at a 15° or 30° angle to the skull surface. In an adult patient, torque of 8 in-lb was found to be safe and effective in lowering the incidence of pin loosening and infection, in comparison with 6 in-lb torque. Pins are tightened in increments of 2 in-lb, until a torque of 8 in-lb is reached. The recommendation for inserting halo pins in children is to use eight pins with 4 in-lb torque to avoid penetrating the skull.[15]

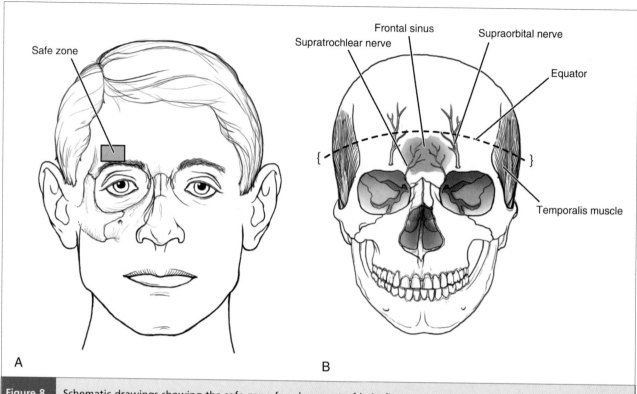

Figure 8 Schematic drawings showing the safe zone for placement of halo fixator pins. **A,** Anterior pins are placed anterolaterally, approximately 1 cm above the orbital rim, below the equator (area of widest circumference) of the skull, and cephalad to the lateral two thirds of the orbit. **B,** The safe zone avoids the temporalis muscle and fossa laterally and the supraorbital and supratrochlear nerves and frontal sinus medially. Posterior pin placement is much less difficult because of the lack of neuromuscular structures and the uniformity and thickness of the skull in that area.

The Subaxial Spine

Anatomy Related to an Anterior Approach to the Cervical Spine

Understanding the important anatomic structures in the vicinity of the anterior approach to the cervical spine can minimize the risk of injury. The recurrent laryngeal nerve is a branch of the vagus nerve. On the right side, this nerve arises anterior to the first part of the subclavian artery, curves back below and behind it, and ascends to the side of the trachea behind the common carotid artery. On the left side, the recurrent laryngeal nerve loops under the arch of the aorta before ascending to the larynx. The loop of the recurrent laryngeal nerve is at the T1-T3 level on the right side and more caudally at the T3-T6 level on the left side. The recurrent laryngeal nerve enters the larynx between the C5 and C7 levels on both sides. At C7 the recurrent laryngeal nerve lies deep within the esophagotracheal groove on the left side but 6.5 mm (±1.2 mm) anterior and 7.3 mm (±0.8 mm) lateral to the esophagotracheal groove on the right side. The recurrent laryngeal nerve supplies all laryngeal muscles except the cricothyroid, which is innervated by the external branch of the superior laryngeal nerve. The superior laryngeal nerve also innervates the mucosa of the larynx below the glottis. Clinical studies found no difference in the incidence of recurrent

laryngeal nerve injury based on whether the cervical spine anterior approach was on the right or left side.[16,17] Injury to the recurrent laryngeal nerve results in a hoarse voice. The superior thyroid vessels above C4 and the inferior thyroid vessels below C6 should be considered during an anterior cervical approach. Although bleeding from the thyroid vessels can be controlled fairly easily, the proximity of these vessels to the superior and recurrent laryngeal nerves often leads to nerve injury during attempted ligation of the thyroid vessels. The ligation must be done as laterally as possible, avoiding inadvertent inclusion of the nerves in the suture.

The superior laryngeal nerve originates from the vagus nerve inferior ganglion in the carotid sheath at the C2 level and descends medially toward the thyrohyoid membrane. It branches into an external and an internal branch deep to the internal carotid artery at the C3 level. The external branch, along with the cricothyroid artery, descends deep to the superior thyroid artery toward the cricothyroid muscle. Injury to the external branch results in paralysis of the cricothyroid muscle, which leaves the patient with voice fatigue or difficulty singing high-pitched notes. The internal branch, accompanied by the superior laryngeal artery, passes deep to the loop of the superior thyroid artery and pierces the thyrohyoid membrane. The distal portion of the internal branch of the superior laryngeal nerve is located between the C3 and C4 vertebral bodies. Both nerves reside in the fascia covering the longus colli muscles and are supplied by the accompanying arteries. The internal branch of the superior laryngeal nerve innervates the mucosa of the larynx above the glottis and forms the afferent limb of the gag reflex. Injury to this nerve causes gagging or choking, and the loss of supraglottic sensation increases the risk of aspiration and pneumonia. Injury most commonly occurs because of excessive retraction or accidental ligation of the nerve.[18]

The sympathetic trunk is situated anterior to the longus capitis muscles and has three ganglia. The superior ganglion is located at C2-C3; the middle ganglion, at C6; and the inferior ganglion, at C7-T1. Awareness of the regional anatomy of the sympathetic trunk may help in identifying and preserving this important structure during exposure of the transverse foramen or uncovertebral joint at the lower cervical levels or during anterior cervical surgery. Self-retaining retractors should be applied deep to the longus colli; if applied superficial to the longus colli, the retractors may damage the sympathetic trunk. This damage leads to the development of Horner syndrome, which is characterized by ptosis, meiosis, and anhidrosis.

The Vertebral Artery

Familiarity with the anatomy of the vertebral artery can lower the risk of injury during cervical spine surgery. Each vertebral artery originates from the subclavian artery and usually enters the C6 transverse foramen, courses cephalad within the transverse foramen of each vertebra, and eventually winds around the lateral mass and posterior arch of the atlas before passing through the posterior atlanto-occipital membrane into the foramen magnum. The mean distance between the two vertebral arteries progressively decreases as the arteries pass cephalad from C3 to C6; the distance between the lateral aspect of the uncinate process and the medial border of the transverse foramen decreases from a mean of 3.3 mm (±1 mm) at C6 to 1.7 mm (±0.8 mm) at C4. The vertebral veins are located medial to the arteries, and consequently they are injured more frequently than the arteries during decompression of the uncovertebral region.

Posteriorly, the lateral aspect of the vertebral foramen is 9 to 12 mm from the midpoint of the lateral mass (Figure 9). Insertion of a lateral mass screw 10° to 15° cephalad in the sagittal plane and 20° to 30° laterally in the horizontal plane avoids nerve root and vertebral artery injury from C3 to C6.[19]

The vertebral artery emerges from the transverse foramen of C2 and courses medially in the vertebral artery grove on the anterior portion of the superior surface of the posterior C1 ring. In adult vertebrae, the distance from the midline of C1 to the medial aspect of the vertebral artery groove ranges from 12 to 23 mm on the posterior aspect of the ring and from 8 to

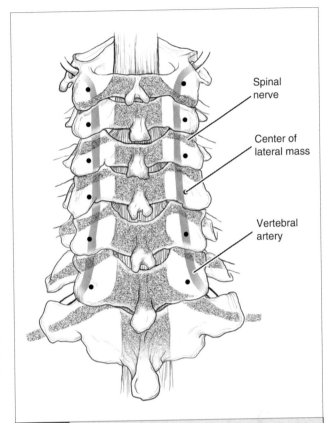

Figure 9 Schematic drawing of the posterior cervical spine, showing the anatomic relationship of the lateral mass, vertebral artery, and spinal nerve root.

13 mm on the superior aspect of the ring (Figure 10). To minimize the risk of injury to the vertebral artery, dissection on the posterior aspect of the ring should remain within 12 mm lateral to the midline, and dissection on the superior aspect of the posterior ring should remain within 8 mm of the midline.[20]

The arcuate foramen, also known as the ponticulus posticus (posterior bridge), is a bony bridge on the atlas posterior ring that covers the groove for the vertebral artery. The arcuate foramen is an anomaly that occurs in approximately 15% of the population; it can be well seen on a lateral plain radiograph of the craniovertebral junction[21] (Figure 11). Preoperative radiographic identification of the arcuate foramen should alert the surgeon not to use the posterior ring as a starting point for a C1 lateral mass screw, so as to avoid injuring the vertebral artery. Instead, a C1 lateral mass screw should be inserted directly into the C1 lateral mass caudal to the C1 posterior ring.

Injury to the vertebral artery leads to Wallenberg syndrome, which involves contralateral pain and temperature impairment all over the body, cerebellar ataxia, ipsilateral Horner syndrome, and ipsilateral cranial nerve injuries. Trigeminal nerve injury causes facial numbness, glossopharyngeal nerve injury causes hoarseness, and vagus nerve injury causes dysphagia.

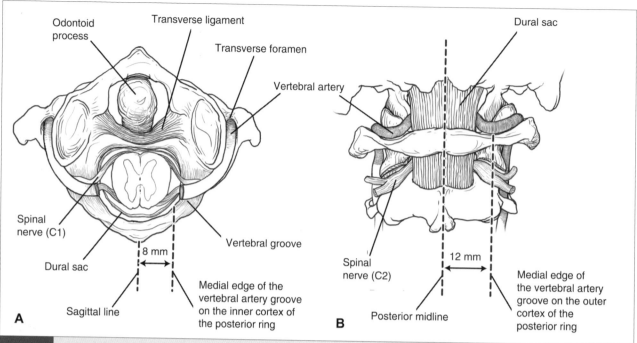

Figure 10 Schematic drawings showing the course of the vertebral artery on the C1 vertebra. To minimize the risk of injury to the vertebral artery, dissection on the superior aspect of the superior ring should remain within 8 mm of the midline (**A**), and dissection on the posterior aspect of the ring should remain within 12 mm of the midline (**B**).

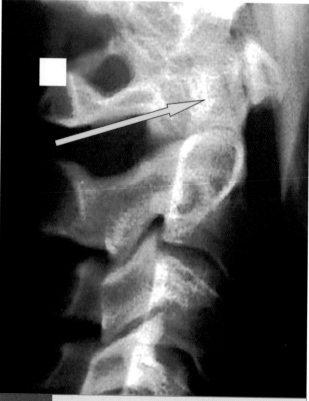

Figure 11 Lateral radiograph showing the arcuate foramen *(white block)*. The arrow indicates the ideal starting point for C1 lateral mass screw insertion to avoid injury to the vertebral artery if an arcuate foramen is present.

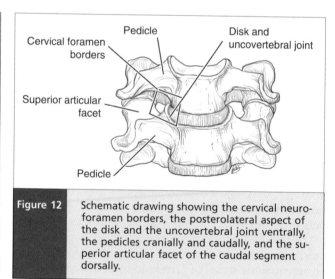

Figure 12 Schematic drawing showing the cervical neuroforamen borders, the posterolateral aspect of the disk and the uncovertebral joint ventrally, the pedicles cranially and caudally, and the superior articular facet of the caudal segment dorsally.

The Cervical Neuroforamen

The cervical neuroforamen is bordered ventrally by the uncinate process, the posterolateral aspect of the intervertebral disk, and the inferior portion of the vertebral body above the disk level. Cranially and caudally, the neuroforamen is bordered by the pedicles. The roof of the foramen is the facet joint, with the superior articular facet of the vertebral body below (Figure 12). A numbered nerve is located above the pedicle of the corresponding cervical vertebral level.

The cervical nerve root occupies one third of the foraminal space in a normal spine, usually in the inferior aspect, with the superior aspect filled with fat and associated veins. The ventral (motor) roots emerge from the dura mater more caudally than the dorsal sensory roots, and the ventral roots course along the caudal border of the dorsal roots within the foramina. Compression of the ventral or dorsal roots or both depends on the anatomic structure around the nerve roots. For example, a prolapsed disk causes ventral root compression, and osteophytes from the facet joints compress the dorsal root. The most likely site of nerve compression is in the entrance zone of the foramen. The medial entrance zone of the foramen is smaller in diameter than the lateral exit zone, in which the nerve root is widest where it leaves the central thecal sac and becomes narrower laterally.

Decompression of the neuroforamen is accomplished by resecting the entire superior articular facet that covers the foramen to the lateral margin of the pedicles. Resection of the superior articular facet lateral to the pedicle is unnecessary and may lead to facet instability.

Cervical and Lumbar Spinal Canal Stenosis

More than 400 specimens from the Hamann-Todd Osteological Collection of the Cleveland Museum of Natural History were examined.[22] The average diameter of the spinal canal from C3 to C7 was 14.1 mm (±1.6 mm). Stenosis was defined as a spinal canal diameter of less than 12 mm. Men had significantly larger cervical canals than women at all levels. Specimens from donors older than 60 years had significantly narrower canals than those from younger donors. No difference was observed based on black or white racial identity. The diameter of the spinal canal changes with spine movement; extension causes the canal diameter to decrease, and flexion causes it to increase. Patients with cervical spinal canal stenosis can be asymptomatic or have myelopathic symptoms. Individuals with a narrow midsagittal cervical spinal canal have a greater risk of neurologic injury from a spine fracture or dislocation than those with a large midsagittal canal diameter. Minor trauma such as hyperextension can lead to central cord syndrome, regardless of overt injury.[23]

The normal lumbar spinal canal has a midsagittal diameter greater than 13 mm. Relative stenosis exists if the anteroposterior canal diameter is 10 to 13 mm. Absolute stenosis of the lumbar canal exists if the measurement is 10 mm or less. Stenosis can be central or foraminal. Disk degeneration with loss of height, facet hypertrophy, and an infolded flaval ligament contributes to central or foraminal stenosis. A patient with lumbar spinal canal stenosis usually has neurologic claudication.

The Cervicothoracic Junction

Pedicle Screw Instrumentation at C7

The C7 pedicle diameter is large, and the vertebral artery does not pass through the C7 transverse process.

Therefore, pedicle screws are commonly used for instrumentation at C7, rather than lateral mass screws. The entry point is at the middle of the C7 lateral mass. Incremental drilling using a 2.4-mm smooth Kirschner wire drill is recommended, in a 35° inward and 10° downward direction. The entry point and the screw trajectory can be identified more securely after a bilateral C7 laminotomy is performed to allow palpation of the pedicle from within the spinal canal and improve the accuracy of screw placement. The length of the screw is approximately 22 to 30 mm, and the recommended screw diameter is 3.5 to 4.0 mm.

Pedicle Screw Instrumentation at T1-T3

The thoracic pedicle angle varies, but the average is 0.3° toward midline at T12 , increasing to 13.9° at T4 and approximately 35° at T1.[24] Therefore the screw entry point is slightly lateral at T1, compared with the entry point for the caudal thoracic spine, and the screw medial convergence trajectory is higher at T1, compared with the trajectory at T12. The anatomic landmark for the entry point is just medial to the lateral border of the facet joint at the upper border of the transverse process. To avoid penetration of the lateral wall of the vertebral body, the the screw trajectories converge 20° to 30° to midline. Fluoroscopic guidance facilitates accurate and safe screw trajectory placement. If the patient's body habitus precludes adequate imaging, a small laminotomy using a Penfield retractor may be helpful for locating the inner border of the pedicle. The length of the screw is approximately 30 to 35 mm, and the diameter is 5.0 mm.

The Thoracolumbar Spine

Lumbar Spine Motion Segments

The borders of the lumbar neuroforamen are shown in Figure 13. A numbered lumbar nerve root traverses the disk space and exits the foramen under the corresponding pedicle (Figure 14). Each lumbar motion segment can be divided from cephalad to caudal into three zones, which together are known as the three-story zone system or three-story house (Figure 15). The pedicular zone is the top floor, for insertion of the pedicle screw; the infrapedicular zone is the main floor, containing the neuroforamen, with the nerve root exiting through the upper part of the foramen); and the diskal zone is the basement, where diskectomy is performed during transforaminal lumbar interbody fusion. Each of these lumbar motion segments has four subzones, from midline to far lateral: central (the region of the thecal sac), lateral recess (between the lateral border of thecal sac and the medial border of the pedicle), foraminal (between the medial and lateral borders of the pedicle), and extraforaminal (lateral to the lateral wall of the pedicle).

Surgical decompression for lumbar spinal canal stenosis is achieved by central decompression through a

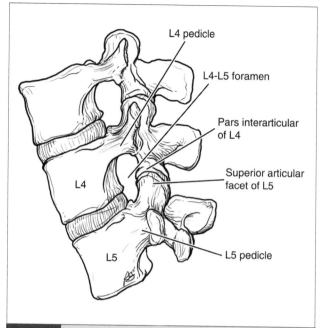

Figure 13   Schematic drawing showing the L4-L5 foramen, which is bordered ventrally by the inferior portion of the L4 vertebral body and the L4-5 disk, superiorly and inferiorly by the L4 and L5 pedicles, and dorsally by the L4 pars and the L5 superior articular process.

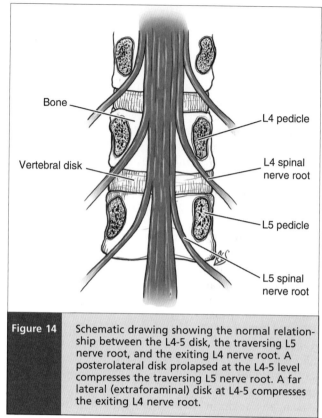

Figure 14   Schematic drawing showing the normal relationship between the L4-5 disk, the traversing L5 nerve root, and the exiting L4 nerve root. A posterolateral disk prolapsed at the L4-5 level compresses the traversing L5 nerve root. A far lateral (extraforaminal) disk at L4-5 compresses the exiting L4 nerve root.

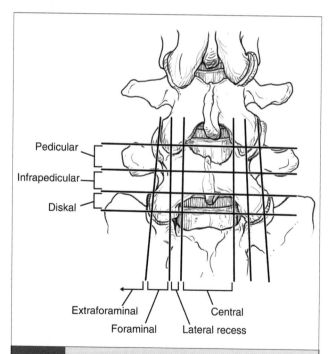

Figure 15   Schematic drawing showing the three lumbar motion segment zones (pedicular, infrapedicular, and diskal) and their four subzones (central, lateral recess, foraminal, and extraforaminal). The three-story zone system is used to identify pathologic processes and helpful landmarks during surgical decompression and posterior instrumentation of the lumbar spine.

laminectomy or a midline-sparing bilateral hemilaminotomy. Lateral recess decompression is achieved by undercutting the facet to allow decompression while maintaining the integrity of the facet. Resecting more than 50% of both facets or 100% of a single facet destabilizes this motion segment.

Anatomy Related to an Anterior Approach to the Lumbar Spine

The anterolateral abdominal wall consists of the muscles and their fascia on each side. Three large, flat muscles (the external oblique, internal oblique, and transverse abdominis) lie laterally. The multigastric, longitudinally oriented rectus abdominis muscle lies medially. The thoracoabdominal nerves, arising from the 7th to the 12th intercostal nerves, supply the abdominal wall muscles. The inferior part of the abdominal wall muscles is innervated by the iliohypogastric and ilioinguinal nerves, arising from the L1 nerve. The neurovascular supply of the internal oblique and transverse abdominis muscles is supplied by segmental neurovascular bundles that run obliquely between these muscles and ends in the lateral border of the rectus abdominis muscle. To spare the neurovascular bundles, a retroperitoneal approach should pass medial to the rectus abdominis muscle.

The psoas major originates on the anterolateral aspect of the lumbar vertebral bodies and transverse processes and the intervertebral disks adjacent to T12 to L5. The distal tendon inserts on the lesser trochanter.

The psoas major is innervated from the anterior rami of L2 to L4. These anterior rami are embedded in the psoas major muscle. The function of the psoas major is flexion and external rotation of the hip. A painful spasm of this muscle during hip flexion and external rotation, called psoitis, can result from a spine infection that extends to the psoas.

The iliacus muscle is a large triangular muscle that originates from the superior two thirds of the iliac fossa, extends across the sacroiliac joint, and inserts on the lesser trochanter of the femur and a portion of the shaft inferior to it. The action of the iliacus muscle is to flex the hip. Its innervation is from the femoral nerve segments L2 to L4. The iliopsoas muscle is surrounded by an aponeurotic sheet; this iliac fascia accompanies the muscle from T12 to the upper part of the thigh. An abscess of the spine can migrate along this sheath and become external at the base of the thigh.

The anterior branches of the lumbar spine nerves, which contribute to the lumbar plexus, lie in a lateral position in the psoas muscle. The anterior branches of the L2, L3, and L4 spinal nerves contribute to the femoral and obturator nerves. The posterior retraction of the muscle required for vertebral body exposure may cause postoperative femoral nerve palsy unless overretraction is avoided. To preclude excessive tension on the lumbar plexus during posterior retraction of the psoas and thereby lower the risk of this complication, the hip should be flexed on the side being operated on.

The level of the bifurcation of the aorta and the origin of the vena cava is variable. The aorta ends at L4 in 45% of individuals, L4-L5 in 25%, L3-L4 in 20%, and L3 and L5 in 5%. The origin of the inferior vena cava is at L5 in 45% of individuals, L4-L5 in 30%, L4 in 20%, and L5-S1 in 5%.

The superior hypogastric plexus has a role in the physiology of ejaculation through its sympathetic components, which come mainly from the first two lumbar splanchnic nerves. The patient should be informed of the risk of retrograde ejaculation before an anterior approach to the lower lumbar spine is used. The risk can be lowered by avoiding the use of sharp dissection or electrocoagulation in the retroperitoneal space.

A transperitoneal or retroperitoneal approach to the lumbar spine can be used. During the transperitoneal approach to L5-S1, the anterior aspect of the disk should be reached first on the right side, medial to the right iliac vein. The superior hypogastric plexus has no relevant links on the right side; the attachment of the superior hypogastric plexus to the inferior mesenteric plexus on the left side makes the left-side approach more challenging. Once the anterior surface of the disk is exposed, blunt dissection is performed, and the retroperitoneal soft tissue is gradually pushed cranially and laterally. A transperitoneal approach to the L4-5 disk is achieved by mobilizing the aorta and its bifurcation to the right side. The superior hypogastric plexus is left in front of the aorta within its surrounding fat tissue. The retroperitoneal approach to the L5-S1 disk can be achieved from either the right or the left side. The advantage of the right-side approach is that the right half of the disk is less covered than the left by the superior hypogastric plexus. If the L5-S1 disk is the only disk to be approached, the right-side approach is preferable. If two or more disks must be approached, the left-side approach should be used. The retroperitoneal approach to the L4-5 disk is performed from the left-side; an approach from the right side is difficult because of the vascular anatomy.

The Blood Supply to the Spinal Cord

Radicular branches of the aorta, the intercostal arteries, and the lumbar arteries enter the spinal canal through the intervertebral foramina and divide into anterior and posterior radicular arteries. The anterior radicular arteries supply the anterior spinal artery, and the posterior radicular arteries supply the posterior spinal artery. The most significant radicular artery to the cervical cord originates from the deep cervical artery accompanying the left C6 spinal nerve root. Other medullary feeders to the cervical cord are commonly present at C3 from the left and at C5 and T1 from the right. The radicular artery of Adamkiewicz is a major contributor to the anterior spinal artery and provides the main blood supply to the lower spinal cord. This artery originates from the left side in 80% of people; usually it accompanies the ventral root of T9, T10, or T11, but it can originate at any point from T5 to L5. The artery of Adamkiewicz usually originates from a segmental artery at the level of the costotransverse joint and enters the intervertebral foramen. Dissection near the foramen and disarticulation of the costotransverse and costovertebral joints can injure the artery. Ligation of the segmental vessels over the midportion of the vertebral body helps to minimize the risk of injury to the artery of Adamkiewicz by allowing the posterior intersegmental anastomoses to remain intact.

The Anatomic Bases of Sagittal Balance

Spinal sagittal balance is an important measure of spinal deformity, and patients' satisfaction after lumbar spine surgery is correlated with restoration of the sagittal balance.[25] Spinal sagittal balance is the result of normal cervical lordosis (20° to 40°), normal thoracic kyphosis (20° to 40°), and normal lumbar lordosis (30° to 60°). As much as 47% is from L5-S1. The normal sagittal vertical axis extends from the center of C2 to the front of T7, to the middle of the T12-LI disk, behind L3, and to the posterosuperior corner of the sacrum. In positive sagittal imbalance, as in flat-back syndrome or fixed hip flexion, the sagittal vertical axis is anterior to the sacrum. In negative sagittal imbalance, as in lumbar hyperlordosis, the sagittal vertical axis is posterior to the sacrum. The sacral inclination is measured as shown in Figure 16. The normal sacral inclination is 30°, but it is smaller in a patient with spondylolisthesis. The average normal pelvic incidence is 50°; in children, this angle is 47°, and in adults it is 57°. Pelvic incidence

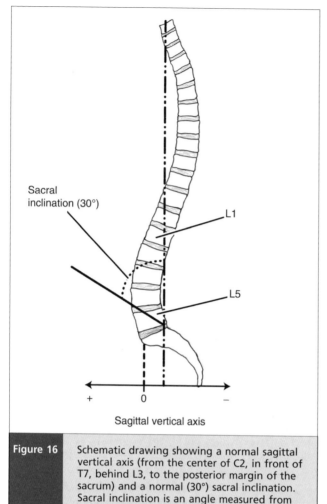

Sacral inclination (30°)

L1

L5

+   0   –

Sagittal vertical axis

Figure 16	Schematic drawing showing a normal sagittal vertical axis (from the center of C2, in front of T7, behind L3, to the posterior margin of the sacrum) and a normal (30°) sacral inclination. Sacral inclination is an angle measured from the posterior surface of the sacrum to a vertical plumb line.

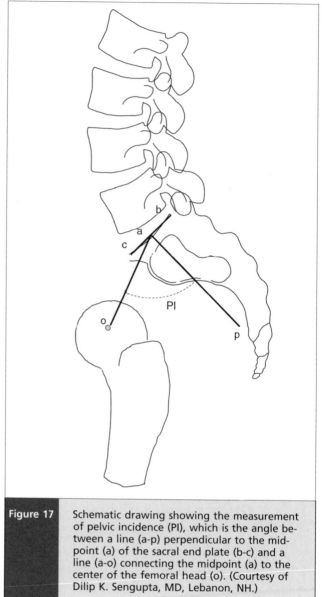

b
a
c
PI
o
p

Figure 17	Schematic drawing showing the measurement of pelvic incidence (PI), which is the angle between a line (a-p) perpendicular to the midpoint (a) of the sacral end plate (b-c) and a line (a-o) connecting the midpoint (a) to the center of the femoral head (o). (Courtesy of Dilip K. Sengupta, MD, Lebanon, NH.)

is measured as shown in Figure 17. A high pelvic incidence occurs with the increase in lumbar lordosis associated with increased shear forces at the lumbosacral junction, which increases the risk of slip progression in spondylolisthesis.

Anatomy Related to Iliac Crest Bone Graft Harvesting

Autogenous iliac crest bone graft frequently is used to promote fusion in spine surgery. The ilium is thickest in two regions: the area extending from a point 2 to 3 cm posterior to the anterosuperior iliac spine a distance of 6 to 8 cm posteriorly along the iliac crest, and the posteroinferior portion (sacroiliac surface area) of the ilium. The neurovascular structures adjacent to the anterior ilium include the lateral femoral cutaneous, iliohypogastric, and ilioinguinal nerves (Figure 18), and the neurovascular structures adjacent to the posterior ilium include the superior cluneal nerves and superior gluteal neurovascular bundle (Figure 19). These struc-

tures are vulnerable to injury during bone graft harvesting.

The iliohypogastric nerve arises from the ventral ramus of L1 and emerges from the lateral border of the psoas major. It perforates the transverse abdominis muscle above the pelvis and supplies the transverse and internal oblique abdominal muscles. Its lateral cutaneous branch supplies the skin of the posterior part of the gluteal region. The ilioinguinal nerve also originates in the ventral ramus of L1 and runs just medial to the iliohypogastric nerve proximally. Distally, the ilioinguinal nerve crosses in front of the upper part of the iliacus muscle and passes into the inguinal canal to supply the skin of the groin area. The lateral femoral cutaneous nerve is the sensory branch from the L2 and L3 ventral rami. In the anterior iliac region, the lateral femoral cutaneous nerve exits the iliac fossa from be-

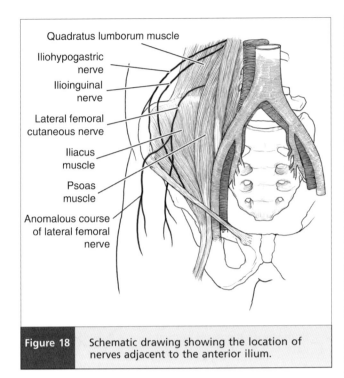

Figure 18 Schematic drawing showing the location of nerves adjacent to the anterior ilium.

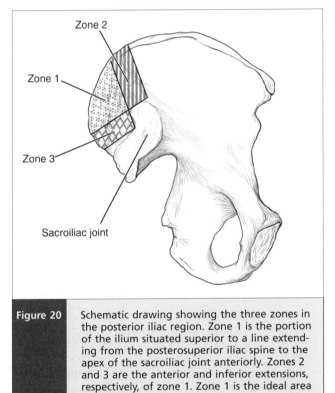

Figure 20 Schematic drawing showing the three zones in the posterior iliac region. Zone 1 is the portion of the ilium situated superior to a line extending from the posterosuperior iliac spine to the apex of the sacroiliac joint anteriorly. Zones 2 and 3 are the anterior and inferior extensions, respectively, of zone 1. Zone 1 is the ideal area for posterior iliac bone graft harvesting, with no risk of sacroiliac joint violation.

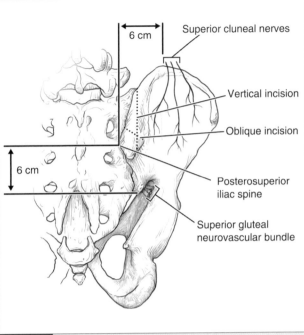

Figure 19 Schematic drawing showing the location of the superior cluneal nerves and the superior gluteal neurovascular bundle in relation to the posterosuperior iliac spine. To avoid the superior cluneal nerves, the posterior ilium can be approached through a vertical incision parallel to the midline or a lateral oblique incision within 6 cm of the posterosuperior iliac spine.

injury during an approach to the anterior iliac region. The superior cluneal nerves originate in the dorsal rami of L1, L2, and L3; they emerge from the lumbodorsal fascia and cross the iliac crest approximately 6 to 8 cm lateral to the posterosuperior iliac spine. These nerves provide sensation to the region of the posterior iliac crest and the cephalad portion of the buttock. The superior gluteal artery is a main branch of the internal iliac artery; it leaves the pelvis through the most proximal portion of the greater sciatic notch, staying against the bony notch and supplying the gluteal muscles.

The posterior ilium can be approached through a vertical incision parallel to the midline or a lateral oblique incision within 6 cm of the posterosuperior iliac spine to avoid the superior cluneal nerves. To avoid injuring the superior cluneal nerves, a curved or transverse incision along the iliac crest in the posterior iliac region should be avoided. It is important to identify the working area before harvesting the bone graft to avoid violating the sacroiliac joint.

The posterior iliac region has three zones (Figure 20). Zone 1 is the portion of the ilium situated superior to a line extending from the posterosuperior iliac spine to the apex of the sacroiliac joint anteriorly. The anterior margin of zone 1 is the superior extension of the posterior border of the superior edge of the articular surface, and the inferior margin is a line extending anteriorly from the posterosuperior iliac spine to the apex

neath the inguinal ligament just inferior to the anterosuperior iliac spine and becomes extrafascial almost immediately over the anterolateral thigh. In some patients, the lateral cutaneous nerve exits the iliac fossa over the anterior iliac crest, placing the nerve at risk for of the sacroiliac joint, oriented perpendicular to the posterior margin of the superior edge. During posterior iliac bone graft harvesting, zone 1 is oriented perpendicular to the plane of the operating table, with an anteroposterior width of 3 to 4 cm. Zones 2 and 3 are the anterior and inferior extensions, respectively, of zone 1. The ideal area for posterior iliac bone graft harvesting is zone 1, as there is no risk of violating the sacroiliac joint. Zone 2 or zone 3 may be considered if a greater quantity of cancellous bone graft is required; however, the surgeon must be aware of the risk of violating the sacroiliac joint.[26]

Annotated References

1. Ebraheim NA, Lu J, Biyani A, Brown JA, Yeasting RA: An anatomic study of the thickness of the occipital bone: Implications for occipitocervical instrumentation. *Spine (Phila Pa 1976)* 1996;21(15):1725-1729.

2. Nadim Y, Lu J, Sabry FF, Ebraheim N: Occipital screws in occipitocervical fusion and their relation to the venous sinuses: An anatomic and radiographic study. *Orthopedics* 2000;23(7):717-719.

3. Jackson RS, Banit DM, Rhyne AL III, Darden BV II: Upper cervical spine injuries. *J Am Acad Orthop Surg* 2002;10(4):271-280.

4. Harris JH Jr, Carson GC, Wagner LK: Radiologic diagnosis of traumatic occipitovertebral dissociation: 1. Normal occipitovertebral relationships on lateral radiographs of supine subjects. *AJR Am J Roentgenol* 1994;162(4):881-886.

5. Harris JH Jr, Carson GC, Wagner LK, Kerr N: Radiologic diagnosis of traumatic occipitovertebral dissociation: 2. Comparison of three methods of detecting occipitovertebral relationships on lateral radiographs of supine subjects. *AJR Am J Roentgenol* 1994;162(4):887-892.

6. Spence KF Jr, Decker S, Sell KW: Bursting atlantal fracture associated with rupture of the transverse ligament. *J Bone Joint Surg Am* 1970;52(3):543-549.

7. Steele HH: Anatomical and mechanical considerations of the atlanto-axial articulations. *J Bone Joint Surg Am* 1968;50:1481-1482.

8. Ebraheim NA, Lu J, Yang H: The effect of translation of the C1-C2 on the spinal canal. *Clin Orthop Relat Res* 1998;351:222-229.

9. Wright NM, Lauryssen C, American Association of Neurological Surgeons/Congress of Neurological Surgeons: Vertebral artery injury in C1-2 transarticular screw fixation: Results of a survey of the AANS/CNS section on disorders of the spine and peripheral nerves. *J Neurosurg* 1998;88(4):634-640.

10. Currier BL, Maus TP, Eck JC, Larson DR, Yaszemski MJ: Relationship of the internal carotid artery to the anterior aspect of the C1 vertebra: Implications for C1-C2 transarticular and C1 lateral mass fixation. *Spine (Phila Pa 1976)* 2008;33(6):635-639.

    The anatomic relation of the internal carotid artery to the anterior aspect of C1 was assessed in a retrospective analysis of 50 random head and neck CT scans with contrast medium.

11. Ebraheim NA, Misson JR, Xu R, Yeasting RA: The optimal transarticular c1-2 screw length and the location of the hypoglossal nerve. *Surg Neurol* 2000;53(3):208-210.

12. Madawi AA, Casey AT, Solanki GA, Tuite G, Veres R, Crockard HA: Radiological and anatomical evaluation of the atlantoaxial transarticular screw fixation technique. *J Neurosurg* 1997;86(6):961-968.

13. Liu J, Shafiq Q, Ebraheim NA, et al: Value of intraoperative true lateral radiograph of C2 pedicle for C1-2 transarticular screw insertion. *Spine J* 2005;5(4):434-440.

    A total of 40 C1-C2 transarticular screws were inserted in 20 embalmed human cadaver cervical spine specimens using the Magerl and Seemann technique. On true lateral radiographs of the C2 pedicle, the height of the area allowing instrumentation of the pedicle was 7.75 mm (±0.92 mm) (right) and 7.64 mm (±0.63 mm) (left). On sagittal CT, the height of pedicles was 7.71 mm (±0.7 mm) (right) and 7.58 mm (±1.01 mm) (left). On 30°-sagittal CT, the height of pedicles was 7.84 mm (±1.00 mm) (right) and 7.76 mm (±1.02 mm) (left). On true lateral radiographs, the pedicles were found to provide useful information for intraoperative definition of screw trajectory.

14. Ebraheim N, Rollins JR Jr, Xu R, Jackson WT: Anatomic consideration of C2 pedicle screw placement. *Spine (Phila Pa 1976)* 1996;21(6):691-695.

15. Botte MJ, Byrne TP, Garfin SR: Application of the halo device for immobilization of the cervical spine utilizing an increased torque pressure. *J Bone Joint Surg Am* 1987;69(5):750-752.

16. Ebraheim NA, Lu J, Skie M, Heck BE, Yeasting RA: Vulnerability of the recurrent laryngeal nerve in the anterior approach to the lower cervical spine. *Spine (Phila Pa 1976)* 1997;22(22):2664-2667.

17. Lu J, Ebraheim NA, Nadim Y, Huntoon M: Anterior approach to the cervical spine: Surgical anatomy. *Orthopedics* 2000;23(8):841-845.

18. Melamed H, Harris MB, Awasthi D: Anatomic considerations of superior laryngeal nerve during anterior cervical spine procedures. *Spine (Phila Pa 1976)* 2002;27(4):E83-E86.

19. Lu J, Ebraheim NA: The vertebral artery: Surgical anatomy. *Orthopedics* 1999;22(11):1081-1085.

20. Ebraheim NA, Xu R, Ahmad M, Heck B: The quantitative anatomy of the vertebral artery groove of the atlas and its relation to the posterior atlantoaxial approach. *Spine (Phila Pa 1976)* 1998;23(3):320-323.

21. Young JP, Young PH, Ackermann MJ, Anderson PA, Riew KD: The ponticulus posticus: Implications for screw insertion into the first cervical lateral mass. *J Bone Joint Surg Am* 2005;87(11):2495-2498.

   A retrospective review of 464 lateral radiographs of the neck identified 72 complete or incomplete arcuate foramina (a prevalence of 15.5%). Identification of the arcuate foramen on preoperative lateral radiographs should alert the surgeon to avoid using the ponticulus posticus as a starting point for a lateral mass screw.

22. Lee MJ, Cassinelli EH, Riew KD: Prevalence of cervical spine stenosis: Anatomic study in cadavers. *J Bone Joint Surg Am* 2007;89(2):376-380.

   In 469 adult skeletal specimens of the cervical spine, cervical stenosis was defined as a canal diameter of less than 12 mm. The canal diameters ranged from 9.0 to 20.9 mm, with a median of 14.4 mm. The authors concluded that cervical stenosis is present in 4.9% of all adults, 6.8% of those 50 years or older, and 9% of those 70 years or older.

23. Dvorak MF, Fisher CG, Hoekema J, et al: Factors predicting motor recovery and functional outcome after traumatic central cord syndrome: A long-term follow-up. *Spine (Phila Pa 1976)* 2005;30(20):2303-2311.

   A prospectively maintained, database-generated retrospective review and cross-sectional outcome analysis was performed at a single academic center to assess improvement in geriatric patients' American Spinal Injury Association motor score as well as health-related quality of life.

24. Cinotti G, Gumina S, Ripani M, Postacchini F: Pedicle instrumentation in the thoracic spine: A morphometric and cadaveric study for placement of screws. *Spine (Phila Pa 1976)* 1999;24(2):114-119.

25. Kim YJ, Bridwell KH, Lenke LG, Cheh G, Baldus C: Results of lumbar pedicle subtraction osteotomies for fixed sagittal imbalance: A minimum 5-year follow-up study. *Spine (Phila Pa 1976)* 2007;32(20):2189-2197.

   A retrospective study reported results at a minimum 5-year follow-up after pedicle subtraction osteotomy for fixed sagittal imbalance in 35 consecutive patients. Ten pseudarthroses occurred in 8 patients (29%). Patients had very good satisfaction (87%), good self-image (76%), good function (69%), and fair pain (66%).

26. Ebraheim NA, Elgafy H, Xu R: Bone-graft harvesting from iliac and fibular donor sites: Techniques and complications. *J Am Acad Orthop Surg* 2001;9(3):210-218.

1: Basic Science of the Spine

Chapter 2

The Biomechanics of the Spinal Column

Mei Wang, PhD   Raj D. Rao, MD

Introduction

The study of spine biomechanics involves the stability, deformation, and motion patterns of the spinal column and its constituent parts, as well as alterations in these properties when the spine is subjected to internal muscular or external applied loads. The spinal column is a complex mechanical structure consisting of several articulations that allow it to undergo substantial rotation in the sagittal, lateral, and axial planes and translation in the anteroposterior, lateral, and axial planes. The structural components that contribute to these mechanical properties include the vertebrae, intervertebral disks, facet joints, and spine ligaments. The study of spine biomechanics uses analytic tools including the equations of newtonian mechanics and mathematical principles from continuum mechanics, fracture mechanics, and computational modeling.

Mechanical Behaviors of Biologic Structures

Elastic Behaviors

When a force is applied to a biologic structure such as a vertebra or a functional spinal unit (FSU), the structure becomes deformed from its initial dimensions. The relative change in the dimensions at any point of the structure is referred to as strain at that point. The applied force also generates an internal force within the structure. The intensity of the internal force acting across a perpendicular plane within the structure is called stress. In the simplified example shown in Figure 1, a cylinder-shaped sample of trabecular bone is subjected to a tensile force until it breaks. Initially, the elongation of the cylinder increases with the applied force in a linear fashion or at a constant rate (Figure 1, A). The slope of

the force-deflection curve is referred to as the stiffness of the cylinder (Figure 1, B). The end point of the initial curve is referred to as the yield point, and it represents the elastic limit of the sample. Loading continued beyond the yield point results in permanent deformation of the structure when the force is removed. In biologic tissues, permanent deformation indicates some level of damage. The force at the yield point is referred to as the yield load. The point of failure is indicated by highest load on the force-deflection plot before a sudden decline; the force at the peak is referred to as the failure load.

The force-deflection plot represents the mechanical behavior of the three-dimensional structure but does not provide information on the material of which the structure is composed. For a structure that can be considered as a uniform material or tissue, such as a block of cancellous bone, the force-deflection plot can be normalized into a stress-strain plot to represent the mechanical behavior of the unit material (Figure 1, C). Several corresponding material properties can be derived from the stress-strain plot. The slope of the plot is referred to as the elastic modulus or Young modulus. The stress at the yield point becomes yield strength, and the stress at the point of failure becomes ultimate strength.

A material is considered anisotropic, rather than isotropic, if its material properties vary in different directions. Most biologic tissues are anisotropic, with an elastic modulus that varies depending on the loading direction. This characteristic makes it challenging and often impossible to completely define the material properties of the tissue. In practice, partial symmetry in the properties of a material is assumed, and the number of independent elastic constants required to define its properties is thereby reduced. Two examples are orthotropic symmetry, in which the tissue has three mutually perpendicular planes of mirror symmetry, and therefore nine independent elastic constants are required to define its properties; and transversely isotropic symmetry, in which the material is symmetric about an axis (usually along the primary loading direction) that is normal to a plane of isotropy.

Dr. Wang or an immediate family member has received research or institutional support from Medtronic. Dr. Rao or an immediate family member serves as a board member, owner, officer, or committee member of the North American Spine Society, the Lumbar Spine Research Society, and the US Food and Drug Administration Orthopaedic and Rehabilitation Devices Scientific Advisory Panel.

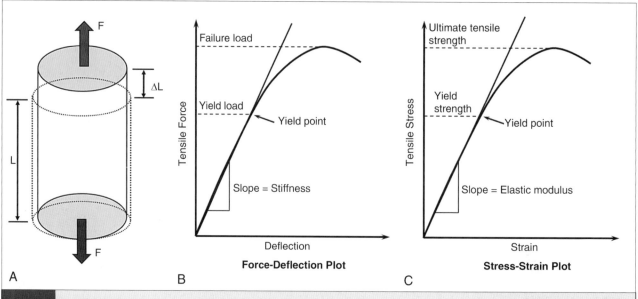

Figure 1 **A,** Schematic drawing showing a cylindrical bone sample subjected to a tensile force (F) and the resulting deflection (ΔL). Dotted lines = the dimensions of the cylinder before force application, L = the original length. **B,** The force-deflection plot, in which the applied tensile force and corresponding deflection are used to determine the structural properties of the cylindrical bone. **C,** The stress-strain plot, in which the tensile force is normalized over the cross-sectional area of the bone sample and the deflection is normalized over the original length to determine the material properties of the bone.

Viscoelastic Behaviors

In many biologic materials, the elastic modulus changes when the material is loaded at different rates. This characteristic is referred to as viscoelastic behavior, and it is manifested in two ways. First, when a viscoelastic material is loaded to a certain stress and held at that stress, the strain within the material continues to increase, although at a gradually reducing rate. This phenomenon is called creep. Second, when a viscoelastic material is deformed to a certain strain and held at that strain, the stress caused by the deflection continues to decline, although at a gradually reducing rate. This phenomenon is called relaxation. When a viscoelastic material is loaded and then unloaded, the stress-strain plots follow a different path, and the difference between the two plots represents the amount of energy dissipated or lost during the loading-unloading cycle. This phenomenon is referred to as hysteresis.

Most biologic materials are viscoelastic to some extent. Viscoelastic materials return to their original shape after any deforming force has been removed (that is, they show an elastic response), even though time is required for this viscous component to respond. During experimental testing of biologic structures, loads often are applied in a quasi-static manner to minimize the variance induced by the viscoelastic behavior of the specimens. In addition, the specimen is normally subjected to several loading-unloading cycles for preconditioning before data collection. This process stabilizes the amount of hysteresis in the tissue and therefore reduces intersample variations resulting from viscoelastic behaviors.

The Functional Biomechanics of the Spinal Column

The spinal column has two biomechanical functions: to stabilize the head and trunk (protecting the contained neural tissues) during the loading that occurs during normal activities of daily living; and to allow the head and trunk to move freely to facilitate daily activities. Loading and kinematics of the spine have been extensively studied, and the resulting knowledge is critical for understanding and treating spine diseases as well as for designing and evaluating new treatments. The basic unit for the study of spinal column biomechanics is the FSU, which is defined as an osteoligamentous structure consisting of two adjacent vertebrae and the intervening intervertebral disk and ligamentous structures.

Spine Kinematics

The spinal column is capable of movement in all six degrees of freedom: rotation in the flexion-extension, lateral bending, and axial directions; and translation in the axial compression-distraction, anterior-posterior, and lateral directions. Single- or multiple-FSU cadaver segments have been subjected to simulated physiologic loading to characterize the load-displacement response and detailed motion patterns of the spine level.

A typical FSU load-displacement plot starts with a lax region of motion, which is referred to as the neutral zone (Figure 2). The neutral zone represents a small-response region in which the spine can undergo relatively large movement with very little muscular effort. An FSU with a degenerated disk tends to have more

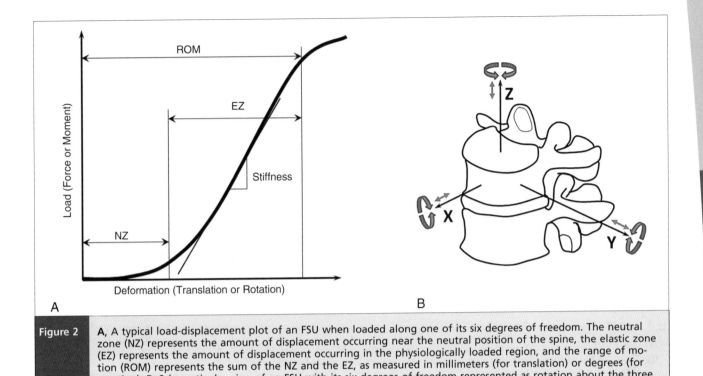

Figure 2 **A,** A typical load-displacement plot of an FSU when loaded along one of its six degrees of freedom. The neutral zone (NZ) represents the amount of displacement occurring near the neutral position of the spine, the elastic zone (EZ) represents the amount of displacement occurring in the physiologically loaded region, and the range of motion (ROM) represents the sum of the NZ and the EZ, as measured in millimeters (for translation) or degrees (for rotation). **B,** Schematic drawing of an FSU with its six degrees of freedom represented as rotation about the three orthogonal axes of X, Y, and Z *(circular arrows)* and translation along the same axes *(straight arrows).*

neutral zone motion than an FSU with a normal disk. The load-displacement plot next enters a stiffening region in which the force needed to generate movement increases significantly. This region sometimes is referred to as the elastic zone, and it represents the behavior of the physiologically loaded spine. The spine movement corresponding to the maximal applied load is referred to as the range of motion. The range of motion varies significantly among the different regions of the spine, depending on their primary function.

The pattern or quality of spine motion also varies, depending on the regional anatomy and the pathologic conditions of the intervertebral disk. The instantaneous axis of rotation (IAR) is often used to describe the pattern of motion; it is the axis around which vertebral rotation occurs at a specific instant of time. In a normal spine, the IAR for each rotational direction (flexion-extension, lateral bending, and axial) is confined to a relatively small area of the FSU.

Because of the complex anatomic shape of the vertebrae, movement of the spine segment about or along one primary axis is always accompanied by movement about or along a secondary axis. This characteristic is known as coupled motion. For example, in the subaxial cervical spine, lateral bending occurs concomitantly with axial rotation in the same direction, primarily because of the orientation of the facets' articular surfaces. In addition, rotation of a spine motion segment almost always is accompanied by translation in some direction.

In vivo spine motion has been characterized using radiographic and other methods. Most early in vivo studies were restricted to evaluating clinical instability and measuring range of motion. The development of more sophisticated motion-tracking systems has led to an increase in information on the patterns of the spine movement, including IAR and out-of-plane coupled motion. A recently proposed approach to tracking in vivo spine motion uses MRI and fluoroscopic imaging.[1] A three-dimensional anatomic model of the vertebrae is first constructed from the patient's MRI studies, and a dual orthogonal fluoroscopic system then is used to capture spatial spine movement while the patient performs unrestricted weight-bearing tasks. The two images are combined to derive measurements of the six degrees of freedom (three rotations and three translations) in intersegmental movement at each spine level.

Spine Loading

As the primary axial support of the head and trunk, the spinal column is subjected to large compression loads during daily activities. These loads are induced by inertia from body weight and internal forces exerted by the trunk musculature as it stabilizes the spinal column. It is both important and challenging to determine these loads, especially in the lumbar region. Most of the existing knowledge has been obtained from indirect computational studies and direct (invasive) intradiskal measurement. There is reasonable agreement between the predictions of spine compression from the direct and indirect approaches.

The computational approach often uses dynamic linked segment models that incorporate electromyelographically measured muscular coactivations to obtain the total loads at the spine level of interest. The total compressive loads are partitioned among the active and passive elements of the spine using computational optimization techniques. These models often are used to estimate the lumbar loads experienced by industrial workers. Using this approach, the estimated compressive force at the L4-L5 level during fast walking was found to exceed three times body weight.[2] Complex coactivation of the trunk muscles was found to result in as much as 1,000 N of anterior-posterior shear force in the L4-5 disk during simulated industrial push-pull tasks.[3]

The gold standard for estimating spine loads may be direct invasive measurement of intradiskal pressure in an individual who has volunteered for the test. A needle with a micropressure transducer is inserted into the lumbar intervertebral disk, and pressure readings are collected while activities of daily living are being performed. The intradiskal pressure data are later converted into compressive force measurements. A seminal study from the 1960s estimated compressive forces at the L3-4 disk in various postures and normalized the data with respect to the posture of relaxed standing.[4] In an average person, the compressive force on the lumbar spine was estimated to be 125 to 200 N while lying down; 500 to 800 N while standing upright; 700 to 1,000 N while sitting upright; and 1,900 to 3,000 N while bending and lifting a 10-kg weight with straight legs. These experiments were repeated 30 years later with an improved flexible pressure transducer.[5,6] The later studies confirmed most of the earlier findings but also reported compressive force of 1,100 to 1,800 N during forward-bend standing and as much as 3,600 N when a 20-kg weight is lifted with straight legs.

The large compressive loads in the lumbar region are primarily resisted by the vertebral bodies and the intervening disk. Most of the compressive load on the vertebral body is absorbed by the trabecular bone. However, with aging and loss of trabecular bone mass, the load share of the vertebral cortex increases. The two facet joints at a motion segment together take up approximately 20% of the compressive loads in the neutral position, but in extension this load share increases significantly. In extension, the articular surfaces of the two facet joints come into contact, limiting rotation and increasing the compressive load. In flexion, the joint opens and the facet joint capsules, in conjunction with the posterior ligaments, are stretched, providing a stable, limited range of motion. Several in vitro biomechanical studies have analyzed the contribution of the capsule and surrounding ligaments to total motion segment stiffness in flexion. These studies found that the facet joint capsule transfers tension, although the diarthrodial facet joints provide sliding articulation and transfer compression and shear loads.[7-9]

Degenerative Changes in the Intervertebral Disk

The unique architecture of the intervertebral disk enables it to act as a major stabilizing structure in the spine. The peripherally located anulus fibrosus is formed of 15 to 20 tightly packed lamellae of collagen fibers, with successive lamellae obliquely oriented in alternating directions. This structure enables the disk to limit movement in multiple directions (such as axial rotation, anterior-posterior translation, lateral translation, and axial distraction) by developing tension in the fibers that are inclined in the direction of movement. The elastic anulus fibrosus, reinforced in the center by the hydrodynamic nucleus pulposus, forms an ideal structure for resisting axial compression. The posterior elements of the FSU, including the facet joints and facet capsular and posterior ligaments, are structured to resist movement in flexion, axial rotation, and anterior translation (Figure 3). In the lumbar region, the oblique orientation of the facets' articular surfaces with respect to the sagittal plane allows some movement in flexion-extension but restricts movement such as axial rotation in the transverse plane.

Disk degeneration generally begins earlier in life than degeneration of other joints. The greater prevalence of disk degeneration at the lower lumbar levels suggests a mechanical origin. Degenerative changes begin in the nucleus pulposus, where breakdown of the large aggregating proteoglycans reduces the capacity of the nucleus to attract and bind water, leading to a loss of disk hydration and decreased hydrostatic pressure. Subsequent structural changes occur in the lamellar microarchitecture of the anulus fibrosus, resulting in tears and progressive loss of disk height. Before the onset of degeneration in the nucleus pulposus, hydrostatic pressures generated in response to compressive loads are equally transmitted throughout the disk. As the disk degenerates, compressive loads are directly transmitted to the peripheral annular contact regions of the disk, rendering the structure even more susceptible to delamination and degenerative change. Disk degeneration can accelerate the degeneration of surrounding tissues such as facet joints. Biomechanical and histologic studies have shown a close functional relationship between degeneration of the lumbar disks and their corresponding facet joints.

Experimental Protocols for Biomechanical Evaluation of the Spine

In vitro testing of single or multiple FSUs forms the basis of much of the available information on the mechanical behavior of the natural intact spine, loss of stability from injury or other pathologic processes involving the spine, and the mechanical performance of different spine implants. The studies typically collect six degrees of motion displacement at each spine level and the corresponding loads. The kinematic variables,

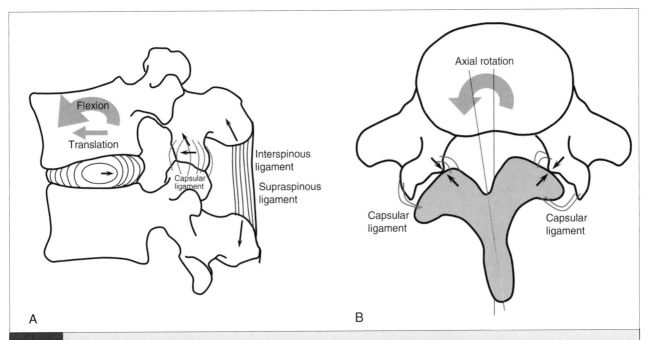

Figure 3 A, Sagittal-view schematic drawing of an FSU illustrating the resistance of posterior elements (facet joints, facet capsular ligaments, and interspinous and supraspinous ligaments *[black arrows]*) to displacement in flexion and anterior translation *(gray arrows)*. **B**, Transverse-view drawing illustrating the resistance of the facet joint and its capsular ligaments *(black arrows)* to axial rotation *(gray arrow)*.

such as the neutral zone, range of motion, IAR, and coupled motion, are analyzed to determine changes caused by spine pathology or a spine implant. By combining motion data with loading information and other parameters (such as stiffness in the elastic zone or viscoelastic behaviors), the spine segment can be studied. The load sharing of the disk or implant can be evaluated by inserting needle-mounted transducers to obtain intradiskal pressure or applying a strain gauge to an implant.

Load- and Displacement-Controlled Testing

A load-controlled flexibility protocol and a displacement-controlled stiffness protocol are commonly used for testing. With the flexibility protocol, a predetermined force in single- or combined-loading modes is applied to an unconstrained end of the spine segment, and the resulting three-dimensional spine motion is recorded. The load is commonly applied through a process known as pure moment loading (Figure 4). When pure moments, rather than direct forces, are applied at the unconstrained end of the spine segment, the resulting loads do not change through the entire length of the testing segment, regardless of the rigidity of the specimens or the amount of deflection that occurs at different spine levels. This factor becomes significant if each specimen is used as its own control, and multiple repeated tests are performed on the specimens at various conditions (such as intact, destabilized, or after fixation or fusion). To simulate physiologic loading levels, maximum moments of 7.5 N·m to 10 N·m often are used for lumbar segments, and maximum moments of

1.5 N·m to 4 N·m are used for cervical segments.

With the stiffness protocol, a predetermined displacement is applied to the spine segment. The loads required to produce this displacement, the resulting changes in internal spine forces (such as intradiskal pressure or load transmitted through an implant), and other kinematic variables are recorded at each level. Although the stiffness protocol is relatively simple to implement, it constrains spine motion into one plane and may thereby impose undefined loads on the out-of-plane degrees of freedom. More complex testing schemes have been proposed, in which a robot replicates the unconstrained motion path that the spine specimen exhibits during the original load-control test.[10] The spine can be compared in different conditions, using data obtained from a series of displacement-controlled tests in which the spine specimen moves along an identical unconstrained motion path.

Adjacent-Level Motion Testing

The selection of a testing protocol is critical in investigations of adjacent-level biomechanical effects, before and after a simulated spine fusion. The specimens used for these studies have multiple motion segments and may be tested repeatedly in their intact and simulated-fusion states. With a stiffness protocol, the multisegment spine with simulated fusion is forced to move to the same predetermined level as before the fusion, despite the increased rigidity of the construct. As a result, the levels adjacent to the fusion inevitably undergo a

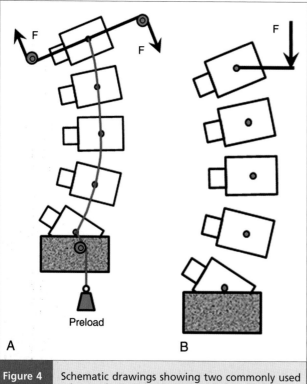

Figure 4	Schematic drawings showing two commonly used schemes for in vitro flexion loading in multilevel spine segments. **A,** Pure moment loading with a preload applied in a follower-load fashion. The pure moment results from the application of a coupled force (F) and stays constant throughout the length of the spine. **B,** Off-center compressive force loading. The off-center compressive force (F) results in varying moments at different spine segments, depending on the distance from the line of action of the force to the curved spine. Arrows = direction(s) of applied force.

protocols evaluate adjacent-level changes at the same global range of motion under all testing conditions. In contrast to the hybrid protocol, the load-limit control protocol sets a common load limit for all test conditions to avoid potential structural damage, especially when loading a rigid posttreatment spine to the level of the intact spine global range of motion.

Long Segment Testing With a Follower Load

Specimens with multiple FSUs are preferred for conducting in vitro mechanical tests on the osteoligamentous spine. At least one free FSU should be present on either side of the tested segment of the spine; these extra FSUs are essential for minimizing the constraints posted by the embedded segment. Long segment testing requires additional stabilization that simulates the agonist and antagonist muscular forces, if possible. Constant compressive preloads have been applied to the unconstrained cranial vertebra of the tested segment as a simplified simulation of the effect of body weight and musculature.

The use of the so-called follower load represents an improved approach in which the compressive preload is applied along the curvature of the spine.[14] The advantages of using a follower load rather than an unconstrained free-hanging weight is that it allows the application of larger, near-physiologic compressive loads and minimizes the resulting extra shear force and bending moment on the spine segments. Finite element study found that applying 500 N of preload in a follower-load fashion is a realistic means of simulating the standing posture.[15]

Animal Models

In vitro testing of human cadaver spine segments is essential for preclinical evaluation of the biomechanical performance of a new spine implant. The use of human cadaver specimens has limitations, however, including availability, degenerative changes associated with the typical older age of donors, and large interspecimen variation in tissue properties. The use of cadaver spines from animal models therefore is an appealing alternative. The commonly accepted animal spine models for in vitro spine implant evaluation are from the calf, pig, sheep, and goat. Cadaver spines from these animals have good comparability with human cadaver spines in terms of major anatomic features, general kinematic parameters, and the characteristics of load sharing between the disk and the posterior elements.[16-19] There are a few distinctive differences from the human spine, however, especially in the porcine and ovine spines, including a flatter sagittal alignment of the spinal column, a greater range of lateral bending motion, and smaller intervertebral dimensions. It is important to use skeletally mature animals, whenever possible, to avoid the possibility of growth plate rupture.

The validity of using quadruped animal models for in vivo spine research has often been questioned. The argument is that the design of a quadruped's horizon-

larger range of motion than they did before the fusion. The use of this protocol may lead to an overestimation of increases in adjacent-level motion after a fusion. In contrast, when the flexibility protocol is used, increased rigidity may prevent the same load from moving the entire segment to the prefusion range of motion.

A hybrid testing protocol has been proposed to facilitate an unbiased evaluation of adjacent-level motion.[11,12] In the hybrid protocol, load-controlled pure moments are applied to the spine in the intact stage and all posttreatment stages. In the posttreatment spine, the magnitude of the applied moment increases until the entire multisegment spine reaches the range of motion of the intact spine. In the displacement-limit control protocol, a comparison of adjacent-level effects is made at this point. In another proposed alternative, the load-controlled test is performed to the same predetermined level of maximum pure moment (the load-limit control), but the adjacent-level parameters are compared at the greatest common global range of motion found under any of the testing conditions used for the specimen.[13] Both displacement-limit and load-limit hybrid tally positioned spinal column may be different from that of the primarily axially loaded bipedal human spine. However, force analysis of standing and walking quadrupeds found that the spine-loading patterns are similar to those of the biped.[19] Substantial bending moment is imposed on the quadruped spinal column from gravitational force. To maintain the quadruped's posture and counterbalance the bending moment, additional forces are recruited from the dorsal muscles. This additional muscular activity causes the spine to be loaded primarily in axial compression. The vertebral trabecular bone architecture of quadrupeds, like that of humans, runs horizontally between the end plates; this factor also indicates that the primary load within the vertebral body is compression. The trabecular bone in quadrupeds tends to be more dense than it is in humans, however, and the interspecies difference may reflect different levels of axial compressive stress.

Small animals such as rabbits and rodents generally are not recommended for the study of spine biomechanics. However, these animals have been extensively used as in vivo models for studying the biologic mechanisms of spine fusion, disk degeneration, and repair. A mouse spine fusion biologic model was developed to allow the use of transgenic mice in evaluating specific genetic responses to spine surgery.[20] This model offers potential for the study of bone transduction pathways and other genetic components involved in producing a local fusion mass. Two types of degenerative disk models have been created in small animals; one uses mechanical intervention, such as sustained or cyclic loading in the rodent tail model, and the other creates superficial stabbing injuries to the annular fibers of the disk.

Finite Element Modeling

Analysis of in vitro experiments provides an abundance of information on spine biomechanics. However, experimental study has its limitations, including interspecimen variability, difficulty in incorporating muscle activities, and inability to monitor and control internal tissue behaviors. Finite element modeling allows the mechanical behaviors of the spine to be studied by segmenting the spine into finite elements that contain the proper material properties and boundary conditions. This type of study is a useful complement to experimental investigation. Complex spine-loading conditions can be simulated, as well as various treatments and surgical interventions. Most computational-model research focuses on internal mechanisms that would be difficult or even impossible to research in laboratory experiments. For example, modeling can be used to examine internal stresses in the intervertebral disk under different physiologic conditions and to provide valuable insight on the functional mechanical roles of individual soft- and hard-tissue components of the FSU.

The creation of finite element models is dependent on knowledge obtained from in vitro experiments on the material properties of different spine components. Because anatomic geometry, material behaviors, and boundary conditions are complex and uncertain, most finite element models are constructed based on averaged geometric and material properties and on simplified, idealized assumptions. The complexity of the nonlinear properties of the constituent materials, especially the collagen fibers, means that finite element modeling of the intervertebral disk requires iterative solutions and significant computing power. It is essential that the spine computational model be validated by comparing its output with experimental data. Experimental laboratory data are limited to global kinematic or loading parameters obtained under simplified loading conditions, however, and validation at this level may not be adequate to allow the computational model to be applied in more complex loading or pathologic situations. Sensitivity analyses must be performed to evaluate the effects of various model parameters and identify the parameters that are particularly critical in each application.

Experimentally validated finite element models are a powerful tool for examining the internal and external behaviors of the components of FSUs and understanding the biomechanical characteristics of the spine. Recent advances in imaging and computational techniques allow the automated generation of finite element models directly from CT or MRI studies, with accurate geometric and material details. These advances enable the development of patient-specific spine models that can be used in the clinical assessment of pathologic spine conditions.[21]

Biomechanical Considerations in Rigid Spine Stabilization

Implant Load Sharing

Rigid spine fixation devices are commonly used in treating a wide variety of spine disorders that lead to pain, neurologic deficit, or clinical instability, including tumors, trauma, and degenerative disk disease. Posterior instrumentation systems using pedicle screws, hooks and rods, or translaminar facet screws are effective in stabilizing and supporting the lumbar and thoracic segments until solid fusion or fracture healing is achieved. In the cervical segments, anterior plate fixation often is used to supplement anterior cervical diskectomy and fusion, with the aim of increasing local rigidity and thereby promoting fusion. Despite the good clinical outcomes, rigid fixation inevitably introduces substantial changes to the natural mechanical interactions among individual spine components. It is therefore important to investigate the characteristics of load sharing between the natural anatomy and the stabilizing hardware, based on specific functional needs.

The optimal patterns of implant load sharing depend on the specific functions of the implant and the biologic condition of the surrounding tissues. In a spine fusion, markedly rigid instrumentation may allow inadequate load transmission through the graft, resulting in stress shielding and affecting the quality of the eventual fusion mass. Experimental studies found that the levels of constraint in an anterior cervical plate significantly influence the loading pattern of an anterior structural graft. For example, a rigid anterior plate may carry more than half of the segmental load, but a dynamic cervical plate may allow 50% or more of the load to be transmitted through the graft. Application of a rigid fixation device also can be problematic if the patient has osteopenia or osteoporosis. The stress concentration from the mismatched mechanical properties can lead to catastrophic failure at the hardware and host-bone interfaces. Using a less constrained dynamic device may avoid this difficulty. In contrast, insufficient rigidity in the posterior instrumentation used to stabilize a deficient anterior column can cause hardware failure from excessive loading.

Adjacent-Segment Effects

The etiology of adjacent-segment disease after fusion has not been clearly established. The assumption is that by stiffening the fused segment, the mechanical stresses in the neighboring mobile disks are increased, and the degeneration process at these levels is thereby accelerated. This consideration is perhaps the most important motivation for the development of motion preservation devices. Adjacent-segment changes also have been reported after nonfusion spine surgery, however, and some researchers believe they are the result of the natural degenerative processes that accompany aging. Adjacent-segment disease occurs more frequently after surgery to treat degenerative disk disease than after surgery for other disorders; this factor supports the theory that the presurgical condition of the adjacent disks creates a predisposition to the adjacent-segment effect.

The segments adjacent to a lumbar fusion have been biomechanically evaluated by assessing their intervertebral motion and intradiskal pressure, and excessive increases in range of motion and intradiskal pressure have been reported.[22-25] In vitro studies of adjacent-segment effects in the cervical spine are less consistent, however.[26-29] The use of different experimental protocols can affect adjacent-segment mechanical findings. The great mobility of the cervical spine makes it more sensitive to loading conditions than the lumbar spine.

Concepts in Spine Instrumentation

Motion Preservation Devices

Several nonfusion stabilization devices for the spinal column have been developed in an attempt to improve surgical outcomes and obviate the adverse sequelae associated with fusion pseudarthrosis and adjacent-level degeneration. So-called softer stabilization devices may avoid the extreme stress concentration at the implant-bone interface that can lead to construct failure. Several dynamic stabilization devices with varying degrees of rigidity are in clinical use. Limited research is available

on the ideal implant rigidity for each clinical application or the long-term outcomes of patients with these implants.

Anterior Motion–Sparing Total Disk Replacement

Artificial disks are designed to replace the intervertebral disk in structure and function. The anatomic structure and biomechanical function of the disk are complex, however, and it has been difficult to design a total disk replacement using materials and dimensions capable of restoring all of the biomechanical functions, mechanical strength, and durability of a natural disk. The prosthesis must be able to sustain an axial compression load from the superior vertebra and transmit it to the inferior vertebra. The prosthesis also must be strong enough to withstand tension, compression, shear, torsion, and crimping. Finally, the prosthesis must allow a physiologic range of motion between the vertebrae and must permit a full range of motion in flexion-extension, lateral bending, axial rotation, and essential translations.

An artificial disk is classified, based on amount of motion allowed, as unconstrained, semiconstrained, or constrained. A device that allows hypermobility beyond the physiologic range and imposes no mechanical constraint in a specific motion direction is classified as unconstrained for that mode. A device that permits unrestricted motion for a specific mode of motion within the physiologic range but restrains motion outside the physiologic range is defined as semiconstrained in that mode. A device that imposes mechanical restrictions for a given mode of motion within the physiologic range is defined as constrained in that mode. A healthy natural disk therefore is a semiconstrained system, as it allows physiologic motion and restrains excessive, pathologic motion in all modes.

Several devices are commercially available for replacing a lumbar or cervical disk (Table 1). The device generally has two or three components, consisting of two disk plates and a core that is either connected onto the lower plate or separated. The movement between the two plates is determined by the core. The core often is made of an elastic material to re-create the flexibility of the natural disk, and the superior and inferior plates are made of a hard metallic material that is strong and can maintain fixation within the vertebra. The shapes of the articular surfaces determine the characteristics of the resulting motion. The conforming ball-and-socket interface of a constrained prosthesis or the spherical interface of a semiconstrained prosthesis imposes a fixed center of rotation on spine motion. The nonconforming ball-and-socket interface or deformable core of an unconstrained prosthesis allows motion around a moving center, as dictated by the kinematic and loading conditions of the spine.

The Charité artificial disk (DePuy Spine, Raynham, MA) is designed for the lumbar vertebrae from L2-L3 to L5-S1. This disk allows coupled rotation and trans-

Table 1

Lumbar and Cervical Disk Prostheses

Device	Manufacturer	Classification	Center of Rotation	Materials
Lumbar				
Activ-L	Aesculap	Semiconstrained	Moving	Metal on polymer
Charité	DePuy Spine	Unconstrained	Moving	Metal on polymer
Maverick	Medtronic	Semiconstrained	Fixed	Metal on metal
ProDisc-L	Synthes	Semiconstrained	Fixed	Metal on polymer
Cervical				
Bryan	Medtronic	Unconstrained	Moving	Metal on polymer
Discover Clinical	DePuy Spine	Semiconstrained	Fixed	Metal on polymer
Prestige	Medtronic	Unconstrained	Moving	Metal on metal
ProDisc-C	Synthes	Semiconstrained	Fixed	Metal on polymer

lation of the spine. A sliding biconvex ultra-high–molecular-weight polyethylene spacer acts as a mobile core to facilitate the translation motion. The Prestige disk (Medtronic Sofamor Danek, Memphis, TN) allows coupled rotation and translation in the cervical spine through an incongruent interface between a hemispherical ball on the upper component and a shallow ellipsoidal saucer in the lower component. This design feature is intended to mimic the kinematics pattern of the natural disk by allowing the axis of rotation to be dictated by the interaction of the posterior facet joints, surrounding ligaments, and geometry of the implant, thereby reducing impingement and stress concentration at the posterior facets.

The spine motion patterns restored by artificial disks have been investigated using in vivo radiographic evaluation, in vitro cadaver testing, and finite element modeling. Range of motion and IAR are the parameters commonly used to characterize the motion of the FSU after disk replacement; range of motion in each direction is used to quantify the level of mobility, and IARs in different planes of motion are used to describe the kinematic trajectory of the motion. Despite the substantial variation in prosthesis designs, the locations of IARs for flexion-extension motion do not significantly differ; all are within or near the natural physiologic range in the posterior third of the intervertebral space. Most in vivo radiographic investigations have reported preserved or partially preserved range of motion after cervical or lumbar disk arthroplasty.[30,31] Several in vitro studies found an increased range of motion after artificial disk implantation, especially in the cervical disks.[32-34] The results of these studies may reflect the testing conditions and loading protocols (specifically, whether a flexibility or stiffness test was used, with or without a compressive preload).

Studies found that facet loads were increased with both semiconstrained and unconstrained artificial disks.[35,36] The anterior-posterior placement of the artificial disk has less effect on the unconstrained design than on the constrained design. Experimental studies to determine the immediate impact of the artificial disk on the adjacent levels found only marginal changes in adjacent-level intradiskal pressure and range of motion.[32,36-38] Further investigation is needed to determine the long-term clinical effects of these devices on the adjacent levels.

Anterior Motion-Sparing Nucleus Replacement

Nucleus pulposus replacement may be a less invasive alternative to total disk replacement in the lumbar spine. An anterior retroperitoneal, lateral, or posterior surgical approach can be used for insertion. The device is intended to replace the presumed pain generator in patients with mild or moderate degenerative disk disease or to provide a prophylactic postdiskectomy measure in relatively young patients with a large disk herniation.

In addition to restoring anatomic disk height, a nucleus replacement device should mimic the hydrostatic load-bearing function and intradiskal load transmission pattern of the natural nucleus under all physiologic loading conditions. The design challenge is to select materials that ensure mechanical integration with the surrounding anulus fibrosus and end plates. Injectable or preformed hydrogel is the natural choice because of its great water-absorbing capacity. Products made with hydrogel include the Prosthetic Disk Nucleus (Raymedica, Minneapolis, MN), the Hydraflex preformed device (Raymedica), the NeuDisc preformed device (Replication Medical, Cranbury, NJ), and the BioDisc injectable device (Cryolife, Kennesaw, GA). Also available is a product using a polyetheretherketone-on-polyetheretherketone inner articulation (NUBAC; Pioneer Surgical Technology, Driebergen, Netherlands).

None of these nucleus replacement devices has been approved by the US Food and Drug Administration. Multidirectional flexibility testing of some of these devices found that their use restored neutral zone motion and range of motion to the levels of the intact spine.[39-41] The inherently deformable nature of devices made from elastomeric materials means that they tend to have the best shock absorbency as well as the most uniform stress distribution among the surrounding tissues. Devices made from hard materials tend to have the best strength and durability. Because nucleus replacement devices are not anchored to the end plates, the risk of extrusion is high; this is especially true for the preformed devices.

The optimal compressive properties of nucleus replacement devices have been investigated using finite element models.[42,43] Devices with a compressive modulus similar to that of the healthy nucleus pulposus (1 to 4 MPa) convert axial stresses to greater radial and circumferential stresses to promote load sharing from the anulus fibrosus. However, this conversion may not be a desirable outcome of nucleus replacement, as the patient may have preexisting degenerative changes of the anulus fibrosus. Devices with an extremely high compressive modulus reduce the stress within the anulus fibrosus but impose greater stress at the end plate contacts, thereby creating a risk of device subsidence.

Posterior Motion-Sparing Facet Replacement

Paired facet joints provide the posterior articulations of a three-joint FSU. The bony lumbar facets have a major role in resisting the shear forces resulting from axial rotation and extension. In flexion, the motion segment is stabilized by the tension that develops in the facet joint capsule and posterior ligaments. Facet replacement systems were developed for the same reasons as total disk arthroplasty systems: to preserve motion, improve the characteristics of load-sharing between spine elements, and reduce the risk of adjacent-segment effects. The functional goal of a facet arthroplasty prosthesis is to restore posterior segmental stability while preserving anatomic or near-anatomic motion characteristics at the spine segment. A prosthesis is more challenging to design for facet joint arthroplasty than for disk arthroplasty because of the facet joint's small articular surfaces, multidirectional joint movement, large transmitted loads, and small device-anchoring points.

The primary indication for facet replacement is the need to treat or prevent iatrogenic instability after surgical decompression involving complete facetectomy. In a patient with significant facet arthritis, disk replacement alone may not be effective in relieving pain, and a facet prosthesis has the potential for augmenting a total disk replacement to form a circumferential motion reconstruction.

Preliminary in vitro biomechanical studies of some of the available facet replacement systems found that implantation restores a normal or near-normal range of spine motion at the surgical and adjacent levels.[44-47] Further research is needed to complete an in-depth evaluation of the load-sharing behavior of the prosthesis and its possible failure mechanisms.

Posterior Motion-Sparing Pedicle-Based Devices

Pedicle-based dynamic stabilization devices such as the Dynesys (Zimmer, Bordeaux, France) and AccuFlex (Globus Medical, Audubon, PA) systems are intended to improve the load-sharing characteristics of the posterior spine segment while preserving some spine motion to avoid the sequelae of rigid spine fixation. Both of these systems have been approved by the US Food and Drug Administration. Decompression of the lateral recess by distraction is followed by stabilization of the motion segment. These devices have been used in an attempt to reduce postoperative instability after partial or complete laminectomy for spinal stenosis, and they also can act as a load-sharing device to reduce the forces on the affected intervertebral disk and reduce discogenic pain. When a posterior dynamic stabilization device is used to augment an interbody fusion, it acts as a posterior tension band to increase the amount of force transmitted through the interbody graft. The long-term viability of these constructs in an unfused spine is unclear.

Summary

The spinal column is a complex multiarticulation construct that enables motion in six degrees of freedom while maintaining spine stability. Understanding the biomechanics of the spinal construct in its normal, healthy state is essential to understanding how each component contributes to the overall function of the spine and how degenerative or other pathologic changes in one component affect the load-sharing behavior of the other components and, thus, the stability and mobility of the entire spinal column. Experimental analysis and validated computational modeling are well-established tools for spine biomechanical investigation. Both have an important role in the design and development of new devices and procedures for managing spine diseases through a fusion or motion-preservation approach.

Annotated References

1. Li G, Wang S, Passias P, Xia Q, Li G, Wood K: Segmental in vivo vertebral motion during functional human lumbar spine activities. *Eur Spine J* 2009;18(7):1013-1021.

   In vivo vertebral motion in six degrees of freedom was measured during unrestricted weight-bearing functional body activities, using a combined MRI and dual fluoroscopic imaging technique.

2. Callaghan JP, Patla AE, McGill SM: Low back three-dimensional joint forces, kinematics, and kinetics during walking. *Clin Biomech (Bristol, Avon)* 1999;14(3):203-216.

3. Marras WS, Knapik GG, Ferguson S: Loading along the lumbar spine as influence by speed, control, load magnitude, and handle height during pushing. *Clin Biomech (Bristol, Avon)* 2009;24(2):155-163.

   Compression, anterior-posterior, and lateral shears acting on the lumbar spine were assessed during pushing and pulling tasks, using a biologically assisted biomechanical model.

4. Nachemson A: The load on lumbar disks in different positions of the body. *Clin Orthop Relat Res* 1966;45:107-122.

5. Wilke HJ, Neef P, Caimi M, Hoogland T, Claes LE: New in vivo measurements of pressures in the intervertebral disc in daily life. *Spine (Phila Pa 1976)* 1999;24(8):755-762.

6. Sato K, Kikuchi S, Yonezawa T: In vivo intradiscal pressure measurement in healthy individuals and in patients with ongoing back problems. *Spine (Phila Pa 1976)* 1999;24(23):2468-2474.

7. Adams MA, Hutton WC, Stott JR: The resistance to flexion of the lumbar intervertebral joint. *Spine (Phila Pa 1976)* 1980;5(3):245-253.

8. Adams MA, Hutton WC: The mechanical function of the lumbar apophyseal joints. *Spine (Phila Pa 1976)* 1983;8(3):327-330.

9. Ianuzzi A, Khalsa PS: Comparison of human lumbar facet joint capsule strains during simulated high-velocity, low-amplitude spinal manipulation versus physiological motions. *Spine J* 2005;5(3):277-290.

10. Walker MR, Dickey JP: New methodology for multi-dimensional spinal joint testing with a parallel robot. *Med Biol Eng Comput* 2007;45(3):297-304.

    A novel method is presented for spine joint testing using a custom-built parallel robot with hybrid load-position control.

11. Panjabi MM: Hybrid multidirectional test method to evaluate spinal adjacent-level effects. *Clin Biomech (Bristol, Avon)* 2007;22(3):257-265.

    A spine testing method designed for the study of adjacent-level effects is described.

12. Goel VK, Panjabi MM, Patwardhan AG, Dooris AP, Serhan H, American Society for Testing and Materials: Test protocols for evaluation of spinal implants. *J Bone Joint Surg Am* 2006;88(suppl 2):103-109.

    Testing protocols for evaluating implantable spine devices are reviewed, and the need for a standardized test protocol is presented.

13. Hongo M, Gay RE, Zhao KD, et al: Junction kinematics between proximal mobile and distal fused lumbar segments: Biomechanical analysis of pedicle and hook constructs. *Spine J* 2009;9(10):846-853.

    An experimental study compared the effect of three different fusion constructs on adjacent-segment motion proximal to lumbar fusion.

14. Patwardhan AG, Havey RM, Meade KP, Lee B, Dunlap B: A follower load increases the load-carrying capacity of the lumbar spine in compression. *Spine (Phila Pa 1976)* 1999;24(10):1003-1009.

15. Rohlmann A, Zander T, Rao M, Bergmann G: Applying a follower load delivers realistic results for simulating standing. *J Biomech* 2009;42(10):1520-1526.

    A finite element study compared in vivo data to the loading modes commonly used in experimental and numerical investigations of the lumbar spine.

16. Kettler A, Liakos L, Haegele B, Wilke HJ: Are the spines of calf, pig and sheep suitable models for pre-clinical implant tests? *Eur Spine J* 2007;16(12):2186-2192.

    The use of calf, pig, or sheep spine specimens was investigated as an alternative to human cadaver specimens in experimental studies.

17. Easley NE, Wang M, McGrady LM, Toth JM: Biomechanical and radiographic evaluation of an ovine model for the human lumbar spine. *Proc Inst Mech Eng H* 2008;222(6):915-922.

    The essential biomechanical behaviors and disk morphology of the ovine lumbar model is compared to those of the human spine.

18. Wilke HJ, Krischak S, Claes L: Biomechanical comparison of calf and human spines. *J Orthop Res* 1996;14(3):500-503.

19. Smit TH: The use of a quadruped as an in vivo model for the study of the spine: Biomechanical considerations. *Eur Spine J* 2002;11(2):137-144.

20. Rao RD, Bagaria VB, Cooley BC: Posterolateral intertransverse lumbar fusion in a mouse model: Surgical anatomy and operative technique. *Spine J* 2007;7(1):61-67.

    A mouse model was developed for biologic evaluation of posterolateral spine fusion.

21. O'Reilly MA, Whyne CM: Comparison of computed tomography based parametric and patient-specific finite element models of the healthy and metastatic spine using a mesh-morphing algorithm. *Spine (Phila Pa 1976)* 2008;33(17):1876-1881.

    A patient-specific finite element model of spine motion segments uses mesh-morphing methods applied to a parametric finite element model.

22. Chow DH, Luk KD, Evans JH, Leong JC: Effects of short anterior lumbar interbody fusion on biomechanics of neighboring unfused segments. *Spine (Phila Pa 1976)* 1996;21(5):549-555.

1: Basic Science of the Spine

23. Esses SI, Doherty BJ, Crawford MJ, Dreyzin V: Kinematic evaluation of lumbar fusion techniques. *Spine (Phila Pa 1976)* 1996;21(6):676-684.

24. Cunningham BW, Kotani Y, McNulty PS, Cappuccino A, McAfee PC: The effect of spinal destabilization and instrumentation on lumbar intradiscal pressure: an in vitro biomechanical analysis. *Spine (Phila Pa 1976)* 1997;22(22):2655-2663.

25. Weinhoffer SL, Guyer RD, Herbert M, Griffith SL: Intradiscal pressure measurements above an instrumented fusion: A cadaveric study. *Spine (Phila Pa 1976)* 1995; 20(5):526-531.

26. Rao RD, Wang M, McGrady LM, Perlewitz TJ, David KS: Does anterior plating of the cervical spine predispose to adjacent segment changes? *Spine (Phila Pa 1976)* 2005;30(24):2788-2793.

27. Fuller DA, Kirkpatrick JS, Emery SE, Wilber RG, Davy DT: A kinematic study of the cervical spine before and after segmental arthrodesis. *Spine (Phila Pa 1976)* 1998; 23(15):1649-1656.

28. Eck JC, Humphreys SC, Hodges SD: Adjacent-segment degeneration after lumbar fusion: A review of clinical, biomechanical, and radiologic studies. *Am J Orthop (Belle Mead NJ)* 1999;28(6):336-340.

29. Pospiech J, Stolke D, Wilke HJ, Claes LE: Intradiscal pressure recordings in the cervical spine. *Neurosurgery* 1999;44(2):379-384.

30. Nabhan A, Ahlhelm F, Shariat K, et al: The ProDisc-C prosthesis: Clinical and radiological experience 1 year after surgery. *Spine (Phila Pa 1976)* 2007;32(18):1935-1941.

   A prospective randomized study analyzed segmental motion during the first year after disk replacement using a disk prosthesis.

31. McAfee PC, Cunningham B, Holsapple G, et al: A prospective, randomized, multicenter Food and Drug Administration investigational device exemption study of lumbar total disc replacement with the CHARITE artificial disc versus lumbar fusion: Part II. Evaluation of radiographic outcomes and correlation of surgical technique accuracy with clinical outcomes. *Spine (Phila Pa 1976)* 2005;30(14):1576-1583.

   A prospective, randomized, multicenter study compared the safety and effectiveness of treating single-level degenerative disk disease with anterior lumbar interbody fusion or with total disk replacement using the Charité artificial disk.

32. Chang UK, Kim DH, Lee MC, Willenberg R, Kim SH, Lim J: Range of motion change after cervical arthroplasty with ProDisc-C and Prestige artificial discs compared with anterior cervical discectomy and fusion. *J Neurosurg Spine* 2007;7(1):40-46.

   In vitro changes in range of motion occurred at the replaced and adjacent segments after implantation of two cervical artificial disks.

33. Goel VK, Grauer JN, Patel TCh, et al: Effects of Charité artificial disc on the implanted and adjacent spinal segments mechanics using a hybrid testing protocol. *Spine (Phila Pa 1976)* 2005;30(24):2755-2764.

   A finite element study determined the effects of the Charité artificial disk on the replaced and adjacent segments.

34. O'Leary P, Nicolakis M, Lorenz MA, et al: Response of Charité total disc replacement under physiologic loads: Prosthesis component motion patterns. *Spine J* 2005; 5(6):590-599.

   An in vitro study determined the effects of the Charité total disk replacement on the mechanical behaviors of a lumbar motion segment.

35. Rousseau MA, Bradford DS, Bertagnoli R, Hu SS, Lotz JC: Disc arthroplasty design influences intervertebral kinematics and facet forces. *Spine J* 2006;6(3):258-266.

   A cadaver study determined the kinematic and load transfer modifications at L5-S1 after total disk replacement using the ProDisc or Charité prosthesis.

36. Chang UK, Kim DH, Lee MC, Willenberg R, Kim SH, Lim J: Changes in adjacent-level disc pressure and facet joint force after cervical arthroplasty compared with cervical discectomy and fusion. *J Neurosurg Spine* 2007;7(1):33-39.

   In vitro adjacent-level intradiskal pressure and facet force after arthroplasty are compared with the fusion model.

37. Demetropoulos CK, Sengupta DK, Knaub MA, et al: Biomechanical evaluation of the kinematics of the cadaver lumbar spine following disc replacement with the ProDisc-L prosthesis. *Spine (Phila Pa 1976)* 2010;35(1): 26-31.

   A cadaver study determined the effects of total disk replacement using the ProDisc-L on the kinematic properties of a motion segment and the adjacent level.

38. Ingalhalikar AV, Reddy CG, Lim TH, Torner JC, Hitchon PW: Effect of lumbar total disc arthroplasty on the segmental motion and intradiscal pressure at the adjacent level: An in vitro biomechanical study. *J Neurosurg Spine* 2009;11(6):715-723.

   A cadaver study compared motion and intradiskal pressure at the surgical and adjacent levels after implantation of a ball-and-socket artificial disk.

39. Tsantrizos A, Ordway NR, Myint K, Martx E, Yuan HA: Mechanical and biomechanical characterization of a polyurethane nucleus replacement device injected and cured in situ within a balloon. *SAS J* 2008;2:28-39.

   A series of preclinical mechanical bench and biomechanical tests assessed the effectiveness of the DASCOR nucleus replacement device.

40. Bao Q, Songer M, Pimenta L, et al: Nubac disc arthroplasty: Preclinical studies and preliminary safety and efficacy evaluations. *SAS J* 2007;1:36-45.

   A series of preclinical studies assessed the safety and effectiveness of the NUBAC nucleus replacement device.

41. Kettler A, Kaps HP, Haegele B, Wilke HJ: Biomechanical behavior of a new nucleus prosthesis made of knitted titanium filaments. *SAS J* 2007;1:125-130.

   An in vitro biomechanical assessment of a new nucleus prosthesis made of knitted titanium filaments is presented.

42. Meakin JR: Replacing the nucleus pulposus of the intervertebral disk: Prediction of suitable properties of a replacement material using finite element analysis. *J Mater Sci Mater Med* 2001;12(3):207-213.

43. Rundell SA, Guerin HL, Auerbach JD, Kurtz SM: Effect of nucleus replacement device properties on lumbar spine mechanics. *Spine (Phila Pa 1976)* 2009;34(19):2022-2032.

   A finite element study assessed the ideal material properties of nucleus replacement devices for a single lumbar motion segment.

44. Phillips FM, Tzermiadianos MN, Voronov LI, et al: Effect of the Total Facet Arthroplasty System after complete laminectomy-facetectomy on the biomechanics of implanted and adjacent segments. *Spine J* 2009;9(1):96-102.

   An in vitro biomechanical study determined the effect of a facet replacement device on the kinematics of the operative and adjacent lumbar segments.

45. Wilke HJ, Schmidt H, Werner K, Schmölz W, Drumm J: Biomechanical evaluation of a new total posterior-element replacement system. *Spine (Phila Pa 1976)* 2006;31(24):2790-2797.

   An in vitro biomechanical study assessed the ability of a facet replacement device to restore the physiologic motion of the spine.

46. Zhu Q, Larson CR, Sjovold SG, et al: Biomechanical evaluation of the Total Facet Arthroplasty System: 3-dimensional kinematics. *Spine (Phila Pa 1976)* 2007;32(1):55-62.

   An in vitro biomechanical study assessed the three-dimensional kinematics of the lumbar spine after facet arthroplasty using a facet replacement device.

47. Goel VK, Mehta A, Jangra J, et al: Anatomic facet replacement system (AFRS) restoration of lumbar segment mechanics to intact: A finite element study and in vitro cadaver investigation. *SAS J* 2007;1:46-54.

   An in vitro study and finite element analysis compared the biomechanical effects of a facet replacement device to the intact spine.

Chapter 3

The Pathophysiology of Axial Neck and Low Back Pain

James D. Kang, MD   Gwendolyn Sowa, MD, PhD   Barrett I. Woods, MD

Introduction

Axial neck pain and low back pain are common, but even the most experienced physician can find these conditions difficult to diagnose and treat. Degenerative changes in the cervical or lumbar spine motion segments cannot be arbitrarily identified as the source of the pain. The anatomy and pathophysiology of axial neck pain and low back pain must be understood. The distinction between acute and chronic pain has significant implications for the patient's response to treatment.

Axial Neck Pain

The neuroanatomy of the cervical spine is important in clinical practice because the muscles, joints, disks, and ligaments of the neck are innervated and thus can be sources of pain (Figure 1). The cervical spine consists of seven vertebral bodies. Below the occipital-atlantoaxial articulation, the cervical vertebrae are interposed with intervertebral disks that disperse compressive forces and protect the posterior elements from excessive tensional stress. The intervertebral disk, and specifically its anulus fibrosus, is innervated by the sinuvertebral nerve, which is formed by contributions from the ventral nerve root and sympathetic plexus.[1] The sinuvertebral nerve also innervates the posterior longitudinal ligament, epidural vasculature, adjacent periosteum of the posterior vertebral body, and medial aspect of the atlantoaxial joint. The posterior neck muscles and cervical zygapophyseal joints are primarily innervated by the cervical dorsal rami. The lateral atlanto-occipital and atlantoaxial joints are supplied by the C1 and C2 ventral rami, respectively. The prevertebral and lateral vertebral muscles are innervated by the ventral rami.[1] The vertebral nerve is composed of branches from the

Dr. Kang or an immediate family member has received research or institutional support from DePuy, a Johnson & Johnson company; and Advanced Technologies and Regenerative Medicine. Neither of the following authors nor any immediate family member has received anything of value from or owns stock in a commercial company or institution related directly or indirectly to the subject of this chapter: Dr. Sowa, Dr. Woods.

cervical gray rami communicans; this nerve provides sensory innervation to the vertebral artery.

Innervation alone does not determine the potential of a structure to generate pain; physiologic capability also is required. Physiologic potential was elucidated by several studies in which pain was caused by administering noxious stimuli or relieved by administering anesthesia to a painful site. Somatic referred pain was first identified more than 50 years ago in classic experiments in which the posterior paravertebral musculature and spine ligaments were injected with saline, and segmental areas of referred pain were mapped.[2,3] Segmental referred pain was produced because of the convergence of nociceptive afferents from target tissues with afferents from distal sites on second-order neurons in the spinal cord. Multiple studies have confirmed that zygapophyseal joints also can cause neck pain and referred somatic pain,[4,5] and a meta-analysis confirmed that anesthetic intra-articular zygapophyseal joint injections and medial branch blocks are useful for identifying the source of chronic neck pain in some patients.[6] These studies have established that noxious stimulation of cervical zygapophyseal joints results in relatively reproducible segmental patterns of referred pain. Similar reproducible segmental patterns have been found by stimulating the cervical intervertebral disk.[7] Therefore it can be concluded that innervation, rather than anatomic structure, dictates the pattern of cervical referred pain (Figure 2).

The distribution of pain can serve as a guide to its source. However, discogenic and zygapophyseal pain are clinically indistinguishable. Suboccipital pain can originate in several structures in the upper cervical spine, including the atlanto-occipital and lateral atlanto-axial joints. As with pain referred from posterior structures, the source of referred suboccipital pain cannot be distinguished clinically; however, the location allows the clinician to focus on a segmental location, namely, the upper cervical spine.

Identifying the segmental origin of pain can be helpful in evaluating axial neck pain. Successfully treating the pain can be challenging because the pain may have multiple sources, including the muscles, ligaments, intervertebral disks, dura, and vertebral artery. Treatment may be confounded by chronic pain or a psychosocial

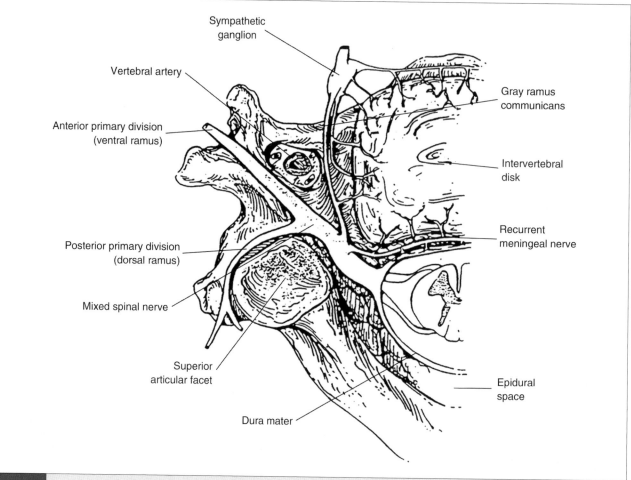

Sympathetic
ganglion

Vertebral artery

Anterior primary division
(ventral ramus)

Gray ramus
communicans

Intervertebral
disk

Posterior primary division
(dorsal ramus)

Recurrent
meningeal nerve

Mixed spinal nerve

Superior
articular facet

Dura mater

Epidural
space

Figure 1 Schematic drawing showing a cross section of the cervical spine, with an exiting cervical nerve root and the recurrent meningeal or sinuvertebral nerve formed by branches of the ventral rami and sympathetic plexus. It is important to consider the proximity of the nerves to the disk space, facet, and uncovertebral joint. (Adapted with permission from Cramer GD, Darby SA, Huff TG, et al: *Basic and Clinical Anatomy of the Spine, Spinal Cord, and ANS*, ed 2. St. Louis, MO, Elsevier Mosby, 2005.)

condition. Some well-established conditions must be ruled out when evaluating a patient with isolated axial neck pain. An understanding of the possible causes of neck pain, as outlined in Table 1, can allow the clinician to quickly narrow the range of diagnoses.

Life-threatening causes of neck pain are rare but initially may be overlooked. Patients with vertebral or carotid artery dissection usually have a headache, and 50% to 90% of patients were found to have neck pain; neck pain was the sole symptom in 6% of patients.[8] Neck pain is rarely reported with a dissecting aortic aneurysm. Tumor and infection should be ruled out through a detailed history, a physical examination, and radiographic studies.

Causes of pain that are not life threatening should be ruled out. Polymyalgia rheumatica and fibromyalgia are systemic conditions that can cause neck pain, although neck pain rarely is the initial symptom. Longus colli tendinitis or retropharyngeal tendinitis causes upper muscle inflammation from C1 to C4 and occasion-

ally to C6, and it may result in anterior neck pain. These conditions can be diagnosed with MRI, which reveals inflammation and edema of the tendinous junction or muscle belly of the longus colli. Conditions such as diffuse idiopathic skeletal hyperostosis and ossification of the posterior longitudinal ligament often are asymptomatic but can be readily identified radiographically. Often the initial symptom of ossification of the posterior longitudinal ligament is myelopathy rather than axial neck pain. Osteoarthritis of the cervical spine is the most common diagnosis related to axial neck pain in patients with radiographic evidence of degenerative change. Although degeneration of the cervical spine occurs with age, almost all patients who are older than 65 years and have radiographic evidence of degeneration are asymptomatic.[9] Degenerative changes of the cervical spine probably result from multiple factors, including aging, and thus should not be assumed to be the source of pain, especially in patients older than 65 years.

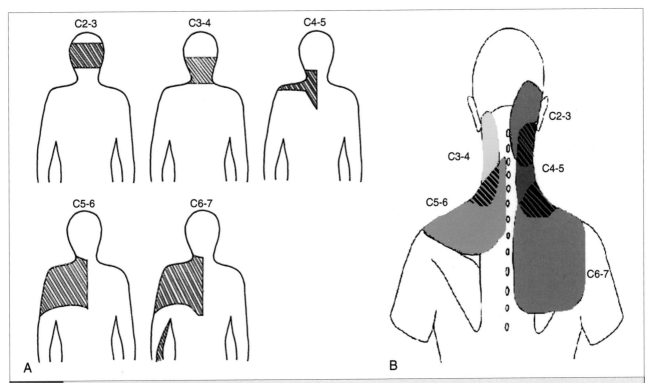

Figure 2 **A,** Schematic drawings showing diskographic patterns of axial neck pain, as provoked by noxious stimulation of C2-3, C3-4, C4-5, C5-6, and C6-7. **B,** Schematic drawing showing a composite of axial pain patterns produced by injection into the cervical facet joints. Similar segmental patterns of referred pain result from noxious stimulation of a cervical intervertebral disk and the corresponding facet joint, suggesting that innervation, rather than structure, dictates the distribution of pain. (Adapted with permission from Dwyer A, Aprill C, Bogduk N: Cervical zygapophyseal joint pain patterns: I. A study in normal volunteers. *Spine [Phila Pa 1976]* 1990;15[6]:453-457; and Grubb SA, Kelly CK: Cervical discography: Clinical implications from 12 years of experience. *Spine [Phila Pa 1976]* 2000;25[11]:1382-1389.)

Low Back Pain

The Lumbar Spine

Most low back pain is transient and likely to improve spontaneously, without intervention. Low back pain has multiple etiologies, the most common of which are musculoligamentous. The segmental patterns of referred pain are less well defined in the lumbar spine than in the cervical spine, probably because of the diffuse innervation patterns of the intervertebral disk and posterior elements of the spine.[10] The intervertebral disk has been identified as one possible source of low back pain.[11] Discogenic back pain has nonspecific symptoms and is difficult to distinguish clinically from low back pain having another etiology. The diagnosis has important treatment implications, however. The bony vibration test has been proposed for distinguishing discogenic low back pain from other types of low back pain,[12] but this test has low sensitivity and specificity. Physical examination alone has limited clinical utility for diagnosing of discogenic low back pain.[13] Diagnostic provocative injections into the disk can help determine whether the disk is the primary pain source.

It was initially thought that nociceptive stimuli were transmitted cephalad directly from a lumbar interverte-bral disk through the ventral rami into the corresponding spinal nerve. Current evidence suggests that afferent fibers from the intervertebral disk are transmitted through the sinuvertebral nerve entering the neuroaxis via the L1-2 dorsal root ganglia before entering the cord. Discogenic pain appears to be referred to the groin partly because this path also is the route by which afferent input from the skin around the groin enters the neuroaxis. Selective anesthetic injection of the L1-2 dorsal root ganglion has had mixed results, and its usefulness for treating discogenic low back pain has yet to be determined.[14,15]

Degenerative changes in the lumbar spine, like those in the cervical spine, are ubiquitous and often are not correlated with symptoms. The presence or severity of lumbar stenosis on MRI is not correlated with the patient's subjective experience of pain.[16] The correlation between radiographic findings and lumbosacral radicular symptoms is similarly poor.[17]

Mechanoreceptors

Mechanoreceptors are important in monitoring joint position and movement, and they may have a role in back pain. These receptors function synergistically with dynamic stabilizers to sense the normal physiologic range

Table 1

Causes of Neck Pain

Infectious
Diskitis
Meningitis
Osteomyelitis
Septic arthritis

Inflammatory
Ankylosing spondylitis
Crystal arthropathies
Diskitis
Longus colli tendinitis
Polymyalgia rheumatica
Rheumatoid arthritis

Musculoskeletal
Cervical sprain
Diffuse idiopathic skeletal hyperostosis
Fracture
Osteoarthritis
Soft-tissue injury
Sternocleidomastoid tendinitis
Torticollis
Whiplash

Neurologic
Fibromyalgia
Myelopathy
Myofascial pain
Nerve injury
Radiculopathy
Spinal cord tumor
Thoracic outlet syndrome

Vascular
Aortic dissection
Carotid artery dissection
Vertebral artery dissection

Adapted with permission from Hardin JG, Halla JT: Cervical spine and radicular pain syndromes. *Curr Opin Rheumatol* 1995;7(2):136-140; and Bogduk N: The anatomy and pathophysiology of neck pain. *Phys Med Rehabil Clin N Am* 2003;14(3):455-472.

of motion and initiate protective muscular reflexes when its limits are reached. The four types of mechanoreceptors were first described in articular cartilage;[18] they are classified based on their response to stimuli, morphology, and function, as outlined in Table 2.

Neuroanatomic, physiologic, and biomechanical studies have identified the mechanoreceptors in the facet joints, intervertebral disks, and ligamentous tissue of the spine.[19] Type IV receptors (free nerve endings) probably have the most important role in nociceptive transmission, although type III receptors also have been implicated. Animal studies of arthritis found that chemical or mechanical sensitization of the fibers in afferent receptors (types III and IV) results in the production of noxious responses to a previously innocuous stimulus such normal range of motion.[20] Patients with chronic back pain were found to have more mechanoreceptors in the lumbar disks; type I, II, and III mechanoreceptors were more common in patients with low back pain than in patients with pain-free scoliosis.[21]

The Dorsal Root Ganglion

The dorsal root ganglion is a key neuroanatomic structure related to afferent input and pain production. The dorsal root ganglion processes sensory information and releases chemical mediators that affect sensation and pain and serve as a link between the physical environment and the perception of afferent stimuli. Each dorsal root ganglion is located on the dorsal root of a spinal nerve; its location varies with respect to the spinal canal and intervertebral foramen. The endoneurial capillaries of the dorsal root ganglion, unlike those of a peripheral nerve, lack a diffusion barrier and are fenestrated. As a result, the microvasculature of a dorsal root ganglion is more permeable than that of a peripheral nerve. This permeability is useful in normal physiologic function but means that the dorsal root ganglion is more susceptible to edema in the face of mechanical compression or vibration.

The dorsal root ganglion was identified as a possible modulator of low back pain more than 60 years ago, when it was observed to be compressed and internally damaged by degenerative processes such as facet arthrosis and dorsolateral disk herniation. The dorsal root ganglion clearly is implicated in some forms of back pain, although its role is not completely understood. The prevailing belief is that the dorsal root ganglion, like the mechanoreceptors, can be sensitized by mechanical or chemical stimuli; the results are prolonged neural discharges and exacerbation of afferent stimuli such as pain. The dorsal root ganglion synthesizes several neuropeptides, including substance P and calcitonin gene-related peptide, which are believed to be transmitters of nociceptive information. When animal models were exposed to whole body vibration, alterations were observed in the concentrations of these neuropeptides and the morphology of the dorsal root ganglion itself.[22] Vibration exposure has been linked to the development of back pain, although the exact mechanism has not been clearly elucidated. Although the dorsal root ganglion certainly has a role in the development and perception of pain, its exact role and the therapeutic implications are yet to be determined.

The Chemical Mediators of Spine Pain

Inflammatory cascade and chemical mediators are believed to be important in pain generation, and specifically in the development of chronic back pain. Neuro-

Table 2

The Classification of Mechanoreceptors

Type	Rate of Adaptation	Threshold	Influence on Muscle Tone	Dynamic/Static
I (Ruffini)	Slow	Low	Continuous	Dynamic and static
II (Pacinian)	Fast	Low	Brief, reflex	Dynamic
III (Golgi tendon)	Slow	High	Reflex	Dynamic
IV (Free nerve endings)	Nonadapting	None	None	None

Adapted with permission from Freeman MA, Wyke B: The innervation of the knee joint: An anatomical and histological study in the cat. *J Anat* 1967;101(pt 3):505-532.

genic chemical mediators of pain released from the cell bodies of sensory neurons and nonneurogenic mediators released from disk tissue may have a role in initiating and perpetuating inflammation and the pain response (Table 3). There is a clear but incompletely understood relationship among degeneration, annular disruption, and the presence of discogenic pain. As degeneration occurs, morphologic alterations to the disk and the catabolic processes intensify. Cytokines including interleukin-6, interleukin-8, nitric oxide, and tumor necrosis factor-α are secreted by annular cells and modulated in the presence of macrophages.[23] The role of nitric oxide in the pain response is not clearly delineated, although persistent activation of nociceptors activates nitric oxide synthases, thereby increasing the levels of nitric oxide. Patients with chronic pain have elevated levels of nitric oxide.[24] Interleukin-6 is thought to be a major cause of neurogenic pain.[25] Interleukin-8 is a chemoattractant for lymphocytes and a potent angiogenic factor that may have a role in neurovascularization of the disk and pain production.[26] Annular cells secrete prostaglandin E₂, which may potentiate inflammation and, when present in great quantity, may lead to increasingly severe osteoarthritis symptoms.[27]

Macrophages probably have a key role in the inflammatory response observed with annular repair or the development of chronic discogenic pain. Macrophages promote reabsorption of diseased or herniated disk tissue through the secretion of growth factors and cytokines. These proinflammatory cells are abundant in painful disk tissues but are not present in normal disk tissue from an asymptomatic host.[28] Histamine, prostaglandin E₂, bradykinin, and serotonin can act as nonneurogenic mediators of pain by exacerbating the inflammatory response and sensitizing nociceptive nerve fibers. This process leads to the release of neuropeptides such as substance P that evoke pain when they are centrally transported.

Neurogenic fibers positive for mediators such as substance P, calcitonin gene-related peptide, somatostatin, and neuropeptide Y are implicated in nociceptive transmission and chronic cervical and lumbar pain. Substance P and calcitonin gene-related peptide have been extensively studied and are believed to be the no-

Table 3

Chemical Mediators of Spine Pain

Nonneurogenic
Acetylcholine
Adenosine triphosphate
Bradykinin
Dihydroxyeicosatetraenoic acid
Histamine
Interleukin-6
Interleukin-8
Leukotrienes
Prostaglandin E₂
Serotonin
Tumor necrosis factor-α
Neurogenic
Angiotensin II
Calcitonin gene-related peptide
Cholecystokinin-like substance
Dynorphin
Enkephalin
Gastrin-releasing peptide
Galanin
Neuropeptide Y
Neurotensin
Somatostatin
Substance P
Vasoactive intestinal peptide

ciceptive mediators found in dorsal root ganglion neurons. The presence of substance P and calcitonin gene-related peptide in patients with pain in the lumbar disks, zygapophyseal joints, and surrounding ligaments suggests that neurogenic mediators may serve as the link between painful spine structures, the dorsal root

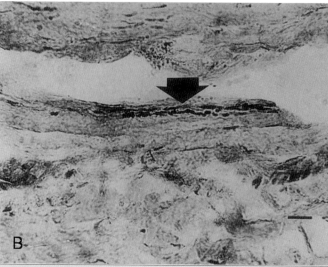

Figure 3 Immunostaining of normal disk tissue (*arrows*) for substance P antibody (**A**) and protein gene product 9.5 (**B**) in the anulus fibrosus of a normal disk. Protein gene product 9.5 is used as a general marker for neurons. The peripheral aspect of the disk is innervated in asymptomatic patients, and a pathologic pain syndrome may result from neovascularization with nerves extending centrally into the disk. (Reproduced with permission from Palmgren T, Grönblad M, Virri J, Kääpä E, Karaharju E: An immunohistochemical study of nerve structures in the anulus fibrosus of human normal lumbar intervertebral discs. *Spine [Phila Pa 1976]* 1999;24[20]:2075-2079.)

ganglion, and chronic pain. Several human and animal studies have identified substance P and calcitonin gene-related peptide nerve fibers in disks, end plates, and facet joints.[21] Stimulation of these tissues altered the concentrations of neuropeptides such as substance P and vasoactive intestinal peptide found in the disk and the dorsal root ganglion.[29] The increasing concentration of nociceptive transmitters in stimulated tissue is one possible means by which discogenic pain is elicited during mechanical stimulation.

The intricate pathways of the inflammatory cascade are not completely understood, but their role in pain production has been documented. The same is true of the transmission of nociceptive stimuli through neurogenic conduction and chemical mediation. An improved understanding of transport methods, pathway signaling, and pain receptor sensitization is paramount for developing new strategies to treat discogenic and chronic back pain syndromes.

Disk Tissue Neovascularization

The structure and morphology of the intervertebral disk changes significantly with age. The immature disk has a relatively dense perivascular network, with adjacent free nerve endings found in the peripheral layers of the anulus fibrosus. This perivascular network recedes during normal aging, and by early adulthood the disk is largely avascular, relying on the peripheral end plates for nutrition and removal of metabolic by-products[30] (Figure 3).

Neovascularization of the peripheral disk, with ingrowth of blood vessels and sensory nerves, is an important feature of a degenerated disk, and it appears to be associated with pain.[21,31] This neovascularization initially was observed in herniated disks, in which radial cracks in the anulus fibrosus had significant capillary ingrowth that was believed to help reabsorb the herniated nucleus pulposus tissue.[32,33] The process may be facilitated by macrophages, which respond to annular injury by secreting powerful growth factors and cytokines.[34] Interleukin-8, which has potent angiogenic properties in other diseases, is increased in the presence of annular injury and macrophages.[23] The newly formed microvessels release neurotrophic growth factors such as nerve growth factor, thus allowing the ingrowth of small, nonmyelinated nerve fibers that extend centrally into the disk.[35] Nerve growth factor also may help sensitize these nerve endings, exacerbating the pain response.[36]

The degenerated disk loses its ability to disperse compressive loads to the peripheral end plates, thus exposing the anulus fibrosus to excessive torsional stresses and predisposing it to mechanical failure. Macrophages respond robustly to anular injury and may be the key to initiating the inflammatory cascade and neovascularization. Discogenic pain may arise because these nociceptive nerve fibers grow centrally into previously aneural areas of the disk. These nerve endings can be sensitized by generation of excessive mechanical forces or by chemical mediators of pain and inflammation, which make normal spine motion painful.

Chronic Back Pain

Chronic pain is complex and often has a multifactorial etiology. Although chronic pain syndromes, specifically chronic back pain, are increasingly well recognized, their pathogenic mechanisms are poorly understood. The transition from acute to chronic back pain may be attributable to increased activity of afferent nociceptive fibers, which results in abnormal central pain processing in the plastic human brain.[37] After a transient insult, primary afferent nociceptors become hyperresponsive to even mild stimuli, resulting in continued pain perception. This hyperalgesic priming or sensitization of nociceptive fibers appears to be critical to the development of chronic pain.

Investigation into the mechanism of receptor priming and development of chronic pain has revealed alterations in intracellular signaling pathways.[38] Mechanical hyperalgesia induced by local cytokines usually is mediated by activation of adenylyl cyclase, cyclic adenosine monophosphate, and protein kinase A, and thus is attenuated by protein kinase A antagonists.[39] This pathway is altered after sensitization, however, when hyperalgesia is no longer attenuated by protein kinase A antagonists but instead is inhibited by the epsilon isoform of protein kinase C. Protein kinase C also appears to have a role in maintaining nociceptive fiber hypersensitivity. In rats, the expression of protein kinase C was decreased by using antisense oligodeoxynucleotide after priming, leading to a reduction in the response to cytokine-induced mechanical hyperalgesia.[40] When these cellular pathways are altered peripherally, the resulting abnormal afferent activity may trigger changes in the central nervous system, resulting in central sensitization.

Chronic back pain has been associated with morphologic alterations in areas of the brain known to play a critical role in pain perception, including the cingulate cortex and thalamocortical processes.[41] In animal models, hyperalgesia was enhanced by stress. Rats had an exacerbated response to mechanical hyperalgesia after receiving local injections of prostaglandin and epinephrine followed by exposure to stressful, nonhabituating sound.[42,43] The altered response to normal mechanical stimuli involved a change in the receptors' G protein coupling (G_s to G_i) and increasing dependence on protein kinase C.[44,45] The reasons some people develop chronic pain and the involved genetic factors remain to be determined. Psychosocial factors such as depression and workers' compensation claims appear to have a significant role in the development of chronic pain.[46,47] Many discoveries remain to be made in the area of chronic pain and its development.

Summary

Determining the etiology of axial neck pain or low back pain requires a detailed understanding of the pa-

tient's symptoms, anatomy, physiology, and psychosocial factors. Spine degeneration is radiographically ubiquitous, especially in patients older than 65 years, and cannot be assumed to be the source of pain. Chemical mediators of pain, their signaling pathways, and the sensitization of nociceptive receptors appear to be crucial in the development of pathologic and chronic back pain. Further investigation into these pathways and their signaling may lead to treatments that prevent pain perception by blunting inflammation, preventing sensitization, and ultimately blocking the transmission of nociceptive information. The identification of psychosocial stressors and risk factors also is likely to dramatically affect the course and treatment of painful spine disorders.

Annotated References

1. Bogduk N, Windsor M, Inglis A: The innervation of the cervical intervertebral discs. *Spine (Phila Pa 1976)* 1988;13(1):2-8.

2. Feinstein B, Langton JN, Jameson RM, Schiller F: Experiments on pain referred from deep somatic tissues. *J Bone Joint Surg Am* 1954;36(5):981-997.

3. Weisengreen HH, Winters SE: Pathways of referred pain with special reference to head and neck: A neuroanatomic study. *Oral Surg Oral Med Oral Pathol* 1952;5: 500-512.

4. Aprill C, Dwyer A, Bogduk N: Cervical zygapophyseal joint pain patterns: II. A clinical evaluation. *Spine (Phila Pa 1976)* 1990;15(6):458-461.

5. Windsor RE, Nagula D, Storm S, Overton A, Jahnke S: Electrical stimulation induced cervical medial branch referral patterns. *Pain Physician* 2003;6(4):411-418.

6. Sehgal N, Shah RV, McKenzie-Brown AM, Everett CR: Diagnostic utility of facet (zygapophysial) joint injections in chronic spinal pain: A systematic review of evidence. *Pain Physician* 2005;8(2):211-224.

   Clinical studies on the efficacy and usefulness of facet joint or nerve injections in diagnosing spine pain from facet joints are systematically reviewed. Level of evidence: III.

7. Grubb SA, Kelly CK: Cervical discography: Clinical implications from 12 years of experience. *Spine (Phila Pa 1976)* 2000;25(11):1382-1389.

8. Silbert PL, Mokri B, Schievink WI: Headache and neck pain in spontaneous internal carotid and vertebral artery dissections. *Neurology* 1995;45(8):1517-1522.

9. Pfirrmann CW, Metzdorf A, Elfering A, Hodler J, Boos N: Effect of aging and degeneration on disc volume and shape: A quantitative study in asymptomatic volunteers. *J Orthop Res* 2006;24(5):1086-1094.

MRI was used in a quantitative investigation of changes in disk height, volume, and shape as a result of aging and/or degeneration in asymptomatic volunteers. Pathologic (painful) disk alterations were omitted. Level of evidence: II.

10. Zhang Y, Kerns JM, Anderson DG, et al: Sensory neurons and fibers from multiple spinal cord levels innervate the rabbit lumbar disc. *Am J Phys Med Rehabil* 2006;85(11):865-871.

    In a prospective observational study, fluorogold particles were injected into the posterior aspect of the L5-6 disk in rabbits, and gold-positive neurons were later traced in the dorsal root ganglion and spinal cord at different levels. Level of evidence: III.

11. Anderson DG, Tannoury C: Molecular pathogenic factors in symptomatic disc degeneration. *Spine J* 2005; 5(6, suppl):260S-266S.

    The biomechanical and molecular alterations that occur during disk degeneration are outlined.

12. Zhang YG, Guo TM, Guo X, Wu SX: Clinical diagnosis for discogenic low back pain. *Int J Biol Sci* 2009;5(7): 647-658.

    The diagnosis of discogenic low back pain is reviewed.

13. Cohen SP, Larkin TM, Barna SA, Palmer WE, Hecht AC, Stojanovic MP: Lumbar discography: A comprehensive review of outcome studies, diagnostic accuracy, and principles. *Reg Anesth Pain Med* 2005;30(2):163-183.

    This retrospective review of lumbar diskography and diskogenic back pain emphasizes the importance of determining whether diskography is accurate and improves surgical outcomes. Level of evidence: III.

14. Simopoulos TT, Malik AB, Sial KA, Elkersh M, Bajwa ZH: Radiofrequency lesioning of the L2 ramus communicans in managing discogenic low back pain. *Pain Physician* 2005;8(1):61-65.

    Five patients with discogenic back pain who were responsive to an L2 rami block were treated with radiofrequency lesioning of the ramus communicans at the L2 level and had partial relief of pain. Level of evidence: IV.

15. Richardson J, Collinghan N, Scally AJ, Gupta S: Bilateral L1 and L2 dorsal root ganglion blocks for discogenic low-back pain. *Br J Anaesth* 2009;103(3):416-419.

    In a prospective cohort study, 12 patients with discogenic back pain underwent bilateral L1-2 dorsal root ganglion blocks with steroids for treatment of chronic lower back pain. Level of evidence: II.

16. Haig AJ, Tong HC, Yamakawa KS, et al: Spinal stenosis, back pain, or no symptoms at all? A masked study comparing radiologic and electrodiagnostic diagnoses to the clinical impression. *Arch Phys Med Rehabil* 2006; 87(7):897-903.

    A prospective, double-controlled study assessed the relationship between clinical lumbar spinal stenosis and the conclusions of radiologists and electrodiagnosticians. Level of evidence: I.

17. van Rijn JC, Klemetso N, Reitsma JB, et al: Symptomatic and asymptomatic abnormalities in patients with lumbosacral radicular syndrome: Clinical examination compared with MRI. *Clin Neurol Neurosurg* 2006; 108(6):553-557.

    A prospective controlled study determined the frequency of symptomatic and asymptomatic herniated disks and root compression in patients with lumbosacral radicular syndrome. The clinical and MRI findings were correlated. Level of evidence: II.

18. Freeman MA, Wyke B: The innervation of the knee joint: An anatomical and histological study in the cat. *J Anat* 1967;101(pt 3):505-532.

19. Cavanaugh JM, Lu Y, Chen C, Kallakuri S: Pain generation in lumbar and cervical facet joints. *J Bone Joint Surg Am* 2006;88(suppl 2):63-67.

    This review article implicates the facet joints and excessive capsule stretching as sources of pain. Level of evidence: III.

20. Birrell GJ, McQueen DS, Iggo A, Coleman RA, Grubb BD: PGI2-induced activation and sensitization of articular mechanonociceptors. *Neurosci Lett* 1991;124(1): 5-8.

21. Roberts S, Eisenstein SM, Menage J, Evans EH, Ashton IK: Mechanoreceptors in intervertebral discs: Morphology, distribution, and neuropeptides. *Spine (Phila Pa 1976)* 1995;20(24):2645-2651.

22. McLain RF, Weinstein JN: Ultrastructural changes in the dorsal root ganglion associated with whole body vibration. *J Spinal Disord* 1991;4(2):142-148.

23. Kim JH, Studer RK, Sowa GA, Vo NV, Kang JD: Activated macrophage-like THP-1 cells modulate anulus fibrosus cell production of inflammatory mediators in response to cytokines. *Spine (Phila Pa 1976)* 2008;33(21): 2253-2259.

    Anulus fibrosus cells obtained from patients undergoing surgery were cocultured with macrophagelike cells, and production of inflammatory mediators was analyzed by quantitative assay. Level of evidence: II.

24. Koch A, Zacharowski K, Boehm O, et al: Nitric oxide and pro-inflammatory cytokines correlate with pain intensity in chronic pain patients. *Inflamm Res* 2007; 56(1):32-37.

    A prospective cohort study investigated the detectability of a range of cytokines and nitric oxide in the plasma of patients with chronic pain and whether cytokine and nitric oxide levels were correlated with pain severity. Level of evidence: II.

25. Kang JD, Georgescu HI, McIntyre-Larkin L, Stefanovic-Racic M, Donaldson WF III, Evans CH: Herniated lumbar intervertebral discs spontaneously produce matrix metalloproteinases, nitric oxide, interleukin-6, and pros-

taglandin E2. *Spine (Phila Pa 1976)* 1996;21(3):271-277.

26. Baggiolini M, Moser B, Clark-Lewis I: Interleukin-8 and related chemotactic cytokines. *Chest* 1994;105(3, suppl):95S-98S.

27. Bonnet CS, Walsh DA: Osteoarthritis, angiogenesis and inflammation. *Rheumatology (Oxford)* 2005;44(1):7-16.

    This review summarizes the evidence that angiogenesis and inflammation play an important role in the pathophysiology of osteoarthritis, with directions for future research on treatments. Level of evidence: III.

28. Peng B, Hao J, Hou S, et al: Possible pathogenesis of painful intervertebral disc degeneration. *Spine (Phila Pa 1976)* 2006;31(5):560-566.

    A prospective cohort study on the pathogenesis of disk degeneration discriminated between non–clinically relevant aging-associated disk degeneration and clinically relevant painful disk degeneration. Level of evidence: II.

29. Weinstein J, Claverie W, Gibson S: The pain of discography. *Spine (Phila Pa 1976)* 1988;13(12):1344-1348.

30. Buckwalter JA: Aging and degeneration of the human intervertebral disc. *Spine (Phila Pa 1976)* 1995;20(11):1307-1314.

31. Virri J, Grönblad M, Savikko J, et al: Prevalence, morphology, and topography of blood vessels in herniated disc tissue: A comparative immunocytochemical study. *Spine (Phila Pa 1976)* 1996;21(16):1856-1863.

32. Hirsch C, Schajowicz F: Studies on structural changes in the lumbar annulus fibrosus. *Acta Orthop Scand* 1953;22(3):184-231.

33. Lindblom K, Hultqvist G: Absorption of protruded disc tissue. *J Bone Joint Surg Am* 1950;32(3):557-560.

34. Freemont AJ, Peacock TE, Goupille P, Hoyland JA, O'Brien J, Jayson MI: Nerve ingrowth into diseased intervertebral disc in chronic back pain. *Lancet* 1997;350(9072):178-181.

35. Freemont AJ, Watkins A, Le Maitre C, et al: Nerve growth factor expression and innervation of the painful intervertebral disc. *J Pathol* 2002;197(3):286-292.

36. Aoki Y, Takahashi Y, Ohtori S, Moriya H, Takahashi K: Distribution and immunocytochemical characterization of dorsal root ganglion neurons innervating the lumbar intervertebral disc in rats: A review. *Life Sci* 2004;74(21):2627-2642.

37. Flor H: Cortical reorganisation and chronic pain: implications for rehabilitation. *J Rehabil Med* 2003;(41, suppl):66-72.

38. Reichling DB, Levine JD: Critical role of nociceptor plasticity in chronic pain. *Trends Neurosci* 2009;32(12):611-618.

    The role of nociceptor plasticity in the development of chronic pain is discussed.

39. Wall PD, Melzack R: *Textbook of Pain*, ed 4. Edinburgh, NY, Churchill Livingstone, 1999.

40. Parada CA, Yeh JJ, Reichling DB, Levine JD: Transient attenuation of protein kinase Cepsilon can terminate a chronic hyperalgesic state in the rat. *Neuroscience* 2003;120(1):219-226.

41. Apkarian AV, Sosa Y, Sonty S, et al: Chronic back pain is associated with decreased prefrontal and thalamic gray matter density. *J Neurosci* 2004;24(46):10410-10415.

42. May A: Chronic pain may change the structure of the brain. *Pain* 2008;137(1):7-15.

    Morphologic changes to the pain transmission pathways of patients with chronic pain are retrospectively analyzed. Level of evidence: III.

43. Khasar SG, Green PG, Levine JD: Repeated sound stress enhances inflammatory pain in the rat. *Pain* 2005;116(1-2):79-86.

    A prospective observational study investigated the effect of sound stress on mechanical analgesia after injection into a rat paw. Level of evidence: III.

44. Dina OA, Khasar SG, Gear RW, Levine JD: Activation of Gi induces mechanical hyperalgesia poststress or inflammation. *Neuroscience* 2009;160(2):501-507.

    A prospective observational study investigated the effect of inflammation and pain on receptor coupling after injection into a rat paw. Level of evidence: III.

45. Khasar SG, Burkham J, Dina OA, et al: Stress induces a switch of intracellular signaling in sensory neurons in a model of generalized pain. *J Neurosci* 2008;28(22):5721-5730.

    A prospective observational study investigated the effect of sound stress on intracellular signaling after injection into a rat paw. Level of evidence: III.

46. Pincus T, Burton AK, Vogel S, Field AP: A systematic review of psychological factors as predictors of chronicity/disability in prospective cohorts of low back pain. *Spine (Phila Pa 1976)* 2002;27(5):E109-E120.

47. Gatchel RJ, Polatin PB, Mayer TG: The dominant role of psychosocial risk factors in the development of chronic low back pain disability. *Spine (Phila Pa 1976)* 1995;20(24):2702-2709.

Chapter 4

The Pathophysiology of Cervical and Lumbar Radiculopathy

Björn Rydevik, MD, PhD   Helena Brisby, MD, PhD   Robert R. Myers, PhD

Introduction

The reported prevalence of lumbar radiculopathy in adults ranges from 2% to 43% in different studies.[1] Cervical radiculopathy has an average annual age-adjusted incidence of 83.5 per 100,000 population, with a peak incidence of 203 per 100,000 population at age 50 to 54 years.[2] Patients typically have pain along the distribution of the L5-S1 dermatomes or the C6-C7 dermatomes, although any motor or sensory nerve root and associated dermatome can be affected (Figure 1). The symptoms can be severe and often include lack of sensation, weakness, and burning or shooting pain that can lead to significant psychological comorbidity with consequences at home and work. The causes of radiculopathy are many and can include metabolic and vascular dysfunction.[3] In most patients, however, the cause is related to traumatic or degenerative changes in the patency of the vertebral foramen or the integrity of the intervertebral disk.

It is important to recognize the sensitivity and vulnerability of nerve roots in their complex and dynamic environment (Figure 2). Nerve roots need to be mobile and within a nurturing environment of cerebrospinal fluid. That environment depends on an intricate vasculature within a space defined by bony passages and semielastic meningeal compartments. Pathophysiologic functioning of a nerve root, like that of any other nerve bundle, often is precipitated by a combination of compressive, inflammatory, and metabolic insults, which are further exacerbated by inflammation within the nerve root. The pathophysiologic and painful consequences of nerve root injury recently have been explained in terms of cytokine-mediated neuropathologic processes.[4] This explanation has provided a unified understanding of nerve root injuries as well as new rationales for pharmacologic therapies targeting painful radiculopathies.

The Effects of Compression and Inflammation on Nerve Roots

The consequences of nerve root injury can be understood in terms of a function deficit manifested as motor weakness and/or sensory abnormalities that range from numbness to paresthesia and burning pain. The distribution of these deficits permits clinical identification of the affected root, and the deficit may be further defined with neural imaging and electrophysiologic tests, especially needle electromyography.[5]

Mechanical compression of a nerve root can occur within the spinal canal, in the spine foramen, or at the lateral border of the disks. Compression most often is caused by a disk bulge or herniation or by expansion within the spine of degenerative tissue such as thickened ligamentum flavum or osteoarthritic facet joints. Such changes commonly appear in spinal stenosis. A traumatic injury, tumor, or infection involving the spine also can cause nerve root compression and give rise to radiculopathy with possible neurologic deficits. The onset of nerve root compression in a disk herniation is more rapid than, for example, in spinal stenosis. Different onset rates as well as differences in the biomechanics of nerve root compression-deformation may explain variations in symptoms and signs among clinically different syndromes such as disk herniation and spinal stenosis.[6] Experimental investigations found that spine nerve roots are more susceptible to mechanical compression than peripheral nerves.[7-9] Mechanical nerve root compression can lead to impairment of the nerve root blood supply and nerve conduction, in addition to structural nerve fiber changes.[10-12] These changes in the nerve root can lead to radicular pain.[13]

Nerve root inflammation can be initiated by an inflammatory disease that affects the nervous system, such as multiple sclerosis, amyotrophic lateral sclerosis,

Dr. Rydevik or an immediate family member serves as a board member, owner, officer, or committee member of the Spine Society of Europe; and has received nonincome support (such as equipment or services), commercially derived honoraria, or other non–research-related funding (such as paid travel) from BioAssets Development Corp. Dr. Brisby or an immediate family member serves as a board member, owner, officer, or committee member of the Swedish Spine Surgery Society and the International Society for Study of the Lumbar Spine. Neither Dr. Myers nor any immediate family member has received anything of value from or owns stock in a commercial company or institution related directly or indirectly to the subject of this chapter.

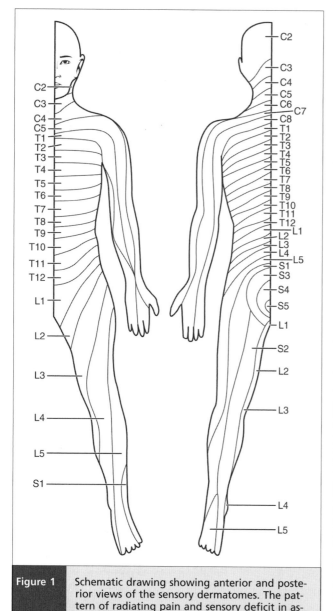

Figure 1 Schematic drawing showing anterior and posterior views of the sensory dermatomes. The pattern of radiating pain and sensory deficit in association with radiculopathy usually follows the dermatomes.

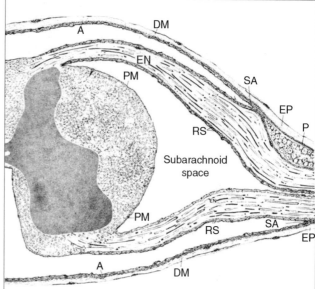

Figure 2 Drawing showing the relationship of the peripheral nerve sheath to the meningeal ensheathment of the spinal cord. The epineurium (EP) is in continuity with the dura mater (DM). The endoneurium (EN) persists from the peripheral nerve through the spinal root to the junction with the spinal cord. At the subarachnoid angle (SA), the greater portion of the perineurium (P) from the distal peripheral nerve bundle passes between the dura and the arachnoid (A), but a few layers appear to continue over the roots as the inner layer of the root sheath (RS). The arachnoid is reflected over the nerve roots at the subarachnoid angle and becomes continuous with the outer layers of the root sheath. At the junction of the spinal cord the outer layers become continuous with the pia mater (PM). (Reproduced with permission from Haller FR, Low FN: The fine structure of the peripheral nerve root sheath in the subarachnoid space in the rat and other laboratory animals. *Am J Anat* 1971;131(1):1-19.)

or a viral infection such as Guillain-Barré syndrome. These diseases most often are not painful. Painful radiculopathy of the spine nerve root involving inflammation is commonly initiated from nonnerve tissue that contains cells expressing cytokines, such as tissue from a herniated intervertebral disk tissue or facet joint arthritis. There is no simple way to determine whether a patient's neural inflammation was induced by nerve root compression or is the result of a primary inflammation. Regardless of the underlying cause of nerve root inflammation, its continuation is facilitated by the recruitment of immunocompetent cells, especially macrophages.[11,13] Macrophages are the most important immune cells with respect to the degeneration of neural tissue and cytokine production.

The Neuropathology of Nerve Root Injury and Mechanisms of Radicular Pain

It has only recently become possible to experimentally link the dynamics of pathologic processes within the nerve root (which begin within minutes of injury) to the protracted changes in clinical pathophysiology and pain (which may slowly shift from acute to chronic). The relationship between etiology and nerve root pathophysiology historically has been studied in the nerve root response to disk degeneration, which provides insight into the mechanical and inflammatory origins of the injury.[12,14] It is now understood that neuroinflammation is a key cause of radiculopathy as well as neuropathic pain in general.[4] Neuroinflammation is a proinflammatory cytokine-mediated process that most often is associated with direct injury to the nervous system but also can be provoked by systemic tissue injury. In general, inflammation is a pathophysiologic state associated with pain. Nociceptive fibers, including the free nerve endings of unmyelinated C fibers, fire spontaneously in an inflammatory environment, including those caused by lowered pH, bradykinin, histamine, or prostaglandins. Neuroinflammation involves immune interactions that activate immune cells, glial cells, and neurons. The process is primarily driven by upregulation and membrane release of the prototypical proinflammatory cytokine tumor necrosis factor–α (TNF-α). TNF-α expression can directly lead to increases in the traditional inflammatory factors including histamine and prostaglandins, as well as upregulation of other proinflammatory cytokines such as interleukin (IL)–1. However, TNF-α by itself can directly induce ectopic activity in nociceptive primary afferent fibers, which is believed to be a principal mechanism in initiating and maintaining neuropathic pain states.[15] This belief recently was reinforced by a finding that TNF-α contributes to upregulation of sodium channels Nav1.3 and Nav1.8 in dorsal root ganglion (DRG) neurons.[16] The expression of these channels was found to persist in the L5 DRG at least 35 days after L5 ventral root transection. This time period overlapped the period in which behavioral signs of neuropathic pain (mechanical allodynia and thermal hyperalgesia) were measured,[17] as well as the period of TNF-α protein and TNF-α receptor-1 upregulation in ipsilateral L4-L5 sensory neurons in the DRG and associated spinal cord dorsal horn.[18] Nav1.3 was found to be upregulated in injured DRG neurons after sensory nerve transection.[19] Thus, ectopic discharges of action potentials in primary afferents resulting from abnormal expression of voltage-gated sodium channels in DRG neurons represent a key pathophysiologic feature of radiculopathy, regardless of whether the primary injury is to motor or sensory fibers. This finding argues for an indirect chemical stimulus of sodium channel upregulation of the kind that was found to occur in cultured DRG neurons stimulated by TNF-α.[16]

Of particular importance is the finding that inflammatory agents from a herniated nucleus pulposus can be a key component of sciatica, in addition to direct nerve root compression.[20] There is significant proinflammatory cytokine expression in degenerated and herniated intervertebral disk tissue.[21,22] Immunoreactivity for TNF-α, IL-4, IL-6, IL-12, IL-17, and interferon-γ is seen in herniated disk material. Some of these cytokines, like TNF-α, are resident but not biologically active in sequestered nucleus pulposus. TNF-α and other cytokines are activated and upregulated in degenerating and herniated disks in part because of the recruitment of macrophages and lymphocytes to the injured tissue, and in part because of the intrinsic pathophysiologic relationship between matrix metalloproteinase (MMP) activity and proinflammatory cytokines, which interact to modulate the tissue environment in a way that rapidly escalates inflammation. MMPs may play a key role in disk degeneration.[23] Disruption of the extracellular disk matrix by MMP enzyme activity is a characteristic sign in disk degeneration. Activated MMPs also perform cell surface activation of TNF-α from its transmembrane precursor and sequestration of TNF-α receptors 1 and 2.[24] In turn, TNF-α induces MMP-9 upregulation in peripheral glial cells and MMP-2 gelatinase activity in nucleus pulposus tissue.[25,26] This interdependence and positive feedback loop has negative consequences in terms of pain and is a target for therapeutic interruption.

A more fundamental understanding of nerve root pathophysiology emerges from knowledge of the pathologic processes of nerve degeneration and regeneration. Injury to nerve roots or distal peripheral nervous system tissues by any mechanism (compression, inflammation, or a viral, ischemic, or metabolic mechanism) results in a pathologic tissue change proportional to the magnitude of the injury.[27] The pathology ranges from changes in barrier permeability (causing edema), through Schwann cell injury (causing primary demyelination of nerve fibers), to axonal injury (causing wallerian degeneration and significant neuropathic pain).[28] Axonal injury is the most serious form of injury, as it is associated with protracted periods of dysfunction and pain. Neural regeneration and restoration of normal motor and sensory function can take considerable time, may not be successful, and depend on resolution of the insult by natural absorptive processes or surgical repair.

All of these forms of injuries are associated with neuroinflammation, which is intrinsic to any neural injury and may supersede extrinsic inflammatory factors (such as exposure to TNF-α from a herniated nucleus pulposus). Extrinsic inflammatory factors by themselves can begin the cascade of neuroinflammation. Thus, an injury to a nerve root, whether initiated by chemical or mechanical factors, within minutes gives rise to upregulation of proinflammatory cytokines such as TNF-α. This upregulation occurs in endothelial cells, Schwann cells, DRG glial cells, fibroblasts, perineurial cells, and, especially, resident macrophages, triggering a cascade of pathologic and pathophysiologic events, such as changes in barrier and endothelial permeability, macrophage invasion, pain, phagocytosis of neural debris, and neural regeneration[29] (Table 1).

Cytokine regulation is dynamic and finely modulated by competing forces seeking to balance the tissue cytokine environment after injury. For example, the upregulation of proinflammatory cytokines in injured tissue initiates changes in molecular signaling that correspondingly increase the production of anti-inflammatory cytokines. Cytokine signaling is complex and can occur through one or more cell-surface receptors that affect autocrine, paracrine, or endocrine signaling. The cytokine signaling occurs primarily through phosphorylation of mitogen-activated protein kinases that regulate critical cellular activities ranging from gene expression to apoptosis.[30] Insight into these pathways has given rise to experimental therapies aimed at reducing the production of proinflammatory cytokines.

1: Basic Science of the Spine

Table 1

The Pathophysiologic Effects of Proinflammatory Cytokine Actions

Proinflammatory Cytokine Action	→	Pathophysiologic Effect
Cellular activation of neurons, glia, Schwann cells, mast cells, endothelial cells, and macrophages	→	Increased sensitivity of cells leading to structural and function changes that can produce pain
Spontaneous electrophysiologic activity	→	Aberrant activity in polymodal nociceptive fibers
Upregulation of voltage-gated sodium channels	→	Aberrant activity in polymodal nociceptive fibers Production of new pain-related sodium channels
Degradation of MMPs	→	Disruption of vascular and perineurial-meningeal barriers, upsetting the local chemical environment and causing edema
Macrophage chemoattraction	→	Powerful signals distributed locally and systemically, attracting macrophages and other immunocompetent cells
Increased activity of vascular adhesion molecules	→	Local upregulation promoting attachment and invasion of immune cells, particularly macrophages, to the site of injury
Proinflammatory cytokine receptor upregulation	→	Upregulation of cytokine receptors, increasing receptor density at the injury site and local effects of the cytokines.
Upregulation of spinal nociceptive mediators	→	Chemical and functional changes in dorsal horn activity and other central neuronal changes

However, the complexity, duplication, and adaptation of the pathways have limited the success of experimental therapy studies and their translation to human testing.

Interference with the cytokine-MMP network also holds promise for understanding the mechanisms of pain signaling along the neuroaxis. TNF-α was found to be physically conveyed by axonal transport to and from sensory neurons in the DRG and spinal cord, where the MMPs are subsequently activated.[31] Because MMPs are the only proteases able to degrade blood-nerve barriers, mediating macrophage infiltration, local neuroinflammation, and pain, their stabilization is of considerable interest. Additionally, it has been shown that other segments of the neuroaxis including the thalamus are activated by application of nucleus pulposus to the DRG.[32] Whether this process occurs through the axonal transport of cytokines, electrophysiologic messaging, or both is not yet entirely clear.

Clinical Implications

The use of oral nonsteroidal anti-inflammatory drugs and epidural steroid injections for treating pain in patients with disk herniation and sciatica is based on the assumption that neuroinflammation is an underlying factor in these conditions. These treatment modalities are used despite the lack of conclusive evidence in support of their effectiveness.[33,34] More specific treatment with intramuscular or subcutaneous injection of an anti–TNF-α substance (infliximab or etanercept) has had promising but conflicting and inconclusive results in nonrandomized clinical studies.[35-37] In a randomized placebo-controlled study, 24 patients were given an epidural injection of etanercept (in a varying dosage) or saline. At 1-month follow-up, 67% to 100% of patients in the treatment group had more than 50% improvement in leg pain, compared with 17% of patients in the control group.[38] The effect, which was statistically significant, persisted in all but one patient at 6-month follow-up. The authors concluded that etanercept is a promising treatment for lumbar radiculopathy. The study was limited in size, however, and anti–TNF-α treatment of radicular pain needs to be evaluated in larger studies. Other cytokines also have been suggested as important factors in sciatica, but the availability of drugs specifically blocking such cytokines, such as anti–IL-6 treatment, has yet to be fully explored.[39]

Summary

The pathophysiology of nerve root involvement in spine disorders is complex and entails mechanical, biochemical, and molecular mechanisms. Recent research has clarified some of these mechanisms. There has been a gradual evolution of the concept that radicular pain radiating from the cervical or lumbar spine most often is based on a combination of mechanical factors and a series of biologic factors that affect the nerve roots. It is important to recognize the role of cytokines such as TNF-α in neural inflammation and radicular pain. Recent clinical research into anti–TNF-α treatment of sciatica and disk herniation has had promising but inconclusive results.

Acknowledgments

This chapter is partly based on research supported by the Swedish Research Council, the US National Institutes of Health, and the US Department of Veterans Affairs.

Annotated References

1. Valat JP, Genevay S, Marty M, Rozenberg S, Koes B: Sciatica. *Best Pract Res Clin Rheumatol* 2010;24(2): 241-252.

   The evidence from basic science and clinical research on lumbar radiculopathy is reviewed.

2. Radhakrishnan K, Litchy WJ, O'Fallon WM, Kurland LT: Epidemiology of cervical radiculopathy: A population-based study from Rochester, Minnesota, 1976 through 1990. *Brain* 1994;117(pt 2):325-335.

3. Benny BV, Nagpal AS, Singh P, Smuck M: Vascular causes of radiculopathy: A literature review. *Spine J* 2011;11(1):73-85.

   The vascular causes of radiculopathy are reviewed, with their impact on the diagnosis and treatment of radicular spine pain.

4. Myers RR, Campana WM, Shubayev VI: The role of neuroinflammation in neuropathic pain: Mechanisms and therapeutic targets. *Drug Discov Today* 2006;11(1-2):8-20.

   This review article details the role of proinflammatory cytokines in orchestrating the pathophysiology and pain of nerve injury. New therapeutic targets for radiculopathy and neuropathy are identified.

5. Watson J: Office evaluation of spine and limb pain: Spondylotic radiculopathy and other nonstructural mimickers. *Semin Neurol* 2011;31(1):85-101.

   The clinical evaluation of patients with radiculopathy is reviewed, including use of imaging and electrodiagnostics.

6. Rydevik B, Lundborg G, Olmarker K, Myers RR: Biomechanics of peripheral nerves, in Nordin M, Frankel VH, eds: *Basic Biomechanics of the Musculoskeletal System*. London, England, Lea & Febiger, 2001, pp 126-146.

7. Rydevik BL, Pedowitz RA, Hargens AR, Swenson MR, Myers RR, Garfin SR: Effects of acute, graded compression on spinal nerve root function and structure: An experimental study of the pig cauda equina. *Spine (Phila Pa 1976)* 1991;16(5):487-493.

8. Olmarker K, Holm S, Rosenqvist AL, Rydevik B: Experimental nerve root compression: A model of acute, graded compression of the porcine cauda equina and an analysis of neural and vascular anatomy. *Spine (Phila Pa 1976)* 1991;16(1):61-69.

9. Cornefjord M, Sato K, Olmarker K, Rydevik B, Nordborg C: A model for chronic nerve root compression studies: Presentation of a porcine model for controlled, slow-onset compression with analyses of anatomic aspects, compression onset rate, and morphologic and neurophysiologic effects. *Spine (Phila Pa 1976)* 1997; 22(9):946-957.

10. Myers RR, Yamamoto T, Yaksh TL, Powell HC: The role of focal nerve ischemia and Wallerian degeneration in peripheral nerve injury producing hyperesthesia. *Anesthesiology* 1993;78(2):308-316.

11. Sommer C, Galbraith JA, Heckman HM, Myers RR: Pathology of experimental compression neuropathy producing hyperesthesia. *J Neuropathol Exp Neurol* 1993;52(3):223-233.

12. Olmarker K, Rydevik B, Kikuchi S, Myers RR: Sciatic and nerve root pain in disc herniation and spinal stenosis: A basic science review and clinical perspective, in Herkowitz HN, Garfin SR, Eismont FJ, Bell GR, Balderston RA, eds: *The Spine*, ed 6. Philadelphia, PA, Elsevier-Saunders, 2011, pp 129-145.

   This book chapter provides a broad overview of the pathophysiology of nerve root involvement in degenerative spine disorders.

13. Myers RR, Shubayev VI, Campana WM: Neuropathology of painful neuropathies, in Sommer C, ed: *Pain in Peripheral Nerve Disease*. Basel, Switzerland, Karger, 2001, pp 8-30.

14. Brisby H: Pathology and possible mechanisms of nervous system response to disc degeneration. *J Bone Joint Surg Am* 2006;88(suppl 2):68-71.

   The relationship of mechanical stimulation and the inflammatory and signaling substances in disk and spine structures is highlighted.

15. Sorkin LS, Xiao W-H, Wagner R, Myers RR: Tumour necrosis factor-alpha induces ectopic activity in nociceptive primary afferent fibres. *Neuroscience* 1997;81(1): 255-262.

16. He X-H, Zang Y, Chen X, et al: TNF-α contributes to up-regulation of Nav1.3 and Nav1.8 in DRG neurons following motor fiber injury. *Pain* 2010;151(2):266-279.

   Proinflammatory cytokines may be responsible for increasing voltage-gated sodium channels in DRG neurons after nerve injury.

17. Li L, Xian CJ, Zhong JH, Zhou XF: Effect of lumbar 5 ventral root transection on pain behaviors: A novel rat model for neuropathic pain without axotomy of primary sensory neurons. *Exp Neurol* 2002;175(1):23-34.

18. Xu JT, Xin WJ, Zang Y, Wu CY, Liu XG: The role of tumor necrosis factor-alpha in the neuropathic pain induced by Lumbar 5 ventral root transection in rat. *Pain* 2006;123(3):306-321.

1: Basic Science of the Spine

The authors report ipsilateral increases in TNF protein and TNF-α receptor-1 immunoreactivity in the L4-5 DRG and spinal cord dorsal horn after associated motor root transection.

19. Waxman SG, Kocsis JD, Black JA: Type III sodium channel mRNA is expressed in embryonic but not adult spinal sensory neurons, and is reexpressed following axotomy. *J Neurophysiol* 1994;72(1):466-470.

20. Omarker K, Myers RR: Pathogenesis of sciatic pain: Role of herniated nucleus pulposus and deformation of spinal nerve root and dorsal root ganglion. *Pain* 1998; 78(2):99-105.

21. Olmarker K, Larsson K: Tumor necrosis factor alpha and nucleus-pulposus-induced nerve root injury. *Spine (Phila Pa 1976)* 1998;23(23):2538-2544.

22. Shamji MF, Setton LA, Jarvis W, et al: Proinflammatory cytokine expression profile in degenerated and herniated human intervertebral disc tissues. *Arthritis Rheum* 2010;62(7):1974-1982.

Surgically obtained intervertebral disk tissue and control tissue from autopsy were analyzed to compare proinflammatory cytokine expression and immune cells, including expression of Th17 lymphocyte lineage and IL-17 expression.

23. Bachmeier BE, Nerlich A, Mittermaier N, et al: Matrix metalloproteinase expression levels suggest distinct enzyme roles during lumbar disc herniation and degeneration. *Eur Spine J* 2009;18(11):1573-1586.

This study provides data on gene and protein levels, highlighting the key role of MMPs, particularly MMP-3, in disk degeneration.

24. Shubayev VI, Myers RR: Upregulation and interaction of TNF-α and gelatinases A and B in painful peripheral nerve injury. *Brain Res* 2000;855(1):83-89.

25. Chattopadhyay S, Myers RR, Janes J, Shubayev V: Cytokine regulation of MMP-9 in peripheral glia: Implications for pathological processes and pain in injured nerve. *Brain Behav Immun* 2007;21(5):561-568.

MMP-9 messenger RNA is upregulated in glia immediately after nerve injury by TNF-α and IL-1, and its removal protects against nerve fiber demyelination and neuropathic pain.

26. Séguin CA, Pilliar RM, Madri JA, Kandel RA: TNF-alpha induces MMP2 gelatinase activity and MT1-MMP expression in an in vitro model of nucleus pulposus tissue degeneration. *Spine (Phila Pa 1976)* 2008; 33(4):356-365.

A mechanism is identified in which TNF-α may contribute to matrix degradation in nucleus pulposus tissue.

27. Myers RR, Heckman HM, Powell HC: Axonal viability and the persistence of thermal hyperalgesia after partial freeze lesions of nerve. *J Neurol Sci* 1996;139(1):28-38.

28. Stoll G, Jander S, Myers RR: Degeneration and regeneration of the peripheral nervous system: From Augustus Waller's observations to neuroinflammation. *J Peripher Nerv Syst* 2002;7(1):13-27.

29. Shubayev VI, Angert M, Dolkas J, Campana WM, Palenscar K, Myers RR: TNF-α–induced MMP-9 promotes macrophage recruitment into injured peripheral nerve. *Mol Cell Neurosci* 2006;31(3):407-415.

Studies with mouse genetic variants link TNF-α and MMP interdependence with macrophage recruitment and expression of these factors.

30. Shubayev VI, Kato K, Myers RR: Cytokines in pain, in Kruger L, Light AR, eds: *Translational Pain Research From Mouse to Man*. Boca Raton, FL, CRC Press, 2010, pp 187-214.

The role of cytokine mechanisms in pain is reviewed, with opportunities for therapeutic intervention.

31. Shubayev VI, Myers RR: Axonal transport of TNF-alpha in painful neuropathy: Distribution of ligand tracer and TNF receptors. *J Neuroimmunol* 2001; 114(1-2):48-56.

32. Brisby H, Hammar I: Thalamic activation in a disc herniation model. *Spine (Phila Pa 1976)* 2007;32(25): 2846-2852.

Using electrophysiologic techniques, the authors found that application of nucleus pulposus but not adipose tissue to DRG caused an increase in evoked thalamic responses after 20 minutes.

33. Herrmann WA, Geertsen MS: Efficacy and safety of lornoxicam compared with placebo and diclofenac in acute sciatica/lumbo-sciatica: An analysis from a randomised, double-blind, multicentre, parallel-group study. *Int J Clin Pract* 2009;63(11):1613-1621.

The results of this study indicate that nonsteroidal anti-inflammatory drugs may have a better analgesic effect than placebo in patients with acute sciatica.

34. Jacobs WC, van Tulder M, Arts M, et al: Surgery versus conservative management of sciatica due to a lumbar herniated disc: A systematic review. *Eur Spine J* 2011; 20(4):513-522.

This systematic review found low-quality evidence that diskectomy is more beneficial than epidural steroid injection in sciatica caused by disk herniation.

35. Karppinen J, Korhonen T, Malmivaara A, et al: Tumor necrosis factor-alpha monoclonal antibody, infliximab, used to manage severe sciatica. *Spine (Phila Pa 1976)* 2003;28(8):750-754.

36. Korhonen T, Karppinen J, Paimela L, et al: The treatment of disc herniation-induced sciatica with infliximab: Results of a randomized, controlled, 3-month follow-up study. *Spine (Phila Pa 1976)* 2005;30(24): 2724-2728.

This randomized controlled study found an equal reduction of leg pain with infliximab treatment or placebo.

1: Basic Science of the Spine

37. Genevay S, Stingelin S, Gabay C: Efficacy of etanercept in the treatment of acute, severe sciatica: A pilot study. *Ann Rheum Dis* 2004;63(9):1120-1123.

38. Cohen SP, Bogduk N, Dragovich A, et al: Randomized, double-blind, placebo-controlled, dose-response, and preclinical safety study of transforaminal epidural etanercept for the treatment of sciatica. *Anesthesiology* 2009;110(5):1116-1126.

    Significant improvements in back and leg pain were seen in patients treated with epidurally injected etanercept, compared with placebo. No drug-related toxicity of epidurally injected etanercept was found.

39. Murakami M, Nishimoto N: The value of blocking IL-6 outside of rheumatoid arthritis: Current perspective. *Curr Opin Rheumatol* 2011;23(3):273-277.

    The role of IL-6 was reviewed in various immune-mediated inflammatory diseases, with the possible role of IL-6 blockade in such conditions.

1: Basic Science of the Spine

Chapter 5

The Pathophysiology of Cervical Spondylotic Myelopathy

S. Babak Kalantar, MD   S. Tim Yoon, MD, PhD

Introduction

The etiologies of cervical myelopathy include spinal cord compression, dynamic factors, and ischemia of the spinal cord. Cervical myelopathy is diagnosed on the basis of the patient's history, physical examination, and imaging findings. The clinical appearance varies substantially and is affected by the severity of compression, the involved spine levels, the chronicity, the patient's age, and any comorbidities. The upper extremity symptoms may include weakness, pain, hand numbness, and clumsiness. The lower extremity symptoms include loss of balance, a tendency to fall, and gait disturbance. Knowledge of the overall pathophysiology of cervical myelopathy is useful for understanding clinical findings based on the location of cord compromise.

Anatomy of the Cervical Spinal Column and Spinal Cord

The subaxial cervical spinal canal from C3 to C7 normally has a midsagittal diameter of 17 to 18 mm. A diameter of less than 13 mm is considered stenotic. Some authors have found a strong association between a stenotic canal and the development of clinically evident myelopathy.[1-6] Compression of the cord within a narrowed canal is believed to cause neural injury and ischemia. Stenosis is not always correlated with neurologic symptoms, however, and therefore other factors must play a role in the pathogenesis of myelopathy. No neurologic deficits were found in 10% of patients who were older than 60 years and had stenosis (defined as a canal diameter of less than 13 mm).[7] Bony canal stenosis can be measured on lateral radiographs with the use of a ratio to eliminate radiographic magnification error[8] (Figure 1). Transient neurapraxia from cord compression was found to be more likely to develop in patients with a spinal canal–vertebral body ratio of less

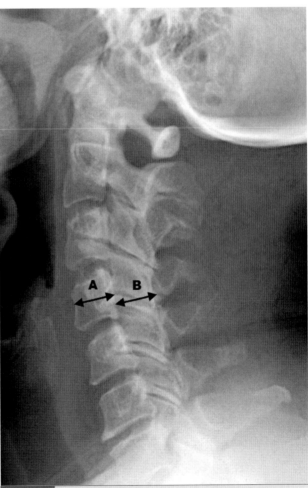

Figure 1   Lateral radiograph showing the measurements used to determine the spinal canal–vertebral body ratio. The ratio is calculated by dividing the sagittal diameter of the spinal canal (B) by the sagittal diameter of the corresponding vertebral body (A).

Dr. Kalantar or an immediate family member has received research or institutional support from Medtronic. Dr. Yoon or an immediate family member is a member of a speakers' bureau or has made paid presentations on behalf of Stryker and Biomet; serves as a paid consultant to or is an employee of MedTech Advisors; serves as an unpaid consultant to Zimmer and Stryker; has received research or institutional support from AOSpine, Medtronic Sofamor Danek, Nuvasive, Johnson & Johnson, Smith & Nephew, and Biomet; and owns stock or stock options in Phygen.

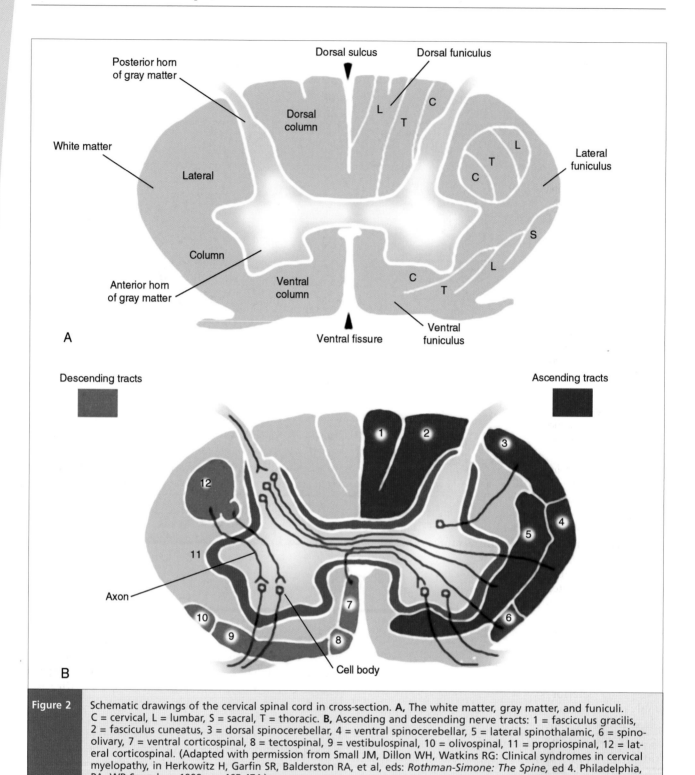

Figure 2   Schematic drawings of the cervical spinal cord in cross-section. **A,** The white matter, gray matter, and funiculi. C = cervical, L = lumbar, S = sacral, T = thoracic. **B,** Ascending and descending nerve tracts: 1 = fasciculus gracilis, 2 = fasciculus cuneatus, 3 = dorsal spinocerebellar, 4 = ventral spinocerebellar, 5 = lateral spinothalamic, 6 = spino-olivary, 7 = ventral corticospinal, 8 = tectospinal, 9 = vestibulospinal, 10 = olivospinal, 11 = propriospinal, 12 = lateral corticospinal. (Adapted with permission from Small JM, Dillon WH, Watkins RG: Clinical syndromes in cervical myelopathy, in Herkowitz H, Garfin SR, Balderston RA, et al, eds: *Rothman-Simone: The Spine*, ed 4. Philadelphia, PA, WB Saunders, 1999, pp 465-474.)

than 0.82.[8] The low specificity of this ratio precludes its use in predicting whether a patient is predisposed to develop symptoms.

The average sagittal diameter of the subaxial cervical spinal cord is 8 mm in adults.[9] In cross-section, the right and left halves of the spinal cord are separated by a ventral median fissure and dorsal sulcus (Figure 2, *A*).

The spinal cord is divided into gray and white matter. The central gray matter is made up of neuron cell bodies, dendrites, and axons, which are divided into posterior, lateral, and anterior horns. The sensory roots and ganglia are within the dorsal horns, and the motor roots are ventral. White matter is made up of myelinated ascending, descending, and transverse axons,

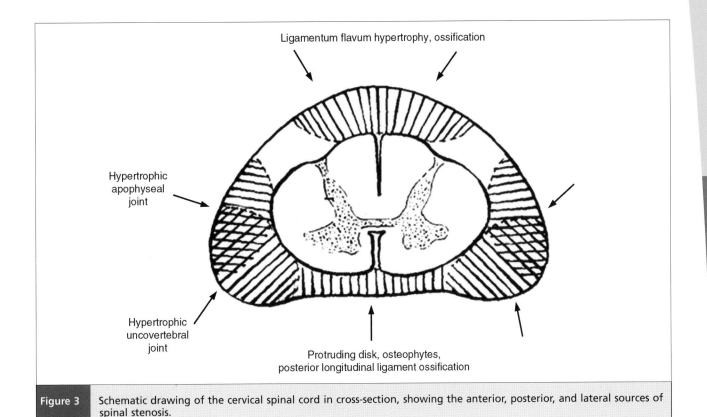

Ligamentum flavum hypertrophy, ossification

Hypertrophic apophyseal joint

Hypertrophic uncovertebral joint

Protruding disk, osteophytes, posterior longitudinal ligament ossification

Figure 3 Schematic drawing of the cervical spinal cord in cross-section, showing the anterior, posterior, and lateral sources of spinal stenosis.

which are divided into ventral, lateral, and dorsal funiculi. These funiculi form tracts responsible for both motor and sensory function. The sensory functions range from proprioception and vibration sense to pain and temperature sensation (Figure 2, B). The spinal nerve arises from dorsal and ventral rootlets that merge laterally.

The vascular supply of the cervical cord is primarily provided by the anterior and paired posterior spinal arteries. The arterial supply is augmented by radicular branches that enter the canal through the neuroforamen. These radicular branches originate in the vertebral artery or branches of the subclavian artery, and they travel with the dorsal and ventral rootlets to the respective dorsal and anterolateral portions of the cord.[10] The anterior spinal artery provides the blood supply of the anterior two thirds of the spinal cord. The paired posterior spinal arteries, which originate from the vertebral artery or posteroinferior cerebellar artery, supply the remaining one third. The anterior sulcal artery branches from the anterior spinal artery, then passes through the ventral median fissure, where it bifurcates into transverse intramedullary branches. Less well-defined branches from the posterior spinal arteries similarly penetrate and supply blood via the dorsal median and dorsolateral sulci.[11] The anterior sulcal branches supply the anterior gray matter and the anterior part of the posterior gray matter, as well as the inner half of the anterior and lateral white columns. The posterior arteries supply the posterior part of the posterior gray matter and the posterior half of the poste-

rior white columns. Pial arteries forming a centripetal arterial system supply the outer half of the white columns.[12]

Pathomechanisms of Cervical Myelopathy

Spinal Cord Compression

Several anatomic structures in the cervical motion segment can be involved in spinal cord compression. Anteriorly, these structures include a protruding disk, posterior osteophytes, and an ossified posterior longitudinal ligament; posteriorly, an infolding of the ligamentum flavum; and laterally, hypertrophic apophyseal and uncovertebral joints (Figure 3). The different modes of cord compression can alter both the sagittal and transverse diameter of the cord. Some authors have attempted to correlate the severity of compression in the sagittal and transverse plane with cord infarction or injury, thus allowing cross-sectional cord morphology to be classified by deformity.[6,13] In this classification, boomerang morphology involves convex lateral surfaces and a concave anterior surface; and triangular morphology involves angular lateral surfaces and a flat anterior surface.[14] Another system similarly classifies cord compression into five types based on intraspinal pathology as reflected by the shape of the cord. Compression of the cord into the shape of a banana was found to lead to the worst prognosis, with 98% of patients having signs and symptoms of myelopathy.[15]

Ossification of the Posterior Longitudinal Ligament

Ossification of the posterior longitudinal ligament (OPLL) is a relatively specific and well-studied form of compression-related myelopathy. It is most common in Asian populations, which have an overall incidence of 2%.[16,17] Scientists have identified several genetic abnormalities that may contribute to ectopic OPLL, including a substitution mutation within the nucleotide pyrophosphatase (NPPS) gene and other abnormalities in the progressive ankylosis (ank) and leptin receptor (LEPR) genes.[18-20] Although the early genetic evaluation studies used a mouse model, a genetic study of humans with OPLL identified a mutation in the human NPPS gene.[21] Specific mutations in the human LEPR gene also are correlated with OPLL, and patients with these mutations tend to have a relatively severe or extensive form of the disease.[22] Based on the pattern of ossification, OPLL is classified as segmental, continuous, localized to the disk space, or mixed. OPLL should be considered a progressive disease that leads to increasingly severe stenosis affecting additional vertebral levels. The progression is believed to be slower if the involved level is fused and more rapid if the level has motion. The natural history and progression of OPLL-related cervical myelopathy has been investigated.[23,24] In a 10-year study of 207 patients with OPLL, myelopathy was diagnosed before or during the study period in 70 patients (34%).[23] Patients with relatively little cervical motion at the stenotic level tended to have less myelopathy progression. This finding supports the belief that a dynamic etiology is involved in the onset and progression of cervical myelopathy.

Ossification of the Ligamentum Flavum

Cord compression can result from ossification of the ligamentum flavum (OLF). OLF is common in Japan, where it is found in as many as 20% of patients older than 65 years.[25] In OLF, the ligamentum flavum fuses adjacent lamina from the ventral aspect of the upper lamina to the dorsal aspect of the lower lamina. The common symptoms include neck pain and arm weakness.[26] Bone morphogenetic protein–2 and transforming growth factor–β were found to contribute to OLF by stimulating progenitor cells to form cartilage and ossify.[27]

Dynamic Factors

Abnormal or excessive motion of the cervical spinal column is associated with progression of myelopathy.[28-30] After laminectomy, a flexion-extension arc of more than 60° was found to increase the risk of developing progressive myelopathy.[29,30] Several other studies found excellent clinical results in patients with myelopathy who were treated with elimination of cervical motion, even without decompression.[29,31,32] During the early phases of canal narrowing by anterior and/or posterior structures, cervical cord compression may occur only transiently during physiologic cervical motion. The effects of compression may resolve or decrease when motion is stopped or limited. The cord and its vascular supply have the ability to adapt to a chronic, slowly progressing compression; therefore, dynamic compression may be more important than static compression in the development of myelopathic symptoms. Patients with canal stenosis also have limited cord excursion, and spinal column motion may increase the strain and shear forces on the spinal cord. MRI studies support the role of motion in the pathogenesis of myelopathy. Dynamic MRI of the cervical spine in flexion, neutral position (0°), and extension in patients with myelopathy found that cord compression increased in flexion and extension because of buckling of the ligamentum flavum or bulging of the anulus fibrosus in the posterior disk.[33,34] In a dynamic MRI evaluation of 46 patients, 22 patients (48%) had more severe spinal stenosis in extension than in neutral position, and 11 patients (24%) had more severe stenosis in flexion than in neutral position.[35] In extension, the observed stenosis was anterior, posterior, or both. In flexion, only anterior encroachment of the spinal cord was observed.[33-35] The role of dynamic MRI in evaluating patients with myelopathy as yet is undetermined.

Sagittal Alignment of the Cervical Spinal Column

A kyphotic deformity can create a tethering effect as the cord drapes over the kyphotic segment. The elongation of the spinal cord in this position, especially if it is subject to additional flexion of the spinal column, can increase internal strain and susceptibility to myelopathy.[36,37] Kyphosis has been identified in several studies as a risk factor for the development and progression of cervical cord compression and myelopathy.[38-40] In 13 patients with kyphosis, the degree of kyphosis at the apex of deformity was found to predict the risk of developing cervical myelopathy.[39] A tethering effect is created that leads to spinal cord elongation and axial strain, perhaps as a result of both sagittal plane deformity and dynamic instability.[39] The actual tethering may occur as the spinal cord is dorsally displaced from ventral structures and the dentate ligament tethers the cord, leading to increased strain. Cadaver studies found that even physiologic flexion leads to stretching of the spinal cord and elongation of the spinal canal.[28] This finding may explain the manner in which focal compression creates excess stretch and elongation at both the level of stenosis and remote levels.

Vascular Factors

Several studies have investigated the role of ischemia in the pathogenesis of cord compromise.[41-43] Autopsies of individuals with OPLL and symptomatic myelopathy revealed that anterior compression had compromised perfusion through the transverse intramedullary branches of the anterior sulcal arteries and that posterior compression had reduced perfusion to the intramedullary branches of the central gray matter.[44] Anatomic cadaver studies found that flattening of the spinal cord resulted in elongation of the terminal branches of the anterior spinal artery and the lateral plexus vessels supplying the lateral corticospinal tracts, making these vessels vulnerable to luminal narrowing. Vessels that penetrated the anterior and posterior columns and ran in an anterior-posterior direction were not affected, except for possible widening secondary to the mechanical forces placed on them. This finding may help explain the patterns of spinal cord lesions that occur with cervical spondylotic myelopathy.[36,41] Although the cord blood supply has an important role, surgical decompression to expand the canal and relieve compressive pressures did not alter the course of symptoms in all patients. This finding suggests that nonvascular factors have a role.[45,46] Hypotension or anemia in the setting of an already-tenuous blood supply also may be a consideration in ischemic compromise of the cervical cord. Four patients with cervical myelopathy had several episodes of transient hypotension during cervical laminectomy with fusion.[47] The patients awoke from anesthesia with new neurologic deficits, although they recovered with the use of steroids and induction of hypertension. The authors concluded that the occurrence of hypotension can contribute to ischemic compromise of the cord.[47]

Histopathology of the Spinal Cord

Spinal cord metabolism and axonal transport can be disrupted by cord deformation, stretching, or blood supply alteration, resulting in axolemmal damage, reactive axonal swelling, and eventual neuronal cell death.[48-50] This disruption also can be associated with myelin edema and eventual demyelination. Oligodendrocytes, which are responsible for the myelin sheath, are extremely sensitive to ischemic injury. Injury to this type of cell may explain the demyelination seen in cervical myelopathy.[51] The critical role of oligodendrocytes in neurologic development, myelin maintenance, and prevention or recovery from axonal injury means that these cells are a critical component of the central nervous system. Damage to oligodendrocytes can be deleterious.[52] Autopsies found that seven patients with cervical myelopathy had significant atrophy and neuronal loss in the anterior horn and intermediate zone, followed by degeneration of the lateral and posterior funiculi. In addition to these gray matter findings, there was profound atrophy in the thin myelinated and demyelinated fibers of the white matter.[53] The histology of the spinal cord was studied in the Yoshimura tiptoeing mouse (which has a mutation causing soft-tissue ectopic ossification of spine) and in a human cadaver specimen from a donor with cervical myelopathy.[54] In both the mouse model and the human cadaver specimen, the researchers found apoptotic cells, with descending degeneration in the anterior and lateral columns and ascending degeneration in the posterior column.[54]

Apoptosis is a process of cellular death involving DNA fragmentation as a result of genetic programming or in response to noxious stimuli. The cells disintegrate into membrane-bound particles that are eliminated by phagocytosis. Apoptosis is believed to be an important mechanism of cell loss in cervical myelopathy. Ischemic compromise of the cord, as occurs with chronic compression, is believed to initiate a cascade that starts with dysfunction of glutamate transporters. Increased extracellular glutamate causes a cationic-mediated cell injury that leads to apoptotic cell death.[55] As seen in the Yoshimura mouse, apoptosis results in descending and ascending degeneration at the level of compression as well as distant levels.[54] The pattern is similar to that of traumatic spinal cord injury, in which the initial insult, which causes cell loss and damage, is followed by secondary injury, with the occurrence of apoptosis causing further cell loss and degeneration along white matter tracts.[56-58] Apoptosis may be a source of continuing cell loss in cervical myelopathy, even after appropriate decompression for stenosis.[54]

Imaging and Cord Signal

The gold standard for evaluating cervical myelopathy is MRI, which can identify areas of stenosis and cord compression and is useful in surgical planning. MRI also can be used to determine the prognosis for neurologic deterioration or recovery. Intramedullary signal changes on T1- and T2-weighted MRI may indicate irreversible damage to the cord. Although these signal changes have been the focus of intense study, controversy remains. High-intensity signal changes on T2-weighted images can be either well demarcated or diffuse and either focal or multisegmental. Many authors have supported the belief that a high-intensity intramedullary signal on T2-weighted images is correlated with a poor prognosis for neurologic recovery and that the absence of this finding or postoperative resolution of signal is correlated with a favorable prognosis.[59,60] In a prospective evaluation of 104 patients, older age, duration of disease, postoperative Japanese Orthopaedic Association score, and intramedullary signal on T2-weighted MRI all were correlated with a poor prognosis for neurologic recovery.[61] However, when MRI was repeated at an average 39.2-month follow-up, no statistically significant correlation was found between an alteration in high-signal intensity on T2-weighted studies and surgical outcome.[62] Other studies found preoperative or postoperative T2-weighted MRI to be an unreliable prognostic indicator; pyramidal signs such as clonus, spasticity, and hypointensity on T1-weighted studies were more reliable predictors. Hypointensity on T1-weighted MRI may indicate irreversible damage to the gray matter and therefore suggests a poor prognosis for neurologic recovery.[63,64] Well-demarcated signal changes on T2-weighted MRI and hypointensity on T1-weighted MRI

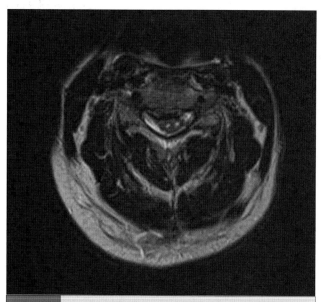

Figure 4   T2-weighted axial MRI of the cervical spine showing the snake-eyes appearance, which represents cystic necrosis of the gray matter.

are believed to occur during the late stages of myelopathy, and they may indicate irreversible damage such as cystic necrosis.[65] Further study is needed to better evaluate these factors.

The so-called snake-eyes appearance on axial T2-weighted MRI is a pathognomonic imaging finding in cervical myelopathy (Figure 4); it indicates cystic necrosis of the gray matter and the anterior horn, probably resulting from mechanical compression and venous infarction.[66] This finding has been identified as a negative predictor of neurologic recovery after a decompressive procedure, though controversy remains.[67] A retrospective study of 47 patients attempted to determine prognostic factors for neurologic recovery by analyzing the influence of patient age, sex, preoperative neurologic grade, duration of symptoms, and radiographic findings.[67] Diabetes mellitus was the only statistically significant negative prognostic factor, although intramedullary signal (the snake-eyes appearance) did trend toward being a negative prognostic indicator.

Summary and Future Research

The pathophysiology of cervical myelopathy is multifactorial. Static factors including stenosis, ligament ossification, and sagittal alignment can place the cord at risk for compression and lead to ischemic and histologic changes such as apoptosis. Dynamic factors such as segmental motion at a stenotic level also may contribute to this pathology. MRI has been used to document and predict the clinical prognosis, but further research is needed.

Acute spinal cord injury has been the focus of an enormous amount of research, but relatively little re-

search has focused on the chronic injury typical of cervical spondylotic myelopathy. Secondary injury reduction may prove to be useful in treating cervical myelopathy. Neuroprotective agents should be evaluated for reducing secondary zone injury and reducing apoptosis in the spinal cord. The timing of surgery in the treatment of cervical myelopathy also requires study. Surgery is beneficial for patients with significant myelopathy and functional deficits. The treatment is unclear for patients with severe cord compression and few or no symptoms, and a better understanding of the pathophysiology of cervical myelopathy may provide useful information. There is still great controversy as to the best surgical approach and technique for treating the myriad manifestations of cervical myelopathy. Research also is needed to better elucidate the biologic mechanisms underlying the progressive cell death that occurs in cervical myelopathy.

Annotated References

1. Wolf BS, Khilnani M, Malis L: The sagittal diameter of the bony cervical spinal canal and its significance in cervical spondylosis. *J Mt Sinai Hosp N Y* 1956;23(3):283-292.

2. Hayashi H, Okada K, Hashimoto J, Tada K, Ueno R: Cervical spondylotic myelopathy in the aged patient: A radiographic evaluation of the aging changes in the cervical spine and etiologic factors of myelopathy. *Spine (Phila Pa 1976)* 1988;13(6):618-625.

3. Edwards WC, LaRocca H: The developmental segmental sagittal diameter of the cervical spinal canal in patients with cervical spondylosis. *Spine (Phila Pa 1976)* 1983;8(1):20-27.

4. Gore DR: Roentgenographic findings in the cervical spine in asymptomatic persons: A ten-year follow-up. *Spine (Phila Pa 1976)* 2001;26(22):2463-2466.

5. Lee MJ, Cassinelli EH, Riew KD: Prevalence of cervical spine stenosis: Anatomic study in cadavers. *J Bone Joint Surg Am* 2007;89(2):376-380.

    An anatomic study analyzed the spectrum of sagittal diameters of the cervical spinal canal, the frequency of cervical stenosis in the general population, and the prevalence of cervical stenosis by age group, race, and sex.

6. Okada Y, Ikata T, Katoh S, Yamada H: Morphologic analysis of the cervical spinal cord, dural tube, and spinal canal by magnetic resonance imaging in normal adults and patients with cervical spondylotic myelopathy. *Spine (Phila Pa 1976)* 1994;19(20):2331-2335.

7. Hayashi H, Okada K, Hamada M, Tada K, Ueno R: Etiologic factors of myelopathy: A radiographic evaluation of the aging changes in the cervical spine. *Clin Orthop Relat Res* 1987;214:200-209.

8. Pavlov H, Torg JS, Robie B, Jahre C: Cervical spinal stenosis: Determination with vertebral body ratio method. *Radiology* 1987;164(3):771-775.

9. Herzog RJ, Wiens JJ, Dillingham MF, Sontag MJ: Normal cervical spine morphometry and cervical spinal stenosis in asymptomatic professional football players: Plain film radiography, multiplanar computed tomography, and magnetic resonance imaging. *Spine (Phila Pa 1976)* 1991;16(6, suppl):S178-S186.

10. Turnbull IM, Brieg A, Hassler O: Blood supply of cervical spinal cord in man: A microangiographic cadaver study. *J Neurosurg* 1966;24(6):951-965.

11. Brockstein B, Johns L, Gewertz BL: Blood supply to the spinal cord: Anatomic and physiologic correlations. *Ann Vasc Surg* 1994;8(4):394-399.

12. Tator CH, Koyanagi I: Vascular mechanisms in the pathophysiology of human spinal cord injury. *J Neurosurg* 1997;86(3):483-492.

13. Koyanagi T, Hirabayashi K, Satomi K, Toyama Y, Fujimura Y: Predictability of operative results of cervical compression myelopathy based on preoperative computed tomographic myelography. *Spine (Phila Pa 1976)* 1993;18(14):1958-1963.

14. Kameyama T, Hashizume Y, Ando T, Takahashi A, Yanagi T, Mizuno J: Spinal cord morphology and pathology in ossification of the posterior longitudinal ligament. *Brain* 1995;118(pt 1):263-278.

15. Houser OW, Onofrio BM, Miller GM, Folger WN, Smith PL: Cervical spondylotic stenosis and myelopathy: Evaluation with computed tomographic myelography. *Mayo Clin Proc* 1994;69(6):557-563.

16. Abe H, Tsuru M, Ito T, Iwasaki Y, Koiwa M: Anterior decompression for ossification of the posterior longitudinal ligament of the cervical spine. *J Neurosurg* 1981;55(1):108-116.

17. Izawa K: Comparative roentgenographical study on the incidence of ossification of the posterior longitudinal ligament and other degenerative changes of the cervical spine among Japanese, Koreans, Americans and Germans. *Nippon Seikeigeka Gakkai Zasshi* 1980;54(5):461-474.

18. Okawa A, Nakamura I, Goto S, Moriya H, Nakamura Y, Ikegawa S: Mutation in Npps in a mouse model of ossification of the posterior longitudinal ligament of the spine. *Nat Genet* 1998;19(3):271-273.

19. Okano T, Ishidou Y, Kato M, et al: Orthotopic ossification of the spinal ligaments of Zucker fatty rats: A possible animal model for ossification of the human posterior longitudinal ligament. *J Orthop Res* 1997;15(6):820-829.

20. Sampson HW: Spondyloarthropathy in progressive an- kylosis (ank/ank) mice: Morphological features. *Spine (Phila Pa 1976)* 1988;13(6):645-649.

21. Nakamura I, Ikegawa S, Okawa A, et al: Association of the human NPPS gene with ossification of the posterior longitudinal ligament of the spine (OPLL). *Hum Genet* 1999;104(6):492-497.

22. Tahara M, Aiba A, Yamazaki M, et al: The extent of ossification of posterior longitudinal ligament of the spine associated with nucleotide pyrophosphatase gene and leptin receptor gene polymorphisms. *Spine (Phila Pa 1976)* 2005;30(8):877-881.

   Through genomic DNA evaluation and radiographic analysis, revealed that *NPPS* and *LEPR* polymorphisms were associated with more extensive OPLL.

23. Matsunaga S, Sakou T, Taketomi E, Yamaguchi M, Okano T: The natural course of myelopathy caused by ossification of the posterior longitudinal ligament in the cervical spine. *Clin Orthop Relat Res* 1994;305:168-177.

24. Morio Y, Nagashima H, Teshima R, Nawata K: Radiological pathogenesis of cervical myelopathy in 60 consecutive patients with cervical ossification of the posterior longitudinal ligament. *Spinal Cord* 1999;37(12):853-857.

25. Yamashita Y, Takahashi M, Matsuno Y, et al: Spinal cord compression due to ossification of ligaments: MR imaging. *Radiology* 1990;175(3):843-848.

26. Mak KH, Mak KL, Gwi-Mak E: Ossification of the ligamentum flavum in the cervicothoracic junction: Case report on ossification found on both sides of the lamina. *Spine (Phila Pa 1976)* 2002;27(1):E11-E14.

27. Ono K, Yonenobu K, Miyamoto S, Okada K: Pathology of ossification of the posterior longitudinal ligament and ligamentum flavum. *Clin Orthop Relat Res* 1999;359:18-26.

28. Bohlman HH: Cervical spondylosis and myelopathy. *Instr Course Lect* 1995;44:81-97.

29. Barnes MP, Saunders M: The effect of cervical mobility on the natural history of cervical spondylotic myelopathy. *J Neurol Neurosurg Psychiatry* 1984;47(1):17-20.

30. Yonenobu K, Okada K, Fuji T, Fujiwara K, Yamashita K, Ono K: Causes of neurologic deterioration following surgical treatment of cervical myelopathy. *Spine (Phila Pa 1976)* 1986;11(8):818-823.

31. Eleraky MA, Llanos C, Sonntag VK: Cervical corpectomy: Report of 185 cases and review of the literature. *J Neurosurg* 1999;90(1, suppl):35-41.

32. Kumar VG, Rea GL, Mervis LJ, McGregor JM: Cervical spondylotic myelopathy: Functional and radiographic long-term outcome after laminectomy and posterior fusion. *Neurosurgery* 1999;44(4):771-778.

33. Rosen CL, Orphanos JR, Nugent RG, Marano G: The use of MR-myelography combining flexion and extension imaging in the diagnosis of cervical myelopathy: A case report. *W V Med J* 2009;105(1):10-14.

Noninvasive magnetic resonance myelography, combining flexion and extension views, was used to reveal causative factors in cervical myelopathy.

34. Guppy KH, Hawk M, Chakrabarti I, Banerjee A: The use of flexion-extension magnetic resonance imaging for evaluating signal intensity changes of the cervical spinal cord. *J Neurosurg Spine* 2009;10(4):366-373.

Dynamic MRI of the cervical spine found spinal cord compression after static studies had not found cord compression.

35. Muhle C, Weinert D, Falliner A, et al: Dynamic changes of the spinal canal in patients with cervical spondylosis at flexion and extension using magnetic resonance imaging. *Invest Radiol* 1998;33(8):444-449.

36. Breig A, Turnbull I, Hassler O: Effects of mechanical stresses on the spinal cord in cervical spondylosis: A study on fresh cadaver material. *J Neurosurg* 1966;25(1):45-56.

37. Smith CG: Changes in length and position of the segments of the spinal cord with changes in posture in the monkey. *Radiology* 1956;66(2):259-266.

38. Zdeblick TA, Bohlman HH: Cervical kyphosis and myelopathy: Treatment by anterior corpectomy and strut-grafting. *J Bone Joint Surg Am* 1989;71(2):170-182.

39. Iwasaki M, Yamamoto T, Miyauchi A, Amano K, Yonenobu K: Cervical kyphosis: Predictive factors for progression of kyphosis and myelopathy. *Spine (Phila Pa 1976)* 2002;27(13):1419-1425.

40. Spivak J, Giordano C: Cervical kyphosis, in Bridwell KH, DeWald RL, eds: *Textbook of Spinal Surgery*, ed 2. Philadelphia, PA, Lippincott-Raven, 1997, pp 1027-1038.

41. Doppman JL: The mechanism of ischemia in anteroposterior compression of the spinal cord. *Invest Radiol* 1975;10(6):543-551.

42. al-Mefty O, Harkey HL, Marawi I, et al: Experimental chronic compressive cervical myelopathy. *J Neurosurg* 1993;79(4):550-561.

43. Gooding MR, Wilson CB, Hoff JT: Experimental cervical myelopathy: Effects of ischemia and compression of the canine cervical spinal cord. *J Neurosurg* 1975;43(1):9-17.

44. Hashizume Y, Iijima S, Kishimoto H, Yanagi T: Pathology of spinal cord lesions caused by ossification of the posterior longitudinal ligament. *Acta Neuropathol* 1984;63(2):123-130.

45. Ebersold MJ, Pare MC, Quast LM: Surgical treatment for cervical spondylitic myelopathy. *J Neurosurg* 1995;82(5):745-751.

46. Nurick S: The pathogenesis of the spinal cord disorder associated with cervical spondylosis. *Brain* 1972;95(1):87-100.

47. Bhardwaj A, Long DM, Ducker TB, Toung TJ: Neurologic deficits after cervical laminectomy in the prone position. *J Neurosurg Anesthesiol* 2001;13(4):314-319.

48. Povlishock JT: Traumatically induced axonal injury: Pathogenesis and pathobiological implications. *Brain Pathol* 1992;2(1):1-12.

49. Maxwell WL, Irvine A, Graham DI, et al: Focal axonal injury: The early axonal response to stretch. *J Neurocytol* 1991;20(3):157-164.

50. Christman CW, Grady MS, Walker SA, Holloway KL, Povlishock JT: Ultrastructural studies of diffuse axonal injury in humans. *J Neurotrauma* 1994;11(2):173-186.

51. Li Y, Field PM, Raisman G: Death of oligodendrocytes and microglial phagocytosis of myelin precede immigration of Schwann cells into the spinal cord. *J Neurocytol* 1999;28(4-5):417-427.

52. Pfeiffer SE, Warrington AE, Bansal R: The oligodendrocyte and its many cellular processes. *Trends Cell Biol* 1993;3(6):191-197.

53. Ito T, Oyanagi K, Takahashi H, Takahashi HE, Ikuta F: Cervical spondylotic myelopathy: Clinicopathologic study on the progression pattern and thin myelinated fibers of the lesions of seven patients examined during complete autopsy. *Spine (Phila Pa 1976)* 1996;21(7):827-833.

54. Yamaura I, Yone K, Nakahara S, et al: Mechanism of destructive pathologic changes in the spinal cord under chronic mechanical compression. *Spine (Phila Pa 1976)* 2002;27(1):21-26.

55. Park E, Velumian AA, Fehlings MG: The role of excitotoxicity in secondary mechanisms of spinal cord injury: A review with an emphasis on the implications for white matter degeneration. *J Neurotrauma* 2004;21(6):754-774.

56. Li GL, Brodin G, Farooque M, et al: Apoptosis and expression of Bcl-2 after compression trauma to rat spinal cord. *J Neuropathol Exp Neurol* 1996;55(3):280-289.

57. Liu XZ, Xu XM, Hu R, et al: Neuronal and glial apoptosis after traumatic spinal cord injury. *J Neurosci* 1997;17(14):5395-5406.

58. Crowe MJ, Bresnahan JC, Shuman SL, Masters JN, Beattie MS: Apoptosis and delayed degeneration after spinal cord injury in rats and monkeys. *Nat Med* 1997;3(1):73-76.

59. Fernández de Rota JJ, Meschian S, Fernández de Rota A, Urbano V, Baron M: Cervical spondylotic myelopathy due to chronic compression: The role of signal intensity changes in magnetic resonance images. *J Neurosurg Spine* 2007;6(1):17-22.

A retrospective study analyzed whether T2-weighted MRI of the cervical cord in patients with compressive myelopathy is useful in determining the prognosis of the disease.

60. Mastronardi L, Elsawaf A, Roperto R, et al: Prognostic relevance of the postoperative evolution of intramedullary spinal cord changes in signal intensity on magnetic resonance imaging after anterior decompression for cervical spondylotic myelopathy. *J Neurosurg Spine* 2007; 7(6):615-622.

Postoperative alterations in MRI signal intensity in the cervical spinal cord were found in patients with cervical spondylotic myelopathy.

61. Yukawa Y, Kato F, Yoshihara H, Yanase M, Ito K: MR T2 image classification in cervical compression myelopathy: Predictor of surgical outcomes. *Spine (Phila Pa 1976)* 2007;32(15):1675-1679.

A prospective imaging study evaluated the relationship of MRI signal intensity, symptom severity, and surgical outcome in patients with cervical compressive myelopathy.

62. Yukawa Y, Kato F, Ito K, et al: Postoperative changes in spinal cord signal intensity in patients with cervical compression myelopathy: Comparison between preoperative and postoperative magnetic resonance images. *J Neurosurg Spine* 2008;8(6):524-528.

Preoperative and postoperative MRI signal intensities in the spinal cord are compared, with consideration of whether postoperative classification and increased signal intensity reflect the postoperative severity of symptoms and the surgical outcome.

63. Alafifi T, Kern R, Fehlings M: Clinical and MRI predictors of outcome after surgical intervention for cervical spondylotic myelopathy. *J Neuroimaging* 2007;17(4): 315-322.

Definition of clinical and MRI predictors of outcome was attempted after intervention for cervical spondylotic myelopathy.

64. Uchida K, Nakajima H, Yayama T, et al: High-resolution magnetic resonance imaging and 18FDG-PET findings of the cervical spinal cord before and after decompressive surgery in patients with compressive myelopathy. *Spine (Phila Pa 1976)* 2009;34(11):1185-1191.

The cervical spinal cord of patients with compressive myelopathy was evaluated using MRI and high-resolution (18F) fluorodeoxyglucose positron emission tomography.

65. Wada E, Ohmura M, Yonenobu K: Intramedullary changes of the spinal cord in cervical spondylotic myelopathy. *Spine (Phila Pa 1976)* 1995;20(20):2226-2232.

66. Mizuno J, Nakagawa H, Inoue T, Hashizume Y: Clinicopathological study of "snake-eye appearance" in compressive myelopathy of the cervical spinal cord. *J Neurosurg* 2003;99(2, suppl):162-168.

67. Choi S, Lee SH, Lee JY, et al: Factors affecting prognosis of patients who underwent corpectomy and fusion for treatment of cervical ossification of the posterior longitudinal ligament: Analysis of 47 patients. *J Spinal Disord Tech* 2005;18(4):309-314.

The clinical and radiologic parameters of patients with OPLL were analyzed to identify factors affecting prognosis after decompression with corpectomy.

1: Basic Science of the Spine

Chapter 6

The Pathobiology and Treatment of Acute Spinal Cord Injury

Brian Hood, MD   James D. Guest, MD, PhD

1: Basic Science of the Spine

Introduction

The tissues of the spinal cord are highly susceptible to injury and have little capacity for self-repair. Because spinal cord injury (SCI) can irreversibly and dramatically change the course of a life, the reversal of SCI continues to be one of the greatest challenges in medicine. Spinal cord salvage and spinal cord repair are two primary goals of therapy. Knowledge of the pathobiology of SCI is rapidly evolving, and components once thought to be entirely detrimental, such as glial scarring and inflammation, now are understood to have beneficial aspects.

Traumatic SCI typically is caused by a contusive force to the spinal cord, leading to the activation of numerous mechanisms that both extend and limit the injury (Figure 1). Abundant experimental data show that tissue-neuroprotective treatment strategies can preserve some spinal cord structure and neurologic function after a contusive injury, but these effects have been difficult to prove clinically. In addition, numerous experimental strategies exist for partial repair of the spinal cord after the injury is established. To design and apply neuroprotective and repair strategies, it is important to understand the temporal evolution of the injury mechanisms. The complex process of translating experimental studies to clinical studies also should be understood.

The prospects for spinal cord repair were regarded with pessimism until three decades ago. Nonetheless, some relevant biologic facts were well known, including the partial natural recovery of damaged peripheral nerves, the ability of some species of fish and other nonmammalian animals to undergo effective spinal cord repair, and the benefit of relieving chronic severe spinal cord compression in patients with myelopathy. The reasons for pessimism included the evident lack of distal recovery after a complete SCI, the histology of

SCI with cavitation, the extensive axonal loss with SCI, and an apparent lack of spontaneous repair. The recent acceleration of clinical and experimental progress has increased hope that new and effective treatments will be developed.

The involvement of a spine surgeon in the care of patients with SCI traditionally has been in acute care, surgical decompression, vertebral stabilization, and management of chronic complications such as syringomyelia, tethering, and progressive deformity. The spine surgeon's role is expanding, however, to include translational clinical studies of neuroprotective and neurorestorative treatments as well as collaboration with the biotechnology industry. Education in designing and conducting preclinical and clinical studies is fundamental to minimizing bias and generating clear answers. There is a continuing need for leaders with surgical and scientific training to take advantage of the many promising therapies that await translation by conducting translation and clinical research studies.

Epidemiology

The US Spinal Cord Injury Model Care System, instituted during the 1970s, required federally funded SCI centers to contribute patient information to a national database. The resulting National Spinal Cord Injury Statistical Center merged with a database from the Centers for Disease Control and Prevention during the 1980s to allow a reasonably thorough description of the epidemiology of SCI in the United States. Formerly, the most common causes of traumatic SCI were low-velocity accident and battlefield trauma, and traumatic SCI probably was less common than infectious SCI. Infections from causes such as tuberculosis now are frequently resolved before they result in spinal cord damage. In contrast, trauma associated with motorized transportation, industry, or sports increasingly involves unprecedented levels of speed and force.

The estimated annual incidence of acute SCI in the United States among those who survive a traumatic event is 40 per 1 million population, or approximately 12,000 per year, and the number of people living with SCI in the United States has been estimated at

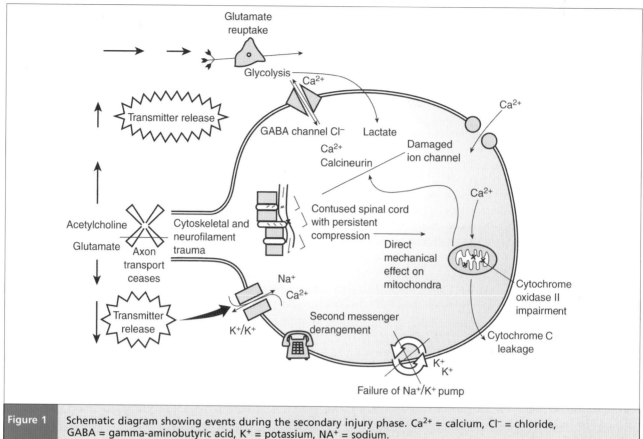

| Figure 1 | Schematic diagram showing events during the secondary injury phase. Ca²⁺ = calcium, Cl⁻ = chloride, GABA = gamma-aminobutyric acid, K⁺ = potassium, NA⁺ = sodium. |

265,000.[1] Traumatic SCI primarily affects young adults; almost 50% of new injuries involve patients age 16 to 30 years. The average age at injury is increasing along with the median age of the US population: from 1973 to 1979, the average age at injury was 28.7 years, but since 2005, the average age has been more than 40 years.[1] The distribution of age at injury has become bimodal. The first peak occurs in young adults and adolescents, and a second peak occurs in adults older than 60 years. Since 1980, the percentage of SCIs occurring in older adults has increased from 4.7% to 11.5%.[1] The US population of adults older than 60 years is expected to double from 34 million in 1999 to 69 million in 2030.[2] Adults older than 60 years are more vulnerable to SCI because of age-related changes in bone quality, the high prevalence of cervical spondylosis and stenosis, the effects of medication and sensory loss, and a relatively high rate of motor vehicle crashes per driven miles. In addition, the clinical outcome of SCI in patients older than 60 years tends to be considerably worse than the outcome in younger patients.

Eighty-one percent of SCIs occur in men and boys, although this percentage has declined since 1980.[1] Motor vehicle crashes account for more than 40% of all reported SCIs, and falls account for 28%. Acts of violence accounted for 25% of SCIs between 1990 and 1999 but currently account for 15%. Sports injuries account for 8%, and the mechanism is unreported for

more than 8% of injuries. Approximately 50% of patients have a cervical injury, 35% have a thoracic or thoracolumbar injury, 11% have a lumbar or lumbosacral injury, and the location of the remaining 4% of injuries is unknown or unreported.[1] The single most common level of injury is C5. The most frequently reported post-SCI neurologic category is incomplete tetraplegia (39.5%); complete paraplegia accounts for 22.1%, complete tetraplegia for 21.7%, and incomplete paraplegia for 16.3%.

The goals of the acute clinical treatment of SCI are to prevent further injury, maintain blood flow, relieve compression, and provide vertebral stabilization to allow early rehabilitation. Initial management of the primary SCI is most challenging in a patient with multiple traumatic injuries. At least 20% of patients with SCI have other major injuries such as cerebral contusions or flail chest; rates as high as 57% have been reported.[3-5] Because autoregulation is not preserved after severe SCI, the cord is susceptible to ischemia during hypotension. Periods of fever or other hyperthermia appear to be detrimental to tissue preservation in patients with acute SCI. Thus, attention to systemic physiology may influence the outcome after SCI.

The cost of caring for a patient with SCI is substantial but differs depending on whether the patient has a complete or incomplete injury. Excluding indirect costs such as lost wages and productivity, the estimated average cost of caring for a patient with a complete, high cervical injury is $985,774 during the first year, with an additional $171,183 for each subsequent year. The lifetime cost of care is approximately $4,373,912 for a patient injured at age 25 years and $2,403,828 for a patient injured at age 50 years. The estimated mortality rate is approximately 6% during the first year after SCI, 2% during the second year, and 1% per year thereafter. However, these rates pertain to countries that offer the best possible care, and patient survival is far less likely in many developing countries.

Efforts to prevent SCI include the installation of motor vehicle safety features such as seatbelts and airbags, improved sports equipment design, workplace safety measures, and school-based education. Think First Foundation and the Foundation for Spinal Cord Injury Prevention, Care and Cure provide school lectures on such risks as contact sports participation, drinking and driving, and diving into shallow water. However, risk taking is inherent to human nature, and SCIs are likely to continue to occur.

Although reconstruction of the spinal cord leading to functional recovery is an exciting prospect, it is important to appreciate the many simple advances in SCI management that have extended patients' quality of life and lifespan. No other single intervention has been more useful than intermittent catheterization, which is believed to have reduced mortality and morbidity among patients with SCI by more than 20%.[6] Prevention of deep venous thrombosis and decubitus ulcers is of similar importance.

Classification

No two SCIs are identical, and therapies are most effective if they can be tailored to the individual patient. Genetic studies are beginning to show that polymorphisms for certain alleles affect the neurologic outcome after SCI, and epigenetic studies are likely to discover an even greater degree of complexity.[7-9] The individual patient's age, preexisting diseases, lesion characteristics, and pharmacokinetic variations may partially account for the failure of large drug studies to show substantial efficacy in treating SCI.

An SCI is clinically defined as complete or incomplete, depending on the presence or absence of motor and/or sensory neurologic function below the neurologic level. At the level of injury, there may be paralysis of the lower motor neuron type resulting from the destruction of gray matter, including motor neurons and nerve roots. Areflexia and hypotonia initially occur after the injury and eventually lead to muscle atrophy. Below the lesion, paralysis is mainly of the upper motor neuron type and is characterized by spasticity, exaggerated stretch reflexes, and clonus. Lesions of the cauda equina affect lower motor neurons and can lead to flaccid paralysis with eventual muscle loss. Lesions of the conus medullaris affect mixed upper and lower motor neurons and can lead to a combination of flaccid paralysis and spasticity. A spinal cord concussion, causing partial or complete loss of function with complete recovery hours or days after injury, presumably results primarily from local axonal depolarization and transient dysfunction.

It is increasingly recognized that an exclusive focus on the motor and sensory components of spinal cord function neglects important autonomic functions. There is evidence of retained autonomic connectivity in some SCIs with complete motor and sensory loss. The International Standards for Classification of Spinal Cord Injury now include clinical testing of autonomic function.[10,11] Autonomic changes such as postural hypotension have serious functional effects on patients with SCI. An SCI higher than T6 disrupts supraspinal sympathetic control of cardiovascular function, including coronary blood flow, cardiac contractility, and heart rate. Unopposed parasympathetic input from the vagus nerve can lead to bradycardia and other cardiac arrhythmias. SCI caudal to T6 permits normal cardiac responses, with decreased regulation of the peripheral vascular response. Postmortem immunohistochemical examination of spinal cord tissue in individuals in whom neurogenic shock developed after acute SCI found significantly fewer preserved axons caudal to the injury site than is found in individuals with no significant symptoms of abnormal cardiovascular control. A clinically complete acute injury can occur without an anatomically complete transection. Even minimal anatomic continuity of central nervous system (CNS) tracts across the lesion is important for the purposes of therapies to promote neuroplasticity and myelin repair. Patients with paraplegia rank the recovery of bladder, bowel, and sexual function as more important than walking.[12]

Pathobiology

The Normal Spinal Cord

The normal spinal cord is a stable structure throughout life, although the number of myelinated axons and neurons modestly decreases with advancing age. Neurons have highly specific connectional complexity, with numerous inputs and often several outputs that are extensively feedback modulated. Neurons are especially vulnerable to injury because of the length, complexity, and specificity of their connections. In addition, the receptor and membrane specializations that enable chemical and electrical neuronal transmission cause a high capacity for and vulnerability to major ionic shifts. The spinal cord's component tissues are rarely exposed to inflammatory cells, and there is a specialized barrier between endothelial cells supported by astroglia that restricts movement of proteins and other molecules. The evolutionary value of the spinal cord's limited ability to undergo axonal regeneration is unknown.

1: Basic Science of the Spine

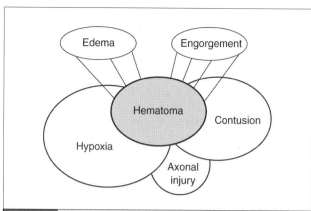

Figure 2	Schematic diagram showing multiple factors that contribute to the ischemic cascade during the secondary injury phase. The spinal cord typically is contused and swollen after injury. The swelling is accompanied by ischemia, and neuronal and axonal damage is accompanied by vascular endothelial damage and hypoxia. Continued compression may exacerbate the ischemic cascade.

The Injured Spinal Cord

Traumatic injury to the spinal cord occurs as the osseoligamentous column fails under loading. The spinal cord may undergo abrupt direct physical deformation. In addition, the spinal cord, nerve roots, and associated vessels may be crushed and lacerated by bone fragments. Central SCI may occur from an abrupt contusion during hyperextension of a stenotic cervical spine, without dislocation or fracture. The distinction between contusion and compression is in the compression rate (as seen, for example, in the acute compression from a cervical fracture-dislocation compared with the slowly progressive nature of cervical spondylotic myelopathy). In acute SCI the compressive force is so rapid that the rate of deformation exceeds the tissue component's tolerance, leading to physical disruption or irreversible injury of the axons, myelinating cells, neuron cell bodies, and vascular endothelium. In a gunshot wound, the spinal cord and nerve roots may be directly injured by the projectile or indirectly injured by fragments of bone or disk. As the projectile's kinetic energy is dissipated, the spinal cord also may undergo abrupt distortion and shearing (blast cavitation) without direct contact by the projectile or tissue fragments. The maximal neurologic deficit usually is observed immediately after an SCI because axonal transmission is blocked by local ionic perturbations. However, tissue damage continues during the secondary injury phase, substantially extending the size of the injury.[13]

After an injury, the spinal cord typically is contused and swollen, may be partially lacerated, but rarely is transected. The first visible sign of injury is swelling caused by the extracellular edema associated with increased endothelial permeability and intracellular edema (astrocytic swelling). Edema and hemorrhage within the cord may extend from the primary site of impact over several rostral and caudal levels (**Figure 2**). Hemorrhage is more evident in the gray matter because of its rich vascularity. Endothelial damage is a key factor in the recruitment of inflammatory cells after SCI.

The initial, primary SCI causes abrupt neuronal cellular damage, endothelial and blood vessel damage, hemorrhage, and massive shifts in membrane potential and ionic concentrations. The secondary injury phase begins immediately and may extend for several days. More protracted injury responses occur over the subsequent months to years. The secondary events include further ionic shifts and membrane channel dysfunction, lipid peroxidation, oxidative stress, glutamatergic excitotoxicity, excessive intracellular calcium levels, ischemia, hemorrhage, edema, apoptotic and necrotic cellular death, and an inflammatory response.[14,15] Continued compression of the injured spinal cord by disk, bone, or blood clot in the epidural space may exacerbate the magnitude of the ischemic and secondary injury cascades. Several counterdestructive mechanisms are initiated, including the birth of new cells, angiogenesis, and the production of trophic molecules. Axonal disruption is the least reversible of the injury effects. The predominately lipid structure of the spinal cord partially accounts for its vulnerability to injury; aside from the pia mater, there is very little connective tissue in the spinal cord in comparison with the peripheral nerves, which are much more resilient.

Experimental Models of SCI

Increasing the precision and reducing the variability of experimental models of SCI have led to important progress. Experiments now require fewer animals than were previously used. Better modeling also allows more accurate comparisons of study results. In the most common experimental injury, the NYU piston impactor is used to create a 12.5 g per cm dorsal contusion.[16] This injury magnitude typically causes an incomplete SCI followed by locomotor function recovery measured as approximately 12 on a widely used 21-point recovery scale. With this extent of recovery, the animal can use the hind limbs but completely lacks coordination and balance. The alternative epidural balloon and spring clip compression methods are more sensitive to the amount and duration of maximal compression. The maximal amount, duration, and rate of compression are the three injury variables that best predict the extent of an SCI. Functional and anatomic damage at a low contact velocity is best predicted by the maximal amount of compression. Because the spinal cord has both viscous and elastic properties, certain deformations can be tolerated without injury. With increasing contact velocity, SCI severity becomes a function of the viscous response, as the suddenly applied forces exceed the spinal cord's ability to absorb energy without injury. The rate of cord deformation was found to be the most reliable predictor of the severity of the lesion, as determined using a weight drop model of experimental

SCI.[17] The amount of energy absorbed or dissipated during rapid deformation is correlated with injury severity.[18] For example, a gunshot produces an extremely rapid rate of tissue deformation, and the resulting injuries are severe.

Persistent Spinal Cord Compression

Persistent compression is common after SCI and may be caused by a ruptured disk, bony fragmentation, or dislocation. Ischemia is the presumptive mechanism of persistent compression. Persistent compression after contusive SCI caused potentially reversible additional injury in numerous animal studies. When the use of a weight drop model of SCI was followed by placement of an epidural spacer to simulate persistent compression, spinal cord decompression improved the outcome; this finding applied to mild or moderate SCI but not to severe SCI.[19] Neurologic recovery was inversely related to the duration of compression.

The Importance of Neuroprotection

The complex and specific organization of the spinal cord is established during prenatal development. No restorative treatment can be as effective as neuroprotection of the tissue not destroyed by the primary injury. The primary injury usually does not transect the entire cord, and postmortem studies of acutely injured spinal cords found that a subpial rim of spared but damaged long tract axons frequently spans the lesion.[14] Animal studies found that significant neurologic function can be maintained if only 1.4% to 12% of the total number of axons are spared across the injury.[20-23] By reinforcing the concept that even small gains in axon preservation can substantially affect functional neurologic recovery, these studies have helped establish a strong theoretical basis for the value of neuroprotection. The potential for neuroprotection to reduce secondary injury has been abundantly supported in diverse experimental studies that found increased tissue preservation. Diverse compounds ranging from hormonal receptor agents such as tamoxifen and estrogen to polyethylene glycol have neuroprotective effects on numerous mechanistic pathways.[23-25]

A clinical neuroprotective effect has been difficult to establish, possibly because of the heterogeneity of human populations in comparison with experimental animals. Neuroprotective drugs and strategies are most beneficial if administered during a therapeutic window soon after the injury. Later administration offers no benefit. Maximal neuroprotection may require a multitargeted approach initiated immediately after the injury. The lack of correlation between the benefits observed in animal and human studies of SCI also is present in studies of other injuries for which neuroprotection is desirable, such as stroke.

After the initial therapeutic window for neuroprotection has ended, repair strategies have been used for treating severe SCI, with the aim of restoring CNS communication above and below the injury. These strategies now include the use of technologic devices to restore some functions, such as bladder emptying and standing, in the absence of a neuronal reconnection to the brain and brainstem. One basis for these technologic approaches is the fact that a completely transected spinal cord is capable of some autonomous function, including stepping, despite its isolation from the brain.[26] The neural networks within the spinal cord that mediate reciprocating locomotor output in vertebrates have been called central pattern generators. In cats with spinal transection, these central pattern generators were potently activated pharmacologically or by sensory input through treadmill training.[27,28] Thus, the spinal cord in mammals is capable of specific autonomous functions under certain conditions and can be trained without a need for input from the brain. However, some key functions, such as balance, remain absent in this state.

Ionic Dysregulation

Ionic homeostasis is lost immediately after SCI, further propagating the injury. Failure of the cell membrane and the transmembrane adenosine triphosphate pumps causes loss of regulation of extracellular concentrations of sodium, glutamate, and other molecules[29] (Figure 1). Excessive glutamate receptor activation leads to a further influx of sodium and calcium through N-methyl-D-aspartate (NMDA), aminoisopropyl propionic acid, and kainate receptors. Activation of the NMDA receptor has been associated with numerous changes in gene regulation and serves as a key signaling event in SCI.[30] Excess calcium influx initiates the activation of calpains as well as mitochondrial breakdown, and it contributes to the production of free radicals. Oligodendrocytes (the myelinating cells of the CNS) possess NMDA receptors and are susceptible to death from glutamate excitotoxicity.[31] The death of oligodendrocytes can leave remnants of poorly myelinated or dysmyelinated axons. Repair of inadequately myelinated residual axons is an important target of therapy aimed at improving conduction of spared axons.

Spinal Cord Inflammation

The inflammatory response has a major role in the expansion and resolution of the SCI lesion and is a key target for neuroprotection. The literature on posttraumatic spinal cord inflammation has developed rapidly during the past 15 years and represents one of the most active areas of current investigation. The spinal cord usually is not exposed to inflammation, in contrast to tissues such as those of the skin, bones, or lungs, which frequently undergo healing processes. Thus, macrophages, lymphocytes, and polymorphonuclear leukocytes (neutrophils) are seldom observed in the normal spinal cord, and the intrinsic microglia usually are quiescent. In an evolutionary sense, infection has been the main disease threat to the CNS and the spinal cord, and the inflammatory responses of the spinal cord appear more suited to infection than trauma. Because an infec-

1: Basic Science of the Spine

tion progresses from a minimal level, there is a possibility of local control and attenuation. In contrast, the inflammation after SCI is severe and appears to exceed the capacity of a spinal cord response adapted to debris removal and new tissue formation. In some mouse models, a reduced intrinsic inflammatory response was associated with reduced tissue injury after SCI.[32] However, there is evidence that components of the inflammatory response also aid in repairing SCI.[33]

The contribution of inflammatory responses to both destructive and reparative processes after SCI is a clear theme of research during the past decade. The inflammatory response to mechanical injury is substantially more severe in the spinal cord than in the brain, as a result of differences in the proinflammatory cytokines secreted after injury. The inflammatory events after SCI were formerly oversimplified to emphasize free-radical liberation, lipid peroxidation promoted by neutrophils, and the removal of cellular debris by macrophages. Some of the early neuroprotective strategies targeted the downstream consequences of cell activities such as lipid peroxidation rather than the potentially more effective interruption of earlier events such as cellular ingress through damaged endothelium. Evolving knowledge indicates that the inflammatory response is complex. Therefore, regulation of the response to enhance repair is more challenging than was appreciated even 2 or 3 years ago. Until recently, it seemed probable that attenuating the inflammatory response, especially by limiting neutrophils, would lead to tissue preservation. However, recent data indicate that neutrophils have key roles in injury resolution.[34]

The four general classes of inflammatory cells that respond to SCI are microglia, neutrophils, macrophages, and lymphocytes. Microglia, neutrophils, and macrophages offer innate immunity, and lymphocytes offer adaptive immunity. Cytokines are potent signaling molecules that affect cell recruitment, activation, and activity. Although all cells release and respond to a variety of cytokines, CNS cells are rarely exposed to inflammatory cytokines. The prominent cytokines present at SCI sites include interleukin (IL)–1, IL-6, tumor necrosis factor–α, and transforming growth factor–1. Early expression of tumor necrosis factor–α and IL-1 by microglia enhances the recruitment of inflammatory cells to the injury site.[35,36] IL-1β is upregulated within 1 hour of injury, peaks at 8 hours after injury, and persists at least 7 days.[37] Nuclear factor κ-β activity is elevated within 30 minutes of injury, undergoes nuclear translocation, and persists at least 72 hours.[38]

The SCI inflammatory response is believed to be composed of nine elements: endothelial damage and activation; activation of resident microglia; in-migration of polymorphonuclear leukocytes; in-migration of macrophages; dysregulated oxidative metabolism and release of free radicals; free-radical–mediated damage of membranes, proteins, and nucleic acids; propagation of excitotoxicity, toxic calcium, and sodium concentrations; necrotic and apoptotic cell death; and local and systemic activation and recruitment of anti-CNS antigen-reactive T and B cells.

Vascular Injury

Endothelial damage appears to be the primary event that initiates the cascade of SCI inflammation because the endothelial cells normally form a barrier that excludes the many active components of blood from the CNS. This blood-CNS barrier is characterized by tight junctions between endothelial cells and strong interactions between the surrounding astrocyte foot processes and basal lamina. SCI causes traumatic disruption of the blood-CNS barrier, initiating microglial activation and leukocyte infiltration.[39] In primates, mechanical gaps between endothelial cells develop within 1.5 minutes of injury, leading to damage in the perivascular basement membrane, red blood cell extravasation, platelet aggregation, and fibrin deposition.[40] Platelet aggregates occlude some vessels, leading to ischemia. Endothelial gaps allow an immediate influx of fluid and proteins, thus promoting edema. Several subsequent events promote movement of leukocytes into the spinal cord, including increased endothelial expression of vascular cell adhesion molecule, which is a ligand for monocyte α4-β1 integrin and upregulation of matrix metalloprotease 9, which degrades the basal lamina.[41] These events exacerbate the loss of endothelial integrity, increasing vascular permeability and leukocyte influx.

Circulating and Endogenous Inflammatory Cell Response

Neutrophils enter the damaged spinal cord immediately after injury and reach peak numbers within 6 hours. Macrophages subsequently enter the cord, reaching peak numbers within 2 to 7 days and persisting as long as 2 weeks after injury.[39,42] Changes in circulating neutrophil and macrophage numbers and activation state parallel these levels in the spinal cord.[43] Lymphocyte entry is delayed and protracted; the cells are detectable several months after the injury. The acute inflammatory response after human SCI lasts approximately 10 days.[39] Inflammatory cell counts generally are not elevated in human cerebrospinal fluid (CSF) later than 3 weeks after injury.

Neutrophil Response

It was formerly believed that the only beneficial activity of neutrophils in the spinal cord after SCI was in the context of infection. Attenuating neutrophil entry and activity therefore was considered desirable. However, neutrophil depletion was found to reduce histologic recovery from injury.[44] The use of strategies designed to deplete neutrophils must be balanced against the essential systemic role of neutrophils if life-threatening pneumonia or urinary tract infection occurs. The systemic neutrophil activation associated with SCI may lead to peripheral organ damage, and SCI may be associated with an increase in circulating inflammatory mediators.

The interplay between systemic and CNS neutrophil activity requires further investigation.

Microglia Response

Microglia are intrinsic inflammatory cells of the spinal cord. Microglial activation begins almost immediately after injury and has been correlated with an increase in tissue damage.[45] Upregulation of proinflammatory tumor necrosis factor-α, IL-β1, and IL-6 is detectable within minutes of injury and increases during the first 1 to 4 days after injury.[45] Microglia have different phases of activation including early acute inflammation and later production of neurotrophins such as glial cell line–derived neutrophilic factor.[46] Blockade of metabotropic glutamate receptor subunit 5 on microglia is associated with reduced microglial activation and improvement in tissue and functional outcome after SCI.

Macrophage Response

Debris removal by macrophages and microglia is a necessary part of postinjury tissue repair. The phagocytic response of inflammatory cells is beneficial for removing cell debris and permitting regeneration because it removes the growth-inhibitory components of myelin debris.[45] Although one experimental study found that reduction of circulating macrophages reduces tissue injury and improves recovery, another study found that in-migrating macrophages contribute to recovery.[47,48] Therapeutic immune manipulation is controversial. In experimental animals, retrograde dieback of axons over months to years involves macrophage release of matrix metalloproteinase. Macrophages also are associated with deposition of chondroitin sulfate proteoglycan, which can inhibit axon growth.

Lymphocyte Response

The role of lymphocytes in SCI a topic of debate. The triggering of a pathologic autoimmune response was found after experimental SCI in mice that lacked T lymphocytes; these mice were found to have less extensive tissue loss than control mice.[49] Antibodies against T lymphocytes were found to decrease secondary injury in animals with SCI, compared with control animals.[50] Blockade of lymphocyte infiltration through peripheral sequestration was associated with reduced tissue damage. However, the concept of protective autoimmunity includes the proposal that T cells that are autoreactive to myelin are advantageous but inefficient.[51] A so-called priming vaccination therefore would be useful in treating SCI.

Free-Radical–Mediated Damage

The term oxidative stress refers to the cytotoxic effects of oxygen free radicals generated as byproducts of normal and atypical metabolic processes using molecular oxygen. Lipid peroxidation has two distinct temporal peaks that coincide with the initial influx of neutrophils and subsequent macrophage and microglia activation. Oxidative damage may continue as long as 5 days.

These cells generate a self-perpetuating chain of reactive oxygen species that cause substantial damage to membranes, proteins, and nucleic acids by lipid peroxidation, protein nitration, and activation of redox-sensitive signaling cascades.[52] Neutrophils and activated microglia are the major source of nicotinamide adenine dinucleotide phosphate oxidase-derived reactive oxygen species in the injured human spinal cord.[39] Xanthine oxidase levels also are elevated, and macrophages produce toxic quinolinic acid.[53] Oxidation of membrane lipids increases permeability to ions and causes failure of the transmembrane adenosine triphosphate–driven pump function.

The Glial Scar

One consequence of SCI is the proliferation of astrocytes and the development of a glial scar, which is a physical and biochemical barrier to regeneration.[14] Transforming growth factor-β2 modulates glial scar formation. The reactive astrocytes that form this scar secrete growth-inhibitory components known as chondroitin sulfate proteoglycans, which consist of a core protein surrounded by glycosaminoglycan side chains and act as a physical barrier to regenerating axons.[54] This physical barrier has been experimentally attenuated by degrading chondroitin sulfate proteoglycans with the enzyme chondroitinase ABC. Injection of chondroitinase ABC partially restored sensory function after SCI by making the CNS environment more permissive for neuroplasticity.[54] It may be possible to use this therapy in combination with other restorative therapies to amplify the capacity for regeneration and plasticity. Activated astrocytes also produce trophic factors;[55] such discoveries reinforce the principle that no cell type has a uniformly detrimental response to SCI activation.

Chronic Changes After SCI

Local disruption of CNS connections after SCI is followed by multiple changes throughout the neuraxis, which can affect repair strategies. These changes include transneuronal degeneration, retrograde neuronal degeneration, segmental sprouting of axons, plasticity, and alterations in neuronal excitability. The clinical sequelae associated with these changes include spasticity, autonomic dysreflexia, and neuropathic pain. The mature lesion may be influenced by other pathologic changes such as syringomyelia, myelomalacia, and spinal cord tethering. In many patients with SCI, a syrinx develops that can cause delayed neurologic dysfunction such as ascending paralysis as well as brainstem symptoms and pain.

Endogenous Reparative Processes

Endogenous reparative tissue responses are present after SCI. For example, an initial wave of angiogenesis appears to fail because of inflammatory factors promoting cavitation. Several studies confirmed that new cells are born around the ependyma.[56] Stem cells born after SCI actively replace some depleted cells, especially oligodendroglia.[57] The number of new cells can be increased through exercise or by administration of transduced transcription factors or intravenous agents such as sonic hedgehog protein.[58] In-migration of Schwann cells can lead to functional myelin repair of CNS axons. Treatments such as methylprednisolone may attenuate the normal endogenous response, which is linked to the presence of inflammatory cells.[59]

Therapies

Clinical Evidence for Early Decompression

Although numerous animal studies have validated the intuitive concept that early decompression is beneficial after SCI with persistent compression, data from human studies are limited.[60] The topic is controversial, mostly because of concern that early surgery could worsen SCI. The Surgical Treatment of Acute Spinal Cord Injury Study attempted to resolve the question beginning in 2003. This prospective observational study of patients with traumatic cervical SCI (age, 16 to 71 years) is focused on surgical decompression within 24 hours of injury. Preliminary results indicate that 24% of patients who received decompressive surgery within 24 hours of injury had an improvement of at least two grades on the American Spinal Injury Association (ASIA) scale, compared with 4% of patients who had later surgery. The overall rate of complications among those who received early intervention was approximately 20% lower than that of patients who received later treatment. Based on current literature and the emerging data from the Surgical Treatment of Acute Spinal Cord Injury Study, the Spine Study Trauma Group recommended that patients with acute SCI but no other life-threatening injuries should receive decompression within 24 hours of injury.[61]

Support of Spinal Cord Perfusion

It is difficult to measure spinal cord blood flow in humans. The assumption is that mean spinal cord perfusion pressure is equivalent to mean arterial pressure minus CSF pressure. The autoregulation of spinal cord blood flow is believed to be altered after SCI so that the cord is increasingly vulnerable to systemic hypotension. Level II evidence supports the prevention and treatment of spinal cord blood hypotension (less than 90 mm Hg) by using early appropriate fluid resuscitation to maintain tissue perfusion and resolve shock.[62] One study found that volume expansion and pressors can increase spinal cord blood flow.[63] Another study found that somatosensory-evoked potentials can be improved by raising blood pressure during spinal cord compression.[64] Before it is assumed that a patient with multiple trauma has a central mechanism for hypotension, an extensive search for other sources must be completed.[62] Neurogenic shock can be treated with fluid resuscitation until the dilated intravascular volume is filled to a normal central venous pressure. The subsequent use of vasopressors may be required to avoid volume overload. The use of vasopressors with both α and β adrenergic actions is recommended to counter the loss of sympathetic tone and provide chronotropic support.

Neuroprotective Drugs

The clinically tested neuroprotective drugs include methylprednisolone, tirilazad mesylate, ganglioside-1 (GM-1), gacyclidine, naloxone, nimodipine, and thyrotropin-releasing hormone; riluzole is under investigation. Methylprednisolone is the most extensively investigated pharmacologic intervention for SCI. Research on methylprednisolone has led to numerous important conclusions. Preclinical experiments, primarily in cats treated with methylprednisolone, found post-SCI improvement in spinal cord blood flow; conduction of somatosensory-evoked potentials; biochemical measures of membrane breakdown, oxidation, and inflammation; and edema.[65] A longer term study failed to find a functional benefit, however.[66]

Phase I of the National Acute Spinal Cord Injury Study (NASCIS) compared the efficacy of a 100-mg or 1,000-mg loading dose of methylprednisolone followed by 25 mg or 250 mg every 6 hours for 10 days. There was no difference in the primary motor and sensory outcome after 6 weeks, 6 months, or 1 year.[67] Phase II of NASCIS compared the efficacy of a much higher initial dose of methylprednisolone (30 mg per kg), followed by 5.4 mg per kg per hour for 23 hours, to the efficacy of naloxone (an opioid antagonist) or a placebo. The intent-to-treat analysis found no difference in primary outcomes among the three groups of patients.[68] However, subset analysis revealed differences based on the timing of the loading dose (before or after 8 hours) and SCI severity (complete or incomplete). Patients with an incomplete injury who were treated within 8 hours had a significantly better outcome after 1 year than other patients. This study provided clinical evidence of a therapeutic window for neuroprotection in patients with SCI. Methylprednisolone can have serious adverse effects, however; patients treated with high-dosage methylprednisolone had an increased incidence of wound infection, pneumonia, sepsis, and death from respiratory complications.[68]

Phase III of NASCIS was designed to further explore the beneficial effects of methylprednisolone using the Functional Independence Measure.[69] All patients received a loading dose of 30 mg per kg within 8 hours of injury and were randomly assigned to receive one of three treatments: methylprednisolone (5.4 mg per kg per hour) for 24 hours, methylprednisolone (5.4 mg per kg per hour) for 48 hours, or intravenous tirilazad mesylate (2.5 mg per kg every 6 hours) for 48 hours. The data indicate that if treatment is initiated within 3 hours of injury, there is no benefit to extending treatment beyond 24 hours. If treatment is initiated later than 3 hours after injury, however, greater motor improvement occurs when infusions are continued for 48 hours. These findings further emphasize the importance of the therapeutic window in treating patients with SCI. Based on the NASCIS results, the American Association of Neurologic Surgeons Joint Section on Disorders of Spine and Peripheral Nerve Guidelines supported the use of methylprednisolone only as an option for treatment.[70]

Tirilazad Mesylate
Tirilazad mesylate, a 21-aminosteroid, is a synthetic glucocorticoid that can inhibit lipid peroxidation without activating glucocorticoid receptors. The proposed neuroprotective mechanisms of tirilazad mesylate include antioxidation, membrane stabilization through inhibition of lipid peroxidation, and preservation of vitamin E. In phase III of NASCIS, tirilazad mesylate was not found to be more efficacious than methylprednisolone or a placebo.[69] Tirilazad mesylate has not been further used to treat SCI in clinical practice.

Gangliosides
The gangliosides are a group of glycosphingolipids with a high concentration in the outer membranes of nerve tissue. Exogenous administration of gangliosides was found to promote neural repair and functional outcome in some animal studies of neural diseases.[71] Gangliosides in SCI were first systematically studied clinically rather than in preclinical models. In patients with cervical or thoracic SCI, GM-1 was found to be efficacious for recovery of the lower extremities compared with a placebo, perhaps because of the enhanced function of axons traversing the damaged area.[72] A much larger subsequent study enrolled 797 patients, each of whom received a loading dose of 30 mg per kg of methylprednisolone followed by 5.4 mg per kg per hour for 23 hours. Patients were then randomly assigned to receive high-dosage GM-1, low-dosage GM-1, or a placebo for 56 days. No group achieved the primary outcome goal (a two-grade improvement from the baseline ASIA impairment score). However patients in the high-dosage group had a more rapid recovery than the placebo group, and they had improvement in bowel and bladder function, sacral sensation, and anal contraction.[73] Because methylprednisolone was considered a standard of care, the impact of treating patients with GM-1 alone was not determined. GM-1 is now rarely used to treat SCI.

Glutamate Antagonists
Glutamate has a well-established role in facilitating excitotoxic cell death. Pharmacologic studies have tested blockade of excess glutamate receptor activation in stroke and head injury. Glutamate is an important neurotransmitter, and direct and competitive antagonization of glutamate has been problematic because of the occurrence of adverse cognitive effects including agitation, sedation, hallucination, and memory deficits.[74] A large French study evaluated gacyclidine, a noncompetitive NMDA antagonist in acute SCI.[75] This study included both early drug administration and surgical decompression. No drug effect was observed at the primary end point. As in the GM-1 study, subgroup analysis revealed an effect for patients with incomplete injury. Future neuroprotection studies should be designed to separately stratify the outcome analysis of initial complete and incomplete SCIs.

Lessons from Completed Pharmacologic Studies
Some well-designed randomized phase III clinical studies, such as NASCIS and the so-called Sygen study of GM-1, did not find that the tested treatment has a robust benefit.[67-69,73] However, the preclinical evidence foundation of the Sygen study, in particular, had important gaps. The trend across the studies is to reveal a more potent effect when incomplete injuries are treated rather than complete injuries. The range of histologic damage in complete injuries probably is underestimated. Many incomplete injuries initially appear to be complete because of the acute ionic dysregulation in focal contusive SCI.

Ongoing Pharmacologic Studies
Rho Kinase Inhibitor BA-210
The CNS environment is substantially inhibitory to regeneration. Component proteins of CNS myelin inhibit the growth of neural processes. For example, cultured neurons fail to enter the optic nerve but rapidly regenerate into the sciatic nerve. Biochemical studies of CNS myelin have identified inhibitory proteins, the most important of which is the Nogo protein.[76] The identification of Nogo led to the discovery of the Nogo receptor (NgR), through which Nogo signals. Subsequent studies of downstream signaling have identified important mediators of NgR signaling including the *Ras* homolog gene family (Rho) and Rho-associated protein kinase (ROCK).[77]

The Rho-ROCK pathway is an important convergence point for multiple proteins that signal through NgR, and the Rho-ROCK pathway therefore is an attractive target for blocking the inhibitory effect of multiple pathways. Rho inactivation enhances CNS regeneration in the optic nerve and after SCI.[78] The initial blockade of Rho was achieved using C3 transferase, a protein toxin produced by *Clostridium botulinum*. BA-210, a recombinant version of C3 transferase with a transport sequence to enhance delivery, has been commercially developed (Cethrin: QSV Biologics, Edmonton, AB; Alseres Pharmaceuticals, Hopkinton, MA). When BA-210 was mixed with Tisseel fibrin sealant (Baxter, Deerfield, IL) and applied to the dura during spinal decompression surgery, patients in early-phase studies had a 27% improvement in ASIA impairment grade conversion rate.[79]

AT-135
In rodent and primate models of SCI, monoclonal antibodies directed against Nogo were associated with in-

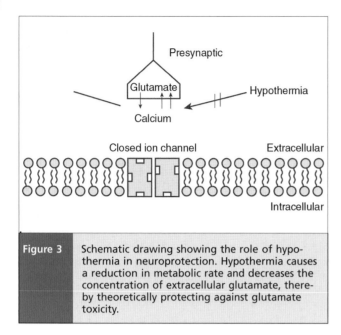

Figure 3 Schematic drawing showing the role of hypothermia in neuroprotection. Hypothermia causes a reduction in metabolic rate and decreases the concentration of extracellular glutamate, thereby theoretically protecting against glutamate toxicity.

creased axonal sprouting and regeneration.[80] Extensive phase I clinical studies of AT-135, a human anti-Nogo antibody infused into the subarachnoid space for 28 days after SCI, are being conducted in Europe and Canada.[81]

Minocycline
Minocycline, a lipophilic synthetic derivative of the antibiotic tetracycline, was found to cross the blood-CNS barrier and reduce excitotoxicity, oxidative stress, caspase-dependent cell death, and levels of proinflammatory mediators.[82] Minocycline also was found to inhibit microglial p38 mitogen-activated protein kinase. Minocycline-associated neuroprotection has been found in animal models of CNS diseases including stroke, Parkinson disease, Huntington disease, amyotrophic lateral sclerosis, and multiple sclerosis. In some but not all animal studies of SCI, the use of minocycline decreased oligodendrocyte apoptosis; reduced the number of activated microglia; and decreased lesion size, neuropathic pain, and neurologic deficit.[83] A prospective randomized placebo-controlled study is investigating the use of intravenous minocycline within 12 hours of injury; an early report suggests efficacy for patients with cervical injury, particularly those with incomplete injury, but no benefit for patients with complete thoracic SCI.[84]

Riluzole
Membrane injury and metabolic dysfunction lead to marked changes in ionic concentrations after SCI. In addition to calcium accumulation, there is a deleterious accumulation of intracellular sodium that leads to membrane depolarization and a further influx of sodium. Blocking sodium channels in experimental models of SCI was found to preserve axons in white matter.[85] Riluzole is an anticonvulsant that antagonizes sodium channels and inhibits calcium-dependent gluta-

mate release.[86] In patients with amyotrophic lateral sclerosis, the use of riluzole has an established safety profile and has been found to prolong life for several months. Riluzole promoted neurologic recovery in rodent models of SCI.[87] A phase I clinical study of orally administered riluzole for patients with acute SCI is under way.[88]

Dosage and Frequency of Administration of Therapeutics
Compounds with biologic activity lack efficacy at an insufficient body fluid concentration but are toxic at an overly high concentration. It is important to determine the drug's serum concentrations and, if possible, the CSF concentrations, especially at the trough level. The clinical dosage of a new compound should be extrapolated from relevant animal studies in which toxic levels have been determined. Computational models for allometric scale-up are available. In the absence of preclinical and clinical pharmacodynamic and pharmacokinetic measures, clinical effects are the only means of surmising the achieved dose. A clinical study may determine that a compound failed to achieve a clinical end point because clinical effects were not observed, but it may not be understood that an adequate dosage was not reached in the study. For this reason, human phase I and IIA studies are designed for dosage finding. These studies should include pharmacokinetic and pharmacodynamic measures.

Nonpharmacologic Interventions
Hypothermia
Hypothermia has been studied in models of SCI for several decades. The efficacy of hypothermia has been proved for neuroprotection during spinal cord ischemia and for survival of out-of-hospital cardiac arrest.[89] The use of hypothermia has had inconsistent results after brain trauma and variable efficacy in experimental studies of SCI.[90] Historically, local hypothermia was used during surgical decompression for SCI.

Hypothermia causes a reduction in the metabolic rate, a decrease in extracellular glutamate (Figure 3), a decrease in macrophage and neutrophil numbers at the injury site, a decrease in vasogenic edema, and reduced cell death through oxidative stress and apoptosis.[90] However, the clinical use of hypothermia is associated with a risk of infection and high myocardial demand during rewarming.[91]

CSF Intrathecal Hypotension
Lowering CSF pressure theoretically could improve spinal cord hemodynamics and reduce ischemic secondary damage. When CSF was drained during thoracoabdominal aortic aneurysm surgery, the results suggested that the incidence of ischemic paraplegia could be significantly reduced by decreasing intrathecal pressure.[92]

Cellular Therapies

The CNS is composed of cells with variable sensitivity to injury; neurons and oligodendroglia are most vulnerable to injury. SCI often causes cavitation of a major portion of the original spinal cord tissue in humans and rodents. Endogenous repair occurs to some extent but is incomplete in adult mammals.[93] Theoretically, there is a role for cells, tissues, or alternatively bioengineered scaffolds in supporting tissue recovery and bridging the lesion. Cell preparations can be better purified and characterized than tissue preparations and therefore are considered to have greater safety and utility. Current research in cellular therapies has four general aims: direct replacement of lost oligodendrocytes and neurons; support of axonal regeneration, plasticity and remyelination; restoration of tissue continuity to provide a vascularized substrate for new axons and neurons; and promotion of endogenous repair through mechanisms such as neurotrophin release. The primary goal is to reconnect the long descending and ascending CNS pathways that were interrupted by injury. The secondary goal is to create local relay networks by promoting plasticity in preserved neurons and axons. The cells currently considered suitable for transplantation include glial cells, stromal cells from various sources, partly differentiated embryonic stem cells, induced pluripotent cells, and neural stem cells. Although neural and glial stem cells originally were derived from brain tissue, it is now apparent that many other tissues (from skin, fat, bone marrow, or umbilical cord blood) also contain stem cells that may be differentiated to show aspects of the neural and glial phenotype.

Remyelination

Segmental axonal demyelination is a clearly established consequence of SCI. It has been believed for several decades that only inadequate myelin repair occurs after SCI and that demyelinated axons are chronically dysfunctional as a result. In experimental models, new oligodendroglia can arise from local precursor cells, and in-migrating peripheral Schwann cells can repair central axons in various glial toxin or radiation injuries.[94] Controversy has arisen regarding the temporal stability of chronic demyelinated axons. By comparison with multiple sclerosis, the belief is emerging that demyelinated axons after SCI may not have long-term survival. Two major clinical studies are planned to test the impact of transplanting myelinating cells in acute and subacute SCI. A study supported by Geron Corporation (Menlo Park, CA) is based on evidence that embryonic stem cell–derived oligodendroglial precursors improve functional and anatomic outcome after transplantation in rodents with SCI.[95] In the Geron study, a human embryonic stem cell–derived cell line differentiated into oligodendrocyte precursors will be transplanted into acutely injured patients who will receive immunosuppressive therapy. In the second study, autologous stem cells will be transplanted into patients with acute or chronic SCI.[96] Stem cells myelinate in peripheral nerves and are essential for nerve regeneration. Stem cell transplantation after experimental SCI can lead to enhanced axonal regeneration and remyelination.[97] This strategy is attractive because stem cells can be obtained from peripheral nerve biopsies, grown and amplified in culture, and autotransplanted into the damaged cord to enhance repair.[98] Autotransplantation obviates the need for immunosuppression.

Olfactory-ensheathing cells (OECs) are specialized glia of the olfactory system that are unique in their lifelong ability to guide axons from newly born olfactory receptor neurons in the peripheral nervous system to the olfactory bulb in the CNS. In the olfactory pathway, OECs do not myelinate. Several studies have indicated that OECs support axonal repair after transplantation and may form myelin in the spinal cord.[99] In Portugal, Australia, China, and Russia, OEC-containing tissue has been transplanted in patients with SCI, with the largest reported experience in China. Clinical autotransplantation of purified cells is hampered by the difficulty of obtaining source tissue, however.

Transplantation of Autologous Macrophages

Macrophages play a key role in successful peripheral nerve regeneration after SCI by removing myelin debris and synthesizing factors that may aid in regeneration. CNS myelin damage exposes axon growth inhibitors such as Nogo, myelin-associated glycoprotein, and myelin-oligodendrocyte glycoprotein. Inadequate clearance of myelin debris by activated microglia and macrophages may be a factor in the poor axonal regenerative response of the CNS after injury. In experimental SCI in rodents, autologous macrophages activated by ex vivo exposure to skin or peripheral nerves were injected into the contused cord, leading to recovery of motor function and reduced cyst formation.[100] Based on success in animal models, a commercial preparation of autologous macrophages is undergoing phase II human studies.[101] Macrophages isolated from the patient's own blood are exposed to autologous skin biopsies, and the activated macrophages are injected into the injured spinal cord at several points below the injury contusion. Substantial criticism has been directed at this study because only one preclinical study was published before US Food and Drug Administration approval and patient enrollment. The growing consensus among SCI researchers is that the preclinical evidence for a promising therapy should meet stringent criteria before human studies are conducted, including verification of efficacy by an independent research laboratory and replication of the effects in a second nonhuman species.[102]

Stem Cells

Before the discovery of stem cells in the nervous system it was believed that the adult CNS had no potential for endogenous replacement of lost neurons. Terminally differentiated neurons were believed to respond to in-

1: Basic Science of the Spine

jury with limited plasticity, but functional replacement was not believed to occur. During the 1990s, stem cells were discovered first in the adult brain and later in the spinal cord. Certain neuronal populations were found to undergo replacement from a stem cell pool throughout life. The best-studied structure is the dentate gyrus of the hippocampus. Other cell types, such as oligodendrocytes, are replaced from a pool of glial-committed precursor cells. Multipotent endogenous progenitor cells exist in the subventricular zone throughout the neuraxis and can be harvested during neurosurgical procedures. Several other types of stem cells have been studied for application to brain and spinal cord disease and injury, including bone marrow stromal cells, umbilical cord stem cells, and precursor cells derived from skin and fat.

Embryonic stem cells are pluripotent cells capable of self-renewal in cell culture and able to produce cells from all three embryonic germ layers. In an undifferentiated state, embryonic stem cells form teratomas after transplantation.[103] These cells were forced to differentiate into oligodendroglial lineage and found to remyelinate after transplantation into the injured spinal cord in experimental SCI models.[104] One exciting recent finding is that fully differentiated adult cells can be made to regress to a state identical to that of totipotent embryonic stem cells.[105] Theoretically, therefore, any tissue can be reactivated from somatic cells. This finding has tremendous implications for autologous tissue repair. However, the difficulty created by the lack of instructive signals in the injury environment should not be underestimated. It is not sufficient to replace cells (or tissues) in the injured spinal cord; the cells also must form appropriate connectivity. The potential for stem cell medicine to deliver fundamental new therapies for CNS disease within the near future may have been exaggerated.

New Insights From Rehabilitation Training

Within the past two decades, an unprecedented degree of plasticity has been identified in the human nervous system. The observation that repetitive activity can drive this neuroplasticity is fundamental to neurorestoration. A spontaneous reorganization of intrinsic propriospinal circuits in the spinal cord and an elaboration of new projections from spared descending fibers occur spontaneously after incomplete SCI and can support functional recovery. The process can be enhanced by locomotor training.[106] Intrinsic neural circuits within the spinal cord respond to afferent sensory information and are capable of self-sustaining patterns of locomotor activity. These central pattern generators can function independently of supraspinal input and show use-dependent plasticity. The effects of training appear to be task specific; for example, training to swim does not improve the ability to walk.[107] Repetitive stimulation of a synapse can lead to changes in structural plasticity, reorganization of receptors, and changes in transmitter properties. Experimental studies have confirmed struc-

tural, biochemical, and neurophysiologic plasticity in response to training.[106] In parallel with the development of neuroprotective and neural repair strategies, the modification of synaptic transmission and plasticity through assisted locomotion may optimize the functionality of spared and regenerating fibers.

Nonbiologic and Hybrid Approaches

Adaptive technologies have the potential to provide functional ability without the need for spinal cord regeneration. It is quite possible that technologic approaches, including such science fiction–like devices as a robotic exoskeleton, in the shorter term may provide patients with more independence and functional ability than biologic strategies.[108] The brain-machine interface is a hybrid technology that can integrate technology, brain activity recording, filtering, and neuroplastic learning mechanisms. The ramifications of such areas of research extend far beyond spinal cord injury into direct decoding of thought processes from cortical activity.[109] Other hybrid approaches are being explored, including the creation of neural relays within the spinal cord using microprocessor relays across the lesion area to allow growth of traumatically severed fibers.[110]

Managing Expectations

There is a strong tendency to generalize and extrapolate concepts pertaining to specific CNS paradigms to SCI, and it is important to avoid a flawed perspective. For example, because new adult neurons can replace lost neurons in the hippocampus, they might be expected to do so after SCI. The comparison is invalid for numerous reasons, one of which is that the presence of external instructive cellular cues is a critical aspect of endogenous repair in the hippocampus but is lacking after SCI. Another example is the assumption that because OECs support and guide new neuronal growth throughout life in the olfactory system, such cells might provide similar benefits in the damaged spinal cord, which is a radically different tissue environment. Restoration of function after SCI almost certainly will not be achieved through any single intervention but is likely to require multiple carefully timed interventions. Given the low efficacy of the agents that have been studied and the frequent inability to replicate initially promising studies, it is important to detect modest but definite changes in neurologic connectivity and function and to progressively build on the findings.

Summary

It is critical to preserve as much spinal cord tissue as possible after SCI. Early decompression and maintenance of blood pressure are important clinical variables. Numerous neuroprotective drugs and strategies have been tested, and exciting restorative therapies are being studied. A combination of agents that accomplish neuroprotection, amplify and augment endogenous repair, and promote and entrain plasticity appear to be needed to achieve substantial neurologic recovery. Alternative technologic approaches are equally important.

Annotated References

1. National Spinal Cord Injury Statistical Center: Spinal cord injury facts and figures at a glance. https://www.nscisc.uab.edu. Updated February 2011.

   The National Spinal Cord Injury Database has existed since 1973 and captures data from an estimated 13% of new instances of SCI in the United States. Twenty-six federally funded SCI Model Systems have contributed to the database.

2. Miller KE, Zylstra RG, Standridge JB: The geriatric patient: A systematic approach to maintaining health. *Am Fam Physician* 2000;61(4):1089-1104.

3. Meguro K, Tator CH: Effect of multiple trauma on mortality and neurological recovery after spinal cord or cauda equina injury. *Neurol Med Chir (Tokyo)* 1988;28(1):34-41.

4. Guttmann L: Organisation of spinal units: History of the National Spinal Injuries Centre, Stoke Mandeville Hospital, Aylesbury. *Paraplegia* 1967;5(3):115-126.

5. Harris P: Associated injuries in traumatic paraplegia and tetraplegia. *Paraplegia* 1968;5(4):215-220.

6. Weld KJ, Dmochowski RR: Effect of bladder management on urological complications in spinal cord injured patients. *J Urol* 2000;163(3):768-772.

7. Jha A, Lammertse DP, Coll JR, et al: Apolipoprotein E epsilon4 allele and outcomes of traumatic spinal cord injury. *J Spinal Cord Med* 2008;31(2):171-176.

   In a retrospective review, patients with cervical SCI who had an apolipoprotein E-epsilon4 allele had a poorer neurologic recovery and a longer rehabilitation length of stay than other patients.

8. Setzer M, Hermann E, Seifert V, Marquardt G: Apolipoprotein E gene polymorphism and the risk of cervical myelopathy in patients with chronic spinal cord compression. *Spine (Phila Pa 1976)* 2008;33(5):497-502.

   A prospective study of patients with stenosis of the cervical spinal canal found that those with an apolipoprotein E-epsilon4 allele were at increased risk of cervical spondylotic myelopathy.

9. Chao MJ, Ramagopalan SV, Herrera BM, et al: Epigenetics in multiple sclerosis susceptibility: Difference in transgenerational risk localizes to the major histocompatibility complex. *Hum Mol Genet* 2009;18(2):261-266.

   Data from a study of inheritance patterns in multiple sclerosis strongly suggest that the increased female risk is mediated through specific alleles or adjacent variation.

10. Krassioukov AV, Karlsson AK, Wecht JM, et al: Assessment of autonomic dysfunction following spinal cord injury: Rationale for additions to International Standards for Neurological Assessment. *J Rehabil Res Dev* 2007;44(1):103-112.

    This preliminary report of a joint American Spinal Injury Association and International Spinal Cord Society committee proposes a comprehensive set of definitions for general autonomic nervous system dysfunction after SCI.

11. Alexander MS, Biering-Sorensen F, Bodner D, et al: International standards to document remaining autonomic function after spinal cord injury. *Spinal Cord* 2009;47(1):36-43.

    A system is described for documenting the impact of SCI on autonomic function, including cardiovascular, bronchopulmonary, sudomotor and thermoregulatory, bladder, bowel, and sexual function.

12. Anderson KD: Targeting recovery: Priorities of the spinal cord-injured population. *J Neurotrauma* 2004;21(10):1371-1383.

13. Bartholdi D, Schwab ME: Methylprednisolone inhibits early inflammatory processes but not ischemic cell death after experimental spinal cord lesion in the rat. *Brain Res* 1995;672(1-2):177-186.

14. Tator CH, Fehlings MG: Review of the secondary injury theory of acute spinal cord trauma with emphasis on vascular mechanisms. *J Neurosurg* 1991;75(1):15-26.

15. Blight AR: Delayed demyelination and macrophage invasion: A candidate for secondary cell damage in spinal cord injury. *Cent Nerv Syst Trauma* 1985;2(4):299-315.

16. Basso DM, Beattie MS, Bresnahan JC, et al: MASCIS evaluation of open field locomotor scores: Effects of experience and teamwork on reliability. Multicenter Animal Spinal Cord Injury Study. *J Neurotrauma* 1996;13(7):343-359.

17. Hung TK, Albin MS, Brown TD, Bunegin L, Albin R, Jannetta PJ: Biomechanical responses to open experimental spinal cord injury. *Surg Neurol* 1975;4(2):271-276.

18. Viano DC, Lau IV: A viscous tolerance criterion for soft tissue injury assessment. *J Biomech* 1988;21(5):387-399.

19. Dimar JR II, Glassman SD, Raque GH, Zhang YP, Shields CB: The influence of spinal canal narrowing and timing of decompression on neurologic recovery after spinal cord contusion in a rat model. *Spine (Phila Pa 1976)* 1999;24(16):1623-1633.

20. Blight AR: Cellular morphology of chronic spinal cord injury in the cat: Analysis of myelinated axons by line-sampling. *Neuroscience* 1983;10(2):521-543.

21. Eidelberg E, Straehley D, Erspamer R, Watkins CJ: Relationship between residual hindlimb-assisted locomotion and surviving axons after incomplete spinal cord injuries. *Exp Neurol* 1977;56(2):312-322.

22. Fehlings MG, Tator CH: The relationships among the severity of spinal cord injury, residual neurological function, axon counts, and counts of retrogradely labeled neurons after experimental spinal cord injury. *Exp Neurol* 1995;132(2):220-228.

23. Tian DS, Liu JL, Xie MJ, et al: Tamoxifen attenuates inflammatory-mediated damage and improves functional outcome after spinal cord injury in rats. *J Neurochem* 2009;109(6):1658-1667.

   The efficacy of tamoxifen for attenuating SCI-induced pathology was determined in a rat study. Blood–spinal cord barrier permeability, tissue edema formation, microglial activation, neuronal cell death, and myelin loss were investigated.

24. Sribnick EA, Wingrave JM, Matzelle DD, Wilford GG, Ray SK, Banik NL: Estrogen attenuated markers of inflammation and decreased lesion volume in acute spinal cord injury in rats. *J Neurosci Res* 2005;82(2):283-293.

   Treatment with estrogen was found to reduce edema and decrease inflammation and myelin loss in the lesion and penumbral areas of rats with SCI. Estrogen has potential as a therapeutic agent, but its neuroprotective mechanism must be elucidated.

25. Baptiste DC, Austin JW, Zhao W, Nahirny A, Sugita S, Fehlings MG: Systemic polyethylene glycol promotes neurological recovery and tissue sparing in rats after cervical spinal cord injury. *J Neuropathol Exp Neurol* 2009;68(6):661-676.

   Polyethylene glycol promoted modest but significant neurobehavioral recovery after SCI. Collectively, the results indicate that polyethylene glycol protects key axonal cytoskeletal proteins after SCI and that the protection is associated with axonal preservation.

26. Guertin PA: The mammalian central pattern generator for locomotion. *Brain Res Rev* 2009;62(1):45-56.

   This is a comprehensive review of findings on the organization and properties of the mammalian central pattern generator. This caudally localized spinal cord network was found to generate the basic command signals to muscles of the limbs for locomotor rhythm and pattern generation.

27. Chau C, Barbeau H, Rossignol S: Early locomotor training with clonidine in spinal cats. *J Neurophysiol* 1998;79(1):392-409.

28. Barbeau H, Rossignol S: Recovery of locomotion after chronic spinalization in the adult cat. *Brain Res* 1987; 412(1):84-95.

29. Lipton SA, Rosenberg PA: Excitatory amino acids as a final common pathway for neurologic disorders. *N Engl J Med* 1994;330(9):613-622.

30. Nesic O, Svrakic NM, Xu GY, et al: DNA microarray analysis of the contused spinal cord: Effect of NMDA receptor inhibition. *J Neurosci Res* 2002;68(4):406-423.

31. Stys PK, Lipton SA: White matter NMDA receptors: An unexpected new therapeutic target? *Trends Pharmacol Sci* 2007;28(11):561-566.

   Uncompetitive NMDA channel blockers such as memantine hold therapeutic promise because they are well tolerated clinically and may be effective for protecting certain white matter elements from a variety of insults.

32. Ma M, Wei P, Wei T, Ransohoff RM, Jakeman LB: Enhanced axonal growth into a spinal cord contusion injury site in a strain of mouse (129X1/SvJ) with a diminished inflammatory response. *J Comp Neurol* 2004; 474(4):469-486.

33. Dal Canto MC, Barbano RL: Remyelination during remission in Theiler's virus infection. *Am J Pathol* 1984; 116(1):30-45.

34. Ghasemlou N, Bouhy D, Yang J, et al: Beneficial effects of secretory leukocyte protease inhibitor after spinal cord injury. *Brain* 2010;133(Pt 1):126-138.

   A beneficial role for secretory leukocyte protease inhibitor was found in mice after spinal cord contusion injury.

35. Bartholdi D, Schwab ME: Expression of proinflammatory cytokine and chemokine mRNA upon experimental spinal cord injury in mouse: An in situ hybridization study. *Eur J Neurosci* 1997;9(7):1422-1438.

36. Pan JZ, Ni L, Sodhi A, Aguanno A, Young W, Hart RP: Cytokine activity contributes to induction of inflammatory cytokine mRNAs in spinal cord following contusion. *J Neurosci Res* 2002;68(3):315-322.

37. Wang CX, Olschowka JA, Wrathall JR: Increase of interleukin-1beta mRNA and protein in the spinal cord following experimental traumatic injury in the rat. *Brain Res* 1997;759(2):190-196.

38. Bethea JR, Castro M, Keane RW, Lee TT, Dietrich WD, Yezierski RP: Traumatic spinal cord injury induces nuclear factor-kappaB activation. *J Neurosci* 1998;18(9): 3251-3260.

39. Fleming JC, Norenberg MD, Ramsay DA, et al: The cellular inflammatory response in human spinal cords after injury. *Brain* 2006;129(Pt 12):3249-3269.

   Endothelial alterations occur as early as 1.5 minutes after an impact injury to the primate spinal cord. Separation of the endothelial junctions and exposure of microvascular basal lamina result in platelet adhesion and aggregations that cover defects in the vessel wall and may progress to complete vascular occlusion.

40. Goodman JH, Bingham WG Jr, Hunt WE: Platelet aggregation in experimental spinal cord injury: Ultrastructural observations. *Arch Neurol* 1979;36(4):197-201.

41. Fleming JC, Bao F, Chen Y, et al: Timing and duration of anti-alpha4beta1 integrin treatment after spinal cord injury: Effect on therapeutic efficacy. *J Neurosurg Spine* 2009;11(5):575-587.

Long-term anti–α4 monoclonal antibody treatment beginning 2 hours after SCI improved neurologic outcomes, with tissue sparing near the lesion and no impairment of the late immune response to injury.

42. Carlson SL, Parrish ME, Springer JE, Doty K, Dossett L: Acute inflammatory response in spinal cord following impact injury. *Exp Neurol* 1998;151(1):77-88.

43. Stirling DP, Yong VW: Dynamics of the inflammatory response after murine spinal cord injury revealed by flow cytometry. *J Neurosci Res* 2008;86(9):1944-1958.

SCI triggers a robust inflammatory response that contributes to secondary degeneration of spared tissue. Flow cytometry was used to quantify the inflammatory response after SCI.

44. Stirling DP, Liu S, Kubes P, Yong VW: Depletion of Ly6G/Gr-1 leukocytes after spinal cord injury in mice alters wound healing and worsens neurological outcome. *J Neurosci* 2009;29(3):753-764.

Although the spectrum of cells affected by anti–Ly6G/Gr-1 antibody treatment cannot be fully ascertained, the correspondence of neutrophil depletion and poor recovery suggests that neutrophils promote recovery after SCI through wound healing and protective events that limit lesion propagation.

45. Donnelly DJ, Popovich PG: Inflammation and its role in neuroprotection, axonal regeneration and functional recovery after spinal cord injury. *Exp Neurol* 2008;209(2):378-388.

Posttraumatic neuroinflammation is described, particularly as related to the spinal cord, with a discussion of controversies and therapies designed to target neuroinflammatory cascades.

46. Hashimoto M, Nitta A, Fukumitsu H, Nomoto H, Shen L, Furukawa S: Inflammation-induced GDNF improves locomotor function after spinal cord injury. *Neuroreport* 2005;16(2):99-102.

Limited activation of microglia and macrophages in the CNS occurs after injury. This finding may explain unsuccessful axonal regeneration. The relationship between lipopolysaccharide-induced inflammation and recovery of locomotor function of rats after SCI was examined.

47. Popovich PG, Guan Z, Wei P, Huitinga I, van Rooijen N, Stokes BT: Depletion of hematogenous macrophages promotes partial hindlimb recovery and neuroanatomical repair after experimental spinal cord injury. *Exp Neurol* 1999;158(2):351-365.

48. Shechter R, London A, Varol C, et al: Infiltrating blood-derived macrophages are vital cells playing an anti-inflammatory role in recovery from spinal cord injury in mice. *PLoS Med* 2009;6(7):e1000113.

Part of the limited recovery after SCI can be attributed to the inadequate and untimely spontaneous recruitment of monocytes.

49. Fee D, Crumbaugh A, Jacques T, et al: Activated/effector CD4+ T cells exacerbate acute damage in the central nervous system following traumatic injury. *J Neuroimmunol* 2003;136(1-2):54-66.

50. Gonzalez R, Glaser J, Liu MT, Lane TE, Keirstead HS: Reducing inflammation decreases secondary degeneration and functional deficit after spinal cord injury. *Exp Neurol* 2003;184(1):456-463.

51. Schwartz M: T cell mediated neuroprotection is a physiological response to central nervous system insults. *J Mol Med (Berl)* 2001;78(11):594-597.

52. Bao F, Liu D: Peroxynitrite generated in the rat spinal cord induces apoptotic cell death and activates caspase-3. *Neuroscience* 2003;116(1):59-70.

53. Xu J, Beckman JS, Hogan EL, Hsu CY: Xanthine oxidase in experimental spinal cord injury. *J Neurotrauma* 1991;8(1):11-18.

54. Cafferty WB, Bradbury EJ, Lidierth M, et al: Chondroitinase ABC-mediated plasticity of spinal sensory function. *J Neurosci* 2008;28(46):11998-12009.

Intact spinal circuits were confirmed to have a profound influence on functional restoration after SCI. A comprehensive understanding of these targets may lead to therapeutic interventions that can be spatially tailored to specific circuitry, thereby reducing unwanted maladaptive axon growth of distal pathways.

55. Faulkner JR, Herrmann JE, Woo MJ, Tansey KE, Doan NB, Sofroniew MV: Reactive astrocytes protect tissue and preserve function after spinal cord injury. *J Neurosci* 2004;24(9):2143-2155.

56. Mothe AJ, Tator CH: Proliferation, migration, and differentiation of endogenous ependymal region stem/progenitor cells following minimal spinal cord injury in the adult rat. *Neuroscience* 2005;131(1):177-187.

A minimal SCI adjacent to the ependyma is sufficient to induce an endogenous ependymal cell response in which ependymal stem-progenitor cells proliferate and migrate from the region of the central canal, differentiating primarily into astrocytes.

57. Yang H, Lu P, McKay HM, et al: Endogenous neurogenesis replaces oligodendrocytes and astrocytes after primate spinal cord injury. *J Neurosci* 2006;26(8):2157-2166.

Natural cell division and replacement were found to be extensive and to contribute to neural repair in adult rhesus monkeys after SCI.

58. Foret A, Quertainmont R, Botman O, et al: Stem cells in the adult rat spinal cord: Plasticity after injury and treadmill training exercise. *J Neurochem* 2010;112(3):762-772.

Endogenous neural stem cells in the normal and injured adult rat spinal cord were differentiated. The effects of treadmill training were investigated using immunohistochemical and behavioral studies.

59. West NR, Leblanc V, Collins GH: Support of axonal regrowth by endogenous mechanisms following spinal cord injury in adult rats. *Neuropathology* 2001;21(3): 188-202.

60. Vaccaro AR, Daugherty RJ, Sheehan TP, et al: Neurologic outcome of early versus late surgery for cervical spinal cord injury. *Spine (Phila Pa 1976)* 1997;22(22): 2609-2613.

61. Lenehan B, Fisher CG, Vaccaro A, Fehlings M, Aarabi B, Dvorak MF: The urgency of surgical decompression in acute central cord injuries with spondylosis and without instability. *Spine (Phila Pa 1976)* 2010;35(21, Suppl)S180-S186.

Expert review of relevant data led to the conclusion that it is reasonable and safe to consider early surgical decompression in patients with a profound neurologic deficit and persistent spinal cord compression.

62. Consortium for Spinal Cord Medicine: Early acute management in adults with spinal cord injury: A clinical practice guideline for health-care professionals. *J Spinal Cord Med* 2008;31(4):403-479.

The protocols developed by the Consortium for Spinal Cord Medicine were used to review the evidence pertaining to care of the patient with a new SCI, focusing on the first 72 hours.

63. Dolan EJ, Tator CH: The effect of blood transfusion, dopamine, and gamma hydroxybutyrate on posttraumatic ischemia of the spinal cord. *J Neurosurg* 1982; 56(3):350-358.

64. Croft TJ, Brodkey JS, Nulsen FE: Reversible spinal cord trauma: A model for electrical monitoring of spinal cord function. *J Neurosurg* 1972;36(4):402-406.

65. Hall ED, Braughler JM: Effects of intravenous methylprednisolone on spinal cord lipid peroxidation and Na+ + K+)-ATPase activity: Dose-response analysis during 1st hour after contusion injury in the cat. *J Neurosurg* 1982;57(2):247-253.

66. Faden AI, Jacobs TP, Patrick DH, Smith MT: Megadose corticosteroid therapy following experimental traumatic spinal injury. *J Neurosurg* 1984;60(4):712-717.

67. Bracken MB, Shepard MJ, Hellenbrand KG, et al: Methylprednisolone and neurological function 1 year after spinal cord injury: Results of the National Acute Spinal Cord Injury Study. *J Neurosurg* 1985;63(5):704-713.

68. Bracken MB, Shepard MJ, Collins WF Jr, et al: Methylprednisolone or naloxone treatment after acute spinal cord injury: 1-year follow-up data. Results of the second National Acute Spinal Cord Injury Study. *J Neurosurg* 1992;76(1):23-31.

69. Bracken MB, Shepard MJ, Holford TR, et al: Administration of methylprednisolone for 24 or 48 hours or tirilazad mesylate for 48 hours in the treatment of acute spinal cord injury: Results of the Third National Acute Spinal Cord Injury Randomized Controlled Trial. National Acute Spinal Cord Injury Study. *JAMA* 1997; 277(20):1597-1604.

70. McCormick P: Pharmacological therapy after acute cervical spinal cord injury. *Neurosurgery* 2002;50(3, Suppl) S63-S72.

71. Bose B, Osterholm JL, Kalia M: Ganglioside-induced regeneration and reestablishment of axonal continuity in spinal cord-transected rats. *Neurosci Lett* 1986;63(2): 165-169.

72. Geisler FH, Dorsey FC, Coleman WP: Recovery of motor function after spinal-cord injury: A randomized, placebo-controlled trial with GM-1 ganglioside. *N Engl J Med* 1991;324(26):1829-1838.

73. Geisler FH, Coleman WP, Grieco G, Poonian D, Sygen Study Group: The Sygen multicenter acute spinal cord injury study. *Spine (Phila Pa 1976)* 2001;26(24, Suppl) S87-S98.

74. Davis SM, Albers GW, Diener HC, Lees KR, Norris J: Termination of Acute Stroke Studies Involving Selfotel Treatment: ASSIST Steering Committed. *Lancet* 1997; 349(9044):32.

75. Tadié M, Mathe JF, et al: Early care and treatment with a neuroprotective drug, gacyclidine, in patients with acute spinal cord injury. *Rachis* 2003;15:363-376.

76. Huber AB, Schwab ME: Nogo-A, a potent inhibitor of neurite outgrowth and regeneration. *Biol Chem* 2000; 381(5-6):407-419.

77. McKerracher L, Higuchi H: Targeting Rho to stimulate repair after spinal cord injury. *J Neurotrauma* 2006; 23(3-4):309-317.

Data are reviewed on the use of Rho antagonists to promote axon regeneration, neuroprotection, and functional recovery after SCI, with a report of efforts to translate rodent studies to clinical studies of patients with acute SCI.

78. Fournier AE, Takizawa BT, Strittmatter SM: Rho kinase inhibition enhances axonal regeneration in the injured CNS. *J Neurosci* 2003;23(4):1416-1423.

79. Fehlings MG, Theodore N, Harrop J, et al: A phase I/IIa clinical trial of a recombinant Rho protein antagonist in acute spinal cord injury. *J Neurotrauma* 2011;28(5): 787-796.

A phase I-IIA clinical study was designed to test the safety and tolerability of a single dose of BA-210 during acute SCI surgery, as well as the neurologic status of patients after drug administration.

© 2012 American Academy of Orthopaedic Surgeons

80. Schnell L, Schwab ME: Axonal regeneration in the rat spinal cord produced by an antibody against myelin-associated neurite growth inhibitors. *Nature* 1990; 343(6255):269-272.

81. Rowland JW, Hawryluk GW, Kwon B, Fehlings MG: Current status of acute spinal cord injury pathophysiology and emerging therapies: Promise on the horizon. *Neurosurg Focus* 2008;25(5):E2.

    The current understanding of SCI pathophysiology is reviewed, with a discussion of emerging regenerative strategies including the use of neural stem cells to remyelinate spared axons.

82. Thomas M, Le WD, Jankovic J: Minocycline and other tetracycline derivatives: A neuroprotective strategy in Parkinson's disease and Huntington's disease. *Clin Neuropharmacol* 2003;26(1):18-23.

83. Lee JH, Tigchelaar S, Liu J, et al: Lack of neuroprotective effects of simvastatin and minocycline in a model of cervical spinal cord injury. *Exp Neurol* 2010;225(1): 219-230.

    Simvastatin and minocycline are known to reduce inflammation and oxidative stress, improve endothelial function, and modulate the immune system in patients with stroke, traumatic brain injury, or SCI. Their neuroprotective properties are evaluated in a model of contusive cervical cord injury.

84. Casha S, Zygun D, McGowan D, Yong VW, Hurlbert RJ: Neuroprotection with minocycline after spinal cord injury: Results of a double blind, randomized, controlled pilot study. *Neurosurgery* 2009;65(2):410-411.

    The biologic basis and translational potential of minocycline on the nervous system is critically reviewed.

85. Rosenberg LJ, Teng YD, Wrathall JR: Effects of the sodium channel blocker tetrodotoxin on acute white matter pathology after experimental contusive spinal cord injury. *J Neurosci* 1999;19(14):6122-6133.

86. Wang SJ, Wang KY, Wang WC: Mechanisms underlying the riluzole inhibition of glutamate release from rat cerebral cortex nerve terminals (synaptosomes). *Neuroscience* 2004;125(1):191-201.

87. Schwartz G, Fehlings MG: Evaluation of the neuroprotective effects of sodium channel blockers after spinal cord injury: Improved behavioral and neuroanatomical recovery with riluzole. *J Neurosurg* 2001;94(2, Suppl) 245-256.

88. National Institutes of Health: Safety of riluzole in patients with acute spinal cord injury. http://clinicaltrials.gov/ct2/show/NCT00876889. Accessed September 21, 2011.

    The primary aim of this ongoing study is to develop safety and pharmacokinetic profiles of riluzole in patients with acute traumatic SCI. The secondary objective is to conduct exploratory analyses of functional outcomes for the purpose of planning a phase II randomized study.

89. Cambria RP, Davison JK, Carter C, et al: Epidural cooling for spinal cord protection during thoracoabdominal aneurysm repair: A five-year experience. *J Vasc Surg* 2000;31(6):1093-1102.

90. Chatzipanteli K, Yanagawa Y, Marcillo AE, Kraydieh S, Yezierski RP, Dietrich WD: Posttraumatic hypothermia reduces polymorphonuclear leukocyte accumulation following spinal cord injury in rats. *J Neurotrauma* 2000; 17(4):321-332.

91. Guest JD, Vanni S, Silbert L: Mild hypothermia, blood loss and complications in elective spinal surgery. *Spine J* 2004;4(2):130-137.

92. Coselli JS, Lemaire SA, Köksoy C, Schmittling ZC, Curling PE: Cerebrospinal fluid drainage reduces paraplegia after thoracoabdominal aortic aneurysm repair: Results of a randomized clinical trial. *J Vasc Surg* 2002; 35(4):631-639.

93. Bambakidis NC, Horn EM, Nakaji P, et al: Endogenous stem cell proliferation induced by intravenous hedgehog agonist administration after contusion in the adult rat spinal cord. *J Neurosurg Spine* 2009;10(2):171-176.

    After SCI in adult rats, an intravenous hedgehog agonist at dosages that upregulate spinal cord Gli1 transcription also increases the population of neural precursor cells.

94. Franklin RJ, Gilson JM, Blakemore WF: Local recruitment of remyelinating cells in the repair of demyelination in the central nervous system. *J Neurosci Res* 1997; 50(2):337-344.

95. Keirstead HS, Nistor G, Bernal G, et al: Human embryonic stem cell-derived oligodendrocyte progenitor cell transplants remyelinate and restore locomotion after spinal cord injury. *J Neurosci* 2005;25(19):4694-4705.

    Evidence that cell transplants can improve recovery outcomes in SCI models substantiates SCI clinical treatment strategies involving cell replacement.

96. David S, Aguayo AJ: Axonal regeneration after crush injury of rat central nervous system fibres innervating peripheral nerve grafts. *J Neurocytol* 1985;14(1):1-12.

97. Xu XM, Guénard V, Kleitman N, Bunge MB: Axonal regeneration into Schwann cell-seeded guidance channels grafted into transected adult rat spinal cord. *J Comp Neurol* 1995;351(1):145-160.

98. Guest JD, Rao A, Olson L, Bunge MB, Bunge RP: The ability of human Schwann cell grafts to promote regeneration in the transected nude rat spinal cord. *Exp Neurol* 1997;148(2):502-522.

99. Ramón-Cueto A, Cordero MI, Santos-Benito FF, Avila J: Functional recovery of paraplegic rats and motor axon regeneration in their spinal cords by olfactory ensheathing glia. *Neuron* 2000;25(2):425-435.

1: Basic Science of the Spine

100. Bomstein Y, Marder JB, Vitner K, et al: Features of skin-coincubated macrophages that promote recovery from spinal cord injury. *J Neuroimmunol* 2003;142 (1-2):10-16.

101. Knoller N, Auerbach G, Fulga V, et al: Clinical experience using incubated autologous macrophages as a treatment for complete spinal cord injury: Phase I study results. *J Neurosurg Spine* 2005;3(3):173-181.

     A phase I study concluded that patients with acute SCI can tolerate incubated autologous macrophage cell therapy. Further clinical study is warranted.

102. Kwon BK, Okon EB, Tsai E, et al: A grading system to evaluate objectively the strength of pre-clinical data of acute neuroprotective therapies for clinical translation in spinal cord injury. *J Neurotrauma* 2011;28(8):1525-1543.

     A system is presented for objectively grading the preclinical literature on neuroprotective treatments for acute SCI. The objective is to evaluate the rationale for translating an individual experimental treatment into human studies.

103. Reubinoff BE, Pera MF, Fong CY, Trounson A, Bongso A: Embryonic stem cell lines from human blastocysts: Somatic differentiation in vitro. *Nat Biotechnol* 2000;18(4):399-404.

104. McDonald JW, Liu XZ, Qu Y, et al: Transplanted embryonic stem cells survive, differentiate and promote recovery in injured rat spinal cord. *Nat Med* 1999; 5(12):1410-1412.

105. Takahashi K, Yamanaka S: Induction of pluripotent stem cells from mouse embryonic and adult fibroblast cultures by defined factors. *Cell* 2006;126(4):663-676.

     Induced pluripotent stem cells were found to be directly generated from fibroblast cultures with the addition of a small number of defined factors.

106. Courtine G, Song B, Roy RR, et al: Recovery of supraspinal control of stepping via indirect propriospinal relay connections after spinal cord injury. *Nat Med* 2008;14(1):69-74.

     Targeted intervention to augment the remodeling of relay connections may be a new therapeutic strategy to bypass lesions and restore function after SCI.

107. Magnuson DS, Smith RR, Brown EH, et al: Swimming as a model of task-specific locomotor retraining after spinal cord injury in the rat. *Neurorehabil Neural Repair* 2009;23(6):535-545.

     Repetition was sufficient to bring about significant improvements in the pattern of hindlimb movement after SCI but did not improve the forces generated, leaving animals with persistent deficits.

108. Hesse S, Schmidt H, Werner C, Bardeleben A: Upper and lower extremity robotic devices for rehabilitation and for studying motor control. *Curr Opin Neurol* 2003;16(6):705-710.

109. Kellis S, Miller K, Thomson K, Brown R, House P, Greger B: Decoding spoken words using local field potentials recorded from the cortical surface. *J Neural Eng* 2010;7(5):056007.

     These results further support using cortical surface potentials (electrocorticography) in brain–computer interfaces.

110. Colicos MA, Syed NI: Neuronal networks and synaptic plasticity: Understanding complex system dynamics by interfacing neurons with silicon technologies. *J Exp Biol* 2006;209(Pt 12):2312-2319.

     Technologies hold tremendous potential for future research into synaptic plasticity as well as strategies for implanting electronic devices into live animals during memory tasks.

Chapter 7

Venous Thromboembolism in Patients With a Spine Disorder

Christopher M. Bono, MD   Michael P. Glotzbecker, MD

Introduction

Venous thromboembolism (VTE) is related to substantial mortality, morbidity, and use of resources. Pulmonary embolism (PE) remains the most common preventable cause of in-hospital deaths.[1] The average cost of an episode of deep venous thrombosis (DVT) or PE is $9,337 or $12,795, respectively, and this cost is compounded by the patient's increased risk of a repeat episode (21.5% or 2.6%, respectively).[2] Most hospitalized patients have at least one risk factor for VTE, and approximately 40% have three or more risk factors.[1] The general risk factors include any of the three classic components of the Virchow triad (hypercoagulability, stasis, and intimal injury). Other common risk factors for thromboembolic disease are listed in Table 1.

Patients with a spine disorder may be at increased risk of VTE.[1] A patient with spinal cord injury and paralysis is at particularly high risk because of stasis and inactivity in the lower extremities. A patient with a spine fracture or dislocation (regardless of neurologic deficit) often has a concomitant long bone or pelvic fracture, head injury, or visceral injury that can result in prolonged recumbency and increased risk of VTE. A patient undergoing elective spine surgery may not be immediately ambulatory after the surgery, depending on the magnitude of the procedure.[1]

Chemical prophylaxis is standard for an elective orthopaedic extremity procedure such as total hip or knee replacement because the risk-benefit ratio is well defined. The data and recommendations are less clear for elective spine surgery. Postoperative hematoma in the spine can lead to catastrophic neurologic sequelae. Decision making is best guided by a thorough understanding of the relative incidence of DVT and PE after specific spine procedures in patients at different levels of risk.

Dr. Bono or an immediate family member serves as a board member, owner, officer, or committee member of the North American Spine Society, Spine Arthroplasty Society, and American Academy of Orthopaedic Surgeons; is a member of a speakers' bureau or has made paid presentations on behalf of Stryker Spine and DePuy Spine; serves as a paid consultant to or is an employee of DePuy Spine, Life Spine, and Stryker; has received research or institutional support from DePuy Spine and Synthes Spine; and has received nonincome support (such as equipment or services), commercially derived honoraria, or other non–research-related funding (such as paid travel) from Stryker. Neither Dr. Glotzbecker nor any immediate family member has received anything of value from or owns stock in a commercial company or institution related directly or indirectly to the subject of this chapter.

Table 1

Risk Factors for Venous Thromboembolism

Acute medical illness

Cancer

Cancer therapy

Central venous catheterization

Earlier DVT-PE

Erythropoiesis-stimulating event

Estrogen-containing oral contraceptives or hormone replacement therapy

Immobility or lower extremity paresis

Increasing age

Inflammatory bowel disease

Inherited or acquired thrombophilia

Myeloproliferative disorder

Nephrotic syndrome

Obesity

Paroxysmal nocturnal hemoglobinuria

Pregnancy or postpartum period

Selective estrogen receptor modulators

Surgery

Trauma

Venous compression

Adapted from Geerts WH, Pineo GF, Heit JA, et al: Prevention of venous thromboembolism: The Seventh ACCP Conference on Antithrombotic and Thrombolytic Therapy. *Chest* 2004;126(suppl 3):338S-400S.

Screening for VTE

Many DVTs are asymptomatic, and screening therefore is important.[3] The ideal screening method has not been determined. The most sensitive and specific test for DVT is venography, but venography is invasive and may be impractical for routine screening. Clinical diagnosis by physical examination is readily completed but inherently less sensitive. A recent systematic review of screening after spine surgery found that DVT was detected by clinical examination, ultrasonography, or venography in 1%, 4%, or 12% of patients, respectively.[4]

It is unclear whether ultrasonography or venography is cost-effective for screening or has a beneficial effect on clinical outcome. A DVT below the knee often is not treated because embolization to a lung is unlikely. The American College of Chest Physicians (ACCP) does not recommend the routine use of duplex ultrasonography when asymptomatic patients are discharged from the hospital after major orthopaedic surgery.[1]

VTE and Spinal Cord Injury

Epidemiology

Patients with spinal cord injury are at high risk for VTE. These patients have all three components of the classic Virchow triad.[5,6] The risk of DVT in a patient with a spinal cord injury is twice that of all patients with trauma; for a patient with a spine fracture, the risk is increased three times.[7] The surveillance technique influences the reported rate of DVT.[1,8] The reported rates of DVT after spinal cord injury range from 5% to 100%.[1,5,6,8-12] Nine studies found rates ranging from 5.3% to 38.6%, with a mean pooled average of 16.9%.[9] Only 10% of patients with an acute spinal cord injury may have clinically evident DVT.[8,13]

A 10-year retrospective cohort study of 16,240 patients with spinal cord injury found that the 91-day cumulative incidence of VTE was 5.4%.[14] Significant predictors of VTE were male sex, African American race, complete paraplegia, and the presence of three or more comorbid conditions. Age younger than 14 years was not a protective factor. VTE was not a predictor of death during the first 3 months after spinal cord injury.

The rate of PE ranges from 0% to 18% in patients with acute spinal cord injury. Most PEs are asymptomatic.[1,6,9,10] Clinically evident PE may be seen in only 3% of patients.[8,13] When PE does occur, it is fatal in as many as 5% of patients.[1,6,9,10] PE accounts for 37% of all deaths in patients not receiving VTE prophylaxis, and it remains the third most common cause of death after a spinal cord injury.[1,8]

Mechanical Prophylaxis

Knee-high compression stockings were found to be sufficient for preventing venous distention in patients with spinal cord injury because they significantly decrease venous capacity.[15] However, there are only limited clinical studies of mechanical prophylaxis for primary prevention of VTE in patients with acute spinal cord injury. Level IV evidence suggests that the use of a pneumatic sequential compression device (PSCD), compression stockings, and low-dosage unfractionated heparin (UFH) reduces the risk of VTE in patients with spinal cord injury.[6] However, the use of a PSCD or compression stockings alone does not provide adequate protection and is not recommended.[16] Patients should be monitored during mechanical prophylaxis for evidence of skin breakdown, and insensate patients should be monitored for skin irritation.[6]

Low-Dosage Unfractionated Subcutaneous Heparin

Few studies have examined the use of UFH as a primary method of prophylaxis in patients with spinal cord injury. No difference was found over a 28-day period in the risk of DVT for 16 patients with acute spinal cord injury who were receiving UFH and 17 patients who were receiving a placebo; however, 15 patients treated with UFH plus electrical stimulation had a significantly lower incidence of DVT.[17] In another study, 75 patients with spinal cord injury were randomly assigned to receive 5,000 international units (IU) of UFH every 12 hours or an adjusted dosage based on activated partial thromboplastin time. Nine of the patients (31%) receiving a fixed dosage and 2 of the patients (7%) receiving an adjusted dosage had a DVT. There were no bleeding events among the patients in the fixed-dosage group, but there were 7 such events among patients in the adjusted-dosage group.[18]

A recent systematic review of 23 studies related to VTE and spinal cord injury found level II evidence that 5,000 IU of UFH every 12 hours is no better than placebo but that UFH in conjunction with electrical stimulation may have a role in preventing VTE. There is level I evidence that adjusted-dosage UFH is more effective than fixed-dosage UFH but is associated with a higher risk of bleeding complications.[6]

Low-Molecular-Weight Heparin

Compared with UFH, low-molecular-weight heparin (LMWH) binds less strongly to protein, has enhanced bioavailability, interacts less with platelets, and has a more predictable dosage response. Thrombocytopenia has not been associated with the short-term use of LMWH.[6] The most commonly used LMWH is enoxaparin, which has a half-life of 4.4 hours, compared with 0.35 hours for UFH, and a bioavailability of 50%, compared with 20% for UFH.[6,19]

Twice-daily screening by clinical examination or ultrasonography found no DVTs in 105 patients who were given 30 mg of enoxaparin, including 66 patients with spinal cord injury.[20] A retrospective study of 111 patients found a 7.1% incidence of DVT and a 2.3% incidence of PE in patients who received prophylaxis with a PSCD alone.[11] When a PSCD was used with

UFH, the incidence of DVT or PE was 11.1% or 2.8%, respectively. With a PSCD plus LMWH, the incidence was 7.4% or 0%, respectively. There were no statistically significant between-group differences.[11]

A randomized controlled study of 119 patients with spinal cord injury compared the use of 5,000 IU of UFH every 8 hours to that of 40 mg of enoxaparin every 24 hours. The rate of DVT was 21.7% or 8.5%, respectively ($P = 0.052$).[6,21] A randomized controlled study of 107 patients compared the use of a PSCD plus UFH to the use of 30 mg of enoxaparin twice daily. The rate of DVT was 63.3% or 65.5%, respectively; the rate of PE was 18.4% or 2.6%, respectively ($P = 0.14$).[6,22] When 41 patients with spinal cord injury were randomly assigned to receive either UFH or LMWH, 5 of the 21 patients who received UFH had a thrombotic event, including two fatal PEs, and 2 patients had bleeding that required discontinuation of the medication.[23] In contrast, patients in the LMWH group had no events. A nonrandomized comparison of enoxaparin dosing found no difference in bleeding complications or DVT risk between patients receiving 40 mg once daily and patients receiving 30 mg twice daily.[6,24]

Several forms of LMWH are available. A retrospective evaluation of 90 patients treated with 5,000 IU of dalteparin once daily or 5,000 IU of UFH twice daily found no difference in the rate of complications, the location of VTE, or the incidence of fatal PE.[8] A randomized controlled study comparing the use of 30 mg of enoxaparin twice daily to that of 5,000 IU of dalteparin once daily found no difference in the rate of DVT or bleeding complications.[10] However, 135 patients undergoing major orthopaedic surgery had a DVT rate of 1.6% with enoxaparin or 9.7% with dalteparin.[25] This finding suggests that dalteparin may not be clinically equivalent to enoxaparin.

A recent systematic review based on two randomized controlled studies found level I evidence that LMWH in the form of enoxaparin is more effective than UFH for reducing VTE.[6] In addition, there is level IV evidence that enoxaparin has equivalent efficacy at 40-mg and 30-mg dosages. There is level I evidence that the efficacy of enoxaparin is equivalent to that of dalteparin.[6]

Inferior Vena Cava Filters

Inferior vena cava (IVC) filters were found to be 98% effective in preventing PE from a lower extremity DVT.[26] However, the risk of DVT may increase after an IVC filter is placed.[14] The data suggest there may be a role for IVC filters in patients who have such a high thromboembolic risk that anticoagulation therapy cannot safely be discontinued before spine surgery. These patients include those with a recent actively treated DVT. IVC filter placement also may be a reasonable means of preventing PE in high-risk patients for whom anticoagulation therapy is contraindicated, such as patients with a gastric ulcer.[27]

Of 21 patients with spinal cord injury who were treated with an IVC filter, 1 patient had a perioperative PE, and 2 patients had a DVT.[28] A retrospective review of 22 patients with spinal cord injury who were treated with an IVC filter found no DVTs, PEs, or other complications.[29] In a comparison of 108 patients with an IVC filter inserted after multiple trauma including spinal cord injury and 216 matched patients who did not have a filter, none of the patients in the IVC filter group had a PE; of the 13 patients in the control group who had a PE ($P < 0.05$), 9 died.[26]

Morbidity related to IVC filter use should be considered. An IVC filter can increase the risk of lower extremity DVT and lead to additional complications including migration or thrombosis of the filter itself. Hematoma at the site of insertion is an uncommon early adverse event.

A recent systematic review found level III evidence that the use of an IVC filter reduces the risk of PE in patients with spinal cord injury.[6] However, it was calculated that prevention of one nonfatal PE would require placing an IVC filter in 50 patients with spinal cord injury who were receiving chemical thromboprophylaxis, at a cost of $250,000.[11] Advances in the use of IVC filters, particularly in the ability to retrieve the filter, have increased their role. The long-term complications and benefits of using retrievable or permanent filters must be evaluated and compared to define the indications for their use.[27]

Recommendations

Sufficient evidence exists to support the routine use of chemical anticoagulation therapy for VTE prophylaxis in patients with spinal cord injury. The ACCP recommends that all patients with acute spinal cord injury receive chemical thromboprophylaxis. LMWH was found to be safe and efficacious in randomized controlled studies, and it is the preferred agent.[1,22-24] If LMWH is contraindicated, mechanical prophylaxis with PSCD is recommended until chemical prophylaxis can be safely initiated. IVC filters are not recommended for primary prophylaxis, but they may have a role if there are contraindications to the use of other modalities.[1] LMWH should be continued during rehabilitation or used as a bridge to oral warfarin therapy (to achieve an International Normalized Ratio of 2.0 to 3.0). Routine thromboprophylaxis should be continued for at least 3 months.[1]

VTE and Routine Spine Surgery

Epidemiology

Many methods of VTE prophylaxis have been used after routine elective spine surgery, including compression stockings, thromboembolic deterrent stockings (TEDS), PSCDs, IVC filters, and chemical anticoagulation.[16,30-44] However, no one method has been found clearly superior to the others, and therefore it is difficult to define actual rates of DVT and PE after spine surgery or to develop standardized prophylaxis

1: Basic Science of the Spine

guidelines. The ambiguity is further increased by the variability of the methods used to detect DVT, including clinical examination, screening duplex ultrasonography, and venography.[16,30-32,35-46] Reflecting these inconsistencies, the reported incidence of DVT after spine surgery ranges from less than 1% to 31%; a systematic review found overall rates of 2.2% and 0.3% for DVT and PE, respectively.[4]

It is difficult to apply the results of individual studies to clinical practice because of the diversity of patient populations, prophylactic protocols, and surveillance methods. However, individual studies can provide a sense of the incidence of VTE in patients who receive no prophylaxis at all. Studies using venography or radionuclide phlebography as the primary method of surveillance found higher rates of postoperative DVT than studies using other methods. In several studies, the rates of DVT were 27% (14 of 51 patients having elective lumbar surgery under spinal anesthesia), 14% (6 of 44 patients having elective lumbar surgery under general anesthesia), 16% (17 of 110 patients having a posterior spine procedure), and 18% (3 of 16 adult patients having a Harrington procedure for scoliosis).[35,46,47] Patients who received no prophylaxis and had a diagnosis based on clinical examination generally were reported to have lower rates of DVT: 2% (2 of 119 patients having an anterior or posterior lumbar interbody fusion), 2.6% (3 of 115 patients having laminectomy or spinal fusion), or 0.7% (8 of 1,229 patients age 14 to 18 years having a Harrington procedure for scoliosis).[45,48,49]

A retrospective study compared complications in two groups of 500 patients after lumbar fusion. Patients with an average postoperative recumbency time of 18.5 days had a 4.2% rate of DVT (21 patients), and patients with an average recumbency time of 10.5 days had a 2.2% rate (11 patients).[50] This finding suggests that a longer recumbency period leads to a greater risk of DVT. Studies of PE after routine spine surgery found rates of 0.2% (1 of 481 patients) after lumbar disk surgery, 0.9% (1 of 115 patients) after laminectomy or spinal fusion, and less than 0.1% (1 of 1,129 patients age 14 to 18 years) after a Harrington procedure.[48,49,51]

Mechanical Prophylaxis
Compression Stockings and TEDS
Three related studies used ultrasonographic surveillance to determine rates of DVT in patients treated with compression stockings and/or TEDS as the primary means of VTE prophylaxis. The rates were similar: 5% (4 of 74 patients) after lumbar laminectomy or fusion, 6% (5 of 86 patients) after spinal decompression, and 5% (3 of 60 patients) after laminectomy or laminotomy.[31-33] A fourth study found no clinically evident proximal DVTs in 42 patients treated with compression stockings and TEDS after a major reconstructive spine procedure.[30] Other studies that included patients treated with compression stockings or TEDS reported only the rate of postoperative PE after spine

surgery. Ten clinically significant PEs occurred with a postoperative protocol that included compression stockings, with or without PSCD, in 1,223 patients undergoing anterior spinal fusion.[39] Other studies reported no clinically significant PEs when similar prophylaxis was used.[30-32]

PSCD
Studies of PSCD for primary prophylaxis found a 3% rate of clinically detected DVT (in 3 of 104 patients) after posterior spine instrumentation, a 4% rate of ultrasonographically detected DVT (in 8 of 200 patients) after cervical spine surgery, a 2.8% rate of ultrasonographically detected DVT (in 4 of 139 patients) after multilevel laminectomy with instrumented fusion, and a 6% rate of venographically detected DVT (in 13 of 211 patients) after elective lumbar spine surgery.[34,35,52,53] In the elective lumbar spine surgery study, DVT rates were compared among four subgroups of patients. DVT occurred in 14% (6 of 44 patients) of those who received general anesthesia with no prophylaxis, 8% (8 of 99 patients) with general anesthesia and PSCD, 27% (14 of 51 patients) with spinal anesthesia and no prophylaxis, and 4.5% (5 of 112 patients) with spinal anesthesia and PSCD.[35] Of 200 patients undergoing cervical spine surgery, 1.5% (3 patients) had a clinical diagnosis of PE.[34] Of 139 patients undergoing multilevel laminectomy and instrumented fusion, 0.7% (1 patient) had a PE.[53]

PSCD Plus TEDS
A randomized prospective study based on ultrasonographic surveillance after major thoracolumbar reconstructive surgery found a 0% rate of DVT in 75 patients who used TEDS plus foot pumps and a 2% rate (1 of 59 patients) in those who used TEDS plus PSCD.[54] The DVT rates were comparable in other studies of PSCD and TEDS use, based on ultrasonographic examination: none of 33 patients after major reconstructive surgery; 0.9% (1 of 116 adult patients) after reconstructive surgery; 0.8% (1 of 126 patients) after consecutive spine procedures at a single institution; and 14% (6 of 41 patients) after fusion and instrumentation (10% [4 of 39] if patients with paraplegia were excluded).[30,38,40,41] A comparative study found no DVTs among 111 patients treated with PSCD after lumbar laminectomy or fusion; 5.4% (4 patients) of 74 patients treated with TEDS alone had a DVT ($P < 0.05$).[31]

In two retrospective studies, DVT was diagnosed by clinical examination alone. The rates were 0% in 202 patients after adult reconstructive spine surgery (excluding cervical spine procedures) and 0.5% (1 of 191 patients) after consecutive spine procedures at a single institution.[38,40]

When patients were treated with TEDS and PSCD, studies found clinically symptomatic PE in 0% (0 of 33 patients), 0.7% (1 of 134 patients), 0% (0 of 111 patients), 1% (2 of 194 patients), and 0.3% (1 of 317 patients).[30,31,36,40,54] In one study, 73 of 318 patients had a

Table 2

Rates of DVT (Number of Patients) by Methods of Prophylaxis and Screening

Prophylaxis Method	Screening Method			Total DVT Rate, by Prophylaxis Method
	Clinical Examination	Ultrasonography	Venography	
None or unknown	1.6% (46 of 2,956)	NR	18% (40 of 221)	2.7% (86 of 3,177)
Compression stockings or TEDS	0.4% (1 of 225)	1% (12 of 262)	NR	2.7% (13 of 487)
PSCD	2.9% (3 of 104)	4% (8 of 200)	6% (13 of 211)	4.6% (24 of 515)
PSCD and TEDS	0.3% (1 of 393)	1.9% (14 of 755)	NR	1.3% (15 of 1,148)
Chemical anticoagulation, with or without compression stockings, TEDS, or PSCD	0.6% (18 of 2,914)	0% (0 of 264)	NR	0.6% (18 of 3,178)
IVC filter, with or without compression stockings, TEDS, or PSCD	0% (0 of 17)	26% (25 of 96)	NR	22% (25 of 113)
Total DVT rate, by screening method	1% (69 of 6,609)	3.7% (59 of 1,577)	12.3% (53 of 432)	2.1% (181 of 8,618)

NR = none recorded.

Adapted with permission from Glotzbecker MP, Bono CM, Wood KB, et al: Thromboembolic disease in spinal surgery: A systematic review. *Spine (Phila Pa 1976)* 2009;34(3):291-303.

ventilation perfusion scan for surveillance, and 7 of these patients were found to have a PE.[38]

Chemoprophylaxis
Limited data are available on the safety and efficacy of chemoprophylaxis after routine elective spine surgery. In a prospective comparative study based on ultrasonographic surveillance, no proximal DVTs or PEs were found in 35 patients being treated with low-dosage warfarin after major reconstructive spine surgery to maintain a prothrombin time 1.3 to 1.5 times the normal value. In comparison, the rate of DVT was 0% in 42 patients treated with TEDS, 0% in 33 patients treated with TEDS and PSCD, and 0.5% (1 patient) in 219 patients variably treated with TEDS and/or PSCD.[30] After spine surgery at a single institution, patients treated with LMWH less than 24 hours after surgery had a rate of DVT lower than 1% (1 of 1,954 patients) and a 0% rate of PE.[16]

Pooled Results
A recent systematic review of VTE after spine surgery included a calculation of pooled rates of DVT and PE based on methods of prophylaxis and screening[4] (Tables 2 and 3). The overall rate of DVT in the 25 reviewed studies was 2.1% (181 of 8,618 patients). In patients with no prophylaxis, the rate was 2.7% (86 of 3,177 patients). The rate for patients treated with compression stockings or TEDS was 2.7% (13 of 487 pa-

tients); with PSCD, 4.6% (24 of 515 patients); with PSCD and TEDS, 1.3% (15 of 1,148 patients); with chemical anticoagulation therapy, 0.6% (18 of 3,178 patients); and with IVC filters (with or without other prophylaxis), 22% (25 of 113 patients). The rates of DVT varied with the screening method: 1% (69 of 6,609 patients) with clinical surveillance, 3.7% (59 of 1,577 patients) with ultrasonographic surveillance, and 12.3% (53 of 432 patients) with venographic surveillance. The overall rate of PE in the 25 reported studies was 0.3% (69 of 21,657 patients).

Recommendations
Most studies found a low rate of DVT or PE, regardless of the type of prophylaxis after elective spine surgery. In patients who received no prophylaxis, the rates of DVT and PE were 2.7% and 0.2%, respectively.[4] Despite this low incidence, most spine surgeons choose to treat patients with some method of noninvasive prophylaxis.

DVT rates may be lower in patients who are treated with PSCD and TEDS than in patients treated with other methods of mechanical prophylaxis,[31] and therefore it is recommended that PSCD and TEDS be used after elective spine surgery. However, the studies that support the use of PSCD and TEDS reported that many of the detected DVTs were distal to the knee, and such DVTs are of unclear clinical significance.[55] The Seventh ACCP Conference on Antithrombotic and Throm-

Table 3

Rates of Pulmonary Embolism by Method of Prophylaxis

Prophylaxis Method	PE Rate (Number of Patients)
None or unknown	0.2% (34 of 15,204)
Compression stockings or TEDS	0.6% (10 of 1,710)
PSCD	1.1% (3 of 304)
PSCD and TEDS	1% (11 of 1,148)
Chemical anticoagulation with or without compression stockings, TEDS, or PSCD	0.3% (10 of 3,178)
IVC filter with or without compression stockings, TEDS, or PSCD	1% (1 of 113)
Total PE rate	**0.3% (69 of 21,657)**

Adapted with permission from Glotzbecker MP, Bono CM, Wood KB, et al: Thromboembolic disease in spinal surgery: A systematic review. *Spine (Phila Pa 1976)* 2009;34(3):291-303.

bolytic Therapy recommends perioperative treatment with an intermittent PSCD alone (grade 1B evidence), graduated compression stockings alone (grade 2B evidence), or a perioperative intermittent PSCD with graduated compression stockings (grade 2C evidence). PSCD, with or without TEDS, may be used for primary prophylaxis after spine surgery in patients with additional thrombotic risk factors because these interventions carry little risk, and the resulting rate of DVT is low. Based on grade II and III evidence, the North American Spine Society recommends that mechanical prophylaxis be used to lower the incidence of VTE after elective spine surgery.[56]

It may be possible to further lower the risk of DVT by treating patients with chemical anticoagulation therapy. However, studies of chemical prophylaxis after spine surgery are sparse, lack appropriate control groups, generally are underpowered, and have significantly heterogeneous study populations. These factors preclude strong conclusions as to whether using chemical anticoagulants leads to a clinically significant reduction in VTE after routine spine surgery. The consensus-based recommendation of the North American Spine Society is that chemoprophylaxis may not be warranted in routine, elective spine surgery because these agents carry a defined risk of complications such as persistent wound drainage and epidural hematoma.[56,57]

VTE and High-Risk Spine Surgery

Epidemiology

Patients with multitrauma or a malignant tumor are at increased risk of VTE disease.[1,36,37,42,44] The few studies that focused on high-risk patients had varying definitions of risk, diverse patient populations, and different methods of prophylaxis and surveillance. These inconsistencies may be partly responsible for the variability found in a recent survey of surgeons' opinions on the

risk of DVT in high-risk spine surgery.[58] The study revealed a considerable range in surgeons' estimates of the risk of DVT, and the perceived risk of DVT influenced the initiation of chemical prophylaxis.

Mechanical and Chemical Prophylaxis

A retrospective study found a 31% rate of DVT and a 1.4% rate of PE in 74 patients who were at high risk for VTE and received IVC filters because of contraindications to prophylactic perioperative anticoagulation therapy.[37] In a retrospective review of 423 patients with a spinal tumor who were treated with compression stockings and PSCD, the rate of DVT detected by screening duplex ultrasonography was 1.2% and the rate of clinically detected PE was 0.7%.[36] None of the 229 patients who also received LMWH had a DVT, and 1 had a PE. Of the 194 patients not receiving chemoprophylaxis, 2.5% (5 patients) had a DVT and 1% (2 patients) had a PE. A review of 978 patients who received chemical prophylaxis after spine surgery for a traumatic injury found a DVT rate of 2.2% (22 patients) and a PE rate of 0.9% (4 patients).[44] A prospective study of 161 high-risk patients who underwent spine surgery found no PEs in the 39 patients with an IVC filter; of the remaining 122 patients, 13.1% (16 patients) had a PE.[42]

Recommendations

The use of chemical anticoagulants for prophylaxis may be indicated for some patients at increased risk of VTE disease. The evidence is sufficient to support chemical anticoagulation in patients with spinal cord injury.[1,22-24] However, patients with an existing neurologic injury are vastly different from other high-risk surgical patients because an epidural hematoma would have less clinical consequence for them. The unusual risk-benefit ratio for patients with spinal cord injury means that recommendations pertaining to them may not be applicable to high-risk patients who are neurologically intact. Except for studies of patients with spinal cord injury, there is a clear void in the research literature on appropriate thromboprophylaxis for high-risk patients after spinal surgery. Defining the risk-benefit ratio may be most important for this subpopulation of patients who undergo spine surgery. Limited studies indicate that high-risk patients have a lower rate of VTE when treated with chemoprophylaxis agents, but there is sufficient variability among surgeons' practices to restrict the ability to make general recommendations.[36,44,58]

The Seventh ACCP Conference on Antithrombotic and Thrombolytic Therapy recommended combining low-dosage UFH or LMWH with graduated compression stockings and/or intermittent PSCD in patients with multiple risk factors for VTE (grade 1C+). Advanced age, a known malignancy, the presence of a neurologic deficit, an earlier VTE, and an anterior surgical approach were identified as risk factors, but an appropriate time for initiating therapy was not identified.[1] The literature does not clearly identify the factors that define a high-risk patient, and there is insufficient evidence to define the risk-benefit ratio for anticoagulation in high-risk patients. Well-controlled prospective studies are needed to better define the true incidence of DVT in specific groups of high-risk patients, the indications for chemical prophylaxis, and the best time for initiating therapy. The current North American Spine Society evidence-based guideline contains a consensus recommendation that LMWH or low-dosage warfarin can be added to PSCD and compression stockings for high-risk patients but that the decision should be based on individual patient factors.[56] Patients considered to be at high risk may have a neoplastic or traumatic condition, hypercoagulable state, or an anticipated prolonged recumbency (for example, after staged anterior-posterior surgery to correct a deformity).

The use of an IVC filter may reduce the risk of PE in a patient who is at increased risk of thromboembolism but who cannot receive anticoagulation therapy. Some surgeons use an IVC filter as a precaution against fatal PE, even if chemical anticoagulants are being administered. Others use IVC filters as the sole means of preventing PE, often if chemical anticoagulation therapy is contraindicated. IVC filter use is not free of complications, and there is insufficient evidence to support their routine use in patients who are at high risk.

Complications of Chemical Prophylaxis

A symptomatic epidural hematoma may be the most serious nonfatal complication associated with early postoperative anticoagulation therapy. Whether, and by how much, prophylactic anticoagulation therapy increases the risk of symptomatic epidural hematoma has been a critical question. A recent systematic review found that during the past 30 years symptomatic epidural hematoma was reported in 133 patients after spine surgery.[59] Although the reported rates of epidural hematoma ranged from 0% to 1%,[59] a recent survey of spine surgeons revealed that most estimated the risk to be higher than 1%.[58]

Noncomparative studies did not find a substantially increased risk of epidural hematoma in patients who received chemoprophylaxis after spine surgery.[16,43,44] Data from studies of small, dissimilar groups of patients revealed no clear relationship between the use of LMWH and the incidence of symptomatic epidural hematoma. A multicenter randomized controlled study compared the use of both LMWH (initiated within 24 hours of surgery) and compression stockings to the use of compression stockings alone after elective neurosurgical procedures.[43] Of the patients who underwent spine surgery, 31 were treated with LMWH and compression stockings, and 15 were treated with compression stockings alone; none of these 46 patients had a postoperative epidural hematoma. The incidence of major or minor bleeding not specific to spine procedures was 18 of 153 patients in the LMWH–compression stockings group and 11 of 154 patients in the compression stockings–alone group ($P = 0.18$). There were four major bleeding events in each group, including intracranial bleeding or melena.[43] A review found an overall 0.4% rate of epidural hematoma (8 patients) when routine treatment with LMWH was initiated within 24 hours of 1,954 consecutive spine procedures affecting different levels.[16]

The incidence of clinically silent epidural hematoma clearly is much higher than that of symptomatic hematoma.[60,61] After lumbar decompression, an epidural hematoma developed in 58% of patients, as diagnosed by MRI 2 to 5 days after surgery; the epidural hematoma was large enough to compress the thecal sac beyond its preoperative level.[61] Also after lumbar decompression, an MRI-diagnosed epidural hematoma developed in 89% of patients without a postoperative drain, and 36% of those treated with a postoperative drain had evidence of an epidural hematoma.[60] In both of these studies, the epidural hematoma was completely asymptomatic.

Complications other than symptomatic epidural hematoma may be more common with anticoagulation therapy, although the literature is limited. Minor bleeding was found more than twice as often as epidural hematoma in a retrospective review of 978 patients who underwent surgery for spine trauma.[44] LMWH was used in 945 of the patients, although the timing of therapy was not reported. Postoperative epidural hematoma was not specifically mentioned, but the rate of major bleeding was 0.6% (6 patients).[44] In a poll of 22 members of the Scoliosis Research Society, nine patients were identified as having been treated for PE after spine surgery with a therapeutic dosage of intravenous UFH.[57] Complications related to the anticoagulation therapy developed in six of these patients (67%), including wound hematoma (two patients), draining hematoma (four patients), deep wound infection (two

1: Basic Science of the Spine

patients), upper gastrointestinal bleeding (one patient), and epidural hematoma (two patients). This report was interpreted as suggesting that therapeutic UFH may be associated with bleeding complications.[57]

Timing of Chemoprophylaxis

If chemoprophylaxis is to be used after spine surgery, the surgeon must decide when it will be initiated. Surgeons use a wide range of timing intervals.[58] Starting chemoprophylaxis too early can lead to bleeding complications at the surgical site, but a delay obviates the benefits of chemoprophylaxis during the initial postoperative stage, when the patient is least mobile. Data are lacking to define a safe, effective protocol for chemoprophylaxis. Two studies found no increased risk when LMWH was administered during the early postoperative period (less than 24 hours after surgery).[16,43] Because the patient populations were small or heterogeneous, the results of these studies have only limited usefulness for general clinical practice. Prospective studies are necessary to define a safe time point for initiating chemical prophylaxis. The North American Spine Society evidence-based guideline makes no recommendation regarding the timing of chemoprophylaxis after spine surgery, except to note that there is level IV evidence that chemoprophylaxis can be started the day of surgery.[56]

Summary

Within a limited group of published studies, the risk of DVT ranged from 0.3% to 31% in patients after spine surgery and from 0% to 100% in patients with spinal cord injury, as detected by different methods of screening. Given the significant variability of the existing studies and the lack of well-designed studies, surgeons use widely varying postoperative prophylaxis protocols, especially for high-risk, neurologically intact patients. For patients with spinal cord injury, there is good evidence to support chemical prophylaxis with LMWH, with or without mechanical prophylaxis. It is reasonable to use PSCD and TEDS after elective spine procedures, particularly if mobilization will be delayed. The available literature is insufficient to precisely guide current clinical practice with regard to VTE prophylaxis in high-risk patients. However, it seems reasonable to use postoperative chemoprophylaxis in some high-risk patients, as determined on an individual basis. Well-designed prospective studies are needed to evaluate postoperative prophylaxis protocols in patients with risk factors for VTE.

Annotated References

1. Geerts WH, Pineo GF, Heit JA, et al: Prevention of venous thromboembolism: The Seventh ACCP Conference on Antithrombotic and Thrombolytic Therapy. *Chest* 2004;126(3, suppl):338S-400S.

   VTE in spine surgery is reviewed. The topics include pathophysiology, incidence, risk factors in elective spine surgery, and spinal column trauma. Anticoagulation prophylaxis and its complications are discussed.

2. Heck CA, Brown CR, Richardson WJ: Venous thromboembolism in spine surgery. *J Am Acad Orthop Surg* 2008;16(11):656-664.

   A systematic review of 25 articles found that the overall rate of DVT was 2.1%. The rate ranged from 0.3% to 31% and varied with patient population and surveillance method. The method of prophylaxis was important: no prophylaxis, 2.7%; compression stockings, 2.7%; PSCD, 4.6%; PSCD and compression stockings, 1.3%; chemical anticoagulation, 0.6%; and IVC filters (with or without another method of prophylaxis), 22%. DVT rate also was influenced by the method of diagnosis (range, 1% to 12.3%).

3. Lindner DJ, Edwards JM, Phinney ES, Taylor LM Jr, Porter JM: Long-term hemodynamic and clinical sequelae of lower extremity deep vein thrombosis. *J Vasc Surg* 1986;4(5):436-442.

4. Glotzbecker MP, Bono CM, Wood KB, Harris MB: Thromboembolic disease in spinal surgery: A systematic review. *Spine (Phila Pa 1976)* 2009;34(3):291-303.

   In a systematic review of asymptomatic DVT in spinal cord injury, DVT was detected in 16.9% of patients (in 25 studies). Only 4 studies reported the occurrence of PE, in 4.4% of patients. There is insufficient evidence to support or refute a recommendation for routine DVT screening in adults with acute traumatic spinal cord injury who are receiving thromboprophylaxis. However, there is level II evidence that screening could detect asymptomatic DVT in 22.7% of these patients.

5. Aito S, Pieri A, D'Andrea M, Marcelli F, Cominelli E: Primary prevention of deep venous thrombosis and pulmonary embolism in acute spinal cord injured patients. *Spinal Cord* 2002;40(6):300-303.

6. Teasell RW, Hsieh JT, Aubut JA, et al: Venous thromboembolism after spinal cord injury. *Arch Phys Med Rehabil* 2009;90(2):232-245.

   A systematic review of 23 studies on VTE in spinal cord injury found strong evidence to support the use of LMWH in reducing VTE. A higher adjusted dosage of UFH was found to be more effective than 5,000 IU administered every 12 hours, although bleeding complications were more common.

7. Velmahos GC, Kern J, Chan LS, Oder D, Murray JA, Shekelle P: Prevention of venous thromboembolism after injury: An evidence-based report. Part II: Analysis of risk factors and evaluation of the role of vena caval filters. *J Trauma* 2000;49(1):140-144.

8. Worley S, Short C, Pike J, Anderson D, Douglas JA, Thompson K: Dalteparin vs low-dose unfractionated heparin for prophylaxis against clinically evident venous

thromboembolism in acute traumatic spinal cord injury: A retrospective cohort study. *J Spinal Cord Med* 2008; 31(4):379-387.

This is a retrospective cohort study of 90 patients who received LMWH (dalteparin, 5,000 IU daily) or low-dosage UFH (5,000 IU twice daily) for VTE prophylaxis after acute traumatic spinal cord injury. There was no statistically significant association between the incidence of VTE (7.78%) and the type of prophylaxis.

9. Furlan JC, Fehlings MG: Role of screening tests for deep venous thrombosis in asymptomatic adults with acute spinal cord injury: An evidence-based analysis. *Spine (Phila Pa 1976)* 2007;32(17):1908-1916.

10. Chiou-Tan FY, Garza H, Chan KT, et al: Comparison of dalteparin and enoxaparin for deep venous thrombosis prophylaxis in patients with spinal cord injury. *Am J Phys Med Rehabil* 2003;82(9):678-685.

11. Maxwell RA, Chavarria-Aguilar M, Cockerham WT, et al: Routine prophylactic vena cava filtration is not indicated after acute spinal cord injury. *J Trauma* 2002; 52(5):902-906.

12. Sugimoto Y, Ito Y, Tomioka M, et al: Deep venous thrombosis in patients with acute cervical spinal cord injury in a Japanese population: Assessment with Doppler ultrasonography. *J Orthop Sci* 2009;14(4):374-376.

A retrospective assessment of 52 patients with acute cervical spinal cord injury found that 21% (11 patients) had DVT, based on ultrasonographic screening, and there were no PEs.

13. Chen D, Apple DF Jr, Hudson LM, Bode R: Medical complications during acute rehabilitation following spinal cord injury: Current experience of the Model Systems. *Arch Phys Med Rehabil* 1999;80(11):1397-1401.

14. Jones T, Ugalde V, Franks P, Zhou H, White RH: Venous thromboembolism after spinal cord injury: Incidence, time course, and associated risk factors in 16,240 adults and children. *Arch Phys Med Rehabil* 2005; 86(12):2240-2247.

A retrospective cohort analysis of 16,240 patients with spinal cord injury found a 91-day cumulative incidence of VTE of 5.4%. In a multivariate model, significant predictors of VTE included male sex, African American racial identity, complete paraplegia rather than tetraplegia, and the presence of three or more comorbid conditions.

15. Rimaud D, Boissier C, Calmels P: Evaluation of the effects of compression stockings using venous plethysmography in persons with spinal cord injury. *J Spinal Cord Med* 2008;31(2):202-207.

Venous capacity and venous outflow were evaluated with and without the use of graduated compression stockings in nine men with spinal cord injury. The study found that 21 mm Hg knee-length graduated compression stockings were sufficient for preventing venous distention.

16. Gerlach R, Raabe A, Beck J, Woszczyk A, Seifert V: Postoperative nadroparin administration for prophylaxis of thromboembolic events is not associated with an increased risk of hemorrhage after spinal surgery. *Eur Spine J* 2004;13(1):9-13.

17. Merli GJ, Herbison GJ, Ditunno JF, et al: Deep vein thrombosis: Prophylaxis in acute spinal cord injured patients. *Arch Phys Med Rehabil* 1988;69(9):661-664.

18. Green D, Lee MY, Ito VY, et al: Fixed- vs adjusted-dose heparin in the prophylaxis of thromboembolism in spinal cord injury. *JAMA* 1988;260(9):1255-1258.

19. Tomaio A, Kirshblum SC, O'Connor KC, Johnston M: Treatment of acute deep vein thrombosis in spinal cord injured patients with enoxaparin: A cost analysis. *J Spinal Cord Med* 1998;21(3):205-210.

20. Harris S, Chen D, Green D: Enoxaparin for thromboembolism prophylaxis in spinal injury: Preliminary report on experience with 105 patients. *Am J Phys Med Rehabil* 1996;75(5):326-327.

21. Spinal Cord Injury Thromboprophylaxis Investigators: Prevention of venous thromboembolism in the rehabilitation phase after spinal cord injury: Prophylaxis with low-dose heparin or enoxaparin. *J Trauma* 2003;54(6): 1111-1115.

22. Spinal Cord Injury Thromboprophylaxis Investigators: Prevention of venous thromboembolism in the acute treatment phase after spinal cord injury: A randomized, multicenter trial comparing low-dose heparin plus intermittent pneumatic compression with enoxaparin. *J Trauma* 2003;54(6):1116-1126.

23. Green D, Lee MY, Lim AC, et al: Prevention of thromboembolism after spinal cord injury using low-molecular-weight heparin. *Ann Intern Med* 1990; 113(8):571-574.

24. Hebbeler SL, Marciniak CM, Crandall S, Chen D, Nussbaum S, Mendelewski S: Daily vs twice daily enoxaparin in the prevention of venous thromboembolic disorders during rehabilitation following acute spinal cord injury. *J Spinal Cord Med* 2004;27(3):236-240.

25. Slavik RS, Chan E, Gorman SK, et al: Dalteparin versus enoxaparin for venous thromboembolism prophylaxis in acute spinal cord injury and major orthopedic trauma patients: 'DETECT' trial. *J Trauma* 2007;62(5):1075-1081.

This retrospective cohort study included patients with traumatic pelvis, femoral shaft, or complex lower extremity fracture and/or acute spinal cord injury, who received LMWH for VTE prophylaxis in the intensive care unit. The rates of clinically symptomatic proximal DVT or PE were 1.6% with enoxaparin and 9.7% with dalteparin (*P* = 0.103).

26. Khansarinia S, Dennis JW, Veldenz HC, Butcher JL, Hartland L: Prophylactic Greenfield filter placement in

selected high-risk trauma patients. *J Vasc Surg* 1995; 22(3):231-236.

27. Johns JS, Nguyen C, Sing RF: Vena cava filters in spinal cord injuries: Evolving technology. *J Spinal Cord Med* 2006;29(3):183-190.

   The authors of a literature review of IVC filters in spinal cord injury concluded that retrievable vena cava filters are safe and feasible for secondary VTE prophylaxis in patients with spinal cord injury. Objective criteria for temporary and permanent placement remain to be defined.

28. Jarrell BE, Posuniak E, Roberts J, Osterholm J, Cotler J, Ditunno J: A new method of management using the Kim-Ray Greenfield filter for deep venous thrombosis and pulmonary embolism in spinal cord injury. *Surg Gynecol Obstet* 1983;157(4):316-320.

29. Wilson JT, Rogers FB, Wald SL, Shackford SR, Ricci MA: Prophylactic vena cava filter insertion in patients with traumatic spinal cord injury: Preliminary results. *Neurosurgery* 1994;35(2):234-239.

30. Rokito SE, Schwartz MC, Neuwirth MG: Deep vein thrombosis after major reconstructive spinal surgery. *Spine (Phila Pa 1976)* 1996;21(7):853-859.

31. Ferree BA, Wright AM: Deep venous thrombosis following posterior lumbar spinal surgery. *Spine (Phila Pa 1976)* 1993;18(8):1079-1082.

32. Ferree BA, Stern PJ, Jolson RS, Roberts JM V, Kahn A III: Deep venous thrombosis after spinal surgery. *Spine (Phila Pa 1976)* 1993;18(3):315-319.

33. Ferree BA: Deep venous thrombosis following lumbar laminotomy and laminectomy. *Orthopedics* 1994;17(1): 35-38.

34. Epstein NE: Intermittent pneumatic compression stocking prophylaxis against deep venous thrombosis in anterior cervical spinal surgery: A prospective efficacy study in 200 patients and literature review. *Spine (Phila Pa 1976)* 2005;30(22):2538-2543.

   In a prospective study, 100 consecutive patients undergoing single-level anterior corpectomy-fusion and 100 patients undergoing multilevel anterior corpectomy-fusion with posterior fusion were treated with intermittent pneumatic compression stockings alone. In the single-level group, 1 patient had DVT-PE; in the multilevel group, 7 patients had DVT, and 2 had PE.

35. Tetzlaff JE, O'Hara J, Bell GR, Boumphrey FR, Graor RA: Influence of anesthetic technique on the incidence of deep venous thrombosis after elective lumbar spine surgery. *Reg Anesth* 1994;19(2S):28.

36. Smith SF, Simpson JM, Sekhon LH: Prophylaxis for deep venous thrombosis in neurosurgical oncology: Review of 2779 admissions over a 9-year period. *Neurosurg Focus* 2004;17(4):E4.

37. Leon L, Rodriguez H, Tawk RG, Ondra SL, Labropoulos N, Morasch MD: The prophylactic use of inferior vena cava filters in patients undergoing high-risk spinal surgery. *Ann Vasc Surg* 2005;19(3):442-447.

   Prophylactic IVC filters were used after spine surgery for 74 patients who had risk factors for DVT and a contraindication to anticoagulation therapy. At a mean 11-month follow-up, PE developed in 1 patient and DVT developed in 27 limbs in 23 patients. Five limbs had an isolated calf DVT and 22 had proximal vein involvement.

38. Dearborn JT, Hu SS, Tribus CB, Bradford DS: Thromboembolic complications after major thoracolumbar spine surgery. *Spine (Phila Pa 1976)* 1999;24(14):1471-1476.

39. Faciszewski T, Winter RB, Lonstein JE, Denis F, Johnson L: The surgical and medical perioperative complications of anterior spinal fusion surgery in the thoracic and lumbar spine in adults: A review of 1223 procedures. *Spine (Phila Pa 1976)* 1995;20(14):1592-1599.

40. Smith MD, Bressler EL, Lonstein JE, Winter R, Pinto MR, Denis F: Deep venous thrombosis and pulmonary embolism after major reconstructive operations on the spine: A prospective analysis of three hundred and seventeen patients. *J Bone Joint Surg Am* 1994;76(7):980-985.

41. West JL III, Anderson LD: Incidence of deep vein thrombosis in major adult spinal surgery. *Spine (Phila Pa 1976)* 1992;17(8, suppl):S254-S257.

42. Rosner MK, Kuklo TR, Tawk R, Moquin R, Ondra SL: Prophylactic placement of an inferior vena cava filter in high-risk patients undergoing spinal reconstruction. *Neurosurg Focus* 2004;17(4):E6.

43. Agnelli G, Piovella F, Buoncristiani P, et al: Enoxaparin plus compression stockings compared with compression stockings alone in the prevention of venous thromboembolism after elective neurosurgery. *N Engl J Med* 1998; 339(2):80-85.

44. Platzer P, Thalhammer G, Jaindl M, et al: Thromboembolic complications after spinal surgery in trauma patients. *Acta Orthop* 2006;77(5):755-760.

   Postoperative systemic prophylaxis was used for 978 patients after spine surgery for traumatic injury. The incidence of symptomatic thromboembolic complications was 2.2% (22 patients). Seventeen patients had clinical signs of DVT, of whom 4 developed PE. PE developed in 5 patients without earlier clinical signs of DVT. Six patients died because of thromboembolic disease.

45. Scaduto AA, Gamradt SC, Yu WD, Huang J, Delamarter RB, Wang JC: Perioperative complications of threaded cylindrical lumbar interbody fusion devices: Anterior versus posterior approach. *J Spinal Disord Tech* 2003;16(6):502-507.

46.	Oda T, Fuji T, Kato Y, Fujita S, Kanemitsu N: Deep venous thrombosis after posterior spinal surgery. *Spine (Phila Pa 1976)* 2000;25(22):2962-2967.

47.	Nillius A, Willner S, Arborelius M Jr, Nylander G: Combined radionuclide phlebography and lung scanning in patients operated on for scoliosis with the Harrington procedure. *Clin Orthop Relat Res* 1980;152: 241-246.

48.	Miller F, Young DC, Wang GJ: The incidence of thromboembolic disease. *Clin Orthop Relat Res* 1983;176: 210-216.

49.	Udén A: Thromboembolic complications following scoliosis surgery in Scandinavia. *Acta Orthop Scand* 1979; 50(2):175-178.

50.	Prothero SR, Parkes JC, Stinchfield FE: Complications after low-back fusion in 1000 patients: A comparison of two series one decade apart. 1966. *Clin Orthop Relat Res* 1994;306:5-11.

51.	Stolke D, Sollmann WP, Seifert V: Intra- and postoperative complications in lumbar disc surgery. *Spine (Phila Pa 1976)* 1989;14(1):56-59.

52.	Dickman CA, Fessler RG, MacMillan M, Haid RW: Transpedicular screw-rod fixation of the lumbar spine: Operative technique and outcome in 104 cases. *J Neurosurg* 1992;77(6):860-870.

53.	Epstein NE: Efficacy of pneumatic compression stocking prophylaxis in the prevention of deep venous thrombosis and pulmonary embolism following 139 lumbar laminectomies with instrumented fusions. *J Spinal Disord Tech* 2006;19(1):28-31.

    Of 139 patients who received PCSD prophylaxis after multilevel lumbar laminectomy with instrumented fusion, DVT developed in 4 (2.8%).

54.	Wood KB, Kos PB, Abnet JK, Ista C: Prevention of deep-vein thrombosis after major spinal surgery: A comparison study of external devices. *J Spinal Disord* 1997; 10(3):209-214.

55.	Cohen JR, Tymon R, Pillari G, Johnson H: Regional anatomical differences in the venographic occurrence of deep venous thrombosis and long-term follow-up. *J Cardiovasc Surg (Torino)* 1988;29(5):547-551.

56.	Bono CM, Watters WC III, Heggeness MH, et al: An evidence-based clinical guideline for the use of antithrombotic therapies in spine surgery. *Spine J* 2009; 9(12):1046-1051.

    The evidence-based clinical guideline of the North American Spine Society is based on the highest quality literature. The updated guideline with references is available at www.spine.org.

57.	Cain JE Jr, Major MR, Lauerman WC, West JL, Wood KB, Fueredi GA: The morbidity of heparin therapy after development of pulmonary embolus in patients undergoing thoracolumbar or lumbar spinal fusion. *Spine (Phila Pa 1976)* 1995;20(14):1600-1603.

58.	Glotzbecker MP, Bono CM, Harris MB, Brick G, Heary RF, Wood KB: Surgeon practices regarding postoperative thromboembolic prophylaxis after high-risk spinal surgery. *Spine (Phila Pa 1976)* 2008;33(26):2915-2921.

    Ninety-four surgeons completed a questionnaire on their perceived risk of DVT, PE, and postoperative epidural hematoma; the safe time point for initiation of chemoprophylaxis; and their preferred chemoprophylactic agents and use of IVC filters in high-risk patients. The responses to the survey varied significantly.

59.	Glotzbecker MP, Bono CM, Wood KB, Harris MB: Postoperative epidural hematoma: A systematic review. *Spine (Phila Pa 1976)* 2010;35(10):E413-E420.

    In this systematic review of 17 articles, symptomatic epidural hematoma was reported after spine surgery in 133 patients. The overall calculated rate was 0.2% (range, 0 to 1%). In patients who received LMWH, the overall rate of epidural hematoma was 0.4% (range, 0 to 0.7%).

60.	Mirzai H, Eminoglu M, Orguc S: Are drains useful for lumbar disc surgery? A prospective, randomized clinical study. *J Spinal Disord Tech* 2006;19(3):171-177.

    Fifty patients undergoing lumbar disk surgery were randomly assigned to receive or not to receive insertion of a drain in the epidural space. MRI revealed epidural hematoma in 36% of patients with a drain and 89% of patients without a drain (P = 0.000).

61.	Sokolowski MJ, Garvey TA, Perl J II, et al: Prospective study of postoperative lumbar epidural hematoma: Incidence and risk factors. *Spine (Phila Pa 1976)* 2008; 33(1):108-113.

    Of 50 patients prospectively evaluated with MRI after lumbar decompression surgery, epidural hematoma of sufficient magnitude to compress the thecal sac developed in 58%. Age older than 60 years, a multilevel procedure, and preoperative International Normalized Ratio were associated with greater hematoma volume.

1: Basic Science of the Spine

Section 2

Nonsurgical Care of the Spine

EDITOR
MATTHEW SMUCK, MD

Chapter 8

The Pharmacologic Management of Spine Pain

Gerard A. Malanga, MD   Amrish D. Patel, MD, PT

Introduction

A thorough evaluation aids in the selection of treatments for a patient's low back pain, even if the exact cause of the pain remains elusive. A comprehensive history and physical examination can lead to a differential diagnosis and provide clues as to contributing biomechanical, infectious, inflammatory, neoplastic, myofascial, and psychologic factors. The pain can be classified as acute, subacute, or chronic and as nociceptive (somatic or visceral) or neuropathic. The medical treatment of spine pain is guided by the patient's type of pain and experience with medications. The many pharmacologic options range from over-the-counter agents to controlled substances.

Medical Treatment by Spine Pain Category

Categorizing a patient's pain based on its duration, source (nociceptive or neuropathic), or severity allows informed decision making regarding pharmacologic treatment.

Duration

The duration of pain is important to determining the stage of healing and likelihood of improvement. Acute pain typically is defined as having less than 1 month's duration, and chronic pain as having more than 3 months' duration.

Source

Nociceptive pain is defined as arising from stimulation or damage to nerve receptors that respond to pressure, touch, heat, or irritant chemicals. Such receptors are found throughout the spine, excluding only the inner

portion of an uninjured, undegenerated anulus fibrosus and nucleus pulposus. Nociceptive pain typically is described as a well-localized aching or throbbing pain. Visceral pain is a subtype of nociceptive pain originating in an internal organ; it is more episodic and less well localized than other nociceptive pain. Neuropathic pain develops from a lesion in the central or peripheral nervous system or from inappropriate peripheral or central nervous system processing in response to somatosensory signals. Neuropathic pain typically is described as burning, shooting, or electric.

Depending on the duration and severity of nociceptive pain, the regimen can include nonsteroidal anti-inflammatory drugs (NSAIDs), muscle relaxants, and opioids. The medical treatment of neuropathic pain involves a wide range of options, from NSAIDs and opioids to the tricyclic antidepressant (TCA) serotonin-norepinephrine reuptake inhibitors, anticonvulsants, gamma-aminobutyric acid agonists, capsaicin, and N-methyl-D-aspartate receptor antagonists.

Severity: The World Health Organization Pain Ladder

A World Health Organization (WHO) cancer unit expert committee developed a pain ladder that classifies acute or chronic pain as mild, moderate, or severe based on a scale of 1 to 10[1] (Figure 1). The WHO pain ladder is intended to aid physicians in assessing the quality and intensity of pain and determining the most appropriate relief measures. The WHO recommends treating cancer patients based on the severity of pain, regardless of acuity, and makes recommendations for each level of pain. The goal is to keep pain to a level of 1 to 4 through continual reassessment of the patient's condition and the effectiveness of the means of control. Several medications are recommended for controlling different levels of acute or chronic pain on the WHO pain ladder. Nonopioid medications such as aspirin, acetaminophen, or the aspirinlike NSAIDs are recommended for treating mild pain (a score of 1 to 4). A combination of NSAIDs or acetaminophen and so-called weak narcotics, such as codeine, hydrocodone, or propoxyphene, is recommended for treating moderate pain (a score of 5 to 7). For severe pain (a score of 8 to 10), a strong opioid such as morphine, meperidine, hydromorphone, fentanyl, or methadone is used in combination with an NSAID.

The WHO pain ladder was developed for treating cancer pain and does not distinguish between the treatment of acute and chronic pain. When the pain ladder is used by medical professionals to guide the treatment of nonmalignant spine pain, the distinction between acute and chronic pain informs treatment. Few dispute the value of short-term use of opioids for acute back pain, but their role in treating chronic low back pain remains controversial.[2] Prescriptions for opioids to treat spine pain increased from 9.4 million to 19.6 million from 1997 to 2004.[3] The adverse effects of chronic opioid use include decreased hormone levels, reduced immunity, and, paradoxically, an increased sensitivity to pain.[4,5] Deaths related to prescription opioid overdose in the United States have increased almost tenfold during the past 30 years.[6]

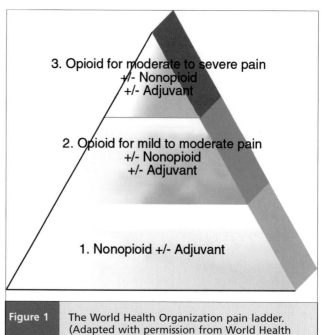

| Figure 1 | The World Health Organization pain ladder. (Adapted with permission from World Health Organization: WHO's Pain Ladder. Geneva, Switzerland, World Health Organization, 2011. http:// www.who.int/cancer/palliative/painladder/en/.) |

Medical Management by Diagnosis

A consensus for the treatment of acute or chronic low back pain has yet to emerge, but the goal of treatment is consistent: to improve function while decreasing pain.[1] Patients with any type of pain should be educated about the medication options, the reasons for preferring some medications to others, and the benefits and risks of the selected medications. A balance should be maintained between the strength of a medication and its adverse effects.[2,7,8] Patient preference always should be considered.

Acute Axial Low Back Pain

For a patient with mild to moderate acute low back pain, there is evidence to support the use of acetaminophen and NSAIDs, with or without the concomitant use of skeletal muscle relaxants.[2] The use of muscle relaxants should be considered if, for example, the patient has painful muscle spasms that limit activity and mobility. However, it is recommended that muscle relaxants not be used for more than 2 weeks.[9] The use of a cyclooxygenase (COX)–2 inhibitor or a nonselective NSAID, in addition to a proton pump inhibitor, may be considered for a patient with a history of gastritis. A scheduled short course of NSAIDs can reduce the potential for adverse effects associated with longer term use.[2,8,9] In a patient with severe acute low back pain, the judicious use of an opioid can reduce pain in the short term, although these medications have not been shown to speed recovery or promote an earlier return to work.

The Quebec Task Force in 1987 published the first guidelines on the treatment of low back pain, and many additional guidelines and protocols have since been published.[10,11] The recommendations differ and sometimes lack an adequate evidence basis. Almost all guidelines for acute low back pain (including those from the United States, New Zealand, Finland, the Netherlands, the United Kingdom, Germany, and Australia) recommend the first-line use of paracetamol, followed by the use of NSAIDs.[10-18] Only the guidelines from the Netherlands, the United Kingdom, and Sweden recommend that prescriptions for muscle relaxants be time limited. Guidelines from Denmark, the Netherlands, and New Zealand do not recommend the use of muscle relaxants because of the risk of physical and psychologic dependence. In contrast, guidelines from Germany, Switzerland, and the United States recommend the use of muscle relaxants if the patient's acute pain is accompanied by prominent muscle spasms. The United Kingdom guidelines recommend adding a short course of a muscle relaxant if paracetamol, NSAIDs, or paracetamol combined with a weak opioid do not adequately control the pain.[11]

Chronic Axial Low Back Pain

A cure for chronic low back pain is elusive, and management to allow improved function is the most reasonable current treatment goal. The WHO pain ladder can guide the medical management of chronic back pain, despite the continuing controversy regarding the long-term use of opioids. Systematic reviews of opioids in the treatment of different chronic conditions found moderate improvement in pain but limited evidence of a concomitant improvement in function.[7,8] Studies on the long-term use of opioids for chronic spine pain have not determined the impact on pain and function. Proponents of using opioids for treating chronic pain believe that patients who are correctly screened before and during treatment can be well managed without sig-

Table 1

The Nonsteroidal Anti-inflammatory Drugs

Subclass	Typical Drugs
Salicylates	Aspirin, diflunisal, salsalate[a]
Phenylacetics	Diclofenac
Indoleacetic acids	Etodolac, indomethacin, sulindac, tolmetin
Oxicams	Piroxicam, meloxicam[a]
Propionic acids	Ibuprofen, naproxen, ketorolac, oxaprozin
Naphthylkanones	Nabumetone
COX-2 selective inhibitors	Celecoxib,[a] rofecoxib, valdecoxib, etoricoxib

[a] Minimal effect on bleeding time.

nificant adverse effects or medication misuse.[19,20] Opponents cite limited evidence of the benefit of opioids, the increase in adverse effects, and the growing social issue of prescription opioid analgesic misuse and abuse.[21-23] Opponents also note that large cross-sectional studies of patients who use opioids over a long time period did not find significant gains in pain and function.[21,22,24]

There is moderate evidence to suggest that antidepressants are beneficial adjunctive analgesic agents for treating chronic low back pain, regardless of the presence of depression.[25] It appears that a comprehensive approach, of which medications are only one part, is required to maximize the outcome in patients with chronic pain. The biopsychosocial model of chronic pain, which takes into account a patient's fears, maladaptive pain behaviors, cultural beliefs, perceived disability, stress, and social support networks, is important in managing chronic low back pain. Incorporating cognitive-behavioral treatment helps patients take an active role in their long-term care and can reduce the fear of becoming dependent on medications.

Radiculopathy

The nonsurgical management of radiculopathy includes medications, physical therapy, and corticosteroid injections. Medications are often used for acute pain control and early mobilization. Analgesic medications are believed to have a greater effect on acute pain if they are taken on a scheduled rather than an as-needed basis.[26] The medications commonly used to treat radiculopathy include acetaminophen, NSAIDs, opioids, and muscle relaxants. Acetaminophen is a first-line therapy in acute pain because of its high safety profile.[27] NSAIDs provide similar analgesia but have a significant potential for gastrointestinal and renovascular adverse effects.[28] Opioid analgesics must be used judiciously for treating moderate to severe pain because of their ad-

verse effects and the risk of dependence and abuse. Muscle relaxants, when used in combination with analgesics for no longer than 1 week, were found to be more effective than placebo for treating the pain of lumbar radiculopathy.[9] A short course of oral corticosteroids can be used to treat acute lumbar radiculopathy, although a placebo-controlled study found no benefit to their use.[27]

Neurogenic Claudication

A wide variety of nonsurgical options are available for treating neurogenic claudication, but none have been well studied. Studies of NSAIDs, opioids, adjuvant analgesics, muscle relaxants, intranasal calcitonin, methylcobalamin, and lipoprostaglandin E_1 have produced insufficient evidence for their benefit in the treatment of neurogenic claudication.[29] Most of the studies combined patients who had spinal stenosis with patients who had other types of back pain. Despite the lack of definite evidence to support their use, NSAIDs and analgesics are typically used in the treatment of spinal stenosis. One small clinical study did find some improvement in function and pain when gabapentin was added to a treatment regimen including NSAIDs, physical therapy, and bracing.[29]

Medications for Treating Spine Pain

Nonsteroidal Anti-inflammatory Drugs

NSAIDs block the COX isoenzymes to prevent the production of prostaglandins. This action leads to both anti-inflammatory and analgesic effects. The many roles of the prostaglandins include mediating inflammation and sensitizing peripheral nociceptors. Table 1 outlines the subclasses of NSAIDs. Each NSAID subclass and individual drug and subclass has distinct characteristics and adverse effects.

When used with drugs that inhibit clotting, such as warfarin, NSAIDs increase the risk of serious bleeding or complications from bleeding. Meloxicam, salsalate, and celecoxib are NSAIDs with minimal effect on bleeding time, and they are recommended if an NSAID must be used before an invasive procedure. There is some evidence that NSAIDs have a negative impact on soft-tissue and bone healing,[30] although animal studies found that many NSAIDs do not have such a detrimental effect.[31] Patients on daily aspirin therapy to reduce cardiovascular or colon cancer risk must be aware that other NSAIDs may block these beneficial effects of aspirin.

A Cochrane review of 51 studies found that after 1 week of treatment of acute mild to moderate low back pain, nonselective NSAIDs were superior to a placebo for global improvement and eliminating the need for additional analgesics.[32] A recent systematic review of 21 studies reached the same conclusions.[33] Ibuprofen was superior to placebo for relieving mild to moderate chronic low back pain in one high-quality study.[33] Another high-quality study found no difference between

Table 2

Antidepressants Used for the Treatment of Spine Pain

Category	Typical Drugs
Tricyclic antidepressants	Amitriptyline, nortriptyline, trazodone, imipramine
Serotonin-norepinephrine reuptake inhibitors	Duloxetine, fenlafaxine
Selective serotonin-noradrenaline reuptake inhibitors	Bupropion, sertraline, paroxetine, escitalopram

NSAIDs and placebo for treating back pain with sciatica.[28]

No evidence was found in the Cochrane review to support the use of any single nonselective NSAID over another for pain relief, and no clear difference in efficacy was found among NSAIDs, opioids, and muscle relaxants.[32] The studies were limited by small sample size, however. Nonselective NSAIDs and placebo were found to have similar adverse effect risks, but the studies did not evaluate the risk of relatively uncommon but serious gastrointestinal and cardiovascular adverse effects. Only 6 of the 51 studies analyzed outcomes beyond 2 weeks, and the longest study period was 6 weeks. The recommendations therefore were restricted to short-term use.[32]

Nonopioid Analgesics

The nonopioid analgesics include acetaminophen, topical medications such as diclofenac and lidocaine, antidepressants, anticonvulsants, and tramadol.

Acetaminophen

Acetaminophen is a para-aminophenol derivative that has both analgesic and antipyretic properties, with mild anti-inflammatory effects. It weakly inhibits the COX isoenzymes, inhibiting prostaglandin synthesis without inhibiting neutrophils. Acetaminophen can be used as a first-line analgesic for mild to moderate acute low back pain.

Liver toxicity is a concern with acetaminophen use. The existing recommendation is to restrict acetaminophen dosage to 4 g per 24 hours.[34] This recommendation is under review, and the acceptable daily amount may be further limited because of the risk of liver toxicity and dysfunction. Acetaminophen was found superior to placebo for treating osteoarthritis pain and is recommended as a first-line agent for osteoarthritis.[19] Many patients are not aware of the maximum daily allowable dosage of acetaminophen or its potential toxicity. Although acetaminophen is effective and is available without a prescription, any discussion of its use

should include instruction as to the maximum dosage and the risk of toxicity.

The longest study of acetaminophen for mild to moderate acute low back pain lasted only 4 weeks.[33] This lower quality study found no difference between 3 g per day of acetaminophen and no treatment. Four studies found no significant difference between as much as 4 g per day of acetaminophen and NSAIDs for relieving mild to moderate acute low back pain.[33] One study found acetaminophen to be inferior to diflunisal after 4 weeks of treatment for mild to moderate chronic low back pain, and several other high-quality systematic reviews of patients with osteoarthritis, not limited to low back pain, found acetaminophen to be slightly inferior to NSAIDs for pain relief.[33]

Antidepressants

Antidepressants are commonly used off label to treat a variety of pain syndromes including migraine, neuropathic pain associated with diabetic neuropathy, postherpetic neuralgia, and pain associated with fibromyalgia, rheumatoid arthritis, or osteoarthritis[33] (Table 2). The connection of pain and depression is believed to be in the neurotransmitters serotonin and norepinephrine, which not only modulate pain transmission through the ascending and descending neural pathways but also act as key neurotransmitters in the pathophysiology of depression.[25] The analgesic abilities of antidepressants have been observed in patients with or without concurrent depression. The use of antidepressants can have a beneficial impact on the patient's functional status and use of the health care system.[25] Antidepressants should be used only with caution in patients with chronic spine pain who have a psychiatric history or are taking other psychotropic medications.

The TCAs have a longer history in the treatment of chronic pain syndromes than other types of antidepressants. The TCA dosages used in clinical studies of patients in pain are less than dosages for the treatment of depression. The advantages of TCAs include their low cost and long-established track record in treating chronic pain. The disadvantages include cardiovascular adverse effects such as hypertension, postural hypotension, and arrhythmias as well as urinary retention, dry mouth, sedation, dizziness, falls in older adults, and the potential for lethal overdose. Serotonin-norepinephrine reuptake inhibitors including selective serotonin-noradrenaline reuptake inhibitors (SNRIs) and selective serotonin reuptake inhibitors (SSRIs) also have been used to treat chronic and neuropathic pain syndromes. SSRIs have been shown to have a limited effect on neuropathic pain and a weak analgesic effect.[25]

Several systematic reviews have evaluated the usefulness of antidepressants in treating chronic pain. Two high-quality reviews found that antidepressants consistently were more effective than placebo for adjunctive relief of mild to moderate chronic low back pain.[35,36] However, the impact on functional outcomes was not consistently reported, and no clear benefits were found.

Table 3

Muscle Relaxants Used for the Treatment of Spine Pain

Category	Typical Drugs
Antispasmodics	Carisoprodol, chlorzoxazone, cyclobenzaprine, metaxalone, methocarbamol
Sedative-hypnotics	Alprazolam, hydroxyzine HCL, clonazepam, flurazepam, diazepam
Antispastics	Baclofen, dantrolene, tizanidine

The effect on pain is not consistent across antidepressants.[36] TCAs were moderately more effective than placebo for pain relief in four of six studies.[37] Paroxetine and trazodone were found to be no more effective than placebo in three studies.[37,38] Antidepressants are associated with a higher rate of adverse events than placebo; drowsiness, dry mouth, dizziness, and constipation are most common.[39] It is important to note that these studies did not assess the risk of serious adverse effects such as suicidality, arrhythmias, or overdose.

Tramadol

Although tramadol is chemically unrelated to opioid analgesics, it provides analgesia through similar mechanisms. It weakly binds to μ and δ opiate receptors and is partially affected by the opiate antagonist naloxone.[40] Tramadol can interfere with serotonin and norepinephrine reuptake in the descending inhibitor pathways.[41] Specific attention should be paid to other comorbid conditions that might interfere with the use of tramadol. Serotonin syndrome may occur if tramadol and an SSRI or SNRI are used concomitantly. The potential for seizures is increased in patients with a history of seizures, and central respiratory depression also can occur.[42]

Tramadol was found to be beneficial for treating mild to moderate acute back pain. A high-quality study found tramadol to be moderately more effective than placebo for relieving pain and improving functional status after 4 weeks of treatment in patients with mild to severe chronic low back pain.[41] Two studies found no significant difference between long-acting and immediate-release tramadol for treating chronic low back pain.[41,43] Tramadol use was discontinued because direct comparisons found that the rate of adverse effects was similar to that of placebo and acetaminophen with codeine.[41,43]

Muscle Relaxants

Muscle relaxants are among the many adjunctive treatments for acute low back pain[40,44,45] (Table 3). Muscle relaxants sometimes are categorized as skeletal or centrally acting. Centrally acting muscle relaxants inhibit central polysynaptic neuronal events, which indirectly act on skeletal muscle.[44] Muscle relaxants also are categorized as antispasmodic or antispastic. Antispasmodic medications frequently are used to decrease muscle spasms associated with painful conditions. Antispasticity medications are used to reduce spasticity that interferes with movement or function, often as a result of centrally acting processes such as cerebral palsy, multiple sclerosis, stroke, or spinal cord injury.[44,45] Antispasmodic medications act centrally by unknown mechanisms. Antispasmodic muscle relaxants approved by the US Food and Drug Administration for treating musculoskeletal conditions include carisoprodol, chlorzoxazone, cyclobenzaprine, metaxalone, methocarbamol, and orphenadrine. Cyclobenzaprine, the most widely studied of these drugs, is believed to act on the brain stem, and metaxalone may work by generally depressing the central nervous system.[44,45] Both drugs inhibit central polysynaptic neuronal events, which indirectly act on skeletal muscle.[45]

Benzodiazepines have both sedative-hypnotic and antispasmodic properties and sometimes are used to treat painful muscle spasms.[46] The mechanisms by which benzodiazepines provide muscle relaxation are unknown but possibly are related to postsynaptic spinal cord transmission of γ-aminobutyric acid. Tolerance to the muscle relaxant effects often develops. The benzodiazepines commonly used for muscle relaxation include alprazolam, hydroxyzine HCL, clonazepam, flurazepam, and diazepam.[45] Baclofen sometimes is used as an alternative to the benzodiazepines.[45]

Antispasticity medications act at various segments of the motor pathways, such as the muscle, spinal cord, or brain levels, to reduce motor neuron activity. The medications approved by the Food and Drug Administration for the treatment of spasticity include baclofen, dantrolene, and tizanidine.[44,45] Research on antispasticity medications has found that various antispasticity medications have general central nervous system depressant effects including sedation, somnolence, ataxia, and respiratory and cardiovascular depression.[45]

Tizanidine is widely used in the treatment of muscle spasticity. This drug is a short-acting α-2 adrenergic agonist that is believed to inhibit presynaptic motor neurons.[47] The α-2 adrenergic agonists are often used in patients with a central nervous system condition such as spinal cord injury or multiple sclerosis. Tizanidine was recently found to have promise for the treatment of myofascial, neuropathic, and low back pain.[47]

A detailed history is required to assess the source of muscle spasms before the optimal medication can be selected. Patients with a musculoskeletal cause of muscle spasms can benefit from treatment with antispasmodics. Patients whose muscle spasms are caused by a central process are better treated with antispasticity agents, with care to avoid reducing functionally beneficial spasticity.[45] Because of the potential for abuse, patients

2: Nonsurgical Care of the Spine

with a history of addiction should avoid sedative hypnotic medications such as benzodiazepines.[46]

Two systematic reviews of skeletal muscle relaxants have been completed.[45,46] The 36 unique studies in these reviews had a study period of 2 weeks or less, except for one study lasting 3 weeks.[37] A high-quality Cochrane review found muscle relaxants to be moderately superior to placebo for short-term relief of mild to severe acute low back pain.[45] No single specific muscle relaxant was found to be more beneficial or harmful than others. There is only sparse evidence of benefit from the use of dantrolene or baclofen for treating low back pain, and therefore these medications are not recommended.[45] Tizanidine was found to be efficacious for treating acute low back pain but not sciatica pain.[37,46] A systematic review of cyclobenzaprine for treating subacute or chronic low back or neck pain had mixed results compared with placebo.[37,46] Muscle relaxants were associated with more overall and central nervous system adverse events than placebo; most of the adverse events were self-limited, and serious adverse effects were rare.

The effectiveness of benzodiazepines was evaluated in a Cochrane review of eight studies with a duration of 5 to 14 days.[45] No differences were found among diazepam, tizanidine, and cyclobenzaprine for treating acute low back pain. One high-quality study found no difference between diazepam and placebo for treating acute low back pain, and another study found diazepam to be inferior to carisoprodol in reducing muscle spasm, leading to lower functional status and global efficacy.[37,45,46] Two studies of patients with chronic low back pain found that, compared with placebo, tetrazepam was associated with less likelihood of pain relief or global relief after 8 to 14 days.[48,49] Central nervous system events such as somnolence, fatigue, and lightheadedness were reported more frequently with benzodiazepines than with placebo.[37]

Anticonvulsants

Anticonvulsants have been used to manage pain for many years. Often anticonvulsants play an important role as an adjuvant treatment of mild to severe pain, especially neuropathic pain. This class of medications acts on neuronal membrane stability to increase inhibitory neuronal transmission or decrease excitatory neuronal transmission. The primary medications used to treat neuropathic pain include gabapentin, pregabalin, lamotrigine, topiramate, valproate, levetiracetam, oxcarbazepine, and carbamazepine.[36] Gabapentin, pregabalin, and topiramate have been studied for treating low back pain, and lamotrigine, valproate, levetiracetam, oxcarbazepine, and carbamazepine have been studied for treating neuropathic pain associated with other pathologies.

Gabapentin and pregabalin are the most studied medications for the treatment of neuropathic pain. Both of these agents act as neuromodulators by binding the α-2 δ subunit of calcium channels in the brain and spinal cord, resulting in the inhibition of excitatory neurotransmitters important in pain production.[29] These medications were found to be better than placebo for treating neuropathic pain.[36] However, gabapentin and topiramate were associated with only small improvements in pain scores in patients with low back pain with radiculopathy.[37] The mechanism of action of topiramate is unknown. This medication was associated with a small improvement in pain scores and is only slightly better than placebo for functional status improvement.[50] Lamotrigine was found to be effective for treating neuropathic pain caused by trigeminal neuralgia, HIV neuropathy, diabetic neuropathy, and central poststroke pain.[36]

The most important concern in the use of anticonvulsants is the potential for inducing central nervous system depression or somnolence. Sedation is a common adverse effect of most anticonvulsants, and patients should be made aware that the effects of sedation can be minimized by administering these medications at night.

The use of antiepileptic drugs for low back pain has not been systematically reviewed. However, gabapentin and topiramate each have been evaluated in two studies of 6 to 10 weeks' duration.[50-52] Three small studies of low back pain associated with radiculopathy found that anticonvulsants were associated with a small improvement in pain score, compared with placebo.[37] One high-quality study of patients with chronic low back pain with or without radiculopathy found topiramate to be moderately superior to placebo for improvement of pain but not functional status.[50] Drowsiness, loss of energy, and dizziness were reported with the use of gabapentin. Topiramate was associated with higher rates of withdrawal because of adverse events such as sedation and diarrhea, compared with diphenhydramine.[37]

Opioid Analgesics

The mechanism of action of opioids occurs through binding to opioid receptors, which are primarily located in the central nervous system. The use of opioids is widely accepted for treatment of cancer-related pain, other moderate to severe acute pain, and palliative care. The use of opioids for treating chronic pain continues to be controversial, however.[10,24]

The analgesic effects of opioids result from a decreased perception of pain, a decreased reaction to pain, and increased pain tolerance.[53] The adverse effects of opioids include sedation, respiratory depression, and constipation. Physical dependence can develop with the ongoing administration of opioids, leading to a withdrawal syndrome if opioids are abruptly discontinued or antagonists are administered. In some patients, opioids produce a feeling of euphoria, and this effect, coupled with physical dependence, can lead to recreational use or abuse. A hereditary predisposition to addiction may be a factor.

Table 4

Opioids Used for the Treatment of Spine Pain

Type	Typical Drugs (Proprietary Names)
Long acting (8-24 h)	Oxycodone (OxyContin), morphine (MS Contin, Kadian, Avinza, Oramorph-SR), oxymorphone (Opana ER), fentanyl (Duragesic), methadone
Short acting (3-6 h)	Oxycodone, fentanyl (Actiq, Fentora), meperidine (Demerol), hydromorphone (Dilaudid), tapentadol (Nucynta), propoxyphene (Darvon)
Combination	Oxycodone (Percocet, Endocet, Combunox), hydrocodone (Vicodin, Vicoprofen), codeine (Tylenol 3 and 4)

The pharmacodynamic response to an opioid depends on which receptor it binds to, its affinity for that receptor, and whether the opioid is an agonist or an antagonist. Each opioid has a unique binding affinity to the different classes of opioid receptors, which are activated at different magnitudes depending on the specific receptor-binding affinities of the opioid[54] (Table 4).

Opioids often are prescribed to treat patients with chronic pain, although the evidence for this use is limited. The adverse effects must be monitored and identified. Constipation is common, and patients should be treated prophylactically with stool softeners and bowel stimulants. Of more concern is the risk of overdose or abuse. The potential for addiction and medication diversion can be decreased by careful monitoring with regular follow-up evaluations every 1 to 3 months to assess benefits, adverse effects, and any indications of aberrant medication use. Random drug testing can be added to monitor for drug abuse or misuse.

Tolerance to chronic opioid therapy develops as a process of neuroadaptation leading to receptor desensitization. The reduction in drug effect is more pronounced for some opioid effects than others.[55] Tolerance has not been a limiting factor in long-term opioid management for patients with chronic cancer or noncancer pain. Tolerance usually can be managed with opioid rotation, dosing changes, or a drug holiday.

Opioid dependence is not a sign of addiction but instead is a normal physiologic response to opioid medications. Symptoms of rapid withdrawal, including severe dysphoria, sweating, nausea, rhinorrhea, depression, severe fatigue, vomiting, and pain, can be expected in any patient who has been maintained on opioid medications. Slowly reducing the patient's intake of opioids over days or weeks can reduce or eliminate the withdrawal symptoms. The speed and severity of withdrawal depends on the opioid half-life. The symptoms of opioid withdrawal can be decreased by using medications such as clonidine, antidepressants, and benzodiazepines.[55]

Addiction is a psychologic process involving physical and/or psychologic dependence on the drug. Addiction is associated with higher-than-prescribed dosages, continued drug use despite physical or psychologic harm, and a decline in social functioning. Often there is misuse or abuse of other drugs such as benzodiazepines or recreational drugs. The use of medications obtained from multiple physicians is common. Psychologic addiction is more common in persons taking opioids recreationally than in patients taking opioids for pain relief.[55] Patients who are suspected of having an addiction should be referred to and treated by an addiction specialist.

The research regarding the effectiveness of opioid medications for chronic low back pain is limited. Sustained-release oxymorphone and sustained-release oxycodone were found to be superior to placebo in the short term for the treatment of mild to severe chronic low back pain.[56] The study was limited because the opioids were titrated to a stable dose before randomization; the poorer outcomes in patients treated with placebo could have partly resulted from the cessation of opioids leading to withdrawal symptoms. Lower quality studies found no difference between propoxyphene and placebo or codeine and acetaminophen for treating acute low back pain.[37] Two systematic reviews of placebo-controlled studies found opioid therapy to be moderately effective for treating pain conditions unrelated to cancer, most commonly osteoarthritis or neuropathy.[57,58] Five lower quality studies of sustained-release opioids for treating low back pain found no evidence of superiority to immediate-release opioid formulations on a variety of outcome measures.[37] One high-quality study of opioid use for low back pain reported that constipation and sedation were the most common adverse effects.[57,58]

Systemic Corticosteroids

Oral corticosteroids are effective for treating inflammatory processes such as allergic reaction to medications, severe asthma exacerbation, and rheumatic or autoimmune disease. These drugs interact with receptor proteins in target tissues to regulate gene expression, thereby affecting protein synthesis. Corticosteroids reduce tissue damage by stabilizing cell membranes, reducing capillary permeability, and limiting the release of proinflammatory substances.[10] Glucocorticoids have anti-inflammatory and immunosuppressive effects secondary to their inhibition of the immune responses of lymphocytes, macrophages, and fibroblasts. This action occurs early in the inflammatory cascade and should reduce the leukotriene- and prostaglandin-mediated inflammatory response.

Inflammation caused by intervertebral disk herniation is known to have an important role in radicular

2: Nonsurgical Care of the Spine

pain.[46,59] Oral corticosteroids for acute low back pain with radiculopathy typically are prescribed in a quick-tapering short course (less than 1 week). The severe adverse effects associated with long-term corticosteroid use are rarely seen with short-term use. However, adverse events, including an increase in blood glucose, water retention, irritability, insomnia, and osteonecrosis, can occur with short courses of corticosteroids.[60,61] Because of their adverse effects, oral corticosteroids should be used with caution in patients who have diabetes or hypertension. These drugs should be avoided in patients who have an active infection or are at risk for infection. Repeated or prolonged use is not recommended.

The efficacy of oral corticosteroids for treating acute low back pain is unproved. There are no identified systemic reviews of systemic corticosteroid treatment of low back pain. Three small, high-quality studies of corticosteroid use in patients with acute sciatica or sciatica of unspecified duration found no clinically significant benefit from a single injection or a short tapered oral course, compared with placebo.[59,62] A comparison of the use of a single intramuscular injection of methylprednisolone or placebo in patients with acute low back pain found no differences in pain relief.[59] No adverse effects were reported, but two patients had transient hyperglycemia and one patient had facial flushing after a single high-dosage intramuscular injection of corticosteroid.

Summary

The use of NSAIDs and nonopioid analgesics is helpful in reducing acute low back pain. Muscle relaxants are effective for improving pain symptoms but must be used with caution because of their sedating effects; a short course of treatment is recommended. No evidence supports the use of oral corticosteroids for treating acute low back pain or radicular pain or the use of NSAIDs for treating radicular low back pain. Short-term analgesics allow patients to be more active during rehabilitation and recovery. The WHO pain ladder can guide the selection of medication for acute pain. Nonetheless, the overall treatment should be tailored to the individual patient (Table 5).

Evidence supports the use of analgesics such as NSAIDs for short-term relief of chronic low back pain, with or without adjunctive medication. The long-term use of NSAIDs is common but not well supported by evidence. The evidence for the benefit of using muscle relaxants alone or in combination with NSAIDs is limited for acute low back pain and nonexistent for chronic low back pain. There appears to be evidence for the benefit of anticonvulsant medications and various antidepressant medications including SNRIs and SSRIs in treating both chronic axial and radicular low back pain. Every medication should be carefully evaluated by weighing its risks, benefits, and effectiveness

for the individual patient. The optimal selection of a medication takes into account the indications, contraindications, adverse effects, treatment goals, and clinical evidence. The overall goal is to afford the patient maximal pain relief with minimal adverse effects and the greatest positive impact on daily function.

Table 5

Summary of Drug Classes Used for the Treatment of Spine Pain

Drug Class	Pain Type	
	Duration	Source
Nonsteroidal anti-inflammatory drugs	Acute Chronic	Somatic
Nonopioid analgesics	Acute Chronic	Somatic
Muscle relaxants	Acute	Somatic
Antidepressants	Chronic	Somatic Neuropathic
Anticonvulsants	Acute Chronic	Neuropathic
Opioids	Acute Chronic	Somatic Neuropathic
Corticosteroids	Acute	Somatic Neuropathic

+ = present, – = not present.

Table 5 (continued)

Adverse Effects				
General	**Sedation**	**Habit Formation**	**Toxicity**	**Relative Cost**
Gastrointestinal upset or bleeding Nausea, vomiting Renal insufficiency Cardiovascular effects	+	–	Renal failure Gastrointestinal bleeding	Low
Nausea, diarrhea Tinnitus	–	–	Renal failure Hepatic failure	Low
Dry mouth Drowsiness Dizziness Fatigue	+	+	Drowsiness Tachycardia Cardiac arrest (rare) Cardiac dysrhythmias Severe hypotension Seizures Neuroleptic malignant syndrome	Moderate
Sedation Hypertension Syncope Depression Mania	+	–	Acute renal failure Acute respiratory distress syndrome QT prolongation, torsades de pointes Refractory hypotension Death	Moderate to high
Sedation Dizziness Peripheral edema Dry mouth Ataxia Fatigue	+	–	Seizure Ataxia Severe drowsiness Arrhythmia	Moderate to high
Constipation Drowsiness Euphoria	+	+	Respiratory suppression Hypotension Convulsions Renal failure Rhabdomyolysis Death	Moderate to high
Hyperglycemia Euphoria	–	–	Burning or itching skin Convulsions Deafness Depression Dry skin High blood pressure Muscle weakness Nervousness Psychosis	Low

Annotated References

1. World Health Organization: *WHO's Pain Ladder.* Geneva, Switzerland, World Health Organization, 2011. http://www.who.int/cancer/palliative/painladder/en/. Accessed June 22, 2011.

The WHO website describes a three-step sequence for the use of medications to control pain in patients with cancer.

2. van Tulder MW, Koes BW, Bouter LM: Conservative treatment of acute and chronic nonspecific low back pain: A systematic review of randomized controlled trials of the most common interventions. *Spine (Phila Pa 1976)* 1997;22(18):2128-2156.

3. Deyo RA, Mirza SK, Turner JA, Martin BI: Overtreating chronic back pain: Time to back off? *J Am Board Fam Med* 2009;22(1):62-68.

The treatment of chronic low back pain is outlined, with treatment trends and outcomes.

4. Sullivan MD, Edlund MJ, Fan MY, Devries A, Brennan Braden J, Martin BC: Risks for possible and probable opioid misuse among recipients of chronic opioid therapy in commercial and medicaid insurance plans: The TROUP Study. *Pain* 2010;150(2):332-339.

This study validated an administrative indicator of opioid misuse among large samples of recipients of chronic opioid therapy and determined the demographic, clinical, and pharmacologic risks associated with opioid misuse.

5. Sjøgren P, Grønbæk M, Peuckmann V, Ekholm O: A population-based cohort study on chronic pain: The role of opioids. *Clin J Pain* 2010;26(9):763-769.

The role of opioid therapy for chronic pain patients is discussed.

6. Warner M, Chen LH, Makuc DM: *Increase in Fatal Poisonings Involving Opioid Analgesics in the United States: 1999-2006.* Hyattsville, MD, National Center for Health Statistics, 2009. National Center for Health Statistics Data Brief 22.

Data from the National Vital Statistics System Mortality File were used to determine the number of fatal poisonings involving opioid analgesics from 1999 through 2006. During this period the number of US deaths rose from 4,000 to 13,800.

7. World Health Organization: *Cancer, Pain Relief and Palliative Care.* Geneva, Switzerland, World Health Organization, 1990. World Health Organization Technical Report Series 408.

8. Malanga G, Nadler S, Agesen T: Epidemiology, in Cole AJ, Herring SA, eds: *Low Back Pain Handbook*, ed 2. Philadelphia, PA, Hanley and Belfus, 2003, pp 1-7.

9. Malanga G, Wolff E: Evidence-informed management of chronic low back pain with nonsteroidal anti-inflammatory drugs, muscle relaxants, and simple analgesics. *Spine J* 2008;8(1):173-184.

The best available evidence on the use of NSAIDs, muscle relaxants, and simple analgesics in the treatment of chronic low back pain is summarized.

10. Arnau JM, Vallano A, Lopez A, Pellisé F, Delgado MJ, Prat N: A critical review of guidelines for low back pain treatment. *Eur Spine J* 2006;15(5):543-553.

This is a critical evaluation and review of the methodologic quality of guidelines for low back pain treatment, including a determination of whether recommendations were based on or explicitly linked to evidence.

11. Bigos S, Bowyer O, Braen G, et al: Acute low back problems in adults. *Clinical Practice Guideline 14.* Rockville, MD, Agency for Health Care Policy and Research, 1994. Publication 95-0642.

12. Royal College of General Practitioners: *Clinical Guidelines for the Management of Acute Low Back Pain.* London, England, Royal College of General Practitioners, 1999.

13. Accident Rehabilitation, Compensation, and Insurance Corporation, National Health Committee: *New Zealand Acute Low Back Pain Guide.* Wellington, New Zealand, 1997.

14. Danish Institute for Health Technology Assessment: *Low Back Pain: Frequency, Management and Prevention from an HTA Perspective.* Copenhagen, Denmark, Danish Institute for Health Technology Assessment, 1999.

15. Faas A, Chavannes AW, Koes BW, et al: Clinical practice guidelines for low back pain. *Huisarts Wet* 1996; 39:18-31.

16. Malmivaara A, Kotilainen E, Laasonen E, Poussa M, Rasmussen M: *Clinical Practice Guidelines: Diseases of the Low Back.* Helsinki, Finland, Finnish Medical Association Duodecim, 1999.

17. Victorian Workcover Authority: *Guidelines for the Management of Employees With Compensable Low Back Pain.* Melbourne, Australia, Victorian Workcover Authority, 1996.

18. Drug Committee of the German Medical Society: Treatment guideline: Backache. *Z Arztl Fortbild Qualitatssich* 1997;91(5):457-460.

19. Schofferman J, Mazanec D: Evidence-informed management of chronic low back pain with opioid analgesics. *Spine J* 2008;8(1):185-194.

The best available evidence on opioid management of chronic low back pain is summarized and made accessible to nonexperts. The theory, evidence of efficacy, harm, and management of opioid use for chronic low back pain are described.

20. Chou R, Fanciullo GJ, Fine PG, et al: Clinical guidelines for the use of chronic opioid therapy in chronic noncancer pain. *J Pain* 2009;10(2):113-130.

The evidence on chronic opioid therapy for chronic noncancer pain was systematically reviewed by a multidisciplinary expert panel and used to formulate recommendations.

21. Noble M, Treadwell JR, Tregear SJ, et al: Long-term opioid management for chronic noncancer pain. *Cochrane Database Syst Rev* 2010;1:CD006605.

The safety, efficacy, and effectiveness of the long-term use of opioids for chronic noncancer pain are assessed.

22. Trescot AM, Glaser SE, Hansen H, Benyamin R, Patel S, Manchikanti L: Effectiveness of opioids in the treatment of chronic non-cancer pain. *Pain Physician* 2008;11(2, suppl):S181-S200.

The relevant English literature on opioid use was evaluated, with pain relief as the primary outcome measure and evidence of addiction and improvement in function, psychologic status, and work status as the secondary outcome measures.

23. Crofford LJ: Adverse effects of chronic opioid therapy for chronic musculoskeletal pain. *Nat Rev Rheumatol* 2010;6(4):191-197.

    The adverse effects of chronic opioid therapy for musculoskeletal pain were evaluated.

24. Noble M, Tregear SJ, Treadwell JR, Schoelles K: Long-term opioid therapy for chronic noncancer pain: A systematic review and meta-analysis of efficacy and safety. *J Pain Symptom Manage* 2008;35(2):214-228.

    A systematic review of opioid therapy for chronic noncancer pain evaluated efficacy and adverse events in patients treated for at least 6 months.

25. Jann MW, Slade JH: Antidepressant agents for the treatment of chronic pain and depression. *Pharmacotherapy* 2007;27(11):1571-1587.

    Antidepressants can have beneficial effects in patients with chronic pain, regardless of whether the patient has depression or another medical condition.

26. Schofferman J: The use of medications in low back pain, in Cole AJ, Herring SA, eds: *Low Back Pain Handbook*, ed 2. Philadelphia, PA, Hanley and Belfus, 2003, pp 133-150.

27. Chou R, Qaseem A, Snow V, et al: Diagnosis and treatment of low back pain: A joint clinical practice guideline from the American College of Physicians and the American Pain Society. *Ann Intern Med* 2007;147(7): 478-491.

    Diagnosis, workup, stratification, and treatment options for patients with low back pain are recommended in a clinical practice guideline.

28. Roelofs PD, Deyo RA, Koes BW, Scholten RJ, van Tulder MW: Non-steroidal anti-inflammatory drugs for low back pain. *Cochrane Database Syst Rev* 2008;1: CD000396.

    The effects of NSAIDs and COX-2 inhibitors in the treatment of nonspecific low back pain are systematically reviewed, with a comparison of the effectiveness of NSAIDs.

29. Yaksi A, Ozgönenel L, Ozgönenel B: The efficiency of gabapentin therapy in patients with lumbar spinal stenosis. *Spine (Phila Pa 1976)* 2007;32(9):939-942.

    A randomized controlled pilot study evaluated the role of gabapentin in the treatment of symptomatic lumbar spinal stenosis.

30. Vuolteenaho K, Moilanen T, Moilanen E: Non-steroidal anti-inflammatory drugs, cyclooxygenase-2 and the bone healing process. *Basic Clin Pharmacol Toxicol* 2008;102(1):10-14.

    The experimental and clinical evidence is presented on the effect of NSAIDs on ectopic bone formation and fracture healing.

31. Mullis BH, Copland ST, Weinhold PS, Miclau T, Lester GE, Bos GD: Effect of COX-2 inhibitors and non-steroidal anti-inflammatory drugs on a mouse fracture model. *Injury* 2006;37(9):827-837.

    The effect of COX-2 inhibitors and NSAIDs on fracture healing in mice was studied.

32. van Tulder MW, Scholten RJ, Koes BW, Deyo RA: Nonsteroidal anti-inflammatory drugs for low back pain: A systematic review within the framework of the Cochrane Collaboration Back Review Group. *Spine (Phila Pa 1976)* 2000;25(19):2501-2513.

33. Kuijpers T, van Middelkoop M, Rubinstein SM, et al: A systematic review on the effectiveness of pharmacological interventions for chronic non-specific low-back pain. *Eur Spine J* 2011;20(1):40-50.

    A review evaluated the effectiveness of pharmacologic interventions for nonspecific chronic low back pain.

34. Larson AM, Polson J, Fontana RJ, et al: Acetaminophen-induced acute liver failure: Results of a United States multicenter, prospective study. *Hepatology* 2005; 42(6):1364-1372.

    A prospective study determined the incidence, risk factors, and outcomes of acetaminophen-induced acute liver failure at 22 tertiary care centers in the United States.

35. Salerno SM, Browning R, Jackson JL: The effect of antidepressant treatment on chronic back pain: A meta-analysis. *Arch Intern Med* 2002;162(1):19-24.

36. Jensen TS, Madsen CS, Finnerup NB: Pharmacology and treatment of neuropathic pains. *Curr Opin Neurol* 2009;22(5):467-474.

    A review of the definition and clinical presentation of neuropathic pain highlighted recent treatment advances.

37. Chou R, Huffman LH, American Pain Society, American College of Physicians: Medications for acute and chronic low back pain: A review of the evidence for an American Pain Society/American College of Physicians clinical practice guideline. *Ann Intern Med* 2007; 147(7):505-514.

    The evidence for medications used to treat acute and chronic low back pain is reviewed.

38. Staiger TO, Gaster B, Sullivan MD, Deyo RA: Systematic review of antidepressants in the treatment of chronic low back pain. *Spine (Phila Pa 1976)* 2003; 28(22):2540-2545.

39. Otto M, Bach FW, Jensen TS, Brøsen K, Sindrup SH: Escitalopram in painful polyneuropathy: A randomized, placebo-controlled, cross-over trial. *Pain* 2008;139(2): 275-283.

    A randomized double-blind placebo-controlled cross-over study tested whether the SSRI escitalopram relieves pain in patients with polyneuropathy.

40. Malanga GA, Dennis RL: Use of medications in the treatment of acute low back pain. *Clin Occup Environ Med* 2006;5(3):643-653.

2: Nonsurgical Care of the Spine

The appropriate use of medications to address the underlying pain generator is described, with current evidence, for the treatment of patients with acute low back pain.

41. Schnitzer TJ, Gray WL, Paster RZ, Kamin M: Efficacy of tramadol in treatment of chronic low back pain. *J Rheumatol* 2000;27(3):772-778.

42. Labate A, Newton MR, Vernon GM, Berkovic SF: Tramadol and new-onset seizures. *Med J Aust* 2005;182(1):42-43.

The association of seizure onset and tramadol use was studied in Australia.

43. McCarberg B: Tramadol extended-release in the management of chronic pain. *Ther Clin Risk Manag* 2007;3(3):401-410.

Tramadol ER is used early in the management of chronic pain because of its efficacy and safety profile.

44. See S, Ginzburg R: Choosing a skeletal muscle relaxant. *Am Fam Physician* 2008;78(3):365-370.

The use of skeletal muscle relaxants is reviewed, with comparable effectiveness data. The choice of agent should be based on the adverse effects profile, patient preference, abuse potential, and possible drug interactions.

45. van Tulder MW, Touray T, Furlan AD, Solway S, Bouter LM, Cochrane Back Review Group: Muscle relaxants for nonspecific low back pain: A systematic review within the framework of the Cochrane Collaboration. *Spine (Phila Pa 1976)* 2003;28(17):1978-1992.

46. Kroenke K, Krebs EE, Bair MJ: Pharmacotherapy of chronic pain: A synthesis of recommendations from systematic reviews. *Gen Hosp Psychiatry* 2009;31(3):206-219.

An evidence-based approach to the pharmacotherapy of chronic pain is described.

47. Malanga G, Reiter RD, Garay E: Update on tizanidine for muscle spasticity and emerging indications. *Expert Opin Pharmacother* 2008;9(12):2209-2215.

Recent findings on the clinical application of tizanidine are reviewed.

48. Arbus L, Fajadet B, Aubert D, Morre M, Goldfinger E: Activity of tetrazepam in low back pain. *Clin Trials J* 1990;27:258-267.

49. Salzmann E, Pforringer W, Paal G, Gierend M: Treatment of chronic low back pain syndrome with tetrazepam in a placebo controlled double-blind trial. *J Drug Dev* 1992;4:219-228.

50. Khoromi S, Patsalides A, Parada S, Salehi V, Meegan JM, Max MB: Topiramate in chronic lumbar radicular pain. *J Pain* 2005;6(12):829-836.

A double-blind randomized two-period crossover study of topiramate and diphenhydramine as active placebo assessed the efficacy of topiramate in the treatment of chronic lumbar radicular pain.

51. McClean GJ: Does gabapentin have an analgesic effect on background, movement and referred pain? A randomized, double-blind, placebo controlled study. *Pain Clin* 2001;13:103-107.

52. Yildirim K, Sisecioglu M, Karatay S, et al: The effectiveness of gabapentin in patients with chronic radiculopathy. *Pain Clin* 2003;15:213-218.

53. Fine PG, Portenoy RK: *A Clinical Guide to Opioid Analgesia.* New York, NY, McGraw Hill, 2004.

54. Corbett AD, Henderson G, McKnight AT, Paterson SJ: 75 years of opioid research: The exciting but vain quest for the Holy Grail. *Br J Pharmacol* 2006;147(suppl 1):S153-S162.

The historical pathway of opioid research leading to the current state of knowledge is described.

55. Fine PG: Opioid insights: Opioid-induced hyperalgesia and opioid rotation. *J Pain Palliat Care Pharmacother* 2004;18(3):75-79.

56. Hale ME, Dvergsten C, Gimbel J: Efficacy and safety of oxymorphone extended release in chronic low back pain: Results of a randomized, double-blind, placebo- and active-controlled phase III study. *J Pain* 2005;6(1):21-28.

A multicenter randomized placebo-controlled double-blind study evaluated the analgesic efficacy and safety of oxymorphone ER and oxycodone CR in opioid-experienced patients with chronic low back pain.

57. Kalso E, Edwards JE, Moore RA, McQuay HJ: Opioids in chronic non-cancer pain: Systematic review of efficacy and safety. *Pain* 2004;112(3):372-380.

58. Furlan AD, Sandoval JA, Mailis-Gagnon A, Tunks E: Opioids for chronic noncancer pain: A meta-analysis of effectiveness and side effects. *CMAJ* 2006;174(11):1589-1594.

A meta-analysis compared the efficacy of opioids for chronic noncancer pain with other drugs and placebo, identified types of chronic noncancer pain that respond well to opioids, and determined the most common adverse effects of opioids.

59. Finckh A, Zufferey P, Schurch MA, Balagué F, Waldburger M, So AK: Short-term efficacy of intravenous pulse glucocorticoids in acute discogenic sciatica: A randomized controlled trial. *Spine (Phila Pa 1976)* 2006;31(4):377-381.

A double-blinded randomized controlled study tested the short-term efficacy of a single intravenous pulse of glucocorticoids on the symptoms of acute discogenic sciatica.

60. Deyo RA: Drug therapy for back pain: Which drugs help which patients? *Spine (Phila Pa 1976)* 1996;21(24):2840-2850.

61. Xiao CS, Lin N, Lin SF, Wan R, Chen WH: Experimental study on avascular necrosis of femoral head in chickens induced by different glucocorticoides. *Zhongguo Gu Shang* 2010;23(3):184-187.

The effects of methylprednisolone and dexamethasone on osteonecrosis of the femoral head were evaluated in chickens.

62. North American Spine Society: *Evidence-Based Clinical Guidelines for Multidisciplinary Spine Care: Diagnosis and Treatment of Degenerative Lumbar Spinal Stenosis.* Burr Ridge, IL, North American Spine Society, 2007. http://www.spine.org/Documents/NASSCG_Stenosis. pdf. Accessed July18, 2010.

The diagnosis, stratification, and treatment of lumbar spinal stenosis are presented in clinical guidelines.

2: Nonsurgical Care of the Spine

Chapter 9

Therapeutic Exercise for Low Back Pain

Venu Akuthota, MD   Joel M. Press, MD   Eric Shoemaker, DO

Introduction

Therapeutic exercise is a cornerstone of treatment for low back pain. The value of physical activity for this ubiquitous and costly condition has been articulated in guidelines, but spine care recommendations in general still do not fully embrace the concept of exercise as medicine.[1] Exercise is beneficial for patients with a low back condition because it can improve general physical fitness, cardiovascular health, strength, flexibility, and endurance. The primary benefit of exercise may be in thwarting the vicious cycle of fear-avoidance behavior. Therapeutic exercise regimens including core strengthening, manual treatments, traction, aerobic exercise, and McKenzie protocols can supplement general exercise.

Properly performed exercise is safe and does not increase the risk of further back injury, despite the misconceptions of some practitioners and patients.[2,3] No single therapeutic exercise regimen is best for all patients, and a specific low back condition may respond better to some regimens than to others.[4] The choice of a particular exercise regimen is largely based on theory. Recently, subgrouping has emerged as an effective way of choosing proper exercise.[5]

The belief that low back pain is self-limited has been debunked by studies showing an unacceptably high rate of recurrence. A review of 36 studies investigating the long-term course of low back pain found that 44% to 78% of patients had relapsing low back pain, leading to work absence in an average 33% of patients.[6-8]

After the initial reduction of pain, the goals of rehabilitation center on prevention of a recurrence. Biomechanical deficits such as insufficient core strength and restricted segmental motion are treated, and self-management techniques are taught.[9] When the patient is able to return to activity, the rehabilitation team and the patient should continue working to achieve and maintain flexibility, strength, and endurance as well as proper posture and ergonomics.

Patient Assessment and Therapeutic Exercise Selection

A thorough assessment is required before an exercise regimen is chosen. The history should include the patient's work and recreational activities to determine the movements and forces the patient's lumbar spine customarily experiences as well as the functional and biomechanical movements affecting pain severity. For example, the clinician might determine whether the patient leans forward while sitting without a lumbar support and whether the patient engages in a proper hip hinge during the transition into different positions.

Often the patient's history leads to a working hypothesis as to the pain generator, which is confirmed or amended by the physical examination. Radicular pain is differentiated from referred pain. A patient often describes radicular pain as numbness or tingling, particularly if the pain is in a dermatomal pattern, but referred pain is less precisely described. Thorough provocation testing is used for the purpose of choosing a therapeutic exercise regimen. Positive dural (neural) tension maneuvers and tests suggest an exercise regimen emphasizing directional preference. Functional maneuvers are used to determine the positions or motor patterns that relieve or exacerbate pain. For example, a patient with spinal stenosis and neurogenic claudication would benefit from a regimen emphasizing flexion-based rather than extension-based exercises. The presence of a midrange motion segment abnormality can be determined using the signs listed in Table 1.

Clinical prediction rules have been developed for determining whether spine manipulation or stabilization exercises are likely to be beneficial (Figure 1). The most important factors predicting improvement with spine manipulation appear to be acute pain of less than 16 days' duration and a nonradicular pattern in which there is no pain distal to the knee.[10] Trunk (core) stabilization programs appear to have a greater chance of

2: Nonsurgical Care of the Spine

success if the patient is younger than 40 years and has a negative straight-leg raise test (in which pain is absent or present only with a straight-leg angle greater than 90°), a positive prone instability test (pain provoked by posteroanterior pressure to the midline of the lumbar spine and relieved with activation of the paraspinal muscles), aberrant motions such as difficulty moving from a flexed into an extended or neutral position, lumbar hypermobility (on spring testing), and minimal fear-avoidance behavior.[11]

McKenzie testing or directional preference assessment of the end lumbar ranges also can be helpful in classifying a patient with low back pain as a candidate for manipulation or stabilization.[5] Lumbar traction can be considered for a patient with radicular pain who does not have pain relief or centralization when placed in a maximal lumbar range of motion. Several factors predict successful lumbar traction, including nonpartic-ipation in manual work activities, a low level of fear-avoidance behavior, an absence of neurologic deficits, and an age older than 30 years.[12] However, a Cochrane review did not find lumbar traction efficacious for treating low back pain.[13]

Therapeutic Exercise Concepts and Methods

Core and Trunk Anatomy

The lumbar core can be thought of as a muscular box in which the abdominal muscles form the front, the paraspinal and gluteal muscles form the back, the diaphragm forms the top, and the pelvic floor and hip girdle musculature forms the bottom.[14] The box comprises 29 pairs of muscles that help to stabilize the spine, pelvis, and kinetic chain during functional movements. Without these muscles, the spine would become mechanically unstable; the compressive forces would be as low as 90 N, which is a load much less than the weight of the upper body.[15] Stability of the spine depends not only on muscular strength but also on sensory input that alerts the central nervous system to interactions between the body and the environment, providing constant feedback and allowing refinement of movement.[16] Research from the Queensland Physiotherapy Group brought a great deal of attention to the importance of the deep core musculature, specifically the transversus abdominis and multifidi, for core stability.[14] However, other researchers have emphasized the importance of the larger so-called prime mover muscles, such as the abdominal obliques and quadratus lumborum, in providing stability.[17] It appears that a coordinated contraction of all deep and superficial core muscles is needed for optimal spine stabilization.[18]

Although a patient with low back pain often is described as having a weak core, stability of the core or trunk is difficult to characterize because of overlapping biomechanical and clinical definitions. The term instability can have several different meanings. Gross spine instability is an obvious radiographic displacement of

Table 1

Physical Examination Signs That May Signify a Midrange Motion Segment Abnormality

Gower sign

Instability catch

McNabb sign

Painful flexion or return from flexion

Positional muscle spasm (for example, transverse band of muscle spasm that decreases when the patient is supine, muscle twitching when patient leans on one leg, shaking during forward flexion)

Posterior shear testing

Posteroanterior testing that produces more spring at one level (passive accessory motion testing)

Prone instability test

Step deformity (listhesis)

Total lumbar flexion greater than 53°

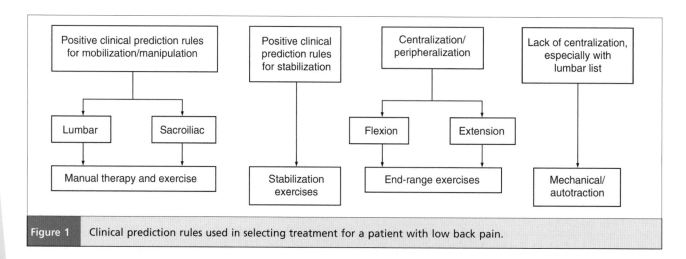

| Figure 1 | Clinical prediction rules used in selecting treatment for a patient with low back pain. |

vertebrae, often with associated neurologic deficit and deformity. Functional or clinical instability is not as easily defined. Clinical instability has been defined as the loss of the spine's ability to maintain its patterns of displacement under physiologic loads and thus avoid creating an initial or additional neurologic deficit, a major deformity, or incapacitating pain.[19]

The spine stability system consists of three interacting subsystems: neuromuscular, provided by the neural elements; passive, provided by the bones and ligaments; and active, provided by the muscles. Core stability requires neuromuscular control, particularly in the neutral zone of the lumbar spine. The term midrange segmental motion abnormality has been proposed to replace the term instability in determining whether a patient can benefit from core stability or strengthening exercises.[20] Therapeutic exercises for core strengthening are more likely to affect midrange motor control deficits than the end-range deficits characteristic of conditions such as progressive spondylolisthesis with dynamic instability.

Muscle Imbalances
Several low back pain syndromes have been described in the context of muscle imbalance. A muscle imbalance occurs when an agonist muscle becomes dominant and short while the antagonist muscle becomes inhibited and weak. One muscle imbalance pattern that affects the lumbar spine involves tightness and overactivity of the primary hip flexor (the iliopsoas), which causes a reciprocal inhibition of the primary hip extensor (the gluteus maximus), leading to increased anterior pelvic tilt and secondarily to increased lumbar extension as well as excessive force on the posterior elements of the spine. Exercises directed at improving such a muscle imbalance pattern can affect the lumbar spine pain generators in the posterior spine and reduce symptoms that are exacerbated by spine extension, such as those of lumbar spinal canal stenosis.

The obvious goal of exercise for a patient with low back pain is to strengthen deficient muscles and improve the range of motion of tight muscles and joints. However, some low back pain primarily results from inadequate motor patterns rather than isolated deficits in muscle strength or flexibility. A patient with chronic or recurrent low back pain may have a pattern of increased spine motion, increased spine muscle strength, poor muscle endurance, poor hip mobility, and gluteal muscle underuse.[21]

A comprehensive lumbar rehabilitation program attempts to restore normal lumbar motion through stretching protocols. Some experts believe that stretching the hip girdle musculature is particularly important for patients with low back pain.[21] Several types of stretching exercises frequently are included in a patient's exercise program. The familiar method of static stretching begins with the muscle at rest, then elongated and held for 30 seconds to 2 minutes. Proprioceptive neuromuscular facilitation techniques add a

short isometric contraction-relaxation period to the stretch; the stretch is facilitated by the augmented postisometric relaxation at the end of the contraction. The antagonist muscle also can be contracted to assist the stretch. Ballistic stretching involves bouncing the muscle against the end of the range of movement and is typically used by athletes before a high-velocity activity. Functional stretching incorporates movement required for a planned future activity. The best stretching method is unknown, although one study found that proprioceptive neuromuscular facilitation and functional stretching provided the greatest increase in range of motion.[22]

Exercise Progression
Patients with low back pain vary greatly in their ability to exercise. Often the patient must learn fundamental exercise and muscle-training techniques or must relearn these techniques in pain-free and relatively unloaded positions. The neutral spine position minimizes the load on the spine ligaments and joints and is an initial position of comfort.[3] The neutral spine position approximates the center of reaction; this relatively stable athletic posture allows quick movement into lumbar flexion or extension. Some patients progress rapidly to more advanced functional tasks. However, many patients need supervision to properly execute functional exercises. A physical therapist or another skilled clinician can provide postural and muscle cues and biofeedback to help the patient improve. Some individuals with chronic or recurrent low back pain may have adequate back extensor muscle strength, as tested by maximal contraction, but lack the muscle endurance required for functional tasks.[23] The clinician's role is to determine the deficit contributing to improper spine loading, as related the patient's spine diagnosis. The clinician also must determine the optimal amount of exercise; for example, a patient with poor endurance may need shorter, more frequent, and less intense sessions than most other patients.

Endurance often improves less rapidly than other parameters. Power and agility exercises using the transverse (rotational) plane are introduced during the final stages of the program for a high-performance athlete or an individual whose functional tasks require rotational motion. Exercises in the transverse plane should be performed with caution because transverse plane movement creates four to five times more force on the spine than sagittal plane movement.[21] Compliance with a continuing home exercise or self-management program is key to preventing a recurrence of low back pain.[9]

Core Strengthening
Core strengthening exercises are particularly important for patients with spine instability. The stability of the spine depends not only on muscular strength but also on sensory input that alerts the central nervous system to body-environment interaction, thus providing constant feedback and allowing refinement of movement.[16]

Table 2

Sample Evidence-Based Progressive Core Stability Program

General Concepts
Active patient participation
Importance of the core anatomy
Core muscle isolation in different positions

Basic and Intermediate Exercises
Transversus abdominis isolation (advanced when patient is able to perform 30 8-second repetitions)
Abdominal bracing with heel slides, leg lifts, bridging, standing, standing row, walking
Paraspinal and multifidus isolation (advanced when patient is able to perform 30 8-second repetitions)
Quadruped arm lifts with bracing
Quadruped leg lifts with bracing
Alternate quadruped arm and legs lifts with bracing
Quadratus lumborum and obliques isolation (advanced when patient is able to perform 30 8-second repetitions)
Side plank with knees flexed
Side plank with knees extended
Trunk curl

Facilitation Techniques (Used as Necessary)
Palpation
Pelvic floor contraction
Substitution patterns
Ultrasonography
Visualization

Advanced Exercise
Endurance building
Functional training with activation of core
Physioball use

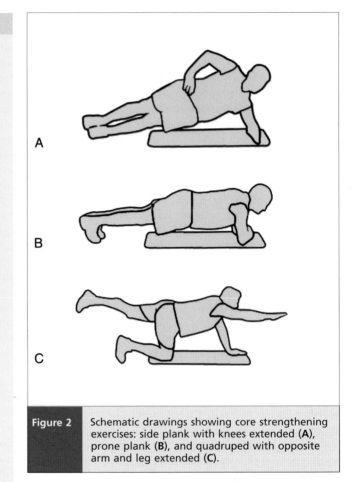

Figure 2 Schematic drawings showing core strengthening exercises: side plank with knees extended (**A**), prone plank (**B**), and quadruped with opposite arm and leg extended (**C**).

A complete core stability program therefore should include both sensory and motor components.

A core strengthening program progresses from one level to the next based on the patient's ability (Table 2). In the first stage, the patient learns and begins to apply the concept of neutral spine position, in which a midpoint is found between lumbar flexion and extension.[24] Core stability training begins with learning to activate the abdominal wall musculature. Patients who are not adept at volitional activation of motor pathways or who have chronic low back pain and fear-avoidance behavior may require extra time and instruction to learn to recruit muscles in isolation or in the correct motor patterns.[25] The technique of abdominal bracing is particularly important for activating multiple core muscles and appears to be more beneficial than abdominal hollowing.[26]

When the patient has become proficient in these skills, she or he is taught more advanced exercises, including the curl-up, side plank (side bridge), prone plank (prone bridge), and quadruped with alternate arm and leg raises (the bird-dog exercise)[27] (Figure 2).

When these static exercises are mastered, the patient is ready to advance to standing exercises that incorporate functional movements in multiple planes. The use of an unstable surface such as a balance board or exercise ball can introduce additional challenges. Maintenance of neutral spine posture should be emphasized in all activities. The goal of a core strengthening program is not absolute strength but instead is coordination and muscle endurance, as well as integration and efficiency of central nervous system control.

Directional Preference Exercises

The McKenzie method is a well-known system of spine pain assessment, classification, and treatment. The centralization phenomenon refers to the "sequential and lasting abolition of all distal referred symptoms and subsequent abolition of any remaining spinal pain in response to a single direction of repeated movements or sustained postures."[28] Using directional preference exercises, peripheral or distal radicular low back pain is centralized into the proximal aspects of the pain pattern and is sequentially abolished through repeated single-direction movements or postures. A standardized assessment of end-range lumbar motion is used. The belief is that impingement of the pain-generating nerve root is lessened in certain end ranges. In the most common scenario, unilateral radicular leg and low back pain from a lumbar paracentral disk herniation is reduced or centralized through the repeated use of end-range extension maneuvers.

A meta-analysis found the McKenzie method to be effective for treating acute low back pain but not clearly proven for relieving chronic low back pain.[29] This method may be more effective than other therapeutic exercise regimens, particularly in the acute pain phase.[30] Centralization of pain was found to predict a superior outcome, but peripheralization predicted a poor outcome.[31] As a clinical classification method based on examination, the McKenzie method probably has diagnostic value for distinguishing discogenic from nondiscogenic pain.[31]

Manual Treatments

Physical therapists as well as medical, chiropractic, and osteopathic clinicians commonly use manual treatments such as manipulation and mobilization to treat low back pain. The use of manual treatment for chronic low back pain is supported by moderate evidence; for acute low back conditions, the evidence is stronger.[32] The effect of spine manipulation therapy appears to be similar to that of exercise and anti-inflammatory medications.

Aerobic Exercise and Functional Restoration

Physical activity and involvement in an exercise program are generally accepted as superior to passive treatment. Intensive exercise can have an important role in the treatment of chronic low back pain disability and was found to be equal in effect to lumbar fusion in a randomized controlled study.[33] Intensive exercise also was found beneficial in 187 patients with subacute low back pain of 4 weeks' to 6 months' duration.[8] Chronic back pain was reduced by 36% in patients who underwent a 3-week intensive exercise program, compared with 20% in patients who received passive treatment.[24] In patients with chronic low back pain, exercise intensity was found to be correlated with the extent of reduction.[34] Patients who participated in active exercise had a 45% reduction in pain, compared with no reduction in those who participated in a passive program.[35] Other studies found that exercise led to a reduction in disability ranging from 8% to 50%.[36-40]

The use of intensive, non–pain-contingent exercises for treating chronic back pain has received recent attention. These so-called functional restoration programs typically extend beyond functional goals to include exercises designed to decrease kinesiophobia. In this "aggressive quota-based exercise approach," objective goals are set and quantifiable tasks and parameters are used to measure patient achievement.[41]

Pain Control

A variety of medications can be used to control pain. Several nonmedicinal tools also can be useful, particu-

larly during the acute phase after a low back injury. However, the use of nonmedicinal tools is supported only by a low level of evidence. For discogenic conditions, bed rest in a position of comfort may be effective if used for less than 48 hours, but prolonged immobilization has numerous adverse effects. A patient with low back pain should be encouraged to move after the acute phase. The patient should receive early instruction on proper body mechanics for sitting, standing, and lifting, perhaps during the initial visit to the physician's office. The use of a neutral spine position of comfort can mitigate acute low back pain. If the patient has a discogenic pathology, flexion within 1 hour of awakening may place the disk at risk.[17]

The use of cold packs within the first 48 hours after injury can reduce muscle guarding, pain, and superficial inflammation. Superficial or deep heat therapy often is used to reduce pain and muscle guarding during the later stages. A continuous low-level heat wrap is effective in relieving low back pain, but erythema ab igne, a dermatologic discoloration, can occur if heat is repeatedly applied for a long period.[42] Transcutaneous electrical nerve stimulation also can be used to relieve low back pain. A Cochrane review found only inconclusive evidence in favor of transcutaneous electrical nerve stimulation, and the parameters for achieving reduction of chronic pain were unclear.[43]

Lumbar orthoses have been used for pain control. Most lumbar orthoses, including corsets, are unlikely to substantially limit lumbar motion but may prevent painful directional motion. However, repeated use of an orthosis may impair core musculature strength and endurance. There is little high-quality evidence for the use of different types of lumbar traction.[44] However, traction was found to be a useful modality in some patients with radicular pain[12]

Evidence-based manual treatments such as mobilization and manipulation can be effective for reducing pain during the first few weeks of a low back pain episode.[32] These manual treatments are believed to be most likely to benefit patients with joint-related low back pain such as facet- or sacroiliac-mediated pain. Some clinicians who are proficient in the McKenzie method can reduce acute pain through repeated directional preference exercise. For example, unilateral radicular pain with lumbar flexion from a posterolateral disk herniation can be mitigated with centralizing repeated extension maneuvers.

Specific Lumbar Diagnoses

A program must be specific to the type of back pain or the pain generator. For example, a patient with joint-related pathology such as facet or sacroiliac joint pain may benefit from manipulation combined with a stabilization program; a patient with sacroiliac pain may particularly benefit from gluteal muscle strengthening designed to achieve force closure.

Imaging evaluation is particularly important for determining the best therapeutic exercise regimen for a patient with disk pain. An annular radial tear or bulge without disk height loss can be treated with extension maneuvers, which may reduce intradiskal pressure. A patient with disk height loss or a circumferential tear may not benefit from extension exercises. A patient with obvious or gross instability (as in spondylolisthesis or on a lateral flexion-extension lumbar radiograph) or a more subtle midrange segmental motion abnormality can benefit from increased lumbar stability and hip mobility and is likely to need a therapeutic exercise regimen based on stabilization exercises. A patient with lumbar stenosis may benefit from flexion-based therapeutic exercises, manual treatment of stiff segments, and an unweighted treadmill-walking program.[45] Stabilization exercises should be emphasized if the stenosis is associated with spondylolisthesis or bilateral facet joint effusions.

At the conclusion of a course of therapy, it is helpful for the patient to discuss options for promoting overall health and maintaining the improvements achieved in therapy. For example, a patient with a condition that benefits from flexion can maintain aerobic conditioning by bicycling or walking on an inclined treadmill. Cross-country skiing or walking on a neutral (flat) treadmill is better for a patient whose condition benefits from extension.

Summary

Therapeutic exercise regimens clearly have an important role in treating low back pain. An individualized exercise regimen can be a far-reaching intervention that can help a patient self-manage low back pain, decrease the pain, and minimize disability.

Annotated References

1. Fritz JM, Cleland JA, Speckman M, Brennan GP, Hunter SJ: Physical therapy for acute low back pain: Associations with subsequent healthcare costs. *Spine (Phila Pa 1976)* 2008;33(16):1800-1805.

   A retrospective study found that adherence to active care recommendations by patients referred to physical therapy for acute low back pain is associated with better outcomes and decreased health care costs.

2. Rainville J, Hartigan C, Martinez E, Limke J, Jouve C, Finno M: Exercise as a treatment for chronic low back pain. *Spine J* 2004;4(1):106-115.

3. Sorosky SC, Sorosky B, Press JM: The management of low back pain: A comprehensive rehabilitation program, in Spivak JM, Connolly PJ, eds: *Orthopaedic Knowledge Update: Spine 3.* Rosemont, IL, American Academy of Orthopaedic Surgeons, 2006, pp 129-139.

   A comprehensive rehabilitation program for lumbar

spine conditions is outlined, with therapeutic exercise regimens and their theoretic constructs.

4. Akuthota V, Ferreiro A, Moore T, Fredericson M: Core stability exercise principles. *Curr Sports Med Rep* 2008; 7(1):39-44.

   The anatomy of the core, the progression of core strengthening, the evidence for the theoretic construct of core strengthening, and its efficacy in musculoskeletal conditions are summarized. Core stability exercises are described.

5. Brennan GP, Fritz JM, Hunter SJ, Thackeray A, Delitto A, Erhard RE: Identifying subgroups of patients with acute/subacute "nonspecific" low back pain: Results of a randomized clinical trial. *Spine (Phila Pa 1976)* 2006; 31(6):623-631.

   A randomized clinical study found that physical therapy for patients with nonspecific low back pain had better functional outcomes when the patients were grouped by treatment categories. Nonspecific low back pain was determined not to be a homogenous condition.

6. Donchin M, Woolf O, Kaplan L, Floman Y: Secondary prevention of low-back pain: A clinical trial. *Spine (Phila Pa 1976)* 1990;15(12):1317-1320.

7. Hides JA, Jull GA, Richardson CA: Long-term effects of specific stabilizing exercises for first-episode low back pain. *Spine (Phila Pa 1976)* 2001;26(11):E243-E248.

8. Moffett JK, Torgerson D, Bell-Syer S, et al: Randomised controlled trial of exercise for low back pain: Clinical outcomes, costs, and preferences. *BMJ* 1999;319(7205): 279-283.

9. Schenkman ML, Jordan S, Akuthota V, et al: Functional movement training for recurrent low back pain: Lessons from a pilot randomized controlled trial. *PM R* 2009; 1(2):137-146.

   A pilot study examined the utility of a functional movement training program for individuals with chronic low back pain. Functional movement and self-management techniques were emphasized.

10. Fritz JM, Childs JD, Flynn TW: Pragmatic application of a clinical prediction rule in primary care to identify patients with low back pain with a good prognosis following a brief spinal manipulation intervention. *BMC Fam Pract* 2005;6(1):29.

    Low back pain that was relatively acute and unlikely to be radicular, as indicated by symptoms of less than 16 days' duration and no symptoms below the knee, was found to have a good outcome when the patient underwent spine manipulative therapy.

11. Hicks GE, Fritz JM, Delitto A, McGill SM: Preliminary development of a clinical prediction rule for determining which patients with low back pain will respond to a stabilization exercise program. *Arch Phys Med Rehabil* 2005;86(9):1753-1762.

    A clinical prediction rule study found that individuals with low back pain who were younger than 40 years or had a negative straight-leg raise test, a positive prone instability test, aberrant motions, lumbar hypermobility, or low fear-avoidance beliefs had good outcomes from a lumbar stabilization program.

12. Cai C, Pua YH, Lim KC: A clinical prediction rule for classifying patients with low back pain who demonstrate short-term improvement with mechanical lumbar traction. *Eur Spine J* 2009;18(4):554-561.

A clinical prediction rule for lumbar traction was identified. The variables predicting a good outcome of lumbar traction included noninvolvement with manual work, a low level of fear-avoidance beliefs, no neurologic deficit, and an age older than 30 years.

13. Clarke JA, van Tulder MW, Blomberg SE, et al: Traction for low-back pain with or without sciatica. *Cochrane Database Syst Rev* 2007;2:CD003010.

A Cochrane review of studies with a mixed population base did not find a significant benefit to lumbar traction.

14. Richardson C, Jull G, Hodges P, Hides J: *Therapeutic Exercise for Spinal Segmental Stabilization in Low Back Pain: Scientific Basis and Clinical Approach*. Edinburgh, NY, Churchill Livingstone, 1999.

15. Crisco JJ, Panjabi MM, et al: Euler stability of the human ligamentous lumbar spine: Part II. Experiment. *Clin Biomech (Bristol, Avon)* 1992;7(1):27-32.

16. Hodges PW: Core stability exercise in chronic low back pain. *Orthop Clin North Am* 2003;34(2):245-254.

17. McGill S: *Low Back Disorders: Evidence-Based Prevention and Rehabilitation*. Champaign, IL, Human Kinetics, 2002.

18. Akuthota V, Nadler SF: Core strengthening. *Arch Phys Med Rehabil* 2004;85(3, suppl 1):S86-S92.

19. Panjabi MM: Clinical spinal instability and low back pain. *J Electromyogr Kinesiol* 2003;13(4):371-379.

20. Reiman MP: Trunk stabilization training: An evidence basis for the current state of affairs. *J Back Musculoskelet Rehabil* 2009;22(3):131-142.

This review of trunk stabilization includes the definition of instability, a history, and physical examination maneuvers for detecting midrange segmental abnormality. The evidence base of particular exercise regimens is provided.

21. McGill SM: *Corrective and Therapeutic Exercise for the Painful Lumbar Spine: Technique Matters*. Rochester, MN, American Academy of Neuromuscular and Electrodiagnostic Medicine, 2009.

The evidence base, proper performance, and scheduling of therapeutic exercise for the lumbar spine are discussed.

22. Fasen JM, O'Connor AM, Schwartz SL, et al: A randomized controlled trial of hamstring stretching: Comparison of four techniques. *J Strength Cond Res* 2009; 23(2):660-667.

The efficacy of four hamstring-stretching techniques is compared. The use of proprioceptive neuromuscular facilitation in the 90/90 active stretch provided better knee range-of-motion improvement than the 90/90 passive methods.

23. McGill S, Grenier S, Bluhm M, Preuss R, Brown S, Russell C: Previous history of LBP with work loss is related to lingering deficits in biomechanical, physiological, personal, psychosocial and motor control characteristics. *Ergonomics* 2003;46(7):731-746.

24. Alaranta H, Rytökoski U, Rissanen A, et al: Intensive physical and psychosocial training program for patients with chronic low back pain: A controlled clinical trial. *Spine (Phila Pa 1976)* 1994;19(12):1339-1349.

25. Klenerman L, Slade PD, Stanley IM, et al: The prediction of chronicity in patients with an acute attack of low back pain in a general practice setting. *Spine (Phila Pa 1976)* 1995;20(4):478-484.

26. Grenier SG, McGill SM: Quantification of lumbar stability by using 2 different abdominal activation strategies. *Arch Phys Med Rehabil* 2007;88(1):54-62.

Abdominal bracing was found to be better than abdominal hollowing for increasing stability to the lumbar spine.

27. O'Sullivan PB, Beales DJ, Beetham JA, et al: Altered motor control strategies in subjects with sacroiliac joint pain during the active straight-leg-raise test. *Spine (Phila Pa 1976)* 2002;27(1):E1-E8.

28. May S, Donelson R: Evidence-informed management of chronic low back pain with the McKenzie method. *Spine J* 2008;8(1):134-141.

McKenzie methods for chronic low back pain are reviewed.

29. Machado LA, de Souza MS, Ferreira PH, Ferreira ML: The McKenzie method for low back pain: A systematic review of the literature with a meta-analysis approach. *Spine (Phila Pa 1976)* 2006;31(9):E254-E262.

Pooled data from 11 high-quality studies revealed some evidence that the McKenzie method is more effective than passive therapy for acute (but not chronic) low back pain. The magnitude of the difference appears to be small.

30. Long A, Donelson R, Fung T: Does it matter which exercise? A randomized control trial of exercise for low back pain. *Spine (Phila Pa 1976)* 2004;29(23):2593-2602.

31. Donelson R, Aprill C, Medcalf R, Grant W: A prospective study of centralization of lumbar and referred pain: A predictor of symptomatic discs and anular competence. *Spine (Phila Pa 1976)* 1997;22(10):1115-1122.

2: Nonsurgical Care of the Spine

32. Bronfort G, Haas M, Evans R, Kawchuk G, Dagenais S: Evidence-informed management of chronic low back pain with spinal manipulation and mobilization. *Spine J* 2008;8(1):213-225.

The evidence for spine manipulation and mobilization is reviewed, and an overall benefit to these treatments is suggested.

33. Brox JI, Sørensen R, Friis A, et al: Randomized clinical trial of lumbar instrumented fusion and cognitive intervention and exercises in patients with chronic low back pain and disc degeneration. *Spine (Phila Pa 1976)* 2003;28(17):1913-1921.

34. Manniche C, Lundberg E, Christensen I, Bentzen L, Hesselsøe G: Intensive dynamic back exercises for chronic low back pain: A clinical trial. *Pain* 1991;47(1):53-63.

35. Kankaanpää M, Taimela S, Airaksinen O, Hänninen O: The efficacy of active rehabilitation in chronic low back pain: Effect on pain intensity, self-experienced disability, and lumbar fatigability. *Spine (Phila Pa 1976)* 1999;24(10):1034-1042.

36. Hazard RG, Fenwick JW, Kalisch SM, et al: Functional restoration with behavioral support: A one-year prospective study of patients with chronic low-back pain. *Spine (Phila Pa 1976)* 1989;14(2):157-161.

37. Mayer TG, Gatchel RJ, Mayer H, Kishino ND, Keeley J, Mooney V: A prospective two-year study of functional restoration in industrial low back injury: An objective assessment procedure. *JAMA* 1987;258(13):1763-1767.

38. Rainville J, Jouve CA, Hartigan C, Martinez E, Hipona M: Comparison of short- and long-term outcomes for aggressive spine rehabilitation delivered two versus three times per week. *Spine J* 2002;2(6):402-407.

39. Risch SV, Norvell NK, Pollock ML, et al: Lumbar strengthening in chronic low back pain patients: Physiologic and psychological benefits. *Spine (Phila Pa 1976)* 1993;18(2):232-238.

40. Taimela S, Diederich C, Hubsch M, Heinricy M: The role of physical exercise and inactivity in pain recurrence and absenteeism from work after active outpatient rehabilitation for recurrent or chronic low back pain: A follow-up study. *Spine (Phila Pa 1976)* 2000;25(14):1809-1816.

41. Cohen I, Rainville J: Aggressive exercise as treatment for chronic low back pain. *Sports Med* 2002;32(1):75-82.

42. Nadler SF, Steiner DJ, Erasala GN, et al: Continuous low-level heat wrap therapy provides more efficacy than Ibuprofen and acetaminophen for acute low back pain. *Spine (Phila Pa 1976)* 2002;27(10):1012-1017.

43. Carroll D, Moore RA, McQuay HJ, Fairman F, Tramèr M, Leijon G: Transcutaneous electrical nerve stimulation (TENS) for chronic pain. *Cochrane Database Syst Rev* 2001;3:CD003222.

44. Gay RE, Brault JS: Evidence-informed management of chronic low back pain with traction therapy. *Spine J* 2008;8(1):234-242.

The evidence for the various types of lumbar traction is reviewed.

45. Whitman JM, Flynn TW, Childs JD, et al: A comparison between two physical therapy treatment programs for patients with lumbar spinal stenosis: A randomized clinical trial. *Spine (Phila Pa 1976)* 2006;31(22):2541-2549.

A novel treatment protocol for lumbar spinal stenosis included unweighted treadmill walking and manual treatments. The program was found to improve functional outcomes more than a traditional physical therapy program.

Chapter 10

Osteopathic Manipulative Treatment

Darren C. Rosenberg, DO   William M. Foley, DO, MSc   George Pasquarello, DO, FAAO

Background

Osteopathy is a system of medicine in which diagnosis and treatment are based on three tenets: structure and function within the body are reciprocally interrelated; the body has self-regulating and self-healing mechanisms; and the body should be treated as an integrated unit incorporating physical, mental, and emotional elements. Hands-on techniques are used to make an accurate diagnosis, support homeostasis, and encourage the body to heal itself.

Andrew Taylor Still, MD, who developed osteopathy in 1874, did not view osteopathy in isolation. Rather, osteopathic principles and techniques were to be integrated into the practice of all physicians as a complementary system of diagnosis and treatment. Complementary and alternative medicine, including osteopathic manipulative treatment (OMT), increasingly is being incorporated into traditional medical training. OMT is included in the National Institutes of Health classification of complementary and alternative medicine. The use of OMT was found to decrease both the number of days of physical therapy and cost of care for patients with various conditions.[1]

Osteopathic Manipulative Treatment

Osteopathic manipulative medicine is the application of the osteopathic philosophy to structural diagnosis and treatment. An osteopathic structural examination focuses on the patient's neuromusculoskeletal system. Close attention is paid to posture, spine motion, and balance. A palpatory examination of the entire body is performed to detect asymmetry, tissue texture, restriction of motion, and tenderness in the ligaments, joints, tendons, muscles, and fascia. An abnormal finding is called a somatic dysfunction. OMT is used to improve or resolve somatic dysfunction.

The ability to palpate for somatic dysfunction is a psychomotor skill that develops with use and is essential for osteopathic diagnosis and treatment. Palpation also is used to monitor improvement from the use of OMT, as well as other treatments such as physical therapy, medications, and injections. The goal of OMT is to reduce pain, remove restrictions in motion, and improve function or support healing of an injury.

The practitioner can determine the presence of somatic dysfunction by testing the patient's range of motion both passively and actively. A physiologic barrier is found at the end point of the active range of motion, and an anatomic barrier is found at the end of the passive range of motion. OMT is directed at decreasing or eliminating these restrictive barriers for the purpose of restoring normal range of motion to the area.[3] The body's ability to heal itself by improving blood flow and lymphatic drainage to the area also may be improved. The alignment of the thoracic-abdominal-pelvic cylinder is maintained to allow proper functioning of the diaphragm, resulting in better oxygenation, blood flow, and lymphatic drainage. Alterations in the thoracic-abdominal-pelvic cylinder are believed to be caused by somatic dysfunction and to interfere with the body's self-regulating mechanisms.

A patient with chronic pain syndrome usually must be treated with an approach that is more inclusive than manipulation or any other single modality.[2] The usefulness of an individual treatment sometimes can be increased if it is combined with other treatments.

Treatment Types

An osteopathic treatment can be classified as direct, indirect, or combination. A direct technique is used to treat a somatic dysfunction by engaging the restrictive barrier and carrying the dysfunctional component into the restrictive barrier. In one direct technique, the mus-

2: Nonsurgical Care of the Spine

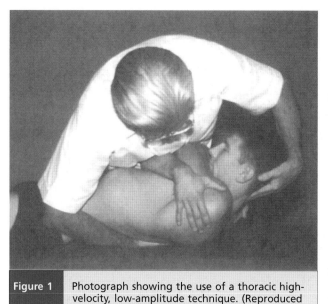

Figure 1 | Photograph showing the use of a thoracic high-velocity, low-amplitude technique. (Reproduced with permission from Greenman PE: *Principles of Manual Medicine*, ed 3. Philadelphia, PA, Lippincott Williams & Wilkins, 2003, p 253.)

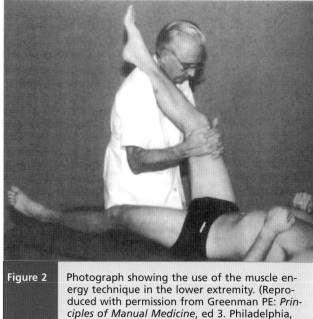

Figure 2 | Photograph showing the use of the muscle energy technique in the lower extremity. (Reproduced with permission from Greenman PE: *Principles of Manual Medicine*, ed 3. Philadelphia, PA, Lippincott Williams & Wilkins, 2003, p 460.)

cle energy treatment, the practitioner engages and holds a restrictive barrier as the patient engages muscles to move the joint against the resistance. The patient relaxes after a few seconds of muscle contraction to allow the restricted area to be moved until a new restrictive barrier is encountered. This process is repeated until the range of motion has been improved. An indirect technique disengages the restrictive barrier, moving the dysfunctional component away from the restrictive barrier until tissue tension is equal in all planes of motion. In counterstrain, an indirect technique, tender points are identified in areas of muscle tension and somatic dysfunction. A segment or joint is moved away from the restrictive barrier to a position that provides comfort and relief of the tender point. This position is maintained for approximately 90 seconds to allow physiologic resetting of the muscle-resting tension and palpable relaxation of the area. The process is repeated until the range of motion and muscle tension has been improved.

Techniques also can be classified as active or passive. An active technique requires the patient to voluntarily perform a practitioner-directed motion. Muscle energy is an active technique, as it requires the patient to contract muscles against practitioner-applied resistance. During a passive technique, the patient refrains from voluntary muscle contraction. Counterstrain is a passive technique, as it requires the patient to relax while the practitioner positions the area or joint. Techniques can be used alone or in combination for the purpose of achieving maximal improvement.

The high-velocity, low-amplitude or thrust technique is a direct passive treatment that involves the application of a high-velocity, low-amplitude force to restore a specific joint motion. The practitioner delivers a quick thrust within the joint's normal range of motion and not exceeding the joint's anatomic barrier. Very little force is required, but for effective mobilization, proper positioning and engagement of the restrictive barrier are necessary before the thrust. The joint regains its normal range of motion by release of the restrictive barrier and resetting of neural reflexes. The thrust may or may not result in the joint producing an audible popping sound. The presence or absence of the popping sound does not indicate whether the dysfunction has been resolved (Figure 1). This treatment has some contraindications because of the thrusting movement, even though it involves little force. The relative contraindications include osteoporosis, rheumatoid arthritis involving the upper cervical spine, carotid or vertebrobasilar vascular disease, and the possibility of an underlying metastatic lesion.

The muscle energy technique is a direct active treatment based on the principle of reciprocal inhibition. In reciprocal inhibition, indirect pressure is believed to always cause agonist muscles on one side of a joint to relax to accommodate the contraction of antagonistic muscles on the other side of the joint. The muscle energy technique is gentle but requires that the patient have the cognitive ability to follow a command to contract muscles. This technique can restore range of motion that might be restricted because of muscle spasm. The patient is asked to contract the muscle gently against the practitioner's counterforce for 5 seconds. After the contraction is complete, the practitioner waits for the patient to relax and then passively moves the joints to the new end point or restrictive barrier. The process is repeated two or three times to increase the range of motion (Figure 2). Improvement is monitored by comparing the treated region to the contralateral

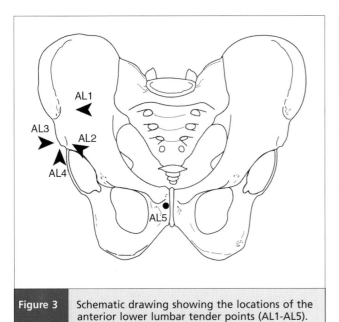

Figure 3 Schematic drawing showing the locations of the anterior lower lumbar tender points (AL1-AL5). (Reproduced with permission from Jones LH, Kusunose R, Goering E: *Jones Strain-Counterstrain*. Boise, ID, Jones Strain-Counterstrain Inc, 1995, p 73.)

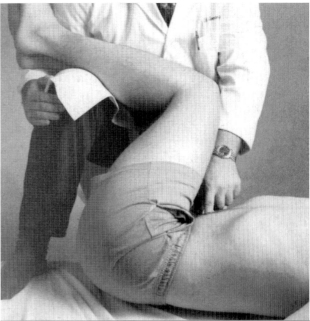

Figure 4 Photograph showing the counterstrain technique for the anterior second lumbar tender point. (Reproduced with permission from Jones LH, Kusunose R, Goering E: *Jones Strain-Counterstrain*. Boise, ID, Jones Strain-Counterstrain Inc, 1995, p 74.)

side. The muscle energy technique is safe and has few contraindications.

Counterstrain is an indirect passive technique used to reduce pain from a tender point related to a muscle. A tender point is unlike a trigger point in that it does not radiate pain. The patient's tender points are identified, and the patient is positioned (Figure 3). Positioning generally involves curling the patient around the tender point to find the position that decreases the pain or discomfort. This position of ease should be held for 90 seconds. It is believed that the position of ease helps normalize the gamma-efferent system, leading to softening of the focal tender point and the restoration of normal function. After the treatment, the practitioner must move the patient back to a neutral position slowly and without assistance from the patient. Care must be taken to treat the most painful tender point first; otherwise, the treatment is unlikely to succeed (Figure 4).

The low-velocity, high-amplitude or articulatory technique is a direct passive technique designed to increase the range of motion of a restricted joint or tissue by gently moving beyond the restrictive barrier. Treatment can involve gently and repetitively engaging the restrictive barrier (called springing) or guiding a patient through passive range of motion while overcoming the restrictive barrier. Respiratory cooperation and active muscle contraction from the patient can be combined with articulatory technique to mobilize the restricted area or spine segment. Articulatory techniques should be avoided if the patient has an acutely inflamed joint or an unhealed fracture.

Myofascial release is a passive technique that can be direct or indirect. The goal of myofascial release is to improve lymphatic flow to all tissues by removing myofascial restrictions. The restricted region is isolated, and indirect compression or traction is applied. A twisting or transverse force is then added. The release can be assisted by patient respiration and muscle contraction. Myofascial release is an extremely safe technique, but it should be avoided in the region of a fracture or lymphatic system malignancy.

Osteopathy in the cranial field, facilitated positional release, balanced ligamentous tension, progressive inhibition of neuromuscular structures, and the Still technique are among the many other osteopathic techniques. The practitioner decides, based on experience, which techniques are best suited to a patient and establishes a treatment plan to maximize their efficacy. An active therapy component often is necessary to achieve the greatest improvement and prevent future dysfunction.

OMT Practice

In a patient with spine pain, OMT is used to restore proper posture and the efficient use of the musculoskeletal system. A manual force generally is applied to release the restricted tissues in an area of somatic dysfunction. The treatments vary with the individual patient's needs, and there are no diagnosis-specific protocols. For example, treatment for acute low back pain depends on findings of the osteopathic examination

2: Nonsurgical Care of the Spine

and therefore differs from patient to patient. Techniques range from gentle to slightly painful.

Every doctor of osteopathy (DO) is trained to use OMT to treat and prevent a range of illness and injury, including chronic pain. Some DOs are certified by the American Osteopathic Board of Neuromusculoskeletal Medicine in neuromusculoskeletal medicine–osteopathic manipulative medicine. A DO who is board certified in this specialty usually practices OMT primarily as a consultant. Many osteopathic family physicians and other primary care specialists treat patients using OMT, and some accept patients on referral. DOs who specialize in osteopathic physical medicine and rehabilitation particularly use OMT for patients with chronic pain.

OMT is prescribed on a visit-to-visit basis. The interval between follow-up appointments depends on the patient's medical condition, whether the condition is chronic or acute, and the patient's overall health. The timing of the next appointment usually is decided upon after each visit; patients whose appointments are scheduled in this manner usually have fewer total manipulation treatments than those who have regularly scheduled appointments.

OMT can be used alone, but it is more effective as part of a comprehensive treatment plan. The treatment plan for a patient with a musculoskeletal disorder should involve a combination of therapies to fully manage the acute injury and prevent future injury. Most treatments of musculoskeletal disorders, including accepted treatments such as nonsteroidal anti-inflammatory drugs and muscle relaxants, have not been proved to be effective when used alone. Clinicians trained in manual therapy use a variety of types of treatment to treat somatic dysfunction, such as medications, injections, and physical therapy. The combination of therapies needs to be arranged and integrated in a manner appropriate to the injury, based on the skill and knowledge of the treating practitioner. Treatment failure can result if the correct treatments are not combined or if they are improperly timed. Further studies that take this factor into consideration are needed and may lead to better outcomes for patients with various musculoskeletal conditions.

Research

Guidelines of the American Osteopathic Association in 2009 stated that "osteopathic physicians use OMT in the care of patients with low back pain. Evidence from systematic reviews and meta-analyses of randomized clinical trials (evidence level IA) supports this."[4] These guidelines for the treatment of patients with low back pain concluded that OMT reduces the level of low back pain significantly more than a placebo and that the effect can persist throughout the first year of treatment. Published studies have supported the use of OMT in patients with spine pain.[5] Guidelines from a multispe-

cialty group recommended a role for OMT in treating back pain.[6]

More than 15 years ago, the existing literature strongly suggested the usefulness of manipulative therapies in treating acute or chronic low back pain. The challenge was to document the effect of such therapies, determine the patient populations for which they are most useful, and fully integrate them into spine rehabilitation programs.[7] When osteopathic spine manipulation was prospectively compared with standard care for subacute low back pain, the patients in both treatment groups had equal pain relief, but those who received OMT required less medication and less physical therapy.[8] Ninety percent of the patients receiving OMT were satisfied with their care.[8] In a prospective randomized study, patients who received OMT reported greater improvement in low back pain, greater satisfaction, and better functioning and mental health than patients who received standard care.[1] However, there were no statistically significant differences when the patients who received OMT were compared with those who received sham manipulation. In patients with acute nonspecific low back pain, there is evidence that the maximum benefit of OMT occurs 1 to 2 weeks after treatment begins.[9]

Back pain secondary to menstrual cramping or dysmenorrhea was found to have an electromyographic pattern similar to that of trauma-induced low back pain. Electromyographic activity, low back pain, and menstrual cramping were significantly decreased during OMT treatment.[10] A randomized placebo-controlled study to measure the efficacy of OMT in relieving back pain during the third trimester of pregnancy found that OMT slows or halts the deterioration of back-specific functioning.[11]

A systematic review and meta-analysis of randomized controlled studies evaluated the role of OMT in low back pain. A stratified analysis found significant pain reduction when OMT was compared with active treatment, placebo, or no treatment.[12] The authors concluded that OMT significantly reduces low back pain and that the benefit persists for at least 3 months. Another meta-analysis found no evidence that the effect of spine manipulative therapy is superior or inferior to that of other recommended therapies, including analgesia, exercise, physical therapy, and "back school."[13] The same analysis concluded that a truly effective therapy for low back pain remains elusive.

A randomized clinical study compared medication, acupuncture, and spine manipulation in patients with chronic spine pain. Manipulation, if not contraindicated, was found to result in greater short-term improvement than acupuncture or medication.[14] The study also concluded that interventions should not be the sole treatment and that a multifaceted approach is needed for managing chronic pain.

OMT has had promising results in treating neck pain. A study of chronic neck pain found that OMT decreased patients' pain intensity and improved their quality of life.[15] Another study compared OMT with intramuscular injection of ketorolac for treating acute neck pain in the emergency department.[16] Patients in both treatment groups reported pain reduction, but those who received OMT had significantly greater immediate pain reduction. One hour after treatment, patients in both groups reported the same pain relief. The authors concluded that OMT is a reasonable alternative to parenteral nonsteroidal anti-inflammatory medication for relieving acute neck pain, that pain relief can be more rapid with OMT, and that OMT decreases the risk of iatrogenic adverse effects from medication use. Serious complications associated with cervical manipulation, such as cerebrovascular accident, were found to be rare.[17] Spine manipulation for patients with low back pain currently is recommended in Denmark, Germany, New Zealand, Sweden, Switzerland, the United Kingdom, and the United States, and the US Agency for Healthcare Research and Quality includes spine manipulation in its guidelines for the treatment of acute low back pain.[18]

The mechanism by which OMT works, its cost effectiveness, and the optimal number of treatments remain unclear for patients with acute or chronic low back pain. The correlation of patient history and physical examination findings with successful OMT also has not been determined. Research is needed to answer these questions.

Summary

The goals of OMT are to reduce pain, remove restrictions to motion, and support the body's inherent self-healing mechanisms or function. During OMT, the osteopathic practitioner palpates tissue restrictions and resolves them using a variety of direct and indirect techniques. Studies support the use of OMT for acute or chronic spine pain, but additional research is needed to establish the evidence base for OMT. OMT generally is considered to be a safe adjunct to conventional care.

Annotated References

1. Licciardone JC, Stoll ST, Fulda KG, et al: Osteopathic manipulative treatment for chronic low back pain: A randomized controlled trial. *Spine (Phila Pa 1976)* 2003;28(13):1355-1362.

2. Stanton DF, Dutes JC: Chronic pain and the chronic pain syndrome: The usefulness of manipulation and behavioral interventions. *Phys Med Rehabil Clin N Am* 1996;7:863-875.

3. Greenman PE: Barrier concepts in structural diagnosis, in *Principles of Manual Medicine*, ed 3. Philadelphia, PA, Lippincott Williams & Wilkins, 2003, pp 39-44.

4. American Osteopathic Association: Guidelines for Osteopathic Manipulative Treatment (OMT) for Patients with Low Back Pain. July 2009. http://www.do-online.org/pdf/AOALowBackPainClinicalPractice Guidelines.pdf. Accessed February 25, 2011.

   The American Osteopathic Association recommends the use of OMT for patients with low back pain. Systematic reviews and meta-analyses of randomized clinical studies provide level I evidence reinforcing this recommendation.

5. Bronfort G, Haas M, Evans RL, Bouter LM: Efficacy of spinal manipulation and mobilization for low back pain and neck pain: A systematic review and best evidence synthesis. *Spine J* 2004;4(3):335-356.

6. Chou R, Qaseem A, Snow V, et al: Diagnosis and treatment of low back pain: A joint clinical practice guideline from the American College of Physicians and the American Pain Society. *Ann Intern Med* 2007;147(7): 478-491.

   This discussion of recommendations for the assessment and treatment of low back pain includes patient evaluation, appropriateness of imaging studies, and therapeutic options. The recommendations are rated according to their strength and the quality of evidence.

7. Mein EA: Low back pain and manual medicine: A look at the literature. *Phys Med Rehabil Clin N Am* 1996;7: 715-729.

8. Andersson GB, Lucente T, Davis AM, Kappler RE, Lipton JA, Leurgans S: A comparison of osteopathic spinal manipulation with standard care for patients with low back pain. *N Engl J Med* 1999;341(19):1426-1431.

9. MacDonald RS, Bell CM: An open controlled assessment of osteopathic manipulation in nonspecific low-back pain. *Spine (Phila Pa 1976)* 1990;15(5):364-370.

10. Boesler D, Warner M, Alpers A, Finnerty EP, Kilmore MA: Efficacy of high-velocity low-amplitude manipulative technique in subjects with low-back pain during menstrual cramping. *J Am Osteopath Assoc* 1993; 93(2):203-208, 213-214.

11. Licciardone JC, Buchanan S, Hensel KL, King HH, Fulda KG, Stoll ST: Osteopathic manipulative treatment of back pain and related symptoms during pregnancy: A randomized controlled trial. *Am J Obstet Gynecol* 2010;202(1):43, e1-e8.

   A randomized, placebo-controlled study compared customary obstetric care alone, with OMT, and with sham ultrasound treatment. OMT was found to retard or stop the deterioration of back-specific functioning during the third trimester of pregnancy.

12. Licciardone JC, Brimhall AK, King LN: Osteopathic manipulative treatment for low back pain: A systematic review and meta-analysis of randomized controlled trials. *BMC Musculoskelet Disord* 2005;6:43.

   A systematic review and meta-analysis of randomized controlled studies was conducted to determine the effi-

2: Nonsurgical Care of the Spine

cacy of OMT as a complementary treatment for low back pain. The use of OMT was found to significantly reduce pain for at least 3 months.

13. Assendelft WJ, Morton SC, Yu EI, Suttorp MJ, Shekelle PG: Spinal manipulative therapy for low back pain: A meta-analysis of effectiveness relative to other therapies. *Ann Intern Med* 2003;138(11):871-881.

14. Giles LG, Muller R: Chronic spinal pain: A randomized clinical trial comparing medication, acupuncture, and spinal manipulation. *Spine (Phila Pa 1976)* 2003; 28(14):1490-1503.

15. Schwerla F, Bischoff A, Nurnberger A, Genter P, Guillaume JP, Resch KL: Osteopathic treatment of patients with chronic non-specific neck pain: A randomised controlled trial of efficacy. *Forsch Komplementmed* 2008; 15(3):138-145.

    A randomized controlled clinical study determined that test-dependent osteopathic interventions may be useful in alleviating chronic nonspecific neck pain. Further studies are needed to determine whether the findings are reproducible and long-term outcomes are achievable.

16. McReynolds TM, Sheridan BJ: Intramuscular ketorolac versus osteopathic manipulative treatment in the management of acute neck pain in the emergency department: A randomized clinical trial. *J Am Osteopath Assoc* 2005;105(2):57-68.

    Patients received a single dose of intramuscular ketorolac or OMT for acute neck pain. OMT was as effective as intramuscular ketorolac for relieving pain and was more effective for reducing pain. OMT is an acceptable alternative to the medication.

17. Haldeman S, Kohlbeck FJ, McGregor M: Unpredictability of cerebrovascular ischemia associated with cervical spine manipulation therapy: A review of sixty-four cases after cervical spine manipulation. *Spine (Phila Pa 1976)* 2002;27(1):49-55.

18. Seefinger MA, Hruby RJ: Mechanical low back pain, in *Evidence-Based Manual Medicine: A Problem-Oriented Approach*. Philadelphia, PA, WB Saunders, 2007, pp 80-81, 127.

Chapter 11
Interventional Spine Care

Michael DePalma, MD   Ben L. Laplante, DO

Introduction

Painful degenerative and low-velocity traumatic spine disorders account for a large health care expenditure because of the associated disability and the costs of diagnosis and therapy.[1] Most patients can be successfully treated using nonsurgical measures.[2] The term nonsurgical spine care is not descriptive because it does not identify the specific components of care. Decisions on nonsurgical care for a specific patient are not straightforward and do not routinely follow traditional orthopaedic, neurosurgical, physiatric, anesthesiologic, neurologic, or psychiatric principles. Diagnosing and treating a painful spine disorder requires a medical model oriented to the specific disease or tissue injury rather than solely to the symptoms. The evaluating clinician must recognize the altered biomechanics and ergonomics, pathophysiology, and neurophysiology responsible for the spine disorder's signs and symptoms. Physical examination and diagnostic imaging findings must be astutely assessed. All of these data must be evaluated in the correct context to obtain an optimal outcome. An evidence- and knowledge-based algorithmic approach should be used for diagnosing and treating (percutaneously or surgically) a disruptive spine condition.

If the imaging data, patient history, and examination findings are inconclusive or conflicting, a precise, fluoroscopically guided spine procedure can elucidate the source of the symptoms and allow definitive percutaneous treatments to be pursued. If such treatments are insufficient, the completed diagnostic procedures can assist in surgical planning. The usefulness of these percutaneous spine procedures depends on adherence to procedural techniques supported by best available

evidence. Deviation from well-supported technique and misguided use of therapeutic procedures resulting from improper diagnosis can explain the poor performance of certain studied procedures. When strict operational criteria and meticulous technique are applied, diagnostic procedures can reveal the source of chronic low back pain in 90% of patients and the source of chronic neck pain in 80% of patients.[3-5] Definitive treatment aimed at the identified source of symptoms then can be used to reduce symptoms, disability, and the need for collateral health care. This perspective underlies the interventional spine care subspecialty.

Lumbosacral Spine Disorders

Axial Low Back Pain Etiologies

Chronic axial low back pain most commonly arises from nonhealing annular fissures, which are the most prevalent source of low back pain in patients age 55 years or younger.[3,6,7] In patients older than 55 years, the most prevalent source of low back pain is a lumbar facet joint, followed by the sacroiliac joint.[3] The intervertebral disk is the source of symptoms in 40% to 42% of adults with low back pain, the facet joint is the source in 32%, and the sacroiliac joint is the source in 18%[3] (Table 1). The prevalence of kissing spinous processes (Baastrup disease) or fusion hardware–mediated low back pain is estimated to be 2% or 3%, respectively.[3] The precise location of the patient's pain and certain physical examination features can be used to predict the source of the pain and thus suggest the highest yield initial diagnostic procedure. The presence of midline low back pain reduces the probability that the patient's symptoms are facet- or sacroiliac-joint related. Low back pain during sustained hip flexion and pelvic rock suggests that the patient's symptoms are discogenic. Multivariate analyses of predictor variables revealed a 94% probability of discogenic low back pain in patients 55 years or younger whose midline pain is exacerbated by sustained hip flexion[8] (Figure 1).

Discogenic Low Back Pain
Diagnosis
Imaging does not discriminate between painful and nonpainful disks. MRI is relatively insensitive (less than 60%) and nonspecific (false-positive rate, 24%; false-negative rate, 38%), and therefore MRI is not useful

Table 1			
Source of Low Back Pain, by Prevalence and Mean Patient Age			
Source	**Number of Patients (N = 170)**	**Prevalence (95% Confidence Interval)**	**Mean Age, in Years (Standard Deviation) (95% Confidence Interval)**
Intervertebral disk	71	41.8% (34.6%-49.3%)	43.7 (10.3) (41.3-46.1)
Lumbar facet joint	52	30.6% (24.2%-37.9%)	59.6 (13.1) (56.0-63.3)
Sacroiliac joint	31	18.2% (13.2%-24.7%)	61.4 (17.7) (54.9-67.9)
Vertebral insufficiency fracture	5	2.9% (1.3%-6.7%)	79.0 (11.8) (64.3-93.7)
Pelvic insufficiency fracture	3	1.8% (0.6%-5.1%)	71.3 (11.7) (42.2-100.4)
Baastrup disease	3	1.8% (0.6%-5.1%)	75.3 (4.7) (63.6-87.1)
Fusion hardware	5	2.9% (1.3%-6.7%)	59.6 (19.4) (35.4-83.8)

Data from DePalma MJ, Ketchum JM, Saullo T: What is the source of chronic low back pain and does age play a role? *Pain Med* 2011;12:228.

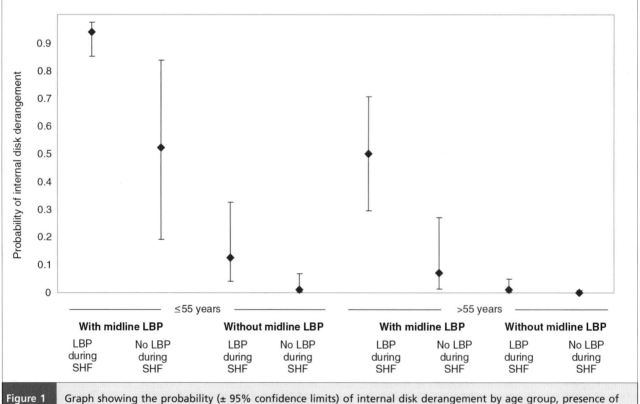

Figure 1	Graph showing the probability (± 95% confidence limits) of internal disk derangement by age group, presence of midline low back pain (LBP), and presence of low back pain during sustained hip flexion (SHF).

for detecting internal disk derangement.[9] High-intensity zone lesions and Modic changes are more predictive of internal disk derangement than disk desiccation, loss of disk height, or herniation. High-intensity zone lesions and moderate to severe Modic type I or II end plate changes are highly specific (79% to 97%), with a positive predictive value of 64% to 87%.[10] A morphologically normal disk on MRI, although relatively unlikely

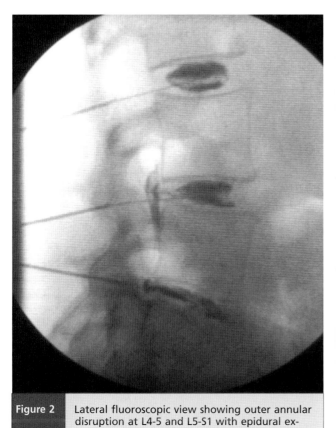

Figure 2 | Lateral fluoroscopic view showing outer annular disruption at L4-5 and L5-S1 with epidural extension at L4-5 when contrast is injected through 22-gauge spinal needles placed in each disk nucleus.

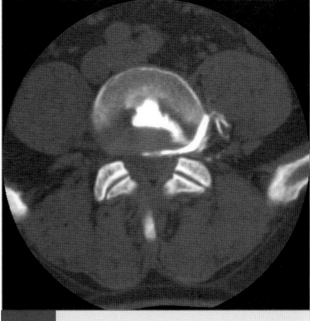

Figure 3 | Postdiskography CT showing a left grade IV annular tear in the L4-5 intervertebral disk (as defined using the modified Dallas diskograph).

to be painful, can contain painful annular fissures.[11] Specific MRI findings of high-intensity zone lesion or Modic changes mean that the involved disks probably are symptomatic. However, provocation lumbar diskography (PLD) traditionally has been performed for confirmation.

Radial annular fissures were first found during the 1940s by intradiskal injection of contrast medium into cadaver intervertebral disks. By the late 1960s, diskography was poised to replace myelography for evaluating axial low back pain in the absence of disk herniation. The growing popularity of PLD was accompanied by growing doubt as to its diagnostic value, however. A study reporting a 37% false-positive rate among prison volunteers was deemed invalid because of poor selection criteria, a high technical failure rate, lack of fluoroscopic guidance, and the use of a known neurotoxic contrast agent.[12] Subsequent evaluation with strict criteria for radiologic abnormality and simultaneous assessment for reproduction of low back pain in asymptomatic individuals revealed a 0% false-positive rate.[12]

Provocation Lumbar Diskography
The purpose of PLD is not to arbitrarily stimulate a disk to produce pain without considering the circumstances under which such pain is elicited. Instead, PLD is intended to determine whether a painful disk con-

tains an annular fissure (Figure 2). For accurately diagnosing internal disk derangement, adherence to strict operational criteria is required: the disk stimulation must produce pain identical or similar to the patient's low back pain, the provoked pain (per patient report) must be more severe than 6 on a 10-point scale, the disk stimulation must reproduce the patient's low back pain at low pressure (less than 50 psi above the opening pressure), stimulation of adjacent disks must not reproduce the pain, and postdiskography CT must reveal a grade III, IV, or V annular fissure in the painful disk[13,14] (Figure 3).

Diskography is a long-standing topic of debate.[15] Opponents argue that PLD is unreliable because of high false-positive rates reported in individuals who were asymptomatic as well as patients with chronic pain who did not have low back pain and patients with a history of somatization disorder. However, these false-positive rates were from studies with small sample sizes, and wide confidence intervals rendered the rates imprecise. In addition, some of these estimates were based on PLD performed without using anatomic control disks or manometric monitoring. A reanalysis of the index data using manometric criteria revealed a clinically acceptable false-positive rate of 10%.[14] Systematic analysis applying strict operational criteria found a false-positive rate of 6% and specificity of 94%.[14]

A 10-year follow-up MRI evaluation found accelerated disk degeneration, Modic changes, and disk herniation in 66% of patients who underwent PLD.[16] These findings shed some light on the long-term risks related to the procedure, but they should be interpreted cau-

2: Nonsurgical Care of the Spine

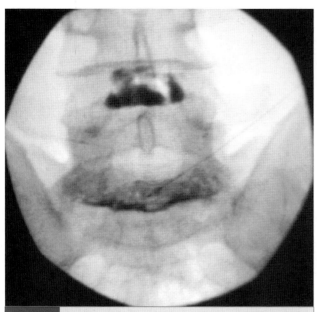

Figure 4 AP fluoroscopic view of a balloon-tipped indwelling catheter anchored in the L5-S1 nucleus. The balloon has been expanded with 0.3 mL of contrast. Local anesthetic of varying pharmacologic duration or placebo can be injected while the patient completes provocative maneuvers.

tiously. The confidence intervals for the proportions of disk degeneration overlapped between the patients who underwent PLD and control subjects, indicating that patients in the two groups were not statistically different. The confidence intervals for disk herniation did not overlap, and therefore, a statistically significant difference seems to exist in the occurrence of disk herniation in patients in the two groups. However, the confidence intervals for patients in each herniation subgroup (broad-based, paracentral, foraminal, and extrusion) did overlap and therefore might not differ between patients in the PLD and control groups. Earlier studies did not find a greater incidence of disk degeneration in patients who had undergone PLD, compared with control subjects.[17] PLD repeated as late as 38 months after the initial procedure led to a 1.3% occurrence of new morphologic intradiskal abnormality.[17] A partial transverse laceration of lamellae fibers, such as occurs with intranuclear placement of the diskography needle, did not progress to a more extensive disruption.

Although surgical fusion outcomes have been improved by the use of PLD, its predictive value has been disputed.[18,19] Only 8 of 30 patients (27%) whose discogenic low back pain was proved by single-level, pressure-controlled diskography met strict criteria for a positive outcome 2 years after fusion surgery.[19] All patients had a presurgical pain score of at least 5 on the 10-point visual analog scale, and 77% had a score higher than 40 on the Oswestry Disability Index. Twenty-four months after surgery, 57% of patients had a score lower than 5 on the visual analog scale, and 73% had a score of 40 or lower on the Oswestry Dis-

ability Index. In other words, most patients had less severe pain, and fewer than one third had a moderate or severe disability 2 years after surgery. No outcome data from the first 12 months after fusion were reported. In the same study, the patients who underwent fusion for unstable spondylolisthesis had even greater improvement. An alternate conclusion based on these data is that single-level 360° fusion is highly effective for treating unstable spondylolisthesis but is less effective for treating discogenic low back pain caused by annular fissures. It is entirely possible that patients with internal disk derangement improved within the first year after fusion but had recurrent low back pain at some point after surgery because of injury to a structure other than the index disk.[20] In another study, patients had a 55% reduction in mean visual analog scale score 6 months after fusion but a statistically significant increase in low back pain during the second year after fusion.[21] Chronic low back pain after fusion may originate in the facet or sacroiliac joints, from adjacent-level internal disk derangement, or from soft-tissue irritation by fusion hardware.[20]

PLD has been found to predict the outcome of fusion. When pressure-controlled manometric diskography was used to isolate highly chemically sensitive disks, significantly better long-term outcomes were achieved with interbody combined fusion than with intertransverse fusion.[18] Patients who did not undergo disk surgery had the least favorable outcome. A separate study found that patients with discogenic low back pain who underwent fusion based on the result of positive PLD using strict criteria were 5 times more likely to return to at least 25% of their daily activities, 3.4 times more likely to return to at least 50% of their daily activities, and 3.3 times more likely to have less low back pain than patients who had positive PLD but did not undergo fusion surgery.[22] Nonsurgical treatment was found to be preferable to fusion in patients with low back pain who had negative PLD.

Analgesic Diskography
A PLD finding that an annular fissure is the source of the patient's pain presumably is confirmed if the pain lessens after intradiskal injection of a local anesthetic. In 80% of painful disks that met positive PLD criteria, low back pain was reduced at least 50% after intradiskal injection of 4% lidocaine.[23] Pain reduction was not statistically significantly different based on the presence of concordant or partially concordant low back pain, one- or two-level painful disks, a negative psychiatric history, or a history of depression. Intradiskal analgesia can be achieved by instilling a local anesthetic within the nucleus, either by direct injection or with a balloon-tipped, small-gauge indwelling catheter (Figure 4).

The predictive usefulness of intradiskal anesthesia or analgesic diskography for the outcome of noninstrumented interbody fusion has been compared with that of PLD.[24] Interbody fusion at levels predicated on the results of intradiskal anesthesia led to a statistically sig-

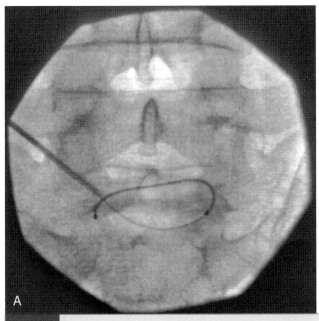
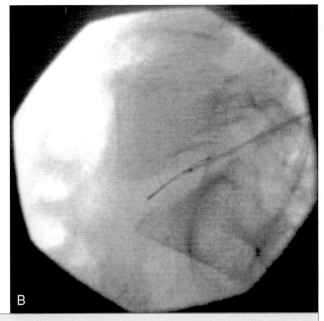

Figure 5   **A,** AP fluoroscopic view of an intradiskal electrothermal annuloplasty catheter threaded into the L5-S1 disk space. **B,** Lateral fluoroscopic view showing placement of the heating element equidistant from the end plates of the L5-S1 disk space.

nificant reduction in low back pain and disability at 1-, 2-, and 3-year follow-up, compared with fusion at levels chosen by PLD.[24] Analgesic diskography needs further evaluation, however. Although analgesic diskography and PLD with strict operational criteria have not been compared, consistent congruence was found between the two diagnostic procedures, and it was concluded that both have face validity when performed using strict guidelines.[25]

Treatment

The percutaneous treatments for lumbar internal disk derangement include strategies to initiate repair of the disk and denervation by heat or chemical neurolytic procedures.

Intradiskal Heating

The application of heat to the injured anulus fibrosus has been evaluated as a means of ablating intradiskal nociceptors and presumably sealing the annular fissure while improving the stiffness of the native collagen. There is no definitive evidence of postheating changes in the mechanical properties of the disk.[26,27] The universal indications for intradiskal therapeutic procedures include low back pain that has persisted at least 6 months despite physical therapy, analgesics, and/or epidural steroid injections; a normal neurologic examination; an absence of neural compressive lesions on MRI; an absence of nonspine conditions that can mimic internal disk derangement; no earlier surgery at the symptomatic intervertebral disk level; and one or two affected levels, as determined by properly performed PLD revealing disk height loss of less than 50%.[28]

Clinical study of intradiskal electrothermal annuloplasty has had positive results[28,29] (Figure 5). Intradiskal electrothermal annuloplasty was more effective than sham treatment for reducing low back pain and disability at 6-month follow-up; however, the number needed to treat to achieve a 75% reduction in low back pain was 5. Although 40% of the patients had a more than 50% reduction in low back pain, 50% had no relief.[29] A second randomized controlled study found no difference between sham treatment and intradiskal electrothermal annuloplasty in a group of patients that included a significant number with a workers' compensation claim; there was no evaluation for psychologic factors or level of baseline disability.[30] Despite its modest therapeutic benefit, the use of intradiskal electrothermal annuloplasty has largely been discontinued.

Transdiskal biacuplasty, in which internal cooling of the intradiskal probes allows greater and more even heat dissipation within annular tissue, recently has been pursued as an alternative to intradiskal electrothermal annuloplasty.[31] The benefits of biacuplasty include minimal disruption of the native tissue architecture; relative ease of electrode placement, compared with threading a flexible heating catheter; and a lower peak disk-heating temperature, allowing better patient tolerance and less risk of stimulating tissue adherence.[27] The pilot data revealed significant improvement in mean low back pain and disability scores after 12 months.[31] A randomized controlled follow-up study is under way.

Intradiskal Neurolytic Procedures

A liquefied neurotoxic agent, presumably following the same tract as PLD contrast dye, in theory can optimally target the nociceptive fibers of the annular fissure. A

2: Nonsurgical Care of the Spine

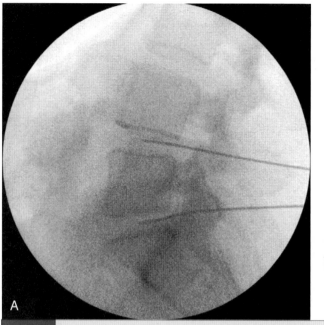
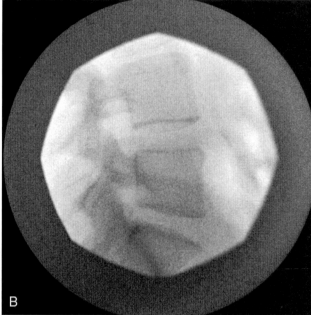

Figure 6 Lateral fluoroscopic views of the L4-5 and L5-S1 intervertebral disks. **A,** Placement of an 18-gauge introducer needle into the nucleus pulposus for injection of 3 mL of fibrin sealant. **B,** The disks after the injection and needle removal.

randomized placebo-controlled study from China recently reported impressive results from the use of methylene blue, a neurotoxic agent that may deactivate a portion of the inflammatory cascade and has been used medicinally for 80 years.[32] Statistically significant improvement in low back pain, disability, patient satisfaction, and analgesic use was observed in patients treated with methylene blue at 6- and 24-month follow-up. Randomized controlled follow-up studies are under way in Australia and Sweden.

Intradiskal Biologic Repair

Cell-based biologic strategies to replace, restore, maintain, or improve the function of injured annular tissue have garnered intense interest.[33,34] Strategies for using intradiskal biologic agents can be grouped into five categories: direct injection of a biologically active factor, modification of the gene expression of resident disk cells in vivo (direct gene therapy), supplementation with autologous implantation of in vitro cultivated and modified cells, stem cell–based gene therapy, and direct repair of annular fissures. Applications in the first four categories aim to deliver biologically active substances to stimulate regeneration or preserve the intradiskal environment. The fifth strategy involves injecting a fibrin sealant to seal the annular tears, stimulate an anabolic state within the disk, and initiate repair of the annular fissure (Figure 6). The nature of the active factor is a function of the molecular mechanisms active within the disk during the stages of degeneration. The appropriateness of each intradiskal agent depends on disk cell biology, disk degeneration stage, and safety concerns. As in PLD, percutaneous delivery of the active agent is

achieved through the posterolateral, parapedicular disk space. Several phase I, II, and III clinical studies are under way to establish the efficacy and safety of intradiskal growth factors, stem cells, and fibrin sealant.[35]

Facet Joint Pain
Diagnosis
Facet joint pain is most likely if a patient with low back pain is at least 55 years old and does not have midline pain.[8] Confirmation that a facet joint is the source of pain requires an appropriate reduction in the patient's index pain after injection of local anesthetic onto the medial branches innervating the joint or into the intra-articular space. Medial branch blockade generally is more appropriate than intra-articular blockade for diagnosis and outcome prediction after medial branch neurotomy (Figure 7). A positive block is defined as reduction of 75% or more in the patient's index low back pain for the duration of the local anesthetic pharmacologic effect. Single diagnostic blocks alone are associated with significant false-positive rates, and dual diagnostic blocks of comparable local anesthetic are required to improve the diagnostic accuracy of the injections.[36] In this scenario, the targeted joint is confirmed as the source of the patient's low back pain if the pain is definitely relieved for at least 2 hours by a short-acting local anesthetic or at least 3 hours by a long-acting local anesthetic. The diagnostic validity of medial branch blocks that adhere to these operational criteria is well documented. Such blocks reliably predict the therapeutic response to medial branch neurotomy and are the gold standard for diagnosing facet joint pain in patients with low back pain[37-39] (Figure 8).

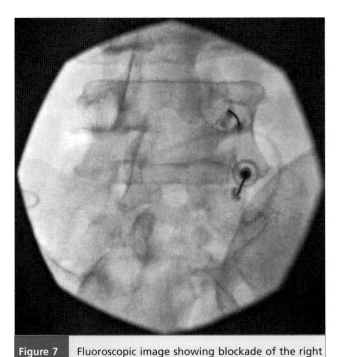

Figure 7 Fluoroscopic image showing blockade of the right L4 medial branch and L5 dorsal ramus. Contrast dispersal at each needle tip is localized to the precise location of the targeted neural element without evidence of intravascular uptake.

Treatment

The percutaneous treatment options for lumbosacral facet joint pain include intra-articular injection of corticosteroids to arrest arthritis-induced inflammation, viscosupplementation to counter the arthritic process, and radiofrequency ablation of the nerve supply to the joint.[40,41]

Intra-articular Injections

Prospective studies have evaluated the efficacy of intra-articular injections of corticosteroid for facet joint pain. Only one study found corticosteroid injections to have value.[40] Six months after receiving one intra-articular steroid injection, 93% of treated patients had a reduction in low back pain; 33% had complete pain relief.[40] In contrast, 53% of patients who received an extra-articular injection had low back pain reduction, but none had complete relief. Diagnostic blocks were not used to determine which joints to treat with intra-articular steroids. Without proper confirmation that the targeted joint was the source of low back pain, a significant number of facet joints may have been erroneously injected. A randomized controlled study found no significant improvement in low back pain 1 and 3 months after one intra-articular steroid injection, but a statistically significant improvement was found at 6 months.[41] The authors concluded that intra-articular steroid injections were not effective for relieving facet joint pain because of the absence of improvement at 1 and 3 months, despite the improvement at 6 months. The improvement observed at 6 months can be attrib-

uted to the intervention, in contrast to any improvement observed in the control subjects, which reflected the natural history of the condition. Although the patients were selected using intra-articular diagnostic blocks, the blocks were not validated, each patient received only one diagnostic injection, and a lenient post-block pain reduction criterion of 50% was used. A 50% reduction of index low back pain is not diagnostically reliable.[42] A clinical study funded by the International Spine Intervention Society is under way to determine the treatment effect of intra-articular steroid injections for lumbar facet joint pain, using an appropriate diagnostic methodology.

Viscosupplementation

Viscosupplementation is an alternative intra-articular facet joint treatment that attempts to treat the arthritic condition itself. Only one study has been completed, using dual local anesthetic blocks. This study found significant improvement in low back pain, disability, bodily function, range of motion, and sitting tolerance at 6-month follow-up but not at 12-month follow-up.[43] Fifteen patients received two injections of hylan G-F 20, including seven patients who received a total of three injections. A transient S1 radiculopathy developed in one patient who had diabetes after injection of the L5-S1 facet joint, but no other adverse events occurred. These pilot data support the pursuit of rigorous controlled studies to better determine the efficacy and safety of viscosupplementation for facet joint pain.

Medial Branch Neurotomy

Direct medial branch laceration and coagulation were early techniques with reported good results for treating facet joint pain. Subsequent dissection studies revealed that these techniques did not adequately reach the neural elements innervating the facet joint. The optimal approach for ablating the medial branches, as validated by cadaver dissection, is to place the heating element parallel to the exposed course of the nerve[44] (Figure 9). The volume of heat dissipation from the probe depends on the girth of the heating element, and large-gauge probes therefore should be used.[38,39] Acceptable probe placement can be achieved by meticulous attention to key radiographic landmarks.[38,39]

A randomized controlled study of radiofrequency medial branch neurotomy did not find significant low back pain relief beyond 6 weeks, but an immediate significant response to the active treatment was observed, compared with sham treatment.[45] The radiofrequency probes were placed perpendicular to the path of the targeted medial branches. Although the correct neural element was targeted, the tangential placement (Figure 9, A) of the heating element only partially coagulated the nerve, and therefore the immediate but short-lived improvement is not surprising.

An anatomically correct technique (Figure 9, B) was used for radiofrequency medial branch neurotomy in patients with low back pain who were properly selected

2: Nonsurgical Care of the Spine

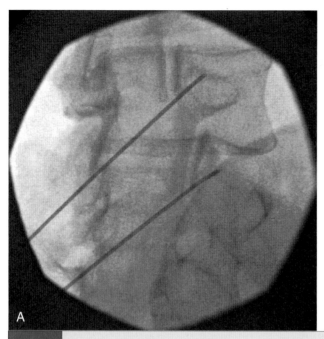
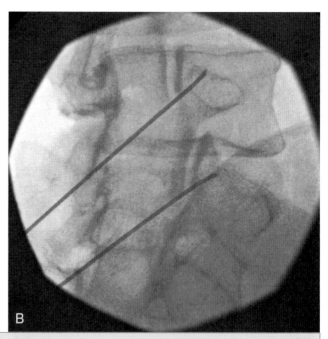

Figure 8 Fluoroscopic views of the patient whose fluorographic image is shown in Figure 7, showing neurotomy of the right L4 medial branch and L5 dorsal ramus. **A,** The initial lesion was created with the curved active needle tip in the groove between the articular process and transverse process. **B,** The second lesion was created by rotating the curved active needle tip cephalad at L5 and withdrawing a few millimeters at S1. Note the upward curve of the probe at L5 and the slightly withdrawn position at S1. (Panel A reproduced with permission from North RA, Shipley J, Taylor R, et al: Generating evidence on spinal cord stimulation for failed back surgery syndrome. *Clin J Pain* 2008;24:757-758. Panel B courtesy of Paul Dreyfuss, MD, Bellevue, WA.)

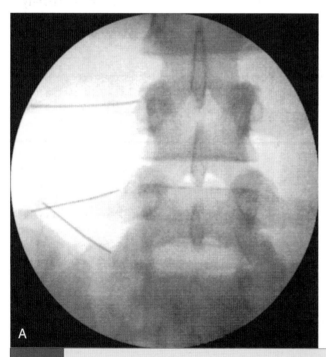
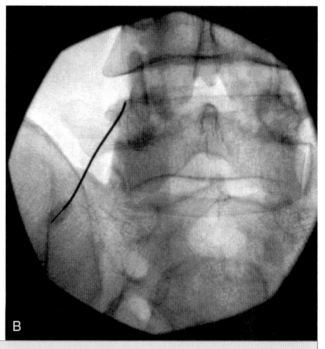

Figure 9 **A,** AP fluoroscopic view of the L4-S1 spine segments in which the neurotomy probes have been placed perpendicular to the target nerve located along the L4, L5, and S1 superior articular pillars. **B,** AP fluoroscopic view of the L5-S1 spine segment in which a radiofrequency probe has been placed parallel to the course of the left L4 medial branch at the junction of the left L5 superior articular process and transverse process. (Reproduced with permission from Bhargava A: Fusion hardware mediated low back pain, in DePalma M, ed: *iSpine: Evidence-Based Interventional Spine Care.* New York, NY, Demos Medical, 2011, pp 151-155.)

using dual diagnostic medial branch blocks. In this uncontrolled clinical study, 80% of the patients had a minimum 60% reduction in low back pain, and 60% had at least 80% relief 12 months after the treatment.[38] This study did not prove the efficacy of radiofrequency medial branch neurotomy, but it did show that this treatment can be successful when the proper procedural technique, as supported by anatomic evidence, is used in properly selected patients.

The first randomized controlled study of radiofrequency medial branch neurotomy in patients accurately diagnosed with lumbar facet joint pain found that pain, disability, and range of motion were significantly improved at 6 months, with no adverse effects.[39] These findings corroborate the earlier work and provide evidence of the efficacy of radiofrequency medial branch neurotomy. This treatment can be reliably used in carefully selected patients with low back pain. Relief of symptoms can be expected to last at least 6 to 12 months.[39,45] Low back pain can recur, however, as the medial branches regenerate. The treatment can be repeated, if necessary, with the expectation of similar pain improvement.

Sacroiliac Joint Pain

Diagnosis
Constellations of certain physical examination findings can help predict the existence of a painful sacroiliac joint, which can be confirmed by fluoroscopically guided intra-articular injection or extra-articular lateral sensory branch blockade with local anesthetic.[47,48] Diagnostic sacroiliac joint blocks have not been well validated or systematically studied for their predictive value relative to treatment interventions. Although prevalence studies estimate that sacroiliac joint pain represents 19% of chronic low back pain, its prevalence increases with older patient age and after lumbosacral fusion.[3,21]

Single intra-articular sacroiliac joint blocks are associated with a significant false-positive rate. The usefulness of diagnostic sacroiliac joint blocks is impaired by the risk of several technical difficulties; these include extra-articular extravasation, which anesthetizes the neural elements; insufficient dispersal of the local anesthetic within the joint cavity; and discomfort from the injection itself, masking postinjection improvement. Extravasation of local anesthetic can spread to the lumbosacral plexus through an aperture in the ventral capsule dorsally toward the sacral foramen or, less commonly, cephalad toward the L5 spinal nerve. Injecting small volumes of local anesthetic (no more than 2 mL) and fluoroscopically monitoring the spread of intra-articular injection of contrast can minimize the likelihood of local anesthetic escaping from the sacroiliac joint or generating a false-positive response. If the patient's low back pain is reduced by 75% for 1 to 8 hours on separate occasions after injection of lidocaine and bupivacaine, intra-articular corticosteroids will provide lasting relief.[49] The value of such diagnostic injections in predicting treatment success after sacroiliac joint fusion has not been assessed.

Blockade of the sacroiliac joint's neural innervation also can be used to block a putatively painful joint and is less susceptible to the technical pitfalls of intra-articular injections.[48] This strategy also may be appropriate for identifying patients with low back pain who will have a good response to radiofrequency neurotomy of the sacroiliac joint lateral sensory branches. Although this technique appears to effectively anesthetize the joint, it may be less successful for reducing painful intra-articular sacroiliac joint pathology.[48]

Treatment
The traditional percutaneous treatment of sacroiliac joint pain is intra-articular corticosteroid injections, with the relatively recent addition of radiofrequency ablation of the sacral lateral sensory branches.

Intra-articular Injections
An initial randomized controlled study enrolled patients with a diagnosis of sacroiliac joint pain (based on history and physical examination findings) and a history of seronegative spondyloarthropathy.[50] The patients who underwent fluoroscopically guided injection of intra-articular corticosteroid had significant improvement in low back pain, compared with those who received saline. Although these results support a role for intra-articular corticosteroid injections in spondyloarthropathic sacroiliac joint pain, they may not apply to patients with nonrheumatologic low back pain.

A retrospective review provided preliminary evidence that intra-articular corticosteroids are beneficial for sacroiliac joint pain.[51] Thirty-one well-selected patients were diagnosed with sacroiliac joint pain based on history, examination, and 80% reduction in low back pain after a single diagnostic intra-articular injection. The patients underwent an average of 2.1 injections and had significant improvement in low back pain and disability at a mean 20.6-month follow-up. Despite the inherent weakness of the retrospective methodology, this study found a treatment benefit warranting more rigorous study. A more recent prospective study included 39 patients with sacroiliac joint pain diagnosed on the basis of two intra-articular injections (lidocaine and bupivacaine) that provided 1 to 8 hours of 75% pain relief.[49] Triamcinolone was injected concurrently with each local anesthetic (total injected volume, 2 mL). In 26 of the 39 patients, the result was a reduction in low back pain of more than 50%, lasting 12 to 60 weeks (mean, 37 weeks). Eight of the 26 patients required a third injection. Thirteen patients had short-lived improvement (mean, 4 weeks) and did not undergo additional injections. Univariate analysis revealed that short-term pain relief was significantly associated with a history of lumbar or lumbosacral fusion. Of the 12 patients with a history of fusion, 5 (42%) responded well to the injections, compared with 21 of the 27 patients without fusion (78%).

Sacroiliac Joint Neurotomy

Radiofrequency denervation of the sacroiliac joint may be a viable treatment for recalcitrant sacroiliac joint pain, particularly after lumbosacral fusion. Although application of radiofrequency energy to ablate the neural innervation of the sacroiliac joint was first reported a decade ago, it entailed intra-articular placement of radiofrequency probes and had a limited effect. Placement of the heating elements adjacent and parallel to the innervating nerves makes more strategic sense than intra-articular positioning. A later report described an alternate technique based on dissection of cadaver pelves to identify the courses of the lateral sensory branches and correlate them with fluoroscopic landmarks of the sacrum.[52] A retrospective review of 14 patients with low back pain who were treated after positive dual diagnostic periarticular sacroiliac joint blocks found that 64% had more than 50% pain relief lasting at least 6 months. A sensory stimulation–guided neurotomy technique was used to identify the targeted sensory nerves. One third of successfully treated patients reported complete pain relief.[52] Sacroiliac joint neurotomy has drawbacks related to technical demands, time consumption, and the necessity for the patient to distinguish dissimilar sensory stimulation and concordant nociception.

Cooled radiofrequency ablation is a relatively new, less demanding treatment modality that maintains a 60°C tissue temperature immediately adjacent to the cooled electrode while the target tissue is heated to 75°C, thus producing a larger lesion diameter. Greater heat dissipation provides a greater lesion depth, increases the distance from the nearby nerve root, and results in less collateral tissue trauma. Cooled radiofrequency denervation of the L4-S3 lateral sensory branches was compared with sham treatment in 28 patients diagnosed with sacroiliac joint pain by rigorous standards.[53] The patients treated with neurotomy had significant improvement in low back pain, functional capacity, and medication use at 6-month follow-up. The median duration of pain relief was 7.9 months. At 6-month follow-up, 57% reported pain relief, in comparison with 0% of the control subjects.[53]

Baastrup Disease

Normal aging-related intervertebral disk degeneration leads to increased facet joint loading and arthropathy. Approximation and eventual hypertrophy of opposing spinous processes can ensue, leading to osteophytosis and neoarthrosis, with or without eventual bursa formation.[54] This potentially painful pseudoarticulation, first described 80 years ago, often is called Baastrup disease. The intervening interspinous ligament can become compromised, innervated, and a source of low back pain. Baastrup disease was found in 1.8% of patients with low back pain who underwent diagnostic spine procedures (95% confidence interval, 0.6–5.1; mean age, 75 years).[3] A patient older than 70 years with strictly midline low back pain aggravated by standing or walking may have Baastrup disease or an injury of the interspinous ligament.[3] The clinical suspicion may be confirmed by symptom alleviation with fluoroscopically guided injection of local anesthetic between the putatively painful spinous processes.[3] Subsequent injection with corticosteroid may provide lasting relief and is an attractive treatment option for interspinous ligament bursitis. Recalcitrant symptoms can be treated using radiofrequency ablation of the bilateral medial branches innervating the affected segmental levels.

Soft-Tissue Irritation by Posterior Fusion Hardware

Fusion hardware–mediated pain can occur in a patient with an instrumented posterior fusion who has paramidline low back pain that can be elicited by single-digit palpation over the hardware.[55] So-called late surgical site pain of unknown etiology, defined as pain around the site of operation beginning at least 6 months after implantation, may be a common reason for reoperation. The symptoms are relatively common in patients with a large spine implant. The precise cause may involve metal allergy, tissue reaction to particulate debris, or low-grade infection in connection with debris. Corrosion, metallic debris, tissue discoloration, and bursa formation have been observed intraoperatively around spine implants.[56] Histologic examination has revealed acute and chronic inflammation with granuloma formation.[57]

Fluoroscopically guided, contrast-confirmed injection of local anesthetic can help identify hardware-related low back pain[3] (Figure 10). After two diagnostic injections with local anesthetics and a placebo injection, a 2.9% prevalence of hardware-related low back pain (95% confidence interval, 1.3%–6.7%) was observed in patients with a mean age slightly younger than 60 years.[3] A stringent diagnostic blockade protocol was used because the remedy for such patients is surgical removal of the hardware.[58]

Lumbosacral Radiculopathy

Lumbosacral radiculopathy is a neurophysiologic condition in which nerve root fibers are hypofunctional, as reflected by reduced muscle stretch reflexes, myotomal weakness, and sensory deficits. Lumbosacral radicular pain represents a hyperexcitable state in which sensory fiber irritation is manifested as pain. The patient's constellation of symptoms usually involves both radicular pain and radiculopathy. Discerning between these two pathophysiologic states is important for the choice of an optimal treatment intervention. Herniation of the intervertebral disk nucleus pulposus is a common cause, especially in a young or middle-aged adult. Radicular signs and symptoms related to spinal stenosis may develop in an older adult. Both scenarios to some extent involve nerve root tension, compression, and inflammation.

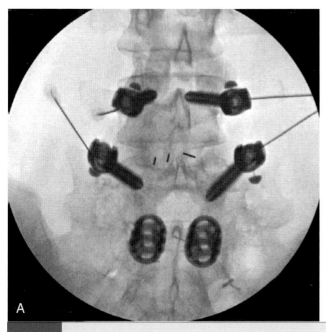 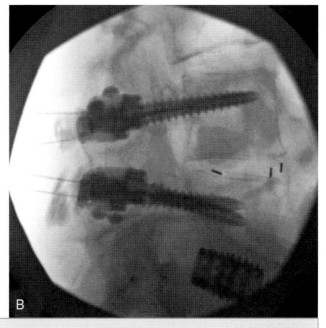

Figure 10 **A,** AP fluoroscopic view showing a needle position over the posterior margin of fusion hardware pedicle screws. **B,** Lateral fluoroscopic view showing contrast over the posterior portions of the pedicle screws after a local anesthetic injection.

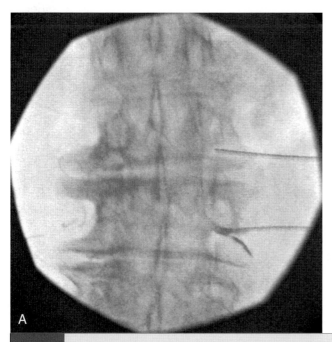 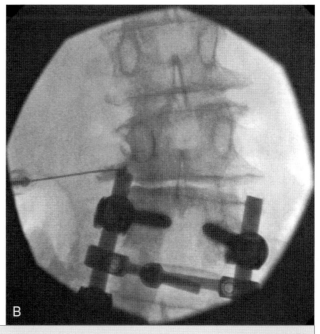

Figure 11 AP fluoroscopic views of selective nerve root blocks at right L4 (**A**) and left L2 adjacent to a previous decompression and fusion (**B**).

Diagnosis

Electrodiagnostic evaluation allows the physician to assess the neurophysiologic correlate to morphologic abnormalities and is an extension of the physical examination. Astute electrodiagnostic testing can rule out other neurologic diagnoses (plexopathy, peripheral neuropathy, entrapment neuropathy, motor neuron dis-

ease), confirm the involved nerve root level, determine the severity of the nerve root injury, and provide prognostic information.[46] Electrodiagnostic studies complement MRI findings in diagnosing lumbosacral radiculopathy.

If electrodiagnostic data are inconclusive, selective blockade of a spine nerve root by injecting a small vol-

2: Nonsurgical Care of the Spine

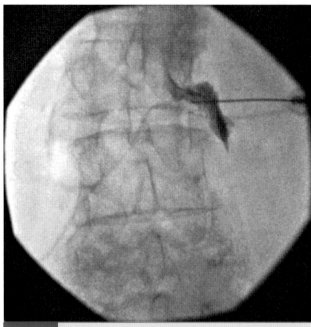

Figure 12 AP fluoroscopic view showing a right L3-4 transforaminal epidural injection of corticosteroid instilled along the exiting L3 root and extending cephalad within the anterior epidural space.

ume of local anesthetic may be used to confirm the involved level (Figure 11). The diagnostic specificity of a selective nerve root block (SNRB) ranges from 87% to 100%.[59-61] In a 1973 study, a corroborative lesion was intraoperatively detected after a positive diagnostic SNRB in 13 of 15 patients (87%).[61] Another study reported good to excellent relief of radicular leg pain after unsuccessful back surgery in 16 patients who had both a positive diagnostic SNRB and a corroborative lesion.[60] Subsequent prospective studies generated similar specificity estimates.[59] In 1993, a corroborative surgical lesion was found in 100% of patients after a positive diagnostic SNRB; specificity of 90% and positive predictive value of 95% were reported with negative diagnostic SNRBs at levels free of radiologic evidence of neurocompressive lesions;[59] the actual positive predictive value may have been 70% to 95% because several patients refused surgical intervention.

The probability of a true-positive result in the presence of disease reflects a test's sensitivity. For diagnostic usefulness, a clinical test must be capable of detecting disease at a rate at least equal to that of other available tests. The sensitivity of diagnostic SNRB has not been rigorously studied. In the 1993 study, a sensitivity of 100% was recorded for diagnostic SNRBs.[59] A retrospective comparison found 99% sensitivity for diagnostic SNRBs, in contrast to 24% and 38% rates of correct identification for myelography and electromyography, respectively.[62] The criteria for determining a positive or negative electrodiagnostic study were not disclosed. If the sensory afferent axon fibers are prefer-

entially affected, rather than motor fibers, electrodiagnostic examination may not determine the segment involved. With S1 involvement, however, H-reflexes will reflect sensory fiber dysfunction despite the absence of motor fiber injury. An asymmetric delay of 1 ms or more in H-reflex latency in the symptomatic limb indicates an S1 radiculopathy.[46]

Since its inception, MRI has shown sensitivity in depicting morphologic spine abnormalities. Determining the clinical significance of these abnormalities requires a complementary diagnostic test of high specificity. Diagnostic SNRBs have great value in confirming whether an MRI abnormality is the patient's pain generator if the symptoms and MRI findings conflict or there is more than one MRI abnormality.[59] Most available studies antedate the routine use of MRI, but several studies have investigated the role of diagnostic SNRB in patients with a complex spine condition. The value of diagnostic SNRBs was established 40 years ago for preoperative evaluation of patients with clinical signs of nerve root irritation but negative imaging studies. Diagnostic SNRB compares favorably with other diagnostic testing modalities (myelography, electromyelography, CT, MRI) for detecting an involved nerve root. The need for decompressive surgery can thus be limited to the clinically affected root, despite imaging evidence of multilevel pathology. Diagnostic SNRBs are valuable in identifying otherwise undetected disk herniations, the symptomatic level in multilevel disk herniations, the primary pain generator in so-called spine-hip syndrome, root irritation in spondylolisthesis, the symptomatic level in multilevel stenosis or anomalous spine segmentation, and the symptomatic root in patients with postoperative fibrosis.

Intrinsic hip joint pathology can mimic upper lumbar radicular pain or somatically referred pain from the lumbar intervertebral disks. The response to diagnostic intra-articular hip injections was retrospectively reviewed in 47 patients with radiographically confirmed hip osteoarthritis.[63] Twenty-four patients had a positive diagnostic block response and subsequent pain relief after total hip replacement. Three of the remaining 23 patients achieved pain relief after total hip arthroplasty 2 years later. The authors concluded that intra-articular hip joint injection of local anesthetic is a valuable diagnostic tool, with calculated sensitivity of 88% and specificity of 100%.[63]

Treatment
Epidural Steroid Injections
Investigation of the optimal route for delivering epidural steroids revealed that interlaminar injections are no more effective than sham injections and that caudal epidural steroid injections are no more effective than injections of local anesthetic alone.[64] Transforaminal epidural steroid injection (TFESI) was found to effectively reduce lumbar radicular pain after a mean 1.8 injections[65] (Figure 12). Critical review of published studies evaluating the efficacy and safety of TFESI found

moderate supporting evidence, although the evidence related to lumbar radicular pain is conflicting. Initial observational studies revealed a surgery-sparing effect or 50% pain relief in more than 70% of treated patients.[65-67] Although TFESI outperformed interlaminar epidural steroid injection for reducing radicular pain and disability, it was no better than transforaminal injection of local anesthetic alone.[68]

A recent prospective randomized study compared the efficacy of TFESI to transforaminal injection of local anesthetic alone, transforaminal injection of normal saline, intramuscular injection of steroid, or intramuscular injection of normal saline in 150 patients with chronic or acute symptoms as well as moderate to severe pain and disability.[69] One month after treatment with one injection, the proportion of patients who had more than 50% pain relief, significant improvement in function and disability, and reduced use of other health care was significantly greater with TFESI than the other treatments. A treatment effect for TFESI was found, with a number needed to treat of 3. One every four patients treated with TFESI retained sufficient relief at 12 months to avoid surgery.[70] Many patients were found to have relief for more than 12 months, although the study was not designed to measure longevity of treatment effect or the value of multiple injections. A follow-up investigation is under development. TFESI led to long-term (12-month) reduction in radicular pain and disability as well as improved walking and standing tolerance in patients with central canal stenosis. Interlaminar epidural steroid injection appears to be similarly effective for reducing radicular pain caused by lumbar spinal stenosis.

Facet Joint Cyst Rupture
Radicular pain caused by a juxtafacet joint cyst (an intraspinal degenerative cyst emanating anterior or anteromedially from the facet joint) has been treated percutaneously by intra-articular facet joint injection of steroids or by aspiration or rupture.[71] Symptomatic improvement obviating the need for surgical excision of the juxtafacet joint cyst occurs in one third of treated patients.[71,72] A retrospective review of 101 patients found statistically significant improvement in pain and disability after juxtafacet joint cyst wall distension and rupture; 46% of treated patients improved sufficiently to avoid surgery.[72] The retrospective questioning of patients as to baseline low back pain and radicular pain possibly led to an overestimate of the treatment effect, however. Prospective follow-up study is warranted to verify the therapeutic role of rupture in treating juxtafacet joint cyst–induced radicular pain.

Percutaneous Diskectomy
Percutaneous strategies can be used to treat lumbar radicular pain caused by focal disk herniation, which is a reversible morphologic abnormality. The term chemonucleolysis describes the injection of chymopapain, a protease derived from the latex of the papaya tree, into the nucleus of herniated intervertebral disks. Chemonucleolysis has become the most extensively evaluated and regulated minimally invasive disk decompression intervention for radicular pain caused by a focal disk protrusion. Chemonucleolysis is superior to and more durable than placebo for reducing radicular pain and disability. Level I evidence supports the short- and long-term efficacy of chemonucleolysis in treating lumbosacral radiculopathy caused by a contained disk herniation.[73] Level II and III evidence suggests that chemonucleolysis is as effective as open surgical diskectomy.[74] Although strong evidence shows the efficacy of chemonucleolysis, it has fallen out of favor because of concerns over catastrophic complications, the most significant of which are transverse myelitis and anaphylactic shock.

Mechanical and thermal technologies were explored beginning in the 1980s.[75] Automated percutaneous lumbar diskectomy did not have favorable results in comparison with conventional open diskectomy and did not become popular as a minimally invasive percutaneous diskectomy technique. A small-gauge mechanical diskectomy probe was approved for clinical use in 2001 (Figure 13). The usefulness of thermal disk decompression using laser wavelengths has not been substantiated by rigorous studies. Nonthermal radiofrequency energy application (nucleoplasty) to decompress a focal herniation was studied as a means of reducing the risk of thermal injury with laser. Initial observational studies supported the benefit of nucleoplasty. A randomized study found that nucleoplasty produced a more significant reduction in radicular pain and disability than TFESI 6 and 12 months after treatment.[76] A prospective audit found a significant reduction in radicular pain and high rates of patient-reported improvement in function, satisfaction, and analgesic use after nucleoplasty.[77] The more recently developed percutaneous diskectomy techniques have not been compared with open surgical diskectomy.

Minimally Invasive Decompression
A recently developed device (*mild;* Vertos Medical, Aliso Viejo, CA) for decompressing the posterior epidural space to treat radicular pain caused by central canal stenosis uses a 5.1-mm trochar for access and a bone rongeur to remove a small portion of the ipsilateral lamina and buckled ligamentum flavum. Preliminary findings suggest that this technique is safe and therapeutic. Prospective observational pilot studies found statistically significant improvement in radicular pain and disability at 6-week follow-up of 75 patients with lumbar spinal stenosis.[78] Additional prospective studies are under way.

Neuromodulation
Spinal cord stimulation relies on the gate-control theory of pain, in which exogenous electrical stimulation obstructs the transmission of impulses that relay nociceptive signals to the brain. By selectively depolarizing large-fiber (A-β) afferents, neuromodulation closes the

2: Nonsurgical Care of the Spine

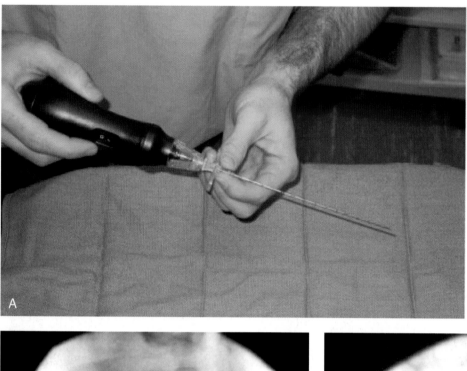
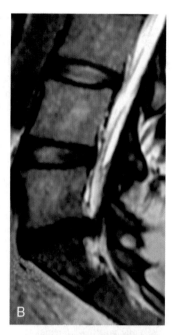
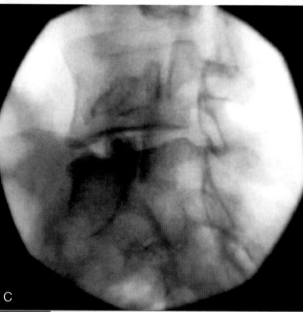
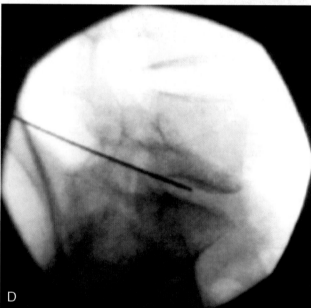

Figure 13   **A,** Photograph of a battery-powered, auger-tipped probe and introducer cannula. **B,** Baseline sagittal T2-weighted MRI showing a left posterolateral broad-based L5-S1 protrusion effacing the traversing left S1 nerve root. The cannula allows intranuclear placement of the probe for removal of nuclear material adjacent to the herniation. **C,** Left lateral–oblique fluoroscopic view showing a 17-gauge introducer cannula entering the left posterolateral L5-S1 disk space. **D,** Lateral fluoroscopic view showing placement of the introducer needle within the posterior one third to one half of the L5-S1 disk space.

gate through which pain sensations pass from the dorsal horn in the spinal cord to the brain without causing undesired motor stimulation. Since the use of a spinal cord stimulator implant was first reported in 1967, neuromodulation has evolved into an advanced technology. The early procedures were open, but percutaneous implantation using an epidural introducer needle was reported in 1974. Multicontact percutaneous leads, effective anchors to reduce lead migration, more

effective programming constructs, smaller and rechargeable generators, multicolumn paddle leads, and physician education were developed during the ensuing three decades.

The use of a spinal cord stimulator was found to reduce low back pain and radicular pain and improve quality of life, functional capacity, and level of satisfaction in patients who underwent lumbar surgery (diskectomy, laminectomy, foraminotomy, or fusion), in

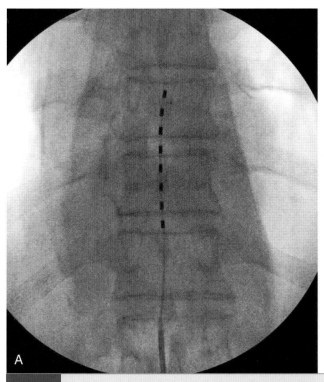
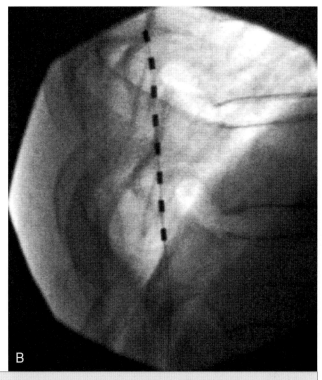

Figure 14 **A,** AP fluoroscopic view showing final positioning of an eight-contact temporary spinal cord stimulation trial lead. The patient had optimal coverage of recurrent left lower limb L5 radicular pain resulting from L5-S1 foraminal stenosis, years after posterolateral fusion. Electromyography did not indicate ongoing root injury, and no instability was seen on motion radiographs. **B,** Lateral fluoroscopic view showing lead placement in the posterior epidural space.

comparison with conventional medical management using physical and psychologic rehabilitation, oral analgesics, nerve root blocks or epidural steroid injections, and chiropractic care.[79] In comparison with repeat spine surgery, a spinal cord stimulator was found to be more successful for reducing postoperative low back pain and radicular pain. In most patients, a spinal cord stimulator eliminated the need for reoperation[80] (Figure 14). A spinal cord stimulator reduced ongoing health care expenditure related to chronic neuropathic pain conditions such as recurrent postoperative low back pain and radicular pain.[81] Retrospective evidence shows that patients with lumbar spinal stenosis have a reduction in radicular pain and oral analgesic use as well as improvement in function.[82]

Depression and pain-catastrophizing behavior can impair the treatment outcome in a patient who is psychologically and physically distressed. A severe psychiatric disorder can impede a patient's ability to discern whether the symptoms originate in the spine condition or in anxiety, depression, or another pathology.

Cervical Spine Disorders

Axial Cervical Pain Etiologies
Chronic neck pain most commonly emanates from a cervical facet joint.[4] Cervical facet joint pain occurs in 36% to 60% of patients with chronic neck pain and can be caused by trauma such as a motor vehicle crash.[5] The most commonly involved joint level is C5-C6, followed by C2-C3.[83] The presence of posterior occipital headaches after trauma strongly suggests upper cervical (C2-C3) joint pain. A combination of facet joint pain and discogenic neck pain occurs in 41% of patients with whiplash injury; facet joint pain or discogenic pain alone occurs in 20% of these patients.[84] The estimated prevalence of isolated cervical discogenic neck pain is 16% to 45%.[4] Morphologic abnormalities on imaging studies are not consistently reliable for detecting painful cervical intervertebral disks or facet joints. Pain referral patterns are consistent and reliable for predicting the segmental source of neck pain, but specific cervical spine structures can be identified as the source of symptoms only with precisely controlled diagnostic procedures.

Cervical Facet Joint Pain
Diagnosis
A putatively painful cervical facet joint can be proved to be the source of symptoms by selective blockade using an injection of a small aliquot of anesthetic onto the corresponding medial branches (Figure 15). Anesthetization of the medial branches innervating the C3-C4 through C6-C7 facet joints predicts whether the patient will respond to definitive treatment with medial branch

neurotomy. The third occipital nerve innervates the C2-C3 joint and is the target of the diagnostic blockade to assess this joint. Single blocks carry a false-positive rate of 27%.[85] Subsequent confirmatory diagnostic me-dial branch blocks should be completed to minimize the false-positive rate. A positive block is defined as re-duction of the patient's index pain by 75% or more for the duration of each anesthetic. Two positive medial branch blocks reliably predict a positive response to treatment with medial branch neurotomy.[86]

Treatment

Intra-articular injection of corticosteroid is no more ef-fective than injection of local anesthetic alone for pro-viding durable pain relief. Application of radiofre-quency energy denatures the protein components of the medial branches by disrupting hydrogen bonds and nonpolar hydrophobic interactions to disrupt the me-dial branches' capacity to convey nociceptive im-pulses.[86,87] Radiofrequency neurotomy is extremely ef-fective for reducing facet joint pain in a well-selected patient who has undergone dual diagnostic medial branch blocks (Figure 16). A randomized placebo-controlled study found a median duration of 263 days until 50% of the index pain returned, compared with 8 days in patients who received a placebo.[86] A patient's active litigation status did not adversely affect the out-come.[86] Subsequent studies found a durable treatment effect, but a randomized controlled study did not find a treatment effect with medial branch neurotomy in pa-tients with cervicogenic headache.[88] However, the study protocol was methodologically flawed. None of the pa-tients reported significant relief in index neck pain after diagnostic blocks; therefore, the structure targeted for treatment was not definitively confirmed as the source of symptoms.

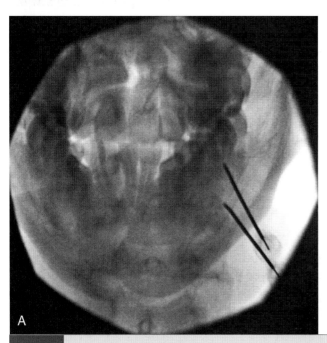

| Figure 15 | Lateral fluoroscopic view showing two 25-gauge needles in position over the left C3 and C4 ar-ticular pillars to anesthetize the left C3 and C4 medial branches. The purpose is to assess the left C3-C4 facet joint as the source of the pa-tient's neck pain after C4-C6 anterior diskec-tomy and fusion. |

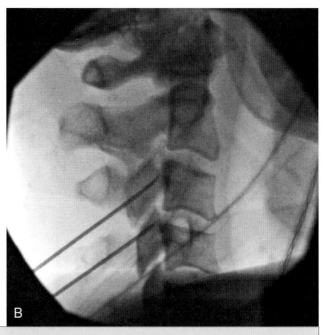

| Figure 16 | AP (A) and lateral (B) fluoroscopic views of a right C3 and C4 medial branch neurotomy. Placement of the C4 radiofrequency probe was predicated on selective blockade of the C4 medial branch. |

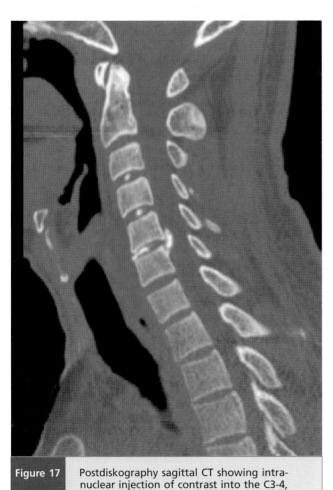

Figure 17 Postdiskography sagittal CT showing intranuclear injection of contrast into the C3-4, C4-5, and C5-6 intervertebral disks. Stimulation of the C5-6 extrusion produced concordant neck pain. There was no baseline neurologic compromise. No neurologic symptoms developed after disk injection.

Cervical Discogenic Pain

Diagnosis

Advanced cervical spine imaging cannot reliably detect a painful cervical disk.[89,90] Disk stimulation has been explored as a diagnostic tool to confirm imaging findings related to painful cervical disks. Cervical diskography was first reported more than 40 years ago to have an unacceptable rate of false-positive responses. This initial report was refuted, however, because an irritating contrast agent was used, image guidance was not used, and the injection needles may not have been placed entirely within the disk nucleus. A retrospective review evaluated the role of diskography in predicting surgical outcomes in patients with axial neck pain who underwent anterior cervical diskectomy and fusion.[91] The authors concluded that surgical outcomes are improved when the levels indicated by diskography are incorporated into the surgical construct; however, the study disregarded 21 of 87 patients who did not undergo diskography, and 15 patients were lost to follow-up. Using a stringent definition, the cervical diskogra-

phy indications of a symptomatic disk have a positive likelihood ratio of 2.6, which does not strongly predict an acceptable outcome.[92] Cervical diskography is useful in presurgical planning, however, because it indicates disks that should not be included in the surgical construct. More rigorous research is necessary to assign a definitive diagnostic value to cervical diskography (Figure 17).

Cervical Radicular Pain

Treatment

Interlaminar Injections

Instillation of corticosteroid into the epidural space can sufficiently alleviate the inflammation irritating the nerve root and/or stabilize its neural membrane, thus quelling the symptoms. Interlaminar epidural steroid injection (ILESI) can be performed without radiographic guidance by relying on tactile feedback from the tissue planes encountered by the needle tip. Although nonguided cervical ILESI has been performed for some time, in trained hands there is a 53% false-positive rate for epidural needle tip placement.[93] Confirmation using image guidance and contrast improves the needle placement.[93] The posterior epidural space is widest at the C6-7 and C7-T1 segmental levels, and cervical ILESI should be performed at these levels after MRI establishes adequate epidural space.[94]

Observational studies found a reduction in cervical radicular pain with ILESI over different time intervals.[95] A randomized controlled study compared ILESI to posterior cervical intramuscular steroid injection (IMSI) in 50 patients, 8 of whom were lost to follow-up.[95] The mean duration of baseline pain was 15 months. After a mean 2.5 injections, 76% of patients treated with ILESI and 36% of patients treated with IMSI reported a 50% or greater reduction in baseline pain at 1 week; 68% of patients treated with ILESI and 12% of patients treated with IMSI reported 50% or greater pain relief at 1 year. Most patients who underwent ILESI had more than 75% pain relief, but only 6% of those treated with IMSI reported 75% pain relief. Overall, at 1 year, the patients treated with ILESI had a statistically significant improvement in cervical range of motion, reduction in analgesic consumption, and increased work capacity compared with those treated with IMSI. This study is evidence that epidural instillation of corticosteroid is effective and necessary, in comparison with nonspecific intra-muscular application of a systemic steroid.

Transforaminal Injections

Transforaminal injections are specific to the targeted nerve root and reliably deposit injectate within the intraforaminal conduit housing the exiting nerve root. Therefore, cervical transforaminal injections can help identify the symptomatic nerve root and assign clinical meaning to a morphologic abnormality seen on diagnostic imaging. During presurgical planning, cervical transforaminal injections can allow a reduction in the

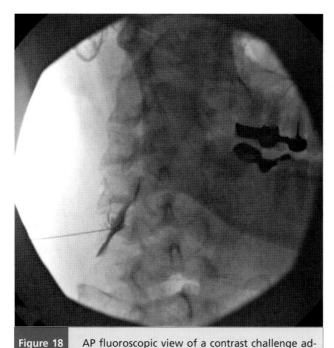

Figure 18 AP fluoroscopic view of a contrast challenge administered before the anesthetic as part of the sequence in a right C6 selective nerve root block. Note the nerve root outline and intraforaminal spread of the contrast agent.

number of spine levels to be treated surgically.

Injection of local anesthetic along a putatively painful cervical nerve root can reveal the source of shoulder girdle and/or upper limb pain (Figure 18). Diagnostic SNRB has been used for 30 years to confirm clinical identification of an affected nerve root.[96] If there is an 80% reduction in the patient's radicular pain after a low volume of local anesthetic (for example, 0.8 mL of 2% lidocaine) is injected directly onto a nerve root suspected of causing symptoms, the blocked root is considered to be the source of symptoms. The reported specificity of cervical diagnostic SNRB is 87% to 100%, with 100% sensitivity.[96]

The usefulness of cervical transforaminal epidural injections lies in allowing surgery to be avoided or improving the surgical outcome.[97,98] A diagnostic cervical transforaminal injection of lidocaine indicates the spine level for surgery and leads to better pain relief after surgery.[96] Surgery was more strongly associated with a good outcome if the surgical level was determined using a cervical transforaminal injection of lidocaine, and the injection was superior to MRI for predicting a poor surgical outcome ($P = 0.01$).[97] Patients undergoing surgery based on relief after cervical transforaminal injection were several times more likely to have a good outcome than those whose surgery affected levels with minimal relief after transforaminal injection ($P = 0.01$).[98]

The therapeutic effect of cervical corticosteroid transforaminal injection on cervical radicular pain was investigated in prospective observational studies that found positive results 1 to 12 months after one to three injections were administered.[97,99-101] A prospective randomized comparison of methylprednisolone and mepivacaine revealed no difference at 3 weeks between patients in the control group, who received a single transforaminal injection of 0.5 mL of 1% mepivacaine and 1 mL saline, and those in the active group, who received a single injection of 0.5 mL of 1% mepivacaine and 1 mL of methylprednisolone (40 mg/mL).[102] Although the addition of methylprednisolone did not improve the outcome, as assessed by patient self-reporting without the use of a validated measurement tool, patients in both groups had improvement after the sole injection. Fewer than 20% of the patients had baseline pain of more than 12 months' duration. Repeat injections obviated the need for surgery in some patients over a 2.5-year period.[97]

The paucity of controlled prospective studies and the conflicting outcomes of retrospective studies preclude a definitive conclusion about the treatment role of cervical transforaminal injections. However, these interventions can be effective in ameliorating or eliminating disabling cervical radicular pain in some patients. Rigorous scientific study of the efficacy and safety of cervical transforaminal injection is necessary.

Percutaneous Diskectomy

Percutaneous diskectomy has been investigated as a nonsurgical treatment for persistent cervical radiculopathy caused by a corroborative focal herniation. Laser, enzymatic, and mechanical means have been studied for decompressing a cervical intervertebral disk herniation, although the posttreatment follow-up intervals have been unspecified or relatively short.[103,104] The two studies with the longest follow-up data had disparate results and included patients with either radicular or axial pain.[103,104]

Nucleoplasty uses energy from Coblation technology (ArthroCare, Austin, TX) to vaporize nuclear tissue into gaseous elementary molecules, which then escape through the introducer cannula. Preliminary investigation found that nucleoplasty and TFESI together can be effective for treating the biomechanical and biochemical causes of cervical intervertebral disk herniation–related radicular pain.[105] The 21 patients had a contained disk herniation without stenosis, as well as persistent radicular pain that had been unresponsive to nonsurgical care; they were considered appropriate surgical candidates. After 6 months, 91% to 95% of the patients had an average 83% reduction in radicular pain, with the greatest rate of reduction within the first 2 weeks. At 12 months, 17 of the 21 patients had a good or excellent result. Two patients ultimately required surgery.[105] These findings were corroborated by subsequent studies of nucleoplasty performed without TFESI. At 6 to 12 months, 81% to 85% of patients had a good to excellent result with significant reduction in radicular pain.[106] More recently, a randomized controlled study of 115 patients found significant reduc-

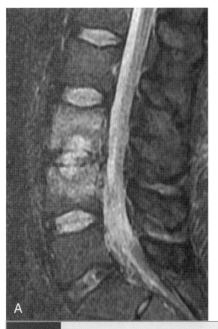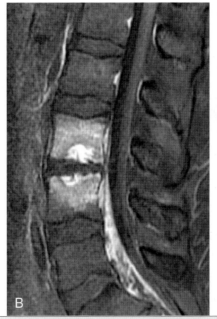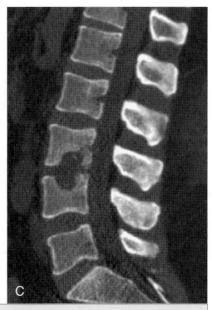

Figure 19 L3-4 diskitis and osteomyelitis. **A,** Sagittal short-tau inversion recovery MRI showing increased intradiskal signal, loss of disk height, and absence of the central disk cleft. **B,** Sagittal MRI with gadolinium enhancement showing contrast uptake in the adjacent end plates and vertebrae without evidence of epidural abscess. **C,** Thin-cut CT showing end plate erosion 8 weeks after provocation diskography.

tion in pain and disability, without complications, at 3, 6, and 12 months after nucleoplasty, in comparison with the use of transcutaneous electrical nerve stimulation, physical therapy, analgesics, or nonsteroidal anti-inflammatory drugs.[107] Percutaneous diskectomy with Coblation technology, with or without TFESI, can be safe and effective for relieving cervical radicular pain caused by a corroborative intervertebral disk protrusion, and it can be offered as an alternative to open surgery if less invasive measures fail.

Complications

Although infection such as meningitis, abscess, or osteomyelitis is rare with percutaneous procedures, it has been reported after epidural, facet joint, and sacroiliac joint injections; diskography; and spinal cord stimulator implantation.[108-110] The risk of infection can be minimized by adherence to aseptic technique, including the sterilization of overlying skin, limited injection instrument contact, and the use of surgical masks. It is appropriate to administer antibiotics before and after intradiskal and indwelling (spinal cord stimulation) procedures. The rate of diskitis after diskography is 0.05% to 1.3% per disk or 0.1% to 2.3% per patient.[110] Cutaneous organisms such as *Staphylococcus aureus* and *Staphylococcus epidermidis* are common sources of lumbar and cervical diskitis (Figure 19). Inadvertent needle tip passage through nearby structures can introduce pharyngeal, esophageal, and bowel organisms (such as *Escherichia coli).*

Injury to central or peripheral neural tissue can occur because of direct trauma or vascular insufficiency resulting from intraluminal obstruction. Brain and spinal cord injury have been reported.[111] These injuries may represent an unrecognized intravascular injection of particulate steroid or misplacement of the needle tip within the cord. The risk of a catastrophic complication can be reduced by meticulous positioning of the injection instrument, accurate fluoroscopic representation of the spine anatomy, contrast confirmation, use of an anesthetic challenge for the transforaminal approach, and injection of nonparticulate steroid preparation. If available, digital subtraction imaging can better elucidate the vascular evacuation of contrast material not easily detectable with routine fluoroscopy.[112] A minor complication occurred in fewer than 10% of lumbar TFESIs, such as transient nonpositional headache (3%), increased back pain (2%), facial flushing (1%), increased radicular pain (0.6%), and vasovagal reaction (0.3%), all of which resolved uneventfully.[113] Similar complications were encountered with cervical injections.

Summary

Painful spine and pelvic disorders without obvious surgical lesions can be accurately diagnosed and optimally treated by percutaneous techniques. Such interventions use an amalgam of findings from imaging, physical examination, electrodiagnostics, and radiographically guided diagnostic injections. Interventional spine care is a subspecialty within spine medicine, and therapeutic interventional spine procedures appropriately treat numerous spine disorders. Diagnostic procedures can clarify the clinical meaning of morphologic imaging abnormalities and be useful in planning therapeutic procedures or surgery. An outcome-oriented perspective is a key feature of the interventional spine care approach. Optimal treatment can only be achieved after an accurate diagnosis.

Interventional spine care was successfully used, for example, in a middle-aged adult with chronic low back pain that persisted after nonsurgical care and limited daily activities. Properly performed provocation diskography revealed a painful grade IV annular fissure at L5-S1, with a nonpainful lobular nucleogram at L4-5. Diagnostic selective nerve root blockade confirmed the patient's significant lateral thigh and leg pain as L5 radicular pain rather than somatic referred pain. Preoperative MRI revealed mild L5 foraminal stenosis in the AP dimension. Assessment of the foramen after successful anterior interbody fusion revealed vascular congestion at the L5 nerve root. The patient was optimally treated by anterior interbody fusion, posterior fixation, and foraminal decompression of the L5 nerve root, leading to resolution of the low back and lower limb pain. A lack of diagnostic nerve root block findings would have led to incomplete surgical treatment and probably to persistent symptoms.

Annotated References

1. Frymoyer JW, Cats-Baril WL: An overview of the incidences and costs of low back pain. *Orthop Clin North Am* 1991;22(2):263-271.

2. DePalma MJ, Slipman CW: Treatment of common neck problems, in Braddom R, ed: *Physical Medicine and Rehabilitation*, ed 3. Philadelphia, PA, Elsevier, 2006, pp 797-824.

   Neck pain is among the most common reasons patients seek medical care. Knowledge of spine biomechanics and pathophysiology is useful for determining the most likely pain generators.

3. DePalma M, Ketchum J, Queler E, et al: What is the etiology of low back pain, and does age effect the prevalence of each etiology? An interim analysis of 170 consecutive cases. *Pain Med* 2009;10(5):949.

   The intervertebral disk is the most common source of chronic low back pain in adults. Discogenic low back pain is more likely in younger adults, and facetogenic or sacroiliac joint pain is more likely in older adults.

4. Yin W, Bogduk N: The nature of neck pain in a private pain clinic in the United States. *Pain Med* 2008;9(2):196-203.

   A pathoanatomic diagnosis can be established in a private practice setting in more than 80% of patients with chronic neck pain, with appropriate investigation.

5. Lord SM, Barnsley L, Wallis BJ, Bogduk N: Chronic cervical zygapophysial joint pain after whiplash: A placebo-controlled prevalence study. *Spine (Phila Pa 1976)* 1996;21(15):1737-1745.

6. Moneta GB, Videman T, Kaivanto K, et al: Reported pain during lumbar discography as a function of anular ruptures and disc degeneration: A re-analysis of 833 discograms. *Spine (Phila Pa 1976)* 1994;19(17):1968-1974.

7. Peng B, Wu W, Hou S, Li P, Zhang C, Yang Y: The pathogenesis of discogenic low back pain. *J Bone Joint Surg Br* 2005;87(1):62-67.

   The zone of granulation tissue with extensive innervation along the tears in the posterior part of the painful disk may be responsible for diskographic and discogenic low back pain.

8. DePalma M, Ketchum J, Queler E, Ruchala M, Kouchouch A, Powell D: Multivariate analysis of predictor variables of low back pain: An interim analysis of a cross sectional analytic study. *Spine J* 2009;9(10S): 143S.

   Multivariate analyses of predictor variables revealed a 94% probability of discogenic low back pain in patients age 55 years or younger with midline pain exacerbated by sustained hip flexion.

9. Zhou Y, Abdi S: Diagnosis and minimally invasive treatment of lumbar discogenic pain: A review of the literature. *Clin J Pain* 2006;22(5):468-481.

   Minimally invasive treatments for discogenic pain can be cost effective and may have relatively few long-term adverse effects.

10. Thompson KJ, Dagher AP, Eckel TS, Clark M, Reinig JW: Modic changes on MR images as studied with provocative diskography: Clinical relevance. A retrospective study of 2457 disks. *Radiology* 2009;250(3):849-855.

    Type I signal intensity changes on MRI have a high positive predictive value in the identification of pain generators.

11. Kang CH, Kim YH, Lee SH, et al: Can magnetic resonance imaging accurately predict concordant pain provocation during provocative disc injection? *Skeletal Radiol* 2009;38(9):877-885.

    A proposed MRI classification is useful identifying a disk with concordant pain.

12. Simmons EH, Segil CM: An evaluation of discography in the localization of symptomatic levels in discogenic disease of the spine. *Clin Orthop Relat Res* 1975;108: 57-69.

13. Derby R, Kim BJ, Chen Y, Seo KS, Lee SH: The relation between annular disruption on computed tomography scan and pressure-controlled diskography. *Arch Phys Med Rehabil* 2005;86(8):1534-1538.

    Annular disruption reaching the outer anulus fibrosus is

a key factor in pain generation. Disk morphology, including annular disruptions extending beyond the outer anulus fibrosus, may increase diskography specificity.

14. Wolfer LR, Derby R, Lee JE, Lee SH: Systematic review of lumbar provocation discography in asymptomatic subjects with a meta-analysis of false-positive rates. *Pain Physician* 2008;11(4):513-538.

   Contrary to recently published studies, diskography has a low false-positive rate for the diagnosis of discogenic pain. Level of evidence: II.

15. Wolfer L, Carragee E, Akuthota V: Lumbar provocation diskography: Helpful or harmful? *PM R* 2010;2(10):957-968.

   This is a review of published lumbar diskography data and the debate regarding its safety and usefulness.

16. Carragee EJ, Don AS, Hurwitz EL, Cuellar JM, Carrino JA, Herzog R: Does discography cause accelerated progression of degeneration changes in the lumbar disc: A ten-year matched cohort study. *Spine (Phila Pa 1976)* 2009;34(21):2338-2345.

   Discography techniques may accelerate disk degeneration, disk herniation, loss of disk height, and the development of reactive end plate changes.

17. Johnson RG: Does discography injure normal discs? An analysis of repeat discograms. *Spine (Phila Pa 1976)* 1989;14(4):424-426.

18. Derby R, Howard MW, Grant JM, Lettice JJ, Van Peteghem PK, Ryan DP: The ability of pressure-controlled discography to predict surgical and nonsurgical outcomes. *Spine (Phila Pa 1976)* 1999;24(4):364-372.

19. Carragee EJ, Lincoln T, Parmar VS, Alamin T: A gold standard evaluation of the "discogenic pain" diagnosis as determined by provocative discography. *Spine (Phila Pa 1976)* 2006;31(18):2115-2123.

   Solid 360° fusion does not appear to be successful for treating discogenic low back pain identified by provocation diskography, when a strict definition for successful outcomes is applied.

20. DePalma MJ, Ketchum JM, Saullo TR: Etiology of chronic low back pain in patients having undergone lumbar fusion. *Pain Med* 2011;12(5):732-739.

   The prevalence of sacroiliac joint pain increases after lumbosacral fusion and probably is 27% to 61% in patients with chronic low back pain.

21. Fritzell P, Hägg O, Wessberg P, Nordwall A, Swedish Lumbar Spine Study Group: Lumbar fusion versus non-surgical treatment for chronic low back pain: A multi-center randomized controlled trial from the Swedish Lumbar Spine Study Group. *Spine (Phila Pa 1976)* 2001;26(23):2521-2534.

22. Cooper G, Kahn S, Lutz GE, et al: Predictive value of provocative lumbar disc stimulation. *16th Annual Scientific Meeting Proceedings*. San Rafael, CA, International Spine Intervention Society, 2007, pp 174-175.

   Patients evaluated with provocation diskography adhering to strict operational criteria have reduced low back pain and disability when treated with fusion surgery at the level indicated by diskography.

23. DePalma MJ, Lee JE, Peterson L, Wolfer L, Ketchum JM, Derby R: Are outer annular fissures stimulated during diskography the source of diskogenic low-back pain? An analysis of analgesic diskography data. *Pain Med* 2009;10(3):488-494.

   Diskogenic pain to a varying extent is caused by the sensitized nociceptors within annular tears.

24. Ohtori S, Kinoshita T, Yamashita M, et al: Results of surgery for discogenic low back pain: A randomized study using discography versus discoblock for diagnosis. *Spine (Phila Pa 1976)* 2009;34(13):1345-1348.

   Pain relief after injection of a small amount of bupivacaine into the painful disk was useful for diagnosing discogenic low back pain, compared with diskography.

25. DePalma M, Derby R, Lee J, Ketchum J, Wolfer L: Do results of provocation lumbar discography and functional anesthetic discography support the face validity of each diagnostic procedure? *Annual Meeting Proceedings*. Toronto, ON, International Society for the Study of the Lumbar Spine, 2009, p 108.

   The results of provocation and analgesic diskography appear to be congruent.

26. Pauza K: Cadaveric intervertebral disc temperature mapping during disc biacuplasty. *Pain Physician* 2008;11(5):669-676.

   The anterior disk and posterolateral ligament remained at a safe temperature (below 45°C) in a cadaver study when temperatures throughout the center posterior and posterolateral disk were increased sufficiently for neuroablation.

27. Kapural L, Mekhail N, Hicks D, et al: Histological changes and temperature distribution studies of a novel bipolar radiofrequency heating system in degenerated and nondegenerated human cadaver lumbar discs. *Pain Med* 2008;9(1):68-75.

   Temperatures in the posterior anulus fibrosus during transdiskal biacuplasty were greater than required for neuroablation. Neural foraminal and epidural temperatures were low enough to avoid neural damage.

28. Saal JA, Saal JS: Intradiscal electrothermal treatment for chronic discogenic low back pain: Prospective outcome study with a minimum 2-year follow-up. *Spine (Phila Pa 1976)* 2002;27(9):966-974.

29. Pauza KJ, Howell S, Dreyfuss P, Peloza JH, Dawson K, Bogduk N: A randomized, placebo-controlled trial of intradiscal electrothermal therapy for the treatment of discogenic low back pain. *Spine J* 2004;4(1):27-35.

30. Freeman BJ, Fraser RD, Cain CM, Hall DJ, Chapple DC: A randomized, double-blind, controlled trial: Intradiscal electrothermal therapy versus placebo for the

2: Nonsurgical Care of the Spine

treatment of chronic discogenic low back pain. *Spine (Phila Pa 1976)* 2005;30(21):2369-2378.

Compared with placebo, intradiskal electrothermal therapy is not effective for reducing low back pain and disability from painful annular fissures.

31. Kapural L: Intervertebral disk cooled bipolar radiofrequency (intradiskal biacuplasty) for the treatment of lumbar diskogenic pain: A 12-month follow-up of the pilot study. *Pain Med* 2008;9(4):407-408.

Improvements in function and pain control persisted 12 months after treatment with bipolar annular radiofrequency.

32. Peng B, Pang X, Wu Y, Zhao C, Song X: A randomized placebo-controlled trial of intradiscal methylene blue injection for the treatment of chronic discogenic low back pain. *Pain* 2010;149(1):124-129.

Injection of methylene blue into a painful disk is a safe, effective, and minimally invasive method of treating intractable and incapacitating discogenic low back pain.

33. Masuda K, Imai Y, Okuma M, et al: Osteogenic protein-1 injection into a degenerated disc induces the restoration of disc height and structural changes in the rabbit anular puncture model. *Spine (Phila Pa 1976)* 2006;31(7):742-754.

The effect on disk height of osteogenic protein-1 injection into degenerative rabbit disks was sustained up to 24 weeks.

34. Chubinskaya S, Kawakami M, Rappoport L, Matsumoto T, Migita N, Rueger DC: Anti-catabolic effect of OP-1 in chronically compressed intervertebral discs. *J Orthop Res* 2007;25(4):517-530.

This study confirmed the anticatabolic activity of osteogenic protein-1, as previously found in human articular cartilage, and provided critical evidence for the potential of this therapy for treating disk degeneration.

35. Patel RK: Intradiscal biologic agents for lumbosacral internal disc disruption, in DePalma M, ed: *iSpine: Evidence-Based Interventional Spine Care*. New York, NY, Demos Medical, 2011.

Recent studies evaluated novel biological approaches to maintaining and improving the structurally compromised intervertebral disk.

36. Schwarzer AC, Aprill CN, Derby R, Fortin J, Kine G, Bogduk N: The false-positive rate of uncontrolled diagnostic blocks of the lumbar zygapophysial joints. *Pain* 1994;58(2):195-200.

37. Pampati S, Cash KA, Manchikanti L: Accuracy of diagnostic lumbar facet joint nerve blocks: A 2-year follow-up of 152 patients diagnosed with controlled diagnostic blocks. *Pain Physician* 2009;12(5):855-866.

Controlled diagnostic lumbar facet joint nerve blocks use the criteria of 80% pain relief and the ability to perform previously painful movements, with a sustained diagnosis of lumbar facet joint pain in at least 89.5% of patients at 2-year follow up.

38. Dreyfuss P, Halbrook B, Pauza K, Joshi A, McLarty J, Bogduk N: Efficacy and validity of radiofrequency neurotomy for chronic lumbar zygapophysial joint pain. *Spine (Phila Pa 1976)* 2000;25(10):1270-1277.

39. Nath S, Nath CA, Pettersson K: Percutaneous lumbar zygapophysial (facet) joint neurotomy using radiofrequency current, in the management of chronic low back pain: A randomized double-blind trial. *Spine (Phila Pa 1976)* 2008;33(12):1291-1298.

Radiofrequency facet denervation is not a placebo and could be used in the treatment of carefully selected patients with chronic low back pain.

40. Lynch MC, Taylor JF: Facet joint injection for low back pain: A clinical study. *J Bone Joint Surg Br* 1986;68(1):138-141.

41. Carette S, Marcoux S, Truchon R, et al: A controlled trial of corticosteroid injections into facet joints for chronic low back pain. *N Engl J Med* 1991;325(14):1002-1007.

42. Bogduk N: Evidence-informed management of chronic low back pain with facet injections and radiofrequency neurotomy. *Spine J* 2008;8(1):56-64.

43. DePalma MJ, Ketchum JM, Queler ED, Trussell BS: Prospective pilot study of painful lumbar facet joint arthropathy after intra-articular injection of hylan G-F 20. *PM R* 2009;1(10):908-915.

Viscosupplementation with hylan G-F 20 for lumbar facet joint arthropathy is associated with modest efficacy lasting up to 6 months.

44. Lau P, Mercer S, Govind J, Bogduk N: The surgical anatomy of lumbar medial branch neurotomy (facet denervation). *Pain Med* 2004;5(3):289-298.

45. van Kleef M, Barendse GA, Kessels A, Voets HM, Weber WE, de Lange S: Randomized trial of radiofrequency lumbar facet denervation for chronic low back pain. *Spine (Phila Pa 1976)* 1999;24(18):1937-1942.

46. Strakowski JA, Redd DD, Johnson EW, Pease WS: H reflex and F wave latencies to soleus normal values and side-to-side differences. *Am J Phys Med Rehabil* 2001;80(7):491-493.

47. Laslett M, Young SB, Aprill CN, McDonald B: Diagnosing painful sacroiliac joints: A validity study of a McKenzie evaluation and sacroiliac provocation tests. *Aust J Physiother* 2003;49(2):89-97.

48. Dreyfuss P, Henning T, Malladi N, Goldstein B, Bogduk N: The ability of multi-site, multi-depth sacral lateral branch blocks to anesthetize the sacroiliac joint complex. *Pain Med* 2009;10(4):679-688.

Multisite, multidepth lateral branch blocks are physiologically effective at a rate of 70% and do not effectively block the intra-articular portion of the sacroiliac joint.

49. Liliang PC, Lu K, Weng HC, Liang CL, Tsai YD, Chen HJ: The therapeutic efficacy of sacroiliac joint blocks with triamcinolone acetonide in the treatment of sacroiliac joint dysfunction without spondyloarthropathy. *Spine (Phila Pa 1976)* 2009;34(9):896-900.

Sacroiliac joint blocks with triamcinolone acetonide are beneficial for some patients with sacroiliac joint pain without spondyloarthropathy. The blocks had long-lasting efficacy.

50. Maugars Y, Mathis C, Berthelot J-M, Charlier C, Prost A: Assessment of the efficacy of sacroiliac corticosteroid injections in spondylarthropathies: A double-blind study. *Br J Rheumatol* 1996;35(8):767-770.

51. Slipman CW, Lipetz JS, Plastaras CT, et al: Fluoroscopically guided therapeutic sacroiliac joint injections for sacroiliac joint syndrome. *Am J Phys Med Rehabil* 2001;80(6):425-432.

52. Yin W, Willard F, Carreiro J, Dreyfuss P: Sensory stimulation-guided sacroiliac joint radiofrequency neurotomy: Technique based on neuroanatomy of the dorsal sacral plexus. *Spine (Phila Pa 1976)* 2003;28(20): 2419-2425.

53. Cohen SP, Hurley RW, Buckenmaier CC III, Kurihara C, Morlando B, Dragovich A: Randomized placebo-controlled study evaluating lateral branch radiofrequency denervation for sacroiliac joint pain. *Anesthesiology* 2008;109(2):279-288.

Preliminary evidence is provided that L4-L5 primary dorsal rami and S1-S3 lateral branch radiofrequency denervation provides intermediate-term pain relief and functional benefit in selected patients with suspected sacroiliac joint pain.

54. Knievel S, Lamer T: Midline posterior element disorders, in DePalma M, ed: *iSpine: Evidence-Based Interventional Spine Care.* New York, NY, Demos Medical, 2011.

There is little literature on definitive interventional treatment of spinous process and associated ligamentous disease. Patients with refractory disease may require surgical removal of the involved spinous processes.

55. Bhargava A: Fusion hardware mediated low back pain, in DePalma M, ed: *iSpine: Evidence-Based Interventional Spine Care.* New York, NY, Demos Medical, 2011, pp 151-155.

It may be appropriate to perform diagnostic injections to rule out lumbar fusion instrumentation as the cause of low back pain.

56. Alanay A, Vyas R, Shamie AN, Sciocia T, Randolph G, Wang JC: Safety and efficacy of implant removal for patients with recurrent back pain after a failed degenerative lumbar spine surgery. *J Spinal Disord Tech* 2007; 20(4):271-277.

Implant removal may be efficient and safe for carefully selected patients. The most consistent predictor of efficacy is pain relief after diagnostic injection on the painful surgical side.

57. Mok JM, Cloyd JM, Bradford DS, et al: Reoperation after primary fusion for adult spinal deformity: Rate, reason, and timing. *Spine (Phila Pa 1976)* 2009;34(8):832-839.

When a strict definition of reoperation was used for a well-defined cohort in the presence of relevant risk factors, many patients undergoing primary fusion for adult spine deformity were found to require reoperation.

58. Martin BI, Mirza SK, Comstock BA, Gray DT, Kreuter W, Deyo RA: Reoperation rates following lumbar spine surgery and the influence of spinal fusion procedures. *Spine (Phila Pa 1976)* 2007;32(3):382-387.

Patients should be informed of the substantial likelihood of reoperation after a lumbar spine operation. For a patient with spondylolisthesis, reoperation is less likely after fusion than after decompression alone.

59. van Akkerveeken PF: The diagnostic value of nerve root sheath infiltration. *Acta Orthop Scand Suppl* 1993;251: 61-63.

60. Krempen JF, Smith BS: Nerve-root injection: A method for evaluating the etiology of sciatica. *J Bone Joint Surg Am* 1974;56(7):1435-1444.

61. Schutz H, Lougheed WM, Wortzman G, Awerbuck BG: Intervertebral nerve-root in the investigation of chronic lumbar disc disease. *Can J Surg* 1973;16(3):217-221.

62. Haueisen DC, Smith BS, Myers SR, Pryce ML: The diagnostic accuracy of spinal nerve injection studies: Their role in the evaluation of recurrent sciatica. *Clin Orthop Relat Res* 1985;198:179-183.

63. Faraj AA, Kumaraguru P, Kosygan K: Intra-articular bupivacaine hip injection in differentiation of coxarthrosis from referred thigh pain: A 10 year study. *Acta Orthop Belg* 2003;69(6):518-521.

64. Valat JP, Giraudeau B, Rozenberg S, et al: Epidural corticosteroid injections for sciatica: A randomised, double blind, controlled clinical trial. *Ann Rheum Dis* 2003; 62(7):639-643.

65. Lutz GE, Vad VB, Wisneski RJ: Fluoroscopic transforaminal lumbar epidural steroids: An outcome study. *Arch Phys Med Rehabil* 1998;79(11):1362-1366.

66. DePalma MJ, Bhargava A, Slipman CW: A critical appraisal of the evidence for selective nerve root injection in the treatment of lumbosacral radiculopathy. *Arch Phys Med Rehabil* 2005;86(7):1477-1483.

TFESI is supported as a minimally invasive and safe procedure for treating painful lumbar radicular symptoms. Level of evidence: III.

67. Riew KD, Park JB, Cho YS, et al: Nerve root blocks in the treatment of lumbar radicular pain: A minimum five-year follow-up. *J Bone Joint Surg Am* 2006;88(8): 1722-1725.

Most patients with lumbar radicular pain who avoid

2: Nonsurgical Care of the Spine

surgery for at least 1 year after receiving a nerve root injection with bupivacaine alone or in combination with betamethasone will continue to avoid surgery for at least 5 years.

68. Tafazal S, Ng L, Chaudhary N, Sell P: Corticosteroids in peri-radicular infiltration for radicular pain: A randomised double blind controlled trial. One year results and subgroup analysis. *Eur Spine J* 2009;18(8):1220-1225.

   Periradicular infiltration of corticosteroids for sciatica does not provide additional benefit compared with local anaesthetic injection alone. Corticosteroids do not obviate the need for subsequent interventions such as root blocks or surgery.

69. Ghahreman A, Ferch R, Bogduk N: The efficacy of transforaminal injection of steroids for the treatment of lumbar radicular pain. *Pain Med* 2010;11(8):1149-1168.

   Transforaminal injection of steroids is effective only in some patients. Its superiority over other injections is obscured when group data are compared but emerges when categorical outcomes are calculated.

70. Baker R: Demystifying lumbar transforaminal epidural steroids: A seminal efficacy study of a specific spinal injection. *Pain Med* 2010;11(8):1141-1143.

   This landmark study vindicated transforaminal steroid injection for lumbar radicular pain as superior to placebo.

71. Allen TL, Tatli Y, Lutz GE: Fluoroscopic percutaneous lumbar zygapophyseal joint cyst rupture: A clinical outcome study. *Spine J* 2009;9(5):387-395.

   Fluoroscopic percutaneous Z-joint cyst rupture appears to be a safe and effective minimally invasive treatment that should be considered before surgical intervention.

72. Martha JF, Swaim B, Wang DA, et al: Outcome of percutaneous rupture of lumbar synovial cysts: A case series of 101 patients. *Spine J* 2009;9(11):899-904.

   Lumbar facet joint steroid injection with attempted cyst rupture is correlated with subsequent avoidance of surgery in half of treated patients. Successful cyst rupture does not appear to add benefit.

73. Gogan WJ, Fraser RD: Chymopapain: A 10-year, double-blind study. *Spine (Phila Pa 1976)* 1992;17(4):388-394.

74. Nordby EJ, Javid MJ: Continuing experience with chemonucleolysis. *Mt Sinai J Med* 2000;67(4):311-313.

75. Bonaldi G: Automated percutaneous lumbar discectomy: Technique, indications and clinical follow-up in over 1000 patients. *Neuroradiology* 2003;45(10):735-743.

76. Gerszten PC, Smuck M, Rathmell JP, et al: Plasma disc decompression compared with fluoroscopy-guided transforaminal epidural steroid injections for symptomatic contained lumbar disc herniation: A prospective, randomized, controlled trial. *J Neurosurg Spine* 2010; 12(4):357-371.

   In patients whose radicular pain was associated with a contained lumbar disk herniation, those treated with plasma disk decompression had significantly reduced pain and better quality of life scores than those treated with repeated TFESI.

77. Alò KM, Wright RE, Sutcliffe J, Brandt SA: Percutaneous lumbar discectomy: One-year follow-up in an initial cohort of fifty consecutive patients with chronic radicular pain. *Pain Pract* 2005;5(2):116-124.

78. Chopko B, Caraway DL: MiDAS I (mild Decompression Alternative to Open Surgery): A preliminary report of a prospective, multi-center clinical study. *Pain Physician* 2010;13(4):369-378.

   In 75 patients, the *mild* procedure proved to be safe and efficacious for improving mobility and reducing pain associated with lumbar spinal canal stenosis.

79. Kumar K, Taylor RS, Jacques L, et al: Spinal cord stimulation versus conventional medical management for neuropathic pain: A multicentre randomised controlled trial in patients with failed back surgery syndrome. *Pain* 2007;132(1-2):179-188.

   In selected patients with failed back surgery syndrome, spinal cord stimulation improves pain relief, health-related quality of life, and functional capacity.

80. North RB, Kidd DH, Farrokhi F, Piantadosi SA: Spinal cord stimulation versus repeated lumbosacral spine surgery for chronic pain: A randomized, controlled trial. *Neurosurgery* 2005;56(1):98-107.

   Spinal cord stimulation was found to be more effective than reoperation for relief of persistent radicular pain.

81. Mekhail NA, Aeschbach A, Stanton-Hicks M: Cost benefit analysis of neurostimulation for chronic pain. *Clin J Pain* 2004;20(6):462-468.

82. Chandler GS III, Nixon B, Stewart LT, Love J: Dorsal column stimulation for lumbar spinal stenosis. *Pain Physician* 2003;6(1):113-118.

83. Cooper G, Bailey B, Bogduk N: Cervical zygapophysial joint pain maps. *Pain Med* 2007;8(4):344-353.

   Pain maps constructed using diagnostic blocks in patients with neck pain or headache were more accurate than those derived from healthy volunteers.

84. Bogduk N, Aprill C: On the nature of neck pain, discography and cervical zygapophysial joint blocks. *Pain* 1993;54(2):213-217.

85. Barnsley L, Lord SM, Wallis BJ, Bogduk N: False-positive rates of cervical zygapophysial joint blocks. *Clin J Pain* 1993;9(2):124-130.

86. Lord SM, Barnsley L, Wallis BJ, McDonald GJ, Bogduk N: Percutaneous radio-frequency neurotomy for chronic

cervical zygapophyseal-joint pain. *N Engl J Med* 1996; 335(23):1721-1726.

87. Barnsley L: Percutaneous radiofrequency neurotomy for chronic neck pain: Outcomes in a series of consecutive patients. *Pain Med* 2005;6(4):282-286.

Radiofrequency neurotomy is an effective palliative treatment for chronic cervical zygapophysial joint pain when performed in routine clinical practice.

88. Stovner LJ, Kolstad F, Helde G: Radiofrequency denervation of facet joints C2-C6 in cervicogenic headache: A randomized, double-blind, sham-controlled study. *Cephalalgia* 2004;24(10):821-830.

89. Parfenchuck TA, Janssen ME: A correlation of cervical magnetic resonance imaging and discography/computed tomographic discograms. *Spine (Phila Pa 1976)* 1994; 19(24):2819-2825.

90. Schellhas KP, Smith MD, Gundry CR, Pollei SR: Cervical discogenic pain: Prospective correlation of magnetic resonance imaging and discography in asymptomatic subjects and pain sufferers. *Spine (Phila Pa 1976)* 1996; 21(3):300-312.

91. Garvey TA, Transfeldt EE, Malcolm JR, Kos P: Outcome of anterior cervical discectomy and fusion as perceived by patients treated for dominant axial-mechanical cervical spine pain. *Spine (Phila Pa 1976)* 2002;27(17):1887-1895.

92. Bogduk N: Point of view. *Spine (Phila Pa 1976)* 2002; 27(17):1895.

93. Stojanovic MP, Vu TN, Caneris O, Slezak J, Cohen SP, Sang CN: The role of fluoroscopy in cervical epidural steroid injections: An analysis of contrast dispersal patterns. *Spine (Phila Pa 1976)* 2002;27(5):509-514.

94. Goel A, Pollan JJ: Contrast flow characteristics in the cervical epidural space: An analysis of cervical epidurograms. *Spine (Phila Pa 1976)* 2006;31(14):1576-1579.

In cervical epidural steroid injections at the C6-C7 and C7-T1 midline, the contrast consistently covers the dorsal cervical epidural space bilaterally, regardless of the volume or neck flexion angle.

95. Stav A, Ovadia L, Sternberg A, Kaadan M, Weksler N: Cervical epidural steroid injection for cervicobrachialgia. *Acta Anaesthesiol Scand* 1993;37(6):562-566.

96. Anderberg L, Annertz M, Brandt L, Säveland H: Selective diagnostic cervical nerve root block: Correlation with clinical symptoms and MRI-pathology. *Acta Neurochir (Wien)* 2004;146(6):559-565.

97. Kolstad F, Leivseth G, Nygaard OP: Transforaminal steroid injections in the treatment of cervical radiculopathy: A prospective outcome study. *Acta Neurochir (Wien)* 2005;147(10):1065-1070.

This prospective cohort study indicates that injection

treatment reduces the need for surgery. The clinical effect is measurable, with a statistically significant improvement in radicular pain.

98. Sasso RC, Macadaeg K, Nordmann D, Smith M: Selective nerve root injections can predict surgical outcome for lumbar and cervical radiculopathy: Comparison to magnetic resonance imaging. *J Spinal Disord Tech* 2005;18(6):471-478.

Diagnostic selective nerve injection can safely and accurately discern the presence or absence of cervical or lumbar radiculopathy.

99. Bush K, Hillier S: Outcome of cervical radiculopathy treated with periradicular/epidural corticosteroid injections: A prospective study with independent clinical review. *Eur Spine J* 1996;5(5):319-325.

100. Cyteval C, Thomas E, Decoux E, et al: Cervical radiculopathy: Open study on percutaneous periradicular foraminal steroid infiltration performed under CT control in 30 patients. *AJNR Am J Neuroradiol* 2004; 25(3):441-445.

101. Dreyfuss P, Baker R, Bogduk N: Comparative effectiveness of cervical transforaminal injections with particulate and nonparticulate corticosteroid preparations for cervical radicular pain. *Pain Med* 2006;7(3):237-242.

The effectiveness of dexamethasone was slightly less than that of triamcinolone, but the difference was not statistically or clinically significant. A theoretically safer nonparticulate agent appears to be a valid alternative to particulate agents.

102. Anderberg L, Annertz M, Persson L, Brandt L, Säveland H: Transforaminal steroid injections for the treatment of cervical radiculopathy: A prospective and randomised study. *Eur Spine J* 2007;16(3):321-328.

Statistical analysis did not reveal an outcome difference depending on whether patients received a local anesthetic block with steroid or saline. Further research is needed before the use of steroids can be excluded.

103. Chiu JC, Clifford TJ, Greenspan M, Richley RC, Lohman G, Sison RB: Percutaneous microdecompressive endoscopic cervical discectomy with laser thermodiskoplasty. *Mt Sinai J Med* 2000;67(4):278-282.

104. Knight MT, Goswami A, Patko JT: Cervical percutaneous laser disc decompression: Preliminary results of an ongoing prospective outcome study. *J Clin Laser Med Surg* 2001;19(1):3-8.

105. Slipman CW, Frey ME, Bhargava A, et al: Outcomes and side effects following percutaneous cervical disc decompression using Coblation technology: A pilot study. *Spine J* 2004;4(5S):71S.

106. Li J, Yan DL, Zhang ZH: Percutaneous cervical nucleoplasty in the treatment of cervical disc herniation. *Eur Spine J* 2008;17(12):1664-1669.

Percutaneous cervical nucleoplasty for the treatment of

cervical disk herniation results in a good outcome without disturbing the stability of the cervical spine.

107. Cesaroni A, Nardi PV, Casilino P, et al: Plasma disc decompression compared to conservative care for treating symptomatic contained cervical disc protrusion: One year results from a prospective randomized controlled study. *Spine J* 2008;8:78S.

108. Hooten WM, Mizerak A, Carns PE, Huntoon MA: Discitis after lumbar epidural corticosteroid injection: A case report and analysis of the case report literature. *Pain Med* 2006;7(1):46-51.

Clinical features and trends of an infectious complication are identified.

109. Bindal M, Krabak B: Acute bacterial sacroiliitis in an adult: A case report and review of the literature. *Arch Phys Med Rehabil* 2007;88(10):1357-1359.

A course of intravenous antibiotics led to complete symptom resolution, thus supporting the diagnosis of bacterial sacroiliitis. Repeat MRI and CT confirmed the complete resolution of the sacroiliitis.

110. Guyer RD, Collier R, Stith WJ, et al: Discitis after discography. *Spine (Phila Pa 1976)* 1988;13(12):1352-1354.

111. Bose B: Quadriparesis following cervical epidural steroid injections: Case report and review of the literature. *Spine J* 2005;5(5):558-563.

Although the evidence is not conclusive, a patient may have sustained a vascular event after a cervical epidural injection.

112. Bogduk N, Dreyfuss P, Baker R, et al: Complications of spinal diagnostic and treatment procedures. *Pain Med* 2008;9(S1):S11-S34.

Strict adherence to published guidelines provides safeguards against complications. Complications are avoided by knowing all anatomy related to a procedure and being able to recognize aberrations as soon as they occur.

113. Botwin KP, Gruber RD, Bouchlas CG, Torres-Ramos FM, Freeman TL, Slaten WK: Complications of fluoroscopically guided transforaminal lumbar epidural injections. *Arch Phys Med Rehabil* 2000;81(8):1045-1050.

Chapter 12
Electrodiagnostic Studies for Suspected Spine Disorders

Nathan D. Prahlow, MD   Ralph Buschbacher, MD

Introduction

The electrical properties of nerve and muscle membranes allow signals to be transmitted from one area of the body to another for the purpose of creating movement or signaling sensory input. Electrodiagnosis is the technique of stimulating nerves by external means to record electrical activity from a nerve or muscle, thus providing an objective measure of neuromuscular function. Electrodiagnostic studies are a useful tool for evaluating a suspected spine disorder. These studies can confirm a diagnosis, reveal an unsuspected neurologic disorder, or, if the diagnosis is not straightforward, define the source of neurologic involvement (Table 1). Needle examination can confirm spine pathology or direct the physician toward another cause of the patient's symptoms. Nerve conduction studies may point to a peripheral nerve disorder mimicking a spine disorder.

Types and Uses of Electrodiagnostic Studies

Although electrodiagnostic studies are routinely referred to as electromyography (EMG), the term EMG specifically refers to the needle examination component of an electrodiagnostic study. A typical electrodiagnostic study includes both nerve conduction studies and needle EMG. Clinicians who order an EMG often expect that both nerve conduction studies and needle examination will be performed. However, the electrodiagnostician may not routinely perform the needle examination. A high-quality electrodiagnostic study requires a systematic, thorough examination that can be adapted as the findings evolve. When placing an order for an electrodiagnostic evaluation, the clinician must detail the suspected disorder to ensure the study results will answer the pertinent questions.

Nerve Conduction Studies

The typical electrodiagnostic evaluation begins with nerve conduction studies. Although there are several types of nerve conduction studies, they all require a similar basic setup. Two recording electrodes are placed at specific locations overlying a muscle or a nerve, along with a ground electrode (Figure 1). The electrodiagnostician uses a specialized stimulator attached to the electrodiagnostic machine to apply an electric shock some distance away from the recording electrodes along the course of the nerve. The machine tracks any electrical signals observed at the recording electrodes and displays them in a waveform that is a quantitative visual depiction of the nerve action potential. The electrodiagnostician interprets the results and determines whether they are abnormal. Waveforms vary from normal to absent in a complete conduction block. Latency (defined as the time required for the signal to reach a given point along the nerve) from stimulation to the appearance of the waveform action potential provides an indication of nerve conduction velocity. The amplitude (defined as the change in height of the waveform from the baseline) and shape of the waveform provide information about the health of the nerve being studied.

Table 1

Common Diagnoses Made Using Electrodiagnostic Studies

Type of Disorder	Example(s)
Mononeuropathy	Carpal tunnel syndrome Ulnar neuropathy at the elbow
Polyneuropathy	Diabetic polyneuropathy
Disorder of the neuromuscular junction	Myasthenia gravis
Motor neuron disease	Amyotrophic lateral sclerosis
Radiculopathy	
Plexopathy	
Muscle disease	Muscular dystrophy

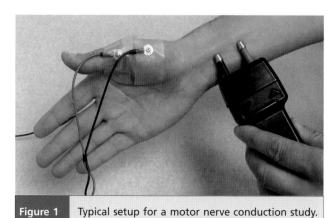

Figure 1 Typical setup for a motor nerve conduction study.

Nerve conduction studies can provide information about a specific nerve and can be used to infer the condition of other nerves, such as in a peripheral neuropathy in a patient with diabetes. Slow conduction along a specific nerve segment may point to a focal problem such as carpal tunnel syndrome. Diffuse slowing across multiple nerves indicates a peripheral polyneuropathy. Low-amplitude potentials can be caused by a focal or diffuse nerve condition. The extent to which conduction is slowed or amplitude is decreased can provide insight into the type and severity of the condition. Comparisons of motor and sensory studies, or of identical studies performed on the contralateral limb, also may be necessary.

Motor nerve conduction studies record the electrical signal generated not by the nerve itself but rather by contraction of a muscle supplied by the nerve. The recorded response is called a compound motor action potential (CMAP). CMAP amplitudes are recorded in the millivolt range. The commonly studied motor nerves include the median and ulnar nerves in the upper limbs and the peroneal and tibial nerves in the lower limbs, but many other motor nerves also can be studied. It is possible to perform a study if both the muscle and its innervating nerve are superficially accessible. The nerve always is stimulated proximal to the muscle recording site so as to study the nerve conduction in its usual direction. This type of study is called orthodromic.

Sensory nerve conduction studies record the action potential in the sensory nerve itself. The recorded result is called the sensory nerve action potential. Smaller amplitudes are seen, in comparison with motor studies, with results in the microvolt range. The commonly performed sensory studies are of the median, ulnar, and radial nerves in the upper limb; and the sural, peroneal, and saphenous nerves in the lower limb. Any accessible sensory nerve can be studied, although small nerve "twigs" may be unidentifiable because their amplitude recordings are too small for differentiation from electrical background noise. In orthodromic sensory nerve stimulation studies, the nerve is stimulated distal to the recording site so as to measure nerve conduction in the direction of sensory transmission. In antidromic stud-

ies, the nerve is stimulated proximal to the recording site to measure nerve conduction in the opposite direction from sensory transmission. The patient's age, height, sex, and body mass index can affect nerve conduction studies.[1] If the patient's skin is too cold, velocity or amplitude may be affected;[2] the limb must be warmed, and the study repeated.

Needle Electromyography
The second part of the typical electrodiagnostic study is the needle EMG (often called the needle examination). A thin metal pin-type electrode or needle is used; often it is Teflon coated except for its tip. The tip is inserted into a muscle and advanced through the muscle in small stages. After each brief advance, the needle tip movement is halted and the examiner observes the muscle's resting electrical activity. To provide a complete picture of motor activity, five to eight muscles are studied in one limb, with numerous studies through each muscle. The passage of the needle tip through a normal muscle irritates the motor fibers, causing a brief burst of electrical activity that quickly resolves. The normal muscle then becomes electrically silent. In contrast, the irritation caused by the needle passage is not quickly quieted in a denervated muscle. The muscle fibers are not silent at rest; instead, they show spontaneous activity in the form of positive waves and fibrillations. This activity is diagnostic for denervation.

As the patient voluntarily contracts the muscle, the electrodiagnostician evaluates the recorded voluntary motor unit action potentials (MUAPs) to determine whether they are normal. Normal MUAPs are brief and narrow, with few electrical phases. The type of abnormal finding provides details about the duration of an axonal injury and allows it to be classified as acute, subacute, or chronic. In the acute and subacute phases of an injury, the MUAP may have a greater-than-normal duration (recorded as increased width) and number of electrical phases. In the chronic phase, the MUAP duration may return to a narrow signal, but amplitude is much greater than normal. The increased amplitude is an electronic reflection of the typical healing process; when distal motor neuron sprouting reinnervates the orphaned motor fibers, a larger group of muscle cells is activated by a given motor neuron.

Earlier spine surgery does not preclude the use of needle EMG. However, the paraspinal muscles generally are studied with caution. It may be impossible to determine whether abnormalities in the paraspinal muscles are the result of perioperative muscle trauma, surgical transaction of the small branches of the dorsal rami that innervate the paraspinal muscles, or a spinal nerve injury.

F-Wave and H-Reflex Studies
In addition to motor and sensory nerve conduction studies, F-wave and H-reflex studies are often performed. The F-wave and the H-reflex studies allow the entire length of a nerve to be studied, from the spinal

cord to the level of the peripheral muscle. The F-wave study is performed in the same manner as a typical motor conduction study, but the machine settings are adjusted to record not only the direct MUAP but also a later signal that results when the stimulus reaches the spinal cord and reflects backward to the target muscle along the same motor nerve. These later signals are variable in their waveform and have small amplitudes in the microvolt range. Proximal nerve lesions, such as radiculopathies, plexopathies, or proximal peripheral neuropathies (for example, Guillain-Barré syndrome), can be evaluated using F-wave studies.[3]

The H-reflex is a true reflex, and it almost always is studied along the sciatic nerve. The stimulus is applied in the popliteal fossa, travels proximally along the sensory nerves, completes the reflex arc in the spinal cord, and causes a distal muscle activation in the calf. An abnormal result often occurs in an S1 radiculopathy.

Somatosensory-Evoked Potential Studies

Somatosensory-evoked potential (SEP) studies are similar to nerve conduction studies in that electrical stimuli are applied at one location and recorded elsewhere. SEP studies differ from nerve conduction studies in that they allow evaluation of the central nervous system structures. SEP studies are not included in typical nerve conduction studies and needle EMG, and they must be ordered separately.

During a SEP study, hundreds of electrical stimuli are applied peripherally and then detected by recording electrodes placed on the scalp or over the spinal cord at standard locations. The detected signals are averaged and compared with expected values for latency. Abnormally slow responses point to pathology somewhere along the pathway, but the study cannot further locate the lesion. Abnormally slow responses may be useful for diagnosing multiple sclerosis, some nerve injuries, plexopathy, or spinal cord injury. Although SEPs have been used in diagnosing radiculopathy, they do not yield as many details as needle EMG.[4] SEPs also are used for intraoperative monitoring of nerve function.

Timing of Electrodiagnostic Studies

After an acute injury, nerve conduction studies can be altered by axonal or myelin damage. Changes may not be seen on needle EMG for several weeks. A complete lesion, such as a nerve transection, does not allow any voluntary muscle activation, however, and it can be seen immediately. Changes in the paraspinal muscles can be seen 2 weeks after the injury, and changes in the peripheral muscles can be seen in 3 weeks. The delays are the result of wallerian degeneration. Motor fibers do not produce spontaneous abnormal electrical activity until wallerian degeneration has progressed to the distal neuromuscular junction. Abnormal needle EMG activity thus is evident first in the most proximal muscles and last in the most distal muscles.[5]

Although there is no clear-cut rule as to when abnormalities can be detected by nerve conduction studies, in some circumstances (as with a suspected transection of a peripheral nerve), a nerve conduction study may be performed soon after the patient is stabilized. The purpose is to determine whether some conduction remains across the injured area. A complete lesion can often be differentiated from an incomplete lesion, and these study results may help direct treatment and surgical options.

Considerations in Performing and Reporting Electrodiagnostic Studies

Performance

The electrodiagnostician must review the patient's symptoms and their onset. A brief physical examination may be performed. A full consultation does not need to accompany an electrodiagnostic study, unless the patient has a complicated condition or a neuromuscular disease. The electrodiagnostician usually should not insist on providing a consultation.

Determining the ideal number of nerves or muscles to be tested is difficult and best done by the electrodiagnostician during the study. As a rule, at least two motor and two sensory studies are performed in the upper limbs, and two motor and one sensory study are performed in the lower limbs. This practice is desirable because it allows an affected nerve to be compared with a control nerve. Side-to-side comparisons sometimes are useful. Many more nerves may need to be tested in complicated studies to detect a condition such as plexopathy or peripheral neuropathy. During needle EMG, usually it is useful to test five to eight muscles per limb. Routine testing of only one or two muscles probably is not sufficient, but testing of more than eight muscles is necessary only for complicated lesions such as plexopathies. The cervical and lumbar paraspinal muscles are important for diagnosing radiculopathy and generally should be tested if a spine condition is suspected. Serial repeat studies sometimes are useful, as in a patient with a compression neuropathy, to allow time for deciding whether a surgical release should be done.

Electrodiagnostic studies primarily are performed by physicians who specialize in neurology or physical medicine and rehabilitation. Subspecialty board certification can be obtained in electrodiagnosis. In some laboratories, nerve conduction studies are performed by a technician who has a graduate degree, and the physician performs the needle EMG. The physician always interprets the data from both the nerve conduction studies and the needle EMG.

Physical therapists sometimes perform a surface EMG study that is purported to be equivalent to a needle EMG. However, surface EMG cannot study deep muscles or differentiate between adjacent muscles with different innervation.[6] Surface EMG is useful for some research applications but is not recommended as a clin-

2: Nonsurgical Care of the Spine

ical replacement for needle EMG. Competence in providing nerve conduction studies and needle EMG requires years of detailed study.

Several companies sell nerve conduction study devices for office use by primary care physicians. These devices typically are worn like a glove. The physician performs the complete nerve conduction study by automatically applying the electrical stimulus and recording the resulting CMAPs or sensory nerve action potentials. No needle EMG is performed. The results are transmitted to an off-site provider, who reviews the data and offers an interpretation. The convenience of an in-office device is outweighed by its limitations, including the risk of inaccurate diagnosis. Although a typical electrodiagnostic study uses a standard group of two to four peripheral nerves, the setup for the study requires precise electrode placement and measurements. The precise sites differ from patient to patient and from side to side in the same patient because of factors such as hand size and finger length. A minor misplacement of an electrode can affect signal changes and alter results. An electrodiagnostician often adjusts the electrode placement for optimal signal acquisition, but the user of the glovelike device cannot make such adjustments. The electrodiagnostician constantly reviews the findings as the study progresses and adjusts the study or pursues additional studies in the interest of obtaining an accurate diagnosis. For example, a suspected routine ulnar neuropathy at the elbow may actually be a lower trunk brachial plexopathy. If an in-office device is used for diagnosis in this example, the best result is the need for a later standard electrodiagnostic study, but the worst result is a missed diagnosis.

Because an in-office device does not allow for a needle EMG, a cervical radiculopathy can be missed if a carpal tunnel syndrome also is present. Although the in-office study might collect F-wave data consistent with a radiculopathy, these data are only a small portion of the information available through a complete study, and they cannot be relied upon to determine whether a radiculopathy is present.

Interpretation and Reporting

It is difficult for a nonelectrodiagnostician to interpret the studies. Different testing techniques for the same nerves make it impossible to look at raw data and come to a definitive conclusion. Nonetheless, clinicians can benefit from understanding the following rules of thumb.

Large differences in latency or amplitude seen when a study is done on the opposite side of the body are likely to be significant. In most studies, a side-to-side drop in amplitude of 50% or more is abnormal. In sensory studies, a latency difference of approximately 0.5 ms may be abnormal. In motor studies, a latency difference of 1.5 to 2.0 ms is often abnormal. Of course, this type of analysis is limited if the abnormalities are bilateral.

Nerves that run along a similar course (for example, the median and ulnar nerves or the peroneal and tibial nerves) can be compared as long as the study distances

are similar. The comparison is valid for differences in latency but usually not for differences in amplitude. A nerve-to-nerve motor latency difference of more than 1.5 to 2.0 ms or a sensory latency difference of more than 0.5 ms generally is considered abnormal.

In needle EMG, it can be very useful to grade denervation fibrillations or positive sharp waves. A grade of 2 or more on a scale of 1 to 4 generally is significant. In contrast, a subjectively described finding such as "polyphasicity" or "abnormal firing pattern" is less likely to be useful.

The electrodiagnostician should interpret the raw study data as specifically as possible, while avoiding erroneous conclusions. Care must be taken to provide only the diagnosis indicated by the results, even at the risk of appearing indecisive, rather than to misdiagnose the patient's condition by providing a definitive but poorly supported diagnosis. The ordering physician should be able to rely on the electrodiagnostician to properly interpret the raw data. Secondary interpretation is fraught with danger unless it is done by an expert who knows exactly which technique was used. For example, latency may differ depending on whether the distance between the stimulating and recording electrodes was 10, 12, or 14 cm. Applying the same latency value to studies in which different distances were used can lead to misinterpretation of a completely normal result as abnormal, or vice versa.

The report of an electrodiagnostic study must state the nerve conduction studies that were performed and the muscles that were sampled during the needle EMG. This statement allows the clinician to determine whether the tests were performed as ordered, whether too few or the wrong nerves and muscles were tested, or whether the testing was excessive. A high-quality study should be reported in a manner that the ordering physician can readily understand and have confidence in. The report should be readily understandable to someone with medical training. For ease of interpretation, the raw data should be presented in the form of tables rather than a narrative. A high-quality report almost always can be presented in one or two pages. A longer report may give an impression of greater thoroughness but in reality is simply harder to read. Printouts of the waveforms may be added to the report but are optional; the clinician should not consider their absence as a sign of a less rigorous study.

It is important for the electrodiagnostician to contact the ordering physician if the study results are ambiguous. The ordering clinician is not an expert on electrodiagnostic studies, and the electrodiagnostician should be ready to explain the results.

Considerations in Ordering Electrodiagnostic Studies

If a clinician's differential diagnosis includes a condition caused by a central or peripheral nerve disorder, an electrodiagnostic study may be indicated. Electrodiagnostic studies can be used to confirm or rule out a diagnosis or to distinguish among multiple possible conditions. If spine pathology is suspected, an electrodiagnostic study may be ordered to confirm radiculopathy or exclude peripheral conditions such as ulnar neuropathy. The common symptoms in patients referred to an electrodiagnostic laboratory include claudication, radiating pain, numbness, tingling, and focal or generalized weakness. The clinician should consider a referral for electrodiagnostic study if the patient's neurologic symptoms are confusing or do not correspond to imaging results. Electrodiagnostic studies also can be considered if the symptoms are not amenable to standard treatment. For example, apparent myofascial pain in the back or neck that is not responsive to physical therapy and medications may indicate the patient has an underlying myopathy, neuropathy, or radiculopathy.

Electrodiagnostic Studies in the Diagnosis of Selected Disorders

Radiculopathy

Radiculopathy should be part of the differential diagnosis for a patient with radiating pain, numbness, or tingling in the arm or leg. Spine MRI often is one of the earliest studies obtained for such a patient. If a small disk protrusion is detected or if the MRI and clinical findings do not correspond, electrodiagnostic studies can be helpful. The sensitivity of electrodiagnostic studies for evaluating radiculopathy is as high as 93% if needle EMG includes testing of five to seven muscles.[7] The needle examination also may provide insight into the chronicity of the nerve injury and reveal whether any healing has occurred. Sensory nerve conduction studies usually are normal in patients with radiculopathy because the lesion is proximal to the postsynaptic sensory cell bodies in the dorsal root ganglion. Motor studies show normal latency, but there may be decreased amplitude if the radiculopathy is severe.

Spinal Stenosis

Signs of radiculopathy may be seen at multiple levels in a patient with spinal stenosis. Motor nerve conduction studies may be affected if the stenosis is severe. However, abnormal sensory studies are not expected in patients with spinal stenosis because the sensory nerve cell body is located in the dorsal root ganglion. A complete study with both nerve conduction studies and needle EMG is needed to differentiate spinal stenosis from peripheral polyneuropathy. Strict EMG criteria can help in differentiating clinically significant spinal stenosis from MRI-positive stenosis.[8]

Spinal Cord Injury

Needle examination may be useful soon after a spinal cord injury to determine whether the patient has any intact voluntary motor activity. However, clinical examination is more typically used for this purpose.

Sacroiliac Joint Pain

Referred sacroiliac joint pain may extend to the level of the knees, but it only occasionally extends below the knees. Sacroiliac joint pain that does extend below the knees can be confused with a low lumbar or sacral radiculopathy.[9] Clinical differentiation can be difficult, especially if MRI shows a possibly incidental noncompressive lumbar disk protrusion. Electrodiagnostic examination usually is less helpful for diagnosis than sacroiliac joint injection under fluoroscopic guidance.[10] If a sacroiliac joint injection does not establish a diagnosis, however, electrodiagnostic studies can be pursued. The results will be normal if the origin of the patient's pain is in the sacroiliac joint.

Piriformis Syndrome

Piriformis syndrome involves a muscle-induced sciatic neuropathy resulting in radiating pain, numbness, and tingling typically extending to the foot. Standard electrodiagnostic studies have normal results, although the condition can affect H-reflex testing.[11] When ordering an EMG to confirm piriformis syndrome, the clinician should specifically request H-reflex testing.

Guillain-Barré Syndrome

The ascending paralysis characterizing Guillain-Barré syndrome initially may appear to be caused by cervical or lumbar spine disease. Unless F-wave studies are obtained, electrodiagnostic studies may fail to identify Guillain-Barré syndrome early in the course of the disease. The clinician should suspect Guillain-Barré syndrome as the patient's symptoms advance, and repeat studies may be warranted because findings evolve with the course of the disease. F-wave studies should be ordered if Guillain-Barré syndrome is suspected.

Plexopathy

Sensory and motor deficits that are not matched to a single nerve or a single nerve root level suggest the presence of a plexopathy. The mechanism of the patient's injury also may lead the clinician to suspect a disorder of the plexus. The nerve conduction studies necessary to determine whether a plexopathy is present are not routinely done. Whenever plexopathy is included in the differential diagnosis, the patient should be referred to an experienced electrodiagnostician. A plexus evaluation can be difficult and time consuming, but often it yields a precise localization of the nerve injury.

Carpal Tunnel Syndrome

The symptoms of numbness and tingling in a median nerve distribution suggest carpal tunnel syndrome but can also be caused by a C6 or C7 radiculopathy. Patients with carpal tunnel syndrome can experience pain, numbness, and tingling proximal to the wrist, mimicking a cervical radiculopathy. The symptoms improve after transverse carpal ligament release.[12] Standard motor and sensory nerve conduction studies of the median and ulnar nerves can lead to the diagnosis of carpal tunnel syndrome. However, some electrodiagnosticians do not routinely perform needle EMG, which is necessary to diagnose a concomitant cervical radiculopathy. Both nerve conduction studies and needle EMG should be specifically ordered if a cervical radiculopathy is suspected.

Long Thoracic Neuropathy

Although long thoracic neuropathy is considered rare, it is found with surprising regularity in patients with muscular injury in the posterior shoulder girdle. The electrodiagnostic studies required to diagnose long thoracic neuropathy are not routinely performed, and testing for this condition must be specified. Long thoracic neuropathy should be differentiated from an injury to cranial nerve XI, which can have a similar appearance. Electrodiagnostic studies can evaluate not only for the presence of the condition but also for its completeness and the progress of any healing.

Peripheral Polyneuropathy and Other Conditions Mimicking a Spine Disorder

The weakness and painful burning, tingling, and numbness associated with peripheral polyneuropathy can mimic a disorder of the spine such as radiculopathy or lumbar spinal stenosis. Peripheral polyneuropathy should be suspected in a patient who has these symptoms, particularly if the patient has diabetes, abuses alcohol or other drugs, or has one of several rheumatologic disorders or nutritional deficits. Nerve conduction studies should be obtained to diagnose and document the severity of the neuropathy. Needle EMG is recommended to evaluate for any concomitant condition.

Numerous other conditions also cause symptoms similar to those of spine pathology. Care must be taken to identify such a condition to ensure optimal treatment of the patient and avoid unnecessary procedures or surgeries.

Summary

Electrodiagnostic studies are of tremendous benefit in the workup of suspected disorders of the spine. These studies can confirm or exclude a possible diagnosis and can yield information on the affected level, injury acuity or chronicity, and extent of neuronal healing.

Annotated References

1. Buschbacher RM, Prahlow ND: *Manual of Nerve Conduction Studies*, ed 2. New York, NY, Demos Medical, 2006.

2. Denys EH: The influence of temperature in clinical neurophysiology. *Muscle Nerve* 1991;14(9):795-811.

3. Fisher MA: H reflexes and F waves: Physiology and clinical indications. *Muscle Nerve* 1992;15(11):1223-1233.

4. Tsao B: The electrodiagnosis of cervical and lumbosacral radiculopathy. *Neurol Clin* 2007;25(2):473-494.

   The basics of electromyography are reviewed, including the technique of SEP studies. An overview of the root-level motor innervation of many limb muscles is included.

5. Koeppen AH: Wallerian degeneration: History and clinical significance. *J Neurol Sci* 2004;220(1-2):115-117.

6. Haig AJ, Gelblum JB, Rechtien JJ, Gitter AJ: Technology assessment: The use of surface EMG in the diagnosis and treatment of nerve and muscle disorders. *Muscle Nerve* 1996;19(3):392-395.

7. Dillingham TR, Lauder TD, Andary M, et al: Identification of cervical radiculopathies: Optimizing the electromyographic screen. *Am J Phys Med Rehabil* 2001;80(2):84-91.

8. Chiodo A, Haig AJ, Yamakawa KS, Quint D, Tong H, Choksi VR: Needle EMG has a lower false positive rate than MRI in asymptomatic older adults being evaluated for lumbar spinal stenosis. *Clin Neurophysiol* 2007;118(4):751-756.

   A prospective masked study compared needle EMG and lumbar MRI for diagnosing symptomatic lumbar spinal stenosis. Abnormal spontaneous activity seen on needle examination is useful as a criterion to lower false-positive rates.

9. van der Wurff P, Buijs EJ, Groen GJ: Intensity mapping of pain referral areas in sacroiliac joint pain patients. *J Manipulative Physiol Ther* 2006;29(3):190-195.

   In a case study, pain diagrams located the most intense sacroiliac joint pain at the joint itself, with progressively less pain radiating to the knee. In some patients, pain radiated past the knee and into the foot.

10. Fortin JD, Aprill CN, Ponthieux B, Pier J: Sacroiliac joint: Pain referral maps upon applying a new injection/arthrography technique. Part II: Clinical evaluation. *Spine (Phila Pa 1976)* 1994;19(13):1483-1489.

11. Fishman LM, Dombi GW, Michaelsen C, et al: Piriformis syndrome: Diagnosis, treatment, and outcome. A 10-year study. *Arch Phys Med Rehabil* 2002;83(3):295-301.

12. Cherington M: Proximal pain in carpal tunnel syndrome. *Arch Surg* 1974;108(1):69.

Chapter 13

Fibromyalgia and Chronic Widespread Pain

Michael C. Hsu, MD   Daniel Clauw, MD

Introduction

Fibromyalgia (FM) and chronic widespread pain (CWP) were once believed to be inflammatory in nature but now are recognized as primarily disorders of central pain processing. Recent epidemiologic and mechanistic research has fundamentally changed the way these syndromes are understood. Evidence-based guidelines can help in choosing the most appropriate treatment for a patient with FM or CWP, from among the variety of available pharmacologic and nonpharmacologic options. Given the considerable overlap between the characteristics of patients with FM or CWP and patients with chronic neck or low back pain, future research is likely to extend the use of many interventions for FM or CWP to other patients with comorbid central sensitivity pain syndromes.

Epidemiology

The definition of CWP is pain of at least 3 months' duration that involves both the left and right sides of the body, regions both above and below the waist, and the axial skeleton. FM, as defined by the American College of Rheumatology (ACR) in 1990, is CWP with the additional presence of at least 11 of 18 possible tender points.[1] In Western countries, CWP affects approximately 4% to 11% of the population.[2] The more narrowly defined FM affects 0.5% to 4%.[3]

The tender points that distinguish FM from CWP have no specific, inherent biologic properties. Research since 1990 has revealed that patients with FM have tenderness not limited to the 18 tender points but throughout their bodies.[4] The tender point count was

Dr. Clauw or an immediate family member serves as a paid consultant to or is an employee of Pfizer, Eli Lilly, Johnson & Johnson, UCB, Cypress Biosciences, Forest Laboratories, and Astra Zeneca; and has received research or institutional support from Eli Lilly, Pfizer, and Forest Laboratories. Neither Dr. Hsu nor any immediate family member has received anything of value from or owns stock in a commercial company or institution related directly or indirectly to the subject of this chapter.

found to partly reflect the patient's level of psychological distress and to be unstable over time.[5] Although the tender point count is helpful in assessing a patient for diffuse tenderness, it should not be used as a criterion for diagnosing FM outside the research setting.

Risk Factors

It appears that any extreme or prolonged physical, immune, or emotional stress increases the risk of development of FM or CWP. Prospective, population-based studies have identified several risk factors for FM or CWP, including earlier illness or trauma, sleep difficulties, poor social support, and workplace bullying[6-10] (Table 1).

Comorbid Overlapping Conditions

Patients with FM or CWP are far more likely than the general population to meet the criteria for a diagnosis of chronic fatigue syndrome, irritable bowel syndrome, temporomandibular joint disorder, vulvodynia, or migraine.[11] Patients with a chronic, disabling occupational disorder of the spine are three to eight times more likely than the general population to meet the ACR criteria for the diagnosis of FM.[12] The terms "central sensitivity syndromes" and "disorders of pain processing" sometimes are used to indicate the coaggregation of these diagnostic entities into a spectrum of disorders.[13]

Familial and Genetic Inheritance

Recent research has revealed that FM and chronic pain in general are to a considerable extent aggregated within families. The first-degree relatives of a person with FM have an 8.5-fold risk of having FM or one of several other pain disorders, and the relatives of patients with FM have more diffuse tenderness than the relatives of control subjects.[14] This familial aggregation appears to have a polygenic component, with the currently identified genes involving catecholamine neurotransmission.[15]

Pathogenesis and Persistence

Despite continuing controversy concerning the pathogenesis of FM and CWP, researchers agree that it is multifactorial, with contributions from both genetic

Table 1		
Research-Supported Risk Factors for the Development of Fibromyalgia or Chronic Widespread Pain		
Risk Factor	**Odds Ratio**	**Research Study**
Preexisting bronchitis (in Gulf War veterans)	4.9	Ang et al[6]
Workplace bullying	4.1	Kivimäki et al[7]
Sleep difficulties	2.7	Gupta et al[8]
Poor social support	2.0	Bergman et al[9]
Maternal death during childhood	2.0	Jones et al[10]
Traffic accident during childhood	1.5	Jones et al[10]

and environmental factors. Recent twin studies suggest that approximately 50% of the risk of development of a functional pain syndrome such as FM, irritable bowel syndrome, or headache is genetic, and 50% is environmental. These studies also found that the pain and sensory amplification traits are clearly distinguishable and separable from the symptoms of depression and anxiety.[11,16] The simplified model shown in Figure 1 integrates the most consistent mechanistic and epidemiologic findings related to this spectrum of illness.

Neurobiologic Factors

If a healthy, asymptomatic individual, perhaps with a genetic predisposition to a functional pain syndrome, is exposed to extreme or prolonged physical or emotional stress, several neurobiologic alterations may occur that increase the risk of development of widespread pain and hyperalgesia. These alterations include general sensory augmentation, long-term potentiation and other neuroplastic changes, and hypothalamic-pituitary-adrenal (HPA) axis dysfunction.

General sensory augmentation is an increased sensitivity to pressure, heat, cold, loud noises, and other sensory stimuli, believed to occur within the central nervous system.[17] Long-term potentiation refers to neuroplastic changes within the brainstem and spinal cord that result in heightened nociceptive neurotransmission, as evidenced by the increased levels of glutamate, nerve growth factor, and brain-derived neurotrophic factor found in the cerebrospinal fluid of patients with FM.[18] In healthy individuals in whom widespread pain subsequently develops, HPA axis dysfunction is a decrease in counterinflammatory cortisol response and diurnal cortisol fluctuation.[19,20] Individuals with this pattern of HPA axis dysfunction typically have chronic psychosocial stress.[21] HPA axis dysfunction may be part of the etiopathogenic link between stress and the subsequent development of widespread pain and hyperalgesia.

Sleep Disruption

Sleep disruption is recognized as a significant risk factor for the development of pain in general and CWP in particular.[9] Healthy volunteers who underwent partial sleep deprivation had an elevated interleukin-6 (IL-6)

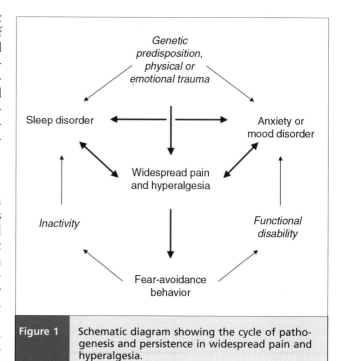

Figure 1   Schematic diagram showing the cycle of pathogenesis and persistence in widespread pain and hyperalgesia.

level, which was correlated with their pain rating.[22] Both the likelihood of sleep difficulties after an emotionally or physically traumatic event and the role of IL-6 in peripheral nerve fiber sensitization to pain suggest that sleep disruption is a mechanistic link between stress and the development of widespread pain.[23] Widespread pain and hyperalgesia can cause further disruption in sleep, thereby leading to the cycle of pain and sleep disruption that is characteristic of FM and CWP.

Anxiety and Mood Disorder

The association between psychiatric conditions and FM is well known; the co-occurrence odds ratio is as high as 6.7 for an anxiety disorder and 2.7 for major depressive disorder.[24] Comorbid anxiety and mood disorder often are considered complications of chronic pain. However, familial studies suggest a shared inheritance between FM and certain psychiatric conditions, and a cause-and-effect relationship is therefore difficult to establish.[14] Nevertheless, both cross-sectional and experimental studies have found that the presence of comorbid depressive symptoms or pain-related anxiety (such as pain-related catastrophizing) predict a heightened pain experience in FM patients.[25,26] These findings underscore the importance of psychiatric comorbidity in the persistence of widespread pain.

Fear-Avoidance Behavior

After widespread pain develops, comorbid sleep and affective disorders contribute to its perpetuation. In addition, avoidance of physical activity because of fear of the resulting pain was found in 39% of patients with FM, and this fear-avoidance behavior can lead to inactivity and disability.[27,28] Inactivity is known to lead to further sleep disruption as well as other negative effects on quality of life.[29] Disability and unemployment contribute to the patient's negative affect.[30] Thus, fear-avoidance behavior can contribute to the persistence of widespread pain and hyperalgesia.

Clinical Presentation and Natural History

Several community-based, cross-sectional studies have improved the ability to characterize patients with FM in general.[31,32] The typical patient is a woman who is 35 to 65 years old at the initial visit. The gender imbalance is an artifact of the ACR criterion requiring the presence of 11 of 18 tender points, in addition to CWP; in population-based studies, women were 10 times more likely than men to meet this criterion.[33] Usually the patient's most important symptoms include pain, fatigue, nonrestorative sleep, morning stiffness, forgetfulness, difficulty in concentrating, and difficulty in initiating sleep. The symptoms typically are exacerbated by emotional distress, changes in the weather, insomnia, and strenuous activity. Most patients report no difficulty in performing routine activities of daily living, but only 18% are able to walk 1 mile without difficulty, and only 7% are able to complete heavy household tasks without difficulty. Only half of patients with FM are able to maintain paid employment.[31]

A diagnosis of low back pain is found in the medical history of 63% of patients with FM. Other common past diagnoses, in descending order of frequency, are headache, arthritis, irritable bowel syndrome, chronic fatigue syndrome, depression, anxiety, sinus condition, restless leg syndrome, and tinnitus (in 30% of patients). Between 32% and 46% of patients also report tingling, numbness, or balance difficulty.[32]

Studies of the natural history of FM and CWP have had conflicting results, perhaps reflecting the different characteristics of patients seen at tertiary care and primary care facilities. Patients seen at a tertiary care facility may have much greater psychological comorbidity than patients seen in a primary care setting. A study of patients treated at a tertiary care facility found little or

no improvement in symptoms, even at 6-year follow-up.[34] In contrast, community-based studies reported that approximately 11% of patients with CWP achieved symptom resolution within 1 year and that an additional one third of patients had only regional pain after 1 year.[7,35]

Treatment Considerations

Diagnosis and Education

Providing the patient with a diagnosis of FM or CWP may reduce any health care–seeking behavior, improve the ability to cope, and relieve tension in interpersonal relationships.[36] Initial counseling should emphasize that the condition is nondestructive and that a substantial percentage of patients have improvement within 1 year. The patient should understand that the primary dysfunction is in the nervous system, even though the pain is felt in the muscles, and the pain does not reflect damage to the tissues.

Patients may seek a single curative treatment, but a multidisciplinary, multimodal approach usually yields a more favorable outcome.[37] As suggested by the pathogenic model (Figure 1), the treatment should include not only pharmacologic management of widespread pain and hyperalgesia but also a program of increased physical activity, sleep improvement, and cognitive-behavioral or cognitive-affective intervention.

Pharmacologic Neuromodulation

Meta-analyses and large randomized controlled studies have established that some medications aimed at altering the neurochemistry of the central nervous system are reasonably successful in the short-term reduction of pain for patients with FM or CWP[38-47] (Table 2). These medications include tricyclic antidepressants, some selective serotonin-reuptake inhibitors, serotonin-norepinephrine reuptake inhibitors, and antiepileptic drugs. To select the most appropriate medication for an individual patient, the physician should consider the benefits, adverse effects, US Food and Drug Administration approval status, titration schedule, and cost. The modest overall effect is the result of a pattern in which some, but not most, patients have a positive response to a particular drug. The modest effect size underscores the lack of analgesics with a strong effect size in any chronic pain state, as well as the importance of multidisciplinary management of FM and CWP.

Ibuprofen and other nonsteroidal anti-inflammatory drugs are widely used but were found to be no better than placebo for the pharmacologic management of FM.[48,49] With the exception of tramadol,[44] the use of opiates for treating FM or CWP has not been supported or refuted by randomized controlled studies.

Increased Physical Activity

Inactivity and functional disability contribute to the perpetuation of pain because of their negative effects

2: Nonsurgical Care of the Spine

Table 2

The Pharmacologic Treatment of Fibromyalgia

Drug Category	Drug Name	Approximate Effect Size for Pain*	Other Benefits	Common Adverse Effects
Tricyclic antidepressant	Cyclobenzaprine	0.5	Sleep	Somnolence Dry mouth Dizziness
	Amitriptyline	0 to 0.7	Sleep	Somnolence Dry mouth Constipation Weight gain
Selective serotonin-reuptake inhibitor	Fluoxetine	0.9	Mood Fatigue	Insomnia Somnolence Nausea
Serotonin-norepinephrine reuptake inhibitor	Duloxetine	0.5	Mood Physical function	Nausea Insomnia Dry mouth Constipation
	Milnacipran	0.3 to 0.5	Cognition Physical function Fatigue	Nausea Constipation Hyperhidrosis Dizziness
	Tramadol-acetaminophen	0.4	Physical function	Nausea Pruritus Constipation
Anticonvulsant	Gabapentin	0.6	Sleep	Lightheadedness Somnolence Dizziness Weight gain
	Pregabalin	0.3 to 0.5	Sleep	Dizziness Somnolence Weight gain Edema
Hypnotic	Sodium oxybate	0.4	Sleep Fatigue	Dizziness Somnolence Nausea

*Calculated using Cohen's d.
qhs = at night.

on the patient's sleep and affect. The treatment plan for a patient with FM or CWP should include a program of increased physical activity. Low- or moderate-intensity exercise of any type was found to yield improvement in pain, fatigue, sleep, and mood in patients with FM.[50] Initially, the exercise regimen should avoid impact movements such as running or jumping, and the initial target heart rate should not exceed 50% of maximum heart rate. Warm-water aquatic training may lead to more rapid improvement than land-based exercise.[51]

An early failure could reinforce the patient's fear-avoidance behavior. The clinician should educate the patient and the patient's exercise trainer about the need for pacing to avoid the extremes of hyperactivity or inactivity.

Sleep Quality Improvement

Sleep disruption and increasing pain can become a destructive cycle. Interventions to improve sleep quality should be part of a multicomponent treatment plan. A recent epidemiologic study found that restorative sleep is predictive of CWP resolution (odds ratio, 2.7).[52] Insomnia often can be treated by using medications that modify neurotransmission (Table 2). Sleep can be further improved through cognitive-behavioral interventions and sleep hygiene education.[53] Targeting inactivity and treating any comorbid anxiety or mood disorder should have a beneficial effect on sleep; for example, studies have found that aquatic therapy and written expression of emotion have a positive effect on sleep.[54,55]

Patients with FM and CWP appear to have a rela-

Table 2 (continued)

US Food and Drug Administration Status for Fibromyalgia Use	Starting Dosage	Target Dosage	Approximate Monthly Cost	Research Study
Not approved	10 mg qhs	10-40 mg daily, over 2-3 doses	$50 or less	Tofferi et al[38]
Not approved	25 mg qhs	25 mg qhs	$50 or less	Nishishinya et al[39]
Not approved	20 mg daily	20 mg every other day–80 mg daily	$50 or less	Arnold, Hess et al[40]
Approved	20 mg daily	60 mg daily–60 mg twice daily	$100-$150	Arnold, Pritchett et al[41]
Approved	25 mg daily	100 mg twice daily	$100-$150	Mease et al[42] Vitton et al[43]
Not approved	37.5 mg daily	150-300 mg daily, over 4 doses	$100-$150	Bennett et al[44]
Not approved	300 mg qhs	1200-2400 mg daily, over 3 doses	$50 or less	Arnold, Goldenberg et al[45]
Approved	150 mg daily	150-300 mg twice daily	$150-$200	Arnold, Russell et al[46]
Not approved	4.5 mg qhs, over 2 doses	4.5-6 mg daily, over 2 doses	$2,000	Russell et al[47]

tively high prevalence of sleep-disordered breathing.[56] Ambulatory plethysmography or overnight polysomnography should be considered for patients who snore excessively or have daytime somnolence. If sleep-disordered breathing is present, continuous positive airway pressure may improve the quality of sleep and prevent circulatory complications.[57] A specialized pillow designed to prevent supine positioning during sleep and subsequent airway obstruction can be used as an alternative first-line empiric treatment.

Interventions Targeting Fear-Avoidance Behavior and Pain-Related Catastrophizing

Several randomized controlled studies found that cognitive-behavioral therapy leads to long-term improvement in physical function and mood in patients with FM.[58,59] The primary goal of cognitive-behavioral interventions for patients with FM and CWP should be to decrease fear-avoidance behavior and reduce pain-related catastrophic thinking.[60] Patient expectations affect the outcome of cognitive-behavioral interventions, and therefore the clinician may need to explain that pain-related beliefs can alter the processing of pain signals in the brain.[61]

Although the term cognitive-behavioral therapy usually refers to individual treatment by a clinical psychologist, group education-discussion sessions led by a psychologist or another qualified clinician can be equally effective.[62] A self-directed written or video program is another cost-effective means of teaching cognitive-behavioral concepts.[63]

Interventions Targeting Anxiety and Mood Disorders

Several pharmacologic agents, such as fluoxetine and duloxetine, have a beneficial effect on comorbid de-

2: Nonsurgical Care of the Spine

pressive symptoms in patients with FM.[40,64] Aerobic exercise also was found to beneficially affect mood in patients with FM.[51,65] Cognitive-affective interventions, such as mindfulness meditation and written emotional expression, were found to have efficacy in improving mood and pain in patients with FM, and they may be particularly beneficial in patients who are willing to confront internal sources of emotional distress.[55,66]

Nonpharmacologic Neuromodulation

Acupuncture and magnetic or electrical brain stimulation are capable of modulating neurotransmission. These two distinct modalities have received increasing attention in recent years. A systematic review concluded that the results were inconsistent in five randomized controlled studies of acupuncture for patients with FM.[67] However, a more recent study found that acupuncture led to a moderate decrease in pain and a slight decrease in fatigue and anxiety that extended as long as 7 months after treatment.[68] It appears that the type of placebo used in each study influenced the results. The effect of acupuncture is highly dependent on the individual clinician and patient, but in general, the use of greater needle stimulation (including electroacupuncture) appears to be correlated with a more beneficial effect.

Transcranial stimulation of different cortical regions of the brain, either with magnetic pulses or direct current, recently has been studied in patients with FM. A randomized, placebo-controlled study using transcranial direct current stimulation found that patients had a significant reduction in pain that was still present at 3-week follow-up.[69] Another recent small randomized, placebo-controlled study found that transcranial direct current stimulation of the left primary cortex had beneficial effects on pain, fatigue, physical function, and sleep.[70] Repetitive transcranial magnetic stimulation and direct current stimulation are typically administered during daily sessions of less than 30 minutes each, for 4 to 6 weeks. The reported adverse effects are minimal. Further research is needed to investigate the efficacy and safety of these neuromodulatory treatments for treating intractable FM and CWP.

Summary

FM and CWP affect a large portion of the population and have characteristics in common with other functional pain syndromes. Recent studies repeatedly have found that the ongoing dysfunction in FM and CWP is in central pain processing, with only minor contributions from the immunologic and peripheral nervous systems. The evidence supports the use of a multicomponent treatment plan that includes pharmacologic neuromodulation, physical activity, improvement of sleep quality, elimination of fear-avoidance behavior and pain-related catastrophizing, and treatment of comorbid anxiety or mood disorder. The usefulness of acupuncture and magnetic or electrical neurostimulation is still being researched.

Annotated References

1. Wolfe F, Smythe HA, Yunus MB, et al: The American College of Rheumatology 1990 Criteria for the Classification of Fibromyalgia. *Arthritis Rheum* 1990;33(2): 160-172.

2. Lindell L, Bergman S, Petersson IF, Jacobsson LT, Herrström P: Prevalence of fibromyalgia and chronic widespread pain. *Scand J Prim Health Care* 2000;18(3):149-153.

3. White KP, Speechley M, Harth M, Ostbye T: The London Fibromyalgia Epidemiology Study: The prevalence of fibromyalgia syndrome in London, Ontario. *J Rheumatol* 1999;26(7):1570-1576.

4. Harden RN, Revivo G, Song S, et al: A critical analysis of the tender points in fibromyalgia. *Pain Med* 2007; 8(2):147-156.

   Compared with control subjects, patients with FM had abnormal pressure-pain, even at points not used in the ACR criteria. Level of evidence: III.

5. Wolfe F: The relation between tender points and fibromyalgia symptom variables: Evidence that fibromyalgia is not a discrete disorder in the clinic. *Ann Rheum Dis* 1997;56(4):268-271.

6. Ang DC, Peloso PM, Woolson RF, Kroenke K, Doebbeling BN: Predictors of incident chronic widespread pain among veterans following the first Gulf War. *Clin J Pain* 2006;22(6):554-563.

   A prospective cohort study of 370 Gulf War veterans found that those with symptoms of bronchitis at baseline had a 4.9-fold greater likelihood of development of CWP within 5 years. Level of evidence: II.

7. Kivimäki M, Leino-Arjas P, Virtanen M, et al: Work stress and incidence of newly diagnosed fibromyalgia: Prospective cohort study. *J Psychosom Res* 2004;57(5): 417-422.

8. Gupta A, Silman AJ, Ray D, et al: The role of psychosocial factors in predicting the onset of chronic widespread pain: Results from a prospective population-based study. *Rheumatology (Oxford)* 2007;46(4):666-671.

   In a 15-month community-based, prospective cohort study involving 3,171 individuals without CWP at baseline, those with a baseline score of 9 or higher on the Sleep Problems Scale had a 2.7-fold greater likelihood of development of CWP. Level of evidence: I.

9. Bergman S, Herrström P, Jacobsson LT, Petersson IF: Chronic widespread pain: A three year followup of pain distribution and risk factors. *J Rheumatol* 2002;29(4): 818-825.

10. Jones GT, Power C, Macfarlane GJ: Adverse events in childhood and chronic widespread pain in adult life: Results from the 1958 British Birth Cohort Study. *Pain* 2009;143(1-2):92-96.

The authors used 1958 British Birth Cohort Study data acquired at age 7 years to assess 7,571 individuals for CWP. Experiencing maternal death in childhood led to a twofold increase in the likelihood of development of CWP by age 45 years. Level of evidence: II.

11. Kato K, Sullivan PF, Evengård B, Pedersen NL: Chronic widespread pain and its comorbidities: A population-based study. *Arch Intern Med* 2006;166(15):1649-1654.

Data were gathered from 44,897 individuals in the Swedish Twin Registry. Using case-control and co-twin designs, significant associations were found between FM and many other chronic pain conditions. Level of evidence: III.

12. Mayer TG, Towns BL, Neblett R, Theodore BR, Gatchel RJ: Chronic widespread pain in patients with occupational spinal disorders: Prevalence, psychiatric comorbidity, and association with outcomes. *Spine (Phila Pa 1976)* 2008;33(17):1889-1897.

Among 2,730 consecutive patients with a chronic, disabling occupational spine disorder treated at a multidisciplinary pain clinic, 32% met the ACR criteria for CWP. Level of evidence: III.

13. Clauw DJ, Williams DA: Relationship between stress and pain in work-related upper extremity disorders: The hidden role of chronic multisymptom illnesses. *Am J Ind Med* 2002;41(5):370-382.

14. Arnold LM, Hudson JI, Hess EV, et al: Family study of fibromyalgia. *Arthritis Rheum* 2004;50(3):944-952.

15. Buskila D, Sarzi-Puttini P, Ablin JN: The genetics of fibromyalgia syndrome. *Pharmacogenomics* 2007;8(1):67-74.

A review of recent landmark studies found an increased prevalence of certain serotonergic, dopaminergic, and catecholaminergic genetic polymorphisms in patients with FM or other chronic pain disorders, compared with control subjects. Level of evidence: III.

16. Kato K, Sullivan PF, Evengård B, Pedersen NL: A population-based twin study of functional somatic syndromes. *Psychol Med* 2009;39(3):497-505.

The Swedish Twin Registry was used to identify 31,318 twins who were interviewed to determine the presence of CWP, irritable bowel syndrome, chronic fatigue syndrome, or recurrent headache. Multivariate analysis revealed a significant genetic influence on the development of each of these syndromes. Level of evidence: III.

17. Kosek E, Ekholm J, Hansson P: Sensory dysfunction in fibromyalgia patients with implications for pathogenic mechanisms. *Pain* 1996;68(2-3):375-383.

18. Sarchielli P, Mancini ML, Floridi A, et al: Increased levels of neurotrophins are not specific for chronic migraine: Evidence from primary fibromyalgia syndrome. *J Pain* 2007;8(9):737-745.

Examination of the cerebrospinal fluid of 20 patients with FM, 20 patients with chronic migraine, and 20 healthy control subjects revealed elevated levels of brain-derived neurotrophic factor, nerve growth factor, and glutamate in the patients with FM or chronic migraine, compared with the control subjects. Level of evidence: III.

19. McBeth J, Silman AJ, Gupta A, et al: Moderation of psychosocial risk factors through dysfunction of the hypothalamic-pituitary-adrenal stress axis in the onset of chronic widespread musculoskeletal pain: Findings of a population-based prospective cohort study. *Arthritis Rheum* 2007;56(1):360-371.

In 267 individuals without CWP, HPA axis function was assessed at baseline and followed for the development of CWP. A deficiency in dexamethose suppression response yielded a 3.53-fold greater likelihood of development of CWP over a 15-month period. Level of evidence: I.

20. Glass JM, Lyden AK, Petzke F, et al: The effect of brief exercise cessation on pain, fatigue, and mood symptom development in healthy, fit individuals. *J Psychosom Res* 2004;57(4):391-398.

21. Simpkiss JL, Devine DP: Responses of the HPA axis after chronic variable stress: Effects of novel and familiar stressors. *Neuro Endocrinol Lett* 2003;24(1-2):97-103.

22. Haack M, Sanchez E, Mullington JM: Elevated inflammatory markers in response to prolonged sleep restriction are associated with increased pain experience in healthy volunteers. *Sleep* 2007;30(9):1145-1152.

In 18 volunteers, a 12-day period of sleeping no more than 4 hours per night led to elevated IL-6 levels, compared with sleeping 8 hours per night. IL-6 level was strongly associated with pain rating. Level of evidence: III.

23. Brenn D, Richter F, Schaible HG: Sensitization of unmyelinated sensory fibers of the joint nerve to mechanical stimuli by interleukin-6 in the rat: An inflammatory mechanism of joint pain. *Arthritis Rheum* 2007;56(1):351-359.

Injection of 20 ng of IL-6 into the knee joints of anesthetized rats was compared to an isotonic control solution injection. IL-6 led to increased C-fiber activity in the medial articular nerve with mechanical rotation of the knee.

24. Arnold LM, Hudson JI, Keck PE, Auchenbach MB, Javaras KN, Hess EV: Comorbidity of fibromyalgia and psychiatric disorders. *J Clin Psychiatry* 2006;67(8):1219-1225.

Data were gathered from 78 individuals with FM and 146 of their relatives. Using a case-control design, significant associations were found between FM and psychiatric disorders including bipolar disorder, major depressive disorder, and any anxiety disorder. Level of evidence: III.

25. Hassett AL, Cone JD, Patella SJ, Sigal LH: The role of catastrophizing in the pain and depression of women with fibromyalgia syndrome. *Arthritis Rheum* 2000; 43(11):2493-2500.

26. Gracely RH, Geisser ME, Giesecke T, et al: Pain catastrophizing and neural responses to pain among persons with fibromyalgia. *Brain* 2004;127(pt 4):835-843.

27. Turk DC, Robinson JP, Burwinkle T: Prevalence of fear of pain and activity in patients with fibromyalgia syndrome. *J Pain* 2004;5(9):483-490.

28. Karsdorp PA, Vlaeyen JW: Active avoidance but not activity pacing is associated with disability in fibromyalgia. *Pain* 2009;147(1-3):29-35.

    The Chronic Pain Coping Inventory, Fibromyalgia Impact Questionnaire, and Pain Disability Index were completed by 409 Dutch patients with FM. Regression analysis revealed that patients who avoided physical activity reported greater physical impairment and disability, even when controlling for pain intensity and catastrophizing. Level of evidence: III.

29. Hague JF, Gilbert SS, Burgess HJ, Ferguson SA, Dawson D: A sedentary day: Effects on subsequent sleep and body temperatures in trained athletes. *Physiol Behav* 2003;78(2):261-267.

30. Frese M, Mohr G: Prolonged unemployment and depression in older workers: A longitudinal study of intervening variables. *Soc Sci Med* 1987;25(2):173-178.

31. Bennett RM, Jones J, Turk DC, Russell IJ, Matallana L: An internet survey of 2,596 people with fibromyalgia. *BMC Musculoskelet Disord* 2007;8:27.

    A questionnaire was completed by 2,569 people with FM to estimate the prevalence of common symptoms and the commonly used treatments for FM.

32. McNally JD, Matheson DA, Bakowsky VS: The epidemiology of self-reported fibromyalgia in Canada. *Chronic Dis Can* 2006;27(1):9-16.

    The prevalence of FM in Canada was calculated to be 1.1%, based on data from the 2000 Canadian Community Health Survey. FM was found to be associated with various somatic and psychological symptoms.

33. Yunus MB: The role of gender in fibromyalgia syndrome. *Curr Rheumatol Rep* 2001;3(2):128-134.

34. Baumgartner E, Finckh A, Cedraschi C, Vischer TL: A six year prospective study of a cohort of patients with fibromyalgia. *Ann Rheum Dis* 2002;61(7):644-645.

35. MacFarlane GJ, Thomas E, Papageorgiou AC, Schollum J, Croft PR, Silman AJ: The natural history of chronic pain in the community: A better prognosis than in the clinic? *J Rheumatol* 1996;23(9):1617-1620.

36. Reich JW, Olmsted ME, van Puymbroeck CM: Illness uncertainty, partner caregiver burden and support, and relationship satisfaction in fibromyalgia and osteoarthritis patients. *Arthritis Rheum* 2006;55(1):86-93.

    Fifty-one patients with FM were surveyed concerning illness uncertainty and partner relationship. In patients with high uncertainty as to diagnosis and illness status, symptom severity was negatively correlated with relationship satisfaction.

37. Häuser W, Bernardy K, Arnold B, Offenbächer M, Schiltenwolf M: Efficacy of multicomponent treatment in fibromyalgia syndrome: A meta-analysis of randomized controlled clinical trials. *Arthritis Rheum* 2009; 61(2):216-224.

    This systematic review included a meta-analysis of nine randomized controlled studies that examined the efficacy of multicomponent treatment of FM. Significant short-term improvement in pain, fatigue, depressive symptoms, health-related quality of life, and pain self-efficacy were found. Level of evidence: I.

38. Tofferi JK, Jackson JL, O'Malley PG: Treatment of fibromyalgia with cyclobenzaprine: A meta-analysis. *Arthritis Rheum* 2004;51(1):9-13.

39. Nishishinya B, Urrútia G, Walitt B, et al: Amitriptyline in the treatment of fibromyalgia: A systematic review of its efficacy. *Rheumatology (Oxford)* 2008;47(12):1741-1746.

    This systematic review included six randomized controlled studies that examined the efficacy of amitriptyline (25 mg daily) administered to treat the symptoms of FM. After 6 to 8 weeks, a consistent short-term benefit was found in pain, sleep, and fatigue. Level of evidence: I.

40. Arnold LM, Hess EV, Hudson JI, Welge JA, Berno SE, Keck PE Jr: A randomized, placebo-controlled, double-blind, flexible-dose study of fluoxetine in the treatment of women with fibromyalgia. *Am J Med* 2002;112(3): 191-197.

41. Arnold LM, Pritchett YL, D'Souza DN, Kajdasz DK, Iyengar S, Wernicke JF: Duloxetine for the treatment of fibromyalgia in women: Pooled results from two randomized, placebo-controlled clinical trials. *J Womens Health (Larchmt)* 2007;16(8):1145-1156.

    The pooled results of two randomized controlled studies comparing the use of duloxetine in 326 patients with the use of a placebo in 212 patients found that duloxetine was effective in improving pain and quality of life after 12 weeks. Level of evidence: I.

42. Mease PJ, Clauw DJ, Gendreau RM, et al: The efficacy and safety of milnacipran for treatment of fibromyalgia: A randomized, double-blind, placebo-controlled trial. *J Rheumatol* 2009;36(2):398-409.

    In a randomized controlled study involving 888 patients with FM, a significantly higher proportion of patients taking milnacipran had improvement in pain, fatigue, cognition, and physical function after 15 weeks, compared with patients taking a placebo. Level of evidence: I.

43. Vitton O, Gendreau M, Gendreau J, Kranzler J, Rao SG: A double-blind placebo-controlled trial of milnacipran in the treatment of fibromyalgia. *Hum Psychopharmacol* 2004;19(suppl 1):S27-S35.

44. Bennett RM, Kamin M, Karim R, Rosenthal N: Tramadol and acetaminophen combination tablets in the treatment of fibromyalgia pain: A double-blind, randomized, placebo-controlled study. *Am J Med* 2003;114(7):537-545.

45. Arnold LM, Goldenberg DL, Stanford SB, et al: Gabapentin in the treatment of fibromyalgia: A randomized, double-blind, placebo-controlled, multicenter trial. *Arthritis Rheum* 2007;56(4):1336-1344.

    In a randomized controlled study involving 150 patients with FM, gabapentin led to significant improvements in pain and sleep after 12 weeks, compared with a placebo. Level of evidence: I.

46. Arnold LM, Russell IJ, Diri EW, et al: A 14-week, randomized, double-blinded, placebo-controlled monotherapy trial of pregabalin in patients with fibromyalgia. *J Pain* 2008;9(9):792-805.

    In a randomized controlled study involving 750 patients with FM, pregabalin led to significant improvements in pain and sleep after 14 weeks, compared with a placebo. Level of evidence: I.

47. Russell IJ, Perkins AT, Michalek JE, Oxybate SXB-26 Fibromyalgia Syndrome Study Group: Sodium oxybate relieves pain and improves function in fibromyalgia syndrome: A randomized, double-blind, placebo-controlled, multicenter clinical trial. *Arthritis Rheum* 2009;60(1):299-309.

    In a randomized controlled study involving 188 patients with FM, a significantly higher proportion of patients taking sodium oxybate had improvement in pain and sleep after 8 weeks, compared with a placebo. Level of evidence: I.

48. Yunus MB, Masi AT, Aldag JC: Short term effects of ibuprofen in primary fibromyalgia syndrome: A double blind, placebo controlled trial. *J Rheumatol* 1989;16(4):527-532.

49. Quijada-Carrera J, Valenzuela-Castaño A, Povedano-Gómez J, et al: Comparison of tenoxicam and bromazepan in the treatment of fibromyalgia: A randomized, double-blind, placebo-controlled trial. *Pain* 1996;65(2-3):221-225.

50. Jones KD, Adams D, Winters-Stone K, Burckhardt CS: A comprehensive review of 46 exercise treatment studies in fibromyalgia (1988-2005). *Health Qual Life Outcomes* 2006;4:67.

    A comprehensive review of 46 exercise treatment studies involving 3,035 patients with FM found strong evidence to support aerobic exercise for improving symptoms and fitness. Level of evidence: I.

51. Assis MR, Silva LE, Alves AM, et al: A randomized controlled trial of deep water running: Clinical effectiveness of aquatic exercise to treat fibromyalgia. *Arthritis Rheum* 2006;55(1):57-65.

    In a study of 60 patients with FM, land-based and deep-water running exercise had similar benefits for improving pain and depression symptoms. Deep-water running led to more rapid improvement than land-based exercise. Level of evidence: I.

52. Davies KA, Macfarlane GJ, Nicholl BI, et al: Restorative sleep predicts the resolution of chronic widespread pain: Results from the EPIFUND study. *Rheumatology (Oxford)* 2008;47(12):1809-1813.

    Of 1,061 subjects with CWP, 300 no longer met the criteria for CWP at 15-month follow-up. Restorative sleep at baseline doubled the likelihood of not having CWP at 15 months. Level of evidence: II.

53. Edinger JD, Wohlgemuth WK, Krystal AD, Rice JR: Behavioral insomnia therapy for fibromyalgia patients: A randomized clinical trial. *Arch Intern Med* 2005;165(21):2527-2535.

    Forty-seven patients with FM were randomly assigned to cognitive-behavioral therapy, sleep hygiene, or usual care. Compared with usual care, cognitive-behavioral therapy led to a significant reduction in nocturnal awake time. Sleep hygiene improved pain and mental well-being. Level of evidence: II.

54. Munguía-Izquierdo D, Legaz-Arrese A: Assessment of the effects of aquatic therapy on global symptomatology in patients with fibromyalgia syndrome: A randomized controlled trial. *Arch Phys Med Rehabil* 2008;89(12):2250-2257.

    A randomized controlled study involving 60 subjects with FM found that a 16-week, three-times-a-week warm-water aquatic training program led to short-term improvement in self-reported physical function, cognitive function, and sleep. Level of evidence: II.

55. Gillis ME, Lumley MA, Mosley-Williams A, Leisen JC, Roehrs T: The health effects of at-home written emotional disclosure in fibromyalgia: A randomized trial. *Ann Behav Med* 2006;32(2):135-146.

    In a randomized controlled study of 83 patients with FM, a 4-day self-directed program of writing about stressful experiences led to greater improvements in sleep and physical function after 3 months than writing about neutral time-management tasks. Level of evidence: I.

56. Shah MA, Feinberg S, Krishnan E: Sleep-disordered breathing among women with fibromyalgia syndrome. *J Clin Rheumatol* 2006;12(6):277-281.

    A case study of 23 patients with FM was conducted in a clinic where patients are routinely offered polysomnograms. Half of the patients had a nadir oxygen saturation lower than 87%. Level of evidence: IV.

57. Gold AR, Dipalo F, Gold MS, Broderick J: Inspiratory airflow dynamics during sleep in women with fibromyalgia. *Sleep* 2004;27(3):459-466.

58. Williams DA, Cary MA, Groner KH, et al: Improving physical functional status in patients with fibromyalgia: A brief cognitive behavioral intervention. *J Rheumatol* 2002;29(6):1280-1286.

59. White KP, Nielson WR: Cognitive behavioral treatment of fibromyalgia syndrome: A followup assessment. *J Rheumatol* 1995;22(4):717-721.

60. Jensen MP, Turner JA, Romano JM: Changes in beliefs, catastrophizing, and coping are associated with improvement in multidisciplinary pain treatment. *J Consult Clin Psychol* 2001;69(4):655-662.

61. Goossens ME, Vlaeyen JW, Hidding A, Kole-Snijders A, Evers SM: Treatment expectancy affects the outcome of cognitive-behavioral interventions in chronic pain. *Clin J Pain* 2005;21(1):18-26, discussion 69-72.

    Pooled data from two randomized controlled studies were used to evaluate the effectiveness of cognitive-behavioral interventions for 171 patients with FM or chronic low back pain. Pretreatment expectancy significantly affected pain coping and quality of life immediately after treatment and 12 months later. Level of evidence: II.

62. Goossens ME, Rutten-van Mölken MP, Leidl RM, Bos SG, Vlaeyen JW, Teeken-Gruben NJ: Cognitive-educational treatment of fibromyalgia: A randomized clinical trial. II. Economic evaluation. *J Rheumatol* 1996;23(7):1246-1254.

63. University of Michigan Health System Chronic Pain and Fatigue Center: Self-management skills and techniques. http://www.med.umich.edu/painresearch/patients/self.htm Accessed February 18, 2010.

    This free, online coping-strategies workbook is designed to teach patients cognitive-behavioral concepts.

64. Arnold LM, Hudson JI, Wang F, et al: Comparisons of the efficacy and safety of duloxetine for the treatment of fibromyalgia in patients with versus without major depressive disorder. *Clin J Pain* 2009;25(6):461-468.

    Pooled data from four randomized controlled studies of patients with FM were analyzed. Of the 350 patients with a comorbid major depressive disorder, the use of duloxetine led to significantly greater improvement than placebo ($P < .05$) on the Hamilton Depression Rating Scale. Level of evidence: II.

65. Gowans SE, Dehueck A, Voss S, Silaj A, Abbey SE: Six-month and one-year followup of 23 weeks of aerobic exercise for individuals with fibromyalgia. *Arthritis Rheum* 2004;51(6):890-898.

66. Broderick JE, Junghaenel DU, Schwartz JE: Written emotional expression produces health benefits in fibromyalgia patients. *Psychosom Med* 2005;67(2):326-334.

    In a randomized, controlled study of 92 patients with FM, three once-a-week, 20-minute private writing sessions on personal traumatic experiences led to significantly greater improvement in pain and psychological well-being after 4 months than a control writing exercise. Level of evidence: I.

67. Mayhew E, Ernst E: Acupuncture for fibromyalgia: A systematic review of randomized clinical trials. *Rheumatology (Oxford)* 2007;46(5):801-804.

    A review of five randomized controlled studies concluded that the use of electroacupuncture was responsible for the beneficial effects of acupuncture in treating FM. However, the methodology was generally poor, and the results were inconsistent.

68. Martin DP, Sletten CD, Williams BA, Berger IH: Improvement in fibromyalgia symptoms with acupuncture: Results of a randomized controlled trial. *Mayo Clin Proc* 2006;81(6):749-757.

    In a randomized controlled study involving 50 patients with FM, true acupuncture led to greater improvements in pain, anxiety, and fatigue at 1-month follow-up than sham acupuncture that did not pierce the skin. Level of evidence: I.

69. Fregni F, Gimenes R, Valle AC, et al: A randomized, sham-controlled, proof of principle study of transcranial direct current stimulation for the treatment of pain in fibromyalgia. *Arthritis Rheum* 2006;54(12):3988-3998.

    In a randomized controlled study involving 32 patients with FM, five daily 20-minute treatments with transcranial direct current stimulation to the primary cortex led to greater short-term improvements in pain than sham stimulation or stimulation over the dorsolateral prefrontal cortex. Level of evidence: I.

70. Passard A, Attal N, Benadhira R, et al: Effects of unilateral repetitive transcranial magnetic stimulation of the motor cortex on chronic widespread pain in fibromyalgia. *Brain* 2007;130(Pt 10):2661-2670.

    In a randomized controlled study involving 30 patients with FM, 10 daily 25-minute treatments with repetitive transcranial magnetic stimulation to the primary cortex led to greater short-term improvement in pain, fatigue, and sleep than sham stimulation. Level of evidence: I.

Chapter 14
Psychosocial Considerations in Spine Disorders

Robert J. Gatchel, PhD, ABPP   Nancy D. Kishino, OTR/L, CVE

Introduction

Spine disorders such as low back pain generally have a good prognosis, and most patients recover within a few weeks or months. Of the 5% to 10% of patients who remain symptomatic after several months, most continue to have pain and associated disability during the subsequent 2 years. These patients account for most of the treatment and indemnity costs associated with spine disorders.[1] Several psychosocial factors have been shown to contribute to or exacerbate these disorders, especially when the disorder becomes chronic.

The Experience of Pain and Suffering

The patient's experience of a disorder such as low back pain is subjective. The pain generator often cannot be unequivocally delineated or relieved, despite the use of increasingly sophisticated diagnostic techniques and surgical procedures. Low back pain initially may be nociceptive, with specific nerve fibers sending a signal to the brain of potential injury or harm. The patient's perception of nociception may be significantly altered by both physical and psychosocial factors. The gate control theory of pain postulated the existence of a gating mechanism in the dorsal horn of the spinal cord that is controlled by peripheral afferent and descending pathways.[2] Modification of pain impulses to the brain by this mechanism of transmission can explain phenomena such as referred pain as well as the influence of psychosocial factors on the patient's pain level and reporting.[3] The suffering that accompanies pain constitutes the patient's emotional reaction to nociceptive input, and it is influenced by preexisting psychosocial variables. A patient may develop specific pain behaviors, such as avoidance of activities, grimacing, guarded walking, or bracing, as a consequence of this suffering as well as past experiences. These experiences continue in the

form of responses from the surrounding environment, including the responses of family and friends, the employer, insurance companies, and health care providers.[4] Secondary and tertiary gain processes also may begin to have an influence.[5]

As the initial acute pain becomes chronic, the suffering and pain behaviors may begin to take on a life of their own, becoming an overlay on or independent of the original nociceptive experience. Any treatment directed solely toward the pain generator and nociception is inadequate for resolving the process of pain and suffering. A comprehensive biopsychosocial approach is required to understand the evolution of a chronic spine disorder and the potential psychosocial barriers to recovery.

The Biopsychosocial Model of Spine Disorders

The biopsychosocial approach has developed rapidly in all areas of medicine, and it is now considered to be the most comprehensive and heuristic approach to the evaluation of medical disorders, including those of the spine.[4,6-9] The biopsychosocial model focuses on the complex interaction among biologic, psychosocial, and medicolegal variables that patients encounter when coping with persistent and distressing medical conditions. This complex interaction may perpetuate or worsen the patient's clinical condition, negatively affecting various aspects of the patient's life. A comprehensive assessment and treatment approach must consider both the biologic and psychosocial aspects of care.

This approach is in striking contrast to the formerly used biomedical reductionist approach, which mistakenly assumed that most medical disorders can be separated into distinct, independent physical and psychosocial components. Every patient experiences a medical condition uniquely, and the complexity of a condition can be especially evident when it persists over time, as a range of psychological, social, and economic factors comes into play. These factors interact with the physical pathology to modulate the patient's discomfort and disability. Individual patients differ significantly in the frequency with which they report physical symptoms,

2: Nonsurgical Care of the Spine

their tendency to visit a physician for identical symptoms, and their response to identical treatment.[10] The nature of a patient's response to treatment frequently has little to do with his or her objective physical condition.

The role of psychosocial factors in spine disorders is being defined in a growing number of studies. Evidence of a "psychosocial disability factor" was found in some patients with low back pain.[11] In this study, a comprehensive assessment of biopsychosocial characteristics was used to characterize patients with acute low back pain who developed chronic pain disability (as measured by job or work status) 1 year after the initial evaluation. A standard battery of psychological assessment tests was administered within 6 weeks of the onset of acute lumbar spine pain, along with a complete physical examination. A structured telephone interview was conducted 1 year after the biopsychosocial assessment to evaluate return-to-work status. In logistic regression analyses to differentiate patients who were back at work at 1 year from those who were not, two psychosocial measures emerged as important: a high level of self-reported pain and disability and an elevated somatization score. Female sex and the existence of a workers' compensation or personal injury insurance claim also were significant variables. The model correctly identified 90.7% of the patients who were considered to be at high or low risk. No difference was found between the two groups in physician-rated severity of the initial back injury or the physical demands of the work to which the patient would return. These study results reveal the existence of a robust psychosocial disability factor in injured workers who have chronic low back pain with disability, confirming that chronic pain and disability reflect more than the presence of physical symptoms or a single psychosocial characteristic. Rather, chronic pain and disability are complex psychosocioeconomic phenomena.

Interdisciplinary Assessment and Treatment Using the Biopsychosocial Model

The biopsychosocial model of spine disorders has been used to develop effective interdisciplinary assessment and treatment methods.[4] Primary, secondary, and tertiary spine pain must be distinguished from the outset because each of these pain types requires substantially different biopsychosocial assessment and treatment.[12] In back pain rehabilitation, the term primary care usually is applied to the treatment of acute pain of limited severity. Basic symptom-control methods are used for relieving pain during the normal early healing period. Basic psychological reassurance that the acute pain is temporary and soon will be resolved frequently is effective. Secondary care represents a reactivation of treatment for a patient whose pain has not improved through the normal healing process. Secondary care is administered during the transition from acute (primary)

<table>
<tr><td>Table 1</td></tr>
</table>

Critical Elements of Tertiary Care for Patients With a Spine Disorder

An interdisciplinary, medically directed team approach with formal staffing of patients, frequent team conferences, and a low staff-to-patient ratio

Formal, repeated quantification of physical deficits for use in individualizing and monitoring the progress of physical training

A psychosocial and socioeconomic assessment for use in individualizing and monitoring disability behavior–oriented interventions and outcomes

A multimodal disability management program using cognitive-behavioral approaches

Psychopharmacologic interventions used for detoxification and psychological treatment

Ongoing outcome assessments using standardized objective criteria

care to the patient's return to work. This treatment is designed to promote a return to productivity before the patient develops advanced physical deconditioning and significant psychosocial barriers to returning to work. A patient whose pain does not appear to be decreasing may need more active psychosocial intervention. Tertiary care is intended for patients who are physically deconditioned and have chronic disability, and it requires an interdisciplinary and comprehensive approach (see chapter 15). In general, tertiary and secondary care differ in intensity of rehabilitation services required, including functional restoration and psychosocial and disability management.[13] Interdisciplinary care involves several critical elements, as listed in Table 1. Interdisciplinary biopsychosocial treatment programs were found to be extremely efficacious and cost-effective for treating patients with chronic pain, compared with less intensive, single-modality treatment programs.[14,15]

When a patient is receiving primary or secondary care, the clinician must be aware of the many psychosocial factors that can contribute as the acute pain episode becomes subacute or chronic. A patient may progress through several stages as the pain and disability become more chronic. Significant psychosocial, functional, legal, and work-related barriers to recovery may develop. Unless they are effectively dealt with, these barriers can greatly interfere with the patient's return to full functioning and a productive lifestyle. While the patient is in treatment, it is important that members of the health care team be knowledgeable about all psychosocial issues, including the potential secondary gains of continued disability. Understanding these factors allows staff members not only to serve the patient better but also to be more effective in problem solving if the patient's physical progress is slow or nonexistent.

For example, an objective difficulty such as lack of transportation or child care can function as an excuse for suboptimal performance or failure to adhere to the treatment regimen. Indeed, failure to make physical progress generally indicates the existence of psychosocial barriers to recovery, which must be effectively assessed and brought to the attention of the entire treatment team. Steps can then be taken to understand the origins of the barriers and avoid their interference with treatment goals.[16-21]

Major Psychosocial Variables

A plethora of studies have found that various psychological factors are related to pain and disability. Several are especially important: emotional factors such as anxiety, depression, and anger; cognitive factors such as appraisal and beliefs; catastrophizing and fear-avoidance beliefs; perceived self-efficacy; and vulnerability and resilience.[22] The importance of psychosocial factors dictates the need for a careful patient assessment before designing a comprehensive pain management intervention. The assessment should proceed from the global biopsychosocial diagnosis of a spine disorder to a detailed evaluation of the interactive factors affecting the patient's condition.[23] It is important to keep in mind that the stress and uncertainty associated with a spine disorder such as low back pain contribute to the severity and duration of pain. Pain perception is augmented through central mechanisms affecting the pain gate, and elevated muscle tension further increases the stress level through a continuous feedback loop.[3] This pain-stress cycle can affect the hypothalamic-pituitary-adrenal axis,[4] as the hypothalamus stimulates corticotrophin-releasing hormone, causing the pituitary gland to release adrenocorticotropic hormones and other substances.[23] Adrenocorticotropic hormone then stimulates the adrenal cortex to release cortisol (a so-called stress hormone). Prolonged stress means a prolonged release of cortisol. To ensure a sufficient supply of glucose to fuel the demand for cortisol during stress, protein in new muscle breaks down, and ongoing replacement of calcium in bones is inhibited. The pain-stress cycle is a possible explanation for the muscle and joint pain that characterizes many chronic pain conditions.[4]

The patient's psychosocial functioning also is affected. The patient learns to limit physical movements that may exacerbate the pain; the result is hypervigilance, avoidance of activity, and pain behaviors. Somatization (the expression of emotional distress through physical symptoms) can appear in any medical disorder, but it is more likely in chronic pain disorders. Symptom magnification (an excessive focusing on physical symptoms and assuming the worst possible explanation for them) reflects emotional distress. As pain and emotional distress become more chronic, the patient often develops a major psychiatric disorder, such as depression, anxiety, or substance abuse.[24,25] A cascade of ever-increasing biopsychosocial consequences can progress

Table 2

Factors in the Clinical Detection of a Developing Psychosocial Barrier

The patient has physical symptoms and/or disabilities inconsistent with the spine injury, particularly if they are associated with nonorganic signs. This pattern suggests somatization and symptom magnification.

The patient or a family member has a history of a mental health condition such as depression or substance abuse.

The patient had a stressful change in lifestyle or marital status, before or after the injury, that could have precipitated the pain.

The patient's pain drawing is grossly nonanatomic or exaggerated.

The patient's answer to a query about preinjury and post-injury levels of income and financial concerns suggests a potential financial secondary gain issue, regardless of whether the answer appears to be straightforward or evasive. The existence of an injury-related litigation or a pending workers' compensation claim also may suggest a secondary financial gain issue.

from pain to stress, hypothalamic-pituitary-adrenal axis reactivity, emotional distress, and psychopathology. A patient with a personality disorder that earlier had not been clinically apparent may begin to have an increasingly inadequate ability to cope and display dysfunctional behaviors such as poor compliance, suspiciousness, emotional lability, and acting out.

Pain-related fear and concern about avoiding additional harm and pain are quite common.[4] The threat of intense pain becomes a focus for most patients, and frequently it is difficult to disengage from. This fear of pain, which is driven by the anticipation of pain and not necessarily by the sensory experience of pain itself, prompts significant avoidance behavior and a retreat from normal functional activities. Avoidance eventually leads to increased fear, activity limitations, and other negative consequences that significantly contribute to prolonged disability and the persistence of pain. Fear of movement and fear of reinjury were found to be better predictors of functional limitation than biomedical parameters.[26] Therefore, it is extremely important to deal with fear-avoidance behavior as part of a comprehensive pain management program. Techniques such as cognitive-behavioral therapy and stress management should be combined with progressive pacing of physical activities. A combination of basic clinical acumen and easily administered screening tests[6] may help in identifying emerging psychosocial barriers to recovery and suggest the need for a formal mental health evaluation. Some of these emerging barriers are listed in Table 2.

Potential psychosocial issues must be considered before treatment planning. The treatment can then be tailored to the specific biopsychosocial characteristics of the patient.[4,27] The current trend in pain management is to move away from the so-called myth of homogeneity and toward an attempt to match the individual patient's treatment to specific assessment outcomes.[28,29] Patients with the same medical diagnosis or set of symptoms, such as chronic low back pain, traditionally have been grouped together and treated in the same manner. However, different patients with the same pain diagnosis have different responses to the same treatment.[4] Thus, it is essential to tailor the treatment based on a careful initial biopsychosocial assessment of the patient.

Efficacy and Cost-Effectiveness

Traditional medical treatments of chronic pain are not consistently efficacious or cost-effective. In contrast, more recent comprehensive pain management programs are both therapeutically efficacious and cost-effective. A substantial body of evidence-based scientific studies has shown that various chronic pain disorders, including those of the spine, can be efficaciously and cost-effectively treated using a comprehensive, interdisciplinary approach based on the biopsychosocial model.[30] In a review of the available evidence, data on the major outcome variables of self-reported pain, function, health care utilization and cost, medication use, work factors, and insurance claims were derived from studies reporting treatment outcome results for patients with chronic pain.[31] When possible, conventional medical treatments were used as the benchmark for evaluating comprehensive interdisciplinary programs. This review clearly showed that comprehensive programs offer more efficacious and cost-effective treatment for patients with chronic pain than conventional treatment programs.

Further evidence of the robustness of interdisciplinary pain management programs is provided by the repeated independent replication of the positive functional restoration outcomes in randomized, controlled studies conducted in the United States, Denmark, Germany, Canada, France, and Japan.[31-37] The robustness and consistency of the research findings, as well as the utility of this approach, have been confirmed by clinical treatment teams functioning in regions and countries having markedly different economic and social conditions and workers' compensation systems. This functional restoration approach also was found to be effective for treating chronic upper extremity disorders and preventing chronic disability.[38] In a randomized controlled study, patients with acute low back pain who were identified as being at high risk for developing chronic back pain disability were randomly assigned to early functional restoration or conventional treatment.[39] At 1-year follow-up, a wide range of work, health care utilization, medication use, and self-reported pain indexes showed less chronic pain disability in the patients who underwent functional restoration. For example, patients in the functional restoration group were less likely to be taking narcotic analgesic drugs (odds ratio = 0.44) or psychotropic drugs (odds

ratio = 0.24). Patients in the conventional treatment group were less likely to have returned to work (odds ratio = 0.55). The cost-comparison data revealed that over the 1-year period the cost of treating the patients in the conventional treatment group was twice that of treating the patients in the functional restoration group.

Summary

There is no doubt that psychosocial factors can play a significant role in spine disorders, especially when such a disorder becomes chronic. The gate control theory of pain and subsequent findings have led to the development and wide acceptance of the biopsychosocial model of pain, which focuses on the complex interaction among biologic, psychosocial, and medicolegal variables that contribute to the pain experience and its treatment. These complex interactions account for the wide differences in patients' initial pain and the process by which it develops into chronic pain. This complexity dictates that a comprehensive biopsychosocial assessment and treatment approach is required for effective management of spine pain disorders.

The use of the biopsychosocial model has led to the development of effective interdisciplinary assessment and treatment methods for managing spine pain disorders. The interdisciplinary approach is a necessity at the tertiary care level because of complexity of treatment resulting from the patient's advanced stage of physical deconditioning and chronic disability, significant psychosocial barriers to recovery (such as symptom magnification, emotional distress, and potential secondary gain), and any comorbid psychiatric disorders. A substantial body of evidence-based scientific studies has documented the treatment- and cost-effectiveness of comprehensive interdisciplinary pain management programs based on the biopsychosocial model. A comprehensive biopsychosocial assessment and treatment program is the treatment of choice for a patient with a chronic pain disorder, including a disorder of the spine.

Annotated References

1. Mayer TG, Gatchel RJ, Polatin PB, eds: *Occupational Musculoskeletal Disorders: Function, Outcomes, and Evidence.* Philadelphia, PA, Lippincott Williams & Wilkins, 2000.

2. Melzack R, Wall PD: Pain mechanisms: A new theory. *Science* 1965;150(699):971-979.

3. Polatin PB, Gatchel RJ: Psychosocial factors in spinal disorders, in Garfin S, Vaccaro R, eds: *Orthopaedic Knowledge Update: Spine.* Rosemont, IL, American Academy of Orthopaedic Surgeons, 1997.

4. Gatchel RJ: *Clinical Essentials of Pain Management.* Washington, DC, American Psychological Association, 2005.

5. Dersh J, Gatchel RJ, Kishino N: The role of tertiary gain in pain disability. *Practical Pain Management* 2005; 5(6):13-28.

   In the assessment and treatment of pain and disability, tertiary gain is defined as a gain from an illness that is sought or attained by someone other than the patient (for example, a health care provider, health care insurer, family member). Tertiary gain issues can be significant in perpetuating illness or disability.

6. Gatchel RJ, Mayer TG: Psychological evaluation of the spine patient. *J Am Acad Orthop Surg* 2008;16(2):107-112.

   The most comprehensive and heuristic approach to assessing a patient with spine pain is the biopsychosocial perspective, which focuses on the complex interaction among biologic, psychological, and social variables affecting a medical condition. The comprehensive biopsychosocial evaluation of patients with a spine disorder is discussed.

7. Block AR, Gatchel RJ, Deardorff W, Guyer RD: *The Psychology of Spine Surgery.* Washington, DC, American Psychological Association, 2003.

8. Gatchel RJ: Comorbidity of chronic pain and mental health disorders: The biopsychosocial perspective. *Am Psychol* 2004;59(8):795-805.

9. Turk DC, Gatchel RJ: Psychosocial assessment of chronic occupational musculoskeletal disorders, in Mayer TM, Gatchel RJ, Polatin PB, eds: *Occupational Musculoskeletal Disorders: Function, Outcomes, and Evidence.* Philadelphia, PA, Lippincott Williams & Wilkins, 2000, pp 587-608.

10. Gatchel RJ, Kishino ND, Strizak A: The importance of outcome assessment in orthopaedics: An overview, in Spivak JM, Connolly PJ, eds: *Orthopaedic Knowledge Update: Spine 3.* Rosemont, IL, American Academy of Orthopaedic Surgeons, 2006, pp 95-102.

    Outcomes monitoring is important for determining treatment efficacy as well as monitoring for institutional quality assurance purposes and developing a potentially important marketing strategy. Considerations in using several outcome measures are discussed.

11. Gatchel RJ, Polatin PB, Mayer TG: The dominant role of psychosocial risk factors in the development of chronic low back pain disability. *Spine (Phila Pa 1976)* 1995;20(24):2702-2709.

12. Mayer TG, Polatin P, Smith B, et al: Spine rehabilitation: Secondary and tertiary nonoperative care. *Spine (Phila Pa 1976)* 1995;20(18):2060-2066.

13. Mayer TG, Gatchel RJ: *Functional Restoration for Spinal Disorders: The Sports Medicine Approach.* Philadelphia, PA, Lea & Febiger, 1988.

14. Deschner M, Polatin PB: Interdisciplinary programs: Chronic pain management, in Mayer TG, Gatchel RJ, Polatin PB, eds: *Occupational Musculoskeletal Disorders: Function, Outcomes, and Evidence.* Philadelphia, PA, Lippincott Williams & Wilkins, 2000, pp 629-637.

15. Mayer TG, Polatin PB: Tertiary nonoperative interdisciplinary programs: The functional restoration variant of the outpatient chronic pain management program, in Mayer TG, Gatchel RJ, Polatin PB, eds: *Occupational Musculoskeletal Disorders: Function, Outcomes, and Evidence.* Philadelphia, PA, Lippincott Williams & Wilkins, 2000, pp 639-649.

16. Gatchel RJ, Mayer TG: Evidence-informed management of chronic low back pain with functional restoration. *Spine J* 2008;8(1):65-69.

    The biopsychosocial evaluation of a patient with spine pain is reviewed in detail.

17. Wright AR, Gatchel RJ: Occupational musculoskeletal pain and disability, in Turk DC, Gatchel RJ, eds: *Psychological Approaches to Pain Management: A Practitioner's Handbook,* ed 2. New York, NY, Guilford, 2002, pp 349-364.

18. Turk DC, Gatchel RJ: Psychosocial factors and pain: Revolution and evolution, in Gatchel RJ, Turk DC, eds: *Psychosocial Factors in Pain: Critical Perspectives.* New York, NY, Guilford, 1999.

19. Gatchel RJ, Lou L, Kishino N: Concepts of multidisciplinary pain management, in Boswell MV, Cole DE, eds: *Weiner's Pain Management: A Practical Guide for Clinicians,* ed 7. Sonora, CA, CRC Press, 2006.

    The philosophy and components of multidisciplinary pain management programs are reviewed. The most effective programs, such as functional restoration, are based on the biopsychosocial approach to chronic pain.

20. Gatchel RJ, Kishino N, Noe C: "Carving-out" services from multidisciplinary chronic pain management programs: Negative impact on therapeutic efficacy, in Schatman M, Campbell A, eds: *A Guidebook for Multidisciplinary Program Development.* New York, NY, Informa Health Care Publishers, 2007.

    So-called carving out of services to outside providers (such as psychological treatment, physical therapy, and occupational therapy) has a negative impact on the efficacy of interdisciplinary team–based pain management programs.

21. Feinberg SD, Feinberg RM, Gatchel RJ: Functional restoration and chronic pain management. *Crit Rev Phys Rehabil Med* 2008;20:221-235.

    Functional restoration has been found to be a therapeutic, cost-effective approach to chronic pain management.

22. Gatchel RJ, ed: *Compendium of Outcome Instruments,* ed 2. LaGrange, IL, North American Spine Society, 2006.

2: Nonsurgical Care of the Spine

The commonly used, valid measures for evaluating treatment outcomes in patients with a spine disorder are evaluated, and recent research is comprehensively reviewed.

23. Melzack R: Pain and stress: A new perspective, in Gatchel RJ, Turk DC, eds: *Psychosocial Factors in Pain: Critical Perspectives*. New York, NY, Guilford, 1999.

24. Dersh J, Mayer T, Theodore BR, Polatin P, Gatchel RJ: Do psychiatric disorders first appear preinjury or postinjury in chronic disabling occupational spinal disorders? *Spine (Phila Pa 1976)* 2007;32(9):1045-1051.

   The temporal relationship between a work-related injury claim and a psychiatric disorder was evaluated in patients with a chronic disabling occupational spine disorder. In general, psychiatric disturbance was not found to be a risk factor for development of such a disorder. Level of evidence: II.

25. Dersh J, Gatchel RJ, Mayer T, Polatin P, Temple OR: Prevalence of psychiatric disorders in patients with chronic disabling occupational spinal disorders. *Spine (Phila Pa 1976)* 2006;31(10):1156-1162.

   In an evaluation of 1,323 patients with a chronic disabling occupational spine disorder, 65% were found to have at least one psychiatric disorder (in addition to pain disorder).

26. Turk DC, Robinson JP, Burwinkle T: Prevalence of fear of pain and activity in patients with fibromyalgia syndrome. *J Pain* 2004;5(9):483-490.

27. Sullivan MJ, Feuerstein M, Gatchel RJ, Linton SJ, Pransky G: Integrating psychosocial and behavioral interventions to achieve optimal rehabilitation outcomes. *J Occup Rehabil* 2005;15(4):475-489.

   A selective review of the literature on psychosocial and behavioral interventions for work-related disability found a need for further research into worker- and workplace-related psychosocial risk factors.

28. Turk DC, Okifuji A: Matching treatment to assessment of patients with chronic pain, in Turk DC, Melzack R, eds: *Handbook of Pain Assessment*, ed 2. New York, NY, Guilford, 2001.

29. Turk DC, Monarch ES: Biopsychosocial perspective on chronic pain, in Turk DC, Gatchel RJ, eds: *Psychological Approaches to Pain Management: A Practitioner's Handbook*, ed 2. New York, NY, Guilford, 2002.

30. Gatchel RJ, Okifuji A: Evidence-based scientific data documenting the treatment and cost-effectiveness of comprehensive pain programs for chronic nonmalignant pain. *J Pain* 2006;7(11):779-793.

   This is a review of evidence on the treatment- and cost-effectiveness of comprehensive interdisciplinary pain management programs for chronic nonmalignant pain.

31. Hazard RG, Fenwick JW, Kalisch SM, et al: Functional restoration with behavioral support: A one-year prospective study of patients with chronic low-back pain. *Spine (Phila Pa 1976)* 1989;14(2):157-161.

32. Patrick LE, Altmaier EM, Found EM: Long-term outcomes in multidisciplinary treatment of chronic low back pain: Results of a 13-year follow-up. *Spine (Phila Pa 1976)* 2004;29(8):850-855.

33. Bendix AF, Bendix T, Vaegter K, Lund C, Frølund L, Holm L: Multidisciplinary intensive treatment for chronic low back pain: A randomized, prospective study. *Cleve Clin J Med* 1996;63(1):62-69.

34. Hildebrandt J, Pfingsten M, Saur P, Jansen J: Prediction of success from a multidisciplinary treatment program for chronic low back pain. *Spine (Phila Pa 1976)* 1997;22(9):990-1001.

35. Corey DT, Koepfler LE, Etlin D, Day HI: A limited functional restoration program for injured workers: A randomized trial. *J Occup Rehabil* 1996;6:239-249.

36. Jousset N, Fanello S, Bontoux L, et al: Effects of functional restoration versus 3 hours per week physical therapy: A randomized controlled study. *Spine (Phila Pa 1976)* 2004;29(5):487-494.

37. Shirado O, Ito T, Kikumoto T, Takeda N, Minami A, Strax TE: A novel back school using a multidisciplinary team approach featuring quantitative functional evaluation and therapeutic exercises for patients with chronic low back pain: The Japanese experience in the general setting. *Spine (Phila Pa 1976)* 2005;30(10):1219-1225.

   A novel back-school component was part of a multidisciplinary functional restoration program for patients with chronic low back pain in Japan. This approach was found to be therapeutically efficacious. Level of evidence: II.

38. Evans RI III, Gergen PJ, Mitchell H, et al: A randomized clinical trial to reduce asthma morbidity among inner-city children: Results of the National Cooperative Inner-City Asthma Study. *J Pediatr* 1999;135(3):332-338.

39. Gatchel RJ, Polatin PB, Noe CE, Gardea MA, Pulliam C, Thompson J: Treatment- and cost-effectiveness of early intervention for acute low-back pain patients: A one-year prospective study. *J Occup Rehabil* 2003;13(1):1-9.

Chapter 15

The Interdisciplinary Treatment of Patients With Chronic Pain

Eric A.K. Mayer, MD   Tom G. Mayer, MD

Introduction

The total expense related to neck and back pain in the United States was estimated in 2005 to be $80 billion to $92 billion.[1] Although a spine condition usually is benign, this cost was comparable to that of arthritis ($80 billion), cancer ($89 billion), or diabetes ($98 billion). From 1997 to 2006 total expenditures related to spine conditions increased 82%, and the proportion of the US population reporting a spine-related physical limitation increased from 20% to almost 30%.[2] From 1992 to 2006 the number of physician visits related to chronic, disabling spine pain increased threefold in North Carolina,[3] approximately 65% of patients who underwent a fusion procedure in Washington state were disabled 2 years later,[4] and there was a nationwide increase in the number of workers who left the workforce because of a spine injury.[5] From 1980 to 2007 the percentage of all Social Security disability benefit recipients who listed musculoskeletal disease as the cause of disability increased from 15% to almost 30%; musculoskeletal disease was second only to mental health as a cause of Social Security disability.[5]

These metrics are an important indicator that physicians, particularly spine specialists, are not providing care that encourages function. The most important reasons for this failure are lack of recognition that different patients require different modes of treatment and that a patient's treatment may require the expertise of more than one provider. However, the most important predictor of a high cost of care is not the patient's level of pain or radiologic findings but the physician's failure to identify related nonmedical circumstances such as job dissatisfaction, opioid use, indemnity payments, family discord, or an earlier unsuccessful workers' compensation or health insurance claim.[6,7]

The Interdisciplinary Care Model

In the United States more than 85% of the total expenditure for neck and back care is devoted to fewer than 10% of patients, whose disability has become chronic.[8,9] Only inadequate data are available concerning these patients, for whom all single-provider interventions (including surgery) often are unsuccessful.[10] The prospect for adding to this knowledge is slim because research studies continue to rely on self-reported numeric pain scales and other subjective measures of function rather than on objective functional outcomes. A more positive development is the waning popularity of some treatments that worsened patient outcomes. Most spine specialists now recognize that limiting bed rest and encouraging an early return to activity can improve the functional outcome of patients with acute low back and/or leg pain more than so-called restful waiting.[11] The use of aggressive, quota-based rehabilitation was found to improve function more rapidly than placebo treatment.[12-14] The term quota-based rehabilitation is used to describe the concept that the intensity of physical therapy should progress according to a physiologic schedule or program, rather than the patient's subjective pain inhibition.

There is consensus that, if initial interventions are not successful, patients with acute nonradicular low back pain improve with "intensive interdisciplinary rehabilitation with a cognitive-behavioral emphasis."[15] Unfortunately, this consensus has not always led to improved outcomes based on common single-specialty modalities.[1,15-17] Progressive resistance exercises favoring extension were found to consistently and measurably improve strength, endurance, and spine muscle cross-sectional area and often to decrease kinesophobia. However, these improvements were not consistently correlated with a reduction in self-reported pain or disability, improvement in quality-of-life measures, or return to work.[18] Although patients who underwent

Dr. Eric A.K. Mayer or an immediate family member serves as a board member, owner, officer, or committee member of the North American Spine Society; is a member of a speakers' bureau or has made paid presentations on behalf of Pfizer and Medtronic; serves as an unpaid consultant to Medtronic; and owns stock or stock options in Life Technology and the Productive Rehabilitation Institute of Dallas for Ergonomics. Dr. Tom G. Mayer or an immediate family member serves as a paid consultant to or is an employee of the Productive Rehabilitation Institute of Dallas for Ergonomics; and owns stock or stock options in the Productive Rehabilitation Institute of Dallas for Ergonomics.

2: Nonsurgical Care of the Spine

| Table 1 | | |

A Comparison of the Interdisciplinary and Multidisciplinary Care Models

Participant or Feature	Interdisciplinary Model	Multidisciplinary Model
Physician	The physician is responsible for integrating disparate information and creating the patient's care plan.	Multiple physician specialists focus on individual parts of the clinical picture.
Nurse, therapist, psychologist, case manager	The specialist presents data as part of an integrated overall plan. Data are collated and priorities are set by the team under supervision.	The specialist treats the patient individually before consulting other specialists.
Organization	A physician director oversees multiple allied health professionals and integrates recommendations from other physicians concerning medications, physical training, and other aspects of care.	Multiple physicians and allied health professionals may treat the patient in a sequential, nonintegrated pattern.
Care plan	The care plan can be adjusted during team meetings if the patient has not improved.	Unsuccessful care by one specialist can lead to transfer of care to another specialist. This pattern usually leads to surgery.
Setting	The costly structure of care usually dictates treatment in a tertiary-level or rehabilitation setting.	Many clinical practices are structured on the multidisciplinary model, with specialists consulting one another only if the patient does not improve.
Medication management	The collaborative nature of the program allows a patient to receive simultaneous detoxification from opioids, titration of psychotropic drugs, and physical reconditioning.	Physical reconditioning may be suspended while a specialist supervises opioid detoxification or medication titration.

surgery for chronic low back pain had quantifiable improvement, surgery as a stand-alone modality was not found to have a greater benefit than cognitive-behavioral interventions.[17,19]

A patient's disability often is rooted in more than the tissue injury. A patient whose condition does not improve with 90 days of any single-provider treatment modality is likely to receive increasingly aggressive and invasive interventions, with variable functional outcomes. Creating a best-practice model for such patients is complicated by the absence of a correlation between pain and functional outcome or radiologic success criteria.[6,20] In the refractory 10% of patients with a spine injury, the pain is multifactorial in origin, deeply entrenched, inaccessible to visual inspection, and subject to diverse influences such as psychologic stress, coping failure, social status forfeiture, and financial collapse. This multifactorial pain must be treated by specialists in multiple disciplines in an interdisciplinary team setting.

The terms multidisciplinary and interdisciplinary often are used interchangeably, but the subtle differences between these terms can have a dramatic effect on outcomes. Historically, multidisciplinary treatment programs involved integrated teams that met regularly in formal patient care conferences to ensure the highest quality of care. Positive published data led to imitation of this model. The term has evolved to include groups of medical professionals from multiple specialities who do not necessarily provide integrated care. Quite often, these multidisciplinary teams include chiropractors, physical therapists, nonsurgical spine specialists, interventionalists, and surgeons whose separate treatment plans may overlap or be repetitious. A patient whose condition does not respond to treatment from one provider is referred to a provider specializing in more invasive and often more expensive treatments. Surgery may be performed before the likelihood of underlying biopsychosocial deficits, fixed thoughts, or pervasive physical deconditioning is considered. This model of multidisciplinary care omits consideration of patient factors that do not fit into a team member's specialty.

In contrast, the term interdisciplinary care has come into favor to describe programs that provide truly integrated care. The integration of disparate practices can be difficult to achieve, and the concept continues to advance. Outcome studies have been uncommon but are now conducted more frequently, as required by a competitive health care marketplace. Although interdisciplinary practices are heterogeneous, the team often is led by a physician. As in the multidisciplinary model, patients are assessed in multiple domains that include medical, physical, psychologic, and occupational and ergonomic barriers, as well as functional goals. The entire interdisciplinary team devises an efficient care plan to treat deficits that are preventing the patient from resuming his or her place in the family, workplace, and community (Table 1).

Interdisciplinary care is not routinely taught in medical schools, nor is it usually part of a formal postgraduate training program. The exception is physical medicine and rehabilitation residency training, which mandates proficiency in physician-directed management of interdisciplinary teams.

Consensus Guidelines

During the past two decades, clinicians increasingly have had access to tiered care algorithms that can provide a means of negotiating a patient's emotional dissonance, contradictory feedback, or frank manipulation.[21] The use of algorithms has led to compelling cost savings and better patient outcomes.[21-23] The concepts underlying the phasic care model were identified by expert panels and formalized in a consensus document of the North American Spine Society.[24,25] The algorithm structure involves three treatment concepts called the primary, secondary, and tertiary modes of treatment. Progression to a higher mode brings greater expense but offers a commensurately greater probability of return to function. Primary care refers to interventions for an acute injury and is intended to modify symptoms. The interventions may include injections, surgery, braces or other assistive devices, manual techniques, early mobilization, and educational programs, usually provided by a single practitioner. The number of treatment sessions is limited, and the intent is to return the patient to full function within the 90-day natural history of most acute spine conditions. Secondary care refers to treatment provided to patients whose condition does not respond to the initial symptom-modification treatment. The patient's postacute or postoperative symptoms require a care plan focused on reactivation, with rehabilitation that includes a quota-based exercise program and education. Additional passive modalities sometimes are required for symptom modification. The primary goal is to prevent or reverse the late-phase deconditioning that typifies the transition from functional impairment to disability. Secondary care sometimes has a component of programmatic consolidation, particularly toward the end of the postacute period (as in back-school programs). Advanced care is not necessary for most patients. Intensive weight training need not be delivered on site but may be used in conjunction with a gymnasium or trainer to reduce the cost. Programmatic consolidation may be interdisciplinary, as in a work-hardening program. Often the program is led by a physical or occupational therapist. Consultation from a physician, psychologist, social worker, disability manager, and/or chiropractor may be necessary and provided in an a la carte fashion to ensure the patient's progress to maximal function.

A few patients require tertiary care after unsuccessful secondary care or a complex surgical procedure. Tertiary care is specifically defined as care provided by a physician-directed interdisciplinary team with on-site representatives of all disciplines available to every patient. Treatment management guidelines (for example, the Official Disability Guidelines or the guidelines of the American College of Occupational and Environmental Medicine[26,27]) increasingly carry the weight of law in compensation cases and increasingly are being used as the minimum standard for secondary and tertiary care programs. Treatment guidelines codify the configuration of tertiary care and the minimal outcome standards, thereby justifying the cost of tertiary care. In addition, the guidelines are useful for clarifying tertiary care–related nomenclature. For example, tertiary care is provided by some but not all pain clinics and work-hardening programs. Although the specific programmatic terminology still is in flux, the use of the concept of levels of care increasingly is statutorily mandated, and the force of evidence-based program definitions is thereby being increased.[26,27]

The concept of best practices as related to third-party payers is somewhat difficult to understand, aside from the billing and coding aspects of medical practice. Most third-party payments to physicians and other health care providers are made by private health insurers, government plans, and workers' compensation plans. The workers' compensation claim system is primarily organized on a statewide basis, with several federal programs; the total is approximately 58 US jurisdictions. In general, workers' compensation plans in states identified as business friendly are most successful in keeping patients at work (by emphasizing job duty modification or rapid return to work after sick leave); a relatively high proportion of their expenditures are for medical care rather than settlement fees. Keeping patients at work has a significant influence on local and federal tax revenues. However, some jurisdictions have policies that encourage injured workers to apply for Social Security disability payments. The workers' compensation system is regulated through several oversight mechanisms that limit the financial and medical benefits to patients. It remains to be seen whether federal health care reform will extend to mandating similar oversight of the much larger private and group health insurance system.

Pain and Function

The Paradox of Pain

The greatest obstacle to effective treatment of chronic pain is the so-called paradox of pain. The construct of pain is subjective and self-perceived. Disabling pain usually is invisible, nonquantifiable, and dramatically intrusive into family, occupational, and societal roles. Patients often perceive pain as causing ongoing harm or damage to tissue. In contrast, the construct of function is visible, quantifiable, relevant to social and health behaviors, and tied to physical performance measurements. Function involves performing activities of daily living that can involve position tolerance, such as

2: Nonsurgical Care of the Spine

walking, climbing, reaching, or squatting, as well as materials handling, as in lifting, pushing, pulling, or carrying. These complex functions are subdivided into various body functions, such as joint range of motion, muscle strength, endurance, and agility. Only the patient experiences pain, but anyone can observe the patient's function and social or health behaviors. Unlike pain, function is intrinsically related to the construct of disability. Disability is defined as inability to perform customary work-related, recreational, or domestic activities. Pain may lead to poor functional performance. During the past several decades, there has been an increasing recognition of the importance of restoring function as well as the need to avoid abetting certain pain behaviors (such as passive waiting for treatment, attention seeking, opioid addiction, failure to maintain social responsibilities). In addition, rehabilitation focused on improving function was found to frequently have the effect of ameliorating pain and its consequences.[28,29]

Patients with chronic musculoskeletal pain often seek external validation (for family, social, or litigation reasons) by making multiple medical appointments, attempting to demonstrate medication need, or displaying surgical scars. This external validation often fails to replace the patient's loss of familial role, loss of money, or loss of function. Chronic pain may become the center of the patient's life, and pain reporting ultimately may become the patient's only remaining means of influencing his or her environment. This behavior becomes frustrating to the patient's family, friends, and care providers and leads to misunderstandings that further isolate the patient from his or her normal roles. Many patients who need tertiary-level care attempt to deflect any objective pain measurement by discussing their suffering. An interdisciplinary team can be crucial to changing the patient's dysfunctional trajectory.

Many of the methods used at lower levels of care have the unfortunate effect of reinforcing disability behaviors; these include an overdependence on self-reported scores, an unproductive focus on suffering, and a reliance on passive treatments. The subjective data provided by self-report measures serve to mirror the patient's perception of pain, depression, anxiety, kinesophobia, and disability. Objective data are required to change the patient's self-fulfilling prophecy of failure. Progressive improvement in objective data scores creates a new and consistent message across all domains that belies the patient's feeling of loss and instead reflects the patient's gains. Gathering useful data is difficult in the face of a patient's fear-avoidance and secondary gain behaviors. Disability is a global phenomenon that is amenable to being broken apart into multiple domains. The interdisciplinary team leader is responsible for collating, synthesizing, and formulating the team's plan. It may take some time for the patient to trust the team approach, however.

The Functional Capacity Evaluation

Functional gains must be tracked using validated, reproducible, quantitative measures of the patient's area of physical dysfunction. This so-called weak link is defined as tissue that has sustained an injury and undergone the normal course of healing but remains below its original physical capacity. Sometimes the patient maintains normal function by allowing stronger motion segments in the biomechanical chain to take over the function of the weak link. However, a patient who compensates for an injured lumbar spine by following the adage "Lift with your legs and not with your back" is prone to reinjury unless the lumbar spine is strengthened. A functional capacity evaluation is used to identify the patient's weak link and track progress toward ameliorating it. The primary goal of the functional capacity evaluation is to measure the performance of relevant occupational, avocational, and domestic activities of daily living. For a manual laborer, the most relevant activities may involve lifting, carrying, pushing, and pulling. For an office worker, the relevant activities may include typing, gripping, pinching, and reaching. The functional capacity evaluation is intended to lead to the development of protocols that will hinder substitution and push the weak link beyond the threshold of pain (while remaining under the threshold of injury). A properly applied functional capacity evaluation can help the interdisciplinary team differentiate the weak link from uninjured tissue that may have become deconditioned secondary to prolonged disuse caused by pain limitations.

The initial functional capacity evaluation may be pain limited and therefore unreliable as a measure of the extent of deconditioning. Nonetheless, the combined effect of weak link deficits will be revealed, as well as psychologic issues such as fear-avoidance, physical inhibition, and kinesophobia. The low, pain-limited quantitative test result should alert the treatment team to the patient's critical physical, psychologic, and pharmaceutical needs. In contrast, the postrehabilitation functional capacity evaluation generally confirms the patient's reacceptance of social and vocational roles and suggests the level of physical demand the patient will be able to tolerate when resuming work or home responsibilities.

There is great variability among the commercially available functional capacity evaluation protocols. Their underlying methodologies differ, and some developers of functional capacity evaluations teach and market principles having questionable validity. Many functional capacity evaluations use a qualitative, observational methodology (traditionally used in physical therapy) and eschew a quantitative approach. Quantifying physical ability requires a physics-based approach that is not part of standard training for physical therapists or physicians.[30] A physics-based approach denotes any numeric measurement system that attempts to integrate speed and motion (often using dynamometers or computerized isokinetic devices) to analyze force through an arc of motion, which may identify momentary strength or motion deficits that differentiate the patient's injury profile from a normal profile.

Chronic pain is a complex and interactive psychophysiologic behavior pattern in which the psychosocial barriers to functional recovery may be as recalcitrant as the physical barriers. Childhood trauma or psychiatric illness such as major depression, substance abuse, anxiety disorder, or personality disorder is more common in patients with chronic pain than in the general US population.[31-33] A good objective assessment of functional barriers should use psychologic as well as physical means of identifying factors that may impede a patient's rehabilitation program or eventual reintegration into societal roles. Functional restoration requires a true quantification of mind and body function. A poor choice of quantitative measures will lead to an inferior outcome.

The Structure of an Interdisciplinary Program

The increasing level of expenditures for spine care in the United States has not led to a commensurate increase in patient function. Interdisciplinary programs are intended to ensure that a patient receives an appropriate level of care, but such programs are not available to all patients. Interdisciplinary programs are heterogenous but share an emphasis on achieving quantifiable social behavior outcomes, such as work return and retention. One tertiary care program, Productive Rehabilitation Institute of Dallas for Ergonomics (PRIDE), over 25 years has published objective, socioeconomically relevant outcome data related to patients with a chronic spine disorder (Table 2). Both authors of this chapter are indirect shareholders in PRIDE; Tom G. Mayer, MD, is the founder and medical director of PRIDE. More than 5,000 patients have completed the PRIDE program (2,000 additional patients began but did not complete the program). Team members, through the PRIDE Research Foundation, have studied the program's prospectively collected database to determine level II and II prognostic and therapeutic evidence as well as program outcome data and have published more than 150 studies in peer-reviewed journals.

Evaluation and Assessment

The structure of an interdisciplinary program must be sufficiently flexible to accommodate patients' objective functional goals. Normally, a patient's entry into an interdisciplinary program begins with an evaluation that is intended to quantify the barriers to recovery. A physician and a nurse perform a standard outpatient medical examination, reviewing the patient's history, physical findings, and relevant radiologic or other diagnostic data. The examination most often leads to the conclusion that the existing tissue damage is unlikely to improve with passive healing or additional surgery. The

Table 2

PRIDE 25-Year Data on Functional Restoration Outcomes

Outcome	Measure
Return to work	>90%
Work retention	>80%
Posttreatment surgery	<4%
Unsettled claim	<15%
Spine-related medical visits (excluding functional restoration or referring physician visits)	<5 visits per year
Recurrent injury resulting in claim or lost work time	<2%

patient's psychosocial distress and nonorganic barriers, such as insomnia, hypomobility, anxiety-related hypertension, and depression, are assessed. The physician initiates the first of many quantitative evaluations by measuring the range of motion of the impaired functional unit, with the corresponding effort factor. The effort factor represents a patient's conscious or unconscious ability to exert a full effort. Evaluation of effort may be as simple as a comparison of sitting and supine straight leg raise tests or as complex as a double goniometric comparison of true lumbar flexion and extension. The physician should identify and document the patient's goals. The use of the patient's own words from this interview is invaluable in later discussions related to the patient's program participation.

Nonphysician team members conduct the functional capacity evaluations. The physical function portion of the evaluation is difficult if the patient's pain and hypomobility are not an accurate guide to ongoing harm or damage. The point of the assessment is to gather quantitative, physics-based information about the numeric extent of injured or deconditioned motion segments. Quantifying function is an important first step; most patients have already undergone a qualitative single-specialty analysis that did not lead to improvement. This portion of the evaluation is intended to "set the speedometer" for the patient's functional training. After the physician assesses mobility and strength around the dysfunctional motion segment (the weak link), physical and occupational therapists evaluate the range of motion, dynamic strength, and endurance of the dysfunctional motion unit. These measurements are checked against one another using both an internally validated effort factor (involving heart rate, signs of pain limitation, and nonorganic pain origin) and an externally validated normative database.[34-37] A wholebody performance assessment usually is the province of the occupational therapist. The important data include cardiovascular measures (to determine the extent of deconditioning), materials-handling performance (to

2: Nonsurgical Care of the Spine

determine ability to compensate), positional tolerance, effort, and tolerance to external forces like repetitive weight. Deconditioning in uninjured segments of the body and paradoxical discrepancies may suggest the presence of nonfunctional compensatory behaviors.

The psychologic assessment (often called a mental health evaluation) includes a complex interplay of tests administered with the help of a staff psychologist. The goal is to identify the psychosocial barriers to functional recovery rather than to treat any premorbid psychiatric distress. At the tertiary care level, patients are largely self-selected and are characterized by a complex psychopathology that allowed them to function in society before the injury but not after the injury. The staff psychologist compares self-reported scores, functional questionnaires, personal interviews, and affective inventories to objectively determine levels of depression, anxiety, fear, inhibition, anger, and, occasionally, antisocial or manipulative traits. Although some self-reported scores have validity for identifying psychologic barriers, it is desirable for the psychologist to make a diagnosis based on the *Diagnostic and Statistical Manual of Mental Disorders,* assist in medication recommendations, and develop a treatment plan for a counselor to implement. Consultation with a psychiatrist is advantageous if a patient's medication issues are complex. Therapeutic intervention with cognitive-behavioral therapy and medication is used if a *Diagnostic and Statistical Manual* Axis I or Axis II diagnosis is identified as a barrier to recovery. The psychologist tallies the quantified data so the physician can use the required psychologic intervention or pharmacologic adjuncts in determining the length of the patient's program.

The disability case manager provides a critically important but often overlooked assessment. The disability assessment helps determine whether any identified physical, psychologic, or social barrier will prevent the patient from returning to his or her preferred job. The vital role of the disability case manager often is not incorporated into a tertiary care program because of its cost and difficulty, but patient outcomes suffer when disability case management is neglected. The disability case manager often is the only team member who has both the time and the knowledge required for assessing the practicality of the patient's vocational or societal goal. Some patients who reach their medical goals persist with unrealistic expectations that lead to failure. In addition, statutory, policy, employer, and union barriers can undermine the patient's work retention. The disability manager establishes links to the family, employer, state agencies, and retraining sites to ensure that external forces do not undermine the patient's reasonable expectations upon program completion.

The second, postevaluation visit with the physician often is more challenging for the physician and the patient than the initial assessment visit. The physician must allot time to integrate the four quantitative domains provided by the physical therapist, occupational therapist, psychologist, and disability case manager to decide on the required length and intensity of the patient's program. Relatively lengthy preprogram training may be necessary if the patient is markedly deconditioned or if work with weights, objects, or material handling is unsafe because of opioid habituation. The second visit enables the physician to review any radiologic or diagnostic studies not available during the first visit. Rarely, an occult fracture, nonunion, neurologic finding, or joint motion impairment may be detected that accounts for the patient's low functional scores. The physician may consult a surgeon, interventionalist, or neurologist for treatment of a newly discovered abnormality before the patient embarks on an expensive tertiary care program. After all relevant diagnostic tests are evaluated and the possibility of a hidden pain generator is eliminated, the physician gauges the patient's desire for functional recovery. Between the first and second meeting, the patient has been through a thorough and probably painful assessment. This arduous assessment should inspire enthusiasm for the program, its goals, and one or more of the individual staff members. However, the patient also may have been influenced by family, friends, clergy, or legal counsel who may not view the patient's functional recovery as a primary goal. The interdisciplinary program offers the possibility of success if the patient is attracted to it rather than if it was promoted to the patient. The team must refocus the patient from looking toward a "good-as-new" recovery toward reaching a plateau at which he or she has the physical strength and endurance for a return to work as well as the psychologic tools for coping with daily stressors.

The Initial Phase

The initial phase of the interdisciplinary program focuses on endurance and mobility. This phase usually extends over 2 to 6 days and consists of all-day activities that include 2 to 4 hours of weight-based isokinetic training and cardiovascular training in a communal gymnasium. Home-based cardiovascular training and muscle-joint stretching programs are established. The staff often observe that attention span, mood, and tolerance for socialization have atrophied along with the body. Patients must rapidly build their tolerance for a full day of activity.

The use of narcotic medications is incompatible with a progressive, quota-based program of resistive exercise. Any necessary detoxification from alcohol, opioids, muscle relaxants, and anxiolytic medications is begun during the first phase. The physician may add nonsteroidal anti-inflammatory drugs or adjuvant medication to control symptoms created by the initial physical activation. Antidepressant, sleep, and, occasionally, long-acting anxiolytic medications may be prescribed to treat barriers to functional improvement identified in the initial assessment.

By the end of the initial phase, a patient should be moving toward tolerating a full day of activity, sleeping through the night, participating in the program's social milieu, finishing any detoxification program, and refining the vocational plan. Adherence to attendance and compliance standards is essential before the patient is allowed to progress to the intensive phase. Patient safety considerations also are important to the transition to the intensive phase. There is a fine balance between management of hyperalgesia-induced fear-avoidance and the masking of opioid use, leading to injury. In the absence of guidance from research studies, the recommendation for the initial phase is to maintain a subthreshold exercise program until the dosage is tapered to less than 15 morphine equivalents per day of opioids. Patient safety can be ensured through monitoring by an addiction treatment specialist or another professional experienced in medication management, with the use of blood or urine toxicology testing.

Interdisciplinary programs earn their outcomes through the quality of interstaff communication. During the intensive phase, the team members conduct several reassessments of quantitative physical and psychologic data and record the patient's daily progress. This information is communicated to the team to create the multimodal disability management that is the hallmark of a tertiary program.

The Intensive Phase
The patient attends the intensive-phase program 8 hours per day and 3 to 5 days per week, depending on work status. The average length of the intensive phase is 20 days and is based on the extent of quantified impairment, the chronicity of the disability, and the assessed psychosocial or vocational barriers. The daily physical portion of the program combines weight-based, quota-adjusted strengthening, aerobic fitness, and stretching exercises with materials handling, positional tolerance, and other work simulation activities. The daily program also includes education in anatomy and physiology, group and individual counseling, assertiveness training, rational and emotive therapy, stress management counseling, repeated quantitative testing, and vocational planning. The educational sessions teach the patient how to make the structural, functional, behavioral, and life trajectory choices that are critical to recovery.

Occupational counseling ensures that the patient attains the established vocational goals. Ideally, assistance is available from the patient's union or a state or federal vocational rehabilitation agency. Although these statutory vocational services are required only for a small number of patients, the participants have high rates of work retention (the metric that often determines provider funding levels). The likelihood of work retention is dramatically enhanced in patients who are both medically rehabilitated and physically and mentally prepared for employment.

The Work-Transition Phase
The work-transition phase is needed by a minority of patients who either are reentering a robustly demanding job or who have had a lengthy period of disability. This phase requires three to eight visits devoted to further strengthening of the injured area and work simulation with materials-handling training. In addition, the patient receives case-closure assistance related to any remaining medication, occupational, legal, and administrative concerns, which can sabotage the patient's outcome if not resolved.

A long-term care plan and outcome-tracking phase are a necessary part of a high-quality program. Patients' perception that the environment of care extends beyond program completion leads to a higher rate of postprogram compliance in testing and outcome tracking.[38] Statutory mandates often affect patients' perception during this challenging phase, as many jurisdictions recognize the benefit of a long-term care plan. During quarterly visits to a physician, the patient receives medications as well as advice for meeting program goals such as a return to work, functional gains, a home exercise program, and a decreasing use of health care resources. Cost-effectiveness is best maintained if the patient is able to return as necessary for management of a symptom exacerbation or a focused intervention consistent with functional restoration. This final phase allows an updated evaluation of the long-term effectiveness of the program from the patient's point of view and for purposes of the facility's continuous quality improvement initiative. The patient is given the opportunity to consolidate gains, obtain feedback, and maintain the physical capacity plateau. After the intensive phase, patients may choose to present themselves for team feedback at one full-team staff meeting. In addition, the staff tracks outcomes by telephone at fixed intervals; the report is communicated to referring physicians, insurance or managed care adjusters, and attorneys. A patient's independence is reinforced when the scope of somatic complaints is minimized, functional gains are emphasized, and a few additional program sessions are available if the need arises.

Quality Assessment
Continuous quality improvement initiatives are paramount to the success of an interdisciplinary tertiary care program, and the data should be published (Table 2). Overall improvement in metrics related to chronic pain–related disability is essential, especially in a health care environment in which reimbursement eventually may be tied to outcome metrics. As the population ages, it becomes increasingly important that individuals in the working-age population continue to work and pay taxes rather than become fully disabled.

There is evidence that a history of unsuccessful surgical or nonsurgical treatment does not decrease patients' ability to return to their original job after completing a functional restoration program.[39] Exercise specifically designed to simulate the motions and loads of a specific work or sports activity was found in multiple studies to be robustly protective against reinjury.[40-43] A functional restoration program should track former patients and their work retention record to develop a database from which prognostic and therapeutic medical evidence can be derived. Publication of such information can positively affect third-party payer policies regarding functional restoration.

Patient feedback at specific intervals (3, 6, and 12 months after program completion) is at the heart of the quality assessment process. The patient's social and medical behaviors should be assessed through a structured telephone interview. A patient with a long-term care plan understands that the benefits of the program remain available and is more likely to remain in contact. The patient's return to the referring physician or primary care plan can create concerns, however. Many physicians have an understanding of chronic pain that is not consistent with continued function.[21] The long-term care plan is useful for avoiding miscommunication.

Medication Management

The overall cost of opioids prescribed for nonmalignant musculoskeletal pain increased more than 400% between 1990 and 2004.[44,45] The number of deaths from misuse of prescription opioid medications surpassed those from heroin and cocaine use beginning in 2003.[44] Opioid tapering presents significant challenges during the medical treatment of a patient with pain in a functional restoration program. It is legal in all US states to taper a patient's pain medications for the purpose of avoiding withdrawal symptoms. (In contrast, detoxification of a person who abuses drugs is legal only if the physician has a special certification.) Patients on high-dosage opioids need significant tapering before they can participate in an aggressive weight-based training program. However, the patient may have considerable distress about the prospect of opioid withdrawal. The practitioner must treat the patient with compassion, dignity, and respect while formulating a tapering protocol. The advice of a psychiatrist or addiction treatment specialist often is required. A patient who is using a low-dosage opioid should be able to tolerate a dosage reduction of 10% per day or 25% every 3 days. However, a patient with chronic pain may need a tapering process extending over 2 to 3 weeks and coinciding with the initial treatment phase.

The severity of withdrawal symptoms can be eased by using a longer acting opioid and/or low-dosage clonidine or a benzodiazepine.[46] Buprenorphine, a partial μ agonist–κ antagonist opiate receptor, is promising for use in opioid substitution and tapering. In comparison with morphine, buprenorphine is less potent and is more tightly bound to and slower to dissociate from the opiate receptor. Buprenorphine is approved by the US Food and Drug Administration (FDA) in sublingual form as an opiate dependence treatment and in intramuscular form as an analgesic. Buprenorphine is available alone or in combination with naloxone.[47] Patients with chronic pain who are treated with buprenorphine experience fewer cognitive, sedative, and euphoric effects than those treated with most other opioids. The drug offers mood enhancement and a smooth, uncomplicated withdrawal process. The patient is able to safely participate in functional physical training with faster integration into the program milieu. Buprenorphine is a moderate analgesic that can enhance the patient's ability to continue in treatment, and it does not appear to create the opioid-induced hyperalgesia that occurs with many other agents. The physician must induce a mild withdrawal before buprenorphine can preferentially displace other opioids from the μ receptor sites, while avoiding precipitation of a full competitive-receptor withdrawal state.[47]

Mental health conditions are becoming more common among patients with a musculoskeletal condition. Nonspecific neuropathic pain, fibromyalgia, widespread pain, chronic headaches, and chronic fatigue are symptoms that cannot be correlated with radiologic findings. These conditions often are best managed with medication and referral to a tertiary-level interdisciplinary program. Because neuropsychiatric illnesses often are comorbid with pain, effective pharmacotherapeutic treatment is necessary in a functional restoration program. Chronic widespread pain or fibromyalgia may be premorbid or comorbid with a traumatic injury.[48] The treatment agents include serotonin-norepinephrine reuptake inhibitors such as high-dosage venlafaxine, desmethylvenlafaxine, duloxetine, and milnacipran; duloxetine and milnacipran are FDA approved for treating both pain and affective disorders.[49] The standard dosage usually is sufficient. These agents generally have a more benign adverse effect profile than the tricyclic antidepressants, which have long been the mainstay treatment for chronic neuropathic pain. Pregabalin, in a higher dosage than is used for neuropathic pain, also is FDA approved. Chronic neuropathic pain often is extremely challenging to treat in the rehabilitation setting because of the patient's difficulty in disassociating hurt and harm. It is a challenge to convince patients with neuropathic pain to try medication they believe will not be effective (for example, an antiseizure medication such as gabapentin, pregabalin, topiramate, or levetiracetam previously received in a subtherapeutic dosage).

All tricyclic antidepressants can be used at low dosages for treating chronic pain.[49] A patient with neuropathic pain and comorbid depression should be given a full, clinically effective dosage. The use of the secondary amine-group tricyclic antidepressants nortriptyline, desipramine, and protriptyline should be considered, as these relatively old agents may not have been prescribed by other providers. These medications primarily act as norepinephrine reuptake inhibitors and may produce fewer sedating, anticholinergic, or orthostatic effects than drugs in the tertiary amine group. The tertiary amine agents amitriptyline, clomipramine, imipramine, and doxepin combine serotonergic and adrenergic effects. There is poor evidence to suggest any efficacy of selective serotonin reuptake inhibitors such as fluoxetine, paroxetine, sertraline, citalopram, escitalopram or bupropion, and mirtazapine in the treatment of chronic pain. These drugs are a mainstay for treating the comorbid affective or adjustment disorders prevalent in patients with chronic pain, however. A neuromodulator such as low-dose oxcarbazepine or topiramate, administered at bedtime, can be an efficacious second-line agent to treat a neuropathic pain disorder. Some patients require treatment with multiple agents having different mechanisms of action. Sodium channel blockers such as mexiletine and lidocaine can be effective for this purpose because they have few adverse effects when used with other drugs.[50]

Panic disorder, generalized anxiety disorder, posttraumatic stress disorder, and obsessive-compulsive disorder are common in patients with chronic pain. Serotonin-norepinephrine reuptake inhibitors, tricyclic antidepressants, and selective serotonin reuptake inhibitors are effective in treating these comorbid anxiety disorders.[51] These agents can reduce anxiety and may secondarily reduce muscular tension and pain perception. The "knock-on effect"' of good pharmacologic management may increase the ease of tapering sedative, benzodiazepine, and opioid use.

Patients who are dependent on high-dosage carisoprodol or a short-acting benzodiazepine can be converted to standard-dosage diazepam and tapered over 4 to 5 weeks. Patients who have taken a high-dosage benzodiazepine for more than 6 months may be able to tolerate a 10% reduction every 1 to 2 weeks.[52] An antispasticity agent such as baclofen or tizanidine may be required for a patient who cannot tolerate functional restoration without a muscle relaxant. These agents also may have analgesic properties. Carisoprodol use can lead to injury during activity and requires tapering or conversion to a benzodiazepine before the patient begins the exercise program.

An atypical neuroleptic drug occasionally is beneficial for a patient with spine pain who has a comorbid personality disorder, comorbid psychotic disorder, refractory chemical dependency disorder, or treatment-resistant affective disorder. The on-staff presence of a strong, clinically minded psychiatrist is important for guiding the medical management of such a patient.

Summary

An interdisciplinary functional restoration program is the most efficacious and least expensive treatment for a patient with chronic pain. Such a program offers an opportunity to restore function before deconditioning,

disability, depression, and drug use permanently alienate the patient from society and destroy the potential for productivity.[53] Treatment for patients with a complex chronic pain condition requires an interdisciplinary team led by a physician. Communication is the most important tool in helping these challenging patients achieve their goals. Repeated imaging reveals tissue pathology, but it cannot measure the patient's suffering and sense of hopelessness. Eventually, the use of quantitative tools should replace imaging in rehabilitation programs. Although quantification of physical and psychologic function has been well described and is important, its specificity, accuracy, and reproducibility are still evolving. Such measures remain underused in the assessment of patients with chronic pain.

Annotated References

1. Martin BI, Deyo RA, Mirza SK, et al: Expenditures and health status among adults with back and neck problems. *JAMA* 2008;299(6):656-664.

   The cost of neck and back pain was estimated through a survey of household and medical expenditure. Self-reported neck and back pain accounted for a large and expanding proportion of health care expenditures from 1997 to 2005, without evidence of improvement in general health status measures.

2. Martin BI, Turner JA, Mirza SK, Lee MJ, Comstock BA, Deyo RA: Trends in health care expenditures, utilization, and health status among US adults with spine problems, 1997-2006. *Spine (Phila Pa 1976)* 2009; 34(19):2077-2084.

   A survey from 1997 to 2005 confirmed a 65% increase in spine-related health care expenditure. A 49% increase in the number of patients seeking spine care was the largest contributing factor to increasing outpatient expenditure. Per-patient inpatient hospitalization increased by 37%, and per-patient medication prescriptions increased 139%.

3. Freburger JK, Holmes GM, Agans RP, et al: The rising prevalence of chronic low back pain. *Arch Intern Med* 2009;169(3):251-258.

   A cross-sectional telephone survey was conducted in North Carolina in 1992 and 2006. The prevalence of chronic low back pain rose to more than 9% of the survey population, with associated disability and cost.

4. Maghout Juratli S, Franklin GM, Mirza SK, Wickizer TM, Fulton-Kehoe D: Lumbar fusion outcomes in Washington State workers' compensation. *Spine (Phila Pa 1976)* 2006;31(23):2715-2723.

   A retrospective cohort study of injured workers in Washington state who underwent lumbar fusion found that 3.6% or 58.1% received cage instrumentation in 1996 or 2001, respectively. The overall disability rate 2 years after lumbar fusion was 63.9%, the reoperation rate was 22.1%, and the overall complication rate was 11.8%. The use of cages or other instrumentation was associated with an increased complication rate without a decrease in disability.

5. Social Security Administration: *Annual Statistical Report on Social Security Disability Insurance Program.* Baltimore, MD, Office of Research Evaluation and Statistics, 2007.

   The two most common diagnostic categories in patients who received Social Security disability income benefits were those related to mental health and musculoskeletal causes. Each of these categories far outpaces combined disability income payments for stroke, spinal cord injury, and traumatic brain injury.

6. Modic MT, Obuchowski NA, Ross JS, et al: Acute low back pain and radiculopathy: MR imaging findings and their prognostic role and effect on outcome. *Radiology* 2005;237(2):597-604.

   MRI alone has no measurable value for planning nonsurgical care. Informing patients of MRI results does not seem to improve functional outcomes and may be associated with decreased mental health scores.

7. Schenk P, Läubli T, Hodler J, Klipstein A: Magnetic resonance imaging of the lumbar spine: Findings in female subjects from administrative and nursing professions. *Spine (Phila Pa 1976)* 2006;31(23):2701-2706.

   Women with persistent low back pain were assessed using MRI. Changes in disk hydration or morphology were not associated with heavy or light work, job type, or characteristics of physical loading.

8. Webster BS, Snook SH: The cost of 1989 workers' compensation low back pain claims. *Spine (Phila Pa 1976)* 1994;19(10):1111-1116.

9. Hashemi L, Webster BS, Clancy EA: Trends in disability duration and cost of workers' compensation low back pain claims (1988-1996). *J Occup Environ Med* 1998; 40(12):1110-1119.

10. Deyo RA, Ciol MA, Cherkin DC, Loeser JD, Bigos SJ: Lumbar spinal fusion: A cohort study of complications, reoperations, and resource use in the Medicare population. *Spine (Phila Pa 1976)* 1993;18(11):1463-1470.

11. Deyo RA, Diehl AK, Rosenthal M: How many days of bed rest for acute low back pain? A randomized clinical trial. *N Engl J Med* 1986;315(17):1064-1070.

12. Kernan T, Rainville J: Observed outcomes associated with a quota-based exercise approach on measures of kinesiophobia in patients with chronic low back pain. *J Orthop Sports Phys Ther* 2007;37(11):679-687.

    In a nonblinded study of non–pain-contingent, progressively advancing physical therapy (called quota-based therapy) to improve flexibility, strength, and lifting capacity, patients who completed the program had decreased fear-avoidance of movement.

13. Scientific approach to the assessment and management of activity-related spinal disorders: A monograph for clinicians. Report of the Quebec Task Force on Spinal Disorders. *Spine (Phila Pa 1976)* 1987;12(7, suppl):S1-S59.

14. Coste J, Delecoeuillerie G, Cohen de Lara A, Le Parc JM, Paolaggi JB: Clinical course and prognostic factors in acute low back pain: An inception cohort study in primary care practice. *BMJ* 1994;308(6928):577-580.

15. Chou R, Loeser JD, Owens DK, et al: Interventional therapies, surgery, and interdisciplinary rehabilitation for low back pain: An evidence-based clinical practice guideline from the American Pain Society. *Spine (Phila Pa 1976)* 2009;34(10):1066-1077.

    A multidisciplinary panel developed eight recommendations for interventional therapies, surgery, and interdisciplinary rehabilitation for low back pain. The strongest recommendation was for intensive, interdisciplinary rehabilitation with a cognitive-behavioral emphasis for patients who do not respond to conventional single-specialty therapy.

16. Chou R, Atlas SJ, Stanos SP, Rosenquist RW: Nonsurgical interventional therapies for low back pain: A review of the evidence for an American Pain Society clinical practice guideline. *Spine (Phila Pa 1976)* 2009; 34(10):1078-1093.

    A multidisciplinary panel found evidence that surgery is superior to nonsurgical intradiskal therapies for axial low back pain. Epidural steroid injection had short-term benefit for radicular symptoms. Spinal cord stimulation had moderate benefit for so-called failed-back syndrome. Insufficient evidence existed for the other sampled injection or surgical modalities.

17. Chou R, Baisden J, Carragee EJ, Resnick DK, Shaffer WO, Loeser JD: Surgery for low back pain: A review of the evidence for an American Pain Society Clinical Practice Guideline. *Spine (Phila Pa 1976)* 2009;34(10): 1094-1109.

    A multidisciplinary panel reviewed the evidence for surgery in patients with low back pain. There was fair evidence that fusion is no better then intensive rehabilitation for nonradicular low back pain. Fewer than half of patients had an optimal outcome after fusion, but fusion may be slightly superior to unknown treatment. Good evidence exists that diskectomy is superior to nonsurgical therapy during the initial 3 months of radicular symptoms. For symptomatic spinal stenosis (neuroclaudication), good evidence exists that decompressive surgery is moderately superior to nonsurgical therapy.

18. Mayer J, Mooney V, Dagenais S: Evidence-informed management of chronic low back pain with lumbar extensor strengthening exercises. *Spine J* 2008;8(1):96-113.

    Lumbar extensor–strengthening exercises can strengthen the lumbar musculature, as supported by varying levels of evidence. There is significant evidence that progressive resistance exercises are more effective than no treatment or passive modalities for improving pain, disability, or other patient-reported outcomes in patients with chronic low back pain.

19. Brox JI, Sørensen R, Friis A, et al: Randomized clinical trial of lumbar instrumented fusion and cognitive intervention and exercises in patients with chronic low back pain and disc degeneration. *Spine (Phila Pa 1976)* 2003; 28(17):1913-1921.

20. Stover B, Wickizer TM, Zimmerman F, Fulton-Kehoe D, Franklin G: Prognostic factors of long-term disability in a workers' compensation system. *J Occup Environ Med* 2007;49(1):31-40.

    Several predictors of long-term disability are noted, including some that confirm other study findings: an occupation involving heavy labor, low job satisfaction (including a high unemployment rate), back injury, delay in first medical treatment, and delay between medical treatment and claim filing.

21. Rainville J, Pransky G, Indahl A, Mayer EK: The physician as disability advisor for patients with musculoskeletal complaints. *Spine (Phila Pa 1976)* 2005;30(22): 2579-2584.

    A literature review noted the preponderant evidence that a physician's opinion (even if contrary to scientific evidence) may significantly affect the patient's eventual decision not to return to a former level of activity or file for disability benefits.

22. Cutler RB, Fishbain DA, Rosomoff HL, Abdel-Moty E, Khalil TM, Rosomoff RS: Does nonsurgical pain center treatment of chronic pain return patients to work? A review and meta-analysis of the literature. *Spine (Phila Pa 1976)* 1994;19(6):643-652.

23. Hazard RG: Spine update: Functional restoration. *Spine (Phila Pa 1976)* 1995;20(21):2345-2348.

24. Mayer TG, Polatin P, Smith B, et al: Spine rehabilitation: Secondary and tertiary nonoperative care. *Spine (Phila Pa 1976)* 1995;20(18):2060-2066.

25. Mayer T, Polatin P, Smith B, et al: Spine rehabilitation: Secondary and tertiary nonoperative care. *Spine J* 2003; 3(3, suppl):28S-36S.

26. Pain (chronic), in Denniston PO, ed: *Official Disability Guidelines: 2008.* Encinitas, CA, Work Loss Data Institute, 2008, pp 1351-1632.

    These widely used guidelines primarily are related to workers' compensation. The use of a "well-established, outcome-confirmed" interdisciplinary functional restoration program is recommended.

27. Chronic pain, in Hegmann K, ed: *Occupational Medicine Practice Guidelines,* ed 2. Elk Grove Village, IL, American College of Occupational and Environmental Medicine, 2008.

    These widely used guidelines primarily describe recommended actions in a workers' compensation setting. The use of chronic pain programs is recommended for patients with a refractory disability or chronic pain syndrome.

28. Rainville J, Hartigan C, Jouve C, Martinez E: The influence of intense exercise-based physical therapy program on back pain anticipated before and induced by physical activities. *Spine J* 2004;4(2):176-183.

29. Long A, Donelson R, Fung T: Does it matter which exercise? A randomized control trial of exercise for low back pain. *Spine (Phila Pa 1976)* 2004;29(23):2593-2602.

30. Genovese E, Galper JS: *Guide to the Evaluation of Functional Ability: How to Request, Interpret, and Apply Functional Capacity Exams.* Chicago, IL, American Medical Association, 2009.

    Multiple chapters discuss the best practice philosophy for a functional capacity evaluation to maximize the patient's ability to remain at work after an injury and minimize the possibility of reinjury.

31. Dersh J, Mayer T, Gatchel RJ, Towns B, Theodore B, Polatin P: Psychiatric comorbidity in chronic disabling occupational spinal disorders has minimal impact on functional restoration socioeconomic outcomes. *Spine (Phila Pa 1976)* 2007;32(17):1917-1925.

    Data were analyzed for 1,323 patients with a psychiatric comorbidity who entered a functional restoration program after an average of more than 19 months of work-precluding disability. An Axis II personality disorder best predicted program noncompletion; the rate in these patients was more than twice as high as in patients with another disorder. Compared with other patients, those with a history of difficult opioid discontinuation were 2.7 times less likely to return to or retain work.

32. Gatchel RJ, Polatin PB, Mayer TG, Garcy PD: Psychopathology and the rehabilitation of patients with chronic low back pain disability. *Arch Phys Med Rehabil* 1994;75(6):666-670.

33. Polatin PB, Kinney RK, Gatchel RJ, Lillo E, Mayer TG: Psychiatric illness and chronic low-back pain: The mind and the spine. Which goes first? *Spine (Phila Pa 1976)* 1993;18(1):66-71.

34. Dvir Z: *Isokinetics: Muscle Testing, Interpretation and Clinical Applications,* ed 2. Philadelphia, PA, Churchill Livingstone, 2004.

35. Newton M, Thow M, Somerville D, Henderson I, Waddell G: Trunk strength testing with iso-machines: Part 2. Experimental evaluation of the Cybex II Back Testing System in normal subjects and patients with chronic low back pain. *Spine (Phila Pa 1976)* 1993;18(7):812-824.

36. Benjamin S, Flood J, Bechtel R: Isokinetic testing prior to and following anterior lumbar interbody fusion surgery: A pilot study. *Isokinet Exerc Sci* 2005;13:159-162.

37. Dervisevica E, Hadzica V, Burger H: Reproducibility of trunk isokinetic strength findings in healthy individuals. *Isokinet Exerc Sci* 2007;15:99-109.

38. Garcy P, Mayer T, Gatchel RJ: Recurrent or new injury outcomes after return to work in chronic disabling spinal disorders: Tertiary prevention efficacy of functional restoration treatment. *Spine (Phila Pa 1976)* 1996; 21(8):952-959.

39. Mayer T, McMahon MJ, Gatchel RJ, Sparks B, Wright A, Pegues P: Socioeconomic outcomes of combined

2: Nonsurgical Care of the Spine

spine surgery and functional restoration in workers' compensation spinal disorders with matched controls. *Spine (Phila Pa 1976)* 1998;23(5):598-606.

40. Hägglund M, Waldén M, Ekstrand J: Lower reinjury rate with a coach-controlled rehabilitation program in amateur male soccer: A randomized controlled trial. *Am J Sports Med* 2007;35(9):1433-1442.

    A randomized controlled study found a reduced rate of injury in European men who were amateur soccer players if they completed a 10-step resistance-based active physical therapy program before return to play was allowed. Level of evidence: I.

41. Ekstrand J, Gillquist J, Liljedahl SO: Prevention of soccer injuries: Supervision by doctor and physiotherapist. *Am J Sports Med* 1983;11(3):116-120.

42. Hägglund M, Waldén M, Ekstrand J: Previous injury as a risk factor for injury in elite football: A prospective study over two consecutive seasons. *Br J Sports Med* 2006;40(9):767-772.

    An inadequately rehabilitated injury may predict injury during the subsequent season, even if the patient has adequate rest between seasons.

43. Askling C, Karlsson J, Thorstensson A: Hamstring injury occurrence in elite soccer players after preseason strength training with eccentric overload. *Scand J Med Sci Sports* 2003;13(4):244-250.

44. Paulozzi LJ, Budnitz DS, Xi Y: Increasing deaths from opioid analgesics in the United States. *Pharmacoepidemiol Drug Saf* 2006;15(9):618-627.

    A trend analysis of drug poisoning deaths used US Centers for Disease Control and Prevention mortality data related to underlying cause of death and multiple causes of death as well as US Drug Enforcement Administration opioid analgesic sales data. The number of deaths from prescription opioid analgesics increased 91.2% from 1990 through 2002, compared with 12.4% and 22.8% increases for heroin and cocaine, respectively. In 2002, prescription opioid analgesic poisoning was responsible for 5,528 deaths (more than cocaine or heroin poisoning).

45. Deyo RA, Mirza SK, Turner JA, Martin BI: Overtreating chronic back pain: Time to back off? *J Am Board Fam Med* 2009;22(1):62-68.

    Medicare expenditures for spine injections, fusion surgery, and opioid analgesia increased over a 10-year period without documented improvement in outcomes or overall improved function.

46. Johnson RE, Strain EC, Amass L: Buprenorphine: How to use it right. *Drug Alcohol Depend* 2003;70(2, suppl): S59-S77.

47. Koppert W, Ihmsen H, Körber N, et al: Different profiles of buprenorphine-induced analgesia and antihyperalgesia in a human pain model. *Pain* 2005;118(1-2): 15-22.

    In a randomized double-blind placebo-controlled crossover study of 15 volunteers, sublingual buprenorphine had serum availability more than 50% longer than intravenous buprenorphine. The half-lives of buprenorphine-induced analgesic and antihyperalgesic effects were 171 and 288 minutes, respectively. In contrast to pure μ-receptor agonists, buprenorphine exerts a lasting antihyperalgesic effect. Buprenorphine may improve the treatment of central sensitization.

48. Mayer TG, Towns BL, Neblett R, Theodore BR, Gatchel RJ: Chronic widespread pain in patients with occupational spinal disorders: Prevalence, psychiatric comorbidity, and association with outcomes. *Spine (Phila Pa 1976)* 2008;33(17):1889-1897.

    Retrospectively collected prognostic data related to 878 patients revealed a convergence of chronic widespread pain and spine disorders in an occupational setting. Thirty-two percent of patients met American College of Rheumatology criteria for chronic widespread pain, compared with 4.1% to 13.5% of the general population.

49. Verdu B, Decosterd I, Buclin T, Stiefel F, Berney A: Antidepressants for the treatment of chronic pain. *Drugs* 2008;68(18):2611-2632.

    The evidence was reviewed for using antidepressant medication for patients with pain. There is good evidence for tricyclic medication to treat neuropathic pain or headache and lower level evidence for selective norepinephrine reuptake inhibitors. No evidence of benefit was found for using selective serotonin reuptake inhibitors for treating chronic pain.

50. Jackson KC II: Pharmacotherapy for neuropathic pain. *Pain Pract* 2006;6(1):27-33.

    This is a discussion of theory that the use of two medications with different mechanisms of action to control pain may be superior to monotherapy in patients with chronic pain.

51. Seidel S, Aigner M, Ossege M, Pernicka E, Wildner B, Sycha T: Antipsychotics for acute and chronic pain in adults. *Cochrane Database Syst Rev* 2008;4: CD004844.

    Antipsychotic medication may provide adjuvant therapy for patients with chronic pain and significant psychologic comorbidity. The risks of using these medications may outweigh the benefits.

52. Smith D, Wesson D, Sabnani S: Benzodiasepine and other sedative hypnotic dependence, in Gabbard GO, ed: *Gabbard's Treatments of Psychiatric Disorders*, ed 4. Arlington, VA, American Psychiatric Publishing, 2007, pp 207-216.

    Withdrawal from sedative or hypnotic medications has multiple complications.

53. Jordan KD, Mayer TG, Gatchel RJ: Should extended disability be an exclusion criterion for tertiary rehabilitation? Socioeconomic outcomes of early versus late functional restoration in compensation spinal disorders. *Spine (Phila Pa 1976)* 1998;23(19):2110-2117.

Chapter 16

Spine Orthoses

Michael H. Heggeness, MD, PhD   John A. Hipp, PhD

Introduction

Braces and external supports have been used since antiquity to treat patients with a spine disorder; the use of braces for spine injuries was described in Egyptian texts as early as 3500 BCE.[1-3] Orthoses continue to be routinely used in numerous clinical conditions to decrease pain, prevent deformity, allow fracture healing, or prevent deformity. Although a significant body of literature describes the effect of braces on asymptomatic volunteers with no known spine disorder, only scant research has assessed and quantified the mechanical effects of braces on patients with chronic or acute spine pathology. Information is essentially nonexistent on the specific influence of orthosis use on clinical outcomes in most spine disorders.

The fundamental goal of a spine brace, as used for most conditions other than scoliosis, is to minimize intervertebral motion, prevent further injury to the spine, or create a biomechanical environment that will facilitate wound healing or fusion. Although many research studies have assessed the ability of spine braces to restrict motion, the braces were worn by healthy volunteers in almost all studies. In general, it is unknown whether the research results apply to patients with a spine disorder. Several variables related to actual brace use are difficult to represent in a laboratory study. Patients must wear a brace for a much longer period of time than used in laboratory studies, and they experience a range of activities in which the effectiveness of a brace may vary. Patients undergoing prolonged brace treatment also may become acclimated to the brace and make modifications to the brace itself or the manner in which it is fitted.

The mechanism by which a spine brace restricts motion is different from that of an extremity brace. A brace used for a fracture usually compresses the soft tissues and applies controlling forces to the bone through the soft tissues. This principle is less applicable to a spine brace, as breathing or the blood supply could be compromised if the force through the soft tissues were

sufficient to effectively immobilize the spine. Instead, spine braces attempt to create an external load-sharing bridge spanning the region of the spine that is to be immobilized. For example, most hard cervical collars contact the head at several points around the base of the skull, creating a rigid bridge that spans the cervical spine and contacts the upper torso at several points around the shoulders, chest, and back.

Cervical Orthoses

The Soft Cervical Collar

A soft cervical collar is a circumferential orthosis constructed of foam rubber covered with soft fabric. A hook-and-loop (Velcro) fastener is used to close the brace (Figure 1). The soft cervical collar is believed to provide little or no mechanical stability to the cervical spine, and its efficacy is supported by few data. In healthy volunteers, a soft collar was found to provide a minimal reduction in head motion and provides no sig-

Dr. Heggeness or an immediate family member has received royalties from Relievant Medsystems; owns stock or stock options in Relievant Medsystems; and is a board member, owner, officer, or committee member of the North American Spine Society. Dr. Hipp or an immediate family member has received research or institutional support from Medtronic.

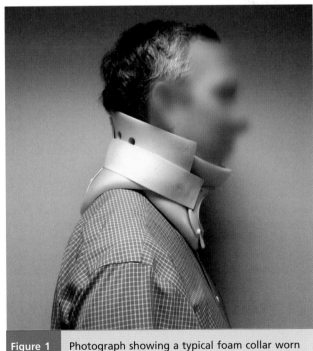

Figure 1 Photograph showing a typical foam collar worn by a healthy volunteer.

2: Nonsurgical Care of the Spine

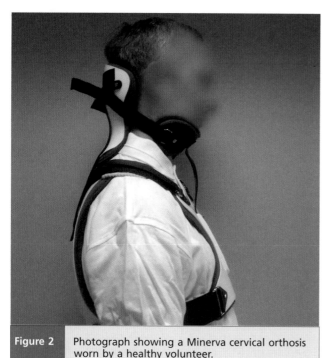

Figure 2 Photograph showing a Minerva cervical orthosis worn by a healthy volunteer.

nificant stability.[4] The soft collar can provide the patient with tactile feedback that may serve as a reminder to restrict head motion but also may provide a false sense of security. A foam collar was found to be least effective for reducing intervertebral motion in healthy volunteers.[5,6] In contrast, another study found that soft and hard collars were similarly effective when a wide range of activities of daily living was tested.[7] These researchers suggested that the most important effect of a collar is to act as a proprioceptive guide to regulating overall head and neck motion. A soft cervical collar can be useful in weaning a patient from brace use. A patient who has worn a restricting brace for an extended period often is transitioned to a soft-collar brace for several days while learning to independently support and move the neck.

The Rigid Cervical Collar
A rigid cervical collar is applied millions of times every year after an accident. The goal is to protect the cervical spine in the unlikely event that the patient has a cervical injury. The efficacy of this practice has never been proved, and evidence exists that the presence of a rigid cervical collar can be detrimental if the patient has a severe dissociative injury.[8,9] A rigid cervical collar can help restrict intervertebral motion and thereby facilitate the formation of bridging bone after fusion surgery. However, the ability of a rigid cervical collar to improve fusion has never been documented.

A rigid cervical collar can be considered a high thoracic orthosis. The anterior aspect of the brace typically does not extend distal to the sternal notch, and the posterior aspect does not extend distal to the level of the

T3 spinous process. Proximally, the commonly used orthoses engage the occiput below the inion posteriorly and the mandible anteriorly. Distally, the cervical collar rests on the trapezial areas posteriorly and laterally and on the clavicles and suprasternal notch anteriorly. The brace may create longitudinal traction between the cranium and skull. This traction can create several millimeters of separation between vertebrae in the presence of a severe dissociative injury.[8] A variety of devices are available, differing in the stiffness of the bracing materials and the characteristics of the padding material. The effectiveness of these devices depends on proper fitting and the geometry of the individual.[10,11] The clinician should assume responsibility for ensuring the collar is properly fitted.

The Sternal-Occipital-Mandibular Immobilizer
A sternal-occipital-mandibular immobilizer (commonly known as a SOMI brace) consists of a padded sternal plate with extensions that rest on the shoulders. Separate occipital and chin pads connect to the sternal plate through adjustable rigid bars. Straps stabilize the sternal and shoulder pieces around the torso. The advantage of the SOMI brace for a patient who is confined to bed is the absence of a back plate to cause discomfort when the patient is supine. When healthy volunteers attempted head and neck flexion-extension, this design was found to be as effective in restricting intervertebral motion as the Minerva and pinless halo braces.[5] The SOMI brace does not prevent all cervical spine motion; it allows an average 5° of intervertebral motion at some levels.[5]

The Minerva Brace
The Minerva brace is constructed of padded hard plastic and is contoured to engage the sternum and anterior chest, with extensions to engage the mandible and occiput (Figure 2). Unlike the SOMI brace, the Minerva brace has a back plate to engage the upper thoracic and periscapular regions of the back. The effectiveness of the Minerva brace is comparable to that of the SOMI and pinless halo braces in reducing head and intervertebral motion. All three designs were found to be more effective than a soft or rigid collar.[5] Dysphagia attributable to the fit of the brace has been reported,[12] and therefore the fit of the device should be assessed around the anterior aspects of the neck, particularly if the patient has had difficulty in swallowing.

The Halo Brace
The halo brace consists of a padded hard plastic vest, usually lined with synthetic sheepskin material, that rigidly attaches by vertical posts to a ring encircling the head. In the back, the ring may be closed or open (for ease of application), and it has perforations that can accommodate four or more pins to penetrate the skin and engage the outer table of the skull. For compatibility with MRI, the ring usually is constructed of graphite and the pins are titanium.

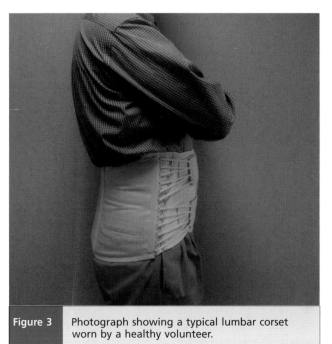

Figure 3   Photograph showing a typical lumbar corset worn by a healthy volunteer.

sion.[16] However, it is not known whether fusion rates could be improved by using a device that maintains an optimal range of intervertebral motion at the surgical site. The best brace for some patients may be the one that allows the least amount of motion, but a moderate amount of controlled motion may optimize healing in other patients. Research to objectively define the goals of bracing will facilitate interpretation of the available data.

Thoracic and Lumbar Orthoses

An external brace must directly or indirectly apply forces to the vertebrae to provide stability or modify the position of the thoracolumbar spine. These forces pass from the brace through the soft tissues and into the spine. A thoracolumbar brace must apply sufficient force to provide the needed stability or correction to the spine, without causing soft-tissue breakdown or interfering with the patient's breathing or gastrointestinal function. The contours of the patient's torso and pelvis contours in the sagittal, coronal, and axial planes are important to the effectiveness of a brace, as are the properties of soft tissue; a thick layer of adipose tissue can affect the manner in which the orthosis applies forces to the body. Compression of the entire abdomen can be used, but only where it does not compromise breathing or gastrointestinal function. Alternatively, a brace can apply forces to the rib cage along the cranial aspects of the brace and to the pelvis at the caudal aspect of the device, thereby indirectly applying forces to the thoracolumbar spine. This type of brace functions as a load-sharing construct that bridges the cranial and caudal regions of contact. Some braces use a combination of force-transfer mechanisms.

A recent systematic literature review found no evidence that lumbar supports can prevent back pain.[17] There was conflicting evidence on the use of any type of lumbar support for treating back pain. The review did not consider the effectiveness of different types of braces.

Lumbar Binders, Belts, and Corsets

Elastic binders and belts designed to support the lumbar area are available in a wide variety of designs. These supports do not rigidly immobilize the spinal column but can be effective in relieving episodic axial pain. Lumbar corsets provide mechanical support that is believed to primarily result from the hydraulic effects of gentle compression on the abdominal contents (Figure 3). A lumbar corset usually is constructed of canvas or a similar fabric and extends from the lower thoracic region to the pelvis. The width and rigidity of the brace usually is adjustable with laces or straps. Some corsets use rigid metal stays or flexible soft stays. The stays are vertical struts that are not primarily intended to provide vertical support but to prevent the corset from sliding or bundling around the waist. Corset use was

The halo brace requires pin fixation to the skull. Pins are placed in safe zones below the equator of the skull, with care to avoid the temporal area (where thin bone increases the risk of pin penetration) and the masseter muscles. The frontal area, cephalad to the medial half of each eyebrow, is avoided because of the risk of injury to the supraorbital nerve. Pins usually are placed with 6 to 8 in-lb of torque and are retightened after 24 hours to compensate for creep. Pin placement generally requires local anesthesia, and sterile technique is used. Pin site loosening and infection, usually occurring together, are frequent but minor complications. Daily pin care and pin site inspection are necessary for the duration of treatment. The halo device was considered a successful component of treatment in 85% of more than 340 patients.[13] Complications were common but minor; the most common was pin tract infection, followed by instability (fracture site motion in follow-up flexion-extension studies). A pinless version of the halo device is available. This device was found to be equivalent to the Minerva and SOMI braces in restricting intervertebral and head motion.[5]

Choosing a Brace

The options for cervical spine bracing can be quantitatively compared using several studies.[4-7,10,14,15] However, most of the study results apply only to a subset of daily activities. A wide range of activities can result in intervertebral motion, and bracing may be more effective during some activities than others. The greatest difficulty in interpreting the clinical significance of intervertebral and head motion data is that the optimal amount of motion during fusion maturation or soft-tissue or fracture healing is not known. Use of a cervical collar after fusion surgery did not improve the rate of fu-

Table 1

Reductions in Sagittal Plane Intervertebral Motion With Brace Use, Relative to Motion Without Bracing[a]

Brace	Average Reduction (SD)[b]					
	C1-C2	C2-C3	C3-C4	C4-C5	C5-C6	C6-C7
Miami-J	7.7 (4.9)	5.8 (3.0)	7.1 (3.9)	8.8 (4.7)	8.9 (5.6)	7.9 (6.1)
Aspen	6.4 (5.1)	5.9 (3.2)	7.1 (4.1)	8.6 (5.7)	9.2 (6.0)	7.7 (6.6)
PMT	7.4 (5.0)	6.3 (3.4)	8.1 (3.7)	9.5 (4.9)	10.0 (6.5)	8.0 (6.6)
Philadelphia	7.4 (5.7)	6.5 (3.0)	8.8 (4.6)	9.9 (5.3)	10.0 (5.6)	7.1 (6.1)
SOMI	7.3 (4.5)	8.0 (2.9)	10.6 (4.3)	12.6 (5.0)	12.3 (6.5)	7.9 (7.7)
Pinless halo	6.8 (5.3)	8.1 (3.3)	10.8 (4.6)	12.7 (5.3)	13.0 (5.2)	10.3 (7.1)
Minerva	8.1 (5.2)	8.2 (2.9)	11.7 (4.7)	14.6 (4.7)	13.9 (5.1)	11.2 (6.0)

[a]Measurements obtained from lateral flexion-extension spine radiographs in 45 healthy volunteers.
[b]Measured in degrees.

Adapted with permission from Schneider AM, Hipp JA, Nguyen L, Reitman CA: Reduction in head and intervertebral motion provided by 7 contemporary cervical orthoses in 45 individuals. *Spine (Phila Pa 1976)* 2007;32(1):E1-E6.

found to have some benefit, based on the outcome scores of patients with low back pain.[18]

The Thoracolumbosacral Orthosis

A thoracolumbosacral orthosis (TLSO) frequently is used in the management of a fracture or another pathology located between T7 and L4. This rigid brace is commercially available in a variety of sizes, or it can be custom molded to an individual patient. A TLSO fitted for an earlier treatment or for a similar-size patient usually is satisfactory. Custom molding is required if the patient has a significant deformity from a fracture or another condition. A custom prosthesis provides more secure immobilization of the spine but is expensive and labor intensive to mold. A plaster cast of the patient's torso is used to create a torso cast, which serves as the template for a custom rigid orthosis, traditionally constructed of thermoplastic material. Creating the mold with the patient in the prone position can provide an extension moment to the spine, which is useful in a flexion-compression or flexion-distraction spine injury.

A TLSO is fabricated as separate rigid front and back plastic shells connected by multiple straps. If immobilization from L4 to S1 is indicated, the TLSO can be fitted with an adjustable, lockable hinge that attaches to a thigh extension. The hinge usually is designed to lock in neutral position to permit standing and in a flexed position to accommodate sitting.

Human Motion Studies

The Cervical Spine

The ability of different braces to control spine range of motion has been investigated. The methodology and findings of the available studies vary slightly, but most involved young, uninjured volunteers. There is general agreement that cervical collars and orthoses variably reduce intervertebral motion from the occipitocervical junction to the C6-C7 level in healthy subjects.[5,6,15] In a study of 45 healthy volunteers, sagittal plane intervertebral motion was measured from lateral fluoroscopic flexion-extension images.[5] Intervertebral motion was measured with the subject first wearing no brace and then wearing each of seven commonly used collars or orthoses. Table 1 compares the reductions in intervertebral motion. These findings suggest that, on average, the choice of brace or orthosis for the upper cervical spine makes little difference. The cervicothoracic orthoses generally were more effective for the mid and lower cervical levels, however. A substantial variation in standard deviations supports the belief that the effectiveness of braces and orthoses depends on several largely unexplored factors.

The effects of cervical orthoses as measured in a controlled laboratory environment may significantly misrepresent the effects of these devices in improving patient activites after injury or surgery. For example, mastication was found to produce little significant cervical motion in research volunteers who were not wearing a collar. In contrast, mastication caused significant cervical spine motion in every patient who was wearing a cervical orthosis or collar, and more occiput-C1 and C1-C2 motion was produced with a collar than without a collar.[19] A collar that is too large or too small allows significant, unpredictable cervical intervertebral motion.[11]

All commonly used high thoracic braces restricted the motion of the mid and lower cervical spine in young volunteers.[5] Rotation is more limited with braces that engage the jaw with well-contoured anterior chin support than with other braces. A low thoracic brace, such as the SOMI or Minerva brace, limits motion at the cervicothoracic junction more than a high thoracic brace.[5]

Cervical braces and backboards are routinely used in the early management of spine injuries, and they are invaluable in protecting an unstable spinal cord from further injury. A comprehensive literature review on the use of cervical collars for all trauma patients concluded that the effect of spine immobilization is uncertain for mortality, neurologic injury, spine stability, and other adverse effects.[20] Airway obstruction is a major cause of preventable death in trauma patients, and spine immobilization, particularly of the cervical spine, can contribute to airway compromise. The possibility that immobilization may increase the risk of mortality and morbidity therefore cannot be excluded.

The Thoracolumbar and Lumbar Spine

In healthy volunteers, thoracolumbar orthoses were found to reduce trunk motion, as detected by skin surface markers.[21-25] It is unclear whether a reduction in motion at the skin surface corresponds to a useful reduction in motion between the targeted vertebrae. It is also not known how these motion restriction data can be used clinically. There are no validated criteria for interpreting the cited studies' quantitative data. For some patients, the brace that best reduces motion may be optimal, but for others a brace that allows reduced but controlled motion may be preferable.

Several small studies used radiographs to study the effect of braces on intervertebral motion, with inconsistent findings.[17,21,22,26,27] Intervertebral motion may actually increase when some patients wear a brace. The level-dependent average reduction in intervertebral motion was approximately 40% with a canvas corset, jacket, or brace incorporating a thigh extension, but there was substantial variability.[22] Four braces, including a corset and a TLSO, were found to more effectively reduce motion in the coronal plane than in the sagittal plane. With lumbar orthoses, the reduction in trunk motion detected during flexion-extension was not observed with the trunk motions that occur during walking.[28] Many lumbar braces may be ineffective in obtaining the desired reduction of motion, particularly if the goal is to promote fusion or healing, such as after fusion surgery or for treatment of a pars defect. Braces may, however, be effective for constantly reminding the patient to avoid trunk motion.

Lumbar braces are often used to protect the lumbar spine in the workplace. Although braces are effective in reducing workplace trunk motion, there is little evidence that the risk of work-related back injury is thereby decreased. In a systematic review of the literature on the use of lumbar supports for workplace spine protection, a lack of high-quality evidence prevented the authors from strongly recommending the clinical use of a lumbar support belt or a more rigid orthosis, such as a TLSO.[29]

Summary

There is no doubt that braces are useful in the treatment of many spine disorders. The ideal means of bracing for different spine conditions has not been extensively investigated, however. The development of more effective brace designs and improved bracing applications will require a better understanding of the mechanism by which an orthosis immobilizes the spine and provides clinical benefits.

Annotated References

1. Sypert GW: External spinal orthotics. *Neurosurgery* 1987;20(4):642-649.

2. Moen KY, Nachemson AL: Treatment of scoliosis: An historical perspective. *Spine (Phila Pa 1976)* 1999; 24(24):2570-2575.

3. Knoeller SM, Seifried C: Historical perspective: History of spinal surgery. *Spine (Phila Pa 1976)* 2000;25(21): 2838-2843.

4. Richter D, Latta LL, Milne EL, et al: The stabilizing effects of different orthoses in the intact and unstable upper cervical spine: A cadaver study. *J Trauma* 2001; 50(5):848-854.

5. Schneider AM, Hipp JA, Nguyen L, Reitman CA: Reduction in head and intervertebral motion provided by 7 contemporary cervical orthoses in 45 individuals. *Spine (Phila Pa 1976)* 2007;32(1):E1-E6.

   The ability of various orthoses to control motion between cervical vertebrae is compared. The data can help justify the selection of a specific orthosis for a patient.

6. Askins V, Eismont FJ: Efficacy of five cervical orthoses in restricting cervical motion: A comparison study. *Spine (Phila Pa 1976)* 1997;22(11):1193-1198.

7. Miller CP, Bible JE, Jegede KA, Whang PG, Grauer JN: Soft and rigid collars provide similar restriction in cervical range of motion during fifteen activities of daily living. *Spine (Phila Pa 1976)* 2010;35(13):1271-1278.

   The range of motion of the cervical spine during common activities of daily living was similar when a volunteer wore a soft collar or a rigid orthosis. This finding suggests that the primary function may be to remind the patient to restrict motion.

8. Ben-Galim P, Dreiangel N, Mattox KL, Reitman CA, Kalantar SB, Hipp JA: Extrication collars can result in abnormal separation between vertebrae in the presence of a dissociative injury. *J Trauma* 2010;69(2):447-450.

   Application of a cervical extrication collar to fresh cadaver specimens with a dissociative injury created grossly abnormal separation between vertebrae at the site of the injury. In the presence of a severe injury, a cervical collar may create secondary injuries.

2: Nonsurgical Care of the Spine

9. Rechtine GR, Del Rossi G, Conrad BP, Horodyski M: Motion generated in the unstable spine during hospital bed transfers. *J Trauma* 2004;57(3):609-612.

10. Sandler AJ, Dvorak J, Humke T, Grob D, Daniels W: The effectiveness of various cervical orthoses: An in vivo comparison of the mechanical stability provided by several widely used models. *Spine (Phila Pa 1976)* 1996; 21(14):1624-1629.

11. Bell KM, Frazier EC, Shively CM, et al: Assessing range of motion to evaluate the adverse effects of ill-fitting cervical orthoses. *Spine J* 2009;9(3):225-231.

    A poorly fitted cervical orthosis could lead to increased motion of the head and neck, affect patient satisfaction and clinical outcome, or, in the presence of instability, lead to secondary injuries.

12. Odderson IR, Lietzow D: Dysphagia complications of the Minerva brace. *Arch Phys Med Rehabil* 1997; 78(12):1386-1388.

13. Bransford RJ, Stevens DW, Uyeji S, Bellabarba C, Chapman JR: Halo vest treatment of cervical spine injuries: A success and survivorship analysis. *Spine (Phila Pa 1976)* 2009;34(15):1561-1566.

    Complications are common during the clinical application of halo vest immobilization. Halo vest treatment was nonetheless successful in 85% of patients, and 74% of patients who survived successfully completed the intended treatment period.

14. Gavin TM, Carandang G, Havey R, Flanagan P, Ghanayem A, Patwardhan AG: Biomechanical analysis of cervical orthoses in flexion and extension: A comparison of cervical collars and cervical thoracic orthoses. *J Rehabil Res Dev* 2003;40(6):527-537.

15. Koller H, Zenner J, Hitzl W, et al: In vivo analysis of atlantoaxial motion in individuals immobilized with the halo thoracic vest or Philadelphia collar. *Spine (Phila Pa 1976)* 2009;34(7):670-679.

    A Philadelphia collar was as effective as a halo vest for controlling C1-C2 sagittal plane motion in healthy volunteers. Data are not provided to help in selecting treatment for an unstable cervical spine.

16. Campbell MJ, Carreon LY, Traynelis V, Anderson PA: Use of cervical collar after single-level anterior cervical fusion with plate: Is it necessary? *Spine (Phila Pa 1976)* 2009;34(1):43-48.

    A cervical brace was not found to be effective for improving fusion rates after anterior cervical fusion with plating.

17. Tuong NH, Dansereau J, Maurais G, Herrera R: Three-dimensional evaluation of lumbar orthosis effects on spinal behavior. *J Rehabil Res Dev* 1998;35(1):34-42.

18. Million R, Nilsen KH, Jayson MI, Baker RD: Evaluation of low back pain and assessment of lumbar corsets with and without back supports. *Ann Rheum Dis* 1981; 40(5):449-454.

19. Chin KR, Auerbach JD, Adams SB Jr, Sodl JF, Riew KD: Mastication causing segmental spinal motion in common cervical orthoses. *Spine (Phila Pa 1976)* 2006; 31(4):430-434.

    Intervertebral motion at the occiput-C1 and C1-C2 levels was higher when healthy volunteers were wearing a cervical collar rather than no collar. All effects of a cervical collar should be considered instead of the effect on one simple type of activity.

20. Kwan I, Bunn F, Roberts I: Spinal immobilisation for trauma patients. *Cochrane Database Syst Rev* 2001;2: CD002803.

21. Axelsson P, Johnsson R, Strömqvist B: Effect of lumbar orthosis on intervertebral mobility: A roentgen stereophotogrammetric analysis. *Spine (Phila Pa 1976)* 1992; 17(6):678-681.

22. Fidler MW, Plasmans CM: The effect of four types of support on the segmental mobility of the lumbosacral spine. *J Bone Joint Surg Am* 1983;65(7):943-947.

23. Lantz SA, Schultz AB: Lumbar spine orthosis wearing: Part I. Restriction of gross body motions. *Spine (Phila Pa 1976)* 1986;11(8):834-837.

24. Buchalter D, Kahanovitz N, Viola K, Dorsky S, Nordin M: Three-dimensional spinal motion measurements: Part 2. A noninvasive assessment of lumbar brace immobilization of the spine. *J Spinal Disord* 1988;1(4): 284-286.

25. Cholewicki J, Alvi K, Silfies SP, Bartolomei J: Comparison of motion restriction and trunk stiffness provided by three thoracolumbosacral orthoses (TLSOs). *J Spinal Disord Tech* 2003;16(5):461-468.

26. Brown T, Norton PL: The immobilizing efficiency of back braces: Their effect on the posture and motion of the lumbosacral spine. *J Bone Joint Surg Am* 1957; 39(1):111-139.

27. Lumsden RM II, Morris JM: An in vivo study of axial rotation and immobilization at the lumbosacral joint. *J Bone Joint Surg Am* 1968;50(8):1591-1602.

28. Willems PC, Nienhuis B, Sietsma M, van der Schaaf DB, Pavlov PW: The effect of a plaster cast on lumbosacral joint motion: An in vivo assessment with precision motion analysis system. *Spine (Phila Pa 1976)* 1997; 22(11):1229-1234.

29. van Duijvenbode IC, Jellema P, van Poppel MN, van Tulder MW: Lumbar supports for prevention and treatment of low back pain. *Cochrane Database Syst Rev* 2008;2:CD001823.

    A systematic review found a lack of high-quality evidence. The existing evidence suggests that lumbar supports do not prevent low back pain. Evidence is conflicting as to whether lumbar supports help in treating low back pain.

Chapter 17

Rehabilitation After Spinal Cord Injury

William P. Waring III, MD, MS

Introduction

The estimated annual incidence of spinal cord injury (SCI) in the United States is 40 per million population, or approximately 12,000 new instances each year.[1] Figure 1 shows the most important causes of injuries resulting in SCI. (Additional epidemiologic data are provided in chapter 6.) The median number of days of acute care hospitalization for those who enter a model system center immediately after injury has declined from 24 days (1973 to 1979) to 12 days since 2005. The trend for days in a rehabilitation unit is similarly downward (from 98 to 37 days).[1]

The Background and Organization of Rehabilitation Services

Until the middle of the 20th century, an SCI almost always led to premature death.[2] The first large-scale application of modern medicine to SCI occurred during World War I. Despite progress in understanding the anatomy, neurology, and complications of SCI, however, treatment remained at a primitive level. The modern era of SCI treatment began during World War II with advances in emergency evacuation, the treatment of infection, rehabilitation, and social attitudes toward disability. The pioneers in delivering service to patients learned from experiences in World War I to expect to treat many patients with SCI, and they understood that social attitudes must be changed to avoid low expectations leading to drug addiction, hopelessness, and dependency among patients.[3,4]

The first facility to combine acute medical care and rehabilitation for patients with SCI was Stoke Mandeville Hospital in England, in 1944. In the United States, the first SCI centers also were established during World War II, as part of the Veterans Administration system.

For the first time, a person with SCI was believed to have the ability to become a healthy, productive member of society.[5] The science of rehabilitation was furthered during the 1940s and 1950s by programs for people with residual paralysis from polio. The medical specialty of physiatry evolved during World War II, as did other rehabilitation specialties, including physical therapy, occupational therapy, vocational counseling, and psychology.

The ways in which rehabilitation services were delivered also evolved. A nonmilitary regional SCI system was started during the early 1970s, partially funded by the National Institute on Disability and Rehabilitation Research. Fourteen Spinal Cord Injury Model Care System centers now receive government funding at major medical centers throughout the United States (Table 1). These programs are committed to a system of care that includes emergency medical services, level I trauma care, comprehensive inpatient SCI rehabilitation, psychosocial and vocational services, and follow-up care. Other SCI rehabilitation programs are accredited by CARF International (formerly the Commission on Accreditation of Rehabilitation Facilities), including the 24 SCI centers of the US Department of Veterans Affairs[6] (Table 2).

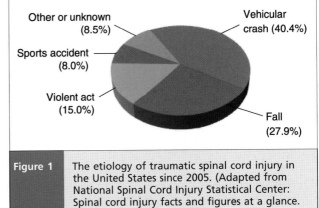

| Figure 1 | The etiology of traumatic spinal cord injury in the United States since 2005. (Adapted from National Spinal Cord Injury Statistical Center: Spinal cord injury facts and figures at a glance. https://www.nscisc.uab.edu.) |

Table 1

Locations of the Spinal Cord Injury Model Care System Centers

Alabama	Birmingham: University of Alabama Birmingham Model SCI Care System, Spain Rehabilitation Center
Colorado	Englewood: Rocky Mountain Regional Spinal Injury System, Craig Hospital
Georgia	Atlanta: Georgia Regional SCI System, Shepherd Center
Illinois	Chicago: Midwest Regional Spinal Cord Injury Care System, Rehabilitation Institute of Chicago
Massachusetts	Boston: New England Regional SCI Center, Boston Medical Center
Michigan	Ann Arbor: University of Michigan Model SCI System, University of Michigan Medical Center
New Jersey	West Orange: Northern New Jersey SCI System, Kessler Institute for Rehabilitation
New York	New York: Mount Sinai SCI Model System, Mount Sinai Medical Center
Ohio	Cleveland: Northeast Ohio Regional Spinal Cord Injury System, MetroHealth Medical Center
Pennsylvania	Philadelphia: Regional SCI System of Delaware Valley, Magee Rehabilitation Hospital, Thomas Jefferson University Hospital
	Pittsburgh: University of Pittsburgh Model System on SCI
Texas	Houston: Texas Model SCI System, Institute for Rehabilitation and Research
Washington	Seattle: Northwest Regional SCI System, Harborview Medical Center
Washington, DC	National Capital Spinal Cord Injury Model System, National Rehabilitation Hospital

Table 2

Locations of the US Department of Veterans Affairs SCI Centers

California	Long Beach, Palo Alto, San Diego
Florida	Miami, Tampa
Georgia	Augusta
Illinois	Hines
Massachusetts	West Roxbury
Minnesota	Minneapolis
Missouri	St. Louis
New Jersey	East Orange
New Mexico	Albuquerque
New York	Bronx, Castle Point
Ohio	Cleveland
Puerto Rico	San Juan
Tennessee	Memphis
Texas	Dallas, Houston, San Antonio
Virginia	Hampton, Richmond
Washington	Seattle
Wisconsin	Milwaukee

Research on Rehabilitation After SCI

Database-oriented research has had a significant impact on medical rehabilitation services for SCI patients. The Uniform Data System for Medical Rehabilitation tracks rehabilitation outcomes for patients with SCI and some other disabilities.[6] The Uniform Data System is a proprietary service, and up-to-date data are available by subscription. One the other hand, the federally funded National Spinal Cord Injury Statistical Center, which manages the world's largest SCI database and is the hub of the Spinal Cord Injury Model Care System, freely disseminates its data and findings.[7]

One reason for establishing dedicated SCI programs was the belief that clinical outcomes can be improved by treating the large number of patients needed to support the development of clinical guidelines and protocols. Institutions participating in Spinal Cord Injury Model Care System have documented the improvements in clinical outcomes for patients with SCI. In particular, the percentage of incomplete SCIs increased from 44% (from 1973 to 1977) to 57% (from 1987 to 1989) of the total number of SCIs, with a corresponding improvement in patients' potential for neurologic recovery.[8] The number of acute hospital admissions was reduced from 0.61 per patient per year (from 1973 to 1975) to 0.31 (from 1986 to 1989). The number of complications such as decubitus ulcer or contracture was reduced for patients admitted to an SCI program within 24 hours of injury, compared with patients admitted later, as was the medical cost of acute care (a $5,000 saving in 1992). The average length of rehabilitation unit stay was reduced to 53% of the average length of stay in 1991.[8]

Improvement in rehabilitation outcomes has been more difficult to document. Many patients in the Spinal Cord Injury Model Care System centers have a severe injury and relatively little potential for gaining function in the areas typically measured by outcome tools such as the Functional Independence Measure, which assesses 18 areas related to mobility, activities of daily living, sphincter control, communication, and social integration. Persons with SCI have especially poor long-term outcomes related to employment. Despite a healthy economy in the mid 1990s, only 20% to 30% of patients with SCI were employed.[7,8]

Principles of SCI Rehabilitation

Many of the people who work with patients undergoing SCI rehabilitation have an uncommon commitment and fervor for their work. The reasons may lie in the unusual opportunity to work with relatively young patients over an extended period of time and to participate in the process through which patients regain their sense of individuality and become active, healthy, and productive members of society.

A patient with SCI should be given the opportunity to undergo rehabilitation in a specialized program. A spine surgeon can have a significant influence on the patient's decision. Despite the benefits of a specialized SCI program, the federally funded Spinal Cord Injury Model Care System regional centers serve only 13% of patients with a new SCI. The possible reasons for the limited use of specialized SCI programs may be related to third-party payer restrictions, patient or family preference for community-based care, community-based referral patterns, and ready access to a community-based spine surgeon.

In the regional specialized program model, specialized SCI services begin the day a patient with SCI is admitted. Physical therapists, occupational therapists, psychologists, social workers, nurses, and nurse case managers provide care regardless of whether the patient is in an acute care or a rehabilitation unit. The goals of early intervention are to minimize complications such as decubitus ulceration and contractures, prepare the patient and family for rehabilitation, and minimize the risk of depression by educating the patient as to the goals of rehabilitation (with a shift in focus from full recovery to realistic goals). Most SCI programs provide long-term medical and rehabilitation care through outpatient SCI clinics staffed by physiatrists and nurses. Follow-up care usually is provided as an annual clinical evaluation that does not include primary care. However, the Veterans Affairs system has promoted holistic SCI clinics as the principal point of service for veterans with SCI.

The mean length of hospital stay for acute care and rehabilitation after SCI was 144.8 days from 1973 to 1977 and 77.5 days from 1989 to 1992.[6] The comparable figure was 36 days in 2008.[7] Part of the decrease in length of stay can be attributed to improved acute care, more efficient rehabilitation, and an earlier transition to outpatient therapy. Other factors include pressure from the health care system to reduce costs, third-party payer limits on reimbursement for care, and the use of clinical pathways designed to standardize inpatient care. Despite concern that shorter hospitalizations would lead to less satisfactory rehabilitation outcomes, there has been little change in outcomes on the Functional Independence Measure for patients with SCI.[7,9,10] Whether shorter lengths of hospital stay lead to increased rates of complications and readmissions is being studied.

Neurologic Cure–Based Treatments for Acute SCI

Despite more than 20 years of intense, well-funded international research, there is no cure for traumatic SCI. Cure-based research has been limited by small numbers of patients, lack of randomization, questionable statistics, varying outcome measures, and lack of studies to reproduce beneficial results. Dubious, fraudulent, and even dangerous treatments have been promoted, often outside the United States, including vitamin injections into the spinal cord during the 1970s, embryonic shark cell transplants during the 1990s, peripheral nerve bridge surgery during the early 2000s, and, most recently, stem cell treatments ranging from intravenous injections to spinal cord implantation. It can be difficult for physicians, patients, and families to rationally assess widely publicized so-called breakthrough strategies.[11] Links to approved research projects can be found on many US consumer and SCI program websites. The National Institutes of Health provides a registry of government and privately funded clinical studies at http://clinicaltrials.gov.

The use of methylprednisolone illustrates the complexity of evaluating a new treatment for SCI. Intravenous corticosteroids became the expected treatment for acute SCI almost overnight after a study with positive results received widespread publicity.[12] After an initial period of acceptance, questions began to arise concerning the study's design, including the choice of sensory outcome measures and the lack of nonparametric statistical analysis. Only one other study reproduced the study findings, and morbidity associated with the use of high-dosage corticosteroids was recognized. There is no current consensus on the use of methylprednisolone therapy, and some institutions no longer routinely use it.[13-18]

In animal studies, autologous bone marrow cell transplantation and administration of activated macrophages have shown promise for treating acute SCI. Eight patients with acute, neurologically complete SCI were treated with autologous incubated macrophages in a phase I study.[19] Within 1 year, three patients recovered significant motor and sensory function, as measured using the American Spinal Injury Association (ASIA) Impairment Scale (Figure 2); the other patients had no change. A subsequent multicenter randomized, controlled phase II study prematurely ended because of lack of funding, but analysis of data collected for 50 patients showed that patients in the control group had a trend toward greater improvement on the ASIA

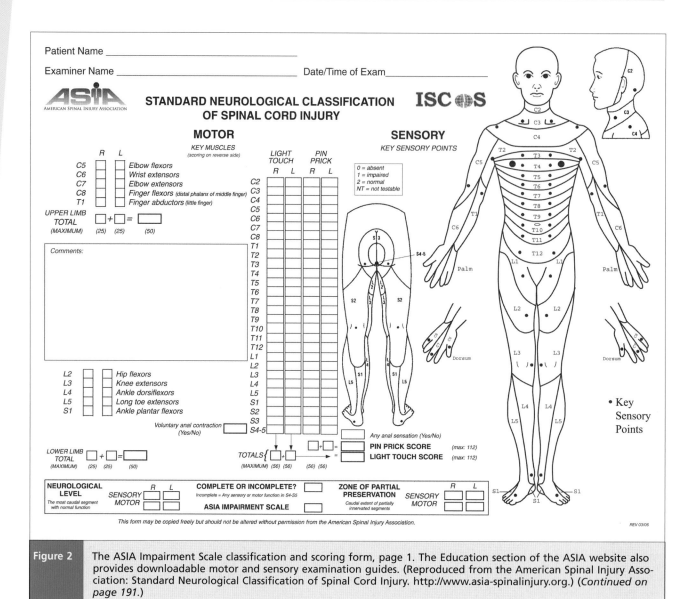

Patient Name _____

Examiner Name _____ Date/Time of Exam_____

STANDARD NEUROLOGICAL CLASSIFICATION OF SPINAL CORD INJURY

| Figure 2 | The ASIA Impairment Scale classification and scoring form, page 1. The Education section of the ASIA website also provides downloadable motor and sensory examination guides. (Reproduced from the American Spinal Injury Association: Standard Neurological Classification of Spinal Cord Injury. http://www.asia-spinalinjury.org.) (*Continued on page 191.*) |

Impairment Scale motor index and a small but significantly greater improvement on the sensory index.[20]

Despite extensive research into stem cell–based treatment for SCI, only one human study has been approved by the US Food and Drug Administration.[21] This stem cell study of patients with new, complete paraplegia was approved in 2010, and enrollment is under way. A second application for approval to study the use of stem cells in treating SCI has been submitted to the Food and Drug Administration; in this proposed study, the patients would be more than 1 year postinjury.[22]

Spinal cord cooling, or hypothermia, was first discussed as a SCI treatment during the late 1950s.[23] However, this treatment has not been tested in clinical studies, and it is not practical for use in patients with multiple trauma. Hypothermia was used in 2008 to treat a professional football player who had a significant recovery after SCI.[24] This patient was relatively young and in excellent health. Despite initial reports

that the injury was complete, the patient appears to have had an incomplete SCI. His recovery therefore cannot be attributed to the hypothermia treatment. The patient began to have sensory return within 3 hours of injury and had a flicker of movement within 8 hours. These early signs suggest an excellent prognosis for recovery. Such changes occur with some frequency soon after SCI, and therefore it is recommended that a prognosis be delayed until a reliable examination can be done 72 hours after the injury.[25]

Rehabilitation and Patient Care During the Acute Medical-Surgical Period

A patient is most likely to have optimal medical and rehabilitation outcomes if rehabilitation begins on the day of the injury.[26] The initial goals are to prevent complications and communicate realistic expectations for

MUSCLE GRADING

0   total paralysis

1   palpable or visible contraction

2   active movement, full range of motion, gravity eliminated

3   active movement, full range of motion, against gravity

4   active movement, full range of motion, against gravity and provides some resistance

5   active movement, full range of motion, against gravity and provides normal resistance

5*   muscle able to exert, in examiner's judgement, sufficient resistance to be considered normal if identifiable inhibiting factors were not present

NT not testable. Patient unable to reliably exert effort or muscle unavailable for testing due to factors such as immobilization, pain on effort or contracture.

ASIA IMPAIRMENT SCALE

☐   **A = Complete**: No motor or sensory function is preserved in the sacral segments S4-S5.

☐   **B = Incomplete**: Sensory but not motor function is preserved below the neurological level and includes the sacral segments S4-S5.

☐   **C = Incomplete**: Motor function is preserved below the neurological level, and more than half of key muscles below the neurological level have a muscle grade less than 3.

☐   **D = Incomplete**: Motor function is preserved below the neurological level, and at least half of key muscles below the neurological level have a muscle grade of 3 or more.

☐   **E = Normal**: Motor and sensory function are normal.

CLINICAL SYNDROMES (OPTIONAL)

☐   Central Cord
☐   Brown-Sequard
☐   Anterior Cord
☐   Conus Medullaris
☐   Cauda Equina

STEPS IN CLASSIFICATION

The following order is recommended in determining the classification of individuals with SCI.

1. Determine sensory levels for right and left sides.

2. Determine motor levels for right and left sides.
   Note: in regions where there is no myotome to test, the motor level is presumed to be the same as the sensory level.

3. Determine the single neurological level.
   This is the lowest segment where motor and sensory function is normal on both sides, and is the most cephalad of the sensory and motor levels determined in steps 1 and 2.

4. Determine whether the injury is Complete or Incomplete (sacral sparing).
   *If voluntary anal contraction = **No** AND all S4-5 sensory scores = **0** AND any anal sensation = **No**, then injury is COMPLETE. Otherwise injury is incomplete.*

5. Determine ASIA Impairment Scale (AIS) Grade:

Is injury **Complete**?   If YES, AIS=A Record ZPP
   NO   (For ZPP record lowest dermatome or myotome on each side with some (non-zero score) preservation)

Is injury motor **incomplete**?   If **NO**, AIS=B
   YES   (Yes=voluntary anal contraction OR motor function more than three levels below the motor level on a given side.)

Are **at least** half of the key muscles below the (single) **neurological** level graded 3 or better?
   NO   YES
   AIS=C   AIS=D

If sensation and motor function is normal in all segments, AIS=E
Note: AIS E is used in follow up testing when an individual with a documented SCI has recovered normal function. If at initial testing no deficits are found, the individual is neurologically intact; the ASIA Impairment Scale does not apply.

Figure 2 *(Continued from page 190.)* The ASIA Impairment Scale classification and scoring form, page 2.

the patient's rehabilitation. The Consortium for Spinal Cord Medicine, a group of health care, payer, and consumer organizations including the American Academy of Orthopaedic Surgeons, publishes a useful series of evidence-based monographs and clinical practice guidelines to guide the acute medical management of patients with SCI.[27] The topics include bladder and bowel management, early acute care, depression, outcomes, pressure ulcers, autonomic hyperreflexia, thromboembolism, respiratory care, upper limb function, and sexual health.

Skin Care

To prevent pressure sores from forming during the acute medical-surgical phase after SCI, the patient should be turned in bed every 2 hours, and the skin should be inspected at least once a day. Fastidious hygiene and the use of an appropriate wheelchair and wheelchair cushion are required. The use of a cardiac chair or a similar device is discouraged to avoid sacral sitting and the consequent risk of developing a sacral pressure sore. During the acute phase, a pressure sore is most likely to develop on the heel, sacrum, or occiput. After the patient starts using a wheelchair, the areas of risk are the heel, sacrum, trochanter, and ischium. The patient should receive pressure relief every 15 to 20 minutes while sitting in a wheelchair. Many products are available for pressure sore healing and dressing, but the first treatment is to remove or minimize weight bearing on the affected area. During the acute phase, specialized heel protection is used, time in the prone position is decreased, and time in a reclined sitting position is minimized to avoid shear stress on the skin overlying the sacrum.

Thromboembolism

A patient with an acute SCI has the classic risk factors for thromboembolic disease: venous stasis, immobility, vascular injury, and hypercoagulability. Low-molecular-weight heparin is superior to unfractionated heparin, warfarin, or a serial compression device for preventing blood clots.[28] Low-molecular-weight heparin is used for 2 to 3 months after the injury (for example, enoxaparin at 40 mg daily or 30 mg twice daily, dalteparin at 5,000 units daily).

The optimal time to begin chemical prophylaxis is controversial because of the risk of bleeding after injury or surgery. There is much less research on prophylaxis after spine surgery than after elective joint arthroplasty. Chemical prophylaxis often is started when the patient's condition is stabilized, or within 1 to 2 days of surgery. Because of the very high incidence of thromboembolic disease after SCI, a delay of more than 72 hours may not comply with current best practice guidelines, unless the patient has a specific contraindication such as a bleeding disorder. However, the surgeon must make the decision on an individual basis.[28]

The use of inferior vena cava filters is controversial because of the risk of embolism, and the availability of retrievable filters has not settled the controversy. The specific indications for using these filters include concurrent cerebral hemorrhage, heparin product allergies, and earlier drug-induced thrombocytopenia. There is no need to use filters for an uncomplicated SCI, however. Even a filter placed during the hyperacute phase of SCI cannot prevent a deep venous thrombosis. If a blood clot develops with a filter, low-molecular-weight heparin should be started as soon as safety allows. Treating clots with a filter will prevent postphlebitic syndrome, which can cause skin breakdown, impede the use of lower extremity orthoses for ambulation, and, because the legs are large and heavy, complicate simple tasks such as transfers.

Bowel and Bladder Care

Adynamic ileus is particularly likely in a patient with an acute SCI because of the patient's immobility, the expected neurogenic bowel hypomotility, and the liberal use of narcotics for pain management. Ogilvie syndrome (toxic dilation of the cecum) can cause bowel death and is diagnosed using abdominal radiographs. The judicious use of a nasogastric tube and minimization of narcotic use are the first-line treatments for adynamic ileus. The daily use of stool softeners, mild laxatives, and suppositories (bisacodyl or docusate) can be combined with digital stimulation and possibly the manual removal of stool to achieve a satisfactory bowel program. It is important to carry out a routine bowel program to promote bowel training, regardless of the results.

Little scientific evidence is available to support the choice of a long-term bladder management method. Indwelling urethral balloon catheters are commonly used after injury. Colonization by resistant urinary bacteria, especially strains of methicillin-resistant *Staphylococcus aureus* and *Pseudomonas*, is common with the use of an indwelling bladder drainage tube, however. The risk of infection can be minimized by intermittent catheterization in the hospital setting. The presence of multiple urinary organisms can make it difficult to treat a presumed urinary tract infection. Changing the catheter before collecting urine for culturing was found to decrease the number of organisms present.[29] The criteria for beginning intermittent catheterization include medical stability, the absence of urethral injury, and a daily urinary output of no more than 2,000 mL. Typically, intermittent catheterization is done every 3 to 6 hours to maintain a volume of approximately 300 to 400 mL. A high urinary output requires more frequent catheterization, which can interfere with sleep or preclude daily activities such as physical therapy sessions.

Pulmonary Function

A patient with acute SCI at or below the T12 neurologic level usually has normal respiratory capacity and function, including a normal cough. The ability to cough becomes progressively weaker and lung capacity decreases with each level of injury above T12. For a patient with neurogenic weakness from a higher level injury, weaning from the ventilator can be challenging and is done by progressively increasing off-ventilator time intervals. In contrast, a patient who is otherwise neurologically intact is weaned from the ventilator by dialing down the intermittent mandatory ventilation control settings.[27] A patient who cannot be weaned from the ventilator should receive a tracheotomy, especially if there are copious secretions.

The best practice for a patient with abnormal pulmonary function includes vaccination against pneumococci and influenza. An elastic abdominal support can be used if the patient has shortness of breath while upright; in a supine position, the abdominal contents naturally push against the diaphragm and help the patient exhale.

Autonomic Function

A condition called spinal shock occurs immediately after SCI. The belief that spinal shock involves motor and somatic sensory recovery is mistaken; instead, there is a loss of the spinal cord–mediated reflex function, which can require days, weeks, or months for recovery.[30] Reflex-mediated SCI conditions such as spasticity, bladder hyperactivity, and autonomic dysreflexia may not be evident during the acute medical-surgical phase after injury. These conditions appear after the spinal shock resolves, often while the patient is in the rehabilitation unit.

Bradycardia, hypotension, and orthostatic hypotension are specific autonomic problems that appear soon after the injury. Bradycardia after an acute mid- or high-level cervical injury can result from unopposed vagal (parasympathetic) cardiac input while spinal cord–mediated sympathetic input is absent because of spinal shock or diffuse cord injury. Bradycardia can be monitored as long as the sinus rhythm is normal, with stable urinary output and blood pressure. However, if asystole, syncope, or hypotension occurs, the use of a cardiac pacemaker should be considered.

Hypotension after SCI can reduce cord perfusion and affect longer term neurologic recovery. Similarly, spinal cord ischemia can occur in a hypertensive patient who has lower blood pressure after elective spine surgery. Hypotension after SCI can be a short-term or long-term difficulty. Hypotension tends to be more severe in a patient with a higher level injury. Maintaining blood pressure based on regulating urinary output may be insufficient to maximize cord perfusion and hence recovery. In addition to hydration monitoring, the use of midodrine (5 to 10 mg three times daily) is safe and appropriate for managing hypotension after SCI.[31]

The symptoms of orthostatic hypotension include dizziness, syncope, nausea, weakness, and fatigue. The treatment can include adequate hydration with the use of an elastic abdominal support, support stockings, or elastic leg wrappings. Midodrine is a suitable medication if nonpharmacologic therapies are insufficient. Ephedrine was used before the discovery of midodrine; it can cause insomnia and loss of appetite, however. Sodium chloride or mineral corticoids such as fludrocortisone also can be used, but they can have adverse effects including peripheral edema and fluid overload, which complicates heart failure.

Prognosis and Expectations for a Patient With SCI

A growing body of published research uses a standard neurologic examination to suggest the prognosis for neurologic recovery after an SCI.[25] The gold standard for an SCI neurologic examination is the International Standards for the Neurological Classification of Spinal Cord Injury.[32,33] This examination includes 10 key muscles and key sensory testing locations for each dermatome. The examination is done with the patient supine, so that testing immediately after an acute injury can be replicated later. A scoring, scaling, and classification system is used to determine the severity of motor and sensory injury. The degree of injury completeness is determined using the ASIA Impairment Scale (Figure 2), which is a modification of the five-category Frankel scale.

A complete SCI, in which there is no clinical finding of motor or sensory function below the level of injury, has a poor prognosis. A complete SCI usually remains complete. Months after injury, however, a small percentage of patients with complete SCI recover some sensation and nonuseful motor activity such as a toe wiggle. A patient with tetraplegia, even with complete SCI, often regains at least one level of function below the level of injury. Weak muscles become stronger, and upper extremity weakness can improve by as much as one or two muscle grades. There is almost always motor improvement after incomplete SCI. The potential for functional ambulation with an incomplete motor injury is highest when the sensory impairment is least, especially if the patient has pinprick sensation and proprioception.

The speed and the extent of a patient's recovery are correlated. As with other neurologic injuries, such as cerebrovascular accident, most of the recovery occurs within the first several months, and particularly within the first 6 to 12 weeks. The first few days to weeks after SCI are the critical time for recovery. Nonetheless, only 1% of patients with SCI who undergo SCI rehabilitation have a normal recovery, based on a standard neurologic examination. A competent standardized neurologic examination is a prerequisite for making a prognosis. The prognosis cannot be made if the patient cannot fully understand or participate in the neurologic examination because of, for example, concurrent brain injury, anxiety, mental illness, or high-dosage psychotropic or narcotic drugs. When any of these impediments exists, serial neurologic testing may be needed.

The methods used to inform patients of their prognosis have received scrutiny.[34] It is important to give a patient an honest appraisal of the SCI and the expected short- and long-term recovery. Some patients begin SCI rehabilitation with a false understanding after being told they "will never walk again" and that they will need to spend several months in an inpatient SCI rehabilitation unit or will require 1 to 2 years for recovery. When rehabilitation providers outline the realistic goals of rehabilitation, the patient and family can begin to focus on functional goals for rehabilitation rather than simply on whether the patient has movement in the legs or feet.

The physician must devote sufficient time to performing a thorough examination and establishing a relationship with the patient before informing the patient of the prognosis in a thoughtful, compassionate manner. Although not every spine surgeon has the time or expertise for a thorough neurologic examination, it is important for the patient to be informed of the severity of the injury. The purpose of giving a prognosis is not to eliminate hope but rather to provide hope while outlining the need for rehabilitation and the expected time for recovery. For example, a physician can tell a patient with complete tetraplegia that the injury is serious and may remain complete, while identifying the root level immediately below the injury and informing the patient that some recovery often occurs at that level. The spine surgeon should be prepared to defer to a specialist in the rehabilitation of patients with SCI for determining the prognosis and the rehabilitation goals.

Patients and their families are increasingly sophisticated about SCI and rehabilitation. Extensive, valuable information is readily available through the Internet and by networking with other patients with SCI and their families. The Internet also can be a source of misinformation and a marketing tool for dubious treatments, however. Some of the websites that offer valid recommendations for patients and their families are listed in Table 3. These sites offer consumer education materials and links to other SCI-related sites. Many accredited SCI rehabilitation programs have a website.

Summary

SCI is one of the more devastating injuries spine surgeons encounter. With appropriate acute medical-surgical care focused on preventing complications and with SCI rehabilitation, patients can live many decades in relatively good health. Many resources for learning about the acute prevention of complications and the availability of specialized SCI rehabilitation programs are available to surgeons, patients, and families. There have been no major breakthroughs in research leading toward a cure of SCI. A new SCI usually has a better

Table 3

Internet-Based Sources of Information on SCI Rehabilitation

Sponsoring Organization	Website
Academy of Spinal Cord Professionals	www.ascipro.org
American Spinal Injury Association	www.asia-spinalinjury.org
Christopher Reeve Foundation	www.paralysis.org
CARF International	www.carf.org
International Spinal Cord Society	www.iscos.org.uk
National Spinal Cord Injury Association	www.spinalcord.org
National Spinal Cord Injury Statistical Center	www.nscisc.uab.edu
Paralyzed Veterans of America	www.pva.org
Spinal Cord Injury Model Care System	www.sci-info-pages.com/model.html
US Department of Veterans Affairs SCI Centers	www1.va.gov/opa/fact/spinalcfs.asp

outcome if the patient is transferred to a facility with an established SCI program.

Annotated References

1. National Spinal Cord Injury Statistical Center: Spinal cord injury facts and figures at a glance. https://www.nscisc.uab.edu. Updated February 2011. Accessed June 16, 2011.

   The University of Alabama–Birmingham Department of Physical Medicine and Rehabilitation is the federally funded operator of the National Spinal Cord Injury Statistical Center and its database.

2. Elsberg CA: The Edwin Smith Surgical Papyrus, and the diagnosis and treatment of injuries to skull and spine 5,000 years ago. *Ann Med Hist* 1931;3:271-279.

3. Cole TM: Spinal cord injury and trauma, in Day SB, ed: *Trauma.* New York, NY, Plenum, 1973, pp 303-327.

4. Dick TB: Traumatic paraplegia pre-Guttmann. *Paraplegia* 1969;7(3):173-178.

5. Guttman L: *Spinal Cord Injuries: Comprehensive Management and Research,* ed 2. Oxford, England, Blackwell Scientific, 1976, p 9.

6. Granger CV, Hamilton BB: The Uniform Data System for Medical Rehabilitation report of first admissions for 1992. *Am J Phys Med Rehabil* 1994;73(1):51-55.

7. National Spinal Cord Injury Statistical Center: Annual Statistical Report. https://www.nscsc.uab.edu/public_content/annual_stat_report.aspx. Accessed June 16, 2011.

   The National Spinal Cord Injury Statistical Center reports collected data on an annual basis.

8. Stover SL, DeLisa LA, Whiteneck GG, eds: *Spinal Cord Injury: Clinical Outcomes from the Model Systems.* Gaithersburg, MD, Aspen, 1995.

9. Lammertse DP, Jackson AB, Sipski ML: Research from the Model Spinal Cord Injury Systems: Findings from the current 5-year grant cycle. *Arch Phys Med Rehabil* 2004;85(11):1737-1739.

10. Morrison SL, Stanwyck D, Daviou P: The effect of shorter lengths of stay on inpatient and outpatient outcomes of spinal cord injury rehabilitation. *Spinal Cord Med* 1997;20:151.

11. Barrett S: The shady side of embryonic stem cell therapy. *Quackwatch* 2006. http://www.quackwatch.org/06/ResearchProjects/stemcell.html. Accessed March 25, 2010.

   This is a report on the most important commercial promoters of dubious stem cell treatments for SCI.

12. Bracken MB, Shepard MJ, Collins WF, et al: A randomized, controlled trial of methylprednisolone or naloxone in the treatment of acute spinal-cord injury: Results of the Second National Acute Spinal Cord Injury Study. *N Engl J Med* 1990;322(20):1405-1411.

13. Bracken MB, Shepard MJ, Hellenbrand KG, et al: Methylprednisolone and neurological function 1 year after spinal cord injury: Results of the National Acute Spinal Cord Injury Study. *J Neurosurg* 1985;63(5):704-713.

14. Bracken MB, Shepard MJ, Holford TR, et al: Administration of methylprednisolone for 24 or 48 hours or tirilazad mesylate for 48 hours in the treatment of acute spinal cord injury: Results of the Third National Acute Spinal Cord Injury Randomized Controlled Trial. National Acute Spinal Cord Injury Study. *JAMA* 1997;277(20):1597-1604.

15. Nesathurai S: Steroids and spinal cord injury: Revisiting the NASCIS 2 and NASCIS 3 trials. *J Trauma* 1998;45(6):1088-1093.

16. Qian T, Campagnolo D, Kirshblum S: High-dose methylprednisolone may do more harm for spinal cord injury. *Med Hypotheses* 2000;55(5):452-453.

17. Miller SM: Methylprednisolone in acute spinal cord injury: A tarnished standard. *J Neurosurg Anesthesiol* 2008;20(2):140-142.

18. Otani K, Abe H, Kadoya S, et al: Beneficial effects of methylprednisolone sodium succinate in the treatment of acute spinal cord injury. *Sekitsui Sekizui* 1994;7:633-647.

19. Knoller N, Auerbach G, Fulga V, et al: Clinical experience using incubated autologous macrophages as a treatment for complete spinal cord injury: Phase I study results. *J Neurosurg Spine* 2005;3(3):173-181.

    A phase I study found that incubated autologous macrophage cells are well tolerated by patients with SCI. Further study is warranted.

20. Lammertse D, Jones L, Charlifue S, et al: Autologous incubated macrophage treatment in complete spinal cord injury: Results of the multicenter trial [abstract]. *J Spinal Cord Med* 2009;32(4):449.

21. Geron Corporation: Safety study of GRNOPC1 in spinal cord injury. http://clinicaltrials.gov/ct2/show/NCT01217008?term=geron&rank=9. Updated April 2011. Accessed June 16, 2011.

    This listing in the National Institutes of Health registry outlines a phase I study of stem cells for the treatment of SCI.

22. Neuralstem files FDA application for first chronic spinal cord injury stem cell trial [news release]. Rockville, MD, PR Newswire/Neuralstem, Inc, August 25, 2010. http://www.prnewswire.com/news-releases/neuralstem-files-fda-application-for-first-chronic-spinal-cord-injury-stem-cell-trial-101460239.html. Accessed June 16, 2011.

    Neuralstem, Inc. filed an investigational new drug application with the Food and Drug Administration to begin a phase I study of stem cells for the treatment of chronic SCI.

23. Albin MS, White RJ, Acosta-Rua GD, Yashon D: Study of functional recovery produced by delayed localized cooling after spinal cord injury in primates. *J Neurosurg* 1968;29(2):113-120.

24. Cappuccino A: Moderate hypothermia as treatment for spinal cord injury. *Orthopedics* 2008;31(3):243-246.

25. Kirshblum SC, O'Connor KC: Levels of spinal cord injury and predictors of neurologic recovery. *Phys Med Rehabil Clin N Am* 2000;11(1):1-27.

26. Heinemann AW, Yarkony GM, Roth EJ, et al: Functional outcome following spinal cord injury: A comparison of specialized spinal cord injury center vs general hospital short-term care. *Arch Neurol* 1989;46(10):1098-1102.

27. Consortium for Spinal Cord Medicine: Clinical practice guidelines for health care professionals. http://www.pva.org. Accessed March 25, 2010.

    The Consortium for Spinal Cord Medicine clinical practice guidelines can be downloaded from the Paralyzed Veterans of America website.

28. Geerts WH, Pineo GF, Heit JA, et al: Prevention of venous thromboembolism: The Seventh ACCP Conference on Antithrombotic and Thrombolytic Therapy. *Chest* 2004;126(3, suppl):338S-400S.

29. Shah PS, Cannon JP, Sullivan CL, Nemchausky B, Pachucki CT: Controlling antimicrobial use and decreasing microbiological laboratory tests for urinary tract infections in spinal-cord-injury patients with chronic indwelling catheters. *Am J Health Syst Pharm* 2005;62(1):74-77.

    A comparison study of 85 patients found that replacing an indwelling catheter before collecting a urine sample for culture reduced the number of identified pathogens as well as the number of prescribed antimicrobial drugs and the laboratory technician time.

30. Ditunno JF, Little JW, Tessler A, Burns AS: Spinal shock revisited: A four-phase model. *Spinal Cord* 2004;42(7):383-395.

31. Krassioukov A, Eng JJ, Warburton DE, Teasell R, Spinal Cord Injury Rehabilitation Evidence Research Team: A systematic review of the management of orthostatic hypotension after spinal cord injury. *Arch Phys Med Rehabil* 2009;90(5):876-885.

    A review of the literature on managing orthostatic hypotension in patients with SCI found that very few treatments recommended for use in the general population have been studied in patients with SCI.

32. American Spinal Injury Association: *Reference manual for the International Standards for Neurological Classification of Spinal Cord Injury.* Chicago, IL, American Spinal Injury Association, 2003.

33. Waring WP III, Biering-Sorensen F, Burns S, et al: 2009 review and revisions of the International Standards for the Neurological Classification of Spinal Cord Injury. *J Spinal Cord Med* 2010;33(4):346-352.

    International standards and related materials were reviewed with a recommendation for future routine published reviews.

34. Kirshblum S, Fichtenbaum J: Breaking the news in spinal cord injury. *J Spinal Cord Med* 2008;31(1):7-12.

    This article describes communications skills specific to discussing prognosis with patients with SCI and their families.

2: Nonsurgical Care of the Spine

Spine Trauma

SECTION EDITOR
PAUL A. ANDERSON, MD

Chapter 18

The Early Management of Spine Injuries

Michael J. Vives, MD   Praveen Yalamanchili, MD

Introduction

The early management of a patient with an identified or a suspected spine injury is a complex undertaking. The diversity of injury patterns, the emergence of new diagnostic and therapeutic technologies, and the need to maximize clinical outcomes while containing costs mean that the field is constantly evolving.

Epidemiology

Although acute spine injuries constitute a relatively small proportion of all traumatic skeletal injuries, their impact on the patient and society is significant. The incidence of spinal cord injury (SCI) in the United States has been estimated at 15 to 40 per million population.[1-3] The incidence of neurologic injury associated with all spine fractures and dislocations is approximately 14%; the incidence is 39% among patients with a cervical-level injury.[4] (Additional epidemiologic data are provided in chapter 6.)

The thoracolumbar junction is the most commonly fractured region of the spine. The most common causes of spine injury are motor vehicle crashes, falls, sports-related accidents, and acts of violence. Patients older than 65 years are most likely to be injured by falling and to sustain SCI after a minor fall. Despite advances in managing SCI before and during hospitalization, SCI is still associated with a significant mortality rate.

Dr. Vives or an immediate family member is a member of a speakers' bureau or has made paid presentations on behalf of Biomet and the Musculoskeletal Transplant Foundation; has received research or institutional support from DePuy, the Musculoskeletal Transplant Foundation, and Zimmer; and owns stock or stock options in Accelalox. Neither Dr. Yalamanchili nor any immediate family member has received anything of value from or owns stock in a commercial company or institution related directly or indirectly to the subject of this chapter.

Evaluation and Provisional Stabilization in the Field

Every patient who sustains multiple traumatic injuries is suspected to have a spine injury until proved otherwise. Oxygenation and intravenous fluid administration are vital to maintaining organ perfusion and mitigating a worsening injury to the spinal cord. The patient's airway is checked, and, if necessary, intubation is performed with minimal movement of the neck. The patient is carefully monitored for signs of shock.

Spine immobilization is a component of the initial field management of these patients, although there is no definite evidence to support the belief that immobilization prevents further injury. A meta-analysis was unable to quantify the effect of spine immobilization on mortality, neurologic injury, spine stability, or adverse effects in patients with trauma.[5] The American College of Surgeons Advanced Trauma Life Support recommendations for transport in the field include the use of a full-length hard backboard, a rigid cervical collar, and lateral support devices with the patient secured by tape. A patient who is wearing a helmet should be transported with the helmet on, unless the face mask is not removable or the helmet prevents airway access. For a child, a cutout board or mild elevation of the torso is used to accommodate the relatively large occiput and prevent hyperflexion. The disadvantages of spine immobilization, including a small increase in intracranial pressure and an increase in required respiratory effort, lead to the question of when spine immobilization can safely be avoided.[6] Protocols have been proposed to allow emergency medical services (EMS) personnel to selectively immobilize patients based on clinical criteria. When EMS personnel performed out-of-hospital assessments using varying criteria such as altered mental status, neurologic deficit, and spine pain, the protocols were found to have sensitivity of 87% to 92% and to lead to lower rates of spine immobilization, with good results.[7,8] Data on the risks of immobilization are limited, however, and the evidence is insufficient to recommend forgoing spine immobilization of a trauma patient.

After initial field management, a patient with SCI is transported to a facility capable of providing definitive care.[9] The mode of transportation (ground or air) does not appear to affect outcome. Early referral to a specialized SCI center can be beneficial.

Emergency Department Evaluation

In the emergency department, the Advanced Trauma Life Support protocol is continued. Any aspects of resuscitation that could not be successfully completed in the field are performed. A higher level SCI is most likely to require intubation and ventilatory assistance. Any patient requiring urgent intubation after trauma should be treated as if a cervical spine injury is present. The airway should be secured with as little movement of the cervical spine as possible. The standard intubation technique for such a patient is a rapid-sequence induction with cricoid pressure and manual in-line stabilization.

Many patients with SCI have associated systemic injuries and therefore are at risk of hemodynamic and neurogenic shock. Neurogenic shock is more common in patients with higher level SCI. A recent study of patients in the emergency department found a 19% incidence of neurogenic shock among those with cervical SCI (compared to a 7% risk with thoracic SCI and a 3% risk with lumbar SCI).[10] Fluid resuscitation is done carefully in a patient with neurogenic shock to avoid fluid overload. The severity of shock can be determined using the initial base deficit or lactate level in addition to standard parameters such as pulse and blood pressure. Maintaining the mean arterial blood pressure at 85 to 90 mm Hg for 7 days after SCI may be beneficial.[11]

After initial stabilization, a secondary survey is performed to identify additional injuries. A complete history is obtained from the patient, the family, witnesses to the incident that caused the patient's injuries, and EMS personnel for purposes of determining the mechanism of injury and guiding management. The patient's medical history may identify an underlying condition predisposing the patient to SCI, such as ankylosing spondylitis or a congenital abnormality. The examination may yield clues pointing to SCI, including areas of tenderness, step-offs of the spinous processes, palpable subcutaneous fluid collections (determined by spinal column palpation), or visually apparent bruising, abrasion, ecchymosis, or subcutaneous hematoma. Although gross motor deficits are identified on the initial examination, a complete neurologic examination is essential in the emergency department to characterize the level and pattern of injury. Preserved perianal sensation, voluntary contraction of the rectal sphincter, and toe flexor function suggest that the patient has an incomplete SCI, which has a much better prognosis for neurologic recovery than a complete injury. The physi-

cian must be aware of spinal shock, which is a transient syndrome of acute sensorimotor dysfunction that develops in patients with SCI and typically lasts 24 to 72 hours. Spinal shock is characterized by flaccid areflexic paralysis and anesthesia. The presence of spinal shock hinders the determination of SCI level and prognosis. The resolution of spinal shock is heralded by a return of reflex activity, specifically the bulbocavernosus reflex, below the level of injury. However, injury to the conus medullaris can result in persistent loss of the bulbocavernosus reflex in the absence of spinal shock.

The most widely used instrument for the assessment and classification of neurologic impairment in an awake, alert patient is the American Spinal Injury Association (ASIA) Standard Neurological Classification of Spinal Cord Injury. (See Chapter 17, Figure 2.) The ASIA system includes bilateral manual muscle testing of 10 key muscle groups, bilateral sensory examination of light touch and dull-sharp discrimination in 28 dermatomes, and a rectal examination for voluntary contraction and sensation. Approximately 10% to 15% of patients initially classified as having a complete injury (ASIA grade A) are later assessed as having an incomplete injury (grade B, C, or D). Within 1 year of injury, approximately 73% of patients initially classified as having a grade B injury and 71% of those initially classified as having a grade C injury are reclassified as improving at least one ASIA grade. Patients initially classified as having a grade D injury typically cannot be reclassified, however.[12]

Patients with incomplete SCI may have distinct clinical syndromes of neurologic deficit, with varying prognoses. Central cord syndrome is the most common incomplete SCI syndrome; it is caused by a hyperextension mechanism, usually occurs in a patient with preexisting stenosis and infolding of the ligamentum flavum, and is characterized by greater weakness in the upper extremities than in the lower extremities. The hands typically are more involved than proximally innervated muscle groups. The prognosis for recovery varies but is relatively favorable. At an average 6-year follow-up, 81% of patients reported bowel and bladder continence, and 86% were capable of ambulation.[13] Anterior cord syndrome may be associated with injury to the anterior spinal artery, which affects both the motor tracts and the spinothalamic tracts and leads to a loss of pain and temperature perception. This syndrome is characterized by a dense motor deficit and dissociated sensory deficit below the level of injury, but posterior column–mediated functions such as position and vibration sense are preserved. The prognosis for recovery is poor. Brown-Séquard syndrome is characterized by ipsilateral loss of motor function and dorsal column sensation and by contralateral loss of pain and temperature below the level of the injury. The prognosis for recovery is favorable.

Radiographic Assessment

The choice of imaging protocols for a patient with spine trauma frequently depends on patient factors as well as the available resources. An awake, alert patient who is asymptomatic and has no pain, tenderness, neurologic symptoms, or potentially distracting injury does not require radiologic evaluation. Distracting injuries include, but are not limited to, a long bone fracture, a visceral injury, a significant laceration, a degloving injury, and a large burn.[14] CT is increasingly used in the initial assessment of suspected cervical spine injury. The sensitivity of CT has led to improved injury detection, especially in the craniocervical and cervicothoracic regions.[15] Spiral or helical CT with sagittal and coronal reconstruction appears to be ideal for detecting cervical fractures because of superior bone visualization. Reports of 100% sensitivity and negative predictive value, with the use of CT as the gold standard, have established a false end point for the true variable in a clinically significant spine injury. The mean effective radiation exposure required for spine CT is higher than that of any other musculoskeletal CT and many times higher than that of plain radiography.[16]

A three-view series of plain radiographs (AP, lateral, and open-mouth odontoid) is commonly used to evaluate the cervical spine. Injuries occasionally are missed when the three-view series is used, however, primarily because of failure to adequately visualize the region of injury, particularly at the extremes of the cervical spine. Even when the entire cervical spine from the occiput to T1 has been adequately visualized, the sensitivity is approximately 60%.[17,18]

The Eastern Association for the Surgery of Trauma has formulated imaging guidelines for patients who have a suspected spine injury or cannot otherwise be evaluated.[19] The most recent guidelines recommend that any patient with a significant injury mechanism who has neck pain, spine tenderness, neurologic deficit, evidence of intoxication, altered mental status, or a co-existing distracting injury should undergo CT from the occiput to T1, with sagittal and coronal reconstructions. Plain radiography is no longer recommended for such patients. For a neurologically intact, awake, alert patient with neck pain and negative CT findings, the options include continued cervical collar use, MRI, and passive flexion-extension fluoroscopy to rule out ligamentous injury. For an obtunded patient with negative CT findings, the use of passive flexion-extension fluoroscopy may be hazardous, as the patient may have spinal cord compression caused by undetected disk herniation or instability. A patient with significant pain may not be able to produce sufficient voluntary excursion for a true dynamic study.

A recent meta-analysis of five level I studies examined the usefulness of MRI for excluding cervical spine injury if the patient's clinical condition is suspicious or the patient cannot otherwise be properly evaluated.[20] MRI was found to have 100% negative predictive value in these patients. The most practical application of these data may be in the use of MRI for definitively excluding spine injury in patients who have significant trauma and negative or equivocal radiographic or CT findings and who are likely to remain obtunded beyond the immediate postinjury period. The cost and logistic considerations related to using MRI in an obtunded patient are outweighed by the risk of skin ulceration, aspiration, or ventilation difficulty resulting from unnecessary external immobilization.

Patients suspected of having thoracolumbar injury traditionally have been evaluated with AP and lateral radiographs. As trauma imaging protocols have evolved to include chest, abdomen, and pelvis CT, some centers have explored whether the use of CT can obviate the need for plain radiographs. Recent studies comparing CT of the chest, abdomen, and pelvis to AP and lateral radiographs found that CT has higher sensitivity and specificity for detecting thoracolumbar fractures.[21,22]

In addition to their role in screening, advanced imaging studies are useful for the definitive evaluation of injuries detected on plain radiographs. CT provides precise information on bone injury patterns, particularly in posterior element fractures and thoracolumbar burst injuries. In a patient with neurologic deficit, MRI can provide information on the nature of the injury, such as the presence of cord contusion, disk injury, or epidural hematoma (particularly in a patient with ankylosing spondylitis). MRI also can be useful in determining spine stability (based on an evaluation of associated disk or ligament injury) and in formulating surgical treatment strategies. When a spine injury is detected in a patient with blunt trauma, the entire spinal column should be evaluated using plain radiographs or CT reconstruction. The rate of noncontiguous spine injuries in these patients is 10% to 40%.[23,24]

The Role of Associated Injuries

The American College of Surgeons recommends completing a tertiary trauma survey after the initial resuscitation and interventions, for the purpose of discovering any initially undetected injuries. All patients with significant traumatic injury should receive a tertiary survey. The survey is especially important for patients with altered mental status or the possibility of a distracting injury. The survey generally is performed within 24 hours of hospital admission and is repeated when the patient is awake, responsive, and able to communicate symptoms. The tertiary trauma survey involves repetition of the primary and secondary surveys, a complete head-to-toe examination, a comprehensive review of the medical record and any pertinent comorbidities, and assimilation of all radiographic and laboratory findings. Many centers use a standard worksheet for cataloging all injuries and helping in the development of a comprehensive care plan.

3: Spine Trauma

From 1973 to 1999, data were prospectively gathered in 24 model systems on more than 18,000 patients with SCI during the first 24 hours after injury.[25] Twenty-eight percent of patients had extraspinal fractures, with higher percentages among motorcyclists (50%) and pedestrians struck by motor vehicles (62%). A study using the National Spinal Cord Injury Statistical Center database found that the five most common anatomic sites for associated extraspinal fracture were the rib and/or sternum (43%), the clavicle and/or scapula (17%), the radius and/or ulna (14%), the face and/or mandible (12%), and the tibia and/or fibula (12%).[26] Some low-energy, minimally displaced extraspinal fractures can be managed nonsurgically. Precautions to protect insensate skin, such as avoidance of an encircling cast or a nonremovable splint, should be followed. A long bone fracture should be surgically treated as soon as possible to facilitate early mobilization.

Patients with traumatic spine injury have a high incidence of closed head and traumatic brain injury. One study reported that 49% of 82 patients with SCI had traumatic brain injury, with the highest risk among patients injured in a motor vehicle crash.[27] A careful evaluation for associated thoracic or abdominal injury should be performed in all patients with acute SCI. The risk of such an injury is higher in a patient with a thoracolumbar fracture than in a patient with a cervical injury.[28,29]

A cervical fracture may be accompanied by a vertebral artery injury. Unilateral vertebral artery occlusion caused by thrombosis may remain asymptomatic because of collateral blood flow. Catheter angiography has been the gold standard for diagnosis, but magnetic resonance angiography and computed tomographic angiography are less invasive and have appropriate sensitivity and specificity. Magnetic resonance angiography at the time of admission detected vertebral artery thrombosis in 83 of 632 patients (13%) with cervical spine fracture after blunt trauma.[30] Patients with SCI were more likely to have vertebral artery thrombosis than neurologically intact patients. The spinal injury patterns that have commonly been associated with vertebral artery injury include upper cervical fracture, facet subluxation, and fracture extending into the transverse foramen. If a unilateral injury is detected, some experts recommend extreme care during placement of any lateral mass or cervical pedicle screws on the contralateral side because a bilateral injury can be fatal. The role of screening is debatable for asymptomatic patients with these injury patterns, but some experts suggest noninvasive testing.[31] There are no absolute recommendations for treating an asymptomatic unilateral vertebral artery injury. Preemptive treatment may be reasonable in selected patients, however. The options include the use of heparin or an antiplatelet agent, although the risk of this treatment after cervical spine surgery must be considered.[32,33]

Closed Reduction

Closed reduction of a cervical spine dislocation or fracture-dislocation typically is performed in a monitored setting using bedside fluoroscopy or radiography. The patient should be alert, understand the purpose of closed reduction, and be able to cooperate with frequent neurologic examination. Gardner-Wells tongs are applied, and traction usually begins at 10 to 15 lb, with early imaging to exclude the possibility of craniocervical distraction from an unrecognized injury. In the absence of clinical or neurologic worsening, 10-lb weights are incrementally added every 10 to 15 minutes. Traction should be halted if overdistraction is noted on radiographic imaging. Reduction often is achieved with 40 to 70 lb of traction, but as much as 140 lb of traction has been required.[34] In the absence of fracture, a flexion moment is applied during the initial phases of traction to unlock dislocated facets. Weight in excess of 80 lb should not be placed on most carbon fiber MRI-compatible tongs, although traditional steel tongs can safely tolerate weight greater than 100 lb. This factor may be a consideration in choosing tongs for a patient with a large body habitus. After successful closed reduction, the cervical spine is immobilized until definitive treatment.

The role of prereduction MRI has been debated. Undetected herniated disk fragments at the injury site can compress the spinal cord during reduction. In patients who are unconscious or cannot be examined, prereduction MRI should be performed to allow a herniated disk to be treated with anterior decompression and open reduction. In an awake, cooperative patient, closed reduction is safe without the need for prereduction MRI. When MRI was used before and after closed reduction in 11 awake patients with cervical spine dislocation, 9 of the patients were found to have successful closed reduction.[35] Two patients had disk herniation before reduction, and five had disk herniation after reduction. None of the patients had neurologic worsening, however, and the link between disk herniation and the safety of closed reduction remains unclear. In a pilot study on closed reduction of cervical spine fracture-dislocation with MRI guidance, 15 of 17 patients (88%) had disk disruption, and 4 (24%) had posterior herniation.[36] Traction led to a return of herniated disk material in all affected patients. All 17 patients tolerated traction without neurologic worsening. Progressive improvement in canal dimensions occurred during reduction, with no intervals of canal narrowing. Timing was found to be important in both the success of reduction and the potential for neurologic recovery. In a retrospective study of patients with cervical dislocation and neurologic injury, the patients with reduction within the first 4 hours of the initial injury had a more successful reduction and greater neurologic recovery than other patients.[37] Awake patients with dense, incomplete injury are probably best indicated for early closed reduction without a delay to allow MRI evaluation.

The role of closed reduction in patients with thoracic or lumbar spine injury is less well defined. Safe, acceptable functional and radiographic results have been reported after closed reduction and casting of thoracolumbar and lumbar burst fractures.[38] Recovery of neurologic function was reported in patients who had a compression or burst-type fracture at the thoracolumbar junction associated with unilateral radicular pain, after treatment with closed reduction and casting.[39] Closed reduction was performed on a fracture table, with a belt used to perform a lordotic reduction maneuver at the level of the fracture, and a thoracolumbar plaster cast was applied.

Medical Management of SCI

A patient with high-level SCI initially is best treated in an intensive care unit because of the need for close neurologic, respiratory, and cardiovascular monitoring. A patient who is likely to remain ventilator dependent or to be slowly weaned from ventilator support should be considered for early tracheotomy.[40] Secretion retention caused by expiratory muscle weakness may be best treated with measures beyond suctioning, such as manually assisted coughing and mechanical insufflation-exsufflation. A critically ill patient should receive stress ulcer prophylaxis, and normoglycemia should be maintained. In a patient with acute SCI, the judicious use of fluids and vasopressors is sometimes recommended to achieve a mean arterial pressure of 85 mm Hg for 7 days, based on the outcomes of uncontrolled studies.[11] A cervical SCI is associated with bradydysrhythmias, which can lead to hypotension and asystole, and intervention with atropine, aminophylline, or a pacemaker may be required.

Venous thromboembolism is a common complication of acute SCI; in the absence of prophylaxis, it develops in as many as half of patients with acute SCI. Venous thromboembolism is uncommon in children, but the risk in adolescents appears similar to that in adults.[41] Although a mechanical compression device should be applied soon after injury, such a device is relatively ineffective as a sole prophylactic measure. Low-molecular-weight heparin or unfractionated heparin plus intermittent pneumatic compression should be instituted if primary hemostasis becomes evident. Intracranial bleeding, perispinal hematoma, hemothorax, and impending surgical intervention are indications for delaying the administration of anticoagulants. Placement of a vena cava filter can be considered in a patient who has active bleeding that is anticipated to persist for more than 72 hours. Anticoagulants should be instituted when the bleeding has stabilized, even if a vena cava filter is in place, because the incidence of lower extremity deep venous thrombosis after filter placement is as high as 36%.[42] These findings have led to recommendations for the temporary use of retrievable filters.

Avoiding pressure changes in the skin and subcutaneous tissues during the acute hospitalization phase after SCI is critical to minimizing skin breakdown. The patient should be repositioned to provide pressure relief every 2 hours, with care to maintain spine precautions. The areas at risk of skin breakdown should be assessed with each repositioning. If the patient's condition permits, a pressure reduction mattress or overlay should be used, and a similar seat cushion should be used when the patient is mobilized to a chair. Early patient and family education on the importance of vigilance and prompt management for skin integrity may be beneficial.[43] A consultation with a physiatrist can be useful in reducing the risk of skin and other complications and facilitating rehabilitation.

Neuroprotective Strategies

The currently used neuroprotective treatment protocols seek to attenuate the secondary pathophysiologic pathways. Many pharmacologic agents have been found to offer some benefit in animal models. During the past several years, clinical studies have evaluated the safety and efficacy of several potential therapies. Large-scale multicenter studies have used agents such as methylprednisolone, monosialotetrahexosylganglioside (GM-1), gacyclidine (an aspartate receptor antagonist), tirilazad (a free radical scavenger), and naloxone. Unfortunately, these agents were not found to be indisputably efficacious, and they may have severe adverse effects. As a result, their use cannot be definitively recommended.

Although the use of methylprednisolone after acute SCI was never approved by the US Food and Drug Administration, it became widespread after the second and third National Acute Spinal Cord Injury Studies reported improvements in ASIA motor and sensory scores in patients who received methylprednisolone.[44,45] Potential confounding variables limited the extent to which these conclusions could be applied to all patients with acute SCI, however, and the failure of subsequent post hoc analyses to find improvement in primary outcome measures (motor, pinprick, and light-touch scores) suggests that their findings represent random events. Both studies documented serious complications of methylprednisolone administration, including infection, respiratory complications, and gastrointestinal hemorrhage.[44,45] Another study found that the prophylactic use of methylprednisolone during spine surgery in patients with acute SCI was associated with a significantly increased risk of complications.[46] Clinical judgment should be used to guide the use of methylprednisolone in SCI, while keeping the risks in mind. Methylprednisolone should not be used as a prophylactic therapy in the absence of a clearly documented SCI or in a patient with penetrating spinal cord injury. Methylprednisolone should be discontinued in a patient whose neurologic symptoms have resolved, and it should be used cautiously in a patient who is elderly or

3: Spine Trauma

has a high cervical injury. A predominantly conus medullaris injury should be considered together with SCI. Methylprednisolone has not been established as a therapy for cauda equina injury. The neuroprotective efficacy of therapeutic hypothermia, including the rapid, stable systemic temperature control achievable with intravascular cooling catheters, is being investigated in patients with spinal cord ischemia.

The Timing of Surgery

The timing of surgery as part of the early management of acute SCI remains controversial. Surveys of practice patterns across North America found a wide variation in the timing of surgical intervention. Data published during the 1980s led to a recommended 5-day delay in surgery to avoid the risk of neurologic deterioration.[47] More recent studies found that early decompressive or stabilizing surgery is not associated with an increased risk of complications.[48] The efficacy of early surgery in promoting neurologic recovery has not been conclusively shown in well-designed, well-executed randomized studies, however. Therefore, early surgery remains an option rather than a practice standard. The multicenter, prospective Surgical Timing in Acute Spinal Cord Injury Study has been undertaken as an attempt to clarify this aspect of early management; data are not yet published.

Summary

The hours and days immediately after trauma are crucial to the outcome of a patient with severe spine injury. Although life-saving interventions may be the focus, instituting preventive measures early in the acute phase can help avoid long-term complications. Ongoing research is essential to clarify the role of existing and emerging diagnostic and treatment strategies.

Annotated References

1. Bracken MB, Freeman DH Jr, Hellenbrand K: Incidence of acute traumatic hospitalized spinal cord injury in the United States, 1970-1977. *Am J Epidemiol* 1981; 113(6):615-622.

2. Sekhon LH, Fehlings MG: Epidemiology, demographics, and pathophysiology of acute spinal cord injury. *Spine (Phila Pa 1976)* 2001;26(24, suppl):S2-S12.

3. National Spinal Cord Injury Statistical Center: Spinal Cord Injury Facts and Figures at a Glance. http://www.spinalcord.uab.edu. Updated July 2010.

   A federally funded online database collected from a network of medical centers serves as a source of statistics on SCI throughout the United States.

4. Riggins RS, Kraus JF: The risk of neurologic damage with fractures of the vertebrae. *J Trauma* 1977;17(2):126-133.

5. Kwan I, Bunn F, Roberts I: Spinal immobilisation for trauma patients. *Cochrane Database Syst Rev* 2001;2:CD002803.

6. Kwan I, Bunn F: Effects of prehospital spinal immobilization: A systematic review of randomized trials on healthy subjects. *Prehosp Disaster Med* 2005;20(1):47-53.

   The evidence on the efficacy and adverse effects of various immobilization methods was evaluated in a review of 17 randomized controlled studies of spine immobilization.

7. Domeier RM, Frederiksen SM, Welch K: Prospective performance assessment of an out-of-hospital protocol for selective spine immobilization using clinical spine clearance criteria. *Ann Emerg Med* 2005;46(2):123-131.

   A 4-year prospective study evaluated an EMS protocol for selective spine immobilization. The protocol required immobilization for patients with altered mental status, intoxication, neurologic deficit, extremity fracture, spine pain, or tenderness, with 92% sensitivity. Level of evidence: II.

8. Burton JH, Dunn MG, Harmon NR, Hermanson TA, Bradshaw JR: A statewide, prehospital emergency medical service selective patient spine immobilization protocol. *J Trauma* 2006;61(1):161-167.

   An EMS spine assessment protocol instituted in Maine was 87% sensitive for acute spine fracture. In approximately 32,000 trauma encounters, there was one patient with a nonimmobilized, unstable spine fracture. Level of evidence: IV.

9. MacKenzie EJ, Rivara FP, Jurkovich GJ, et al: A national evaluation of the effect of trauma-center care on mortality. *N Engl J Med* 2006;354(4):366-378.

   A comparative study examined mortality outcomes among patients treated in 18 hospitals with a level I trauma center and 51 nontrauma centers in 14 states. The in-hospital mortality rate and 1-year mortality rate were significantly lower in the trauma centers. Level of evidence: III.

10. Guly HR, Bouamra O, Lecky FE, Trauma Audit and Research Network: The incidence of neurogenic shock in patients with isolated spinal cord injury in the emergency department. *Resuscitation* 2008;76(1):57-62.

    The Trauma Audit and Research Network in England and Wales was used to determine the incidence of neurogenic shock in patients arriving in the emergency department with SCI. Level of evidence: IV.

11. Hadley M: Blood pressure management after acute spinal cord injury. *Neurosurgery* 2002;50(3, 1 suppl):S58-S62.

12. Marino RJ, Ditunno JF Jr, Donovan WH, Maynard F Jr: Neurologic recovery after traumatic spinal cord injury: Data from the Model Spinal Cord Injury Systems. *Arch Phys Med Rehabil* 1999;80(11):1391-1396.

13. Dvorak MF, Fisher CG, Hoekema J, et al: Factors predicting motor recovery and functional outcome after traumatic central cord syndrome: A long-term follow-up. *Spine (Phila Pa 1976)* 2005;30(20):2303-2311.

     A retrospective database review compared improvement in ASIA motor score and functional status in patients with traumatic central cord syndrome when assessed within 72 hours of injury and at an average 6-year follow-up. Most patients had improvement but a lower functional level than the general population. Level of evidence: III.

14. Stiell IG, Clement CM, McKnight RD, et al: The Canadian C-spine rule versus the NEXUS low-risk criteria in patients with trauma. *N Engl J Med* 2003;349(26): 2510-2518.

15. McCulloch PT, France J, Jones DL, et al: Helical computed tomography alone compared with plain radiographs with adjunct computed tomography to evaluate the cervical spine after high-energy trauma. *J Bone Joint Surg Am* 2005;87(11):2388-2394.

     A prospective study compared helical CT of the cervical spine with standard three-view plain radiography after high-energy trauma. Helical CT was found to be safely used without plain radiography to evaluate the cervical spine for osseous abnormalities. Level of evidence: I.

16. Biswas D, Bible JE, Bohan M, Simpson AK, Whang PG, Grauer JN: Radiation exposure from musculoskeletal computerized tomography scans. *J Bone Joint Surg Am* 2009;91(8):1882-1889.

     Effective radiation dosages for musculoskeletal CT were calculated using dosimetry software. The highest mean effective dosages were found in studies of the spine (4.26, 17.99, 19.15 mSv for the cervical, thoracic, and lumbar spines, respectively).

17. Ajani AE, Cooper DJ, Scheinkestel CD, Laidlaw J, Tuxen DV: Optimal assessment of cervical spine trauma in critically ill patients: A prospective evaluation. *Anaesth Intensive Care* 1998;26(5):487-491.

18. Berne JD, Velmahos GC, El-Tawil Q, et al: Value of complete cervical helical computed tomographic scanning in identifying cervical spine injury in the unevaluable blunt trauma patient with multiple injuries: A prospective study. *J Trauma* 1999;47(5):896-903.

19. Como JJ, Diaz JJ, Dunham CM, et al: Practice management guidelines for identification of cervical spine injuries following trauma: Update from the Eastern Association for the Surgery of Trauma Practice Management Guidelines Committee. *J Trauma* 2009;67(3):651-659.

     This retrospective review provides guidelines for the identification of cervical spine injury following trauma. The major changes since the previous publication include the increased role of CT for patients who require imaging.

20. Muchow RD, Resnick DK, Abdel MP, Munoz A, Anderson PA: Magnetic resonance imaging (MRI) in the clearance of the cervical spine in blunt trauma: A meta-analysis. *J Trauma* 2008;64(1):179-189.

     In a meta-analysis of prospective and retrospective diagnostic studies of MRI of the cervical spine, negative MRI was found to conclusively exclude cervical spine injury in a patient with blunt trauma. Level of evidence: I.

21. Hauser CJ, Visvikis G, Hinrichs C, et al: Prospective validation of computed tomographic screening of the thoracolumbar spine in trauma. *J Trauma* 2003;55(2): 228-235.

22. Smith MW, Reed JD, Facco R, et al: The reliability of nonreconstructed computerized tomographic scans of the abdomen and pelvis in detecting thoracolumbar spine injuries in blunt trauma patients with altered mental status. *J Bone Joint Surg Am* 2009;91(10):2342-2349.

     The reliability of nonreconstructed CT of the abdomen and pelvis was evaluated as a screening tool for thoracolumbar spine injuries in patients with blunt trauma and altered mental status. Nonreconstructed CT was found to detect fractures of the thoracolumbar spine more accurately than plain radiographs. Level of evidence: I.

23. Vaccaro AR, An HS, Lin S, Sun S, Balderston RA, Cotler JM: Noncontiguous injuries of the spine. *J Spinal Disord* 1992;5(3):320-329.

24. Qaiyum M, Tyrrell PN, McCall IW, Cassar-Pullicino VN: MRI detection of unsuspected vertebral injury in acute spinal trauma: Incidence and significance. *Skeletal Radiol* 2001;30(6):299-304.

25. Chen Y, DeVivo MJ: Epidemiology of extraspinal fractures in acute spinal cord injury: Data from Model Spinal Cord Injury Care systems, 1973-1999. *Top Spinal Cord Inj Rehabil* 2005;11:18-29.

     A review of a consecutive sample of 5,711 patients admitted to the National SCI Database between 1973 and 1999 found a 28% incidence of associated extraspinal fractures. The most common patterns and associations are described. Level of evidence: III.

26. Wang CM, Chen Y, DeVivo MJ, Huang CT: Epidemiology of extraspinal fractures associated with acute spinal cord injury. *Spinal Cord* 2001;39(11):589-594.

27. Davidoff G, Thomas P, Johnson M, Berent S, Dijkers M, Doljanac R: Closed head injury in acute traumatic spinal cord injury: Incidence and risk factors. *Arch Phys Med Rehabil* 1988;69(10):869-872.

28. Albuquerque F, Wolf A, Dunham CM, Wagner R, Spagnolia T, Rigamonti D: Frequency of intra-abdominal injury in cases of blunt trauma to the cervical spinal cord. *J Spinal Disord* 1992;5(4):476-480.

29. Rabinovici R, Ovadia P, Mathiak G, Abdullah F: Abdominal injuries associated with lumbar spine fractures in blunt trauma. *Injury* 1999;30(7):471-474.

30. Torina PJ, Flanders AE, Carrino JA, et al: Incidence of vertebral artery thrombosis in cervical spine trauma:

Correlation with severity of spinal cord injury. *AJNR Am J Neuroradiol* 2005;26(10):2645-2651.

A retrospective study of 1,283 patients with nonpenetrating cervical injuries, with or without SCI, found that vertebral artery thrombosis was common in patients with relatively severe SCI. Patients without SCI also were at risk. Magnetic resonance angiography was used. Level of evidence: II.

31. Fassett DR, Dailey AT, Vaccaro AR: Vertebral artery injuries associated with cervical spine injuries: A review of the literature. *J Spinal Disord Tech* 2008;21(4):252-258.

A literature review identified publications on vertebral artery injuries associated with cervical spine trauma. Approximately 0.5% of all trauma patients were found to have a vertebral artery injury, and 70% of all traumatic vertebral artery injuries were found to have an associated cervical spine fracture. Screening and treatment of asymptomatic injuries may be considered, but the recommendations are unclear. Level of evidence: III.

32. Hadley MN: Management of vertebral artery injuries after nonpenetrating cervical trauma. *Neurosurgery* 2002;50(3, suppl):S173-S178.

33. Inamasu J, Guiot BH: Vertebral artery injury after blunt cervical trauma: An update. *Surg Neurol* 2006;65(3):238-246.

A literature review found a 0.20% to 0.77% rate of vertebral artery injury among patients admitted with blunt trauma. Most patients remained asymptomatic, but sudden and unexpected deterioration was often reported. No definitive treatment recommendations could be made. Level of evidence: III.

34. Lee AS, MacLean JC, Newton DA: Rapid traction for reduction of cervical spine dislocations. *J Bone Joint Surg Br* 1994;76(3):352-356.

35. Vaccaro AR, Falatyn SP, Flanders AE, Balderston RA, Northrup BE, Cotler JM: Magnetic resonance evaluation of the intervertebral disc, spinal ligaments, and spinal cord before and after closed traction reduction of cervical spine dislocations. *Spine (Phila Pa 1976)* 1999;24(12):1210-1217.

36. Darsaut TE, Ashforth R, Bhargava R, et al: A pilot study of magnetic resonance imaging-guided closed reduction of cervical spine fractures. *Spine (Phila Pa 1976)* 2006;31(18):2085-2090.

A prospective case study of 17 patients with cervical fracture-dislocation who underwent reduction with MRI guidance found that canal dimensions did not diminish at any time, even during sequential traction application. Level of evidence: IV.

37. Reinhold M, Knop C, Lange U, Rosenberger R, Schmid R, Blauth M: Reduction of traumatic dislocations and facet fracture-dislocations in the lower cervical spine. *Unfallchirurg* 2006;109(12):1064-1072.

A retrospective review of 117 patients with cervical dislocation suggested that the success of reduction and po-

tential for recovery are improved if reduction is performed within 4 hours of injury. Level of evidence: III.

38. Tropiano P, Huang RC, Louis CA, Poitout DG, Louis RP: Functional and radiographic outcome of thoracolumbar and lumbar burst fractures managed by closed orthopaedic reduction and casting. *Spine (Phila Pa 1976)* 2003;28(21):2459-2465.

39. Weninger P, Schultz A, Hertz H: Conservative management of thoracolumbar and lumbar spine compression and burst fractures: Functional and radiographic outcomes in 136 cases treated by closed reduction and casting. *Arch Orthop Trauma Surg* 2009;129(2):207-219.

A review of 136 patients found that closed reduction and casting of thoracolumbar and lumbar compression and burst fractures can be safe and effective and can help restore function in patients with unilateral radicular pain. Level of evidence: III.

40. Griffiths J, Barber VS, Morgan L, Young JD: Systematic review and meta-analysis of studies of the timing of tracheostomy in adult patients undergoing artificial ventilation. *BMJ* 2005;330(7502):1243.

A meta-analysis of critically ill patients found that early tracheotomy is associated with a reduction in length of intensive care unit stay and duration of mechanical ventilation.

41. Jones T, Ugalde V, Franks P, Zhou H, White RH: Venous thromboembolism after spinal cord injury: Incidence, time course, and associated risk factors in 16,240 adults and children. *Arch Phys Med Rehabil* 2005;86(12):2240-2247.

A review of California hospital discharge data found that venous thromboembolism developed in 6% of all patients admitted with SCI. Level of evidence: IV.

42. PREPIC Study Group: Eight-year follow-up of patients with permanent vena cava filters in the prevention of pulmonary embolism: The PREPIC (Prevention du Risque d'Embolie Pulmonaire par Interruption Cave) randomized study. *Circulation* 2005;112(3):416-422.

In a randomized study of anticoagulation treatment with or without the use of a filter, deep venous thrombosis had developed in 35.7% of patients with filters at 8-year follow-up. Level of evidence: IV.

43. Consortium for Spinal Cord Medicine: *Pressure ulcer prevention and treatment following spinal cord injury: A clinical practice guideline for health care professionals.* Washington, DC, Paralyzed Veterans of America, 2000.

44. Bracken MB, Shepard MJ, Collins WF Jr, et al: Methylprednisolone or naloxone treatment after acute spinal cord injury: 1-year follow-up data. Results of the Second National Acute Spinal Cord Injury Study. *J Neurosurg* 1992;76(1):23-31.

45. Bracken MB, Shepard MJ, Holford TR, et al: Administration of methylprednisolone for 24 or 48 hours or tirilazad mesylate for 48 hours in the treatment of acute

spinal cord injury: Results of the Third National Acute Spinal Cord Injury Randomized Controlled Trial. *JAMA* 1997;277(20):1597-1604.

46. Molano Mdel R, Broton JG, Bean JA, Calancie B: Complications associated with the prophylactic use of methylprednisolone during surgical stabilization after spinal cord injury. *J Neurosurg* 2002;96(3, suppl):267-272.

47. Marshall LF, Knowlton S, Garfin SR, et al: Deterioration following spinal cord injury: A multicenter study. *J Neurosurg* 1987;66(3):400-404.

48. Fehlings MG, Perrin RG: The timing of surgical intervention in the treatment of spinal cord injury: A systematic review of recent clinical evidence. *Spine (Phila Pa 1976)* 2006;31(11, suppl):S28-S36.

A 10-year systematic review of clinical studies examining the timing of surgery was limited to level II and III evidence.

3: Spine Trauma

Chapter 19

Upper Cervical Spine Injuries

Paul A. Anderson, MD

Introduction

Spine injuries between the occiput and C2 are common. Usually these injuries are the result of a rapid head deceleration or an impact to the face or cranium, with downward-directed forces to the atlas and axis. The impact forces can vary in direction from directly axial to bending in the sagittal and coronal planes or, rarely, in rotation. Shear is the most dangerous force, especially in the anterior-to-posterior direction, and it results in highly unstable injuries. The complex anatomy and variable mechanisms of injury lead to a wide spectrum of often-confusing injuries. An understanding of anatomy, kinematics, and radiographic findings is essential for the diagnosis and treatment of an upper cervical spine injury.

Anatomy

The Occipitoatlantal Articulation

The occipital condyles are semilunar projections from the inferior surface of the skull that together lie within shallow concavities of the atlas, creating a ball-and-socket configuration. The slope of the concavities is highest anteriorly and laterally. The articulation is stabilized by the alar ligaments, which project laterally from the dens tip to the inner aspect of each occipital condyle; and by the tectorial membrane, which is a continuation of the posterior longitudinal ligament to the anterior aspect of the foramen magnum. The paired alar ligaments and the tectorial membrane are essential for craniocervical stability. Structures such as the apical ligament and the occipitocervical membrane and joint capsules provide little intrinsic stability. Approximately 25° of flexion-extension and 5° to 10° of lateral bending and rotation occur at the occipitoatlantal articulation. Normally the occipitoatlantal joints have a per-

fectly congruous relationship, and any displacement should be considered abnormal. Mechanical studies found that more than 2 mm of diastasis suggests a ligamentous disruption and an unstable injury.[1]

The Atlas

The atlas is a ring structure with large lateral masses and small anterior-posterior connecting arches. The lateral masses articulate with the occipital condyle and the corresponding lateral masses of the axis. The transverse ligament, which passes behind the dens, originates at tubercles on the medial side of the lateral masses. The anterior arch, dens, and transverse ligament form an important complex that prevents anterior-to-posterior atlantoaxial shear. The rotation of the atlantoaxial articulation is approximately 45° in each direction. The rotation is further limited by tightening of the opposite alar ligaments, which act as restraints to rotation.

The Axis

The axis has a unique anatomy because a large cranial projection, the odontoid process, lies behind the anterior arch of the atlas and in front of the transverse ligament. The superior facet of the axis, which articulates with the atlas, is located anteriorly; its flat or slightly convex shape facilitates rotation. The inferior facet, which articulates with C3, is located posteriorly and is connected to the body with small tubular structures called the pars interarticularis. A large bifid spinous process and heavy lamina serve as an attachment for the nuchal ligament. Maintenance of the attachments of the nuchal ligament and the short cervical muscles that attach to the axis is important for preventing chin-on-chest deformity.

Diagnosis

Physical Examination

The upper cervical spine requires careful scrutiny, as it is the most common site of missed spine injury. Many incidences of neurologic deterioration or death have been reported as a consequence of such missed injuries.[1-3] The patient may have an altered level of consciousness as a consequence of skull impact. An alert patient usually reports upper cervical pain or occipital neuralgia and has upper cervical tenderness to

Dr. Anderson or an immediate family member has received royalties from Pioneer Surgical and Stryker; serves as a paid consultant to or is an employee of Medtronic Sofamor Danek, Pioneer Surgical, Expanding Orthopedics, and Aesculap/B.Braun; has received research or institutional support from Medtronic Sofamor Danek and Titan; and owns stock or stock options in Titan Surgical, Pioneer Surgical, Expanding Orthopedics, Crosstrees, and Titan.

3: Spine Trauma

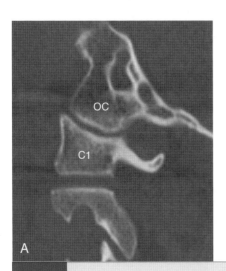
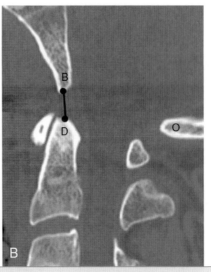
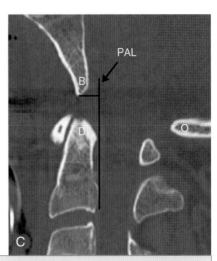

Figure 1 CT showing the relationship between the occipital condyles (OC) and the C1 lateral masses. **A,** The normal congruent relationship. More than 2 mm of joint diastasis or joint incongruity indicates rupture of the alar ligaments and probable occipitocervical instability. **B,** The basion (B) lies no more than 12 mm above the tip of the dens (D). The opisthion (O) is the posterior margin of the foramen magnum. **C,** The posterior axial line (PAL) should lie within a 12-mm anterior-posterior distance of the basion. Greater displacement indicates occipitocervical subluxation.

palpation. Although a variety of neurologic syndromes can occur in these patients, the relative wideness of the upper cervical spinal canal usually prevents neurologic injury. Cranial nerve examination is important, as injuries to cranial nerves IX, X, XI, and XII are common.[4] A patient with a spinal cord or brain stem injury may have impaired ventilation and require lifesaving intervention.

Radiographic Examination

The upper cervical spine is best seen on CT, which is especially cost-effective if cervical spine and head CT scans are obtained at the same time.[5] The alignment of the occipitoatlantal articulation should be congruous (Figure 1, *A*). Diastasis of more than 2 mm indicates a ligamentous injury.[6] Asymmetry may indicate a mild injury. The basion (the terminal end of the clivus) should lie directly above and no further than 12 mm from the dens tip[7,8] (Figure 1, *B*). The basion also should lie within 12 mm of the posterior axial line[7,8] (Figure 1, *C*). Soft-tissue swelling also is an indication of craniocervical injury. MRI with fat suppression sometimes is useful for identifying soft-tissue injuries and edema.

The atlas normally is positioned symmetrically around the dens. However, an offset to one side is common and usually represents poor head positioning during scanning. The anterior atlantodens interval (ADI) normally is less than 3 mm in adults and less than 5 mm in children. A greater displacement indicates a transverse ligament injury. The dens should be carefully examined, as a nondisplaced fracture can easily be overlooked. In children, the dental synchondrosis may be present and confused with a fracture; this synchondrosis usually ossifies by age 7 years.

Occipital Condyle Fractures

Occipital condyle fractures are being diagnosed with increasing frequency as a result of the increased use of head CT. Except when associated with craniocervical instability, these fractures are relatively benign and easily treated. Most patients have sustained a blow to the cranium with a traumatic brain injury.

Classification

Occipital condyle fractures are classified as type I, a comminuted fracture without displacement; type II, associated with a skull base fracture; and type III, an alar ligament avulsion fracture[9] (Figure 2, Table 1). Type I fractures are stable. Type II fractures usually are stable; in rare instances, however, the entire condyle is detached, rendering the craniocervical articulation unstable. Type III fractures may be associated with an occipitoatlantal dislocation. Careful evaluation of the alignment between the occipital condyles and the atlantolateral masses is essential to determining the integrity of the alar ligaments and the stability of the injury. Occipital injuries can be unilateral or bilateral; bilateral injuries suggest the presence of greater instability.[4]

Treatment

A stable injury, in which there is no displacement of the occipitoatlantal articulation, can be treated using a rigid collar (Table 1). An unstable injury with minimal displacement can be treated using a halo vest. An unstable injury with displacement should be reduced and surgically treated with occipitocervical fusion.

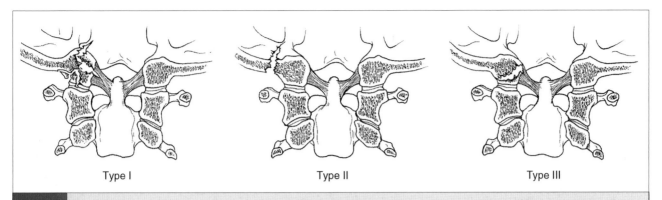

| Type I | Type II | Type III |

Figure 2 Schematic drawings showing the classification of occipital condyle fractures. (Reproduced with permission from Anderson PA: Injuries to the atlanto-occipital cervical articulation, in Clark CR, Dvorak J, Ducker TB, et al, eds: *The Cervical Spine*, ed 3. Philadelphia, PA, Lippincott-Raven, 1998, pp 587-606.)

Table 1

Occipital Condyle Fractures

Type	Description	Stability	Treatment Options
I	Comminuted fracture	Stable	Cervical orthosis
II	Basilar skull fracture	Stable	Cervical orthosis
		Unstable	Halo vest*
			Occipitocervical fusion (rarely)
III	Alar ligament avulsion fracture	Stable	Cervical orthosis
		Unstable	Occipitocervical fusion

*Preferred treatment

Craniocervical Instability

Craniocervical instability (also called occipitoatlantal instability) results in dramatic injury and is the cause of death in as many as 15% of fatal injuries from motor vehicle crashes.[10] An increasing number of patients are surviving these injuries. Improvements in imaging have allowed variation in the severity of injury to be identified. Unfortunately, the diagnosis often is delayed, with resulting neurologic deterioration or even death.[1,2]

Classification

Craniocervical instability formerly was classified by the direction of displacement (vertical, anterior, or posterior). Most injuries are unstable in all directions, however, and this classification is not useful for determining whether a patient should be treated nonsurgically or surgically. More clinically useful classification systems are based on MRI and CT findings[1,11] (Table 2). In a retrospective review of 28 patients, a type I injury was described as having normal alignment on CT but increased MRI signal in the craniocervical ligaments, and a type II injury was described as having displacement on CT and MRI, with evidence of disruption of the alar ligaments and/or tectorial membrane.[11] Another retrospective study described a type I injury as MRI positive, with normal CT findings. Type II represents dynamic instability, with positive MRI and normal CT findings but distraction testing showing a basion-dens interval at least 2 mm larger than normal.[1] In a type III injury, CT or MRI also reveals a basion-dens interval at least 2 mm larger than normal in any direction. Associated injuries are common and can include atlantoaxial distraction, occipital condyle fracture, atlas fracture, transverse ligament injury, or vascular injury to the vertebral and carotid arteries.

Treatment
Initial Treatment
The goal of initial treatment should be to protect the neural tissues by stabilization with sandbags, tape, reverse Trendelenburg positioning, and minimization of transfers. A halo vest should be applied as soon as possible. Tong traction should be avoided because it can cause longitudinal displacement, harming the spinal cord or brain stem. After the halo vest has been applied, reduction can be obtained under fluoroscopic guidance by manually adjusting the head relative to the thorax. The alignment is confirmed by assessing the position of the basion relative to the dens.[7]

Definitive Treatment
A type I injury probably is stable and can be treated with a collar. An occipital surgical fusion is recom-

3: Spine Trauma

Table 2

Occipitocervical Instability

Type	Description	Stability	Treatment Options
I	Normal CT findings Positive MRI finding: ligament injury without displacement	Stable	Cervical orthosis
II	Normal CT findings Positive MRI finding but a traction test showing more than 2 mm of diastasis	Unstable	Halo vest* Occipitocervical fusion
III	Positive CT and MRI findings 2 mm of displacement	Unstable	Occipitocervical fusion

*Preferred treatment

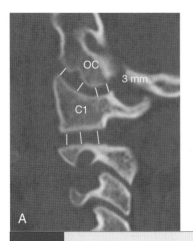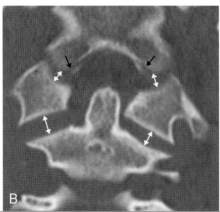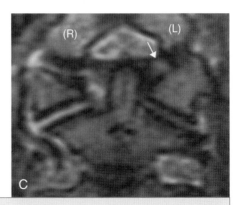

Figure 3 Craniocervical instability in a 10-year-old boy. **A,** CT showing type II occipitoatlantal subluxation. There is a 3-mm diastasis between the occipital condyles (OC) and the C1 lateral masses, and a vertical diastasis is present at C1-C2. **B,** Coronal CT reconstruction showing bilateral type III occipital condyle fractures *(black arrows)* and diastasis of both the occipitoatlantal and atlantoaxial articulations *(white arrows)*. **C,** MRI confirming the injury to both alar ligaments. The left ligament (L) has increased signal and a complete tear *(arrow)*; the right ligament (R) appears attenuated at its insertion on the occipital condyle. The patient was treated with closed reduction and a halo vest. Six months later, the upper cervical alignment was normal, and the patient had no pain or neurologic symptoms.

mended for a type II or III injury.[1] Rigid stabilization with screw fixation is recommended and is usually possible even for a child. Treatment with a halo vest may be satisfactory for some type II injuries, especially in pediatric patients (**Figure 3**).

Atlas Fractures

Classification

Fractures of the atlas are classified by location[12] (**Figure 4**). A type I injury is a fracture of the posterior arches. An unstable anterior arch is called a plough fracture; it occurs as a result of a posterior shear that forces the dens to plow through the anterior atlas, with continuing force causing a posterior atlantoaxial dislocation.[13] A type II injury is a burst-type (Jefferson) fracture secondary to downward-directed forces from the cranium; the resulting excessive hoop stresses in the atlas cause

multiple fractures of the atlas ring, which displace outward in a radial direction. The transverse ligament attached to the medial aspect of the lateral masses is progressively tensioned and fails by bony avulsion or a midsubstance tear. Biomechanical studies found that a transverse ligament injury occurs when the combined lateral displacement of the lateral masses relative to the axis is at least 6.9 mm.[14] When the transverse ligament ruptures, further lateral displacement can occur during immobilization. The height of the axis is reduced with displacement of the lateral masses, and the dens migrates cranially, sometimes causing brain stem compression. The stability of a type II fracture is determined by the status of the transverse ligament; lateral mass displacement of less than 7 mm represents stability.

A type III fracture involves the lateral mass. Its stability, like that of a type II fracture, depends on the integrity of the transverse ligament. Significant lateral displacement suggests transverse ligament disruption. A

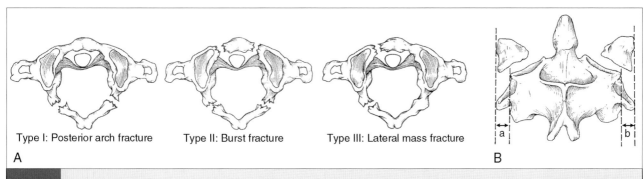

Figure 4 **A,** Schematic drawings showing the classification of atlas fractures. (Adapted with permission from Heller J, Pedlow F: Anatomy of the cervical spine, in Clark CR, Dvorak J, Ducker TB, et al, eds: *The Cervical Spine,* ed 3. Philadelphia, PA, Lippincott-Raven, 1998.) **B,** Schematic drawing showing lateral displacement of the atlantolateral masses in the open mouth view. If the total measured displacement on both sides (a and b) is more than 6.9 mm, the transverse ligament is disrupted and the fracture is unstable. (Adapted with permission from Anderson PA: Injuries to the atlanto-occipital cervical articulation, in Clark CR, Dvorak J, Ducker TB, et al, eds: *The Cervical Spine,* ed 3. Philadelphia, PA, Lippincott-Raven, 1998, pp 587-606.)

Table 3

Atlas Fractures

Type	Description	Stability	Treatment Options
I	Isolated arch fractures Plough fracture of anterior atlantal arch	Stable Unstable	Rigid cervical orthosis Posterior C1-C2 fusion* Halo vest
II	Bursting-type fracture	Stable Unstable	Halo vest* Cervical orthosis Halo vest* Osteosynthesis Occipitocervical fusion
III	Lateral mass fracture	Stable Unstable	Cervical orthosis Halo vest* Occipitocervical fusion Osteosynthesis

*Preferred treatment

recent study described sagittal fracture in the lateral mass, sometimes with instability caused by loss of lateral mass integrity to the ring.[15] A coronal split is a rare type of lateral mass fracture in which the occipital condyles displace posteriorly, essentially creating a posterior occipitocervical dislocation.

Treatment

A stable injury can be treated by simple immobilization in a collar[16] (Table 3). A stable type II injury usually is treated with a halo vest; 96% of patients healed after treatment with a halo vest, and none had functional disability.[16]

No consensus has been reached as to the best treatment of an unstable burst fracture. A retrospective study found that the patient's long-term quality of life was negatively affected, especially with significant displacement or associated injuries.[17] The treatment options include a rigid cervical orthosis, a cervicothoracic brace, a halo vest, and posterior fusion with screw fixation and osteosynthesis (anterior or posterior). In theory, osteosynthesis allows reduction of the displaced fracture and avoids atlantoaxial fusion, thus preserving motion.[18] However, only small case studies are available, and evidence is lacking to clearly indicate an improvement over nonsurgical care. Instead, traction is recommended to reduce the fracture, followed by 12 weeks of halo vest immobilization. Atlantoaxial stability is then assessed, and if residual instability is present, a posterior C1-C2 fusion is performed, provided there has been bony healing of the C1 arch fragments. During healing, open mouth radiographs are scrutinized for progressive lateral displacement of the lateral masses. Lateral mass fractures are treated in a manner similar to that of bursting fractures, depending on whether the transverse ligament is disrupted. A plough fracture or a lateral mass fracture associated with a posterior occipitoatlantal dislocation is reduced, provisionally treated

Table 4

Atlantoaxial Instability

Type	Description	Stability	Treatment Options
Lateral	Atlas fracture with lateral displacement Displacement of C1 lateral masses > 7 mm	Stable Unstable	Halo vest* Cervical orthosis* Halo vest Osteosynthesis Occipitocervical fusion
Rotatory I	Intact transverse ligament C1-C2 subluxation	Stable	Reduction and cervical orthosis* Observation
Rotatory II	5- to 7-mm ADI Possible transverse ligament rupture C1-C2 subluxation	Unstable	Cervical orthosis Halo vest* Cervicothoracic brace Posterior C1-C2 fusion
Rotatory III	ADI > 7 mm C1-C2 dislocation	Unstable	Posterior C1-C2 fusion* Halo vest Cervicothoracic brace Cervical orthosis
Rotatory IV	Posterior C1-C2 dislocation	Unstable	Posterior C1-C2 fusion*
Anterior shear	Adult ADI > 3 mm Transverse ligament rupture Pediatric ADI > 5 mm Transverse ligament rupture	Unstable	Posterior C1-C2 fusion* Halo vest Cervicothoracic brace Posterior C1-C2 Fusion Halo vest Cervicothoracic brace
Posterior shear	Type IV rotatory subluxation Plough fracture of anterior atlantal arch	Unstable Unstable	Posterior C1-C2 fusion* Posterior C1-C2 fusion* Halo
Anterior-to-posterior shear	Type II odontoid fracture	Unstable	Posterior C1-C2 fusion* Odontoid screw fixation* Halo
Vertical	Tear of alar ligaments Probable occipitoatlantal instability Diastasis > 2 mm between C1-C2	Unstable	Occipitocervical fusion*

*Preferred treatment

with a halo vest, and definitively treated with posterior fusion.[19]

Atlantoaxial Instability

Atlantoaxial instability implies an actual or potential displacement of the atlantolateral masses relative to the axis. This displacement can occur along any of the three axes (vertical, anterior-posterior, or lateral) (Table 4). Biomechanically, the atlantoaxial articulation is stabilized by the transverse ligament and its attachment to the atlantolateral masses and, secondarily, by the alar ligaments. Atlantoaxial stability also requires an intact anterior ring of C1 and dens.

Classification

Vertical atlantoaxial instability is caused by functional loss of the alar ligaments, either from ligamentous disruption or bony avulsion (a type III occipital condyle fracture or a type I dens fracture). Alar ligament incompetency often occurs in association with an occipitoatlantal dislocation and should be considered a variant of that injury. Lateral instability is seen with type II and III atlas fractures and less commonly with a lateral mass fracture of the axis. Rotatory atlantoaxial instability most commonly occurs in children who have the so-called cock-robin head position. There are four types[20] (Figure 5). Type I is rotation of the atlas relative to the axis, with an intact transverse ligament; this rotation type can be difficult to differentiate from normal physiologic motion. In type II, the ADI is as large as 5 mm, and there is some disruption of the transverse ligament. In type III, the ADI is larger than 5 mm, with complete transverse ligament disruption. Type IV is rare; it is a posterior dislocation of the anterior atlantal arch that causes the arch to lie posterior to the dens.

Anterior-to-posterior shear, the most common mechanism of atlantoaxial instability, is the result of disruption of the transverse ligament, fracture of the dens

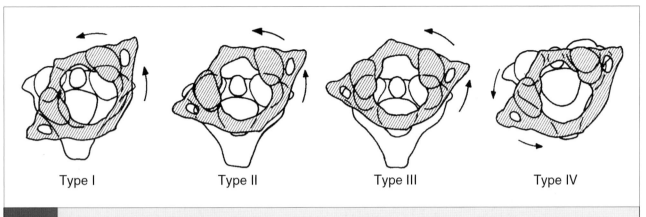

Type I   Type II   Type III   Type IV

Figure 5   Schematic drawings showing the classification of atlantoaxial rotatory instability, with the direction of rotation *(arrows)*. (Adapted from Copley LA, Dormans JP: Cervical spine disorders in infants and children. *J Am Acad Orthop Surg* 1998;6:204-214.)

(usually a type II fracture), or fracture of the anterior atlantal arch (a plough fracture).

Treatment

The treatment of atlantoaxial instability often is dictated by other injury components, such as an atlas or dens fracture.

Isolated Transverse Ligament Injuries

The treatment of an isolated transverse ligament rupture depends on the amount of displacement, whether the injury is a bony avulsion or a midsubstance tear, and the patient's age.[21] The indications for nonsurgical treatment, usually with a halo vest, are patient age younger than approximately 15 years, a combined lateral mass displacement of less than 7 mm, and a bony avulsion.[21-23] In such an injury, immobilization with a halo vest can be attempted to allow healing and return of stability. An adult patient or a patient with greater displacement is best treated with a posterior C1-C2 fusion.

Rotatory Subluxation

A type I injury should be reduced, and usually it is sufficient to use simple pain control and muscle relaxation or traction with a halter, followed by a short period of immobilization in a collar. A type II or III injury involves the transverse ligament and should be reduced with traction. Because these injuries commonly occur in children, a trial of nonsurgical treatment with a halo vest can be considered. Careful attention to alignment is continued during mobilization after halo vest removal.[22] A posterior C1-C2 fusion is another option, especially for a purely ligamentous injury or in an adult patient. Recurrent deformity or anterior translation is not uncommon, and it requires a posterior C1-C2 fusion. A type IV injury has transverse ligament and alar ligament disruption, and therefore it should be reduced and treated with occipitocervical fusion.

Axis Fractures

An axis fracture is the most common cervical spine injury. The types are odontoid fracture, traumatic spondylolisthesis of the axis, and C2 body fracture. Many patients have a combination of two or three of these injury patterns.

Odontoid Fractures

The odontoid process is an axle around which the atlas rotates, and therefore it is subject to many forces that can cause fractures (**Table 5**). Odontoid fractures occur at a high rate in a bimodal age distribution, with peak incidences in young adults age 20 to 30 years (from a high-energy mechanism), and, increasingly more commonly, in adults older than 65 years (from a fall).

Classification

Odontoid fractures are classified by location[24] (**Figure 6**). A type I fracture occurs at the dens tip and is a bony avulsion of the alar ligament. A type II fracture is through the dens waist, cranial to the facet articulations. A type III fracture is a transverse fracture that extends into the body and involves the articulations. A further classification of type II fractures is useful in treatment decision making: type IIA is nondisplaced, type IIB has fracture lines that run obliquely downward in the anterior-to-posterior direction, and type IIC is comminuted or has fracture lines that run obliquely upward in the anterior-to-posterior direction.[25]

Treatment

Multiple systematic reviews have outlined the management of odontoid fractures.[26-28] A type I injury is a functional impairment of the alar ligament, and it has the potential for occipitocervical instability. If alignment between the occipital condyles and the atlantolateral masses is normal, cervical orthosis immobilization is sufficient. If there is associated occipitoatlantal instability, occipitocervical fusion is recommended.

Table 5

Odontoid Fractures

Type	Description	Stability	Treatment Options
I	Avulsion at dens tip	Stable	Cervical orthosis
	Associated occipitoatlantal instability	Unstable	Occipitocervical fusion*
			Halo vest
II	Dens waist fracture	Unstable	
	IIA: Nondisplaced		Halo vest*
			Cervicothoracic brace
			Cervical orthosis
			Odontoid screw
			Posterior C1-C2 fusion
	IIB: Oblique, favorable for screw fixation		Odontoid screw fixation*
			Posterior C1-C2 fusion
			Halo vest
			Cervicothoracic brace
			Cervical orthosis
	IIC: Oblique, unfavorable for screw fixation		Posterior C1-C2 fusion*
			Halo vest
			Cervicothoracic brace
			Cervical orthosis
	II in patients older than approximately 65 years		Posterior C1-C2 fusion*
			Cervical orthosis*
			Odontoid screw
			Cervicothoracic brace
III	Transverse fracture extending into body	Unstable	Cervicothoracic brace*
			Halo
			Cervical orthosis
			Odontoid screw fixation
			Posterior C1-C2 fusion

*Preferred treatment

A type II injury is the most unstable and has the poorest prognosis. The risk factors for nonunion with halo vest treatment, as determined using bivariate and multivariate analysis, include a large fracture displacement (5 to 6 mm), a fracture gap larger than 1 mm, a residual displacement larger than 2 mm, and a patient age older than 65 years.[28,29] Determining these risk factors is important for developing a treatment strategy, although there is no consensus regarding the best treatment. Systematic reviews have found that approximately 68% of fractures heal with halo vest treatment, but only half of fractures heal with a less rigid form of immobilization.[27] Other surgical options are posterior C1-C2 fusion and anterior odontoid screw fixation. Posterior C1-C2 fusion using modern screw techniques has a success rate higher than 90%, at the cost of loss of C1-C2 motion.[28] Odontoid screw fixation is an osteosynthesis, and theoretically it maintains C1-C2 rotation. Rotation after fixation was found not to be maintained, however, with the loss of approximately 50% of C1-C2 motion.[30] Although healing occurs in approximately 85% of patients, odontoid screw fixation is as-

sociated with significant dysphagia and occasional loss of fixation.[31]

The risk factors for nonunion should be determined in a type II odontoid fracture. In a low-risk patient, a trial halo vest immobilization is recommended. If the reduction can be maintained, the halo vest is used for 12 weeks, after which flexion-extension radiographs are assessed to determine healing. If there is nonunion, posterior C1-C2 fusion is performed. In a high-risk patient, either an odontoid screw or posterior C1-C2 fusion is performed, depending on the fracture type. An odontoid screw is preferred for a type IIB fracture, as the fracture line is favorable for screw fixation (it is relatively orthogonal to the screw direction). In a type IIC fracture, a posterior C1-C2 fusion using screw fixation is recommended because the fracture pattern is unfavorable.

Nonsurgical treatment is indicated for a type III fracture unless the alignment cannot be maintained or nonunion occurs. There are no differences in fusion rate between a cervical orthosis and a halo vest. Therefore, an attempt using a cervical orthosis is recommended; if

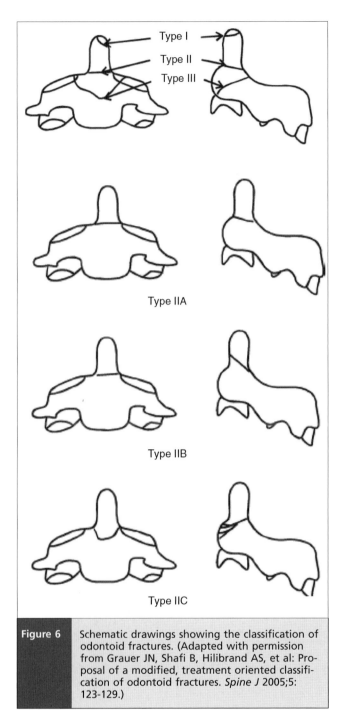

Figure 6 Schematic drawings showing the classification of odontoid fractures. (Adapted with permission from Grauer JN, Shafi B, Hilibrand AS, et al: Proposal of a modified, treatment oriented classification of odontoid fractures. *Spine J* 2005;5: 123-129.)

Type I

Type II

Type III

Type IIA

Type IIB

Type IIC

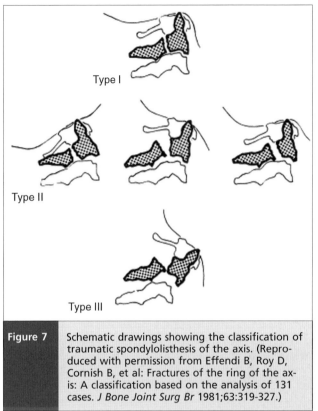

Type I

Type II

Type III

Figure 7 Schematic drawings showing the classification of traumatic spondylolisthesis of the axis. (Reproduced with permission from Effendi B, Roy D, Cornish B, et al: Fractures of the ring of the axis: A classification based on the analysis of 131 cases. *J Bone Joint Surg Br* 1981;63:319-327.)

it is unsuccessful, a halo vest is used or surgery is performed.

Odontoid Fractures in Older Patients
Odontoid fracture in patients older than approximately 65 years is associated with significant morbidity and mortality similar to those of hip fracture. The morbidities include the development of dysphagia, aspiration, pulmonary failure, and decubitus ulceration. The goal of treatment should be rapid mobilization with minimal bracing. Use of the halo vest was found to increase risk of death and usually should be avoided in geriatric patients.[32,33] The realistic options include the use of a rigid cervical orthosis, with an expectation of nonunion and a small risk of catastrophic displacement or the need for surgical stabilization. This treatment is recommended for patients who have a cognitive impairment, another disabling condition, or significant comorbidities. Patients who are active and have no significant medical comorbidities are candidates for surgical intervention. The goal of surgery is stabilization to allow minimal mobilization and early ambulation. Either anterior odontoid screw fixation or C1-C2 posterior fusion can be used, with the latter more likely to lead to healing and having a lower overall mortality rate.[34] If odontoid screw fixation is chosen, two screws should be used; healing does not occur in almost half of geriatric patients.[34]

Traumatic Spondylolisthesis of the Axis
Traumatic spondylolisthesis of the axis, also known as hangman's fracture, is a relatively benign injury. The injury is created by hyperextension force concentrated on the pars interarticularis until failure. The force is then transferred to the C2-3 disk, which is progressively injured in an anterior-to-posterior direction.

Classification
Traumatic spondylolisthesis of the axis is classified by the displacement across the C2-3 disk and C2-C3 facet articulations[35] (Figure 7). In many patients, fracture lines extend into the body or out into the lamina. A

3: Spine Trauma

type I injury is a nondisplaced fracture. The fractures of the posterior arch may not be symmetric on the right and left sides, and sometimes they even extend into the posterior vertebral body. Type II is a C2-3 discoligamentous injury that may result in subluxation or excessive kyphotic angulation. Type III is rare and has an associated C2-C3 facet dislocation.

Treatment

A type I injury can be successfully treated with simple orthotic immobilization. No consensus is available as to the best treatment of a type II fracture. The options include immobilization with a simple orthosis or a halo vest, anterior C2-C3 fusion, and posterior osteosynthesis with screw or posterior C1-C3 fusion. Systematic reviews indicate that most type II injuries heal with simple immobilization, although the healing may be in a displaced position.[26,36] A type III injury is associated with a C2-C3 facet dislocation; it cannot be reduced with traction and should be surgically treated. An open reduction and fusion of the C2-C3 facet dislocation is performed, and the pars fracture is stabilized using either a C2 pedicle screw or adjunctive external immobilization.

C2 Body Fractures
Classification

Many C2 fractures do not fit the pattern of odontoid fracture or traumatic spondylolisthesis of the axis, and they are grouped together as C2 body fractures. Type I is an avulsion fracture of the anteroinferior corner of the C2 body, type II is a low transverse body fracture, type III is a comminuted body fracture, and type IV is a sagittal plane fracture with extension into the lateral masses.[37]

Treatment

The C2 body fractures all occur in cancellous bone and generally have a good prognosis. Nonsurgical therapy therefore should be considered. A cervical orthosis is indicated for a nondisplaced fracture. A displaced fracture should be reduced and treated with a trial halo vest immobilization.[38]

Complications

Adverse events are common after an upper cervical spine injury, and they often lead to significant morbidity and mortality. A missed or delayed diagnosis is all too common. The cause is likely to be failure to perform adequate imaging in a timely fashion or misreading of images, especially if the injury is at the craniocervical junction.[2,3] Most injuries are unstable or have the potential for instability, and displacement with resultant neurologic injury may occur. It is essential to carefully attend to orthotic principles and to radiographically verify the maintenance of alignment over time. Epidural hematoma from these injuries is rare, al-

though a vertebral artery injury is common. The anatomy of the vertebral artery should be reviewed before surgery, and CT angiography should be considered if bony anomalies or fractures are present in areas around the vascular foramen. Airway obstruction and significant dysphagia can occur because of swelling, retropharyngeal hematoma, malalignment, immobilization, or bracing.[39] These complications appear to be more common and severe in patients older than approximately 65 years, and they can be fatal. Surgery-related adverse events including failure of proper screw placement (especially around C2), iatrogenic vascular injury, and loss of fixation are related to improper alignment. They increase the risk of spinal cord injury. Loss of fixation is most likely in a geriatric patient.

Summary

Upper cervical spine injuries are common and often associated with a delayed or missed diagnosis, with the possibility of neurologic deterioration. CT is the most sensitive imaging modality; occiput-C1 and C1-C2 alignment should be carefully assessed on CT in all blunt trauma patients. Atlanto-occipital injury with displacement of more than 2 mm should be treated surgically, with the occasional exception of injury to a child younger than 15 years. Except in a burst-type fracture of the atlas, most injuries associated with transverse ligament rupture should be treated with posterior C1-C2 fusion. A type II odontoid fracture has a high incidence of nonunion; the most important risk factor is initial displacement of more than 4 mm. Patients older than 65 years are at high risk for morbidity and mortality after an odontoid fracture, and new treatment strategies for these injuries need to be developed and tested. The literature suggests that a cervical orthosis is sufficient for management of a type III odontoid fracture or a type I or II traumatic spondylolisthesis of the axis.

Annotated References

1. Bellabarba C, Mirza SK, West GA, et al: Diagnosis and treatment of craniocervical dislocation in a series of 17 consecutive survivors during an 8-year period. *J Neurosurg Spine* 2006;4(6):429-440.

   A retrospective analysis described a functional classification of craniocervical injuries. Type I injuries are nondisplaced, with abnormal MRI, and can be treated nonsurgically. Type II injuries have displacement under a traction test. Type III injuries have initial displacement of more than 2 mm. Posterior occipitocervical fusion is recommended for types II and III.

2. Levi AD, Hurlbert RJ, Anderson P, et al: Neurologic deterioration secondary to unrecognized spinal instability following trauma: A multicenter study. *Spine (Phila Pa 1976)* 2006;31(4):451-458.

   A multicenter retrospective analysis of patients with blunt trauma identified 24 who had deterioration secondary to unrecognized spine injury. The most common causes were failure to obtain proper imaging, inadequate images, and incorrect diagnosis.

3. Platzer P, Hauswirth N, Jaindl M, Chatwani S, Vecsei V, Gaebler C: Delayed or missed diagnosis of cervical spine injuries. *J Trauma* 2006;61(1):150-155.

A delay in diagnosis occurred in 4.9% of 367 patients who had cervical spine fracture, resulting from misinterpretation, incomplete radiographs, or inadequate radiographs. The consequence of missed injury was significant; 44% of the patients had neurologic deterioration.

4. Mann FA, Cohen W: Occipital condyle fracture: Significance in the assessment of occipitoatlantal stability. *AJR Am J Roentgenol* 1994;163(1):193-194.

5. Blackmore CC, Mann FA, Wilson AJ: Helical CT in the primary trauma evaluation of the cervical spine: An evidence-based approach. *Skeletal Radiol* 2000;29(11):632-639.

6. Werne S: Studies in spontaneous atlas dislocation. *Acta Orthop Scand Suppl* 1957;23:1-150.

7. Harris JH Jr, Carson GC, Wagner LK: Radiologic diagnosis of traumatic occipitovertebral dissociation: 1. Normal occipitovertebral relationships on lateral radiographs of supine subjects. *AJR Am J Roentgenol* 1994;162(4):881-886.

8. Harris JH Jr, Carson GC, Wagner LK, Kerr N: Radiologic diagnosis of traumatic occipitovertebral dissociation: 2. Comparison of three methods of detecting occipitovertebral relationships on lateral radiographs of supine subjects. *AJR Am J Roentgenol* 1994;162(4):887-892.

9. Anderson PA, Montesano PX: Morphology and treatment of occipital condyle fractures. *Spine (Phila Pa 1976)* 1988;13(7):731-736.

10. Adams VI: Neck injuries: I. Occipitoatlantal dislocation: A pathologic study of twelve traffic fatalities. *J Forensic Sci* 1992;37(2):556-564.

11. Horn EM, Feiz-Erfan I, Lekovic GP, Dickman CA, Sonntag VK, Theodore N: Survivors of occipitoatlantal dislocation injuries: Imaging and clinical correlates. *J Neurosurg Spine* 2007;6(2):113-120.

Injuries were classified based on a retrospective review: type I, without atlanto-occipital displacement but with abnormal MRI; and type II, with more than 2 mm of displacement. Nonsurgical treatment was recommended for a type I injury, and posterior surgery was recommended for a type II injury.

12. Gehweiler JA, Duff DE, Martinez S, et al: Fractures of the atlas vertebra. *Skeletal Radiol* 1976;1:97-102.

13. Mohit AA, Schuster JA, Mirza SK, Mann FA: "Plough" fracture: Shear fracture of the anterior arch of the atlas. *AJR Am J Roentgenol* 2003;181(3):770.

14. Spence KF Jr, Decker S, Sell KW: Bursting atlantal fracture associated with rupture of the transverse ligament. *J Bone Joint Surg Am* 1970;52(3):543-549.

15. Bransford R, Falicov A, Nguyen Q, Chapman J: Unilateral C-1 lateral mass sagittal split fracture: An unstable Jefferson fracture variant. *J Neurosurg Spine* 2009;10(5):466-473.

Six patients developed a cock-robin head position after a coronal split fracture of the atlantolateral mass with intact transverse ligament. All patients had successful occipitocervical fusion. The authors concluded that the initial treatment should be surgery or prolonged traction.

16. Kontautas E, Ambrozaitis KV, Kalesinskas RJ, Spakauskas B: Management of acute traumatic atlas fractures. *J Spinal Disord Tech* 2005;18(5):402-405.

In an observational prospective study of 29 patients with an atlas fracture, patients with a nondisplaced fracture were successfully treated with a cervical orthosis. The halo vest was used in patients with a displaced fracture, with healing in 96%.

17. Dvorak MF, Johnson MG, Boyd M, Johnson G, Kwon BK, Fisher CG: Long-term health-related quality of life outcomes following Jefferson-type burst fractures of the atlas. *J Neurosurg Spine* 2005;2(4):411-417.

The long-term outcome (mean, 75 months) of 34 patients with atlas fracture was retrospectively assessed using the Medical Outcomes Study Short Form-36 and American Academy of Orthopaedic Surgeons–North American Spine Society instruments. The patients scored significantly poorer than normative patients on both instruments. Displacement of more than 7 mm and the presence of associated injuries were correlated with a relatively poor outcome.

18. Koller H, Kammermeier V, Ulbricht D, et al: Anterior retropharyngeal fixation C1-2 for stabilization of atlantoaxial instabilities: Study of feasibility, technical description and preliminary results. *Eur Spine J* 2006;15(9):1326-1338.

CT anatomic analysis was used to determine the feasibility of anterior fixation of the atlantoaxial articulation in 42 patients. Sufficient bone stock was available to achieve satisfactory screw purchase, and the technique was safe for the vertebral artery.

19. Howard JJ, Duplessis SJ: Posterolateral dislocation of the C1-C2 articulation associated with fracture of the anterior arch of C1: A case report. *Spine (Phila Pa 1976)* 2004;29(24):E562-E564.

20. Fielding JW, Cochran GB, Lawsing JF III, Hohl M: Tears of the transverse ligament of the atlas: A clinical and biomechanical study. *J Bone Joint Surg Am* 1974;56(8):1683-1691.

21. Dickman CA, Greene KA, Sonntag VK: Injuries involving the transverse atlantal ligament: Classification and treatment guidelines based upon experience with 39 injuries. *Neurosurgery* 1996;38(1):44-50.

3: Spine Trauma

22. Rahimi SY, Stevens EA, Yeh DJ, Flannery AM, Choudhri HF, Lee MR: Treatment of atlantoaxial instability in pediatric patients. *Neurosurg Focus* 2003;15(6):ECP1.

23. Vilela MD, Peterson EC: Atlantal fracture with transverse ligament disruption in a child: Case report. *J Neurosurg Pediatr* 2009;4(3):196-198.

A 5-year old child with a displaced atlantolateral mass and transverse ligament rupture was treated for 11 weeks in a halo vest. At 6 months, the child had normal neck motion and alignment on radiographs.

24. Anderson LD, D'Alonzo RT: Fractures of the odontoid process of the axis. *J Bone Joint Surg Am* 1974;56(8):1663-1674.

25. Grauer JN, Shafi B, Hilibrand AS, et al: Proposal of a modified, treatment-oriented classification of odontoid fractures. *Spine J* 2005;5(2):123-129.

A classification was proposed for use in treatment decision making for type II dens fractures. Interobserver and intraobserver agreement was excellent in a review by four expert surgeons of 55 patients with a C2 fracture. Prospective evaluation of the usefulness of this system is required.

26. Isolated fractures of the axis in adults. *Neurosurgery* 2002;50(3, suppl):S125-S139.

27. Julien TD, Frankel B, Traynelis VC, Ryken TC: Evidence-based analysis of odontoid fracture management. *Neurosurg Focus* 2000;8(6):e1.

28. Nourbakhsh A, Shi R, Vannemreddy P, Nanda A: Operative versus nonoperative management of acute odontoid Type II fractures: A meta-analysis. *J Neurosurg Spine* 2009;11(6):651-658.

A meta-analysis compared surgical and nonsurgical treatment of odontoid fractures in 26 retrospective studies. The conclusions were limited by poor study quality and especially by nonstandard descriptions of radiologic outcomes and variable follow-up time points.

29. Koivikko MP, Kiuru MJ, Koskinen SK, Myllynen P, Santavirta S, Kivisaari L: Factors associated with nonunion in conservatively-treated type-II fractures of the odontoid process. *J Bone Joint Surg Br* 2004;86(8):1146-1151.

30. Jeanneret B, Vernet O, Frei S, Magerl F: Atlantoaxial mobility after screw fixation of the odontoid: A computed tomographic study. *J Spinal Disord* 1991;4(2):203-211.

31. Dailey AT, Hart D, Finn MA, Schmidt MH, Apfelbaum RI: Anterior fixation of odontoid fractures in an elderly population. *J Neurosurg Spine* 2010;12(1):1-8.

A retrospective study evaluated 57 patients older than 70 years with a type II odontoid fracture treated with odontoid screw. Bony healing was observed in 57%, fibrous union in 24%, and nonunion in 19% of patients. Patients treated with two screws had a significantly higher fusion rate than those treated with one screw.

32. Chapman J, Bransford R: Geriatric spine fractures: An emerging healthcare crisis. *J Trauma* 2007;62(6, suppl):S61-S62.

This review documents the emerging crisis of spine fractures in older adults, including osteoporotic fractures, type II odontoid fractures, and fractures in ankylosed spine. All of these fractures are associated with significant morbidity and mortality.

33. Kuntz C IV, Mirza SK, Jarell AD, Chapman JR, Shaffrey CI, Newell DW: Type II odontoid fractures in the elderly: Early failure of nonsurgical treatment. *Neurosurg Focus* 2000;8(6):e7.

34. Bednar DA, Parikh J, Hummel J: Management of type II odontoid process fractures in geriatric patients: A prospective study of sequential cohorts with attention to survivorship. *J Spinal Disord* 1995;8(2):166-169.

35. Effendi B, Roy D, Cornish B, Dussault RG, Laurin CA: Fractures of the ring of the axis: A classification based on the analysis of 131 cases. *J Bone Joint Surg Br* 1981;63(3):319-327.

36. Li XF, Dai LY, Lu H, Chen XD: A systematic review of the management of hangman's fractures. *Eur Spine J* 2006;15(3):257-269.

A systematic review of the effectiveness of hangman's fracture management found that the classification system of Effendi and Levine was adequate for directing treatment. Nonsurgical treatment was appropriate for most fractures, except for fractures with C2-C3 facet dislocation or those that were unstable despite nonsurgical treatment.

37. Chiba K, Fujimura Y, Toyama Y, Fujii E, Nakanishi T, Hirabayashi K: Treatment protocol for fractures of the odontoid process. *J Spinal Disord* 1996;9(4):267-276.

38. Fujimura Y, Nishi Y, Kobayashi K: Classification and treatment of axis body fractures. *J Orthop Trauma* 1996;10(8):536-540.

39. Cognetti DM, Enochs WS, Willcox TO: Retropharyngeal pseudomeningocele presenting as dysphagia after atlantooccipital dislocation. *Laryngoscope* 2006;116(9):1697-1699.

A rare incidence is described of retropharyngeal pseudomeningocele resulting in dysphagia associated with an atlanto-occipital dislocation. Because of persistent dysphagia, MRI was performed, revealing a large pseudomeningocele that was treated successfully with a lumbar-peritoneal shunt.

Chapter 20

Subaxial Cervical Spine Injuries

A. Jay Khanna, MD, MBA   Brian K. Kwon, MD, PhD, FRCSC

Introduction

Subaxial cervical spine injuries include fractures, dislocations, and ligamentous injuries between C3 and T1. Subaxial cervical spine injury most frequently occurs in young men in association with a motor vehicle crash, a fall from a height, or a sports injury. This injury also is likely to occur in patients who are elderly, particularly those with an underlying degenerative condition, spinal stenosis, or osteoporosis.

The protocols for clearance of the cervical spine in patients with blunt trauma were recently described.[1] Along with a careful history and physical examination, the evaluation of a patient with a known or suspected cervical spine injury begins with imaging. The imaging studies typically include conventional radiographs, CT, and MRI. Conventional radiography is widely and quickly available and therefore has been the first-used modality. However, conventional radiographic studies have low sensitivity, ranging from 52% to 85%.[1-3] Flexion-extension cervical spine radiographs occasionally are used to evaluate patients with suspected cervical spine instability, typically in a subacute setting, but they are not cost-effective or efficacious in the acute setting, especially given the risk associated with their acquisition.[1,4-7]

With the widespread availability of multidetector imaging, CT increasingly is accepted as a first-line imaging modality for patients with a known or suspected cervical spine injury. Only 0.7% of cervical, thoracic, and lumbar fractures in 3,537 patients were missed on CT, and these were fractures requiring minimal or no treatment.[8] The disadvantages of CT include the relatively high cost and radiation exposure.[9]

Dr. Khanna or an immediate family member serves as a board member, owner, officer, or committee member of the North American Spine Society and the American Academy of Orthopaedic Surgeons; is a member of a speakers' bureau or has made paid presentations on behalf of AO Spine North America; serves as a paid consultant to or is an employee of Orthofix, Inc.; has received research or institutional support from Zimmer and Orthofix, Inc; and owns stock or stock options in New Era Orthopaedics, LLC. Dr. Kwon or an immediate family member serves as a paid consultant to or is an employee of Medtronic Sofamor Danek and has received research or institutional support from Medtronic Sofamor Danek.

Although CT provides excellent anatomic detail and spatial resolution, MRI provides optimal visualization of soft-tissue structures, allowing identification of any ligamentous injury and the type and extent of a neural compression or spinal cord injury. The primary indication for MRI of the cervical spine after trauma is the presence of a neurologic deficit. MRI can effectively be used to evaluate compression of the neural elements by osseous fragments, disk material, or epidural hematomas. The excellent visualization of the spinal cord on MRI reveals the presence and extent of any cord signal changes. Ligamentous injury is best evaluated on short tau inversion recovery or fat-suppressed T2-weighted MRI.[10,11] MRI is most sensitive for detecting ligamentous injury within the first 24 to 72 hours after injury.[12-14]

Five level I studies enrolled a total of 464 patients with cervical spine trauma who were evaluated with MRI, CT, or conventional radiography. Meta-analysis found an overall sensitivity of 97.2%, an overall specificity of 98.5%, and a negative predictive value of 100%.[15] The incidence of abnormalities detected on MRI but not on conventional radiographs or CT was 20.9%. MRI and CT allow optimal evaluation of the occipitocervical and cervicothoracic junctions, which are not well visualized on conventional radiographs.

It is important to keep in mind that MRI cannot always be obtained in the acute trauma setting because of specific limitations relating to the treatment of patients with severe multisystem trauma, such as potential hemodynamic instability; the presence of traction, other stabilizing devices, and ventilators; difficulty of access to an unstable patient during imaging studies; and lack of 24-hour MRI availability.

Classification

Allen-Ferguson Classification

The Allen-Ferguson classification originally was described in 1982 based on static radiographs of 165 patients.[16] The categories of fractures refer to the postulated position of the spine at the time of injury and the presumed dominant mechanism of spine failure: compressive flexion, vertical compression, distractive flexion, compressive extension, distractive extension, or lateral flexion. Each category is subclassified into stages based on the extent of anatomic disruption.

3: Spine Trauma

Table 1

The Subaxial Cervical Spine Injury Classification Scale

Category	Points
Injury morphology	
No abnormality	0
Compression	1
Burst	+1 = 2
Distraction (eg, facet perch, hyperextension)	3
Translation or rotation (eg, facet dislocation, unstable teardrop, or advanced staged flexion-compression injury)	4
Diskoligamentous complex integrity	
Intact	0
Indeterminate (eg, isolated interspinous widening, MRI signal change only)	1
Disrupted (eg, widening of disk space, facet perch, or dislocation)	2
Neurologic impairment	
Intact	0
Root injury	1
Complete cord injury	2
Incomplete cord injury	3
Continuous cord compression in setting of neurologic deficit (neuromodifier)	+1

Reproduced with permission from Vaccaro AR, Hulbert RJ, Patel AA, et al: The subaxial cervical spine injury classification system: A novel approach to recognize the importance of morphology, neurology, and integrity of the disco-ligamentous complex. *Spine (Phila Pa 1976)* 2007;32:2365-2374.

Subaxial Spine Injury Classification

The recently described Subaxial Spine Injury Classification (known as the SLIC) is based on an assessment of three major injury characteristics that are critical to clinical decision making: injury morphology or major pattern of injury; the integrity of the diskoligamentous complex (DLC), comprising the soft tissues of the motion segment; and the patient's neurologic status.[17] Subgroups are identified and graded within each category (Table 1).

Conventional radiography, CT, and MRI are used to classify the injury morphology as compression, distraction, or translation-rotation. The integrity of the DLC can be evaluated on the same imaging studies; T2-weighted and fat-suppressed T2-weighted MRI may show increased signal along the course of ligamentous structures, suggesting the presence of edema[18] (Figure 1). The SLIC scale is used to assign numeric values based on injury morphology, DLC integrity, and neurologic compromise. A patient with a relatively high score is more likely to require a surgical procedure than a patient with a low score. An evidence-based algorithm has been proposed based on the SLIC to guide decision making regarding surgical intervention as well as the type of surgical approach.[19]

The SLIC was found to be both reliable and valid. Interrater agreement, as evaluated by the intraclass correlation coefficient of the morphology, DLC, and neurologic status categories, was 0.66, 0.75, and 0.90, respectively, which compares favorably with that of the Allen-Ferguson system.[17] The raters agreed with the treatment recommendation of the algorithm in 93.3% of the cases, suggesting high validity.[17]

Instability After Cervical Spine Trauma

Clinical instability of the spine has been defined as the inability of the spine to maintain a normal relationship between vertebral segments under physiologic loads, with possible subsequent deformity, pain, or neurologic deficit.[20,21] Instability can be caused by injury to the osseous and/or ligamentous structures that provide stability to the subaxial cervical spine. Checklist point systems for the cervical, thoracic, and lumbar spines have been developed using anatomic, biomechanical, and clinical considerations to help determine the presence and extent of spine instability.[21,22] The checklist for the diagnosis of clinical instability in the middle and lower cervical spine includes evaluation of the anterior and posterior elements, neurologic findings, radiographic translation of more than 3.5 mm or 20%, relative sagittal plane angulation of more than 11° on static radiographs, congenital stenosis, and other factors.[21,22] The SLIC emphasizes the importance of the posterior capsuloligamentous structures, which provide the spine with the ability to resist kyphosis. The SLIC fracture morphology and neurologic status categories describe the two other essential factors in evaluating the instability of the injured cervical spine.

Treatment

The goals of surgical intervention for a patient with subaxial cervical spine injury are to relieve any spinal canal or foraminal neural compression and to provide long-term mechanical stability to the injured motion segment. Many authors have published guidelines based on experience and literature review to help spine surgeons decide between surgical and nonsurgical treatment.[17,19,23,24] Although algorithms and guidelines can help the surgeon select the optimal treatment of the fracture, the optimal treatment of an individual patient also requires consideration of factors such as medical comorbidities, concomitant injuries, and patient preference.

Flexion-Compression Injuries

A flexion-compression injury results from axial loading of the cervical spine in combination with a flexion mo-

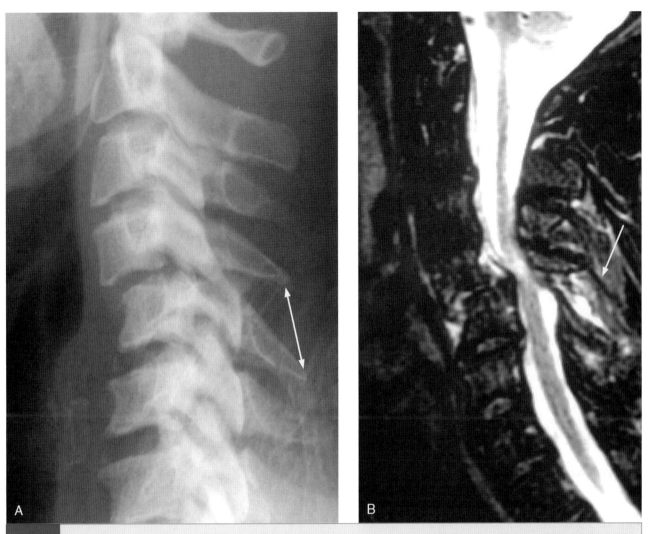

Figure 1 A DLC injury. **A,** Lateral radiograph showing bilateral facet subluxation at C4-C5, with widening of the interspinous process space *(between arrowheads)*. **B,** Sagittal short tau inversion recovery MRI showing edema in the region of the interspinous and supraspinous ligaments between C4 and C5 *(arrow)*, which is compatible with a DLC injury.

ment. These injuries range from a relatively stable minor compression fracture of the anterosuperior end plate to a highly unstable flexion teardrop or quadrangular fracture with associated dislocation and disruption of the DLC. A patient with an end plate compression fracture typically is neurologically intact. Usually there is no involvement of the middle column (the posterior vertebral body). These patients typically are treated using a rigid cervical orthosis. An end plate compression fracture typically has an SLIC morphology score of 1 or 2 and a DLC score of 0. In a patient with an end plate compression fracture and a neurologic injury, the examiner should suspect an acute disk herniation or a gross disruption through the DLC that has allowed substantial spinal displacement followed by reduction back to near-anatomic alignment. In either case, the presence of neurologic compromise in the setting of such a morphologic injury should prompt further investigation using MRI. If substantial neural compression from a disk protrusion or extrusion is found,

an anterior decompression and stabilization procedure can be considered.

Flexion teardrop fracture results from severe flexion forces that lead to a triangular fracture from the anterior aspect of the rostral vertebral body, with or without associated retrolisthesis of the vertebral body into the spinal canal.[10,25] A quadrangular fracture is differentiated from a flexion teardrop fracture in that a larger fragment of the anterior vertebral body is fractured, with a greater likelihood of associated circumferential soft-tissue injury, kyphosis, and retrolisthesis (Figure 2). A teardrop or quadrangular fracture typically occurs in conjunction with a sagittal split of the vertebral body posterior to the teardrop or quadrangular fragment. A teardrop or quadrangular fracture often is associated with incomplete or complete neurologic injuries and advanced injury to the osseous structures and DLC; surgical intervention is almost always indicated. Anterior neural decompression in the form of corpectomy, followed by reconstruction with bone

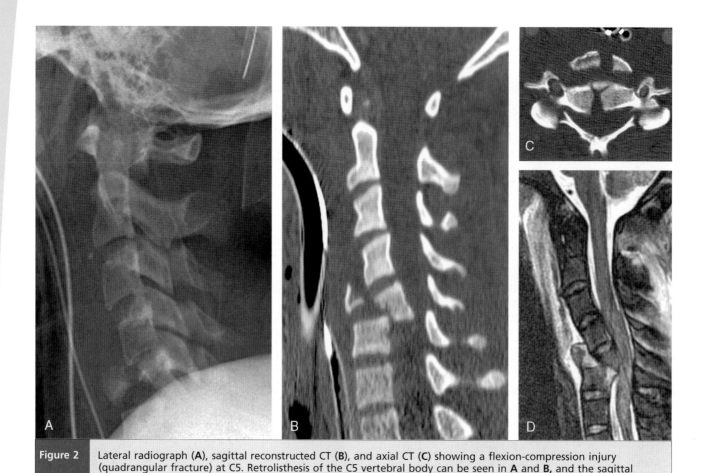

Figure 2 Lateral radiograph (**A**), sagittal reconstructed CT (**B**), and axial CT (**C**) showing a flexion-compression injury (quadrangular fracture) at C5. Retrolisthesis of the C5 vertebral body can be seen in **A** and **B**, and the sagittal plane fracture can be seen in **C**. Sagittal T2-weighted MRI showing similar features (**D**) as well as associated spinal cord compression and prevertebral edema.

graft as well as static plating and posterior-instrumented arthrodesis, is required for most of these injuries.[19,26,27]

Burst Fractures

Cervical burst fractures result from pure axial loading of the spine, with fracture of the vertebral body (including the posterior aspect), and retropulsion of osseous fragments into the spinal canal[10] (Figure 3). True burst fractures are rare in the cervical spine and tend to occur in the lower cervical and cervicothoracic region. Although burst fractures technically result from a pure axial load, they typically occur in association with a component of flexion; therefore, there may be injury to the posterior ligamentous complex. Sagittal and axial MRI allows evaluation of the presence and extent of spinal cord and nerve root compression. The MRI studies should be carefully inspected for the absence, presence, and extent of injury to the DLC. Axial and reconstructed CT provide optimal osseous detail, including the fracture pattern and configuration.

The optimal treatment of cervical burst fractures is anterior corpectomy, decompression, reconstruction, and plating.[19,27-30] Posterior-instrumented arthrodesis can be considered for patients who do not need anterior decompression of the spinal cord.[28] The other

treatment option is nonsurgical intervention with traction and halo or other bracing. A retrospective review of 69 patients with a cervical burst or teardrop fracture found that the 35 patients treated with anterior decompression and fusion had markedly better overall sagittal alignment and neurologic recovery than the 34 patients treated nonsurgically with skull traction or a halo vest.[29] In patients with substantial concomitant injury to the DLC, posterior-instrumented fusion should be considered after the anterior reconstruction. Nonsurgical treatment always should be considered if the patient has a medical comorbidity or other factor that may decrease the chance of a good outcome with surgical intervention.

Flexion-Distraction Injuries

Flexion-distraction forces can cause a spectrum of osteoligamentous abnormalities including capsular strain, facet subluxation, perched facet, unilateral or bilateral facet dislocation, and fracture. In the Allen-Ferguson classification, flexion-distraction injuries are differentiated into four categories of increasing severity: facet subluxation, unilateral facet dislocation, bilateral facet dislocation with 50% displacement, and complete dislocation.[10,16] In the SLIC, these injuries may be classi-

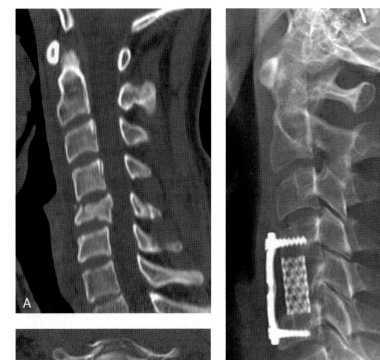

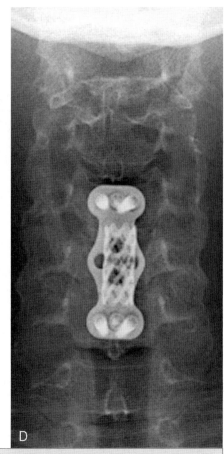

Figure 3 **A,** Sagittal reconstructed CT showing a burst fracture of the C5 vertebral body, with minimal retropulsion of the posterosuperior aspect of the vertebral body into the spinal canal. **B,** Axial CT showing fracture of the posterior wall of the vertebral body. Lateral (**C**) and AP (**D**) radiographs after a corpectomy of C5 and anterior reconstruction and fusion with a titanium mesh cage and plate.

fied as purely distractive in nature or as distractive with a flexion component: unilateral facet subluxation or bilateral perched facets receive a morphology score of 3, and bilateral or unilateral facet dislocation receives a score of 4 (because a rotational component is present). Both types receive a DLC score of 2. The neurologic impairment score can vary from 0 to 4. Almost all high-grade flexion-distraction injuries require surgical intervention. CT and MRI are essential for completely evaluating a cervical flexion-distraction injury. CT provides excellent osseous detail, particularly if the patient is obese or the lower cervical spine radiographs are suboptimal. CT allows evaluation of the relative position of the facet joints; differentiates subluxation from fully dislocated or locked facets; and facilitates the detection of associated fractures of the lamina, lateral mass, or pedicles. MRI allows optimal evaluation of the soft tissues, including the DLC. Disruption of the supraspinous and intraspinous ligaments and the facet capsules frequently can be detected on MRI. MRI also allows the extent of spinal stenosis to be assessed.[31]

The role of closed reduction for patients with facet subluxation or dislocation has been debated over the years because there is a small but potentially cata-strophic risk of displacing a herniated disk posteriorly into the spinal cord and causing iatrogenic cord injury.[19,31-33] This topic remains controversial, with varying opinions and only weak consensus.[34] In a neurologically intact patient with a facet dislocation, there is little to be gained by performing a closed reduction without first using MRI to confirm the absence of a disk herniation. However, in a neurologically impaired patient who can be reliably examined, a closed reduction with careful clinical monitoring of neurologic status during the procedure is considered by many to be safe. In a patient with complete quadriplegia and residual compression because of the spinal malalignment, there is little to be lost by reducing the dislocation, realigning the spine, and indirectly decompressing the cord as soon as possible, without waiting for MRI.

If the patient has an incomplete neurologic injury, the risk of displacing a disk fragment into the cord during a closed reduction must be weighed against the potential benefit of quickly relieving compression on the cord by realigning the spinal canal. Unfortunately, there are no guidelines to definitively direct treatment in this circumstance. Weighing in favor of proceeding with an expeditious closed reduction are small case studies that

3: Spine Trauma

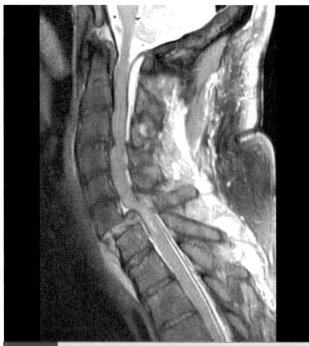

Figure 4 Sagittal T2-weighted MRI showing a large disk protrusion in a patient who sustained bilateral facet dislocations with a herniated nucleus pulposus at C6-7.

A closed reduction in a conscious patient requires adequate analgesia, sedation, and supervision of respiratory function. Radiographic imaging must be available for visualizing the injury. Traction for the weight of the head usually is applied as 10 to 15 lb, with an additional 5 to 10 lb for each level below C1.[10] Substantially heavier weights (up to 140 lb) have been described, however.[37] A component of cervical spine flexion helps to disengage the facets and facilitate reduction.

If the patient has neurologic deterioration during a closed reduction or if prereduction MRI reveals a disk herniation that is displaced into the spinal canal (Figure 4), an anterior cervical decompression with an attempt at open reduction, fusion, and plating is indicated.[19,38-40] If open reduction cannot be accomplished after the diskectomy, the surgeon should proceed with a posterior open reduction by applying distraction through the spinous processes and partially resecting the superior facets, if needed. The procedure concludes with a posterior instrumented fusion and, finally, an anterior reconstruction and plating.[10,19,41]

If there is no evidence of a substantial-size disk herniation or a free disk fragment in the canal, either an anterior or posterior reduction of the dislocation is a valid option. In a prospective randomized controlled study of 42 patients, anterior and posterior stabilization of unilateral facet injury were both found to be valid treatment options.[42] A similar study of 52 patients with unstable cervical spine injury and associated spinal cord injury also found no significant differences between the two approaches.[28]

Extension Injuries

The three distinct types of extension injuries are based on whether the cervical spine is mobile, ankylosed, or spondylotic and stenotic. If the cervical spine is mobile, extension-compression injury may be manifested by multiple spinous process fractures without substantial disruption of the anterior longitudinal ligament. T2-weighted or fat-suppressed MRI often shows high signal in the posterior ligamentous complex, but this finding is a result of compressive failure of the spinous processes and bleeding rather than tensile disruption of the ligaments. Because the spine is loaded in compression, the anterior longitudinal ligaments theoretically should be intact. More commonly, the extension is accompanied by distractive forces to the anterior column. The anterior disk space and anterior longitudinal ligament fail in tension, as manifested by subtle radiographic signs such as edema in the anterior soft tissues and small avulsion fractures off the anteroinferior end plate (Figure 5). In a more extreme injury, the disk can be totally disrupted, with acute lordosis across the interspace (Figure 6).

Distraction-extension injury also commonly occurs in association with an ankylosing condition of the spine, such as ankylosing spondylitis or diffuse idiopathic skeletal hyperostosis (DISH). In ankylosing

found a closed reduction to be safe, even when a disk herniation is known to exist.[35,36] Conversely, a patient with an incomplete spinal cord injury (in contrast with a patient who is neurologically intact) is more likely to have a disk fragment trapped behind the body of the dislocated vertebra. A trapped disk fragment is particularly likely if the disk space appears collapsed on radiographic images; the implication is that the disk material not present between the two vertebral end plates must be somewhere else. The surgeon must make the decision to proceed with one of three treatment options: immediate closed reduction, if the patient is neurologically examinable or is neurologically impaired but might benefit from expeditious indirect decompression; MRI to determine whether the patient has a disk herniation, followed by closed reduction or surgical intervention; or immediate anterior cervical diskectomy and fusion, under the premise that any disk herniation would be treated with this procedure. Because there is no standard protocol, the decision-making process must include consideration of the resources available at the surgeon's institution. For example, MRI can require more time than simply bringing the patient to the operating room and performing an anterior diskectomy and fusion; closed reduction in the emergency department is particularly hazardous for the patient unless the necessary staff is available to manage analgesia, sedation, and oxygenation; and it might not be possible to obtain timely access to an operating room.

3: Spine Trauma

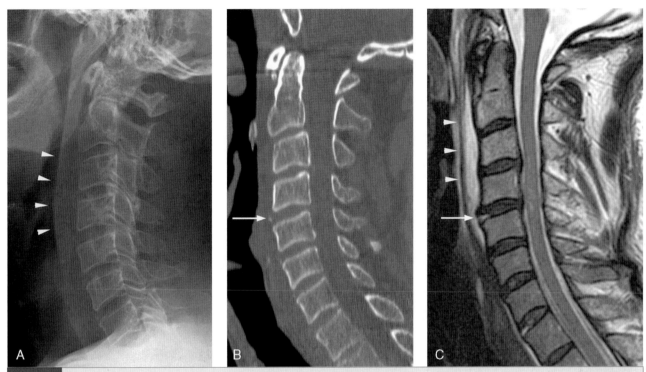

Figure 5 Extension-distraction injury with incomplete spinal cord injury in a 35-year-old man who was injured in a fall from a scaffold, with forcible extension of the neck. **A,** Lateral radiograph showing substantial edema in the anterior soft tissues *(arrowheads)*. **B,** Sagittal reconstructed CT showing avulsion from the C4 inferior end plate *(arrow)*. **C,** Sagittal T2-weighted MRI showing the acute tensile failure of the C4-5 disk, with bright signal within the disk *(arrow)*; anterior soft-tissue edema also is visible *(arrowheads)*. The patient was treated nonsurgically because of the absence of severe instability or cord compression.

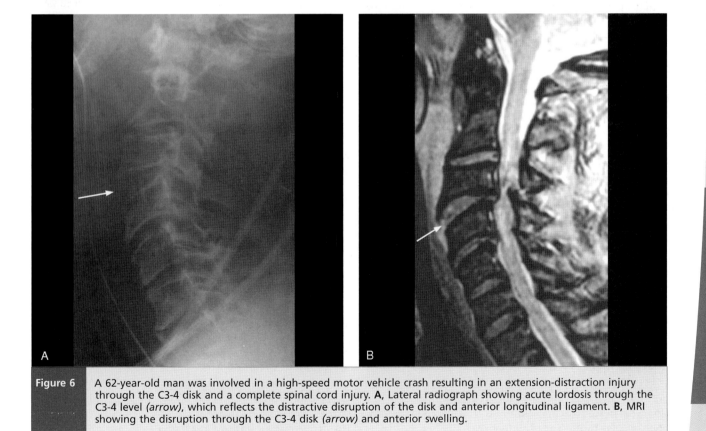

Figure 6 A 62-year-old man was involved in a high-speed motor vehicle crash resulting in an extension-distraction injury through the C3-4 disk and a complete spinal cord injury. **A,** Lateral radiograph showing acute lordosis through the C3-4 level *(arrow)*, which reflects the distractive disruption of the disk and anterior longitudinal ligament. **B,** MRI showing the disruption through the C3-4 disk *(arrow)* and anterior swelling.

3: Spine Trauma

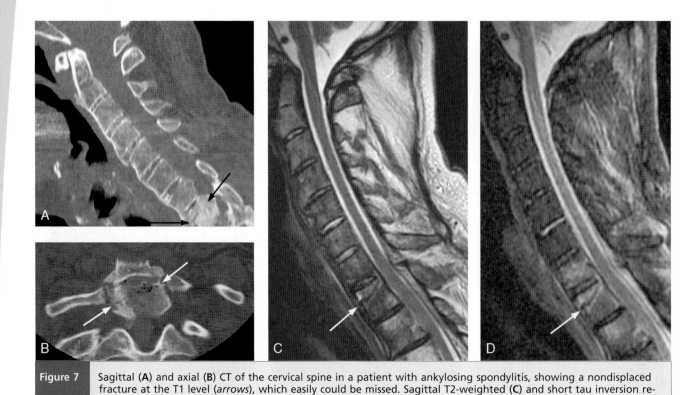

Figure 7   Sagittal (**A**) and axial (**B**) CT of the cervical spine in a patient with ankylosing spondylitis, showing a nondisplaced fracture at the T1 level (*arrows*), which easily could be missed. Sagittal T2-weighted (**C**) and short tau inversion recovery MRI (**D**) showing the same fracture (*arrows*). In **D**, edema at the fracture site indicates a relatively acute injury.

spondylitis, the stabilizing ligaments of the spine, including the anterior and posterior longitudinal ligaments, are ossified. Despite minimal displacement, the fracture can lead to substantial structural instability. A common and yet potentially catastrophic mistake is to miss a subtle fracture in a patient with ankylosing spondylitis who has neck pain after a low-energy injury; or to fail to detect a small fracture line in the anterior column, erroneously concluding that the spine is stable because the posterior elements are intact. The spine is like a long bone in a patient with an ankylosing spondylitis fracture; therefore, an obligatory fracture must exist through the posterior elements, although sometimes it is detectable only with CT or MRI[42] (Figure 7). Errors in diagnosing these fractures or misinterpreting their instability can have devastating neurologic consequences. Historically, these fractures have been treated nonsurgically with a halo vest, but complications are associated with the application of these orthoses. More recently, treatment has been with anterior, posterior, or circumferential fusion.[42-44] A recent study evaluated 122 spine fractures in 112 patients with an ankylosing spine disorder (primarily ankylosing spondylitis or DISH) and suggested that multilevel posterior segmental instrumentation (typically three levels above and below the injury) allows effective fracture stabilization and healing.[45]

Extension-distraction injury can occur in patients with DISH. The posterior elements typically are not ossified, as in ankylosing spondylitis. However, the segments above and below the injury may be fused, impos-

ing major lever-arm stresses on the injury site and making it quite unstable (Figure 8).

Hyperextension injuries commonly occur in patients who are elderly. Although many such low-energy injuries are not accompanied by substantial disruption of the spinal column, preexisting spinal stenosis related to chronic degenerative changes places the spinal cord at risk as the posterior lamina kinks the cord. The patient may have tripped and fallen forward, striking the head and sustaining quadriplegia without an unstable spinal column injury.

The timing of surgical intervention has been discussed for patients with chronic spondylosis who sustain a cervical spinal cord injury related to hyperextension; however, there appear to be no prospective randomized studies.[19,46-51] Consensus also is lacking as to the timing of decompressive surgery for patients with a central cord pattern of incomplete quadriplegia and a stable cervical spine. Many patients who are disproportionately impaired in the upper extremity achieve substantial motor recovery regardless of the timing of decompression, although their ultimate functioning often is limited by pain and spasticity.[47] When the decision is made to proceed with surgery, the number of spine levels involved and the overall alignment of the cervical spine help determine whether an anterior or posterior approach is preferable.[19,52] For a patient with multilevel stenosis and lordotic alignment, most surgeons prefer to proceed with a posterior-approach laminectomy and fusion or laminoplasty.[53] For a pa-

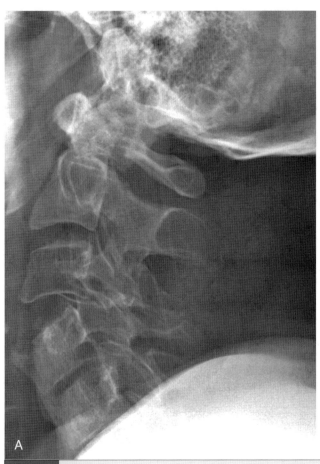
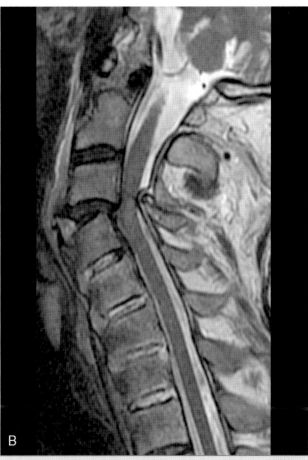

Figure 8 The patient sustained an extension-distraction injury through the C3-4 disk space. **A,** Lateral radiograph suggesting DISH ossification of the spinal column anteriorly at C3-C6. **B,** MRI showing that the fracture ruptured the bridging osteophyte at the C3-4 disk.

tient with a neutral spine or only mild kyphosis, lordosis can be obtained after laminectomy via intraoperative positioning and maintained with posterior fixation and fusion.[19] For a patient with focal or severe kyphosis or a patient with anterior compression from disk herniations or spondylosis at one or two levels, the preferred procedure is an anterior approach with diskectomies or corpectomies and anterior reconstruction and plate fixation.[19]

Summary

A subaxial cervical spine injury occurs after high- or low-energy trauma to the cervical spine, leading to fracture, dislocation, and ligamentous injury between C3 and T1. A patient with such an injury must be treated expeditiously and carefully, with stabilization and protection of the cervical spine. A careful history and physical examination are necessary. Conventional and advanced imaging techniques allow excellent visualization of the injury and classification using the Allen-Ferguson or SLIC system. Recognition of the spectrum of injury within each category helps the spine

surgeon avoid missing an injury. The selection of nonsurgical or surgical treatment is based on the goals of providing mechanical stability to the spinal column and neurologic stability or decompression of the associated neural elements. When surgical intervention is selected, an anterior, posterior, or combined approach can be used. The decision is based on the type of injury and the neurologic status of the patient. Published guidelines are useful, but selecting the optimal treatment for the fracture also requires considering patient-related factors including medical comorbidities, concomitant injuries, and patient preference.

Annotated References

1. Anderson PA, Gugala Z, Lindsey RW, Schoenfeld AJ, Harris MB: Clearing the cervical spine in the blunt trauma patient. *J Am Acad Orthop Surg* 2010;18(3): 149-159.

    The Advanced Trauma Life Support protocol for initial assessment of the cervical spine trauma patient is reviewed. Patients with blunt cervical spine trauma are classified as asymptomatic, temporarily unassessable, symptomatic, or obtunded. Evaluation algorithms are provided for the four groups. Level of evidence: V.

2. Gale SC, Gracias VH, Reilly PM, Schwab CW: The inefficiency of plain radiography to evaluate the cervical spine after blunt trauma. *J Trauma* 2005;59(5):1121-1125.

Retrospective review of the radiographic evaluation of 848 patients with blunt trauma, most of whom underwent conventional radiography and CT of the cervical spine, concluded that conventional radiographs are inadequate to fully evaluate the cervical spine. Supplemental CT is commonly required. Level of evidence: IV.

3. Holmes JF, Akkinepalli R: Computed tomography versus plain radiography to screen for cervical spine injury: A meta-analysis. *J Trauma* 2005;58(5):902-905.

A meta-analysis of seven studies that met multiple inclusion criteria concluded there is ample evidence that CT is significantly better than conventional radiography for evaluating patients at high risk for cervical spine injury. Level of evidence: III.

4. Anglen J, Metzler M, Bunn P, Griffiths H: Flexion and extension views are not cost-effective in a cervical spine clearance protocol for obtunded trauma patients. *J Trauma* 2002;52(1):54-59.

5. Hadley MN, Walters BC, Grabb PA, et al: Radiographic assessment of the cervical spine in symptomatic trauma patients. *Neurosurgery* 2002;50(3, suppl):S36-S43.

6. Knopp R, Parker J, Tashjian J, Ganz W: Defining radiographic criteria for flexion-extension studies of the cervical spine. *Ann Emerg Med* 2001;38(1):31-35.

7. Pollack CV Jr, Hendey GW, Martin DR, et al: Use of flexion-extension radiographs of the cervical spine in blunt trauma. *Ann Emerg Med* 2001;38(1):8-11.

8. Brown CV, Antevil JL, Sise MJ, Sack DI: Spiral computed tomography for the diagnosis of cervical, thoracic, and lumbar spine fractures: Its time has come. *J Trauma* 2005;58(5):890-896.

Retrospective review of spiral CT of the spine in 3,537 patients with blunt trauma found that this imaging modality detected 99.3% of all fractures. Level of evidence: IV.

9. Brenner DJ, Hall EJ: Computed tomography: An increasing source of radiation exposure. *N Engl J Med* 2007;357(22):2277-2284.

The radiation doses, mechanism of biologic damage, and cancer risks associated with CT are comprehensively reviewed. Level of evidence: V.

10. Kwon BK, Vaccaro AR, Grauer JN, Fisher CG, Dvorak MF: Subaxial cervical spine trauma. *J Am Acad Orthop Surg* 2006;14(2):78-89.

The epidemiology, anatomy, biomechanics, and classification of common but often missed subaxial cervical spine injuries are described, with treatment methods and possible complications.

11. Zebala LP, Buchowski JM, Daftary AR, O'Brien JR, Carrino JA, Khanna AJ: The cervical spine, in Khanna AJ, ed: *MRI for Orthopaedic Surgeons*. New York, NY, Thieme, 2010, pp 229-268.

Standard MRI of the cervical spine for degenerative pathologies usually includes sagittal T1-weighted spin-echo, sagittal T2-weighted fast spin-echo, axial gradient-echo, and axial T2-weighted fast spin-echo. These images help visualize fracture lines, edema, hemorrhage, and extent of cord compression, respectively.

12. D'Alise MD, Benzel EC, Hart BL: Magnetic resonance imaging evaluation of the cervical spine in the comatose or obtunded trauma patient. *J Neurosurg* 1999;91(1, suppl):54-59.

13. Mirvis SE: Use of MRI in acute spinal trauma, in Uhlenbrock D, ed: *MR Imaging of the Spine and Spinal Cord*. New York, NY, Thieme, 2004, pp 437-465.

14. Stassen NA, Williams VA, Gestring ML, Cheng JD, Bankey PE: Magnetic resonance imaging in combination with helical computed tomography provides a safe and efficient method of cervical spine clearance in the obtunded trauma patient. *J Trauma* 2006;60(1):171-177.

A new cervical spine clearance guideline to assess obtunded patients with blunt trauma is evaluated. Cervical spine CT, when used in combination with MRI, provides a safe and efficient method for cervical spine clearance in these patients. Level of evidence: II.

15. Muchow RD, Resnick DK, Abdel MP, Munoz A, Anderson PA: Magnetic resonance imaging (MRI) in the clearance of the cervical spine in blunt trauma: A meta-analysis. *J Trauma* 2008;64(1):179-189.

MRI showed that 97 (20.9%) of 464 patients with blunt trauma had cervical spine abnormalities unidentified by radiographs and/or CT. MRI is the gold standard for clearing the cervical spine in a patient with blunt trauma who is clinically suspicious or unevaluable.

16. Allen BL Jr , Ferguson RL, Lehmann TR, O'Brien RP: A mechanistic classification of closed, indirect fractures and dislocations of the lower cervical spine. *Spine (Phila Pa 1976)* 1982;7(1):1-27.

17. Vaccaro AR, Hulbert RJ, Patel AA, et al: The subaxial cervical spine injury classification system: A novel approach to recognize the importance of morphology, neurology, and integrity of the disco-ligamentous complex. *Spine (Phila Pa 1976)* 2007;32(21):2365-2374.

A multicenter study using a literature review and expert opinion was the basis of a comprehensive classification system for subaxial cervical spine trauma. The SLIC conveys information about injury pattern, severity, treatment considerations, and prognosis. The reliability and validity of the scale was assessed. Level of evidence: III.

18. Takhtani D, Melhem ER: MR imaging in cervical spine trauma. *Magn Reson Imaging Clin N Am* 2000;8(3):615-634.

19. Dvorak MF, Fisher CG, Fehlings MG, et al: The surgical approach to subaxial cervical spine injuries: An evidence-based algorithm based on the SLIC classification system. *Spine (Phila Pa 1976)* 2007;32(23):2620-2629.

Using a literature review and expert opinion, the authors designed a treatment algorithm for subaxial cervical spine trauma based on the SLIC. The algorithm is designed to answer the most common questions in managing subaxial cervical spine trauma: Should the patient be treated surgically? If so, by which approach? Level of evidence: III.

20. White AA, Southwick WO, Panjabi MM: Clinical instability in the lower cervical spine: A review of past and current concepts. *Spine (Phila Pa 1976)* 1976;1:15-27.

21. White AA III, Panjabi MM: *Clinical Biomechanics of the Spine.* Philadelphia, PA, Lippincott Williams & Wilkins, 1990.

22. White AA III, Panjabi MM: Update on the evaluation of instability of the lower cervical spine. *Instr Course Lect* 1987;36:513-520.

23. Anderson PA, Moore TA, Davis KW, et al: Cervical spine injury severity score: Assessment of reliability. *J Bone Joint Surg Am* 2007;89(5):1057-1065.

The authors developed a method of quantifying the stability of subaxial cervical spine injuries and found the SLIC to have excellent intraobserver and interobserver reliability. Quantifying stability on the basis of fracture morphology would allow surgeons to better characterize the injuries. Level of evidence: II.

24. Glaser JA, Jaworski BA, Cuddy BG, et al: Variation in surgical opinion regarding management of selected cervical spine injuries: A preliminary study. *Spine (Phila Pa 1976)* 1998;23(9):975-983.

25. Ianuzzi A, Zambrano I, Tataria J, et al: Biomechanical evaluation of surgical constructs for stabilization of cervical teardrop fractures. *Spine J* 2006;6(5):514-523.

This biomechanical study of cervical flexion teardrop fracture fixation found that all five tested constructs (one or two levels; anterior, posterior, or combined approach) restored stability.

26. Cybulski GR, Douglas RA, Meyer PR Jr, Rovin RA: Complications in three-column cervical spine injuries requiring anterior-posterior stabilization. *Spine (Phila Pa 1976)* 1992;17(3):253-256.

27. Toh E, Nomura T, Watanabe M, Mochida J: Surgical treatment for injuries of the middle and lower cervical spine. *Int Orthop* 2006;30(1):54-58.

Retrospective review of the anatomic and neurologic outcomes of patients with a burst or teardrop dislocation fracture in the middle or lower cervical spine found that anterior decompression and fusion better restored spinal canal diameter and neurologic function than a posterior or combined approach. Level of evidence: III.

28. Brodke DS, Anderson PA, Newell DW, Grady MS, Chapman JR: Comparison of anterior and posterior approaches in cervical spinal cord injuries. *J Spinal Disord Tech* 2003;16(3):229-235.

29. Koivikko MP, Myllynen P, Karjalainen M, Vornanen M, Santavirta S: Conservative and operative treatment in cervical burst fractures. *Arch Orthop Trauma Surg* 2000;120(7-8):448-451.

30. Ripa DR, Kowall MG, Meyer PR Jr, Rusin JJ: Series of ninety-two traumatic cervical spine injuries stabilized with anterior ASIF plate fusion technique. *Spine (Phila Pa 1976)* 1991;16(3, suppl):S46-S55.

31. Vaccaro AR, Madigan L, Schweitzer ME, Flanders AE, Hilibrand AS, Albert TJ: Magnetic resonance imaging analysis of soft tissue disruption after flexion-distraction injuries of the subaxial cervical spine. *Spine (Phila Pa 1976)* 2001;26(17):1866-1872.

32. Hart RA: Cervical facet dislocation: When is magnetic resonance imaging indicated? *Spine (Phila Pa 1976)* 2002;27(1):116-117.

33. Lee JY, Nassr A, Eck JC, Vaccaro AR: Controversies in the treatment of cervical spine dislocations. *Spine J* 2009;9(5):418-423.

The literature on cervical spine dislocation is reviewed. The major controversies are choice of imaging, closed or open reduction, and surgical approach. Evidence-based management guidelines are provided.

34. Grauer JN, Vaccaro AR, Lee JY, et al: The timing and influence of MRI on the management of patients with cervical facet dislocations remains highly variable: A survey of members of the Spine Trauma Study Group. *J Spinal Disord Tech* 2009;22(2):96-99.

Twenty-five spine surgeons were asked to decide whether closed or open reduction was preferable for cervical facet dislocation in the same 10 patients, both with and without the use of MRI. The authors found that the timing and use of MRI for patients with these injuries remains variable.

35. Darsaut TE, Ashforth R, Bhargava R, et al: A pilot study of magnetic resonance imaging-guided closed reduction of cervical spine fractures. *Spine (Phila Pa 1976)* 2006;31(18):2085-2090.

Seventeen patients with fracture-dislocation of the subaxial cervical spine underwent traction with MRI guidance. All patients tolerated the traction without neurologic worsening, and canal dimensions improved in 11 patients. The closed reduction appeared to be safe and effective in achieving immediate spinal cord decompression. Level of evidence: IV.

36. Vaccaro AR, Falatyn SP, Flanders AE, Balderston RA, Northrup BE, Cotler JM: Magnetic resonance evaluation of the intervertebral disc, spinal ligaments, and spinal cord before and after closed traction reduction of cervical spine dislocations. *Spine (Phila Pa 1976)* 1999; 24(12):1210-1217.

37. Cotler JM, Herbison GJ, Nasuti JF, Ditunno JF Jr, An H, Wolff BE: Closed reduction of traumatic cervical spine dislocation using traction weights up to 140 pounds. *Spine (Phila Pa 1976)* 1993;18(3):386-390.

38. Aebi M, Zuber K, Marchesi D: Treatment of cervical spine injuries with anterior plating: Indications, techniques, and results. *Spine (Phila Pa 1976)* 1991;16(3, suppl):S38-S45.

39. Goffin J, Plets C, Van den Bergh R: Anterior cervical fusion and osteosynthetic stabilization according to Caspar: A prospective study of 41 patients with fractures and/or dislocations of the cervical spine. *Neurosurgery* 1989;25(6):865-871.

40. Razack N, Green BA, Levi AD: The management of traumatic cervical bilateral facet fracture-dislocations with unicortical anterior plates. *J Spinal Disord* 2000; 13(5):374-381.

41. Payer M: Immediate open anterior reduction and antero-posterior fixation/fusion for bilateral cervical locked facets. *Acta Neurochir (Wien)* 2005;147(5):509-514.

    In patients with traumatic bilateral cervical locked facets, immediate open anterior reduction and circumferential fixation-fusion was safe and reliable, avoided time loss and patient discomfort from attempted closed reduction, obviated the need for external immobilization, and resulted in an excellent fusion rate. Level of evidence: IV.

42. Kwon BK, Fisher CG, Boyd MC, et al: A prospective randomized controlled trial of anterior compared with posterior stabilization for unilateral facet injuries of the cervical spine. *J Neurosurg Spine* 2007;7(1):1-12.

    A prospective randomized controlled study compared the postoperative outcomes of patients with unilateral facet injury who were treated with anterior cervical diskectomy and fusion or with posterior fixation. Both methods were found to be valid, with no statistical difference in primary outcome measure and variable secondary outcome measures. Level of evidence: I.

43. Westerveld LA, Verlaan JJ, Oner FC: Spinal fractures in patients with ankylosing spinal disorders: A systematic review of the literature on treatment, neurological status and complications. *Eur Spine J* 2009;18(2):145-156.

    The literature was reviewed on the treatment, neurologic status, and complications of patients with a preexisting ankylosed spine who sustained spine trauma. The clinical outcomes of patients with fracture from ankylosing spondylitis or advanced diffuse idiopathic skeletal hyperostosis were considerably worse than those of the general trauma population.

44. Whang PG, Goldberg G, Lawrence JP, et al: The management of spinal injuries in patients with ankylosing spondylitis or diffuse idiopathic skeletal hyperostosis: A comparison of treatment methods and clinical outcomes. *J Spinal Disord Tech* 2009;22(2):77-85.

    Retrospective review of treatment methods for spine in-jury in patients with ankylosing spondylitis or diffuse idiopathic skeletal hyperostosis found that the rate of neurologic injury was high for both groups, but that patients in the former group were more likely to have neurologic deficit and undergo surgery. Stable fractures without neurologic deficit often were successfully managed with immobilization. Level of evidence: III.

45. Caron T, Bransford R, Nguyen Q, Agel J, Chapman J, Bellabarba C: Spine fractures in patients with ankylosing spinal disorders. *Spine (Phila Pa 1976)* 2010;35(11): E458-E464.

    Retrospective review of 122 spine fractures in 112 consecutive patients with ankylosing spine disorders led to the conclusion that patients with spine fracture are at high risk for complications and death. Multilevel posterior segmental instrumentation led to effective fracture healing. Level of evidence: III.

46. Chen TY, Dickman CA, Eleraky M, Sonntag VK: The role of decompression for acute incomplete cervical spinal cord injury in cervical spondylosis. *Spine (Phila Pa 1976)* 1998;23(22):2398-2403.

47. Dvorak MF, Fisher CG, Hoekema J, et al: Factors predicting motor recovery and functional outcome after traumatic central cord syndrome: A long-term follow-up. *Spine (Phila Pa 1976)* 2005;30(20):2303-2311.

    Retrospective review of the database records of patients with cervical trauma identified possible predictors of motor recovery and functional outcome. The significant predictive variables included initial motor score, formal education, comorbidities, age at injury, and development of spasticity. More than the motor score was required for valid assessment. Level of evidence: III.

48. Guest J, Eleraky MA, Apostolides PJ, Dickman CA, Sonntag VK: Traumatic central cord syndrome: Results of surgical management. *J Neurosurg* 2002;97(1, suppl):25-32.

49. Ishida Y, Tominaga T: Predictors of neurologic recovery in acute central cervical cord injury with only upper extremity impairment. *Spine (Phila Pa 1976)* 2002;27(15): 1652-1658.

50. McKinley W, Meade MA, Kirshblum S, Barnard B: Outcomes of early surgical management versus late or no surgical intervention after acute spinal cord injury. *Arch Phys Med Rehabil* 2004;85(11):1818-1825.

51. Pollard ME, Apple DF: Factors associated with improved neurologic outcomes in patients with incomplete tetraplegia. *Spine (Phila Pa 1976)* 2003;28(1):33-39.

52. Harrop JS, Sharan A, Ratliff J: Central cord injury: Pathophysiology, management, and outcomes. *Spine J* 2006;6(6, suppl):198S-206S.

    The literature through 2005 on the pathophysiology of and treatment options for central cord injuries was reviewed. Medical management and surgical decompression and stabilization provided improved neurologic recovery in this heterogeneous population.

53. Uribe J, Green BA, Vanni S, Moza K, Guest JD, Levi AD: Acute traumatic central cord syndrome. Experience using surgical decompression with open-door expansile cervical laminoplasty. *Surg Neurol* 2005;63(6):505-510.

Retrospective review of the records of 29 patients with acute traumatic central cord syndrome found that open-door expansile cervical laminoplasty was effective and safe (without postoperative neurologic changes) for a subset of these patients without instability but with substantial cervical spondylosis or stenosis. Level of evidence: III.

3: Spine Trauma

Chapter 21

Thoracic and Lumbar Fractures

Kris Radcliff, MD   Christopher K. Kepler, MD   Jeremy S. Smith, MD   Alexander Vaccaro, MD, PhD

Introduction

Thoracic and lumbar fractures range from low-energy osteoporotic vertebral compression fractures (which affect 700,000 patients every year in the United States) to high-energy fractures and dislocations associated with spinal cord injury.[1] These common fractures are classified anatomically by the involved spine region as pure thoracic (T1 to T9), thoracolumbar (T10 to L2), or low lumbar (L3 to L5). The thoracolumbar spine is the most common site of spine fracture. Morphologically, thoracolumbar fractures are classified as compressive, distractive, or translational-rotational.

Surgical treatment is indicated for a patient with an unstable thoracolumbar fracture to protect the neural elements, restore skeletal alignment, facilitate mobilization and rehabilitation, avoid complications associated with prolonged immobilization, and prevent progressive deformity.

Anatomy

The thoracic spine is relatively immobile and has anterior biomechanical support from the rib cage and sternum. The coronal facet orientation of the thoracic

Dr. Vaccaro or an immediate family member serves as a board member, owner, officer, or committee member of the North American Spine Society, American Spinal Injury Association, and Cervical Spine Research Society; has received royalties from Aesculap/B.Braun, Globus Medical, Medtronic Sofamor Danek, K2M, Stout Medical, Progressive Spinal Technology, Applied Spinal Intellectual Properties, and DePuy, a Johnson & Johnson company; serves as a paid consultant to or is an employee of K2M; has received research or institutional support from AO North America, Medtronic Sofamor Danek, Stryker, and DePuy, a Johnson & Johnson company; and owns stock or stock options in Globus Medical, Disk Motion Technology, Progressive Spinal Technologies, Advanced Spinal Intellectual Properties, Computational Biodynamics, Stout Medical, Paradigm Spine, K2M, Replication Medica, Spinology, Spine Medica, Orthovita, Vertiflex, Small Bone Technologies, NeuCore, Crosscurrent, Syndicom, In Vivo, Flagship Surgical, Pearl Driver, Location Based Intelligence, and Gamma Spine. None of the following authors nor any immediate family member has received anything of value from or owns stock in a commercial company or institution related directly or indirectly to the subject of this chapter: Dr. Radcliff, Dr. Kepler, Dr. Smith.

spine blocks flexion and extension. The main function of the thoracic spine appears to be protection of the thoracic spinal cord, which in most individuals terminates at L1.

The thoracolumbar junction biomechanically is a transitional region between the immobile thoracic segments and the mobile lumbar segments. In an upright posture, the thoracolumbar junction has a straight alignment between T10 and L2. The ideal center of the head, arm, and trunk weight is anterior to T10, and therefore the thoracolumbar junction is exposed to a flexion moment. Because positive sagittal balance after a thoracolumbar fracture has been associated with a poor outcome, the goal of a reconstruction of the thoracolumbar junction is to maintain upright posture.[2] The thoracolumbar junction is characterized by a transition of facet joint orientation from the coronal plane of the thoracic spine to the oblique sagittal plane of the lumbar spine. As a result, the facet morphology of the thoracolumbar junction is optimal for flexion, extension, and rotational movements. The main ligamentous stabilizers of the thoracolumbar junction include the supraspinous ligament, the facet capsules, the interspinous ligament, and the intervertebral disk.[3] The thoracolumbar junction also is characterized by a transition of the neurologic elements from the conus medullaris to the cauda equina, which in adults usually is posterior to the body of L1.

The low lumbar spine is defined as beginning at L3, which usually is the apex of lumbar lordosis. The lumbar facets are sagittally oriented to permit maximal flexion and extension of the lumbar spine. The lumbar vertebrae are the largest in the body, and the spinal canal has its largest diameter in the lumbar spine. As a result, most low lumbar fractures do not cause a neurologic deficit. The neural elements in the low lumbar spine are in the cauda equina, which is generally more resilient than the spinal cord or conus medullaris. Biomechanically, the gravity line intersects the midlumbar spine, and in most individuals it terminates at the posterior aspect of the S1 vertebral body.

Epidemiology

Approximately 90% of all thoracic and lumbar fractures occur at the thoracolumbar junction, and 10% to 20% of thoracolumbar fractures are burst fractures.[4] A burst fracture occurs in as many as 60% of individuals who sustain a high-energy blunt traumatic injury.[5] A fall from a height is a common cause of burst fracture.[6] Thoracolumbar burst fracture is most common in boys and men in the second or third decade of life. Approximately 50% of patients with a thoracolumbar burst fracture have a resulting neurologic deficit, particularly if they have spinal canal compression of more than 50%.[7]

Clinical Evaluation

History and Physical Examination

The clinical evaluation of a patient with a thoracic or lumbar fracture begins with the Advanced Trauma Life Support protocol. Additional injuries (particularly noncontiguous spine injury) should be identified if possible, and airway, ventilation, and cardiovascular support should be provided. Although a thoracic spinal cord injury does not lead to complete respiratory arrest, a concomitant injury such as pneumothorax, diaphragmatic rupture, or rib fracture can affect ventilation. If possible, a history should be elicited, including the details of the trauma, pain sites, and possible incontinence. An associated injury such as a calcaneus fracture resulting from a fall should prompt attention to the spine. During a motor vehicle crash, the flexion moment over a seat belt commonly causes a hollow viscus abdominal injury as well as a Chance fracture. Other relevant elements of the history include spondyloarthropathy, earlier spine surgery, concomitant injuries, or the presence of a pacemaker or other metallic foreign body contraindicating the use of MRI. A patient with spondyloarthropathy commonly develops significant instability in extension and has multiple fractures that may be difficult to detect on plain radiographs or CT. All patients should be directly queried as to any coagulopathy (therapeutic or historical).

The patient should be turned once, using the logroll maneuver, to examine for ecchymosis, induration, or other signs of significant spine instability. The physical examination should include palpation of the thoracolumbar spine for ecchymosis or a degloving injury, manual muscle strength testing of the torso and lower extremities, sensory pinprick testing, and deep tendon reflex testing. Sacral nerve root function, including voluntary rectal tone and the bulbocavernosus reflex, should be assessed with a rectal examination. Care should be taken to distinguish voluntary control of the anal musculature from the anal wink reflex, which is a reflexive contraction of the external anal sphincter.

In a patient with neurologic deficits, an intact pinprick sensation in the lower sacral dermatome distribution may portend a favorable prognosis for recovery of bladder function. Priapism signifies a complete spinal cord injury because it indicates loss of sympathetic tone to the genitalia in the presence of intact, unregulated parasympathetic input. The most important predictor of a favorable neurologic outcome is retention of sacral (S4-S5) sensation 72 hours to 1 week after the injury.[8]

Spinal cord shock is a cessation of neurologic function in the torso and extremities causing flaccid paralysis after an injury to the spinal cord. This clinical diagnosis is made on the basis of physical examination. Spinal cord shock ends with the return of the bulbocavernosus reflex, which indicates that the arc between the pelvic afferent nerves and sacral cord efferent nerves is once again intact. Technically, a spinal cord injury syndrome cannot be classified until the bulbocavernosus reflex returns to signify the end of spinal shock.

Hemodynamic status should be carefully assessed to detect neurogenic or hypovolemic shock. Hypovolemic shock is much more common than neurogenic shock in patients with spinal cord injury because of the hemorrhage associated with high-energy trauma. Patients in hypovolemic shock have cold and clammy skin and are tachycardic. The incidence of neurogenic shock is greater in patients with a cervical injury than in those with an isolated thoracic injury.[9] Neurogenic shock consists of a combination of hypotension and bradycardia caused by loss of sympathetic tone from a spinal cord injury.[10] Volume resuscitation should be combined with vasopressors and chronotropic agents, as necessary, to treat neurogenic shock.[10] Studies of cervical and thoracic cord injury suggest that patient outcomes after spinal cord injury are improved by maintaining the mean arterial pressure above 85 mm Hg. Prophylaxis for skin decubitus ulcer, gastrointestinal ulcer, pneumonia, and deep venous thrombosis should be considered immediately. Patients with spondyloarthropathy who have an extension-distraction injury should be carefully monitored for delayed development of an epidural hematoma.

Imaging

Imaging studies should be obtained in all patients who have sustained a traumatic injury and have thoracic or lumbar pain, neurologic deficit, bowel or bladder dysfunction, a high-energy mechanism of injury, or an injury indicative of a high-energy mechanism. High-resolution CT is the study of choice in many centers. In other centers, however, the evaluation of spine traumatic injury begins with plain radiography. Radiographs are highly specific for identifying a spine injury, although CT provides superior resolution of bony injury. Because the patient is supine, CT may not reveal instability that is apparent in an upright position. Many physicians use both upright radiographs and CT to avoid basing the treatment decision on CT alone.[11] However, a retrospective study found that the information provided by CT alone was equivalent to that of the CT–upright radiography combination for evaluating thoracolumbar fracture.[12]

The substantial difference in radiation exposure during radiography and CT should be considered. CT of the chest is estimated to expose the patient to approximately 100 times the radiation necessary for standard

3: Spine Trauma

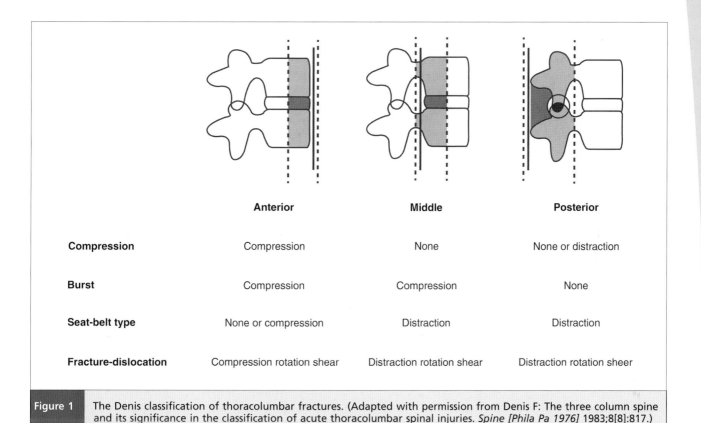

	Anterior	Middle	Posterior
Compression	Compression	None	None or distraction
Burst	Compression	Compression	None
Seat-belt type	None or compression	Distraction	Distraction
Fracture-dislocation	Compression rotation shear	Distraction rotation shear	Distraction rotation sheer

Figure 1 The Denis classification of thoracolumbar fractures. (Adapted with permission from Denis F: The three column spine and its significance in the classification of acute thoracolumbar spinal injuries. *Spine [Phila Pa 1976]* 1983;8[8]:817.)

AP and lateral radiographs of the chest.[13] The relative effective radiation dosage is slightly different in spine radiographs and CT because CT can be collimated to exclude anterior structures. Nonetheless, the dosage is significantly larger for CT than for radiographs. It is estimated that for women in their 20s, one radiation-induced cancer results from every 500 abdominal-pelvic CT scans or every 2,300 cervical spine CT scans.[13] The number of thoracolumbar CT scans necessary to induce one cancer is likely to fall between these two estimates, as thoracolumbar CT exposes the patient to less radiation exposure than abdominal CT but more than cervical CT. Dosage-modulation techniques should be used whenever possible to decrease the radiation exposure in spine CT by more than one third while maintaining image quality.[14]

Most physicians focus on midsagittal CT for evaluating thoracolumbar traumatic injury. The intervertebral facet joints should be carefully evaluated on parasagittal radiographs and CT. The images also should be examined for the global angular spine alignment, the causes of a pathologic fracture, and the presence of spondyloarthropathy. A thoracolumbar injury should prompt imaging to detect any additional spine injury.

MRI is used to detect a disk herniation, damage to the posterior ligamentous complex (PLC), a pathologic fracture, or a mass lesion in the spinal canal. MRI is highly sensitive for ligamentous injury. PLC injury was found in 100% of fracture-dislocation injuries, 42% of

burst fractures, and 26% of compression injuries.[15] The presence of a spreading epidural hematoma or deep subcutaneous edema can be a sign of PLC injury.[16] MRI has estimated sensitivity and specificity of 89.4% and 92.3%, respectively, for identifying supraspinous ligament injury; and 98.5% and 87.2%, respectively, for identifying interspinous ligament injury.[17] A prospective study found that the extent of injury was overestimated on MRI, in comparison with open surgical findings.[18]

Thoracolumbar Injury Classification

Thoracolumbar injuries were first classified by the mechanism and severity of injury. In the Denis system, thoracolumbar burst fractures were classified by surgical reconstruction prognosis and outcome[3] (Figure 1). The critical concept of the Denis classification is the contribution of the middle column of the spine to overall vertebral body stability. The four subtypes of thoracolumbar fracture, based on anterior, middle, or posterior column involvement, are compression fracture, burst fracture, seat belt fracture, and fracture-dislocation. Under this scheme, the characteristics of a compression injury are compression of the anterior column, no injury to the middle column, and either no injury or distraction (in severe injury) of the posterior column. Compression fracture is subclassified as occurring after anterior or lateral flexion and as fracturing the upper or lower end plate.

3: Spine Trauma

Injury morphology		Qualifier	Points
Compression	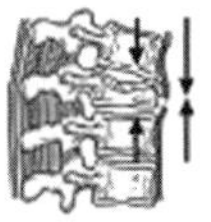	-	1
		Burst	+1
Rotation-translation	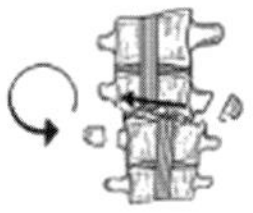	-	3
		-	4
Distraction	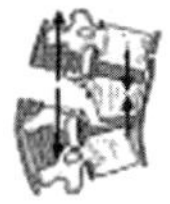		
Neurologic status			
Intact		-	0
Nerve root		-	2
Spinal cord/conus medullaris		Incomplete	3
		Complete	2
Cauda equina		-	3
Posterior ligaments			
Intact		-	0
Suspected/indeterminate		-	1
Disrupted		-	2

Figure 2   The Thoracolumbar Injury Classification System. The schematic drawings show compression, rotation-translation, and distraction injury morphology; the arrows indicate the directions of force. The overall score consists of the total of the injury morphology, neurologic status, and PLC status subscores. (Adapted with permission from Vaccaro AR, Lehman RA Jr, Hurlbert RJ, et al: A new classification of thoracolumbar injuries: The importance of injury morphology, the integrity of the posterior ligamentous complex, and neurologic status. *Spine [Phila Pa 1976]* 2005;30[20]:2325.)

There are four types of Denis burst fractures. Type A involves comminution of both end plates; 16% of burst fractures were classified as type A.[3] The mechanism of injury is axial compression resulting in pedicle and posterior element comminution. Type B involves only the superior end plate and represents 62% of all burst fractures.[3] The type B fracture is believed to result from axial compression with concomitant flexion moment, as the result of retropulsion of a bony fragment into the spinal canal at the level of the pedicles. The type C fracture is rare and is predominantly located at the inferior end plate. Type D results from both axial loading and rotation, leading to significant translation. Type E results from axial loading and lateral flexion and differs from lateral compression fracture in that the posterior

cortex of the vertebral body is affected, allowing retropulsion of bone into the canal. A seat belt injury (now called a flexion-distraction injury) is created through distraction of the middle and posterior elements, causing bony or ligamentous injury with minimal or no compression of the anterior column. A fracture-dislocation injury results from a rotational injury, accompanied by distraction of the middle and posterior columns and compression of the anterior column; or from a shearing mechanism across all three columns. A burst fracture, like a compression fracture, is characterized by compression of the anterior column, with the addition of a compressed middle column; the posterior column is intact.

The limitation of the Denis classification is that injuries resulting from different mechanisms can have a similar radiographic appearance, particularly in the presence of severe bony destruction. This factor was not considered in the first classification systems, nor did these systems consider ligamentous complex or neurologic injury, which are important markers of instability. The Thoracolumbar Injury Classification System (TLICS) categorizes injuries by morphology (rather than by injury mechanism), ligamentous injury, and neurologic injury[19] (Figure 2). Interobserver reliability for discrimination among compression, distraction, and translation-rotation injuries was found to be improved when lesion morphology was included.[20]

In the TLICS, compression injury includes compression and burst fractures, both of which commonly result from axial loading. These injuries cause a significant loss of vertebral body height and comminution, without translation or rotation deformity. This injury group includes typical compression and burst fractures but not fracture-dislocations. Translation-rotation injuries, including facet fracture or dislocation, bilateral pedicle fracture, and pars fracture with vertebral subluxation, involve significant translation or rotation of the proximal aspect of the vertebral column relative to the distal aspect. The spine elements are designed to resist these motions while permitting flexion-extension. Such a dislocation may occur in isolation or in combination with vertebral body fracture. TLICS scoring assigns three points to translation-rotation injury patterns. In the presence of significant ligamentous damage or neurologic injury, a translational injury is considered unstable and requires surgical intervention. Rotatory injuries are relatively rare but extremely unstable. Rotational instability can be best seen as a horizontal rotation of the spinous processes and pedicles on an AP radiograph or axial CT.

Distraction injuries involve separation of the vertebral elements and are assigned four points in the TLICS. The typical morphology includes a fracture line in the axial plane traversing the bony or soft-tissue elements at one or more adjacent levels, typically accompanied by low-grade comminution. The two subsets of distraction injury are flexion-distraction injury, called a Chance fracture, involving rotation around an axis an-

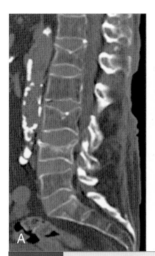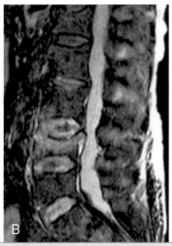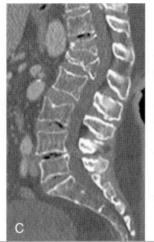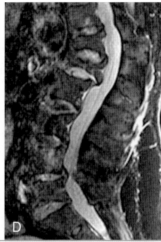

Figure 3   An L4 compression fracture in two patients. **A** and **B**, A 78-year-old patient had acute low back pain after a fall from standing height. Midsagittal CT (**A**) showing mild deformities at L1 and L3, which were not easily seen on plain radiographs; the intact posterior vertebral body wall indicates that the injury is a compression fracture rather than a burst fracture. T2-weighted midsagittal MRI (**B**) showing high signal at L4 consistent with an acute fracture; the low signal at L3 suggests that the mild compression fracture is old. **C** and **D**, A 62-year-old patient had pain after a fall; the patient also had severe back pain after a fall 1 year earlier. Midsagittal CT (**C**) showing an incidental finding of an earlier L1 chronic compression. Midsagittal short tau inversion recovery MRI (**D**) showing no acute increased signal intensity in the L1 fracture and increased signal in the L4 end plate consistent with an acute fracture.

terior to the spine; and extension-distraction injury. Flexion-distraction injury typically occurs in a young, healthy person after high-energy trauma, and extension-distraction injury typically occurs after low-energy trauma in an older person with spondyloarthropathy.

Compression Fractures

A compression fracture involves damage to the anterior vertebral body only, with an intact posterior vertebral body wall (**Figure 3**). A compression fracture usually is a stable, isolated injury that does not cause neurologic compromise and can be treated nonsurgically. Bracing can be used if deformity progression or pseudarthrosis is a concern. Thoracic compression fractures may not require bracing because of the inherent stability provided by the rib cage, but most physicians prescribe an external orthosis for patient comfort as well as stability. Thoracolumbar or lumbar burst fractures are treated with bracing for control of symptoms. Some isolated compression fractures are treated with corset bracing, primarily for patient comfort. A prospective randomized study found that bracing for 6 weeks, with subsequent physical therapy, led to a better outcome than postural education or casting for 6 to 12 weeks.[21] A retrospective study found no difference in the radiographic outcomes of thoracolumbar compression fractures based on treatment with bracing.[22]

Pathologic causes of vertebral compression fracture should be ruled out, particularly if the injury was atraumatic or low energy. Careful inspection for extensive osteolysis, an abnormal soft-tissue mass, or an atypical fracture morphology or signal on MRI is mandatory for identification of a pathologic compression fracture. The common causes of pathologic fracture include multiple myeloma, metastatic disease (originating in the lung, breast, prostate, or thyroid, or as renal cell carcinoma), osteoporosis, or osteomalacia. The spine surgeon should counsel the patient as to the possibility of osteoporosis and, in concert with the primary care physician, recommend a diagnostic workup and treatment.

Burst Fractures

The relative contributions of vertebral body height loss, kyphosis, and PLC injury to the stability of a thoracolumbar burst fracture are a subject of controversy.[23] Burst fractures with more than 50% height loss, 20° of kyphosis, or a neurologic deficit originally were identified as unstable and requiring surgical treatment.[24] However, subsequent studies found that PLC injury is associated with late kyphosis and a poor outcome and emphasized the importance of the PLC in determining the stability of a thoracolumbar fracture.[25]

Thoracolumbar burst fractures, particularly Denis type B fractures, can result in significant bony retropulsion (**Figure 4**). The long-term significance of canal compromise in a burst fracture is not well understood. Canal compromise of more than 50% at T12-L1 is associated with persistent neurologic deficit after fracture healing.[7] Canal compromise after fracture healing carries less risk of neurologic deficit in the lumbar spine than in the thoracic spine; a compromise of 45% at L1 or 35% at T11 is tolerated.[26] Another study found no

3: Spine Trauma

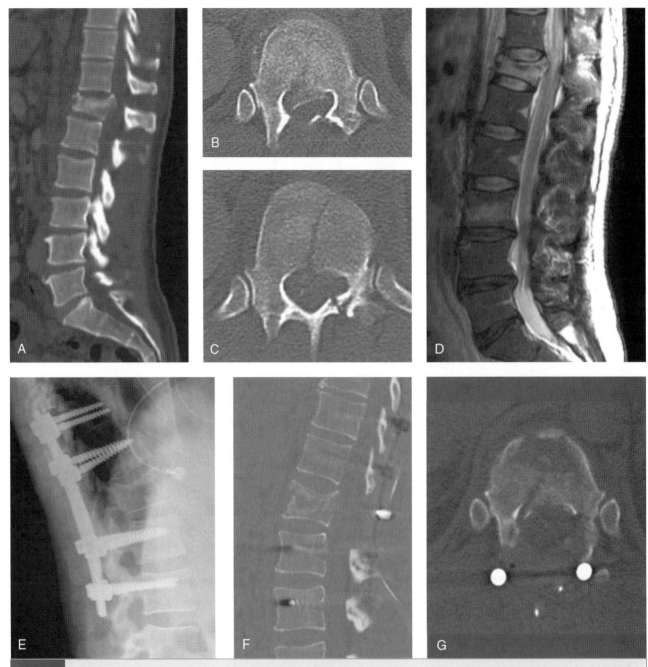

Figure 4 Diagnosis and treatment of a T12 burst fracture in a 31-year-old man with an incomplete spinal cord injury after a fall from a height. Midsagittal (**A**) and axial (**B**) CT showing fracture with fragment retropulsion into the neural canal and approximate 50% canal compromise. **C**, Axial CT showing an associated lamina fracture. **D**, T2-weighted midsagittal MRI showing increased signal at T12 and high signal in the posterior element, which suggest a PLC injury. **E**, Lateral radiograph after posterior spine instrumentation with fixation two levels cranial and caudal to the fracture. **F**, Midsagittal CT showing successful spinal cord decompression after indirect fracture reduction and direct posterior decompression. **G**, Axial CT showing improvement in canal compromise after indirect reduction and instrumentation.

relationship between canal compromise and local kyphotic angle.[27] Bony reabsorption leads to a decrease in canal compromise after fracture healing over time.

The goal of treatment of a burst fracture is to prevent the progression of deformity and neurologic injury. The supra-adjacent disk loses height after a thoracolumbar burst fracture, and collapse of the supra-adjacent disk may contribute to late kyphotic deformity. Therefore, particular attention should be given to restoring vertebral body height. Contradictory results have been reported concerning the effect of progressive kyphosis on patient-reported outcomes. In a retrospective study, progressive kyphosis (mean, 9.4° over 25.5 months) was not associated with change in patient-reported pain scores or outcomes.[28] A retrospective study of 27 patients who underwent posterior short-segment instrumentation found that patients with a sagittal index of more than 15° had a higher incidence of moderate to severe pain compared with patients with a sagittal index of less than 15.[29] There is a correlation among spinopelvic parameters, progression of kyphosis, and outcome of treatment for a thoracolumbar burst fracture. Patients had a worse outcome if they were unable to fully compensate for fracture kyphosis by adjusting their lumbar lordosis or thoracic kyphosis (within the ranges allowed by the pelvic incidence).[2]

The absolute indications for surgical treatment of a thoracolumbar burst fracture include progressive neurologic deficit, cauda equina syndrome with thecal sac impingement, and significant spine instability during bracing. A fracture that changes in alignment while positioned upright in a brace may be considered unstable and suitable for surgical stabilization. Surgical treatment also is considered if the intervertebral disk has herniated into the vertebral body, diminishing the potential for fracture healing and increasing the risk of nonunion. The presence of organ system injuries that would complicate the use of bracing is a relative indication for surgical intervention in a patient with a thoracolumbar burst fracture. A prospective randomized study found no difference in radiographic or clinical outcomes after thoracolumbar burst fractures were surgically or nonsurgically treated in patients who were neurologically intact, although the complication rate was higher after surgical treatment.[30]

Nonsurgical Treatment

Nonsurgical treatment may be considered for a thoracolumbar burst fracture if the patient is neurologically intact or has only radicular symptoms with an intact PLC.[31] Two points are assigned on the TLICS. Nonsurgical treatment of a thoracolumbar burst fracture with PLC disruption, end plate involvement, or extensive vertebral body comminution carries a risk of kyphotic failure.[5] A prospective case study found that patients usually return to their prereduction local kyphotic angle and develop significant adjacent-disk degeneration after nonsurgical treatment, even if the PLC is intact.[32] The nonsurgical treatment may consist of a plaster cast molded with the patient prone on a Risser table and an anterior force applied to reduce the kyphosis, or a thoracolumbosacral orthosis molded in extension. The brace is used for approximately 8 to 12 weeks, depending on patient comfort. A prospective randomized study found that the outcomes of treatment with a hyperextension cast or thoracolumbosacral orthosis were equivalent to those of surgical treatment in patients who were neurologically intact.[30] Other studies found no difference in the outcomes of thoracolumbar burst fracture treated with or without an orthosis.[21,33]

Surgical Treatment
Posterior Approach
The advantages of the posterior surgical approach for decompression of a burst fracture include the comparatively low risk to visceral and vascular structures, surgeon familiarity, and ease of surgical reexploration. Fracture fragments can be indirectly reduced through ligamentotaxis using distraction instrumentation.[34] Ligamentotaxis is effected through tension on the posterior longitudinal ligament, which results in anterior translation of the retropulsed fragments. Indirect decompression is most successful within 3 days of injury, and it provides an average 15% increase in canal diameter.[35] If surgery is delayed or the fracture fragments are markedly retropulsed or rotated, the patient may be a poor candidate for indirect decompression. If indirect decompression does not provide adequate reduction, direct decompression may be performed through a posterior transpedicular corpectomy approach.[36-38] Laminectomy alone provides inadequate decompression because the neural elements continue to be compressed by the retropulsed vertebral body elements. Laminectomy can be used to directly repair traumatic dural tears and reduce entrapped lumbar rootlets, which may be associated with lamina fracture in thoracolumbar burst fracture.[5,39,40] A posterior approach allows direct visualization for this procedure.

In the standard instrumentation construct, pedicle screw stabilization extends three levels cephalad and two levels caudal to the fusion level, for the purpose of resisting the cantilever ending moment on the rods. A clinical study found that short-segment posterior instrumentation one or two levels cephalad and caudal to the fracture led to an unacceptably high rate of failure.[41] In a biomechanical study, instrumentation spanning two spine segments was found to be less rigid than the intact spine.[42] These studies suggest that a short-segment posterior instrumentation construct may require prolonged bedrest or buttressing (using fixation of the fractured vertebra or anterior column support).

The load-sharing score (LSS) was designed to predict the outcome of short-segment posterior instrumentation in thoracolumbar burst fractures.[43] The LSS quantifies vertebral body damage, including vertebral communication, fragment diastasis, and kyphosis, to predict the ability of the vertebral body to support axial loading after a burst fracture. The LSS initially was designed to determine whether a fracture should be treated with long-segment instrumentation or anterior column support. An LSS higher than 6 of 9 possible points was found to predict construct failure in short-segment posterior instrumentation.[44] Such a fracture may be better treated with a combined anterior-posterior approach or a long-segment posterior fixation.

Open instrumentation without arthrodesis is another treatment option. Some studies found that open reduction and internal fixation of spine fractures without intersegmental arthrodesis was associated with successful outcomes in patients with thoracolumbar burst fracture.[45] There were no significant differences in clinical or radiographic outcomes after long-segment posterior instrumentation, with or without posterolateral fusion, but patients with fusion had a significantly longer surgical time, greater blood loss, and greater donor site morbidity.[46] A prospective randomized study comparing fusion using short-segment posterior instrumentation with nonfusion techniques using short-segment posterior instrumentation found no differences in outcomes.[45] The thoracolumbar burst fractures in this study primarily involved the superior vertebral end plate and had an LSS of 6 of lower. Loss of correction and screw breakage are significant concerns with nonfusion techniques.[46]

Percutaneous posterior instrumentation, with or without fusion, has been studied as an alternative treatment for thoracolumbar burst fracture. Limited percutaneous skeletal stabilization immediately after trauma has been described as a form of damage control orthopaedics. Percutaneous spine instrumentation may be thought of as an application of damage control orthopaedics to achieve early fracture stabilization, early patient mobilization, and, if subsequent anterior surgery is necessary, a shorter surgical time. Percutaneous posterior instrumentation was found to have acceptable clinical outcomes, with less blood loss and fewer wound complications than open treatment of thoracolumbar burst fractures.[47]

Posterior short-segment instrumentation has been studied in conjunction with anterior column augmentation with cement, bone graft, or bone morphogenetic protein for treating thoracolumbar burst fracture. Short-segment percutaneous pedicle screw instrumentation with balloon-augmented polymethylmethacrylate cement vertebroplasty was associated with minimal kyphosis and height loss at 2-year follow-up.[48] Percutaneous vertebral augmentation with calcium phosphate cement or transpedicular bone grafting to prevent late kyphosis and facilitate vertebral body healing had mixed results as an adjunct to open short-segment posterior reduction and fixation.[49] The long-term risks, such as nonunion, cement extravasation and migration, and instrumentation failure, have not yet been studied. Biologic products to augment fusion or fracture healing have been used in association with percutaneous methods. However, the use of bone morphogenetic protein 2 as a fusion adjunct may be limited because it can penetrate intrathecally and may cause scarring and gliosis after spinal cord injury.[50] Anterior corpectomy and reconstruction from a posterior approach is possible with the use of a costotransversectomy and placement of an expandable cage.[51]

Anterior Approach
Anterior surgery for a thoracolumbar burst fracture involves a retroperitoneal approach, a corpectomy, and anterior stabilization with plates and screws. The ante-

rior approach may offer superior neural decompression, particularly at the conus medullaris level, and include fewer motion segments than the posterior approach. The relative indications for the anterior approach include severe vertebral body comminution, kyphosis of more than 30°, and severe canal compromise (more than 70%).[52] Some but not all studies found that the anterior approach led to a better neurologic recovery, compared with a posterior approach, because of the potential for superior decompression.[53] Isolated anterior decompression may lead to a higher failure rate in the presence of PLC damage,[54] although good results have been reported even after anterior fixation in the context of PLC injury.[55] The major disadvantage of an anterior approach is the excessive blood loss associated with an acute fracture and, at many centers, the necessity of involving an approach surgeon. Some biomechanical studies indicate that anterior corpectomy and instrumentation are superior or equivalent to posterior reconstruction for thoracolumbar burst fractures.[56-58] Other studies have found that the anterior approach is biomechanically inferior to a posterior-only approach.[59]

Combined Anterior-Posterior Approach
The relative indications for an anterior-posterior approach include injuries at the conus medullaris level if the patient has a neurologic deficit or severe canal compression with PLC injury; or has a neurologic deficit with persistent, significant anterior thecal sac compression after surgery through a posterior approach. In the presence of an injury to the spinal cord or conus medullaris, anterior decompression may have a better result than posterior decompression.[60] Biomechanical studies found that combined anteroposterior instrumentation was superior to single-side instrumentation in all motion planes (flexion, extension, rotation, and lateral bending).[61] A combined surgical reconstruction may be best for long-term kyphosis correction and reconstruction of the posterior tension band, although this practice is not universally accepted.[62] The anterior-posterior approach also allows the preservation of motion levels by shortening the fusion segments; this is a particularly relevant consideration in an L2 burst fracture, which otherwise would require fusion to L4.

Translation-Rotation Injuries

A translation-rotation injury is treated from a posterior approach if the vertebral rotation or translation has led to abnormal spinal canal alignment. An isolated bilateral facet fracture or dislocation with translation frequently results in a complete spinal cord injury secondary to the pincer effect of the intact but displaced neural arches. This injury is most common in the thoracolumbar or lumbosacral spine. Reduction and instrumented fusion from a posterior approach is the usual treatment[63] (Figure 5). Bilateral pedicle or pars fracture with vertebral subluxation results in spon-

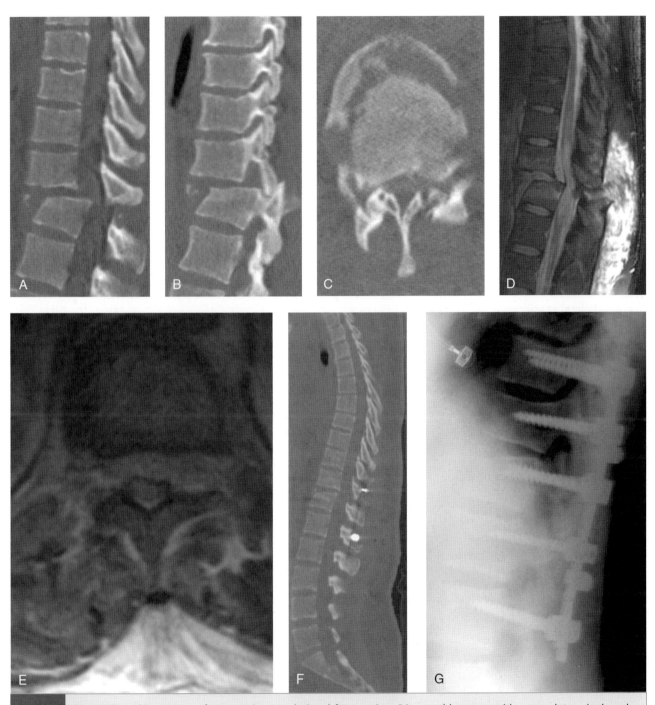

Figure 5 Diagnosis and treatment of an anterior translational fracture in a 24-year-old woman with a complete spinal cord injury after a high-speed, head-on motor vehicle crash in which she was a restrained driver. **A,** Midsagittal CT showing an anterolisthesis of approximately 25% of the vertebral body width, with an associated flexion-teardrop injury. **B,** Parasagittal CT through the facet joints showing acute facet dislocation with the inferior facet of T11 anterior to the superior articular process of T12, which was present bilaterally. **C,** Axial CT showing spinal stenosis resulting from the so-called cigar-cutter effect of the translation of adjacent vertebrae, with intact neural elements. **D,** Midsagittal short tau inversion recovery MRI showing translational injury with disk disruption and high signal in the PLC, indicating an unstable injury. **E,** Axial T1-weighted MRI showing canal stenosis. **F,** CT after posterior reduction and instrumentation restored alignment. **G,** Lateral radiograph after reduction of the translational injury, showing alignment maintained with a pedicle screw construct.

3: Spine Trauma

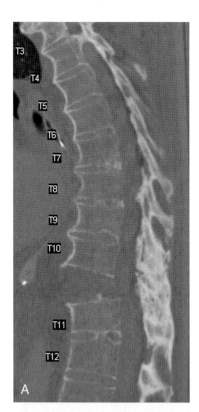

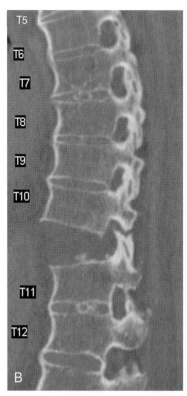

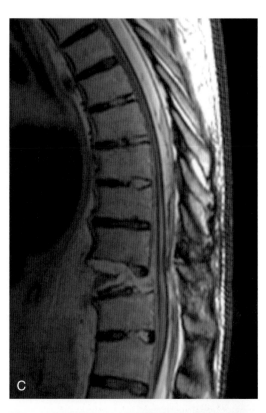

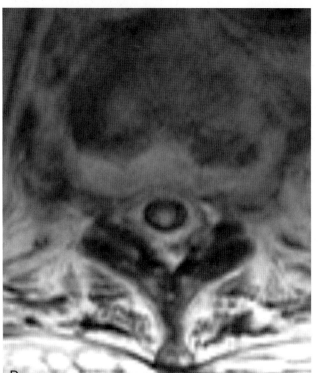

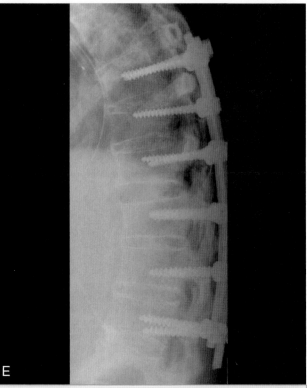

Figure 6　Diagnosis and treatment of an extension-distraction fracture in an 81-year-old man with a complete spinal cord injury after a fall from a standing height. **A,** Midsagittal CT showing distraction at T10-T11 with fusion of the posterior elements; no posterior element discontinuity is seen. **B,** Parasagittal CT showing distraction between the vertebral bodies of T10 and T11 as well as bilateral fracture and distraction across the pars interarticularis. **C,** Midsagittal T2-weighted MRI with evidence of anterior and middle column distraction as well as high signal indicating disk disruption. The posterior elements are intact in this midline image. **D,** Axial T2-weighted MRI showing high signal within the spinal cord, indicating neurologic injury related to the translational injury. **E,** Lateral radiograph after posterior reduction and instrumentation; the defect in the T10 pars is still visible.

dylolisthesis and may require interbody fusion because extreme instability or a discontinuity between the vertebral body and the posterior elements creates a challenging environment for fusion.[64]

Distraction Injuries

A distraction injury is characterized by a separation of elements that results in destruction of bony or soft-tissue structures (Figure 6). On the TLICS, a ligamentous or neurologic injury is documented by an overall score higher than 5, which indicates that surgical intervention is necessary. Isolated bony distraction lesions heal reliably and can be managed nonsurgically using an extension orthosis for 3 months. A soft-tissue distraction injury or a hybrid injury of bone and soft tissue through the disk or PLC is at increased risk of late instability because of nonunion and therefore usually is managed surgically. The injury may be simultaneously distracted and translated or rotated. Radiographic evidence of interspinous widening denotes a distraction or rotational component.[65] An injury with translation only and no interspinous widening is considered a translation-only injury and is assigned 3 points on the TLICS. A retrospective study of flexion-distraction injuries identified a 25% incidence of neurologic deficit and a 30% incidence of associated abdominal injury.[66] Thoracolumbar facet dislocation can involve significant bony instability and may be associated with severe neurologic injury. The outcome of a pure thoracolumbar facet dislocation is worse if the residual canal diameter is less than 10 mm.[67] These injuries can be treated with posterior short-segment instrumentation because the load-bearing capacity of the anterior vertebral body has not been damaged.[68] Posterior reduction can be achieved by manipulating the spinous process or pedicle screw instrumentation. Facetectomy can be a useful tool for reduction, but it leaves only a limited fusion surface. Anterior-posterior reconstruction can be considered for a vertebral body fracture associated with a flexion-distraction injury.[69]

An extension-distraction injury is assigned 4 points on the TLICS. This injury usually occurs through the intervertebral disk space or the vertebral body and often is associated with neurologic injury. A patient with an extension-distraction injury may have preexisting spondyloarthropathy and be susceptible to epidural hematoma. Short-segment instrumentation may be appropriate for a distraction injury with intact bony elements because the ability of the anterior column to bear axial loads has not been compromisd.

Surgical Timing

There is no consensus regarding timing of surgery for thoracolumbar fractures. A retrospective review of 361 patients who underwent surgery for a spine fracture found a higher mortality rate in patients treated less than 24 hours after injury than in those treated more than 24 hours after injury (7.6% or 2%, respectively).[70] Most of the deaths were in patients with a cervical fracture. Another retrospective review found that patients who underwent early surgery had a shorter period of intensive care, a shorter period of ventilator dependence, a lower mortality rate, and a shorter hospitalization stay than patients treated later.[71] Patients with a thoracic fracture who underwent surgery within 24 hours of injury also were found to have a higher rate of neurologic recovery.[72] A systematic review of these and other studies of thoracic and lumbar fractures determined that early fixation leads to a lower complication rate and shorter intensive care and hospital stays but does not necessarily improve the neurologic outcome.[73] Despite equivocal study findings, the general recommendation is that surgery should be performed as soon as the patient is medically stable.

Spinal Cord Injury Prognosis

Patients with an incomplete spinal cord injury have a better prognosis for neurologic recovery than those with a complete injury. In one case study, 28 of 54 patients (52%) with incomplete paraplegia were ambulatory 1 year after spinal cord injury.[74] In a study of 142 patients with complete paraplegia, none of the patients with injury above T9 and only 20% of patients with injury below T12 were ambulatory at 1 year.[75] A more recent study reported that 44% of patients with complete neurologic injury and 73% of patients with incomplete injury recovered at least one grade on the American Spinal Injury Association scale.[53] Traumatic injury to the thoracolumbar spine, particularly a thoracolumbar burst fracture, typically causes contusion to the conus medullaris and cauda equina, with a mixed prognosis.

Summary

Thoracolumbar fracture is a common injury with complex biomechanical and technical diagnostic and reconstruction challenges. The status of the PLC and neurologic elements should be considered as well as the injury to the bony elements. Surgical reconstruction, if necessary, should include the site of neurologic compression and provide skeletal stability.

Annotated References

1. Johnell O, Kanis JA: An estimate of the worldwide prevalence and disability associated with osteoporotic fractures. *Osteoporos Int* 2006;17(12):1726-1733.

   A study designed to quantify the global burden of osteoporotic fracture found significant morbidity and mortality, particularly in developed countries.

3: Spine Trauma

2. Koller H, Acosta F, Hempfing A, et al: Long-term investigation of nonsurgical treatment for thoracolumbar and lumbar burst fractures: An outcome analysis in sight of spinopelvic balance. *Eur Spine J* 2008;17(8): 1073-1095.

   At long-term follow-up of patients who underwent nonsurgical treatment of a burst fracture, sagittal plane deformity and a 62% rate of good or excellent outcomes were found. Level of evidence: IV.

3. Denis F: The three column spine and its significance in the classification of acute thoracolumbar spinal injuries. *Spine (Phila Pa 1976)* 1983;8(8):817-831.

4. Wood KB, Bohn D, Mehbod A: Anterior versus posterior treatment of stable thoracolumbar burst fractures without neurologic deficit: A prospective, randomized study. *J Spinal Disord Tech* 2005;18(suppl):S15-S23.

   A prospective randomized study compared anterior-only and posterior-only instrumented fusion for thoracolumbar burst fractures. The results were similar, but anterior surgery had fewer complications.

5. Oner FC, van Gils AP, Faber JA, Dhert WJ, Verbout AJ: Some complications of common treatment schemes of thoracolumbar spine fractures can be predicted with magnetic resonance imaging: Prospective study of 53 patients with 71 fractures. *Spine (Phila Pa 1976)* 2002; 27(6):629-636.

6. Meves R, Avanzi O: Correlation between neurological deficit and spinal canal compromise in 198 patients with thoracolumbar and lumbar fractures. *Spine (Phila Pa 1976)* 2005;30(7):787-791.

   A retrospective study found that progressive stenosis of the thoracolumbar and lumbar spine caused by retropulsed bony fragments after spine fracture increased the likelihood of neurologic deficit; 78% or 68% of patients had 75% canal stenosis after a thoracolumbar or lumbar fracture, respectively. Level of evidence: IV.

7. Caffaro MF, Avanzi O: Is there a difference between narrowing of the spinal canal and neurological deficits comparing Denis and Magerl classifications? *Spinal Cord* 2011;49(2):297-301.

   A retrospective CT reivew of thoracolumbar and lumbar burst fractures in 227 patients found that the likelihood of neurologic deficit was correlated with bone fragment size, regardless of the classification system used.

8. Marino RJ, Ditunno JF Jr, Donovan WH, Maynard F Jr: Neurologic recovery after traumatic spinal cord injury: Data from the Model Spinal Cord Injury Systems. *Arch Phys Med Rehabil* 1999;80(11):1391-1396.

9. Vale FL, Burns J, Jackson AB, Hadley MN: Combined medical and surgical treatment after acute spinal cord injury: Results of a prospective pilot study to assess the merits of aggressive medical resuscitation and blood pressure management. *J Neurosurg* 1997;87(2):239-246.

10. Levi L, Wolf A, Belzberg H: Hemodynamic parameters in patients with acute cervical cord trauma: Description, intervention, and prediction of outcome. *Neurosurgery* 1993;33(6):1007-1017.

11. Lee JY, Vaccaro AR, Schweitzer KM Jr, et al: Assessment of injury to the thoracolumbar posterior ligamentous complex in the setting of normal-appearing plain radiography. *Spine J* 2007;7(4):422-427.

    In patients with normal-appearing plain radiographs, the most common determinants of PLC injury were ligament disruption on T1-weighted MRI and diastasis of the facet joints on CT. Level of evidence: V.

12. Dai LY, Wang XY, Jiang LS, Jiang SD, Xu HZ: Plain radiography versus computed tomography scans in the diagnosis and management of thoracolumbar burst fractures. *Spine (Phila Pa 1976)* 2008;33(16):E548-E552.

    Radiographs and CT of thoracolumbar burst fractures were reviewed retrospectively. Although radiographs provide sufficient detail for gross preoperative planning, CT is useful for selection of the appropriate treatment strategy and detailed planning. Level of evidence: IV.

13. Smith-Bindman R, Lipson J, Marcus R, et al: Radiation dose associated with common computed tomography examinations and the associated lifetime attributable risk of cancer. *Arch Intern Med* 2009;169(22):2078-2086.

    Radiation dosages from common diagnostic CT examinations are higher and more variable than generally thought. There is a need for greater standardization across institutions. Level of evidence: IV.

14. Smith AB, Dillon WP, Lau BC, et al: Radiation dose reduction strategy for CT protocols: Successful implementation in neuroradiology section. *Radiology* 2008; 247(2):499-506.

    The use of dosage modulation techniques for neuroradiology CT offers a significant dose reduction while maintaining image quality. Level of evidence: IV.

15. Terk MR, Hume-Neal M, Fraipont M, Ahmadi J, Colletti PM: Injury of the posterior ligament complex in patients with acute spinal trauma: Evaluation by MR imaging. *AJR Am J Roentgenol* 1997;168(6):1481-1486.

16. Kim NR, Hong SH, Choi JY, et al: Spreading epidural hematoma and deep subcutaneous edema: Indirect MRI signs of posterior ligamentous complex injury in thoracolumbar burst fractures. *Skeletal Radiol* 2010;39(8): 767-772.

    Spreading epidural hematoma and deep subcutaneous edema were significantly associated with injury to the PLC after thoracolumbar trauma. Level of evidence: III.

17. Haba H, Taneichi H, Kotani Y, et al: Diagnostic accuracy of magnetic resonance imaging for detecting posterior ligamentous complex injury associated with thoracic and lumbar fractures. *J Neurosurg* 2003;99(1, suppl):20-26.

18. Rihn JA, Fisher C, Harrop J, Morrison W, Yang N, Vaccaro AR: Assessment of the posterior ligamentous complex following acute cervical spine trauma. *J Bone Joint Surg Am* 2010;92(3):583-589.

    MRI was sensitive for evaluating injury to the PLC after acute cervical trauma but had a relatively low positive predictive value and specificity. Injury to the PCL may be overread on MRI. Level of evidence: II.

19. Vaccaro AR, Lehman RA Jr, Hurlbert RJ, et al: A new classification of thoracolumbar injuries: The importance of injury morphology, the integrity of the posterior ligamentous complex, and neurologic status. *Spine (Phila Pa 1976)* 2005;30(20):2325-2333.

    A classification system is proposed for fracture morphology, neurologic status, and evidence of injury to the PLC. Application of the system to typical fractures is described. Level of evidence: II.

20. Harrop JS, Vaccaro AR, Hurlbert RJ, et al: Intrarater and interrater reliability and validity in the assessment of the mechanism of injury and integrity of the posterior ligamentous complex: A novel injury severity scoring system for thoracolumbar injuries. Invited submission from the Joint Section Meeting on Disorders of the Spine and Peripheral Nerves, March 2005. *J Neurosurg Spine* 2006;4(2):118-122.

    The use of the TLICS is validated, and its interobserver and intraobserver reliability is presented. Level of evidence: III.

21. Stadhouder A, Buskens E, Vergroesen DA, Fidler MW, de Nies F, Öner FC: Nonoperative treatment of thoracic and lumbar spine fractures: a prospective randomized study of different treatment options. *J Orthop Trauma* 2009;23(8):588-594.

    A prospective randomized study compared the use of physical therapy alone, a removable brace, or a plaster cast for treating burst and compression fractures. Brace treatment with supplementary physical therapy is the treatment of choice for patients with compression fractures of the thoracic and lumbar spine. More than 20% of all patients had moderate or severe back pain at long-term follow-up. Level of evidence: I.

22. Ohana N, Sheinis D, Rath E, Sasson A, Atar D: Is there a need for lumbar orthosis in mild compression fractures of the thoracolumbar spine? A retrospective study comparing the radiographic results between early ambulation with and without lumbar orthosis. *J Spinal Disord* 2000;13(4):305-308.

23. Holdsworth F: Fractures, dislocations, and fracture-dislocations of the spine. *J Bone Joint Surg Am* 1970;52(8):1534-1551.

24. McAfee PC, Yuan HA, Lasda NA: The unstable burst fracture. *Spine (Phila Pa 1976)* 1982;7(4):365-373.

25. Oner FC, van Gils AP, Dhert WJ, Verbout AJ: MRI findings of thoracolumbar spine fractures: A categorisation based on MRI examinations of 100 fractures. *Skeletal Radiol* 1999;28(8):433-443.

26. Hashimoto T, Kaneda K, Abumi K: Relationship between traumatic spinal canal stenosis and neurologic deficits in thoracolumbar burst fractures. *Spine (Phila Pa 1976)* 1988;13(11):1268-1272.

27. Dai LY, Wang XY, Jiang LS: Neurologic recovery from thoracolumbar burst fractures: Is it predicted by the amount of initial canal encroachment and kyphotic deformity? *Surg Neurol* 2007;67(3):232-238.

    Neurologic recovery from thoracolumbar burst fracture was not predicted by the amount of initial canal encroachment or kyphotic deformity. Therefore, both neurologic function and spine stability should be taken into account. Level of evidence: III.

28. Lakshmanan P, Jones A, Mehta J, Ahuja S, Davies PR, Howes JP: Recurrence of kyphosis and its functional implications after surgical stabilization of dorsolumbar unstable burst fractures. *Spine J* 2009;9(12):1003-1009.

    Even without implant removal, there was a progressive loss of correction of the angle of kyphosis after posterior stabilization with instrumentation, primarily corresponding to the decrease in the anterior segment height of the fractured vertebral body. Level of evidence: IV.

29. Wang XY, Dai LY, Xu HZ, Chi YL: Kyphosis recurrence after posterior short-segment fixation in thoracolumbar burst fractures. *J Neurosurg Spine* 2008;8(3):246-254.

    The use of a posterior-only construct for burst fractures led to late kyphosis. Anterior column reconstruction is necessary if the wedge angle cannot be restored after posterior instrumentation. Level of evidence: IV.

30. Wood K, Buttermann G, Mehbod A, et al: Operative compared with nonoperative treatment of a thoracolumbar burst fracture without neurological deficit: A prospective, randomized study. *J Bone Joint Surg Am* 2003;85-A(5):773-781. [Erratum, *J Bone Joint Surg Am* 2004 86(6):1283.]

    A prospective randomized study compared surgical and nonsurgical treatment for thoracolumbar burst fractures. The results were similar, but nonsurgical treatment had fewer complications.

31. Weninger P, Schultz A, Hertz H: Conservative management of thoracolumbar and lumbar spine compression and burst fractures: Functional and radiographic outcomes in 136 cases treated by closed reduction and casting. *Arch Orthop Trauma Surg* 2009;129(2):207-219.

    A retrospective study found closed reduction and casting to be safe and effective for treating compression and burst-type fractures at the thoracolumbar junction and to restore neurologic function in patients with unilateral radicular pain. This method was less effective in lumbar and burst-type fractures with posterior column involvement. Level of evidence: IV.

32. Alanay A, Yazici M, Acaroglu E, Turhan E, Cila A, Surat A: Course of nonsurgical management of burst fractures with intact posterior ligamentous complex: An MRI study. *Spine (Phila Pa 1976)* 2004;29(21):2425-2431.

33. Bailey CS, Dvorak MF, Thomas KC, et al: Comparison of thoracolumbosacral orthosis and no orthosis for the treatment of thoracolumbar burst fractures: Interim analysis of a multicenter randomized clinical equivalence trial. *J Neurosurg Spine* 2009;11(3):295-303.

A prospective randomized study found no significant difference at 1- to 2-year follow-up between patients with a type A3 burst fracture treated with or without a thoracolumbosacral orthosis for any outcome measure at any stage. Level of evidence: II.

34. Shi J, Yang H: Comparison of radiography and computed tomography in evaluating posterior indirect reduction of spinal canal bone fragment. *Orthopedics* 2010;159-164.

A retrospective case study of indirect reduction and posterior-only instrumentation for patients with a burst fracture and canal compromise found that canal compromise improved after indirect reduction. Level of evidence: IV.

35. Willén J, Lindahl S, Irstam L, Nordwall A: Unstable thoracolumbar fractures: A study by CT and conventional roentgenology of the reduction effect of Harrington instrumentation. *Spine (Phila Pa 1976)* 1984;9(2):214-219.

36. Kaya RA, Aydin Y: Modified transpedicular approach for the surgical treatment of severe thoracolumbar or lumbar burst fractures. *Spine J* 2004;4(2):208-217.

37. Kong W, Sun Y, Hu J, Xu J: Modified posterior decompression for the management of thoracolumbar burst fractures with canal encroachment. *J Spinal Disord Tech* 2010;23(5):302-309.

The clinical and radiographic results of posterior reduction and instrumentation of burst fracture for a transpedicular decompression using a surgical instrument developed by the authors. Level of evidence: IV.

38. Viale GL, Silvestro C, Francaviglia N, et al: Transpedicular decompression and stabilization of burst fractures of the lumbar spine. *Surg Neurol* 1993;40(2):104-111.

39. Tisot RA, Avanzi O: Laminar fractures as a severity marker in burst fractures of the thoracolumbar spine. *J Orthop Surg (Hong Kong)* 2009;17(3):261-264.

40. Cammisa FP Jr, Eismont FJ, Green BA: Dural laceration occurring with burst fractures and associated laminar fractures. *J Bone Joint Surg Am* 1989;71(7):1044-1052.

41. McLain RF, Sparling E, Benson DR: Early failure of short-segment pedicle instrumentation for thoracolumbar fractures: A preliminary report. *J Bone Joint Surg Am* 1993;75(2):162-167.

42. Kim HS, Lee SY, Nanda A, et al: Comparison of surgical outcomes in thoracolumbar fractures operated with posterior constructs having varying fixation length with selective anterior fusion. *Yonsei Med J* 2009;50(4):546-554.

The results of treating thoracolumbar burst fractures with intermediate segment fixation were worse than the results of intermediate segment fixation with instrumentation at the fracture level or long-segment fixation. Level of evidence: III.

43. McCormack T, Karaikovic E, Gaines RW: The load sharing classification of spine fractures. *Spine (Phila Pa 1976)* 1994;19(15):1741-1744.

44. Dai LY, Jiang LS, Jiang SD: Conservative treatment of thoracolumbar burst fractures: A long-term follow-up results with special reference to the load sharing classification. *Spine (Phila Pa 1976)* 2008;33(23):2536-2544.

Nonsurgical treatment of patients with a thoracolumbar burst fracture is described. The LSS can be used in surgical decision making. Level of evidence: IV.

45. Dai LY, Jiang LS, Jiang SD: Posterior short-segment fixation with or without fusion for thoracolumbar burst fractures: A five to seven-year prospective randomized study. *J Bone Joint Surg Am* 2009;91(5):1033-1041.

No difference in radiographic or clinical results was found at 5-year follow-up of patients treated with or without posterolateral bone grafting after posterior instrumentation for a Denis B burst fracture. Level of evidence: I.

46. Tezeren G, Bulut O, Tukenmez M, Ozturk H, Oztemur Z, Ozturk A: Long segment instrumentation of thoracolumbar burst fracture: Fusion versus nonfusion. *J Back Musculoskelet Rehabil* 2009;22(2):107-112.

Patients treated for a thoracolumbar burst fracture with long-segment instrumentation, with or without bone grafting and fusion, had similar radiographic and clinical results. Level of evidence: III.

47. Palmisani M, Gasbarrini A, Brodano GB, et al: Minimally invasive percutaneous fixation in the treatment of thoracic and lumbar spine fractures. *Eur Spine J* 2009;18(suppl 1):71-74.

48. Fuentes S, Blondel B, Metellus P, Gaudart J, Adetchessi T, Dufour H: Percutaneous kyphoplasty and pedicle screw fixation for the management of thoraco-lumbar burst fractures. *Eur Spine J* 2010;19(8):1281-1287.

A prospective case study describes the treatment of patients with a Magerl A3 fracture using vertebral augmentation and percutaneous pedicle screw fixation. Level of evidence: IV.

49. Marco RA, Kushwaha VP: Thoracolumbar burst fractures treated with posterior decompression and pedicle screw instrumentation supplemented with balloon-assisted vertebroplasty and calcium phosphate reconstruction. *J Bone Joint Surg Am* 2009;91(1):20-28.

Clinical and radiographic results are presented for patients treated with short-segment posterior spine fixation and anterior column support using cement augmentation. Level of evidence: II.

50. Dmitriev AE, Farhang S, Lehman RA Jr, Ling GS, Symes AJ: Bone morphogenetic protein-2 used in spinal fusion with spinal cord injury penetrates intrathecally

and elicits a functional signaling cascade. *Spine J* 2010; 10(1):16-25.

An in vivo rat study describes the signaling cascade that results from intrathecal diffusion of bone morphogenetic protein, which can occur in humans whenever bone morphogenetic protein is used in conjunction with dural compromise.

51. Sasani M, Özer AF: Single-stage posterior corpectomy and expandable cage placement for treatment of thoracic or lumbar burst fractures. *Spine (Phila Pa 1976)* 2009;34(1):E33-E40.

52. Kirkpatrick JS: Thoracolumbar fracture management: Anterior approach. *J Am Acad Orthop Surg* 2003; 11(5):355-363.

53. Reinhold M, Knop C, Beisse R, et al: Operative treatment of 733 patients with acute thoracolumbar spinal injuries: Comprehensive results from the second, prospective, internet-based multicenter study of the Spine Study Group of the German Association of Trauma Surgery. *Eur Spine J* 2010;19(10):1657-1676.

The report of a survey of German spine trauma surgeons describes injury patterns, surgical patterns, and outcomes at 2-year follow-up. Level of evidence: IV.

54. Vaccaro AR, Lim MR, Hurlbert RJ, et al: Surgical decision making for unstable thoracolumbar spine injuries: Results of a consensus panel review by the Spine Trauma Study Group. *J Spinal Disord Tech* 2006;19(1): 1-10.

A survey of a panel of experts provided insight into spine trauma decision making and surgical strategies. Level of evidence: V.

55. Dai LY, Ding WG, Wang XY, Jiang LS, Jiang SD, Xu HZ: Assessment of ligamentous injury in patients with thoracolumbar burst fractures using MRI. *J Trauma* 2009;66(6):1610-1615.

In a retrospective case study, there was no correlation between the extent of injury to the PLC of the spine and fracture severity. Level of evidence: IV.

56. Schultheiss M, Hartwig E, Kinzl L, Claes L, Wilke HJ: Thoracolumbar fracture stabilization: Comparative biomechanical evaluation of a new video-assisted implantable system. *Eur Spine J* 2004;13(2):93-100.

57. Gurr KR, McAfee PC, Shih CM: Biomechanical analysis of anterior and posterior instrumentation systems after corpectomy: A calf-spine model. *J Bone Joint Surg Am* 1988;70(8):1182-1191.

58. Gurwitz GS, Dawson JM, McNamara MJ, Federspiel CF, Spengler DM: Biomechanical analysis of three surgical approaches for lumbar burst fractures using short-segment instrumentation. *Spine (Phila Pa 1976)* 1993; 18(8):977-982.

59. Kallemeier PM, Beaubien BP, Buttermann GR, Polga DJ, Wood KB: In vitro analysis of anterior and posterior fixation in an experimental unstable burst fracture model. *J Spinal Disord Tech* 2008;21(3):216-224.

An in vitro cadaver burst fracture study found that the most rigid fixation was provided by circumferential instrumentation, followed by posterior fixation with anterior strut grafting, posterior fixation alone, and anterior fixation with strut grafting.

60. Bradford DS, McBride GG: Surgical management of thoracolumbar spine fractures with incomplete neurologic deficits. *Clin Orthop Relat Res* 1987;218(218): 201-216.

61. Wilke HJ, Kemmerich V, Claes LE, Arand M: Combined anteroposterior spinal fixation provides superior stabilisation to a single anterior or posterior procedure. *J Bone Joint Surg Br* 2001;83(4):609-617.

62. Rousseau MA, Lazennec JY, Saillant G: Circumferential arthrodesis using PEEK cages at the lumbar spine. *J Spinal Disord Tech* 2007;20(4):278-281.

A case study of polyetheretherketone cages used for circumferential spine fusion found a high fusion rate but a loss of lordosis, especially at caudal levels. Level of evidence: IV.

63. Levine AM, Bosse M, Edwards CC: Bilateral facet dislocations in the thoracolumbar spine. *Spine (Phila Pa 1976)* 1988;13(6):630-640.

64. Yadla S, Lebude B, Tender GC, et al: Traumatic spondyloptosis of the thoracolumbar spine. *J Neurosurg Spine* 2008;9(2):145-151.

Traumatic spondyloptosis, which is a rare condition, and its treatment are described. Level of evidence: IV.

65. Lee HM, Kim HS, Kim DJ, Suk KS, Park JO, Kim NH: Reliability of magnetic resonance imaging in detecting posterior ligament complex injury in thoracolumbar spinal fractures. *Spine (Phila Pa 1976)* 2000;25(16):2079-2084.

66. Chapman JR, Agel J, Jurkovich GJ, Bellabarba C: Thoracolumbar flexion-distraction injuries: Associated morbidity and neurological outcomes. *Spine (Phila Pa 1976)* 2008;33(6):648-657.

The characteristics of flexion-distraction injury in patients at a major trauma center are described. The incidence of neurologic deficit was 25%, and the incidence of associated abdominal injuries was 30%. Level of evidence: IV.

67. Gellad FE, Levine AM, Joslyn JN, Edwards CC, Bosse M: Pure thoracolumbar facet dislocation: Clinical features and CT appearance. *Radiology* 1986;161(2):505-508.

68. Finkelstein JA, Wai EK, Jackson SS, Ahn H, Brighton-Knight M: Single-level fixation of flexion distraction injuries. *J Spinal Disord Tech* 2003;16(3):236-242.

69. Tezer M, Ozturk C, Aydogan M, Mirzanli C, Talu U, Hamzaoglu A: Surgical outcome of thoracolumbar burst fractures with flexion-distraction injury of the posterior elements. *Int Orthop* 2005;29(6):347-350.

3: Spine Trauma

Consecutive patients with a flexion-distraction injury were treated using circumferential fusion, with an average 70-month follow-up. Level of evidence: IV.

70. Kerwin AJ, Frykberg ER, Schinco MA, et al: The effect of early surgical treatment of traumatic spine injuries on patient mortality. *J Trauma* 2007;63(6):1308-1313.

    Analysis of a large database indicated that early treatment of traumatic spinal injury is associated with elevated mortality, compared with fixation 48 hours or more after injury. Level of evidence: III.

71. Schinkel C, Frangen TM, Kmetic A, Andress HJ, Muhr G: German Trauma Registry: Timing of thoracic spine stabilization in trauma patients: Impact on clinical course and outcome. *J Trauma* 2006;61(1):156-160.

    Analysis of a large database indicated that surgical treatment of spine fractures within 72 hours of injury is associated with decreased mortality. Level of evidence: III.

72. Cengiz SL, Kalkan E, Bayir A, Ilik K, Basefer A: Timing of thoracolomber spine stabilization in trauma patients; impact on neurological outcome and clinical course: A real prospective (rct) randomized controlled study. *Arch Orthop Trauma Surg* 2008;128(9):959-966.

    A prospective randomized study found more favorable results in patients treated within 8 hours of injury than in those treated 3 to 15 days after injury. Level of evidence: II.

73. Rutges JP, Oner FC, Leenen LP: Timing of thoracic and lumbar fracture fixation in spinal injuries: A systematic review of neurological and clinical outcome. *Eur Spine J* 2007;16(5):579-587.

    A systematic review concluded that early fixation leads to a lower complication rate but does not necessarily improve the outcome of thoracolumbar trauma.

74. Waters RL, Adkins RH, Yakura JS, Sie I: Motor and sensory recovery following incomplete paraplegia. *Arch Phys Med Rehabil* 1994;75(1):67-72.

75. Waters RL, Yakura JS, Adkins RH, Sie I: Recovery following complete paraplegia. *Arch Phys Med Rehabil* 1992;73(9):784-789.

3: Spine Trauma

Chapter 22

Fractures of the Sacrum

Carlo Bellabarba, MD   Thomas A. Schildhauer, MD   Jens R. Chapman, MD

Introduction

A sacral fracture may be intrinsic to the sacrum, involve injury to the pelvic ring or lumbosacral junction, or be a combination of these injury patterns. The cause usually is a high-energy trauma, as in an automobile or motorcycle crash, a fall from a height, or an industrial accident with a crushing mechanism. Insufficiency fractures resulting from a low-impact or chronic force in a patient with a metabolic bone disorder are a separate entity not discussed in this chapter. Sacral fracture as part of pelvic ring injury is caused by an anterior or lateral compression force or a vertical shear mechanism; the fracture line generally is longitudinal, in a plane parallel to the long axis of the sacrum. In a sacral fracture-dislocation associated with spinopelvic dissociation, the spinal column typically creates a flexion or extension moment arm on the posterior pelvic ring, often with an associated axial loading vector. The result often is a comminuted and complex multiplanar sacral fracture pattern with functional dissociation of the spine from the pelvis, with associated pelvic instability.

The evaluation and treatment of a sacral injury must take into account the complexity of the spinopelvic junction, the challenges associated with fixation of the sacrum and posterior pelvic ring, and the relatively large forces that must be neutralized to achieve and maintain a reduction across the spinopelvic junction. The difficulty of achieving adequate skeletal stabilization after extensive lumbosacral neural decompression has been attributed to the limitations of previously available implants, which were primarily designed for

thoracolumbar deformity surgery or extremity trauma. The osteosynthesis techniques developed for pelvic ring injuries often are not suited to stabilizing the multidirectional instabilities that characterize many sacral fracture-dislocations with spinopelvic dissociation. The treatment often was nonsurgical, with acceptance that the patient would require long-term immobilization and have residual sacral deformity, chronic pain, and unchanged or mildly improved neurologic symptoms. Advances in imaging and stabilization techniques now permit more standardized, biomechanically advantageous surgical treatment of patients with sacral fracture.

Anatomy

The sacrum acts as a V-shaped keystone between the lower lumbar spine and the pelvic ring. Its integrity guarantees the maintenance of normal spinopelvic alignment. The overall kyphotic shape of the five fused sacral vertebral bodies is the basis of lumbar lordosis. The 45° slope of the S1 superior end plate relative to the horizontal plane is critical in determining the amount of shear force to which the lumbosacral junction is subjected.[1] On either side, the lateral portions of S1 and S2 articulate with the ilium through the sacroiliac joints, reinforced by strong anterior and posterior sacroiliac ligaments. Additional support to the sacroiliac joints is provided by the sacrospinous and sacrotuberous ligaments.

In cross-section, the sacral spinal canal changes from a capacious triangular structure at S1 to a flat, narrow structure at the lower sacral segments. The sacrum protects the lumbosacral plexus, whose L5, S1, and lower sacral roots provide bowel and bladder control as well as sexual function. The sacral roots course through the sacrum itself, but the L5 root exits rostral to the sacrum, coursing along the shoulder of the sacral ala in close proximity to its ventral surface. The cerebrospinal fluid–containing dural sac usually ends at the S2 segment. Sacral motor roots emerge through the ventral foramina to their target organs. A relatively narrow channel is available for passage of the S1 roots, which occupy one third of their respective foramina. Each lower sacral root is of progressively smaller size and occupies a progressively smaller space within its foramen; the S4 root occupies only one sixth of its ventral foraminal space.[2] The cutaneous posterior rami of the sacral

Dr. Bellabarba or an immediate family member serves as a board member, owner, officer, or committee member of AOSpine North America; is a member of a speakers' bureau or has made paid presentations on behalf of Synthes; and has received research or institutional support from Stryker and Synthes. Dr. Schildhauer or an immediate family member is a member of a speakers' bureau or has made paid presentations on behalf of Smith & Nephew and Zimmer; and serves as a paid consultant to or is an employee of Smith & Nephew and Zimmer. Dr. Chapman or an immediate family member serves as a board member, owner, officer, or committee member of AOSpine North America; is a member of a speakers' bureau or has made paid presentations on behalf of Synthes; and has received research or institutional support from Medtronic and Stryker.

3: Spine Trauma

roots pass through the posterior sacral foramina before contributing to the cluneal nerves. The ventral rami of the S2-S5 roots, with S3 as the main neural branch of the so-called pudendal plexus, comprise the pelvic splanchnic nerves, which provide parasympathetic control to the bladder and the rectum. Sympathetic input to the inferior hypogastric plexus primarily is derived from the sympathetic ganglia located on the anterolateral aspect of the L5 and S1 vertebral bodies, which course caudally along the ventral surface of the sacrum just medial to the ventral S2-S4 foramina.

Classification

The AO/Orthopaedic Trauma Association (OTA) classification (the most commonly used fracture classification for orthopaedic and trauma surgery) categorizes sacral fractures in the context of overall pelvic stability as 61-A3, 61-B1 to 61-B3, and 61-C1 to 61-C3 (Figure 1). A 61-A3 fracture does not compromise the integrity of the posterior pelvic ring and generally involves a direct-impact injury to the caudal aspect of the sacrum, below the sacroiliac joints. A 61-B injury represents an incomplete disruption of the osseoligamentous integrity of the posterior pelvic ring, with an intact pelvic floor and therefore no vertical displacement. More specifically, a 61-B1 injury involves unilateral dislocation of the sacroiliac joint, a 61-B2 injury involves unilateral sacral fracture associated with an open-book or lateral compression pelvic injury, and a 61-B3 injury is bilateral, with a pattern similar to that of 61-B2. A 61-C injury is a so-called vertical shear injury and involves the complete loss of osseoligamentous stability of the posterior arch and disruption of the pelvic floor. A 61-C1 injury affects one hemipelvis, a 61-C2 injury also includes a contralateral (B-type) incomplete injury, and a 61-C3 injury is a bilateral C-type injury.

The Denis classification specifically focuses on sacral fractures (Figure 2). This widely used system correlates anatomic factors with neurologic injury risk on a progressive severity scale. The Denis system differentiates alar fracture (zone 1), transforaminal fracture (zone 2), and central fracture, which includes any fracture extending into the spinal canal (zone 3).[3] Lumbosacral stability is not taken into account, however. The Isler classification recognizes that a vertical sacral fracture extends rostrally lateral to, through, or medial to the S1 superior facet and that a fracture involving or extending medial to the L5-S1 facet may cause lumbosacral instability[4] (Figure 3).

Sacral fracture-dislocation associated with spinopelvic dissociation is characterized by bilateral vertical fracture, often connected by a somewhat transverse fracture line or a series of comminuted fracture lines. In descriptive terms, the result is a U-type fracture, or, if the vertical fracture lines extend and exit caudal to the sacroiliac joint, an H-type (bilateral pelvic instability) or Y-type (unilateral pelvic instability) fracture or a similar permutation. H- and Y-type fracture patterns

disrupt the posterior pelvic ring and cause pelvic instability. Typically they also are associated with an anterior pelvic ring injury. The L-, T-, and λ-type fracture patterns are less commonly encountered[5] (Figure 4). U-type and H-type sacral fracture-dislocations are summarized in the AO/OTA system as the type 61-C3.3 pelvic fracture. In the Denis classification, such fracture-dislocations are zone 3 injuries because they involve the sacral canal.

Unfortunately, these classifications do not take into account the mechanism of injury or the type, magnitude, or direction of fracture displacement. The helpful Roy-Camille subclassification of Denis zone 3 injuries and sacral fracture-dislocations associated with spinopelvic dissociation describes three types of transversely oriented sacral fractures that are classified according to injury severity and presumed likelihood of neurologic injury.[6] The model of a single transverse fracture line connecting two longitudinally oriented fractures is overly simple; the fracture pattern usually is more complex, and the comminution is more extensive. A type 1 injury consists of a simple flexion deformity of the sacrum without translation and is believed to result from an axial-loading injury with the spine in flexion. A type 2 injury is characterized by flexion and posterior translation of the upper sacrum, also presumably caused by an axial-loading injury with the spine in flexion. A type 3 injury has complete anterior translation of the upper sacrum, typically caused by an axial-loading force in extension. A type 4 injury was later added; it consists of a segmental comminuted S1 vertebral body caused by axial implosion of the lumbar spine into the upper sacrum[7] (Figure 5). All of these injuries are caused by indirect force to the lumbosacral junction. A direct impact force, as in impalement or gunshot injury, can result in a completely disrupted sacrum with lumbosacral instability.[8] These injuries can be classified as type 5.

The spinopelvic junction typically is not compromised by a vertical sacral fracture extending rostrally lateral to the facet joint or by a transverse sacral fracture distal to the sacroiliac joint. Sacral fracture associated with functional instability of the spinopelvic junction primarily occurs under two circumstances: if a vertical sacral fracture, which constitutes the posterior component of a pelvic ring injury, extends rostrally into or medial to the S1 superior facet, thereby disarticulating the L5-S1 facet from the stable (medial) sacral fracture fragment; or if a multiplanar sacral fracture (with many possible fracture patterns but often composed of bilateral longitudinal fractures and a transverse fracture component) separates the upper central sacrum and remainder of the spine from the peripheral sacrum and attached pelvis. The result of this fracture pattern and its variants is dissociation of the spine from the pelvic ring and functional spinopelvic instability. Treatment of these complex sacral fractures necessitates a combined approach that merges conventional concepts of spinal and pelvic trauma surgery.

Pelvis, ring, stable (61-A)
1. Fracture of innominate bone, avulsion (61-A1)

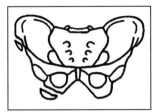

2. Fracture of innominate bone, direct blow (61-A2)

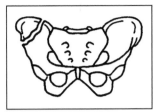

3. Transverse fracture of sacrum and coccyx (61-A3)

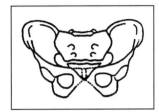

Pelvis, ring, partially stable (61-B)
1. Unilateral, partial disruption of posterior arch, external rotation ("open-book" injury) (61-B1)

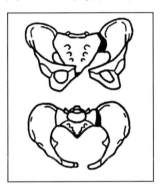

2. Unilateral, partial disruption of posterior arch, internal rotation (lateral compression injury) (61-B2)

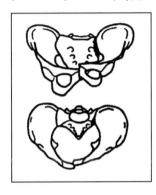

3. Bilateral, partial lesion of posterior arch (61-B3)

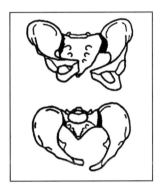

Pelvis, ring, complete disruption of posterior arch unstable (61-C)
1. Unilateral, complete disruption of posterior arch (61-C1)

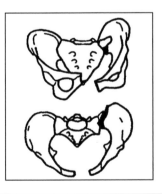

2. Bilateral, ipsilateral complete, contralateral incomplete (61-C2)

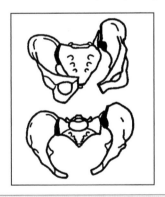

3. Bilateral, complete disruption (61-C3)

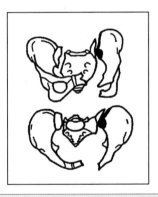

Figure 1 The AO/OTA classification of pelvic fractures. (Adapted with permission from Marsh JL, Slongo TF, Agel J, et al: Orthopaedic Trauma Association Classification, Database and Outcomes Committee: Fracture and dislocation classification compendium: 2007. *J Orthop Trauma* 2007;21[10, suppl]:S60.)

Clinical Evaluation

Examination
The initial physical examination follows the Advanced Trauma Life Support protocol for recording of vital signs and cognitive status. A formal log-rolling technique is required to allow inspection and palpation of the patient's posterior spine and integument. Sentinel examination includes the following findings in the sacral region and surrounding posterior soft tissues: tenderness, swelling, ballottable subcutaneous fluid, overt soft-tissue disruption, crepitus, and atypical bony prominences or step-offs. Severe subcutaneous degloving can involve several of these findings, including soft-

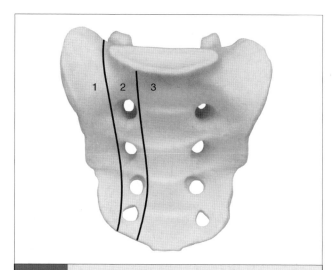

Figure 2   Schematic drawing showing the Denis classification of sacral fractures, in which zone 1 is alar, zone 2 is transforaminal, and zone 3 extends into the spinal canal.

tissue crepitus and formation of subcutaneous fluid collections at a considerable distance from the fracture, in association with extensive contusion of the skin.

Formal testing of neurologic function should be performed using American Spinal Injury Association principles.[9] The rectal examination should include specific assessment of motor, reflex, and sensory components of the lumbosacral and sacral plexus as well as screening for overt or occult blood in the meatus, rectum, or vaginal vault.[10,11] Bowel, bladder, or sexual dysfunction generally requires bilateral injury to the S2-S4 roots. In unilateral Denis zone 1 and 2 fractures the neurologic deficits generally are limited to the lower extremities. Six percent of zone 1 injuries are associated with sensorimotor deficits and primarily involve the L5 nerve root distribution, which is in a vulnerable position along the sacral ala. Lower extremity neurologic deficits occur in 28% of zone 2 injuries and may affect multiple nerve roots, depending on the involved foramina. The likelihood of neurologic deficits in a zone 3 injury is 57%;

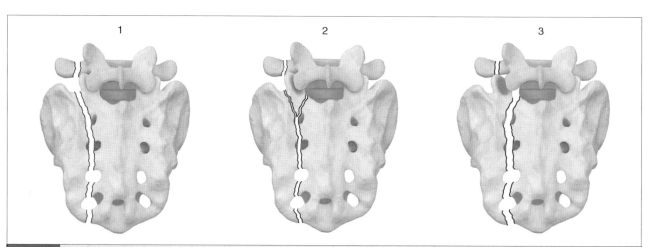

Figure 3   Schematic drawings showing the Isler classification of lumbosacral injuries. In type 1 the sacral fracture extends lateral to the L5-S1 facet joint, in type 2 the sacral fracture involves the L5-S1 facet joint, and in type 3 the sacral fracture extends medial to the L5-S1 facet joint. In types 2 and 3, there is a risk of instability at the lumbosacral junction.

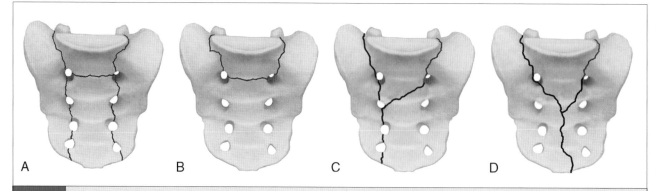

Figure 4   Schematic drawings showing the descriptive classification of multiplanar sacral fractures: the H-, U-, λ-, and Y-type fracture patterns (A, B, C, and D, respectively).

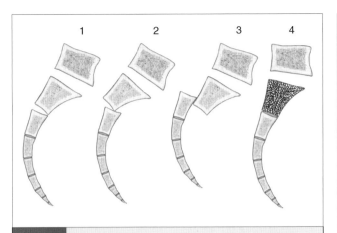

Figure 5 | Schematic drawings showing the Roy-Camille/Strange-Vognsen subclassification of Denis zone 3 sacral fractures. Type 1 is a simple flexion deformity of the sacrum without translation, type 2 is a posterior translation of the upper sacrum with kyphosis, type 3 is an anterior translation of the upper sacrum with extension deformity, and type 4 is a segmental comminution of the S1 vertebral body caused by axial loading of the lumbar spine into the cephalad sacrum.

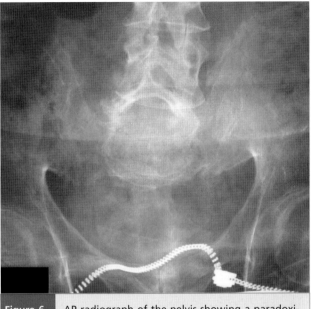

Figure 6 | AP radiograph of the pelvis showing a paradoxical inlet view resulting from sacral kyphosis.

three fourths of these deficits involve a loss of bowel, bladder, or sexual function, probably because of bilateral root injury.[3]

Imaging

The initial evaluation of a patient with a traumatic injury often includes an AP pelvic radiograph. A U- or H-type sacral fracture should be suspected if the radiograph shows bilateral vertical fracture lines or a sacral inclination so great as to give the appearance of an inlet view of the S1 vertebral body on an AP view of the pelvic ring (a so-called paradoxical inlet) (Figure 6). A lateral radiograph of the sacrum may help identify a transverse sacral fracture or fracture-dislocation not visible on standard plain pelvic radiographs (Figure 7).

If there is suspicion of a sacral fracture on plain radiographs, pelvic CT is needed (Figure 8). CT is becoming the primary radiographic screening tool, precluding the need for plain radiography. Axial images often are sufficient for identifying a simple fracture pattern such as a vertical Denis zone 1 or 2 injury, although CT reconstruction of inlet and outlet pelvic views may be useful. A sacral CT may provide additional insight into a complex sacral fracture pattern.[12] The acquisition of 2-mm or thinner slices allows high-quality sagittal and coronal reformation, which provides comprehensive visualization of the sacral anatomy and identification of lumbosacral pathology. Abdominopelvic CT increasingly is used as a screening tool for visceral injury in patients with trauma; if a fracture is identified, similar multiplanar reconstruction allows high-resolution CT evaluation of the sacrum.

MRI can be helpful for determining the etiology of a neurologic deficit and ruling out associated spinal cord

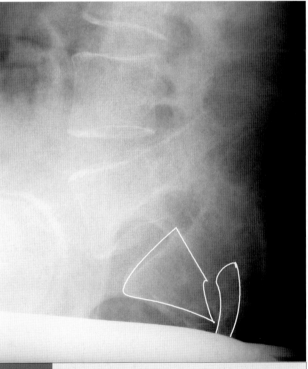

Figure 7 | Lateral radiograph of the pelvis showing a displaced zone 3 sacral fracture (outlined).

injury or hematoma, for which the neurologic findings may be more rostral. Recent advances in MRI neurography allow visualization of acute or chronic lumbosacral plexus injuries. Retrograde cystourethrograms or a diatrizoic acid enema can be useful for identifying associated bladder, urethral, or rectal injury.

3: Spine Trauma

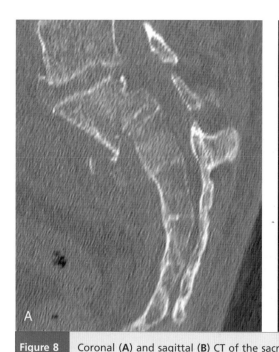
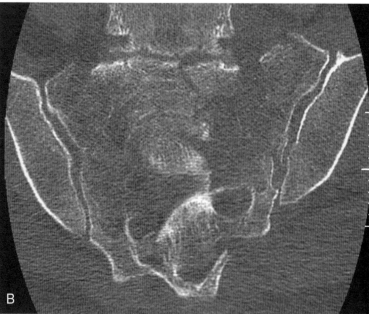

Figure 8   Coronal (**A**) and sagittal (**B**) CT of the sacrum showing a zone 3 sacral insufficiency fracture in a patient with progressively increasing low back pain and cauda equina deficits.

Treatment

Emergency resuscitation is the first priority for a patient with acute traumatic injury, following the Advanced Trauma Life Support protocol for treating immediately life-threatening conditions and maintaining hemodynamic stability. If the patient has a sacral fracture as part of an unstable pelvic ring injury, the application of a circumferential pelvic antishock sheet or anterior external fixator may be indicated during the early resuscitative phase to reduce pelvic volume and provide provisional pelvic stability.[13,14] Severe soft-tissue injuries such as abrasions, lacerations, and internal degloving (Morel-Lavallée) lesions must be identified because of their significance for further management of the lumbosacral injury.

Neurologic Recovery

Approximately 80% of patients have neurologic improvement after sacral fracture-dislocation, regardless of treatment.[2,15] Several small studies described better neurologic outcomes with surgical treatment, particularly in patients with bowel or bladder impairment.[3,16-18] These studies had significant shortcomings, however; in addition to small cohort sizes and selection bias, the type and severity of neural encroachment were not reported for patients who were nonsurgically treated. The significance and reliability of the reported recovery rates are limited by study variability in injury types, persistence of pelvic instability, timing of intervention, adequacy of decompression, type of pelvic stabilization, extent of improvement, and outcome criteria.[3,19]

Patients with a predominantly neurapraxic-type single-root lesion, with no significant bony encroachment of the neural elements, can be expected to have spontaneous neurologic improvement over time. The currently used neuroimaging and electrophysiologic tests do not allow for conclusive preoperative differentiation among sacral root traction, compression, transection, and avulsion. Preoperative determination of the type of neural injury remains a matter of clinical judgment. In general, a traction injury to peripheral nerves has a worse prognosis than a compression injury.[10] A traction injury to the lumbosacral plexus and sacral roots in the presence of trauma generally occurs in conjunction with significant posterior pelvic ring disruption. Surgical intervention under such circumstances is primarily aimed at establishing a stable fracture reduction for structural purposes, with possible neurologic recovery a secondary goal. Surgical intervention to achieve neurologic improvement may be futile in a patient with transected sacral roots or neural elements exposed to significant traction or shear injury. Because of the large zone of injury associated with sacral fractures, surgical root end-to-end repair or reconstruction with interposition graft is rarely feasible. Aggressive intervention may be favored, however, based on the observation that restoration of even unilateral sacral root function can lead to a return of voluntary continence.[20]

Nonsurgical Treatment

Nonsurgical treatment generally is recommended for neurologically intact patients with a sacral fracture that does not compromise pelvic or spinopelvic stability, such as a transverse fracture below the sacroiliac joints

(AO/OTA 61-A3). Nonsurgical treatment is appropriate for an incomplete, unilateral AO/OTA 61-B sacral fracture (Denis zone 1 or 2) involving either the ventral or dorsal cortex, but not both. The nonsurgical treatment consists of a short period of bed rest followed by early mobilization and protected weight bearing on the injured side, with or without the use of an orthotic device.[7,15,17,21] Unfortunately, there is little consensus on the tolerable extent of fracture displacement or the definition of instability. An analysis of long-term functional outcomes after surgical or nonsurgical treatment of sacral fracture found a high rate of fair or poor results unrelated to the magnitude of residual displacement and believed to result from pain or a radicular lesion.[22] Displacement of 5 mm sometimes is considered to be the threshold for mandatory surgical stabilization of a complete Denis zone 1 or 2 fracture involving both the ventral and dorsal cortices. This threshold varies considerably in clinical practice, however. The significant potential for late displacement of a complete fracture may justify percutaneous stabilization even if the fracture is minimally displaced.

Severe comminution, relative osteopenia of the sacral ala, the anatomic complexity of the sacrum, and the absence of instrumentation well suited to this region are among the specific challenges associated with achieving stable fixation of the sacrum in a zone 3 sacral-U fracture variant (AO/OTA 61-C3.3). In the past, such factors may have contributed to a reluctance to treat the fracture surgically. However, surgical intervention is recommended for these injuries because nonsurgical treatment probably would require 8 to 12 weeks of bed rest and distal femoral skeletal traction, with a high risk of complications including skin breakdown at the apex of the sacral kyphosis.[10]

Surgical Treatment

The treatment of choice for a patient with a displaced sacral fracture and neurologic deficits is neural decompression by fracture reduction, with or without sacral laminectomy or foraminotomy.[18,23,24] Early fracture reduction with fixation can facilitate neural decompression and lumbosacral deformity correction.[23,24]

Open Fractures

An open fracture or a significant soft-tissue injury requires special consideration. The wound should be débrided as soon as the patient's hemodynamic condition is stable. If there is perineal involvement, a urologic or gynecologic consultation should be considered. Rectal involvement requires an early loop colostomy, preferably of the transverse colon, followed by a distal colonic washout. The patient should receive prophylactic broad-spectrum antibiotics for 24 to 48 hours. Nonviable tissue requires early and sometimes repeated débridement, followed by meticulous dead space closure and drainage. Depending on the fracture type, the initial fracture stabilization may include anterior pelvic ring external fixation and percutaneous iliosacral screw

fixation of the posterior pelvis.[5,25] Definitive sacral fracture stabilization can be performed when the soft tissues are viable and progressively healing. Stabilization of the fracture is of the utmost importance in the treatment of soft-tissue injury. The degree of mechanical stability was identified as the only variable statistically associated with infection in open pelvic fractures; a mechanically unstable pelvis, as determined by physical examination, was associated with a tenfold increase in the risk of infection.[26]

Neural Decompression

Decompression of neural elements can be accomplished by several techniques. Nerve root decompression may occur indirectly with fracture reduction, most effectively before fracture hematoma consolidation. Direct neural decompression requires a laminectomy, followed by decompression of each involved sacral root to its ventral foraminal exit. A multilevel sacral laminectomy is necessary for a complex sacral fracture involving extensive areas of the sacral spinal canal. Ventral canal and foraminal decompression can be accomplished by freeing the sacral roots in the injury zone from their epidural venous cuff and proceeding with ventral disimpaction or direct removal of protruding bone fragments. Ventral disimpaction is facilitated by placing an elevator into the fracture as a lever or by using an impactor to directly push the dorsal wall of the injured sacral vertebral bodies and thus correct the posterior displacement. Lateral C-arm control is helpful during sacral root decompression surgery for orientation and assessment of sacral alignment and associated decompression of the spinal canal.

Decompression of the sacral roots through an anterior approach is rarely indicated. Anterior access is difficult because of the sacral inclination, visceral structures, fracture hematoma, and extensive venous plexus overlying the anterior sacrum. If fragments of the anterior sacral ala impinge on the L5 nerve root, however, direct access for fracture reduction and decompression of the nerve root can only be gained by an anterior approach through the Olerud window.[10]

Traumatic dural tears are relatively common. Suture repair is undertaken if possible. Otherwise, the patching technique should involve the use of a dural allograft, collagen matrix, or biologic sealant.

Most displaced, complete Denis zone 1 and 2 sacral fractures are treated with closed reduction using distal femoral traction, followed by percutaneous iliosacral screw fixation in the supine position. Stabilization of associated displaced anterior pelvic ring injuries can facilitate the subsequent reduction of the sacral fracture. For this purpose, the techniques include open plating of the symphysis pubis or parasymphyseal pubic fracture as well as percutaneous techniques such as antegrade or retrograde pubic ramus screw fixation or application of an anterior pelvic external fixator.[27] The indications for open reduction of a sacral fracture include inability to obtain an acceptable reduction by closed means and the

3: Spine Trauma

presence of foraminal debris that requires direct decompression. Open reduction is most commonly performed through a paramedian incision.

A Denis zone 3 fracture-dislocation of the sacrum is associated with severe multidirectional instability caused by functional dissociation of the spine from the pelvis. The instability is compounded by the presence of pelvic ring instability, as in an H-type variant fracture. The fracture stabilization therefore must counteract the forces associated with upper body weight as well as motion in all directions. These forces and moments must be bilaterally transferred directly from the lumbosacral spine to the ilium by bridging or bypassing the sacral fracture. The ability to span the sacral fracture is a valuable feature of lumbopelvic fixation techniques because of increased instability at the fracture site from neural decompression and removal of the posterior sacral elements essential for fixation techniques such as local plate osteosynthesis.

If there is associated pelvic ring involvement, anterior stabilization of the anterior pelvic ring may facilitate indirect reduction of the posterior pelvic ring and partial pelvic stability, and it provides a helpful fulcrum during attempts at sacral fracture reduction. If an acceptable posterior pelvic ring reduction is achieved with these techniques and the first sacral vertebral body is intact, percutaneous iliosacral screw fixation completes the stabilization of the pelvic ring. Percutaneous iliosacral screw fixation alone has also been recommended for minimally displaced Roy-Camille type 1 and 2 U-shaped sacral fractures, with no need for neurologic decompression.[5] Several types of sacral U-shaped fractures are not amenable to percutaneous iliosacral screw fixation: highly displaced (and irreducible by closed means) fractures, in which the safe zone for iliosacral screw placement is prohibitively narrow; extensively comminuted fractures, in which iliosacral screw fixation may not be sufficiently stable; and fractures with cauda equina syndrome, in which the need for extensive decompression is expected to further destabilize the fracture. No specific criteria have established the acceptable extent of sacral fracture comminution or displacement, and it must be determined as a matter of clinical judgment. The additional disadvantages of using percutaneous iliosacral screw fixation alone in U-shaped sacral fractures are that this technique does not allow correction of the traumatic sacral deformity or early postsurgical weight bearing. Bilateral iliosacral screws alone biomechanically stabilize the posterior pelvic ring by compression of the longitudinal fracture lines, but their orientation parallel to the transverse fracture plane and associated lumbosacral flexion moment results in considerable sagittal-plane rotational instability. Iliosacral screw fixation therefore may need to be augmented with lumbopelvic fixation when the patient's overall condition allows more extensive open posterior pelvic ring surgery.[28] Lumbopelvic fixation generally is accomplished by connecting pedicle screws in L5 to long iliac screws (diameter, 7 to 8 mm) inserted

along the bony column between the posterosuperior and anteroinferior iliac spine.[29] The purpose is to counteract multiplanar forces in the vertical direction as well as in flexion and bending moments at the lumbosacral junction.[30]

Timing of Surgical Intervention
The timing of surgical intervention depends on the patient's neurologic function and comorbidities. A sacral fracture often is accompanied by soft-tissue contusion or an internal degloving (Morel-Lavallée) lesion, and there is an increased likelihood of postoperative wound infection. Cerebrospinal fluid leakage from a traumatic dural tear adds to the infection risk. The increased blood loss typical of early surgical intervention may affect the ability to carry out a procedure. The patient's perioperative morbidity also must be considered. Emergency surgical intervention is recommended only if the patient has an open fracture, dorsal soft-tissue compromise caused by displaced fracture fragments, or a deteriorating neurologic examination.[1,3,31] Otherwise, the timing of surgical intervention should be determined based on improvement in the patient's physiologic status. The ideal timing is 48 hours to 2 weeks after injury. If the patient has bony encroachment with concordant neurologic deficit, however, late surgical intervention may lead to a poor neurologic recovery or an increased likelihood of permanent radicular pain and dysesthesias.[10]

Lumbopelvic Fixation
Screw application in the ilium is performed under C-arm visualization, primarily using the lateral pelvic view and the combined obturator-oblique outlet view[29] (Figure 9). A starting point is established along the medial aspect of the posterior ilium, and a screw is placed after a channel is cannulated in a lateral direction between the inner and outer tables superior to the sciatic notch and the acetabulae, using a 3.5-mm drill or a pedicle awl. The iliac oblique view and combined obturator-oblique inlet view may be useful in confirming appropriate screw position and length. Supplementary S1 pedicle screw fixation should be considered if there is substantial instability and if the S1 comminution permits. If the fracture is highly unstable, particularly with extensive fracture involvement of the S1 vertebral body, the lumbopelvic fixation may need to be extended to the L4 pedicles and may need to include two long iliac screws bilaterally.[8,32] After application of lumbopelvic fixation, the vertical connecting rods should be compressed toward each other by one or two transversely placed cross-connector rods to improve overall stability and reestablish posterior pelvic ring alignment. Care should be taken to ensure that this transverse compression does not compromise the sacral neuroforamina. Soft-tissue coverage and viability are a constant concern with these injuries, and particular care should be taken to avoid iliac screw prominence. It is advisable to recess the iliac screws by preparing a bony window at the insertion point on the posterior ilium (Figure 10). Figure 11 shows variations of the lum-

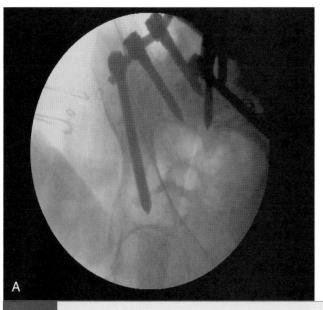

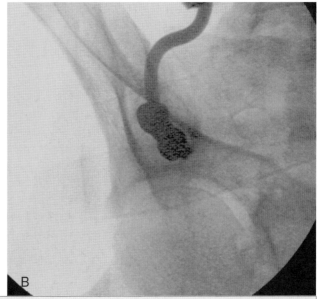

Figure 9 | Obturator-oblique outlet (**A**) and inlet (**B**) fluoroscopic projections used to guide or confirm the accuracy of iliac screw placement.

bopelvic fixation technique in an acute lumbosacral fracture-dislocation and a pathologic fracture at the lumbosacral junction.

For a unilateral sacral fracture with rostral extension into and medial to the L5-S1 facet (usually a Denis zone 2 injury), a so-called triangular osteosynthesis results in stable fracture fixation and allows early weight bearing. Triangular osteosynthesis consists of lumbopelvic fixation between the pedicle of L5 and the ilium, usually with ipsilateral iliosacral screw fixation (Figure 12). This technique is particularly valuable if mobilization without restricted weight bearing is not possible; if the fracture is highly displaced or comminuted; or if decompression will cause further destabilization and eliminate the possibility of anatomic, interdigitated fracture reduction.[28,30] Iliosacral screw fixation is done percutaneously at the S1 and/or S2 level with cannulated screws (diameter, 7.0 to 7.3 mm), using a combination of lateral, inlet, and outlet fluoroscopic views. For a bilateral sacral fracture, added stability typically is sought by extending the S2 screws across the contralateral sacroiliac joint to engage both cortices of the ilium. Local bone graft from the sacral laminectomy is applied to the decorticated posterolateral elements from the posterolateral elements of the most rostral instrumented lumbar vertebra to the sacral ala. The pelvis and posterior ilium are not included in the arthrodesis, and the sacroiliac joints therefore are not formally fused.

Complications

Wound-related complications are relatively common after the surgical treatment of sacral fractures. A 16% incidence of postoperative infection was reported in a

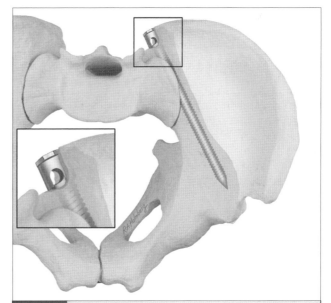

Figure 10 | Schematic drawing showing a bony window *(inset)* used to recess the iliac screw at the posterosuperior iliac spine insertion point, for the purpose of avoiding complications related to screw prominence.

study of patients with surgically treated high-grade sacral fracture-dislocation.[33] The treatment usually involves surgical wound débridement, intravenous antibiotics for at least 6 weeks, and nutritional support. Wound drainage resulting from seroma and pseudomeningocele formation requires surgical reexploration.[33]

Decubitus ulcers may develop over prominent bone or hardware. Precautions including appropriate skin

3: Spine Trauma

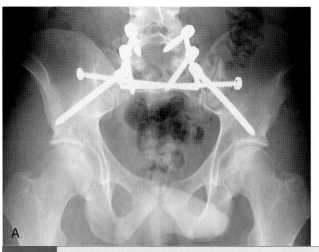
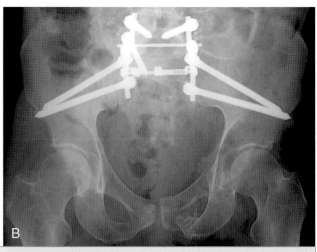

Figure 11 AP radiographs of the pelvis after lumbopelvic fixation to treat a high-energy U-type sacral fracture (**A**) and a low-energy U-type sacral insufficiency fracture with associated anterior pelvic ring insufficiency fractures (**B**).

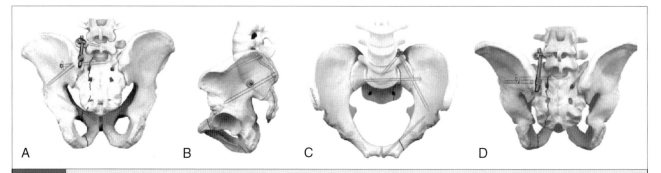

Figure 12 Schematic drawings showing unilateral combined iliosacral and lumbopelvic fixation, also known as triangular osteosynthesis, based on the appearance of the fixation construct on inlet radiographs (posterior [**A**], lateral [**B**], inlet [**C**], and outlet [**D**] views). Triangular osteosynthesis is among the most stable known methods for fixation of a unilateral Denis zone 2 sacral fracture.

care and recessed screw positioning at the posterosuperior iliac spine are essential. Early iliac screw removal or exchange may be indicated if prominence causes a severe decubitus ulcer.

Neurologic deterioration may occur after sacral laminectomy, foraminotomy, indirect fracture reduction, or direct removal of bony fragments. To prevent this complication, it is recommended that sacral decompression and stabilization be performed under lateral radiographic C-arm control with intraoperative electromyography and monitoring of somatosensory-evoked potentials. CT and MRI must be used to identify the cause of any postoperative neurologic deterioration including a treatable condition such as postoperative hematoma within the sacral canal.

Hardware failure can occur before or long after fracture healing and has been reported in as many as 30% of patients.[34] In one study, all instances of broken hardware were identified after fracture healing and were related to persistent motion of the sacroiliac joint, which had not undergone formal arthrodesis.[34] Rod breakage was not associated with clinical symptoms and was in-

cidentally identified on routine follow-up radiographs. Nonetheless, hardware removal after fracture healing at 6 to 12 months may be indicated to prevent late hardware failure or symptoms caused by prominent hardware under the skin.

Loss of reduction and pseudarthrosis have not been reported after the use of lumbopelvic stabilization techniques for sacral fracture-dislocation.[33] However, malreduction may contribute to persistent neurologic symptoms from bony encroachment on neural elements. Reduction of the lumbar spine to the pelvis determines the sacral incidence and the need for compensatory lumbar lordosis; malreduction resulting in changes in sacral incidence may cause chronic low back pain because of muscular imbalance at the lumbopelvic junction.

Scoliotic deformity at the lumbosacral junction may be caused by overdistraction during unilateral lumbopelvic fixation.[35] The risk can be minimized if fracture fixation is first performed in the transverse plane (for example, with iliosacral screw osteosynthesis) and is followed by lumbopelvic fixation for the purpose of neutralization.

Persistent pain after fracture healing can have multifactorial causes but is most likely to be caused predominantly by persistent neurologic deficits. Patients with sexual dysfunction and dysesthesias in the distribution of the lumbosacral plexus have consistently worse outcomes than other patients.[33]

Summary

The evaluation and treatment of sacral fractures have evolved considerably as imaging standards have improved and new fracture stabilization concepts and techniques have been developed. Nonsurgical care remains appropriate for treating a minimally displaced longitudinal zone 1 or 2 sacral fracture in a neurologically intact patient. Reduction and stabilization, possibly with direct decompression, usually are required for a displaced injury or in the presence of neurologic deficits. Percutaneous supine iliosacral stabilization techniques can be used for most zone 1 and 2 sacral fractures, although prone open treatment through a paramedian exposure may be required if closed reduction is unsuccessful or decompression is necessary. The additional stability provided by unilateral lumbopelvic fixation sometimes is useful. Bilateral lumbopelvic fixation is recommended for multiplanar zone 3 sacral fractures resulting in functional discontinuity of the spine from the pelvis. In the presence of cauda equina deficits, neural decompression may improve the likelihood of neurologic recovery. The benefits of surgical treatment of a complex sacral fracture must be weighed against the relatively high risk of wound-related complications.

Annotated References

1. Stagnara P, De Mauroy JC, Dran G, et al: Reciprocal angulation of vertebral bodies in a sagittal plane: Approach to references for the evaluation of kyphosis and lordosis. *Spine (Phila Pa 1976)* 1982;7(4):335-342.

2. Schmidek HH, Smith DA, Kristiansen TK: Sacral fractures. *Neurosurgery* 1984;15(5):735-746.

3. Denis F, Davis S, Comfort T: Sacral fractures: An important problem. Retrospective analysis of 236 cases. *Clin Orthop Relat Res* 1988;227:67-81.

4. Isler B: Lumbosacral lesions associated with pelvic ring injuries. *J Orthop Trauma* 1990;4(1):1-6.

5. Nork SE, Jones CB, Harding SP, Mirza SK, Routt ML Jr: Percutaneous stabilization of U-shaped sacral fractures using iliosacral screws: Technique and early results. *J Orthop Trauma* 2001;15(4):238-246.

6. Roy-Camille R, Saillant G, Gagna G, Mazel C: Transverse fracture of the upper sacrum: Suicidal jumper's fracture. *Spine (Phila Pa 1976)* 1985;10(9):838-845.

7. Strange-Vognsen HH, Lebech A: An unusual type of fracture in the upper sacrum. *J Orthop Trauma* 1991;5(2):200-203.

8. Schildhauer TA, Chapman JR, Mayo KA: Multisegmental open sacral fracture due to impalement: A case report. *J Orthop Trauma* 2005;19(2):134-139.

A 15-year-old patient sustained an open pelvic fracture from a sacral impalement injury. Treatment with triangular osteosynthesis led to primary wound healing, immediate mobilization, and a return of bowel and bladder control.

9. American Spinal Injury Association, International Medical Society of Paraplegia: *Standard for Neurologic and Functional Classification of Spinal Cord Injury*. Atlanta, GA, American Spinal Injury Association, 1992.

10. Chapman JR, Schildhauer TA, Bellabarba C, Nork SE, Mirza SK: Treatment of sacral fractures with neurologic injuries. *Top Spinal Cord Inj Rehabil* 2002;8:59-78.

11. Tseng S, Tornetta P III: Percutaneous management of Morel-Lavallee lesions. *J Bone Joint Surg Am* 2006;88(1):92-96.

No deep wound infections occurred in 19 patients treated with percutaneous drainage and debridement of Morel-Lavallée degloving lesions within 3 days of pelvic and acetabular fracture.

12. Rommens PM, Vanderschot PM, Broos PL: Conventional radiography and CT examination of pelvic ring fractures: A comparative study of 90 patients. *Unfallchirurg* 1992;95(8):387-392.

13. Routt ML Jr, Falicov A, Woodhouse E, Schildhauer TA: Circumferential pelvic antishock sheeting: A temporary resuscitation aid. *J Orthop Trauma* 2002;16(1):45-48.

14. Routt ML Jr, Simonian PT, Swiontkowski MF: Stabilization of pelvic ring disruptions. *Orthop Clin North Am* 1997;28(3):369-388.

15. Phelan ST, Jones DA, Bishay M: Conservative management of transverse fractures of the sacrum with neurological features: A report of four cases. *J Bone Joint Surg Br* 1991;73(6):969-971.

16. Gibbons KJ, Soloniuk DS, Razack N: Neurological injury and patterns of sacral fractures. *J Neurosurg* 1990;72(6):889-893.

17. Sabiston CP, Wing PC: Sacral fractures: Classification and neurologic complications. *J Trauma* 1986;26(12):1113-1115.

18. Fountain SS, Hamilton RD, Jameson RM: Transverse fractures of the sacrum: A report of six cases. *J Bone Joint Surg Am* 1977;59(4):486-489.

3: Spine Trauma

19. Fisher RG: Sacral fracture with compression of cauda equina: Surgical treatment. *J Trauma* 1988;28(12):1678-1680.

20. Gunterberg B: Effects of major resection of the sacrum: Clinical studies on urogenital and anorectal function and a biomechanical study on pelvic strength. *Acta Orthop Scand Suppl* 1976;162(suppl):1-38.

21. Ferris B, Hutton P: Anteriorly displaced transverse fracture of the sacrum at the level of the sacro-iliac joint: A report of two cases. *J Bone Joint Surg Am* 1983;65(3):407-409.

22. Dujardin FH, Hossenbaccus M, Duparc F, Biga N, Thomine JM: Long-term functional prognosis of posterior injuries in high-energy pelvic disruption. *J Orthop Trauma* 1998;12(3):145-151.

23. Fardon DF: Displaced fracture of the lumbosacral spine with delayed cauda equina deficit: Report of a case and review of literature. *Clin Orthop Relat Res* 1976;120:155-158.

24. Carl A, Delman A, Engler G: Displaced transverse sacral fractures: A case report, review of the literature, and the CT scan as an aid in management. *Clin Orthop Relat Res* 1985;194:195-198.

25. Bellabarba C, Stewart JD, Ricci WM, DiPasquale TG, Bolhofner BR: Midline sagittal sacral fractures in anterior-posterior compression pelvic ring injuries. *J Orthop Trauma* 2003;17(1):32-37.

26. Woods RK, O'Keefe G, Rhee P, Routt ML Jr, Maier RV: Open pelvic fracture and fecal diversion. *Arch Surg* 1998;133(3):281-286.

27. Routt ML Jr, Nork SE, Mills WJ: Percutaneous fixation of pelvic ring disruptions. *Clin Orthop Relat Res* 2000;375:15-29.

28. Schildhauer TA, Josten C, Muhr G: Triangular osteosynthesis of vertically unstable sacrum fractures: A new concept allowing early weight-bearing. *J Orthop Trauma* 1998;12(5):307-314.

29. Schildhauer TA, McCulloch P, Chapman JR, Mann FA: Anatomic and radiographic considerations for placement of transiliac screws in lumbopelvic fixations. *J Spinal Disord Tech* 2002;15(3):199-205.

30. Schildhauer TA, Ledoux WR, Chapman JR, Henley MB, Tencer AF, Routt ML Jr: Triangular osteosynthesis and iliosacral screw fixation for unstable sacral fractures: A cadaveric and biomechanical evaluation under cyclic loads. *J Orthop Trauma* 2003;17(1):22-31.

31. Scoles PV, Linton AE, Latimer B, Levy ME, Digiovanni BF: Vertebral body and posterior element morphology: the normal spine in middle life. *Spine (Phila Pa 1976)* 1988;13(10):1082-1086.

32. Schildhauer TA, Bellabarba C, Selznick HS, McRoberts D, Vedder NB, Chapman JR: Unstable pediatric sacral fracture with bone loss caused by a high-energy gunshot injury. *J Trauma* 2007;63(4):E95-E99.

Soft-tissue management and musculoskeletal reconstruction with spinopelvic stabilization are described for a pediatric sacral fracture caused by a close-range shotgun blast, with extensive bone loss and soft-tissue injury.

33. Bellabarba C, Schildhauer TA, Vaccaro AR, Chapman JR: Complications associated with surgical stabilization of high-grade sacral fracture dislocations with spinopelvic instability. *Spine (Phila Pa 1976)* 2006;31(11,suppl):S80-S88, discussion S104.

In a retrospective review of complications associated with spinopelvic fixation, an absence of pseudarthrosis or postoperative loss of alignment was found in 19 patients with a sacral U-type fracture variant and spinopelvic dissociation. The major complications were primarily related to infection, wound healing, hardware prominence, and asymptomatic rod breakage, often requiring additional surgical intervention but without long-term sequelae.

34. Schildhauer TA, Bellabarba C, Nork SE, Barei DP, Routt ML Jr, Chapman JR: Decompression and lumbopelvic fixation for sacral fracture-dislocations with spino-pelvic dissociation. *J Orthop Trauma* 2006;20(7):447-457.

In a retrospective review of the results of spinopelvic fixation, all patients with a sacral U-type fracture variant and spinopelvic dissociation had healed at 31-month follow-up, without loss of reduction. Average sacral kyphosis improved from 43° to 21°. Fifteen patients had full or partial recovery from bowel and bladder deficits. All patients with incomplete deficits had full recovery of cauda equina function, but only 20% of those with complete deficits had full recovery (*P* = 0.024). The authors concluded that lumbopelvic fixation provided reliable fracture stability and allowed consistent fracture union without loss of alignment and that neurologic outcome was influenced by completeness of injury and presence of sacral root disruption.

35. Sagi HC, Militano U, Caron T, Lindvall E: A comprehensive analysis with minimum 1-year follow-up of vertically unstable transforaminal sacral fractures treated with triangular osteosynthesis. *J Orthop Trauma* 2009;23(5):313-321.

Forty patients underwent triangular osteosynthesis of a comminuted vertical shear transforaminal (Denis zone 2) sacral fracture. At a minimum 1-year follow-up, triangular osteosynthesis was found to be a reliable form of fixation. Postoperative alignment was maintained in 95% of patients despite full weight bearing 6 weeks after surgery. The significant technical difficulties and complications included iatrogenic nerve injury, coronal plane malalignment, and the need for a second surgery to remove painful instrumentation. Selective use of this technique is recommended for comminuted transforaminal sacral fractures in which reliable iliosacral or transsacral screw fixation cannot be performed.

Chapter 23

Spine Injuries in Sports

Reginald S. Fayssoux, MD   John M. Rhee, MD

Introduction

An injury involving the spine is among the most feared injuries related to athletic competition because of its potential for significant disability. Proper care is predicated on an understanding of the mechanisms and patterns of spine injury as well as their sport-specific relationships. Spine injuries occurring in the context of adult athletic competition have unique aspects related to injury patterns, on-the-field management, prevention, and return to play.

Sport-Specific Epidemiology

Almost 15% of spine injuries in the United States are related to participation in a sport or recreational activity. The type of injury to a large extent depends on the mechanisms of load application to the spine, and as a result different sports are associated with different patterns of susceptibility to spine injury.

Diving is the water sport most commonly associated with cervical spinal cord injury (SCI) and is responsible for 5% of all water-related accidents in children.[1] The incidence of diving-related cervical SCI in the United States is decreasing as a result of preventive efforts, and most injuries now occur in unsupervised settings. The typical mechanism of injury is a headfirst dive into shallow water. Normal cervical lordosis allows the intervertebral disks to absorb shock and the paravertebral musculature to dissipate energy. If cervical lordosis is reversed by neck flexion, the straightened cervical spine is unable to effectively dissipate energy. Axially directed forces are transferred directly to the spinal column, which acts as a segmented column and fails in compression by buckling. Tissue tolerances are ex-

ceeded, resulting in catastrophic failure either through the intervertebral disk or by fracture or dislocation, with possible injury to the spinal cord (Figure 1).

Full-contact collision sports, such as American football, are responsible for a significant number of sports-related spine injuries. The common injuries include cervical sprain, cervical strain, and brachial plexus injury. The incidence of brachial plexus injury is as high as 2.2 per 100 players.[2] The incidence of spine injuries in full-contact sports has decreased with the proper use of shoulder rolls and pads to bolster the cervical spine. Catastrophic cervical spine injury, defined as unstable fracture, dislocation, disk herniation, or cervical cord neurapraxia (CCN), is rare. The reported incidence is 1.1 per 100,000 high school football players and 4.7 per 100,000 college football players.[3] Traumatic quadriplegia complicates one third of these injuries. Paradoxically, the introduction of protective headgear in the early 1970s initially led to an increase in the incidence of catastrophic cervical spine injuries. The increase probably was related to a decreased fear of head injury, leading to an increase in tackling maneuvers using the crown of the head (so-called spear tackling). Spear tackling was banned in 1976, and the incidence of catastrophic cervical injuries dropped 80% by 1987.[4] This example underscores the importance of understanding injury mechanisms as well as the value of using a national injury tracking registry such as that of the National Center for Catastrophic Sports Injury Research in designing prevention programs. Lumbar spine injury occasionally occurs in American football; a classic example is spondylolysis in linemen resulting from repeated lumbar hyperextension.

Spine injuries are common in ice hockey players, accounting for 9% of all collegiate ice hockey injuries during the 2001-2002 season.[5] During the 1980s, the introduction of head and face protection is believed to have led to more aggressive play and an increased incidence of catastrophic spine injury.[6] Injury most commonly occurs when a check to the back sends a player headfirst into the boards. (Often the player was looking down and not anticipating being hit.) Because of the high speeds at which the game is played, the injury may be serious.

Rugby is similar to American football in that the style of play is aggressive. No protective gear is worn in rugby, however. Ten percent of injuries involve the cervical spine. These injuries most frequently occur during

Dr. Rhee or an immediate family member has received royalties from Biomet; is a member of a speakers' bureau or has made paid presentations on behalf of Biomet and Synthes; serves as a paid consultant to or is an employee of Synthes; has received research or institutional support from Synthes and Medtronic Sofamor Danek; and owns stock or stock options in Phygen. Neither Dr. Fayssoux nor any immediate family member has received anything of value from or owns stock in a commercial company or institution related directly or indirectly to the subject of this chapter.

3: Spine Trauma

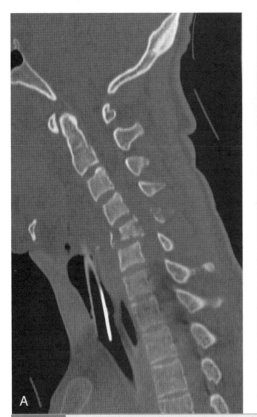
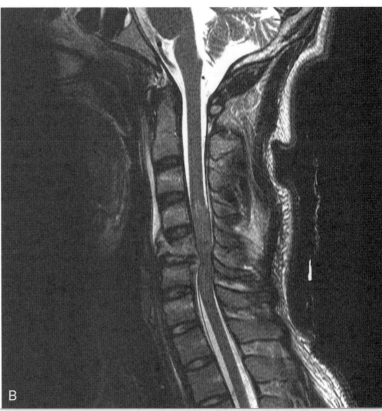

| Figure 1 | A young man sustained a high-grade flexion-compression injury at C5 by hitting his head on a submerged rock while diving into a shallow river. **A,** Midsagittal cervical spine CT showing significant canal compromise. **B,** Midsagittal cervical spine MRI showing spinal cord deformation at the level of injury. |

the scrum, and the central player on the front row (the hooker) most commonly sustains injury.[7,8]

The annual incidence of catastrophic spine injury among high school and collegiate wrestlers is 1 per 100,000 participants.[9] The injury typically involves the cervical spine and most commonly occurs during takedown of a standing opponent in the defensive position, typically in lightweight and middleweight matches.

Cheerleading was responsible for half of all catastrophic spine injuries among female high school and college athletes from 1982 to 2005.[10] Injury most commonly occurs to a cheerleader who falls to the ground from the top of a pyramid formation or after being thrown into the air during a basket toss. Trampolines often are used to practice cheerleading stunts. Trampoline use was a common cause of spine injury until an American Academy of Pediatrics policy statement called for a ban in schools, competitive sports, and home or recreational settings. The result was a dramatic decrease in the incidence of injury.[11,12]

The overall incidence of spine injury among baseball players is low. The incidence of catastrophic cervical injury (0.43 per 100,000 participants) is relatively high, however, when compared with other sports.[13] These injuries most commonly occur when a base runner collides with a fielder (typically the catcher) during a headfirst slide into base.

High-speed sports such as downhill skiing and snowboarding are relatively common causes of spine injury. The impact speed typically is much higher in skiing than in other sports. The reported incidence of SCI is 0.01 per 1,000 skier days, with injuries evenly distributed among all spine levels.[14,15] The risk factors for injury include poorly groomed slopes, equipment failure, unfavorable weather conditions, overcrowding, skier error, and skier loss of control.[16] The reported incidence of spine injuries among snowboarders is three to four times higher than among skiers. Jumping is responsible for as many as 80% of spine injuries among snowboarders and typically affects the thoracolumbar region.[15,17]

Types of Injuries

The spine injuries incurred by participants in athletic competition vary from a relatively benign cervical sprain or strain to a life-threatening SCI.

Musculoligamentous Injury

Cervical musculoligamentous injuries are common in sports and are akin to the whiplash injuries that occur in motor vehicle crashes. The cause typically is a violent bending or rotational force to the head or neck, leading to sprain or strain of a ligament or muscle. Concomitant injury to the facet capsules is associated with a relatively poor prognosis. These soft-tissue injuries can occur in any sport but are most common in full-contact sports and high-speed sports such as skiing. Participants in a full-contact sport in which helmets are used without protective neck gear are especially vulnerable because force is transmitted to the neck.

Neck pain usually is not noticed until 12 to 24 hours after the traumatic event, presumably because of the timing of the inflammatory cascade. Paravertebral spasm may be evident on examination, and painful resisted motion may help in isolating a specific muscle. The patient's range of motion may be limited because of protective guarding. Tenderness is identified in the musculature of the neck. Tenderness of the articular pillars sometimes is present and may suggest a facet capsule injury. No neurologic signs or symptoms should be evident. The radiographic findings typically are normal but may reveal a loss of normal cervical lordosis. It is important to avoid missing a nondisplaced fracture or ligamentous instability in a persistently symptomatic patient. Muscular spasms may protect against ligamentous instability early after injury. Therefore, flexion-extension radiographs obtained immediately after injury are less likely to reveal ligamentous instability than those obtained 2 to 3 weeks later. CT scans can identify an occult fracture. MRI can detect both ligamentous injury and bony fracture.

The initial treatment of musculoligamentous injury is to manage pain and inflammation. Subsequent rehabilitation is aimed at regaining normal range of motion and strength. The mainstay of therapy is to avoid the injury-provoking activity. Ice is used at the outset to reduce inflammation, followed by moist heat for muscle relaxation. When the pain is tolerable, range-of-motion and strengthening exercises encourage a return to normal flexibility and strength. Formal physical therapy may be used as symptoms improve and active participation becomes possible. Muscle relaxants and nonsteroidal anti-inflammatory drugs can be useful adjuncts to treatment. A rigid cervical orthosis should be used for a patient with acute pain until ligamentous injury can be ruled out. A soft collar can be used to limit painful motion in the acute setting, provided that significant ligamentous instability or occult fracture is considered unlikely. Cervical immobilization tends to prolong the period of disability, and its use therefore should be limited. The prognosis of cervical musculoligamentous injury typically is good but depends on the extent of injury. Return to play is allowed when the patient is asymptomatic and has a normal cervical range of motion, typically within 1 to 2 weeks.

Thoracolumbar musculoligamentous injuries also are common. These injuries are caused by significant rotational and bending forces to the trunk, commonly during a full-contact or high-speed sports activity. The patient typically reports back strain. As with cervical musculoligamentous injury, the onset of pain typically

is delayed and the physical examination is consistent with musculoligamentous injury. The algorithm for the radiographic workup is the same as for a cervical injury. Patients older than approximately 40 years with arthritic facets overloaded in a traumatic event may have symptoms mimicking those of musculoligamentous back pain; facet blocks may be useful in the diagnosis and treatment of these patients. In the absence of significant injury, the treatment proceeds along the same lines as for cervical musculoligamentous injury. Bracing can provide back support in the acute setting, but its long-term use should be discouraged. Instead, stretching and core-strengthening exercises should be encouraged.

Disk Herniation

Disk herniation is not a common sports injury, but it can lead to significant morbidity. Disk herniation can appear as isolated axial pain, radiculopathy, or, in rare circumstances, injury to the spinal cord or cauda equina. In the neck, the mechanism of injury usually involves axial loading and rotation of the flexed (straightened) cervical spine, which result in traumatic herniation of the nucleus pulposus through an annular defect. Disk herniation typically occurs in an already-degenerated disk and is most likely in an athlete older than approximately 40 years. Disk herniation in younger patients is classified into one of two subgroups: herniation without earlier disk degeneration, which typically occurs at C3-4 or C4-5; or herniation with premature disk degeneration, which typically occurs in athletes who use their head to strike an object.

In a patient with isolated axial neck pain, the symptoms of disk herniation may resemble those of musculoligamentous injury and may include neck pain, paravertebral spasm, tender musculature, and loss of range of motion. Loss of disk height is seen on plain radiographs, but the diagnosis is made on MRI when symptoms persist. An increased T2-weighted signal in the herniated disk component suggests a traumatic disk herniation. Because of the prevalence of abnormal MRI findings in asymptomatic individuals, it is important to correlate the findings of the patient history and physical examination with MRI findings before arriving at a diagnosis.[18]

Posterolateral disk herniation can appear as a radiculopathy, with dermatomal arm pain accompanied by neck pain, numbness, or weakness. A brachial plexus injury may have similar symptoms, but because a brachial plexus injury is a neurapraxia, the symptoms typically resolve within 1 to 2 weeks with nonsurgical management. It is important to rule out SCI by carefully determining whether the symptoms are present in more than one extremity and examining for the presence of long tract signs. MRI can aid in the diagnosis, and electrodiagnostic studies occasionally are useful.

Isolated axial neck pain and radiculopathies from disk herniation are initially treated with nonsurgical modalities including rest, ice, heat, nonsteroidal anti-

Table 1

Absolute Contraindications to Return to Play

Ankylosing spondylitis

Asymptomatic ligamentous laxity (more than 11° of kyphotic deformity)

Basilar invagination

C1-C2 fixed rotary subluxation

C1-C2 fusion

C1-C2 instability

Cervical cord abnormality

Cervical cord neurapraxia (more than two episodes)

Cervical disk herniation (symptomatic)

Cervical fusion of three or more levels

Cervical laminectomy

Cervical myelopathy

Continuing cervical discomfort, decreased range of motion, and neurologic deficit

Cord encroachment after fracture

Diffuse idiopathic skeletal hyperostosis

Distraction-extension injury

Healed subaxial spine fracture with deformity

Multilevel Klippel-Feil syndrome

Occipitocervical assimilation

Rheumatoid arthritis

Spear tackler spine*

*Developmental narrowing of the cervical spinal canal, with straightening or reversal of the normal lordotic curvature and posttraumatic radiographic cervical spine abnormalities, in an athlete with a history of headfirst contact tackling.

Adapted from Vaccaro AR, Harrop JS, Daffner SD, Berta SC: Acute cervical spine injuries in the athlete: Diagnosis, management, and return-to-play. *Int J Sports Med* 2003;4(1):1-5.

Table 2

Relative Contraindications to Return to Play

Prolonged symptomatic burner or cervical cord neurapraxia of more than 24 hours' duration

Three or more burners without return to baseline

Two-level cervical fusion (not including lateral mass fixation)

Adapted from Vaccaro AR, Harrop JS, Daffner SD, Berta SC: Acute cervical spine injuries in the athlete: Diagnosis, management, and return-to-play. *Int J Sports Med* 2003;4(1):1-5.

Table 3

Noncontraindications to Return to Play

C7 spinous process fracture

Healed C1 or C2 fracture with normal range of motion

Healed subaxial fracture

One or two burners

One episode of cervical cord neurapraxia

Single-level fusion

Single-level Klippel-Feil syndrome not involving the occiput-C1

Single or multilevel laminoforaminotomy

Spina bifida occulta

Torg ratio lower than 0.8

Adapted from Vaccaro AR, Harrop JS, Daffner SD, Berta SC: Acute cervical spine injuries in the athlete: Diagnosis, management, and return-to-play. *Int J Sports Med* 2003;4(1):1-5.

inflammatory drugs, physical therapy, and tapered steroids. Epidural steroid injections may be useful if radicular pain is persistent. Surgical intervention is considered if nonsurgical measures are unsuccessful or the neurologic symptoms progress. In deciding on a surgical option, it is important to consider the athlete's desire to return to play, as some procedures, such as multilevel fusion, preclude a safe return to play (Tables 1, 2 and 3).

The mechanism of injury in lumbar disk herniation in athletes is similar to that of cervical disk herniation, consisting of axial loading and rotation of the flexed lumbar spine. Lumbar disk herniation is most likely to occur in obese athletes, who have an increased risk of premature disk degeneration. Patients with low back pain related to disk herniation often observe a more sudden onset of symptoms than patients with a musculoligamentous injury, but the symptoms otherwise are similar. Radiculopathy may be present. Bowel and bladder findings related to cauda equina compression

should be ruled out. Plain radiographs typically are unrevealing but may show a loss of disk height. MRI with increased T2-weighted signal may show acute traumatic herniation, but the prevalence of abnormal MRI findings in asymptomatic individuals should be recognized.[19] The initial treatment is nonsurgical. Surgical intervention is considered after unsuccessful nonsurgical therapy or progression of neurologic symptoms.

Fracture, Subluxation, and Dislocation

The spectrum of vertebral fracture, subluxation, and dislocation resulting from sports activity ranges from a benign spinous or transverse process fracture to a cervical fracture-dislocation with complete SCI. These injuries are described elswhere in this section.

Burners

Neurapraxia of one or more cervical nerve roots or the brachial plexus is commonly called a burner or a stinger. Multiple mechanisms have been implicated. A burner is believed to occur in a younger athlete when the head is forced laterally to one side while the contralateral shoulder is depressed, causing a traction injury to the upper cervical roots or brachial plexus trunk. Other mechanisms include axial loading of the extended, laterally rotated neck, resulting in neuroforaminal compression (usually in an older athlete with foraminal stenosis from degenerative changes of the disk and facet joint); a direct impact at the Erb point with upper trunk involvement; and, less commonly, forced shoulder hyperabduction affecting the lower roots or trunk. Intracanal, foraminal, or extraforaminal pathology (posterolateral disk herniation, foraminal stenosis, or extraforaminal disk bulge, respectively) can aggravate root involvement from a traction mechanism. Burners are common in contact-sport athletes. As many as 65% of college football players reportedly are affected over the course of a 4-year career,[20] but the true incidence is unknown because many such injuries are not reported. Burners also can occur in noncontact sports. In baseball, they can occur when a player slides headfirst into a base.

The clinical symptoms of a burner include unilateral transient lancinating, burning, or dysesthetic pain that typically lasts 10 to 15 minutes. Motor weakness occasionally is present. The Spurling test often is negative if the injury resulted from traction, but it can be positive if the injury resulted from neuroforaminal compression. The key to managing burners and stingers is to rule out a radiculopathy or an underlying SCI. The appearance of a burner may closely resemble that of a radiculopathy, as stimulation of a single nerve root can provoke symptoms outside the classic dermatomal distribution.[21,22] Careful analysis of the patient's symptoms, physical examination findings, and pertinent imaging is essential to making an accurate diagnosis. A burner can be distinguished from a more significant SCI by its unilaterality and the absence of long tract signs; this distinction is useful in on-the-field management. Although most burners are neurapraxias, higher grade neural injuries can occur. If the symptoms persist, electrodiagnostic studies may be helpful in distinguishing neurapraxia from axonotmesis and neurotmesis. For a neurapraxia, the treatment is nonsurgical. The symptoms are self-limited and usually resolve within 1 to 2 weeks. A tapered steroid may be used for relief of symptoms. Return to play is expected after 1 to 2 weeks, when the player is asymptomatic and has full cervical range of motion. Persistent symptoms related to axonotmesis or neurotmesis of the brachial plexus can be difficult to diagnose and treat. These higher grade injuries require careful counseling with regard to prognosis and timely referral to a hand surgeon for possible repair.

Reinjury is not uncommon and may be associated with development of proximal arm weakness and chronic pain syndrome.[23] In American football players, the incidence of these injuries can be reduced by training in proper blocking and tackling techniques as well as equipment modifications such as high shoulder pads, soft cervical rolls, or a total-contact neck-shoulder-chest orthosis (a cowboy collar) worn beneath the shoulder pads.[24] A persistent or recurrent burner

should prompt a careful reevaluation to rule out a radiculopathy.

Spinal Cord Injury

Sports and other recreational activities are the second most common cause of acute SCI in developed countries. Nonetheless, SCI resulting from sports is rare, with an estimated prevalence of 4.5 to 9.5 per 100,000 population.[25] Almost 80% of sports-related SCIs are in men or boys. However, in North America, most SCIs related to horseback riding occur in women or girls.

The appearance of SCI can be dramatic, but subtle forms can easily be misdiagnosed. Injury to the spinal cord or cauda equina can be devastating because of the significant resulting dysfunction and the often-poor prognosis for recovery. The compressive pathologies of these injuries are similar to those of non–sports-related injuries and include a midline herniated disk, fracture, or dislocation. An SCI can be complete, with no motor or sensory function below the level of injury, or incomplete. Incomplete injury can involve central cord, anterior cord, or Brown-Séquard syndrome. In burning hand syndrome, which is a relatively uncommon variant of central cord syndrome, the principal symptom is burning dysesthetic pain in the hands.[26] Burning hand syndrome can be misdiagnosed as a brachial plexus injury if the bilateral upper extremity involvement is not appreciated.

In CCN, also known as transient quadriplegia, the patient has a temporary loss of cervical spinal cord function after injury. The typical symptoms are sensory changes and weakness or paralysis in at least two extremities. CCN has an incidence of fewer than 1.3 per 100,000 sports participants.[4] The pincer mechanism is commonly believed to be responsible: during cervical hyperextension, the cord is compressed between the posteroinferior corner of the vertebral body and the superior edge of the lower subjacent lamina.[27] Cervical hyperextension can lead to thickening of the spinal cord, buckling of the ligamentum flavum, or narrowing of the subarachnoid space, all of which increase the pressure on the spinal cord.[28] The neurologic symptoms typically last 10 to 15 minutes but may require 48 hours to fully resolve. Immediately after the injury, many patients have full, painless range of motion, with no pain referable to the neck. Bony injury is uncommon. The primary predisposing factor is believed to be cervical canal stenosis; at least one study found a strong correlation between the extent of stenosis and the likelihood of a recurrence, which occurs in as many as 50% of patients with CCN. Spine precautions should be instituted acutely until an unstable cervical spine fracture or dislocation is ruled out. Radiographs and MRI are useful in determining the presence and extent of cervical spinal stenosis and spinal cord signal changes. Because CCN and permanent SCI are unusual, research has not determined whether a single episode of CCN substantially increases the risk of permanent SCI and therefore should restrict the patient's return to

Table 4

Important Considerations in the Prevention of Sports-Related Spine Injury

Supervision

Safe rules of play

Appropriate refereeing

Protective Equipment for Collision Sports

Head gear with removable face mask

Neck roll and lifters (also known as a cowboy collar) for American football players to decrease allowable cervical spine range of motion

Properly fitting shoulder pads to absorb shock, protect shoulders, fit chest, fix midcervical spine to trunk

Sport-Specific Athletic Training

Proper technique (for example, proper tackling technique in American football)

Situational awareness (for example, awareness of pool depth before diving)

Education on mechanisms of injury (for example, spear tackling)

Preparation

Situational practice

Helmet check for ease of face mask removal

Tools to remove face masks and helmets

Transport equipment

  Spine board

  Cervical collars

  Head bolsters

Medical equipment

  Intravenous access

  Defibrillator

Methylprednisolone

Medically trained personnel

---

are most likely during a high-speed activity such as downhill skiing or snowboarding. Conus medullaris syndrome results from injury to the conus medullaris, which is the terminal expansion of the spinal cord responsible for innervation of the lower lumbar and sacral levels. There are both upper motor neuron findings from conus involvement and lower motor neuron findings from root involvement. In contrast, cauda equina syndrome results from more caudal compression of only the cauda equina nerve roots. Both syndromes are typified by perianal sensation deficits and sphincter dysfunction, resulting in bowel and bladder symptoms. Urinary retention, with or without overflow incontinence, is characteristic. Fecal incontinence is less common but is associated with a relatively poor prognosis. In the acute setting, the use of high-dosage steroids, although controversial, may be considered to treat conus medullaris syndrome because of the spinal cord involvement. High-dosage steroids have not been shown to be of benefit in treating cauda equina syndrome.

Injury Prevention

Prevention measures aimed at decreasing the incidence and severity of spine injuries in sports participants are the key to significantly affecting overall outcomes. The education of athletes, coaches, and referees in sport-specific dangers, the use of proper athletic equipment and safe venues, and the preparation of the medical staff are all important to providing a safe environment for athletic competition (Table 4).

On-the-Field Management

When a spine injury occurs during a sports event, the first goal is to prevent further damage.[32] Early recognition is key; there should be a high index of suspicion for unstable spine injury if an appropriate injury mechanism is involved. Any patient with acute, severe neck or back pain or neurologic symptoms, as well as any unconscious patient, should be treated as if an unstable spine injury is present until proved otherwise. Protocols for acute management of spine trauma by emergency medical personnel have led to improved outcomes; these algorithms should be the standard of care in dealing with injured athletes.[33]

Preparation probably is the most critical aspect of on-the-field management.[34] Athletic equipment should be carefully inspected (for example, for ease of face mask removal). During a high-energy or contact-sport event, qualified emergency medical personnel should be available for the initial assessment and stabilization of an injured athlete. The athletic training staff should have the ability and tools for removing protective equipment. The standard trauma protocols apply. The helmet or shoulder pads should be left on, provided that the head is being securely held, the face mask can

play. In one study, no patient with a history of CCN later experienced a catastrophic spine injury, and no patient with an SCI had a history of CCN.[29] The researchers therefore argued that CCN and catastrophic cervical spine injury are unrelated and that a history of CCN should not predispose an athlete to catastrophic cervical spine injury. This viewpoint was challenged by a subsequent report of a quadriplegic injury in an athlete with an earlier CCN.[30,31]

A large traumatic midline disk herniation or, less commonly, a thoracolumbar fracture can cause thecal sac compression in the thoracolumbar and lumbar spine at the level of the conus medullaris and cauda equina, leading to distinct clinical syndromes. These injuries require significant force, and consequently they be removed, and the airway can be controlled. If removal is necessary, the helmet and pads should be removed together to prevent cervical hyperextension. Cervical spine alignment should be checked, as there is a tendency for unintended neck flexion if the helmet remains in place, especially in the absence of shoulder pads. The face mask should be removed to allow access to the airway. Jaw thrust and chin lift maneuvers, rather than cervical hyperextension, should be used to control the airway, if necessary. After the patient's airway is stabilized, a directed history and physical examination (with particular attention to the neurologic examination) are used to determine whether the patient can be safely moved. For a patient suspected of having an unstable spine injury, spine precautions should be instituted immediately and the emergency medical protocol should be activated.

The responsible personnel should routinely practice removing an injured player from the playing field. A patient with a suspected spine injury or an unconscious patient must be transported from the field using a rigid backboard for thoracolumbar spine immobilization. A cervical collar must be applied, with bolsters to support the sides of the head or manual splinting to immobilize the cervical spine and achieve neutral alignment. A previously designated team leader should be in charge of controlling the patient's head and directing the transfer. A multiperson carry, ideally with six team members, is the safest method of transport.

If the patient is suspected of having an SCI, attention must be directed toward maintaining oxygenation and blood pressure (a minimum mean arterial pressure of 85 mm Hg) to maximize spinal cord perfusion. The use of systemic hypothermia via infusion of cooled saline garnered national attention after it was used in the prehospital treatment of a National Football League player who sustained a cervical SCI during a game.[35] However, clinical evidence is lacking to prove the efficacy of systemic hypothermia, and its routine use has not been supported.[36] High-dose methylprednisolone may be instituted according to the National Acute Spinal Cord Injury Study protocol, although this practice is controversial and the true benefit-risk balance is unclear.[37,38] After initial resuscitation, the patient should be transported to a level I or tertiary referral trauma center.

Return-to-Play Guidelines

The decision as to an athlete's return to play after a spine injury is complex. Although athletes often are highly compliant with the physician's postsurgical orders, they may be less compliant if the physician decides that abstaining from sports activity is necessary for a prolonged time. This requirement can be frustrating for the physician as well as the patient. Opinions vary widely as to return-to-play criteria, and there is no strong evidence to guide clinical decision making. The primary goal of the physician is to identify whether an athlete is at an increased risk of injury; if so, counseling and activity restriction may be necessary. The basic criteria for return to play are normal strength, painless range of motion, a stable vertebral column, and adequate spine space for the neurologic elements. The decision is multifaceted and includes consideration of the injury, any anatomic factors that create a predisposition to further injury, posttraumatic injury status, postsurgical procedural restrictions, the nature of the sport or recreational activity, and the extent of risk that is acceptable to the patient and the physician.

Cervical Spine Injury

Cervical canal stenosis theoretically confers an increased risk of neurologic injury, and it probably is the most controversial topic in return-to-play decision making. The radiographic ratio of the spinal canal diameter to the vertebral body diameter (the Torg ratio) is used to identify developmental stenosis. A decreased Torg ratio formerly was believed to be a risk factor for neurologic injury, but it was found to have a poor positive predictive value for detecting cervical spinal stenosis and is not recommended as a screening mechanism for determining whether an athlete can participate in contact sports.[29,39] The concept of functional stenosis may be more useful for evaluating canal stenosis.[30,40] The MRI assessment of functional stenosis takes into consideration the canal dimensions, the thickness of the cord, and the amount of intervening cerebrospinal fluid. This direct assessment of the physiologic buffer available for the spinal cord is believed to better predict the risk of neurologic injury, compared with the Torg ratio.

The upper cervical spine is anatomically unique in being designed for mobility at the expense of stability. Almost 50% of flexion-extension and rotation occur between the occiput and C1 and between C1 and C2, respectively. An anomaly in this region (such as a fusion), whether it is congenital, developmental, caused by injury, or postsurgical, can affect stability, risk neurologic injury, and contraindicate return to play.[41] The significant limitations to range of motion that result from a cervical fusion can limit the athlete's ability to compete and increase the risk of injury. Before return to play is allowed, the athlete should be screened for upper cervical spine fusion or conditions particularly associated with instability, including trisomy 21 (Down syndrome), skeletal dysplasias, os odontoideum, and rheumatoid arthritis (in which atlantoaxial instability is a particular concern). In Klippel-Feil syndrome, which is characterized by a congenital failure of segmentation in the cervical spine, the patient may have a fusion involving the occipitocervical junction. A patient with Klippel-Feil syndrome has a classic triad of a stiff neck, low hairline, and webbed neck.

In the subaxial cervical spine, the primary considerations in determining an increased risk of injury are the stability of the spine and the presence of a fusion, which could restrict motion or lead to junctional injury at the levels subjacent to the fusion. Posterior cervical foraminotomy should not destabilize the spine enough to compromise spine stability. Posterior cervical laminectomy can lead to instability as a result of the loss of the posterior tension band. Multilevel procedures can denervate the paraspinal musculature, thus compromising its ability to share the load within the cervical spine and resulting in a transfer of energy to the osseous and ligamentous structures.[42] Cervical laminoplasty preserves the posterior tension band better than cervical laminectomy, but the concerns regarding return to play are similar. Cervical laminoplasty and laminectomy are most commonly performed for cervical myelopathy, which is itself a contraindication to return to play. The consensus within the literature is that a one-level anteroposterior cervical fusion is not a contraindication to return to play. A two-level fusion is controversial, however, and a three-level fusion is a contraindication to return to play. Patients returning to play after a one-level anterior cervical diskectomy and fusion for cervical cord neurapraxia were found to have an increased risk of repeated herniation above or below the level of fusion.[43] The literature on cervical disk replacement is insufficient to provide guidance for the use of this procedure in athletes and subsequent return to play. In military personnel, cervical disk arthroplasty had favorable results compared with arthrodesis and allowed an earlier return to active duty.[44]

Thoracic Spine Injury

The stability of the thoracic spine is augmented by the sternum and rib cage. Thus, significant instability after thoracic laminectomy is rare, and return to play is not absolutely contraindicated. A fusion extending across the cervicothoracic and thoracolumbar junctions increases the stresses at the transitions between the stiff thoracic spine and the flexible cervical and lumbar spines, respectively. Some experts prefer to restrict return to play after such a fusion.[42]

Lumbar Spine Injury

The stability of the lumbar spine is aided by the stout supporting musculoligamentous structures. The spinal canal in the lumbar region is relatively capacious and encloses the spinal nerve roots, which are more tolerant of compression than the spinal cord. In one study, an average of 5 months was required until return to play after nonsurgical management of lumbar disk herniation.[45] Single-level lumbar disk surgery did not appear to limit or compromise sports activity in relatively young adult patients.[46,47] Fusion in the lumbar spine does not contraindicate a return to sports. Compared with cervical spine injury, lumbar spine injury is less common, junctional issues are less important, and the risk of significant neurologic injury is lower. The data on lumbar disk replacement are insufficient for a consensus on clinical decision making. However, a study including professional athletes and athletes in extreme

sports found that 95% of patients returned to sports activity after lumbar disk replacement.[48]

Summary

A delicate balance is required for the human spine to carry out two opposing goals: providing spine motion and protecting the nervous system. Any injury to the spinal column risks damaging the ability of the spine to carry out these disparate functions. Prevention remains the most effective way to reduce the incidence of potentially devastating sports-related spine injury. Not all injuries can be prevented, however, and an understanding of sport-specific risk factors, along with appropriate patient history, physical examination, and diagnostic testing can help identify the injury and guide treatment. On the field, in the office, and in the operating room, a thorough understanding of treatment algorithms is necessary for an optimal outcome.

Annotated References

1. Hwang V, Shofer FS, Durbin DR, Baren JM: Prevalence of traumatic injuries in drowning and near drowning in children and adolescents. *Arch Pediatr Adolesc Med* 2003;157(1):50-53.

2. Clarke KS: Epidemiology of athletic neck injury. *Clin Sports Med* 1998;17(1):83-97.

3. Boden BP, Tacchetti RL, Cantu RC, Knowles SB, Mueller FO: Catastrophic cervical spine injuries in high school and college football players. *Am J Sports Med* 2006;34(8):1223-1232.

   The epidemiology and mechanisms of almost 200 catastrophic high school and college football injuries were retrospectively identified using data reported to the National Center for Catastrophic Sports Injury Research over a 13-year period.

4. Torg JS, Guille JT, Jaffe S: Injuries to the cervical spine in American football players. *J Bone Joint Surg Am* 2002;84(1):112-122.

5. Flik K, Lyman S, Marx RG: American collegiate men's ice hockey: An analysis of injuries. *Am J Sports Med* 2005;33(2):183-187.

   Prospectively collected data on 113 injuries in eight Division I teams during a single season were used to identify the most common injuries and mechanisms of injury in American men's collegiate ice hockey.

6. Stuart MJ, Smith AM, Malo-Ortiguera SA, Fischer TL, Larson DR: A comparison of facial protection and the incidence of head, neck, and facial injuries in Junior A hockey players: A function of individual playing time. *Am J Sports Med* 2002;30(1):39-44.

7. Scher AT: Rugby injuries to the cervical spine and spinal cord: A 10-year review. *Clin Sports Med* 1998;17(1):195-206.

8. Wetzler MJ, Akpata T, Laughlin W, Levy AS: Occurrence of cervical spine injuries during the rugby scrum. *Am J Sports Med* 1998;26(2):177-180.

9. Boden BP, Lin W, Young M, Mueller FO: Catastrophic injuries in wrestlers. *Am J Sports Med* 2002;30(6):791-795.

10. Mueller FO, Cantu RC; National Center for Catastrophic Sports Injury Research: *Twenty-Third Annual Report: Fall 1982-Spring 2005.* Chapel Hill, NC, National Center for Catastrophic Sports Injury Research, 2005.

11. American Academy of Pediatrics, Committee on Accident and Poison Prevention, and Committee on Pediatric Aspects of Physical Fitness, Recreation and Sports: Trampolines II. *Pediatrics* 1981;67:438-439.

12. American Academy of Pediatrics, Committee on Injury and Poison Prevention, and Committee on Sports Medicine and Fitness: Trampolines at home, school, and recreational centers. *Pediatrics* 1999;103(5, pt 1):1053-1056.

13. Boden BP, Tacchetti R, Mueller FO: Catastrophic injuries in high school and college baseball players. *Am J Sports Med* 2004;32(5):1189-1196.

14. Morrow PL, McQuillen EN, Eaton LA Jr, Bernstein CJ: Downhill ski fatalities: The Vermont experience. *J Trauma* 1988;28(1):95-100.

15. Levy AS, Smith RH: Neurologic injuries in skiers and snowboarders. *Semin Neurol* 2000;20(2):233-245.

16. Boden BP, Jarvis CG: Spinal injuries in sports. *Neurol Clin* 2008;26(1):63-78, viii.

    This review of spine injuries in athletic competition includes sports activities with the highest risk of catastrophic spine injury. A brief overview of the common mechanisms of injury, preventive measures, and on-the-field management are provided.

17. Tarazi F, Dvorak MF, Wing PC: Spinal injuries in skiers and snowboarders. *Am J Sports Med* 1999;27(2):177-180.

18. Boden SD, McCowin PR, Davis DO, Dina TS, Mark AS, Wiesel S: Abnormal magnetic-resonance scans of the cervical spine in asymptomatic subjects: A prospective investigation. *J Bone Joint Surg Am* 1990;72(8):1178-1184.

19. Boden SD, Davis DO, Dina TS, Patronas NJ, Wiesel SW: Abnormal magnetic-resonance scans of the lumbar spine in asymptomatic subjects: A prospective investigation. *J Bone Joint Surg Am* 1990;72(3):403-408.

20. Sallis RE, Jones K, Knopp W: Burners: Offensive strategy for an underreported injury. *Phys Sportsmed* 1992;20(11):47-55.

21. Slipman CW, Plastaras CT, Palmitier RA, Huston CW, Sterenfeld EB: Symptom provocation of fluoroscopically guided cervical nerve root stimulation: Are dynatomal maps identical to dermatomal maps? *Spine (Phila Pa 1976)* 1998;23(20):2235-2242.

22. Kelly JD IV, Aliquo D, Sitler MR, Odgers C, Moyer RA: Association of burners with cervical canal and foraminal stenosis. *Am J Sports Med* 2000;28(2):214-217.

23. Cantu RC: Head and spine injuries in youth sports. *Clin Sports Med* 1995;14(3):517-532.

24. Markey KL, Di Benedetto M, Curl WW: Upper trunk brachial plexopathy: The stinger syndrome. *Am J Sports Med* 1993;21(5):650-655.

25. Clarke K, Jordan B: Sports neuroepidemiology, in Jordan B, Tsairis P, Warren R, eds: *Sports Neurology*, ed 2. Philadelphia, PA, Lippincott-Raven, 1998, pp 3-13.

26. Maroon JC: 'Burning hands' in football spinal cord injuries. *JAMA* 1977;238(19):2049-2051.

27. Penning L: Some aspects of plain radiography of the cervical spine in chronic myelopathy. *Neurology* 1962;12: 513-519.

28. Muhle C, Weinert D, Falliner A, et al: Dynamic changes of the spinal canal in patients with cervical spondylosis at flexion and extension using magnetic resonance imaging. *Invest Radiol* 1998;33(8):444-449.

29. Torg JS, Naranja RJ Jr, Pavlov H, Galinat BJ, Warren R, Stine RA: The relationship of developmental narrowing of the cervical spinal canal to reversible and irreversible injury of the cervical spinal cord in football players. *J Bone Joint Surg Am* 1996;78(9):1308-1314.

30. Cantu RC: Cervical spine injuries in the athlete. *Semin Neurol* 2000;20(2):173-178.

31. Castro FP Jr: Stingers, cervical cord neurapraxia, and stenosis. *Clin Sports Med* 2003;22(3):483-492.

32. Swartz EE, Boden BP, Courson RW, et al: National athletic trainers' association position statement: Acute management of the cervical spine-injured athlete. *J Athl Train* 2009;44(3):306-331.

    The National Athletic Trainers Association provides a thorough overview of the acute management of an athlete with a cervical spine injury, with evidence-based recommendations on prevention strategies, on-the-field management, and emergency department management.

33. Bohrer S: Improving care for cervical spine injuries. *Ann Emerg Med* 1988;17(2):188-189.

34. Banerjee R, Palumbo MA, Fadale PD: Catastrophic cervical spine injuries in the collision sport athlete, part 2: Principles of emergency care. *Am J Sports Med* 2004; 32(7):1760-1764.

3: Spine Trauma

35. Cappuccino A, Bisson LJ, Carpenter B, Marzo J, Dietrich WD III, Cappuccino H: The use of systemic hypothermia for the treatment of an acute cervical spinal cord injury in a professional football player. *Spine (Phila Pa 1976)* 2010;35(2):E57-E62.

   A National Football League player sustained an SCI and was treated with expedient conventional care in addition to modest systemic hypothermia. The patient's injury and clinical course are described.

36. Kwon BK, Mann C, Sohn HM, et al: Hypothermia for spinal cord injury. *Spine J* 2008;8(6):859-874.

   This review by the North American Spine Society Section on Biologics describes state-of-the-art (2008) treatment with local modest systemic hypothermia for SCI.

37. Bracken MB, Shepard MJ, Holford TR, et al: Administration of methylprednisolone for 24 or 48 hours or tirilazad mesylate for 48 hours in the treatment of acute spinal cord injury: Results of the Third National Acute Spinal Cord Injury Randomized Controlled Trial. National Acute Spinal Cord Injury Study. *JAMA* 1997; 277(20):1597-1604.

38. Coleman WP, Benzel D, Cahill DW, et al: A critical appraisal of the reporting of the National Acute Spinal Cord Injury Studies (II and III) of methylprednisolone in acute spinal cord injury. *J Spinal Disord* 2000;13(3): 185-199.

39. Herzog RJ, Wiens JJ, Dillingham MF, Sontag MJ: Normal cervical spine morphometry and cervical spinal stenosis in asymptomatic professional football players: Plain film radiography, multiplanar computed tomography, and magnetic resonance imaging. *Spine (Phila Pa 1976)* 1991;16(6, suppl):S178-S186.

40. Bailes JE: Experience with cervical stenosis and temporary paralysis in athletes. *J Neurosurg Spine* 2005;2(1): 11-16.

   The findings of this case study of 10 athletes suggest that a single episode of transient SCI should not substantially increase the risk of catastrophic SCI, if MRI shows preservation of cerebrospinal fluid.

41. Torg JS, Ramsey-Emrhein JA: Management guidelines for participation in collision activities with congenital, developmental, or postinjury lesions involving the cervical spine. *Clin J Sport Med* 1997;7(4):273-291.

42. Burnett MG, Sonntag VK: Return to contact sports after spinal surgery. *Neurosurg Focus* 2006;21(4):E5.

   This focused review describes return-to-play guidelines and their evidence-based rationale, as used at Barrow Neurological Institute (Phoenix, AZ).

43. Maroon JC, El-Kadi H, Abla AA, et al: Cervical neurapraxia in elite athletes: evaluation and surgical treatment: Report of five cases. *J Neurosurg Spine* 2007;6(4):356-363.

   Five elite football players returned to play after treatment with anterior cervical diskectomy and fusion for CCN from a single-level disk herniation. Two patients developed recurrent adjacent-segment herniation, and one required repeat surgical decompression.

44. Tumialán LM, Ponton RP, Garvin A, Gluf WM: Arthroplasty in the military: A preliminary experience with ProDisc-C and ProDisc-L. *Neurosurg Focus* 2010;28(5): E18.

   This retrospective review describes preliminary outcomes of 12 cervical and 12 lumbar disk arthroplasties in active-duty military personnel. Return to duty was more rapid than in matched patients who underwent fusion.

45. Iwamoto J, Takeda T, Sato Y, Wakano K: Short-term outcome of conservative treatment in athletes with symptomatic lumbar disc herniation. *Am J Phys Med Rehabil* 2006;85(8):667-677.

   A retrospective review found that conservative treatment for symptomatic lumbar disk herniation led to return to play at an average of 4.7 months in 56 of 71 patients (79%) at a sports medicine clinic.

46. Dollinger V, Obwegeser AA, Gabl M, Lackner P, Koller M, Galiano K: Sporting activity following discectomy for lumbar disc herniation. *Orthopedics* 2008;31(8): 756.

   A telephone questionnaire was used to determine the return-to-play experience of 67 patients (average age, 30 years) after diskectomy for lumbar disk herniation. Single-level surgery did not appear to limit sports activity in these young patients.

47. Watkins RG IV, Williams LA, Watkins RG III: Microscopic lumbar discectomy results for 60 cases in professional and Olympic athletes. *Spine J* 2003;3(2):100-105.

48. Siepe CJ, Wiechert K, Khattab MF, Korge A, Mayer HM: Total lumbar disc replacement in athletes: Clinical results, return to sport and athletic performance. *Eur Spine J* 2007;16(7):1001-1013.

   The return-to-play experience of 39 athletic patients was reviewed after lumbar total disk replacement. Ninety-five percent resumed sporting activity, with 85% noting improvement in athletic performance. Minor subsidence of the implant was noted in 30%.

Chapter 24
Whiplash-Associated Disorders

Vladimir Sinkov, MD   P. Justin Tortolani, MD

Introduction

The US National Highway Traffic Safety Administration estimates that 800,000 whiplash injuries occur each year in the United States.[1] These injuries represent 70% of all motor vehicle insurance claims for bodily injury. The direct costs are approximately $2.7 billion per year, and the total costs, including those related to litigation, are as much as $29 billion per year.

The term whiplash was originally used in 1928 to describe head and neck motion during a rear-impact motor vehicle crash, causing indirect soft-tissue injury.[2] The term now refers to any indirect injury to the cervical spine, other than a fracture or dislocation. Whiplash-associated disorder (WAD) is the term used for the combination of symptoms caused by a whiplash injury, including neck pain, stiffness, upper extremity symptoms, headache, and memory loss. Despite extensive research, substantial controversy exists regarding the diagnosis, prognosis, and treatment of WAD. A thorough understanding of biomechanics, pathoanatomy, and therapeutic options is crucial for successful treatment of whiplash injuries.

Classification

The Quebec Task Force on Whiplash-Associated Disorders in 1995 developed a classification system to improve communication, documentation, and research on whiplash injury[3] (Table 1). This simple system consists of five mutually exclusive grades indicating progressively greater severity. Most whiplash injuries fall into grade I or II. Fracture and/or dislocation is included in grade IV, and therefore grade IV is outside the scope of properly defined whiplash injury.

Dr. Tortolani or an immediate family member serves as a board member, owner, officer, or committee member of Towson Orthopaedic Associates; has received royalties from Globus Medical; is a member of a speakers' bureau or has made paid presentations on behalf of Globus Medical; serves as a paid consultant to or is an employee of Globus Medical; and has received research or institutional support from DePuy and Globus Medical. Neither Dr. Sinkov nor any immediate family member has received anything of value from or owns stock in a commercial company or institution related directly or indirectly to the subject of this chapter.

Biomechanics

Biomechanical studies have provided an understanding of the forces and motion involved in whiplash injuries.[4-7] The classic kinematics occur in three stages[8,9] (Figure 1). The first stage of the whiplash motion occurs during the first 100 milliseconds (ms) after a rear impact. The torso is driven forward and upward. The cervical spine, which has a lordotic alignment at rest, is forced into a straight alignment within the first 20 ms and into flexion within the first 50 ms. During this time the cervical spine sustains compressive and shear forces, followed by tensile forces. The second stage occurs between 100 and 130 ms after the rear impact. The torso moves backward; the lower vertebrae extend; and, as the head lags behind, the cervical spine assumes an S shape. The vertebrae quickly rotate from flexion into extension. It is believed that most injuries occur during this deformation. The third stage occurs as the head swings back, extending the entire cervical spine. The shear and tensile forces are the greatest during the third stage, especially in the lower segments. The entire motion occurs within 500 ms. The neck muscles begin to respond only in the third stage, as the sternocleidomastoid contracts in eccentric fashion to limit excessive extension.

The biomechanics of whiplash injuries originally were studied in a cadaver model.[10] A subsequent human-volunteer study using live cineradiography and electromyography found similar kinematics and time ranges.[11] This study emphasized that most of the axial loads and shear forces occur when the spine is in an S shape and before muscles are activated.[8]

A cadaver study found that a minimum vehicle acceleration of 3.5 g is needed to cause facet joint compression beyond physiologic limits.[12] The lower cervical segments were found to experience the greatest forces. An in vivo study found that more force was required to produce whiplash symptoms. In this study, human volunteers were subjected to rear impact while seated in an automobile equipped with crash recorders.[13] No injuries occurred when the peak acceleration was 6 g or less. Short-term disability was caused by a peak acceleration of 10 g. Long-term WAD-like symptoms occurred after collisions with a peak acceleration of 13 to 15 g.[13]

Although most biomechanical research on WAD has used a rear-impact model, impact from another direction can lead to similar symptoms (Table 2).

Table 1	

The Classification of Whiplash-Associated Disorders

Grade	Clinical Presentation
0	No report of neck pain or physical signs
I	Neck pain, stiffness, tenderness
II	Neck pain and musculoskeletal signs (decreased range of motion and point tenderness)
III	Neck pain and neurologic signs (decreased or absent deep tendon reflexes, weakness, sensory deficits)
IV	Neck pain and fracture-dislocation

Adapted with permission from Spitzer WO, Skovron ML, Salmi LR, et al: Scientific monograph of the Quebec Task Force on Whiplash-Associated Disorders: Redefining "whiplash" and its management. *Spine (Phila Pa 1976)* 1995;20(8, suppl):1S-73S.

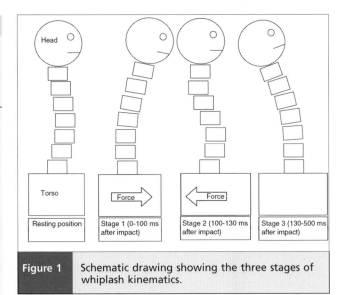

Figure 1	Schematic drawing showing the three stages of whiplash kinematics.

Pathoanatomy

The facet joints and their capsules have been implicated as the source of pain in cervical spine conditions including WAD. These structures are innervated by the medial branches of the dorsal primary rami. Whiplash injury may cause a nonphysiologic stretching of the capsules during the first and second stages and a pinching of the posterior synovial folds during the third stage. The greatest strains usually are seen at C5-C6 and C6-C7. The nociceptive nerve fibers in the capsules are believed to be susceptible to damage, with subsequent abnormal responses to normal joint loading. Damage to the collagen network of the joint capsule can start an inflammatory response. These two mechanisms may explain the persistent pain patients with chronic WAD have during normal neck motion. This theory is supported by evidence that facet blocks and medial branch neurotomies are effective in relieving chronic WAD pain.[14,15]

The cervical ligaments and intervertebral disks provide passive stability as well as proprioceptive feedback to the neck. The structures extending from C3-C4 to C7-T1 were found to be at greatest risk of whiplash injury.[16] Patients with WAD were found to have poor coordination of head movements, with resulting dizziness, probably because of poor proprioceptive feedback from injured mechanoreceptors in the passive restraints of the cervical spine.[17] The alar and transverse ligaments in the upper cervical spine usually are not subjected to the forces that result in WAD, but they are more susceptible if the head is rotated during impact.[16,18,19]

Vertebral arteries can be stretched beyond their physiologic limits in whiplash injury. The resulting intimal damage can cause insufficient brainstem perfusion, which may be the cause of WAD symptoms such as headache, dizziness, and vertigo.[16,20] The nerve roots and dorsal root ganglia are more susceptible to compression injury than the peripheral nerves because they lack an epineurium. Concomitant foraminal narrowing is present in 20% of cadaver whiplash models.[21] Permanent nerve root damage from compression or stretching of the neuroforamina may cause abnormal neural responses to external stimuli, such as some patients' general hypersensitivity and decreased thermal pain thresholds in the skin around the neck.[16,21,22]

Eccentric loading of the neck during whiplash injury also can injure the paraspinal musculature. Although the direct muscle damage is expected to heal over the course of several weeks, the indirect effect of the trauma may explain some chronic symptoms of WAD. The multifidus muscles are in the deepest layer of posterior musculature and insert into the facet capsules; these muscles or their tendon attachments can be injured during forceful eccentric contraction. Muscle injury can lead to poor neuromuscular control and inappropriate movement, which can contribute to chronic neck pain.[17] Considerable debate remains as to whether direct muscle damage causes abnormal neuromuscular patterns or, instead, pain avoidance strategies cause a patient to move the neck in an abnormal manner.[16]

Table 2	

Whiplash-Associated Disorders Differentiated by Impact Direction and Vehicle Occupant

	Vehicle Occupant	
Injury Mechanism	Driver	Passenger
Rear impact	51.9%	54.3%
Front impact	27.2%	21.3%
Side impact	16.4%	12.2%

Data from Chen HB, Yang KH, Wang ZG: Biomechanics of whiplash injury. *Chin J Traumatol* 2009;12(5):305-314.

Table 3

Patients With a Whiplash-Associated Disorder Who Experience Individual Symptoms

Symptom	Patients With Symptom
Neck pain*	100%
Shoulder symptoms	22%
Low back pain	30%-42%
Acute stress syndrome	20%
Posttraumatic stress disorder	5%
Travel anxiety	18%

*Time from injury to onset of pain (cumulative): none, 37%; less than 12 hours, 62% to 65%; less than 24 hours, 90%.

Data from Bannister G, Amirfeyz R, Kelley S, Gargan M: Whiplash injury. *J Bone Joint Surg Br* 2009;91(7):845-850; and Schofferman J, Bogduk N, Slosar P: Chronic whiplash and whiplash-associated disorders: An evidence- based approach. *J Am Acad Orthop Surg* 2007;15(10):596-606.

Clinical Evaluation

Only 37% of patients with WAD develop pain immediately after the motor vehicle crash, but 90% are symptomatic within 24 hours of the crash.[23] The most common symptoms include neck, shoulder symptoms, and low back pain as well as psychologic disturbances[14,23] (Table 3). Occipital headache and arm paresthesias in a nondermatomal pattern are also common, but the reported incidences vary widely.[14] Shoulder impingement, brachial plexopathy, otologic and vestibular disturbances, and temporomandibular joint pain also may be present. Although 14% to 50% of patients develop chronic pain, usually the pain is mild; 5% to 12% of patients become permanently disabled, however.[14,23]

The initial clinical findings are nonspecific and usually include a decreased, painful range of motion as well as posterior midline and paraspinal tenderness to palpation. The neurologic symptoms, if present, usually arise several days after the injury and include numbness, weakness, and occasionally hyporeflexia in a nondermatomal distribution. The hyporeflexia is believed to be caused by pain inhibition. WAD cannot be identified by a specific clinical examination finding. The diagnosis is usually made by using the clinical history and eliminating other causes of posttraumatic neck pain.

No specific imaging modality or finding has been correlated with WAD or the likelihood of developing chronic symptoms. A loss of cervical lordosis caused by muscle spasm is often seen on lateral radiographs. Multiple studies have evaluated the efficacy of MRI after a whiplash injury.[14,23,24] Early MRI was not found to lead to clinically relevant findings in most whiplash patients and was not correlated with outcomes.[24]

Psychosocial factors have been found to significantly affect the severity and chronicity of symptoms.[14,23,25] The patient's expectations of recovery, coping skills,

Table 4

Risk Factors for Chronic Pain in a Whiplash-Associated Disorder

Significant
Initial pain severity
Relatively large number of initial symptoms
Severity of initial disability
Absence of active head restraint and seat back system
Female sex
Legal system favorable for litigation or compensation

Possible*
Head restraint position
Body position during impact
Direction of impact
Cultural differences
Age
Involvement in litigation
Vehicle type

Not Significant
Level of education

*Conflicting or inconclusive evidence

and social support network should be noted, as well as the presence of depression and the potential for litigation.

Predisposing Factors for Chronic Pain

Because of the significant socioeconomic impact of whiplash injuries, there is great interest in elucidating factors that predispose the patient to longer duration and greater severity of pain and other WAD symptoms. Unfortunately, most studies have had inconclusive or conflicting findings. Thorough literature reviews have identified general risk factors for chronic WAD, which are categorized as injury related or patient related (Table 4). In multiple studies, the strongest injury-related predictors of chronic severe pain and poor outcome are severe initial pain, a large number of symptoms, and extensive disability.[26] These symptoms probably represent a more severe injury to the neck structures. The significance of collision-related factors such as the direction of impact, the person's position in the vehicle during impact, and the vehicle type were found to conflict in the findings of multiple studies, and these factors are no longer considered useful for predicting the severity or duration of symptoms.[26] Some evidence suggests that the use of an active vehicular head restraint and seat back system can reduce the incidence of WAD.

3: Spine Trauma

Table 5

Supporting and Opposing Evidence for Treatments of Whiplash-Associated Disorders

Treatment	Supporting Evidence		Opposing Evidence	
	Study	Level of Evidence	Study	Type or Level of Evidence
Early mobilization	Borchgrevink et al[31] Kongsted et al[32]	Level I Level I	Haines et al[33]	Meta-analysis
Early multidisciplinary evaluation			Pape et al[34]	Case-control study
Cognitive-behavioral therapy	Wicksell et al[25]	Level II		
Trigger point injections			Scott et al[35]	Meta-analysis
Botulinum toxin injections			Carroll et al[36]	Level I

The multifactorial nature of WAD is underscored by the presence of patient-related physical, psychologic, and social factors that affect the severity and length of symptoms. In most studies, a history of neck pain appears to predict relatively severe WAD symptoms.[14,23,26] Women were found to be at greater risk for WAD (accounting for 69% of all incidences) and to have a longer duration of symptoms than men;[26-28] anatomic differences in neck musculature may contribute to this difference. Multiple psychologic factors have been shown to affect recovery time, chronicity, and the risk of permanent disability in patients with WAD. Depression, passive coping skills, fear-avoidance behavior, pain catastrophizing, and low expectations for recovery have been identified as possible risk factors for more severe and chronic symptoms. The presence of a legal system that is likely to award monetary damages after a whiplash injury was found to increase the incidence and severity of WAD in some studies.[28,29] However, other studies suggested that patients' symptoms did not improve after the litigation ended.[26,30]

Treatment

Recent studies have provided evidence to support some treatments for WAD (Table 5). Patients with a whiplash injury have highly variable symptoms that range in severity, and the treatment must be individualized. After a serious injury to the neck has been ruled out, neck pain after a whiplash injury initially should be treated with early mobilization and patient education on the nature of injury and the probable good outcome. Early mobilization was found to be more beneficial than short-term immobilization at 6-month follow-up after injury, and it was as effective as formal physical therapy.[31,32] A recent meta-analysis found no benefit to early formal physical therapy, however.[33] A thorough initial medical evaluation and early multidisciplinary medical intervention can be detrimental, possibly because they can enhance the patient's concern about the

injury and encourage the patient to take on the role of a whiplash injury "victim."[34] Initial pain severity is a definite predictor of chronic symptoms, and therefore pain control should be optimized by relying on nonsteroidal anti-inflammatory drugs and the short-term use of corticosteroids.[23]

The treatment options for a patient with chronic WAD are limited and relatively ineffective. Neck exercises directed by a physical therapist remain the mainstay of treatment. Both acute and chronic neck pain has been shown to respond to nonsteroidal anti-inflammatory drugs, opioid analgesics, and muscle relaxants. Because of the lack of clear anatomic defects, it is very difficult to direct therapies to relieve the pain and disability. The facet joints are frequently suspected to be the injured structures in WAD, and pain relief after injection of the suspected facets may be diagnostic as well as therapeutic. The injection can be followed by radiofrequency neurotomy of the medial branches, which has been reported to provide relief for 9 to 13 months and can be repeated as needed.[14] The evidence on the effectiveness of trigger point injections is conflicting, and botulinum toxin injection was not found to be effective.[14,35,36] Cervical fusion should be limited to refractory WAD with radicular symptoms that are correlated with MRI evidence of a structural abnormality. The patient should be counseled that the effectiveness of cervical surgery in the setting of WAD is less predictable than in patients with no history of WAD.[14] Cognitive behavioral therapy emphasizing exposure and acceptance strategies was found to be effective in early reports, although long-term studies are needed.[25] A patient with WAD who has psychologic or psychiatric symptoms should also receive care from a mental health professional.

Prevention

WAD is common and potentially devastating. The socioeconomic impact is significant, but there is a paucity of good treatment options. The prevention of whiplash injury should be emphasized, including the use of a properly positioned automobile head restraint. Positioning of the headrest within 3 inches of the occiput is important for preventing excessive neck extension during the third stage of a whiplash incident. An active head restraint system is designed to react to the movement of the torso against the seat by causing the headrest to move to a higher and more forward position. Such a system can limit the backward motion of the head but is not sufficient to eliminate the cervical strain associated with the S-curve formation in the second stage.[37]

An energy-absorbing automobile seat design uses several strategies to absorb the energy of the impact and limit body and neck motion. A rotational spring damper in the seat back and a translational spring damper in the seat pan are activated only when the level of vehicle deceleration is sufficient to produce a whiplash injury. In cadaver studies and real-world crashes, these designs were found to lower the incidence of whiplash injury.[38,39] Accident avoidance mechanisms such as a laser-initiated braking system are under development.[23]

Summary

WAD is a common, multifactorial condition that begins with a whiplike injury to the neck and is classically associated with a rear-impact motor vehicle crash. The cervical spine undergoes an uncontrolled, passive movement that places multiple anatomic structures at risk. Facet capsules, paraspinal muscles, and interspinous ligaments are most vulnerable. The evaluation and management of WAD can be frustrating because of the paucity of physical examination or imaging findings correlated with the symptoms. After a more severe injury is ruled out, the early treatment should focus on pain management, active mobilization, and perhaps cognitive behavioral therapy. If chronic pain develops, the use of facet blocks and medial branch rhizotomy may be helpful. Multiple psychosocial factors seem to be associated with the patient's pain level, duration of symptoms, and response to treatment. Surgery should be limited to patients with clear-cut neurologic findings that are confirmed by appropriate imaging. Measures to prevent whiplash injury through crash avoidance and advanced automotive technology may reduce the future socioeconomic burden of WAD.

Annotated References

1. US Department of Transportation National Highway Traffic Safety Administration: Final rule: Head restraints. 49 CFR 571.202. http://www.nhtsa.dot.gov/cars/rules/rulings/HeadRest/update/202FinalRule.html. December 7, 2004. Accessed August 11, 2010.

2. Crowe HD: Whiplash injuries of the cervical spine, in *Proceedings of the Section of Insurance Negligence and Compensation Law*. Chicago, IL, American Bar Association, 1928, pp 176-184.

3. Spitzer WO, Skovron ML, Salmi LR, et al: Scientific monograph of the Quebec Task Force on Whiplash-Associated Disorders: Redefining "whiplash" and its management. *Spine (Phila Pa 1976)* 1995;20(8, suppl):1S-73S.

4. Ivancic PC, Panjabi MM, Ito S, Cripton PA, Wang JL: Biofidelic whole cervical spine model with muscle force replication for whiplash simulation. *Eur Spine J* 2005;14(4):346-355.

   A new in vitro whiplash model is incorporates all muscle forces in the neck. Experimental evaluation found that the model closely replicates kinematic data from in vivo human volunteer experiments. The authors concluded that the model can be used to reliably produce biomechanical whiplash data.

5. Panjabi MM, Pearson AM, Ito S, Ivancic PC, Wang JL: Cervical spine curvature during simulated whiplash. *Clin Biomech (Bristol, Avon)* 2004;19(1):1-9.

6. Panjabi MM, Cholewicki J, Nibu K, Grauer JN, Babat LB, Dvorak J: Mechanism of whiplash injury. *Clin Biomech (Bristol, Avon)* 1998;13(4-5):239-249.

7. Cholewicki J, Panjabi MM, Nibu K, Babat LB, Grauer JN, Dvorak J: Head kinematics during in vitro whiplash simulation. *Accid Anal Prev* 1998;30(4):469-479.

8. Chen HB, Yang KH, Wang ZG: Biomechanics of whiplash injury. *Chin J Traumatol* 2009;12(5):305-314.

   This review of recent literature describes whiplash pathoanatomy and kinematics in cadaver and live human cervical spines, with mechanisms believed to contribute to whiplash injury. Mathematical models of injury are reviewed.

9. Grauer JN, Panjabi MM, Cholewicki J, Nibu K, Dvorak J: Whiplash produces an S-shaped curvature of the neck with hyperextension at lower levels. *Spine (Phila Pa 1976)* 1997;22(21):2489-2494.

10. Luan F, Yang KH, Deng B, Begeman PC, Tashman S, King AI: Qualitative analysis of neck kinematics during low-speed rear-end impact. *Clin Biomech (Bristol, Avon)* 2000;15(9):649-657.

11. Kaneoka K, Ono K, Inami S, et al: The human cervical spine motion during rear impact collisions: A proposed cervical facet injury mechanism during whiplash trauma. *J Whiplash Relat Disord* 2002;1(1):85-97.

12. Pearson AM, Ivancic PC, Ito S, Panjabi MM: Facet joint kinematics and injury mechanisms during simulated whiplash. *Spine (Phila Pa 1976)* 2004;29(4):390-397.

13. Krafft M, Kullgren A, Lic A: Soft tissue injury of the cervical spine in rear-end car collisions. *J Traffic Med* 1997;25(3-4):89-96.

14. Schofferman J, Bogduk N, Slosar P: Chronic whiplash and whiplash-associated disorders: An evidence-based approach. *J Am Acad Orthop Surg* 2007;15(10):596-606.

    This review summarizes whiplash biomechanics, natural history, and prognostic factors, as well as the clinical symptoms of WAD. Treatment options for acute and chronic neck pain are described, with an emphasis on medial branch rhizotomy.

15. Ivancic PC, Ito S, Tominaga Y, et al: Whiplash causes increased laxity of cervical capsular ligament. *Clin Biomech (Bristol, Avon)* 2008;23(2):159-165.

    Cervical facet joint capsular ligaments from whiplash-exposed cadaver spines were found to elongate to a significantly greater extent than specimens from uninjured spines. This laxity could contribute to persistent pain after whiplash injury.

16. Siegmund GP, Winkelstein BA, Ivancic PC, Svensson MY, Vasavada A: The anatomy and biomechanics of acute and chronic whiplash injury. *Traffic Inj Prev* 2009;10(2):101-112.

    This review describes the biomechanical rationale of injury to cervical anatomic structures and how they may contribute to the development of WAD. The clinical evidence of injury, relevant anatomy, injury mechanism, and direction of future research related to each anatomic site are discussed.

17. Woodhouse A, Stavdahl Ø, Vasseljen O: Irregular head movement patterns in whiplash patients during a trajectory task. *Exp Brain Res* 2009;201(2):261-270.

    In a clinical study, head movement patterns were analyzed in patients with WAD, patients with chronic nontraumatic neck pain, and asymptomatic control subjects. Patients with WAD had irregular head movements that could be attributed to altered central sensorimotor processing.

18. Tominaga Y, Ndu AB, Coe MP, et al: Neck ligament strength is decreased following whiplash trauma. *BMC Musculoskelet Disord* 2006;7:103.

    In a cadaver model, whiplash-exposed neck ligamentous structures had significantly lower force to failure and a trend to lower energy absorption capacity, in comparison with control data.

19. Panjabi MM, Ito S, Pearson AM, Ivancic PC: Injury mechanisms of the cervical intervertebral disc during simulated whiplash. *Spine (Phila Pa 1976)* 2004;29(11):1217-1225.

20. Nibu K, Cholewicki J, Panjabi MM, et al: Dynamic elongation of the vertebral artery during an in vitro whiplash simulation. *Eur Spine J* 1997;6(4):286-289.

21. Tominaga Y, Maak TG, Ivancic PC, Panjabi MM, Cunningham BW: Head-turned rear impact causing dynamic cervical intervertebral foramen narrowing: Implications for ganglion and nerve root injury. *J Neurosurg Spine* 2006;4(5):380-387.

    A rear-impact cadaver whiplash model was evaluated, and increased foraminal width narrowing was found in the head-turned position, especially at C5-C6 and C6-C7. This factor could result in greater cervical ganglion compression when the head is turned during a rear-impact whiplash injury.

22. Ito S, Panjabi MM, Ivancic PC, Pearson AM: Spinal canal narrowing during simulated whiplash. *Spine (Phila Pa 1976)* 2004;29(12):1330-1339.

23. Bannister G, Amirfeyz R, Kelley S, Gargan M: Whiplash injury. *J Bone Joint Surg Br* 2009;91(7):845-850.

    Information on the socioeconomic costs, history, and mechanism of whiplash injury is provided. An overview of clinical presentation, outcomes, and factors affecting outcomes in WAD is synthesized from 100 publications.

24. Kongsted A, Sorensen JS, Andersen H, Keseler B, Jensen TS, Bendix T: Are early MRI findings correlated with long-lasting symptoms following whiplash injury? A prospective trial with 1-year follow-up. *Eur Spine J* 2008;17(8):996-1005.

    In 178 patients, most MRI findings 2 weeks and 3 months after whiplash injury were degenerative in nature and not correlated with outcomes 3 and 12 months after injury.

25. Wicksell RK, Ahlqvist J, Bring A, Melin L, Olsson GL: Can exposure and acceptance strategies improve functioning and life satisfaction in people with chronic pain and whiplash-associated disorders (WAD)? A randomized controlled trial. *Cogn Behav Ther* 2008;37(3):169-182.

    Twenty-one volunteers with chronic WAD were randomly assigned to observation or cognitive behavioral therapy. The treated patients had significantly more improvement in pain disability, life satisfaction, fear of movement, depression, and psychologic inflexibility, persisting for more than 7 months.

26. Carroll LJ, Holm LW, Hogg-Johnson S, et al: Course and prognostic factors for neck pain in whiplash-associated disorders (WAD): Results of the Bone and Joint Decade 2000-2010 Task Force on Neck Pain and Its Associated Disorders. *Spine (Phila Pa 1976)* 2008;33(4, suppl):S83-S92.

    A thorough review of research on neck pain between 1980 and 2006 found that 70 of 226 articles related to WAD satisfied the inclusion criteria. The clinical course of WAD and its prognostic factors were reviewed.

27. Storvik SG, Stemper BD, Yoganandan N, Pintar FA: Population-based estimates of whiplash injury using NASS CDS data: Biomed 2009. *Biomed Sci Instrum* 2009;45:244-249.

    The authors acquired data on all rear-impact motor vehicle crashes from 1998 to 2007. The National Automotive Sampling System was used to analyze populationwide estimates on whiplash injuries. Women were found to be most susceptible to developing WAD after a crash.

28. Represas C, Vieira DN, Magalhães T, et al: No cash no whiplash? Influence of the legal system on the incidence of whiplash injury. *J Forensic Leg Med* 2008;15(6):353-355.

   The incidence of whiplash in Spain and Portugal was retrospectively analyzed. Spain has a mandatory legal compensation system, whereas Portugal does not. The higher odds ratio for WAD in Spain (24.57) suggests that legal context may alter the frequency and severity of whiplash complaints.

29. Obelieniene D, Schrader H, Bovim G, Miseviciene I, Sand T: Pain after whiplash: A prospective controlled inception cohort study. *J Neurol Neurosurg Psychiatry* 1999;66(3):279-283.

30. Leth-Petersen S, Rotger GP: Long-term labour-market performance of whiplash claimants. *J Health Econ* 2009;28(5):996-1011.

   Data from the Netherlands on whiplash injuries from 1996 to 1998 were analyzed with respect to return to work. After settlement, patients with a severe injury who were awarded compensation were unable to return to work at the preinjury level.

31. Borchgrevink GE, Kaasa A, McDonagh D, Stiles TC, Haraldseth O, Lereim I: Acute treatment of whiplash neck sprain injuries: A randomized trial of treatment during the first 14 days after a car accident. *Spine (Phila Pa 1976)* 1998;23(1):25-31.

32. Kongsted A, Qerama E, Kasch H, et al: Neck collar, "act-as-usual" or active mobilization for whiplash injury? A randomized parallel-group trial. *Spine (Phila Pa 1976)* 2007;32(6):618-626.

   Patients with acute whiplash injury were randomly assigned to immobilization, advice to "act as usual," or an active mobilization program. At 1-year follow-up, there were no significant differences in outcomes.

33. Haines T, Gross A, Burnie SJ, Goldsmith CH, Perry L: Patient education for neck pain with or without radiculopathy. *Cochrane Database Syst Rev* 2009;21;(1): CD005106.

   A review of studies on the effects of patient education strategies for neck disorders found no conclusive evidence that these interventions are effective for treating neck pain.

34. Pape E, Hagen KB, Brox JI, Natvig B, Schirmer H: Early multidisciplinary evaluation and advice was ineffective for whiplash-associated disorders. *Eur J Pain* 2009; 13(10):1068-1075.

   A retrospective comparison of Norwegian patients with whiplash injuries that occurred before or after the implementation of mandatory multidisciplinary team evaluation found that significantly more patients who underwent the intervention developed chronic neck pain.

35. Scott NA, Guo B, Barton PM, Gerwin RD: Trigger point injections for chronic non-malignant musculoskeletal pain: A systematic review. *Pain Med* 2009;10(1): 54-69.

   A review of the literature on the effectiveness of trigger point injections for chronic pain found moderate pain improvement after trigger point injections for chronic pain in whiplash injury, but the effects were short lived.

36. Carroll A, Barnes M, Comiskey C: A prospective randomized controlled study of the role of botulinum toxin in whiplash-associated disorder. *Clin Rehabil* 2008; 22(6):513-519.

   Patients with symptoms of WAD 2 months after injury were randomly assigned to receive trigger point injections with botulinum toxin or a placebo. Both groups had improvement, but there were no significant difference in outcomes.

37. Ivancic PC, Sha D, Panjabi MM: Whiplash injury prevention with active head restraint. *Clin Biomech (Bristol, Avon)* 2009;24(9):699-707.

   A cadaver study of neck motion during a simulated rear impact, with or without an active head restraint, found that the active restraint reduced peak spine rotations between segments but that the peak rotation still exceeded physiologic limits.

38. Himmetoglu S, Acar M, Bouazza-Marouf K, Taylor AJ: Energy-absorbing car seat designs for reducing whiplash. *Traffic Inj Prev* 2008;9(6):583-591.

   Several antiwhiplash car seat designs were tested using a human body model. The designs that had, at a minimum, a back with a rotational spring damper and a seat pan with a translational spring damper were effective at reducing whiplash.

39. Jakobsson L, Isaksson-Hellman I, Lindman M: WHIPS (Volvo cars' Whiplash Protection System): The development and real-world performance. *Traffic Inj Prev* 2008;9(6):600-605.

   This retrospective review compared whiplash injuries to front seat occupants in Volvo automobiles with and without an injury protection system. The system was found to reduce the risk of whiplash injury 21% to 47%. Occupants facing straight ahead, with the head close to the headrest, also had a lower risk of whiplash.

Section 4

The Adult Spine

SECTION EDITOR
EERIC TRUUMEES, MD

Chapter 25

The Evaluation and Management of Axial Neck and Low Back Pain

Shawn Hermenau, MD   Jonathan N. Grauer, MD

Introduction

Axial pain in the neck or low back is among the most common reasons for seeking medical attention. The lifetime prevalence of low back pain exceeds 80% in the United States, and as many as 15% of adults seek medical attention for low back pain every year. Within a 3-month survey period, 43% to 60% of adults were reported to have back or neck pain.[1,2] Although neck pain and back pain have many causes, most patients are diagnosed with a strain injury or symptomatic degeneration.

Axial back pain is a major public health issue.[3] In the United States, back pain is the primary reason adults younger than 45 years limit their physical activities, the second most common reason for missing work or a physician visit, the third most common reason for a surgical procedure, and the fifth most common reason for hospitalization.[4-9] The statistics for neck pain are lower but similar in nature.[1] The incidence of neck pain has been consistent during the past decade; in one study, the lifetime incidence of neck pain was found to be greater than 66%.[10] The prevalence of neck pain appears to be similar in other countries.

Neck and back pain are responsible for a substantial economic burden, including the direct costs of physician and caregiver services, medications, physical therapy, braces, diagnostic imaging, hospitalization, and surgical intervention. The indirect costs include missed workdays, disability payments, and lost productivity. Each year, 2% of the entire US workforce receives some form of compensation related to low back disability.[11] In the United Kingdom, workers with neck pain missed

an average of 13 workdays per claim.[12] The estimated annual direct cost of treating low back pain in the United States ranges from $20 to $50 billion dollars, in addition to $28 billion in lost productivity.[13] These costs are borne by health care insurers, corporations and other private payers, health insurance purchasers, patients, government agencies, and, ultimately, taxpayers. The consequences for the financial health of the nation are significant.

Evaluation

Axial Neck Pain

Axial neck pain is defined as pain occurring in the cervical, occipital, or posterior scapular areas but not radiating into the upper extremities. The etiology may be multifactorial and often is elusive. The terms axial neck pain, neck strain, neck sprain, whiplash, mechanical neck disorder, and neck and shoulder pain all have been used to define a group of patients who report similar symptoms. Pain is considered acute if it has been present for less than 4 weeks, subacute if it has been present for 4 to 12 weeks, and chronic if it has been present for more than 12 weeks.[13] Cervical disks, facet joints, joint capsules, muscles, tendons, and neurologic structures have all been implicated as generators of axial neck pain.

Axial neck pain typically is considered to be self-limiting and to resolve within 6 weeks.[14] However, one study of the natural history of untreated mechanical neck pain found that 21% of patients had complete relief, 49% had partial relief, and 22% had no relief.[15] Another study found that 23% of patients with axial neck pain remained partially or totally disabled after 5 years.[16]

Certain occupations seem to be associated with a particularly high risk of neck pain. The reported prevalence was 41% to 52% in dentists, 54% to 76% in miners, and 84% in butchers or meat carriers.[17] A literature review identified several significant risk factors: female sex; a pattern of repetitive movements or heavy lifting; an extreme, prolonged work posture; prolonged computer use; and a highly quantitative, mentally demanding occupation.[18] There was insufficient evidence

Dr. Hermenau or an immediate family member serves as an unpaid consultant to DePuy, a Johnson & Johnson company. Dr. Grauer or an immediate family member is a member of a speakers' bureau or has made paid presentations on behalf of Alphatec Spine, Stryker, and DePuy, a Johnson & Johnson company; serves as a paid consultant to or is an employee of Affinergy, Alphatec Spine, KCI, Stryker, Smith & Nephew, Vital 5, and DePuy, a Johnson & Johnson company; and has received research or institutional support from Stryker and Medtronic Sofamor Danek.

to support a causal relationship between vibration exposure and neck pain.

History and Physical Examination

A thorough history and physical examination are the cornerstones of the evaluation and management of axial neck pain. The patient's pain quality, duration, onset, and associated activities are relevant for identifying potential etiologies. The examination should include areas of tenderness, overall alignment, and motion as well as a complete neurologic evaluation. Axial posterior neck pain that worsens with prolonged flexion may be secondary to muscle fatigue or a discogenic etiology. Conversely, posterior neck pain that worsens with extension may be facetogenic in origin. Neurologic examination of the upper and lower extremities can be useful for ruling out concurrent cervical radiculopathy or myelopathy.

The possibility of a serious underlying condition such as tumor, infection, or traumatic injury can be identified through simple questioning. If the patient has night pain, night sweats, weight loss, or a recent history of trauma or acute neurologic changes, further exploration is required to avoid a delay in diagnosis, refine the examination, and guide possible diagnostic imaging. The presence of a condition with known cervical sequelae, such as rheumatoid arthritis or Down syndrome, also should trigger a targeted evaluation. The shoulder joint should be examined to rule out a source of referred pain. The findings of a vascular test such as the Adson maneuver or Wright test may raise suspicion for thoracic outlet syndrome.

A nonorganic pathology may be suggested by severe sensitivity to touch in a nondermatomal distribution, variation in examination findings, cogwheeling or jerky motor testing, disproportionate pain, or an exaggerated expression. The possibility of secondary gain should be considered.

Imaging

Because most axial neck pain is self-limiting, early imaging is not warranted unless the history or physical examination findings are of concern. Standing AP and neutral lateral radiographs should be obtained if the patient's symptoms persist after 6 weeks of simple nonsurgical treatment. Degenerative changes frequently are seen on plain radiographs. In a patient with cervical pain, there may be a loss of normal lordosis or kyphosis. Plain radiographs showed at least one degenerative change in 95% of asymptomatic men and 70% of asymptomatic women who were age 65 years or older.[19] Degeneration is most common at C5-C6, followed by C6-C7 and C4-C5.[19] Oblique radiographs may be most useful for visualizing the facet joints and the cervicothoracic junction. Flexion and extension lateral radiographs can be considered for assessing cervical instability. Open-mouth odontoid radiographs can be useful for visualizing C1-C2 pathology.

Advanced imaging studies may better define the pain generators or rule out a specific diagnosis. MRI is the imaging study of choice for a patient with persistent neck pain. MRI studies provide a clear picture of soft-tissue structures, neural elements, and vertebral bodies as well as the hydration of the intervertebral disk. Because of the high incidence of degenerative changes in asymptomatic patients, thoughtful interpretation of imaging studies is necessary. It is crucial to closely correlate imaging findings with the patient's clinical appearance.[20] CT is excellent for imaging of the bony anatomy and detecting spondylosis. However, CT generally is used only for planning surgery, assessing a bony pathology such as a fracture or tumor, or defining the ossification of structures associated with a degenerative pathology.

Cervical diskography has been used to assess the discogenic component of chronic axial neck pain but is controversial. In provocative diskography, disks are stimulated from an anterior approach, a contrast medium is injected, and symptomatic disks are identified. The resulting data have limited sensitivity and specificity, and complications including diskitis, subdural empyema, neurologic injury, vascular injury, and prevertebral abscess can occur. Accelerated disk degeneration has been reported after lumbar diskography.[21] This effect has not been documented in the cervical spine, but the risk appears to be real. Incorrect needle localization during cervical spine surgery was found to increase the risk of progressive disk degeneration at the affected adjacent levels.[22]

Axial Low Back Pain

Axial low back pain is the second most common reason patients visit a physician, after the common cold.[6,11] Low back pain is the most common cause of disability in people younger than 45 years, and it accounts for 25% of all lost workdays.[11] The direct costs of low back pain disability in the United States have been estimated to be more than $50 billion per year.[11]

Axial low back pain is defined as pain in the lumbar, lumbothoracic, or lumbosacral area that does not radiate into the lower extremities. As with axial neck pain, a direct correlation to an anatomic structure or pathologic condition is not always possible. Low back pain is a multifactorial condition that may be related to mechanical, neurophysiologic, or psychologic factors. The natural course of low back pain generally is favorable; most patients report resolution of symptoms within 4 to 6 weeks. As with neck pain, axial low back pain can be classified based on its duration as acute (less than 4 weeks), subacute (4 to 12 weeks), or chronic (more than 12 weeks).

The risk factors for axial back pain include increasing age; heavy physical work; long periods of static posture, lifting, or twisting; obesity; smoking; depression; and work dissatisfaction. Leg-length inequality, poor posture, and scoliosis probably have only a limited effect.[11,23]

History and Physical Examination

The evaluation of a patient with low back pain begins with a focused history and physical examination. The goal is to identify any specific etiology or underlying condition contributing to the pain. As in the evaluation of neck pain, any recent weight loss, fever, trauma, or neurologic symptom may suggest an underlying condition and warrant a targeted diagnostic evaluation.

A patient with discogenic low back pain typically reports pain that worsens with sitting and often increases with forward flexion or a prolonged axial loading activity. The pain may be poorly localized to the low back area, often in a bandlike distribution. The pain usually is dull in nature and can be decreased by shifting to a different position. Facet-related pain often is better localized, activity related, and more severe when the back is extended. Patients may report morning stiffness that initially improves but later worsens during the course of the day, particularly with walking. The quality of pain may be described as sharp. A specific spine level may be the source of both axial and radicular symptoms.

A thorough examination includes a gait analysis as well as an assessment of overall alignment, motion, and tenderness. The examination should include areas from which pain can be referred, such as the hip and sacroiliac joints. Provocative and neurologic testing should be performed. Provocative testing of the hips with internal-external rotation and flexion-abduction–external rotation may point to a pain origin in the hip or sacroiliac joint.

The presence of Waddell signs may indicate that the patient's low back pain has a nonorganic component and often is found in patients with secondary gain issues. These signs include diminished sensation or motor weakness in an atypical dermatomal or nonanatomic distribution, exaggerated response to light touch, distraction test findings such as a straight leg raise test that is positive in the supine position but negative in the seated position, simulation test findings such as low back pain that is elicited by axial compression of the head, and exaggerated response or emotional overreaction to simple nonprovocative maneuvers. Any patient involvement in litigation, a workers' compensation claim, or excessive narcotic use may require consideration.

Imaging

Because of the generally favorable natural history of acute low back pain as well as the high incidence of asymptomatic degenerative changes and normal variations, imaging studies are not useful unless there is concern that a serious, specific etiology is present. Imaging can be considered if the symptoms persist beyond 6 weeks. The initial radiographs should include standing AP and neutral lateral views of the lumbar spine. Coronal alignment is best seen on an AP radiograph; sagittal alignment and disk height loss should be assessed on lateral radiographs. Diffuse degenerative changes often can be seen on plain radiographs. The most common levels of degeneration are L4-L5 and L5-S1. Oblique radiographs may be useful for visualizing the pars region if spondylolysis is suspected. Flexion and extension lateral radiographs may be considered for assessing dynamic instability.

MRI is indicated if a patient's chronic axial back pain does not improve with basic nonsurgical treatment. MRI is the most sensitive and specific study for identifying disk degeneration and herniation, spinal stenosis, neural compression, soft-tissue injury, neoplasm, or infection.[21,24,25] Because of the likelihood of asymptomatic degeneration, careful clinical correlation is required for an accurate diagnosis. CT has largely been replaced by MRI for evaluating chronic low back pain but can be considered if MRI is contraindicated because the patient has an implant such as a pacemaker. The excellent bone definition provided by CT is useful for defining bony pathologies such as spondylolysis and facet joint degeneration. CT myelography can be considered if further definition of possible neural element compression is needed.

Lumbar diskography is a controversial test that is used in patients with presumed discogenic back pain if surgical intervention is being considered. Contrast medium is injected directly into the disk being tested as well as one or more control disks. The key findings include injection pressures, dye distribution or leakage, and pain provocation. The goal of the study is to correlate imaging findings with pain provocation and correlate the provoked pain with the patient's typical symptoms. A recent study suggested an association of annular puncture for the diskogram with accelerated disk degeneration, loss of disk height, and a higher incidence of disk herniation on the side of the annular puncture, compared with control subjects at 7- to 10-year follow-up.[26] Another study reported end plate degeneration as well as disk degeneration after diskography.[27] Nonetheless, lumbar diskography is one of the only means of directly correlating imaging findings with clinical symptoms.

Anesthetic diskography, in which pain relief is assessed after bupivacaine is injected into the disk, is a potential alternative to provocative diskography. A recent comparison of provocative and anesthetic diskography found that pain relief was a better predictor of surgical outcome than pain provocation.[28] Anesthetic diskography often is limited to the presumed painful level. The risk of accelerating the degeneration of adjacent disks may be limited to the presumed painful level, and restricting the diskography to the presumed painful level reduces the risk of progressive degeneration at adjacent disk levels.

Management

Axial low back pain initially is managed with a brief period of relative rest, a cessation of pain-provoking activities, and a limited course of medications. The possible adjunctive treatments include physical therapy, a brief

4: The Adult Spine

period of immobilization, and local modalities such as heat, ice, massage, ultrasonography, and transcutaneous electrical nerve stimulation. Spine injections or surgery may be considered for recurrent or severe chronic axial pain. Many of these modalities have mixed reported outcomes, and their effectiveness depends on an accurate diagnosis of the pain generators.[29-33]

Lifestyle modifications can lead to improvement in chronic low back pain. In particular, smoking cessation and weight loss are associated with relief of chronic low back pain in a patient who is obese. The time required for reversing the effects of smoking or obesity or achieving clinical improvement have yet to be determined.[29] The complementary or alternative modalities for treating axial spine pain include spine manipulation, acupuncture, yoga, and other exercise-based physical therapies. There is a lack of scientific support for these treatments, but isolated studies show potential benefits.[32,34]

Medication
Nonsteroidal anti-inflammatory drugs (NSAIDs), acetaminophen, tramadol, muscle relaxants, antidepressants, and opioids are used to treat chronic axial pain. In patients with chronic axial pain, the use of a simple analgesic, such as acetaminophen or tramadol, in combination with an antidepressant appears to have the greatest efficacy.[30] Muscle relaxants may help some patients, but there is only weak evidence for their efficacy, and the benefits must be balanced against the potential for adverse effects. Long-term opioid use appears to be safe but only modestly effective for patients with refractory chronic low back pain. The adverse effects of opioids, including aberrant behavior and central nervous system depression leading to decreased alertness and manual dexterity, make these drugs less than ideal for long-term therapy.[31] Patients receiving long-term opioid therapy have only modest functional improvements, despite the pain improvement. The adverse effects of opioids as well as the development of tolerance must be discussed with the patient.

NSAIDs are among the most common medications used for treating chronic low back pain, although the outcome data are mixed.[35] NSAIDs were found to be effective for treating acute or chronic low back pain without sciatica but were no more effective than acetaminophen, narcotics, muscle relaxants, or any other commonly used drug. The increased risks for patients with hypertension or a cardiac condition should be considered before an NSAID is prescribed for long-term use.

Exercise Programs
Exercise programs generally are based on core strengthening and aerobic conditioning. There is moderate-quality evidence that such exercise programs provide better reduction in pain and disability than rest and medications alone.[36] No difference has been found in the effectiveness of supervised and home-based exercise

programs. With regard to work outcomes, a literature review found that exercise programs reduced the duration of sick leave and increased the percentage of patients returning to work within the first year of disability.[32] Yoga or Pilates exercise programs may be appropriate for conditioning.

No clear benefit has been found for using traction in patients with axial low back pain. A meta-analysis found insufficient evidence to support the use of cervical traction in patients who have chronic mechanical neck pain, with or without radiculopathy.[37] Many studies with poor reporting and inadequate outcome measures were excluded from the review.

Local and Alternative Treatment Modalities
Acupuncture or dry needling has become a mainstream adjunctive treatment for patients with chronic low back pain. The science behind acupuncture is not well understood, but many patients have testified to its benefits. As a complementary therapy for axial pain, acupuncture is well tolerated and has a low risk of serious adverse effects. A meta-analysis to assess the efficacy of acupuncture found a limited number of studies with high-quality data; these data suggest that acupuncture leads to a modest improvement in symptoms and overall function.[34]

A recent prospective cohort study of cervical chiropractic manipulation for patients with neck pain found that patients with a self-reported benign adverse event had significantly more pain and disability at short-term follow-up.[38] These data as well as reports of serious adverse effects and even death suggest that cervical manipulation should not be considered a standard treatment.[39,40] Chiropractic manipulation was found to be moderately superior to sham manipulation for patients with chronic axial back pain, but it was no better than the standard modalities.[32]

Work Hardening
Work hardening is a form of physical rehabilitation designed to restore a patient's physical capacity and function as required for a return to work. Work hardening restores systemic and neurologic function as well as musculoskeletal function (strength, endurance, movement, flexibility, and motor control). Real or simulated work activities can be used to restore physical, behavioral, and vocational functions. Work hardening has been found to be more effective than other programs for treating chronic back pain. Work hardening for a patient with chronic back pain is most effective in combination with cognitive-behavioral therapy, which typically is focused on exercise-related beliefs or behaviors, coping mechanisms, and/or methods of relaxation.[41]

Injections
Injections are minimally invasive and may provide relief for patients whose axial spine pain has not improved with noninvasive modalities. Injections are not intended as a definitive treatment. One goal of injec-

© 2012 American Academy of Orthopaedic Surgeons

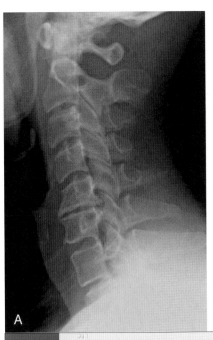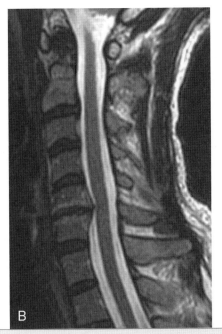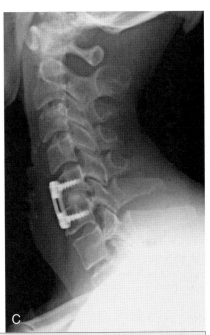

Figure 1	A 54-year-old man had predominantly axial neck pain that did not respond to extensive nonsurgical treatment. **A,** Sagittal radiograph of the cervical spine showing significant degenerative changes at C5-C6. **B,** Sagittal T2-weighted MRI corroborating the presence of significant degenerative changes at C5-C6 with no significant degenerative changes at other levels. **C,** Sagittal radiograph showing an anterior cervical diskectomy and fusion at the C5-C6 level, which was associated with significant symptom improvement. The patient returned to work with no defined restrictions and has only occasional posterior cervical discomfort.

tions is to provide a period of pain relief so that the patient can focus on relatively aggressive noninvasive modalities. Often patients find that repeated injections lead to a diminished quality and duration of pain relief. The use of trigger point or botulinum toxin injections to relieve chronic axial pain is not supported by evidence.[42]

Cervical epidural and foraminal injections may offer some relief to patients with chronic axial pain, with a low risk of adverse effects.[43] In a double-blinded study, patients with axial neck pain without radiculopathy or disk herniation received steroid injections or bupivacaine injections into the facet joints of the cervical spine.[43] Patients in both groups had similar pain improvement, duration of relief, and functional improvement, with low complication rates. Such injections appear to be a relatively safe option for treating refractory axial neck pain. There was no clear benefit to the addition of steroid to the injected solution.

Interlaminar epidural steroid injections appear to be an effective short-term treatment of nonspecific axial low back pain. A series of one to three injections is supported by evidence of improved pain and function.[44] Several patient factors are predictive of a negative outcome when interlaminar epidural steroid injections are used to treat chronic axial back pain, including constant pain, a psychologic disturbance, a relatively low education level, tobacco use, and unemployment.[44] The use of facet blocks can be both diagnostic and therapeutic in patients with chronic back pain.

Surgery

Neck Pain
If extensive nonsurgical intervention has not returned function and decreased pain, a properly selected patient with chronic axial neck pain at a limited number of levels may be a candidate for cervical fusion or disk replacement. Patient selection is the key to a successful surgical outcome (Figure 1). The patient evaluation should exclude all other potential sources of pain as well as pain generators related to a psychologic disturbance. Any possible secondary gain issue should be assessed, and the patient's motivation should be determined. Some surgeons refer patients to a psychiatrist or therapist for a mental health evaluation to further improve patient selection.

Realistic expectations related to the surgical outcome should be an integral part of presurgical counseling, along with the standard risks and benefits of surgery. Surgical intervention was reported to have a moderate benefit in patients in whom intractable, debilitating discogenic neck pain has been properly diagnosed.[45,46] More than 80% of patients who underwent anterior cervical fusion for axial neck pain rated the outcome as good or excellent. More than 90% of these patients had less pain, and at least 50% had improvement in their ability to perform activities of daily living.[46] Another study found insufficient evidence to support surgical intervention for treating axial neck pain unless the patient had radicular symptoms or clear pathology.[43]

4: The Adult Spine

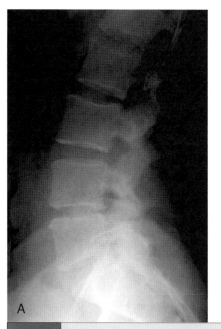
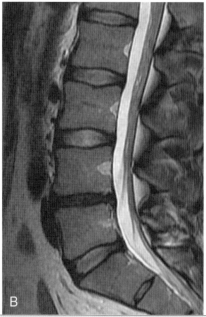
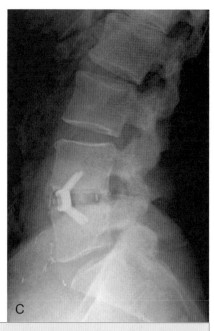

Figure 2 A 40-year-old man had axial low back pain that did not respond to extensive nonsurgical treatment. **A,** Sagittal radiograph of the lumbar spine showing isolated loss of disk height at L4-5. **B,** Sagittal T2-weighted MRI showing loss of disk height and hydration at L4-5. The patient had marked improvement of symptoms after a stand-alone anterior lumbar interbody fusion. **C,** Sagittal radiograph at 1-year follow-up showing bony incorporation consistent with fusion. At most recent follow-up, the patient had returned to full activities, including manual labor, with no residual symptoms.

Back Pain

The question of surgical intervention for chronic axial back pain often is raised if nonsurgical treatment does not lead to sufficient improvement (Figure 2). The key to a good surgical outcome is patient selection. The evaluation of a patient with chronic axial back pain should exclude any other source of pain, assess any secondary gain issue, and determine the patient's motivation. Studies of the outcome of surgery for chronic axial back pain have found mixed results.[44,47-49] A Swedish comparison study of the outcomes of lumbar fusion and nonsurgical therapy found moderate improvement in pain and function in the patients treated with fusion and little change in the patients treated nonsurgically.[50] Patients in the two groups had similar return-to-work rates, but patient satisfaction was twice as high among the surgically treated patients. At 2-year follow-up, nonsurgical treatment was found to be more costly than surgery for patients with axial back pain.[51]

The surgical options for lumbar fusion vary. As surgical techniques improve, less invasive procedures may be found clearly superior to earlier procedures or to nonsurgical treatment. Minimally invasive surgery, which avoids stripping the posterior muscles, has had clinical and radiographic outcomes similar to those of standard open lumbar fusions. The additional benefits of minimally invasive surgery are decreased initial postsurgical pain, decreased length of hospitalization, and early rehabilitation.[52] Anterior lumbar interbody fusion also avoids posterior muscle stripping to improve overall postsurgical back pain. Dynamic stabilization recently has generated interest, but no evidence supports its use in the management of chronic low back pain.[51]

Emerging technologies such as lumbar disk replacement have led to outcomes that appear comparable to those of fusion for patients with chronic low back pain. One study found that lumbar disk replacement has an overall lower cost than lumbar fusion.[50] The limited available long-term data support 2-year follow-up data as to the efficacy of lumbar disk replacement.[53] Disk replacement has several contraindications, including facet arthrosis, osteopenia, spondylolisthesis, lumbar deformity, and lateral recess stenosis. These contraindications limit the use of disk replacement to a small percentage of the patients with chronic low back pain who are candidates for lumbar fusion.

As the technologies evolve and are further studied, it may become clear whether surgery or continued nonsurgical treatment provides a superior long-term outcome in the treatment of chronic low back pain.

Summary

Axial neck and back pain are common and generally self-limiting conditions that are multifactorial in etiology. The economic burden of these conditions is enormous and expected to rise as the US population ages. The evaluation of axial pain begins with a focused history and physical examination. Imaging studies are obtained only if the symptoms do not improve with nonintensive therapies. Imaging generally should be used for confirmation of a diagnosis because the general degenerative processes of aging may lead to a high rate of false-positive results.

The treatment should focus on relief of symptoms and a rapid return to work and normal activities. Brief periods of rest and analgesics can improve acute symptoms, but chronic pain is best treated with an exercise program, lifestyle modifications, work rehabilitation and hardening, behavior modification therapy, and alternative therapies such as acupuncture, yoga, and, for some patients, spine manipulation. Surgery has had mixed outcomes and is reserved for chronic severe pain that has not improved with the use of any other modality. The surgical outcome is most predictable if the patient has been carefully selected.

Annotated References

1. National Center for Health Statistics: *Health, United States, 2008*. Hyattsville, MD, US Department of Health and Human Services, 2009, pp 278-279. http://www.cdc.gov/nchs/data/hus/hus08.pdf. Accessed March 8, 2011.

2. Haralson RH III, Zuckerman JD: Prevalence, health care expenditures, and orthopedic surgery workforce for musculoskeletal conditions. *JAMA* 2009;302(14): 1586-1587.

    This commentary discusses future health care needs and demands, particularly as they concern the practice of orthopaedics.

3. Deyo RA: Low-back pain. *Sci Am* 1998;279(2):48-53.

4. Bratton RL: Assessment and management of acute low back pain. *Am Fam Physician* 1999;60(8):2299-2308.

5. Lively MW: Sports medicine approach to low back pain. *South Med J* 2002;95(6):642-646.

6. Hart LG, Deyo RA, Cherkin DC: Physician office visits for low back pain: Frequency, clinical evaluation, and treatment patterns from a U.S. national survey. *Spine (Phila Pa 1976)* 1995;20(1):11-19.

7. Wolsko PM, Eisenberg DM, Davis RB, Kessler R, Phillips RS: Patterns and perceptions of care for treatment of back and neck pain: Results of a national survey. *Spine (Phila Pa 1976)* 2003;28(3):292-298.

8. Praemer A, Furner S, Rice DP: *Musculoskeletal Conditions in the United States*. Park Ridge, IL, American Academy of Orthopaedic Surgeons, 1992.

9. Taylor VM, Deyo RA, Cherkin DC, Kreuter W: Low back pain hospitalization: Recent United States trends and regional variations. *Spine (Phila Pa 1976)* 1994; 19(11):1207-1213.

10. Côté P, Cassidy JD, Carroll L: The Saskatchewan Health and Back Pain Survey: The prevalence of neck pain and related disability in Saskatchewan adults. *Spine (Phila Pa 1976)* 1998;23(15):1689-1698.

11. Devereaux M: Low back pain. *Med Clin North Am* 2009;93(2):477-501, x.

    Salient points related to low back pain include its prevalence, clinical presentation, differential diagnosis, and treatment options. Nonsurgical and surgical treatments are described as supported by medical literature.

12. Health and Safety Executive: Estimated days (full-day equivalent) off work and associated average days lost per (full-time equivalent) worker and per case due to a self-reported work-related illness or workplace injury. http://www.hse.gov.uk/statistics/lfs/lfs0708.pdf. Accessed March 8, 2011.

    A report of the British Labour Force Survey details lost productivity from self-reported and work-related injuries, with a comparison to past years.

13. Nachemson AL, Jonsson E, eds: *Neck and Back Pain: The Scientific Evidence of Causes, Diagnosis and Treatment*. Philadelphia, PA, Lippincott Williams & Wilkins, 2000.

14. Ahn NU, Ahn UM, Ipsen B, An HS: Mechanical neck pain and cervicogenic headache. *Neurosurgery* 2007; 60(1, suppl 1):S21-S27.

    The presentation, differential diagnosis, and workup of patients with mechanical neck pain are reviewed.

15. DePalma AF, Rothman RH, Lewinnek GE, Canale ST: Anterior interbody fusion for severe cervical disc degeneration. *Surg Gynecol Obstet* 1972;134(5):755-758.

16. Rothman RH, Rashbaum RF: Pathogenesis of signs and symptoms of cervical degenerative disc degeneration. *Instr Course Lect* 1978;27:203-215.

17. Jensen I, Harms-Ringdahl K: Strategies for prevention and management of musculoskeletal conditions: Neck pain. *Best Pract Res Clin Rheumatol* 2007;21(1):93-108.

    Interventions for nonspecific neck pain are summarized. Based on the evidence, different forms of exercise and other nonsurgical treatment are recommended for patients with acute or chronic nonspecific neck pain. The risk factors for axial neck pain are described.

18. Larsson B, Søgaard K, Rosendal L: Work related neck-shoulder pain: A review on magnitude, risk factors, biochemical characteristics, clinical picture and preventive interventions. *Best Pract Res Clin Rheumatol* 2007; 21(3):447-463.

19. Wieser ES, Wang JC: Surgery for neck pain. *Neurosurgery* 2007;60(1, suppl 1):S51-S56.

    The clinical approach to treating patients with axial neck pain without radiculopathy and myelopathy is described, with a discussion of controversy related to diagnostic evaluation and diskography. Surgical management strategies and patient selection are addressed.

20. Boden SD, McCowin PR, Davis DO, Dina TS, Mark AS, Wiesel S: Abnormal magnetic-resonance scans of the cervical spine in asymptomatic subjects: A prospective investigation. *J Bone Joint Surg Am* 1990;72(8):1178-1184.

21. Carragee EJ, Hannibal M: Diagnostic evaluation of low back pain. *Orthop Clin North Am* 2004;35(1):7-16.

22. Nassr A, Lee JY, Bashir RS, et al: Does incorrect level needle localization during anterior cervical discectomy and fusion lead to accelerated disc degeneration? *Spine (Phila Pa 1976)* 2009;34(2):189-192.

Incorrect needle localization of levels during surgery was found to lead to progressive disk degeneration in a retrospective study. The odds ratio was increased to 3.2 for patients with progressive disk degeneration at an adjacent segment after incorrect level identification. Level of evidence: III.

23. Gremeaux V, Casillas JM, Fabbro-Peray P, Pelissier J, Herisson C, Perennou D: Analysis of low back pain in adults with scoliosis. *Spine (Phila Pa 1976)* 2008;33(4):402-405.

A prospective study compared patients with chronic low back pain with or without scoliosis. Patients had similar duration and intensity of pain. In patients with scoliosis, pain severity was correlated with Cobb angle and rotatory listhesis.

24. Jensen MC, Brant-Zawadzki MN, Obuchowski N, Modic MT, Malkasian D, Ross JS: Magnetic resonance imaging of the lumbar spine in people without back pain. *N Engl J Med* 1994;331(2):69-73.

25. Beattie PF, Meyers SP, Stratford P, Millard RW, Hollenberg GM: Associations between patient report of symptoms and anatomic impairment visible on lumbar magnetic resonance imaging. *Spine (Phila Pa 1976)* 2000;25(7):819-828.

26. Carragee EJ, Don AS, Hurwitz EL, Cuellar JM, Carrino JA, Herzog R: Does discography cause accelerated progression of degeneration changes in the lumbar disc: A ten-year matched cohort study. *Spine (Phila Pa 1976)* 2009;34(21):2338-2345.

A prospective study compared the 10-year progression of disk degeneration based on whether patients had undergone diskography. Patients who had diskography had greater disk degeneration, herniation, loss of height, and reactive end plate changes than control subjects.

27. Saifuddin A, Renton P, Taylor BA: Effects on the vertebral end-plate of uncomplicated lumbar discography: An MRI study. *Eur Spine J* 1998;7(1):36-39.

28. Ohtori S, Kinoshita T, Yamashita M, et al: Results of surgery for discogenic low back pain: A randomized study using discography versus discoblock for diagnosis. *Spine (Phila Pa 1976)* 2009;34(13):1345-1348.

A randomized controlled study assigned patients with discogenic low back pain with disk degeneration at L4-5 or L5-S1 to standard diskography or bupivacaine block. Outcomes were assessed after interbody fusion. During the first 3 years after surgery, outcome improvements were significantly greater in patients who received bupivacaine than in those who received diskography.

29. Wai EK, Rodriguez S, Dagenais S, Hall H: Evidence-informed management of chronic low back pain with physical activity, smoking cessation, and weight loss. *Spine J* 2008;8(1):195-202.

An evidence-based review of the literature on nonsurgical interventions for nonspecific chronic low back pain focused on physical activity, smoking cessation, and weight loss. There is moderate evidence that physical activity is beneficial, compared with a sedentary lifestyle. Pain and disability decreased with physical activity. No evidence of efficacy was found for smoking cessation or nonsurgical weight loss.

30. Malanga G, Wolff E: Evidence-informed management of chronic low back pain with nonsteroidal anti-inflammatory drugs, muscle relaxants, and simple analgesics. *Spine J* 2008;8(1):173-184.

An evidence-based literature review of nonsurgical interventions for nonspecific chronic low back pain focused on analgesics, NSAIDs, and muscle relaxants. The use of simple analgesics (such as tramadol), antidepressants, or both was recommended. NSAIDs and muscle relaxants were effective but have adverse effect profiles that need to be better understood. Cannabinoids have potentially useful properties for treating chronic low back pain.

31. Schofferman J, Mazanec D: Evidence-informed management of chronic low back pain with opioid analgesics. *Spine J* 2008;8(1):185-194.

The literature regarding use of opioids for chronic low back pain was assessed. Opioids are safe and effective for short-term use but less effective for long-term treatment, with no evidence of functional improvements. Adverse effects are common, and high withdrawal rates are reported.

32. Chou R, Huffman LH, American Pain Society, American College of Physicians: Nonpharmacologic therapies for acute and chronic low back pain: A review of the evidence for an American Pain Society/American College of Physicians clinical practice guideline. *Ann Intern Med* 2007;147(7):492-504.

The literature on medications prescribed for low back pain was reviewed, with a comparison of the effectiveness of different pharmaceutical agents. There is good evidence of pain relief with the use of NSAIDs, acetaminophen, muscle relaxants (short-term use), and tricyclic antidepressants (for chronic back pain); and fair evidence with opioids, tramadol, and benzodiazepines. Most studies were of limited length, and no comparisons of combination medications were available.

33. DePalma MJ, Slipman CW: Evidence-informed management of chronic low back pain with epidural steroid injections. *Spine J* 2008;8(1):45-55.

The literature on the treatment of chronic low back pain with epidural steroids is systematically reviewed.

34. Kelly RB: Acupuncture for pain. *Am Fam Physician* 2009;80(5):481-484.

The published evidence suggests that acupuncture is most likely to benefit patients with nonspecific low back pain or neck pain, chronic idiopathic or tension headache, migraine, or knee osteoarthritis. The limitations of the review and the analysis of acupuncture are identified.

35. Roelofs PD, Deyo RA, Koes BW, Scholten RJ, van Tulder MW: Nonsteroidal anti-inflammatory drugs for low back pain: An updated Cochrane review. *Spine (Phila Pa 1976)* 2008;33(16):1766-1774.

A review of 65 randomized controlled studies found evidence that NSAIDs provide minor short-term pain relief in patients with low back pain without sciatica.

36. Chiu TT, Hui-Chan CW, Chein G: A randomized clinical trial of TENS and exercise for patients with chronic neck pain. *Clin Rehabil* 2005;19(8):850-860.

Patients with chronic axial neck pain were randomly assigned to treatment twice a week for 6 weeks with transcutaneous electrical nerve stimulation plus irradiation, exercise training plus irradiation, or irradiation alone. At 6-month follow-up, patients in the transcutaneous electrical nerve stimulation and exercise groups had better outcome scores related to disability, muscle strength, and pain compared with those in the irradiation-alone group.

37. Graham N, Gross AR, Goldsmith C; Cervical Overview Group: Mechanical traction for mechanical neck disorders: A systematic review. *J Rehabil Med* 2006;38(3):145-152.

A systematic review of the literature on mechanical traction for neck disorders found 10 studies, one of which was considered good quality. Limited data suggest that intermittent traction is beneficial in reducing pain and improving function. Continuous traction probably is not beneficial.

38. Rubinstein SM, Knol DL, Leboeuf-Yde C, van Tulder MW: Benign adverse events following chiropractic care for neck pain are associated with worse short-term outcomes but not worse outcomes at three months. *Spine (Phila Pa 1976)* 2008;33(25):E950-E956.

A prospective cohort study of patients undergoing supervised chiropractic treatment for neck pain in the Netherlands was based on a self-reported survey of benign adverse events, neck pain, and disability after chiropractic treatment. At 3-month follow up, there was no difference in outcome based on whether patients had a benign adverse event.

39. Tinel D, Bliznakova E, Juhel C, Gallien P, Brissot R: Vertebrobasilar ischemia after cervical spine manipulation: A case report. *Ann Readapt Med Phys* 2008;51(5):403-414.

Vertebrobasilar ischemia occurred after chiropractic manipulation of the cervical spine. Eight months later, the patient still had persistent paralysis of the right upper extremity and cranial nerves and a cerebellar syndrome. Risk factors, clinical presentation, and treatment are discussed.

40. Leon-Sanchez A, Cuetter A, Ferrer G: Cervical spine manipulation: An alternative medical procedure with potentially fatal complications. *South Med J* 2007;100(2):201-203.

This case report describes an incident of fatal cerebrovascular accident after cervical spine manipulation therapy. Risk factors, clinical presentation, and treatments of infrequent but serious complications after cervical spine manipulation are discussed.

41. Schonstein E, Kenny DT, Keating J, Koes BW: Work conditioning, work hardening and functional restoration for workers with back and neck pain. *Cochrane Database Syst Rev* 2003;1:CD001822.

A review of 18 randomized controlled studies found that physical conditioning programs appear to be effective for some patients with chronic back pain.

42. Devereaux M: Neck pain. *Med Clin North Am* 2009;93(2):273-284.

Salient points related to neck pain include its prevalence, clinical presentation, differential diagnosis, and treatment options. Nonsurgical and surgical treatments are described as supported by medical literature.

43. Carragee EJ, Hurwitz EL, Cheng I, et al: Treatment of neck pain: Injections and surgical interventions. Results of the Bone and Joint Decade 2000-2010 Task Force on Neck Pain and Its Associated Disorders. *Spine (Phila Pa 1976)* 2008;33(4, suppl):S153-S169.

A best evidence synthesis of the literature from 1980 to 2006 evaluated injections and surgical interventions in the treatment of neck pain with or without radiculopathy. More than 1,200 studies were reviewed. Treatment with certain injections and surgery is supported for patients with neck pain and radicular symptoms. There is a paucity of evidence for these procedures in patients with axial neck pain without radicular symptoms.

44. Fritzell P, Hägg O, Wessberg P, Nordwall A; Swedish Lumbar Spine Study Group: Lumbar fusion versus nonsurgical treatment for chronic low back pain: A multicenter randomized controlled trial from the Swedish Lumbar Spine Study Group. *Spine (Phila Pa 1976)* 2001;26(23):2521-2534.

45. Garvey TA, Transfeldt EE, Malcolm JR, Kos P: Outcome of anterior cervical discectomy and fusion as perceived by patients treated for dominant axial-mechanical cervical spine pain. *Spine (Phila Pa 1976)* 2002;27(17):1887-1895.

46. Jaramillo-de la Torre JJ, Grauer JN, Yue JJ: Update on cervical disc arthroplasty: Where are we and where are we going? *Curr Rev Musculoskelet Med* 2008;1(2):124-130.

Motion preservation surgery in the cervical spine is discussed, including indications, surgical technique, and

2-year outcome data. Long-term issues include wear, heterotopic ossification-fusion, and deformity. Future directions include improvements in biomaterials and technique.

47. Brox JI, Reikerås O, Nygaard Ø, et al: Lumbar instrumented fusion compared with cognitive intervention and exercises in patients with chronic back pain after previous surgery for disc herniation: A prospective randomized controlled study. *Pain* 2006;122(1-2):145-155.

In a single-blinded randomized study, patients with evidence of disk degeneration at L4-5 or L5-S1 and chronic low back pain of more than 1 year's duration were assigned to posterior spinal fusion followed by physical therapy or to cognitive intervention and exercises. At 1-year follow-up, no statistically significant differences existed between the two patient groups with respect to Oswestry Disability Index scores, pain, use of analgesics, life satisfaction, or return to work. The patients who underwent surgery had less lower limb pain, and those who had cognitive intervention had fewer fear-avoidance beliefs. The success rate was 70% after surgery and 76% after cognitive intervention. The surgical complication rate was 18%.

48. Brox JI, Sørensen R, Friis A, et al: Randomized clinical trial of lumbar instrumented fusion and cognitive intervention and exercises in patients with chronic low back pain and disc degeneration. *Spine (Phila Pa 1976)* 2003; 28(17):1913-1921.

49. Fairbank J, Frost H, Wilson-MacDonald J, et al: Randomised controlled trial to compare surgical stabilisation of the lumbar spine with an intensive rehabilitation programme for patients with chronic low back pain: The MRC spine stabilisation trial. *BMJ* 2005; 330(7502):1233.

In a randomized controlled study, patients with generalized chronic low back pain of more than 1 year's duration were assigned to receive posterior spinal fusion or intense physical therapy. At 2-year follow-up, there was very little difference in outcomes.

50. Fritzell P, Hägg O, Jonsson D, Nordwall A; Swedish Lumbar Spine Study Group: Cost-effectiveness of lumbar fusion and nonsurgical treatment for chronic low back pain in the Swedish Lumbar Spine Study: A multicenter, randomized, controlled trial from the Swedish Lumbar Spine Study Group. *Spine (Phila Pa 1976)* 2004;29(4):421-434 [discussion, Z3].

51. Don AS, Carragee E: A brief overview of evidence-informed management of chronic low back pain with surgery. *Spine J* 2008;8(1):258-265.

An evidence-based review of the literature on the effectiveness of surgical and nonsurgical interventions for nonspecific chronic low back pain found insufficient evidence on the effectiveness of fusion, dynamic fusion, and disk arthroplasty for chronic low back pain without structural disease or a clearly identifiable pain generator.

52. Peng CW, Yue WM, Poh SY, Yeo W, Tan SB: Clinical and radiological outcomes of minimally invasive versus open transforaminal lumbar interbody fusion. *Spine (Phila Pa 1976)* 2009;34(13):1385-1389.

A prospective study compared the clinical and radiologic outcomes of minimally invasive and open transforaminal lumbar interbody fusion. The outcomes were similar, but patients who underwent minimally invasive surgery had fewer complications and several other benefits.

53. Fritzell P, Berg S, Borgström F, Tullberg T, Tropp H: Cost effectiveness of disc prosthesis versus lumbar fusion in patients with chronic low back pain: Randomized controlled trial with 2-year follow-up. *Eur Spine J* 2011;20(7):1001-1011.

A randomized controlled study compared the effectiveness of lumbar fusion and lumbar disk replacement from the health care and economic standpoints. Two-year follow-up of 152 patients revealed essentially no between-group differences. Patients who had disk replacement returned to work more quickly, but there was no overall cost savings.

Chapter 26

The Evaluation and Treatment of Cervical Radiculopathy and Myelopathy

Garrick W. Cason, MD   Edward Radcliffe Anderson III, MD   Harry N. Herkowitz, MD

Introduction

Patients with cervical degenerative disease must be systematically evaluated for axial neck pain, radiculopathy, myelopathy, or myeloradiculopathy. Axial neck pain may be mechanical; it is exacerbated by motion and alleviated by rest and avoidance of inciting maneuvers. Cervical radiculopathy commonly appears as dermatomal upper extremity sensory or motor changes, but it can appear as a cervicogenic headache. Pure cervical myelopathy involves gait disturbance and long tract signs (pathologic reflexes, hyperreflexia, and spasticity from spinal cord compression). Myeloradiculopathy (upper extremity, lower motor neuron deficits combined with lower extremity, upper motor neuron deficits) is more common clinically than cervical myelopathy alone.

Cervical Radiculopathy

Epidemiology and Natural History

As many as 66% of all adults experience neck pain at some time.[1] Neck pain is the most prevalent symptom

Dr. Anderson or an immediate family member has received research or institutional support from DePuy, a Johnson & Johnson company. Dr. Herkowitz or an immediate family member serves as a board member, owner, officer, or committee member of the American Board of Orthopaedic Surgery, the American Orthopaedic Association, the Cervical Spine Research Society, the North American Spine Society, the Orthopaedic Research and Education Foundation, the Orthopaedic Research Society, and the International Society for the Study of the Lumbar Spine; has received royalties from Medtronic and Stryker; serves as a paid consultant to or is an employee of Magnifi IEP; has received research or institutional support from Stryker, DePuy, and Medtronic; and owns stock or stock options in Globus Medical. Neither Dr. Cason nor any immediate family member has received anything of value from or owns stock in a commercial company or institution related directly or indirectly to the subject of this chapter.

in patients with cervical spondylosis. The age-adjusted annual incidence of cervical radiculopathy is 83 per 100,000 individuals between age 13 and 91 years.[2] Several studies suggest that symptoms resolve in as many as 45% of patients when they are treated with a soft collar, rest, physical therapy, traction, manipulation, or a combination of these modalities.[3,4] The prognosis is less favorable if a patient with neck pain does not have cervical radiculopathy. Two thirds of patients with neck pain and radicular symptoms may benefit from surgical decompression.[4]

Clinical Findings

Patients with cervical radiculopathy often describe sharp pain, tingling, or burning of the upper extremities in a dermatomal distribution. They also may report motor weakness. The patient may keep the head tilted to the side opposite the painful arm or may rest the affected arm over the head, as these maneuvers relieve tension on the irritated cervical nerve roots. A thorough physical examination of the cervical spine should be performed, including an inspection of posture, nuchal tenderness, range of motion, sensory and motor function, and normal and pathologic reflexes. Peripheral pulses should be evaluated, and shoulder and elbow pathology should be ruled out as the cause of the upper extremity symptoms. The Spurling and shoulder abduction tests are useful for confirming the presence of cervical rather than shoulder pathology. The Adson, Wright, and Roos tests can be used to assess for thoracic outlet syndrome. In patients with peripheral neuropathy or distal compressive neuropathy, the double-crush phenomenon lowers the threshold for symptomatic compression.

Radiographic Evaluation

Standard AP, flexion-extension lateral, and oblique radiographs are used to evaluate overall alignment, disk space narrowing, facet arthrosis, osteophytes of the uncovertebral joints, and translational or angular instability. On a lateral radiograph, the possibility of

4: The Adult Spine

Table 1			
MRI Findings as Related to Patient Age in Asymptomatic Patients			
MRI Finding*	All Patients (N = 63)	Patients Younger Than 40 Years (n = 40)	Patients Older Than 40 Years (n = 23)
Herniated disk	8%	10%	5%
Bulging disk	2%	0%	3%
Foraminal stenosis	9%	4%	20%
Total	**19%**	**14%**	**28%**

*The abnormality was graded as major for at least one disk level.

Adapted with permission from Boden SD, McCowin PR, Davis DO, Dina TS, Mark AS, Weisel S: Abnormal magnetic-resonance scans of the cervical spine in asymptomatic subjects: A prospective investigation. *J Bone Joint Surg Am* 1990;72(8):1178-1184.

congenital stenosis is evaluated using the Pavlov or Torg ratio (the distance from the midposterior vertebral body to the nearest point on the spinal laminar line, divided by the width of the corresponding vertebral body); a ratio lower than 0.8 may indicate congenital stenosis. On CT or MRI, a sagittal central canal diameter of less than 10 mm indicates a congenitally reduced space available for the spinal cord. MRI provides excellent resolution of the cervical soft tissues, disks, and neural elements, and it is the study of choice for evaluating cervical soft disk herniations, sequestered disk fragments, and acquired stenosis. Spinal cord compression, intrinsic cord changes of myelomalacia, posttraumatic changes, and syrinx can also be seen on MRI. As many as 19% of asymptomatic patients have major cervical abnormalities on MRI, and the pathology seen on imaging studies must be carefully correlated with the patient's symptoms and physical examination findings[5] (Table 1).

CT myelography can show both bony detail and neural compression in patients with a contraindication to MRI (such as the presence of a pacemaker). If the etiology is difficult to discern, electrodiagnostic studies can be used to differentiate between neuropathy and cervical or peripheral compression. With nerve root compression, the electromyelographic changes are a decrease in motor unit potentials and the presence of fibrillation potentials.

Treatment

There is no clear evidence to support or refute the use of cervical traction for neck pain with or without radiculopathy.[6] The efficacy of nonsteroidal anti-inflammatory drugs has been proved for treating acute low back pain but not cervical spine pain.[7] Physical therapy using range of motion exercises and modalities such as electrical stimulation, ultrasonography, and heat may provide short-term relief but cannot alter the natural history of the disease or provide long-term relief.[8,9] Anecdotal evidence suggests that cervical epidural steroid injections and selective nerve root blocks

may provide temporary relief, but any improvement over the course of the natural history has not been proved.[10]

The surgical indications for cervical radiculopathy include persistent or recurrent arm pain refractory to at least 3 months of nonsurgical treatment with physical therapy, nonsteroidal anti-inflammatory drugs, and epidural steroid injections; progressive neurologic deficits; static neurologic deficits with significant arm pain; and imaging studies correlated with the physical examination findings.

Anterior Cervical Diskectomy and Corpectomy

Surgery for cervical radiculopathy most frequently is performed using the Smith-Robinson anterior technique. An anterior approach is specifically recommended for central or broad disk herniation, spondylotic disease, loss of lordosis, and disease involving three or fewer levels. The anterior approach allows pathologic disk removal and both direct and indirect foraminal decompression by means of osteophyte resection and increased disk space height. In disease involving more than three levels, anterior cervical diskectomy and fusion (ACDF) using autograft or allograft and plating has led to fusion rates of 97% to 100%, with 90% of patients (including those who were smokers) having a good or excellent result[11-14] (Figure 1).

Anterior cervical corpectomy allows simultaneous decompression at two disk levels and facilitates safe removal of any large adjacent osteophytes compressing the neural structures. If the compressive pathology is directly posterior to the vertebral body, a corpectomy may be necessary to decompress the spinal cord and nerve roots. Corpectomy is more commonly necessary in patients with myelopathy or myeloradiculopathy, however. Autologous iliac crest and fibular struts traditionally have been used to provide mechanical support in the trough that is created. Equivalent fusion rates and clinical outcomes were reported after allograft bone or titanium cages and plates were used.[15,16]

The use of plating increased the fusion rate in multilevel ACDF and decreased the graft-related complica-

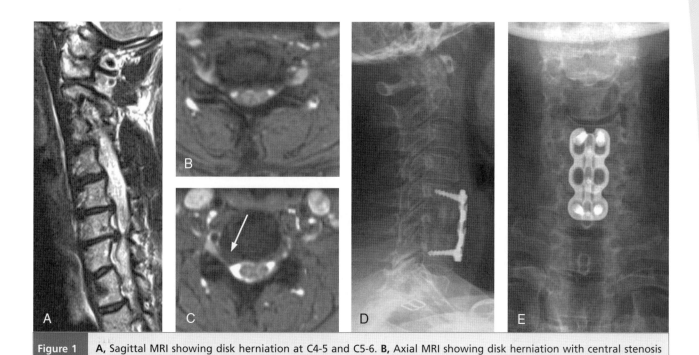

Figure 1 **A,** Sagittal MRI showing disk herniation at C4-5 and C5-6. **B,** Axial MRI showing disk herniation with central stenosis at C4-C5. **C,** Axial MRI showing right foraminal stenosis caused by disk herniation *(arrow)* at C5-6. Postoperative lateral **(D)** and AP **(E)** radiographs showing C5-C7 ACDF with fibular allograft and an anterior plate.

tion rate. In particular, graft dislodgement was prevented in multilevel anterior cervical corpectomy and fusion (ACCF). Adjacent-level disease has been reported to occur at a rate of 2.9% per year, with the risk inversely related to the number of levels treated.[17]

Complications are rare after a single-level ACDF. When autograft is used, donor site complications are most common. Nine percent to 27% of patients have a transient sore throat and dysphagia, which usually resolves within 12 weeks. A perforating injury to the esophagus is rare (affecting 0.3% of patients), but it can be life threatening. An esophageal perforation noted intraoperatively should be repaired acutely; a nasogastric tube should be placed, and parenteral nutrition should be administered. The risk of esophageal perforation can be minimized by avoiding excessive retraction and using blunt retractors. The most common neurologic complication is recurrent laryngeal nerve palsy (affecting 3% of patients).[18]

The rates of pseudarthrosis after single-level ACDF range from 0% to 5%, and the rate approaches 17% after multilevel fusion. An anterior or posterior approach can be used for repair or augmentation of pseudarthrosis, with 87% to 100% success. The application of anterior plates for ACDF and ACCF has led to improved fusion rates of 90% to 100% and has reduced the need for postoperative rigid immobilization.[11-14]

Posterior Laminoforaminotomy

Posterior cervical laminoforaminotomy is indicated if the anterior approach is contraindicated or the patient has predominantly radicular symptoms from posterolateral soft disk herniation, spondylosis, cervical foram-

inal stenosis, facet arthropathy with foraminal compression, or persistent radiculopathy after ACDF. Laminoforaminotomy is contraindicated in a patient with central canal stenosis, central disk herniation, cervical myelopathy, instability, ossification of the posterior longitudinal ligament (OPLL), or kyphotic deformity. Laminoforaminotomy avoids fusion of the motion segment and obviates the risk of injury to the soft tissues and neurovascular structures, as encountered during the anterior approach.

The neural foramen is narrowest in its entrance zone, where the nerve root often is compressed anteriorly by the disk and osteophytes of the uncovertebral joint and posteriorly by the superior articular process, ligamentum flavum, and periarticular fibrous tissue. Decompression using laminoforaminotomy requires resection of 25% to 50% of the facet joint to expose 2.7 to 5.9 mm of the nerve root.[19] An attempt to resect anterior uncovertebral osteophytes often leads to iatrogenic nerve injury; as a result, some authors recommend using laminoforaminotomy alone for these patients.[20,21] Far lateral disks, which may be missed from the anterior approach, are clearly accessible from this posterior approach. Unilateral complete facetectomy or a bilateral resection of more than 50% leads to instability.[19]

Cervical laminoforaminotomy provides relief of 93% to 97% of significant radicular arm pain and a 93% to 98% recovery of motor function.[20,21] The best results follow the treatment of soft disk herniations or a combination of hard and soft disk herniations. After microendoscopic foraminotomy, 97% of patients had a good or excellent result, and more than 90% had im-

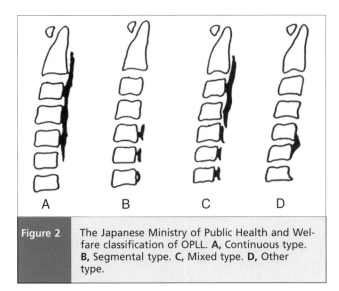

Figure 2 The Japanese Ministry of Public Health and Welfare classification of OPLL. **A,** Continuous type. **B,** Segmental type. **C,** Mixed type. **D,** Other type.

provement in their symptoms.[22] In comparison with traditional open techniques, microendoscopic foraminotomy requires less surgical time, less blood loss, a shorter hospital stay, and less narcotic use.[22,23] The most common complications are pain and spasm from paraspinal muscle dissection and increased epidural bleeding. Air embolism and dural tears occur less frequently, but they can be more clinically significant.

Cervical Spondylotic Myelopathy

Cervical spondylotic myelopathy (CSM) is the development of long tract signs secondary to degenerative changes in the cervical spinal column. CSM is the most common cause of myelopathy in patients older than 50 years. In general, insidious symptom onset precedes a stepwise progression and functional decline. A careful patient history and physical examination allow early diagnosis and treatment, can prevent neurologic deterioration, and can lead to an optimal clinical outcome.

A congenitally narrow cervical canal creates a predisposition to myelopathy after early spondylotic changes or an acute disk herniation. Compressive pathology may arise from the anterior or posterior canal and span one or more levels. Degenerative changes are most common at C5-C6 and C6-C7. It is likely that the greater motion at these segments parallels their propensity to degeneration. Disk protrusions, olisthesis, osteophytes, hypertrophy of the facets, and infolding of the ligamentum flavum contribute to spinal canal narrowing. The resulting spinal cord compression leads to myelopathy.

The posterior longitudinal ligament ossifies when heterotopic lamellar bone is formed from enchondral and intramembranous ossification. The highest prevalence of OPLL was found in Japan (1.9% to 4.3% of individuals older than 30 years).[24] In the United States and Germany, the prevalence ranges from 0.1% to 0.7%.[24] OPLL has been associated with ankylosing

spondylitis and diffuse idiopathic skeletal hyperostosis. Diabetes mellitus is an independent risk factor; there is a positive association between an abnormal insulin secretory response and the severity of the patient's OPLL. OPLL may be associated with ossification of the ligamentum flavum.[24] OPLL is morphologically classified into four types: continuous, segmental, mixed, or other (Figure 2). Myelopathy was found to develop in 100% of patients with stenosis of more than 60% or space available for the cord of less than 6 mm.[25] Patients with hypermobility of the cervical spine between C2 and C7 and 6 mm to 14 mm of space available for the cord also were relatively likely to develop myelopathy. Increased cervical range of motion, the segmental type, age older than 50 years, and a high T2-weighted cord signal intensity on MRI are other risk factors for the development of myelopathy in patients with OPLL.[25-27]

Epidemiology and Natural History

The studies evaluating the natural history of CSM are inconsistent with regard to clinical evaluation.[28] The natural history of cervical myelopathy most frequently involves a stepwise deterioration in neurologic function, with stable plateau periods. The natural history has been described as mixed, with many patients experiencing a slow, stepwise decline; others experiencing a slow, steady, progressive decline; and some improving over time.[28] The most common interventions were activity modification and immobilization. In patients younger than 75 years with mild myelopathy (a score higher than 12 on the modified Japanese Orthopaedic Association [JOA] scale) nonsurgical management may lead to a stable 36-month clinical course before further deterioration. Symptom duration of more than 18 months, greater than normal cervical spine range of motion, and female sex portend a poor prognosis.[28]

Clinical Findings

Patients with myelopathy usually have upper extremity symptoms including hand clumsiness, difficulty in performing fine motor tasks, and diffuse numbness (exemplified, respectively, by a tendency to drop objects, difficulty in buttoning a shirt, and inability to differentiate coins by palpation). Patients may have lower extremity symptoms that appear to require a lumbar spine evaluation. These patients typically have a wide-based gait with spasticity, ataxia, or weakness. They may report electric shocklike sensations that travel down the spine or extremities when the neck is in certain provocative positions (the Lhermitte sign). Neck pain and radicular symptoms may accompany the lower extremity symptoms. Subjective weakness and bowel or bladder dysfunction, typically, are late findings and indicators of a poor prognosis.

A thorough neurologic examination should be performed. The gait should be assessed for spasticity and ataxia. Hyperreflexia of the extremities is typically present but may be masked by peripheral nerve disease or concomitant nerve root compression. The Lhermitte sign is positive when neck flexion causes electric shock-like sensations down the spine and/or the upper and lower extremities. The Hoffman sign is positive if flexion of the thumb and index finger results when the examiner extends the distal phalanx of the long finger and suddenly releases it. The crossed radial reflex is positive if both biceps and wrist extension responses are elicited when the biceps reflex is tested. The inverted radial reflex is positive if both wrist extension and finger flexion are elicited by tapping the brachioradialis. The finger escape sign is positive if the patient is unable to hold the ulnar digits in extension and adduction. In the lower extremities, a Babinski sign and sustained clonus may indicate cord compression. The severity of myelopathy was found to be correlated with the result of the 10-second grip-and-release test and the time required to walk 10 steps.[29]

Radiographic Evaluation

AP and flexion-extension lateral radiographs are used to evaluate overall alignment, disk space narrowing, facet arthrosis, osteophytes of the uncovertebral joints, and translational and angular instability. Congenital stenosis is evaluated using the Pavlov or Torg ratio (as for cervical radiculopathy), with a ratio below 0.8 suggesting congenital stenosis. On CT or MRI, a central canal sagittal diameter of less than 10 mm indicates a congenitally reduced space available for the cord. In the absence of extrinsic compressive pathology, dynamic radiographs may show degenerative instability responsible for spinal cord trauma.

MRI and CT myelography can reveal the source of cord compression and evaluate the ratio of the smallest sagittal cord diameter to the largest transverse diameter at one level. A ratio below 0.4 is an indicator of a poor prognosis, but spinal cord expansion to a postoperative ratio above 0.4 is correlated with a better prognosis.[30] Patients with low-intensity signal changes in the spinal cord on T1-weighted MRI (representing myelomalacia and necrosis) and multisegment high-intensity signal changes on T2-weighted images (representing edema and gliosis) have a significantly poorer functional recovery rate than patients with focal changes on T2-weighted images and no changes on T1-weighted images.[31]

CT is required before surgery for OPLL to identify the morphologic type, which has prognostic implications; and to reveal details such as the double-layer sign, which is highly suggestive of dural penetration by the OPLL.

Treatment

Nonsurgical management with activity modification, a soft collar, and anti-inflammatory nonsteroidal drugs may be useful in patients with mild myelopathy, such as those with only hyperreflexia and no functional impairment; and in patients whose medical comorbidities preclude surgery. Patients with mild myelopathy who are younger than 75 years may remain clinically stable for as long as 36 months, but many such patients have pro-gressive neurologic decline and ensuing functional impairment.[28] The goals of surgical intervention are to increase the space available for the cord and stabilize the spinal column, thereby halting the progression of neurologic dysfunction. Patients with severe or rapidly progressive neurologic deterioration or severe spinal cord compression may be offered urgent surgery. The choice of surgical approach is based on the location of compression, the number of involved cervical levels, the severity of instability, the sagittal alignment, and the surgeon's experience.

The commonly used procedures from the anterior approach include single- and multiple-level ACDF and ACCF. Large anterior osteophytes can cause substantial cord compression, and anterior approaches are well suited to address this pathology. Patients with loss of cervical lordosis or frank kyphosis should be treated using an anterior approach, which provides better sagittal alignment correction and maintenance of the correction.[16,32,33] Osteophytes, disk herniations, and OPLL extending above or below the disk space may be more completely decompressed by a corpectomy and fusion. The defect is reconstructed using autograft, allograft, or cages, at the surgeon's discretion. Although autograft may be considered the gold standard, allograft combined with anterior plate fixation offers equivalent results, eliminates the need for postoperative collar immobilization, and reduces donor site morbidity.[11-14] In multilevel ACCF, anterior plating decreases the risk of graft dislodgement or pseudarthrosis, especially if two additional screws are placed in the middle of the construct to reduce the cantilever bending forces.

The risk of strut graft dislodgement, fracture, or pistoning is proportional to the number of corpectomy levels. The graft most commonly dislodges at its lower end. An 11% rate of early graft dislodgement was reported in multilevel corpectomy with fibular allograft and either plate or halo immobilization. The only predictive factor for graft complications was the number of corpectomies performed.[34] The dislodgement rates were 9% and 50% after two- and three-level corpectomies, respectively, even with plate fixation and external immobilization.[35] There is an increased risk of dural tearing in patients with OPLL, especially if CT reveals a double-layer sign indicative of dural penetration by the OPLL.[36]

Anterior decompression and fusion procedures for CSM result in a significant improvement in pain and Nurick Myelopathy Scale grade. At 2- to 17-year follow-up, 81% of patients had returned to strenuous work or sports activity.[32,37] Increasing age and symptom duration of more than 1 year are associated with a relatively poor prognosis. The results of ACCF were excellent in patients who had myelopathy with kyphosis, with an average deformity correction of 32° and improvement of at least one grade on the Nurick Scale; 97% of patients still had solid fusion at 18-month follow-up.[32] The predictors of a good or excellent clinical outcome after single-level ACDF were found to be

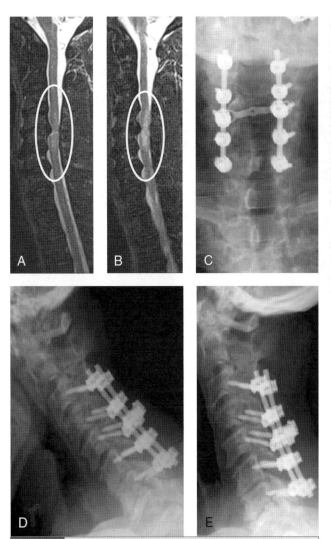

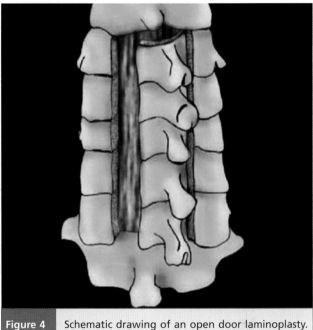

Figure 4 Schematic drawing of an open door laminoplasty.

Figure 3 Sagittal short tau inversion recovery MRI showing the most significant stenosis at C4-C5 (A) and multilevel cervical stenosis with myelomalacia behind C5 (B). The area of myelomalacia is circled. Postoperative AP (C), flexion lateral (D), and extension lateral (E) radiographs of a C3-C7 laminectomy and fusion. The loss of lordosis has resulted in a straighter cervical spine.

Posterior Cervical Laminectomy

The posterior approach is primarily indicated for patients with multilevel disease superimposed on a congenitally narrow spinal canal. Dorsal spinal cord compression from buckling of the ligamentum flavum, shingling of the laminae, or synovial cysts can be addressed by posterior decompression. Posterior decompression in a lordotic cervical spine allows posterior spinal cord migration. In a kyphotic cervical spine, posterior drift of the spinal cord is less likely, alignment is more difficult to correct, and progression of the kyphosis is more likely with posterior decompression alone.[39-41] The significant limiting factors of laminectomy include postoperative loss of lordosis, progression of kyphosis, segmental instability, and progression of OPLL. Adding an instrumented fusion with lateral mass screws to the laminectomy maintains the decompressive effect and the lordotic alignment, and it halts OPLL progression[41] (Figure 3).

Laminoplasty

Cervical laminoplasty can be used in patients with multilevel myeloradiculopathy. Laminoplasty ideally avoids postoperative instability or the need for fusion at multiple levels. Loss of lordosis occurs after laminoplasty in 10% to 50% of patients, and cervical range of motion usually continues to decrease up to 18 months postoperatively. Laminoplasty is contraindicated in patients who have less than 10° of lordosis or significant axial pain.[42]

Commonly used types of laminoplasty include the expansive open door technique, in which the arch is opened on one side and hinged on the contralateral side (Figure 4), and the French door technique, in which the lamina are opened in the midline and bilaterally

a normal preoperative sensory examination, gainful (paid) employment, and relatively severe preoperative neck disability. In contrast, the negative predictors were described as unemployment, a workers' compensation claim, and litigation.[38] At 10-year follow-up after ACCF for multilevel myelopathy, 54% of patients with CSM and 56% of those with OPLL had neurologic improvement. Adjacent-level degeneration had occurred in 23%, neurologic deterioration in 3%, and transient C5 radiculopathy in 5%.[33] At 2-year follow-up, patients with two-level ACDF had better maintenance of lordosis and segmental height than those with ACCF; the patients with two-level ACDF also had less bleeding, shorter surgical time, and greater improvement on the neck visual analog scale.[16]

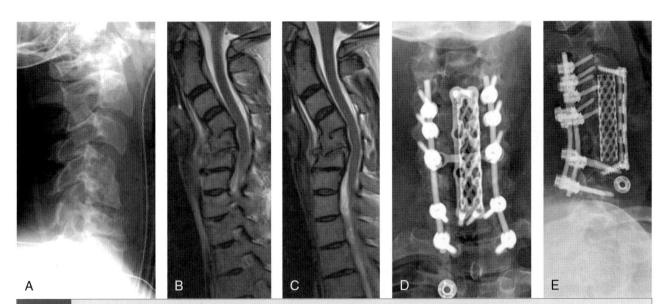

Figure 5 **A,** Preoperative lateral radiograph showing central kyphosis. **B,** Sagittal T2-weighted MRI showing cervical kyphosis with the spinal cord draped over the vertebral bodies. **C,** Sagittal T2-weighted MRI showing the central myelomalacia. AP **(D)** and lateral **(E)** postoperative radiographs showing C4-C6 corpectomy and reconstruction with a titanium mesh cage and plate and supplemental C3-T1 posterior instrumented fusion.

hinged. Laminoplasty provides a good or excellent result in 80% of patients with continuous-type OPLL or CSM affecting at least three levels. Laminoplasty has a poor result in patients with hill-shaped OPLL and a canal-occupying ratio (defined as the maximum AP OPLL thickness divided by the AP canal diameter) above 60%. Patients with plateau-shaped OPLL and a canal-occupying ratio below 60% have better results.[25,27,43] At 10- to 14-year follow-up, approximately 30% of results were found to have deteriorated more than 5 years after expansive open door laminoplasty for OPLL.[26,27] Long-term follow-up also found spontaneous fusion in 85% to 97% of patients, frank kyphosis in 10%, loss of lordosis in 40% to 50%, and OPLL progression (associated with increased mobility between C2 and C7) in 60% to 70%.[26,27] OPLL progression has not been found to affect outcome. Increasing age, a relatively low preoperative JOA score, and a longer preoperative duration of symptoms are predictors of a relatively low postoperative JOA score and a poor outcome.[25-27] The outcomes of laminoplasty in segmental-type OPLL are significantly worse than those of continuous- or mixed-type OPLL.[44] The complications of laminoplasty include transient radiculopathy in 5% to 7% of patients, usually at C5 or C6; and symptomatic kyphosis in 10%. Loss of cervical range of motion occurs within 12 to 18 months after surgery in as many as 97% of patients, although 30% to 50% of patients have late-onset neurologic deterioration (in 10 to 14 years).[42,45-47]

Combined Anterior-Posterior Procedures
Combining an anterior decompression and fusion with a posterior fusion improves the likelihood of fusion and decreases the risk of graft extrusion, especially with corpectomies at three or more levels. This approach is frequently recommended for a patient with kyphosis after earlier laminectomy. Correction of a fixed kyphotic alignment often requires extensive anterior releases (**Figure 5**). A combined anterior-posterior procedure also is beneficial in a patient who requires revision surgery; has a condition affecting bone quality, such as diabetes mellitus, osteoporosis, rheumatoid arthritis, or kidney failure requiring renal dialysis; or is a smoker.[48] Posterior fusion and instrumentation increases rigidity over an anterior plate alone. This circumferential procedure achieved fusion in almost 100% of patients, with relatively few graft dislodgements and plate failures.[49] A recent meta-analysis found that circumferential procedures were better for deformity correction and maintenance of correction than an anterior or posterior procedure alone. Complications occur in as few as 3% of patients and often are related to the anterior surgery.[49,50]

Total Disk Replacement for Cervical Radiculopathy and Myelopathy

The US Food and Drug Administration (FDA) recently approved cervical arthroplasty devices to be used in treating cervical radiculopathy and myelopathy. The perceived benefit of these devices is to preserve motion, diminish adjacent-level stress, and prevent symptomatic adjacent-level degeneration. Two- to 4-year follow-up data on several devices are available from FDA investigational device exemption studies.[51-53] The biomechanics of several devices also have been studied.[54-60] Disk replacement devices were found to maintain motion at the index level and to lead to kinematics that mimic the native intact spine more closely than fusion does.[54-61]

At 2- to 6-year follow-up, randomized controlled comparison studies of the use of cervical disk replacement (CDR) and ACDF for treating radiculopathy found that CDR led to significant improvement in the Neck Disability Index, the arm pain scale of the visual analog scale, the Medical Outcomes Study Short Form-36 Health Survey (SF-36), and overall success. These studies found that CDR had results that were statistically similar to those of ACDF with respect to symptom relief and overall neurologic and clinical success.[51-53,62-64] The patients who underwent CDR specifically for myelopathy had no worsening of myelopathy and no difference in gait or neurologic function, but their blood loss and surgical time were greater than those of comparable patients who underwent ACDF. There were fewer complications after CDR than after ACDF.[65] An analysis of adverse events in one study found more dysphagia and dysphonia in patients treated with ACDF; the patients treated with CDR and ACDF had an equal incidence of implant-related complications.[66] Only short-term outcome data are available for CDR used to treat cervical radiculopathy and CSM, but the results are promising and the complication rates are low.

Summary

The evaluation and treatment of cervical radiculopathy and myelopathy begins with a systematic patient history and physical examination. The treatment is based on clinical findings that are correlated with radiographic and MRI or CT myelographic findings. Factors that contribute to the choice of an anterior or posterior approach include the location of the compressive pathology, cervical spine alignment, stability, and the surgeon's experience. Most of the procedures have similar efficacy. However, there is a high rate of progression to kyphosis after laminectomy alone, requiring revision surgery, and therefore laminectomy should be accompanied by an instrumented fusion. Cervical disk arthroplasty has had good short-term results, but long-term data are not yet available.

Annotated References

1. Côté P, Cassidy JD, Carroll L: The Saskatchewan Health and Back Pain Survey: The prevalence of neck pain and related disability in Saskatchewan adults. *Spine (Phila Pa 1976)* 1998;23(15):1689-1698.

2. Radhakrishnan K, Litchy WJ, O'Fallon WM, Kurland LT: Epidemiology of cervical radiculopathy: A population-based study from Rochester, Minnesota, 1976 through 1990. *Brain* 1994;117(pt 2):325-335.

3. Lees F, Turner JW: Natural history and prognosis of cervical spondylosis. *Br Med J* 1963;2(5373):1607-1610.

4. Gore DR, Sepic SB, Gardner GM, Murray MP: Neck pain: A long-term follow-up of 205 patients. *Spine (Phila Pa 1976)* 1987;12(1):1-5.

5. Boden SD, McCowin PR, Davis DO, Dina TS, Mark AS, Wiesel S: Abnormal magnetic-resonance scans of the cervical spine in asymptomatic subjects: A prospective investigation. *J Bone Joint Surg Am* 1990;72(8):1178-1184.

6. Graham N, Gross A, Goldsmith CH, et al: Mechanical traction for neck pain with or without radiculopathy. *Cochrane Database Syst Rev* 2008;3:CD006408.

   Seven randomized controlled studies with a total of 958 patients were reviewed to compare the effects of continuous or intermittent traction with those of placebo in patients with neck pain of more that 3 months' duration, with or without radicular symptoms. Only one study (with 100 patients) had a low risk of bias; this study and several others found no statistical difference between continuous traction and placebo.

7. Deyo RA: Drug therapy for back pain: Which drugs help which patients? *Spine (Phila Pa 1976)* 1996;21(24):2840-2850.

8. Levine MJ, Albert TJ, Smith MD: Cervical radiculopathy: Diagnosis and nonoperative management. *J Am Acad Orthop Surg* 1996;4(6):305-316.

9. Santiesteban AJ: The role of physical agents in the treatment of spine pain. *Clin Orthop Relat Res* 1983;179:24-30.

10. Rhee JM, Yoon T, Riew KD: Cervical radiculopathy. *J Am Acad Orthop Surg* 2007;15(8):486-494.

    The nonsurgical and surgical treatments for cervical radiculopathy are summarized. Physical therapy, manipulation, and cervical epidural steroid injections were not found to alter the natural history of cervical radiculopathy.

11. Samartzis D, Shen FH, Matthews DK, Yoon ST, Goldberg EJ, An HS: Comparison of allograft to autograft in multilevel anterior cervical diskectomy and fusion with rigid plate fixation. *Spine J* 2003;3(6):451-459.

12. Bose B: Anterior cervical instrumentation enhances fusion rates in multilevel reconstruction in smokers. *J Spinal Disord* 2001;14(1):3-9.

13. Matz PG, Ryken TC, Groff MW, et al: Techniques for anterior cervical decompression for radiculopathy. *J Neurosurg Spine* 2009;11(2):183-197.

    A database search found that anterior cervical diskectomy and ACDF result in equivalent clinical outcomes and arm pain in patients with cervical radiculopathy. One study found ACDF to provide quicker relief of arm and neck pain, with better fusion and avoidance of post-operative kyphosis. Cervical plates improve lordosis, reduce the risk of pseudarthrosis, and reduce the incidence of graft-related complications. Dynamic plated fixation was not found to increase fusion rates, compared with rigid plates. Cervical arthroplasty is as effective as ACDF and plating for controlling neck and arm pain.

14. Fraser JF, Härtl R: Anterior approaches to fusion of the cervical spine: A metaanalysis of fusion rates. *J Neurosurg Spine* 2007;6(4):298-303.

This meta-analysis identified 21 studies that evaluated fusion rates for diskectomy alone, ACDF without a plate, and ACDF with a plate. The studies had at least 25 patients and an average 12-month follow up. The fusion rate for ACDF with a plate at one, two, or three levels was 97%, 94.6%, or 82%, respectively. All of these rates were significantly higher than those for ACDF without plating.

15. Hilbrand AS, Fye MA, Emery SE, Palumbo MA, Bohlman HH: Increased rate of arthrodesis with strut grafting after multilevel anterior cervical decompression. *Spine (Phila Pa 1976)* 2002;27(2):146-151.

16. Oh MC, Zhang HY, Park JY, Kim KS: Two-level anterior cervical discectomy versus one-level corpectomy in cervical spondylotic myelopathy. *Spine (Phila Pa 1976)* 2009;34(7):692-696.

A retrospective outcome comparison of one- and two-level ACDF for treating two-level CSM in 31 patients found similar clinical outcomes at 26-month follow-up. Patients with two-level ACDF had shorter surgical times, less blood loss, and better maintenance of segmental height and cervical lordosis.

17. Hilibrand AS, Carlson GD, Palumbo MA, Jones PK, Bohlman HH: Radiculopathy and myelopathy at segments adjacent to the site of a previous anterior cervical arthrodesis. *J Bone Joint Surg Am* 1999;81(4):519-528.

18. Fountas KN, Kapsalaki EZ, Nikolakakos LG, et al: Anterior cervical discectomy and fusion associated complications. *Spine (Phila Pa 1976)* 2007;32(21):2310-2317.

In a retrospective review of 1,015 patients who underwent primary ACDF through a Smith-Robinson approach for treatment of cervical radiculopathy resulting from degenerative disk disease, the most common complications were dysphagia and hematoma (affecting 9.5% and 5.6% of patients, respectively). The most lethal complication was esophageal perforation, which affected 0.3% of patients.

19. Zdeblick TA, Zou D, Warden KE, McCabe R, Kunz D, Vanderby R: Cervical stability after foraminotomy: A biomechanical in vitro analysis. *J Bone Joint Surg Am* 1992;74(1):22-27.

20. Krupp W, Schattke H, Müke R: Clinical results of the foraminotomy as described by Frykholm for the treatment of lateral cervical disc herniation. *Acta Neurochir (Wien)* 1990;107(1-2):22-29.

21. Ziedman SM, Ducker TB: Posterior laminoforaminotomy for radiculopathy: Review of 172 cases. *Neurosurgery* 1993;33(3):356-362.

22. Adamson TE: Microendoscopic posterior cervical laminoforaminotomy for unilateral radiculopathy: Results of a new technique in 100 cases. *J Neurosurg* 2001;95(1, suppl):51-57.

23. Fessler RG, Khoo LT: Minimally invasive cervical microendoscopic foraminotomy: An initial clinical experience. *Neurosurgery* 2002;51(5, suppl):S37-S45.

24. Kim TJ, Bae KW, Uhm WS, Kim TH, Joo KB, Jun JB: Prevalence of ossification of the posterior longitudinal ligament of the cervical spine. *Joint Bone Spine* 2008; 75(4):471-474.

A 3-year radiologic review of 11,774 Koreans older than 16 years evaluated the prevalence and type of OPLL in the cervical spine. A literature review evaluated the prevalence in other countries. The 0.6% prevalence in Korea was lower than the 1.9% to 4.3% reported in Japan but higher than the 0.1% to 0.07% reported in the United States.

25. Matsunaga S, Kukita M, Hayashi K, et al: Pathogenesis of myelopathy in patients with ossification of the posterior longitudinal ligament. *J Neurosurg* 2002;96(2, suppl):168-172.

26. Matsunaga S, Sakou T, Taketomi E, Komiya S: Clinical course of patients with ossification of the posterior longitudinal ligament: A minimum 10-year cohort study. *J Neurosurg* 2004;100(3, suppl):245-248.

27. Matsunaga S, Nakamura K, Seichi A, et al: Radiographic predictors for the development of myelopathy in patients with ossification of the posterior longitudinal ligament: A multicenter cohort study. *Spine (Phila Pa 1976)* 2008;33(24):2648-2650.

A retrospective multicenter cohort study with 10-year follow-up reported the radiographic predictors of myelopathy in patients with OPLL. Myelopathy developed in 100% of patients with more than 60% canal stenosis but only 49% of patients with less than 60% canal stenosis. An increased C2-C7 range of motion was a risk factor for the development of myelopathy.

28. Matz PG, Anderson PA, Holly LT, et al: The natural history of cervical spondylotic myelopathy. *J Neurosurg Spine* 2009;11(2):104-111.

A database search for studies relevant to the natural history of CSM found selection bias and inconsistent selection criteria for nonsurgical therapy. Many patients have a slow stepwise decline with long periods of quiescence. Although some patients have improvement, pathologic studies found an association between CSM and severe stenosis with demyelination of white matter and necrosis of both gray and white matter. Patients older than 75 years can be managed nonsurgically with a stable clinical course for as long as 36 months before deterioration.

29. Yukawa Y, Kato F, Ito K, et al: "Ten second step test" as a new quantifiable parameter of cervical myelopathy. *Spine (Phila Pa 1976)* 2008;34(1):82-86.

    JOA scores as well as the results of the 10-second grip-and-release and maximum-steps tests were compared in 163 patients with cervical myelopathy and 1,200 healthy volunteers. The patients performed fewer steps than the control subjects. One year after surgery, the performance of the patients had significantly improved.

30. Ono K, Ota H, Tada K, Yamamoto T: Cervical myelopathy secondary to multiple spondylotic protrusion: A clinico-pathologic study. *Spine (Phila Pa 1976)* 1977;2: 109-125.

31. Fernández de Rota JJ, Meschian S, Fernández de Rota A, Urbano V, Baron M: Cervical spondylotic myelopathy due to chronic compression: The role of signal intensity changes in magnetic resonance images. *J Neurosurg Spine* 2007;6(1):17-22.

    A prospective case study of 67 patients correlated MRI characteristics and functional recovery after surgical treatment for chronic spinal cord compression. Poor functional recovery was found in patients whose MRI signal was low intensity with T1 weighting and high intensity over multiple levels with T2 weighting.

32. Zdeblick TA, Bohlman HH: Cervical kyphosis and myelopathy: Treatment by anterior corpectomy and strut-grafting. *J Bone Joint Surg Am* 1989;71(2):170-182.

33. Ikenaga M, Shikata J, Tanaka C: Long-term results over 10 years of anterior corpectomy and fusion for multi-level cervical myelopathy. *Spine (Phila Pa 1976)* 2006; 31(14):1568-1575.

    Clinical and radiographic results were reviewed in 31 patients more than 10 years after multilevel corpectomies and strut grafting for myelopathy. The constructs remained stable, as did the patients' neurologic status. Only 3 patients had lost 1 point for numbness on the JOA score. Adjacent disk degeneration did not affect the clinical outcome.

34. Macdonald RL, Fehlings MG, Tator CH, et al: Multi-level anterior cervical corpectomy and fibular allograft fusion for cervical myelopathy. *J Neurosurg* 1997;86(6): 990-997.

35. Vaccaro AR, Falatyn SP, Scuderi GJ, et al: Early failure of long segment anterior cervical plate fixation. *J Spinal Disord* 1998;11(5):410-415.

36. Min JH, Jang JS, Lee SH: Significance of the double- and single-layer signs in the ossification of the posterior longitudinal ligament of the thoracic spine. *Neurosurgery* 2007; 61(1):118-122.

    Retrospective review determined the association of double- and single-layer signs on CT and type of OPLL with dural penetration in 197 patients treated with anterior decompression and fusion for OPLL. Dural penetration was found in 52% of those with double-layer signs and 50% of those with nonsegmental-type OPLL.

37. Bernard TN Jr, Whitecloud TS III: Cervical spondylotic myelopathy and myeloradiculopathy: Anterior decompression and stabilization with autogenous fibula strut graft. *Clin Orthop Relat Res* 1987;221:149-160.

38. Anderson PA, Subach BR, Riew KD: Predictors of outcome after anterior cervical discectomy and fusion: A multivariate analysis. *Spine (Phila Pa 1976)* 2009;34(2): 161-166.

    In a retrospective study of 488 patients after ADCF, the predictors of overall success were a high Neck Disability Index score and a normal sensory examination; negative predictors were a workers' compensation claim and "weak" narcotic use. Predictors of an improved Neck Disability Index score were older age, a high preoperative Neck Disability Index score, and gainful (paid) employment; litigation was a negative predictor.

39. Kato Y, Iwasaki M, Fuji T, Yonenobu K, Ochi T: Long-term follow-up results of laminectomy for cervical myelopathy caused by ossification of the posterior longitudinal ligament. *J Neurosurg* 1998;89(2):217-223.

40. Epstein NE: An argument for traditional posterior cervical fusion techniques: Evidence from 35 cases. *Surg Neurol* 2008;70(1):45-52.

    Clinical and radiographic success was described in 35 patients with cervical myelopathy and spinal cord compression over one to three levels and preserved lordosis. Two patients had transient root palsy, all patients had fusion, and 29 patients had a good or excellent outcome on the Odom criteria.

41. Chen Y, Guo Y, Chen D, Wang X, Lu X, Yuan W: Long-term outcome of laminectomy and instrumented fusion for cervical ossification of the posterior longitudinal ligament. *Int Orthop* 2009;33(4):1075-1080.

    In 83 patients with OPLL who were treated with laminectomy and instrumented fusion, JOA scores had improved 62% at 4.8-year follow-up. Correction of loss of lordosis may contribute to neurologic deficits.

42. Iwasaki M, Okuda S, Miyauchi A, et al: Surgical strategy for cervical myelopathy due to ossification of the posterior longitudinal ligament: Part 1. Clinical results and limitations of laminoplasty. *Spine (Phila Pa 1976)* 2007;32(6):647-653.

    The surgical results of laminoplasty were retrospectively reviewed in 66 patients with OPLL-caused myelopathy. Patients with an occupying ratio greater than 60%, hill-shaped OPLL, and age older than 60 years had a poor result.

43. Li H, Jiang LS, Dai LY: A review of prognostic factors for surgical outcome of ossification of the posterior longitudinal ligament of cervical spine. *Eur Spine J* 2008; 17(10):1277-1288.

    The literature was reviewed on clinical factors that predict the outcome after surgical intervention for OPLL. The transverse area of the spinal cord, spinal cord–evoked potentials, increased range of motion, diabetes, history of trauma, onset of ossification of the ligament flavum in the thoracic spine, snake-eyes appearance, and incomplete decompression may predict a poor prognosis.

44. Ogawa Y, Chiba K, Matsumoto M, et al: Long-term results after expansive open-door laminoplasty for the segmental-type of ossification of the posterior longitudinal ligament of the cervical spine: A comparison with nonsegmental-type lesions. *J Neurosurg Spine* 2005; 3(3):198-204.

   A long-term clinical follow-up study of 57 patients with symptomatic OPLL treated with open door laminoplasty found that after 5 years patients with segmental-type OPLL began to have more deterioration than other patients, possibly because of hypermobility.

45. Iwasaki M, Kawaguchi Y, Kimura T, Yonenobu K: Long-term results of expansive laminoplasty for ossification of the posterior longitudinal ligament of the cervical spine: More than 10 years follow up. *J Neurosurg* 2002;96(2, suppl):180-189.

46. Ogawa Y, Toyama Y, Chiba K: Long-term results of expansive open-door laminoplasty for ossification of the posterior longitudinal ligament of the cervical spine. *J Neurosurg Spine* 2004;1(2)168-174.

47. Chiba K, Ogawa Y, Ishii K, et al: Long-term results of expansive open-door laminoplasty for cervical myelopathy: Average 14-year follow-up study. *Spine (Phila Pa 1976)* 2006;31(26):2998-3005.

   A retrospective review of 80 patients treated with open door laminoplasty found that JOA scores improved up to 3 years after surgery but began to decline after 5 years. A loss of lordosis and range of motion was noted, as well as OPLL progression after 5 years.

48. Kim PK, Alexander JT: Indications for circumferential surgery for cervical spondylotic myelopathy. *Spine J* 2006;6(6, suppl):299S-307S.

   A review of indications, techniques, and results for circumferential cervical fusion in the treatment of cervical myelopathy suggests that patients with conditions such as osteoporosis, renal failure requiring dialysis, corpectomies of three or more levels, and more than three levels of ACDF can benefit from circumferential fusion.

49. Sembrano JN, Mehbod AA, Garvey TA, et al: A concomitant posterior approach improves fusion rates but not overall reoperation rates in multilevel cervical fusion for spondylosis. *J Spinal Disord Tech* 2009;22(3): 162-169.

   Seventy-eight patients who underwent anterior or anterior-posterior surgery for multilevel CSM (55 or 23 patients, respectively) were compared at 2-year follow-up. Fusion was assessed by surgical exploration, CT, and flexion-extension radiographs. No patients had pseudarthrosis after circumferential fusion. Early and overall reoperation rates did not differ, but there were significantly more late reoperations in the patients who underwent anterior-only surgery. Reoperation in the patients who underwent circumferential surgery was for redecompression, posterior hardware complications, adjacent segment disease, infection, and evacuation of hematomas.

50. Etame AB, Wang AC, Than KD, La Marca F, Park P: Outcomes after surgery for cervical spine deformity: Review of the literature. *Neurosurg Focus* 2010;28(3):E14.

   In 14 retrospective studies with a total of 399 patients who underwent anterior, posterior, or circumferential surgery to treat neck pain and myeloradiculopathy with concomitant cervical kyphosis, posterior approaches with osteotomies and circumferential approaches provided greater deformity correction than anterior-only approaches. Overall, horizontal gaze was improved and patients were satisfied with their outcomes.

51. Murrey D, Janssen M, Delamarter R, et al: Results of the prospective, randomized, controlled multicenter Food and Drug Administration investigational device exemption study of the ProDisc-C total disc replacement versus anterior discectomy and fusion for the treatment of 1-level symptomatic cervical disc disease. *Spine J* 2009;9(4):275-286.

   The FDA investigational device exemption comparison study of the ProDisc-C (Synthes, West Chester, PA) and ACDF with plate for single-level cervical disk disease found significantly better neurologic success for the ProDisc-C after 6 months but not after 2 years. The ProDisc-C had significantly better device success and fewer secondary surgical procedures. There were no between-group statistical differences for adverse events and success measures. The ad hoc analysis of minimal clinically important difference in health-related quality of life measures showed the ProDisc-C to be statistically superior to ACDF.

52. Garrido BJ, Taha TA, Sasso RC: Clinical outcomes of Bryan Cervical Disc Arthroplasty: A prospective, randomized, controlled, single site trial with 48-month follow-up. *J Spinal Disord Tech* 2010;23(6):367-371.

   The Bryan cervical disk (Medtronic Sofamor Danek, Memphis, TN) randomized controlled study provided level I evidence on functional outcomes. The prosthesis maintained Neck Disability Index, SF-36, and visual analog scale improvements at 48 months, with only one secondary surgery related to adjacent-level disease.

53. Burkus JK, Haid RW, Traynelis VC, Mummaneni PV: Long-term clinical and radiographic outcomes of cervical disc replacement with the Prestige disc: Results from a prospective randomized controlled clinical trial. *J Neurosurg Spine* 2010;13(3):308-318.

   Five-year clinical and radiographic outcomes from the Prestige (Medtronic Sofamor Danek, Memphis, TN) randomized controlled study are presented. Patients treated with arthroplasty maintained clinical success, as measured by the Neck Disability Index, SF-36, and visual analog scale, as well as angular motion of the device. The rate of adjacent-level surgery was lower in patients treated with arthroplasty, but not significantly.

54. DiAngelo DJ, Roberston JT, Metcalf NH, McVay BJ, Davis RC: Biomechanical testing of an artificial cervical joint and an anterior cervical plate. *J Spinal Disord Tech* 2003;16(4):314-323.

55. Wigfield CC, Skrzypiec D, Jackowski A, Adams MA: Internal stress distribution in cervical intervertebral

4: The Adult Spine

discs: The influence of an artificial cervical joint and simulated anterior interbody fusion. *J Spinal Disord Tech* 2003;16(5):441-449.

56. Dmitriev AE, Cunningham BW, Hu N, Sell G, Vigna F, McAfee PC: Adjacent level intradiscal pressure and segmental kinematics following a cervical total disc arthroplasty: An in vitro human cadaveric model. *Spine (Phila Pa 1976)* 2005;30(10):1165-1172.

   A cadaver study compared kinematics and intradiskal pressures in the native spine, levels adjacent to disk replacement, a bone dowel, and a bone dowel plus plate. Intradiskal pressures were no different adjacent to disk replacement or in the intact state and were significantly less than in all other conditions tested.

57. Puttlitz CM, Rousseau MA, Xu Z, Hu S, Tay BK, Lotz JC: Intervertebral disc replacement maintains cervical spine kinetics. *Spine (Phila Pa 1976)* 2004;29(24):2809-2814.

58. Sasso R, Best NM, Metcalf NH, Anderson PA: Motion analysis of Bryan cervical disc arthroplasty versus anterior discectomy and fusion: Results from a prospective, randomized, multicenter, clinical trial. *J Spinal Disord Tech* 2008;21(6):393-399.

   A motion analysis subset from the Bryan disk randomized controlled study found that the Bryan disk maintained its motion at 24 months and did not subside or migrate.

59. Sasso RC, Best NM: Cervical kinematics after fusion and Bryan disc arthroplasty. *J Spinal Disord Tech* 2008;21(1):19-22.

   A comparison of motion parameters in single-level disk replacement or fusion revealed that after 6 months there was significantly more translation at levels above the fusion than at the disk replacement. This difference was no longer significant at 12 months.

60. Chang UK, Kim DH, Lee MC, Willenberg R, Kim SH, Lim J: Range of motion change after cervical arthroplasty with ProDisc-C and Prestige artificial discs compared with anterior cervical discectomy and fusion. *J Neurosurg Spine* 2007;7(1):40-46.

   A cadaver comparison of range of motion adjacent to ProDisc-C, Prestige II, or ACDF surgery revealed that both disk replacements had more motion at the index level than in the intact state. The adjacent-level ranges of motion were less than in intact state, except in extension.

61. Eck JC, Humphreys SC, Lim TH, et al: Biomechanical study on the effect of cervical spine fusion on adjacent-level intradiscal pressure and segmental motion. *Spine (Phila Pa 1976)* 2002;27(22):2431-2434.

62. Mummaneni PV, Burkus JK, Haid RW, Traynelis VC, Zdeblick TA: Clinical and radiographic analysis of cer-

vical disc arthroplasty compared with allograft fusion: A randomized controlled clinical trial. *J Neurosurg Spine* 2007;6(3):198-209.

   The clinical and radiographic results of the Prestige ST study were reported at 24-month follow up. Patients treated with arthroplasty had a significantly better neurologic outcome, fewer revisions, a more rapid return to work, and less symptomatic adjacent-level disease. There were no implant failures or migrations.

63. Heller JG, Sasso RC, Papadopoulos SM, et al: Comparison of Bryan cervical disc arthroplasty with anterior cervical decompression and fusion: Clinical and radiographic results of a randomized, controlled, clinical trial. *Spine (Phila Pa 1976)* 2009;34(2):101-107.

   At 2-year follow-up in a randomized controlled comparison of 242 Bryan cervical disk replacements and 221 ACDFs to treat radiculopathy or myelopathy from single-level cervical disk disease, the patients with the Bryan disk had significantly more improvement in the primary outcome variables, with fewer device- and surgery-related events. These patients returned to work 2 weeks earlier than those with ACDF.

64. Goffin J, van Loon J, Van Calenbergh F, Lipscomb B: A clinical analysis of 4- and 6-year follow-up results after cervical disc replacement surgery using the Bryan Cervical Disc Prosthesis. *J Neurosurg Spine* 2010;12(3):261-269.

   Long-term results of Bryan disk implantation were reported from Belgium. The device maintained its motion, with only six device-related complications. Patients maintained their improvement as measured on the SF-36, Neck Disability Index, and Odom classification.

65. Riew KD, Buchowski JM, Sasso R, Zdeblick T, Metcalf NH, Anderson PA: Cervical disc arthroplasty compared with arthrodesis for the treatment of myelopathy. *J Bone Joint Surg Am* 2008;90(11):2354-2364.

   In the patients with myelopathy from the Bryan and Prestige FDA investigational device exemption randomized controlled studies, improvement from disk replacement was found to be similar to that from fusion, with no worsening of symptoms.

66. Anderson PA, Sasso RC, Riew KD: Comparison of adverse events between the Bryan artificial cervical disc and anterior cervical arthrodesis. *Spine (Phila Pa 1976)* 2008;33(12):1305-1312.

   Adverse events from the randomized controlled study of the Bryan disk were compared with those from fusion. There was no difference in overall medical events, but there were more severe events in the patients treated with fusion. Patients in the fusion group had more reoperations, but there was more dysphagia in those treated with the Bryan disk.

Chapter 27

Lumbar Disk Herniation

Eugene Carragee, MD   S. Raymond Golish, MD, PhD

Introduction

Lumbar disk herniation is common in adults and sometimes is directly associated with symptoms of nerve root irritation or injury. Disk herniation can be caused by massive trauma to a normal disk but more commonly is the result of annular disruption associated with degenerative disk disease. The classic presentation of a symptomatic lumbar herniated nucleus pulposus (HNP) is a period of increased back pain, followed by an acute onset of gluteal and leg pain with some resolution of the back pain. An acute disk herniation may be superimposed on other spine pathology, such as spinal stenosis, spondylolisthesis, or other lumbar disk degeneration.

Most disk herniations detected by imaging are not symptomatic. Symptomatic HNP is most clearly diagnosed if leg pain predominates over back pain; if radicular pain can be provoked by a maneuver that stretches the nerve, such as the straight leg raise or femoral stretch test; and if the imaging evidence of neurocompression is correlated with a radicular pattern of pain, sensory loss, or weakness.

The natural history of symptomatic HNP is favorable. Most patients improve with nonsurgical care alone.[1,2] The rate of precipitous neurologic decline with nonsurgical care is low.[1,3] On the other hand, surgical treatment is clearly effective in providing more rapid relief of severe symptoms.[4,5] Mainstream surgical techniques have evolved gradually, and, despite numerous innovations and purported improvements, only a few new techniques have proved their value over time.

Clinical Evaluation

The radicular pain syndrome associated with disk herniation usually does not result from a specific injury. In a prospective study of 154 consecutive patients with new lumbar disk herniation, 95 (62%) reported that the symptoms began spontaneously, and 40 (26%) reported that the symptoms began after a common nonlifting activity of daily living or household task.[6] Fewer than 8% perceived their new-onset sciatica as related to heavy lifting or physical trauma.

Although most patients with a symptomatic lumbar HNP have both back and leg pain, only a small proportion of low back pain syndromes stem from HNP or another potentially serious cause. Low back pain episodes require a careful workup. The presence of an indicator of serious underlying disease or injury, a serious motor loss, or intolerable disability requires more aggressive evaluation. In the absence of such a red flag, the initial nonsurgical treatment is similar, regardless of the etiology of pain.

The confirmatory diagnosis of a symptomatic HNP usually is made from MRI. Because of the high rate of spontaneous recovery and the likelihood of irrelevant imaging findings, 6 weeks of nonsurgical care is a reasonable guideline before advanced imaging is undertaken. The diagnosis and management of HNP is most straightforward in patients whose leg pain is greater than their back pain and whose MRI findings are correlated with a dermatomal pattern of pain or distributional weakness. On physical examination, tension signs such as the straight leg raise and femoral stretch test are believed to be most specific for HNP.

A disk herniation is defined as a focal displacement of nuclear and annular material beyond the normal peripheral margin of the disk. The four classic morphologic categories of herniations are based on increasing severity: a bulge is a general outpouching of the anulus fibrosus without focal displacement of the nucleus pulposus; a protrusion is displacement of the nucleus pulposus within a partially torn or thinned anulus fibrosus, in which the base of the herniation is broader than the apex; an extrusion is a displacement of the nucleus pulposus through a complete defect of the anulus fibrosus, often subligamentous but possibly transligamentous relative to the posterior longitudinal ligament; and a sequestered herniation has separated from its origin

4: The Adult Spine

Table 1

Classification of Lumbar Disk Herniations Based on Intraoperative Findings

Type	General Description	Disk Fragment	Anulus Fibrosus	Treatment Implications
I	Fragment: fissure	Extruded or sequestered	Small defect	Good outcome Low reherniation rate
II	Fragment: defect	Extruded or sequestered	Large defect	Good initial outcome High reherniation rate
III	Fragment: contained	Subannular detached	Intact	Good outcome Intermediate reherniation rate
IV	No fragment: contained	No subannular detached fragment	Intact but protruding	Inferior outcome Associated with negative psychosocial factors

Adapted with permission from Carragee EJ, Han MY, Suen PW, Kim D: Clinical outcomes after lumbar discectomy for sciatica: The effects of fragment type and anular competence. *J Bone Joint Surg Am* 2003;85-A(1):102-108.

and is a completely free fragment. Bulges and protrusions are contained herniations; extrusions and sequestered fragments are noncontained herniations. Although this traditional system of classifying disk herniations is accurate at a gross anatomic level, it is not well validated for predicting outcomes using MRI or gross anatomic criteria.

A classification system correlated with clinical surgical outcomes, including the risk of reherniation and reoperation, is outlined in Table 1.[7,8] Group I disks were associated with a low risk and the best outcomes, whereas group III disks were associated with high rates of reherniation and reoperation. Group IV disks had poor overall outcomes. Numerous other factors have been identified as predictive of the clinical course of HNP and are relevant to management (Table 2).

Special Considerations

The anatomic location of the disk herniation dictates the neurologic symptoms. A herniation in the central zone may affect the traversing nerve roots or the nerve roots caudal to the herniation. The most common herniation is in the subarticular region (the lateral recess between the pedicle and center of the spinal canal). This type of herniation impinges on the anterolateral traversing nerve root. Foraminal and extraforaminal (far lateral) herniations are less common; they impinge on the exiting nerve root. Far lateral herniations are best diagnosed by correlating MRI and clinical findings. In the past, these herniations may have been underdiagnosed. When surgical treatment is indicated, there is a significant trend toward the use of tubular retractors and endoscopic techniques, which appear well suited to the surgical anatomy of a far lateral herniation.[9]

Lumbar disk herniation rarely appears as cauda equina syndrome. A high index of suspicion must be maintained for timely diagnosis and treatment of cauda

equina syndrome. To a varying extent, most patients have bladder dysfunction, bowel dysfunction, and motor or sensory loss. The prognosis for a full return to function is guarded. Emergency surgical treatment within 24 to 48 hours of diagnosis still is a mainstay of management, although some studies have cast doubt on the correlation of surgical timing and return of function.[10-12]

Lumbar disk herniation is uncommon in adolescents or children and rarely requires surgical management. The patients are most likely to be teenagers. An extensive period of nonsurgical management is warranted, with a high expectation of success. Microdiskectomy can be used if nonsurgical management is truly unsuccessful. In a large study, the mean age of patients undergoing microdiskectomy was 16 years, and 60% of the patients were girls. The patients had symptoms for a mean of 12 months, with 25% reporting weakness.[13] The complications of microdiskectomy include infection, durotomy, and a need for reoperation.

Imaging

The interpretation of imaging studies requires correlation with the patient's history and physical examination findings. Isolated, noncorrelated imaging findings must be interpreted with caution.

MRI

Two hundred patients with symptoms of varying severity underwent baseline MRI followed by a 5-year observation period.[14] MRI was repeated for the 51 patients who had new, severe episodes of low back pain (defined as a score of at least 6 on a 10-point visual analog scale) lasting more than 1 week. There was progression of MRI findings in 84%. The patients whose findings had progressed were mostly likely to have age-related changes such as disk height loss, facet arthrosis,

---

Table 2

Patient Variables Predicting the Risk of Lumbar Disk Herniation, Risk of Reherniation, and Response to Treatment

Variable	Risk of Lumbar Disk Herniation	Risk of Reherniation	Response to Nonsurgical Treatment	Response to Surgical Treatment	Psychosocial Outcome of Treatment
Demographic	—	—	Sex Age	Sex	—
History and physical examination	—	—	Leg pain Severity Duration	—	—
Psychosocial	Smoking Obesity Distress Work requiring heavy manual labor	—	Treatment expectations Educational level	Smoking Workers' compensation claim Distress	Smoking Workers' compensation claim Treatment expectations Distress
Imaging	Sagittal alignment	Size of annular defect Volume of surgical disk removal	—	Spine level Sequestration	—
Rehabilitation	—	—	—	Physical therapy is *not* a factor.	
Surgical	—	Limited diskectomy	—	Limited diskectomy Surgical method is *not* a factor.	—
Molecular	Some genetic loci	—	Inflammatory markers	—	

or end plate changes. Only two of the 51 patients had MRI changes that were correlated with physical examination findings, and both of these patients had primarily radicular symptoms. Demographic factors involving chronic pain, psychologic distress, a compensation claim, or smoking predicted the new, severe episodes of pain. Although patients with early disk degeneration are at risk of radiographic progression (degeneration or herniation), this risk does not predict the likelihood of long-term pain or surgery.[15] Over time, both symptomatic and asymptomatic disk herniations decrease in size on MRI. It is difficult to predict using imaging alone whether a herniation will be intractably symptomatic.[16]

The scientific basis and clinical utility of an MRI finding of changes in the end plate (Modic changes) continue to be obscure. For example, the presence of type I (edema) or II (fatty infiltration) Modic changes was found not to affect the outcome of diskectomy.[17] Although type I changes are associated with earlier lumbar herniation, they also may be associated with nonspecific low back pain.[18] Type I changes are not associated with increased positron emission tomography uptake.[19]

The use of three tesla magnets, novel pulse sequences such as T1(rho)-weighted studies, and upright imaging are among the MRI technical improvements under in-

vestigation. The use of dynamic MRI in flexion and extension may increase or decrease the appearance of disk bulges relative to supine MRI in a neutral posture.[20,21] A weight-bearing upright MRI study may better reveal posterior disk herniation and anterolisthesis than a supine MRI study, but with unknown clinical significance.[22] Large-scale studies are required to determine whether these novel MRI technologies not only improve image characteristics but also have a positive impact on functional outcomes.

Molecular Imaging

The future of disk disease imaging may rely on molecular imaging. An improved understanding of the molecular pathogenesis of disk disease can be used in molecular imaging of disk pathology as well as molecular biomarkers to predict clinical outcomes and sharpen surgical indications. In principle, numerous molecular mediators of disk degeneration could act as biomarkers for the purposes of molecular imaging. Table 3 presents a partial list of molecular mediators associated with disk degeneration. The ability to use molecular imaging to assess musculoskeletal diseases is already anticipated for rheumatoid arthritis.[23]

In summary, the ability to image specific molecular

Table 3

Molecular Mediators of Disk Disease

Category	Molecule	Published Studies		
		Disk	Articular Cartilage[a]	Human[b]
Inflammatory	Interleukin-6 (IL-6)	X	X	X
	Prostaglandin E2	X	X	X
	Nitric oxide (NO)	X	X	X
	Interferon-γ (IFN-γ)	X	X	X
	5-hydroxytryptamine (5HT)	X		
	RANTES	X		
	Microphage inflammatory protein–1a (MIP-1a)	X	X	X
	Monocyte chemotactic protein–1 (MCP-1)	X	X	X
	Interleukin-1ra (IL-1ra)	X	X	X
	Tumor necrosis factor–α (TNF-α)	X	X	X
Extracellular matrix	Procollagens	X	X	
	Type II collagen telopeptide (CTX II)	X	X	
	ARGS/aggrecan fragments	X	X	
	Fibronectin fragments	X	X	
	Fibronectin-aggrecan complex (FAC)	X	X	X
	Cartilage oligomeric matrix protein (COMP)	X		X
	CS 846/chondroitin fragments		X	
	sRAGE	X	X	
Protease	Matrix metalloproteinase-3 (MMP-3)	X	X	X
	MMP-13 and other MMPs	X	X	X
	ADAMTS-4/aggrecanases	X	X	
Signal transduction	NF-κB	X		
	p38 mitogen-activated protein kinase	X	X	
	DR5/DcR2	X		

[a] Studied in the articular cartilage of synovial joints as well as the disk.
[b] Identified in vivo or ex vivo in humans.

pathogenic pathways is likely to exceed the diagnostic capabilities of other imaging technologies such as MRI spectroscopy and T1(rho)-weighted studies. Disease-specific probe development and the correlation of imaging findings with clinical outcomes will be expensive and time consuming, however.[24]

Nonsurgical Treatment

Epidural Injections

The usefulness of epidural steroid injections as a nonsurgical treatment of radiculopathy is still being defined. With the use of current clinical selection criteria, there is only fair evidence that epidural steroid injection

has moderate, short-term effectiveness for pain relief related to radiculopathy from HNP.[25] The evidence related to chronic pain, back pain (not leg pain), and functional improvement is poorer.[26,27] The role of steroids compared with local anesthetics for symptom relief remains in doubt. Clinical and animal studies found no significant difference between infiltration with corticosteroids and a local anesthetic alone for treating radiculopathy from HNP.[28-30] This result is counterintuitive, in light of the pharmacologic half-life of these agents.

The future use of epidural steroid injections for radiculopathy from HNP will be determined when research identifies biomarkers that can predict clinical response and improved techniques for controlled delivery of steroids, local anesthetics, and novel agents such as antibody therapies. The MRI parameters that predict a favorable response to epidural steroid injection include a foraminal location and a high-grade root compression. High-sensitivity C-reactive protein levels can predict the response but may not be sufficiently specific.[31] Epidural molecular markers are correlated with pain relief after epidural steroid injection, but the sampling technique requires cannulation of the epidural space.[32]

Microparticles of steroids, local anesthetics, and other drugs have been developed. The combined effects of different drugs are important, as is the selection of polymers (including traditional polymers such as polylactic-co-glycolic acid and advanced polymers such as polyphosphazenes).[33-38] The novel pharmaceutical agents include tumor necrosis factor–α (TNF-α). Despite the failure of systemic TNF-α therapy in a randomized controlled study, there is considerable experimental evidence in support of a role for this agent.[39-41] In the future, the numerous molecular mediators of disk disease may be developed for specific injection therapies.

Intradiskal Injections and Diskography

The prototype of intradiskal injection therapies is chymopapain chemonucleolysis. This procedure was supported by multiple studies before it fell out of favor because of the complications associated with its use.[42] The use of intradiskal chemonucleolysis with collagenase and, increasingly, with oxygen-ozone, has been reported, despite the risk of serious complications.[43-45] Additional evidence is required to support the routine use of this therapy. The proposed intradiskal treatments include gene therapy, stem cell therapy, and the inhibition of molecular mediators of degeneration.[46-48] The focus of many of these approaches is to identify and treat early degenerative disk disease rather than end-stage degeneration or radiculopathy from HNP. The success of advanced intradiskal therapies will require the use of diagnostic molecular biomarkers. Some biomarkers have been clinically validated through lavage of the intradiskal space.[49] If further validated, biomarkers obtained by disk cannulation could direct surgical decision making or the use of intradiskal injections. Many molecular mediators of disk degeneration conceivably could serve as targets for intradiskal pharmacotherapy, if identified as causing the degenerative cascade (Table 3).

Diskography is an invasive procedure requiring disk puncture and injection, with possible long-term morbidity. In a matched study with 10-year follow-up, diskography was correlated with a risk of disk herniation, annular rupture at the diskogram site, and accelerated disk degeneration.[50] These effects must be considered during the future development of intradiskal biochemical assays or treatments.

Systemic Therapy and TNF-α Inhibitors

Systemic anti–TNF-α antibody therapy has been investigated for managing radiculopathy from HNP. However, a placebo-controlled randomized controlled study of infliximab reported no benefit.[41] The negative results were remarkable in light of the experimental and clinical evidence supporting the role of TNF-α.[39,40,51]

Surgical Treatment

The Spine Patient Outcomes Research Trial

The publication of data from the Spine Patient Outcomes Research Trial (SPORT) has rejuvenated the debate on managing lumbar HNP with radiculopathy. In 13 centers, 501 patients who had radiculopathy for longer than 6 weeks were randomly assigned to diskectomy or nonsurgical treatment.[1] The Medical Outcomes Study Short Form-36 Health Survey (SF-36) bodily pain and physical function scales and the Oswestry Disability Index were used as the primary outcome measures at several points over 2 years. Only 60% of patients randomly assigned to surgery ultimately underwent surgery, and 45% of patients randomly assigned to nonsurgical treatment crossed over to surgical treatment. This factor has severely limited the value of SPORT as a randomized controlled study because statistical methods for the analysis of partial compliance were not widely used.[52-54]

As an observational study, SPORT offers compelling data.[1] Of the 743 patients in the observational cohort, 528 underwent surgery. At 3-month follow-up, all primary outcome measures revealed highly significant differences in favor of surgery. These differences persisted, with diminished but significant magnitude, at 2-year follow-up. A combined as-treated analysis of the randomized and observational groups at 4-year follow-up found that the surgically treated patients had a superior result on all primary outcome measures.[4]

SPORT found that patients who had surgery differed demographically from those who did not. Those who did not have surgery on average were older, were better educated, and reported milder symptoms.[55] This observation suggests that patients' ability to cope with prolonged nonsurgical management may vary by demographic status and that earlier surgical relief may be most attractive to patients who have severe symptoms and fewer social resources to support a prolonged disabling illness.[5] In this and other studies, the relatively low rate of minor complications observed in all groups of surgical patients is counterbalanced by the absence of documented serious neurologic deterioration with continued nonsurgical management.[3] Most patients, in the absence of serious neurologic loss, may decide on surgery or nonsurgical management as it best suits their goals and resources.[55]

Other Studies and Cost Analysis

In a study of 283 patients who were randomly assigned to microdiskectomy or nonsurgical treatment,[5] sciatica improved more rapidly with surgery; however, there were no differences in outcomes at 1- or 2-year follow-up.[2] Unsuccessful nonsurgical treatment leading to delayed surgery was more likely in patients who had more intense leg pain or a higher disability score.[56] At 2-year follow-up of 50 patients randomly assigned to surgery or nonsurgical treatment, the patients who underwent surgery tended to have a more rapid recovery, but there was no difference in longer term leg pain. In another study, 169 patients were randomly assigned to diskectomy or epidural steroid injection. A comparison of scores on the visual analog scale revealed that the patients who underwent surgery had a higher rate and quicker onset of relief, with successful treatment over the study period; patients with incomplete relief after epidural steroid injection went on to diskectomy without detriment.[57]

The cost of surgical management per quality-adjusted life year (QALY) is relatively high for diskectomy compared with other interventions. The estimated increased cost per QALY of surgical care over nonsurgical care ranges from $34,000 to $69,000 depending on the method of estimating costs. In comparison, the traditional benchmark for a cost-effective treatment is $50,000 per QALY.[58,59] In European studies, however, the greater cost per QALY appeared to be well offset by lower total societal costs.[60,61]

Microdiskectomy and Open Diskectomy

Mainstream surgical techniques have evolved only gradually. The accepted procedure still is the traditional open laminotomy and diskectomy, with or without microscope illumination and magnification.[62] A review of all surgical treatments concluded that traditional open surgery and microdiskectomy are broadly similar and effective.[42] The extent of diskectomy is controversial; specifically, whether the preferred procedure is limited diskectomy (in which only the herniated fragment and any loose intervertebral fragments are removed) or more extensive subtotal diskectomy. Limited diskectomy usually leads to better pain relief and satisfaction than subtotal diskectomy, but this procedure increases the chance of reherniation in a large annular defect.[8,63,64] Removal of more disk material results in a greater loss of disk height.[65] If there is a recurrence after a limited or subtotal primary procedure, revision diskectomy usually has a satisfactory outcome, although it is costly and has associated morbidity.[7,66,67]

Despite the success of well-established procedures, numerous innovations and modifications have been proposed, including the use of nuclear replacement devices, annular repair devices, local and systemic injections, and minimally invasive procedures and surgeries.[41,43,68-70] No high-level evidence has established that new procedures have better outcomes than the mainstream procedures.[42,71]

Minimally Invasive Techniques

Numerous minimally invasive diskectomy and decompression technologies are commercially available. The marketing of these products using terms such as "percutaneous," "laser," and "endoscopic" may impede the surgeon's ability to distinguish their fundamental design features. With few exceptions, the value of these new technologies and the overall cost of using them (including the cost of achieving proficiency) are not yet known. These products and techniques fall into four broad categories: tubular retractors, interlaminar endoscopy, foraminal endoscopy and diskoscopy, and intradiskal procedures.

Tubular Retractors

The most studied approach involves the use of various soft-tissue retractors that are claimed to be less invasive than similar products. The geometry may be tubular, conical, or quadrangular, with the size of the working cannulae ranging from 7 to 18 mm. Tubular retractors originally were developed for use with an integrated endoscope in a microendoscopic diskectomy. In practice, many surgeons use tubular retractors during a conventional laminotomy and diskectomy, thus blurring the distinction between this and conventional microdiskectomy methods. A multicenter randomized controlled study compared microendoscopic diskectomy using a tubular retractor with conventional microdiskectomy in 328 patients. At 1-year follow-up, the results of conventional microdiskectomy were statistically superior in terms of pain metrics and functional outcome, as measured on the Roland-Morris Disability Questionnaire.[72] These findings may be clinically important.[73] In another study, 60 patients were randomly assigned to standard microdiskectomy or microdiskectomy through an 11.5-mm trocar. Scores on the visual analog scale, Oswestry Disability Index, and SF-36 were compared at a minimum 6-month follow-up.[74] There were no significant differences in outcome measures, complication rates, or operating room time. The learning curve for microendoscopic diskectomy has been investigated in multiple studies; surgeons were found to achieve proficiency after approximately 20 procedures.[75-77]

Interlaminar Endoscopy

Interlaminar endoscopic diskectomy uses a traditional posterior interlaminar interval. Interlaminar diskectomy using a small integrated endoscope represents a greater departure from conventional microdiskectomy than microendoscopic diskectomy using a microscope or endoscope through a tubular retractor. Of 331 patients treated using a 6.9-mm endoscope in combination with foraminal endoscopy, 178 were randomly assigned to full endoscopic diskectomy and 153 were assigned to conventional microdiskectomy.[78,79] Even with experienced surgeons, there were no differences in patients' functional outcomes at 2-year follow-up. However, patients who underwent endoscopy had an earlier return to work than those who underwent microdiskectomy. The significance of this finding is unknown; patients in both groups returned to work later than patients in other microdiskectomy studies.[7]

Foraminal Endoscopy and Diskoscopy

A foraminal endoscopy begins extraforaminally and proceeds to the neural foramen from the outside in. Decompression proceeds intradiskally or transforaminally to the epidural space. Instruments are passed through a posterolateral working portal created under fluoroscopic guidance. Foraminoplasty can be accomplished through a cannula under direct visualization. Special cannulae and instruments protect the exiting nerve root from the working instruments. Decompression of neuroforaminal stenosis can be achieved, and diskectomy is accomplished from the outside in. Diskoscopy, for which the working portal is introduced into the nucleus pulposus, can be performed for a relatively central disk herniation. In contrast to intradiskal procedures, a video endoscope allows direct visualization. To retrieve an extruded fragment from the epidural space, an annulotomy can be extended around the base of the extruded fragment from the inside out. In practice, foraminal endoscopy and diskoscopy overlap; most systems and surgical techniques use a combination of these approaches.

The clinical evidence regarding foraminal endoscopy does not fully support its marketing claims. Foraminal and extraforaminal herniations appear to be especially amenable to the use of this technique.[80] Higher failure rates are reported when foraminal endoscopy is used for large, central, or migrated herniations.[81] Conversely, a far lateral approach may be required for herniations inaccessible with posterolateral endoscopy, including central herniations and sequestrations.[82] In a randomized study of 178 patients to compare interlaminar and transforaminal endoscopic diskectomy with conventional microdiskectomy, there were no differences in pain metrics, functional outcomes metrics, or recurrence rate at 2-year follow-up, and no neurologic deficits were reported.[79] The risks, complications, and expense of developing proficiency in the technique are unknown.

Intradiskal Procedures

The use of intradiskal procedures is confined to the nucleus pulposus. From a posterolateral approach, a large-gauge needle or a small-gauge cannula acts as a working portal to the central nucleus pulposus. Various instruments, catheters, shavers, lasers, radiofrequency probes, and suction, lavage, and cautery devices indirectly decompress the nucleus pulposus under fluoroscopic guidance. Although nucleus pulposus removal can globally reduce intradiskal pressure, disk bulging and rim forces may increase.[83] These techniques do not permit retrieval of extruded nuclear material and therefore are indicated only for contained herniations. It may be difficult to predict disk extrusion preoperatively because the MRI grading system for disk herniation is not well validated.[7]

Percutaneous diskectomy has a low clinical level of evidence and a conflicting scientific rationale.[84-88] There is a possibility of serious complications.[89,90] A multicenter randomized clinical study is under way to compare conventional open diskectomy to percutaneous laser disk decompression.[91]

Summary

The natural history of HNP is favorable. With nonsurgical care, which is the mainstay of treatment, patients are unlikely to experience a precipitous neurologic decline. The current evidence supports diskectomy to achieve more rapid improvement in well-selected patients with persistent, severe symptoms. Numerous factors contribute to the response to both surgical and nonsurgical therapy, including demographic and psychosocial factors as well as clinical factors such as a predominance of leg pain.

The relationship between HNP and discogenic pain (chronic axial pain in the setting of degenerative disk disease) remains unclear. Numerous technologic advances have been proposed related to injection, stem cell, and gene therapy as well as intradiskal and minimally invasive surgery. None of these advances has been proved to offer advantages in safety and efficacy over current methods of management.

Annotated References

1. Weinstein JN, Lurie JD, Tosteson TD, et al: Surgical vs nonoperative treatment for lumbar disk herniation: The Spine Patient Outcomes Research Trial (SPORT) observational cohort. *JAMA* 2006;296(20):2451-2459.

   Patients in the observation cohort of the SPORT study were treated without randomization. The outcomes of diskectomy were favorable.

2. Peul WC, van den Hout WB, Brand R, Thomeer RT, Koes BW; Leiden-The Hague Spine Intervention Prognostic Study Group: Prolonged conservative care versus early surgery in patients with sciatica caused by lumbar disc herniation: Two year results of a randomised controlled trial. *BMJ* 2008;336(7657):1355-1358.

   Diskectomy had favorable outcomes in a European randomized controlled study.

3. Cribb GL, Jaffray DC, Cassar-Pullicino VN: Observations on the natural history of massive lumbar disc herniation. *J Bone Joint Surg Br* 2007;89(6):782-784.

   The natural history of lumbar HNP is relatively favorable, with a low rate of neurologic emergency.

4. Weinstein JN, Lurie JD, Tosteson TD, et al: Surgical versus nonoperative treatment for lumbar disc herniation: Four-year results for the Spine Patient Outcomes Research Trial (SPORT). *Spine (Phila Pa 1976)* 2008; 33(25):2789-2800.

4: The Adult Spine

Four-year follow-up of the full SPORT study group, including patients in both the randomized and observational cohorts, revealed that relief of symptoms was more rapid with surgery.

5. Peul WC, van Houwelingen HC, van den Hout WB, et al: Surgery versus prolonged conservative treatment for sciatica. N Engl J Med 2007;356(22):2245-2256.

A European study found that relief of symptoms was more rapid after surgery than after nonsurgical treatment.

6. Suri P, Hunter DJ, Jouve C, et al: Inciting events associated with lumbar disc herniation. Spine J 2010;10(5):388-395.

Most disk herniations are not traumatic but are associated with activities of daily living.

7. Carragee EJ, Han MY, Suen PW, Kim D: Clinical outcomes after lumbar discectomy for sciatica: The effects of fragment type and anular competence. J Bone Joint Surg Am 2003;85-A(1):102-108.

8. Wera GD, Marcus RE, Ghanayem AJ, Bohlman HH: Failure within one year following subtotal lumbar discectomy. J Bone Joint Surg Am 2008;90(1):10-15.

This study sought to confirm and expand the Carragee classification of disk herniations.

9. Foley KT, Smith MM, Rampersaud YR: Microendoscopic approach to far-lateral lumbar disc herniation. Neurosurg Focus 1999;7(5):e5.

10. Ahn UM, Ahn NU, Buchowski JM, Garrett ES, Sieber AN, Kostuik JP: Cauda equina syndrome secondary to lumbar disc herniation: A meta-analysis of surgical outcomes. Spine (Phila Pa 1976) 2000;25(12):1515-1522.

11. Olivero WC, Wang H, Hanigan WC, et al: Cauda equina syndrome (CES) from lumbar disc herniations. J Spinal Disord Tech 2009;22(3):202-206.

The outcomes of diskectomy for cauda equina syndrome were examined.

12. Qureshi A, Sell P: Cauda equina syndrome treated by surgical decompression: The influence of timing on surgical outcome. Eur Spine J 2007;16(12):2143-2151.

Time to surgery was correlated with neurologic improvement after cauda equina syndrome.

13. Cahill KS, Dunn I, Gunnarsson T, Proctor MR: Lumbar microdiscectomy in pediatric patients: A large single-institution series. J Neurosurg Spine 2010;12(2):165-170.

This is a case study of microdiskectomy in adolescents after unsuccessful nonsurgical management.

14. Carragee E, Alamin T, Cheng I, Franklin T, van den Haak E, Hurwitz E: Are first-time episodes of serious LBP associated with new MRI findings? Spine J 2006;6(6):624-635.

New episodes of low back pain are not well correlated with MRI changes.

15. Waris E, Eskelin M, Hermunen H, Kiviluoto O, Paajanen H: Disc degeneration in low back pain: A 17-year follow-up study using magnetic resonance imaging. Spine (Phila Pa 1976) 2007;32(6):681-684.

Early disk degeneration predicts MRI progression but not symptoms.

16. Masui T, Yukawa Y, Nakamura S, et al: Natural history of patients with lumbar disc herniation observed by magnetic resonance imaging for minimum 7 years. J Spinal Disord Tech 2005;18(2):121-126.

17. Chin KR, Tomlinson DT, Auerbach JD, Shatsky JB, Deirmengian CA: Success of lumbar microdiscectomy in patients with modic changes and low-back pain: A prospective pilot study. J Spinal Disord Tech 2008;21(2):139-144.

Modic changes are not well correlated with the outcome of diskectomy.

18. Albert HB, Manniche C: Modic changes following lumbar disc herniation. Eur Spine J 2007;16(7):977-982.

Modic changes are related to both herniation and nonspecific back symptoms.

19. Albert H, Pedersen H, Manniche C, Høilund-Carlsen PF: PET imaging in patients with Modic changes. Nuklearmedizin 2009;48(3):110-112.

Type I Modic changes are not associated with increased positron emission tomography uptake.

20. Zou J, Yang H, Miyazaki M, et al: Missed lumbar disc herniations diagnosed with kinetic magnetic resonance imaging. Spine (Phila Pa 1976) 2008;33(5):E140-E144.

Dynamic MRI was claimed to increase the rate of diagnosed HNP.

21. Parent EC, Videman T, Battié MC: The effect of lumbar flexion and extension on disk contour abnormality measured quantitatively on magnetic resonance imaging. Spine (Phila Pa 1976) 2006;31(24):2836-2842.

The appearance of disk herniation varied on MRI in a flexed, extended, or neutral position.

22. Ferreiro Perez A, Garcia Isidro M, Ayerbe E, Castedo J, Jinkins JR: Evaluation of intervertebral disc herniation and hypermobile intersegmental instability in symptomatic adult patients undergoing recumbent and upright MRI of the cervical or lumbosacral spines. Eur J Radiol 2007;62(3):444-448.

Herniation with listhesis is more apparent on upright MRI than on recumbent MRI, but the clinical significance is unclear.

23. Massoud TF, Gambhir SS: Molecular imaging in living subjects: Seeing fundamental biological processes in a new light. Genes Dev 2003;17(5):545-580.

24. Wunder A, Straub RH, Gay S, Funk J, Müller-Ladner U: Molecular imaging: Novel tools in visualizing rheumatoid arthritis. *Rheumatology (Oxford)* 2005;44(11): 1341-1349.

This is a position paper on the use of molecular imaging with a known pathogenesis of rheumatoid arthritis.

25. Chou R, Atlas SJ, Stanos SP, Rosenquist RW: Nonsurgical interventional therapies for low back pain: A review of the evidence for an American Pain Society Clinical Practice Guideline. *Spine (Phila Pa 1976)* 2009; 34(10):1078-1093.

The evidence for epidural steroid injection as a treatment for radiculopathic pain secondary to HNP is comprehensively reviewed.

26. Staal JB, de Bie RA, de Vet HC, Hildebrandt J, Nelemans P: Injection therapy for subacute and chronic low back pain: An updated Cochrane review. *Spine (Phila Pa 1976)* 2009;34(1):49-59.

The evidence for epidural steroid injection as a treatment for back pain but not leg pain is comprehensively reviewed.

27. Buenaventura RM, Datta S, Abdi S, Smith HS: Systematic review of therapeutic lumbar transforaminal epidural steroid injections. *Pain Physician* 2009;12(1):233-251.

The treatment indications for epidural steroid injection in lumbar pain syndromes are reviewed.

28. Manchikanti L, Singh V, Cash KA, Pampati V, Damron KS, Boswell MV: Preliminary results of a randomized, equivalence trial of fluoroscopic caudal epidural injections in managing chronic low back pain: Part 2. Disc herniation and radiculitis. *Pain Physician* 2008;11(6): 801-815.

This is a clinical study of epidural steroid injection and corticosteroids for lumbar pain syndromes from the caudal approach.

29. Tafazal S, Ng L, Chaudhary N, Sell P: Corticosteroids in peri-radicular infiltration for radicular pain: A randomised double blind controlled trial. One year results and subgroup analysis. *Eur Spine J* 2009;18(8):1220-1225.

Corticosteroids were studied for radicular pain syndromes relevant to steroid efficacy.

30. Tachihara H, Sekiguchi M, Kikuchi S, Konno S: Do corticosteroids produce additional benefit in nerve root infiltration for lumbar disc herniation? *Spine (Phila Pa 1976)* 2008;33(7):743-747.

A model system of steroid infiltration for pain relief was studied.

31. Ackerman WE III, Zhang JM: Serum hs-CRP as a useful marker for predicting the efficacy of lumbar epidural steroid injections on pain relief in patients with lumbar disc herniations. *J Ky Med Assoc* 2006;104(7):295-299.

The sensitivity, but not specificity, of high-sensitivity C-reactive protein was evaluated as a biomarker for response to epidural steroid injection for the indication of radiculopathy.

32. Scuderi GJ, Brusovanik GV, Anderson DG, et al: Cytokine assay of the epidural space lavage in patients with lumbar intervertebral disk herniation and radiculopathy. *J Spinal Disord Tech* 2006;19(4):266-269.

The technique of epidural cannulation and lavage was documented for purposes of biomarker investigation.

33. Kohane DS, Smith SE, Louis DN, et al: Prolonged duration local anesthesia from tetrodotoxin-enhanced local anesthetic microspheres. *Pain* 2003;104(1-2):415-421.

34. Palmer GM, Cairns BE, Berkes SL, Dunning PS, Taylor GA, Berde CB: The effects of lidocaine and adrenergic agonists on rat sciatic nerve and skeletal muscle blood flow in vivo. *Anesth Analg* 2002;95(4):1080-1086.

35. Dräger C, Benziger D, Gao F, Berde CB: Prolonged intercostal nerve blockade in sheep using controlled-release of bupivacaine and dexamethasone from polymer microspheres. *Anesthesiology* 1998;89(4):969-979.

36. Castillo J, Curley J, Hotz J, et al: Glucocorticoids prolong rat sciatic nerve blockade in vivo from bupivacaine microspheres. *Anesthesiology* 1996;85(5):1157-1166.

37. Krogman NR, Singh A, Nair LS, Laurencin CT, Allcock HR: Miscibility of bioerodible polyphosphazene/ poly(lactide-co-glycolide) blends. *Biomacromolecules* 2007;8(4):1306-1312.

This is a chemical engineering reference for combined preparations of novel and traditional polymers for controlled drug delivery.

38. Ibim SM, el-Amin SF, Goad ME, Ambrosio AM, Allcock HR, Laurencin CT: In vitro release of colchicine using poly(phosphazenes): The development of delivery systems for musculoskeletal use. *Pharm Dev Technol* 1998;3(1):55-62.

39. Murata Y, Nannmark U, Rydevik B, Takahashi K, Olmarker K: The role of tumor necrosis factor-alpha in apoptosis of dorsal root ganglion cells induced by herniated nucleus pulposus in rats. *Spine (Phila Pa 1976)* 2008;33(2):155-162.

An animal model was used in a study of the role of TNF-α in the dorsal root ganglion for HNP.

40. Murata Y, Nannmark U, Rydevik B, Takahashi K, Olmarker K: Nucleus pulposus-induced apoptosis in dorsal root ganglion following experimental disc herniation in rats. *Spine (Phila Pa 1976)* 2006;31(4):382-390.

An animal model was used in a study of the role of TNF-α in the dorsal root ganglion for HNP.

41. Korhonen T, Karppinen J, Paimela L, et al: The treatment of disc-herniation-induced sciatica with infliximab: One-year follow-up results of FIRST II, a randomized controlled trial. *Spine (Phila Pa 1976)* 2006; 31(24):2759-2766.

A commercially available TNF-α inhibitor for the indication of HNP was evaluated in a randomized clinical study.

42. Gibson JN, Waddell G: Surgical interventions for lumbar disc prolapse: Updated Cochrane Review. *Spine (Phila Pa 1976)* 2007;32(16):1735-1747.

   An updated Cochrane review of the world literature on surgical treatment of HNP includes the history of chymopapain chemonucleolysis.

43. Wu Z, Wei LX, Li J, et al: Percutaneous treatment of non-contained lumbar disc herniation by injection of oxygen-ozone combined with collagenase. *Eur J Radiol* 2009;72(3):499-504.

   The combined use of ozone and collagenase for HNP was studied.

44. Muto M, Ambrosanio G, Guarnieri G, et al: Low back pain and sciatica: Treatment with intradiscal-intraforaminal O(2)-O (3) injection: Our experience. *Radiol Med* 2008;113(5):695-706.

   This is a clinical report of oxygen-ozone intradiskal therapy for HNP.

45. Gazzeri R, Galarza M, Neroni M, Esposito S, Alfieri A: Fulminating septicemia secondary to oxygen-ozone therapy for lumbar disc herniation: Case report. *Spine (Phila Pa 1976)* 2007;32(3):E121-E123.

   A serious complication from intradiskal oxygen-ozone therapy was reported.

46. Vadalà G, Sowa GA, Kang JD: Gene therapy for disc degeneration. *Expert Opin Biol Ther* 2007;7(2):185-196.

   A leading group in the pursuit of gene therapies for disk degeneration presents a comprehensive review.

47. Sobajima S, Vadala G, Shimer A, Kim JS, Gilbertson LG, Kang JD: Feasibility of a stem cell therapy for intervertebral disc degeneration. *Spine J* 2008;8(6):888-896.

   This is a pilot study on intradiskal therapy of stem cells.

48. Anderson DG, Risbud MV, Shapiro IM, Vaccaro AR, Albert TJ: Cell-based therapy for disc repair. *Spine J* 2005;5(6, suppl):297S-303S.

   This is a report and review of the prospects for using stem cells for intradiskal regeneration and repair.

49. Cuellar JM, Golish SR, Reuter MW, et al: Cytokine evaluation in individuals with low back pain using discographic lavage. *Spine J* 2010;10(3):212-218.

   A proteomic study of inflammatory biomarkers in the epidural space in humans was conducted.

50. Carragee EJ, Don AS, Hurwitz EL, Cuellar JM, Carrino JA, Herzog R: Does discography cause accelerated progression of degeneration changes in the lumbar disc? A ten-year matched cohort study. *Spine (Phila Pa 1976)* 2009;34(21):2338-2345.

   An award-winning study presented the long-term effect of cannulation of the intradiskal space for provocative diskography.

51. Karppinen J, Korhonen T, Malmivaara A, et al: Tumor necrosis factor-alpha monoclonal antibody, infliximab, used to manage severe sciatica. *Spine (Phila Pa 1976)* 2003;28(8):750-754.

52. Greenland S: An introduction to instrumental variables for epidemiologists. *Int J Epidemiol* 2000;29(4):722-729.

53. Greenland S, Pearl J, Robins JM: Causal diagrams for epidemiologic research. *Epidemiology* 1999;10(1):37-48.

54. Hernán MA, Robins JM: Instruments for causal inference: An epidemiologist's dream? *Epidemiology* 2006;17(4):360-372.

   Causality and its relationship to the analysis of studies with partial compliance are conceptually reviewed.

55. Carragee E: Surgical treatment of lumbar disk disorders. *JAMA* 2006;296(20):2485-2487.

56. Peul WC, Brand R, Thomeer RT, Koes BW: Improving prediction of "inevitable" surgery during non-surgical treatment of sciatica. *Pain* 2008;138(3):571-576.

57. Buttermann GR: Treatment of lumbar disc herniation: Epidural steroid injection compared with discectomy. A prospective, randomized study. *J Bone Joint Surg Am* 2004;86(4):670-679.

58. Tosteson AN, Skinner JS, Tosteson TD, et al: The cost effectiveness of surgical versus nonoperative treatment for lumbar disc herniation over two years: Evidence from the Spine Patient Outcomes Research Trial (SPORT). *Spine (Phila Pa 1976)* 2008;33(19):2108-2115.

   A SPORT analysis indicated that the cost of surgical treatment was greater than that of nonsurgical management.

59. Golish SR, DeHart MM: Principles of practice and statistics, in Miller MD, ed: *Review of Orthopaedics*, ed 5. New York, NY, Elsevier, 2008, pp 661-687.

60. van den Hout WB, Peul WC, Koes BW, et al: Prolonged conservative care versus early surgery in patients with sciatica from lumbar disc herniation: Cost utility analysis alongside a randomised controlled trial. *BMJ* 2008;336(7657):1351-1354.

   A European estimate of the total cost of surgical management included the societal costs of nonsurgical management.

61. Hansson E, Hansson T: The cost-utility of lumbar disc herniation surgery. *Eur Spine J* 2007;16(3):329-337.

   A European study included the societal cost of lumbar disk disease and its management.

62. Katayama Y, Matsuyama Y, Yoshihara H, et al: Comparison of surgical outcomes between macro discectomy and micro discectomy for lumbar disc herniation: A prospective randomized study with surgery performed by the same spine surgeon. *J Spinal Disord Tech* 2006; 19(5):344-347.

A single-surgeon randomized study found that both traditional open diskectomy and microdiskectomy are safe and effective.

63. Carragee EJ, Spinnickie AO, Alamin TF, Paragioudakis S: A prospective controlled study of limited versus subtotal posterior discectomy: Short-term outcomes in patients with herniated lumbar intervertebral discs and large posterior anular defect. *Spine (Phila Pa 1976)* 2006;31(6):653-657.

Subtotal diskectomy has lower recurrence rates than total diskectomy, with good early outcomes but poorer ultimate outcomes.

64. McGirt MJ, Ambrossi GL, Datoo G, et al: Recurrent disc herniation and long-term back pain after primary lumbar discectomy: Review of outcomes reported for limited versus aggressive disc removal. *Neurosurgery* 2009;64(2):338-345.

The effect of disk removal extent on pain and recurrence rate is examined.

65. McGirt MJ, Eustacchio S, Varga P, et al: A prospective cohort study of close interval computed tomography and magnetic resonance imaging after primary lumbar discectomy: Factors associated with recurrent disc herniation and disc height loss. *Spine (Phila Pa 1976)* 2009;34(19):2044-2051.

The radiographic parameters after diskectomy include a loss of height as the extent of disk removal increases.

66. Papadopoulos EC, Girardi FP, Sandhu HS, et al: Outcome of revision discectomies following recurrent lumbar disc herniation. *Spine (Phila Pa 1976)* 2006;31(13): 1473-1476.

Revision diskectomy has acceptable outcomes but a higher complication rate than primary surgery.

67. Ambrossi GL, McGirt MJ, Sciubba DM, et al: Recurrent lumbar disc herniation after single-level lumbar discectomy: Incidence and health care cost analysis. *Neurosurgery* 2009;65(3):574-578.

Revision diskectomy is associated with higher costs and more complications than primary surgery.

68. Boelen EJ, Koole LH, van Rhijn LW, van Hooy-Corstjens CS: Towards a functional radiopaque hydrogel for nucleus pulposus replacement. *J Biomed Mater Res B Appl Biomater* 2007;83(2):440-450.

A bioengineering approach to a nucleus pulposus replacement procedure is presented.

69. Hegewald AA, Knecht S, Baumgartner D, et al: Biomechanical testing of a polymer-based biomaterial for the restoration of spinal stability after nucleotomy. *J Orthop Surg Res* 2009;4:25.

The development of a polymer-engineered nucleus pulposus replacement device is described.

70. Bron JL, Helder MN, Meisel HJ, Van Royen BJ, Smit TH: Repair, regenerative and supportive therapies of the annulus fibrosus: Achievements and challenges. *Eur Spine J* 2009;18(3):301-313.

Trends in the repair of a ruptured anulus fibrosus are described.

71. Chou R, Baisden J, Carragee EJ, Resnick DK, Shaffer WO, Loeser JD: Surgery for low back pain: A review of the evidence for an American Pain Society Clinical Practice Guideline. *Spine (Phila Pa 1976)* 2009;34(10): 1094-1109.

The evidence is comprehensively reviewed for all types of surgical interventions related to lumbar decompression, including percutaneous procedures.

72. Arts MP, Brand R, van den Akker ME, et al: Tubular diskectomy vs conventional microdiskectomy for sciatica: A randomized controlled trial. *JAMA* 2009;302(2): 149-158.

A European study found similar but somewhat poorer results for microdiskectomy with a tubular retractor compared with a typical microdiskectomy.

73. Jordan K, Dunn KM, Lewis M, Croft P: A minimal clinically important difference was derived for the Roland-Morris Disability Questionnaire for low back pain. *J Clin Epidemiol* 2006;59(1):45-52.

An estimate of the minimum clinically important difference on the Roland-Morris Questionnaire is relevant to the study presented by Arts et al.[72]

74. Ryang YM, Oertel MF, Mayfrank L, Gilsbach JM, Rohde V: Standard open microdiscectomy versus minimal access trocar microdiscectomy: Results of a prospective randomized study. *Neurosurgery* 2008;62(1): 174-182.

A study of microdiskectomy with and without a tube found no differences in multiple process and outcome measures.

75. McLoughlin GS, Fourney DR: The learning curve of minimally-invasive lumbar microdiscectomy. *Can J Neurol Sci* 2008;35(1):75-78.

The learning curve for single-surgeon experience is formally assessed.

76. Ikuta K, Tono O, Tanaka T, et al: Surgical complications of microendoscopic procedures for lumbar spinal stenosis. *Minim Invasive Neurosurg* 2007;50(3):145-149.

The rate of complications as a function of number of procedures is investigated.

77. Rong LM, Xie PG, Shi DH, et al: Spinal surgeons' learning curve for lumbar microendoscopic discectomy: A prospective study of our first 50 and latest 10 cases. *Chin Med J (Engl)* 2008;121(21):2148-2151.

4: The Adult Spine

Complication rates of a group of surgeons at the outset of their surgical experience are prospectively assessed.

78. Ruetten S, Komp M, Godolias G: A New full-endoscopic technique for the interlaminar operation of lumbar disc herniations using 6-mm endoscopes: Prospective 2-year results of 331 patients. *Minim Invasive Neurosurg* 2006;49(2):80-87.

The experience of surgeons in a leading endoscopic group with an interlaminar all-endoscopic approach without tubular retractors experience is presented.

79. Ruetten S, Komp M, Merk H, Godolias G: Full-endoscopic interlaminar and transforaminal lumbar discectomy versus conventional microsurgical technique: A prospective, randomized, controlled study. *Spine (Phila Pa 1976)* 2008;33(9):931-939.

A randomized study compared typical diskectomy with all-endoscopic treatment using interlaminar and transforaminal approaches.

80. Jang JS, An SH, Lee SH: Transforaminal percutaneous endoscopic discectomy in the treatment of foraminal and extraforaminal lumbar disc herniations. *J Spinal Disord Tech* 2006;19(5):338-343.

Foraminal endoscopy was used for specifically foraminal and extraforaminal herniations.

81. Lee SH, Kang BU, Ahn Y, et al: Operative failure of percutaneous endoscopic lumbar discectomy: A radiologic analysis of 55 cases. *Spine (Phila Pa 1976)* 2006;31(10):E285-E290.

Foraminal diskectomy was less likely to be successful if herniation was relatively large, more central, or migrated.

82. Ruetten S, Komp M, Godolias G: An extreme lateral access for the surgery of lumbar disc herniations inside the spinal canal using the full-endoscopic uniportal transforaminal approach-technique and prospective results of 463 patients. *Spine (Phila Pa 1976)* 2005;30(22):2570-2578.

In a large case study, disk herniations were treated with foraminal endoscopy.

83. Brinckmann P, Grootenboer H: Change of disc height, radial disc bulge, and intradiscal pressure from discectomy: An in vitro investigation on human lumbar discs. *Spine (Phila Pa 1976)* 1991;16(6):641-646.

84. Singh V, Manchikanti L, Benyamin RM, Helm S, Hirsch JA: Percutaneous lumbar laser disc decompression: A systematic review of current evidence. *Pain Physician* 2009;12(3):573-588.

The evidence for the percutaneous lumbar laser disk decompression technique was comprehensively reviewed.

85. Singh V, Benyamin RM, Datta S, Falco FJ, Helm S II, Manchikanti L: Systematic review of percutaneous lumbar mechanical disc decompression utilizing Dekompressor. *Pain Physician* 2009;12(3):589-599.

The evidence for the Dekompressor technique (Stryker, Kalamazoo, MI) was comprehensively reviewed.

86. Manchikanti L, Derby R, Benyamin RM, Helm S, Hirsch JA: A systematic review of mechanical lumbar disc decompression with nucleoplasty. *Pain Physician* 2009;12(3):561-572.

The evidence for the nucleoplasty technique was comprehensively reviewed.

87. Hirsch JA, Singh V, Falco FJ, Benyamin RM, Manchikanti L: Automated percutaneous lumbar discectomy for the contained herniated lumbar disc: A systematic assessment of evidence. *Pain Physician* 2009;12(3):601-620.

The evidence for the automated percutaneous lumbar diskectomy technique was comprehensively reviewed.

88. Tassi GP: Comparison of results of 500 microdiscectomies and 500 percutaneous laser disc decompression procedures for lumbar disc herniation. *Photomed Laser Surg* 2006;24(6):694-697.

A comparative study found good outcomes for percutaneous laser-assisted decompressive diskectomy.

89. Nau WH, Diederich CJ: Evaluation of temperature distributions in cadaveric lumbar spine during nucleoplasty. *Phys Med Biol* 2004;49(8):1583-1594.

90. Cuellar VG, Cuellar JM, Vaccaro AR, Carragee EJ, Scuderi GJ: Accelerated degeneration after failed cervical and lumbar nucleoplasty. *J Spinal Disord Tech* 2010;23(8):521-524.

Patients who underwent nucleoplasty had marked disk degeneration compared with control subjects.

91. Brouwer PA, Peul WC, Brand R, et al: Effectiveness of percutaneous laser disc decompression versus conventional open discectomy in the treatment of lumbar disc herniation. Design of a prospective randomized controlled trial. *BMC Musculoskelet Disord* 2009;10:49.

A planned randomized controlled study was designed to compare percutaneous to traditional diskectomy.

Chapter 28

Thoracic Disk Herniation and Stenosis

Gregory Gebauer, MD, MS   Alexander Vaccaro, MD, PhD

4: The Adult Spine

Introduction

Thoracic disk herniation has a confusing spectrum of symptoms and a low incidence. Often it is an incidental finding. These factors are responsible for a continuing lack of consensus as to the optimal treatment methods, even though the condition has been described for 200 years. In addition, the surgical strategies for treating thoracic disk herniation are challenging because of the proximity of the spinal cord and the technical difficulty of anterior thoracic approaches.

Anatomy

The unique anatomy of the thoracic spine affects its biomechanics. Each thoracic vertebra articulates with a rib. The 2nd through 10th ribs connect anteriorly to form the rib cage, thus adding rigidity to the thorax. The facet joints in the upper portion of the thoracic spine are oriented vertically, with only slight coronal angulation. This configuration resists flexion-extension movement while allowing lateral bending. The facet

Dr. Vaccaro or an immediate family member serves as a board member, owner, officer, or committee member of the North American Spine Society, American Spinal Injury Association, and Cervical Spine Research Society; has received royalties from Aesculap/B.Braun, Globus Medical, Medtronic Sofamor Danek, K2M, Stout Medical, Progressive Spinal Technology, Applied Spinal Intellectual Properties, and DePuy, a Johnson & Johnson company; serves as a paid consultant to or is an employee of K2M; has received research or institutional support from AO North America, Medtronic Sofamor Danek, Stryker, and DePuy, a Johnson & Johnson company; and owns stock or stock options in Globus Medical, Disk Motion Technology, Progressive Spinal Technologies, Advanced Spinal Intellectual Properties, Computational Biodynamics, Stout Medical, Paradigm Spine, K2M, Replication Medica, Spinology, Spine Medica, Orthovita, Vertiflex, Small Bone Technologies, NeuCore, Crosscurrent, Syndicom, In Vivo, Flagship Surgical, Pearl Driver, Location Based Intelligence, and Gamma Spine. Neither Dr. Gebauer nor any immediate family member has received anything of value from or owns stock in a commercial company or institution related directly or indirectly to the subject of this chapter.

orientation in the lower thoracic region allows greater flexion-extension movement.

The anatomic features of the thoracic spine may predispose the spinal cord to injury. Both the cord and the spinal canal narrow in the thoracic region; the spinal cord occupies 25% of the canal area in the cervical spine but occupies 40% in the thoracic region. Patients with congenital or acquired canal stenosis are at additional risk for injury. The thoracic spine is curved in kyphosis, which causes the spinal cord to drape over the posterior portion of the vertebral bodies and the posterior longitudinal ligaments. The dentate ligaments tether the cord and limit posterior displacement. These factors may increase the cord's vulnerability to injury from an anterior impingement such as a disk herniation or bone spur. In the T4-T9 middle portion of the thoracic spine, the relatively tenuous blood supply of the spinal cord means that the cord is more susceptible to injury than in other areas of the spine.

Etiology and Natural History

Thoracic disk herniation, like herniation in the cervical or lumbar spine, is believed to result from disk degeneration. The lower incidence of degenerative disk disease in the thoracic spine, in comparison with the cervical or lumbar spine, may be a result of the greater structural support provided by the rib cage. Most thoracic disk herniations occur below T8, where the ribs provide less structural support. Several risk factors for disk disease in the cervical or lumbar spine presumably also increase the risk of thoracic disk disease; they include genetic factors, nicotine use, exposure to high-frequency vibration, and heavy lifting. Thoracic disk herniation also has been associated with Scheuermann kyphosis.

The location of the herniation is important in surgical planning. Central and paracentral thoracic herniations are most common. These herniations typically cause myelopathy. Lateral herniations are less common; they produce radiculopathy symptoms. Rarely, disk material extrudes intradurally, where it can be mistaken for a tumor. Calcification may be present within the herniated disk, and its presence may indicate that the disk is adhering to the dura.

Table 1

The Differential Diagnosis of Thoracic Pain

Musculoskeletal Pain
Neoplastic
Degenerative
  Spondylosis
  Spinal stenosis
  Degenerative disk disease
  Facet syndrome
  Costochondritis
Metabolic
  Osteoporosis
  Osteomalacia
Traumatic
Inflammatory: Ankylosing spondylitis
Deformity-related
  Scoliosis
  Kyphosis
Muscular
  Strain
  Fibromyalgia
  Polymyalgia rheumatica

Neurogenic Pain
Thoracic disk herniation
Neoplastic
  Extradural
  Intradural
    Extramedullary
    Intramedullary
Arteriovenous malformation
Inflammatory: Herpes zoster
Postthoracotomy syndrome
Intercostal neuralgia

Referred Pain
Intrathoracic
  Cardiovascular
  Pulmonary
  Mediastinal
Intra-abdominal
  Gastrointestinal
  Hepatobiliary
Retroperitoneal
  Renal
  Tumor
  Aneurysm

Sociopsychogenic Pain
Depression
Malingering
Münchausen syndrome

Adapted from Garfin SR, Vaccaro AR, eds: *Orthopaedic Knowledge Update: Spine.* Rosemont, IL, American Academy of Orthopaedic Surgeons, 1997, pp 87-96.

Most thoracic disk herniations are asymptomatic, with imaging abnormalities observed only incidentally in as many as 37% of patients.[1] Often a patient is asymptomatic even if there is evidence of herniation compressing the cord. Symptomatic thoracic disk herniation occurs only in 1 of 1 million people and accounts for 0.25% to 1% of all symptomatic disk herniations.[2]

Most patients are 30 to 50 years old. Men and women are affected in equal numbers.

Longitudinal studies of thoracic disk herniation found minimal change over time. Small or medium-size disk herniations tend to be relatively constant in size, with small herniations having a slight tendency to increase in size and only a small percentage of medium-size herniations increasing or decreasing in size. Large herniations tend to decrease in size.

Clinically, the natural course of thoracic herniation is similar to that of lumbar or cervical herniations, with most symptoms resolving over time. In one study, 77% of patients with a symptomatic thoracic disk herniation had symptom improvement and returned to their baseline level of function.[3] Even large herniations causing myelopathy were observed to decrease in size, with concomitant symptom improvement. Because of the infrequency with which thoracic disk herniations occur and the poor understanding of their natural history, the ability to identify patients who are likely to improve with nonsurgical treatment remains limited.

Clinical Evaluation

Examination and Classification

Most patients with symptomatic thoracic disk herniation have axial or radicular pain. Thoracic radiculitis wraps around the chest or abdomen in a dermatomal distribution. An upper thoracic disk herniation can cause arm pain similar to that of a cervical herniation. Similarly, a lower thoracic herniation may mimic a lumbar herniation by causing leg pain. Any neurologic dysfunction appears as lower extremity sensory or motor dysfunction. Signs of myelopathy, including clumsiness of gait and frequent falling, also may be present. These symptoms often are insidious, although in rare instances they occur acutely. Pain is present in 76% of patients with symptomatic thoracic disk herniation and is the most common symptom, followed by sensory and motor impairment, each of which is present in 61% of patients.[4] Bowel or bladder dysfunction appears in 24% of patients. Similar symptoms can arise from several other disorders that must be considered during clinical evaluation[5-8] (Table 1).

Patients with a thoracic disk herniation may have tenderness to palpation over the thoracic spine. Pain may radiate around the ribs to the sternum. Altered sensation in the affected dermatome may be present. Focal, myotomal weakness in the arms or legs is more likely to be related to a cervical or lumbar herniation than to a thoracic herniation. Diffuse weakness and even paralysis in the legs may be related to thoracic myelopathy.[9] Rectus abdominis weakness may occur during truncal flexion, but it is difficult to assess clinically.[5]

Lower extremity hyperreflexia and clonus may suggest thoracic cord compression. Thoracic disk herniation can cause abnormal abdominal reflexes, with asymmetric contracture of the rectus abdominis to gen-

4: The Adult Spine

Table 2

The Anand and Regan Classification of Thoracic Disk Herniation

Grade	Presenting Symptom	Percentage of Patients
I	Predominant thoracic central (axial) pain	28
II	Predominant thoracic radicular pain	5
IIIA	Significant axial and thoracic radicular pain	38
IIIB	Significant axial and lower leg pain, with or without thoracic radicular pain	19
IV	Myelopathy without significant motor weakness	8
V	Paresis or paralysis with significant motor weakness	2

Adapted from Anand N, Regan JJ: Video-assisted thoracoscopic surgery for thoracic disk disease classification and outcome study of 100 consecutive cases with a 2-year minimum follow-up period. *Spine (Phila Pa 1986)* 2002;27(8):871-879.

tle stimulation. Decreased or absent lower extremity reflexes are more suggestive of a lumbar root or cauda compression than a thoracic disk herniation. The presence of the Hoffman sign or upper extremity hyperreflexia suggests a cervical lesion.

The Anand and Regan classification of thoracic disk herniation is based on clinical presentation[10] (Table 2). Axial pain with thoracic radicular symptoms, found in 38% of patients, was the most common symptom, followed in frequency by axial pain only and then by axial and leg pain. A total of 85% of patients had some axial pain.

Imaging

Plain radiographs should be obtained during the initial evaluation. Chest and abdominal radiographs may help in determining any nonspine causes of the patient's symptoms. Spine radiographs may show a degenerative condition such as disk height narrowing, end plate sclerosis, facet arthrosis, or osteophyte formation. Calcification of the disk also may be present.

MRI is the imaging study of choice for evaluating symptomatic thoracic disk herniation (Figure 1). MRI allows direct visualization of the neural elements and disks. Degenerated and extruded disk material generally appears as an intermediate signal on T1-weighted sequences and a decreased signal on T2-weighted sequences. Rarely, extruded disk fragments can be confused with certain spine tumors, and gadolinium contrast may be helpful in making the distinction.

MRI is sensitive but has low specificity, and many asymptomatic disk protrusions are seen incidentally. There is no clinical correlation between the size and pattern of the herniation and the patient's symptoms. No difference in size, location, or cord compression was found among patients with symptomatic or asymptomatic thoracic disk herniation.[1] A symptomatic disk is further assessed on an axial MRI through the herniation. A central or midline herniation is most prominent at the midsagittal line and extends equally on both sides. A paracentral or paramidline herniation is centered slightly to one side but remains medial to the lateral spinal cord margin. A lateral herniation extends laterally beyond the edge of the cord. MRI studies including the thoracic and lumbar spine may be helpful for presurgical localization of the herniation (Figure 2).

CT is much more sensitive than MRI for detecting disk calcification, and it should be considered when planning for surgery, especially when a calcified disk herniation is suspected.[11] The addition of myelography allows the neural elements to be seen and compressive lesions to be identified (Figure 3). The sensitivity and specificity of CT myelograms are similar to those of MRI, with high false-positive rates. Myelography is invasive and carries a small but significant risk of complications.[12] CT myelography is most useful in patients who have a significant spine deformity or are unable to undergo MRI because of a metal susceptibility or the presence of a pacemaker or other implant.

Additional testing occasionally is required to determine whether the patient's symptoms are caused by a thoracic disk herniation or another condition, with the herniation an incidental finding. Electromyography can confirm nerve root involvement, and somatosensory and motor-evoked potentials can exclude a spinal cord lesion. Injections at the level of the suspected nerve root can be both diagnostic and therapeutic. Thoracic diskography has questionable sensitivity and specificity but may be helpful in evaluating the source of pain if the patient's symptoms are primarily thoracic. Recently, there has been concern about possible long-term acceleration of disk degeneration if the anulus fibrosus is penetrated by the needle used in diskography.[13]

Nonsurgical Treatment

Most thoracic disk herniations follow a benign clinical course and are responsive to nonsurgical treatment.[9] Nonsteroidal anti-inflammatory drugs should be used as an initial treatment. A short course of oral corticosteroids can be considered, but the patient should be aware of the associated risks, including osteonecrosis. If the patient has severe pain, narcotic pain medications and muscle relaxants can be used judiciously.

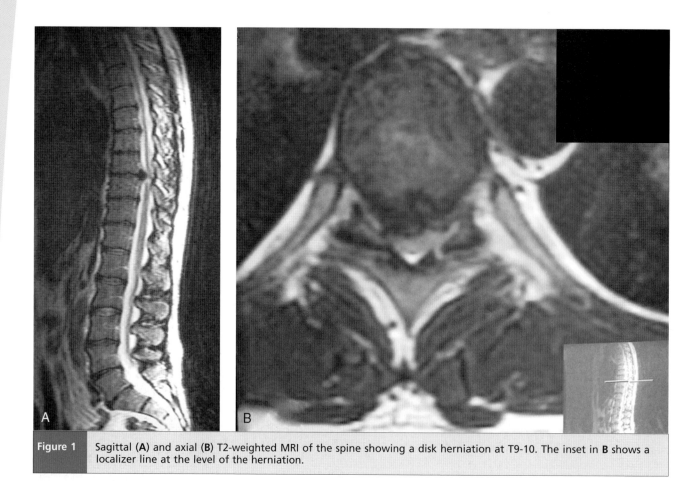

Figure 1   Sagittal (**A**) and axial (**B**) T2-weighted MRI of the spine showing a disk herniation at T9-10. The inset in **B** shows a localizer line at the level of the herniation.

Physical therapy can provide some pain relief.[14] Initially, massage, thermal care, and transcutaneous electrical nerve stimulation can be used to minimize the pain. As the pain abates, the therapy focuses on range of motion, flexibility, and strengthening, with an emphasis on extension-based exercises. Core strengthening and a home exercise program can help to prevent future episodes. Corticosteroid injections may provide some pain relief. These injections are placed into the epidural space, at the nerve root, or into the intercostal space, depending on the patient's symptoms and the morphology of the herniation.

Surgical Treatment

Surgery is indicated if the patient has more than 6 to 8 weeks of severe, recalcitrant radiculopathy or neurologic compromise, especially with signs and symptoms of myelopathy and lower extremity weakness. Because nonsurgical care can be effective in a patient with mild myelopathy, it may be reasonable to observe such a patient for a period of time before proceeding to surgery.

It is estimated that 23% of patients with a symptomatic thoracic disk herniation eventually require surgery.[3] Surgery for axial back pain caused by thoracic disk herniation, like surgery for back pain related to lumbar disk disease, has not been found to provide re-

liable pain relief.[14,15] Therefore, it should be undertaken only with extreme caution.

When a decision in favor of surgery is made, careful preoperative planning and intraoperative vigilance are needed to prevent wrong-site surgery. The level of the herniation should be verified using a preoperative CT myelogram or MRI. A recommended technique is to place the axial image showing the herniation next to a sagittal MRI of the entire spine as a reference for visualizing the sacrum, with a localizer line placed at the level of the herniation. In the operating room, lateral fluoroscopy is then used to count the vertebrae from the sacrum up to the level of the herniation. Other methods of identifying the correct level include counting the ribs on an AP radiograph; identifying disk calcification or bone spurs intraoperatively; or placing a metallic sphere above or below the herniated disk preoperatively under CT or fluoroscopic guidance, then identifying the sphere intraoperatively on plain radiographs.

Surgical Approaches

Thoracic disk herniation traditionally was treated with a laminectomy performed through a direct posterior approach. This approach has been abandoned because of high rates of neurologic decline related to difficult access to the disk space. Several other open or mini-

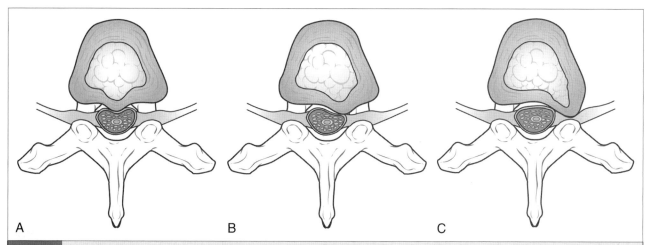

Figure 2 Schematic drawings showing three types of thoracic disk herniation. **A,** Midline or central herniation; the most prominent portion of the disk herniation is at the midline. **B,** Paracentral herniation; the most prominent portion of the herniation is lateral to the midline but medial to the lateral edge of the spinal cord. **C,** Lateral herniation; the most prominent portion of the herniation is lateral to the lateral edge of the spinal cord.

mally invasive approaches have been used. The optimal approach depends on the morphology and location of the disk, the presence or absence of calcifications, and the surgeon's experience. Generally, a better exposure requires more soft-tissue dissection and has a higher associated morbidity (Table 3 and Figure 4). The patient's overall health must be assessed, as some patients may not be able to tolerate a relatively invasive approach.

The Anterior Approach

The anterior approach is most commonly used because it allows excellent visualization of the disk space and anterior thecal sac. Above the T3 level, a transsternal approach is required. Below T3, a thoracotomy is performed. This approach is favored for a large central herniation or a calcified disk that may be adherent to the dura.

An open thoracotomy is carried through the rib space two levels above the pathologic disk level. Dissection is performed through the parietal pleura, necessitating the use of a postoperative chest tube. A portion of the rib may be excised if necessary for the exposure. Midthoracic exposures often require the placement of a double-lumen endotracheal tube to collapse the ipsilateral lung. The approach generally is from the left side, as the thicker walled aorta is more resilient than the vena cava, but it can be altered for a right-side herniation. For a lower thoracic herniation, the diaphragm may have to be incised. After the correct level has been verified, the caudal pedicle is identified and removed to expose the spinal cord underneath (Figure 5). Resection of the rib head and transverse process may help in visualization. Some authors suggest removal of the posterior portion of the vertebral body from the caudal level, which allows a plane to be developed between the dura and the spinal column, away from the compression caused by the disk; this plane can be developed cephalad to aid in disk removal.[16,17]

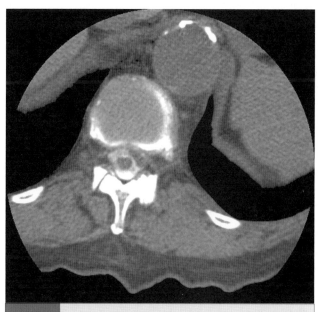

Figure 3 CT myelogram showing a thoracic disk herniation. The calcified disk is impinging on the spinal cord.

Fusion of the level can be considered, based on the amount of disk and bone removed from the cephalad and caudal vertebrae. Below T10, the motion segment is not supported by the rib cage, and fusion is more likely to be required. Arthrodesis generally is performed using an interbody graft, possibly with anteriorly placed instrumentation. Fusion can minimize the risk of future collapse and the development of sagittal imbalance.

Multiple studies reported good to excellent outcomes after an anterior approach was used.[16,17] The anterior approach allows more direct visualization of the disk space and neural elements than other approaches.

Table 3

Comparison of Surgical Approaches to Thoracic Disk Herniation

Surgical Approach	Advantages	Disadvantages
Traditional		
Anterior (transthoracic)	Provides best exposure Can be used for all types of herniations Leaves posterior column intact Is best for calcified disk	Requires a thoracotomy May require a takedown of the diaphragm May not be suitable for a high-risk patient Causes significant postoperative pain
Posterior (transpedicular, costotransversectomy, fenestrated laminectomy)	Causes less soft-tissue disruption Avoids a thoracotomy Is useful for upper thoracic herniation Involves familiar anatomy	Provides poor exposure Can be used only for a lateral herniation Is difficult to use for a calcified disk Cannot be used to treat the ventral dura
Lateral	Is excellent for lateral herniation May allow treatment of central herniation Avoids a thoracotomy Causes less soft-tissue disruption	Disrupts paraspinal muscle Is difficult to use for a calcified disk Requires significant bone resection Requires a longer operating time
Minimally Invasive		
Video-assisted thoracoscopy, endoscopic diskectomy, percutaneous laser diskectomy	Causes less postoperative pain Allows a shorter hospitalization Has a lower rate of complications May be useful for a high-risk patient	Is technically challenging May not adequately treat the pathology Provides poor visualization Is difficult to use for a calcified disk

Adapted from Vanichkachorn J, Vaccaro A: Thoracic disk disease: Diagnosis and treatment. *J Am Acad Orthop Surg* 2000;8(3):159-169.

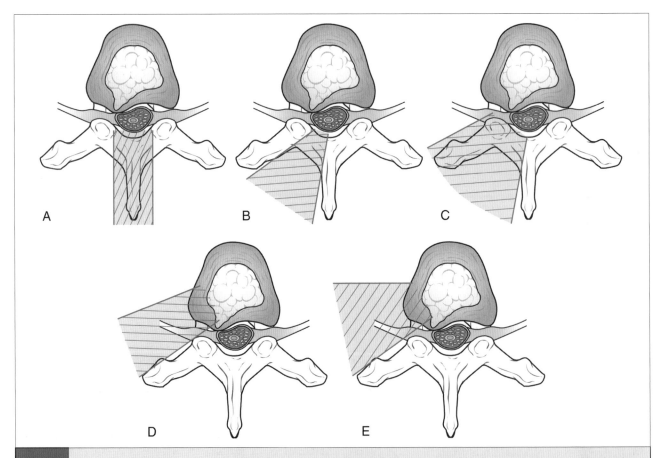

Figure 4   Schematic drawings comparing the relative exposures (diagonal lines) provided by five surgical approaches: laminectomy (**A**), transpedicular (**B**), costotransversectomy (**C**), lateral extracavitary (**D**), and transthoracic (**E**). As the exposure angle becomes more anterior and visualization of the ventral structures improves, the amount of dissection increases.

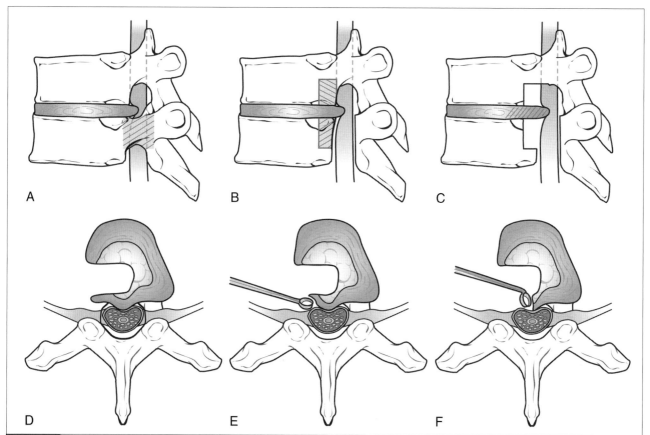

| Figure 5 | Schematic drawings showing steps in the surgical removal of a thoracic disk herniation from an anterior or a lateral approach. Sagittal-view drawings showing removal of the pedicle at the caudal level (A), removal (with a burr) of the posteroinferior aspect of the cranial vertebral body and the posterosuperior aspect of the caudal vertebral body to allow a plane to be developed between the disk and the spinal cord (B), and removal of the disk anterior to the herniation (C). Axial-view drawings showing the initial cavity created in the central portion of the disk (D), the disk elevated anteriorly off the curet (E), and the far side of the disk herniation elevated anteriorly using a reverse-angled curet (F). |

Multiple levels can be treated, if necessary. The incidence of neurologic complications is lower, and the rate of successful disk excision is higher than with other approaches. The disadvantages of the anterior approach are related to the morbidity of thoracotomy. The large incision and retraction and/or the removal of ribs can be extremely painful for the patient and may lead to prolonged limb-girdle dysfunction or respiratory complications.

The Posterolateral Approach
The posterolateral approach includes the transpedicular and costotransversectomy techniques, both of which are performed with the patient prone. Compared with the anterior approach, the relevant anatomy and surgical techniques are familiar to most spine surgeons.

In a transpedicular procedure, the facet joint at the level of the herniation is first removed, followed by the caudal pedicle (Figure 6). The disk space is entered lateral to the spinal cord, and the central disk material is removed. Reverse-angled curets are used to push the herniated disk away from the spinal cord and into the

previously created lateral disk space cavity. If necessary, fusion can be performed using posterior fixation.

A transpedicular approach is best suited for soft, lateral herniations. Its advantages include minimal soft-tissue dissection and little approach-associated morbidity. The disadvantages include limited ability to see the anterior surface of the spinal cord and inability to see the plane between the dura and the herniated disk. This approach therefore is ill suited for a central or paracentral herniation or a relatively large calcified herniation that may be adherent to the dura.

A costotransversectomy is similar to the transpedicular approach, with the addition of a resection of the transverse process and medial portion of the rib. The rib resection allows more lateral angulation and better visualization of the anterior spinal canal than the transpedicular approach. The improved visualization comes at the cost of greater soft-tissue and bone dissection and increased risk of pleural and lung injury. As in the transpedicular approach, the disk is entered laterally, and the central disk material is removed. Reverse-angled curets are used to push the herniation back into

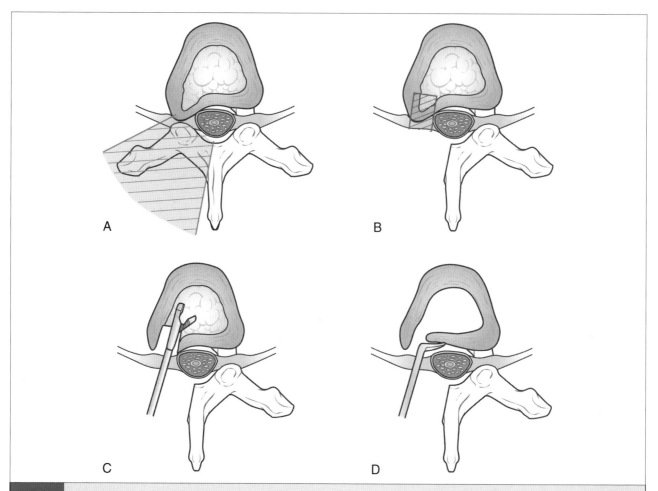

Figure 6 Schematic drawings showing thoracic disk removal from a posterolateral transpedicular approach. **A,** The medial facet, transverse process, and pedicle of the caudal level are removed. **B,** The disk is entered laterally. **C,** The central disk space is cleared using a pituitary rongeur. **D,** The herniated disk is pushed anteriorly away from the spinal cord and into the cavity at the center of the disk space, using a reverse-angled curet.

the disk space. The costotransversectomy technique allows less visualization than an anterior approach, but it avoids the morbidity of a thoracotomy.

In the recently described fenestrated posterior approach, the pedicle is spared, and a burr is used to open the lamina above and below the level of the herniation.[18] This technique spares the facet joint and provides limited access that may be appropriate for a soft lateral herniation. There is only minimal visualization, however, and any concerns as to the adequacy of the exposure should lead to conversion to a transpedicular or costotransversectomy approach. Only very limited experience with this approach has been reported.[18]

The Lateral Approach

The lateral approach to the thoracic spine is a modification of a standard thoracotomy. The medial rib is removed at the surgical level. The approach remains extrapleural, and no postoperative chest tube is required. The facet joint and pedicle are removed to allow access to the spinal canal. The lateral approach allows excellent access to a lateral or paracentral herniation. Although the exposure of a midline herniation is limited, the lateral approach may be appropriate if a formal thoracotomy is contraindicated. In addition, it may be difficult to repair dural injuries over the anterior portion of the spinal cord. The lateral approach should be selected only with caution if the herniation is large and calcified.

The advantages of the lateral approach are that it avoids pleural cavity violation or a diaphragmatic incision at a lower thoracic level, while allowing better exposure than a posteriorly directed approach, especially for a lateral herniation. Its disadvantages include the disruption of the paraspinal muscles and the need to resect the intercostal neurovascular bundle, which can cause postoperative pain.

Minimally Invasive Surgery

Video-Assisted Thoracoscopic Surgery

Video-assisted thoracoscopic surgery (VATS) is a minimally invasive technique that was first used for draining perivertebral abscesses and later was adapted for anterior releases in deformity correction, osteotomies, corpectomies, and disk herniation procedures. The patient is positioned laterally, generally onto the right side, and leaning slightly forward. A double-lumen endotracheal tube is used, and the left lung is deflated. Three or four working portals are used to contain trocars and cannulas through which instruments can be passed into the thoracic cavity. The surgical level is visually confirmed by counting the ribs from inside the thoracic cavity and is reconfirmed fluoroscopically. The diskectomy technique is similar to that of a standard anterior approach. The pedicle and portions of the posterior vertebral bodies are burred away. An experienced surgeon can use VATS to treat midline, paramedial, or lateral herniations. Treatment of 100 herniations using VATS led to a 70% to 83% clinical success rate and an 84% patient satisfaction rate.[10,19]

The advantages of VATS include minimal soft-tissue injury with excellent disk space visualization. The smaller incisions cause relatively little pain, blood loss, and intercostal neuralgia, with fewer pulmonary complications than a thoracotomy. VATS provides more direct visualization of the anterior portion of the spinal canal than the posterior or lateral approach, and endoscope-provided magnification also aids visualization. The disadvantages of VATS include its technical difficulty; few spine surgeons are familiar with the technique. In addition, not all patients can tolerate the required one-lung ventilation. VATS does not easily allow an implant or structural bone graft to be placed, and access for dural repair is limited.

Microendoscopic Diskectomy

The microendoscopic diskectomy is an adaptation of the standard posterior approach to a minimally invasive technique. Fluoroscopic imaging is used to locate the surgical level, where a starting guidewire is positioned at the transverse process. A 3- to 4-cm incision is made, and serial dilators are used to open up the space. The soft tissue is removed from the bone. Depending on the technique and the extent of required exposure, at least part of the facet joint, transverse process, and/or pedicle is removed. The disk is then entered laterally, and its herniated portion is pushed into the void created by the diskectomy. A 30° or 70° endoscope can provide better medial visualization and minimize the need to manipulate the neural elements.

This approach may be appropriate for lateral and some paracentral herniations but should not be considered for central herniations. In two studies, a good or excellent result was found in 22 of 25 patients or all 10 patients treated with microendoscopic diskectomy.[20-22] Neither study reported any surgical complications. The primary advantage of this technique is the limited soft-tissue dissection required. The primary disadvantage is that, despite the use of side-looking endoscopes, the overall exposure is minimal, and there is limited working space. Access to the anterior surface of the spinal cord also is limited.

Percutaneous Laser Diskectomy

Intradiskal laser use has been described for treating thoracic disk herniation in patients with axial or radicular symptoms.[23,24] A neodymium-yttrium aluminum garnet (Nd-YAG) 1,064-Nm laser is placed into the disk space percutaneously, with the patient under local anesthesia and sedation. A maximal dose is used, at 15 W per 1-second dose and a total per-level dose of 1,000 J. Good results were reported when 68 disks in 42 patients were treated with this technique.[24] The complications included spondylodiskitis, pleural irritation, and pneumothorax. Although percutaneous laser diskectomy is the least invasive means of treating disk herniation, the use of lasers for spine pathology is not universally accepted.

Complications

Neurologic deterioration is the most devastating complication of surgical as well as nonsurgical treatment of thoracic disk herniation. The use of laminectomy was abandoned because more than 50% of patients treated with the technique had later worsening of neurologic status.[25] The use of more modern techniques has lowered the rate of iatrogenic neurologic injury, but it remains a concern during any of these procedures. To minimize the risk of neurologic injury, it is imperative to carefully select the surgical approach so as to ensure adequate visualization. Poor exposure also risks inadequate decompression and a continuation of the patient's symptoms.

Late instability and kyphosis can occur after thoracic diskectomy. This collapse is more common after an anterior approach is used, and it may be associated with aggressive vertebral body resection. Fusion may be an option to minimize this risk. Wrong-level surgery is a concern with all thoracic surgeries. The transthoracic and lateral approaches are associated with severe incisional pain and intercostal neuralgia. Additional reported complications include cerebrospinal fluid leakage, infection, pneumonia, pulmonary embolism, and pleural effusion.

Surgical Outcomes

Overall outcomes can be difficult to compare based on specific techniques, and the few comparative studies have been relatively small. Patients generally can expect good results from surgery, however. Pain was found to improve in 67% to 100% of patients and myelopathic symptoms to improve in 75% to 100%.[25,26] Good or excellent outcomes were described in as many as 64% of studies.[10,17] Although outcome definitions vary among studies, generally they are similar to those listed in Table 4. Study results are summarized by surgical approach in Table 5. The study results also varied by patients' initial symptoms. When clinical success was defined as a 20-point improvement on the Oswestry Disability Index, patients with myelopathy were the most likely to improve (100% of patients), and these

4: The Adult Spine

patients also had the greatest score improvement (from an average 44.75 before surgery to 17.66 at final follow-up). Clinical success was achieved in 68% of patients with purely axial pain, 73% of those with both axial back pain and leg pain, and 82% of those with axial pain and thoracic radicular pain. None of the patients with purely thoracic radicular pain improved.[10] Patients with a larger disk herniation had poorer outcomes than those with a medium-size or small herniation.[29]

Thoracic Stenosis

Thoracic stenosis is much rarer than cervical canal stenosis. Its congenital causes include achondroplasia and other skeletal dysplasias. Thoracic stenosis may be related to Scheuermann kyphosis, Paget disease, diffuse skeletal hyperostosis, or renal osteodystrophy. The acquired conditions causing thoracic stenosis include disk herniation, ossification of the posterior longitudinal ligament, hypertrophy or ossification of the ligamentum flavum, and facet hypertrophy.

Depending on the level of disease, the patient may have both upper and lower motor neuron symptoms. The lower thoracic canal houses the lumbosacral enlargement, from which the lower thoracic, lumbar, and sacral nerve roots arise. Concomitant lumbar stenosis can mask some upper motor neuron findings. The stenosis may be intermittent because of dynamic instability or variation in spinal cord blood flow.

As with thoracic disk herniation, thoracic stenosis is diagnosed by careful, thorough examination and advanced imaging. MRI and CT myelography can identify canal compromise. Often there are multiple levels of compression, and identifying an isolated level or region of stenosis therefore can be difficult. The surgeon may need to decide between performing a smaller surgery or decompressing multiple levels to ensure that all disease levels are treated. Cervical and lumbar imaging studies should be obtained.

The options for treating thoracic stenosis are both nonsurgical and surgical. Nonsurgical treatment can include physical therapy, bracing, anti-inflammatory drugs, and activity modification. The use of thoracic epidural injections for severe stenosis should be avoided because the available information is inadequate.

Surgery is indicated for a patient with myelopathy and neurologic dysfunction if nonsurgical treatment is unsuccessful. A decompressive laminectomy is the procedure of choice.[30] Concomitant lumbar stenosis also can be treated through this extensile approach. An adjuvant fusion should be considered if the patient has severe kyphosis, especially with Scheuermann disease, or a need for extensive bony resection.

Table 4

Terms Used to Define Outcomes

Term	Definition (Patient Status)
Excellent	No symptoms; full recovery
Good	Slight pain or weakness; ability to return to usual activities
Fair	Persistent moderate pain or weakness that interferes with activities
Poor	No improvement from preoperative status
Failure	Worse pain or function than before surgery

Table 5

Reported Patient Outcomes by Surgical Approach

Surgical Approach	Study	Neurologic Improvement	Pain Improvement	Functional Outcome	Patient Satisfaction
Anterior	Bohlman and Zdeblick[17]	12 of 14 patients	18 of 19 patients	NR	16 of 19 (good or excellent)
Transpedicular	Bilsky[27]	13 of 14 patients	4 of 6 patients	NR	NR
Fenestrated posterior	Nasser[18]	5 of 5 patients	4 of 5 patients	NR	NR
Thoracoscopic	Johnson et al[28]	Average = two Frankel grades	75%	NR	NR
Thoracoscopic	Anand and Regan[10]	NR	NR	73% had > 20-point improvement on Owestry Disability Index	84%
Microendoscopic	Jho[20]	12 of 13 patients	9 of 10 patients	NR	NR
Percutaneous laser	Hellinger et al[24]	NR	41 of 42 patients	NR	NR

NR = not reported.

The data on surgical outcomes for thoracic stenosis are limited to small case studies, which have reported generally good results. At an average 5-year follow-up after surgery for thoracic or thoracolumbar stenosis, 8 of 12 patients had decreased pain, 7 of 11 patients had improved gait and ambulation, and 8 of 10 patients had improved motor function.[31] Five of the 12 patients required additional surgery for recurrent stenosis or instability.

Summary

Thoracic disk herniation and thoracic stenosis are uncommon conditions that present both diagnostic and therapeutic challenges. A thorough examination and MRI or CT myelography are needed to establish the diagnosis. Surgery is indicated if the patient has neurologic compromise or myelopathy or if nonsurgical treatment has been unsuccessful. It is essential to carefully determine the pathologic level during surgery to prevent wrong-site surgery. Several surgical approaches can be used for thoracic disk herniation. The selection of the most appropriate technique depends on patient-related factors including overall health, the size and location of the herniation, and whether the herniation is calcified; and surgeon-related factors including ease and experience with each technique. Surgical treatment of thoracic disk herniation or thoracic stenosis can be expected to provide good results in terms of both pain relief and improved neurologic function.

Annotated References

1. Awwad EE, Martin DS, Smith KR Jr, Baker BK: Asymptomatic versus symptomatic herniated thoracic discs: Their frequency and characteristics as detected by computed tomography after myelography. *Neurosurgery* 1991;28(2):180-186.

2. Arce CA, Dohrmann GJ: Thoracic disc herniation: Improved diagnosis with computed tomographic scanning and a review of the literature. *Surg Neurol* 1985;23(4):356-361.

3. Brown CW, Deffer PA Jr, Akmakjian J, Donaldson DH, Brugman JL: The natural history of thoracic disc herniation. *Spine (Phila Pa 1976)* 1992;17(suppl 6):S97-S102.

4. Stillerman CB, Chen TC, Couldwell WT, Zhang W, Weiss MH: Experience in the surgical management of 82 symptomatic herniated thoracic discs and review of the literature. *J Neurosurg* 1998;88(4):623-633.

5. Stetkarova I, Chrobok J, Ehler E, Kofler M: Segmental abdominal wall paresis caused by lateral low thoracic disc herniation. *Spine (Phila Pa 1976)* 2007;32(22):E635-E639.

Two patients with thoracic disk herniation had abdominal pain and paresis of the oblique abdominis muscle. Electromyelograms confirmed nerve root involvement. Both patients responded to nonsurgical treatment. Level of evidence: IV.

6. Ozturk C, Tezer M, Sirvanci M, Sarier M, Aydogan M, Hamzaoglu A: Far lateral thoracic disc herniation presenting with flank pain. *Spine J* 2006;6(2):201-203.

In a patient with far-lateral disk herniation causing flank pain, the symptoms mimicked those of a urinary tract infection. The patient responded to nonsurgical care, with complete relief of symptoms.

7. Paolini S, Ciappetta P, Guiducci A, Principi M, Missori P, Delfini R: Foraminal deposition of calcium pyrophosphate dihydrate crystals in the thoracic spine: Possible relationship with disc herniation and implications for surgical planning. Report of two cases. *J Neurosurg Spine* 2005;2(1):75-78.

Thoracic radiculopathy in two patients was thought to be caused by a hard, calcified herniated disk. During surgical decompression the lesions were found to be soft and to contain calcium pyrophosphate crystals. Level of evidence: IV.

8. Rohde RS, Kang JD: Thoracic disc herniation presenting with chronic nausea and abdominal pain: A case report. *J Bone Joint Surg Am* 2004;86(2):379-381.

9. Sasaki S, Kaji K, Shiba K: Upper thoracic disc herniation followed by acutely progressing paraplegia. *Spinal Cord* 2005;43(12):741-745.

A 37-year-old man had acute paraplegia after 5 days of antecedent back pain. A T2-3 disk herniation was found on MRI, and he underwent emergency surgical decompression. The patient's neurologic status was improved 4 weeks after surgery. Level of evidence: IV.

10. Anand N, Regan JJ: Video-assisted thoracoscopic surgery for thoracic disc disease: Classification and outcome study of 100 consecutive cases with a 2-year minimum follow-up period. *Spine (Phila Pa 1976)* 2002;27(8):871-879.

11. Barbanera A, Serchi E, Fiorenza V, Nina P, Andreoli A: Giant calcified thoracic herniated disc: Considerations aiming a proper surgical strategy. *J Neurosurg Sci* 2009;53(1):19-26.

Six of seven patients with a giant calcified herniated thoracic disk were treated with an anterior approach, and one was treated with a costotransversectomy. The American Spinal Injury Association grade improved in five patients, was unchanged in one, and was worse in one. Level of evidence: IV.

12. Cordier D, Wasner MG, Gluecker T, Gratzl O, Merlo A: Acute paraplegia after myelography: Decompensation of a herniated thoracic disc. *Br J Neurosurg* 2008;22(5):684-686.

A 71-year-old man developed acute paraplegia after a myelogram, and a T10-11 disk herniation was found. The patient improved after surgical decompression. Level of evidence: IV.

13. Carragee EJ, Don AS, Hurwitz EL, Cuellar JM, Carrino JA, Herzog R: 2009 ISSLS Prize Winner: Does discography cause accelerated progression of degeneration changes in the lumbar disc. A ten-year matched cohort study. *Spine (Phila Pa 1976)* 2009;34(21):2338-2345.

A 10-year study found that diskography using modern techniques had negative disk degeneration consequences, compared with the progression in matched control subjects.

14. Derby R, Chen Y, Lee SH, Seo KS, Kim BJ: Nonsurgical interventional treatment of cervical and thoracic radiculopathies. *Pain Physician* 2004;7(3):389-394.

15. Haro H, Domoto T, Maekawa S, Horiuchi T, Komori H, Hamada Y: Resorption of thoracic disc herniation: Report of 2 cases. *J Neurosurg Spine* 2008;8(3):300-304.

Two patients with acute myelopathy from thoracic disk herniation were treated nonsurgically with nonsteroidal anti-inflammatory drugs, steroids, and physical therapy. The herniations resorbed over time, and the patients had clinical improvement. Level of evidence: IV.

16. Ohnishi K, Miyamoto K, Kanamori Y, Kodama H, Hosoe H, Shimizu K: Anterior decompression and fusion for multiple thoracic disc herniation. *J Bone Joint Surg Br* 2005;87(3):326-360.

Of 12 patients with multiple thoracic disk herniations treated through an anterior thoracotomy, 4 had a good or excellent result, 6 had a fair result, and 2 had a poor result. Three patients had neurologic improvement.

17. Bohlman HH, Zdeblick TA: Anterior excision of herniated thoracic discs. *J Bone Joint Surg Am* 1988;70(7):1038-1047.

18. Nasser MJ: Standard fenestration approach to thoracic disc herniation. *Br J Neurosurg* 2009;23(4):418-421.

A fenestration technique was used to treat six thoracic disk herniations in five patients, with a 6-month to 3-year follow-up. The authors concluded that the technique is safe and reported good clinical outcomes. Level of evidence: IV.

19. Gille O, Soderlund C, Razafimahandri HJ, Mangione P, Vital JM: Analysis of hard thoracic herniated discs: Review of 18 cases operated by thoracoscopy. *Eur Spine J* 2006;15(5):537-542.

Of 18 patients operated on for hard thoracic disk herniation, 83% had neurologic improvement. Eleven patients had no plane separating the dura from the herniation. Three herniations were intradural. In four patients, the adherent portion of the disk was left to avoid a dural tear. Level of evidence: IV.

20. Jho HD: Endoscopic transpedicular thoracic discectomy. *Neurosurg Focus* 2000;9(4):e4.

21. Lidar Z, Lifshutz J, Bhattacharjee S, Kurpad SN, Maiman DJ: Minimally invasive, extracavitary approach for thoracic disc herniation: Technical report and preliminary results. *Spine J* 2006;6(2):157-163.

A minimally invasive posterolateral approach to the thoracic spine was used in four cadavers, then in 10 patients with a disk herniation. All patients had clinical success, with no complications; 3 of the 10 had an improved American Spinal Injury Association score. Level of evidence: IV.

22. Sheikh H, Samartzis D, Perez-Cruet MJ: Techniques for the operative management of thoracic disc herniation: Minimally invasive thoracic microdiscectomy. *Orthop Clin North Am* 2007;38(3):351-361.

The surgical technique for minimally invasive thoracic diskectomy is described, with a review of the literature.

23. Choy DS: Percutaneous laser disc decompression: A 17-year experience. *Photomed Laser Surg* 2004;22(5):407-410.

24. Hellinger J, Stern S, Hellinger S: Nonendoscopic Nd-YAG 1064 nm PLDN in the treatment of thoracic discogenic pain syndromes. *J Clin Laser Med Surg* 2003;21(2):61-66.

25. Chen TC: Surgical outcome for thoracic disc surgery in the postlaminectomy era. *Neurosurg Focus* 2000;9(4):e12.

26. Aizawa T, Sato T, Sasaki H, et al: Results of surgical treatment for thoracic myelopathy: Minimum 2-year follow-up study in 132 patients. *J Neurosurg Spine* 2007;7(1):13-20.

At 2-year follow-up of 132 patients treated surgically for thoracic myelopathy, the patients who had better preoperative function and a short duration of symptoms before surgery had better postoperative results. Ossification of the posterior longitudinal ligament was associated with poorer outcomes. Level of evidence: IV.

27. Bilsky MH: Transpedicular approach for thoracic disc herniations. *Neurosurg Focus* 2000;9(4):E3.

28. Johnson JP, Filler AG, Mc Bride DQ: Endoscopic thoracic discectomy. *Neurosurg Focus* 2000;9(4):e11.

29. Hott JS, Feiz-Erfan I, Kenny K, Dickman CA: Surgical management of giant herniated thoracic discs: Analysis of 20 cases. *J Neurosurg Spine* 2005;3(3):191-197.

Retrospective view of giant herniated thoracic disks in 20 patients found neurologic improvement in 11, progression arrest in 8, and worsening in 1. These results were less favorable than those of patients with a smaller herniation. Level of evidence: IV.

30. Barnett GH, Hardy RW Jr, Little JR, Bay JW, Sypert GW: Thoracic spinal canal stenosis. *J Neurosurg* 1987;66(3):338-344.

31. Palumbo MA, Hilibrand AS, Hart RA, Bohlman HH: Surgical treatment of thoracic spinal stenosis: A 2- to 9-year follow-up. *Spine (Phila Pa 1976)* 2001;26(5):558-566.

Chapter 29
Lumbar Spinal Stenosis and Degenerative Spondylolisthesis

Louis G. Jenis, MD

Introduction

Lumbar spinal stenosis is defined as narrowing of the spinal canal with compression of the nerve root or cauda equina in one or multiple segments. Lumbar spinal stenosis most often is degenerative, although a congenital etiology may contribute. Spinal stenosis is a very common cause of functional disability in the aging population.

Lumbar degenerative spondylolisthesis is caused by osteoarthritis affecting the intervertebral disk and bilateral facet joints, leading to translation of one vertebral body onto the subjacent vertebral body. The condition is most common in individuals older than 50 years, women, and individuals of African descent[1-4] (Figure 1). The listhesis most often occurs at the L4-L5 level, with a lower incidence at L3-L4 and L5-S1. The extent of slippage typically is less than 30%. Degenerative spondylolisthesis often accompanies spinal stenosis.[5]

Pathogenesis

Degeneration of the intervertebral disk is the initiating event in the development of spinal stenosis and degenerative spondylolisthesis. Loss of disk height leads to infolding and buckling of the ligamentum flavum and bulging of the posterior anulus fibrosus. The abnormal segmental mobility resulting from laxity of the disk and ligamentous structures may allow anterolisthesis, retrolisthesis, or lateral listhesis of the vertebral body, leading to narrowing of the spinal canal. The alignment of the facet joints may create a predisposition to listhesis.[6-8] The sagittal orientation of the facet's articular surfaces may promote listhesis or may represent a response to slippage and osteoarthritic change.[5] As the slip progresses and the disk space continues to narrow and collapse, a series of secondary compensatory changes occurs. These biomechanical responses include hypertrophy of the facet joints secondary to abnormal loads, vertebral body osteophyte formation along the circumference of the anulus fibrosus–end plate junction, and hypertrophy of the ligamentum flavum. The combination of these compensatory stabilizing events further narrows the spinal canal and compresses the nerve roots.

Anatomic Considerations

In patients with spinal stenosis, with or without degenerative spondylolisthesis, the symptoms typically are correlated with nerve root compression at specific anatomic regions within the lumbar spine. The recognized anatomic types of spinal stenosis are central, lateral

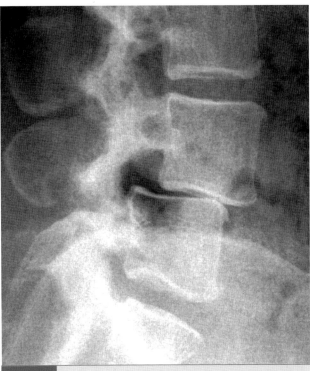

Figure 1 Lateral radiograph of the lumbar spine showing degenerative spondylolisthesis at L4-L5.

Dr. Jenis or an immediate family member is a member of a speakers' bureau or has made paid presentations on behalf of Nuvasive and has received royalties from Stryker.

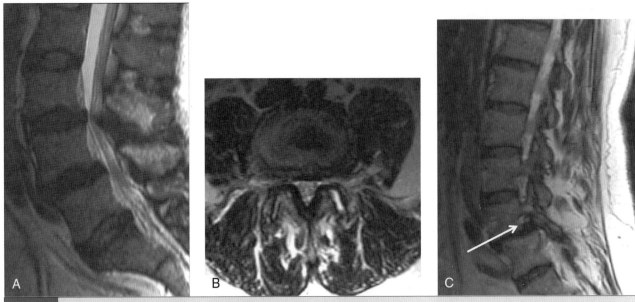

Figure 2   MRI in a patient with spinal stenosis secondary to ligamentum flavum hypertrophy and spondylolisthesis. **A**, Sagittal T2-weighted MRI showing central spinal stenosis at L3-L4 and L4-L5. **B**, Axial MRI at the level of the L4-5 disk space, showing the extent of central canal stenosis. **C**, Parasagittal MRI at the level of the L4-5 intervertebral foramen, showing narrowing related to osteophyte formation from the vertebral end plate (arrow).

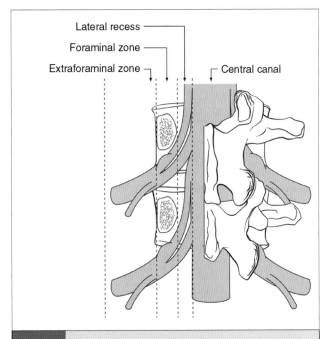

Figure 3   Schematic drawing showing lateral recess stenosis, in which the superior articular process impinges on the traversing lumbar nerve root. (Reproduced from Rao RD, David KS: Lumbar degenerative disorders, in Vaccaro AR, ed: *Orthopaedic Knowledge Update*, ed 8. Rosemont, IL, American Academy of Orthopaedic Surgeons, 2005, p 540.)

Labels in Figure 3: Lateral recess, Foraminal zone, Extraforaminal zone, Central canal

body and disk space. The dimensions at the disk level also vary by lumbar spine level. In general, a midsagittal diameter of less than 13 mm at the disk level is considered relatively stenotic, and a diameter of less than 10 mm constitutes absolute stenosis. A disk area of less than 77 mm² generally is considered critical, but this is not a steadfast value.[11] Central stenosis can cause leg pain and discomfort. The numerous theories regarding the etiology of central stenosis and related lower extremity symptoms include an increase in epidural pressure or intraneural venous hypertension.[9,12,13] Compression of the nerve root at two anatomic sites, whether at the level of the thecal sac, the lateral recess, or the foramen, leads to vascular pooling within the root sleeve with subsequent elevation of venous pressure.[14] The venous hypertension may impair neurophysiologic signaling within the nerve root, leading to symptoms.[12-14] Anterolisthesis, with associated facet joint and ligamentum flavum hypertrophy, contributes to central stenosis (Figure 2).

The lateral recess is the area medial to the pedicle where the nerve root leaves the thecal sac; the lateral recess extends to the medial aspect of the foramen (Figure 3). The height of the lateral recess, as measured from the posterior vertebral body to the anterior aspect of the superior articular process, normally is at least 5 mm. The lateral recess is considered stenotic if the height is less than 3 to 4 mm. Stenosis in this region often is the result of hypertrophy of the superior articular facet of the inferior vertebra. The intervertebral foramen or exit zone of the spine is the region of the nerve root canal from the medial aspect to the lateral aspect of the pedicle. The foramen has the shape of an inverted teardrop; it is bounded cranially and caudally by

recess, and foraminal. Often the patient has nerve root compression at a combination of sites.[9,10] The central canal dimensions differ at the levels of the midvertebral the pedicles, posteriorly by the pars interarticularis and ligamentum flavum, and anteriorly by the posterior disk and vertebral bodies.[15] Symptomatic foraminal stenosis typically is encountered in spondylolytic spondylolisthesis, but it occasionally results from a combination of foraminal disk bulging and osteophyte formation in patients with degenerative spondylolisthesis (Figure 2, C). Extraforaminal nerve root compression is relatively uncommon in degenerative spondylolisthesis.

Congenital lumbar stenosis differs from typical degenerative stenosis in many ways. Congenital stenosis is attributed to abnormal anatomic development of the spinal canal. The narrowing often is uniform over several segmental levels, and relatively few degenerative changes are present at symptom onset. The anterior-to-posterior pedicle is relatively short. The central canal is ovoid in shape and has a relatively small cross-sectional area.[11]

Clinical Syndromes

Most patients with lumbar spinal stenosis remain asymptomatic despite the changes in spine alignment and extensive degeneration. Some patients report lower extremity symptoms, with or without low back pain. Patients with spinal stenosis and degenerative spondylolisthesis most commonly report symptoms of neurogenic claudication including vague weakness and/or lower extremity pain associated with activities requiring lumbar extension, such as prolonged standing or walking. Claudicatory symptoms may be accompanied by reports of numbness, paresthesias, or pain in a nondermatomal distribution. Forward bending or sitting often relieves the symptoms by partly decompressing the thecal sac.

Patients with stenosis may report radiculopathic leg pain in a specific dermatomal distribution. These patients are more likely to have lateral recess stenosis than clinically significant central canal stenosis. The leg pain may be less related to posture than in central canal stenosis. Instead, the pain results from a combination of mechanical compression and chemical irritation of the nerve root, and it may be almost constantly present.

Claudicatory and radicular symptoms also can be caused by hip or knee osteoarthritis, polyneuropathy, a peripheral nerve condition, or deep venous thrombosis. The differential diagnosis should be considered during the clinical evaluation. A patient with a lower extremity vascular insufficiency may describe a burning, painful dysesthesia similar to that of neurogenic claudication. In a patient with vascular claudication, the symptoms uniformly, reproducibly worsen when the patient stands or walks for a specific time or distance.[9] Unlike neurogenic claudication symptoms, the symptoms of vascular claudication are lessened by standing still and are not affected by bending forward. A patient with neurogenic claudication may be able to pedal a bicycle in a forward-bending posture, but a patient with vascular claudication is able to pedal only for a limited

time, regardless of spinal posture. On examination, absent pulses, loss of hair, or poor capillary refill may be noted in the lower extremity.

Patients with spinal stenosis and/or degenerative spondylolisthesis have mechanical low back pain to a varying extent. Claudicatory low back pain is related to prolonged standing and walking and is diminished by sitting. This is a cramping, tight pain in the lumbar paraspinal musculature that is very similar to the more common lower extremity claudication. Significant facet joint arthropathy may lead to localized low back pain that worsens on extension as the facet joints are loaded. The pain may be unilateral or bilateral and often can be relieved by bending forward. Some patients describe a catching sensation in which a sudden, sharp pain, possibly accompanied by a muscle spasm, occurs with bending or rising from a forward-flexed position. Momentarily stopping the movement often relieves the pain, and the patient then can proceed through the range of motion. This type of pain, often described as an instability catch, may not be reflected on radiographs. A patient also may have the more typical low back pain stemming from disk degeneration, described as a low-grade, dull aching sensation in the midlumbar area. This pain is associated with prolonged sitting and is relieved by mobility.

Natural History

The natural course of patients with lumbar spinal stenosis appears favorable. Most patients have stable symptoms. The response to nonsurgical treatments tends to be limited and temporary. At 4-year follow-up after nonsurgical treatment, 70% of patients with spinal stenosis had symptom stability at the baseline level, 15% had greater pain, and 15% had slight improvement.[16] Data comparing the natural history of single- and multiple-level stenosis are limited. Subanalysis of data from the Spine Patient Outcomes Research Trial (SPORT) revealed that patients with single- or multiple-level stenosis had similar baseline clinical characteristics and treatment outcomes.[17] A nonrandomized study of patients with nonsurgically treated single- or multiple-level stenosis found that patients with multiple-level stenosis had poorer outcomes at 3-year follow-up.[18] Whether some of these patients had concomitant degenerative spondylolisthesis was not reported. No other studies have identified any differences in the outcomes of patients with single- or multiple-level stenosis, especially after adequate surgical treatment of multiple-level stenosis.[19] No published studies have compared the natural history of central stenosis with that of stenosis in the lateral recess or foramen.

The natural history of spinal stenosis with degenerative spondylolisthesis is insufficiently understood. No significant correlation has been found between the extent of anterolisthesis and the severity of symptoms. Few prospective studies have been completed, but there are numerous retrospective studies. Patients with symptoms of spinal stenosis and degenerative spondylolisthesis underwent a nonsurgical treatment program consisting of symptomatic treatment of their pain.[20] At an average 15.8-year follow-up, spontaneous resolution of symptoms was rare, and most patients had recurrent symptoms. Ten percent of patients had clinical deterioration without a corresponding change in radiographic alignment, and 30% had developed progressive spondylolisthesis without a corresponding change in their clinical symptoms. A SPORT subanalysis suggested that surgical treatment has a worse prognosis if degenerative spondylolisthesis is accompanied by multiple-level rather than single-level stenosis.[17]

Nonsurgical Treatment

The mainstay treatments for spinal stenosis, with or without degenerative spondylolisthesis, are nonsurgical and focus on function and pain management.[18,21,22] Patients initially are counseled regarding the natural history of spinal stenosis and the warning signs of cauda equina syndrome and progressive radiculopathy. Although physical therapy commonly is prescribed for patients with spinal stenosis, few data are available to determine its efficacy. Physical therapy and functional restoration programs are directed toward flexion-based lumbar spine strengthening and range-of-motion exercises. Patients are taught to identify symptom-precipitating factors such as hyperextension. Bed rest is recommended only for periods of severe pain exacerbation. Aerobic conditioning and a light weight-training exercise regimen often are advised. The ultimate purpose of the functional restoration program is to assist the patient to work within the limits of the pain and disability.

Specific treatments focused on managing pain include nonsteroidal anti-inflammatory drugs, oral steroids, injection therapies, and physical therapy modalities such as traction, ultrasonography, and massage. Nonsteroidal anti-inflammatory drugs are frequently prescribed, and it is critical to advise the patient of their risks. Oral steroids are reserved for patients with severe radiculopathy or back pain. The number of trial treatments with oral steroids should be limited. Epidural, facet, or selective nerve root injections are frequently prescribed for patients with significant pain or disability. The injected local anesthetic often is combined with a steroid. Retrospective studies and case reports have extensively evaluated the impact of injections on pain and function; most suggest that injections are indicated only for short-term use and primarily for leg pain. In a patient with multiple-level stenosis, diagnostic nerve blocks may identify a symptomatic level requiring surgical treatment. Injections for the treatment of nonspecific low back pain are controversial, with only limited evidence available to suggest a favorable long-term effect on outcomes.[23]

Surgical Treatment

Surgical treatment is reserved for patients with spinal stenosis, with or without degenerative spondylolisthesis, who have incapacitating symptoms after unsuccessful nonsurgical treatment for at least 3 to 6 months. Leg pain, neurogenic claudication, or leg weakness is the most common indication for surgery. Cauda equina syndrome and progressive neurologic dysfunction are relatively rare. Surgery should be reserved for patients who are experiencing lower extremity symptoms from spinal stenosis. Surgery for recalcitrant back pain is controversial in the absence of lower extremity symptoms. Neurologic decompression, with or without stabilization, is the primary goal of surgically treating a patient with spinal stenosis. The surgical options include laminectomy, bilateral laminotomy, or laminoplasty.

Lumbar Spinal Stenosis

Spinal stenosis most often is surgically treated with a thorough decompression or laminectomy over the narrowed segments. Pedicle-to-pedicle confirmation of decompression is required to ensure adequate neurologic recovery. Resecting the lamina with the associated interspinous and supraspinous ligaments and undercutting the superior facet process ensure decompression of the thecal sac in the central canal and the nerve root in the lateral recess, respectively. Decompression of the exiting root in the intervertebral foramen often is hampered by the need to maintain the integrity of the facet joint complex. Undercutting the facet articular process, identifying the nerve root, and carefully resecting compressive structures allow effective foraminotomy. A failure to adequately decompress the foramen is among the most common reasons for the persistence of leg pain after surgery. Care must be taken to preserve the pars interarticularis to prevent iatrogenic instability. If concomitant disk herniation is contributing to the stenosis, care also must be taken to avoid overzealous excision of the anulus fibrosus so as to prevent iatrogenic instability and rapid disk degeneration.

Other options for decompression include bilateral laminotomy, in which the midline ligamentous structures are left intact; and unilateral laminotomy, in which the contralateral side of the spinal canal is decompressed by resecting the undersurface of the lamina. These procedures require only limited bone and ligament removal, with the goal of maintaining stability, but this advantage adds complexity to the surgery and makes it more challenging. Unilateral laminotomy or hemilaminectomy also is appropriate for treating patients with symptomatic unilateral stenosis. In decompression for spinal stenosis without degenerative spondylolisthesis, fusion is indicated only to treat iatrogenic instability (as in a total facetectomy or revision decompression requiring resection of more than 50% of the bilateral facet joints).

Surgical treatment of lumbar spinal stenosis usually has a very favorable result. The literature is limited, however, and consists primarily of retrospective case reports and few prospective randomized studies. At 1-year follow-up, the Maine Lumbar Spine Study found improvement of symptoms in 55% of patients after laminectomy and 28% of patients after nonsurgical treatment. At 4-year follow-up, 63% of patients who underwent surgery were satisfied with the outcome, and 70% reported pain improvement.[24] However, these studies implied that 25% to 40% of surgically treated patients and 50% to 60% of nonsurgically treated patients had continuing symptoms at 4-year follow-up and were dissatisfied with their level of disability and pain. The SPORT prospective data show that symptom improvement after surgery was maintained at 2-year follow-up.[25] In SPORT, 289 patients were randomly assigned to surgical treatment, and 365 were observed. Although there was some crossover between patients in the two treatment groups, data analysis for as-treated or intent-to-treat outcomes revealed no differences. The surgically treated patients were found to have superior outcomes.[25] Surgical treatment of one-, two-, or three-level spinal stenosis led to significant improvement in all outcome measures, including low back pain, satisfaction, self-rated progress, and the Medical Outcomes Study Short Form-36 Health Survey mental and physical composite scores.[25]

Degenerative Spondylolisthesis

The use of laminectomy alone for degenerative spondylolisthesis has long been regarded as increasing the risk of postsurgical segmental instability and slippage.[26,27] However, not all patients are at risk. Patients with a stable spondylolisthesis, as suggested by lack of motion on dynamic presurgical radiographs, are likely to have a satisfactory outcome without a concomitant fusion procedure. A significantly collapsed disk space, as seen on radiographs, may be stable after removal of the posterior elements and may allow effective decompression, especially in an older patient with relatively low physical demands. Coronal plane alignment of the facet joints at the level of the listhesis also can contribute to stability.[5]

Maintaining facet joint integrity is critical for preventing postsurgical instability. Good or excellent clinical results were reported at 2- to 7-year follow-up in 33% of patients who underwent laminectomy and total facetectomy and in 80% of patients who underwent laminectomy with preservation of the facet joints.[26] A bilateral laminotomy or fenestration procedure was found to achieve neural decompression while maintaining the interspinous stabilizing ligaments, but no study has proved the clinical outcomes to be superior to those of laminectomy.[28] In 290 patients with stable spondylolisthesis and spinal stenosis who were treated with laminectomy or a fenestration procedure, 82% had a good or excellent result at 10-year follow-up; there was no significant difference in the results of the two techniques.[29]

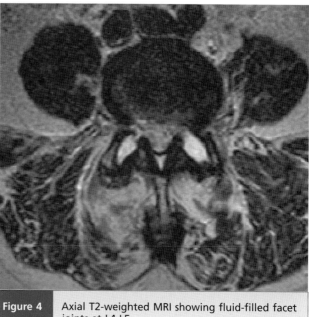

Figure 4 Axial T2-weighted MRI showing fluid-filled facet joints at L4-L5.

The presurgical presence of fluid-filled facet joints may contribute to progressive instability after surgery (Figure 4). On presurgical MRI, the risk of positional translation was correlated with the presence of hypertrophic, distended facet joints at the level of the spondylolisthesis.[30] This finding, as well as a finding of sagittal-aligned facet joints, may be a relative indication for fusion. Careful attention must be given to preserving the integrity of the facet joints during a laminectomy for spinal stenosis with degenerative spondylolisthesis, while avoiding a compromise in the extent of decompression.

Lumbar Fusion

The indications for fusion and instrumentation for degenerative spondylolisthesis are controversial. The benefits are believed to be a diminished risk of instability after a wide decompression, with better clinical outcomes than laminectomy without fusion. In perhaps the best known randomized clinical study in spine surgery, 50 patients with degenerative spondylolisthesis were assigned to decompression using laminectomy or to laminectomy with concomitant noninstrumented posterolateral fusion (PLF) using autogenous iliac crest autograft.[31] The patients treated with fusion had better pain relief and a better functional outcome at a mean 3-year follow-up, although there was no correlation with radiographic arthrodesis. Nine of the 25 patients treated with fusion developed a radiographic nonunion. In a follow-up prospective randomized study, patients were treated with decompression or PLF with or without pedicle screw instrumentation.[32] At 2-year follow-up of 68 patients, 83% of those treated with instrumentation had fusion, in comparison with 45% of those treated without instrumentation. There were no significant differences in early clinical outcomes, however. The investigators subsequently evaluated 47 patients who had undergone noninstrumented fusion during the two earlier studies; patients who had undergone instrumented fusion were not evaluated.[33] At an average 8-year follow-up, 86% of patients who eventually went on to solid arthrodesis had a good or excellent clinical outcome, but only 45% of those who developed pseudarthrosis had similar improvement in function and pain. The investigators concluded that the early and long-term outcomes of surgery may be affected by pseudarthrosis and that the use of stabilizing instrumentation diminishes the risk. This view still is controversial.

SPORT provided further evidence concerning the roles of surgical and nonsurgical treatment as well as the most effective surgical treatment for degenerative spondylolisthesis.[34] The study enrolled 607 patients. In the randomized arm of the study (304 patients), 66% of those randomized to surgery and 54% of those randomized to nonsurgical care received surgery within 4 years. In the observational cohort (303 patients), 97% of those who chose surgical treatment underwent surgery within 4 years, and 33% of those who initially chose nonsurgical care also underwent surgery within 4 years. The intent-to-treat analysis revealed no differences in the outcomes of the two groups of patients, but the as-treated analysis found that at 2- and 4-year follow-up patients who were surgically treated had substantially greater pain improvement than patients who were nonsurgically treated (based on the Medical Outcomes Study Short Form-36 Health Survey and the Oswestry Disability Index bodily pain and satisfaction questionnaires).[34]

SPORT was not designed to evaluate specific interventions in degenerative spondylolisthesis, but the data allow subgroup analysis.[35] Patients in the study were offered a specific surgical procedure based on their surgeon's preference. Of the patients in both arms of the study, 23 had laminectomy alone, 80 had laminectomy and noninstrumented PLF, 213 had laminectomy with pedicle screw fixation, and 63 had laminectomy and circumferential interbody fusion (posterior lumbar interbody fusion [PLIF] or anterior lumbar interbody fusion [ALIF]) combined with posterior pedicle screw fixation. Laminectomy alone was not statistically analyzed because few patients had this treatment. The early analysis revealed inconsistent, variable outcomes at 3- and 4-year follow-up after the three procedures, with no statistically significant differences. Higher rates of radiographic fusion were found in the patients who received instrumentation, although no formal rating system was used.

Numerous other studies have been designed to evaluate the role of instrumentation for use in fusion for degenerative spondylolisthesis. The results have been inconsistent, with conclusions that argue both for and against supplemental fixation in PLF.[36-43] The use of instrumentation has been associated with increases in surgical time, blood loss, and infection rate, as well as a risk of nerve root injury or vascular injury from malpositioning. The use of instrumentation in patients with degenerative spondylolisthesis is limited. The slip must be unstable, based on presurgical dynamic radiographic assessment; segmentally kyphotic (especially if the slip angle is to be reduced); accompanied by severe stenosis requiring extensive bilateral facetectomy; or classified as Meyerding grade II or higher.

Evidence emphasizing the importance of solid fusion in patients with degenerative spondylolisthesis has prompted more aggressive approaches to arthrodesis. PLIF or transforaminal lumbar interbody fusion (TLIF) may lead to better fusion rates than PLF because of the larger end plate surface area available for graft incorporation as well as the compression of the graft in the anterior column of the spine. Distraction of the interbody disk space contributes to foraminal decompression and a possible reduction of anterolisthesis. There is a paucity of data evaluating the role of PLIF and TLIF in degenerative spondylolisthesis. One prospective study randomly assigned 62 patients with degenerative spondylolisthesis to laminectomy, instrumented PLF, or PLIF.[44] There were no differences in clinical or radiographic outcomes at an average 32.6-month follow-up, but the patients treated with PLIF had a higher risk of surgical complications. Most other studies of PLIF did not include PLF and did not find clinical results superior to those of less aggressive approaches.[45,46] PLIF and TLIF are technically demanding procedures and are associated with a higher complication rate than PLF. These factors are important when PLIF or TLIF is being considered as a means of increasing the radiographic fusion. The indications for PLIF or TLIF probably are limited to situations where slip reduction is indicated or an asymmetrically collapsed disk space would benefit from distraction (as with severe unilateral foraminal stenosis) and maintenance of disk height and stability would be enhanced. PLIF or TLIF usually is indicated for a patient who requires slip reduction or a patient who has an asymmetrically collapsed disk space that would benefit from distraction, disk height maintenance, and stability enhancement (as with severe unilateral foraminal stenosis).

The use of ALIF for treating degenerative spondylolisthesis has been studied in Japan but rarely reported in the United States. ALIF provides segmental stabilization by distraction and intersegmental realignment, allowing indirect central canal and foraminal decompression. The published reports are limited but reveal satisfactory clinical outcomes. The use of ALIF is rarely indicated, however, especially because of the relatively advanced age of most patients with degenerative spondylolisthesis.[47-49]

Alternatives to Lumbar Fusion

The varied indications and inconsistent clinical outcomes of arthrodesis for degenerative spondylolisthesis have led to interest in the role of dynamic stabilization. Numerous dynamic stabilization devices have been developed and tested biomechanically and clinically. Dynamic stabilization in the degenerative lumbar spine is intended to restrict abnormal motion rather than to restore individual segments to normal motion. Maintaining motion theoretically lessens the stress on the adjacent levels. The many types of devices for dynamic stabilization can be classified as based on either pedicle screws or interspinous process distraction (IPD). The function of a pedicle screw–based device is provided by its longitudinal connecting element, which ranges from an elastic band to a semirigid bumper. Most studies of pedicle screw–based fixation have focused on lumbar degenerative disk disease but allow subgroup analysis of degenerative spondylolisthesis.[50,51] One randomized study comparing laminectomy and laminectomy with dynamic stabilization found no significant differences in patients' visual analog scores for back or leg pain.[52] Clinical improvement has also been found, however.[53] Spontaneous facet joint fusion and clinical or radiographic screw loosening are two areas of concern after screw fixation. Some data suggest a high incidence of these phenomena.[53] A 17% rate of asymptomatic implant failure was reported at a minimum 2-year follow-up, but the longer term consequences were not reported.[51]

Posterior IPD devices are a possible alternative to laminectomy. In a cadaver model, distraction to induce a kyphotic moment increased the central, lateral recess, and foraminal area, as well as the sagittal-plane canal diameter.[54] Few clinical studies have reported the use of IPD devices in patients with degenerative spondylolisthesis. A multicenter randomized controlled study by the designers of one IPD device reported that the use of the device led to better results than continued nonsurgical treatment.[55] A slight increase in anterolisthesis occurred in patients in both groups but was not believed to be significant.

Numerous questions remain regarding the role of dynamic stabilization in degenerative spondylolisthesis. Although compelling preclinical and biomechanical data are available, clinical long-term data are lacking. No recommendation can be made as to the indications for using these devices as an alternative to laminectomy or laminectomy with fusion.

The Spine Patient Outcomes Research Trial

The SPORT investigation of three of the most common diagnoses leading to low back or leg pain (intervertebral herniated disk, spinal stenosis, and degenerative spondylolisthesis) has received much attention. The study was designed to assess the relative clinical efficacy and cost-effectiveness of treatment approaches. Patient characteristics and treatment outcomes are being compared at 13 spine centers in the United States. The study includes both a randomized cohort and an observational cohort of patients. The project has a sound scientific rationale and will fill a significant void

in spine research. The published SPORT data have some limitations that will affect future long-term outcome analyses, including the high level of patient crossover and the nonadherence to randomization among treatment groups. Direct comparisons also are limited by inconsistencies in surgical and nonsurgical treatment that reflect differences in clinical practice.

Future Directions

The number of patients with symptoms of degenerative spondylolisthesis and spinal stenosis is expected to rise as the population ages. The standards of care in terms of lumbar decompression and concomitant fusion, with or without instrumentation, will continue to be refined as techniques evolve and clinical effectiveness data become available. Alternatives to autograft as well as the use of bone graft substitutes in fusion procedures are currently being investigated, and methods to improve the success of arthrodesis procedures are being evaluated. As minimally invasive decompression procedures are refined, their role is likely to evolve. A nonfusion treatment alternative may be identified that will provide a satisfactory outcome in both the short and long term.

Annotated References

1. Jacobsen S, Sonne-Holm S, Rovsing H, Monrad H, Gebuhr P: Degenerative lumbar spondylolisthesis: An epidemiological perspective. The Copenhagen Osteoarthritis Study. *Spine (Phila Pa 1976)* 2007;32(1):120-125.

   A cross-sectional survey of 4,151 patients identified the prevalence and risk factors for lumbar degenerative spondylolisthesis. Increasing age, body mass index, and angle of lordosis were strong associations.

2. Matsunaga S, Sakou T, Morizono Y, Masuda A, Demirtas AM: Natural history of degenerative spondylolisthesis: Pathogenesis and natural course of the slippage. *Spine (Phila Pa 1976)* 1990;15(11):1204-1210.

3. Love TW, Fagan AB, Fraser RD: Degenerative spondylolisthesis: Developmental or acquired? *J Bone Joint Surg Br* 1999;81(4):670-674.

4. Cummins J, Lurie JD, Tosteson TD, et al: Descriptive epidemiology and prior healthcare utilization of patients in the Spine Patient Outcomes Research Trial's (SPORT) three observational cohorts: Disc herniation, spinal stenosis, and degenerative spondylolisthesis. *Spine (Phila Pa 1976)* 2006;31(7):806-814.

   Baseline data from a prospective multicenter observational cohort described surgical candidates with the three most common diagnoses causing low back and leg pain.

5. Iguchi T, Wakami T, Kurihara A, Kasahara K, Yoshiya S, Nishida K: Lumbar multilevel degenerative spon-

dylolisthesis: Radiological evaluation and factors related to anterolisthesis and retrolisthesis. *J Spinal Disord Tech* 2002;15(2):93-99.

6. Dai LY: Orientation and tropism of lumbar facet joints in degenerative spondylolisthesis. *Int Orthop* 2001; 25(1):40-42.

7. Grobler LJ, Robertson PA, Novotny JE, Pope MH: Etiology of spondylolisthesis: Assessment of the role played by lumbar facet joint morphology. *Spine (Phila Pa 1976)* 1993;18(1):80-91.

8. Boden SD, Riew KD, Yamaguchi K, Branch TP, Schellinger D, Wiesel SW: Orientation of the lumbar facet joints: Association with degenerative disc disease. *J Bone Joint Surg Am* 1996;78(3):403-411.

9. Spivak JM: Degenerative lumbar spinal stenosis. *J Bone Joint Surg Am* 1998;80(7):1053-1066.

10. Jenis LG, An HS: Spine update: Lumbar foraminal stenosis. *Spine (Phila Pa 1976)* 2000;25(3):389-394.

11. Singh K, Samartzis D, Vaccaro AR, et al: Congenital lumbar spinal stenosis: A prospective, control-matched, cohort radiographic analysis. *Spine J* 2005;5(6):615-622.

    A prospective, control-matched, radiographic analysis is presented to quantify and assess the anatomy of congenital lumbar stenosis. Short pedicle length and small cross-sectional area were the identified anatomic features.

12. Takahashi K, Miyazaki T, Takino T, Matsui T, Tomita K: Epidural pressure measurements: Relationship between epidural pressure and posture in patients with lumbar spinal stenosis. *Spine (Phila Pa 1976)* 1995; 20(6):650-653.

13. Takahashi K, Kagechika K, Takino T, Matsui T, Miyazaki T, Shima I: Changes in epidural pressure during walking in patients with lumbar spinal stenosis. *Spine (Phila Pa 1976)* 1995;20(24):2746-2749.

14. Porter RW, Ward D: Cauda equina dysfunction: The significance of two-level pathology. *Spine (Phila Pa 1976)* 1992;17(1):9-15.

15. Hasegawa T, An HS, Haughton VM, Nowicki BH: Lumbar foraminal stenosis: Critical heights of the intervertebral discs and foramina. A cryomicrotome study in cadavera. *J Bone Joint Surg Am* 1995;77(1):32-38.

16. Johnsson KE, Rosén I, Udén A: The natural course of lumbar spinal stenosis. *Clin Orthop Relat Res* 1992; 279:82-86.

17. Park DK, An HS, Lurie JD, et al: Does multilevel lumbar stenosis lead to poorer outcomes? A subanalysis of the Spine Patient Outcomes Research Trial (SPORT) lumbar stenosis study. *Spine (Phila Pa 1976)* 2010; 35(4):439-446.

SPORT data suggest that the number of levels operated upon does not affect the patient's outcome, in the absence of degenerative spondylolisthesis.

18. Simotas AC, Dorey FJ, Hansraj KK, Cammisa F Jr: Nonoperative treatment for lumbar spinal stenosis: Clinical and outcome results and a 3-year survivorship analysis. *Spine (Phila Pa 1976)* 2000;25(2):197-204.

19. Yukawa Y, Lenke LG, Tenhula J, Bridwell KH, Riew KD, Blanke K: A comprehensive study of patients with surgically treated lumbar spinal stenosis with neurogenic claudication. *J Bone Joint Surg Am* 2002;84(11): 1954-1959.

20. Matsunaga S, Ijiri K, Hayashi K: Nonsurgically managed patients with degenerative spondylolisthesis: A 10- to 18-year follow-up study. *J Neurosurg* 2000;93(2, suppl):194-198.

21. Mirza SK, Deyo RA: Systematic review of randomized trials comparing lumbar fusion surgery to nonoperative care for treatment of chronic back pain. *Spine (Phila Pa 1976)* 2007;32(7):816-823.

    A literature review led to the conclusion that most published studies are limited by methodologic concerns and that a structured cognitive-behavioral therapy program may be as effective as surgical intervention for treating chronic back pain.

22. Malmivaara A, Slätis P, Heliövaara M, et al: Surgical or nonoperative treatment for lumbar spinal stenosis? A randomized controlled trial. *Spine (Phila Pa 1976)* 2007;32(1):1-8.

    A randomized study of 94 patients found that patients who had undergone surgery had less back and leg pain and disability at 2-year follow-up.

23. Abdi S, Datta S, Trescot AM, et al: Epidural steroids in the management of chronic spinal pain: A systematic review. *Pain Physician* 2007;10(1):185-212.

    A literature review found primarily moderate evidence for the use of injected corticosteroids for long-term relief of spine pain.

24. Atlas SJ, Keller RB, Robson D, Deyo RA, Singer DE: Surgical and nonsurgical management of lumbar spinal stenosis: Four-year outcomes from the Maine Lumbar Spine Study. *Spine (Phila Pa 1976)* 2000;25(5):556-562.

25. Weinstein JN, Tosteson TD, Lurie JD, et al: Surgical versus nonsurgical therapy for lumbar spinal stenosis. *N Engl J Med* 2008;358(8):794-810.

    Patients with spinal stenosis without spondylolisthesis were enrolled in a randomized or observational cohort. Despite a high level of crossover, both the intent-to-treat and as-treated surgical patients had more improvement in all outcomes than the nonsurgically treated patients.

26. Lombardi JS, Wiltse LL, Reynolds J, Widell EH, Spencer C III: Treatment of degenerative spondylolisthesis. *Spine (Phila Pa 1976)* 1985;10(9):821-827.

27. Johnsson KE, Willner S, Johnsson K: Postoperative instability after decompression for lumbar spinal stenosis. *Spine (Phila Pa 1976)* 1986;11(2):107-110.

28. Kleeman TJ, Hiscoe AC, Berg EE: Patient outcomes after minimally destabilizing lumbar stenosis decompression: The "port-hole" technique. *Spine (Phila Pa 1976)* 2000;25(7):865-870.

29. Epstein NE: Lumbar laminectomy for the resection of synovial cysts and coexisting lumbar spinal stenosis or degenerative spondylolisthesis: An outcome study. *Spine (Phila Pa 1976)* 2004;29(9):1049-1056.

30. Ben-Galim P, Reitman C: The distended facet sign: An indicator of position-dependent spinal stenosis and degenerative spondylolisthesis. *Spine J* 2007;7:245-248.

    In six patients with spinal stenosis, the presence of large fluid-filled facet joints on supine MRI suggested positional translation that could be confirmed by upright MRI.

31. Herkowitz HN, Kurz LT: Degenerative lumbar spondylolisthesis with spinal stenosis: A prospective study comparing decompression with decompression and intertransverse process arthrodesis. *J Bone Joint Surg Am* 1991;73(6):802-808.

32. Fischgrund JS, Mackay M, Herkowitz HN, Brower R, Montgomery DM, Kurz LT: Degenerative lumbar spondylolisthesis with spinal stenosis: A prospective, randomized study comparing decompressive laminectomy and arthrodesis with and without spinal instrumentation. *Spine (Phila Pa 1976)* 1997;22(24):2807-2812.

33. Kornblum MB, Fischgrund JS, Herkowitz HN, Abraham DA, Berkower DL, Ditkoff JS: Degenerative lumbar spondylolisthesis with spinal stenosis: A prospective long-term study comparing fusion and pseudarthrosis. *Spine (Phila Pa 1976)* 2004;29(7):726-734.

34. Weinstein JN, Lurie JD, Tosteson TD, et al: Surgical compared with nonoperative treatment for lumbar degenerative spondylolisthesis: Four-year results in the Spine Patient Outcomes Research Trial (SPORT) randomized and observational cohorts. *J Bone Joint Surg Am* 2009;91(6):1295-1304.

    Data from SPORT confirm that superior surgical outcomes were maintained at 4-year follow-up when patients in the intent-to-treat and as-treated groups were combined and that surgical treatment had better outcomes than nonsurgical treatment.

35. Abdu WA, Lurie JD, Spratt KF, et al: Degenerative spondylolisthesis: Does fusion method influence outcome? Four-year results of the spine patient outcomes research trial. *Spine (Phila Pa 1976)* 2009;34(21):2351-2360.

    The results of the multicenter SPORT are presented. Subgroup analysis revealed no consistent differences in clinical outcomes at 4-year follow-up after various surgical interventions.

36. Bridwell KH, Sedgewick TA, O'Brien MF, Lenke LG, Baldus C: The role of fusion and instrumentation in the treatment of degenerative spondylolisthesis with spinal stenosis. *J Spinal Disord* 1993;6(6):461-472.

37. France JC, Yaszemski MJ, Lauerman WC, et al: A randomized prospective study of posterolateral lumbar fusion: Outcomes with and without pedicle screw instrumentation. *Spine (Phila Pa 1976)* 1999;24(6):553-560.

38. Mochida J, Suzuki K, Chiba M: How to stabilize a single level lesion of degenerative lumbar spondylolisthesis. *Clin Orthop Relat Res* 1999;368:126-134.

39. Kimura I, Shingu H, Murata M, Hashiguchi H: Lumbar posterolateral fusion alone or with transpedicular instrumentation in L4-L5 degenerative spondylolisthesis. *J Spinal Disord* 2001;14(4):301-310.

40. Mardjetko SM, Connolly PJ, Shott S: Degenerative lumbar spondylolisthesis: A meta-analysis of literature 1970-1993. *Spine (Phila Pa 1976)* 1994;19(20, suppl):2256S-2265S.

41. Yuan H, Garfin S, Dickman C, et al: A historical cohort study of pedicle screw fixation in thoracic, lumbar and sacral spinal fusions. *Spine (Phila Pa 1976)* 1994;19(20, suppl):2279S-2296S.

42. Phillips FM: The argument for noninstrumented posterolateral fusion for patients with spinal stenosis and degenerative spondylolisthesis. *Spine (Phila Pa 1976)* 2004;29(2):170-172.

43. Booth KC, Bridwell KH, Eisenberg BA, Baldus CR, Lenke LG: Minimum 5-year results of degenerative spondylolisthesis treated with decompression and instrumented posterior fusion. *Spine (Phila Pa 1976)* 1999;24(16):1721-1727.

44. Kitchel S, Matteri R: Prospective randomized evaluation of posterior lumbar interbody fusion in degenerative spondylolisthesis patients over 60 years old. *Spine J* 2002;2:21S.

45. Sears W: Posterior lumbar interbody fusion for degenerative spondylolisthesis: Restoration of sagittal balance using insert-and-rotate interbody spacers. *Spine J* 2005;5(2):170-179.

    In a prospective, single-cohort study, 34 patients with degenerative spondylolisthesis were treated with posterior distraction and reduction. The clinical and radiographic outcomes were satisfactory, with limited surgical complications.

46. Zhao J, Wang X, Hou T, He S: One versus two BAK fusion cages in posterior lumbar interbody fusion to L4-L5 degenerative spondylolisthesis: A randomized, controlled prospective study in 25 patients with minimum two-year follow-up. *Spine (Phila Pa 1976)* 2002;27(24):2753-2757.

47. Inoue S, Watanabe T, Goto S, Takahashi K, Takata K, Sho E: Degenerative spondylolisthesis: Pathophysiology

4: The Adult Spine

and results of anterior interbody fusion. *Clin Orthop Relat Res* 1988;227:90-98.

48. Satomi K, Hirabayashi K, Toyama Y, Fujimura Y: A clinical study of degenerative spondylolisthesis: Radiographic analysis and choice of treatment. *Spine (Phila Pa 1976)* 1992;17(11):1329-1336.

49. Takahashi K, Kitahara H, Yamagata M, et al: Long-term results of anterior interbody fusion for treatment of degenerative spondylolisthesis. *Spine (Phila Pa 1976)* 1990;15(11):1211-1215.

50. Nockels RP: Dynamic stabilization in the surgical management of painful lumbar spinal disorders. *Spine (Phila Pa 1976)* 2005;30(16, suppl):S68-S72.

    A systematic literature review of clinical and load transmission data suggests that fusion techniques have comparable benefit.

51. Schnake KJ, Schaeren S, Jeanneret B: Dynamic stabilization in addition to decompression for lumbar spinal stenosis with degenerative spondylolisthesis. *Spine (Phila Pa 1976)* 2006;31(4):442-449.

    In a prospective cohort analysis, 26 patients treated with the Dynesys system in addition to decompression were found to have clinical outcomes comparable to those of decompression with fusion and instrumentation.

52. Konno S, Kikuchi S: Prospective study of surgical treatment of degenerative spondylolisthesis: Comparison between decompression alone and decompression with Graf system stabilization. *Spine (Phila Pa 1976)* 2000;25(12):1533-1537.

53. Kanayama M, Hashimoto T, Shigenobu K, Togawa D, Oha F: A minimum 10-year follow-up of posterior dynamic stabilization using Graf artificial ligament. *Spine (Phila Pa 1976)* 2007;32(18):1992-1997.

    A 10-year retrospective study found Graf ligamentoplasty to be effective for treating low-grade degenerative spondylolisthesis and flexion instability.

54. Siddiqui M, Karadimas E, Nicol M, Smith FW, Wardlaw D: Influence of X Stop on neural foramina and spinal canal area in spinal stenosis. *Spine (Phila Pa 1976)* 2006;31(25):2958-2962.

    Preoperative and postoperative MRI found significant increase in foraminal and central canal area in 26 patients with spinal stenosis who were undergoing treatment with the X-Stop device.

55. Zucherman JF, Hsu KY, Hartjen CA, et al: A multicenter, prospective, randomized trial evaluating the X STOP interspinous process decompression system for the treatment of neurogenic intermittent claudication: Two-year follow-up results. *Spine (Phila Pa 1976)* 2005;30(12):1351-1358.

    A prospective, randomized study of 191 patients treated nonsurgically or with the X-Stop device suggested that those treated with the X-Stop had better outcomes (based on the Zurich Claudication Questionnaire).

Chapter 30

Isthmic Spondylolisthesis in Adults

Alan S. Hilibrand, MD   Harvey E. Smith, MD

Epidemiology

The prevalence of radiographic spondylolysis among adults in the United States is estimated at 5% to 6%, with a 2:1 ratio of men to women.[1,2] Spondylolysis is believed to begin in childhood; the estimated prevalence in the pediatric population is 4.4%.[1] The etiology of spondylolysis may have a genetic component, as the incidence increases significantly among near relatives.[3,4] In some ethnic populations, the incidence of radiographic spondylolysis may be as high as 53%.[5-7]

In bilateral spondylolysis the posterior elements are disconnected from the anterior column. The result can be spondylolisthesis (anterior translation of the cephalad vertebrae). Isthmic spondylolisthesis (IS) most commonly occurs at L5-S1, with a decreasing incidence at L4-L5 and L3-L4 (Figures 1 and 2). Understanding of the true incidence of spondylolysis is somewhat limited because historical studies primarily relied on plain radiographs. More recent CT studies of the lumbar spine found an 8.2% prevalence of IS.[7] Among symptomatic adults, equal numbers of men and women are affected. Twenty percent of adults with IS were reported to have slip progression of 9% to 30%, beginning during the fourth decade of life.[2,8,9] Slip progression may be correlated with degenerative changes and loss of disk space height at L5-S1.[2,10]

There is no evidence of in utero pars defects,[1] and spondylolysis generally is believed to develop after birth. However, a congenital lesion such as absence of the posterior elements may increase the forces on the pars interarticularis, creating a risk factor for spondylolysis or spondylolisthesis. An association between IS and spina bifida occulta has been observed.[3] IS has not been observed in mammals other than humans. The unique lumbosacral forces of upright ambulation probably lead to the development of stress lesions in the pars. Facet joint orientation may have a role; a more coronal facet orientation cephalad to the level of IS is believed to concentrate forces in the pars interarticularis.

The initial spondylolisthesis slip occurs in childhood or adolescence and possibly is exacerbated by the pubertal growth spurt. Participants in sports requiring repetitive hyperextension, particularly football linemen and gymnasts, have an increased incidence of IS.[11] Repetitive hyperextension creates a predisposition to stress fracture of the pars interarticularis. In an athlete the initial symptom is low back pain that is exacerbated by the sport activity and alleviated with rest. The incidence of IS is 50% among adolescent athletes with a history of persistent low back pain.[12-14]

Classification

There are three types of IS.[15] Type A is a classic lytic lesion of the pars interarticularis, representing a nonunion. In type B the isthmus is elongated but without a defect, probably representing the remodeling that occurs with healing of an acute fracture. Type C is an acute fracture of the pars. The Meyerding classification is most commonly used to grade spondylolisthesis. This system describes the percentage of anterior subluxation of the cephalad vertebral body relative to the caudal level: the subluxation is 25% or less in grade I, 26% to 50% in grade II, 51% to 75% in grade III, and 76% to 100% in grade IV. Grade V is a complete translation (more than 100%) and is referred to as spondyloptosis.[16]

Clinical Findings

An adult with IS usually has a history of progressive low back pain that is exacerbated with activity and alleviated with rest. The back pain may radiate into the posterior thigh or farther down the leg. The back pain may have a muscular pathogenesis, as a result of IS alterations in the lumbopelvic anatomy. An acute stress lesion of the pars interarticularis is the source of mechanical pain in an active lesion, and hyperextension maneuvers are provocative. Hamstring tightness and

Dr. Hilibrand or an immediate family member serves as a board member, owner, officer, or committee member of the American Orthopaedic Association, Cervical Spine Research Society, and North American Spine Society; has received royalties from Biomet, Zimmer, Stryker, Aesculap, Amedica, and Alphatech; has received research or institutional support from Medtronic and DePuy; and owns stock or stock options in Amedica, Vertiflex, Nexgen, Benvenue, Pioneer, Lifespine, Paradigm Spine, PSD, and Syndicom. Dr. Smith or an immediate family member has received nonincome support (such as equipment or services), commercially derived honoraria, or other non–research-related funding (such as paid travel) from Stryker.

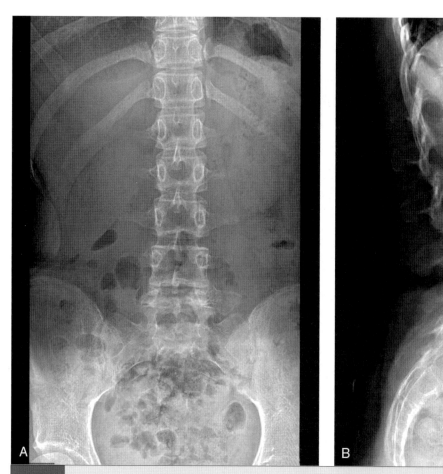

Figure 1 AP (**A**) and lateral (**B**) radiographs showing isthmic spondylolysis at L5-S1 in an 18-year-old ballet dancer who had significant back pain with extension. CT confirmed bilateral L5-S1 spondylolysis.

posterior buttock and thigh pain frequently are associated with IS. A patient with a chronic spondylolisthesis may have a compensatory hyperlordosis cephalad to the slip, with associated paraspinal muscle spasms and hamstring tightness.[17] Buttock and thigh pain also may be muscular. The associated paraspinal spasms and decreased popliteal angles may decrease the forces transmitted to the pars interarticularis. Neurogenic leg pain may result from compression of the dorsal root ganglion or the exiting nerve root. A chronic IS lesion can lead to hypertrophic scar tissue where the pars interarticularis lesion impinges the foramen. Thus, the radicular pain is correlated with the exiting nerve root at the level of the lesion (for example, in IS at L4-L5, the pain is at L4). The dorsal root ganglion is in the superolateral region of the neural foramen,[18] and sometimes it is compressed by direct impingement from hypertrophic fibrous scar tissue or relative anteroposterior narrowing of the foramen with anterior listhesis.

Back pain may be an incidental finding in a patient with radiographic spondylolysis or listhesis. The constellation of associated symptoms, such as hamstring tightness, neurogenic pain from the exiting nerve root, compensatory hyperlordosis cephalad to the IS, and pain with lumbar extension, may indicate that the back

pain is related to the radiographic finding. Low back pain is more prevalent among adults with IS than in the general population, particularly if the slip is greater than 10 mm or disk degeneration is present.[19-21] The listhesis usually is not progressive in adults. Several case studies reported significant slip progression, however, generally in the setting of disk degeneration and loss of disk height.[9,21,22]

Imaging

The radiologic evaluation includes standing lumbar AP, lateral, and oblique views. If a spondylolisthesis is identified on lateral radiographs, flexion-extension views should be considered to determine whether the translation has a dynamic component. There is some controversy regarding motion of the listhetic segment in IS. In theory, the loss of posterior column structural integrity allows abnormal flexion and extension motion at the affected level, but excessive translation of the listhetic level has not been identified. Nonetheless, analysis of the instantaneous centers of rotation of the affected motion segments can identify paradoxical translation of the cephalad segment. Instead of moving forward

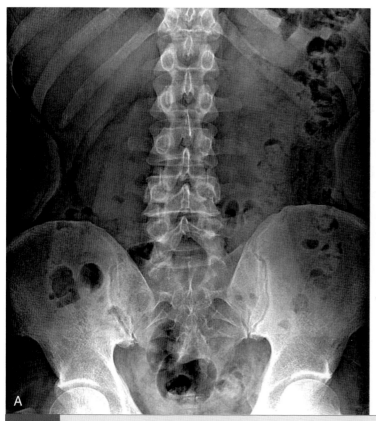
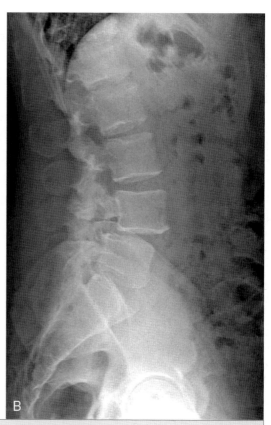

Figure 2 AP (**A**) and lateral (**B**) radiographs showing bilateral spondylolysis with spondylolisthesis at L4-L5. The patient had been in a motor vehicle crash 4 years earlier and subsequently had significant, progressive back pain.

during flexion, the superior level translates backward. This paradoxical translation appears to be small and is of unknown clinical significance, but its existence suggests that adjacent-level biomechanics may be altered in a patient with IS.[23]

CT with fine cuts through the pars interarticularis and sagittal and coronal reconstruction is the most specific method for identifying spondylolysis.[7,24] Single-photon emission computed tomography may be useful for distinguishing a symptomatic from an asymptomatic spondylolisthesis.[25] MRI can be used to assess neural element compression in a patient with radicular symptoms, and it provides information on the extent of intervertebral disk degeneration at the level of the IS and the adjacent levels. A thorough understanding of the anatomy of the nerve root and its course through the neural foramen is important for correlating the anatomic pathology of IS with individual physical findings and clinical symptoms and signs. A chronic pars defect produces hypertrophic fibrous scar tissue that beaks anteriorly, causing direct impingement on the exiting nerve root in the superior recess of the neural foramen.

The importance of sagittal balance and pelvic anatomy for the management of spine deformity is increasingly recognized.[26] No consensus exists regarding the radiographic measurements that are correlated with clinical outcome. It is important for the physician to understand and properly describe the patient's pelvic anatomy, not only for the sake of clinical management but also for correlation with outcomes research.

The spinopelvic anatomy and the resulting orientation of the sacrum and L5 with respect to the horizontal axis generally is based on the anatomic shape of the ilium and sacrum and the rotation of the pelvis about the femoroacetabular axis. Pelvic incidence is defined as the angle formed by a line drawn from the femoral head to the midpoint of the sacral end plate and a line drawn perpendicular to that end plate. The pelvic incidence is a unique, unvarying descriptor of the pelvic anatomy that does not change after an individual reaches adulthood. A greater pelvic incidence was associated with spondylolisthesis in several studies,[26-30] although it may not be the primary factor in the etiology of spondylolysis.[31]

Sacral slope is defined as the angle subtended by a line drawn along the superior end plate of S1 and the horizontal axis. The sacral slope is a position-dependent variable that changes as the pelvis rotates about the axis of the femoroacetabular joint. Pelvic tilt is defined as the angle subtended by a line drawn from the center of the femoral head to the midpoint of the S1 end plate (the pelvic radius) and a vertical reference line. Like sacral slope, pelvic tilt is position dependent.

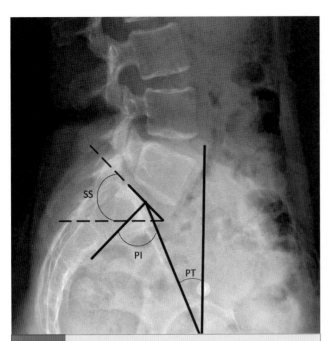

Figure 3 Lateral radiograph showing representative measurements of pelvic incidence (PI), pelvic tilt (PT), and sacral slope (SS). The constant PI is related to PT and SS by the relationship PI = PT + SS. PI is an anatomic constant that does not change after skeletal maturity. SS and PT are variables that can be affected by spondylolisthesis and its surgical management. Standing radiographs are imperative for evaluating the spinopelvic anatomy of a patient with IS.

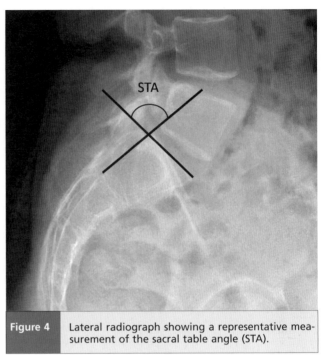

Figure 4 Lateral radiograph showing a representative measurement of the sacral table angle (STA).

The pelvic incidence angle is equal to the sum of the sacral slope and pelvic tilt angles (Figure 3).

The sacral table angle is a constant anatomic descriptor used to characterize the sacral anatomy without regard to its orientation to the ilium. The sacral table angle is subtended by a line drawn along the superior end plate of S1 and a line drawn from the posterosuperior corner of S1 to the posteroinferior edge of S1 in the midline plane. A genetic component may influence the sacral table angle; a study of a genetically homologous group found that a lower mean sacral table angle was associated with an increased occurrence of spondylolysis[31] (Figure 4).

The sacropelvic morphology is useful for predicting the progression of spondylolisthesis; it may be correlated with the clinical outcome and should be considered in surgical planning. Consequently, sacropelvic measurements should be included in the evaluation of any IS patient. At least 6% of asymptomatic adults have a pars defect.[7] A relatively small CT analysis found no statistically significant association among spondylolysis, IS, and low back pain. Almost all symptoms attributed to low-grade IS (Meyerding grade I or II) were found to respond well to a dedicated course of nonsurgical management, the foundations of which were physical therapy, aerobic conditioning, and antilordotic bracing. Continued repetitive loading and ex-

tension were found to predispose patients to low back pain.[7]

Nonsurgical Management

A dedicated course of nonsurgical management is successful for most patients with symptomatic IS.[20,32] Activity modification, physical therapy, and aerobic conditioning are the mainstays of nonsurgical management for adult patients. Anti-inflammatory medication and temporary bracing in 8° to 15° of lumbar flexion can be used until the symptoms subside.[33,34] The goal of bracing in flexion is to offload the pars lesion during the symptomatic flare. Most studies of bracing pertain to the management of acute lesions of the pars interarticularis in adolescents and children. Rigid bracing for up to 3 months generally is recommended for adolescents with acute lesions,[32,35-37] but it is reasonable to end brace treatment in an adult when the symptoms have resolved. The exception is the rare patient with an acute pars fracture. In an adult with acute spondylolysis, as seen on single-photon emission computed tomography, brace treatment may result in healing, with a good outcome maintained even if there is a nonunion.[38] Steroid injections of the pars defect and the exiting nerve root may provide symptomatic relief; the efficacy of this treatment primarily is supported by expert opinion, however.[32] During the acute episode, the patient should be taught to avoid maneuvers that exacerbate symptoms, such as lumbar extension and torsion. As the symptoms subside, physical therapy is used to develop the core musculature and relieve hamstring and anterior hip capsule tightness.[34] Exercises that focus on flexion have better results than extension-based exercises.[34] The overall nonsurgical management strategy is similar to the strategy for other chronic conditions, in which management of a symptomatic flare is followed by a dedicated program of maintenance physical exercises intended to reduce chronic symptoms to a level acceptable to the patient.

Surgical Management

If a comprehensive nonsurgical management program is not successful, surgical arthrodesis can be considered, with decompression of the neural elements if needed. Decompression with removal of the Gill fragment was widely performed in the past, but currently there is a clear consensus that isolated decompression leads to a worse outcome than fusion. In the absence of neurologic symptoms, some evidence suggests that the addition of a decompression to the fusion procedure may decrease the likelihood of successful arthrodesis.[39] Successful arthrodesis at the level of the IS leads to significant improvement in symptoms.[40] The factors associated with a poor outcome include smoking, female sex, a history of lack of exercise, an active workers' compensation claim, and pending litigation.[41]

Controversy remains as to the optimal arthrodesis technique.[42] A strict comparison of outcomes reported in the available studies is confounded by a lack of standard reporting, the retrospective nature of the studies, and inclusion of surgeon-reported fusion rates and outcomes. Data from a single-center study may have limited applicability to other centers because inherent referral-pattern inclusion biases limit the statistical validity of the extrapolated results. In the absence of prospective, multicenter randomized studies, a meta-analysis is useful for widening the applicability of statistically significant findings. A meta-analysis found that individual studies of adult patients with IS had conflicting results, but the pooled data nonetheless revealed that a good clinical result is correlated with a successful fusion; anterior-posterior procedures yielded the highest rates of fusion.[42,43]

Posterolateral fusion (PLF) is the historical standard for the surgical management of IS. It is widely recognized that the addition of pedicle screw instrumentation increases the rate of successful fusion. However, there is no clear consensus that successful posterior arthrodesis is correlated with a good clinical outcome. Multiple studies have suggested a correlation between successful fusion and good outcomes.[42,44] There is a trend toward the use of instrumentation, but noninstrumented in situ fusion with autologous bone graft remains a reasonable option. If decompression and removal of the Gill fragment are deemed necessary, the case for instrumentation may be stronger because of the risk of pseudarthrosis.[39] The use of instrumentation increases surgical time and blood loss.[45] Most available studies of PLF are retrospective, although several prospective studies of posterior fusion have been published.[39,45-48] These prospective studies did not find that clinical outcomes improved when instrumentation was added to PLF for low-grade IS. A prospective, randomized comparison study of adult patients with IS found that successful posterolateral arthrodesis improved the clinical outcome.[47] At 2-year follow-up, patients with IS had better scores on the Oswestry Disability Index and visual analog back and leg pain scales than patients with degenerative spondylolisthesis.[9] This result to some extent may be confounded by the older age of the patients with degenerative spondylolisthesis, which creates a predisposition to adjacent-level degeneration.[49]

Anterior lumbar interbody fusion (ALIF) offers a direct approach to the disk space, places an interbody graft that is under compression and thus biomechanically more conducive to successful arthrodesis, and allows restoration of disk space height. The published fusion rates after isolated ALIF for IS are from retrospective case studies and range from 53% to 90%;[43] the reported outcome success rates range from 80% to 95%.[43] No prospective studies have specifically compared stand-alone ALIF to other fusion techniques for treating IS.

Circumferential (combined anterior-posterior) fusion can be accomplished using ALIF, followed by instrumented PLF; or using posterior transforaminal lumbar interbody fusion (TLIF) or posterior lumbar interbody fusion (PLIF), followed by instrumented PLF. Circumferential fusion is recommended by some experts over PLF because it offers a better rate of successful arthrodesis. TLIF and PLIF avoid the morbidity of anterior approach and are increasingly used to treat patients with IS. No level I data are available to compare TLIF or PLIF to PLF. The use of TLIF and PLIF primarily is based on the belief that successful arthrodesis and a good clinical outcome are correlated, as well as a desire to avoid the potential morbidity of an anterior approach. A prospective comparison study of PLIF and PLF (with or without instrumentation) found no significant difference in outcomes at 2-year follow-up.[50] The only prospective controlled study directly comparing circumferential and PLF found that circumferential fusion had better outcomes at 2-year follow-up.[51] Retrospective case studies reported fusion rates ranging from 88% to 98% with combined anterior-posterior procedures.[43]

Reduction of the listhetic segment in IS remains controversial. In a patient with a high-grade slip, in situ fusion does not treat the sacropelvic deformity, and the slip angle may progress. Reduction restores a more normal spinopelvic alignment and decreases lumbosacral kyphosis. Reduction of a high-grade slip creates a larger bony area for interbody fusion; in addition, it may improve sagittal balance and to some extent protect the adjacent cephalad levels from accelerated degeneration. Slip reduction of a high-grade spondylolisthesis may improve the fusion rate.[52] The patients were adolescents in most of the long-term follow-up studies on the outcomes of reduction. For an adult patient with low-grade IS, postural reduction may be achieved with patient positioning, and anterior placement of the interbody graft is correlated with restoration of lumbar lordosis.[53] No long-term outcome studies have reported the reduction of low-grade IS in adult patients. The role of reduction is controversial in patients with high-grade IS (grade III or higher). In patients with high-grade IS, pseudarthrosis rates were lower after instrumented reduction and fusion than after in situ fusion.[52] Instrumented reduction and fusion were reported to significantly increase the average disk space height as well as the sacral inclination, consistent with an average increase in lordosis. Some case studies found that instrumented reduction with TLIF at 2-year follow-up maintained a statistically significant slip reduction, sacral inclination improvement, and increased disk space height.[54] The extent to which these improved radiographic parameters affect the long-term outcome has not been determined. Conversely, the reduction of high-grade IS has been associated with neurologic injury, including cauda equina syndrome.[55] The reported rate of injury is as high as 19%.[56] If reduction of a high-grade slip is clinically indicated, the use of intraoperative monitoring with free-running electromyography should be considered. Adequate visualization of the neural elements is essential.

The stability of the listhetic segment must be considered during surgical planning or outcome analysis. Many studies comingle relatively common stable slips with the less stable listhesis. Comparative analysis of the surgical treatment techniques used for unstable IS motion segments suggests that combined anterior-posterior fusion leads to better outcomes than instrumented PLF.[51] The heterogeneity of the reported results of surgical management of adult IS suggests that each of the techniques may have a role for properly selected patients. The stability of the motion segment may be the most pertinent clinical factor in the decision between posterior and circumferential fusion. With the increasing biomechanical strength of modern instrumentation constructs, there has been a concomitant improvement in slip angle reduction, restoration of disk space height, and fusion rates. An anterior-posterior procedure may improve the stability of IS motion segments that are unstable on preoperative flexion-extension radiographs.

Summary

The baseline prevalence of spondylolysis in the adult population is 5% to 6%. Most patients are asymptomatic. Spondylolisthesis develops during childhood, and most slips in adults are stable and nonprogressive. Progressive spondylolisthesis and its symptoms are related to degenerative changes and loss of disk space height, and they may be correlated with sacropelvic morphology. Most patients can be successfully treated with a program of physical therapy and aerobic condi-

tioning. For patients who cannot be successfully treated without surgery, fusion of the listhetic segment is recommended. A concomitant decompression is performed if the patient has radicular symptoms or signs. For an unstable, higher grade slip, anterior column interbody support is recommended. The surgical techniques vary, and most reports are limited by the inherent confounding factors of any single-center study. The role of reduction is more controversial than that of the fusion technique. Instrumented reduction can be achieved and maintained, but its role remains to be defined. There is a need for prospective, multicenter outcomes data with standardized reporting of sacropelvic morphology and listhetic segment stability to define the optimal surgical technique and the variables that are correlated with outcomes.

Annotated References

1. Fredrickson BE, Baker D, McHolick WJ, Yuan HA, Lubicky JP: The natural history of spondylolysis and spondylolisthesis. *J Bone Joint Surg Am* 1984;66(5): 699-707.

2. Beutler WJ, Fredrickson BE, Murtland A, Sweeney CA, Grant WD, Baker D: The natural history of spondylolysis and spondylolisthesis: 45-year follow-up evaluation. *Spine (Phila Pa 1976)* 2003;28(10):1027-1035.

3. Ganju A: Isthmic spondylolisthesis. *Neurosurg Focus* 2002;13(1):E1.

4. Wynne-Davies R, Scott JH: Inheritance and spondylolisthesis: A radiographic family survey. *J Bone Joint Surg Br* 1979;61-B(3):301-305.

5. Simper LB: Spondylolysis in Eskimo skeletons. *Acta Orthop Scand* 1986;57(1):78-80.

6. Tower SS, Pratt WB: Spondylolysis and associated spondylolisthesis in Eskimo and Athabascan populations. *Clin Orthop Relat Res* 1990;250:171-175.

7. Kalichman L, Kim DH, Li L, Guermazi A, Berkin V, Hunter DJ: Spondylolysis and spondylolisthesis: Prevalence and association with low back pain in the adult community-based population. *Spine (Phila Pa 1976)* 2009;34(2):199-205.

   Abdominal CT, lumbar spine findings, and a back pain questionnaire revealed no significant association among spondylolysis, spondylolisthesis, and back pain in patients in the Framingham Heart Study. Level of evidence: IV.

8. Seitsalo S, Osterman K, Hyvärinen H, Tallroth K, Schlenzka D, Poussa M: Progression of spondylolisthesis in children and adolescents: A long-term follow-up of 272 patients. *Spine (Phila Pa 1976)* 1991;16(4): 417-421.

9. Floman Y: Progression of lumbosacral isthmic spondylolisthesis in adults. *Spine (Phila Pa 1976)* 2000; 25(3):342-347.

10. Osterman K, Schlenzka D, Poussa M, Seitsalo S, Virta L: Isthmic spondylolisthesis in symptomatic and asymptomatic subjects, epidemiology, and natural history with special reference to disk abnormality and mode of treatment. *Clin Orthop Relat Res* 1993;297:65-70.

11. Tallarico RA, Madom IA, Palumbo MA: Spondylolysis and spondylolisthesis in the athlete. *Sports Med Arthrosc* 2008;16(1):32-38.

   Genetic factors and repetitive trauma contribute to the risk of spondylolysis and/or spondylolisthesis. The athlete's desire for an early return to sports may become an issue in treatment decision making.

12. DePalma MJ, Bhargava A: Nonspondylolytic etiologies of lumbar pain in the young athlete. *Curr Sports Med Rep* 2006;5(1):44-49.

   Adolescent athletes are at risk of persistent back pain from IS or injury as a result of the adolescent growth spurt and skeletal immaturity. An accurate diagnosis is essential before treatment.

13. Micheli LJ, Wood R: Back pain in young athletes: Significant differences from adults in causes and patterns. *Arch Pediatr Adolesc Med* 1995;149(1):15-18.

14. Radcliff KE, Kalantar SB, Reitman CA: Surgical management of spondylolysis and spondylolisthesis in athletes: Indications and return to play. *Curr Sports Med Rep* 2009;8(1):35-40.

   No high-level studies provide specific recommendations for treating IS in competitive athletes. Most such patients can be successfully treated without surgery, but a pars repair or fusion can be considered if necessary and can allow a return to sports at the preinjury level.

15. Wiltse LL, Newman PH, Macnab I: Classification of spondylolisis and spondylolisthesis. *Clin Orthop Relat Res* 1976;117:23-29.

16. Meyerding HW: Spondylolisthesis. *Surg Gynecol Obstet* 1932;54:371-377.

17. Cassidy RC, Shaffer WO, Johnson DL: Spondylolysis and spondylolisthesis in the athlete. *Orthopedics* 2005; 28(11):1331-1333.

   Despite the possibility of returning to sports after treatment of spondylolysis or spondylolisthesis, the goal should be prevention of back injury in athletes at high risk.

18. Shen J, Wang HY, Chen JY, Liang BL: Morphologic analysis of normal human lumbar dorsal root ganglion by 3D MR imaging. *AJNR Am J Neuroradiol* 2006; 27(10):2098-2103.

   The anatomy of the dorsal root ganglion was assessed in 115 lumbar spine MRI studies. The size of the dorsal root ganglion was found to increase in a cranial-to-caudal direction. As many as 6% are not located within the foramen. In the cephalad levels the dorsal root ganglion is larger and more centrally located, creating a predisposition to compression with foraminal narrowing. Level of evidence: IV.

19. Saraste H, Nilsson B, Broström LA, Aparisi T: Relationship between radiological and clinical variables in spondylolysis. *Int Orthop* 1984;8(3):163-174.

20. Lauerman WC, Cain JE: Isthmic spondylolisthesis in the adult. *J Am Acad Orthop Surg* 1996;4(4):201-208.

21. Saraste H: Long-term clinical and radiological follow-up of spondylolysis and spondylolisthesis. *J Pediatr Orthop* 1987;7(6):631-638.

22. Floman Y, Millgram MA, Ashkenazi E, Smorgick Y, Rand N: Instrumented slip reduction and fusion for painful unstable isthmic spondylolisthesis in adults. *J Spinal Disord Tech* 2008;21(7):477-483.

   No instrumentation failures were observed at 38-month follow-up after 12 instrumented reductions for IS using PLIF, and there was a 95% maintenance of reduction. Scores improved on the visual analog back and leg pain scales as well as the Oswestry Disability Index.

23. Schneider G, Pearcy MJ, Bogduk N: Abnormal motion in spondylolytic spondylolisthesis. *Spine (Phila Pa 1976)* 2005;30(10):1159-1164.

   A retrospective study compared 13 patients with symptomatic IS and 20 asymptomatic patients. Motion analysis of the instantaneous centers of rotation suggested the abnormality is in the type of motion with abnormal translation of the cephalad level rather than an absolute change in the magnitude of flexion-extension. Level of evidence: III.

24. Krupski W, Majcher P: Radiological diagnostic of lumbar spondylolysis. *Ortop Traumatol Rehabil* 2004;6(6): 809-818.

25. Collier BD, Johnson RP, Carrera GF, et al: Painful spondylolysis or spondylolisthesis studied by radiography and single-photon emission computed tomography. *Radiology* 1985;154(1):207-211.

26. Labelle H, Roussouly P, Berthonnaud E, Dimnet J, O'Brien M: The importance of spino-pelvic balance in L5-s1 developmental spondylolisthesis: A review of pertinent radiologic measurements. *Spine (Phila Pa 1976)* 2005;30(6, suppl):S27-S34.

   Analysis of standing lateral radiographs for IS at L5-S1 found that postoperative improvement in the L5 pelvic incidence angle and lumbosacral angle were correlated with better outcome. A higher preoperative grade was correlated with a poor outcome. Level of evidence: III.

27. Duval-Beaupere G, Marty C, Barthel F, et al: Sagittal profile of the spine prominent part of the pelvis. *Stud Health Technol Inform* 2002;88:47-64.

28. Labelle H, Roussouly P, Berthonnaud E, et al: Spondylolisthesis, pelvic incidence, and spinopelvic balance: A correlation study. *Spine (Phila Pa 1976)* 2004;29(18): 2049-2054.

29. Hanson DS, Bridwell KH, Rhee JM, Lenke LG: Correlation of pelvic incidence with low- and high-grade isthmic spondylolisthesis. *Spine (Phila Pa 1976)* 2002; 27(18):2026-2029.

30. Marty C, Boisaubert B, Descamps H, et al: The sagittal anatomy of the sacrum among young adults, infants, and spondylolisthesis patients. *Eur Spine J* 2002;11(2): 119-125.

31. Whitesides TE Jr, Horton WC, Hutton WC, Hodges L: Spondylolytic spondylolisthesis: A study of pelvic and lumbosacral parameters of possible etiologic effect in two genetically and geographically distinct groups with high occurrence. *Spine (Phila Pa 1976)* 2005;30(6, suppl):S12-S21.

   Analysis of anatomic specimens from three relatively distinct genetic populations found that the sacral table angle varied within the populations and was correlated with spondylolysis. Remodeling after spondylolysis may cause changes in pelvic incidence. Level of evidence: IV.

32. Hu SS, Tribus CB, Diab M, Ghanayem AJ: Spondylolisthesis and spondylolysis. *J Bone Joint Surg Am* 2008; 90(3):656-671.

33. Bell DF, Ehrlich MG, Zaleske DJ: Brace treatment for symptomatic spondylolisthesis. *Clin Orthop Relat Res* 1988;236:192-198.

34. Sinaki M, Lutness MP, Ilstrup DM, Chu CP, Gramse RR: Lumbar spondylolisthesis: Retrospective comparison and three-year follow-up of two conservative treatment programs. *Arch Phys Med Rehabil* 1989;70(8): 594-598.

35. Fujii K, Katoh S, Sairyo K, Ikata T, Yasui N: Union of defects in the pars interarticularis of the lumbar spine in children and adolescents: The radiological outcome after conservative treatment. *J Bone Joint Surg Br* 2004; 86(2):225-231.

36. Steiner ME, Micheli LJ: Treatment of symptomatic spondylolysis and spondylolisthesis with the modified Boston brace. *Spine (Phila Pa 1976)* 1985;10(10):937-943.

37. Blanda J, Bethem D, Moats W, Lew M: Defects of pars interarticularis in athletes: A protocol for nonoperative treatment. *J Spinal Disord* 1993;6(5):406-411.

38. Sys J, Michielsen J, Bracke P, Martens M, Verstreken J: Nonoperative treatment of active spondylolysis in elite athletes with normal X-ray findings: Literature review and results of conservative treatment. *Eur Spine J* 2001; 10(6):498-504.

39. Carragee EJ: Single-level posterolateral arthrodesis, with or without posterior decompression, for the treatment of isthmic spondylolisthesis in adults: A prospective, randomized study. *J Bone Joint Surg Am* 1997;79(8): 1175-1180.

40. L'Heureux EA Jr, Perra JH, Pinto MR, Smith MD, Denis F, Lonstein JE: Functional outcome analysis including preoperative and postoperative SF-36 for surgically treated adult isthmic spondylolisthesis. *Spine (Phila Pa 1976)* 2003;28(12):1269-1274.

   Thirty-one adult patients with IS were treated with fusion, with significant functional improvement after arthrodesis. Level of evidence: IV.

41. Ekman P, Möller H, Hedlund R: Predictive factors for the outcome of fusion in adult isthmic spondylolisthesis. *Spine (Phila Pa 1976)* 2009;34(11):1204-1210.

   In a prospective study of 164 adult patients with IS who underwent fusion, 74% were "much better" or "better" at 2-year follow-up. The outcomes were quantified with the visual analog scale, Oswestry Disability Index, and Disability Rating Index. Level of evidence: II.

42. Jacobs WC, Vreeling A, De Kleuver M: Fusion for low-grade adult isthmic spondylolisthesis: A systematic review of the literature. *Eur Spine J* 2006;15(4):391-402.

   A systematic review of the literature found that fusion for low-grade adult IS has good outcomes, but there is no consensus regarding the method of fusion (PLF or anterior-posterior) or the use of instrumentation. Level of evidence: III.

43. Kwon BK, Hilibrand AS, Malloy K, et al: A critical analysis of the literature regarding surgical approach and outcome for adult low-grade isthmic spondylolisthesis. *J Spinal Disord Tech* 2005;18(suppl):S30-S40.

   Most of the literature on the surgical treatment of adult low-grade spondylolisthesis was retrospective and heterogenous. A combined anterior-posterior procedure most reliably achieved fusion and a satisfactory clinical outcome.

44. Zdeblick TA: A prospective, randomized study of lumbar fusion: Preliminary results. *Spine (Phila Pa 1976)* 1993;18(8):983-991.

45. Möller H, Hedlund R: Instrumented and noninstrumented posterolateral fusion in adult spondylolisthesis: A prospective randomized study. Part 2. *Spine (Phila Pa 1976)* 2000;25(13):1716-1721.

46. McGuire RA, Amundson GM: The use of primary internal fixation in spondylolisthesis. *Spine (Phila Pa 1976)* 1993;18(12):1662-1672.

47. Möller H, Hedlund R: Surgery versus conservative management in adult isthmic spondylolisthesis: A prospective randomized study. Part 1. *Spine (Phila Pa 1976)* 2000;25(13):1711-1715.

48. Bjarke Christensen F, Stender Hansen E, Laursen M, Thomsen K, Bünger CE: Long-term functional outcome

of pedicle screw instrumentation as a support for posterolateral spinal fusion: Randomized clinical study with a 5-year follow-up. *Spine (Phila Pa 1976)* 2002; 27(12):1269-1277.

49. Lauber S, Schulte TL, Liljenqvist U, Halm H, Hackenberg L: Clinical and radiologic 2-4-year results of transforaminal lumbar interbody fusion in degenerative and isthmic spondylolisthesis grades 1 and 2. *Spine (Phila Pa 1976)* 2006;31(15):1693-1698.

    In a prospective study, 19 adult patients with degenerative spondylolisthesis and 19 with IS were treated with TLIF. The fusion rate was 95%. The patients with IS had significantly better results. The Oswestry Disability Index score for the patients with IS improved from 20.5 to 10.95 at 2-year follow-up. Level of evidence: II.

50. Ekman P, Möller H, Tullberg T, Neumann P, Hedlund R: Posterior lumbar interbody fusion versus posterolateral fusion in adult isthmic spondylolisthesis. *Spine (Phila Pa 1976)* 2007;32(20):2178-2183.

    A prospective study of 86 patients with adult IS found that type of fusion (PLIF or PLF) did not affect the 2-year outcome.

51. Swan J, Hurwitz E, Malek F, et al: Surgical treatment for unstable low-grade isthmic spondylolisthesis in adults: A prospective controlled study of posterior instrumented fusion compared with combined anterior-posterior fusion. *Spine J* 2006;6(6):606-614.

    A prospective controlled study of sequential patients compared posterior instrumented and anterior-posterior fusion. Anterior-posterior fusion led to clinically significant better outcomes at 2-year follow-up. Level of evidence: II.

52. Transfeldt EE, Mehbod AA: Evidence-based medicine analysis of isthmic spondylolisthesis treatment including reduction versus fusion in situ for high-grade slips. *Spine (Phila Pa 1976)* 2007;32(19, suppl):S126-S129.

    A review of the literature on reduction of high-grade spondylolisthesis in the pediatric population found insufficient evidence to formulate evidence-based guidelines. Level of evidence: III.

53. Kwon BK, Berta S, Daffner SD, et al: Radiographic analysis of transforaminal lumbar interbody fusion for the treatment of adult isthmic spondylolisthesis. *J Spinal Disord Tech* 2003;16(5):469-476.

54. Goyal N, Wimberley DW, Hyatt A, et al: Radiographic and clinical outcomes after instrumented reduction and transforaminal lumbar interbody fusion of mid and high-grade isthmic spondylolisthesis. *J Spinal Disord Tech* 2009;22(5):321-327.

    A retrospective study of 13 patients with mid-grade or high-grade IS who underwent instrumented reduction and TLIF found minimal loss of reduction at 2-year follow-up. The fusion rate was 90%. Disk height restoration was maintained, and there was a significant increase in sacral inclination. Level of evidence: IV.

55. Ani N, Keppler L, Biscup RS, Steffee AD: Reduction of high-grade slips (grades III-V) with VSP instrumentation: Report of a series of 41 cases. *Spine (Phila Pa 1976)* 1991;16(6, suppl):S302-S310.

56. Hu SS, Bradford DS, Transfeldt EE, Cohen M: Reduction of high-grade spondylolisthesis using Edwards instrumentation. *Spine (Phila Pa 1976)* 1996;21(3):367-371.

Chapter 31

Adult Spine Deformity

Dilip Kumar Sengupta, MD

Introduction

Adult spine deformity affects as many as 60% of the older adult population but generally is asymptomatic.[1] The incidence of symptomatic adult scoliosis reportedly is 6%, and the average age of those first seeking medical care is 60 to 69 years. Cosmesis tends to be the primary concern among adolescents with scoliosis. In contrast, the significant and measurable impact on health-related quality of life is most important to adults with spine deformity. Cosmetic correction is not a concern, but restoration of global balance is important for achieving pain relief. Several features distinguish adult from adolescent spine deformity: pain rather than cosmetic deformity as the predominant symptom, a different rate of deformity progression, different causes of progression, the presence of degenerative components such as stenosis and spondylolisthesis, the rigidity of the deformity, and the frequent association of osteoporosis or a medical comorbidity. The gradual demographic shift toward an older population and the unwillingness of many older adults to accept the limitations of deformity and pain have made adult spine deformity a much more frequently encountered clinical entity.

Classification

Adult scoliosis traditionally has been classified as primary degenerative scoliosis (type I, sometimes called de novo scoliosis); progressive childhood idiopathic scoliosis in an adult, with secondary degenerative changes (type II); or scoliosis secondary to another pathologic condition (type III)[2] (Table 1). Type III has two subtypes. Type IIIA is scoliosis in the lumbosacral spine caudal to a long fusion for an earlier spine deformity; it results from adjacent-segment degeneration or pelvic obliquity secondary to limb-length discrepancy or hip pathology. Type IIIB is scoliosis secondary to metabolic bone disease (usually osteoporosis) combined with asymmetric degenerative disease and/or vertebral fracture. This classification structure offers a relatively simple means of classifying adult deformity based on cause and general treatment strategies. However, the complexity of specific deformities is not adequately reflected for use in detailed surgical planning.

The classification of adult spine deformity continues to evolve. The Scoliosis Research Society Adult Spinal Deformity Committee in 2006 presented a classification system with seven curve types (six coronal and one sagittal) and three modifiers (regional sagittal, lumbar degenerative, and global balance).[3] This system has been found reliable but is difficult to use in daily practice because it is primarily descriptive and does not take clinical parameters into account.

Recent studies have underlined the importance of sagittal plane analysis and the impact of the pelvis on spinopelvic alignment as well as pain and disability.[4] These factors are considered in the recently proposed Scoliosis Research Society–Schwab Adult Deformity Classification, which includes four curve types and three sets of modifiers[5] (Table 2). This system relies on full-length coronal and sagittal radiographs obtained with the patient in a free-standing posture with the fingers on the clavicles and the shoulders in 45° of forward elevation.

The curve type is determined based on maximal coronal Cobb angle. All curves greater than 30° are categorized by apical level. The modifiers describe the sagittal components of the deformity. One modifier represents the difference between the pelvic incidence and the lumbar lordosis (Figure 1 and Figure 2). In normal sagittal alignment, lumbar lordosis should be almost the same as the pelvic incidence. In adult spine deformity, the lumbar lordosis may be less than the pelvic incidence (a flat back). The pelvic tilt modifier assesses the extent of pelvic retroversion, and the global balance modifier categorizes the global sagittal alignment as indicated by the sagittal vertical axis (Figure 1).

The rationale for the Scoliosis Research Society–Schwab Adult Deformity Classification is the strong correlation of pelvic incidence–lumbar lordosis, pelvic

Dr. Sengupta or an immediate family member serves as a board member, owner, officer, or committee member of the Scoliosis Research Society, the Spine Arthroplasty Society, and the Dartmouth-Hitchcock Medical Center; has received royalties from Globus Medical; is a member of a speakers' bureau or has made paid presentations on behalf of Globus Medical; serves as a paid consultant to or is an employee of Globus Medical; has received research or institutional support from Globus Medical; owns stock or stock options in Globus Medical; and has received nonincome support (such as equipment or services), commercially derived honoraria, or other non–research-related funding (such as paid travel) from Globus Medical.

Table 1

Comparison of Type I and Type II Adult Scoliosis

Characteristic	Type I	Type II
General description	Primary degenerative (de novo) scoliosis	Progressive idiopathic scoliosis
Location	Thoracolumbar or lumbar spine	Thoracic, thoracolumbar, or lumbar spine
Type of curve	Short, sharp	Long segment
Flexibility	Rigid	Relatively flexible
Predominant pathomechanism	Asymmetric disk collapse, lateral listhesis, wedging of vertebra	Rotation and tilting of the vertebra
Symptoms	Back pain, radicular pain, claudication pain, fatigue, loss of global balance	Back pain, loss of global balance, fatigue

Table 2

The Scoliosis Research Society–Schwab Adult Deformity Classification

1. Curves

Curve Type	Description
T	Thoracic curve only: major curve >30°, apical level T9 or higher, lumbar curve <30°
L	Lumbar (L) or thoracolumbar (TL) curve only: major curve >30°, apical level T10 or lower, thoracic curve <30°
D	Double major curve: at least one T and one TL or L curve, both >30°
S	Primarily sagittal deformity: coronal curve <30°

2. Modifiers

Modifier Type	Subclassification
Pelvic incidence minus lumbar lordosis	A: <10° B: 10° to 20° (moderate) C: >20° (marked)
Pelvic tilt	L: <20° M: 20° to 30° H: >30°
Global balance (sagittal vertical axis)	N: <45 mm P: 45 to 90 mm VP: >90 mm

tilt, and sagittal vertical axis with scores on measures of health-related quality of life.[4] Pelvic tilt is a crucial parameter in assessing spine deformity; a high pelvic tilt (increased pelvic retroversion) is a compensatory mechanism that can reduce the apparent extent of global sagittal malalignment. The modifiers of the spino-pelvic parameters are intended to set the thresholds of correction for sagittal realignment procedures (sagittal vertical axis less than 50 mm, pelvic tilt less than 25°, and lumbar lordosis within −10° of pelvic incidence) to achieve a harmonious alignment after surgical correction.[6]

Diagnostic Imaging

Standing full-length AP and lateral radiographs should be obtained on a 36-inch-long cassette with the patient in a free-standing posture and with the fingers on the clavicles and shoulders in 45° of forward elevation.[7] Cervical spine and spinopelvic alignment is assessed on a radiograph taken with the knees in extension, the hips relaxed, and the feet no more than shoulder width apart; this posture allows assessment of pelvic compensation for sagittal imbalance.

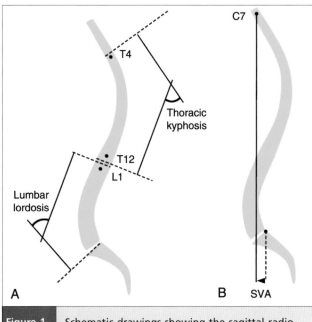

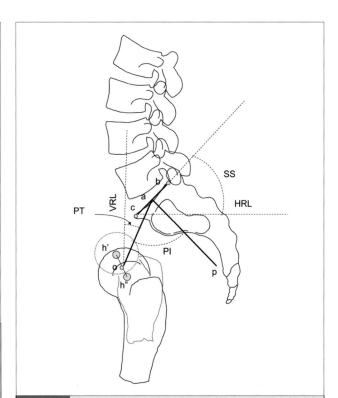

Figure 1 Schematic drawings showing the sagittal radiographic parameters. **A,** Thoracic kyphosis is measured from the superior end plate of T4 to the inferior end plate of T12 *(top dashed lines)*. Lumbar lordosis measured from the superior end plate of L1 to the superior end plate of S1 *(bottom dashed lines)*. **B,** The sagittal vertical axis (SVA) is defined as the horizontal offset from the posterosuperior corner of S1 to the C7 vertebral body.

Figure 2 Schematic drawing showing the pelvic parameters. The line a-p is the perpendicular drawn on the sacral end plate (b-c) at its midpoint (a). The femoral heads axis (o) is the center of the line connecting each femoral head (h', h") when the two femoral heads are not perfectly superimposed on a lateral radiograph. Pelvic incidence (PI) is defined as the angle between the perpendicular line a-p drawn at the midpoint (a) of the sacral end plate (b-c) and the line o-a connecting this point to the center of the femoral heads axis (o). Sacral slope (SS) is defined as the angle between the horizontal reference line (HRL) and the sacral end plate (b-c). Pelvic tilt (PT) is defined as the angle between the vertical reference line (VRL) originating from the center of the femoral head or femoral heads axis (o) and the line a-o joining this point to the midpoint of the sacral end plate. Pelvic tilt increases with retroversion and decreases with anteversion of the pelvis. The relationship between these three parameters is such that PI = PT + SS.

Curve magnitude, curve flexibility, and global sagittal and coronal balance also are assessed on radiographs. The Cobb angle is measured on the full-length AP or lateral radiograph to determine the magnitude of scoliosis or kyphosis, respectively. Curve flexibility is determined from side-bending or hyperextension radiographs. For a curve exceeding 60°, push-prone-traction radiographs are most predictive of curve flexibility. A structural curve is defined by a Cobb angle of at least 25° on a side-bending radiograph.[8] A 36-inch lateral or hyperextension lateral radiograph taken with the patient supine over a bolster may be indicated to assess flexibility of the kyphosis in a primary sagittal plane deformity.

MRI is useful in assessing the extent of degenerative changes in the disk and facet joints as well as the location of central and lateral canal stenosis. CT myelography can be used to assess spinal stenosis in patients with a contraindication to MRI such as a pacemaker. CT with three-dimensional reconstruction may help complete the assessment of complex and severe curves. CT is particularly useful for understanding the anatomy, size, and orientation of the pedicles before pedicle screw instrumentation. Diskography occasionally is helpful in an adult younger than 50 years with idiopathic (type II) scoliosis to rule out the presence of a painful disk and select a caudal instrumentation level in the midlumbar spine. Diskography is not as useful in patients with primary degenerative (type I) scoliosis because the degeneration involves multiple levels and the fixation often must be extended to L5 or the sacrum. Dual-energy x-ray absorptiometry is useful for assessing bone density in these patients, who often have osteopenia or osteoporosis.

The Pathomorphology of Primary Degenerative Scoliosis

Primary degenerative (type I) scoliosis develops secondary to asymmetric disk collapse, anteroposterior or lateral listhesis, or vertebral wedging. The curve is short,

4: The Adult Spine

sharp, and relatively stiff, with minimal rotation. In contrast, idiopathic scoliosis (type II) is characterized by rotation of the apical vertebra toward the convexity of the curve and usually extends over a longer segment of the spine. The loss of sagittal and coronal balance (the plumb line shift) is greater in primary degenerative scoliosis because the seat of the deformity is toward the caudal end of the spine in the lumbar or thoracolumbar region. The spondylolisthesis in the sagittal plane may lead to loss of lumbar lordosis (flat back). Instability in the frontal plane may lead to lateral listhesis, which aggravates the scoliosis. The biologic reaction to an unstable segment is the formation of osteophytes at the facet joints and the vertebral end plates, which contribute to the increasing narrowing of the spinal canal. In addition, hypertrophy and calcification of the ligamentum flavum and joint capsules lead to central and lateral recess stenosis. The collapse of the disk height and lateral listhesis may cause foraminal stenosis, particularly in the concavity of the curve. The convex side, where the nerve roots may be stretched, is not immune to radicular symptoms.

Clinical Features

Pain
Pain is the most common presenting symptom, in several forms. Axial back pain is characterized by a constant dull aching around the lower back. In activity-related mechanical back pain, typically there is an instability catch, defined as a sharp pain in the back or buttock during forward bending or, more often, while returning to erect posture. Pain in the leg may be referred from the back, or it may be typical radicular pain in a dermatomal distribution, resulting from nerve root compression in the stenotic foramen or dynamic overstretching on the convex side of the curve. Patients with a decompensated curve and loss of global balance may have diffuse muscular pain secondary to fatigue during daily activities. Spinal stenosis can cause neurogenic claudication, which is precipitated by standing or walking a short distance and relieved by sitting or leaning forward while supported by, for example, a shopping cart. Neurogenic claudication must be distinguished from vascular claudication, which often is present in these older patients. Claudication pain typically appears as diffuse bilateral leg pain, but occasionally it appears as back pain during standing or walking. A neurologic deficit is uncommon and may represent a radicular condition or, rarely, cauda equina syndrome from a herniated disk in a tight spinal canal.

It is important to note that adult spine deformity is not always associated with pain or disability, particularly after the deformity becomes fixed or rigid.

Curve Progression
Idiopathic scoliosis with a curve smaller than 30° at skeletal maturity tends not to progress. A curve larger than 40° generally progresses 1° to 2° per year but may progress more rapidly as its magnitude progresses. In patients older than approximately 70 years who have secondary degenerative changes, curve progression can exceed 3° per year. Lumbar curves progress more rapidly and to a greater extent than thoracic curves. The risk of curve progression in the lumbar spine is greater if the curve is larger than 30°, rotation of the apical vertebra is greater than 33°, and lateral listhesis is greater than 6 mm and includes an oblique takeoff of L5 on S1.[9] Curve progression often is perceived by the patient as a progressive loss of height. In a decompensated lumbar curve, the loss of height may be secondary to global imbalance. Curve progression is an indicator of an unstable deformity that often is symptomatic and may constitute an indication for surgical intervention. Occasionally, the collapse of the lumbar segment in a severe lumbar curve may lead to the rib cage resting on the pelvis. This occurrence may achieve secondary stabilization of curve progression, sometimes with symptom relief, or the pressure may cause a different kind of pain at the rib–iliac crest junction (Figure 3).

Cosmesis
In contrast to patients with adolescent idiopathic scoliosis, older adult patients usually are not overly concerned about cosmesis. Loss of balance may be the primary presenting symptom; the patient leans forward and requires a walking aid to stand upright. Cosmesis occasionally is a factor for an adult patient younger than 40 years, if pain develops as a result of early secondary degeneration of the disk below an idiopathic thoracolumbar or lumbar scoliosis.

Cardiopulmonary Symptoms
The patient's presenting symptom is rarely cardiopulmonary. In severe thoracic scoliosis (greater than 90°), the cardiorespiratory reserve may decrease secondary to the rib hump as the vertebral bodies on the convex side rotate into the chest cavity.

Coronal and Sagittal Spine Alignment
In adult spine deformity, the restoration of global balance is more important than the absolute degree of coronal curve correction. Global coronal balance is measured as the lateral shift of the C7 plumb line from the center sacral vertical line (CSVL) and apical vertebral translation (Figure 4). Vertebral, pelvic, and shoulder tilt angles can be directly measured relative to a horizontal reference line. Vertebral tilt typically is measured relative to the proximal end plate. Shoulder tilt is measured using the clavicular heads. The sacral ala, sacral sulci, or iliac crests are used to determine pelvic tilt.

There is a wide variation in the normal range of thoracic kyphosis and lumbar lordosis measurements. Thoracic kyphosis normally increases with age, with a greater increase in women.[10] The range in 95% of the adult population is +25° to +65° (mean ± standard

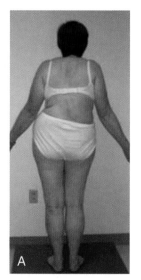
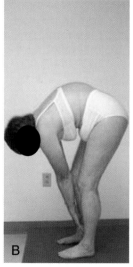
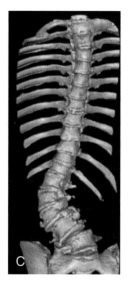
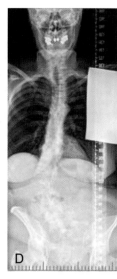
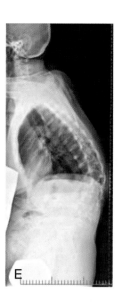

4: The Adult Spine

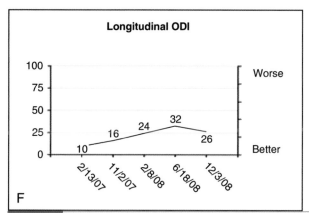
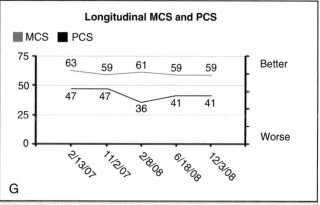

Figure 3   **A** and **B**, Photographs showing a 66-year-old woman with severe kyphoscoliosis of the thoracolumbar spine and both sagittal and coronal imbalance. She had excellent flexibility in her spine. **C**, CT reconstruction showing the magnitude of deformity and bony changes in the lumbar spine. AP (**D**) and lateral (**E**) radiographs showing the rib cage resting on the iliac crest, providing secondary stabilization of the curve and preventing curve progression as well as pain. Over a 22-month period, the patient had minimal pain and disability, as reflected on the Oswestry Disability Index (ODI) (**F**) and the Medical Outcomes Study Short Form-36 mental and physical component summaries (MCS, PCS) (**G**).

deviation) for thoracic kyphosis (T4-T12) and −40° to −84° for lumbosacral lordosis (T12-S1).[11] Approximately 70% of the total lumbosacral lordosis occurs from the superior end plate of L4 to the superior end plate of S1.[11] The lumbosacral lordosis should exceed the thoracic kyphosis by a minimum of 10° to 20°.[12] Despite wide variations in regional sagittal curves, normal upright balance is maintained with the head over the pelvis. The global sagittal balance is measured as the sagittal vertical axis (SVA), which is the offset between the C7 plumb line and the posterosuperior corner of S1 (Figure 3). In normal adults, the range of the SVA is from +48 mm (anterior) to −48 mm (posterior).[11] Although the C7 plumb line is the best means of assessing global sagittal balance, it is not perfect because it is not always directly correlated with the patient's center of gravity, which is the element actually being assessed. A patient's center of gravity always should fall through the hip joints or somewhat behind

it. Usually the center of gravity is in front of the C7 plumb line.

Spinopelvic alignment is measured in terms of pelvic incidence, pelvic tilt, and sacral slope (Figure 2). Pelvic incidence is a morphologic parameter that defines lumbar alignment. Pelvic tilt is a positional parameter that measures pelvic version or rotation in the sagittal plane. In some patients, pelvic tilt serves as a compensatory mechanism for maintaining an upright posture despite age-related changes in sagittal alignment. Sacral slope quantifies the sagittal sacral inclination and completes the geometric relationship (pelvic incidence = pelvic tilt + sacral slope).

The Relationship of Sagittal Balance and Spinopelvic Alignment

In the presence of sagittal malalignment, such as loss of lumbar lordosis (flat-back syndrome), there is positive shift in the C7 plumb line as the SVA moves more than

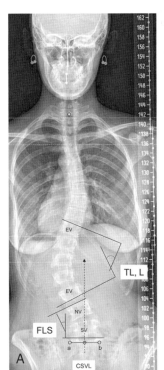

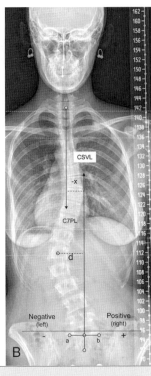

Figure 4 Standing AP radiographs with the patient's left side shown to the left. **A,** Measurement of the Cobb angle. The end vertebra (EV) is the most tilted vertebra and is at the cephalad or caudal end of a curve. The neutral vertebra (NV) is minimally rotated and is the most cephalad vertebra below the apex of the major curve (with symmetric pedicles). The stable vertebra (SV) is the most cephalad vertebra bisected by the CSVL. The CSVL is a vertical reference line through the midline of S1 *(dashed line)*. Line a-b represents the sacral end plate. The CSVL normally is perpendicular to the sacral end plate, but it may deviate in presence of pelvic or sacral obliquity. The Cobb angle is measured between the upper end plate of the proximal (cranial) EV and the lower end plate of the distal (caudal) EV. In adult deformity the curves may transgress the usual boundaries of the spine segments, so that the curve extends from the lumbar region (L) into the lower thoracic region (TL); there may also be a fractional lumbosacral curve (FLS). **B,** Measurement of coronal balance and apical vertical translation. Coronal balance is measured as the horizontal displacement (± x) of the C7 plumb line (C7PL) relative to the CSVL; a shift toward the left is denoted as negative, and toward the right is positive. Apical vertebral translation is measured as the horizontal distance (d) between the centroid of the apical vertebra of the curve *(dot)* and the CSVL.

50 mm in front of the sacral promontory. As a compensatory mechanism, the pelvis rotates into retroversion (the increase in pelvic tilt often is more than 25°) to restore a more normal SVA. This pelvic rotation may lead to hip hyperextension and knee flexion. Therefore, an abnormally great pelvic tilt may be associated with in-

creased difficulty in walking. A true assessment of sagittal balance requires recognition of such compensatory mechanisms. After surgical correction of kyphosis, a normal SVA alone may not indicate an adequate correction of the sagittal malalignment; the pelvic tilt also must be corrected to less than 25°.

In the outcome study that first pointed out the importance of spinopelvic alignment and residual pain after lumbosacral fusion, the patients with a relatively large postsurgical pelvic tilt (increased pelvic retroversion) were found to be most likely to have residual pain.[13] The principle also was valid in adult spine deformity. SVA and pelvic tilt are the key parameters correlated with pain and health-related quality of life scores. A high pelvic tilt was defined as an angle greater than 25°, and a high SVA was defined as greater than 50 mm. A high pelvic tilt and/or a high SVA is associated with a loss of lumbar lordosis (flat back), increased pain, and decreased function.[4]

Nonsurgical Management

The efficacy of any form of physical therapy or chiropractic manipulation for treating adult degenerative scoliosis is supported only by very weak (level IV) evidence, and the evidence for epidural steroid injection also is weak (level III).[14] Nonetheless, it is mandatory to try nonsurgical treatment for every patient before considering surgical intervention. Nonnarcotic pain medications, activity modification, the use of walking aids and braces, physical therapy, and spine injection procedures can be used. Weight reduction and smoking cessation can help prepare the patient for surgical treatment, if necessary.

Surgical Decision Making

The goals of surgery for adult deformity are to treat the patient's pain and relieve any neurologic symptoms while maintaining or restoring three-dimensional balance. The absolute degree of coronal curve correction is less important than the restoration and maintenance of good sagittal balance. The decision to intervene surgically is reached through an informed process between the patient and the surgeon and must be viewed in terms of balancing the risks of surgery against the patient's quality of life. The reported complication rates range from 56% to 75%, and rates of unplanned reoperation range from 18% to 58%.[15] Issues that must be considered in the presurgical decision-making process for an individual patient include the natural history of nonsurgical care, the surgical risk stratification, the presurgical workup, the timing of the surgery, the surgical approach, the location of the end of the construct, and the postsurgical rehabilitation plan. In general, the indications for surgery include intractable back and/or leg pain, neurologic symptoms, documented curve progression, loss of sagittal or coronal balance, and/or decompensation.

Patient Preparation

The purpose of the presurgical workup is to identify any modifiable conditions that may affect the outcome or the risk of perioperative complications. The preparation for surgery involves optimizing these modifiable conditions. The relative risk of respiratory complications in the presence of chronic obstructive pulmonary disease is 4.7. Smokers have a 4.3 times greater risk than nonsmokers, but smoking cessation at least 8 weeks before surgery was found to decrease the risk.[16] The cardiac risk factors include a history of coronary artery disease, diabetes, age older than 64 years, hypertension, smoking, and high cholesterol levels. A patient with a cardiac risk factor may require preoperative cardiac evaluation and stress testing; the use of β blockers can be considered before surgery, if appropriate. Nutritional depletion is not uncommon in thin, older patients as well as patients with chronic disease, infection, alcohol abuse, or spinal cord injury. Nutritional supplementation may be considered, with an assessment of total lymphocyte count as well as albumin and prealbumin levels. The presence of osteoporosis may complicate an instrumentation procedure, and it is preferable to assess a patient at high risk using dual-energy x-ray absorptiometry.

Surgical Options

The selection of the most appropriate surgical procedure for a patient with degenerative adult scoliosis is complex. The procedures include decompression, fusion, and instrumentation for correction of deformity and restoration of balance. Decompression is performed primarily to treat leg pain, whether it is radicular or related to claudication. Fusion is performed primarily to treat axial back pain and provide stability to the unstable motion segment. Fusion also may be performed to prevent instability after decompression. Instrumentation is used to correct deformity, restore balance, and promote fusion. Correction of a rigid deformity may require additional procedures such as anterior or posterior release or osteotomy.

Direct decompression is achieved by laminectomy and undercutting facetectomy and foraminotomy. This procedure may destabilize the spine and therefore should be limited to the properly identified segments and extended to the sides only where the neural elements are compressed. Disk herniation is relatively uncommon, and a diskectomy, if required, may further destabilize the segment. Indirect decompression of the foramen in the concavity of the curve can be achieved by distraction with instrumentation and correction of the scoliosis. Stand-alone decompression procedures without fusion carry the risk of destabilizing the segment and worsening the deformity, and they are rarely indicated. The exceptions are for patients who are frail, older than approximately 75 years, and possibly unable

to tolerate an operation such as instrumented fusion; and for patients who have large anterior osteophytes that provide adequate stability to the motion segment. In general, the destabilization effect is more pronounced when the decompression is performed at the apex of a curve. It may be preferable to add a short-segment stabilization with instrumented fusion during the same procedure, to rebalance the spine and prevent deterioration of the scoliosis (Figure 5). The destabilization effect also may occur if an isolated decompression is done at the bottom of a rigid curve in the lumbar spine, usually at L4-L5 or L5-S1; the rigid curve above the decompression may decompensate these segments in translation, and the spine may fall off balance.

Selection of Fusion Levels

The ideal length of a fusion in adult spine deformity remains unclear. The goal is to fuse the minimal number of motion segments necessary to achieve a balanced spine in the sagittal and coronal planes. The following principles were proposed more than 50 years ago: all vertebrae within the primary or major (structural) curve should be fused, plus an additional vertebra at both ends; the fusion should extend from the cephalad neutral vertebra to the caudal neutral vertebra; and the caudal end of the fusion should lie within the stable zone.[17] A curve is defined as structural if the Cobb angle is measured as at least 25° on a side-bending radiograph. Such a long fusion may maintain the correction well, but it often leads to secondary degenerative changes at the caudal adjacent segment.[18] The advent of segmental instrumentation, particularly pedicle screws, has allowed a greater correction involving fewer segments. Saving the motion segments is particularly important in the lumbar spine but carries the risk of accelerated degeneration and junctional deformity. The extent of fusion depends on the type of curve, the flexibility of the primary and secondary curves, and the extent of sagittal and coronal imbalance or decompensation.

Several generally accepted rules apply to both coronal and sagittal deformity. The construct should not end at the apex of a curve, either cranially or caudally. The construct should not stop adjacent to a severely degenerated disk. In the thoracolumbar region, the cranial end vertebra should be horizontal in the coronal plane and lordotic in the sagittal plane. The caudal end vertebra in the lumbar spine should be horizontal and in the stable zone. In the correction of a thoracic kyphotic deformity, such as Scheuermann kyphosis, the distal fusion should not end at the thoracolumbar junction (T11 or T12); instead, it should extend to the first lordotic segment, which usually is L1 or L2.

Fusion Levels Based on Curve Type

In an adult, a single or double thoracic curve usually represents idiopathic scoliosis. The patient typically is younger than 40 years. Posterior fusion alone is adequate for a relatively flexible curve or a curve smaller

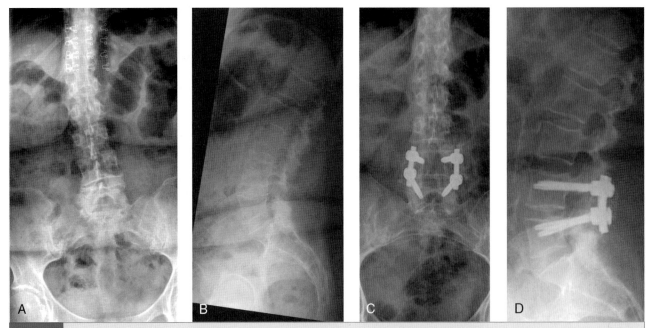

Figure 5 The role of minimal segment fusion in degenerative scoliosis. AP (**A**) and lateral (**B**) radiographs showing primary (type I) scoliosis in a 79-year-old woman. Asymmetric disk and facet degeneration has caused L4 to tilt on L5. AP (**C**) and lateral (**D**) radiographs showing correction of the tilt and restoration of spine balance after decompression and single-level instrumented fusion of L4-L5.

than 70°. A rigid curve larger than 75° usually requires anterior release followed by posterior instrumentation. Anterior instrumentation alone may be adequate for a flexible thoracic curve smaller than 60°, but this type of curve is rare in an adult patient. The fusion should be extended to neutral and stable vertebrae at the proximal and distal ends. In a double thoracic curve, the cranial extension of the fusion should not stop distal to the structural proximal thoracic curve. The proximal thoracic curve is stiffer in adults than in adolescents and therefore should always be included in the fusion to restore shoulder balance.

Double and triple major curves are differentiated by their Cobb angle, apical deviation, and relative rotation. A selective thoracic fusion can be performed if the major thoracic curve is much larger, stiffer, rotated, and deviated than the lumbar curve; the lumbar curve is not structural; and the rotation is less than 30°. The caudal extension of the selective thoracic fusion should include all vertebrae within the thoracic curve, and the fusion should end on a neutrally rotated vertebra in the stable zone. A too-short fusion (stopping short of the caudal end vertebra in the thoracic Cobb angle) may lead to further distal extension of the thoracic curve. On the other hand, a too-long fusion (extension of the fusion halfway into the lumbar curve) may result in decompensation of a previously balanced curve. In a true double major curve where the lumbar curve is structural, larger, and stiffer than the thoracic curve, both curves should be fused. In adolescents, the distal fusion often extends to L3 or L4 based on the stable and neutral vertebra and the tilt at the lowest instrumented verte-

bra. However, adults frequently have associated L4-L5 and/or L5-S1 degeneration. If the disks at these levels are healthy and horizontal, the fusion can be ended at L4. If there is a fixed tilt or subluxation at L4-L5, L5 should be included in the distal fusion. The decision to end the fusion at L5 or extend it to the pelvis is important.

A thoracolumbar or lumbar curve in an adult may originate in adolescent idiopathic scoliosis but is more likely to represent primary degenerative scoliosis. Typically, a degenerated lumbar curve in an adult includes a Cobb angle from L1 to L5, rotatory subluxation at L3-L4, an L4-L5 tilt, and L5-S1 disk degeneration. Fusion can extend from T12 or L1 above the curve to L5 or S1 below the curve. The key question is whether there is a need for the fusion to cross the thoracolumbar or lumbosacral junction. In general, the fusion should be extended to the midthoracic level (T10) rather than to the thoracolumbar junction (T11-L2). The thoracolumbar junction is anatomically unique: it is the point of transition from the immobile thoracic spine to the mobile lumbar spine; the point at which the orientation of the facet joint changes from the coronal plane proximally to the sagittal plane distally; and the junction of thoracic kyphosis and lumbar lordosis. The thoracolumbar junction is characterized by floating ribs at T11 and T12 that do not provide as much stability as the T1-T10 vertebrae. Several difficulties may arise if the upper end of the instrumented fusion is at the thoracolumbar junction, including proximal adjacent-segment degeneration, compression fracture proximal to the fusion mass, screw failure at the upper instrumented vertebra, and proximal junctional kyphosis. These difficulties can be avoided if the fusion is extended to the midthoracic level. However, proximal extension of the fusion has the disadvantages of loss of the motion segment and an incrementally increased risk from extension of the thoracic spine instrumentation. T12 occasionally is selected as the proximal instrumented level if several conditions are met: T12 is neutrally rotated and in the stable zone, in both the sagittal and coronal planes; the T11-T12 motion segment shows no degeneration or instability and is not included in the decompression; and there is no segmental kyphosis at T11-T12. If T12 is close to the apex of the sagittal or coronal plane deformity, the fusion must be extended to T10 or a higher vertebra.[19]

The choice of L5 for the lower end of the fusion requires a relatively normal L5-S1 disk (normal disk height and hydration, no listhesis) and normal lumbar lordosis (normal sagittal balance). The advantages of stopping the fusion at L5 rather than S1 are a smaller extent of operation, a smaller risk of complications, and preservation of L5-S1 motion to permit a normal gait. The clinical outcomes are no different than with fusion extension to the sacrum.[20] The greatest disadvantage is that in many patients the L5-S1 disk subsequently degenerates and causes pain. The absolute indications for extending the fusion to the sacrum in adults include a degenerated L5-S1 disk, L5-S1 spondylolisthesis, an earlier L5-S1 laminectomy, or an oblique takeoff at L5. Occasionally in a patient with advanced degeneration of L5-S1 (complete collapse and disk calcification), the level may be inherently stable and not require fusion. The perceived disadvantages of extending the fusion to the sacrum rather than ending it at L5 are the larger extent of operation; the loss of L5-S1 motion, which may alter gait; the need for iliac screws, which can lead to pain and ultimately require removal in many patients; the high rate of pseudarthrosis (24%);[21] and the high rate of sacral screw breakage or loosening. However, no significant gait difference was found after fusion stopping at L5 or the sacrum.[21] On the contrary, gait is adversely affected if a positive sagittal balance is left uncorrected. Only approximately 15% of patients report pain or iliac screw prominence; these patients may benefit from screw removal, which is a relatively minor procedure.[22] Pseudarthrosis at L5-S1 can be prevented by complete sacropelvic fixation, which requires bilateral and bicortical S1 screws, bilateral iliac screws, and anterior column support (L5-S1 interbody fusion through an anterior, posterior, or transforaminal procedure).[22]

Primary Sagittal Plane Deformity

A predominantly sagittal plane imbalance may appear as a primary or secondary kyphotic deformity. The primary deformities include degenerative kyphoscoliosis, postinfection (diskitis, vertebral osteomyelitis, tubercu-

losis) or posttraumatic kyphosis, Scheuermann kyphosis or neurofibromatosis, or ankylosing spondylitis. Secondary kyphotic deformities (occurring after a spinal fusion) include distal junctional kyphosis in the lumbar spine below a long fusion for adolescent scoliosis; proximal junctional kyphosis in upper thoracic spine above a long fusion for a primary kyphosis or scoliosis; and lumbar or thoracolumbar kyphosis above a distal lumbar fusion for a degenerative lumbar spine with a flat back. The goals of surgical treatment are to restore regional segmental spine alignment in thoracic kyphosis, lumbar lordosis, or spinopelvic alignment and to restore global sagittal balance (the SVA). The restoration of thoracic kyphosis and lumbar lordosis should be balanced so that lumbar lordosis exceeds thoracic kyphosis by at least 10° to 20°. A patient with less thoracic kyphosis requires less lumbar lordosis to maintain balance. Loss of sagittal balance (a forward shift of SVA) normally is compensated for by retroversion of the pelvis (increased pelvic tilt), depending on spine flexibility. A patient with an earlier spinal fusion may not be able to use this compensatory mechanism for secondary kyphotic deformity. The forward gaze is affected by kyphosis with global ankylosis involving the cervical spine, as in ankylosing spondylitis. In addition to SVA, the loss of visual angle should be assessed during surgical planning. The conventional parameter is a measurement of the chin-brow–to–vertical line angle (Figure 6).

Sagittal imbalance can be classified by the ability of the spine or pelvis to compensate for the deformity.[4,23] Type I, compensated sagittal imbalance, is a segmental kyphosis in which the normal SVA has been restored by hyperextension of the adjacent spine segment above or below the kyphosis. Often the pelvis is retroverted to contribute to the compensation, and therefore the pelvic tilt is high (at least 25°). Type II, decompensated sagittal imbalance, is common if the cranial or caudal adjacent spine segment is stiff secondary to severe degeneration or earlier fusion. The stiffness prevents compensatory hyperextension to correct the high SVA (more than 50 mm). The pelvis fails to produce compensatory rotation, and the pelvic tilt may be normal (Figure 7). In a severe deformity, both the SVA and pelvic tilt may be high; despite pelvic retroversion (a high pelvic tilt), the patient is not able to maintain the head over the pelvis (a high SVA).

Surgical Techniques

Anesthesia and Positioning

Most surgical procedures for scoliosis are performed with the patient prone, preferably on a Jackson table. It is essential to fully extend the hips to allow the lumbar spine to achieve the maximum lordosis. Hip flexion during surgery may lead to instrumentation of the lumbosacral spine in kyphosis or flat back. The eyes must be carefully protected to prevent postsurgical vision

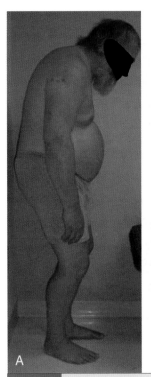
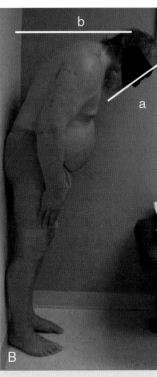

Figure 6   Photographs showing compensation of global imbalance by knee flexion (**A**), as unmasked when the patient stands with the knees fully extended and hips relaxed (**B**). In a patient with global ankylosis in ankylosing spondylitis, the loss of forward gaze can be measured as the chin-brow–to–vertical angle (a); the occiput-to-wall distance (b) is used for clinical assessment of loss of sagittal balance, as an alternative to SVA.

loss. An anterior approach can be used, with the patient in the lateral or supine position, depending on the spine level to be exposed. In the lateral position, the thigh is flexed to relax the ipsilateral iliopsoas muscle, thus improving access to the lateral aspect of the thoracolumbar vertebrae. Prone positioning is more critical for correcting severe kyphosis with a spinal osteotomy. The table should be adjusted to a jackknife position, and the apex of the kyphosis should be positioned over the bend of the table. After the spinal osteotomy, the kyphosis correction may be helped by a gradual straightening of the table, which can slowly and safely achieve closure of the osteotomy gap (Figure 8).

The use of hypotensive anesthesia can limit blood loss but is risky in an adult patient with comorbidities. Hypotension may interfere with motor neuromonitoring and increase the risk of postsurgical vision loss. Most surgeons recommend monitoring both motor- and somatosensory-evoked potentials during any deformity surgery involving the thoracic or upper lumbar (L1-L2) spine in an adult. Surgery below the L2 level does not involve the spinal cord, and spinal cord monitoring is not essential. Nerve root and electromyographic monitoring may be more useful.

Surgical Approaches

Posterior surgery alone, with long-segment instrumentation, generally is adequate for relatively flexible curves and most double major curves (in which the residual scoliotic curves may balance each other). A combined approach is required for more rigid curves, with anterior diskectomy and release followed by a posterior procedure and instrumentation. The parts of a combined procedure can be performed on the same day or staged 5 to 7 days apart if a large blood loss or long duration (more than 12 hours) is required. Only a limited number of segments can be instrumented through most anterior approaches. Anterior fusion is useful for stabilizing the lumbosacral junction. A few surgeons increasingly are using a direct lateral approach through the psoas muscle; this limited-incision technique may be effective for curves limited to the lumbar spine, but neurologic complications are common.

Instrumentation

Pedicle screws generally offer better pullout strength than hooks, unless osteoporosis is present. The pullout strength can be increased by triangulation, in which two screws placed in the same vertebra are pointed medially to converge toward the anterior end of the vertebral body. At the cranial end of fixation, relatively caudally directed pedicle screws approaching the inferior end plate may be more effective for preventing screw pullout and proximal junctional kyphosis than screws directed forward and parallel to the superior end plate (Figure 9). Thoracic pedicle screw insertion requires greater technical skill, particularly close to the apex of the deformity, because of the rotation of the vertebrae. The use of a navigation system is limited by cost and availability. The dimensions and direction of each pedicle of the individual vertebrae in the instrumented region must be carefully templated before surgery. Hooks may be easier and safer to insert than screws, but they provide weaker fixation except against pull in only one direction. A caudally directed laminar hook may be useful at the cranial end of fixation to prevent proximal junctional kyphosis, in a manner similar to a caudally directed pedicle screw. Toward the cranial end of the instrumentation, a claw construct (a laminar hook–pedicle hook or hook-screw combination) may provide a stronger anchor point than a screw or hook alone. The use of cross-links may increase the rotational stability of the fixation and significantly increase the strength of the overall construct.

Correction Maneuvers

Three correction maneuvers can be used for applying the rods to the anchor points: distraction, rod rotation, and lateral translation. Distraction, the simplest technique, is most effective in a relatively large curve. Because distraction lengthens the spine, it has the potential to cause cord damage. In the lumbar spine, distraction has the advantage of indirectly decompressing foraminal stenosis, but it tends to produce kyphosis

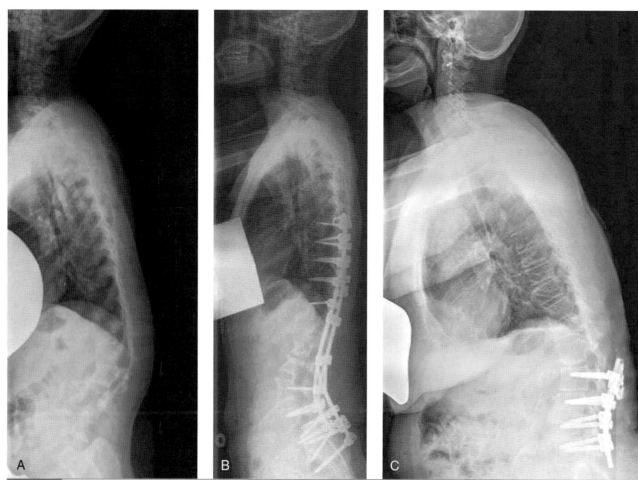

Figure 7 Lateral radiographs showing type I and type II deformities. **A,** In type I, the patient is able to maintain global balance (the C7 plumb line is over the lumbosacral disk) by substantially hyperextending segments above and below the kyphotic segment. The thoracic spine is hypokyphotic, and the lumbosacral junction is hyperlordotic. **B,** Global balance is restored by osteotomy at the apex of the kyphosis. The regional segmental alignment has been restored, with normal thoracic kyphosis and lumbar lordosis exceeding the thoracic kyphosis by 10° to 20°. **C,** In type II, the patient is unable to hyperextend the segments below the kyphosis because of fusion and severe degeneration of the L5-S1 disk; the C7 plumb line falls more than 25 cm in front of the lumbosacral disk.

of the segment. Compression between the pedicle screws at the convex side may restore lumbar lordosis but can cause foraminal stenosis; it may be preferable to achieve lordosis by appropriate rod contouring. Rod rotation usually is performed on one side for maximum curve correction, with the rod on the other side applied to hold the correction. A contoured rod is applied to all the anchor points, usually with pedicle screws, and then is rotated to transfer some of the curvature into the sagittal plane. Screw or hook migration can occur during rotation. The vertebrae are rotated toward the convexity, and the derotation of an individual vertebra should be done in the opposite direction from the rod rotation. Lateral translation is less frequently used; it requires side-opening pedicle screws or hooks. In this technique, the contoured rod is held in the sagittal plane, with both concave and convex rods applied to the anchor points in strategic sequence to help the reduction maneuver. Individual vertebral rotation is done

separately at the end of the procedure, before final tightening. Regardless of the reduction technique, in situ rod bending may be used for fine-tuning the curve correction both in the coronal and sagittal planes.

For correction of kyphotic deformity, contoured rods are connected to anchor points at the cranial or caudal end, then pushed down sequentially against the apex of the kyphosis to the anchor points at the other end. Substantial pullout forces may act on individual anchor points until the load is evenly distributed by attaching the rod to all anchor points. An alternative is to use four rods; one pair is connected to all anchor points cranial to the apex of kyphosis, and the other pair is connected to all anchor points caudal to the apex. The deformity is corrected by pushing the rods from both ends over the apex of the kyphosis and finally connecting each pair with a rod-to-rod connector. Because the rods are connected to multiple anchor points before the deformity reduction is started, anchor pullout is less

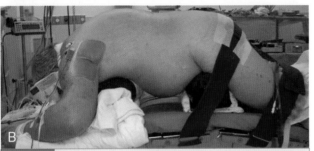

Figure 8 Photographs showing kyphosis correction with osteotomy for rigid deformity. **A,** The patient is positioned with the bend of the table *(arrow)* at the level of the intended osteotomy site. **B,** After completion of the osteotomy, the posterior wedge-shaped gap between the spinous processes is closed by flattening the table gradually to achieve correction of kyphosis.

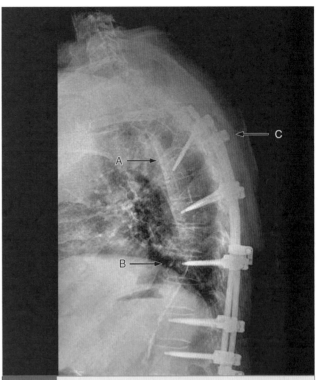

Figure 9 Lateral radiograph showing the cranial end of a long spinal instrumentation. A caudally directed pedicle screw at the proximal end of thoracic fixation (A) provides greater pullout strength than screws placed parallel to the end plate in the lower thoracic vertebrae (B). A caudally directed laminar hook at the cranial end of the other rod (C) also provides better fixation for preventing proximal junctional kyphosis.

common than with other techniques (Figure 10). The correction is fine-tuned by compression between the pedicle screws and in situ rod bending. An average of 5° of kyphosis correction can be expected for each segment of instrumentation, without osteotomy, depending on the flexibility of the spine.

Spinal Osteotomies

The cantilever maneuver alone may not be effective for correcting a deformity through a rigid or fused spine segment, and spinal osteotomy is required. The types include the Smith-Peterson, Ponte, and pedicle subtraction osteotomies as well as vertebral column resection.

The Smith-Peterson osteotomy involves a monosegmental posterior closing wedge resection osteotomy and osteoclasis to open up the anterior column. This is a true osteotomy; it is performed on a fused segment of the spine and can achieve 30° to 40° of angular correction. The anterior column lengthening maneuver has been associated with severe complications including aortic rupture, cauda equina syndrome, paraplegia, and superior mesenteric artery syndrome. This procedure is rarely performed in its original format (Figure 11). The Ponte osteotomy is a polysegmental posterior closing-wedge resection osteotomy. The bony resection is performed in the shape of a V or chevron; it can be limited to an aggressive facetectomy or be as radical as a complete resection of the posterior elements from pedicle to pedicle at each level (Figure 12). The angular correction occurs through the disk, which acts as a hinge. Approximately 10° of angular correction can be achieved at

each level; spread over several segments, this is a more harmonious correction of the kyphosis. The Ponte osteotomy is most effective in a long, rounded, flexible thoracic kyphosis, as with Scheuermann kyphosis. Some authors refer to the Ponte or chevron osteotomy as a Smith-Peterson osteotomy, and it is important to be aware of the confusing nomenclature.

The pedicle subtraction osteotomy is a monosegmental posterior closing wedge resection osteotomy used for treating kyphosis in ankylosing spondylitis (Figure 13). In contrast to the Smith-Peterson osteotomy, the wedge in the pedicle subtraction osteotomy hinges on the anterior wall of the vertebral body. All of the spinal columns are shortened, thus minimizing the risk of damage to the anterior structures and the spinal cord. Pedicle subtraction osteotomy can be performed through the apex of a deformity in the presence of substantial rotation or scoliosis and can simultaneously correct both kyphosis and scoliosis deformity by asymmetric resection (Figure 14). The preferred site of osteotomy is below the level of the cord, at L2 or L3. The osteotomy can accomplish 30° to 40° of angular correction and 12 to 15 cm of posterior shift of the C7 plumb line. Pedicle subtraction osteotomy is ideal for correcting a sharp, angular kyphosis with a substantial

Figure 10   Intraoperative photographs showing the instrumentation steps and the cantilever maneuver for kyphosis correction using the four-rod technique. **A,** The spine is exposed, and pedicle screws are inserted cranial and caudal to the apex. **B,** Chevron osteotomies are performed at multiple segments near the apex to loosen the rigid deformity, and rods are applied to the cranial and caudal anchor points (the pedicle screws) on each side. **C,** The deformity is corrected by completing the osteotomies as the cranial and caudal pairs of rods are pushed downward against the apex of the kyphosis. **D,** The rods are connected with dominos (rod-to-rod connectors). (Courtesy of O. Boachie, MD, New York, NY.)

sagittal imbalance (at least 10 to 12 cm). Pedicle subtraction osteotomy is technically more demanding but more effective than the Ponte osteotomy, particularly in revision surgery through a fused spine. A pedicle subtraction osteotomy for severe thoracic kyphosis may cause too much shortening of the spinal column, raising concern about cord kinking and damage. This complication can be prevented by inserting a structural graft or cage between the vertebral bodies before closing the posterior gap (Figure 15).

Vertebral column resection involves a complete resection of one or more vertebral segments, including all anterior and posterior elements. This procedure is indicated if the patient has a severe, rigid deformity; a tumor; or a hemivertebra. The procedure can be performed through a combined anterior and posterior approach or a posterior approach alone.

The effect of spinal osteotomy in correcting sagittal imbalance depends on the size and location of the angular correction. The posterior shift of the C7 plumb line increases with a larger angular correction, but more importantly, it increases as the location of the osteotomy is moved lower (distal) in the spine. The effect of a planned osteotomy can be assessed before surgery by using tracing paper, as described in Figure 16. For ankylosing spondylitis with global ankylosis of the

spine (when the cervical spine also is ankylosed), the presurgical planning requires attention to correcting the visual angle and sagittal imbalance (Figure 17). A large pedicle subtraction osteotomy (30° to 40°) at the L2 or L3 level usually can achieve most of the needed sagittal balance correction. Additional osteotomies at the upper thoracic spine can fine-tune the visual angle correction without a significant additional posterior shift of the plumb line.

Special Considerations

Revision and Salvage Procedures
Revision of earlier surgery for spine deformity is technically demanding. The most common indications for revision surgery are pseudarthrosis with instrumentation failure, proximal or distal junctional kyphosis, hardware prominence, progression of scoliotic deformity above or below a successful fusion; flat back occurring after a successful fusion for deformity (such as Harrington rod fixation for adolescent idiopathic scoliosis or lumbar fixation for degenerative scoliosis); or overcorrection or undercorrection of deformity. The patient may have recurrent pain, progressive deformity,

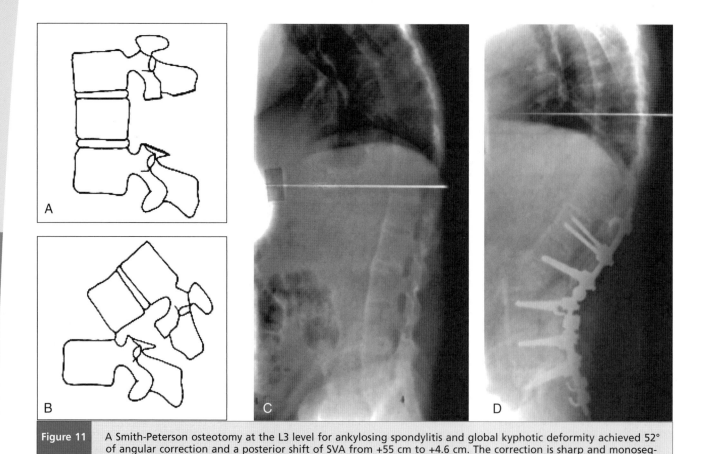

Figure 11 A Smith-Peterson osteotomy at the L3 level for ankylosing spondylitis and global kyphotic deformity achieved 52° of angular correction and a posterior shift of SVA from +55 cm to +4.6 cm. The correction is sharp and monosegmental, resulting in a large anterior opening at the osteotomy site. Schematic drawings showing resection of the posterior elements and pedicles (**A**) and completion of the osteotomy by disruption of the anterior element, usually through a calcified disk (**B**). Lateral radiographs of a patient with ankylosing spondylitis before (**C**) and after (**D**) osteotomy through the L2-3 ossified disk and posterior instrumentation from T12 to S1.

or neurologic deficit after successful deformity surgery. Less commonly, crepitus after a fall may indicate implant breakage. Pain without an obvious mechanical cause should raise suspicion of a deep infection. The surgical strategy should consider the fusion status; possible hardware removal or extension with a compatible rod-to-rod connector; and correction of the residual or recurrent deformity and global balance, which often requires a major osteotomy procedure (Figure 18).

Osteoporosis

Osteoporosis is most likely if the patient is older than 70 years and/or a woman. Fixation strength in osteoporotic bone can be enhanced by using multiple fixation points, augmenting screw fixation with the off-label use of cement, using hydroxyapatite-coated screws, using larger diameter screws, or accepting a smaller correction.

Complications

The rates of major complications after adult lumbar scoliosis surgery with fusion to the sacrum range from 56% to 75%, and the rates of unplanned reoperation range from 18% to 58%.[15] The complication rates are increased in patients older than 75 years and patients with a medical comorbidity. The incidence of perioperative complications (within 3 months of surgery) is 34%, and late complications occur in 37% of patients.[24] The infection rates after deformity surgery are greater in adults (3% to 5%) than in adolescents (1% to 2%). Early revision may be required if there is an epidural hematoma, an early fixation failure, graft dislodgement, vena cava thrombosis, or foraminal stenosis with radicular pain. The late complications include pseudarthrosis (17% of adult patients); painful hardware requiring removal, often involving a loose iliac screw (15%); junctional kyphosis (8%); and painful collapse at an unfused lumbosacral junction.[24] Neurologic complications of adult deformity surgery are relatively uncommon, occurring in 1% to 5% of patients.[24] With osteotomies, particular attention should be paid while correcting the deformity and closing the osteotomy gap. A neurologic deficit can appear several hours after surgery. Postsurgical visual loss is a devastating but rare complication, occurring in 0.5% to 1% of patients.[25]

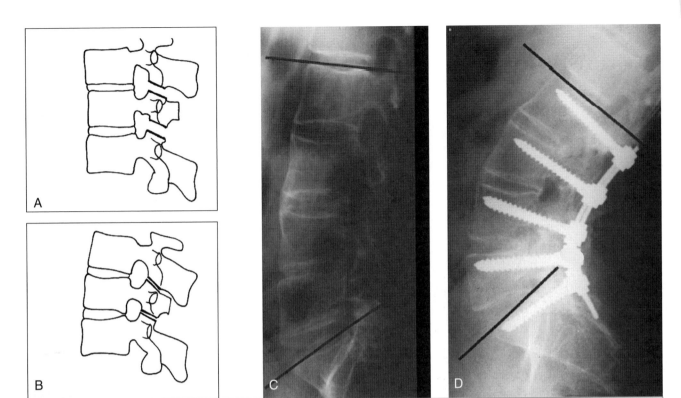

Figure 12 The Ponte osteotomy is a polysegmental wedge osteotomy (similar in appearance to a chevron) that achieves approximately 10° of angular correction at each level through the flexible disk in front, without any significant anterior opening. Schematic drawings before (**A**) and after (**B**) Ponte osteotomies between L2 and S1. Lateral radiographs before (**C**) and after (**D**) Ponte osteotomies between L2 and S1 and posterior instrumented fusion to achieve a significant correction of kyphosis. The correction can be seen by comparing the angle between the two lines in **C** and **D**.

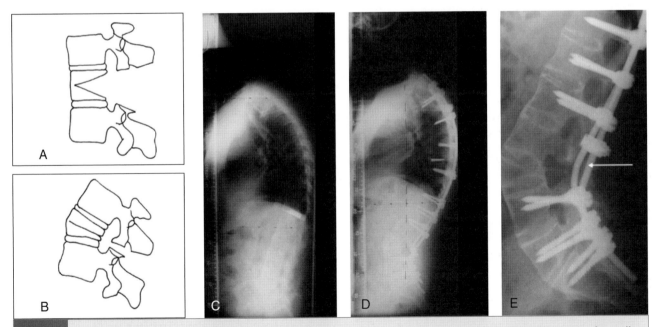

Figure 13 Pedicle subtraction osteotomy at the L3 level. Schematic drawings showing the extent of bone resection from all three columns before (**A**) and after (**B**) closing of the osteotomy. The angular correction hinge is on the anterior wall of the vertebra. Full-length standing lateral radiographs before (**C**) and after (**D**) global sagittal balance correction. **E**, Postoperative lateral lumbar radiograph showing the extent of osteotomy at L3 vertebra; the L3 pedicles are absent (*arrow*).

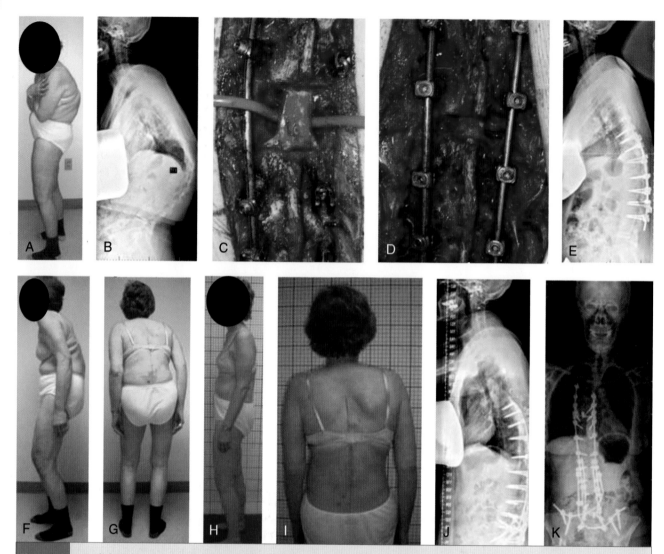

Figure 14 Pedicle subtraction osteotomy at the thoracic level. Photograph (**A**) and lateral radiograph (**B**) showing a 69-year-old woman with lower thoracic kyphosis. The patient had an earlier uninstrumented thoracic spine fusion for scoliosis, which precluded a Ponte osteotomy. Intraoperative photographs showing correction of the thoracic kyphosis by pedicle subtraction osteotomy through the apex of the deformity (**C**), with temporary fixation on one side to prevent subluxation during closure of the osteotomy; and buckling of the dural sac noted with closure of the osteotomy, limiting the extent of kyphosis correction (**D**). The initial correction of sagittal balance was inadequate, as seen by comparing preoperative (**B**) and postoperative (**E**) lateral radiographs. Because the distal fixation was stopped in the lumbar spine, the patient's condition further deteriorated. Photographs showing the subsequent development of lumbar kyphosis (**F**) and scoliosis (**G**). Lateral (**H**) and posterior (**I**) photographs showing correction of both sagittal and coronal imbalance by one osteotomy in the lumbar spine and extension of instrumentation to the pelvis, as seen on lateral (**J**) and AP (**K**) radiographs.

Outcome- and Evidence-Based Medicine

A literature review found no level I evidence that surgery for adult spine deformity improves health-related quality of life.[26] A prospective study of 81 patients who underwent primary surgery for adult spine deformity and 30 patients who declined surgery found that the surgically treated patients had better outcomes.[27] This study was limited by lack of randomization, the use of Harrington rods, and the use of unvalidated outcome questionnaires. In a review of 28 patients who underwent primary corrective surgery for adult idiopathic scoliosis, third-generation instrumentation techniques were found to provide significant clinical improvement, scoliosis correction, maintenance of sagittal alignment, and patient satisfaction, with an acceptable complication rate.[28] A current multicenter study is evaluating the effectiveness of nonsurgical and surgical treatments for improving quality of life in patients with adult symptomatic lumbar scoliosis. The investigators plan to identify important clinical and radiographic determinants of outcome.[29]

The SRS classification of adult deformity can be used to predict a satisfactory surgical outcome.[30] The

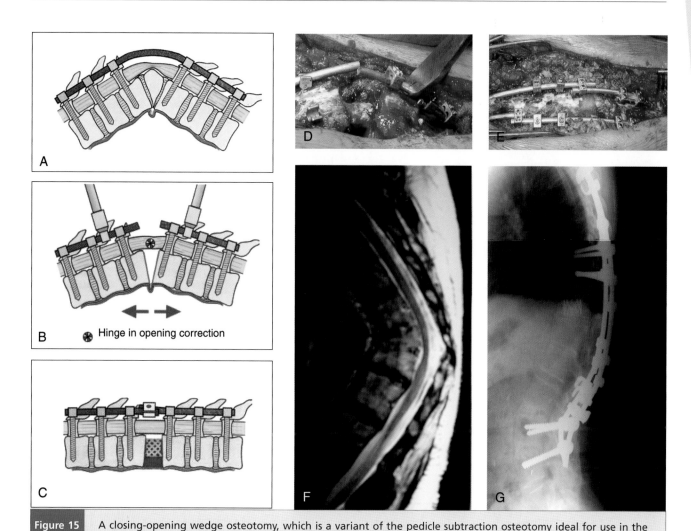

Figure 15 A closing-opening wedge osteotomy, which is a variant of the pedicle subtraction osteotomy ideal for use in the thoracic spine. Schematic drawings showing the effect of moving the hinge from the anterior wall of the vertebral body (A) backward to the level of the cord (B and C). As the hinge of angular correction is moved closer to the dural sac by placing a cage between the vertebral bodies, the correction increases without overshortening of the spinal cord. Intraoperative photographs taken before (D) and after (E) the osteotomy was closed. Postoperative lateral MRI (F) and radiograph (G) of the same patient showing correction of the deformity without overshortening of the cord.

patients most likely to achieve significant improvement had a higher grade deformity, as identified by classification modifiers including lost lumbar lordosis, intervertebral subluxation, and positive sagittal balance. These patients had significant disability before surgery, as indicated by Oswestry Disability Index, SRS, and Medical Outcomes Study Short Form-12 scores. A patient with a baseline score lower than 35 on the Short Form-12 physical component summary was six times more likely to have a 5.2-point improvement (the minimal clinically important difference) than a patient with a higher baseline score.[30]

Summary

Spine deformity can have a significant and measurable impact on an adult's health-related quality of life. The patient often has an associated comorbidity or osteoporosis. The goals of surgery are to treat pain, relieve neurologic symptoms, and maintain or restore global balance. The absolute degree of coronal curve correction and cosmesis is less important than the restoration of sagittal balance.

The surgery is technically demanding and associated with significant risk and morbidity. Surgical decision making should be shared between the patient and the surgeon, with a clear understanding of the balance of risks and benefits between quality of life and surgical complications. The key questions in surgical planning are the choice of fixation levels, extension of fusion across the thoracolumbar junction, choice of an L5 or sacral end point, need for anterior release, and instrumentation technique for the correction maneuver. Revision surgery is more complicated than primary surgery. The surgical approaches to adult deformity continue to

4: The Adult Spine

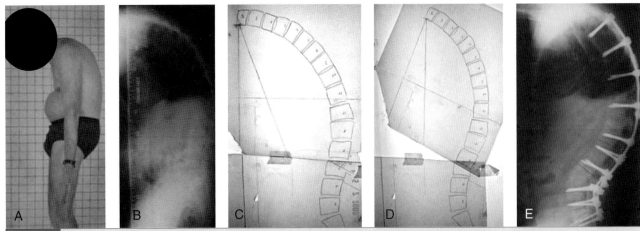

Figure 16 Preoperative planning of the location and type of osteotomy, using a template. Photograph (**A**) and lateral radiograph (**B**) of a man with ankylosing spondylitis causing global ankylosis and loss of sagittal balance as well as loss of forward gaze. On the template, a tracing of the spine is cut at the desired location of osteotomy (**C**) and rotated to observe the effect of angular correction on the posterior shift of the plumb line (**D**). **E**, Postoperative lateral radiograph showing the desired correction, as predicted by preoperative planning.

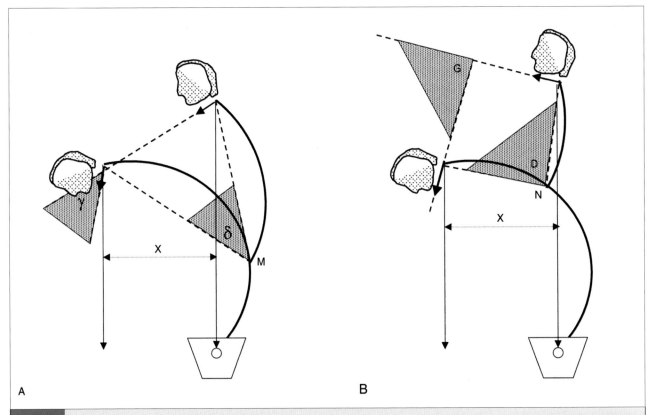

Figure 17 Schematic drawings comparing the effect of size and level of osteotomy. The correction of the gaze angle (γ or G) is always the same as the corresponding osteotomy angle (δ or D), respectively ($\delta = \gamma$ and D = G). **A**, Osteotomy performed at a lower level (M) requires an osteotomy angle δ for restoration of the sagittal balance (X). **B**, Osteotomy performed at a higher level (N) requires a larger osteotomy angle (D). D > δ for the same degree of sagittal balance restoration (X). Because the osteotomy angle always is the same as the gaze angle correction (D = G), the correction of the gaze angle is larger with a higher osteotomy level (G > γ). The result may be an upward overcorrection of the gaze angle. A balanced correction of both gaze angle and sagittal balance can be achieved with pedicle subtraction osteotomy at a lower level, and a smaller Ponte osteotomy at an upper (thoracic) level can fine-tune the gaze angle correction. (Reproduced with permission from Sengupta DK, Khazin R, Grevitt MP, Webb JK: Flexion osteotomy of the cervical spine: A new technique for correction of iatrogenic extension deformity in ankylosing spondylitis. *Spine [Phila Pa 1976]* 2001;26:1068-1072.)

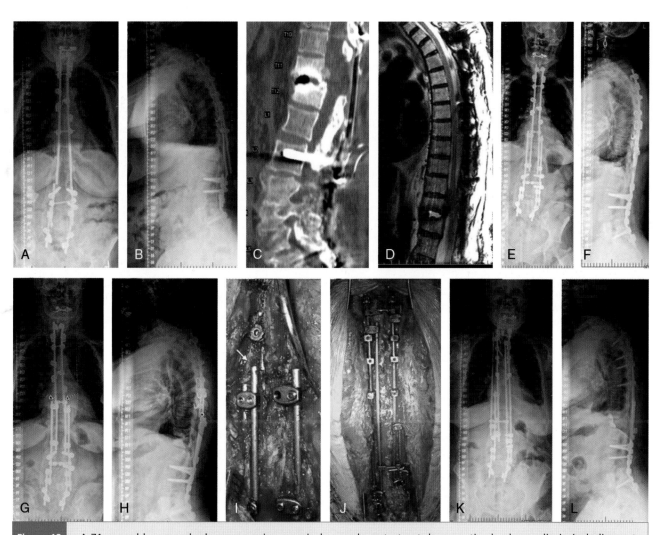

Figure 18 A 71-year-old woman had seven previous surgical procedures to treat degenerative lumbar scoliosis, including anterior and posterior fusions, hardware removals and exchange, and extension of fusions. Over the preceding 3 months, she had developed pseudarthrosis at T10-T11, broken rods, and progressive paraparesis, as seen on AP (**A**) and lateral (**B**) radiographs. CT (**C**) and MRI (**D**) raised suspicion of infection and cord compression. The hardware was revised by connecting the proximal and distal rods with rod-to-rod connectors, after decompression of the spinal cord and bone grafting (AP [**E**] and lateral [**F**] radiographs). The patient fully recovered from the neurologic deficit and had good pain control. Five months later, a fall while dancing caused rod breakage but no pain (preoperative AP [**G**] and lateral [**H**] radiographs, intraoperative photograph [**I**]). Further revision included replacing all hooks cranial to the pseudarthrosis with pedicle screws, reinforcing the fixation with four supplemental rods across the pseudarthrosis, and repairing the pseudarthrosis (intraoperative photograph [**J**] and postoperative AP [**K**] and lateral [**L**] radiographs).

evolve. New techniques and technologies are welcome, but caution is required to determine the indications and safety. There is a significant need for research to provide compelling data for developing an evidence-based approach specific to deformity patterns and treatment strategies.

Annotated References

1. Schwab F, Dubey A, Gamez L, et al: Adult scoliosis: Prevalence, SF-36, and nutritional parameters in an elderly volunteer population. *Spine (Phila Pa 1976)* 2005; 30(9):1082-1085.

A prospective self-assessment analysis and evaluation of nutritional and radiographic parameters in healthy adult volunteers older than 60 years found no significant correlation between adult scoliosis and visual analog scale scores or nutritional status.

2. Aebi M: The adult scoliosis. *Eur Spine J* 2005;14(10): 925-948.

The classification, treatment options, complications, and outcomes of adult spine deformities are reviewed from a European perspective.

3. Lowe T, Berven SH, Schwab FJ, Bridwell KH: The SRS classification for adult spinal deformity: Building on the King/Moe and Lenke classification systems. *Spine (Phila Pa 1976)* 2006;31(19, suppl):S119-S125.

The SRS classification of adult spine deformity is described. A 19-surgeon evaluation of spine deformities in 25 adults using the SRS system revealed good interobserver reliability and prediction in surgical strategies.

4. Lafage V, Schwab F, Patel A, Hawkinson N, Farcy JP: Pelvic tilt and truncal inclination: Two key radiographic parameters in the setting of adults with spinal deformity. *Spine (Phila Pa 1976)* 2009;34(17):E599-E606.

    This study confirms that pelvic position measured as pelvic tilt is better correlated than SVA shift with health-related quality of life in patients with adult deformity. High values of pelvic tilt express compensatory pelvic retroversion for sagittal spine malalignment, with lower quality-of-life scores.

5. Schwab F, Lafage V, Blondel B, et al: Validation of the SRS-Schwab adult deformity classification. *Final Program: 18th International Meeting on Advanced Spine Techniques.* Milwaukee, WI, Scoliosis Research Society, 2011, p 104. www.srs.org/imast/2011/program. Accessed October 12, 2011.

6. Schwab F, Patel A, Ungar B, Farcy JP, Lafage V: Adult spinal deformity-postoperative standing imbalance: How much can you tolerate? An overview of key parameters in assessing alignment and planning corrective surgery. *Spine* (Phila Pa 1976)2010;35:2224-2231.

7. Horton WC, Brown CW, Bridwell KH, Glassman SD, Suk SI, Cha CW: Is there an optimal patient stance for obtaining a lateral 36″ radiograph? A critical comparison of three techniques. *Spine (Phila Pa 1976)* 2005; 30(4):427-433.

    Twenty-five patients with scoliosis were prospectively studied on 36-inch lateral radiographs taken with the arm in three positions (straight, partially flexed, and in the clavicle position). Use of the clavicle position may allow more accurate radiographic measurement and minimize the need for repeated radiograph exposure.

8. Lenke LG, Betz RR, Harms J, et al: Adolescent idiopathic scoliosis: A new classification to determine extent of spinal arthrodesis. *J Bone Joint Surg Am* 2001;83(8): 1169-1181.

9. Korovessis P, Piperos G, Sidiropoulos P, Dimas A: Adult idiopathic lumbar scoliosis: A formula for prediction of progression and review of the literature. *Spine (Phila Pa 1976)* 1994;19(17):1926-1932.

10. Fon GT, Pitt MJ, Thies AC Jr: Thoracic kyphosis: Range in normal subjects. *AJR Am J Roentgenol* 1980; 134(5):979-983.

11. Kuntz C IV, Levin LS, Ondra SL, Shaffrey CI, Morgan CJ: Neutral upright sagittal spinal alignment from the occiput to the pelvis in asymptomatic adults: A review and resynthesis of the literature. *J Neurosurg Spine* 2007;6(2):104-112.

    The literature was reviewed to evaluate neutral upright sagittal spine alignment (occiput-pelvis) in asymptomatic adult volunteers with no spine disease. Despite wide variation in regional lordotic and kyphotic curves, sagittal spine balance is maintained in a narrow range for alignment of the spine over the pelvis and femoral heads.

12. Bernhardt M, Bridwell KH: Segmental analysis of the sagittal plane alignment of the normal thoracic and lumbar spines and thoracolumbar junction. *Spine (Phila Pa 1976)* 1989;14(7):717-721.

13. Lazennec JY, Ramaré S, Arafati N, et al: Sagittal alignment in lumbosacral fusion: Relations between radiological parameters and pain. *Eur Spine J* 2000;9(1): 47-55.

14. Everett CR, Patel RK: A systematic literature review of nonsurgical treatment in adult scoliosis. *Spine (Phila Pa 1976)* 2007;32(19, suppl):S130-S134.

    The evidence as to the effectiveness of any nonsurgical care option for adult scoliosis is insufficient and indeterminate. Specifically, there is level IV evidence for the role of physical therapy, chiropractic care, or bracing. There is level III evidence for injections.

15. Akbarnia BA, Ogilvie JW, Hammerberg KW: Degenerative scoliosis: To operate or not to operate. *Spine (Phila Pa 1976)* 2006;31(19, suppl):S195-S201.

    Controversies related to surgical decision making for typical patients with adult spine deformity are described in debate form.

16. Warner MA, Offord KP, Warner ME, Lennon RL, Conover MA, Jansson-Schumacher U: Role of preoperative cessation of smoking and other factors in postoperative pulmonary complications: A blinded prospective study of coronary artery bypass patients. *Mayo Clin Proc* 1989;64(6):609-616.

17. Moe JH: The management of idiopathic scoliosis. *Clin Orthop* 1957;9:169-184.

18. Brand RA: 50 years ago in CORR: The management of idiopathic scoliosis. [Moe JH: *Clin Orthop Rel Res* 1957;9:169-184.] *Clin Orthop Relat Res* 2010;468(3): 910-912.

    A landmark article described principles of treatment for idiopathic scoliosis, many of which remain valid 50 years later.

19. Shufflebarger H, Suk SI, Mardjetko S: Debate: Determining the upper instrumented vertebra in the management of adult degenerative scoliosis: Stopping at T10 versus L1. *Spine (Phila Pa 1976)* 2006;31(19, suppl): S185-S194.

    Controversies related to determining the uppermost instrumented vertebra (T10 or L1) in the management of adult degenerative scoliosis are described.

20. Edwards CC II, Bridwell KH, Patel A, et al: Thoracolumbar deformity arthrodesis to L5 in adults: The fate of the L5-S1 disc. *Spine (Phila Pa 1976)* 2003; 28(18):2122-2131.

21. Engsberg JR, Bridwell KH, Reitenbach AK, et al: Preoperative gait comparisons between adults undergoing long spinal deformity fusion surgery (thoracic to L4, L5, or sacrum) and controls. *Spine (Phila Pa 1976)* 2001; 26(18):2020-2028.

22. Polly DW Jr, Hamill CL, Bridwell KH: To fuse or not to fuse to the sacrum: The fate of the L5-S1 disc. *Spine (Phila Pa 1976)* 2006;31(19, suppl):S179-S184.

    Controversies are discussed related to the decision to fuse or not to fuse to the sacrum (the fate of the L5-S1 disk) in adult deformity surgery.

23. Booth KC, Bridwell KH, Lenke LG, Baldus CR, Blanke KM: Complications and predictive factors for the successful treatment of flatback deformity (fixed sagittal imbalance). *Spine (Phila Pa 1976)* 1999;24(16):1712-1720.

24. Emami A, Deviren V, Berven S, Smith JA, Hu SS, Bradford DS: Outcome and complications of long fusions to the sacrum in adult spine deformity: Luque-Galveston, combined iliac and sacral screws, and sacral fixation. *Spine (Phila Pa 1976)* 2002;27(7):776-786.

25. Goepfert CE, Ifune C, Templehoff R: Ischemic optic neuropathy: Are we any further? *Curr Opin Anaesthesiol* 2010;23(5):582-587.

    Postoperative visual loss is poorly understood, and the risk factors remain speculative. There is no known treatment. Increased understanding is needed for prevention of this complication.

26. Bridwell KH, Berven S, Edwards C II, Glassman S, Hamill C, Schwab F: The problems and limitations of applying evidence-based medicine to primary surgical treatment of adult spinal deformity. *Spine (Phila Pa 1976)* 2007;32(19, suppl):S135-S139.

    This literature review explores the evidence related to primary adult spine deformity to answer the question of whether surgical treatment benefits patients. No ideal study was found, and a multicenter study is needed.

27. Dickson JH, Mirkovic S, Noble PC, Nalty T, Erwin WD: Results of operative treatment of idiopathic scoliosis in adults. *J Bone Joint Surg Am* 1995;77(4):513-523.

28. Ali RM, Boachie-Adjei O, Rawlins BA: Functional and radiographic outcomes after surgery for adult scoliosis using third-generation instrumentation techniques. *Spine (Phila Pa 1976)* 2003;28(11):1163-1170.

29. Bridwell KH, Lurie J, Shaffrey CI, Weinstein JN: *A Multicenter Prospective Study of Quality of Life in Adult Scoliosis (ASLS)*. St Louis, MO, Washington University School of Medicine, 2010.

    The purpose and protocol of a multicenter evaluation of the effectiveness of nonsurgical and surgical treatments are described. The investigators' intent is to identify important clinical and radiographic determinants of outcomes in the management of adults with symptomatic lumbar scoliosis.

30. Schwab FJ, Lafage V, Farcy JP, Bridwell KH, Glassman S, Shainline MR: Predicting outcome and complications in the surgical treatment of adult scoliosis. *Spine (Phila Pa 1976)* 2008;33(20):2243-2247.

    A prospective multicenter study found that models for predicting outcome can be established by applying the classification of adult deformity and considering patients' baseline health status.

4: The Adult Spine

Chapter 32

Cervical and Lumbar Disk Replacement

Eeric Truumees, MD

Introduction

Spine disease can affect any of the three primary mechanical functions of the spine: load bearing, controlled motion, and neural element protection. Surgical or nonsurgical treatment seeks to restore function while minimizing risk. Specifically, the goal of total disk arthroplasty is to maintain motion, allow the spine to find appropriate sagittal balance, and avoid the complications of fusion such as adjacent segment degeneration, pseudarthrosis, and graft harvest morbidity.

Any surgery for axial spine pain is controversial because the outcome often is unsatisfactory.[1] This controversy is critical in any discussion of total disk replacement (TDR) and many insurers refuse to cover the procedure. The few randomized studies have found surgery to be superior to nonsurgical care for axial pain. However, the magnitude of axial pain relief is smaller than is seen with diskectomy. There is no consensus as to the preferred surgical procedure.[2]

Lumbar TDR is an alternative to fusion for treating discogenic pain, and cervical systems are being studied for patients with radiculopathy and myelopathy.[3] Mechanical and alignment considerations limit the suitability for TDR to a subset of the patients who can be treated using fusion techniques.[4] For carefully selected patients who undergo TDR at a select high-volume center, the surgical outcomes are not inferior to those of fusion. The incidence of early postoperative complications is within the acceptable range.

At least 15 manufacturers are producing a total of 13 cervical and 9 lumbar TDR systems. These systems vary by material, method of spine fixation, constraint, size, implantation technique, and structural properties. It has yet to be determined whether TDR is qualitatively better than fusion and whether some devices are better suited than others to specific clinical scenarios.

Rationale and Design Goals

Both cervical and lumbar arthroplasty systems act as mobile anterior interbody spacers. Axial spine pain may be reduced when the nociceptor-rich degenerative disk is removed and abnormal point loading is dissipated. Segmental height restoration also may decrease pain through indirect neuroforaminal decompression and improvement in stability and sagittal balance. Donor site morbidity and the possibility of pseudarthrosis are avoided, as are the risk of viral transmission and the even greater risk of allograft collapse. Patients do not need post-TDR immobilization.

The earliest systems were low-friction sliding implants, like those for total knee arthroplasty. For an active patient, motion preservation represents an important goal. Maintaining segmental motion after surgery may decrease axial pain by allowing the patient to establish normal sagittal balance. More importantly, maintaining motion is a means of decreasing the degeneration of adjacent segments.

When any motion-preserving spine procedure is being considered, it is important to recognize that spine motion is coupled. Flexion and extension necessarily occur with translation.[5] During flexion, the center of the nucleus pulposus moves dorsally while the cranial vertebral body translates ventrally. The facets guide the coupled motion. Facet joint degeneration impairs this function.[6] In the cervical spine, the uncovertebral joints also participate in guiding coupled motion; their exact role in maintaining rotational stability after arthroplasty remains unclear, however.

Although posteriorly inserted lumbar TDR devices have been described, all current cervical and lumbar systems require an anterior approach. The anterior approach has both advantages and disadvantages. Anterior-column load bearing promotes bony ingrowth into the device end plates. Anterior insertion allows wide implant docking with the apophyseal ring to establish and maintain optimal segmental lordosis. Anterior spine surgery reduces the morbidity associated with extensor muscle stripping.[7,8] The disadvantages of an anterior approach include the risk of retrograde ejaculation and sterility in men because of the

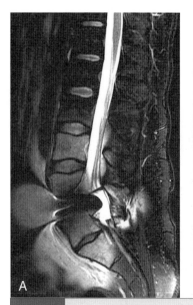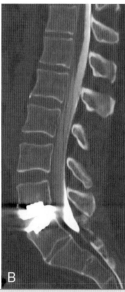

Figure 1 **A,** Sagittal T2-weighted MRI reveals significant metal artifact in the spine of a patient with ongoing pain. **B,** Sagittal CT-myelogram reconstruction of the same patient's spine shows a well-seated ProDisc-L implant (Synthes Spine, Paoli, PA), with no evidence of canal compromise.

erate. A meticulous decompression is needed.[14] The posterior compressive pathology remains in patients with myelopathy, particularly those with spondylosis rather than a focal disk herniation, and anterior spurs may recur.[15] In considering TDR for a patient with myelopathy, it should be recognized that the likelihood of symptom progression is affected by the congenital stenosis and a host metabolic factor such as diffuse idiopathic skeletal hyperostosis or ankylosing spondylitis.[16] Many TDR systems are constructed of cobalt-chromium, which frustrates postoperative imaging[17] (Figure 1). In a patient with postoperative axial pain, implant stability is more difficult to evaluate after TDR than after fusion.

The technical requirements of TDR, such as precise midline placement for optimal mechanical effectiveness, can be challenging (Figure 2). Unfortunately, the midline cervical viscera and the anterior lumbar vascular tree impede a straight anterior insertion vector. Some systems require precise bone cuts, often without the use of jigs such as those used to standardize total knee replacement.

Selecting an Arthroplasty Design

The available implant designs offer varying degrees of freedom or several independent axes of movement. The planes of spine motion, including rotation, translation, and axial compression, occur around a center of rotation. The center of rotation is the point about which the vertebral body can be rotated without translation. Further rotation is coupled with translation, and the center of rotation moves with the arc of spinal motion; the term instantaneous axis of rotation describes this movement. Some TDR systems seek to mimic the mobility of the center of rotation, typically by using mobile cores.

Constraint refers to the extent to which an implant limits motion, in terms of degrees of freedom or total allowed motion. The competing cervical and lumbar TDR systems markedly differ in their device constraint. Proponents of unconstrained devices cite their ability to allow the facets to guide normal, coupled motion.[18] In a constrained prosthesis, segmental motion is guided by the implant itself and may protect the facet joints from shear. The amount of facet joint protection depends on how well the prosthesis and the segmental instantaneous axis of rotations match. Proponents of constrained TDR also cite polyethylene core extrusions from implantations of the Charité Artificial Disc as evidence that constraint is needed.[18] The instantaneous axis of rotation varies markedly from C3-4 to C7-T1 and from L3-4 to L5-S1.[19] The ideal level of constraint and the variability of this ideal across spine levels remain unknown.

A constrained prosthesis progressively opposes motion as the displacement from neutral increases. As the amount of constraint increases, the implant-bone interface is subjected to additional shear. Therefore, the implants that provide the most constraint require the

proximity of the hypogastric plexus. The use of an anterior lumbar approach is especially difficult in patients who are obese, have had earlier surgery through a retroperitoneal approach, or have an active peritoneal or pelvic infection. An earlier anterior approach may have scarred the access plane for either a cervical or lumbar procedure, thereby increasing the risk to adjacent vascular and soft-tissue structures. Cervical arthroplasty has a significant advantage over lumbar arthroplasty in that the surgical approach is familiar to all spine surgeons. A spine surgeon who is not completely familiar with anterior lumbar anatomy should work with an access surgeon. Unlike appendicular total joint arthroplasty, TDR requires reconstruction only of the anterior column. In this way, TDR is more akin to a unicompartmental knee arthroplasty than to a total knee arthroplasty. Disk replacement is not suitable for patients with significant facet degeneration or instability.

The consequences of ongoing motion are not always favorable. Motion generates wear debris, which can lead to loss of bone stock and implant failure. The implants appear to be durable in the short term, but failure of the bone-implant interface is a concern.[9-11] Wear particles, whether polyethylene or metal-on-metal, can migrate into the periprosthetic space and, through the epidural spaces, to the brain.[9,12] Over time, metal ions may be carcinogenic. Ongoing vigilance is required.[13] Proponents of metal-on-metal designs cite concerns about polyethylene, including wear, particle-induced osteolytic reactions, creep, and cracking.[11]

Continued motion also increases the risk of symptom recurrence as osteophytes enlarge or facets degen-

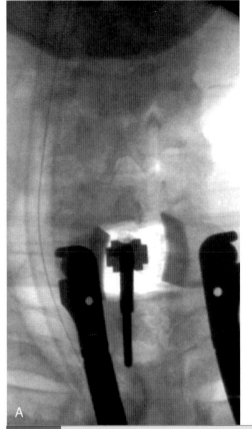
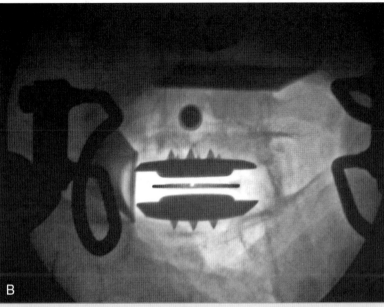

Figure 2 Precise midline placement is critical for optimal functioning of most cervical and lumbar TDR designs. **A,** Intraoperative fluoroscopic image of a localizer used in cervical TDR with the PCM device (NuVasive, San Diego, CA). **B,** AP fluoroscopic image after implantation of a Charité lumbar TDR device (DePuy Spine, Raynham, MA) with the midline marking screw still in place.

most elaborate end plate fixation.[18] A less constrained TDR system may use serrations or teeth to resist extrusion. Finite element models suggest that focal loading at the teeth is greater than required to initiate bone resorption.[20] A very constrained system may use a sport keel, which can improve long-term stability but complicates any attempt at removal. An arthroplasty procedure adjacent to a keeled implant risks a sagittal split fracture of the vertebral body.[21,22]

Constraint is distinguished from stability, which measures an implant's tendency to remain in a given position with minimal muscle contraction. An unstable prosthesis requires significant energy expenditure to maintain its position. Poorly matched motion may be worse than no motion.[23] A poorly placed TDR accelerates the degeneration of the index-level facet joint and the adjacent segments. The resulting excessive loading during motion also can cause a pars or pedicle stress fracture.

Device Evolution

The modern history of disk arthroplasty dates from the early 1980s.[24] The use of the early AcroFlex (DePuy-AcroMed, Raynham, MA) and Charité devices led to

subsidence and other types of failures. The AcroFlex was abandoned, but the Charité gradually was modified into the SB Charité III, which has enlarged end plates with an ingrowth surface and improved insertion instrumentation.[25] The next-developed disk arthroplasty system was the ProDisc. Unlike the Charité, the ProDisc has titanium end plates containing a fixed polyethylene core. Motion occurs when only the upper plate articulates on the convex superior surface of the constrained core.[26] The Charité and ProDisc currently are the only devices for lumbar TDR approved by the US Food and Drug Administration (FDA). The FDA has approved these devices for treating single-level disease from L4 to S1. Newer lumbar systems such as the Kineflex (SpinalMotion, Mountain View, CA) and Maverick (Medtronic, Minneapolis, MN) are metal-on-metal designs with a fixed or mobile core. These systems do not allow significant axial shock absorption. The AcroFlex was composed of two titanium end plates with a rubber core fused between them to allow shock, and the rubber core was believed to be a major cause of failure. The advanced polymers used in some newer designs withstand the high loads in the spinal interspace.

Devices for cervical disk arthroplasty have undergone a shorter evolution, with several design iterations. The key differences between cervical and lumbar biomechanics, as well as the difference in the size of the bony elements, meant that a cervical device could not be merely a miniaturization of a lumbar arthroplasty system. The proximity of the spinal cord and airway compounded the risks associated with displacement. One of the original designs, the Cummins-Bristol disk (Medtronic Sofamor Danek, Memphis, TN), led to dysphagia. This device has been renamed and redesigned several times to correct screw failure and implant subluxation complications.[14] Its current incarnation, the Prestige Cervical Disc System (Medtronic Sofamor Danek), consists of two L-shaped metal wafers. The implant has a ball-in-groove design (a mating of convex and concave surfaces). In the US version, vertical extensions attach to the anterior vertebral body with screws. The version used outside the United States does not require screws. The Bryan disk (Medtronic Sofamor Danek) has a very different design concept from that of the Prestige disk. A polyurethane nucleus articulates with two titanium surface shells to allow load dampening as well as the more typical coupled motions.[27]

Indications and Contraindications

Indications

In general, surgery is indicated only after unsuccessful nonsurgical management. Patients with weakness or progressive neurologic deficits require a more aggressive approach, however. Cervical or lumbar disk arthroplasty is intended to replace fusion for the reconstruction of the degenerative spine. In general, it is important to adhere to the strictest indications for a new technology. European surgeons, who have had more experience with TDR than North American surgeons, gradually have widened the indications for these procedures. For example, in the United States lumbar TDR is indicated as an alternative to anterior, posterior, or 360° fusion for axial pain in a patient with stable single-level degenerative disk disease. In Europe, TDR has been used for patients with recurrent disk herniation, mild spinal stenosis, or multiple-level degenerative disk disease. Nonetheless, over time a seeming contradiction has emerged, in which fewer and fewer patients are considered to be "ideal" candidates for lumbar TDR. The ideal candidate for TDR is a highly motivated, psychologically stable individual with single-level disk degeneration between L3 and S1 and intact facet joints (Table 1).

Cervical TDR primarily has been studied as an alternative to anterior decompression and fusion procedures in patients with radiculopathy or myelopathy. Cervical TDR is indicated as primary surgery for mechanically stable degenerative disease at one or two adjacent levels between C3 and C7. A patient with intractable arm pain, single-level disk herniation, and minimal spondylosis is an ideal candidate for cervical disk arthroplasty

(Figure 3). As in the lumbar spine, the indications are likely to be modified as experience with these devices is gained.[28-30]

Contraindications

The contraindications to cervical and lumbar TDR are evolving (Table 2). There is increased risk with any permanent implant if the patient has mechanical instability, osteoporosis, or an active infection. The anterior approach may be specifically contraindicated if the patient has a soft-tissue or vascular condition. A motion-preserving technique offers little benefit if the patient does not have motion at the intended segment.

Instability remains poorly quantified. TDR is an acceptable option for a patient with subtle retrolisthesis accompanying disk collapse, but it should be avoided in a patient with greater translation or deformity (Figure 4). TDR is best avoided if the patient has had posterior decompression with a facetectomy of more than one third on one side.[31] Severe disk height loss results either in the use of undersized implants or limited post-implantation segmental motion.[32] On plain radiographs, at least 30% bone mass loss is required to reliably identify osteopenia; therefore, dual-energy x-ray absorptiometry screening is recommended if the patient is at risk for bone mass loss.[33] Because trabecular bone has eight times more metabolic activity than cortical bone, osteoporosis mechanically affects the posterior vertebral body before the pedicles.[34]

TDR should be avoided in segments with significant facet osteoarthritis.[32] The facets normally serve to guide segmental motion, but facet degeneration disrupts normal kinematics.[6] In a prospective clinical study of 64 patients, low-grade facet arthrosis did not influence outcomes after implantation of a semiconstrained metal-on-metal TDR device.[35] Surgeons accustomed to fusing the entire motion segment are not completely consistent in assessing facet degeneration.[35] Facet arthrosis can be more accurately evaluated with CT than with MRI.[36] CT also is useful for a possible pars injury.

The tissue planes in the abdomen or anterior neck may be scarred from earlier surgery or infection. Scarring increases the difficulty of dissection and the risk of vessel or soft-tissue injury. In addition, TDR is more difficult and probably less appropriate if the patient is markedly obese; the FDA investigational device exemption studies included strict exclusion criteria, typically based on a body mass index above 20.[28,29] Retraction of the anterior vessels adds to the additional risk for a patient with atherosclerosis or a history of deep venous thrombosis. A posterior approach should be considered if a patient with cervical disease has a tracheal or esophageal abnormality.

Discogenic pain often is described as a deep midline ache that worsens with sitting. The more diffuse the symptoms are, the less likely it is that lumbar TDR will be beneficial. A patient who reports at least temporary relief from injections or other nonsurgical measures is more likely to be satisfied with the surgical outcome

Table 1

Indications for Lumbar Disk Arthroplasty

Strength of Indication	Number of Disk Levels	Accompanying Features
Prime	1	> 4 mm remaining disk height No facet joint osteoarthritis No adjacent-level degeneration Intact posterior elements
Good	1 or 2	> 4 mm remaining disk height No facet joint osteoarthritis Minimum adjacent-level degeneration Minimal posterior-element incursion (eg, microdiskectomy)
Borderline	1, 2, or 3	< 4 mm remaining disk height Primary osteoarthritis to facets Minimum adjacent-level degeneration Minimal posterior-element incursion (eg, microdiskectomy) Adjacent to fusion
Poor	1, 2, or 3	Gross spondylosis Secondary facet joint osteoarthritis < 4 mm remaining disk height at adjacent levels Posterior column instability or facetectomy

Adapted from Bertagnoli R, Kumar S: Indications for full prosthetic disc arthroplasty: A correlation of clinical outcome against a variety of indications. *Eur Spine J* 2002;11(suppl 2):S131-S136.

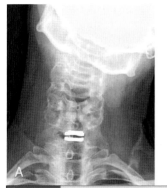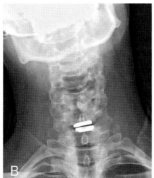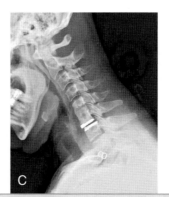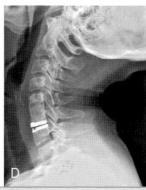

Figure 3 A 42-year-old patient underwent C5-6 anterior cervical diskecomy and fusion (ACDF), with excellent relief of neck and arm pain. Six years later, the symptoms recurred. Nonsurgical management failed to alleviate the symptoms, and the patient underwent a C6-7 disk arthroplasty using the PCM device. TDR is not FDA approved adjacent to a cervical fusion. **A** and **B,** PA side-bending radiographs. **C,** Lateral flexion radiograph. **D,** Lateral extension radiograph.

than a patient who reports worsening symptoms after every treatment attempt. Patients with lumbar disk disease who had dramatic symptoms and very high preoperative Oswestry Disability Index scores at a mean 4-year follow-up reported significantly worse outcomes than patients with more typical symptoms.[37] Elective surgical intervention should be avoided if the patient has an unresolved secondary gain issue, abnormal psychometrics, or exaggerated pain behavior.[38] Patients who had not worked for the preceding 3 months or more tended to have a relatively poor result, and psychosocial variables had a similar impact in patients with cervical radiculopathy.[39] In a patient with axial symptoms only, a multilevel procedure is associated with a poor outcome.[40,41]

The preferred procedure for a patient with neutral or kyphotic alignment probably is fusion to improve or maintain lordosis. Some implants may be more kyphogenic than others.[42,43] A comparison of patients with cervical or lumbar disease found that fewer patients

with cervical disease had a contraindication to arthroplasty.[44] Presurgical evidence of fatty infiltration of the extensor musculature was associated with a relatively poor outcome after lumbar disk replacement.[35]

Technical Considerations

Disk arthroplasty techniques vary with the implant system and its mechanical rationale. A Smith-Robinson anteromedial approach is used for cervical TDR as well as anterior cervical diskectomy and fusion (ACDF). The miniopen retroperitoneal anterior lumbar interbody fusion (ALIF) approach is modified for lumbar TDR, with reliance on the experience of the access surgeon as well as powerful self-contained retractor systems.[45] A transperitoneal approach is best reserved for an obese patient or a patient who has undergone an earlier retroperitoneal exposure.[46] Typically, a short vertical incision is made just off of midline. Alternatively, a Pfannenstiel incision can be used.

When the disk space has been widely exposed, a radical anterior annulotomy is performed. In the cervical spine, the exposure is carried from uncus to uncus. Most systems require a wide diskectomy to allow meticulous midline and posterior positioning of the implant within the disk space. Improper placement limits motion or produces motion outside of the normal axis, which excessively loads the facets.[47] Preservation of the bony end plate avoids postoperative subsidence. Most systems are designed for a wide end plate footprint because the lateral portions of the vertebral body best resist axial loading.[48]

Sacrifice of the posterior longitudinal ligament continues to be a topic of debate.[49] An aggressive resection

Table 2

Contraindications to Lumbar Disk Arthroplasty

Central or lateral spinal stenosis

Compromised vertebral body (irregularly shaped end plate)

Facet joint arthrosis or pain

Iatrogenic spine instability

Major deformity or curvature deviation (eg, scoliosis)

Metabolic bone disease

Metal allergy

Posttraumatic segment

Predominant radiculopathy

Previous or latent infection

Previous surgery with severe scarring and radiculopathy

Spine tumor

Spondylolysis or spondylolisthesis

Adapted from Siepe CJ, Tepass A, Hitzl W, et al: Dynamics of improvement following total lumbar disc replacement: Is the outcome predictable? *Spine (Phila Pa 1976)* 2009;34(23):2579-2586.

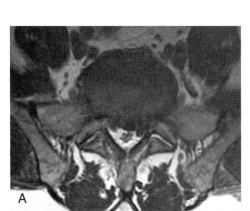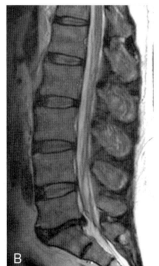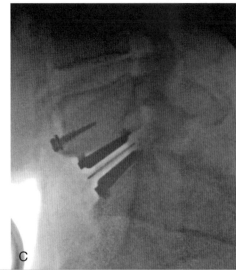

Figure 4

Aggressive nonsurgical management was unsuccessful in a 35-year-old patient with a 3-year history of increasing axial low back pain. MRI revealed a central disk herniation with preserved facet joints (**A**) and segmental collapse (**B**). The patient had approximately 80% relief of pain within the first 2 weeks after Charité lumbar TDR, which was preserved at 5-year follow-up, as seen on a fluoroscopic image (**C**).

4: The Adult Spine

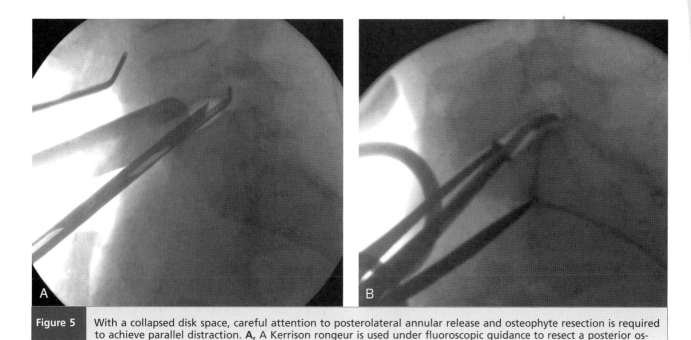

Figure 5   With a collapsed disk space, careful attention to posterolateral annular release and osteophyte resection is required to achieve parallel distraction. **A,** A Kerrison rongeur is used under fluoroscopic guidance to resect a posterior osteophyte. **B,** A curet is used to scratch through the anulus fibrosus.

of posterior osteophytes, the posterior longitudinal ligament, and the anulus fibrosus allows a more parallel distraction of the disk space (Figure 5). Overdistraction decreases index and adjacent segment motion. Insufficient distraction leads to the use of an undersized implant, which carries a risk of extravasation. Small polyethylene cores may exhibit cold flow in which the thin polyethylene deforms over time under loading. In the data submitted for FDA approval of the cervical Pro-Disc, the optimal range of motion was measured with implants between 5 and 7 mm high.[50] Appropriate distraction and implant placement are progressively more difficult in multilevel procedures.[51]

Keeled devices use a box and keel cutter, which must be introduced with great care to avoid injury to the surrounding soft tissues or a posterior vertebral avulsion fracture.[52] The Bryan cervical disk and some other devices use a gravitational referencing system to establish the disk center; a milling fixture then precisely prepares end plate concavities to exactly match the implant geometry.[27]

The postoperative protocols avoid or minimize the need for bracing. Many patients can benefit from postoperative physical therapy for core and neck strengthening. A patient typically returns to work more quickly after cervical or lumbar TDR than after fusion.[53]

Outcomes

The most important concern for a patient is whether the procedure relieves the symptoms that led to the choice of surgical treatment. Most studies answer this question by using validated pain and function instruments as well as satisfaction scores. From the surgeon's

perspective, the measures of success include radiographic range of motion and adjacent-segment degeneration. The focus of interest recently has shifted from the earlier smaller retrospective studies to multicenter randomized prospective data from FDA studies. The FDA data are of higher quality, but their generalizability has several limitations. The FDA studies were designed as noninferiority trials for reasons of power and study size. Critics believe that, at least for the lumbar studies, the procedures used for patients in the control groups were suboptimal. For example, in the Charité study the reference procedure (stand-alone ALIF with paired cylindrical threaded titanium interbody cages) was criticized as having dubious efficacy.[54] In the Pro-Disc study, the control subjects underwent a formal anterior-posterior procedure, which critics believed to be overly aggressive.[54] Patient satisfaction is believed to be affected if a patient specifically sought study inclusion, and patients receiving a "new and improved" treatment typically report greater satisfaction than control subjects. The measures of success used in the FDA-approval studies were less ambitious than, for example, those reported in the Spine Patient Outcomes Research Trial of lumbar diskectomy outcomes. In the FDA lumbar TDR studies, four criteria defined success at 2-year follow-up: an absence of device failure, a major complication, or neurologic deterioration and a more-than-25% improvement on the Oswestry Disability Index. In the Charité study, only 57% of patients with TDR and 46% of patients with ALIF met all four of these criteria. Furthermore, 64% of patients with TDR and 84% of patients with fusion still were using narcotic drugs 2 years after surgery that was considered successful.[54]

Data from the FDA and other available studies do

not establish any early outcome variability based on the differences in constraint systems. A recent 57-patient comparative study found that patients had statistically similar improvement in scores on the Oswestry Disability Index and the visual analog scale after the Charité or the ProDisc system was used.[23]

As with other new technologies, the outcomes of TDR are likely to deteriorate over time and as the use of the procedure is extended to less-than-ideal patients and to lower volume centers. Older, smaller studies may hint at the effects of broader implementation. Device designers reported the difficulty of achieving a good outcome in patients with an axial pain syndrome; 63% to 76% of patients were found to have a good to excellent result.[32,55,56] Authors have suggested that unsatisfactory outcomes primarily result from using improper surgical indications to choose patients.[56]

Cervical disk arthroplasty is intended to replace ACDF, which historically has had high success rates. Proponents of cervical TDR cite FDA study data on outcomes and complications for patients in the ACDF control group as proof that earlier assessments of ACDF were overly optimistic. The private and government payer response to lumbar arthroplasty led to reconfiguration of data sets in the later cervical studies, in an attempt to demonstrate superiority.[53,57] The current FDA investigational device exemption study data include 2- to 4-year outcomes from the Bryan, Prestige-ST, and ProDisc-C arthroplasty systems. The reported primary outcomes are slightly superior or equivalent to those of ACDF. A comparison of the Bryan cervical disk with ACDF (in 242 and 221 patients, respectively) found that both groups of patients had improvement in all outcome measures at 24-month follow-up.[53] The patients with TDR reported statistically greater improvement in the Neck Disability Index ($P = 0.025$) and in overall success ($P = 0.010$). Studies of other devices have reported similar outcomes.[57,58]

Complications

Some device failures, such as device wear, loosening, displacement, and failure to maintain motion, are specific to TDR. The FDA study data are tightly controlled by the sponsoring manufacturers and remain unavailable for meta-analysis. However, up-to-date information from the FDA studies is available on the website of the FDA Center for Devices and Radiological Health.[59] In FDA study submissions, overall serious adverse event rates have been low for both cervical and lumbar TDR, ranging from 0% to 4.9%.[26,29,32,53,60] In most studies, the complication rates for patients who underwent TDR were equal to or lower than those of control subjects.

Extrusion of removable polyethylene liners can lead to radiculopathy, cord compression, and esophageal or vascular compromise in a cervical or lumbar system.[61] The use of an anterior approach for a revision procedure compounds the vascular risks of the anterior approach. In one study, 8 of 46 patients required revision surgery. One implant was removed anteriorly, and seven were left in situ and posteriorly stabilized. Only three of the eight patients improved clinically.[56] Other studies reported similar technical difficulties and poor outcomes after revision.[55,62-64]

Patients who undergo arthroplasty, unlike those who undergo fusion, are vulnerable to index-level mechanical failure for the rest of their life. The possible failure mechanisms include prosthesis subsidence, dislodgement, and segmental kyphosis. The risk of these complications is greater with a multilevel procedure. For example, a small deviation from midline positioning, combined with a two-level implantation, confers an increased risk of coronal plane instability.[65] With aging, the loss of core muscle strength and bone quality affects spine kinematics and may allow implant subsidence.[23,66,67] The patient should be encouraged to take vitamin D and calcium dietary supplements and to undergo regular dual-energy x-ray absorptiometry screening. A late hematogenous infection also may occur.

The extent to which TDR restores normal segmental motion is a topic of controversy. Normal lumbar segmental motion is approximately 14° in flexion-extension. Successful fusion was defined as motion of 5° or less.[68] The average reported motion after TDR ranges from 4° to 9°.[32,56,57] Of 178 patients with lumbar TDR, 70 (39.3%) had motion of 5° or less at 24-month follow-up.[68] Limited postoperative motion may increase the degeneration rate at adjacent levels.[69] In a recent retrospective study with more than 8 years of follow-up, 38 patients with one- or two-level TDR were categorized as having more or less than 5° of postoperative motion. Improvement on the Oswestry Disability Index was described as modest for both groups of patients, but patients with more than 5° of motion reported outcomes superior to those of patients with less motion.[69] At a mean 42.4 months after TDR with a ProDisc II device, a study of 62 patients found the highest satisfaction scores among those with a preoperative disk space height of less than 4.5 mm.[37] After TDR, the mean disk height increased from 5.7 to 11.2 mm. There was a decrease in range of motion from 8.1° to 5.1°. Greater preoperative motion and disk height predicted greater postoperative motion.

In addition to the quantitative aspects of motion, the qualitative aspects must be considered. So-called unnatural motion accelerates facet degeneration and possibly adjacent-segment degeneration. The mechanical impact of an adjacent fusion on nearby degenerative segments is not well understood.[15,70] There is no proof that TDR protects adjacent segments, despite decades of European experience. Midterm results suggest that patients have lower rates of adjacent-segment surgery after TDR than after fusion, but long-term data are limited. A recent literature synthesis resulted only in a weak recommendation for TDR on the basis of a decreased incidence of adjacent-segment disease.[71] The available randomized studies were limited by differences in patient age and other variables.

The impact of TDR motion preservation perhaps may be best compared with the risk of device failure by examining rates of subsequent surgery. Some studies found similar rates, but others found significant differences, depending on length of follow-up.[53] In a study with 2-year follow-up, 17 of 50 patients who underwent TDR had undergone additional surgery; 11 of the procedures were at the adjacent level.[55] In another study, 9 of 106 patients (8.5%) who underwent fusion had secondary surgery, compared with 2 of 103 patients (1.8%) with a ProDisc implant (P = 0.033).[57] Postoperative facet degeneration had occurred in 12 of 33 patients (36.4%) with a Charité implant and 8 of 24 patients (32%) with a ProDisc implant at 3-year follow-up. The percentages for adjacent segment degeneration were statistically similar (19.4% and 28.6%, respectively).[23]

Heterotopic ossification has been reported after both cervical and lumbar disk procedures; it has been found in as many as 17% of cervical arthroplasties and may be more common when certain disk designs are used.[27] Heterotopic ossification also decreases motion. The study with the longest follow-up period is from the Charité hospital, where 63 lumbar TDRs in 53 patients were followed for a mean of 17 years.[72] Implant failures occurred in 13% of patients, 23% of TDRs had to be revised to fusion, and 78% of patients went on to spontaneous ankylosis. Satisfaction was highest in the patients who progressed to autofusion.

During the FDA evaluation of the Charité lumbar TDR, a study of 58 unsuccessful procedures received considerable attention.[13,30,54] The manufacturers and their consultants cited errors in surgical technique as the cause.[73,74] Critics suggested that such failures, which came from expert surgeons in high-volume research centers, could not be dismissed. Perhaps the devices require a level of technical precision that often is precluded by individual local anatomy and biomechanical demands. The anterior soft tissues and the collapsed disk space together may prevent ideal midline placement and the use of the ideal-size implant. Even after five training procedures per surgeon, 17% of the implants were found to be in a suboptimal location.[73]

Patients are more likely to have swallowing difficulty after cervical TDR than after ACDF. The cause probably is the greater and longer retraction required for most TDR systems. The esophagus and other anterior soft tissues should be carefully assessed before closure. Wound infection can occur with any spine reconstruction, but the reported rates have been less than 2%.[27,53,57]

The reported rates of vascular injury range from 3% to 15%, depending on the experience of the access surgeon, the craniocaudal surgical level, and the use of sharp retractors.[55,56,75] At the L4-5 surgical level, patients who were smokers or had atherosclerosis were more likely to sustain injury.[55,56,75] Cervical disk arthro-

plasty carries a slight risk of injury to the vertebral and carotid artery and the internal and external carotid vein. In the lower cervical spine, the thoracic duct is vulnerable on the left. In the lumbar spine, iliac vein tearing occurs in as many as 1 of 20 patients and is the most common complication. The inferior vena cava, ascending lumbar vein, and aorta also are at risk.[76]

Nerve injury can occur with cervical or lumbar TDR. Anterior TDR or ALIF carries significantly less risk to the nerve roots than posterior or transforaminal interbody fusion. Nerve root injury typically results from lateral implant placement, the use of sharp retractors, overaggressive diskectomy with canal intrusion, or aggressive iliac vessel or psoas muscle retraction affecting the lumbar plexus.[77] Postoperative femoral nerve or lumbar plexus dysfunction can result from psoas or iliacus hematoma.[78] Transient L5 radicular pain is most common.[32]

In cervical disk arthroplasty, spinal cord or root injury may occur during decompression, end plate preparation, or final implant impaction. Significant postoperative myelopathy or radiculopathy occurs in less than 0.3% of ACDF procedures.[27,53,57] Persistent neural compression from inadequate osteophyte resection or regrowth is more likely.

In the lower lumbar levels, the preaortic sympathetic autonomic plexus lies on the lateral aspect of the spine, just medial to the psoas. The fibers lie within the aortic bifurcation and along the left iliac artery as it arches over the L5-S1 disk space. This superior hypogastric plexus is particularly susceptible to injury at L5-S1. Disruption of the sympathetic plexus results in retrograde ejaculation and sterility. Men should be specifically counseled about this risk. In the cervical spine, injury to the sympathetic chain occurs from overretraction of the longus colli and leads to a Horner syndrome of ptosis, miosis, and anhidrosis. Vocal cord paralysis occurs after 1% to 11% of procedures secondary to recurrent laryngeal nerve injury.[53,57,58,60]

Summary

When the Charité implant was approved by the FDA in 2004, many observers predicted a revolution in spine care. This revolution has failed to occur. The concept of spine motion preservation remains attractive, but disk arthroplasty has failed to capture a significant percentage of either the cervical or lumbar spine market in the United States. Several important scientific questions remain, the most important of which is the long-term fate of disk arthroplasty systems in the aging spine. With experience, the proposed indications for TDR have contracted. Currently, these procedures are considered only for a small subset of the patients who are appropriate for fusion surgery. The indications for cervical TDR (particularly radiculopathy) are less controversial than the indication for lumbar TDR (axial disease). The outcomes of both procedures seem to be more closely linked to the disease state than to the technology itself. In most US regions, payers will not cover the cost of TDR, citing its great expense and the lack of evidence of long-term benefit.

Longer follow-up, larger data sets, fourth-generation devices, and a bundling of procedural codes for predicate procedures are likely to lead to a niche for disk arthroplasty in the spine surgery armamentarium. It is important to recognize the marked differences among implant designs when considering TDR. Constraint, fixation, bearing surface, and technical insertion difficulty may affect the long-term performance of the device.

Annotated References

1. Deyo RA, Gray DT, Kreuter W, Mirza S, Martin BI: United States trends in lumbar fusion surgery for degenerative conditions. *Spine (Phila Pa 1976)* 2005;30(12): 1441-1447.

   An administrative database was used to compare lumbar fusion rates during the 1990s with rates of other major musculoskeletal procedures. From 1996 to 2001, the number of lumbar fusions increased 113%, compared with 13% to 15% increases for hip replacement and knee arthroplasty.

2. Fritzell P, Hägg O, Jonsson D, Nordwall A, Swedish Lumbar Spine Study Group: Cost-effectiveness of lumbar fusion and nonsurgical treatment for chronic low back pain in the Swedish Lumbar Spine Study: A multicenter, randomized, controlled trial from the Swedish Lumbar Spine Study Group. *Spine (Phila Pa 1976)* 2004;29(4):421-434.

3. Guyer RD, Ohnmeiss DD: Intervertebral disc prostheses. *Spine (Phila Pa 1976)* 2003;28(15, suppl):S15-S23.

4. Huang RC, Lim MR, Girardi FP, Cammisa FP Jr: The prevalence of contraindications to total disc replacement in a cohort of lumbar surgical patients. *Spine (Phila Pa 1976)* 2004;29(22):2538-2541.

5. Pearcy MJ, Bogduk N: Instantaneous axes of rotation of the lumbar intervertebral joints. *Spine (Phila Pa 1976)* 1988;13(9):1033-1041.

6. Gunzburg R, Mayer HM, Szpalski M, Aebi M: Arthroplasty of the spine: The long quest for mobility. Introduction. *Eur Spine J* 2002;11(suppl 2):S63-S64.

7. Nachemson A, Zdeblick TA, O'Brien JP: Lumbar disc disease with discogenic pain: What surgical treatment is most effective? *Spine (Phila Pa 1976)* 1996;21(15): 1835-1838.

8. Zdeblick TA: The treatment of degenerative lumbar disorders: A critical review of the literature. *Spine (Phila Pa 1976)* 1995;20(24, suppl):126S-137S.

9. Anderson PA, Rouleau JP, Bryan VE, Carlson CS: Wear analysis of the Bryan Cervical Disc prosthesis. *Spine (Phila Pa 1976)* 2003;28(20):S186-S194.

10. Anderson PA, Sasso RC, Rouleau JP, Carlson CS, Goffin J: The Bryan Cervical Disc: Wear properties and early clinical results. *Spine J* 2004;4(6, suppl):303S-309S.

11. Hallab N, Link HD, McAfee PC: Biomaterial optimization in total disc arthroplasty. *Spine (Phila Pa 1976)* 2003;28(20):S139-S152.

12. Santos EG, Polly DW Jr, Mehbod AA, Saleh KJ: Disc arthroplasty: Lessons learned from total joint arthroplasty. *Spine J* 2004;4(6, suppl):182S-189S.

13. van Ooij A, Kurtz SM, Stessels F, Noten H, van Rhijn L: Polyethylene wear debris and long-term clinical failure of the Charité disc prosthesis: A study of 4 patients. *Spine (Phila Pa 1976)* 2007;32(2):223-229.

    A clinical case study tested polyethylene liners and periprosthetic tissues in four patients undergoing revision surgery after TDR failure. Implant wear was found to a varying extent, with wear debris and surrounding inflammatory fibrous tissue. In three patients, wear was associated with an unfavorable biomechanical environment.

14. Wigfield CC, Gill SS, Nelson RJ, Metcalf NH, Robertson JT: The new Frenchay artificial cervical joint: Results from a two-year pilot study. *Spine (Phila Pa 1976)* 2002;27(22):2446-2452.

15. Goffin J, Geusens E, Vantomme N, et al: Long-term follow-up after interbody fusion of the cervical spine. *J Spinal Disord Tech* 2004;17(2):79-85.

16. Riew KD, Buchowski JM, Sasso R, Zdeblick T, Metcalf NH, Anderson PA: Cervical disc arthroplasty compared with arthrodesis for the treatment of myelopathy. *J Bone Joint Surg Am* 2008;90(11):2354-2364.

    A cross-sectional analysis of the Bryan and Prestige FDA studies found that ongoing motion did not affect recovery in 199 patients with myelopathy with disk-level cord compression.

17. Sekhon LH, Duggal N, Lynch JJ, et al: Magnetic resonance imaging clarity of the Bryan, Prodisc-C, Prestige LP, and PCM cervical arthroplasty devices. *Spine (Phila Pa 1976)* 2007;32(6):673-680.

    A double-blinded imaging study analyzed the Bryan, Prodisc-C, Prestige LP, and PCM cervical arthroplasty devices in 20 patients (5 patients with each device). Postoperative visualization at the surgical level and adjacent levels was affected by all devices. Titanium created fewer artifacts than cobalt-chromium-molybdenum alloys.

18. Huang RC, Girardi FP, Cammisa FP Jr, Wright TM: The implications of constraint in lumbar total disc replacement. *J Spinal Disord Tech* 2003;16(4):412-417.

19. Pearcy MJ: Stereo radiography of lumbar spine motion. *Acta Orthop Scand Suppl* 1985;212:1-45.

20. Lin CY, Kang H, Rouleau JP, Hollister SJ, Marca FL: Stress analysis of the interface between cervical vertebrae end plates and the Bryan, Prestige LP, and ProDisc-C cervical disc prostheses: An in vivo image-based finite element study. *Spine (Phila Pa 1976)* 2009; 34(15):1554-1560.

Finite element analysis of end plate stress patterns after implantation of the Bryan, Prestige LP, or ProDisc-C cervical disk prosthesis found that the rigid nucleus of the Prestige and ProDisc implants improved maintenance of disk height at the expense of high-contact stresses at the bone–end plate junction.

21. Shim CS, Lee S, Maeng DH, Lee SH: Vertical split fracture of the vertebral body following total disc replacement using ProDisc: Report of two cases. *J Spinal Disord Tech* 2005;18(5):465-469.

In two patients with a lumbar ProDisc replacement, the device's tall keel was associated with postoperative vertebral body fracture and prolonged back pain.

22. Datta JC, Janssen ME, Beckham R, Ponce C: Sagittal split fractures in multilevel cervical arthroplasty using a keeled prosthesis. *J Spinal Disord Tech* 2007;20(1): 89-92.

An intraoperative vertebral fracture was associated with implantation of a keeled cervical disk arthroplasty device in this case report.

23. Shim CS, Lee SH, Shin HD, et al: CHARITE versus ProDisc: A comparative study of a minimum 3-year follow-up. *Spine (Phila Pa 1976)* 2007;32(9):1012-1018.

A retrospective study found statistically similar clinical outcomes in 33 patients with the Charité and 24 with the ProDisc device. In both groups of patients, degeneration of the index-level facet and adjacent-level disk was common.

24. Enker P, Steffee A, McMillin C, Keppler L, Biscup R, Miller S: Artificial disc replacement: Preliminary report with a 3-year minimum follow-up. *Spine (Phila Pa 1976)* 1993;18(8):1061-1070.

25. Mihara H, Cheng BC, David SM, Ohnari K, Zdeblick TA: Biomechanical comparison of posterior cervical fixation. *Spine (Phila Pa 1976)* 2001;26(15):1662-1667.

26. Zigler JE: Lumbar spine arthroplasty using the ProDisc II. *Spine J* 2004;4(6, suppl):260S-267S.

27. Goffin J, Van Calenbergh F, van Loon J, et al: Intermediate follow-up after treatment of degenerative disc disease with the Bryan Cervical Disc Prosthesis: Single-level and bi-level. *Spine (Phila Pa 1976)* 2003;28(24): 2673-2678.

28. Blumenthal S, McAfee PC, Guyer RD, et al: A prospective, randomized, multicenter Food and Drug Administration investigational device exemptions study of lumbar total disc replacement with the CHARITE artificial disc versus lumbar fusion: Part I. Evaluation of clinical outcomes. *Spine (Phila Pa 1976)* 2005;30(14):1565-1575.

A prospective, randomized, multicenter, FDA investigational device exemption study compared the Charité lumbar disk implant with anterior cage fusion in 304 patients. At 2-year follow-up, the clinical outcomes of the patients treated with TDR were not inferior to those of the patients treated with cage fusion. The length of hospital stay and rate of reoperation were lower in the patients treated with TDR.

29. Zigler J, Delamarter R, Spivak JM, et al: Results of the prospective, randomized, multicenter Food and Drug Administration investigational device exemption study of the ProDisc-L total disc replacement versus circumferential fusion for the treatment of 1-level degenerative disc disease. *Spine (Phila Pa 1976)* 2007;32(11):1155-1163.

A prospective, randomized, FDA investigational device exemption study compared the ProDisc-L device with anterior-posterior spine fusion in 286 patients. The clinical outcomes of TDR were not inferior to those of arthroplasty, but measures including neurologic outcome, complication rate, and recovery rate favored TDR.

30. van Ooij A, Oner FC, Verbout AJ: Complications of artificial disc replacement: A report of 27 patients with the SB Charité disc. *J Spinal Disord Tech* 2003;16(4): 369-383.

31. Goel VK, Nishiyama K, Weinstein JN, Liu YK: Mechanical properties of lumbar spinal motion segments as affected by partial disc removal. *Spine (Phila Pa 1976)* 1986;11(10):1008-1012.

32. Bertagnoli R, Kumar S: Indications for full prosthetic disc arthroplasty: A correlation of clinical outcome against a variety of indications. *Eur Spine J* 2002; 11(suppl 2):S131-S136.

33. Syed FI, Oza AL, Vanderby R, Heiderscheit B, Anderson PA: A method to measure cervical spine motion over extended periods of time. *Spine (Phila Pa 1976)* 2007; 32(19):2092-2098.

Volunteers were used to validate the results of a motion sensor system over time in two benchmarks (a material-testing machine and an optical-tracking system). Axial rotation was the least accurately measured motion.

34. Knöller SM, Meyer G, Eckhardt C, Lill CA, Schneider E, Linke B: Range of motion in reconstruction situations following corpectomy in the lumbar spine: A question of bone mineral density? *Spine (Phila Pa 1976)* 2005;30(9):E229-E235.

An in vitro biomechanical study of 24 cadaver spine specimens found that bone mineral density and, by extension, osteoporosis had a significant impact on postreconstruction range of motion.

35. Le Huec JC, Basso Y, Aunoble S, Friesem T, Bruno MB: Influence of facet and posterior muscle degeneration on clinical results of lumbar total disc replacement: Two-year follow-up. *J Spinal Disord Tech* 2005;18(3):219-223.

A prospective study analyzed the 2-year outcomes of 64

patients with Maverick lumbar disk arthroplasty as a function of facet and lumbar extensor muscle status. Patients with grade I or II facet arthrosis had a good clinical outcome. Fatty degeneration of the extensors was associated with a poorer outcome.

36. Stieber J, Quirno M, Cunningham M, Errico TJ, Bendo JA: The reliability of computed tomography and magnetic resonance imaging grading of lumbar facet arthropathy in total disc replacement patients. *Spine (Phila Pa 1976)* 2009;34(23):E833-E840.

  Prospective interrater and intrarater reliability analysis of CT and MRI facet arthropathy data found only fair agreement in the current grading systems. CT was more reliable than MRI.

37. Siepe CJ, Tepass A, Hitzl W, et al: Dynamics of improvement following total lumbar disc replacement: Is the outcome predictable? *Spine (Phila Pa 1976)* 2009; 34(23):2579-2586.

  Retrospective analysis of prospectively gathered data from 62 patients with the ProDisc device found that preoperative disk space height, postoperative range of motion, and clinical outcomes were closely correlated at a mean 42.4-month follow-up. Patients with the greatest disk collapse had the least postoperative range of motion but the highest level of satisfaction.

38. Newman MH, Grinstead GL: Anterior lumbar interbody fusion for internal disc disruption. *Spine (Phila Pa 1976)* 1992;17(7):831-833.

39. Anderson PA, Subach BR, Riew KD: Predictors of outcome after anterior cervical discectomy and fusion: A multivariate analysis. *Spine (Phila Pa 1976)* 2009;34(2): 161-166.

  A retrospective cohort study analyzed 488 patients from the fusion control groups of two FDA investigational device exemption cervical disk replacement studies. Work status, impaired sensory function, involvement in litigation, and low disability scores predicted a poor outcome.

40. Goldner JL, Urbaniak JR, McCollum DE: Anterior disc excision and interbody spinal fusion for chronic low back pain. *Orthop Clin North Am* 1971;2(2):543-568.

41. Siepe CJ, Mayer HM, Wiechert K, Korge A: Clinical results of total lumbar disc replacement with ProDisc II: Three-year results for different indications. *Spine (Phila Pa 1976)* 2006;31(17):1923-1932.

  A prospective nonrandomized study examined outcomes of 92 patients at a mean 34.2-month follow-up after ProDisc lumbar disk arthroplasty. Better outcomes were found in patients who were relatively young, had single-level surgery, and had degeneration associated with disk herniation.

42. Sears WR, Sekhon LH, Duggal N, Williamson OD: Segmental malalignment with the Bryan Cervical Disc prosthesis: Does it occur? *J Spinal Disord Tech* 2007;20(1): 1-6.

  A retrospective study assessed postoperative alignment in 67 patients who underwent 88 Bryan cervical disk ar-

throplasty procedures. The median loss of lordosis was 2°, in comparison with preoperative imaging. The results of the three surgeons differed significantly.

43. Johnson JP, Lauryssen C, Cambron HO, et al: Sagittal alignment and the Bryan cervical artificial disc. *Neurosurg Focus* 2004;17(6):E14.

44. Auerbach JD, Jones KJ, Fras CI, Balderston JR, Rushton SA, Chin KR: The prevalence of indications and contraindications to cervical total disc replacement. *Spine J* 2008;8(5):711-716.

  In a retrospective case study, 167 consecutive patients undergoing cervical spine surgery were assessed to determine whether they were candidates for arthroplasty. Forty-three percent met strict inclusion criteria and had no exclusion criteria. This percentage was higher than was found in a similar study of patients undergoing lumbar surgery.

45. Dewald CJ, Millikan KW, Hammerberg KW, Doolas A, Dewald RL: An open, minimally invasive approach to the lumbar spine. *Am Surg* 1999;65(1):61-68.

46. Scaduto AA, Gamradt SC, Yu WD, Huang J, Delamarter RB, Wang JC: Perioperative complications of threaded cylindrical lumbar interbody fusion devices: Anterior versus posterior approach. *J Spinal Disord Tech* 2003;16(6):502-507.

47. Lemaire JP, Skalli W, Lavaste F, et al: Intervertebral disc prosthesis: Results and prospects for the year 2000. *Clin Orthop Relat Res* 1997;337:64-76.

48. Grant JP, Oxland TR, Dvorak MF: Mapping the structural properties of the lumbosacral vertebral endplates. *Spine (Phila Pa 1976)* 2001;26(8):889-896.

49. McAfee PC, Cunningham B, Dmitriev A, et al: Cervical disc replacement-porous coated motion prosthesis: A comparative biomechanical analysis showing the key role of the posterior longitudinal ligament. *Spine (Phila Pa 1976)* 2003;28(20):S176-S185.

50. Peng CW, Quirno M, Bendo JA, Spivak JM, Goldstein JA: Effect of intervertebral disc height on postoperative motion and clinical outcomes after Prodisc-C cervical disc replacement. *Spine J* 2009;9(7):551-555.

  Prospectively gathered data on 166 patients enrolled in the FDA ProDisc-C investigational device exemption study were retrospectively reviewed. Patients with more than 5 mm of preoperative disk height had greater postoperative range of motion than those with a more collapsed disk. The ideal postoperative disk height was found to be 5 to 7 mm. Disk height and range of motion were not correlated with clinical outcome.

51. David T: Lumbar disc prosthesis: Surgical technique, indications and clinical results in 22 patients with a minimum of 12 months follow-up. *Eur Spine J* 1993;1(4): 254-259.

52. Shim CS, Shin HD, Lee SH: Posterior avulsion fracture at adjacent vertebral body during cervical disc replacement with ProDisc-C: A case report. *J Spinal Disord Tech* 2007;20(6):468-472.

In this case report, the posterior vertebral bodies of C6 and C7 were fractured during insertion of a keeled ProDisc-C implant, with resultant cord compression.

53. Heller JG, Sasso RC, Papadopoulos SM, et al: Comparison of BRYAN cervical disc arthroplasty with anterior cervical decompression and fusion: Clinical and radiographic results of a randomized, controlled, clinical trial. *Spine (Phila Pa 1976)* 2009;34(2):101-107.

A prospective, randomized, multicenter study of 465 patients compared the safety and efficacy of the Bryan cervical arthroplasty system with anterior cervical fusion. The patients treated with arthroplasty had statistically greater improvement in neck disability and greater overall success. The complication rate was higher in the patients treated with fusion.

54. Mirza SK: Commentary on the research reports that led to Food and Drug Administration approval of an artificial disc. *Spine (Phila Pa 1976)* 2005;30(14):1561-1564.

This is a commentary on the deficiencies of the FDA lumbar disk arthroplasty studies.

55. Zeegers WS, Bohnen LM, Laaper M, Verhaegen MJ: Artificial disc replacement with the modular type SB Charité III: 2-year results in 50 prospectively studied patients. *Eur Spine J* 1999;8(3):210-217.

56. Cinotti G, David T, Postacchini F: Results of disc prosthesis after a minimum follow-up period of 2 years. *Spine (Phila Pa 1976)* 1996;21(8):995-1000.

57. Murrey D, Janssen M, Delamarter R, et al: Results of the prospective, randomized, controlled multicenter Food and Drug Administration investigational device exemption study of the ProDisc-C total disc replacement versus anterior discectomy and fusion for the treatment of 1-level symptomatic cervical disc disease. *Spine J* 2009;9(4):275-286.

A prospective, randomized, multicenter study of 209 patients compared the safety and efficacy of the ProDisc-C system with anterior cervical fusion. Although a noninferiority design was used, the patients treated with arthroplasty had superior outcomes in several clinical measures, including pain medication usage. Reoperation rates were higher in the patients treated with fusion.

58. Mummaneni PV, Burkus JK, Haid RW, Traynelis VC, Zdeblick TA: Clinical and radiographic analysis of cervical disc arthroplasty compared with allograft fusion: A randomized controlled clinical trial. *J Neurosurg Spine* 2007;6(3):198-209.

A prospective, randomized, multicenter study of 541 patients compared the safety and efficacy of the Prestige cervical arthroplasty system with that of anterior cervical fusion. The Prestige system was found to maintain physiologic segmental motion at 24 months and was associated with improved neurologic success, improved clinical outcomes, and a reduced rate of secondary surgeries, compared with anterior cervical fusion.

59. US Food and Drug Administration: Medical Devices. http://www.fda.gov/MedicalDevices/default.htm. Accessed June 14, 2011.

60. Sasso RC, Smucker JD, Hacker RJ, Heller JG: Clinical outcomes of BRYAN cervical disc arthroplasty: A prospective, randomized, controlled, multicenter trial with 24-month follow-up. *J Spinal Disord Tech* 2007;20(7):481-491.

Three-center, 24-month data from a study of 115 patients with the Bryan cervical disk found improved neck pain and disability.

61. Mayer HM: Total lumbar disc replacement. *J Bone Joint Surg Br* 2005;87(8):1029-1037.

The rationale and goals of lumbar TDR are examined.

62. Leary SP, Regan JJ, Lanman TH, Wagner WH: Revision and explantation strategies involving the CHARITE lumbar artificial disc replacement. *Spine (Phila Pa 1976)* 2007;32(9):1001-1011.

In a case study of anterior revision of Charité disk replacement in 18 patients, most revisions were necessitated by technical error during the index procedure. Anterior revision can be challenging but was accomplished in all 18 patients.

63. Patel AA, Brodke DS, Pimenta L, et al: Revision strategies in lumbar total disc arthroplasty. *Spine (Phila Pa 1976)* 2008;33(11):1276-1283.

A literature review collated the many case studies of anterior-posterior revision after lumbar disk arthroplasty. The use of adhesion barriers during the primary procedure is recommended to decrease the risk to the great vessels during revision.

64. Ross ER: Revision in artificial disc replacement. *Spine J* 2009;9(9):773-775.

This is a commentary on revision strategies in lumbar disk arthroplasty.

65. Ching AC, Birkenmaier C, Hart RA: Short segment coronal plane deformity after two-level lumbar total disc replacement. *Spine (Phila Pa 1976)* 2010;35(1):44-50.

In this case study, four two-level disk arthroplasty procedures were complicated by coronal plane instability.

66. Rosen C, Kiester PD, Lee TQ: Lumbar disk replacement failures: Review of 29 patients and rationale for revision. *Orthopedics* 2009;32(8):32.

Increasing pain after Charité disk replacement was associated with facet degeneration and stress fracture in 29 patients. Successful posterior fusion led to improvement.

67. Le Huec J, Basso Y, Mathews H, et al: The effect of single-level, total disc arthroplasty on sagittal balance parameters: A prospective study. *Eur Spine J* 2005;14(5):480-486.

A prospective study of 35 patients who underwent Maverick lumbar disk arthroplasty found that sagittal balance markers such as sacral tilt and pelvic tilt were maintained postoperatively.

68. McAfee PC, Cunningham B, Holsapple G, et al: A prospective randomized, multicenter Food and Drug Administration investigational device exemption study of

lumbar total disc replacement with the CHARITE artificial disc versus lumbar fusion: Part II. Evaluation of radiographic outcomes and correlation of surgical technique accuracy with clinical outcomes. *Spine (Phila Pa 1976)* 2005;30(14):1576-1583.

The FDA Charité investigational device exemption study examined postoperative radiographic parameters. Disk height restoration and maintenance were found to be significantly better in patients treated with the Charité device than in those treated with a stand-alone ALIF with paired cylindrical threaded titanium interbody cages.

69. Huang RC, Tropiano P, Marnay T, Girardi FP, Lim MR, Cammisa FP Jr: Range of motion and adjacent level degeneration after lumbar total disc replacement. *Spine J* 2006;6(3):242-247.

A retrospective review of 42 patients who underwent lumbar disk arthroplasty found that almost 25% had adjacent-level degeneration at a mean 8.7-year follow-up. Many of the affected patients had relatively low postoperative range of motion.

70. Hilibrand AS, Carlson GD, Palumbo MA, Jones PK, Bohlman HH: Radiculopathy and myelopathy at segments adjacent to the site of a previous anterior cervical arthrodesis. *J Bone Joint Surg Am* 1999;81(4):519-528.

71. Harrop JS, Youssef JA, Maltenfort M, et al: Lumbar adjacent segment degeneration and disease after arthrodesis and total disc arthroplasty. *Spine (Phila Pa 1976)* 2008;33(15):1701-1707.

A literature review concluded that there was only low-level evidence for the use of arthroplasty to treat adjacent-segment degeneration, in comparison with arthrodesis.

72. Putzier M, Funk JF, Schneider SV, et al: Charité total disc replacement: Clinical and radiographical results after an average follow-up of 17 years. *Eur Spine J* 2006;15(2):183-195.

A retrospective study reported mean 17-year outcomes of 53 patients with a Charité disk replacement. There was progression to spontaneous ankylosis in 60% of patient. Those with ongoing motion had less adjacent-segment degeneration but also significantly lower satisfaction than those who had fusion.

73. McAfee PC: Comments on the van Ooij article. *J Spinal Disord Tech* 2005;18(1):116-117.

This is a commentary on the flaws of the van Ooij et al study of unsuccessful TDA procedures.[30]

74. McAfee PC, Geisler FH, Saiedy SS, et al: Revisability of the CHARITE artificial disc replacement: Analysis of 688 patients enrolled in the U.S. IDE study of the CHARITE Artificial Disc. *Spine (Phila Pa 1976)* 2006; 31(11):1217-1226.

Prospectively collected data from the FDA Charité investigational device exemption study were retrospectively reviewed. Of 589 patients who underwent TDR, 52 (8.8%) required revision. One third received another disk arthroplasty system, and two thirds underwent fusion.

75. Brau SA: Mini-open approach to the spine for anterior lumbar interbody fusion: Description of the procedure, results and complications. *Spine J* 2002;2(3):216-223.

76. McAfee PC, Regan JR, Zdeblick T, et al: The incidence of complications in endoscopic anterior thoracolumbar spinal reconstructive surgery: A prospective multicenter study comprising the first 100 consecutive cases. *Spine (Phila Pa 1976)* 1995;20(14):1624-1632.

77. Brau SA, Spoonamore MJ, Snyder L, et al: Nerve monitoring changes related to iliac artery compression during anterior lumbar spine surgery. *Spine J* 2003;3(5): 351-355.

78. Tonetti J, Vouaillat H, Kwon BK, et al: Femoral nerve palsy following mini-open extraperitoneal lumbar approach: Report of three cases and cadaveric mechanical study. *J Spinal Disord Tech* 2006;19(2):135-141.

This is a case study of three patients with postoperative femoral nerve injury after an extraperitoneal exposure. The recommendations include avoiding the use of self-retaining retractors for a long time period and maintaining hip flexion to decrease nerve tension.

Chapter 33

Dynamic Stabilization in the Lumbar Spine

Krzysztof B. Siemionow, MD   Howard An, MD

Introduction

Spinal arthrodesis is a versatile and effective option for managing spine instability, deformity, and painful conditions.[1] However, an increasing body of biomechanical and clinical evidence suggests that the relative immobility of fused spine segments alters the transfer of stress and accelerates adjacent-level degeneration.[2] Animals with fused spine segments were found to have greater disk degeneration at adjacent levels than control subjects,[3,4] and several in vitro experiments using human and nonhuman specimens found increased mobility at levels adjacent to a fusion.[5-9]

The development of nonfusion spine implants has been driven by concern about arthrodesis-related morbidity related to graft site harvest, pseudarthrosis, and adjacent-level degeneration.[10-12] Posterior dynamic stabilization devices are intended to avoid creating fusion-related stresses on neighboring levels. Currently there is no evidence that the use of a dynamic stabilization device leads to a lower rate of adjacent-segment disease than instrumented fusion. Pedicle-based, interspinous

Dr. Siemionow or an immediate family member serves as a board member, owner, officer, or committee member of Tolera Therapeutics Inc.; has received royalties from Tolera Therapeutics Inc.; serves as a paid consultant to or is an employee of Tolera Therapeutics Inc. and Synthes; serves as an unpaid consultant to MAZOR Surgical Technologies and AxioMed; and owns stock or stock options in Tolera Therapeutics Inc. Dr. An or an immediate family member serves as a board member, owner, officer, or committee member of the Scoliosis Research Society, the North American Spine Society, the American Academy of Orthopaedic Surgeons, the International Society for the Study of the Lumbar Spine, and Articular Engineering LLC; receives royalties from U & I, Inc.; serves as a paid consultant to or is an employee of Johnson & Johnson (DePuy Spine), Zimmer Spine, Alphatech Inc., Life Spine Inc., and Baxter Inc.; has received research or institutional support from Medtronic Sofamor Danek, Johnson & Johnson, and Synthes; owns stock or stock options in U & I, Inc., Articular Engineering Inc., Pioneer Inc., Spinal Kinetics, and Annulex Inc.; and has received nonincome support (such as equipment or services), commercially derived honoraria, or other non–research-related funding (such as paid travel) from Spinal Kinetics Inc., Pioneer Surgical Inc., and DePuy Spine Biologics Inc.

process, and facet replacement devices should be used judiciously, with careful patient selection, until outcomes studies are available to establish the efficacy of these motion-sparing implants.

The Effects of Dynamic Stabilization on Spine Kinetics

Adjacent-segment disease after a lumbar fusion is assumed to be partly or wholly the result of increased biomechanical stress on the level adjacent to the fused segment. Finite element analysis was used to compare lumbar motion segment loads after implantation of a bilateral posterior dynamic device modeled on the Dynesys (Zimmer, Warsaw, IN) and after rigid, pedicle-based instrumentation.[13] The simulated procedures were performed on both healthy and slightly degenerated disks at the L3-4 level, and distraction of the bridged segment also was simulated. Compared with the motion of an intact spine, a spine with a dynamic implant was found to have less intersegmental rotation, less intradiskal pressure during extension and standing, and lower facet joint forces at the implanted level. These decreases were more pronounced in spines with a rigid implant. If the affected disk had mild degeneration, intersegmental rotation at the implanted level was mildly increased during extension and axial rotation, with significant reduction in intradiskal pressure. In a rigid system, in contrast with a dynamic construct, motion-segment distraction markedly reduced intradiskal pressure. At adjacent levels, a posterior rigid implant had a minor effect on intradiskal pressure, but it increased cephalad-level facet joint forces during axial rotation and extension.

Posterior implants characteristically are loaded in compression. The forces borne by the implant generally are greater in a rigid system than in a dynamic implant. Distraction was found to strongly increase both axial and shear forces through the implant.[13] Greater implant stiffness (more than 1,000 N/mm) had only a minor effect on intersegmental rotation. Range of motion was assessed at the instrumented level and the adjacent levels after Dynesys instrumentation and was compared with range of motion after implantation of a rigid

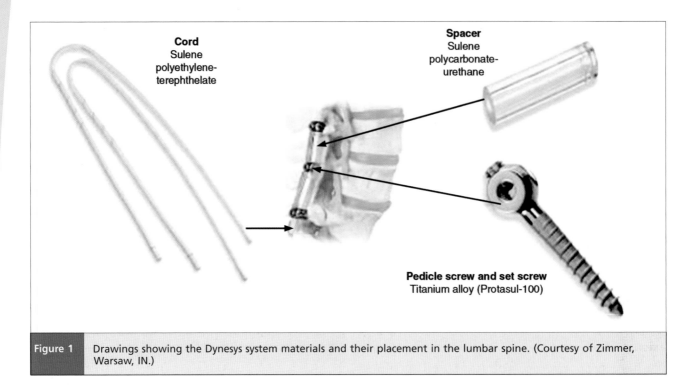

Cord
Sulene
polyethylene-
terephthelate

Spacer
Sulene
polycarbonate-
urethane

Pedicle screw and set screw
Titanium alloy (Protasul-100)

Figure 1	Drawings showing the Dynesys system materials and their placement in the lumbar spine. (Courtesy of Zimmer, Warsaw, IN.)

internal fixator.[14] Both the Dynesys implant and the rigid fixator reduced the range of motion in flexion, relative to an intact spine. Spines with the Dynesys implant had an extension range of motion equal to that of an intact spine. The extension range of motion was decreased in the rigid fixator–implanted spine. Neither instrumentation type affected adjacent-level range of motion.

In vivo, the spine is subjected to a combination of muscular and external forces and moments of unknown magnitudes. In vivo analysis therefore is critical for determining the impact of rigid or semirigid stabilization on adjacent segments. Positional MRI was used to measure the range of motion of the entire lumbar spine, the index level, and the adjacent levels in 24 patients before and after Dynesys instrumentation.[15] Eight of the procedures were monosegmental, 10 were bisegmental, 5 were three-level, and 1 was four-level. After the procedure, range of motion in the whole lumbar spine and the instrumented level was significantly reduced (from 38° to 25°). The motion of the adjacent segments cranial and caudal to the instrumentation site was not significantly reduced. Another study found a nonsignificant change in total lumbar range of motion (from 18° to 14°) after monosegmental Dynesys instrumentation.[16] Both studies indicate that patients who undergo Dynesys instrumentation must expect a less-than-normal range of motion in the lumbar spine.

Posterior Stabilization Devices

Posteriorly implanted devices that reduce but do not eliminate segmental motion have been widely investigated in Europe for treating mechanical back pain and spinal stenosis.[17-19] Unlike total disk replacement, which ablates painful disk tissues, a posterior motion-limiting device leaves the pain-generating disk tissues in situ but restricts certain types of motion and alters load transfer through the functional spinal unit.[20]

Pedicle-Based Systems

Ideally, a dynamic stabilizing device allows pain-free segmental motion and withstands static and dynamic loads on the spine. The longest clinical experience is with the Graf artificial ligamentoplasty system (SEM, Montrouge, France). In an all–pedicle-based system, titanium pedicle screws are connected by prosthetic ligaments that are tensioned to maintain the functional spinal unit in lordosis. Painful lumbar instability is believed to be caused by pathologic facet distraction and subluxation during axial rotation. Although posterior overloading of the anulus fibrosus initially was a concern, no progressive posterior disk height loss was detected at a mean 3.4-year follow-up.[21] However, forced extension has the potential to lead to iatrogenic lateral recess stenosis.

North American surgeons are more familiar with the Dynesys system than with the Graf system (Figure 1). This implant was first used in 1994 and received a Conformité Européene mark in 1999 for use as a nonfusion stabilization system.[22] The Dynesys system received US Food and Drug Administration (FDA) clearance in 2005 as a substantially equivalent pedicle screw system for lumbar fusion, but in 2009, the FDA decided not to grant approval for its use as a nonfusion stabilization system. More than 25,000 Dynesys devices have been implanted worldwide.

The Dynesys and Graf systems are similar, except that compression-resistant polycarbonate urethane sleeves surround the prosthetic ligaments in the Dynesys system. The prosthetic ligaments provide restraint to flexion, and the sleeves prevent excessive lordosis, bear compressive loads, and unload the disk when the patient's musculature exerts a net lordotic moment on the functional spinal unit. The Dynesys system has three potential drawbacks, however.[23,24] First, the compression-resistant sleeves limit the amount of lordosis that can be achieved; this is of concern because an implant placed with excessive distraction becomes kyphogenic. Second, compressive loads on the sleeves produce bending moments on the pedicle screws that could lead to breakage or loosening. Finally, the introduction of compression-resistant sleeves significantly increases construct rigidity, thus affecting its ability to prevent adjacent-level degeneration.

Biomechanics

A cadaver study found that the Dynesys system reduced flexion to less than 20% of the flexion of an intact spine at the affected level.[25] Extension and lateral bending were reduced to approximately 40% of that of the intact spine level. Total range of motion in torsion was not significantly different from that of the intact level. Another cadaver study tested the biomechanical effects of Dynesys implantation after a wide laminectomy.[26] Dynesys restricted range of motion after decompression in all investigated planes. Flexion-extension was most affected, lateral bending was somewhat restricted, and rotation was only mildly affected.

The impact of polymer spacer length on three-dimensional kinematic behavior at the implanted level was assessed using a cadaver model.[27] Injured segments were simulated by sectioning the facet joint capsules and the supraspinous and interspinous ligaments, and a posterolateral nucleotomy was performed. The use of a standard-length Dynesys implant significantly reduced range of motion in comparison with intact and injured specimens. The least significant changes were seen in axial rotation. Injury typically increased the spine's neutral zone of low-stiffness behavior, and Dynesys implantation reduced the neutral zone to less than that of the intact spine. No significant changes in the neutral zone were found with different spacer lengths. Spacer length had a significant effect on range of motion, however, with a long spacer allowing the greatest range of motion in all loading directions. The greatest differences related to spacer length were in axial rotation; a 4-mm increase in spacer length increased the average intersegmental motion 30% in axial rotation, 23% in extension, 14% in flexion, and 11% in lateral bending. In another study, the same researchers evaluated the effects of the Dynesys system on facet joint loading.[28] Dynesys implantation was found not to affect peak facet-contact forces in extension or axial rotation, compared with an intact specimen, but it did alter loads borne by the facet joints in flexion and lateral bending.

Spacer length affected posterior element compression, with a shorter spacer producing greater loads on the facet than a longer spacer.

Outcomes

In a prospective study, 26 consecutive patients with symptomatic lumbar spinal stenosis and degenerative spondylolisthesis underwent interlaminar decompression and Dynesys stabilization.[29] Three patients subsequently underwent lumbar fusion. Significant improvements in walking distance and scores on the visual analog scale at 2-year follow-up were unchanged at 4-year follow-up of 19 patients. There was no radiographic progression of spondylolisthesis, and the motion segments remained stable even in three patients who had screw loosening. One patient reported low back pain; flexion-extension radiographs showed screw breakage and motion at the instrumented level. At 4-year follow-up, 47% of the patients had adjacent-segment degeneration. Eighteen of the patients (95%) stated they would undergo the same procedure again.

In a retrospective analysis of 26 patients with low back pain, claudication from spinal stenosis, and concomitant spondylolisthesis at L4-L5, 15 underwent decompression and monosegmental fusion and 11 underwent decompression and posterior dynamic stabilization with the Dynesys system.[16] All patients had flexion-extension radiographs before surgery and at latest follow-up. Range of motion was assessed at the index level (L4-L5), the adjacent cranial and caudal levels (L3-L4 and L5-S1), and the global lumbar spine (L2-S1). The patients who underwent fusion had significant reduction in global lumbar and index-level range of motion. Adjacent-level range of motion did not change significantly. The patients treated using the Dynesys system had change in global lumbar or segmental (index and adjacent-level) range of motion. The authors concluded that neither instrumented fusion nor Dynesys posterior dynamic stabilization altered cranial or caudal adjacent-level range of motion.

The long-term effect of dynamic stabilization was investigated in vivo by quantifying glycosaminoglycan concentration in instrumented and adjacent spine levels, using delayed gadolinium-enhanced magnetic resonance imaging of cartilage (dGEMRIC).[30] In 10 patients whose low back pain had not responded to nonsurgical treatment, the dGEMRIC protocol was used to quantify glycosaminoglycan concentration before and 6 months after Dynesys implantation at one to three lumbar levels. Six months after implantation, all patients had improved scores on the visual analog scale, Prolo Scale, and Oswestry Disability Index. At the instrumented levels, dGEMRIC revealed a 61% increase in glycosaminoglycan. At the adjacent noninstrumented levels, there was a 68% decrease in glycosaminoglycan, primarily in the posterior disk. The authors concluded that lumbar dynamic stabilization stops and partially reverses disk degeneration while increasing adjacent-level stress.

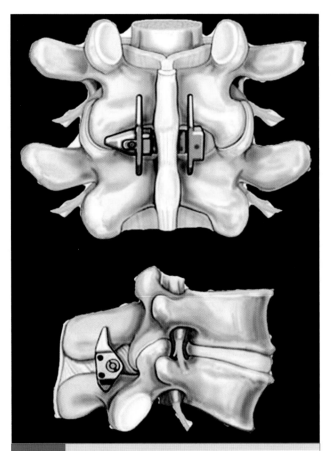

Figure 2	Drawings showing the posterior *(top)* and lateral *(bottom)* lumbar motion segment after implantation of an X-STOP device. The implant is placed posterior to the lamina and away from the nerve roots and spinal cord. The supraspinous ligament is retained to prevent posterior migration. The implant is not fixed to any bony structures.

Interspinous Process Devices

The first interspinous process implant for nonrigid lumbar stabilization was developed in 1986,[19] and several other devices subsequently were developed. The clinical indications for the use of an intraspinous process implant remain poorly defined. Case studies of device outcomes have involved varied indications and incomplete patient follow-up. An interspinous process implant acts as a shock absorber, in a manner comparable to an automobile bumper.[19,31] The available devices include the Device for Intervertebral Assisted Motion (DIAM; Medtronic Sofamor Danek, Memphis, TN), X-STOP Spacer (Medtronic Spine, Memphis, TN), Coflex (Paradigm Spine, New York, NY), and Wallis Interspinous Stabilizer System (Abbott Spine, Austin, TX). These interspinous process implants are designed to provide facet distraction, decrease intradiskal pressure, and reduce abnormal segmental motion and alignment[32] (Figure 2). Interspinous implants are designed to maintain foraminal distraction, expand the central canal, restore

posterior column height, and share in load transmission. Interspinous implants are designed to reduce motion, thus theoretically decreasing pain. In contrast, disk arthroplasty can preserve the motion of a degenerated spine segment.

Biomechanics

A bilateral hemifacetectomy defect was created in intact cadaver lumbar spines to test the Coflex, Wallis, DIAM, and X-STOP devices.[33] Range of motion was determined in flexion-extension, lateral bending, and axial rotation, and intradiskal pressure was measured. The defect caused increases in range of motion ranging from approximately 8% in lateral bending to 18% in axial rotation. Implantation had a similar effect, regardless of the specific device. In extension, the devices overcompensated for the instability caused by the defect, producing a range of motion approximately 50% less than that of the intact spine. The tested devices did not constrain flexion, lateral bending, or axial rotation beyond the range of motion observed in the created defect. Intradiskal pressure after implantation was similar to that of the intact specimens in all directions except extension, in which the implants reduced intradiskal pressure. Another study found that the DIAM device reduced the increased segmental flexion-extension and lateral bending motions observed after diskectomy.[34] In flexion-extension the DIAM restored postdiskectomy motion to below-intact values ($P < 0.05$). The DIAM did not reduce the increased axial rotation motion observed after diskectomy.

Outcomes

A randomized, controlled, prospective, multicenter FDA study compared nonsurgical treatment with X-STOP implantation in 191 patients with intermittent neurogenic claudication.[35] At each time point, the 100 patients treated with the X-STOP device reported significantly better results in all domains of the Zurich Claudication Questionnaire than the 91 nonsurgically treated patients. At 2-year follow-up, the mean symptom severity scores of patients in the X-STOP group had improved 45.4% over baseline, compared with a 7.4% improvement in the nonsurgically treated patients. In the physical function domain, patients in the X-STOP group had a mean improvement of 44.3%, compared with −0.4% in the nonsurgically treated patients. In the X-STOP group, 73.1% of the patients were satisfied with their treatment, compared with 35.9% of the nonsurgically treated patients.

A retrospective review of experience with the X-STOP, Wallis, and DIAM interspinous devices found that use of the X-STOP implant led to improvement in radiographic parameters including foraminal height, width, and cross-sectional area, compared with the DIAM and Wallis implants.[36] However, there were no significant differences in symptom relief at a mean 527-day follow-up (± 377 days). During the follow-up period, the radiographic parameters moved toward preoperative values without a concomitant increase in scores on the visual analog scale. Patient age and symptom improvement were not correlated. A review of experience with one- or two-level X-STOP implantation in 175 patients reported that the mean visual analog scale score for leg pain decreased from 61.2% before surgery to 39.0% 6 weeks after surgery.[37] The mean Oswestry Disability Index score was 32.6% before surgery, 22.7% at 6 weeks after surgery, and 20.3% at 24 months after surgery. Eight patients (4.5%) required X-STOP removal with decompression because of inadequate symptom relief. A favorable outcome was better predicted by position-dependent claudication, with symptom relief during flexion, than by any radiographic feature. The authors found that the use of an interspinous device could replace decompression in patients with severe stenosis and continuous claudication, and they concluded that interspinous device implantation is a safe, effective, and less invasive alternative to decompression in well-selected patients with spinal stenosis.

In a study of 12 patients with symptomatic lumbar spinal stenosis caused by degenerative spondylolisthesis, the revision rate was 58% (7 patients).[38] Four of the 12 patients had no postoperative symptom relief, and 3 patients had recurrent claudicatory pain and worsening of neurologic symptoms within 24 months. A prospective observational study involving 24 patients with moderate stenosis found that the X-STOP device offered significant improvement over a 1-year period.[39] At an average 4.2-year follow-up, X-STOP interspinous process decompression was found to be successful in 14 of 18 patients (78%), as measured using the Oswestry Disability Index.[40] A nonrandomized prospective observational study found that patients with a Wallis interspinous implant cephalad to a lumbar fusion were protected from developing adjacent-segment disease at 60-month follow-up.[41]

Facet Replacement Technology

The Total Posterior Spine (TOPS) system (Impliant, Princeton, NJ) is a pedicle screw–based facet arthroplasty implant in which a titanium layer encloses an interlocking polycarbonate-urethane articulating construct (Figure 3). The flexible polycarbonate urethane elements allow relative movement between the titanium plates to create axial rotation, lateral bending, extension, and flexion. The internal construct mechanically restricts motion to 1.5° of axial rotation, 5° of lateral bending, 2° of extension, and 8° of flexion. The implant also blocks excessive posterior and anterior sagittal translation. Four standard hydroxyapatite-coated polyaxial pedicle screws are used for fixation to the vertebrae. The TOPS device is considered investigational in the United States.

Biomechanics

Several biomechanical studies have evaluated facet replacement technologies. A cadaver study of the biome-

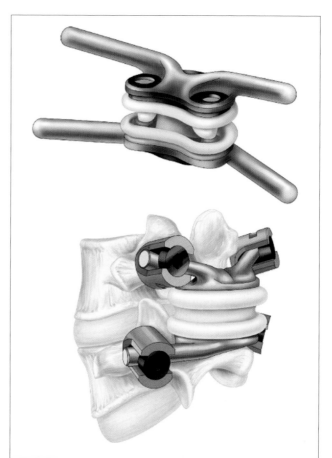

Figure 3 Drawings showing the TOPS facet arthroplasty system. The flexible polycarbonate-urethane elements (top) allow relative movement between the titanium plates to create axial rotation, lateral bending, extension, and flexion (bottom). (Reproduced with permission from Khoo L, Amin U: TOPPS total posterior arthroplasty system, in Yue JJ, Bertagnoli R, McAfee PC, An HS: *Motion Preservation Surgery of the Spine: Advanced Techniques and Controversies.* Philadelphia, PA, Saunders, 2008.)

chanics of the TOPS system used intact specimens; specimens with a bilateral laminectomy of L4, including facetectomy of the lower facet joints; and specimens with device implantation.[42] Range of motion, the neutral zone, and intradiskal pressure were determined. The destabilizing effects of the laminectomy-facetectomy were found to be reversed by device implantation. The authors concluded that the TOPS implant almost ideally restored range of motion in lateral bending and axial rotation, compared with the intact specimen.

Outcomes

In a nonrandomized, multicenter, prospective pilot study of the TOPS system, 29 patients were treated outside the United States for L3-L5 spinal stenosis and/or spondylolisthesis caused by facet arthropathy.[43] All patients underwent a bilateral total laminectomy and facetectomy at L4-L5 or L3-L4. At 1-year follow-up, the mean score on the Oswestry Disability Index had improved 41% over baseline, and the mean score on the 100-mm visual analog scale had improved by 76 mm. Radiographic analysis found that lumbar motion was maintained, disk height was preserved, and no screw loosening was evident. No device malfunctions or migrations and no device-related adverse events were reported.

Disadvantages of Nonfusion Implants

Nonfusion implants are subject to continuous motion, which can lead to late mechanical failure or loosening. Posterior pedicle-based devices such as the Dynesys are subject to screw loosening or breakage. In one study, 7 of 73 patients (10%) were found to have radiographically evident screw loosening at a mean 38-month follow-up;[44] screw loosening usually occurred within the first 6 months, and none of the patients who had well-fixed screws at 1-year follow-up developed late loosening. In two other studies, a 15% rate of screw loosening (3 of 19 patients) was reported at 4-year follow-up,[28] and a 4% rate (3 of 68 patients) was reported at 3-year follow-up.[45] Screw breakage has not been reported but is likely to be found at long-term follow-up.

Different approaches to dynamic stabilization may affect the long-term vulnerability of the screws. A comparison of pedicle screw loads found that the bending moments of Dynesys screws were 56% higher in flexion-extension and 86% higher in lateral bending than those of TOPS screws.[46]

Summary

Fusion remains one of the most useful and versatile tools in the spine surgeon's armamentarium. In some patients, nonfusion implants may be an attractive alternative for relieving pain, restoring motion, and withstanding repetitive loads. The etiology of the pain and need for decompression must be determined as accurately as possible before implant type is considered. Improvements in minimally invasive decompression techniques may limit the risk of iatrogenic destabilization and thus obviate both fusion and dynamic stabilization. Many patients with spinal stenosis and degenerative spondylolisthesis have little preoperative motion, and the use of motion-preserving implants may not make sense for these patients.

Less-than-optimal relief of axial low back pain has been reported with fusion, disk arthroplasty, and posterior dynamic stabilization. The judicious use of motion-sparing implants is warranted until clinical studies are available to validate their safety and efficacy.

Annotated References

1. Bridwell KH, Sedgewick TA, O'Brien MF, Lenke LG, Baldus C: The role of fusion and instrumentation in the treatment of degenerative spondylolisthesis with spinal stenosis. *J Spinal Disord* 1993;6(6):461-472.

2. Hilibrand AS, Robbins M: Adjacent segment degeneration and adjacent segment disease: The consequences of spinal fusion? *Spine J* 2004;4(6, suppl):190S-194S.

3. Olsewski JM, Schendel MJ, Wallace LJ, Ogilvie JW, Gundry CR: Magnetic resonance imaging and biological changes in injured intervertebral discs under normal and increased mechanical demands. *Spine (Phila Pa 1976)* 1996;21(17):1945-1951.

4. Phillips FM, Reuben J, Wetzel FT: Intervertebral disc degeneration adjacent to a lumbar fusion: An experimental rabbit model. *J Bone Joint Surg Br* 2002;84(2): 289-294.

5. Chow DH, Luk KD, Evans JH, Leong JC: Effects of short anterior lumbar interbody fusion on biomechanics of neighboring unfused segments. *Spine (Phila Pa 1976)* 1996;21(5):549-555.

6. Esses SI, Doherty BJ, Crawford MJ, Dreyzin V: Kinematic evaluation of lumbar fusion techniques. *Spine (Phila Pa 1976)* 1996;21(6):676-684.

7. Nagata HS, Schendel MJ, Transfeldt EE, Lewis JL: The effects of immobilization of long segments of the spine on the adjacent and distal facet force and lumbosacral motion. *Spine (Phila Pa 1976)* 1993;18(16):2471-2479.

8. Panjabi MH, Henderson G, Abjornson C, Yue J: Multidirectional testing of one- and two-level ProDisc-L versus simulated fusions. *Spine (Phila Pa 1976)* 2007; 32(12):1311-1319.

   The ProDisc-L preserved physiologic motions at all spine levels, but fusion simulations resulted in significant adjacent-level biomechanical changes.

9. Panjabi MM, Malcolmson G, Teng E, Tominaga Y, Henderson G, Serhan H: Hybrid testing of lumbar Charité discs versus fusions. *Spine (Phila Pa 1976)* 2007;32(9):959-967.

   Charité disks preserved motion at both the surgical and adjacent levels. Fusion affected motion redistribution at the adjacent levels.

10. Ambrosio L, De Santis R, Nicolais L: Composite hydrogels for implants. *Proc Inst Mech Eng H* 1998;212(2): 93-99.

11. Guyer RD, Ohnmeiss DD: Intervertebral disc prostheses. *Spine (Phila Pa 1976)* 2003;28(15, suppl):S15-S23.

12. Sagi HC, Bao QB, Yuan HA: Nuclear replacement strategies. *Orthop Clin North Am* 2003;34(2):263-267.

13. Rohlmann AB, Burra NK, Zander T, Bergmann G: Comparison of the effects of bilateral posterior dynamic and rigid fixation devices on the loads in the lumbar spine: A finite element analysis. *Eur Spine J* 2007;16(8): 1223-1231.

    A dynamic implant does not reduce axial spine loads in comparison with the uninstrumented spine.

14. Schmoelz WH, Huber JF, Nydegger T, Dipl-Ing, Claes L, Wilke HJ: Dynamic stabilization of the lumbar spine and its effects on adjacent segments: An in vitro experiment. *J Spinal Disord Tech* 2003;16(4):418-423.

15. Beastall JK, Karadimas E, Siddiqui M, et al: The Dynesys lumbar spinal stabilization system: A preliminary report on positional magnetic resonance imaging findings. *Spine (Phila Pa 1976)* 2007;32(6):685-690.

    MRI revealed no increase in mobility at adjacent segments when the Dynesys was used. There was a reduction in anterior disk height without a significant increase in posterior disk height.

16. Cakir BC, Carazzo C, Schmidt R, Mattes T, Reichel H, Käfer W: Adjacent segment mobility after rigid and semirigid instrumentation of the lumbar spine. *Spine (Phila Pa 1976)* 2009;34(12):1287-1291.

    Monosegmental posterior dynamic stabilization with Dynesys had no effect on adjacent-segment mobility, compared with monosegmental fusion.

17. Guizzardi G, Petrini P, Morichi R, Paoli L: The use of DIAM (intraspinous stress-breaker device) in the prevention of chronic low back pain in young patients operated on for large dimension lumbar disc herniation. *12th European Congress of Neurosurgery Proceedings.* Bologna, Italy, Monduzzi International Proceedings Division, 2003, pp 835-839.

18. Sénégas J: Mechanical supplementation by non-rigid fixation in degenerative intervertebral lumbar segments: The Wallis system. *Eur Spine J* 2002;11(suppl 2):S164-S169.

19. Schiavone AM: The use of disc assistance prosthesis (DIAM) in degenerative lumbar pathology: Indications, techniques and results. *Italian J Spinal Dis* 2003;3:105-111.

20. Dubois G, Schwarzenbach O, Speccia N, Stoll TM: Treatment of mobile vertebral instability with Dynesys, in Kim DH, Cammisa FP, Fessler RG, eds: *Dynamic Reconstruction of the Spine.* New York, NY, Thieme, 2006, pp 299-304.

21. Kanayama MH, Hashimoto T, Shigenobu K, Oha F, Ishida T, Yamane S: Non-fusion surgery for degenerative spondylolisthesis using artificial ligament stabilization: Surgical indication and clinical results. *Spine (Phila Pa 1976)* 2005;30(5):588-592.

    Artificial ligament stabilization was an effective alternative to spinal arthrodesis in the treatment of symptomatic degenerative spondylolisthesis, with minimal disk space narrowing and coronal facet tropism.

22. Dubois GB, Schaerer N, Fennema P: Dynamic neutralization: A new concept for restabilization of the spine, in Szpalski M, Gunzburg R, Pope MH, eds: *Lumbar Segment Instability.* Philadelphia, PA, Lippincott Williams & Wilkins, 1999, pp 233-240.

23. Mulholland RC, Sengupta DK: Rationale, principles and experimental evaluation of the concept of soft stabilization. *Eur Spine J* 2002;11(suppl 2):S198-S205.

24. Sengupta DK, Mulholland RC: Fulcrum assisted soft stabilization system: A new concept in the surgical treatment of degenerative low back pain. *Spine (Phila Pa 1976)* 2005;30(9):1019-1030.

    A fulcrum-assisted soft stabilization system is described as a means of unloading the disk, controlling range of motion, and maintaining lordosis.

25. Gédet P, Haschtmann D, Thistlethwaite PA, Ferguson SJ: Comparative biomechanical investigation of a modular dynamic lumbar stabilization system and the Dynesys system. *Eur Spine J* 2009;18(10):1504-1511.

    Because the device is placed at a location removed from the natural rotation center of the intervertebral joint, the assumption that a device compliant in bending allows substantial intersegmental motion cannot be supported.

26. Schulte TL, Hurschler C, Haversath M, et al: The effect of dynamic, semi-rigid implants on the range of motion of lumbar motion segments after decompression. *Eur Spine J* 2008;17(8):1057-1065.

    The Wallis and Dynesys devices were found to restrict not only isolated extension but also flexion. The biomechanical results support the hypothesis that the semirigid implants directly provide a primary stabilizing function after surgery.

27. Niosi CA, Zhu QA, Wilson DC, Keynan O, Wilson DR, Oxland TR: Biomechanical characterization of the three-dimensional kinematic behaviour of the Dynesys dynamic stabilization system: An in vitro study. *Eur Spine J* 2006;15(6):913-922.

    The length of the Dynesys spacer was found to affect segment position and kinematic behavior.

28. Niosi CA, Wilson DC, Zhu Q, Keynan O, Wilson DR, Oxland TR: The effect of dynamic posterior stabilization on facet joint contact forces: An in vitro investigation. *Spine (Phila Pa 1976)* 2008;33(1):19-26.

    Dynesys does not affect peak facet contact forces in extension or axial rotation compared with intact specimens. These loads are altered in flexion and lateral bending. Spacer length is important: shorter spacers produce greater facet loads than longer ones.

29. Schaeren SB, Broger I, Jeanneret B: Minimum four-year follow-up of spinal stenosis with degenerative spondylolisthesis treated with decompression and dynamic stabilization. *Spine (Phila Pa 1976)* 2008;33(18):E636-E642.

    Older adult patients with spinal stenosis and degenerative spondylolisthesis have excellent clinical and radiologic results after decompression and dynamic stabilization. Although dynamic stabilization prevents progression of spondylolisthesis, the degenerative disease is progressive; degeneration at adjacent motion segments remains an issue.

30. Vaga SB, Brayda-Bruno M, Perona F, et al: Molecular MR imaging for the evaluation of the effect of dynamic stabilization on lumbar intervertebral discs. *Eur Spine J* 2009;18(suppl 1):40-48.

Dynamic stabilization of the lumbar spine was found to be able to stop and partially reverse disk degeneration, especially in seriously degenerated disks, while incrementally increasing the stress on the adjacent levels, where it induces early degeneration.

31. Taylor JR: Technical and anatomical considerations for the placement of a posterior interspinous stabilizer. *Medtronic Sofamor Danek Technique Guide.* Memphis, TN, Medtronic Sofamor Danek, 2004.

32. Lee JH, Hida K, Seki T, Iwasaki Y, Minoru A: An interspinous process distractor (X STOP) for lumbar spinal stenosis in elderly patients: Preliminary experiences in 10 consecutive cases. *J Spinal Disord Tech* 2004;17(1): 72-78.

33. Wilke HJ, Drumm J, Häussler K, Mack C, Steudel WI, Kettler A: Biomechanical effect of different lumbar interspinous implants on flexibility and intradiscal pressure. *Eur Spine J* 2008;17(8):1049-1056.

The Coflex, Wallis, DIAM, and X-STOP interspinous implants were compared in terms of three-dimensional flexibility and the intradiskal pressure. All of the implants stabilized and reduced intradiskal pressure in extension but had almost no effect in flexion.

34. Phillips FM, Voronov LI, Gaitanis IN, Carandang G, Havey RM, Patwardhan AG: Biomechanics of posterior dynamic stabilizing device (DIAM) after facetectomy and discectomy. *Spine J* 2006;6(6):714-722.

The effects of the DIAM device on the biomechanical response of the lumbar spine in flexion-extension, lateral bending, and axial rotation were analyzed after partial facetectomy and diskectomy. The DIAM device was found effective for stabilizing the unstable segment.

35. Zucherman JF, Hsu KY, Hartjen CA, et al: A multicenter, prospective, randomized trial evaluating the X STOP interspinous process decompression system for the treatment of neurogenic intermittent claudication: Two-year follow-up results. *Spine (Phila Pa 1976)* 2005; 30(12):1351-1358.

The safety and efficacy of the X-STOP device was evaluated at 2-year follow-up. Patients had a mean 45.4% improvement over baseline. The X-STOP was found to be effective for patients with lumbar spinal stenosis.

36. Sobottke R, Schlüter-Brust K, Kaulhausen T, et al: Interspinous implants (X Stop, Wallis, Diam) for the treatment of LSS: Is there a correlation between radiological parameters and clinical outcome? *Eur Spine J* 2009; 18(10):1494-1503.

An interspinous implant offers significant, long-lasting symptom control, even if initially significant radiologic changes appear to revert toward their initial values over time.

37. Kuchta J Sr, Sobottke R, Eysel P, Simons P: Two-year results of interspinous spacer (X-Stop) implantation in 175 patients with neurologic intermittent claudication due to lumbar spinal stenosis. *Eur Spine J* 2009;18(6): 823-829.

In 175 patients, the X-STOP device was used to treat intermittent claudication from spinal stenosis at one or two levels. A good effect was found at 2-year follow-up.

38. Verhoof OJ, Bron JL, Wapstra FH, van Royen BJ: High failure rate of the interspinous distraction device (X-Stop) for the treatment of lumbar spinal stenosis caused by degenerative spondylolisthesis. *Eur Spine J* 2008; 17(2):188-192.

Symptomatic lumbar spinal stenosis caused by degenerative spondylolisthesis in 12 patients was treated using the X-STOP device. The X-STOP device is not recommended for this purpose.

39. Siddiqui MS, Smith FW, Wardlaw D: One-year results of X Stop interspinous implant for the treatment of lumbar spinal stenosis. *Spine (Phila Pa 1976)* 2007;32(12): 1345-1348.

The clinical outcome of patients with symptomatic lumbar spinal stenosis after X-STOP implantation was prospectively assessed. The X-STOP was found to offer significant improvement over a 1-year period.

40. Kondrashov DG, Hannibal M, Hsu KY, Zucherman JF: Interspinous process decompression with the X-STOP device for lumbar spinal stenosis: A 4-year follow-up study. *J Spinal Disord Tech* 2006;19(5):323-327.

At 4-year follow-up after implantation, 18 patients had a mean improvement of 29 points on the Oswestry Disability Index. Fourteen patients (78%) had a successful outcome, defined as a 15-point improvement.

41. Korovessis PR, Repantis T, Zacharatos S, Zafiropoulos A: Does Wallis implant reduce adjacent segment degeneration above lumbosacral instrumented fusion? *Eur Spine J* 2009;18(6):830-840.

The Wallis interspinous implant changed the natural history of adjacent-segment degeneration, saving the two adjacent cephalad vertebrae from fusion and lowering the radiographic incidence of adjacent-segment degeneration 5 years after surgery.

42. Wilke HJ, Schmidt H, Werner K, Schmölz W, Drumm J: Biomechanical evaluation of a new total posterior-element replacement system. *Spine (Phila Pa 1976)* 2006;31(24):2790-2797.

The TOPS implant almost ideally restored range of motion in lateral bending and axial rotation, compared with intact specimens. In the sagittal plane, 85% of the intact range of motion could be obtained.

43. McAfee P, Khoo LT, Pimenta L, et al: Treatment of lumbar spinal stenosis with a total posterior arthroplasty

prosthesis: Implant description, surgical technique, and a prospective report on 29 patients. *Neurosurg Focus* 2007;22(1):E13.

Preliminary surgical data and clinical outcomes in patients treated with the TOPS system indicate that the TOPS system has low surgical morbidity and excellent 1-year functional and radiographic outcomes.

44. Stoll TM, Dubois G, Schwarzenbach O: The dynamic neutralization system for the spine: A multi-center study of a novel non-fusion system. *Eur Spine J* 2002; 11(suppl 2):S170-S178.

45. Sapkas GS, Themistocleous GS, Mavrogenis AF, Benetos IS, Metaxas N, Papagelopoulos PJ: Stabilization of the lumbar spine using the dynamic neutralization system. *Orthopedics* 2007;30(10):859-865.

Evaluation of spine stabilization with a dynamic neutralization system in 68 patients found that the overall results were comparable to those of fusion procedures.

46. Meyers KT, Tauber M, Sudin Y, et al: Use of instrumented pedicle screws to evaluate load sharing in posterior dynamic stabilization systems. *Spine J* 2008;8(6): 926-932.

The effect of the Dynesys and TOPS systems on pedicle screw load was evaluated. The design of the posterior stabilization device influences the amount of load borne by the pedicle screws.

4: The Adult Spine

Chapter 34

Alternatives to Autogenous Bone Graft in Spine Surgery

Kamran Majid, MD   Jeff Fischgrund, MD

Introduction

Bone grafts are used to reconstruct or replace skeletal defects, augment fracture repair, and fill defects after bone tumor treatment. More than 500,000 bone graft procedures are performed annually in the United States, including spine fusion, internal fixation of fractures, treatment of bone defects, and other types of procedures.[1]

Autologous cancellous bone grafting has been the gold standard. Autologous bone graft is the preferred material because of its unique complement of live cells and its osteogenic, osteoinductive, and osteoconductive properties (Table 1). Ossification (osteogenesis) is synonymous with bone tissue formation; it is the process by which cells called osteoblasts lay down new bone material. Normal, healthy bone tissue is formed by intramembranous ossification, which is the direct laying down of bone into the primitive connective tissue (mesenchyme); and endochondral ossification, which involves cartilage as a precursor. Autologous bone graft harvest is associated with morbidities including postoperative donor site pain and potential injury to local neurovascular structures. Infection, hematoma formation, and gait disturbances have been reported after iliac bone graft harvest.[2]

The substitution of materials with equivalent osteoconductive and osteoinductive properties ideally could eliminate the need to harvest autograft bone. The term osteoinduction refers to the stimulation of mesenchymal stem cells to proliferate and differentiate into osteoprogenitor cells with the capacity to form bone.[3] Osteoconduction refers to the ingrowth of sprouting capillaries and perivascular tissues as well as osteoprogenitor cells into the three-dimensional structure of an implant or graft.[4] Synthetic osteoconductive materials include calcium phosphate, calcium sulfate, and calcium hydroxyapatite as well as composites of collagen and calcium salts that imitate autologous bone graft. These materials' osteoconductive properties are believed to result from their microscopic and chemical structure and their surface charge.

Bone Morphogenetic Proteins

Bone morphogenetic proteins (BMPs) are multifunctional growth factors that belong to the transforming growth factor–β superfamily of proteins. The roles of BMPs in the embryonic development and cellular functions of postnatal and adult animals have been extensively studied in recent years. Signal transduction studies revealed that *SMAD1*, *SMAD5*, and *SMAD8* are the immediate downstream molecules of BMP receptors and have a central role in BMP signal transduction.[5,6] Studies from transgenic and knockout mice and from animals and humans with naturally occurring mutations in BMPs and related genes found that BMP signaling has a critical role in heart, neural, and cartilage development.[7,8]

Several small studies and case reports from the 1980s introduced demineralized bone matrix (DBM) and purified human BMPs as having potential clinical efficacy for bone induction.[9-13] In 2002 the US Food and Drug Administration (FDA) approved recombinant human BMP-2 (rhBMP-2) as a substitute for autologous bone in anterior interbody spine fusion. Specifically, rhBMP-2 carried on a type I collagen sponge is approved for use in conjunction with a threaded intervertebral cage (LT-Cage; Medtronic Sofamor Danek, Minneapolis, MN) to obtain anterior lumbar spine fusion. This narrow approval was largely based on a

Dr. Fischgrund or an immediate family member serves as a board member, owner, officer, or committee member of the Cervical Spine Research Society, the Spine Arthroplasty Society, the Spine Study Group, the Lumbar Spine Research Society, and the North American Spine Society; has received royalties from Stryker and DePuy, a Johnson & Johnson company; is a member of a speakers' bureau or has made paid presentations on behalf of Smith & Nephew, Stryker, and DePuy, a Johnson & Johnson company; serves as a paid consultant to or is an employee of Smith & Nephew, Stryker, ApaTech, and DePuy, a Johnson & Johnson company; serves as an unpaid consultant to Fziomed; and has received research or institutional support from Smith & Nephew, Stryker, and DePuy, a Johnson & Johnson company. Neither Dr. Majid nor any immediate family member has received anything of value from or owns stock in a commercial company or institution related directly or indirectly to the subject of this chapter.

Table 1

Properties of Bone Graft Materials

Material	Osteogenic Cells	Osteoinductive Factors	Osteoconductive Matrix	Initial Biomechanical Strength	Donor-Site Morbidity
Allograft, frozen	-	+	+	++	–
Allograft, lyophilized	–	+	+	+	–
Autogenous bone, cancellous	+++	++	+++	–	++
Autogenous bone, cortical	+	+	+	+++	++
Autologous platelet concentrate	–	++	–	–	–
Ceramic	–	–	+++	+	–
Demineralized bone matrix	–	++	+	–	–
Gene therapy, in vivo	–	+++	–	–	–
Gene therapy, ex vivo	++	+++	-	–	+
Mesenchymal stem cells	+++	–	–	–	+
Osteoinductive growth factor	–	+++	–	–	–
Unfractionated bone marrow	++	+	–	–	+

– = none, + = minimal, ++ = moderate, +++ = abundant.

Adapted with permission from Whang PG, Wang JC: Bone graft substitutes for spinal fusion. *Spine J* 2003;3(2):155-165.

prospective, randomized 2-year clinical study of 279 patients with degenerative lumbar disk disease.[14] All patients underwent interbody fusion using two tapered threaded fusion cages. The 143 patients in the investigational group received rhBMP-2 on an absorbable collagen sponge, and the 136 patients in the control group received autogenous iliac crest bone graft. Plain radiographs and CT were used to evaluate the spine fusion 6, 12, and 24 months after surgery. At 24 months, the fusion rate of the patients in the investigational group was 94.5% and that of the patients in the control group was 88.7%. Patients in the two groups had similar outcomes at all postoperative evaluation points, with improved back pain, leg pain, neurologic status, and mean Oswestry Disability Index scores. The researchers concluded that lumbar fusion using rhBMP-2 and a tapered titanium fusion cage can yield a solid union and eliminate the need for harvesting iliac crest bone graft. BMP-7 (recombinant human osteogenic protein-1) has been approved by the FDA for revision posterolateral lumbar spine fusion under a humanitarian device exemption.[15] The use of rhBMP-2 for posterior lumbar fusion is in the process of being evaluated by the FDA.

The use of BMP is associated with several concerns including ectopic bone formation in the spinal canal, postoperative soft-tissue swelling with airway compro-

mise in the cervical spine, and antibody formation.[16,17] The FDA has reported concern regarding an increased incidence of cancers found in a large prospective study, but the clinical relevance of this finding remains unclear.[18] Harmful clinical sequelae related to antibody formation have not yet been found. BMP should not be used in pregnant women. The repeated use of BMP in serial surgeries has not been studied and should be avoided. BMPs should not be used in the presence of a local tumor because of the potential for angiogenesis and cell differentiation.

The delivery of BMP at a fusion site is affected by multiple factors, including the anatomic location, characteristics of the local soft-tissue envelope, and mechanical forces on the bone. Metallic spine implants such as screws and rods alter the local strain environment and affect signaling through bone. The delivery system ideally provides an appropriately timed local release of BMP, maintains an appropriate BMP dosage, and acts as a substrate to enhance cell recruitment and attachment.[19] The delivery system should not generate immune or inflammatory responses that inhibit osteogenesis. The delivery systems currently available for recombinant BMPs include DBM, synthetic polymers, type I collagen, hyaluronic acid gels, and a variety of bone graft substitutes including hydroxyapatite, coralline hydroxyapatite, and tricalcium phosphate.

Several BMPs are being investigated for their therapeutic potential. It appears that a combination of BMPs and other growth factors may be more effective for bone formation than high dosages of a single protein. Implantation of BMP-2–BMP-7 and BMP-4–BMP-7 heterodimers improved bone formation in comparison with their homodimer counterparts.[20]

Alternative Bone Graft Materials

The currently used alternatives to autologous bone graft include allograft bone, DBM, recombinant growth factors, and synthetic products. Each of these alternatives can be combined with autologous bone marrow or various growth factors. None of the alternatives provides all three of the fundamental properties of autograft bone (osteogenicity, osteoconductivity, and osteoinductivity), but all are clinically useful in some circumstances. If the supply of autologous bone graft is limited, one of the alternatives can be used to extend the autogenous bone. In some clinical situations, satisfactory fusion can be achieved without autologous bone graft, and the morbidity of autograft harvest thus can be avoided.[2,21,22] Existing and evolving technologies may allow materials to be combined to cumulatively provide the patient with all three cardinal properties of an ideal bone graft.

Bone graft extenders act as osteoconductive materials to provide a scaffold for new bone formation. These materials lack cellular elements and therefore cannot initiate new bone formation (osteoinduction). Bone graft extenders function solely in a passive role by providing a matrix into which bone can form. The commonly used graft extenders include calcium phosphates, calcium phosphate and collagen composites, and calcium sulfate granules.

Bone Marrow Aspirate

Bone marrow is a readily available source of osteoprogenitor cells, which act in a manner similar to that of autogenous bone graft. Marrow cells typically are aspirated from the iliac crest or a pedicle and are combined with other bone graft substitutes to add osteogenic potential. In a typical patient's bone marrow, approximately 1 of 50,000 nucleated cells is an osteoprogenitor cell.[23] The concentration can be increased by aspiration limited to 2 or 3 mL per site followed by centrifugation.[24] The use of bone marrow aspirate has been studied alone and in combination with other bone graft substitutes.[25] Healing of long bone nonunions was acceptable when bone marrow injection was used.[26] Marrow bone extender material stimulated both spine arthrodesis and long bone fusion in animal and clinical studies.[27,28]

Allograft Bone

The use of allograft bone in spine fusion has increased as procurement, preparation, and storage methods have improved. The risk of associated infection with human

immunodeficiency virus is less than 1 per million.[29] Allograft bone is available fresh, fresh frozen, and freeze dried (lyophilized), in the form of strips, cubes, wedges, shafts, or machined dowels. Allograft bone has both osteoconductive and weakly osteoinductive properties. Its osteoinductivity varies with the preparation and sterilization method. These methods include low-dosage irradiation (less than 20 kGy), physical débridement, ultrasonic or pulsatile water washes, ethanol treatment, and antibiotic soaking (at 4°C for at least 1 hour).[30] The goals of processing are to remove the antigenic components of the graft and thus to avoid induction of a host immune response, ensure sterility, and retain certain biologic and biomechanical functions. If contamination is present, terminal sterilization by gamma irradiation, electron beam irradiation, or ethylene oxide treatment can be used, but the mechanical strength of the graft may be compromised by the dose-dependent effect of these treatments. Sterilization must also kill bacterial spores, using a method such as gamma irradiation.

In comparison with autograft, the disadvantages of allograft include a slower rate of fusion, a greater risk of resorption, and an increased risk of infection.[31] Allograft bone can provoke a spectrum of immunogenic responses from the host. The strength of the immune response depends on the extent of processing-related enzymatic degradation of the native allograft protein.[32] Fresh allograft bone produces a powerful immune response, and its use therefore is limited to particular applications in which the structural properties of the graft are important, such as joint surface replacement. Fresh-frozen allograft bone has less immunogenicity, with biomechanical properties similar to those of fresh allograft. Its immunogenicity is halfway between those of fresh and freeze-dried allograft. Freeze-dried allograft is created by removing water through a vacuum process that substantially reduces its immunogenicity. Freeze-dried bone has diminished compression resistance. In comparison with fresh-frozen allograft bone, which provides optimal strength with intermediate immunogenicity, lyophilized tissue provides less strength and has markedly reduced immunogenicity but allows an extended storage time. Higher rates of fusion have been reported when allograft bone graft is placed under compression for anterior column applications. With neutral load placement for posterior or posterolateral applications, allograft bone graft is associated with slower incorporation, more resorption, and a greater risk of infection than autologous bone graft.[33]

Demineralized Bone Matrix

DBM is a type of bone graft extender that contains trace amounts of naturally occurring BMPs and is mildly osteoinductive. Cortical allograft is processed to make DBM. Acid extraction decalcifies the bone, leaving a composite of collagen with noncollagenous proteins and a low concentration of growth factors. This process renders DBM the least immunogenic form of allograft. In clinical practice, DBM generally is added to autograft to allow the surgeon to increase its volume and improve the likelihood of healing success.

DBM is sold in the form of powder, crushed granules, putty, chips, or gel-packed syringes. Processing, batch variability, and other product-specific factors can significantly affect bone formation, however.[34,35] Enzyme-linked immunosorbent assay was used to compare the quantity of BMP-2 and BMP-7 in three manufacturers' DBM formulations.[36] Concentrations of BMP-2 and BMP-7 were found to be low in all DBM formulations. Each gram of DBM yielded only nanograms of BMP (20.2 to 120.6 ng of BMP-2, 54.2 to 226.8 ng of BMP-7). BMP concentrations differed markedly across lots of the same formulation. Intraproduct variability was found to be higher than interproduct variability.

DBM does not directly induce the formation of bone in subcutaneous or submuscular tissues. After implantation, mesenchymal stem cells do not differentiate into osteoblasts. Instead, DBM induces chondrogenesis, whereby mesenchymal cells differentiate into chondroblasts. The chondroblasts create cartilage, which is resorbed and eventually replaced by bone. In this setting, bone formation differs from so-called true enchondral osteogenesis. The chronological differentiation of cartilage cells into hypertrophic, proliferative, and reserve zone layers, followed by osteoclast resorption of calcified cartilage and the creation of bone on calcified cartilage, does not occur. Instead, bone formation by DBM occurs only after cartilage is resorbed and not concomitant with its resorption.[37,38]

The osteoinductive potential of DBMs has been studied in a range of animal intervertebral and posterolateral spine fusion models. In animals, DBMs promote spine arthrodesis when used alone or in conjunction with autograft, bone marrow, or ceramic materials.[39-41] In spine applications, DBMs may have limited efficacy as an autogenous bone graft substitute but usefulness as a bone graft extender.

Ceramics

A ceramic is an inorganic, nonmetallic solid prepared by the action of heat and subsequent cooling. The structure of ceramic materials can be crystalline, partly crystalline, or amorphous (as in glass). Because most common ceramics are crystalline, the term ceramic often is restricted to inorganic crystalline materials, as opposed to noncrystalline glasses. Crystalline ceramics have three distinct classes of materials: oxides (alumina, zirconia), nonoxides (carbides, borides, nitrides, silicides), and composites (particulate reinforced, combined oxide-nonoxide). Because of their crystalline structure, each of the classes can develop unique material properties.

Ceramics function primarily as an osteoconductive matrix in spine surgery. Most currently used calcium phosphate ceramics are synthetic and are composed of hydroxyapatite ($Ca_{10}[PO_4]_6[OH]_2$), tricalcium phos-

phate ($Ca_3[PO_4]_2$), or a combination of the two. These biomaterials are commercially manufactured as porous implants, nonporous dense implants, and granular, porous particles (Table 2). The three types of ceramics are sintered, replamiform, and collagen mesh. Sintered ceramic is composed of hydroxyapatite and is porous but lacks the interconnectivity of trabecular bone. Replamiform ceramic is made from sea coral and is structurally similar to bone.

Ceramics contain no protein and do not provoke an inflammatory response. However, some ceramics can incite a nonimmune inflammatory response such as a seroma.[42] Because they incorporate no human tissue, ceramics carry no risk of infectious disease spread. Ceramics may be biodegradable and well matched with new bone remodeling, but the resorbing cell is a foreign body giant cell, not an osteoclast.[43] True cutting cone formation does not occur, and bony replacement is restricted to the outer 2 to 10 μm of the implant. Large segments of the ceramic material remain as long as 10 years.[44] In spine applications, coralline implants or graft extenders have been used in both anterior and posterior spine fusion procedures, with mixed results.[45,46]

Graft composites combine the beneficial properties of several materials and are the most quickly expanding category of bone graft alternatives. Composites are regularly combined with various active biologic substances to enhance their osteogenic potential. The synthetic material typically provides osteoconductivity. The organic material adds induction or living cells. Together, a biologically synergistic effect promotes new bone formation. Collagraft (NeuColl, Palo Alto, CA) is a collagen-ceramic composite in the form of porous beads composed of 60% hydroxyapatite and 40% tricalcium phosphate. Healos (DePuy Spine, Raynham, MA) combines autogenous bone marrow aspirate with hydroxyapatite-coated, cross-linked type I collagen fibrils. Actifuse (ApaTech, Foxborough, MA) uses silicate groups to selectively substitute for phosphate groups in the calcium phosphate lattice and had a demonstrable osteogenic response in the rabbit distal femur.[47,48]

Gene Therapy

Gene therapy involves the translocation of a specific DNA sequence in target cells that subsequently express therapeutic proteins such as growth factors and cytokines. This approach allows genetically modified cells to stimulate spinal column fusion through the ongoing delivery of endogenous osteoinductive growth factors. The sustained release of osteogenic proteins at more physiologic levels, compared with larger single doses of exogenous growth factors, may result in more potent osteoinductive signals.

Gene therapy has three basic components: the DNA encoding the protein of interest, the target cells into

Table 2

Calcium-Based Ceramic Bone-Graft Substitutes Approved for Marketing in the United States or Europe

Product	Company	Type
Actifuse	ApaTech Foxborough, MA	Silicate-substituted calcium phosphate
Allomatrix	Wright Medical Technology Arlington, TN	Demineralized human bone matrix in an Osteoset medium
Bio-Oss	Geistlich Biomaterials Wolhusen, Switzerland	Particulate using hydroxyapatite as bone graft material
Collagraft	NeuColl Palo Alto, CA	Hydroxyapatite and tricalcium phosphate Available in granular and strip forms
Endobon	Merck Darmstadt, Germany	Sintered bovine cancellous bone blocks
Healos	DePuy Spine Raynham, MA	Synthetic matrix (80% type I bovine collagen and 20% hydroxyapatite)
Norian SRS	Synthes West Chester, PA	Calcium phosphate (carbonated apatite) Injectable cement
NovaBone	US Biomaterials Jacksonville, FL	Bioactive glass (SiO_2 and minerals)
OsteoGraf	DENTSPLY Friadent CeraMed Lakewood, CO	Hydroxyapatite used as bone graft material in a block form
Osteoset	Wright Medical Technology Arlington, TN	Calcium sulfate pellets
ProOsteon	Interpore Cross Irvine, CA	Based on sea coral converted from calcium carbonate to calcium hydroxyapatite
Vitoss	Orthovita Malvern, PA	Synthetic matrix (80% β-tricalcium phosphate and 20% type I bovine collagen) Porosity and pore size favorable for bony ingrowth

which this DNA sequence is inserted, and a vector to transfer the gene into the cells. Both viral and nonviral vectors deliver genetic material into target cells by transduction. Nonviral vectors are easier to produce, more stable, less antigenic, and theoretically safer than viral vectors. Examples of nonviral vectors include liposomes (DNA suspended in lipid vesicles that are able to bind to cell membranes) and gene-activated matrices (osteoconductive scaffolds loaded with genetic material). Viral vectors provide superior transduction efficiency. Retroviruses, adenoviruses, and adeno-associated viruses have been used to transmit DNA sequences to target cells. Viral vectors elicit a substantial host inflammatory response, and their long-term systemic effects have not been well characterized. Some viruses insert their DNA randomly into the target cell's genome, introducing the possibility of malignant transformation. Safety and economic issues may ultimately determine the viability of gene therapy as a suitable alternative to autogenous bone graft.

Summary

Although it is generally agreed that bone graft, in some form, has a vital role in promoting bony healing in spine fusion surgery, the grafting materials and methods are diverse. Historically, autograft bone has been the most reliable route to successful fusion, although the morbidity associated with graft harvest is well established and often dampens otherwise positive clinical results. Each of the bone graft alternatives has advantages and disadvantages. As the mechanisms underlying the biology of these alternatives and the understanding of spine fusion continue to increase, it is likely that bone graft substitutes will become even more specialized. Future graft materials may be custom made to suit the unique biologic and biomechanical conditions at the fusion site. Randomized, controlled, multicenter clinical studies eventually will be necessary to confirm the efficacy, safety, and cost-effectiveness of these options.

Annotated References

1. Boden SD: Osteoinductive bone graft substitutes: Burden of proof. *AAOS Online Bulletin* 2003;51(1).

2. Younger EM, Chapman MW: Morbidity at bone graft donor sites. *J Orthop Trauma* 1989;3(3):192-195.

3. Urist MR: Bone transplants and implants, in Urist MR, ed: *Fundamental and Clinical Bone Physiology*. Philadelphia, PA, JB Lippincott, 1980, pp 331-368.

4. Carlisle E, Fischgrund JS: Bone morphogenetic proteins for spinal fusion. *Spine J* 2005;5(6, suppl):240S-249S.

   Basic science, animal studies, and clinical studies involving BMPs are reviewed.

5. Retting KN, Song B, Yoon BS, Lyons KM: BMP canonical Smad signaling through Smad1 and Smad5 is required for endochondral bone formation. *Development* 2009;136(7):1093-1104.

   Combined loss of *SMAD1, SMAD5,* and *SMAD8* leads to severe chondrodysplasia. Indian hedgehog (Ihh) is a direct target of BMP pathways in chondrocytes, and fibroblast growth factor (FGF) exerts antagonistic effects on Ihh expression. The results of testing whether FGF exerts its antagonistic effects directly through *SMAD* linker phosphorylation support the alternative conclusion that the in vivo effects of FGFs on BMP signaling are indirect.

6. Ebisawa T, Tada K, Kitajima I, et al: Characterization of bone morphogenetic protein-6 signaling pathways in osteoblast differentiation. *J Cell Sci* 1999;112(pt 20):3519-3527.

7. Choi M, Stottmann RW, Yang YP, Meyers EN, Klingensmith J: The bone morphogenetic protein antagonist noggin regulates mammalian cardiac morphogenesis. *Circ Res* 2007;100(2):220-228.

   The functions of Noggin, a dedicated BMP antagonist, were studied in the developing mouse heart. Evidence of increased BMP signal transduction was found in the myocardium and endocardium, and the cardiac defects of Noggin mutants were rescued by halving the gene dosage of BMP4. The data indicate that antagonism of BMP signaling by Noggin is critical in ensuring proper levels of cell proliferation and epithelial-to-mesenchymal transformation during cardiac morphogenesis in the mouse.

8. Araya R, Kudo M, Kawano M, et al: BMP signaling through BMPRIA in astrocytes is essential for proper cerebral angiogenesis and formation of the blood-brain-barrier. *Mol Cell Neurosci* 2008;38(3):417-430.

   The role of BMP signaling through BMP type IA receptor in early neural development was examined using a conditional knockout mouse model in which BMP 1A is selectively disrupted in telencephalic neural stem cells. The results suggested that this signaling in astrocytes regulates the expression of vascular endothelial growth factor for proper cerebrovascular angiogenesis and has a role in the formation of the blood-brain barrier.

9. Upton J, Boyajian M, Mulliken JB, Glowacki J: The use of demineralized xenogeneic bone implants to correct phalangeal defects: A case report. *J Hand Surg Am* 1984;9(3):388-391.

10. Kaban LB, Mulliken JB, Glowacki J: Treatment of jaw defects with demineralized bone implants. *J Oral Maxillofac Surg* 1982;40(10):623-626.

11. Johnson EE, Urist MR, Finerman GA: Bone morphogenetic protein augmentation grafting of resistant femoral nonunions: A preliminary report. *Clin Orthop Relat Res* 1988;230:257-265.

12. Johnson EE, Urist MR, Finerman GA: Repair of segmental defects of the tibia with cancellous bone grafts augmented with human bone morphogenetic protein: A preliminary report. *Clin Orthop Relat Res* 1988;236(236):249-257.

13. Johnson EE, Urist MR, Finerman GA: Distal metaphyseal tibial nonunion: Deformity and bone loss treated by open reduction, internal fixation, and human bone morphogenetic protein (hBMP). *Clin Orthop Relat Res* 1990;250:234-240.

14. Burkus JK, Gornet MF, Dickman CA, Zdeblick TA: Anterior lumbar interbody fusion using rhBMP-2 with tapered interbody cages. *J Spinal Disord Tech* 2002;15(5):337-349.

15. Vaccaro AR, Patel T, Fischgrund J, et al: A pilot study evaluating the safety and efficacy of OP-1 putty (rhBMP-7) as a replacement for iliac crest autograft in posterolateral lumbar arthrodesis for degenerative spondylolisthesis. *Spine (Phila Pa 1976)* 2004;29(17):1885-1892.

16. Wong DA, Kumar A, Jatana S, Ghiselli G, Wong K: Neurologic impairment from ectopic bone in the lumbar canal: A potential complication of off-label PLIF/TLIF use of bone morphogenetic protein-2 (BMP-2). *Spine J* 2008;8(6):1011-1018.

   A complication of BMP use with interbody fusion is described.

17. Smucker JD, Rhee JM, Singh K, Yoon ST, Heller JG: Increased swelling complications associated with off-label usage of rhBMP-2 in the anterior cervical spine. *Spine (Phila Pa 1976)* 2006;31(24):2813-2819.

   Postoperative swelling with the use of BMP in anterior cervical spine surgery is described.

18. Thawani JP, Wang AC, Than KD, Lin CY, La Marca F, Park P: Bone morphogenetic proteins and cancer: Review of the literature. *Neurosurgery* 2010;66(2):233-246.

   The basic scientific and clinical background of BMPs is reviewed with their role in tumorigenesis and metastasis. Multiple in vitro and in vivo studies suggest that BMPs are significant in promoting cancer, but comparable studies imply that BMPs has a negative effect on cancer. The association between BMPs and the promotion of tumorigenesis or metastasis is not definitive, but the relatively large number of studies reporting a positive effect of BMPs on cancer suggests the need for caution in using BMPs for patients with primary or metastatic spine tumors.

19. Majid K, Baker K, Fischgrund JS, Herkowitz HN: Abstract: Biomimetic calcium phosphate films as BMP delivery systems in posterolateral lumbar fusion. *2010 Annual Meeting Proceedings.* Rosemont, IL, American Academy of Orthopedic Surgeons Annual Meeting, 2010.

20. Israel DI, Nove J, Kerns KM, et al: Heterodimeric bone morphogenetic proteins show enhanced activity in vitro and in vivo. *Growth Factors* 1996;13(3-4):291-300.

21. Arrington ED, Smith WJ, Chambers HG, Bucknell AL, Davino NA: Complications of iliac crest bone graft harvesting. *Clin Orthop Relat Res* 1996;329(329):300-309.

22. Banwart JC, Asher MA, Hassanein RS: Iliac crest bone graft harvest donor site morbidity: A statistical evaluation. *Spine (Phila Pa 1976)* 1995;20(9):1055-1060.

23. Burwell RG: The function of bone marrow in the incorporation of a bone graft. *Clin Orthop Relat Res* 1985; 200:125-141.

24. Salama R, Weissman SL: The clinical use of combined xenografts of bone and autologous red marrow: A preliminary report. *J Bone Joint Surg Br* 1978;60(1):111-115.

25. Begley CT, Doherty MJ, Hankey DP, Wilson DJ: The culture of human osteoblasts upon bone graft substitutes. *Bone* 1993;14(4):661-666.

26. Connolly JF, Guse R, Tiedeman J, Dehne R: Autologous marrow injection as a substitute for operative grafting of tibial nonunions. *Clin Orthop Relat Res* 1991;266: 259-270.

27. Muschler GF, Nitto H, Matsukura Y, et al: Spine fusion using cell matrix composites enriched in bone marrow-derived cells. *Clin Orthop Relat Res* 2003;407:102-118.

28. Ploumis A, Albert TJ, Brown Z, Mehbod AA, Transfeldt EE: Healos graft carrier with bone marrow aspirate instead of allograft as adjunct to local autograft for posterolateral fusion in degenerative lumbar scoliosis: A minimum 2-year follow-up study. *J Neurosurg Spine* 2010;13(2):211-215.

   In 28 patients with degenerative scoliosis after posterolateral instrumented fusion and decompression, Healos hydroxyapatite sponge and bone marrow aspirate plus local allograft led to significantly slower fusion but equivalent clinical outcomes compared with cancellous allograft plus local autograft. Level of evidence: III.

29. Buck BE, Malinin TI, Brown MD: Bone transplantation and human immunodeficiency virus: An estimate of risk of acquired immunodeficiency syndrome (AIDS). *Clin Orthop Relat Res* 1989;240:129-136.

30. Khan SN, Cammisa FP Jr, Sandhu HS, Diwan AD, Girardi FP, Lane JM: The biology of bone grafting. *J Am Acad Orthop Surg* 2005;13(1):77-86.

   Bone graft incorporation into any host depends on factors including transplant site, type of graft (autogenous or allogeneic, vascular or nonvascular), quality of the host and transplanted bone, preservation techniques, systemic and local disease, and mechanical properties of the graft.

31. Sim FH, Frassica FJ: Use of allografts following resection of tumors of the musculoskeletal system. *Instr Course Lect* 1993;42:405-413.

32. Gazdag AR, Lane JM, Glaser D, Forster RA: Alternatives to autologous bone graft: Efficacy and indications. *J Am Acad Orthop Surg* 1995;3(1):1-8.

33. Jorgenson SS, Lowe TG, France J, Sabin J: A prospective analysis of autograft versus allograft in posterolateral lumbar fusion in the same patient: A minimum of 1-year follow-up in 144 patients. *Spine (Phila Pa 1976)* 1994;19(18):2048-2053.

34. Martin GJ Jr, Boden SD, Titus L, Scarborough NL: New formulations of demineralized bone matrix as a more effective graft alternative in experimental posterolateral lumbar spine arthrodesis. *Spine (Phila Pa 1976)* 1999;24(7):637-645.

35. Morone MA, Boden SD: Experimental posterolateral lumbar spinal fusion with a demineralized bone matrix gel. *Spine (Phila Pa 1976)* 1998;23(2):159-167.

36. Bae HW, Zhao L, Kanim LE, Wong P, Delamarter RB, Dawson EG: Intervariability and intravariability of bone morphogenetic proteins in commercially available demineralized bone matrix products. *Spine (Phila Pa 1976)* 2006;31(12):1299-1308.

   The variability of BMPs in different DBM preparations is described.

37. Wang J, Glimcher MJ: Characterization of matrix-induced osteogenesis in rat calvarial bone defects: I. Differences in the cellular response to demineralized bone matrix implanted in calvarial defects and in subcutaneous sites. *Calcif Tissue Int* 1999;65(2):156-165.

38. Wang J, Yang R, Gerstenfeld LC, Glimcher MJ: Characterization of demineralized bone matrix-induced osteogenesis in rat calvarial bone defects: III. Gene and protein expression. *Calcif Tissue Int* 2000;67(4):314-320.

39. Bostrom MP, Yang X, Kennan M, Sandhu H, Dicarlo E, Lane JM: An unexpected outcome during testing of commercially available demineralized bone graft materials: How safe are the nonallograft components? *Spine (Phila Pa 1976)* 2001;26(13):1425-1428.

40. Edwards JT, Diegmann MH, Scarborough NL: Osteoinduction of human demineralized bone: Characterization in a rat model. *Clin Orthop Relat Res* 1998;357:219-228.

4: The Adult Spine

41. Frenkel SR, Moskovich R, Spivak J, Zhang ZH, Prewett AB: Demineralized bone matrix: Enhancement of spinal fusion. *Spine (Phila Pa 1976)* 1993;18(12):1634-1639.

42. Bucholz RW, Carlton A, Holmes R: Interporous hydroxyapatite as a bone graft substitute in tibial plateau fractures. *Clin Orthop Relat Res* 1989;240:53-62.

43. Lane JM, Bostrom MP: Bone grafting and new composite biosynthetic graft materials. *Instr Course Lect* 1998; 47:525-534.

44. Jarcho M: Calcium phosphate ceramics as hard tissue prosthetics. *Clin Orthop Relat Res* 1981;157:259-278.

45. Neen D, Noyes D, Shaw M, Gwilym S, Fairlie N, Birch N: Healos and bone marrow aspirate used for lumbar spine fusion: A case controlled study comparing healos with autograft. *Spine (Phila Pa 1976)* 2006;31(18): E636-E640.

    Compared with iliac crest autograft, the clinical and radiographic performance of Healos soaked in bone marrow aspirate was not inferior in a posterolateral lumbar spine fusion model. However, Healos and bone marrow aspirate were radiographically ineffective in lumbar interbody fusions. Level of evidence: III.

46. Carter JD, Swearingen AB, Chaput CD, Rahm MD: Clinical and radiographic assessment of transforaminal lumbar interbody fusion using HEALOS collagen-hydroxyapatite sponge with autologous bone marrow aspirate. *Spine J* 2009;9(6):434-438.

    Bone marrow aspirate and collagen-hydroxyapatite sponge were implanted in 20 patients undergoing transforaminal lumbar interbody fusion with posterolateral fusion using interbody cages and posterior pedicle screws. Clinical and radiographically assessed fusion rates were acceptable at 2-year follow-up. Level of evidence: IV.

47. Hing KA, Saeed S, Annaz B, Buckland T, Revell PA: Variation in the rate of bone apposition within porous hydroxyapatite and tricalcium phosphate bone graft substitutes. *Transactions of the 50th Annual Meeting.* Rosemont, IL, Orthopaedic Research Society, 2004, poster 1038.

48. Hing KA, Saeed S, Annaz B, Buckland T, Revell PA: Silicate substitution alters the progression of bone apposition within porous hydroxyapatite bone graft substitutes. *Transactions of the 50th Annual Meeting.* Rosemont, IL, Orthopaedic Research Society, 2004, poster 1041.

The Pediatric Spine

SECTION EDITOR
JOHN B. EMANS, MD

Chapter 35

Congenital Anomalies of the Spinal Column and Spinal Cord

John P. Dormans, MD   Christopher Hydorn, MD

Introduction

Anomalies of the spinal column and spinal cord are caused by abnormalities in fetal segmentation or formation. Such anomalies can occur at any spine level, from the occipitocervical junction to the sacrum. Some anomalies do not lead to disability or progression, but others are more severe and require careful monitoring to detect progression and the need for surgical intervention.

Congenital Cervical Anomalies

Klippel-Feil Syndrome

Klippel-Feil syndrome (KFS) was first described in 1912 in a patient with a short neck, low posterior hairline, and limited range of motion in the neck.[1] This classic triad of anomalies occurs in fewer than 50% of patients with KFS, however. The spectrum of anomalies associated with KFS is immense. The unifying entity is congenital synostosis of some or all of the cervical vertebrae. Because of a lack of population screening studies, the incidence of KFS is unknown, but it is estimated to occur in 1 of every 40,000 births.[2]

KFS is believed to originate in a lack of normal segmentation of the cervical somites during fetal development. Between the third and fourth weeks of gestation, the paraxial mesoderm is segmented into discrete somites from cephalad to caudal. These somites give rise to sclerotomes, myotomes, and dermatomes at each spine segment. The sclerotomes undergo resegmenta-

tion, with the caudal end of one somite fusing to the cephalad end of the adjacent somite to form a vertebral body. Failure of this process in the cervical spine causes the congenital fusions characteristic of KFS.[2] Although the existence of a genetic component has been suggested, no gene or genetic process has been definitively identified as being involved in the development of KFS.

The clinical manifestations of KFS are variable. The classic triad may be seen at birth, but often the diagnosis is more difficult. Many patients have a stable fusion pattern and probably will not develop cervical symptoms. However, these patients may later develop a decreased cervical range of motion and/or webbing of the neck, leading to a diagnosis of KFS. If the child is more severely affected, neurologic, myelopathic, and biomechanical symptoms may lead to early identification of cervical instability between or adjacent to the fused segments.[3]

Other anomalies, such as Sprengel deformity, may be associated with KFS. Sprengel deformity is caused by a failure of segmentation within the cervical somites that leaves omovertebral bone as an aberrant connection between the scapula and the cervical spine. Sprengel deformity was found to occur in 5 of 30 patients with KFS (16.7%) but did not appear to be associated with a patient's pattern of fusion, number of fused segments, or extent of cervical involvement.[4] Congenital cardiac, neurologic, and genitourinary anomalies also may be associated with KFS and necessitate a general workup. Patients also may have abnormality of the thoracic and lumbar spine, which places them at risk for scoliosis.[5]

The neurologic symptoms of KFS generally result from hypermobility adjacent to and between fused cervical segments. Congenital fusion can occur at the occipitocervical junction or the atlantoaxial or subaxial portions of the cervical spine. Three patterns of cervical vertebral anomalies are classically associated with neurologic symptoms: C2-C3 fusion with occipitocervical synostosis, extensive cervical fusions with an abnormal occipitocervical junction, and two fused segments separated by a single open joint.[6] A classification system has been developed to describe the relationship between cervical spine fusion patterns: type I (a single fused segment) is predominantly associated with axial neck pain; type II (multiple noncontiguous fused segments) and

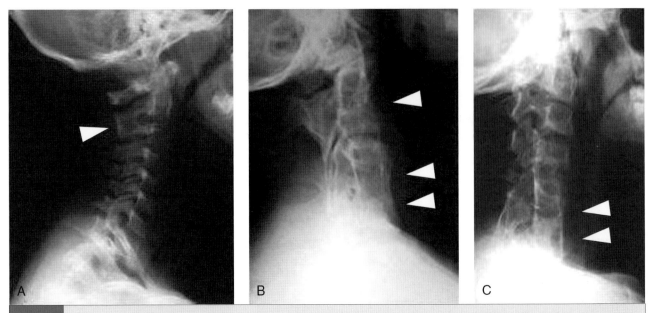

Figure 1 Lateral radiographs showing Klippel-Feil congenital cervical fusion patterns *(arrowheads).* **A,** Type I. **B,** Type II. **C,** Type III. (Reproduced with permission from Samartzis D, Herman J, Lubicky JP, Shen FH: Classification of congenitally fused cervical patterns in Klippel-Feil patients: Epidemiology and role in the development of cervical spine-related symptoms. *Spine [Phila Pa 1976]* 2006;31[21]:E798-E804.)

type III (multiple contiguous fused segments) are associated with radicular and myelopathic symptoms (Figure 1). The rate of neurologic symptoms is highest in type III.[7]

The development of neurologic injury within the cervical segments appears to be age dependent and related to the fusion pattern. A study comparing radiographic and neurologic findings in patients with KFS found that the width of the vertebral bodies is significantly less than normal within fused cervical segments longer than four vertebrae. The result is a larger-than-normal spinal canal over the fused segment. This so-called wasp-waist deformity increases the space available for the spinal cord.[8] A second study to evaluate the axial diameter of the spinal cord and cerebrospinal fluid column found that the axial diameter of the spinal cord was statistically smaller than normal in a fused segment.[9] The relatively small spinal cord and large canal dimensions make it unlikely that neurologic symptoms emanate from within the fused segment. The hypermobile disk space adjacent to or between fusions does not have a decreased vertebral body width.[8] The mechanical stresses at the hypermobile segment lead to disk and facet degeneration and possibly to cervical disk herniation, which lead to stenosis and possibly to spinal cord compromise.[10] The combination of cervical stenosis and instability is especially risky. Athletes with KFS developed central cord syndromes after falling during winter sports.[11] Limiting the patient's involvement in sports and other activities that could lead to cervical injury may help decrease the risk of neurologic injury.

It is safe for the orthopaedic surgeon to follow a patient with KFS who is asymptomatic and has no insta-

bility or stenosis. A patient who develops cervical symptoms may require activity modification, bracing, or traction to reduce the symptoms or delay surgery. A patient with progressive segmental instability or neurologic compromise is a candidate for cervical decompression and fusion of the abnormal region of the cervical spine.

Congenital Muscular Torticollis

Congenital muscular torticollis (CMT) is more common than KFS and may have similar manifestations. A muscular etiology was found in 235 of 288 children with torticollis (82%); the remaining 18% had KFS or another neurologic disorder.[12] Rarely, CMT is caused by a congenital hemiatlas.[13] CMT usually is associated with contracture of the sternocleidomastoid muscle and is painless. The condition may not be present at birth and in that respect it is not a typical congenital disorder. Usually there is a progressive onset within the first 2 months of life. Contracture of the affected sternocleidomastoid muscle causes the patient's head to tilt toward and rotate away from the muscle. CMT often is associated with a musculoskeletal disorder such as hip dysplasia, metatarsus adductus, or clubfoot.

Among the many theories as to the etiology of CMT is fibrosis of the sternocleidomastoid muscle with a cause such as peripartum intramuscular bleeding or compartment syndrome of the sternocleidomastoid muscle. Intrauterine crowding or primary myopathy of the muscle also has been proposed. In patients with CMT, the sternocleidomastoid muscle at birth contains a benign mass composed of myoblasts, fibroblasts, myofibroblasts, and other mesenchymal-like cells. The mass reaches its maximum size at approximately age 4 weeks and then regresses. In 26 infants with torticollis, the mass regressed and disappeared between age 2 weeks and 8.5 weeks; this disappearance lagged behind the clinical disappearance of torticollis by 2 weeks.[14] Severe and/or long-standing torticollis may cause plagiocephaly.

The treatment of CMT has included formal physical therapy and home exercises focused on stretching the sternocleidomastoid muscle by rotating the head toward the ipsilateral shoulder and tilting it toward the contralateral shoulder. Surgical treatment may be indicated if the patient has a residual head tilt, rotation, or tight band within the sternocleidomastoid muscle after 6 months of range-of-motion and stretching exercises. The surgery involves unipolar or bipolar release of the sternocleidomastoid muscle, depending on the surgeon's preference and the severity of the deformity. A study of 47 patients with CMT found that surgery in children younger than 4 years did not affect outcome measures including range of cervical motion, facial asymmetry, head tilt, residual contracture, and subjective outcome.[15] This finding supports the usefulness of surgical intervention for patients of any age, as long as the patient can comply with the required postsurgical physical therapy.

Cervical Instability

Cervical instability is associated with congenital disorders such as Down syndrome, odontoid hypoplasia and aplasia, and basilar invagination. Despite the varying characteristics of these disorders, the treatment of associated cervical instability is similar. The approach differs based on the cervical levels requiring treatment. Down syndrome is a common pattern of malformation caused by trisomy 21 or, rarely, a translocation or mosaicism. Down syndrome is diagnosed before or at birth. Most patients have developmental delays and general ligamentous laxity.[16] Cervical instability associated with Down syndrome usually occurs at the atlantoaxial junction but also can occur at the atlanto-occipital junction. Cervical instability is of particular concern in patients with Down syndrome because of the neurologic sequelae that can result from trauma or athletic injury.[16,17] Odontoid hypoplasia and aplasia cause atlantoaxial instability as a result of the loss of the odontoid's stabilization of the atlas through the transverse and alar ligaments. The fetal development of the atlas and axis is from three separate centra: the proatlas, atlas, and axis. During segmentation, the proatlas and atlas centra fuse to eventually form the odontoid process, which then fuses with the axis centrum. Errors in this process can result in the formation of an os odontoideum (accessory ossicle) and can explain the watershed region at the base of the odontoid process, which may lead to atlantoaxial instability. Basilar invagination is migration of the odontoid proximally into the foramen magnum, possibly encroaching onto the brainstem. The associated anomalies and syndromes include KFS, occipitocervical synostosis, osteogenesis imperfecta, and achondroplasia.[18]

A patient who may have cervical or occipitocervical instability should undergo a radiographic evaluation, specifically including supervised lateral radiographs in flexion and extension. The anterior and posterior atlantodens interval (ADI) can be determined from these radiographs. The anterior ADI is useful for assessing atlantoaxial stability; it should measure 3.5 mm or less in normal children (age 1 to 12 years).[19] The posterior ADI is correlated with the space available for the spinal cord. In normal children, the posterior ADI or space available for the spinal cord should be at least 14 mm. A significant deviation from the normal measurement in the anterior or posterior ADI suggests instability, and MRI of the cervical spine in flexion and extension may be indicated to look for spinal cord changes. In a patient with Down syndrome, an anterior ADI greater than 4 to 5 mm or a posterior ADI smaller than 14 mm often is used as an indication for MRI. Patients with an anterior ADI greater than 7 mm may be at increased risk for symptomatic instability.[20] A comparison of 102 children with Down syndrome to normal control subjects found that the children with Down syndrome had C1 hypoplasia and a smaller area for the spinal cord. This finding may explain the increased risk of myelopathy in these children.[21] The governing body of the Special Olympics requires preparticipation screening radiographs of participants with Down syndrome. The usefulness of this screening is unclear, however, because radiographic findings in asymptomatic individuals have not been found to predict neurologic problems.

Atlantocervical stability is assessed on lateral radiographs using the McRae, Chamberlain, and McGregor lines (Figure 2). The Powers ratio and the Wiesel-Rothman method also are useful in establishing a diagnosis. A Powers ratio greater than 1.0 or a Wiesel-Rothman difference of 1 mm on flexion and extension radiographs indicates atlanto-occipital instability. MRI should be obtained if the patient has neurologic symptoms or if surgery is being considered. CT is useful in some patients to better delineate osseous abnormalities. Only observation is subsequently required in most patients who are asymptomatic. Surgical intervention may be necessary for a patient with symptomatic cervical instability, severe stenosis, excessive asymptomatic instability, or increased spinal cord signal on MRI.

Atlanto-occipital instability also occurs in children with Down syndrome. Laxity at the occiput-C1 level can result from laxity of the joint capsules or of the tectorial and anteroposterior atlanto-occipital membranes. The Powers ratio or Wiesel-Rothman method often is used on a lateral radiograph to define the presence and amount of instability (Figure 3). The Powers ratio is not affected by the size of the patient, and therefore it is especially useful in a younger patient. Instability at the atlanto-occipital junction is defined as a Powers ratio greater than 1.0 or a deviation from normal of more than 1 mm in the flexion-extension distance using the

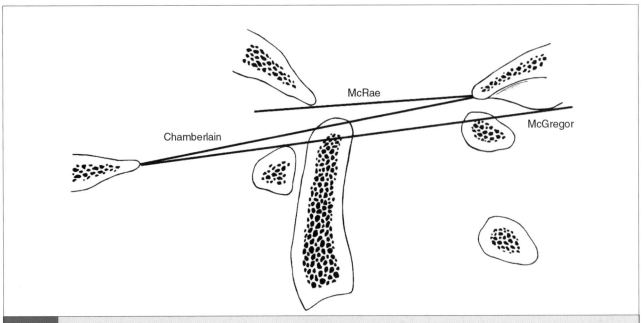

Figure 2 Schematic diagram showing methods of determining basilar invagination. The McGregor line is drawn from the hard palate to the lowest point on the occiput. Protrusion of the tip of the dens more than 4.5 mm above this line is abnormal. The Chamberlain line extends from the dorsal margin of the hard palate to the dorsal lip of the foramen magnum. The normal position of the dens is within 1 mm below this line and 0.6 mm above it. The McRae line extends from the basion to the posterior lip of the foramen magnum. Protrusion of the tip of the dens above the McRae line indicates basilar invagination. (Reproduced from Hosalkar HH, Drummond DS: Pediatric cervical spine, in Spivak JM, Connolly PJ, eds: *Orthopaedic Knowledge Update: Spine 3*. Rosemont, IL, American Academy of Orthopaedic Surgeons, 2006, p 411.)

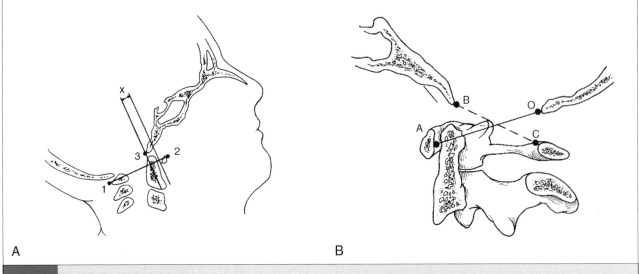

Figure 3 Schematic drawings showing methods of determining atlanto-occipital instability. **A,** In the Wiesel-Rothman measurement, the distance x should not vary more than 1 mm during flexion and extension. Atlantal line = point 1 to point 2; basion = point 3. **B,** In the Powers ratio, BC is divided by OA; a ratio above 1.0 is diagnostic of anterior occipitoatlantal dislocation. (Adapted from Copley LA, Dormans JP: Cervical spine disorders in infants and children. *J Am Acad Orthop Surg* 1998;6[4]:206.)

Wiesel-Rothman method. Surgical treatment of atlanto-occipital instability is rarely necessary but requires occipitocervical arthrodesis. Many methods are available, most of which involve the use of an iliac crest cortico-cancellous graft fixed posteriorly. Additional stabilization also may be used. Because the occiput is relatively large in young patients, an iliac crest graft may not be long enough to cross the gap, and two structural rib autografts can be used with success.[22]

Atlantoaxial arthrodesis is rarely required to treat

atlantoaxial instability. Wire, transarticular screw, and lateral mass or pedicle screw fixation can be used effectively.[23-26] The type of construct is determined based on the surgeon's experience as well as the anatomy and size of the spine elements to be fused. The decision to fuse the occiput to C2 rather than C1 to C2 is based on the presence or absence of instability at the occiput-C1 junction, as defined by the Powers ratio, the need to decompress the C1 level, and the surgeon's preference. In the presence of spinal cord changes or cervical stenosis, decompression may be required, especially at the C1 level. Upper cervical fusions often are supplemented with halo stabilization. The proper use of a halo and vest is safe in a child younger than 3 years, with multiple pins at lower torques.[27,28] A review of 10 patients younger than 3 years found no neurologic injuries, and the only halo-related complications were a superficial pin tract infection and minor pin loosening.[29]

Other Spine Dysraphisms

Myelodysplasia

The myelodysplasias represent a spectrum of neural tube defects that range from benign to severe. The two broad divisions are spina bifida occulta and spina bifida cystica. Spina bifida occulta usually is a benign defect of the posterior elements of the lower lumbar and first sacral vertebrae. Rarely, it is associated with tethered cord and lipomeningocele malformations, which can have progressive neurologic symptoms. Spina bifida cystica is the protrusion of the meninges, with or without neural elements, through a defect in the posterior spine elements. In a meningocele, the meninges protrude through the posterior vertebral elements without involvement of underlying spinal cord or nerve roots. In a myelomeningocele, a portion of the spinal cord and/or nerve roots is included in the meninges. The most severe form of spina bifida cystica is a myelocele, in which the neural plate is exposed with no overlying tissue coverage.[30]

These neural tube defects occur during the second to fourth weeks of gestation. At the beginning of this period, the embryo is a flattened disk with three germ layers. It develops a neural groove that appears in the neural plate, and during the third gestational week this groove deepens and the adjacent tissues fuse over the neural plate to form the neural tube that ultimately forms the brain and spinal cord. The neural tube closes in both a cephalad and caudal direction from the midportion of the fetus, with the caudal end closing at the end of the fourth week. Myelomeningocele, the most common form of spina bifida cystica, results from a failure or reopening of the caudal closure because of distention from cerebrospinal fluid.

A deficiency in folate (folic acid), an important essential vitamin during the early development of the neural tube, has been associated with an increased risk of neural tube defects. Folate supplementation is recommended for women of childbearing age. In addition, the myelodysplasias also are associated with an earlier affected pregnancy, pregestational diabetes, and in utero valproate or carbamazepine exposure. A myelomeningocele usually is discovered through prenatal screening ultrasonography and the maternal serum α-fetoprotein level. The myelomeningocele usually is closed by a neurosurgeon in utero or within 48 hours of birth.

Myelomeningocele is a complicated disorder with numerous clinical manifestations. A patient should be treated by a dedicated multidisciplinary team including a neurosurgeon, urologist, orthopaedic surgeon, and pediatrician. The role of the orthopaedic surgeon primarily involves the treatment of scoliosis and kyphosis. A baseline history and physical examination are required to document function and neurologic status, followed by a regularly scheduled examination every 6 months to identify any deformity progression or neurologic compromise. The examination should include an assessment of truncal and sitting balance, particularly if the patient is nonambulatory. The patient's skin should be monitored for breakdown or ulcers, with wheelchair or prosthesis adjustments made as needed.[31] A rapid scoliosis curve progression or any deterioration in gait, strength, continence, or spasticity may indicate cord tethering.

Radiographs of the entire spine should be obtained at baseline and regular intervals thereafter. The AP and lateral views are obtained with the patient standing (if ambulatory) or sitting (if nonambulatory). A baseline MRI of the spinal cord and brain usually is obtained within the first 2 years of life to identify any intraspinal pathology such as hydrocephalus, syringomyelia, or tethered cord. MRI is repeated if neurologic symptoms arise or progress.[31]

The progression of spine deformity has been associated with myelomeningocele located above L5. In a study of 163 patients with myelomeningocele, those with spine involvement at L5 or lower had a low rate of spine deformity development. Those with L1-L4 involvement had an increased rate of scoliosis, and those with involvement at T12 or higher had a high rate of kyphosis development.[32] These findings support earlier studies that found an increased prevalence of spine deformity with higher level spine involvement.[33]

A patient with myelomeningocele typically has a long C-shaped scoliotic curve that is usually associated with kyphosis rather than lordosis. The curve results from muscle imbalance from the paralysis and eventually leads to pelvic obliquity. A curve smaller than 20° usually is observed with radiographs every 4 to 6 months. Bracing can be attempted for a curve larger than 20°, although such a curve often is refractory to bracing.

Surgical correction is undertaken based on factors including Cobb angle, sitting imbalance, curve progression, and loss of function. The patient may want to achieve sitting balance without needing to use a hand. The surgeon must consider the timing and type of sur-

5: The Pediatric Spine

gery in a young child with a progressive curve. The use of a growing-rod construct may be indicated to allow further growth. When fusion is desired, anterior and/or posterior constructs may be used, at the discretion of the surgeon. As posterior fusion constructs improve, however, there is a trend toward the use of posterior instrumentation and fusion. Whether to fuse to the pelvis also is an important consideration. If the patient is non-ambulatory, the fusion should extend from the upper thoracic vertebrae to the sacrum and include all curves. Sacral fixation can be accomplished using screws (Dunn-McCarthy fixation). A Galveston technique may be used if the ilia are not too small or dysplastic. If the patient is ambulatory, it is preferable to stop the construct in the lower lumbar vertebrae to preserve some lumbar motion and flexibility during ambulation.[31]

Kyphosis associated with myelomeningocele often is rigid and usually is progressive. Untreated kyphosis can lead to loss of truncal height, decreased respiratory capability, and skin breakdown at the apex of a gibbus. Kyphosis results from a lack of erector spinae muscles and anteriorly displaced quadratus lumborum muscles that act as flexors. As the deformity progresses, the osseous structures gradually remodel to form wedge-shaped vertebrae. These patients have long thighs and a protuberant belly, with a sitting position on the posterior aspect of the sacrum.

Nonsurgical treatment does little to prevent or slow the nearly universal progression of kyphosis in patients with myelomeningocele. Skin breakdown and loss of hand function (because the hand is needed for sitting support) are the most compelling reasons for surgical correction, although the absolute indications for surgical intervention are not well established.[31] Kyphectomy has been the surgical procedure of choice at many institutions. An anterior and posterior spine approach is used, with osteotomy or resection of the proximal portion of the apical vertebrae of the gibbus and the distal portion of the adjacent apical lordotic vertebrae.[34,35] There is a recent trend toward a posterior-only approach. A 10-year follow-up study of 24 patients who underwent kyphectomy found excellent maintenance of correction, with an average loss of correction of only 7°. The complication rate was high, however; 18 patients required surgery for a prominent implant, and 13 had wound complications.[36]

Other Spine Dysraphisms

Congenital lipomatous malformations of the spinal cord usually are seen with tethering of the spinal cord. There are two broad groups. The lipomas without a dural defect include filum lipoma, caudal lipoma without dural defect, and intramedullary lipoma. Patients often develop sphincter disturbance at age 5 years or older. If treatment is required, caudal debulking and untethering without duroplasty produce reliable results. The lipomas with a dural defect include dural lipoma, caudal lipoma with a dural defect, lipomyelocele, and lipomyelomeningocele. The patients usually have cuta-

neous markers, are younger than 2 years, and have a relatively pronounced neurologic defect. Duroplasty is required, but retethering or cerebrospinal fluid leakage sometimes occurs.[37,38]

Diastematomyelia is a splitting of the spinal cord, usually caused by fibrous tissue or bone in a longitudinal direction within the spinal cord. The condition is most common between the lower thoracic and upper sacral levels. Asymmetric neurologic symptoms are related to tethering of the spinal cord. Like lipomyelomeningocele, diastematomyelia usually is treated by a neurosurgeon with resection and possibly repair of the spinal cord. Diastematomyelia may be associated with other spine deformities and syndromes, which often can be treated during the same surgical procedure.[39]

Spinal cord tethering occurs with many spine dysraphisms and is particularly associated with myelomeningocele, lipomyelomeningoceles, diastematomyelia, and earlier intraspinal surgery. The spinal cord is tethered in the canal and is unable to ascend within the growing and lengthening spinal column. The resulting tension and distortion within the spinal cord produces neurologic changes in the patient. Signs and symptoms of tethered cord often appear during a growth spurt, particularly the adolescent growth spurt. The posterior spine may have skin changes including dimples, lipomas, skin tags, and hypertrichosis. The orthopaedic changes include rapid progression of scoliosis, gait disturbances, distal motor weakness, neurologic changes, and foot deformities. Urologic and bowel changes also may appear. MRI is the preferred means of evaluating the intraspinal pathology. The appearance of tethering can be seen on MRI in many patients with myelomeningocele who are otherwise asymptomatic, and the clinical evaluation is therefore important for determining the treatment.

The treatment of a tethered cord involves untethering the spinal cord distally, usually from a posterior approach, with careful hemostasis to prevent arachnoiditis from blood products within the dura. The filum terminale is either coagulated or hemoclipped to prevent bleeding before dividing. Any other intradural conditions are treated as indicated, and the dura is repaired. Intraoperative neuromonitoring and intradural nerve root stimulation are essential to ensure the neural elements are not divided during filum terminale division. At 4-year follow-up of 31 patients with symptomatic tethering, untethering had stopped symptom progression and improved sphincter dysfunction and muscle weakness.[40] The response of a scoliotic curve to untethering is less predictable. A study of 27 patients with scoliosis found that curves assessed as Risser grade III to V with a Cobb angle greater than 40° had little progression after untethering, but curves with a lower Risser grade and Cobb angle had continued progression.[41]

Regular follow-up is required after tethered cord release to identify retethering, particularly in a patient with a lipomatous malformation within the dura. These patients have neurologic progression with symptoms similar to the initial symptoms, and a revision untethering procedure may be indicated. Spine-shortening osteotomy and vertebral column subtraction have been investigated for treating multiple recurrences.[42,43]

Caudal Regression Syndrome

Caudal regression syndrome is a spectrum of disorders that includes lumbosacral and sacral agenesis. This condition is characterized by the absence of the axial skeleton and neural elements at the sacral and possibly the lumbar levels. Most patients also have anomalies of the genitourinary and gastrointestinal tracts. The cardiac, renal, and gastrointestinal systems must be evaluated in any patient with a significant congenital spine deformity. The severity of caudal regression syndrome ranges from an absent coccyx to complete absence of the lumbar and sacral spine. In its most severe form, the condition is incompatible with life.

Caudal regression syndrome is associated with maternal diabetes, caudal vascular compromise in utero, and a possible genetic etiology including an association with HLA-type histocompatibility genes. An exact etiology has yet to be proved, however. Continued regression of the postsacral somites in normal fetal development may be implicated. Caudal regression syndrome has been discovered ultrasonographically as early as 14 weeks' gestation.

The clinical appearance of patients with caudal regression varies depending on the extent of involvement. An absent coccyx may be incidentally discovered on a radiograph in an otherwise asymptomatic patient. More severe forms of the syndrome are evident at birth. The child may have a Buddha-like posture of hypoplastic lower extremities with flexed, abducted, and externally rotated hips and flexion contractures of the knees. The neurologic function of the lower extremities typically involves more significant motor loss than sensory loss. The patient often is nonambulatory, with significant sacral agenesis. The upper extremities are well preserved. Unlike the myelodysplasias, caudal regression syndrome usually does not produce clinical effects proximal to the malformation.[44] However, there is an association with Chiari I malformation in some patients, and a full examination of the spine is warranted.

The initial Renshaw classification of caudal regression was based on the amount of sacral and lumbar agenesis and whether the remaining most caudal vertebrae articulated with the ilia.[45] A study of 16 patients with sacral agenesis found that the Renshaw classification did not predict pain, patient satisfaction, or function.[46] The Guille classification is an attempt to better predict the patient's ambulatory potential. In type A, the caudal vertebrae articulate with the ilia; in type B, a portion of the caudal vertebrae articulates with the ilia; and in type C, there is a gap between the caudal vertebrae and the ilia.[47] A lower extremity procedure is re-

quired to facilitate ambulation in patients with a type C deformity who have the potential ability to walk. Stabilization of the pelvis to the residual spine rarely is indicated if a patient who has a type C deformity with a gap between the caudal vertebrae and the pelvis is unable to sit comfortably.

Summary

An orthopaedic spine surgeon may encounter a wide variety of congenital anomalies affecting the spine, from the cervical spine to the sacrum. A detailed understanding of the anatomy, physiology, and biomechanics of the spine is important for treating these patients. A thorough history and physical examination, and particularly a neurologic and radiographic assessment, are critical to the diagnosis and treatment of these anomalies.

Annotated References

1. Klippel M, Feil A: The classic: A case of absence of cervical vertebrae with the thoracic cage rising to the base of the cranium (cervical thoracic cage). *Clin Orthop Relat Res* 1975;109:3-8.

2. Tracy MR, Dormans JP, Kusumi K: Klippel-Feil syndrome: Clinical features and current understanding of etiology. *Clin Orthop Relat Res* 2004;424:183-190.

3. Herring JA: Disorders of the neck, in Herring JA, ed: *Tachdjian's Pediatric Orthopaedics*, ed 4. Philadelphia, PA, Saunders Elsevier, 2008, pp 221-233.

   This textbook review of pediatric neck disorders includes congenital disorders and KFS.

4. Samartzis D, Herman J, Lubicky JP, Shen FH: Sprengel's deformity in Klippel-Feil syndrome. *Spine (Phila Pa 1976)* 2007;32(18):E512-E516.

   A retrospective study of 30 patients with KFS found no factors relating Sprengel deformity to fusion levels or clinical parameters. No risk factor for Sprengel deformity was found in patients with KFS.

5. Copley LA, Dormans JP: Cervical spine disorders in infants and children. *J Am Acad Orthop Surg* 1998;6(4):204-214.

6. Guille JT, Miller A, Bowen JR, Forlin E, Caro PA: The natural history of Klippel-Feil syndrome: Clinical, roentgenographic, and magnetic resonance imaging findings at adulthood. *J Pediatr Orthop* 1995;15(5):617-626.

7. Samartzis DD, Herman J, Lubicky JP, Shen FH: Classification of congenitally fused cervical patterns in Klippel-Feil patients: Epidemiology and role in the development of cervical spine-related symptoms. *Spine (Phila Pa 1976)* 2006;31(21):E798-E804.

5: The Pediatric Spine

A retrospective review of 28 patients with KFS compared radiographic and clinical symptoms to develop a classification system for use in predicting the neurologic outcome based on the radiographic cervical fusion pattern.

8. Samartzis D, Kalluri P, Herman J, Lubicky JP, Shen FH: The role of congenitally fused cervical segments upon the space available for the cord and associated symptoms in Klippel-Feil patients. *Spine (Phila Pa 1976)* 2008;33(13):1442-1450.

   A prospective radiographic and retrospective clinical review of 29 patients with KFS evaluated the role of the fused segments and the space available for the cord in the clinical neurologic symptoms.

9. Auerbach JD, Hosalkar HS, Kusuma SK, Wills BP, Dormans JP, Drummond DS: Spinal cord dimensions in children with Klippel-Feil syndrome: A controlled, blinded radiographic analysis with implications for neurologic outcomes. *Spine (Phila Pa 1976)* 2008;33(12):1366-1371.

   A retrospective case study evaluated the spinal cord and cerebrospinal fluid column dimensions in children with KFS, compared with matched control subjects.

10. Samartzis D, Lubicky JP, Herman J, Kalluri P, Shen FH: Symptomatic cervical disc herniation in a pediatric Klippel-Feil patient: The risk of neural injury associated with extensive congenitally fused vertebrae and a hypermobile segment. *Spine (Phila Pa 1976)* 2006;31(11):E335-E338.

    After high-impact activity, a pediatric patient with KFS had cervical disk herniation that was treated with decompression and fusion. A review of the related literature is included.

11. Matsumoto K, Wakahara K, Sumi H, Shimizu K: Central cord syndrome in patients with Klippel-Feil syndrome resulting from winter sports: Report of 3 cases. *Am J Sports Med* 2006;34(10):1685-1689.

    A high-impact sports fall induced central cord syndrome in three patients with KFS. A review of the literature is included.

12. Ballock RT, Song KM: The prevalence of nonmuscular causes of torticollis in children. *J Pediatr Orthop* 1996;16(4):500-504.

13. Dubousset J: Torticollis in children caused by congenital anomalies of the atlas. *J Bone Joint Surg Am* 1986;68(2):178-188.

14. Dudkiewicz I, Ganel A, Blankstein A: Congenital muscular torticollis in infants: Ultrasound-assisted diagnosis and evaluation. *J Pediatr Orthop* 2005;25(6):812-814.

    The authors describe their experience with the use of ultrasonography to diagnose and follow the disappearance of a benign mass within the sternocleidomastoid muscle in infants.

15. Shim JS, Jang HP: Operative treatment of congenital torticollis. *J Bone Joint Surg Br* 2008;90(7):934-939.

A retrospective review of 47 patients who underwent release of the sternocleidomastoid muscle before or after age 4 years revealed no clinical difference in outcome measures.

16. Caird MS, Wills BP, Dormans JP: Down syndrome in children: The role of the orthopaedic surgeon. *J Am Acad Orthop Surg* 2006;14(11):610-619.

    This review of the orthopaedic care of patients with Down syndrome discusses instability at each cervical level as well as the development and treatment of scoliosis.

17. Mik G, Gholve PA, Scher DM, Widmann RF, Green DW: Down syndrome: Orthopedic issues. *Curr Opin Pediatr* 2008;20(1):30-36.

    The orthopaedic treatment of patients with Down syndrome is reviewed, with an update on their participation in sports activities.

18. David KM, Crockard A: Congenital malformations of the base of the skull, atlas, and dens, in Clark CR, ed: *The Cervical Spine*, ed 4. Philadelphia, PA, Lippincott Williams and Wilkins, 2005, pp 415-426.

    This textbook review discusses congenital malformations involving the base of the skull and upper cervical vertebrae, including odontoid hypoplasia and aplasia.

19. Douglas TS, Sanders V, Machers S, Pitcher R, van As AB: Digital radiographic measurement of the atlantodental interval in children. *J Pediatr Orthop* 2007;27(1):23-26.

    Lateral cervical radiographs of 101 children were used to determine intraobserver and interobserver reliability as well as a maximum ADI of 3.5 mm in normal children.

20. Peuschel SM, Scola FH, Pezzullo JC: A longitudinal study of the atlanto-dens relationships in asymptomatic individuals with Down syndrome. *Pediatrics* 1992;89(6, pt 2):1194-1198.

21. Matsunaga S, Imakiire T, Koga H, et al: Occult spinal canal stenosis due to C-1 hypoplasia in children with Down syndrome. *J Neurosurg* 2007;107(6, suppl):457-459.

    A smaller C1 and a smaller area for the spinal cord were found in 102 children with Down syndrome, compared with control subjects. This finding may explain the increased incidence of myelopathy in children with Down syndrome.

22. Cohen MW, Drummond DS, Flynn JM, Pill SG, Dormans JP: A technique of occipitocervical arthrodesis in children using autologous rib grafts. *Spine (Phila Pa 1976)* 2001;26(7):825-829.

23. Reilly CW, Choit RL: Transarticular screws in the management of C1-C2 instability in children. *J Pediatr Orthop* 2006;26(5):582-588.

    A technique for C1-C2 arthrodesis and its results are described in a review of 12 patients at 5-year follow-up.

24. Heuer GG, Hardesty DA, Bhowmick DA, Bailey R, Magge SN, Storm PB: Treatment of pediatric atlantoaxial instability with traditional and modified Goel-Harms fusion constructs. *Eur Spine J* 2009;18(6):884-892.

A technique is described for C1-C2 fusion using C1 lateral mass screws and C2 pedicle screws in six patients, all of whom had solid fusion at follow-up.

25. Goel A: Treatment of basilar invagination by atlantoaxial joint distraction and direct lateral mass fixation. *J Neurosurg Spine* 2004;1(3):281-286.

26. Dormans JP, Drummond DS, Sutton LN, Ecker ML, Kopacz KJ: Occipitocervical arthrodesis in children: A new technique and analysis of results. *J Bone Joint Surg Am* 1995;77(8):1234-1240.

27. Copley LA, Dormans JP, Pepe MD, Tan V, Browne RH: Accuracy and reliability of torque wrenches used for halo application in children. *J Bone Joint Surg Am* 2003;85(11):2199-2204.

28. Dormans JP, Criscitiello AA, Drummond DS, Davidson RS: Complications in children managed with immobilization in a halo vest. *J Bone Joint Surg Am* 1995;77(9): 1370-1373.

29. Arkader A, Hosalkar HS, Drummond DS, Dormans JP: Analysis of halo-orthoses application in children less than three years old. *J Child Orthop* 2007;1(6):337-344.

In a retrospective review, 10 patients younger than 3 years had a good outcome, with only 2 complications, after pin-halo fixation to treat cervical instability. Recommendations are made for use of a halo in patients younger than 3 years.

30. Thomson J: Myelomeningocele, in Abel M, ed: *Orthopaedic Knowledge Update: Pediatrics 3*. Rosemont, IL, American Academy of Orthopaedic Surgeons, 2006, pp 111-122.

The orthopaedic aspects of myelomeningocele are reviewed.

31. Guille JT, Sarwark JF, Sherk HH, Kumar SJ: Congenital and developmental deformities of the spine in children with myelomeningocele. *J Am Acad Orthop Surg* 2006; 14(5):294-302.

Congenital anomalies associated with myelodysplasia are reviewed, with sections on scoliosis and kyphosis.

32. Glard Y, Launay F, Viehweger E, Hamel A, Jouve JL, Bollini G: Neurological classification in myelomeningocele as a spine deformity predictor. *J Pediatr Orthop B* 2007;16(4):287-292.

Myelomeningocele patients were classified by the level of the malformation to predict future spine deformity.

33. Trivedi J, Thomson JD, Slakey JB, Banta JV, Jones PW: Clinical and radiographic predictors of scoliosis in patients with myelomeningocele. *J Bone Joint Surg Am* 2002;84(8):1389-1394.

34. Odent T, Arlet V, Ouellet J, Bitan F: Kyphectomy in myelomeningocele with a modified Dunn-McCarthy technique followed by an anterior inlayed strut graft. *Eur Spine J* 2004;13(3):206-212.

35. Smith JT, Gollogly S, Dunn HK: Simultaneous anterior-posterior approach through a costotransversectomy for the treatment of congenital kyphosis and acquired kyphoscoliotic deformities. *J Bone Joint Surg Am* 2005; 87(10):2281-2289.

A technique for correcting and fusing kyphotic spine curves is described. Level of evidence: IV.

36. Niall DM, Dowling FE, Fogarty EE, Moore DP, Goldberg C: Kyphectomy in children with myelomeningocele: A long-term outcome study. *J Pediatr Orthop* 2004;24(1):37-44.

37. Muthukumar N: Congenital spinal lipomatous malformations: Part I. Classification. *Acta Neurochir (Wien)* 2009;151(3):179-188, discussion 197.

The first part of a two-part article describes a new classification of lipomeningoceles of the spine.

38. Muthukumar N: Congenital spinal lipomatous malformations: Part II. Clinical presentation, operative findings, and outcome. *Acta Neurochir (Wien)* 2009;151(3): 189-197.

The second part of a two-part article describes the clinical appearance and treatment of lipomeningoceles of the spine.

39. Hamzaoglu A, Ozturk C, Tezer M, Aydogan M, Sarier M, Talu U: Simultaneous surgical treatment in congenital scoliosis and/or kyphosis associated with intraspinal abnormalities. *Spine (Phila Pa 1976)* 2007;32(25):2880-2884.

A retrospective clinical study showed the safety of repairing multiple intraspinal abnormalities in a single surgical setting.

40. Tseng JH, Kuo MF, Kwang Tu Y, Tseng MY: Outcome of untethering for symptomatic spina bifida occulta with lumbosacral spinal cord tethering in 31 patients: Analysis of preoperative prognostic factors. *Spine J* 2008;8(4):630-638.

A retrospective study compared presurgical clinical findings and postsurgical outcomes in patients with tethered cord, with 4-year follow-up.

41. McGirt MJ, Mehta V, Garces-Ambrossi G, et al: Pediatric tethered cord syndrome: Response of scoliosis to untethering procedures. Clinical article. *J Neurosurg Pediatr* 2009;4(3):270-274.

A retrospective study of 27 patients with tethered cord and scoliosis found that the degree of curvature and the age of the patient were related to the risk of further progression.

42. Hsieh PC, Ondra SL, Grande AW, et al: Posterior vertebral column subtraction osteotomy: A novel surgical approach for the treatment of multiple recurrences of teth-

5: The Pediatric Spine

ered cord syndrome. *J Neurosurg Spine* 2009;10(4): 278-286.

Vertebral column subtraction and tethered cord release are described as an option in multiple recurrences of tethered cord syndrome.

43. Miyakoshi N, Abe E, Suzuki T, Kido T, Chiba M, Shimada Y: Spine-shortening vertebral osteotomy for tethered cord syndrome: Report of three cases. *Spine (Phila Pa 1976)* 2009;34(22):E823-E825.

Spine shortening is described as an option for treating multiple recurrences of tethered cord in a retrospective case study of three patients followed for 3 years.

44. Herring JA: Disorders of the spinal cord, in Herring JA, ed: *Tachdjian's Pediatric Orthopaedics*, ed 4. Philadelphia, PA, Saunders Elsevier, 2008, pp 1466-1471.

This textbook review describes caudal regression syndrome and its clinical manifestations.

45. Renshaw TS: Sacral agenesis. *J Bone Joint Surg Am* 1978;60(3):373-383.

46. Caird MS, Hall JM, Bloom DA, Park JM, Farley FA: Outcome study of children, adolescents, and adults with sacral agenesis. *J Pediatr Orthop* 2007;27(6):682-685.

In a retrospective study, pain and functional outcomes were compared with the radiographic Renshaw classification in 16 patients with sacral agenesis.

47. Guille JT, Benevides R, DeAlba CC, Siriram V, Kumar SJ: Lumbosacral agenesis: A new classification correlating spinal deformity and ambulatory potential. *J Bone Joint Surg Am* 2002;84(1):32-38.

Chapter 36

Congenital and Infantile Idiopathic Early-Onset Scoliosis

Michael P. Glotzbecker, MD   John B. Emans, MD

Introduction

Scoliosis that begins before age 5 years is referred to as early-onset scoliosis (EOS), regardless of the underlying cause.[1] EOS reflects the physiologic consequences of spine deformity at a very young age, when the spine, thorax, and surrounding structures are rapidly growing and developing. Among the commonly encountered EOS etiologies are congenital and idiopathic infantile scoliosis. In congenital scoliosis, the vertebral column partially fuses or insufficiently develops.[2-5] Infantile idiopathic scoliosis is an idiopathic scoliosis that develops by age 3 years.[6] Other etiologies of EOS are similar in natural history and treatments; they include neuromuscular scoliosis, congenital kyphosis, Klippel-Feil syndrome and other cervical abnormalities, spinal dysgenesis, congenital spinal dislocation, lumbosacral agenesis, Jarcho-Levin syndrome, and spondylothoracic and spondylocostal dysplasia.

Development of the Spine and Lungs

Somites (precursors of the vertebral column) form in utero during gestational weeks 3 to 5 weeks, and they segment during weeks 6 to 8.[7] The spinal column develops at the same time as other major organ systems. This factor explains the frequent association of abnormalities of the spinal column with those of other organ systems. The spine grows rapidly during infancy and early childhood; two thirds of an individual's adult sitting height is achieved by age 5 years. The growth of the spine between T1 and L5 is more than 2 cm per year before age 5 years, with a marked deceleratation between ages 5 and 10 years.[8] The thorax undergoes a simultaneous rapid increase in size; 50% of adult thoracic volume is achieved by age 10 years.[8] Eighty-five percent of alveoli develop after birth, with the most rapid increase in number and volume occurring from birth to age 3 years.[8-10]

The rapid growth and expansion of the spine, thorax, and respiratory tree in a young child has significance for the treatment of children with EOS. Scoliosis has been associated with abnormal pulmonary development. The inability of the thorax to support normal respiration or lung growth in patients with EOS is called thoracic insufficiency syndrome.[11] Early distortion or restriction of thoracic volume can disturb pulmonary function and prevent normal lung parenchyma development. Alveolar development appears to occur only during the first few years of childhood. Respiratory function depends on both thoracic volume (which is dependent on adequate thoracic height, width, and depth) and thoracic function (the ability to change thoracic volume, which is dependent on diaphragmatic contraction and active thoracic expansion). In addition, normal respiration depends on the presence of healthy, appropriately perfused lung parenchyma.

Thoracic Insufficiency Syndrome

Thoracic insufficiency syndrome, defined as "inability of the thorax to support normal respiration or lung growth,"[11] is common in patients with EOS and can develop in several ways. The fused ribs and short spine associated with congenital scoliosis contribute to constriction of the thorax, which causes diminished thoracic volume and motion. Progressive infantile idiopathic scoliosis with vertebral rotation typically produces a shortened thorax on the concave side and a collapsed thorax on the convex side (called a windswept thorax).[11] Thoracic volume also is adversely affected by thoracic lordosis, in which there is a progressive loss of anteroposterior depth as the spine moves forward toward the sternum; the spinal penetration index was developed to describe this condition.[12] The thoracic deformity may not be proportionate to the spine deformity or Cobb angle.

Chest cage abnormalities present during a child's early growth may affect lung development. Histologic studies found that alveoli in patients with EOS are

Dr. Emans or an immediate family member has received royalties from Synthes, serves as an unpaid consultant to Medtronic Sofamor Danek and Synthes, and has received research or institutional support from Synthes. Neither Dr. Glotzbecker nor any immediate family member has received anything of value from or owns stock in a commercial company or institution related directly or indirectly to the subject of this chapter.

normal in shape and outline but diminished in number.[13] The severity of lung hypoplasticity is correlated with the early onset of scoliosis.[14]

Thoracic insufficiency syndrome should be distinguished from respiratory insufficiency. An infant with severe congenital scoliosis and multiple bilateral fused ribs certainly has thoracic insufficiency syndrome and most likely has respiratory insufficiency. However, an infant with progressive infantile idiopathic scoliosis has thoracic insufficiency syndrome but initially has normal respiratory function. Unless the progressive spine and thoracic deformity are successfully treated, the normal development of the thoracic cage and lungs will be impaired, and respiratory insufficiency will develop during later childhood or adolescence. The thorax is unable to support normal lung growth in either child, but respiratory insufficiency is present early in the development only of the child with congenital scoliosis.

The EOS-associated clinical signs of abnormal thoracic function include loss of chest wall expansion (seen as a limited thumb excursion test), an elevated respiratory rate, clipped speech, failure to thrive (delayed growth and poor weight gain), worsening thoracic deformity based on three-dimensional radiographic studies, and a decline in pulmonary function tests.[1,11] The patient may have restrictive lung disease, with a reduction in vital capacity and total lung capacity, which can lead to alveolar hypoventilation, hypoxic vasoconstriction, and eventually pulmonary artery hypertension or cor pulmonale.[1] Hypoxia during sleep and elevated serum hemoglobin also can reflect chronic respiratory insufficiency.

Patients with severe scoliosis diagnosed before age 5 years are at greatest risk for cardiopulmonary complications. Even without associated cardiac or pulmonary disease, life-threatening respiratory failure is relatively common later in life.[14,15] These patients are smaller than average at maturity. The shortening of the spine is exacerbated by the effects of surgery.[16] Although spine fusion may prevent a local progression, the overall deformity progression may not be controlled.[17] When considering treatment of early scoliosis, surgeons must weigh the effect of untreated progressive deformity on pulmonary function against the pulmonary growth inhibition resulting from spine fusion. Patients who have a spine fusion at a young age are at risk for restrictive lung disease and decreased pulmonary function.[18]

Management Principles for Early-Onset Spine Deformity

The general goal of treatment for EOS is to achieve the maximum spine length and mobility as well as the maximum thoracic volume and function by the end of the child's growth, while exposing the patient to a minimum number of hospitalizations. Two decisions are frequently required for a patient who has EOS with progressive deformity: the selection of treatment and the timing of intervention. If the deformity is localized, a local surgical correction may be definitive. Most EOS deformities involve large sections of the spine, however, and a difficult choice must be made between continuing nonsurgical treatment with resulting progression of deformity or surgical intervention, typically using growth-sparing instrumentation such as the vertical expandable prosthetic titanium rib (VEPTR) or growing rods. Although surgical intervention may be triggered by a worsening spine or thoracic deformity, the development of the thorax usually should be more heavily weighed in the decision to intervene. Spine fusion and instrumentation near the end of growth can resolve most of the spine imbalance and prevent deformity progression, but no similar solution exists for the impairment of thoracic shape and function resulting from EOS. Impaired pulmonary function persists throughout life and usually becomes more limiting with increasing body mass and the normal pulmonary aging process.

Congenital Scoliosis

Etiology

Congenital scoliosis has no clearly identifiable etiology. Environmental and genetic causes have been proposed, including in utero hyperthermia or exposure to valproic acid, boric acid, cigarette smoke, or alcohol.[5,7,19] Based on animal studies, low maternal oxygen tension has been proposed as an environmental cause of congenital vertebral malformations.[19-22]

Most instances of congenital scoliosis are sporadic. The familial recurrence rate of congenital vertebral malformations is only 3%.[5] Studies have identified genes that may have a role in congenital spine abnormalities, including *PAX1*, *WNT3A*, *DLL3*, *SLC35A3*, *T*, and *TBX6*, although no definitive genetic etiology has yet been found.[3,5,23,24] The discovery of mutations in genes of the notch family and their association with spondylocostal dysostosis and Alagille syndrome lends credence to the possibility of a genetic influence on congenital scoliosis.[7] Delineation of the role of *HOX* genes in the differentiation of the axial and appendicular skeleton may further support a genetic influence.[7]

Classification

Congenital spine abnormalities generally are classified based on whether the vertebrae are properly formed or segmented.[25] The first type of abnormality is a failure of formation (Figure 1). A wedge vertebra has two pedicles but asymmetric growth on one side, and a hemivertebra represents a complete unilateral failure of formation.[26] A hemivertebra can be further classified as nonsegmented, partially segmented, or fully segmented based on the number of adjacent disk spaces (none, one, or two, respectively).[4,27] A hemimetameric shift represents a counterbalanced spine in which there is one hemivertebra on each side, separated by at least one healthy vertebra.[28] The second type of abnormality is a failure of segmentation, which is characterized by abnormal connections between adjacent vertebrae[26]

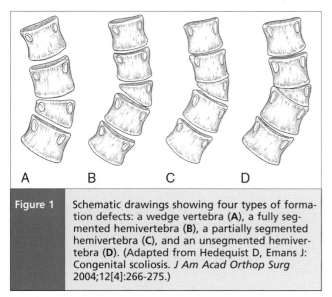

Figure 1   Schematic drawings showing four types of formation defects: a wedge vertebra (**A**), a fully segmented hemivertebra (**B**), a partially segmented hemivertebra (**C**), and an unsegmented hemivertebra (**D**). (Adapted from Hedequist D, Emans J: Congenital scoliosis. *J Am Acad Orthop Surg* 2004;12[4]:266-275.)

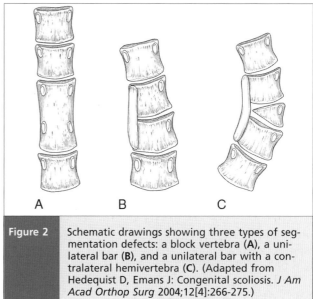

Figure 2   Schematic drawings showing three types of segmentation defects: a block vertebra (**A**), a unilateral bar (**B**), and a unilateral bar with a contralateral hemivertebra (**C**). (Adapted from Hedequist D, Emans J: Congenital scoliosis. *J Am Acad Orthop Surg* 2004;12[4]:266-275.)

(Figure 2). With block vertebrae, the connection between adjacent vertebrae is symmetric. With unilateral bars, the connection is asymmetric. Often a patient has a combination of these abnormalities (a mixed deformity).[4,25,26] Rib anomalies are found in 19% of patients with spine abnormalities. Most frequently, the abnormal ribs are located on the concave side because of a unilateral failure of vertebral segmentation.[29]

Typical two-dimensional classifications are based on plain radiographic findings. The classification of vertebral body abnormalities generally is straightforward. Defining abnormalities of the posterior elements can be much more difficult, however, because the posterior elements cannot be well seen on plain radiographs.[30] A classification system based on three-dimensional characteristics has not yet gained clinical acceptance because rotational deformity often is not evident until a curve has progressed substantially.[30] CT is useful for defining anomalies not seen on plain radiographs. Preoperative CT was found to be 100% accurate when correlated with intraoperative anatomic findings.[31]

Natural History

The natural history of congenital scoliosis depends on the type and location of the malformation.[32] The presence of a disk and its width generally are correlated with the growth potential at each level associated with a congenital deformity. The potential for asymmetric, unbalanced growth and the presence of a tethering deformity such as a unilateral bar are correlated with the likelihood of scoliosis progression. The progression of specific anomalies in congenital scoliosis has been characterized as shown in Table 1.[25] A unilateral bar with a contralateral hemivertebra has the greatest potential for progression, followed by a unilateral bar, a hemivertebra, a wedge vertebra, and a block vertebra. The progression of a mixed deformity with growth is unpredictable.[32] Rib anomalies do not appear to have an adverse effect on the curve size or rate of progression.[29]

Progression occurs with rapid growth of the spine during the first few years of life but also can occur during the preadolescent growth acceleration phase, when rapid growth and the effect of gravity can combine to cause progression in a previously stable deformity. The deformity tends to be clinically more visible if the abnormality is in the cervicothoracic, thoracolumbar, or lumbosacral region. Even if the congenital scoliosis is nonprogressive, the patient usually has a shorter-than-normal spine.[16] The patient may have other long-term effects such as diminished spine motion and adjacent-segment degeneration leading to spinal stenosis.

Clinical Features and Associated Syndromes

A patient with congenital scoliosis should be thoroughly examined for strength, sensation, reflexes (including abdominal reflexes), spine or trunk imbalance in the sagittal and coronal planes, head tilt, pelvic tilt, limb-length discrepancy, and rib cage abnormality. The inspiratory and expiratory capacity of the chest wall should be assessed using the thumb excursion test or appropriate pulmonary function tests.[33] Neural axis abnormalities are found in as many as 35% of patients with congenital scoliosis. The most common abnormalities are diastematomyelia (split cord), tethered cord, Chiari malformation, Dandy-Walker malformation, and intradural lipomas.[4,7,33,34] Therefore, the skin should be evaluated for signs of spinal dysraphism such as abnormal pigmentation, hairy patches, and skin tags. Asymmetric calves, cavus feet, clubfeet, vertical tali, or abnormal neurologic findings also may be found.[33] Any of these features should prompt further evaluation of the neural axis.

Congenital scoliosis may be associated with a musculoskeletal abnormality such as Klippel-Feil syndrome, Sprengel deformity, radial hypoplasia, clubfoot, or dislocated hip.[5,7,29,35,36] Other associations include cranial

5: The Pediatric Spine

Table 1

Median Yearly Deterioration of Congenital Scoliosis Curvature, by Type of Defect and Patient Age (*N* = 251)

Affected Spine Segment	Block Vertebra		Wedge Vertebra		Single Hemivertebra	
	<10 years	10+ years	<10 years	10+ years	<10 years	10+ years
Upper thoracic	<1°	1°		2°	1°	2°
Lower thoracic	<1°	1°	2°	2°	2°	2.5°
Thoracolumbar	<1°	1°	1.5°	2°	2°	3.5°
Lumbar	<1°		<1°		<1°	1°
Lumbosacral					<1°	1.5°

Key to Related Treatment

    = No treatment required   = Spine fusion may be required

Adapted with permission from McMaster MJ, Ohtsuka K: The natural history of congenital scoliosis: A study of two hundred and fifty-one patients. *J Bone Joint Surg Am* 1982;64(8):1128-1147.

nerve palsy, imperforate anus, and hemifacial microsomia.[5,7,36] Goldenhar syndrome (characterized by facial asymmetry and eye and ear deformities), vertebral-anal-cardiac-tracheal-esophageal-renal defect (VATER) association, and vertebral-anal-cardiac-tracheal-esophageal-renal-limb defect (VACTERL) association also are associated with congenital scoliosis.[5,7,36]

Congenital heart disease is found in as many as 25% of patients with congenital scoliosis.[7,33,35] The most common cardiac abnormalities are ventral septal defects, atrial septal defects, tetralogy of Fallot, and transposition of the great vessels. The patient can be asymptomatic or substantially impaired. A patient who is undergoing surgery for a congenital spine deformity should receive a screening echocardiogram, with a cardiology referral if appropriate.[4,33] A urologic or müllerian duct abnormality is found in as many as 33% of patients. The common findings are a horseshoe kidney, renal aplasia, duplicate ureters, and hypospadias.[7,33,35] Screening ultrasonography is the standard practice, with referral to a urologist if an abnormality is found. Alternatively, MRI can be used to detect urologic abnormalities.[33] Auditory anomalies also are associated with congenital vertebral anomalies; the most severe of these appears as Goldenhar syndrome. A routine neonatal hearing screening usually is sufficient for detecting an auditory deficit.

Imaging

Plain radiographs are used for diagnosing the deformity and following its progression. The standard radiographs include PA and lateral films of the spine, often with the addition of traction and/or bending views.[33]

Quantification of a congenital deformity can be difficult. The Cobb angle often dictates the choice of treatment for an idiopathic deformity but has less significance for a congenital deformity. Apical vertebral deviation, truncal imbalance, chest asymmetry, and disturbance of normal sagittal balance are more important in assessing congenital deformity.

The assessment of deformity progression is relatively complex in patients with congenital scoliosis and kyphosis. The effect of weight bearing should be factored into the radiographic evaluation when patients are followed longitudinally. Supine and upright radiographs taken before and after the patient reaches walking age may be mistakenly interpreted as showing curve progression because weight bearing alone can affect the Cobb angle. The same landmarks must be used to accurately assess curve progression on serial radiographs.[37] However, the normal measurement landmarks may be absent, distorted, or ambiguous in a patient with congenital scoliosis. A curve in the normally segmented part of the spine may progress in response to or independent of an adjacent congenital curve. If deformity progression is noted, MRI is indicated to detect any spinal cord tethering or another neural axis abnormality that may be causing or contributing to deformity progression.

The use of CT and MRI has improved the ability to define spine, chest wall, and rib anomalies and to screen for spinal dysraphism.[33] CT is useful for identifying complex anomalies not visible on plain radiography.[31] CT can define lung volume in patients who are too young for pulmonary function tests and is used after expansion thoracoplasty to measure improvement

Table 1 (continued)

Double Hemivertebra		Unilateral Unsegmented Bar		Unilateral Unsegmented Bar and Congenital Hemivertebrae	
<10 years	10+ years	<10 years	10+ years	<10 years	10+ years
2°	2.5°	2°	4°	5°	6°
2°	3°	5°	6.5°	6°	7°
5°		6°	9°	>10°	
		>5°			

= Spine fusion required   = Insufficient data

in chest wall, lung volume, and spine growth.[38,39] Radiation exposure is a concern in young children, and protocols to minimize radiation should be followed.[4,40]

Because of the high incidence of intraspinal abnormalities, some experts recommend a screening MRI for all patients with a congenital spine malformation.[4,7,33,34] Sedation or general anesthesia usually is required for MRI in a child younger than 5 years. General anesthesia carries a particular risk for infants, and it may be preferable to defer a screening MRI until the child is at least 3 to 6 months old. MRI is recommended for patients who are undergoing surgery or have curve progression, abnormal reflexes, limb deformity, incontinence, or a neurologic abnormality.[4] If congenital vertebral anomalies are noted at birth, spine ultrasonography is useful before extensive posterior element ossification occurs at age 6 to 8 weeks.

Nonsurgical Management

There is little evidence to support nonsurgical treatment of congenital scoliosis. Curves that have a symmetric abnormality (a hemimetameric shift) on either side of the spine may not require intervention, however. Bracing was found to be useful for some long, flexible curves as well as flexible compensatory curves adjacent to a congenital segment.[41] A short, sharp, rigid curve does not respond well to nonsurgical treatment. Bracing or casting may delay the need for surgery in a patient with congenital scoliosis but is less successful than bracing in patients with idiopathic scoliosis and cannot serve as the definitive treatment. The long-term risk of bracing to the developing chest cavity is unknown, and therefore the brace should not constrict the chest.

Surgical Management
Principles

In general, the surgical treatments for congenital spine deformity in young patients are in situ fusion to prevent deformity progression, hemiepiphysiodesis or hemiarthrodesis to gradually correct the deformity, hemivertebra or wedge vertebra resection with instrumentation and fusion to acutely correct the deformity, and growth-sparing surgery. The surgical risk of neurologic injury is higher in patients with congenital scoliosis than in patients with idiopathic scoliosis.[42] MRI should be used to define intraspinal anomalies that can be treated before or during the procedure. Intraoperative spinal cord lengthening should be prevented by avoiding distraction and using a spinal column–shortening procedure if appropriate. Controlled hypotension to avoid blood loss should be monitored closely to avoid cord ischemia during correction.[4] Motor- and somatosensory-evoked potentials should be monitored if possible.[42,43] The risk of perioperative neurologic injury is increased in the absence of baseline monitoring.[44] Neurologic status also can be assessed using the wake-up test, which is effective in young patients and is especially useful if changes during monitoring do not resolve.[45]

Spine instrumentation is a challenging aspect of the treatment of congenital anomalies. The use of instrumentation was found to be effective and safe in a study of pediatric patients with congenital spine abnormalities.[46] In another study, screw insertion was found to be safe and feasible in 1-year-old patients, and there were no instances of canal stenosis associated with instrumentation crossing the neurocentral synchondrosis.[47]

5: The Pediatric Spine

Usually, patients younger than 2 years require a 3.2-mm or 3.5-mm rod system, patients age 2 to 8 years require a 4.5-mm rod system, and patients age 8 years or older require a 5.5-mm rod system.[48] The use of titanium implants is beneficial to allow MRI to be used postoperatively for monitoring associated abnormalities or intraspinal anomalies.[4]

Preoperative traction can be used to gradually achieve partial correction of a severe deformity. Postoperative traction can be used after an anterior release.[49,50] In 24 patients who received traction after spine release, the average pretraction Cobb angle was 95°, the posttraction angle was 44°, and the final curve correction was 71%.[49] One patient had a temporary sensory disturbance. Spine release and halo-femoral traction were found to be a safe means of treating a severe congenital spine deformity before fusion.

Although early surgical treatment may reduce the severity of the spine deformity, conventional spine fusion can inhibit spine growth, shorten the spine, and exacerbate pulmonary dysfunction.[51] Patients who underwent early spine fusion had significantly lower pulmonary function tests than healthy children.[18,52] Strategies have been developed to prevent or correct deformity without spine fusion. Guided-growth anterior vertebral stapling can be used on a limited basis in patients at Risser stage 0 or 1 with an idiopathic deformity.[53] Distraction-based techniques based on growing rods or VEPTR are commonly used for patients with EOS. The Shilla growing-rod technique involves complete correction, instrumentation, and fusion of the central portion of an early-onset curve. The rods extend cephalad and caudad beyond the fusion and are attached to sliding screws.[54] There is no need for periodic distraction. Only preliminary results were reported, however. The goals of growth-sparing spine surgery are to achieve maximal spine length, spine mobility, and thoracic function, while minimizing the number of procedures and the surgical risk.[51] Spine growth is asymmetric in congenital deformities, and curve straightening theoretically encourages symmetric spine growth by normalizing the muscle and gravity forces.[51,55]

In Situ Fusion
Radiographic curve progression may be evident only over a long time period. The progression should exceed 5° to 7° before the curve is considered progressive. In situ fusion to prevent deformity progression is indicated for a progressive deformity that has not yet caused a significant truncal imbalance or chest deformity because it leads to only limited loss of spine height and has good long-term results.[4,56] In situ fusion does not provide deformity correction, and therefore the residual deformity must not be large enough to cause a progressive secondary deformity or imbalance with growth and the passage of time. In situ fusion can be anterior, posterior, or both. Anterior-only in situ fusion is useful for a patient with progressive congenital lordosis, and posterior-only in situ fusion is appropriate

for a patient with kyphotic deformity.[4] If posterior-only fusion is planned, the need for a concurrent anterior fusion primarily depends on the growth potential of the disks at the level of the deformity. If the disks associated with the anomaly are healthy, crankshaft progression of the curvature and lordosis may occur even after a solid posterior fusion.[57] An anterior arthrodesis can be done using an open anterior, thoracoscopic, or posterior pedicle approach, depending on the location and the surgeon's preference.[58] Instrumentation helps stabilize the fusion bed and may eliminate the need for other immobilization.[48]

Hemiepiphysiodesis
Anteroposterior hemiepiphysiodesis can provide gradual correction of a congenital deformity. This procedure has been recommended for patients younger than 5 years with a curve smaller than 70°, no significant sagittal abnormality, and concave growth potential at the site of the anomaly.[59] The rationale for the procedure is that arresting growth on the abnormal convex side allows gradual correction of the normal concave side with growth. Postoperative immobilization in a corrective cast is needed. A deformity caused by a failure of segmentation cannot be treated using this procedure because of the lack of concave-side growth potential.

Although the theory supporting hemiepiphysiodesis is attractive, patients have had less than 15° total correction in the long term, and many patients have had no correction.[60] Convex spine epiphysiodesis, with or without Harrington rod instrumentation, was not found to reverse the established deformity.[61] In 32 patients with congenital scoliosis, the mean Cobb angle was 55° before treatment and 50° at follow-up; 47% of these patients had subsequent fusion, and 12% had progression.[62] Hemiepiphysiodesis may slow the rate of deformity progression, although generally it does not achieve significant correction.[62] Transpedicular hemiepiphysiodesis with posterior instrumentation was successful in halting curve progression in 7 of 10 patients with a hemivertebra, but the average curve correction in the segmental area was only 21° to 30°.[63]

Hemivertebra Excision
Hemivertebra excision traditionally has been indicated for a patient who is younger than 5 years and has a significant, progressive deformity caused by an isolated thoracolumbar, lumbar, or lumbosacral hemivertebra, particularly if the deformity is associated with truncal imbalance. Hemivertebra excision also is indicated for a nonprogressive curve with significant deformity, particularly with associated truncal imbalance; or a large curve in the normally segmented spine above or below the hemivertebra. Successful hemivertebra excision restores spine balance and improves a nonstructural curve above or below the hemivertebra. Hemivertebra-associated kyphotic deformity also can be corrected. Hemivertebra excision is less commonly used for a tho-

racic or cervicothoracic hemivertebra. An incarcerated, nonsegmented, or semisegmented hemivertebra may cause little or no overall deformity, despite a large local Cobb angle, and no treatment or only in situ fusion may be needed.[27] Hemivertebra excision can be done using a variety of approaches, most of which involve a combined anterior-posterior approach in a single or staged procedure.[64-70] A single lateral posterior approach also has been used with success.[69] The availability of pediatric-size implants and the increased use of segmental fixation have led to increased interest in posterior-only approaches.[67,71]

A combined anterior-posterior approach allows circumferential exposure and excellent visualization, although a relatively long surgical time is required.[66] At 8.6-year follow-up, 21 patients treated with a combined approach had a mean curve improvement of 71.4%, with improvement in segmental scoliosis from 32.9° to 9.4°.[66] A similar study of 18 patients treated with excision and instrumentation using a simultaneous anterior-posterior exposure found an average 70% curve correction, with no neurologic complications and a 100% fusion rate.[68]

A posterior-only approach can be useful particularly if the patient has associated kyphosis, but it can be technically challenging.[4] At follow-up more than 6 years after posterior resection, osteotomy, and transpedicular instrumentation in 41 children age 1 to 6 years, the patients without bar formation had curve improvement from 36° to 7°, and those with bar formation had improvement from 69° to 23°. Three patients had implant failure, and three additional patients had overloading and breakage of the convex pedicle requiring fusion to the next level.[64] Ten patients who were treated with posterior-only resection and the three-rod technique had curve correction from 44° to 8°, with no implant-related complications or revisions.[67]

Fusion With Correction
In general, acute fusion with deformity correction is indicated for a patient with congenital abnormalities that have led to an unacceptable coronal or sagittal deformity, after the patient has achieved sufficient thoracic cavity size.[4] Three-dimensional CT is helpful for defining the patient's anatomy in preparation for acute correction. Spine shortening rather than distraction should be attempted.[4] If insufficient deformity flexibility is seen on bending or traction radiographs, releases or osteotomies may be added to achieve sufficient curve correction. Anterior surgery may be required in addition to posterior surgery if the disk spaces are well defined or there is significant remaining growth, particularly in a patient with a lordotic deformity or well-defined disks but limited flexibility on bending radiographs.[57] A posterior-only procedure such as a pedicle subtraction osteotomy or vertebral column resection can offer correction of a severe deformity without a separate anterior procedure.[72] Osteotomies of a congenital fusion may improve the correction but are associated with in-

creased risk of neurologic loss and intraoperative bleeding.[72]

Growth-Sparing Surgery Using Growing Rods
Growing rods ideally are used for a growing patient who has a progressive congenital spine deformity involving a large segment of the spine, but no congenital rib fusions. Growing rods essentially are a means of internal bracing; they allow continued spine growth while controlling the spine deformity. Growing rods also are valuable for treating infantile idiopathic scoliosis. The technique involves inserting dual growing rods based on anchor points placed proximally and distally, with limited fusion at these sites. A thoracolumbosacral orthosis may or may not be used for the first 6 months after surgery. Rod lengthening is required every 6 months until the patient reaches age 10 to 12 years and is ready for definitive fusion.[73] Routine, scheduled lengthening appears to be more effective than lengthening only after curve progression is noted.

Several reports have described the techniques for and results of using growing rods in patients with congenital and infantile idiopathic scoliosis. In one study, limited-exposure placement of single-rod implants was used to maximize growth in instrumented areas of the spine.[74] Hook sites were not fused, and a Milwaukee brace was used postoperatively. Patients treated in this manner (the Moe technique) had curve improvement, but 50% had a complication such as rod breakage or hook dislodgment from the rod or lamina. A report of 20 years' experience with the Moe technique found that 44 of 67 patients had an average 30% curve reduction, and the remaining 23 patients had an average 33% curve progression.[75] The patients had segmental growth, but an implant-related complication occurred after 33 of 402 procedures (8%). The use of a similar technique used in patients with heterogeneous characteristics led to an improved Cobb angle and sagittal contouring, but the complication rate was 24%.[76]

Rod breakage and hook dislodgement with the use of single growing rods led to the development of a dual-rod technique.[77,78] A multicenter study found that the use of dual rods was associated with a Cobb angle improvement from 82° to 38° and an average growth of 1.2 cm per year. The ratio of space available for the lung also increased, but 11 of 23 patients had a complication such as infection, rod breakage, hook dislodgement, or screw pullout.[78] In 13 patients with a noncongenital curve, the Cobb angle improved from 81° to 35.7° after a dual-rod procedure; patients whose lengthening procedures were less than 6 months apart had a higher annual growth rate and significantly greater scoliosis correction. Only 6 of 134 patients had a complication.[77] A comparison of single- and dual-rod techniques found that patients treated with a dual-rod technique had better initial correction, maintenance of correction, and growth.[79]

In the available studies of growing-rod techniques, the patient populations were heterogeneous, and only a

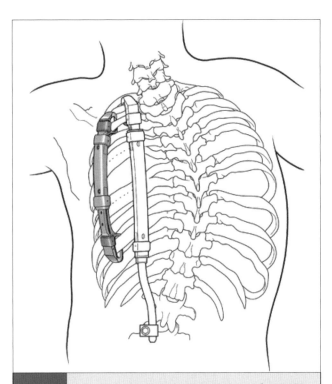

Figure 3 Schematic drawing showing the use of a VEPTR after opening wedge thoracostomy in a patient with congenital vertebral anomalies and fused ribs. A rib-to-rib device *(shaded)* or hybrid rib prosthesis *(unshaded)* can be used to promote thoracic growth by lengthening the concave hemithorax. (Adapted with permission from Campbell RM Jr, Smith MD, Hell-Vocke AK: Expansion thoracoplasty: The surgical technique of opening-wedge thoracostomy. Surgical technique. *J Bone Joint Surg Am* 2004;86[suppl 1]: 51-64.)

limited number of patients had congenital scoliosis. Some studies did not follow the patients until skeletal maturity. A recent multicenter study of distraction-based growing rods suggests that lengthening is not reliably continued during growth.[80] Inadvertent spontaneous posterior spine fusion beneath the growing rods is common and may prompt early fusion and instrumentation. However, it appears that the growing-rod technique provides a means of correcting curves and preventing progression until definitive fusion, while fostering continued spine and thoracic growth. Kyphotic deformity often is incompletely controlled with this distraction-based technique, and the normal sagittal contour is commonly lost.

Growth-Sparing Surgery Using a VEPTR

A VEPTR ideally is used for a patient who has a progressive congenital spine deformity with an associated hemithoracic constriction caused by multiple fused ribs. In addition, a deformity with absent posterior elements, poor soft-tissue coverage, or a recent spine infection does not allow safe or satisfactory spine anchor placement and may be best treated using a VEPTR.[4] Con-

genital scoliosis with rib fusions has been associated with a constricted thorax and thoracic insufficiency syndrome. The tethering effect of the ribs, in addition to the spine abnormalities, alters normal chest growth and leads to insufficient lung development and function.[11,29] Before proceeding with surgery, the surgeon should document the patient's lung volume and pulmonary function tests. Three-dimensional CT can be used to measure lung volume in a young child who cannot perform pulmonary function tests.[58,81]

The VEPTR is attached proximally to the ribs and distally to the ribs, spine, or pelvis. If the hemithoracic constriction is severe or associated with fused ribs, an expansion thoracostomy usually accompanies VEPTR insertion. Early fusion in a patient with congenital abnormalities and fused ribs may compound the existing thoracic insufficiency.[39] To prevent this difficulty, osteotomy of segments of congenitally fused ribs can allow expansion of the hemithorax.[82] The technique involves a standard thoracotomy incision, osteotomy or lysis of adhesions between the fused ribs, and placement of a rib-to-rib VEPTR between the spanning ribs or a rib-to-spine, rib-to-pelvis hybrid VEPTR[82] (Figure 3). Like growing rods, the VEPTR is lengthened on a scheduled basis, typically every 6 months.

A CT study revealed that the use of VEPTR led to a postoperative increase in lung volume.[83] In 27 patients with congenital scoliosis and congenital rib fusions, the Cobb angle improved from 74° to 49°, there was 8 mm of growth per year in both the convex and concave sides of the spine, and pulmonary vital capacity increased.[84] In 31 patients with thoracic insufficiency, spine growth was similar to that of healthy control subjects after treatment with VEPTR.[38] The increased volume of the lungs and the constricted hemithorax was maintained at follow-up.[85]

The complications of VEPTR use include device migration, infection, and brachial plexus palsy.[38] A systematic review of the evidence concluded that chest and lung volumes are increased when a VEPTR is used to treat congenital scoliosis, but there is no evidence of increases in pulmonary function parameters.[9]

Infantile Idiopathic Scoliosis

Etiology

Infantile idiopathic scoliosis accounts for fewer than 1% of all instances of idiopathic scoliosis in the United States.[86] It is important to rule out another cause of early scoliosis, such as a neuromuscular condition, an associated syndrome, or an underlying spinal cord abnormality (a syringomyelia, Chiari malformation, tethered cord, or diastematomyelia).[1] Infantile idiopathic scoliosis has no clear underlying etiology.[1] Intrauterine molding may be a factor, as suggested by an association between infantile idiopathic scoliosis and metatarsus adductus or developmental hip dysplasia. A supine sleep position may have a role. The incidence of infan-

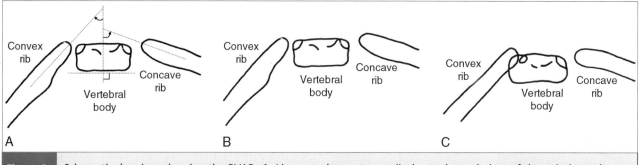

Figure 4 Schematic drawings showing the RVAD. **A,** Lines are drawn perpendicular to the end plate of the apical vertebra and from the midpoint of the head of the rib to the midpoint of the neck of the rib on the concave and convex sides (*dotted lines*). The angle is calculated on each side (*solid lines with arrows*). The RVAD is the difference between these two measurements. **B,** A phase 1 relationship between the rib head and vertebral body is defined by no overlap between the rib and the vertebral body. The RVAD can be calculated. **C,** In a phase 2 relationship between the rib head and vertebral body, the rib overlaps the vertebral body, indicating curve progression. (Adapted with permission from Mehta MH: The rib-vertebra angle in the early diagnosis between resolving and progressive infantile scoliosis. *J Bone Joint Surg Br* 1972;54[2]:230-243.)

tile scoliosis was higher in the United Kingdom, where supine positioning is common, than in the United States until the US practice of placing infants prone for sleeping was replaced by supine positioning as a means of preventing sudden infant death syndrome.[25] There is concern that the "back to sleep" initiative may lead to an increased incidence of infantile idiopathic scoliosis. The genetic component is undefined, but affected children were found to be 30 times more likely than control subjects to have a parent or sibling with scoliosis.[86]

Natural History

The natural history of infantile idiopathic scoliosis is diverse. Although the curve resolves in many patients, other patients have progressive deformity. A systematic review found progression in 333 infantile scoliosis curves and resolution in 573.[87] Early studies found a low incidence of curve resolution, but later studies reported a better outcome.[88,89] After progressive thoracic infantile scoliosis was treated with bracing or surgery, a curve greater than 70° was found in 23 of the 47 patients 5 years or younger at follow-up and 27 of the 37 patients age 6 to 10 years at follow-up.[90] Other studies found that 92 of 100 patients with a structural curve during the first year of life had spontaneous resolution and that only 26 of 99 patients had curve progression.[88,89]

Age at onset, sex, family history, associated developmental anomalies, and curve location, type, and magnitude all have been proposed as predictors of curve progression.[1] A systematic review found that spontaneously resolving curves were associated with a younger age (mean, 5.5 months) than progressive curves (mean, 12 months).[87] Double curves appeared to have a high likelihood of progression.[89] A curve that resolves during infancy is unlikely to reappear and progress during the preadolescent growth spurt.[87]

The rib-vertebral angle difference (RVAD) is the most reliable indicator of curve progression[91] (Fig-

ure 4). The curve is likely to resolve if the RVAD is less than 20°. If there is rib head overlap at the level of the apical vertebra, progression is certain and the RVAD is not measured. In the original study, 46 of 86 patients with no rib head overlap had resolution.[91] The RVAD was less than 20° in 83% of the patients whose curve resolved. The RVAD was greater than 20° in 84% of the patients whose curve progressed. The usefulness of the RVAD for predicting progression was confirmed by subsequent studies.[92] A systematic review of infantile scoliosis found that 91% of patients whose RVAD was lower than 20° had curve resolution, but only 27.5% of patients with a progressive curve had an RVAD lower than 20°.[87]

Clinical Features and Associated Syndromes

Infantile scoliosis predominantly occurs in boys (the ratio of boys to girls is approximately 3:1). A left convexity is typical and is found in 56% to 93% of patients.[87] The primary curve usually is in the thoracic region. The most common pattern is a low thoracic curve with compensatory curves above and below the primary curve.[87] Every patient should be thoroughly examined for strength, sensation, and reflexes, including abdominal reflexes. The patient should be assessed for chest wall and shoulder height asymmetry, trunk imbalance, and pelvic obliquity.[1,86] Lower extremity limb length should be measured to rule out nonstructural scoliosis.[1] The patient also should be examined for cutaneous markers of a systemic disorder or spinal dysraphism. A pulmonary function examination is critical, as it is for patients with congenital scoliosis.

Plagiocephaly is extremely common with EOS, and there also is an increased incidence of developmental dysplasia of the hip, inguinal hernia, and congenital heart disease.[1,86,87,93-95] Studies of patients with an infantile idiopathic scoliosis curve greater than 20° found rates of neural axis abnormality between 13% and 22%, despite a normal neurologic examination and the absence of associated syndromes.[96,97] Many patients

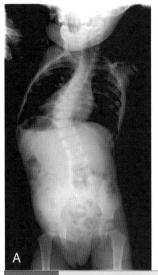
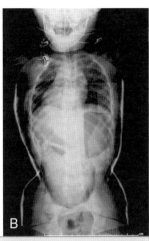

Figure 5   PA radiographs showing infantile idiopathic scoliosis in a child age 1 year 10 months before (A) and during (B) cast treatment. There is excellent in-cast correction of the deformity.

with a neural axis abnormality require neurosurgical intervention.

Imaging
The standard radiographic examination includes full-length PA and lateral radiographs for evaluating the Cobb angle and RVAD.[1] Bending radiographs are used to assess flexibility. A comparison of radiographs taken before and after walking age may mistakenly appear to indicate curve progression. MRI is useful for evaluating the spinal cord because of the high incidence of occult central nervous system abnormalities in patients with infantile scoliosis. Because of the risk associated with administering general anesthesia to infants, close observation rather than immediate MRI may be reasonable.[97] However, many experts recommend MRI examination if the patient's curve exceeds 20° to allow early detection of treatable conditions such as tethered cord or syrinx associated with Chiari I malformation.[87]

Nonsurgical Management
Patients whose RVAD is lower than 20° have a low risk of progression, and reevaluation with serial radiographs every 4 to 6 months is appropriate.[1,86] If there is curve resolution, the patient should be followed every 1 to 2 years until skeletal maturity.[1] A completely resolved curve is unlikely to reappear during the prepubertal growth spurt.[1] If there is progression despite a low RVAD, reevaluation and possibly treatment are required. If the patient's RVAD is greater than 20° or overlapping of the rib and vertebral body at the point of deformity, there is a high likelihood of progression, and treatment should be considered, especially if the Cobb angle progresses.[1]

The patient can be treated with casting, bracing, or a combination. Brace or cast treatment formerly was considered at most to slow the progression of infantile scoliosis deformity. However, lasting and sometimes complete correction has been achieved with modified cast treatment of variable duration; the treatment emphasizes deformity derotation without restrictive pressure on the thorax[98] (Figure 5). This Mehta casting technique has become the standard nonsurgical treatment for infantile scoliosis. In general, cast treatment begins when the patient is as young as 6 months to take advantage of the period of maximum growth velocity for curve correction. If possible, the cast is changed at 6- to 12-week intervals, with the patient under anesthesia, until complete correction. Bracing is then used for at least 2 years, until there is no further evidence of progression.[1,86] Inadvertent thoracic pressure, with the potential for long-term rib cage distortion, should be avoided during brace treatment.[1]

A systematic review found only limited studies focusing on infantile idiopathic scoliosis.[9] Bracing at an early age was found to reverse the course of infantile scoliosis, and treatment at a later age was found to postpone eventual posterior fusion. In 22 patients with progressive infantile scoliosis who were treated with an Edinburgh modification of the Milwaukee brace, a final correction of 11% was achieved.[99]

Surgical Management
Surgical treatment is considered after unsuccessful nonsurgical treatment for a patient with a progressive infantile scoliosis curve.[86] In a child with a large amount of growth remaining, growing rods are the most common choice. As with any EOS, repeated surgical interventions involve a trade-off between stopping curve progression and maximizing the growth and development of the spine, lungs, and thoracic cage.[86] Surgery at a young age involves the complex use of implants in a small, developing spinal column as well as the risk of inadvertent fusion and growth arrest.

Early spine fusion procedures for infantile scoliosis generally were unsuccessful, with resulting curve progression and crankshaft phenomenon.[100,101] Studies found that convex growth arrest procedures at best slow the progression of infantile scoliosis deformity.[60-62] Minimally invasive hemiepiphysiodesis slows curve progression in adolescents but has not been used in small children.[102] Growing-rod techniques are most commonly used for patients with severe infantile scoliosis. Growing rods are intended to allow spine growth while lessening or preventing further deformity; they are especially useful in patients with infantile scoliosis, who do not have inherent vertebral or rib abnormalities. Growing rods provide a means of correcting the curve and preventing progression until eventual fusion while fostering spine and thoracic growth. A comparative study of single- and dual-rod techniques found that dual-rod techniques may allow better initial correction, maintenance of correction, and growth.[79]

Outcomes and Complications of EOS Treatment

The treatment of EOS rarely results in a normal spine at the end of growth. The only exception to this rule may be successful Mehta casting or bracing for infantile scoliosis, which can lead to a mobile, normal-length spine. Definitive spine fusion otherwise is required. Early, growth-friendly surgical treatment of EOS may lessen the deformity at the time of final fusion but requires repeated lengthening and exchange procedures that have direct and indirect costs for the patient and family. The risk of complications such as infection, scarring, and spontaneous spine fusion increases with repeated surgical procedures throughout growth.[73,103] A multicenter study of growing rods found diminishing incremental change after successive lengthening procedures.[80] Some complications, such as severe infection or extensive fusion, may necessitate an end to treatment well before the patient enters the preadolescent growth phase, particularly if surgical treatment was initiated early. However delaying treatment of a progressive curve may worsen the final chest and spine deformity and increase the extent of definitive spine fusion. The need for early deformity control must be balanced against the risk of a severe complication requiring early termination of lengthening.

Summary

Understanding of the etiology, natural history, and clinical appearance of EOS, including congenital and infantile idiopathic scoliosis, continues to improve. Increased appreciation of the association between pulmonary function and early growth of the spinal column and thorax has led to treatment strategies aimed at maximizing spine and pulmonary growth while slowing curve progression.[54,104] Newer techniques include the Shilla system and guided vertebral growth. Such systems have the potential to allow spine growth while avoiding repeated surgery for lengthening. Further study is required to advance these and other developing surgical techniques.

Annotated References

1. Gillingham BL, Fan RA, Akbarnia BA: Early onset idiopathic scoliosis. *J Am Acad Orthop Surg* 2006;14(2): 101-112.

   The presentation, evaluation, imaging, and management of EOS are outlined.

2. Shands AR Jr, Bundens WD: Congenital deformities of the spine: An analysis of the roentgenograms of 700 children. *Bull Hosp Joint Dis* 1956;17(2):110-133.

3. Giampietro PF, Blank RD, Raggio CL, et al: Congenital and idiopathic scoliosis: Clinical and genetic aspects. *Clin Med Res* 2003;1(2):125-136.

4. Hedequist D, Emans J: Congenital scoliosis: A review and update. *J Pediatr Orthop* 2007;27(1):106-116.

   The classification, natural history, evaluation, and treatment of pediatric vertebral anomalies are outlined.

5. Giampietro PF, Dunwoodie SL, Kusumi K, et al: Progress in the understanding of the genetic etiology of vertebral segmentation disorders in humans. *Ann N Y Acad Sci* 2009;1151:38-67.

   Recent advances in molecular embryology related to vertebral malformations, genetic contributions, and the complex interrelationships between genetic and environmental factors are discussed.

6. James JI: Idiopathic scoliosis: The prognosis, diagnosis, and operative indications related to curve patterns and age of onset. *J Bone Joint Surg Br* 1954;36(1):36-49.

7. Hensinger RN: Congenital scoliosis: Etiology and associations. *Spine (Phila Pa 1976)* 2009;34(17):1745-1750.

   An overview of congenital scoliosis and associated conditions is provided. The origin of scoliosis may be environmental, genetic, or a combination.

8. Dimeglio A: Growth in pediatric orthopaedics. *J Pediatr Orthop* 2001;21(4):549-555.

9. Sponseller PD, Yazici M, Demetracopoulos C, Emans JB: Evidence basis for management of spine and chest wall deformities in children. *Spine (Phila Pa 1976)* 2007;32(19, suppl):S81-S90.

   Studies relevant to the treatment of deformities of the chest wall and spine are reviewed, with a comparison of treatment methods and outcomes. Most studies have level III or IV evidence.

10. Emery JL, Mithal A: The number of alveoli in the terminal respiratory unit of man during late intrauterine life and childhood. *Arch Dis Child* 1960;35:544-547.

11. Campbell RM Jr, Smith MD, Mayes TC, et al: The characteristics of thoracic insufficiency syndrome associated with fused ribs and congenital scoliosis. *J Bone Joint Surg Am* 2003;85(3):399-408.

12. Dubousset J, Wicart P, Pomero V, Barois A, Estournet B: Spinal penetration index: New three-dimensional quantified reference for lordoscoliosis and other spinal deformities. *J Orthop Sci* 2003;8(1):41-49.

13. Davies G, Reid L: Effect of scoliosis on growth of alveoli and pulmonary arteries and on right ventricle. *Arch Dis Child* 1971;46(249):623-632.

14. Branthwaite MA: Cardiorespiratory consequences of unfused idiopathic scoliosis. *Br J Dis Chest* 1986;80(4): 360-369.

15. Pehrsson K, Larsson S, Oden A, Nachemson A: Long-term follow-up of patients with untreated scoliosis: A study of mortality, causes of death, and symptoms. *Spine (Phila Pa 1976)* 1992;17(9):1091-1096.

5: The Pediatric Spine

16. Goldberg CJ, Fallon MC, Moore DP, Fogarty EE, Dowling FE: Growth patterns in children with congenital vertebral anomaly. *Spine (Phila Pa 1976)* 2002; 27(11):1191-1201.

17. Goldberg CJ, Moore DP, Fogarty EE, Dowling FE: Long-term results from in situ fusion for congenital vertebral deformity. *Spine (Phila Pa 1976)* 2002;27(6):619-628.

18. Karol LA, Johnston C, Mladenov K, Schochet P, Walters P, Browne RH: Pulmonary function following early thoracic fusion in non-neuromuscular scoliosis. *J Bone Joint Surg Am* 2008;90(6):1272-1281.

    Twenty-eight patients had spinal fusion at a mean age of 3.3 years and were an average 14.6 years old at follow-up. Patients with proximal thoracic deformity, especially those with rib anomalies, were at the highest risk of developing restrictive pulmonary disease.

19. Loder RT, Hernandez MJ, Lerner AL, et al: The induction of congenital spinal deformities in mice by maternal carbon monoxide exposure. *J Pediatr Orthop* 2000; 20(5):662-666.

20. Ingalls TH, Curley FJ: Principles governing the genesis of congenital malformations induced in mice by hypoxia. *N Engl J Med* 1957;257(23):1121-1127.

21. Rivard CH: Effects of hypoxia on the embryogenesis of congenital vertebral malformations in the mouse. *Clin Orthop Relat Res* 1986;208:126-130.

22. Farley FA, Loder RT, Nolan BT, et al: Mouse model for thoracic congenital scoliosis. *J Pediatr Orthop* 2001; 21(4):537-540.

23. Maisenbacher MK, Han JS, O'Brien ML, et al: Molecular analysis of congenital scoliosis: A candidate gene approach. *Hum Genet* 2005;116(5):416-419.

    A molecular study of congenital scoliosis by analysis of the candidate gene *DLL3* (which is known to be associated with spondylocostal dysostosis type I) found one novel missense variant.

24. Erol B, Tracy MR, Dormans JP, et al: Congenital scoliosis and vertebral malformations: Characterization of segmental defects for genetic analysis. *J Pediatr Orthop* 2004;24(6):674-682.

25. McMaster MJ, Ohtsuka K: The natural history of congenital scoliosis: A study of two hundred and fifty-one patients. *J Bone Joint Surg Am* 1982;64(8):1128-1147.

26. Hedequist D, Emans J: Congenital scoliosis. *J Am Acad Orthop Surg* 2004;12(4):266-275.

27. McMaster MJ, David CV: Hemivertebra as a cause of scoliosis: A study of 104 patients. *J Bone Joint Surg Br* 1986;68(4):588-595.

28. Shawen SB, Belmont PJ Jr, Kuklo TR, et al: Hemimetameric segmental shift: A case series and review. *Spine (Phila Pa 1976)* 2002;27(24):E539-E544.

29. Tsirikos AI, McMaster MJ: Congenital anomalies of the ribs and chest wall associated with congenital deformities of the spine. *J Bone Joint Surg Am* 2005;87(11): 2523-2536.

    A retrospective study of 620 consecutive patients with congenital deformities of the spine found that 119 patients had rib anomalies, most commonly associated with congenital scoliosis and a unilateral failure of vertebral segmentation.

30. Kawakami N, Tsuji T, Imagama S, et al: Classification of congenital scoliosis and kyphosis: A new approach to the three-dimensional classification for progressive vertebral anomalies requiring operative treatment. *Spine (Phila Pa 1976)* 2009;34(17):1756-1765.

    Three-dimensional CT of more than 150 patients with congenital spine deformities were compared with plain radiographs. The analysis revealed several types of laminae and clarified the definition of each type of anomalous vertebrae. This information can be useful in developing a strategy for surgical treatment.

31. Hedequist DJ, Emans JB: The correlation of preoperative three-dimensional computed tomography reconstructions with operative findings in congenital scoliosis. *Spine (Phila Pa 1976)* 2003;28(22):2531-2534.

32. Marks DS, Qaimkhani SA: The natural history of congenital scoliosis and kyphosis. *Spine (Phila Pa 1976)* 2009;34(17):1751-1755.

    This is a review of the literature on the natural history of congenital spine deformities.

33. Chan G, Dormans JP: Update on congenital spinal deformities: Preoperative evaluation. *Spine (Phila Pa 1976)* 2009;34(17):1766-1774.

    Congenital scoliosis is a multifaceted condition. A thorough preoperative evaluation is necessary, and all medical conditions must be considered. The treatment should be tailored to the patient, taking into account the patient's age and the effect on pulmonary function.

34. Prahinski JR, Polly DW Jr, McHale KA, Ellenbogen RG: Occult intraspinal anomalies in congenital scoliosis. *J Pediatr Orthop* 2000;20(1):59-63.

35. Basu PS, Elsebaie H, Noordeen MH: Congenital spinal deformity: A comprehensive assessment at presentation. *Spine (Phila Pa 1976)* 2002;27(20):2255-2259.

36. Beals RK, Robbins JR, Rolfe B: Anomalies associated with vertebral malformations. *Spine (Phila Pa 1976)* 1993;18(10):1329-1332.

37. Facanha-Filho FA, Winter RB, Lonstein JE, et al: Measurement accuracy in congenital scoliosis. *J Bone Joint Surg Am* 2001;83(1):42-45.

38. Emans JB, Caubet JF, Ordonez CL, Lee EY, Ciarlo M: The treatment of spine and chest wall deformities with fused ribs by expansion thoracostomy and insertion of vertical expandable prosthetic titanium rib: Growth of thoracic spine and improvement of lung volumes. *Spine (Phila Pa 1976)* 2005;30(17, suppl):S58-S68.

In a prospective clinical study of VEPTR in 31 patients with combined spine and chest wall deformity, the spine deformity was controlled and the thoracic spine grew at a near-normal rate. The complications are discussed.

39. Campbell RM Jr, Hell-Vocke AK: Growth of the thoracic spine in congenital scoliosis after expansion thoracoplasty. *J Bone Joint Surg Am* 2003;85(3):409-420.

40. Brenner D, Elliston C, Hall E, Berdon W: Estimated risks of radiation-induced fatal cancer from pediatric CT. *AJR Am J Roentgenol* 2001;176(2):289-296.

41. Winter RB, Moe JH, MacEwen GD, et al: The Milwaukee brace in the nonoperative treatment of congenital scoliosis. *Spine (Phila Pa 1976)* 1976;1(2):85-96.

42. MacEwen GD, Bunnell WP, Sriram K: Acute neurological complications in the treatment of scoliosis: A report of the Scoliosis Research Society. *J Bone Joint Surg Am* 1975;57(3):404-408.

43. Hedequist DJ: Instrumentation and fusion for congenital spine deformities. *Spine (Phila Pa 1976)* 2009; 34(17):1783-1790.

A systematic review of spine implant use for congenital deformities concluded that instrumentation can be safely and effectively used in patients with spine deformity.

44. Thuet ED, Padberg AM, Raynor BL, et al: Increased risk of postoperative neurologic deficit for spinal surgery patients with unobtainable intraoperative evoked potential data. *Spine (Phila Pa 1976)* 2005;30(18): 2094-2103.

A retrospective review of 4,310 patients who underwent spine surgery at a single institution found no data on intraoperative motor- and/or somatosensory-evoked potentials for 59 patients. Patients with unobtainable data are at a much higher risk of postoperative neurologic deficits.

45. Polly DW Jr, Klemme WR, Fontana JL, Sterbis MD: A modified wake-up test for use in very young children undergoing spinal surgery. *J Pediatr Orthop* 2000; 20(1):64-65.

46. Hedequist DJ, Hall JE, Emans JB: The safety and efficacy of spinal instrumentation in children with congenital spine deformities. *Spine (Phila Pa 1976)* 2004; 29(18):2081-2087.

47. Ruf M, Harms J: Pedicle screws in 1- and 2-year-old children: Technique, complications, and effect on further growth. *Spine (Phila Pa 1976)* 2002;27(21):E460-E466.

48. Hedequist D, Yeon H, Emans J: The use of allograft as a bone graft substitute in patients with congenital spine deformities. *J Pediatr Orthop* 2007;27(6):686-689.

A retrospective review of 107 pediatric patients who underwent instrumentation and arthrodesis using allograft for congenital spine deformity found a pseudarthrosis rate of 2.8% and an infection rate of 0.9%. Freeze-dried allograft is a safe and effective alternative to iliac crest bone graft.

49. Mehlman CT, Al-Sayyad MJ, Crawford AH: Effectiveness of spinal release and halo-femoral traction in the management of severe spinal deformity. *J Pediatr Orthop* 2004;24(6):667-673.

50. Rinella A, Lenke L, Whitaker C, et al: Perioperative halo-gravity traction in the treatment of severe scoliosis and kyphosis. *Spine (Phila Pa 1976)* 2005;30(4):475-482.

Halo-gravity traction for severe spine deformity was studied in 33 patients. The major coronal curve was reduced 38° (46%), compared with pretreatment radiographs. Halo-gravity traction is a safe, well-tolerated, and effective way to apply gradual sustained traction and maximize postoperative correction.

51. Yazici M, Emans J: Fusionless instrumentation systems for congenital scoliosis: Expandable spinal rods and vertical expandable prosthetic titanium rib in the management of congenital spine deformities in the growing child. *Spine (Phila Pa 1976)* 2009;34(17):1800-1807.

A review of the literature on growing-rod and thoracic expansion techniques in patients with congenital spine deformity contrasts the advantages and limitations.

52. Vitale MG, Matsumoto H, Bye MR, et al: A retrospective cohort study of pulmonary function, radiographic measures, and quality of life in children with congenital scoliosis: An evaluation of patient outcomes after early spinal fusion. *Spine (Phila Pa 1976)* 2008;33(11):1242-1249.

A retrospective cohort study evaluated pulmonary function and quality of life in children treated with early fusion for progressive congenital scoliosis. Pulmonary function tests and quality of life scores had declined at 6.9-year follow-up.

53. Betz RR, Ranade A, Samdani AF, et al: Vertebral body stapling: A fusionless treatment option for a growing child with moderate idiopathic scoliosis. *Spine (Phila Pa 1976)* 2010;35(2):169-176.

At a mean 3.2-year follow-up of vertebral body stapling in 28 children with idiopathic scoliosis, the success rate was 87% in patients with lumbar curve and 79% in those with a thoracic curve smaller than 35°. Larger thoracic curves require alternative treatment.

54. McCarthy RE, Sucato D, Turner JL, Zhang H, Henson MA, McCarthy K: Shilla growing rods in a caprine animal model: A pilot study. *Clin Orthop Relat Res* 2010; 468(3):705-710.

In the Shilla growth guidance system, the apex of the curve is corrected and growth continues in the normal

5: The Pediatric Spine

spine. There were no implant failures in 11 2-month-old goats, and all spines had growth with implants.

55. Aronson J, Harrison BH, Stewart CL, Harp JH Jr: The histology of distraction osteogenesis using different external fixators. *Clin Orthop Relat Res* 1989;241:106-116.

56. Winter RB, Moe JH: The results of spinal arthrodesis for congenital spinal deformity in patients younger than five years old. *J Bone Joint Surg Am* 1982;64(3):419-432.

57. Kesling KL, Lonstein JE, Denis F, et al: The crankshaft phenomenon after posterior spinal arthrodesis for congenital scoliosis: A review of 54 patients. *Spine (Phila Pa 1976)* 2003;28(3):267-271.

58. Newton PO, White KK, Faro F, Gaynor T: The success of thoracoscopic anterior fusion in a consecutive series of 112 pediatric spinal deformity cases. *Spine (Phila Pa 1976)* 2005;30(4):392-398.

    This is a retrospective review of a single surgeon's experience with 112 consecutive thorascopic anterior release and fusion procedures with open posterior instrumentation and fusion. Thoracoscopic anterior release and fusion was found to be safe and effective in combination with a posterior procedure.

59. Winter RB, Lonstein JE, Denis F, Sta-Ana de la Rosa H: Convex growth arrest for progressive congenital scoliosis due to hemivertebrae. *J Pediatr Orthop* 1988;8(6):633-638.

60. Roaf R: The treatment of progressive scoliosis by unilateral growth-arrest. *J Bone Joint Surg Br* 1963;45:637-651.

61. Marks DS, Iqbal MJ, Thompson AG, Piggott H: Convex spinal epiphysiodesis in the management of progressive infantile idiopathic scoliosis. *Spine (Phila Pa 1976)* 1996;21(16):1884-1888.

62. Uzumcugil A, Cil A, Yazici M, et al: Convex growth arrest in the treatment of congenital spinal deformities, revisited. *J Pediatr Orthop* 2004;24(6):658-666.

63. Ginsburg G, Mulconrey DS, Browdy J: Transpedicular hemiepiphysiodesis and posterior instrumentation as a treatment for congenital scoliosis. *J Pediatr Orthop* 2007;27(4):387-391.

    A retrospective radiographic evaluation of 10 hemivertebrae in nine patients found that seven patients had no progression or improvement at 2-year follow-up. Two patients older than 9 years 10 months progressed to posterior spine fusion.

64. Ruf M, Jensen R, Letko L, Harms J: Hemivertebra resection and osteotomies in congenital spine deformity. *Spine (Phila Pa 1976)* 2009;34(17):1791-1799.

    A retrospective study of posterior hemivertebrae resection and osteotomy with posterior instrumentation in 41 children age 1 to 6 years found that the average

Cobb angle improved from 36° to 7° in patients without a bar, and from 69° to 23° in those with a bar.

65. Bollini G, Docquier PL, Viehweger E, Launay F, Jouve JL: Thoracolumbar hemivertebrae resection by double approach in a single procedure: Long-term follow-up. *Spine (Phila Pa 1976)* 2006;31(15):1745-1757.

    Thirty-four consecutive patients (mean age, 3.5 years) were treated with a combined anterior-posterior approach for thoracolumbar hemivertebrae. A retrospective review found a mean 69% improvement in the local curve and a mean 33% improvement in the global curve at 6-year follow-up.

66. Bollini G, Docquier PL, Viehweger E, Launay F, Jouve JL: Lumbar hemivertebra resection. *J Bone Joint Surg Am* 2006;88(5):1043-1052.

    Twenty-one consecutive patients with congenital scoliosis or kyphoscoliosis from lumbar vertebrae (mean age, 3.3 years) were treated with resection through a combined anterior-posterior approach. The mean improvement was 71% at 8.6-year follow-up.

67. Hedequist D, Emans J, Proctor M: Three rod technique facilitates hemivertebra wedge excision in young children through a posterior only approach. *Spine (Phila Pa 1976)* 2009;34(6):E225-E229.

    A retrospective review of 10 young children treated with hemivertebrae excision from a posterior-only approach using a three-rod system found that fusion was obtained in all patients. There were no implant-related complications or revisions.

68. Hedequist DJ, Hall JE, Emans JB: Hemivertebra excision in children via simultaneous anterior and posterior exposures. *J Pediatr Orthop* 2005;25(1):60-63.

    A retrospective study of 18 patients who had hemivertebra excision and deformity correction using unilateral compression instrumentation found that all had fusion and an average Cobb correction of 71% at 35-month follow-up.

69. Li X, Luo Z, Li X, Tao H, Du J, Wang Z: Hemivertebra resection for the treatment of congenital lumbarspinal scoliosis with lateral-posterior approach. *Spine (Phila Pa 1976)* 2008;33(18):2001-2006.

    Twenty-four patients (mean age, 9.4 years) with congenital scoliosis from a lumbar hemivertebra were treated through a lateral posterior approach. A retrospective review found a mean curve improvement of 61% at a mean 43-month follow-up.

70. Hosalkar HS, Luedtke LM, Drummond DS: New technique in congenital scoliosis involving fixation to the pelvis after hemivertebra excision. *Spine (Phila Pa 1976)* 2004;29(22):2581-2587.

71. Ruf M, Harms J: Hemivertebra resection by a posterior approach: Innovative operative technique and first results. *Spine (Phila Pa 1976)* 2002;27(10):1116-1123.

72. Suk SI, Kim JH, Kim WJ, Lee SM, Chung ER, Nah KH: Posterior vertebral column resection for severe spinal

deformities. *Spine (Phila Pa 1976)* 2002;27(21):2374-2382.

73. Thompson GH, Akbarnia BA, Campbell RM Jr: Growing rod techniques in early-onset scoliosis. *J Pediatr Orthop* 2007;27(3):354-361.

    The available systems for treating EOS include a single growing rod, dual growing rods, and the VEPTR implant.

74. Moe JH, Kharrat K, Winter RB, Cummine JL: Harrington instrumentation without fusion plus external orthotic support for the treatment of difficult curvature problems in young children. *Clin Orthop Relat Res* 1984;185:35-45.

75. Klemme WR, Denis F, Winter RB, Lonstein JW, Koop SE: Spinal instrumentation without fusion for progressive scoliosis in young children. *J Pediatr Orthop* 1997;17(6):734-742.

76. Blakemore LC, Scoles PV, Poe-Kochert C, Thompson GH: Submuscular Isola rod with or without limited apical fusion in the management of severe spinal deformities in young children: Preliminary report. *Spine (Phila Pa 1976)* 2001;26(18):2044-2048.

77. Akbarnia BA, Breakwell LM, Marks DS, et al: Dual growing rod technique followed for three to eleven years until final fusion: The effect of frequency of lengthening. *Spine (Phila Pa 1976)* 2008;33(9):984-990.

    Thirteen patients underwent dual growing-rod treatment and final fusion. The average correction was from 81° to 35.8°, and the average number of lengthenings was 5.2. Patients who underwent lengthening at intervals of less than 6 months had a 1.8-cm growth rate, compared with 1.0 cm in patients with less frequent lengthening.

78. Akbarnia BA, Marks DS, Boachie-Adjei O, Thompson AG, Asher MA: Dual growing rod technique for the treatment of progressive early-onset scoliosis: A multicenter study. *Spine (Phila Pa 1976)* 2005;30(17, suppl):S46-S57.

    The treatment of 23 patients with a variety of diagnoses was retrospectively reviewed. The patients underwent a total of 189 procedures, of which 151 were lengthenings. The mean scoliosis improved from 82° to 26° at last follow-up or after final fusion. Eleven patients had a complication. T1-S1 length increased across the treatment period.

79. Thompson GH, Akbarnia BA, Kostial P, et al: Comparison of single and dual growing rod techniques followed through definitive surgery: A preliminary study. *Spine (Phila Pa 1976)* 2005;30(18):2039-2044.

    The treatment of 28 consecutive patients was analyzed from growing-rod implantation through definitive spinal fusion. The use of dual growing rods was compared with that of a single growing rod and a submuscular rod with short apical fusion. Time to fusion was similar in all patients. Patients with dual rods had better frontal and sagittal plane balance and the lowest complication rate.

80. Sankar WN, Skaggs DL, Yazici M, et al: Lengthening of dual growing rods and the law of diminishing returns. *Spine (Phila Pa 1976)* 2011;36(10):806-809.

    A retrospective study of 38 patients treated with dual rods found that the average T1-S1 gain was 1.76 cm per year but that the gain decreased significantly with repeated lengthenings ($P = 0.007$).

81. Gollogly S, Smith JT, Campbell RM: Determining lung volume with three-dimensional reconstructions of CT scan data: A pilot study to evaluate the effects of expansion thoracoplasty on children with severe spinal deformities. *J Pediatr Orthop* 2004;24(3):323-328.

82. Campbell RM Jr, Smith MD, Hell-Vocke AK: Expansion thoracoplasty: The surgical technique of opening-wedge thoracostomy. Surgical technique. *J Bone Joint Surg Am* 2004;86(suppl 1):51-64.

83. Gollogly S, Smith JT, White SK, Firth S, White K: The volume of lung parenchyma as a function of age: A review of 1050 normal CT scans of the chest with three-dimensional volumetric reconstruction of the pulmonary system. *Spine (Phila Pa 1976)* 2004;29(18):2061-2066.

84. Campbell RM Jr, Smith MD, Mayes TC, et al: The effect of opening wedge thoracostomy on thoracic insufficiency syndrome associated with fused ribs and congenital scoliosis. *J Bone Joint Surg Am* 2004;86(8):1659-1674.

85. Motoyama EK, Deeney VF, Fine GF, et al: Effects on lung function of multiple expansion thoracoplasty in children with thoracic insufficiency syndrome: A longitudinal study. *Spine (Phila Pa 1976)* 2006;31(3):284-290.

    Thoracic insufficiency syndrome was studied in 10 children. Multiple expansion thoracoplasties were found to be beneficial over time because they allow the lungs to expand with body growth and avoid further deterioration in lung function.

86. Akbarnia BA: Management themes in early onset scoliosis. *J Bone Joint Surg Am* 2007;89(suppl 1):42-54.

87. Fernandes P, Weinstein SL: Natural history of early onset scoliosis. *J Bone Joint Surg Am* 2007;89(suppl 1):21-33.

88. Lloyd-Roberts GC, Pilcher MF: Structural idiopathic scoliosis in infancy: A study of the natural history of 100 patients. *J Bone Joint Surg Br* 1965;47:520-523.

89. Ceballos T, Ferrer-Torrelles M, Castillo F, Fernandez-Paredes E: Prognosis in infantile idiopathic scoliosis. *J Bone Joint Surg Am* 1980;62(6):863-875.

90. James JI, Lloyd-Roberts GC, Pilcher MF: Infantile structural scoliosis. *J Bone Joint Surg Br* 1959;41:719-735.

5: The Pediatric Spine

91. Mehta MH: The rib-vertebra angle in the early diagnosis between resolving and progressive infantile scoliosis. *J Bone Joint Surg Br* 1972;54(2):230-243.

92. Ferreira JH, de Janeiro R, James JI: Progressive and resolving infantile idiopathic scoliosis: The differential diagnosis. *J Bone Joint Surg Br* 1972;54(4):648-655.

93. Hooper G: Congenital dislocation of the hip in infantile idiopathic scoliosis. *J Bone Joint Surg Br* 1980;62(4):447-449.

94. Wynne-Davies R: Infantile idiopathic scoliosis: Causative factors, particularly in the first six months of life. *J Bone Joint Surg Br* 1975;57(2):138-141.

95. Conner AN: Developmental anomalies and prognosis in infantile idiopathic scoliosis. *J Bone Joint Surg Br* 1969;51(4):711-713.

96. Gupta P, Lenke LG, Bridwell KH: Incidence of neural axis abnormalities in infantile and juvenile patients with spinal deformity: Is a magnetic resonance image screening necessary? *Spine (Phila Pa 1976)* 1998;23(2):206-210.

97. Pahys JM, Samdani AF, Betz RR: Intraspinal anomalies in infantile idiopathic scoliosis: Prevalence and role of magnetic resonance imaging. *Spine (Phila Pa 1976)* 2009;34(12):E434-E438.

    In a retrospective review of 54 patients with a diagnosis of infantile idiopathic scoliosis at a single institution, a neural axis abnormality was found on MRI in 7 patients, 5 of whom required intervention.

98. Mehta MH: Growth as a corrective force in the early treatment of progressive infantile scoliosis. *J Bone Joint Surg Br* 2005;87(9):1237-1247.

    In a prospective study, 136 patients younger than 4 years were treated with serial casting for progressive infantile scoliosis. Those treated at a mean age of 1 year 7 months had better correction than those treated at a mean age of 2 years 6 months. The likelihood of reversal was higher in the patients treated at a younger age, and reduction was more likely in the patients treated later.

99. McMaster MJ, Macnicol MF: The management of progressive infantile idiopathic scoliosis. *J Bone Joint Surg Br* 1979;61(1):36-42.

100. Hefti FL, McMaster MJ: The effect of the adolescent growth spurt on early posterior spinal fusion in infantile and juvenile idiopathic scoliosis. *J Bone Joint Surg Br* 1983;65(3):247-254.

101. Dubousset J, Herring JA, Shufflebarger H: The crankshaft phenomenon. *J Pediatr Orthop* 1989;9(5):541-550.

102. Betz RR, Kim J, D'Andrea LP, Mulcahey MJ, Balsara RK, Clements DH: An innovative technique of vertebral body stapling for the treatment of patients with adolescent idiopathic scoliosis: A feasibility, safety, and utility study. *Spine (Phila Pa 1976)* 2003;28(20):S255-S265.

103. Yang JS, McElroy MJ, Akbarnia BA, et al: Growing rods for spinal deformity: Characterizing consensus and variation in current use. *J Pediatr Orthop* 2010;30(3):264-270.

    A survey of preferences on growing rod use and a case-based survey found significant practice variation. Some consensus exists on the indications for surgery, including curve size, diagnosis, and age as well as lengthening intervals and final fusion methods.

104. Newton PO, Upasani VV, Farnsworth CL, et al: Spinal growth modulation with use of a tether in an immature porcine model. *J Bone Joint Surg Am* 2008;90(12):2695-2706.

    Spinal growth modulation was tested in minipigs. Mechanical tethering during growth altered spine morphology in the coronal and sagittal planes, leading to vertebral and disk wedging in proportion to the duration of tethering.

Chapter 37

Juvenile and Adolescent Idiopathic Scoliosis

Joshua M. Pahys, MD   Lawrence G. Lenke, MD

Introduction

Idiopathic scoliosis is a structural, three-dimensional curvature of the spine for which no definitive etiology has been established. The categorization typically is chronologic, based on the age of the patient at initial diagnosis: infantile (birth to age 2 years, 11 months), juvenile (age 3 years to 9 years, 11 months), or adolescent (age 10 years to 17 years, 11 months). It is useful to understand both the historical and current methods of evaluating, classifying, and treating the spectrum of juvenile and adolescent idiopathic spine deformities, from benign to severe.

Juvenile Idiopathic Scoliosis

Epidemiology and Natural History

Patients with juvenile idiopathic scoliosis (JIS) account for 12% to 21% of all patients with idiopathic scoliosis.[1] JIS is diagnosed when the patient is 3 to 9 years old. This age span represents a time of transition between the periods of rapid spine growth in which infantile idiopathic scoliosis or adolescent idiopathic scoliosis (AIS) develops. The ratio of girls to boys is 1:1 in patients age 3 to 6 years, 2:1 to 4:1 in patients age 7 to 9 years, and 8:1 in patients age 10 years.[2] Boys typically are diagnosed at approximately age 5 years, and girls at approximately age 7 years. This difference in age at diagnosis is particularly significant because boys reach skeletal maturity later than girls, and boys with JIS thus are more likely than girls to have curve progression.

Dr. Lenke or an immediate family member serves as a board member, owner, officer, or committee member of the Scoliosis Research Society; has received royalties from Medtronic; serves as an unpaid consultant to Medtronic; and has received research or institutional support from Axial Biotech and DePuy, a Johnson & Johnson company. Neither Dr. Pahys nor any immediate family member has received anything of value from or owns stock in a commercial company or institution related directly or indirectly to the subject of this chapter.

The early age of onset of JIS portends a high risk of progression to severe deformity, despite the typically slow or moderate rate of curve progression. Approximately 70% of patients have spine deformity progression requiring treatment with an orthotic device and/or surgery.[3] Although curve regression was noted in 12 patients who had an untreated JIS curve smaller than 25°, curve regression without treatment is much less common in JIS than in infantile idiopathic scoliosis.[3,4]

Evaluation and Classification

A spine deformity initially is evaluated using standard PA and lateral standing long-cassette radiographs of the entire spine and pelvis. Standard Cobb angles are measured to determine the curve magnitude and the location of apices. The rib–vertebral angle difference, which is used to evaluate curves in infantile idiopathic scoliosis, is less efficacious in predicting JIS curve progression.[5]

A thorough assessment, including a neurologic examination, is necessary for identifying the etiology of the patient's spine deformity. Intraspinal anomalies including Chiari malformation and syringomyelia have been identified in approximately 20% of patients with JIS, including patients with a normal neurologic examination. MRI can be used for patients with a curve of 20° or more to identify any intraspinal pathology related to the deformity.[6] An atypical curve pattern, thoracic hyperkyphosis, reflex asymmetry, a cutaneous sign of spinal dysraphism, a foot deformity, or, possibly, pain should prompt MRI investigation.

The original Lenke AIS classification (Figure 1) can be used to identify curve patterns in JIS, with several slight modifications.[7] The six curve types, three lumbar coronal modifiers, and three thoracic sagittal modifiers are identical to those used in the Lenke AIS classification system. The curve with the largest Cobb angle magnitude is called the major curve. Right thoracic and double major curves are the predominant spine deformity patterns in both JIS and AIS. In JIS, however, side-bending radiographs are not used to determine whether a curve is structural. Instead, the C7 plumbline is used to measure the deviation of the curve apex of the main thoracic region, and the center sacral vertical line (CSVL) is used to measure the deviation of the

The Lenke Classification System for AIS				
Curve Type	Proximal Thoracic	Main Thoracic	Thoracolumbar/Lumbar	Description
1	Nonstructural	Structural*	Nonstructural	Main thoracic (MT)
2	Structural†	Structural*	Nonstructural	Double thoracic (DT)
3	Nonstructural	Structural*	Structural†	Double major (DM)
4	Structural†	Structural§	Structural§	Triple major (TM)
5	Nonstructural	Nonstructural	Structural*	Thoracolumbar/lumbar (TL/L)
6	Nonstructural	Structural†	Structural*	Thoracolumbar/lumbar–main thoracic (TL/L-MT)

*Major curve: largest Cobb measurement, always structural †Minor curve: remaining structural curves §Type 4: MT or TL/L can be the major curve.

Structural Criteria
(Minor curves)

Proximal thoracic - Side-bending Cobb angle ≥25°
- T2-T5 kyphosis ≥+20°

Main thoracic - Side-bending Cobb angle ≥25°
- T10-L2 kyphosis ≥+20°

Thoracolumbar/lumbar - Side-bending Cobb angle ≥25°
- T10-L2 kyphosis ≥+20°

Location of Apex
(Scoliosis Research Society definition)

Curve	Apex
Thoracic	T2 to T11-12 disk
Thoracolumbar	T12-L1
Lumbar	L1-2 disk to L4

Modifiers

Lumbar Coronal Modifier	Center Sacral Vertical Line to Lumbar Apex
A	Between pedicles
B	Touches apical body(ies)
C	Completely medial

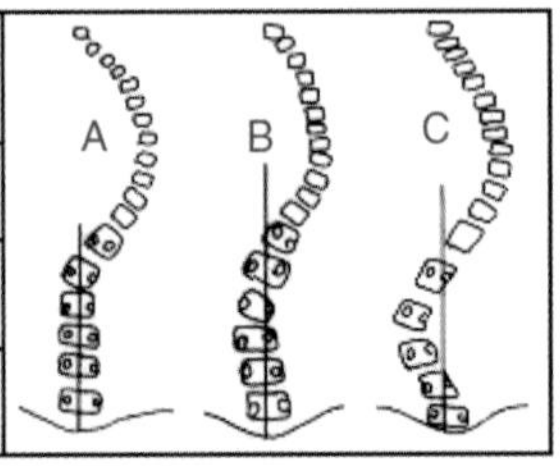

Thoracic Sagittal Profile (T5-T12)	
Modifier	Cobb Angle
– (Hypo)	<10°
N (Normal)	10° - 40°
+ (Hyper)	>40°

Curve type (1-6) + Lumbar coronal modifier (A, B, C) + Thoracic sagittal modifier (–, N, +) = curve classification (eg, 1B+): _____

Figure 1 The Lenke classification of AIS. (Adapted with permission from Lenke LG, Betz RR, Harms J, et al: A new classification to determine extent of spinal arthrodesis. *J Bone Joint Surg Am* 2001;83[8]:1169-1181.)

thoracolumbar/lumbar region. A structural minor curve is thus defined as having an apical vertebra or disk space completely off the midline. In contrast, a nonstructural minor curve has some portion of the apical vertebra or disk space overlying the midline of the thoracic or thoracolumbar/lumbar region. A slightly different definition of a structural curve is used in the proximal thoracic spine. A proximal thoracic curve is structural if the contralateral first rib (the left rib in a right proximal thoracic curve) is elevated; the proximal thoracic curve is nonstructural if the two first ribs are even or if the first rib is higher on the ipsilateral side.

Treatment

Observation

Observation is appropriate if a JIS curve is no larger than 25°. Radiographs initially are warranted every 4 to 6 months to assess for progression, but the follow-up interval may be expanded to as long as 12 months depending on the patient's age, the severity of the clinical deformity, and the magnitude of the curve.[8] More frequent observation may be needed as the pre-

adolescent growth acceleration phase approaches. A curve that was nonprogressive or minimally progressive during the steady growth of childhood can quickly worsen during the rapid growth of early adolescence.[9]

Orthotic Treatment and Physical Therapy

Management with a bracing program is indicated for a curve from 20° to 25° up to 50° to 60°. Multiple braces usually are required because of the prolonged period of treatment. A cervicothoracolumbosacral orthosis (Milwaukee brace) traditionally was used for flexible thoracic and double major curves in patients with JIS. This orthosis consists of a plastic pelvic section with one anterior and two posterior upright bars connected superiorly to a contoured neck ring. In contrast, the thoracolumbosacral underarm brace uses corrective molds fabricated into the plastic of the body jacket as well as pressure from a lumbar pad to manipulate the curve.[10] The thoracolumbosacral orthosis must be used with caution because rib cage compression may occur over a long treatment period. This effect may be undesirable during long-term brace wear by a young patient.[7]

The nighttime-only overcorrection brace, such as the custom-molded Charleston brace, was developed in an effort to improve patient compliance. Casting for the Charleston brace is done with the patient supine in a bending position opposite the curvature while a corrective force is applied at the apex of the curve. The Providence brace is fabricated from computer-aided measurements or a plaster impression generated with the patient placed supine on an acrylic frame while controlled direct, lateral, and rotational forces are applied to the trunk to move the spine toward or beyond the midline.[10]

The prognosis was excellent when part-time bracing was used for patients with a JIS curve no larger than 35°, but patients with a curve of 45° or more had a relatively poor prognosis.[11] There was a 70% success rate when nighttime-only bracing was used for patients with a JIS curve smaller than 45°.[12] Brace treatment success was statistically correlated with the best in-brace correction; successfully treated patients had an average in-brace curve correction of 102%, compared with an average in-brace correction of 73% in patients who later required surgical intervention.[12] A rigid curve in a patient younger than 5 years may require serial casting using a Risser cast changed every 6 to 12 weeks. When the curve is stabilized, a standard orthosis can be used.[8]

Some centers in the United States and Europe recommend specific training exercises for trunk rotational strength.[13] However, there is no clear evidence as to the long-term efficacy of physical therapy designed to halt or correct a spine deformity.

Surgical Treatment

JIS affects patients over a broad age range and with varying characteristics. The indications for surgical treatment therefore are not clearly defined. Fusion has the potential for causing a loss of spine height, thus affecting the patient's overall height and, more importantly, the patient's chest wall and lung growth. A formula has been developed to estimate the spine shortening likely to result from a fusion procedure: the number of fused vertebral segments is multiplied by 0.07 cm, and the product is multiplied by the number of years of remaining spine growth.[14] More comprehensive means of calculating spine growth have been developed in recent years.[15]

There is a risk of crankshaft phenomenon (continued anterior growth and curvature of the spine in a skeletally immature patient, despite a solid posterior fusion).[16] The risk of crankshaft deformity is greatest if the fusion is done when the patient has a large amount of remaining growth, has not reached the peak height velocity phase, is at Risser grade 0, is younger than 10 years, and has open triradiate cartilage.[17] After the patient has passed the peak height velocity phase and the triradiate cartilage is closed, posterior-only fusion is associated with a markedly lower risk of crankshaft deformity.[18] Historically, anterior release and fusion was performed in conjunction with a posterior spinal fusion

in an effort to reduce the risk and severity of crankshaft phenomenon in younger patients.[19] However, methods have been devised to allow continued spine and chest wall growth while controlling progressive spine deformity in skeletally immature patients.

Growing-rod posterior instrumentation should be considered if the patient is younger than 8 to 10 years and has a curve larger than 60° (Figure 2). Other considerations for surgical intervention include a rigid curve that continues to progress despite brace wear and patient intolerance of brace wear.[20] Growing-rod constructs have been in use since 1962. The earliest constructs consisted of a proximal and a distal claw hook connected to a single Harrington distraction rod. No formal fusion was performed during implantation, but autofusion was observed over time at the uninstrumented levels between the proximal and distal fixation points.[21] The early instrumentation systems had complications including instrumentation failure, implant pullout, and rod breakage.[21] More recently developed submuscular dual growing-rod implants have had promising short-term results.[22-24] Pedicle screws are used in the caudal and/or cranial portions of the construct to reduce the incidence of instrumentation failure.[22] A comparison study of apical anterior-posterior fusion with a single or dual growing-rod construct found that the use of dual growing rods without an apical fusion provided the best initial correction and maintenance of correction.[23] At 2-year follow-up, patients with an apical fusion had curve stiffening, crankshaft deformity, and other complications.[23] In another study, 13 patients had promising maintenance of curve correction and increased spine growth, from initial growing-rod implantation to definitive spinal fusion at 3- to 11-year follow-up; the average spine growth was 5.7 cm over 4.4 years.[24] Instrumentation lengthening at intervals of less than 6 months led to a statistically significant greater rate of growth than lengthening at longer intervals.

A growing-rod system is designed to allow spine growth while maintaining apical curve control and obviating the need for repeat surgical procedures. In the Shilla technique, the apex of the deformity is fixed and fused with pedicle screws, and the ends of the deformity are instrumented with screws that are not locked to dual growing rods (Figure 3). Animal and early clinical studies of the Shilla technique found that curve correction is maintained and spine growth continues without the need for formal surgical lengthening procedures.[7,25] Remote-controlled lengthening using the polarity of external magnets was efficacious in animal studies and an early European clinical study.[26-28] One device involves a rod attached to a direct-current motorized gearbox controlled by a radio receiver.[26] Another system uses a magnetic gear device within an expandable rod modeled on an existing expandable prosthesis.[27,28] This device was implanted in 27 patients in Europe.[28] The child's parent used an external handheld magnetic device to perform noninvasive, at-home

5: The Pediatric Spine

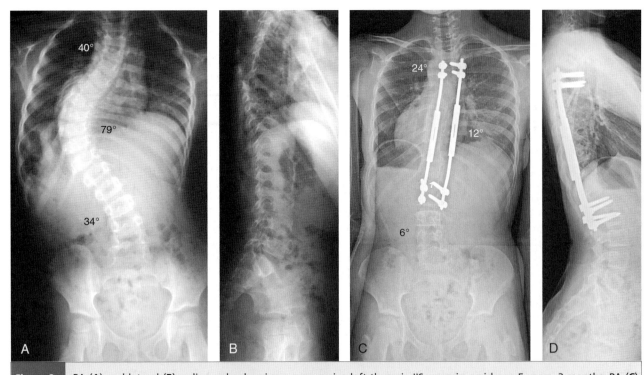

Figure 2 PA (A) and lateral (B) radiographs showing a progressive left thoracic JIS curve in a girl age 5 years, 2 months. PA (C) and lateral (D) radiographs showing excellent curve correction with continued lengthening 6 years after application of a posterior growing rod from T3 to L2.

sequential rod lengthening. The results of formal clinical studies have yet to be published.

The vertical expandable prosthetic titanium rib (VEPTR) is another recent growing-rod system. Implants that extend from rib to rib, from rib to spine, and/or from rib to pelvis are used to simultaneously control progressive juvenile spine deformity and expand the chest. Claw hooks are applied laterally to the ribs cranial to the curve, with caudal implants attached to the ribs, spine, or pelvis. The VEPTR originally was designed to promote chest wall expansion in patients with thoracic insufficiency syndrome secondary to fused ribs in congenital scoliosis. The use of the VEPTR in correcting and maintaining spine growth in early-onset scoliosis has been described in one study of 11 patients.[29]

Children with a severe scoliotic curve (larger than 80°) may benefit from 2 to 6 weeks of preoperative halo-gravity traction. This technique provides slow correction of severe spine deformity and pulmonary compromise. The patient is placed in upright halo-gravity traction with weight progressively added until 32% to 50% of body weight has been applied. The risk of neurologic deficits during the period of traction and the subsequent surgical correction can be reduced by increasing the amount of traction in small increments while the patient is awake.[30]

Spinal fusion may be considered for a patient with JIS who is at least 10 years old.[7,20] Combined anterior-posterior spinal fusion generally is performed to prevent the crankshaft phenomenon. Anterior release and/or fusion using an open or endoscopic technique can be combined with posterior fusion and instrumentation during one procedure. An attempt to minimize the number of fusion levels in a skeletally immature patient often leads to deformity progression cephalad or caudal to the instrumentation levels, requiring subsequent revision and extension of the fusion construct.[7]

Segmental bilateral pedicle screw fixation provides three-column stability but has not yet been proved to prevent crankshaft phenomenon in patients with JIS. Transpedicular three-column fixation was studied as a means of controlling the crankshaft phenomenon in an immature canine model. The use of pedicle screws led to a mechanical epiphysiodesis, thus limiting anterior column growth without supplemental anterior fixation or fusion.[31] Crankshaft deformity did not develop in two patients who underwent fusion with segmental hooks or screws before the peak height velocity phase.[17] Another, slightly larger study retrospectively reported that progressive crankshaft deformity (not requiring reoperation) developed in two of seven patients with JIS after posterior spinal fusion with segmental pedicle screw fixation.[32]

Growing-rod systems require repeated lengthening procedures, and therefore alternative techniques have been developed to modulate spine growth. Results have yet to be reported for patients with JIS.

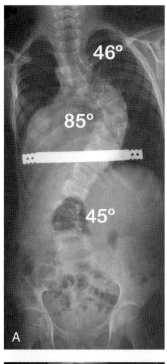

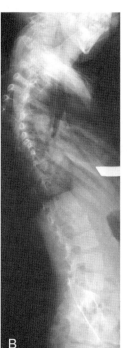

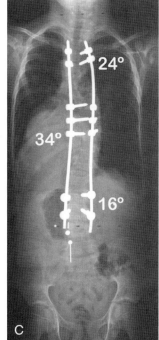

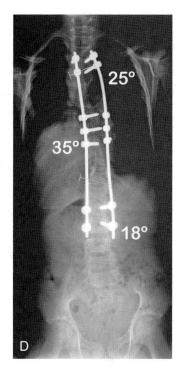

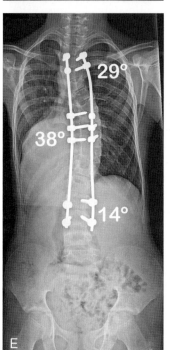

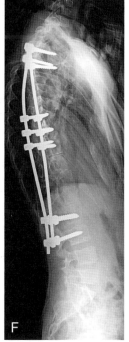

Figure 3 PA (**A**) and lateral (**B**) radiographs showing a progressive 85° thoracic JIS curve in a boy age 5 years, 11 months. The apical three vertebrae (T8-T10) were fixed with a Shilla construct and fused with pedicle screws; the cranial and caudal end segments (T3-T4 and L2-L3, respectively) were instrumented with screws but not fused, to allow the rod to slide through with continued growth. Spine lengthening on the construct and good realignment are seen on PA radiographs at 1-year follow-up (**C**), with 34° of correction; and at 2-year follow-up (**D**), with 35° of correction. PA (**E**) and lateral (**F**) radiographs at 4-year follow-up, when the correction in the thoracic region was 38°. The patient is asymptomatic, continues to grow off the construct, and has required only one surgical procedure.

Adolescent Idiopathic Scoliosis

Etiology

Extensive laboratory and clinical research has attempted to determine the etiology of idiopathic scoliosis. The role of melatonin in the development of human spine deformity was investigated after it was discovered that scoliosis develops in animals after pinealectomy, with subsequent melatonin dysfunction.[33] A defect of varying extent was found in the melatonin signal transduction pathway of all 41 patients undergoing surgery for AIS, and three distinct groups of patients were identified based on the extent of the melatonin signal transduction deficiency.[34] This information led to the first scoliosis screening assay, which is designed to identify children at high risk for AIS. The association of melatonin synthesis and signal transduction in AIS recently was challenged, however.[35]

5: The Pediatric Spine

A multitude of genetic factors may play a role in the development of spine deformity. A multiple-gene inheritance pattern was postulated based on examination of patients and their families, with identification of possible candidate regions on chromosomes 6, 9, 16, 17, and 19.[36] The goal of this research is to develop the ability to predict whether a patient's curve will progress and eventually require surgery.

Genetic markers may be usable for predicting the likelihood of progression to severe AIS. A genomewide association comparison study of 1,200 patients with severe AIS (defined as a curve larger than 40° in a skeletally immature patient or a curve larger than 50° in a skeletally mature patient) and 1,500 control subjects identified 30 genetic markers as useful prognostic markers for progression to severe AIS.[37] This research data set also was used to identify patients whose AIS curve of 25° to 40° may eventually require surgical intervention, despite standard bracing.[38] In 54 of 57 patients (95%), the 30-marker genetic panel was found to accurately calculate the probability that a curve would prove brace resistant, based on genetic profile, age, and curve magnitude at initial presentation. This study also reported on 500 patients with an initial curve smaller than 25° and found that only 9% of the curves predicted by genetic analysis to progress into the surgical range remained smaller than 25° at the final evaluation.[38] The panel has been expanded to more than 50 markers and is being marketed for clinical use.[39]

Genetic testing eventually may prove to be of clinical value. A patient with a mild curve and a low probability of progression based on genetic testing may be spared from multiple follow-up radiographs to monitor curve progression or from a long course of brace treatment. A patient with a similar curve pattern but a high probability of progression based on genetic testing can be closely monitored and counseled on the probable future need for surgical intervention.[40]

Epidemiology and Natural History

AIS is a structural lateral, rotated curvature of the spine beginning at puberty, for which no specific cause can be established. The diagnosis is confirmed by a Cobb angle measurement of at least 10° on erect long-cassette AP and lateral radiographs of the spine. An estimated 1% to 3% of children age 10 to 16 years have spine curvature of 10° or more, but only 0.15% to 0.3% have a curve of more than 30° that requires treatment. AIS is much more common in girls than in boys. This disparity increases with curve magnitude; the female-to-male ratio is 9:1 for curves larger than 40°.[41]

The natural history of AIS depends on several factors. The greatest risk of spine deformity progression is in patients who are skeletally immature and have a relatively large curve at presentation. Skeletal maturity can be evaluated using chronologic age, bone age on wrist radiographs, Risser grade, closure of the triradiate cartilage, onset of menses, and peak height velocity. The peak height velocity phase (occurring in girls ap-

proximately 6 to 12 months before menarche) is a more accurate predictor of skeletal maturity and spine growth than chronologic age or Risser grade.[42] However, sometimes peak height velocity can be determined only in retrospect. The risk of progression in a patient at Risser grade 0 or 1 who has a curve of 20° to 29° is approximately 70%; the comparable risk in a patient at Risser grade 2, 3, or 4 who has a curve of a similar magnitude is 25%.[43]

Long-term follow-up revealed that patients with AIS are at increased risk for back pain and degenerative disk disease. An increased incidence of degenerative lumbar disk changes was found in 127 patients with AIS 22 years after brace treatment, compared with matched control subjects.[44] At 50-year follow-up, 71 of 117 untreated patients with AIS (61%) had back pain, but 70% of those patients reported little physical impairment.[45]

Evaluation and Classification

AIS is a diagnosis of clinical and radiographic exclusion. Neuromuscular, genetic, and connective tissue disorders also are associated with scoliosis, and these pathologies must be ruled out by the patient's history and physical examination. The spine deformity initially is evaluated with standard PA and lateral standing long-cassette radiographs of the entire spine and pelvis. Standard Cobb angles are measured to assess the curve magnitude and the location of apices. The radiographic evaluation should exclude a congenital anomaly of the spine and an atypical curve pattern such as a left thoracic curve, a short-segment curve over four to six levels, apical thoracic kyphosis, or rapid progression. The presence of an atypical curve pattern suggests an underlying intraspinal anomaly and a need for MRI evaluation.[46] Routine MRI is unnecessary for a patient with a normal neurologic examination who is presumed to have AIS, even if the curve is 70° or greater.[46-48] MRI may be obtained if the patient has hyperreflexia, clonus, weakness, paresthesia, abnormal abdominal reflexes, or significant pain.[47,48]

The five-tier King-Moe surgical classification of thoracic curves was the gold standard for nearly 20 years.[49] However, the King-Moe system has only fair to poor interobserver and intraobserver reliability, and it does not include many of the AIS curve patterns.[50] The more recent Lenke classification is more comprehensive and includes both coronal and sagittal planes[51] (Figure 1). In the Lenke system, the curve with the largest Cobb angle is considered surgically structural and is called the major curve. Other, minor curves are categorized as surgically structural or nonstructural based on whether flexibility in the coronal plane is limited to 25°, as seen on a side-bending radiograph.

The lumbar coronal modifier is used to evaluate the apex of the lumbar curve in relation to the CSVL, which is drawn from the center of the sacrum directly vertical in the cephalad direction. In lumbar coronal modifier type A, the CSVL falls between the pedicles of the lumbar spine up to the stable vertebra, indicating the absence of a significant translation or rotation of the lumbar curve. In type B, the CSVL touches the apex of the lumbar curve, indicating moderate translation or rotation of the lumbar curve. In type C, the CSVL is distinctly medial to the apex of the lumbar curve. The thoracic sagittal modifier evaluates the sagittal alignment of the T5-T12 vertebrae based on the Cobb angle, as seen on a lateral radiograph: less than 10° (hypokyphotic), 10° to 40° (normal), or more than 40° (hyperkyphotic).

The Lenke curve classification is useful for describing AIS and, more importantly, for guiding surgical planning. All major and structural minor curves usually are included in the fusion, but nonstructural minor curves are not included. A type 1 (main thoracic) or type 5 (thoracolumbar/lumbar) curve can be treated with selective anterior or posterior instrumentation and fusion. A type 2 (double thoracic), type 3 (double major), type 4 (triple major), or type 6 (thoracolumbar/lumbar–main thoracic) curve should be treated with posterior spinal fusion.[51]

The classification systems are based only on the coronal and sagittal planes of the spine deformity. The rotational component of scoliosis-associated deformity is the subject of increasing attention, however. The use of torsion and axial rotation to evaluate spine deformity is being assessed in research studies.

A cluster analysis technique has recently been used to evaluate stereoradiographic measurements.[52,53] By using six anatomic landmarks for each vertebra, four morphologic parameters of a curve are identified: the Cobb angle, the apical vertebra, the axial rotation of the apical vertebra, and the orientation of the plane of maximum curvature with respect to the sagittal plane.[52] The plane of maximum curvature is defined as the plane passing through the vertebral body centers of the two end vertebrae and the apical vertebrae of each curve segment.[53] The deformity can be assessed in the coronal, sagittal, and axial planes using these parameters. This three-dimensional model may provide a better description of overall spine shape in scoliosis but cannot directly guide treatment decisions. As-yet unpublished long-term studies will further delineate the validity of three-dimensional assessments and their applicability to clinical practice.

Treatment
Observation
The traditional treatment of AIS is to observe a skeletally immature patient with a curve smaller than 25° or a skeletally mature patient with a curve smaller than 50°. Because a curve rarely progresses more rapidly than 1° per month, a 6-month follow-up evaluation generally is appropriate for a curve smaller than 20° to 25°.[51]

Orthotic Treatment
The purpose of bracing in patients with AIS is to apply an external force to the trunk to prevent or slow the progression of spine deformity during the adolescent growth phase. Bracing is recommended for a skeletally immature patient with a curve of approximately 25° to 50°. Daytime, nighttime, or full-time brace wear may be prescribed. The initial prescription usually is for full-time brace wear, but nighttime-only wear was effective in curves smaller than 35° and with an apex below T9.[10,54] A recent evidence-based review reported that skeletally immature patients younger than 15 years with a curve between 20° and 45° had similar rates of surgical intervention regardless of whether they were treated with a brace or observed.[43] A prospective study from Sweden found curve progression requiring brace wear in 20% of patients who were initially observed.[44] Surgical intervention was required in 10% of the patients who were only observed and none of the patients treated with bracing. These results can be interpreted to emphasize that brace treatment was successful or that 70% of patients who were only observed did not require surgical intervention.

The SpineCor dynamic corrective brace (SpineCorp, Chesterfield, Derbyshire, England) attempts to maintain a "curve-specific corrective movement" and thereby create neuromuscular integration through biofeedback.[10] The brace is worn 20 hours a day. One study reported deformity stabilization in 59.4% of patients using the SpineCor brace,[55] but no prospective, large-volume, long-term studies have evaluated its use.

Outcome studies of bracing in AIS may be limited by patient compliance. One study reported a mean compliance rate of only 47% with brace wear (range, 8% to 90%).[56] A relatively small prospective study of 34 patients sought to objectively evaluate the potential for brace wear to halt curve progression.[57] Based on a 90% criterion for high or low compliance with brace wear, the study found that only 1 of the 9 patients with high compliance (11%) had a significant curve progression; in contrast, 14 of 25 patients with low compliance (56%) had significant curve progression.

Physical Therapy
Some centers in the United States and Europe recommend specific training exercises for trunk rotational strength.[13] However, there is no clear evidence as to the long-term efficacy of physical therapy designed to halt or correct spine deformity.

Surgical Treatment
Methods of controlling spine deformity progression without fusion are being investigated. The principles of lower extremity physeal stapling using nitinol staples (which are open when cool but crimp when warmed in the body) have been applied to convex disk stapling. The procedure is called vertebral body stapling.[58] A thoracoscopic technique is used for placing cooled nitinol staples to span each disk space on the convexity of the spine deformity. As they warm, the tines of the staples achieve bony purchase by crimping to a 70° to 80° angle relative to the base. The staples temporarily arrest

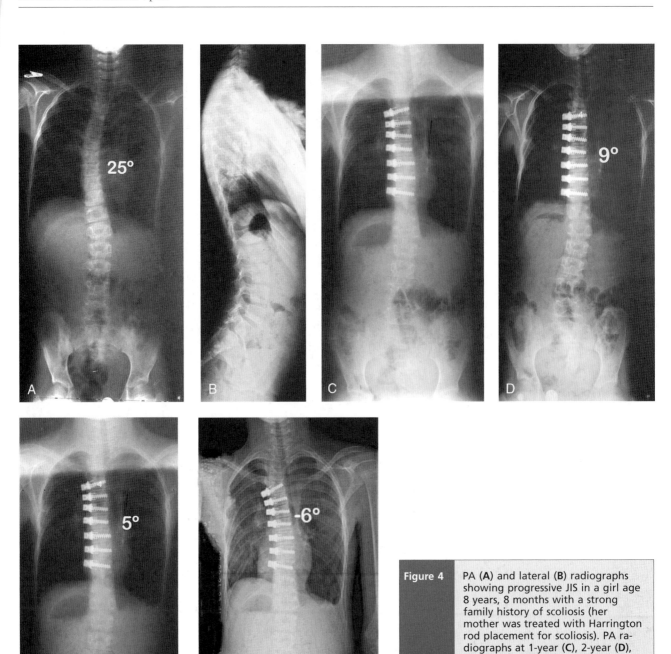

Figure 4 PA (**A**) and lateral (**B**) radiographs showing progressive JIS in a girl age 8 years, 8 months with a strong family history of scoliosis (her mother was treated with Harrington rod placement for scoliosis). PA radiographs at 1-year (**C**), 2-year (**D**), 3-year (**E**), and 4-year (**F**) follow-up after placement of a polypropylene tether from T4 to T10. Full correction of the scoliosis can be seen in (**F**), with slight overcorrection resulting in a –6° deformity in the opposite direction. The patient maintained excellent thoracic sagittal alignment during growth.

spine growth along the convexity of the curve and create the potential for straightening the overall alignment by allowing continued growth of the concavity. Only 1 of 21 patients who underwent vertebral body stapling had progression to a curve greater than 50°, subsequently requiring formal fusion.[58] A 2-year follow-up study of 28 patients found that thoracic curves smaller than 35° were most successfully treated with vertebral body stapling and that correction was inadequately maintained in thoracic curves greater than 35°.[59]

Anterior tethering is another developing technology for systematically controlling spine growth. To restrict motion on the spine convexity to less than 5° without affecting the disk space, single screws are placed anteriorly in the vertebral bodies, and a polypropylene tether

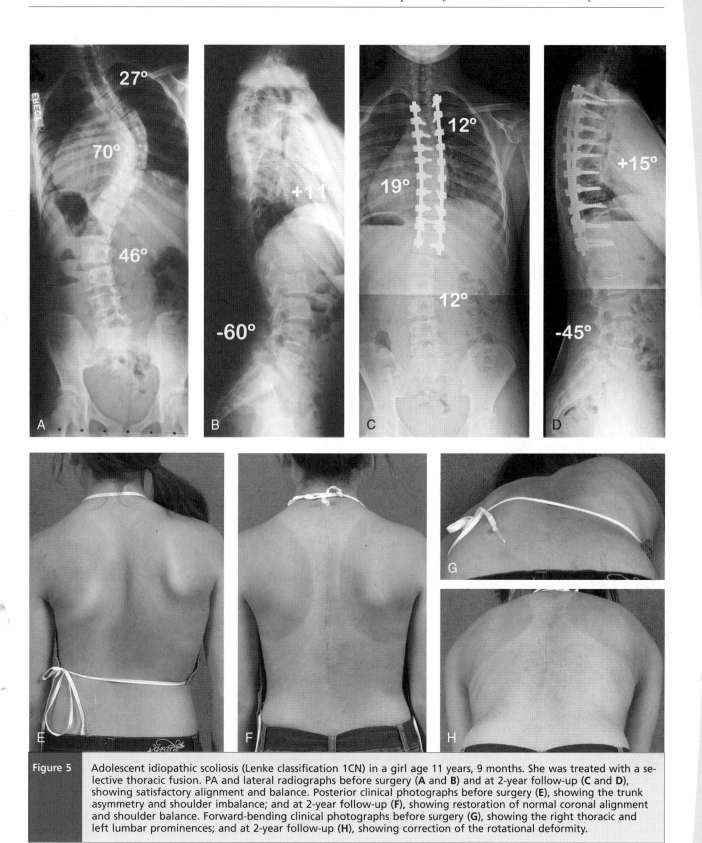

Figure 5 Adolescent idiopathic scoliosis (Lenke classification 1CN) in a girl age 11 years, 9 months. She was treated with a selective thoracic fusion. PA and lateral radiographs before surgery (**A** and **B**) and at 2-year follow-up (**C** and **D**), showing satisfactory alignment and balance. Posterior clinical photographs before surgery (**E**), showing the trunk asymmetry and shoulder imbalance; and at 2-year follow-up (**F**), showing restoration of normal coronal alignment and shoulder balance. Forward-bending clinical photographs before surgery (**G**), showing the right thoracic and left lumbar prominences; and at 2-year follow-up (**H**), showing correction of the rotational deformity.

is attached to the screw heads A goat-model study of experimental scoliosis found that the coronal deformity was slightly improved with the use of an anterior tether construct, but the sagittal plane deformity slightly progressed. Clinical validation of this technique has been reported only in one case study[60] (Figure 4).

Anterior instrumentation and fusion can be performed for a Lenke type 1 (main thoracic) or type 5

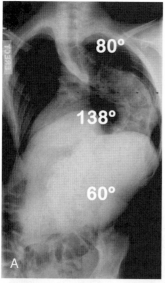
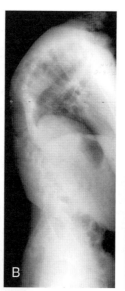
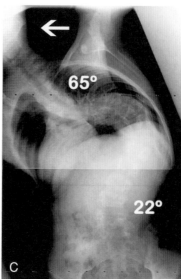
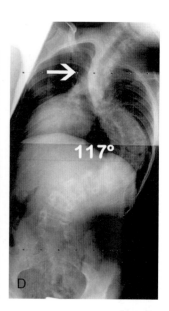

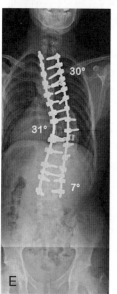
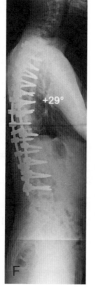

Figure 6   PA (**A**), lateral (**B**), left supine-bending (**C**), and right supine-bending (**D**) radiographs showing severe 138° right thoracic idiopathic scoliosis (Lenke classification 4C+) in a boy age 16 years, 5 months. The patient also had a rigid structural proximal thoracic curve of 80°, with minimal side-bending correction to 65°, as seen in **C**. He underwent a posterior reconstruction from T2 to L4 with an apical T11 vertebral column resection. PA (**E**) and lateral (**F**) radiographs showing correction of the main thoracic curve to 31°, with excellent coronal and sagittal alignment and balance, at 2-year follow-up. No thoracoplasty was performed during the reconstruction; all truncal realignment occurred as a result of the spine realignment. (*Continued on page 11.*)

(thoracolumbar/lumbar) AIS deformity. Indications for treating a type 1 curve anteriorly are a normokyphotic thoracic sagittal modifier and a type C lumbar coronal modifier, which may lead to spontaneous lumbar curve correction. In a type 5 curve, an instrumented anterior fusion from the upper to the lower end vertebrae fuses all convex disks with a single or dual rod construct.[51] Anterior fusion alone might decrease the number of levels requiring fusion and reduce the risk of crankshaft deformity in a skeletally immature patient, compared with posterior spinal fusion without apical pedicle screws.

Multiple studies found that violation of the chest wall for anterior fusion causes a temporary decline in pulmonary function. Two years after thoracotomy and anterior fusion, patients' pulmonary function was slightly depressed or had returned to its baseline level. However, patients treated with posterior-only fusion had a significant postoperative improvement in pulmonary function.[61] Patients had a significant decline in pulmonary function 2 years after open thoracotomy and anterior fusion. In contrast, anterior fusion through a thoracoabdominal approach had no adverse effect on pulmonary function in patients with a type 5 curve at 2-year follow-up.[62]

Thoracoscopic anterior instrumentation techniques were developed in an effort to reduce the pulmonary insult of an open thoracotomy. Patients who underwent thoracoscopic anterior fusion had a return to baseline pulmonary function at 1-year follow-up.[63] The radiographic results, clinical outcome, and complication rate of patients who underwent thoracoscopic fusion compared favorably with those of patients who underwent posterior fusion with an all-pedicle screw construct.[64] The thoracoscopically treated patients had significantly fewer fusion levels than the patients treated with poste-

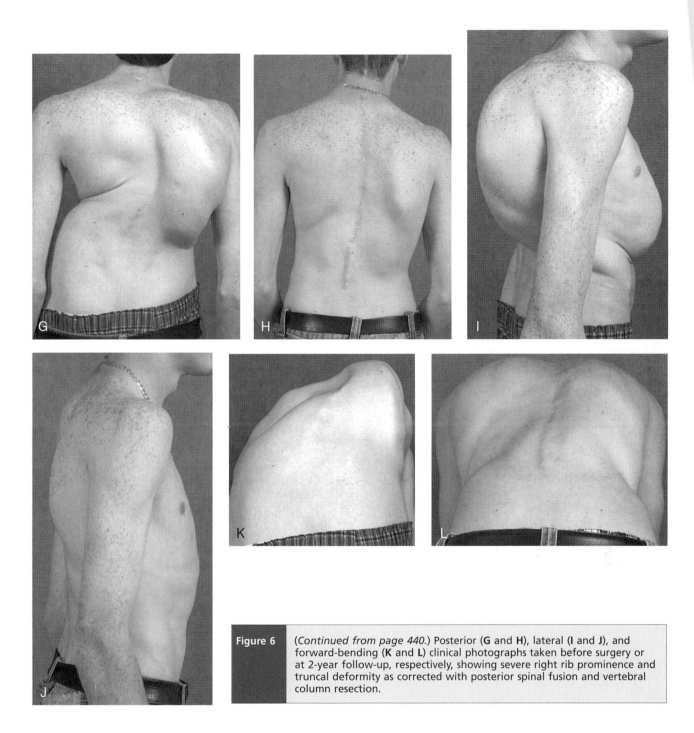

Figure 6 (*Continued from page 440.*) Posterior (**G** and **H**), lateral (**I** and **J**), and forward-bending (**K** and **L**) clinical photographs taken before surgery or at 2-year follow-up, respectively, showing severe right rib prominence and truncal deformity as corrected with posterior spinal fusion and vertebral column resection.

rior fusion (5.9 or 8.9 levels, respectively), with less intraoperative blood loss. However, a longer surgical time was required for the thoracoscopic approach, and these patients had diminished pulmonary function improvement at 2-year follow-up.[64] Another study found stable pulmonary function at 5-year follow-up after thoracoscopic surgery.[65] However, the treatment was unsuccessful in 12% of patients, and revision to a posterior spinal fusion was required.[65] The popularity of stand-alone thoracoscopic procedures for spine deformity has declined because of the potential for treatment

failure, the pulmonary insult, and the steep surgical learning curve, as well as the advent of strong three-column fixation with pedicle screw constructs.

The mainstay of surgical treatment for AIS remains posterior instrumentation and fusion rather than anterior fusion. Posterior spinal fusion can be performed for all types of AIS curves. Posterior surgical techniques have progressed from Harrington rod instrumentation to the current all–pedicle screw constructs and hybrid hook-and-screw constructs. Pedicle screws offer more powerful three-column vertebral fixation than hooks,

5: The Pediatric Spine

allowing greater corrective forces and vertebral derotation. A comparative analysis found significantly better major curve correction and pulmonary function without neurologic complications when all–pedicle screw instrumentation was used, compared with hybrid constructs.[66] Correction rates for AIS curves as large as 70° to 100° were found to be similar regardless of whether a posterior-only all–pedicle screw construct or a combined anterior-posterior procedure was used.[67] Pedicle screw insertion was safe and effective even in curves larger than 90°.[68]

Although all–pedicle screw constructs have been criticized because of their cost, a recent study comparing anterior-posterior to posterior-only surgery for AIS curves of 70° to 100° found no significant difference in total cost or radiographic outcome.[69] The rate of pseudarthrosis and the need for revision surgery were found to be significantly lower when an all–pedicle screw construct was used, compared with a hook or hybrid construct.[70]

Direct vertebral rotation is an adjuvant intraoperative technique to improve curve correction in all three planes. A rotational force is transmitted through the pedicle screws from the posterior pedicle to the anterior vertebral body. The transverse rotation is corrected using long lever-arm screw derotators fixed to both the concave and convex sides. The rotational torque is thereby distributed among several pedicles to prevent pedicle breakage.[71] In a study of eight patients with AIS, those treated with direct vertebral rotation had significantly better sagittal and coronal curve correction as well as axial derotation than those treated with standard rod derotation.[71] The distal fusion levels sometimes could be spared because correction of the thoracic axial rotation led the compensatory lumbar curve to unwind and often to spontaneously correct (Figure 5). Patients who underwent direct vertebral rotation had significantly better three-dimensional correction of an uninstrumented lumbar curve than patients who underwent standard rod derotation.

The correction of severe AIS deformities through a posterior-only approach has been expanded by the use of several types of osteotomies along with pedicle screw fixation. A Smith-Petersen osteotomy involves resection of the superior and inferior articular processes and midline ligaments. A pedicle subtraction osteotomy incorporates a transpedicular vertebral wedge resection extending from the posterior elements through the pedicles and into the anterior cortex of the vertebral body. These maneuvers usually are efficacious for significant sagittal plane correction. Vertebral column resection, which involves the removal of one or more entire vertebrae via a posterior approach, can provide significant coronal, sagittal, and axial curve correction. Although technically challenging, this procedure is a safe and effective means of providing dramatic curve correction in severe spine deformity, possibly obviating the need for a circumferential approach[72] (Figure 6).

Summary

JIS and AIS are common pediatric spine deformities. Both are diagnoses of exclusion based on the absence of any other clinical or radiographic abnormality. Nonsurgical and surgical treatments continue to evolve based on clinical research. The goal of surgery remains to perform the shortest possible spinal fusion to achieve an optimal spine balance, with stability over time, no complications, and an optimal patient-perceived outcome.

Annotated References

1. Ponseti IV, Friedman B: Prognosis in idiopathic scoliosis. *J Bone Joint Surg Am* 1950;32(2):381-395.

2. Pehrsson K, Larsson S, Oden A, Nachemson A: Long-term follow-up of patients with untreated scoliosis: A study of mortality, causes of death, and symptoms. *Spine (Phila Pa 1976)* 1992;17(9):1091-1096.

3. Tolo VT, Gillespie R: The characteristics of juvenile idiopathic scoliosis and results of its treatment. *J Bone Joint Surg Br* 1978;60(2):181-188.

4. Mannherz RE, Betz RR, Clancy M, Steel HH: Juvenile idiopathic scoliosis followed to skeletal maturity. *Spine (Phila Pa 1976)* 1988;13(10):1087-1090.

5. Mehta MH: The rib-vertebra angle in the early diagnosis between resolving and progressive infantile scoliosis. *J Bone Joint Surg Br* 1972;54(2):230-243.

6. Evans SC, Edgar MA, Hall-Craggs MA, Powell MP, Taylor BA, Noordeen HH: MRI of 'idiopathic' juvenile scoliosis: A prospective study. *J Bone Joint Surg Br* 1996;78(2):314-317.

7. Lenke LG, Dobbs MB: Management of juvenile idiopathic scoliosis. *J Bone Joint Surg Am* 2007;89(Suppl 1): 55-63.

   The natural history, epidemiology, classification, and treatment of JIS are discussed.

8. Dobbs MB, Weinstein SL: Infantile and juvenile scoliosis. *Orthop Clin North Am* 1999;30(3):331-341, vii.

9. Charles YP, Daures JP, de Rosa V, Diméglio A: Progression risk of idiopathic juvenile scoliosis during pubertal growth. *Spine (Phila Pa 1976)* 2006;31(17):1933-1942.

   Retrospective evaluation of 205 patients with JIS at skeletal maturity found that the curve pattern (primary thoracic), the Cobb angle at onset (larger than 30°), and the curve progression velocity (greater than 10° per year) were strong predictors of an eventual need for surgery. Level of evidence: IV.

10. Schiller JR, Thakur NA, Eberson CP: Brace management in adolescent idiopathic scoliosis. *Clin Orthop Relat Res* 2010;468(3):670-678.

Types of braces are reviewed, with the indications and efficacy of different brace treatment regimens for AIS.

11. Kahanovitz N, Levine DB, Lardone J: The part-time Milwaukee brace treatment of juvenile idiopathic scoliosis: Long-term follow-up. *Clin Orthop Relat Res* 1982; 167:145-151.

12. Jarvis J, Garbedian S, Swamy G: Juvenile idiopathic scoliosis: The effectiveness of part-time bracing. *Spine (Phila Pa 1976)* 2008;33(10):1074-1078.

A retrospective review of nighttime brace treatment in 34 patients with JIS found a 70% success rate for curves smaller than 45°, most significantly in patients with relatively high in-brace radiographic correction. Level of evidence: IV.

13. McIntire KL, Asher MA, Burton DC, Liu W: Treatment of adolescent idiopathic scoliosis with quantified trunk rotational strength training: A pilot study. *J Spinal Disord Tech* 2008;21(5):349-358.

In a prospective clinical study of 15 patients with AIS, trunk rotational strength training led to stabilization of curves of 20° to 40° at 8-month follow-up, but significant curve progression was noted at 24 months. Exercises were ineffective for curves larger than 50° to 60°. Level of evidence: III.

14. Winter RB: Scoliosis and spinal growth. *Orthop Rev* 1977;6:17-20.

15. Dimeglio A: Growth of the spine before age 5 years. *J Pediatr Orthop B* 1992;1(2):102-107.

16. Dubousset J, Herring JA, Shufflebarger H: The crankshaft phenomenon. *J Pediatr Orthop* 1989;9(5):541-550.

17. Burton DC, Asher MA, Lai SM: Scoliosis correction maintenance in skeletally immature patients with idiopathic scoliosis: Is anterior fusion really necessary? *Spine (Phila Pa 1976)* 2000;25(1):61-68.

18. Sanders JO, Little DG, Richards BS: Prediction of the crankshaft phenomenon by peak height velocity. *Spine (Phila Pa 1976)* 1997;22(12):1352-1357.

19. Sanders JO, Herring JA, Browne RH: Posterior arthrodesis and instrumentation in the immature (Risser-grade-0) spine in idiopathic scoliosis. *J Bone Joint Surg Am* 1995;77(1):39-45.

20. Yang JS, McElroy MJ, Akbarnia BA, et al: Growing rods for spinal deformity: Characterizing consensus and variation in current use. *J Pediatr Orthop* 2010;30(3):264-270.

In a multi-institution survey, surgeons in the Growing Spine Study Group recommended the use of growing rods for curves larger than 60° in patients younger than 10 years.

21. Fisk JR, Peterson HA, Laughlin R, Lutz R: Spontaneous fusion in scoliosis after instrumentation without arthrodesis. *J Pediatr Orthop* 1995;15(2):182-186.

22. Mahar AT, Bagheri R, Oka R, Kostial P, Akbarnia BA: Biomechanical comparison of different anchors (foundations) for the pediatric dual growing rod technique. *Spine J* 2008;8(6):933-939.

In vitro laboratory investigation of fixation points for dual growing rods in immature porcine spines found that a foundation of four pedicle screws in two adjacent vertebrae provided the strongest construct in pullout testing.

23. Akbarnia BA, Marks DS, Boachie-Adjei O, Thompson AG, Asher MA: Dual growing rod technique for the treatment of progressive early-onset scoliosis: A multicenter study. *Spine (Phila Pa 1976)* 2005;30(17, suppl):S46-S57.

Retrospective review of early-onset scoliosis in 23 patients found that dual growing rods without apical fusion provided the best curve correction. Patients with an apical fusion had curve stiffening, crankshaft deformity, and a higher complication rate at 2-year follow-up. Level of evidence: IV.

24. Akbarnia BA, Breakwell LM, Marks DS, et al: Dual growing rod technique followed for three to eleven years until final fusion: The effect of frequency of lengthening. *Spine (Phila Pa 1976)* 2008;33(9):984-990.

Retrospective review of 13 patients treated with dual growing rods found that average spine growth was significantly greater with lengthening at an interval of less than 6 months (1.8 cm per year) rather than a longer interval (1.0 cm per year). Level of evidence: IV.

25. McCarthy RE, Sucato D, Turner JL, Zhang H, Henson MA, McCarthy K: Shilla growing rods in a caprine animal model: A pilot study. *Clin Orthop Relat Res* 2010;468(3):705-710.

Shilla growing rods were implanted in 11 goats for 6 months. All spines grew an average of 48 mm at both the thoracic and lumbar ends of the construct, with no instrumentation failures.

26. Takaso M, Moriya H, Kitahara H, et al: New remote-controlled growing-rod spinal instrumentation possibly applicable for scoliosis in young children. *J Orthop Sci* 1998;3(6):336-340.

27. Akbarnia BA, Mundis GM, Salari P, Yaszay B: Innovation in growing rod technique: Study of safety and efficacy of remotely expandable rod in animal model. *46th Annual Meeting and Course*. Milwaukee, WI, Scoliosis Research Society, 2010, paper 28. http://www.srs.org. Accessed January 24, 2011.

Remotely expandable growing rods were implanted into six pigs, with three control subjects. The implants were effectively distracted using an external magnet, without significant complications, thus negating the need for standard invasive lengthening procedures.

28. Soubeiran A, Miladi L, Dubousset J: A technical report on the Phenix M rod, an expandable rod linkable to the spine, ribs or the pelvis and controllable at home by hand through the skin with a palm size permanent magnet for the treatment of severe early onset scoliosis. *2nd*

5: The Pediatric Spine

Annual Meeting of the International Congress on Early Onset Scoliosis. Wheaton, IL, Growing Spine Meeting, 2008, paper 23. http://www.growingspine.org. Accessed January 24, 2011.

The Phenix M rod (an expandable rod linked to the spine, ribs, and/or pelvis) was implanted into 27 patients with severe early-onset scoliosis. The device was sequentially lengthened by parents at home, using a handheld magnet. The maximum total lengthening achieved with the construct was 60 mm over 3 years.

29. Samdani AF, Ranade A, Dolch HJ, et al: Bilateral use of the vertical expandable prosthetic titanium rib attached to the pelvis: A novel treatment for scoliosis in the growing spine. *J Neurosurg Spine* 2009;10(4):287-292.

A retrospective review of bilateral VEPTR treatment from rib to pelvis in 11 patients with early-onset scoliosis found an average curve correction from 81.7° to 58°, with an average spine growth of 6.3 cm.

30. Rinella A, Lenke L, Whitaker C, et al: Perioperative halo-gravity traction in the treatment of severe scoliosis and kyphosis. *Spine (Phila Pa 1976)* 2005;30(4):475-482.

Retrospective review of preoperative halo-gravity traction (32% to 50% of body weight) over two 6-week periods in 33 patients with severe scoliosis found a decreased risk of postoperative neurologic complications, with subsequent improvement in surgical correction. Level of evidence: IV.

31. Kioschos HC, Asher MA, Lark RG, Harner EJ: Overpowering the crankshaft mechanism: The effect of posterior spinal fusion with and without stiff transpedicular fixation on anterior spinal column growth in immature canines. *Spine (Phila Pa 1976)* 1996;21(10):1168-1173.

32. Sarlak AY, Atmaca H, Buluç L, Tosun B, Musaoğlu R: Juvenile idiopathic scoliosis treated with posterior arthrodesis and segmental pedicle screw instrumentation before the age of 9 years: A 5-year follow-up. *Scoliosis* 2009;4:1-11.

A retrospective review of seven patients with JIS (Risser grade 0) treated with posterior segmental pedicle screw instrumentation found that the average curve correction was 57%, with no reported coronal decompensation at an average 5-year follow-up. Level of evidence: IV.

33. Machida M, Dubousset J, Imamura Y, Iwaya T, Yamada T, Kimura J: An experimental study in chickens for the pathogenesis of idiopathic scoliosis. *Spine (Phila Pa 1976)* 1993;18(12):1609-1615.

34. Moreau A, Wang DS, Forget S, et al: Melatonin signaling dysfunction in adolescent idiopathic scoliosis. *Spine (Phila Pa 1976)* 2004;29(16):1772-1781.

35. Nelson LM, Ward K, Ogilvie JW: Genetic variants in melatonin synthesis and signaling pathway are not associated with adolescent idiopathic scoliosis. *Spine (Phila Pa 1976)* 2011;36(1):37-40.

Genetic analysis of 589 patients with AIS and 1,533 control subjects revealed no significant difference in melatonin synthesis or signaling pathways.

36. Miller NH, Justice CM, Marosy B, et al: Identification of candidate regions for familial idiopathic scoliosis. *Spine (Phila Pa 1976)* 2005;30(10):1181-1187.

Genomic screening and statistical linkage analysis of 202 families having multiple members with idiopathic scoliosis led to identification of regions on chromosomes 6, 9, 16, and 17 as the strongest candidates for idiopathic scoliosis linkage.

37. Ward K, Nelson LM, Chettier R, Braun J, Ogilvie J: Genetic profile predicts curve progression in adolescent idiopathic scoliosis. *43rd Annual Meeting and Course.* Milwaukee, WI, Scoliosis Research Society, 2008, paper 4. http://www.srs.org. Accessed January 24, 2011.

A genomewide association study compared 1,200 patients with severe AIS (defined as a curve larger than 40° in a skeletally immature patient or larger than 50° in a skeletally mature patient) with 1,500 control subjects. Thirty genetic markers were identified as useful prognostic markers for progression to severe AIS. Level of evidence: I.

38. Ogilvie JW, Nelson LM, Chettier R, Smith-Berry T, Ward K: Predicting brace-resistant adolescent idiopathic scoliosis. *43rd Annual Meeting and Course.* Milwaukee, WI, Scoliosis Research Society, 2008, paper 6. http://www.srs.org. Accessed January 24, 2011.

A 30-marker genetic panel was used to accurately predict whether AIS curves between 25° and 40° would progress into the surgical range in 54 of 57 patients (95%). The genetic panel also was 91% accurate in predicting whether AIS curves initially measuring less than 25° in 500 patients would progress at final evaluation. Level of evidence: I.

39. Ward K, Ogilvie JW, Singleton MV, Chettier R, Engler G, Nelson LM: Validation of DNA-based prognostic testing to predict spinal curve progression in adolescent idiopathic scoliosis. *Spine (Phila Pa 1976)* 2010;35(25):E1455-E1464.

A 53-marker genetic panel was used to evaluate the risk of curve progression in 700 Caucasian patients with AIS. Patients were identified as being at low, intermediate, or high risk for curve progression based on the scoring system. Level of evidence: I.

40. Ogilvie JW: Update on prognostic genetic testing in adolescent idiopathic scoliosis (AIS). *J Pediatr Orthop* 2011;31(1, suppl):S46-S48.

This review article examined the innovations in genetic testing implemented in an effort to predict curve progression in patients with AIS. Level of evidence: III.

41. Weinstein SL, Dolan LA, Cheng JC, Danielsson A, Morcuende JA: Adolescent idiopathic scoliosis. *Lancet* 2008;371(9623):1527-1537.

The etiology, natural history, and nonsurgical and surgical treatment of AIS are reviewed. Level of evidence: III.

42. Little DG, Song KM, Katz D, Herring JA: Relationship of peak height velocity to other maturity indicators in idiopathic scoliosis in girls. *J Bone Joint Surg Am* 2000;82(5):685-693.

43. Dolan LA, Weinstein SL: Surgical rates after observation and bracing for adolescent idiopathic scoliosis: An evidence-based review. *Spine (Phila Pa 1976)* 2007; 32(19, suppl):S91-S100.

    A meta-analysis of 18 level III and IV studies compared rates of surgery for patients with AIS after brace treatment or observation (22% or 23%, respectively) and found that neither treatment had a clear advantage. Level of evidence: III.

44. Danielsson AJ, Hasserius R, Ohlin A, Nachemson AL: A prospective study of brace treatment versus observation alone in adolescent idiopathic scoliosis: A follow-up mean of 16 years after maturity. *Spine (Phila Pa 1976)* 2007;32(20):2198-2207.

    A prospective study of 106 patients with AIS who were treated with bracing or observation found that none of the patients treated with bracing had required surgery at a mean 16-year follow-up. Six of the 65 patients who were observed (10%) eventually required surgical correction. Level of evidence: II.

45. Weinstein SL, Dolan LA, Spratt KF, Peterson KK, Spoonamore MJ, Ponseti IV: Health and function of patients with untreated idiopathic scoliosis: A 50-year natural history study. *JAMA* 2003;289(5):559-567.

46. O'Brien MF, Lenke LG, Bridwell KH, Blanke K, Baldus C: Preoperative spinal canal investigation in adolescent idiopathic scoliosis curves > or = 70 degrees. *Spine (Phila Pa 1976)* 1994;19(14):1606-1610.

47. Do T, Fras C, Burke S, Widmann RF, Rawlins B, Boachie-Adjei O: Clinical value of routine preoperative magnetic resonance imaging in adolescent idiopathic scoliosis: A prospective study of three hundred and twenty-seven patients. *J Bone Joint Surg Am* 2001; 83(4):577-579.

48. Davids JR, Chamberlin E, Blackhurst DW: Indications for magnetic resonance imaging in presumed adolescent idiopathic scoliosis. *J Bone Joint Surg Am* 2004;86(10): 2187-2195.

49. King HA, Moe JH, Bradford DS, Winter RB: The selection of fusion levels in thoracic idiopathic scoliosis. *J Bone Joint Surg Am* 1983;65(9):1302-1313.

50. Richards BS, Sucato DJ, Konigsberg DE, Ouellet JA: Comparison of reliability between the Lenke and King classification systems for adolescent idiopathic scoliosis using radiographs that were not premeasured. *Spine (Phila Pa 1976)* 2003;28(11):1148-1157.

51. Lenke LG, Betz RR, Harms J, et al: Adolescent idiopathic scoliosis: A new classification to determine extent of spinal arthrodesis. *J Bone Joint Surg Am* 2001;83(8): 1169-1181.

52. Sangole AP, Aubin CE, Labelle H, et al: Three-dimensional classification of thoracic scoliotic curves. *Spine (Phila Pa 1976)* 2009;34(1):91-99.

    Three-dimensional spine reconstructions were used in a radiographic review of thoracic curves in 172 patients to identify two subgroups of curves initially classified as Lenke type I. Not all of these thoracic curves were hypokyphotic. Level of evidence: III.

53. Stokes IA, Sangole AP, Aubin CE: Classification of scoliosis deformity three-dimensional spinal shape by cluster analysis. *Spine (Phila Pa 1976)* 2009;34(6):584-590.

    Cluster analysis was used to classify curves based on three-dimensional shape in 110 patients who underwent radiography of the spine over a 12-year period. No treatment strategies were provided. Level of evidence: III.

54. D'Amato CR, Griggs S, McCoy B: Nighttime bracing with the Providence brace in adolescent girls with idiopathic scoliosis. *Spine (Phila Pa 1976)* 2001;26(18): 2006-2012.

55. Coillard C, Vachon V, Circo AB, Beauséjour M, Rivard CH: Effectiveness of the SpineCor brace based on the new standardized criteria proposed by the scoliosis research society for adolescent idiopathic scoliosis. *J Pediatr Orthop* 2007;27(4):375-379.

    A prospective observational study of SpineCor brace treatment for AIS found that 59.4% of patients had curve stabilization. Level of evidence: II.

56. Morton A, Riddle R, Buchanan R, Katz D, Birch J: Accuracy in the prediction and estimation of adherence to bracewear before and during treatment of adolescent idiopathic scoliosis. *J Pediatr Orthop* 2008;28(3):336-341.

    Actual brace compliance was prospectively studied in 124 patients with AIS who were treated with a Boston brace equipped with a temperature sensor. Patients were found to wear the brace an average of 47% of the prescribed time, compared with a patient-estimated average of 75%.

57. Rahman T, Bowen JR, Takemitsu M, Scott C: The association between brace compliance and outcome for patients with idiopathic scoliosis. *J Pediatr Orthop* 2005; 25(4):420-422.

    Embedded temperature sensors were used in a prospective study of the relationship between brace compliance (defined as more or less than 90%) and curve progression. In patients with high compliance, 11% of curves progressed; in patients with low compliance, 56% of curves progressed. Level of evidence: II.

58. Betz RR, Kim J, D'Andrea LP, Mulcahey MJ, Balsara RK, Clements DH: An innovative technique of vertebral body stapling for the treatment of patients with adolescent idiopathic scoliosis: A feasibility, safety, and utility study. *Spine (Phila Pa 1976)* 2003;28(20):S255-S265.

59. Betz RR, Ranade A, Samdani AF, et al: Vertebral body stapling: A fusionless treatment option for a growing child with moderate idiopathic scoliosis. *Spine (Phila Pa 1976)* 2010;35(2):169-176.

    A retrospective review of 28 patients with AIS who were treated with vertebral body stapling found a success rate of 87% for lumbar curves and 79% for thoracic curves

5: The Pediatric Spine

smaller than 35° at a minimum 2-year follow-up. Vertebral stapling alone did not sufficiently halt progression of preoperative thoracic curves larger than 35°.

60. Crawford CH III, Lenke LG: Growth modulation by means of anterior tethering resulting in progressive correction of juvenile idiopathic scoliosis: A case report. *J Bone Joint Surg Am* 2010;92(1):202-209.

An 8.4-year-old patient with a 40° thoracic JIS curve underwent an anterior tethering procedure using vertebral body screws connected by a 4.5-mm diameter polypropylene tether on the curve convexity. Curve correction was achieved and maintained at 48-month follow-up, with 2 cm of growth through the segment alone.

61. Vedantam R, Lenke LG, Bridwell KH, Haas J, Linville DA: A prospective evaluation of pulmonary function in patients with adolescent idiopathic scoliosis relative to the surgical approach used for spinal arthrodesis. *Spine (Phila Pa 1976)* 2000;25(1):82-90.

62. Kim YJ, Lenke LG, Bridwell KH, Cheh G, Sides B, Whorton J: Prospective pulmonary function comparison of anterior spinal fusion in adolescent idiopathic scoliosis: Thoracotomy versus thoracoabdominal approach. *Spine (Phila Pa 1976)* 2008;33(10):1055-1060.

A prospective study of anterior spinal fusion in 119 patients with AIS found that open thoracotomy resulted in a significant decrease in pulmonary function at 2-year follow-up but that a thoracoabdominal approach did not decrease pulmonary function. Level of evidence: II.

63. Yaszay B, Jazayeri R, Lonner B: The effect of surgical approaches on pulmonary function in adolescent idiopathic scoliosis. *J Spinal Disord Tech* 2009;22(4):278-283.

A retrospective review of pulmonary function in 61 patients with AIS found that pulmonary function returned to baseline within 3 months of posterior thoracoplasty or open anterior lumbar fusion and within 1 year of video-assisted thoracoscopic anterior-only surgery. Level of evidence: IV.

64. Lonner BS, Auerbach JD, Estreicher M, Milby AH, Kean KE: Video-assisted thoracoscopic spinal fusion compared with posterior spinal fusion with thoracic pedicle screws for thoracic adolescent idiopathic scoliosis. *J Bone Joint Surg Am* 2009;91(2):398-408.

A matched-pair analysis of 34 consecutive patients with AIS who were treated with video-assisted thoracoscopic surgery or traditional posterior spinal fusion found that those treated with video-assisted thoracoscopic surgery had less blood loss and fewer total fusion levels but longer surgical time, less improvement in pulmonary function, and slightly less curve correction. Level of evidence: III.

65. Newton PO, Upasani VV, Lhamby J, Ugrinow VL, Pawelek JB, Bastrom TP: Surgical treatment of main thoracic scoliosis with thoracoscopic anterior instrumentation: Surgical technique. *J Bone Joint Surg Am* 2009;91(suppl 2):233-248.

In a prospective study, 41 patients were treated with anterior-only fusion through a thoracoscopic approach. Fusion was identified at 97% of the instrumented segments, but 3 patients (12% of the 25 patients available for 5-year follow-up) required subsequent posterior fusion because of instrumentation failure. Level of evidence: III.

66. Kim YJ, Lenke LG, Kim J, et al: Comparative analysis of pedicle screw versus hybrid instrumentation in posterior spinal fusion of adolescent idiopathic scoliosis. *Spine (Phila Pa 1976)* 2006;31(3):291-298.

In a retrospective matched-cohort study, 58 patients with AIS were treated using pedicle screw instrumentation or hybrid posterior instrumentation and fusion. At 2-year follow-up, those treated using pedicle screws had better average curve correction and pulmonary function than those who received the hybrid treatment. Level of evidence: III.

67. Luhmann SJ, Lenke LG, Kim YJ, Bridwell KH, Schootman M: Thoracic adolescent idiopathic scoliosis curves between 70 degrees and 100 degrees: Is anterior release necessary? *Spine (Phila Pa 1976)* 2005;30(18):2061-2067.

A retrospective review of 84 patients with AIS found that pedicle screw–only and anterior-posterior fusion procedures led to similar correction rates in severe curves (larger than 70°). Level of evidence: III.

68. Kuklo TR, Lenke LG, O'Brien MF, Lehman RA Jr, Polly DW Jr, Schroeder TM: Accuracy and efficacy of thoracic pedicle screws in curves more than 90 degrees. *Spine (Phila Pa 1976)* 2005;30(2):222-226.

Twenty patients with a curve larger than 90° were treated using a posterior-only pedicle screw construct. Retrospective review found an average curve correction of 68% at 2-year follow-up. Two of the screws (0.57%) were significantly medially placed, with no neurologic complications. Level of evidence: IV.

69. Luhmann SJ, Lenke LG, Kim YJ, Bridwell KH, Schootman M: Financial analysis of circumferential fusion versus posterior-only with thoracic pedicle screw constructs for main thoracic idiopathic curves between 70 degrees and 100 degrees. *J Child Orthop* 2008;2(2):105-112.

Forty-three patients with an AIS curve of 70° to 100° were treated with anterior-posterior fusion or posterior-only all–pedicle screw fusion. A retrospective review found no statistically significant difference in total cost or radiographic correction. Level of evidence: III.

70. Kuklo TR, Potter BK, Lenke LG, Polly DW Jr, Sides B, Bridwell KH: Surgical revision rates of hooks versus hybrid versus screws versus combined anteroposterior spinal fusion for adolescent idiopathic scoliosis. *Spine (Phila Pa 1976)* 2007;32(20):2258-2264.

A retrospective review of 1,428 patients with AIS who were treated at two institutions found that patients treated with a hook or hybrid construct had a significantly higher rate of revision surgery than those treated with an all–pedicle screw or combined anterior-posterior fusion construct. Level of evidence: IV.

71. Lee SM, Suk SI, Chung ER: Direct vertebral rotation: A new technique of three-dimensional deformity correction with segmental pedicle screw fixation in adolescent idiopathic scoliosis. *Spine (Phila Pa 1976)* 2004;29(3): 343-349.

72. Lenke LG, O'Leary PT, Bridwell KH, Sides BA, Koester LA, Blanke KM: Posterior vertebral column resection for severe pediatric deformity: Minimum two-year follow-up of thirty-five consecutive patients. *Spine (Phila Pa 1976)* 2009;34(20):2213-2221.

A retrospective review of a prospectively accrued cohort of patients with severe scoliosis or kyphoscoliosis found that considerable correction was attained using all-posterior vertebral column resection and fusion. No permanent neurologic deficits were reported. Level of evidence: III.

5: The Pediatric Spine

Chapter 38

Neuromuscular Scoliosis

Benjamin J. Davis, MD   Geoffrey S. Marecek, MD   John F. Sarwark, MD

Introduction

A patient with neuromuscular scoliosis is unable to counteract deforming forces across the spinal column. The patient may have abnormal muscle tone or control, weakness, or paralysis. Many varied conditions can lead to such an abnormality, most notably cerebral palsy, spinal muscular atrophy, Duchenne muscular dystrophy, Rett syndrome, poliomyelitis, and spinal cord injury. Although the neuromuscular scoliosis associated with each of these etiologies has common features and treatment principles, the surgeon must understand the natural history of the patient's disease, the associated comorbidities, and possible treatment difficulties. The goals for treatment of neuromuscular scoliosis must be individualized to the patient's abilities, deformities, and social situation. With appropriate treatment and family education, a patient with neuromuscular scoliosis can gain an improved quality of life.

Etiology

The underlying pathology in patients with neuromuscular scoliosis is believed to be muscle weakness, imbalance, and loss of motor tone and control, all of which affect trunk alignment. Thus, a patient with a flaccid paralysis (from Duchenne muscular dystrophy or poliomyelitis) and a patient with spasticity (from cerebral palsy or spina bifida) both may develop spine deformity, but with a different mechanism of deformity and clinical appearance.[1] The extent of scoliosis can be affected by whether the patient is ambulatory, restricted to a wheelchair, or able to leave bed. In a growing, upright patient the spine deformity may be accentuated through stimulation of vertebral end plate growth on the tensile side of the curve and suppression of growth on the concave side. Preadolescent growth acceleration is associated with increased curve progression. Many patients with neuromuscular scoliosis have an atypical growth pattern in which growth continues into their early 20s.

None of the following authors or any immediate family member has received anything of value from or owns stock in a commercial company or institution related directly or indirectly to the subject of this chapter: Dr. Davis, Dr. Marecek, Dr. Sarwark.

Clinical Appearance

The primary care provider should screen every patient with a neuromuscular disease for spine deformity. The physician should learn the details of the patient's neuromuscular disorder, neurologic status, and disease progression. It is important to obtain birth, growth, and developmental histories. The physical examination should consist of a complete neurologic examination assessing the patient's tone and motor strength. Examination of the hips is important because muscle contractures are associated with coronal and sagittal deformity. Hamstring tightness may be associated with increased lumbar lordosis. The spine examination should include overall balance as well as curve deformity and rigidity. Pelvic obliquity is important to assess because severe obliquity can necessitate fusion to the pelvis.[2]

In comparison with idiopathic scoliosis, neuromuscular scoliosis typically appears at a younger age, progresses more rapidly, and is characterized by curves of larger magnitude.[1,3] A patient with neuromuscular scoliosis may have rigid deformity even before the adolescent growth spurt. Curve progression accelerates during the adolescent growth spurt, and a fixed deformity usually develops. Curve progression may occur earlier in a patient with neuromuscular scoliosis. Skeletal maturity may be delayed in these patients. A patient with cerebral palsy, especially one who is quadriplegic, may have curve progression even after skeletal maturity.[4] Patients with quadriplegia have more severe curves, as do patients who are nonambulatory or who have a thoracolumbar curve.[4,5] A curve larger than 40° is at increased risk for progression during adulthood.[5] In contrast to idiopathic scoliosis, neuromuscular scoliosis often entails impairments and discomfort that interfere with basic functions such as sitting, breathing, and personal hygiene.[1] The extent of deformity is correlated with functional decline and the presence of decubiti.[6]

Pulmonary function is of vital importance in a patient with neuromuscular scoliosis who plans to undergo surgery. The extent of pulmonary impairment varies greatly with the severity of the curve and the underlying disease. A restrictive lung disease pattern develops in patients with Duchenne muscular dystrophy, and pulmonary impairment related to muscle weakness develops in those with spinal muscular atrophy.[7] A

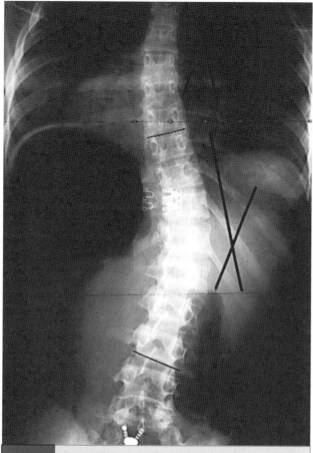

Figure 1 PA long-cassette radiograph of the entire spine in a patient with neuromuscular scoliosis, showing the use of the Cobb method to measure curve magnitude. (Reproduced from Sarwark JF, ed: *Essentials of Musculoskeletal Care*, ed 4. Rosemont, IL, American Academy of Orthopaedic Surgeons, 2010, p 1166.)

severe curve and rib cage deformity lead to further decreases in pulmonary function.[8] A patient with decreased presurgical pulmonary function is at risk for needing prolonged postsurgical mechanical ventilation.[9] However, preexisting respiratory failure is not a contraindication to a safe surgical procedure.[10] The presurgical evaluation should include lung function tests, if possible, and appropriate pulmonary consultation.

Nutritional status should be evaluated before spine surgery in a patient with neuromuscular scoliosis. Presurgical serum albumin levels higher than 3.5 g/dL and a total blood lymphocyte count higher than 1.5 g/L have been associated with lower rates of infection, a shorter period of postsurgical endotracheal intubation, and a shorter hospital stay.[11] Patients with abnormal laboratory values should attempt to improve their nutritional status before surgery. Gastric tube placement and feedings may be necessary to improve nutritional parameters.

A patient with neuromuscular scoliosis may have underlying hematologic disease or use medications that increase the risk of blood loss during surgery. Valproate, a commonly used antiepileptic drug, can cause platelet dysfunction and thrombocytopenia. Bleeding abnormalities should be ruled out or corrected before surgery.

Imaging

All patients should have PA and lateral radiographs of the entire spine. A neuromuscular curve is classically described as long and C shaped, but analysis has shown that most neuromuscular curves are similar to idiopathic curves and include a right thoracic and left lumbar curve.[12] The Cobb angle is a reliable method of measuring deformity in a patient with neuromuscular scoliosis[13] (Figure 1). Curve rigidity is assessed on bending or traction radiographs. Remaining spine growth is assessed on radiographs by determining the patient's Risser stage and the status of the triradiate cartilage. CT or MRI generally is not indicated, although MRI may be needed if the patient has neurologic changes or rapid curve progression.[2]

Treatment

The treatment of neuromuscular scoliosis requires careful planning and frank discussion with the patient, family, and other caregivers. The use of bracing, the timing of an intervention, and the appropriate procedure must be discussed. The natural history of neuromuscular scoliosis varies by disorder, but some guidelines are useful. For example, a patient with spastic cerebral palsy is more likely to have progression if the curve is larger than 40° and the patient is younger than 15 years.[5] If the patient is skeletally mature, a curve larger than 50° is more likely to progress.[4]

Nonsurgical Treatment

The goals of nonsurgical treatment include preserving sagittal and coronal balance when the patient is upright or sitting, halting the progression of spine deformity, and improving the patient's function. Bracing is inadequate for preventing curve progression but can improve the patient's sitting control or delay the need for surgical intervention.[14] A total-contact thoracolumbosacral orthosis is most common, but a soft Boston orthosis also can be used.[15] Bracing is contraindicated if the patient has a stiff curve with pelvic obliquity, is obese, has difficulty with temperature regulation or respiration, or has an unreliable family situation.[1]

Surgical Treatment

The surgical indications are specific to the individual patient and the underlying disorder. Surgery is often indicated if the patient has a large, stiff, and progressive curve that causes functional impairment. The surgical goals include restoring sagittal and coronal balance, correcting spinal curvature, halting curve progression, obtaining a solid fusion, and improving patient function.

Spinal fusion often is the standard treatment for neuromuscular scoliosis, most commonly using a posterior approach and instrumentation. The traditional instrumentation consists of sublaminar wires and hooks, but pedicle screws recently have become popular and successful.[16,17] Unlike sublaminar wires, pedicle screws provide three-column fixation and can control rotation.[14,17] Purchase may be limited in osteopenic bone, however. Fixed deformities may require extensive releases and osteotomies, which can be performed with pedicle screws from a posterior-only approach.[14,16]

Fixed pelvic obliquity is common in patients with neuromuscular scoliosis, with the curve extending to the sacrum. As a result, long constructs with pelvic fixation are frequently necessary. Multiple techniques for sacropelvic fixation have been described, but it is unclear whether any one construct is superior.[18-25] The use of Galveston rods, unit rods, sacral screws, iliac screws, M-W constructs, or pedicle screws has been fairly successful. However, sacropelvic fixation requires extensive dissection that can increase the risk of complications.[14] With a stable lumbosacral articulation, the surgeon may be able to end the fusion construct at L5 with stability equivalent to that of unit rod fixation.[20] A mobile lumbosacral joint can help the patient in sitting and other activities, especially in the presence of hip contractures.[14]

Anterior fusion has a limited role in treating neuromuscular scoliosis, but if indicated it can be effective. Anterior surgery is best considered if the patient has minimal pelvic obliquity and lumbosacral motion can be preserved.[26] However, anterior fusion may not obviate the need for a combined or staged posterior procedure.[27,28] For a severe, rigid curve, anterior surgery can be used to supplement the standard posterior approaches, or an all-posterior approach with vertebral osteotomies can be used.[29] The use of halo-femoral traction was found to improve surgical correction in patients with neuromuscular scoliosis.[30,31]

It may be advisable to delay posterior-only spinal fusion in a skeletally immature patient because of the risk of crankshaft phenomenon, in which the untethered anterior vertebral physes continue to grow after posterior arthrodesis, causing recurrent spine deformity. Few studies have specifically examined crankshaft phenomenon in patients with neuromuscular scoliosis, but most experts believe the risk is reduced by the strength of modern posterior instrumentation and patients' limited growth potential.[32]

Some surgeons recommend the use of a vertical expandable prosthetic titanium rib or growing-rod construct in very young patients with a large or progressive curve.[33-35] Both constructs involve an initial surgery for instrumentation followed by serial expansions to straighten the curve as the patient grows. Few data are

available to help surgeons identify ideal candidates, but a large survey indicated that most spine deformity surgeons consider a curve larger than 60° in a patient younger than 8 to 10 years to be an indication for the use of growing rods.[36]

Outcomes

Patients who undergo surgery for neuromuscular scoliosis have longer hospital stays, significantly higher hospital charges, more total procedures, and more postsurgical complications than patients with idiopathic scoliosis, and they are more likely to be insured under the Medicaid program.[37,38] The reported complication rates after surgery for neuromuscular scoliosis range from 28% to 68%.[39-41] The most common complications are pulmonary, abdominal, or wound related; less common are hardware failure, cardiovascular collapse, neurologic changes, and death.[39,40,42,43] The risk factors for a major complication are nonambulatory status and a presurgical curve larger than 60°.[41] The risk factors for infection include a ventriculoperitoneal shunt, skin breakdown, and a high postsurgical Cobb angle.[44,45]

Despite the overall high rate of complications, long-term studies found that spinal fusion in patients helps restore spine balance, correct the curve, halt curve progression, and improve function.[42,43,46-49]

Summary

The treatment of patients with neuromuscular scoliosis can be challenging. Surgery is often necessary and can involve long, complicated procedures. The surgeon must pay careful attention to the patient's presurgical medical condition. Postsurgical vigilance is key for identifying and treating complications. However, successful surgery can lead to long-term improvement in quality of life for patients and their families.

Annotated References

1. Lubucky J: Neuromuscular scoliosis, in Heary R, ed: *Spinal Deformities: The Essentials.* New York, NY, Thieme, 2007, pp 124-144.

   The treatment of neuromuscular scoliosis is reviewed.

2. McCarthy JJ, D'Andrea LP, Betz RR, Clements DH: Scoliosis in the child with cerebral palsy. *J Am Acad Orthop Surg* 2006;14(6):367-375.

   This review of the natural history of scoliosis in cerebral palsy includes surgical and nonsurgical treatment options, with a focus on the unique challenges of these patients.

3. Chuah SL, Kareem BA, Selvakumar K, Oh KS, Borhan Tan A, Harwant S: The natural history of scoliosis: Curve progression of untreated curves of different

aetiology, with early (mean 2 year) follow up in surgically treated curves. *Med J Malaysia* 2001;56(suppl C): 37-40.

4. Thometz JG, Simon SR: Progression of scoliosis after skeletal maturity in institutionalized adults who have cerebral palsy. *J Bone Joint Surg Am* 1988;70(9):1290-1296.

5. Saito N, Ebara S, Ohotsuka K, Kumeta H, Takaoka K: Natural history of scoliosis in spastic cerebral palsy. *Lancet* 1998;351(9117):1687-1692.

6. Majd ME, Muldowny DS, Holt RT: Natural history of scoliosis in the institutionalized adult cerebral palsy population. *Spine (Phila Pa 1976)* 1997;22(13):1461-1466.

7. Marsh A, Edge G, Lehovsky J: Spinal fusion in patients with Duchenne's muscular dystrophy and a low forced vital capacity. *Eur Spine J* 2003;12(5):507-512.

8. Inal-Ince D, Savci S, Arikan H, et al: Effects of scoliosis on respiratory muscle strength in patients with neuromuscular disorders. *Spine J* 2009;9(12):981-986.

   A comparison of pulmonary function in 39 patients with neuromuscular disease and 24 healthy age- and sex-matched control subjects found that the patients had worse pulmonary function than the control subjects. Patients with neuromuscular disease and scoliosis had worse function than patients with neuromuscular disease but no scoliosis. Respiratory muscle weakness may be independent of scoliosis but should be considered in surgical decision making.

9. Udink ten Cate FE, van Royen BJ, van Heerde M, Roerdink D, Plötz FB: Incidence and risk factors of prolonged mechanical ventilation in neuromuscular scoliosis surgery. *J Pediatr Orthop B* 2008;17(4):203-206.

   A retrospective review of 46 patients who underwent spinal fusion and instrumentation for neuromuscular scoliosis determined the incidence and risk of mechanical ventilation lasting more than 72 hours. Prolonged mechanical ventilation was required in 7 patients (15%). The only risk factor was impaired presurgical pulmonary function.

10. Gill I, Eagle M, Mehta JS, Gibson MJ, Bushby K, Bullock R: Correction of neuromuscular scoliosis in patients with preexisting respiratory failure. *Spine (Phila Pa 1976)* 2006;31(21):2478-2483.

    Eight patients with preexisting respiratory failure and neuromuscular scoliosis were supported with noninvasive ventilation after surgical deformity correction. Noninvasive ventilation was found to be a useful surgical adjunct.

11. Jevsevar DS, Karlin LI: The relationship between preoperative nutritional status and complications after an operation for scoliosis in patients who have cerebral palsy. *J Bone Joint Surg Am* 1993;75(6):880-884.

12. Kouwenhoven JW, Van Ommeren PM, Pruijs HE, Castelein RM: Spinal decompensation in neuromuscular disease. *Spine (Phila Pa 1976)* 2006;31(7):E188-E191.

Radiographs of 198 patients with neuromuscular scoliosis were analyzed for curve shape and direction. Right thoracic, right thoracolumbar, and left lumbar curves predominated. This finding did not significantly differ from known values for idiopathic scoliosis.

13. Gupta MC, Wijesekera S, Sossan A, et al: Reliability of radiographic parameters in neuromuscular scoliosis. *Spine (Phila Pa 1976)* 2007;32(6):691-695.

    The interobserver and intraobserver reliability of the Cobb angle, C7 balance, Ferguson angle, kyphotic Cobb angle, and pelvic obliquity was assessed using radiographs of 48 patients with neuromuscular scoliosis. Cobb angle intraobserver variability was 5.7°, and interobserver variability was 14.8°. The Cobb angle was found to be more reliable than the Ferguson angle. The horizontal method was recommended for determining pelvic obliquity, and dedicated AP radiographs were recommended for determining skeletal maturity.

14. Sarwark J, Sarwahi V: New strategies and decision making in the management of neuromuscular scoliosis. *Orthop Clin North Am* 2007;38(4):485-496, v.

    This review article describes the workup and treatment of a patient with neuromuscular scoliosis. Families and caregivers have high levels of satisfaction after corrective surgery for scoliosis.

15. Letts M, Rathbone D, Yamashita T, Nichol B, Keeler A: Soft Boston orthosis in management of neuromuscular scoliosis: A preliminary report. *J Pediatr Orthop* 1992; 12(4):470-474.

16. Modi HN, Hong JY, Mehta SS, et al: Surgical correction and fusion using posterior-only pedicle screw construct for neuropathic scoliosis in patients with cerebral palsy: A three-year follow-up study. *Spine (Phila Pa 1976)* 2009;34(11):1167-1175.

    The outcomes of 52 patients with neuromuscular scoliosis and cerebral palsy were retrospectively reviewed at a minimum 2-year follow-up. The patients had significant improvement in Cobb angle and pelvic obliquity after posterior-only pedicle screw fixation. Two perioperative deaths and one transient neurologic deficit occurred. Posterior-only pedicle screw constructs were found to offer satisfactory correction without increasing the risk of complications.

17. Modi HN, Suh SW, Song HR, Lee SH, Yang JH: Correction of apical axial rotation with pedicular screws in neuromuscular scoliosis. *J Spinal Disord Tech* 2008; 21(8):606-613.

    A retrospective review determined apical derotation in 24 patients with neuromuscular scoliosis who underwent posterior fusion and pedicle screw instrumentation. The presurgical mean apical rotation was 42°. Surgery led to a mean of 9° improvement. There were no differences based on curve severity or diagnosis.

18. Carroll EA, Shilt JS, Jacks L: MW construct in fusion for neuromuscular scoliosis. *Eur Spine J* 2007;16(3): 373-377.

    A retrospective comparison of 12 patients who underwent posterior spinal fusion included 6 with an M-W construct for spinopelvic fixation and 6 with a Galveston construct. Patients were matched on presurgical Cobb angle and pelvic obliquity. The M-W construct was found to be superior to the Galveston construct for curve correction (18%) and pelvic obliquity (30%).

19. Early S, Mahar A, Oka R, Newton P: Biomechanical comparison of lumbosacral fixation using Luque-Galveston and Colorado II sacropelvic fixation: Advantage of using locked proximal fixation. *Spine (Phila Pa 1976)* 2005;30(12):1396-1401.

   Biomechanical testing on eight cadaver spines found equivalent stiffness with the Colorado II and Galveston constructs. The Colorado II construct had less L5-S1 motion during flexion and extension loading, and the Galveston construct tended to have greater stiffness in torsional loading.

20. McCall RE, Hayes B: Long-term outcome in neuromuscular scoliosis fused only to lumbar 5. *Spine (Phila Pa 1976)* 2005;30(18):2056-2060.

   Thirty patients with cerebral palsy underwent fusion with unit rod instrumentation and sacral fixation, and 25 underwent fusion with a U-rod and fusion ending at L5. A retrospective comparison of outcomes found similar curve correction and pelvic obliquity. Fusion ending at L5 was found to be technically simpler and faster, with equivalent outcome.

21. Peelle MW, Lenke LG, Bridwell KH, Sides B: Comparison of pelvic fixation techniques in neuromuscular spinal deformity correction: Galveston rod versus iliac and lumbosacral screws. *Spine (Phila Pa 1976)* 2006;31(20):2392-2399.

   Retrospective comparison of the results of posterior spinal fusion for neuromuscular scoliosis in 20 patients treated with the Galveston technique and 20 treated with iliac screws for spinopelvic fixation found no difference in Cobb angle at any time point. Pelvic obliquity was similar before and immediately after surgery in both groups but was statistically better with iliac screws at a mean 3.1-year follow-up. There were more episodes of broken hardware and reoperation in patients treated with the Galveston rod.

22. Phillips JH, Gutheil JP, Knapp DR Jr: Iliac screw fixation in neuromuscular scoliosis. *Spine (Phila Pa 1976)* 2007;32(14):1566-1570.

   Outcomes were reviewed in 50 patients with neuromuscular scoliosis who underwent posterior spinal fusion using the modified Luque-Galveston technique with two or four iliac screws. Screw fixation to the ilium was found to be safe and effective. The use of two screws in each wing provided a more stable implant with fewer complications.

23. Tsirikos AI, Lipton G, Chang WN, Dabney KW, Miller F: Surgical correction of scoliosis in pediatric patients with cerebral palsy using the unit rod instrumentation. *Spine (Phila Pa 1976)* 2008;33(10):1133-1140.

   A review of 287 children with cerebral palsy treated with unit rod instrumentation for neuromuscular scoliosis found good correction and a low rate of complications. There was no difference in the outcomes of children with an idiopathic or a neuromuscular curve. The major complication was infection (6.7%).

24. Wimmer C, Wallnöfer P, Walochnik N, Krismer M, Saraph V: Comparative evaluation of luque and isola instrumentation for treatment of neuromuscular scoliosis. *Clin Orthop Relat Res* 2005;439:181-192.

   A review of 52 children treated for neuromuscular scoliosis with either Isola-Asher or Luque instrumentation found significant correction in curve magnitude and pelvic tilt, with minimal loss of correction and similar questionnaire-based outcomes.

25. Zahi R, Vialle R, Abelin K, Mary P, Khouri N, Damsin JP: Spinopelvic fixation with iliosacral screws in neuromuscular spinal deformities: Results in a prospective cohort of 62 patients. *Childs Nerv Syst* 2010;26(1):81-86.

   The results of surgical correction with iliosacral screws for spinopelvic fixation were prospectively recorded in 62 patients with neuromuscular scoliosis. In patients with pelvic obliquity, the iliosacral screws were connected to the main construct with short connecting rods. This technique reduced surgical difficulty and time but was associated with a high infection rate.

26. Tokala DP, Lam KS, Freeman BJ, Webb JK: Is there a role for selective anterior instrumentation in neuromuscular scoliosis? *Eur Spine J* 2007;16(1):91-96.

   Nine patients had selective anterior fusion for neuromuscular scoliosis. The mean Cobb angle improved from 52° to 20°. Two patients required subsequent posterior surgery. There were no complications. Subjective results were excellent in six patients and good in three patients.

27. Hopf CG, Eysel P, Dubousset J: Operative treatment of scoliosis with Cotrel-Dubousset-Hopf instrumentation: New anterior spinal device. *Spine (Phila Pa 1976)* 1997;22(6):618-628.

28. Sarwahi V, Sarwark JF, Schafer MF, et al: Standards in anterior spine surgery in pediatric patients with neuromuscular scoliosis. *J Pediatr Orthop* 2001;21(6):756-760.

29. Suh SW, Modi HN, Yang J, Song HR, Jang KM: Posterior multilevel vertebral osteotomy for correction of severe and rigid neuromuscular scoliosis: A preliminary study. *Spine (Phila Pa 1976)* 2009;34(12):1315-1320.

   One center's experience with multilevel posterior vertebral osteotomies for severe curves (larger than 100°) was prospectively recorded in seven patients with neuromuscular scoliosis. The mean Cobb angle improved from 118.2° to 48.8°. The technique was found to allow anterior column release without a separate approach and offered outstanding results.

30. Takeshita K, Lenke LG, Bridwell KH, Kim YJ, Sides B, Hensley M: Analysis of patients with nonambulatory neuromuscular scoliosis surgically treated to the pelvis with intraoperative halo-femoral traction. *Spine (Phila Pa 1976)* 2006;31(20):2381-2385.

   Spinal fusion with intraoperative halo-femoral traction was compared with fusion without traction in patients with neuromuscular scoliosis who were nonambulatory. Traction provided significantly greater lumbar curve and pelvic obliquity correction, with no traction-related complications

31. Vialle R, Delecourt C, Morin C: Surgical treatment of scoliosis with pelvic obliquity in cerebral palsy: The influence of intraoperative traction. *Spine (Phila Pa 1976)* 2006;31(13):1461-1466.

Patients in two continuous groups had posterior spinal fusion with instrumentation for neuromuscular scoliosis: 59 patients were placed in the knee-chest position for pelvic obliquity correction using various reduction maneuvers, and 51 were placed supine for intraoperative halo traction. Those with supine positioning and halo traction had shorter duration of anesthetic and better correction of curve magnitude and pelvic obliquity.

32. Westerlund LE, Gill SS, Jarosz TS, Abel MF, Blanco JS: Posterior-only unit rod instrumentation and fusion for neuromuscular scoliosis. *Spine (Phila Pa 1976)* 2001; 26(18):1984-1989.

33. Hell AK, Campbell RM, Hefti F: The vertical expandable prosthetic titanium rib implant for the treatment of thoracic insufficiency syndrome associated with congenital and neuromuscular scoliosis in young children. *J Pediatr Orthop B* 2005;14(4):287-293.

The authors describe their experience with the use of the vertical expandable prosthetic titanium rib prosthesis in patients with thoracic insufficiency syndrome and neuromuscular scoliosis. There was good improvement in scoliosis and hemithorax expansion, with few complications.

34. White KK, Song KM, Frost N, Daines BK: VEPTR™ Growing Rods for early-onset neuromuscular scoliosis: Feasible and effective. *Clin Orthop Relat Res* 2011; 469(5):1335-1341.

Fourteen patients were treated with a vertical expandable prosthetic titanium rib placed posteriorly in spine-to-spine fashion as a growing-rod construct. The Cobb angle improved from 74° to 57° after an average of three expansions. The six complications included rod fracture and infections.

35. Sponseller PD, Shah SA, Abel MF, et al: Scoliosis surgery in cerebral palsy: Differences between unit rod and custom rods. *Spine (Phila Pa 1976)* 2009;34(8):840-844.

A review of 36 patients with growing rods anchored in the pelvis using iliac screws, iliac rods, S-rods, or sacral fixation found iliac screws to be superior to pelvic fixation with respect to correction of the Cobb angle and pelvic obliquity. The use of bilateral rods resulted in better correction than unilateral rods. Bilateral growing rods with iliac fixation provided the best correction.

36. Yang JS, McElroy MJ, Akbarnia BA, et al: Growing rods for spinal deformity: Characterizing consensus and variation in current use. *J Pediatr Orthop* 2010;30(3): 264-270.

Survey responses from pediatric spine surgeons were compared with actual practice in a large series from a national database. In the survey, surgeons noted that growing rods were preferable for curves larger than 60° in patients younger than 8 to 10 years. Curve rigidity and brace intolerance were also important. Skeletal maturity, measured as Risser grade III or higher, was most commonly cited as the indicator for definitive fusion.

37. Murphy NA, Firth S, Jorgensen T, Young PC: Spinal surgery in children with idiopathic and neuromuscular scoliosis: What's the difference? *J Pediatr Orthop* 2006; 26(2):216-220.

Patients in a national health care database who underwent spinal fusion for neuromuscular scoliosis and idiopathic scoliosis were compared. Those with neuromuscular scoliosis had longer hospital stays, higher total charges, more diagnoses, and more total procedures than those with idiopathic scoliosis. They also had pneumonia, respiratory failure, urinary tract infection, and wound infection more frequently.

38. Barsdorf AI, Sproule DM, Kaufmann P: Scoliosis surgery in children with neuromuscular disease: Findings from the US National Inpatient Sample, 1997 to 2003. *Arch Neurol* 2010;67(2):231-235.

A cross-sectional study of the Kids Inpatient Database compared children undergoing scoliosis surgery between 1997 and 2003. Children with neuromuscular disease had a longer hospital stay and a higher mortality rate.

39. Modi HN, Suh SW, Yang JH, et al: Surgical complications in neuromuscular scoliosis operated with posterior- only approach using pedicle screw fixation. *Scoliosis* 2009;4:11.

The major complications of spinal fusion in 50 patients with neuromuscular scoliosis included hemothorax, pneumothorax, pleural effusion, pulmonary edema, complete spinal cord injury, deep wound infection, and death. Blood loss, curve magnitude, and pelvic fixation did not increase the complication rate.

40. Mohamad F, Parent S, Pawelek J, et al: Perioperative complications after surgical correction in neuromuscular scoliosis. *J Pediatr Orthop* 2007;27(4):392-397.

A review of 175 patients who underwent surgical treatment of neuromuscular scoliosis found an overall complication rate of 33.1%. Patients with a single-stage procedure had fewer complications (37.4%) than those with staged procedures (57.1%). Pulmonary complications were most common (19.1%), followed by infection (9.7%) and intraoperative neurologic changes (4.6%).

41. Master DL, Poe-Kochert C, Son-Hing J, Armstrong DG, Thompson GH: Wound infections following surgery for neuromuscular scoliosis: Risk factors and treatment outcomes. *Spine (Phila Pa 1976)* 2011;36(3):E179-E185.

A review of 131 patients who underwent surgery for neuromuscular scoliosis determined risk factors for complications. Patients who were nonambulatory were four times more likely to have a major complication than those who were ambulatory. A major curve larger than 60° was the most accurate predictor of major complications.

42. Gitelman A, Joseph SA Jr, Carrion W, Stephen M: Results and morbidity in a consecutive series of patients undergoing spinal fusion with iliac screws for neuromuscular scoliosis. *Orthopedics* 2008;31(12):31.

A retrospective review of 12 patients who underwent surgical correction with Luque instrumentation and iliac screw fixation for neuromuscular scoliosis found that deformity improved significantly, lumbar lordosis remained stable, and there were four minor complications. This method was found to be satisfactory, with stable lumbar lordosis that may improve sitting balance.

43. Modi HN, Suh SW, Hong JY, Cho JW, Park JH, Yang JH: Treatment and complications in flaccid neuromuscular scoliosis (Duchenne muscular dystrophy and spinal muscular atrophy) with posterior-only pedicle screw instrumentation. *Eur Spine J* 2010;19(3):384-393.

A review of 27 patients with flaccid neuromuscular scoliosis who underwent posterior-only pedicle screw instrumentation found significant improvement in Cobb angle and pelvic obliquity. There were five major complications (four respiratory complications and one death), with a 48.1% overall complication rate.

44. Master DL, Connie PK, Jochen SH, Armstrong DG, Thompson GH: Wound infections after surgery for neuromuscular scoliosis: Risk factors and treatment outcomes. *Spine (Phila Pa 1976)* 2011;36(3):E179-E185.

Eight patients who had a wound infection after surgery for neuromuscular scoliosis were compared with 72 patients who did not have a wound complication. The presence of a ventriculoperitoneal shunt was associated with an increased risk of infection, which increased the risk of pseudarthrosis and increased the length of stay.

45. Mohamed Ali MH, Koutharawu DN, Miller F, et al: Operative and clinical markers of deep wound infection after spine fusion in children with cerebral palsy. *J Pediatr Orthop* 2010;30(8):851-857.

The records of 236 patients with cerebral palsy who underwent spinal fusion revealed a 9.3% infection rate. After adjustment, regression modeling revealed that skin breakdown and residual curve magnitude were the best predictors of postsurgical infection.

46. Larsson EL, Aaro S, Ahlinder P, Normelli H, Tropp H, Oberg B: Long-term follow-up of functioning after spinal surgery in patients with Rett syndrome. *Eur Spine J* 2009;18(4):506-511.

In 23 girls with Rett syndrome and neuromuscular scoliosis, spine stabilization was found to lead to a better sitting position, fewer seating adjustments, less daytime resting, fewer pressure sores, less pneumonia, and better overall health.

47. Larsson EL, Aaro SI, Normelli HC, Oberg BE: Long-term follow-up of functioning after spinal surgery in patients with neuromuscular scoliosis. *Spine (Phila Pa 1976)* 2005;30(19):2145-2152.

At 1-year follow-up after surgery in 82 patients with neuromuscular scoliosis, there was improvement in Cobb angle, lung function, seating position, activities of daily living, and time used for resting. At 84.5-month follow-up, all areas had continued to improve except the Cobb angle, which increased.

48. Mercado E, Alman B, Wright JG: Does spinal fusion influence quality of life in neuromuscular scoliosis? *Spine (Phila Pa 1976)* 2007;32(19, suppl):S120-S125.

A meta-analysis of 198 publications from 1980 to 2006 concluded that spinal fusion improves quality of life in patients with cerebral palsy and muscular dystrophy but not in patients with spina bifida.

49. Watanabe K, Lenke LG, Daubs MD, et al: Is spine deformity surgery in patients with spastic cerebral palsy truly beneficial? A patient/parent evaluation. *Spine (Phila Pa 1976)* 2009;34(20):2222-2232.

A survey of 84 patients with spastic cerebral palsy and their families found an overall satisfaction rate of 92% after spinal fusion for neuromuscular scoliosis. Patients who were less satisfied had more late complications, less curve correction, a greater residual curve after correction, and hyperlordosis. Improvement in quality of life was reported in 71%.

5: The Pediatric Spine

Chapter 39

Scheuermann Kyphosis

John Thometz, MD

Introduction

Scheuermann kyphosis is a rigid thoracic kyphotic deformity that most often occurs in adolescents. Scheuermann kyphosis must be distinguished from the more common postural kyphosis (so-called round back) as well as congenital kyphosis, skeletal dysplasia, connective tissue disorders, posttraumatic kyphosis, and kyphosis related to a neuromuscular disorder (Table 1). Scheuermann kyphosis was first described in 1920. A mechanical etiology was proposed in which anterior stress on the vertebral bodies causes growth inhibition and vertebral wedging. Transient osteoporosis, nutrient malabsorption, osteonecrosis of the vertebral ring apophyses, and abnormalities in growth hormone levels also have been proposed as the etiology of Scheuermann kyphosis.[1] A familial incidence has been noted; the condition is inherited through a major gene allele model in which all male carriers of the mutant gene and approximately half of female carriers develop kyphosis. A recent study of Danish twins concluded that the etiology of Scheuermann kyphosis has a major genetic component.[2]

The prevalence of Scheuermann kyphosis is estimated to be 0.4% to 8.3%. The greatest spine deformity can develop during the peak growth period of the spine. Boys age 10 to 14 years are most commonly affected; as many as 90% of patients are male.[1] Histologic examination reveals a thickened anterior longitudinal ligament, disorganized endochondral ossification in the ring apophysis, and decreased collagen and increased proteoglycan in the physis. The histologic abnormalities are variable and do not reveal the cause of Scheuermann kyphosis. Herniations of the disk tissue into the vertebral body (Schmorl nodes) occur with end plate irregularities.

The natural history of untreated Scheuermann kyphosis in skeletally immature patients is progressive deformity with multiple wedged vertebrae. Most patients have mild deformity and low-grade symptoms, however.[1,3] Unless the deformity is greater than 75°, it results in little long-term disability or pain. Adult patients appear to have more back pain than healthy control subjects, but the difference is significant only if the kyphosis is greater than 75°. Adults are more likely to have lumbar pain secondary to degenerative changes caused by the hyperlordotic position. A long-term study found an increased incidence of low back pain in patients with Scheuermann kyphosis, but this pain had no major effect on their activities of daily living.[1] As many as 50% of patients with Scheuermann kyphosis develop spondylolysis or spondylolisthesis because of stress on the hyperlordotic lumbar spine.[4]

Neither Dr. Thometz nor an immediate family member has received anything of value from or owns stock in a commercial company or institution related directly or indirectly to the subject of this chapter.

Table 1

The Etiology of Kyphotic Conditions

Congenital Kyphosis
Failure of formation
Failure of segmentation
Mixed failure
Progressive noninfectious anterior fusion
Connective Tissue Disorder
Neuromuscular Condition
Paralytic
Spastic
Spinal cord tumor
Postinfectious Disorder (Tuberculosis)
Postlaminectomy Kyphosis
Posttraumatic Kyphotic Deformity
Postural Kyphosis
Scheuermann Kyphosis
Thoracic
Thoracolumbar
Skeletal Dysplasia
Achondroplasia
Mucopolysaccharidosis
Neurofibromatosis
Traumatic Kyphosis
Structural bone or ligament failure
Secondary to paralysis

Adapted from Arlet V, Schlenzka D: Pediatric kyphosis, in Abel MF, ed: *Orthopaedic Knowledge Update: Pediatrics 3.* Rosemont, IL, American Academy of Orthopaedic Surgeons, 2006, p 361.

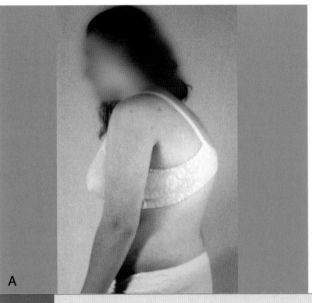
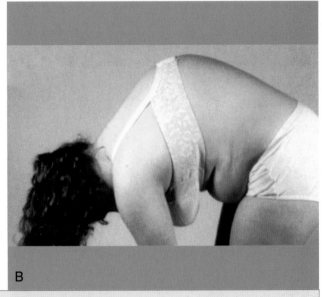

Figure 1 Photographs of a patient with a localized Scheuermann kyphotic deformity. **A,** Standing. **B,** Forward-bending. (Reproduced with permission from Sucato D: Kyphosis, in Herring J, ed: *Tachdjian's Pediatric Orthopaedics*, ed 4. Philadelphia, PA, Saunders Elsevier, 2007, pp 413-441.)

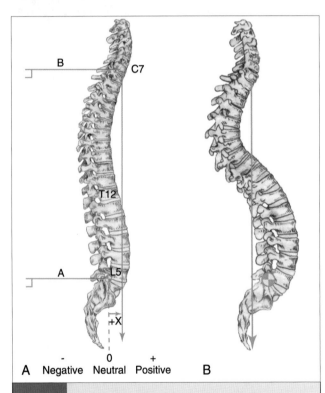

Figure 2 Schematic drawings showing the determination of sagittal balance. **A,** In neutral balance, the distance (X) from the sacral promontory (A) to a plumb line from the C7 vertebral body (B) is 2 cm or less. **B,** In negative sagittal balance, the line from C7 is more than 2 cm posterior to the sacral promontory. (Reproduced with permission from O'Brien MF, Kuklo TR, Blanke KM, Lenke LG: Adolescent idiopathic scoliosis, in *Radiographic Measurement Manual: Spinal Deformity Study Group.* Memphis, TN, Medtronic Sofamor Danek USA, 2004, pp 47-70.)

Clinical Evaluation

The child and the parents may be concerned about the appearance of the kyphotic spine as well as the symptoms. Although symptoms are common, usually they decrease in late adolescence. An adolescent patient often has pain at the apex of the deformity, which usually is in the interscapular region. The pain is exacerbated by standing or strenuous activity and is relieved with rest. Standing increases the thoracic kyphosis and lumbar lordosis, with a forward posture of the head and neck (Figure 1). It is important to observe the child from the side during forward bending because in this position the thoracic kyphosis is exaggerated and localized; often there is a relatively sharply angulated segment in the distal thoracic spine, with a relative flattening of the upper thoracic spine.

Any rigidity in the child's deformity on examination should raise suspicion for Scheuermann kyphosis. A patient with Scheuermann kyphosis cannot voluntarily correct the deformity when prone or supine. Small scoliotic curvatures often are present and should be assessed by the Adams forward bend test. Contractures of the pectoralis, hip flexor, and hamstring muscles are common. Even though patients with Scheuermann kyphosis rarely develop a neurologic deficit, a careful neurologic examination is necessary.

Thoracic kyphosis results in increased lordosis in both the lumbar and cervical spine. The head tends to protrude forward in a goose neck position, frequently causing a negative sagittal balance and an unstable stance. The patient's sagittal balance is determined by measuring the distance from a plumb line extending from the center of the C7 vertebral body to the sacral

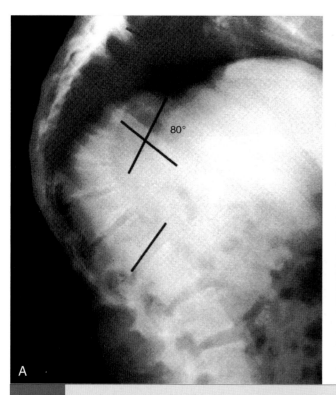
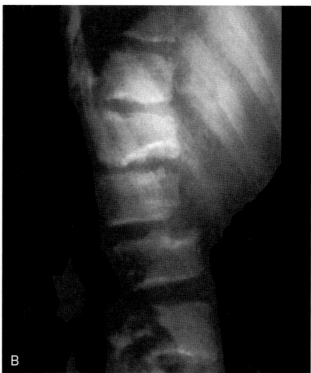

Figure 3 **A,** Standing lateral radiograph of a patient with thoracic Scheuermann kyphosis showing anterior vertebral wedging, irregular end plates, and disk space narrowing. The Cobb angle is 80°. **B,** Lateral radiograph of a patient with lumbar Scheuermann kyphosis showing end plate irregularities, disk narrowing, and Schmorl nodules in the upper lumbar spine. (Reproduced with permission from Warner WC Jr: Kyphosis, in Morrissy RT, Weinstein SL, eds: *Lovell and Winter's Pediatric Orthopaedics*, ed 6. Philadelphia, PA, Lippincott Williams & Wilkins, 2005, pp 797-837.)

promontory (Figure 2). The normal sagittal balance value is within 2 cm of the sacral promontory; in a negative sagittal balance, the plumb line from C7 lies more than 2 cm posterior to the sacral promontory.

Patients with Scheuermann kyphosis rarely develop signs of spastic paraparesis secondary to anterior cord compression or disk herniation. A neurologic deficit associated with thoracic disk herniation is rare but requires surgical decompression. Atypical pain, such as night pain, requires MRI to rule out pathology such as a syrinx. The pulmonary function of patients with Scheuermann kyphosis usually is normal or slightly increased, and pulmonary function tests are not needed unless the deformity is severe (greater than 100°).

Normal thoracic kyphosis (from T5 to T12) ranges from 20° to 45°, and normal lumbar lordosis (from L1 to L5) is 20° to 55°. Difficulty in obtaining the appropriate radiographic exposure can make the anatomic landmarks difficult to identify on radiographs, particularly at the proximal end of the curvature. The standard positioning for radiographs is with hips and knees in extension and the arms resting at shoulder height on a crossbar placed directly in front of the patient. A standing lateral radiograph of an adolescent with Scheuermann kyphosis reveals evidence of increased thoracic kyphosis and anterior wedging of more than 5° in three or more vertebral bodies, as well as end plate irregularities, disk space narrowing, and Schmorl

nodes (Figure 3, *A*). Scheuermann kyphosis sometimes is diagnosed if there is wedging of only one vertebral body, particularly if other typical radiographic signs are present. The apex of the deformity usually is between T7 and T9. If the apex of the deformity is in the distal thoracic spine, the clinical deformity can be significant with a relatively small radiographic deformity. Scheuermann kyphosis is not radiographically detectable in patients younger than 10 years because the ring apophysis has not yet ossified and vertebral wedging is therefore difficult to determine. The flexibility of the curve can be assessed using a cross-table stress lateral radiograph, for which the kyphosis is passively extended over a buttress placed at the apex of the deformity. Determining the flexibility of the spine is important for formulating a nonsurgical or surgical treatment plan.

A lumbar form of Scheuermann kyphosis may develop in adolescents who are very athletic or perform hard manual labor. This condition also is described as epiphysitis or limbus vertebrae. The patient almost always is male, and the primary symptom is backache. The patient has little or no deformity and rarely has a progressive form of kyphosis. Radiographic signs of Scheuermann kyphosis are present, including irregular vertebral end plates and anterior Schmorl nodules (Figure 3, *B*). A patient who is symptomatic is treated with physical therapy or bracing.

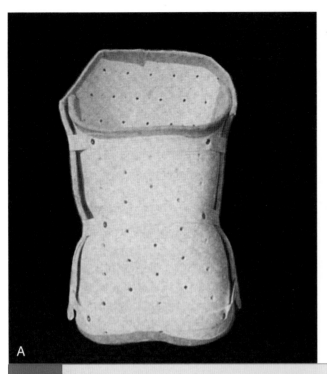
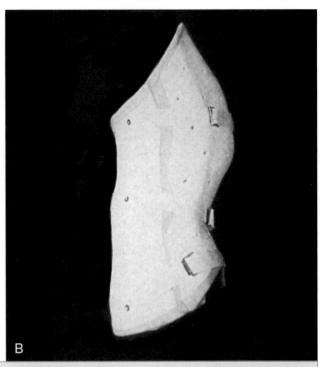

Figure 4   Photographs showing a clamshell thoracolumbosacral orthosis from the front (**A**) and side (**B**), as molded to decrease lumbar lordosis and dorsal kyphosis. (Reproduced from Pizzutillo PD: Nonsurgical treatment of kyphosis, in Birch JG, ed: *Instructional Course Lectures: Pediatrics*. Rosemont, IL, American Academy of Orthopaedic Surgeons, 2006, pp 181-187.)

Nonsurgical Treatment

The natural history of Scheuermann kyphosis usually is painless and nonprogressive, and surgical treatment is not necessary. Physical therapy is helpful for a patient with pain in the thoracic or lumbar spine. Although any postural component of the deformity can be corrected and tight hamstring and pectoralis muscles can be stretched, the magnitude of the kyphosis cannot be decreased through physical therapy. If the patient is skeletally immature, bracing or casting is indicated for a curve larger than 50°. A moderate curve (less than 75°) in a skeletally immature patient is more likely than a more severe curve to respond to treatment with a cast or a brace. A brace is most likely to be effective in a patient with a moderate deformity that is flexible and diffuse, with a relatively distal apex. The patient also should have significant remaining growth and be willing to comply with treatment. Correction of the deformity within the brace must be documented.

Casting is reserved for decreasing the magnitude of a relatively large, rigid curve so that bracing can be used. Rigid deformities can be treated with a series of localizer casts to obtain gradual improvement. In the United States, casting currently is used at only a few centers because of the required physical restrictions and the effect on the patient's skin.

The child must have at least 1 year of growth remaining to benefit from brace treatment. If brace treatment is initiated when the child is skeletally immature, theoretically the brace hyperextension forces allow reconstitution of the anterior vertebral body height and some correction of the deformity. Bracing can lead to reversal of the wedging of the vertebrae in a skeletally immature patient, but only if the brace is worn at least 18 months. Some loss of correction often occurs after bracing is discontinued. Some children develop an adverse psychologic reaction to brace use. For the purpose of improving these patients' brace compliance, individual psychologic support is more effective than peer group support.[5]

The few long-term follow-up studies of treatment with the Milwaukee brace indicate that patients who comply with treatment achieve curve stability or a small correction of deformity.[6] Although the Milwaukee brace has been commonly used for the control of Scheuermann kyphosis deformity, a properly molded thoracolumbosacral orthosis also can provide adequate corrective forces (Figures 4 and 5). An adolescent may better accept the use of a thoracolumbosacral orthosis. The Milwaukee brace may be more beneficial for a patient with a curve apex at T8 or higher, a patient who is obese, or a girl with large breasts.

Surgical Treatment

If nonsurgical treatment is unsuccessful, a patient may be considered for surgery if the curve is larger than 75°

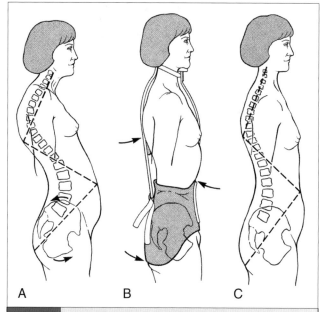

| Figure 5 | Schematic drawings of a patient with Scheuermann kyphosis before (**A**), during (**B**), and after (**C**) treatment with a Milwaukee brace, showing corrective forces generated by the brace (*arrows*) and the extent of deformity before and after treatment (*dashed lines*). (Reproduced with permission from Warner WC Jr: Kyphosis, in Morrissy RT, Weinstein SL, eds: *Lovell and Winter's Pediatric Orthopaedics*, ed 6. Philadelphia, PA, Lippincott Williams & Wilkins, 2005, pp 797-837.) |

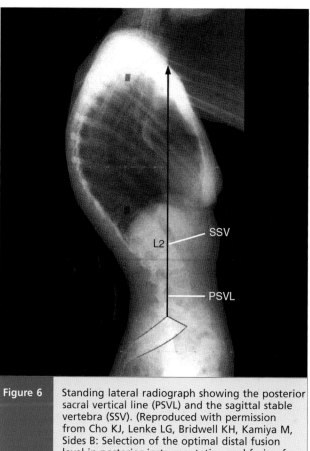

| Figure 6 | Standing lateral radiograph showing the posterior sacral vertical line (PSVL) and the sagittal stable vertebra (SSV). (Reproduced with permission from Cho KJ, Lenke LG, Bridwell KH, Kamiya M, Sides B: Selection of the optimal distal fusion level in posterior instrumentation and fusion for thoracic hyperkyphosis. *Spine [Phila Pa 1976]* 2009;34[8]:765-770.) |

and rigid as well as cosmetically unacceptable or painful. Planning is required to determine the optimal surgical technique for correcting a severe rigid deformity. The goal of surgery is to achieve a stable, balanced spine. The entire deformity must be fused to prevent progressive deformity or junctional kyphosis.[7-9] A too-short fusion, either proximally or distally, can lead to junctional kyphosis, which can cause the global sagittal balance to become more negative than before surgery. Rates of junctional kyphosis as high as 20% to 30% have been reported.[3,8,10] Proximal junctional kyphosis is more common than distal junctional kyphosis. Distal junctional kyphosis is more often associated with pain, however, and is more likely to require revision surgery. The instrumentation and fusion should extend from T2 proximally to the level above the first lordotic disk distally. It has been recommended that the vertebral body touched by a vertical line from the posterosuperior aspect of S1 should be included in the fusion to prevent distal junctional kyphosis[11] (Figure 6).

The indications for supplementary anterior release are limited. Anterior release is needed if a bony fusion is present across the anterior aspect of the disk space, and it can be useful in correcting a severe rigid deformity that primarily involves only a few levels. In the past, the curve was believed to require preliminary anterior diskectomy and fusion unless it could bend to

less than 50° when the patient was placed supine over a buttress beneath the thoracic spine. When diskectomy and fusion are needed, thorascopic release and fusion have the advantage of causing less lung function impairment than open thoracotomy. An adequate diskectomy may be more difficult to achieve, however. Thoracotomy had a notable effect on pulmonary function even at 2-year follow-up.[12] If possible, the segmental vessels should be preserved during an anterior release to provide adequate perfusion of the spinal cord. Equivalent results have been reported for matched groups treated with anterior-posterior or posterior-only spine fusion.[12]

Posterior-only techniques using segmental pedicle screws have had excellent results, with stable fixation and little long-term loss of correction. Complications are rare but include neurologic compromise, loss of fixation, pseudarthrosis with rod breakage, and recurrent deformity. The most common difficulty after surgery is proximal or distal junctional kyphosis. Long-term outcomes of the currently used surgical techniques are unknown. Segmental fixation with pedicle screws provides strong three-column correction of the deformity. A posterior shortening procedure helps eliminate the need for anterior release and allows greater correction

5: The Pediatric Spine

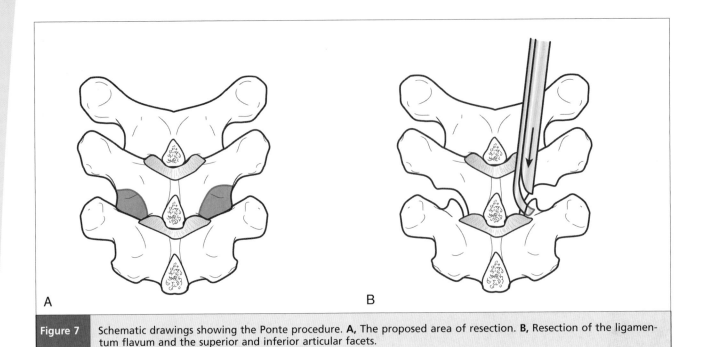

Figure 7 Schematic drawings showing the Ponte procedure. **A,** The proposed area of resection. **B,** Resection of the ligamentum flavum and the superior and inferior articular facets.

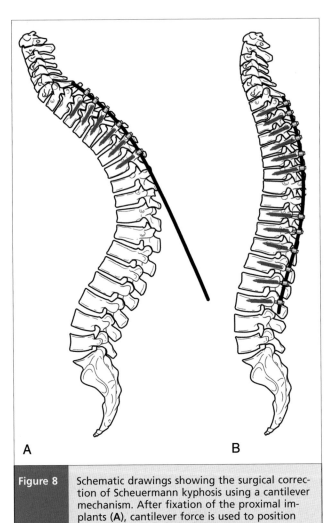

Figure 8 Schematic drawings showing the surgical correction of Scheuermann kyphosis using a cantilever mechanism. After fixation of the proximal implants (**A**), cantilever force is used to position the distal implants for fixation (**B**).

of the deformity; in particular, Ponte osteotomies at multiple levels allow correction of a rigid deformity[13] (Figure 7). This procedure requires removal of the ligamentum flavum as well as the superior and inferior articular facets at the apex of the deformity. Rods large enough to allow correction of a rigid deformity must be used. The goal is to achieve a physiologic sagittal kyphosis of approximately 45°. Care must be taken not to overcorrect the deformity. Deformity correction to less than 50% of the original magnitude has been associated with an increased risk of proximal kyphosis.[14] Correction generally is achieved with a combination of a cantilever mechanism and segmental compression (Figure 8). A minimum of eight anchors should be placed above and below the apex of the kyphosis. After proximal implant fixation, correction is obtained through cantilever force into the distal implants. This process can result in large lever forces at the end of the curve, leading to instrumentation pullout or junctional kyphosis. Incremental segmental correction, beginning at the apex of the deformity and extending proximally and distally, decreases the cantilever forces at the end of the instrumented area (Figures 9 and 10). The use of a distal lumbar hook helps prevent distal pullout, and the use of a proximal transverse process hook helps prevent proximal junctional kyphosis. The interspinous ligaments between the most proximal instrumented and noninstrumented spinous processes should be preserved. After correction has been achieved with instrumentation, copious bone graft with autogenous bone, allograft bone, or a combination is used to achieve fusion. Postoperative bracing is rarely used with rigid fixation systems. A painful prominence or another complication may require late removal of instrumentation, leading to a gradual recurrence of deformity even if the fusion is solid.

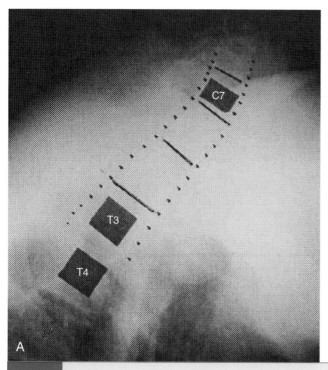
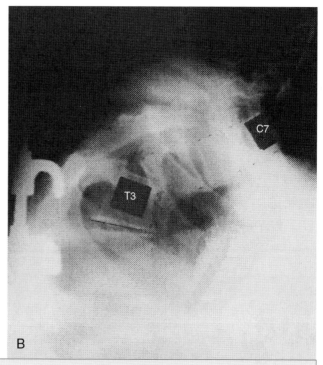

Figure 9 | Lateral radiographs of a patient with Scheuermann kyphosis showing the cervicothoracic junction before surgery (**A**) and proximal junctional kyphosis 2 years after surgery (**B**). (Reproduced with permission from Denis F, Sun EC, Winter RB: Incidence and risk factors for proximal and distal junctional kyphosis following surgical treatment of Scheuermann kyphosis: Minimum five-year follow-up. *Spine [Phila Pa 1976]* 2009;34[20]:E729-E734.)

A patient with a long-standing rigid deformity may have an ossified ligament or disk requiring anterior release. Preoperative MRI is helpful to ensure there is no abnormality such as thoracic disk herniation, congenital spinal stenosis, or epidural cyst, which could increase the risk of neurologic compromise during surgical correction.[15]

For a severe rigid deformity or in a salvage or revision procedure, vertebral column resection has been recommended for its ability to provide marked correction of the deformity and eliminate the need for an anterior procedure.[16] A rigid localized deformity is ideal for vertical column resection. Vertebral column resection entails removal of the posterior elements of the vertebral body, then the vertebral body and adjacent disk material. The spine is completely unstable at this point and must be stabilized with a temporary rod. Care must be taken to avoid excessively distracting or compressing the spinal column. Neurologic loss may result from cord buckling, subluxation, or laminar impingement. Because of the significant potential for neurologic injury, this procedure is best done in a center with trained and experienced personnel.

Intraoperative neuromonitoring is important for avoiding significant neurologic complications. Some form of motor tract assessment must be included because deficits in motor tract function are observable before changes in somatosensory-evoked potentials. Alterations in neuromonitoring data have been reported in

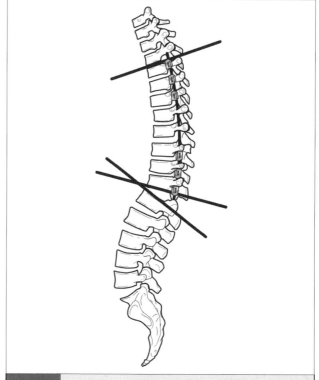

Figure 10 | Schematic drawing showing distal junctional kyphosis (*intersecting lines*) caused by an insufficient fusion, with maintenance of normal proximal kyphosis (*single line*).

association with prolonged intraoperative hypotension, and such alterations should prompt hypotension reversal to increase spinal cord perfusion. Other recommended interventions include release of corrective forces, additional bony decompression, elimination of subluxation, and restoration of anterior column height.[17] Prompt intervention can help prevent a potentially catastrophic neurologic deficit.

Some patients develop a superior mesenteric artery syndrome after correction of spine alignment. A superior mesenteric artery syndrome should be suspected if gastrointestinal symptoms or sepsis of unknown origin develops after correction. A taut superior mesenteric artery may result in duodenal obstruction or even intestinal necrosis.[18] A mild syndrome usually can be managed nonsurgically.

Summary

Appropriate treatment decision making requires an understanding of the natural history of Scheuermann kyphosis. A skeletally immature patient with a Scheuermann kyphotic curve should be treated with bracing. In a skeletally immature patient, brace treatment usually results in stabilization of the curve, but appreciable improvement is rare. A large, rigid curve is relatively unlikely to respond to bracing. A patient with a progressive curve of more than 75°, a curve that is progressing significantly despite bracing, or persistent pain that has not responded to nonsurgical treatment should be considered for surgery. The cosmetic appearance of the curve also should be considered in making the decision for surgery. Anterior release is rarely indicated, except for a severe, localized, and rigid deformity.

The current surgical treatments require major intervention and carry significant risks, but they offer an opportunity for excellent deformity correction with significant relief of discomfort. Most surgical patients report marked improvement in back discomfort after surgical stabilization and are satisfied with the cosmetic appearance of the spine.

Annotated References

1. Murray PM, Weinstein SL, Spratt KF: The natural history and long-term follow-up of Scheuermann kyphosis. *J Bone Joint Surg Am* 1993;75(2):236-248.

2. Damborg F, Engell V, Andersen M, Kyvik KO, Thomsen K: Prevalence, concordance, and heritability of Scheuermann kyphosis based on a study of twins. *J Bone Joint Surg Am* 2006;88(10):2133-2136.

   A major genetic contribution to etiology was found in a study of twins with symptomatic Scheuermann kyphosis.

3. Soo CL, Noble PC, Esses SI: Scheuermann kyphosis: Long-term follow-up. *Spine J* 2002;2(1):49-56.

4. Ogilvie JW, Sherman J: Spondylolysis in Scheuermann's disease. *Spine (Phila Pa 1976)* 1987;12(3):251-253.

5. Korovessis P, Zacharatos S, Koureas G, Megas P: Comparative multifactorial analysis of the effects of idiopathic adolescent scoliosis and Scheuermann kyphosis on the self-perceived health status of adolescents treated with brace. *Eur Spine J* 2007;16(4):537-546.

   Brace treatment affects the patient's self-perceived health status related to quality of life and may require psychologic support.

6. Bradford DS, Moe JH, Montalvo FJ, Winter RB: Scheuermann's kyphosis and roundback deformity: Results of Milwaukee brace treatment. *J Bone Joint Surg Am* 1974;56(4):740-758.

7. Otsuka NY, Hall JE, Mah JY: Posterior fusion for Scheuermann's kyphosis. *Clin Orthop Relat Res* 1990;251:134-139.

8. Denis F, Sun EC, Winter RB: Incidence and risk factors for proximal and distal junctional kyphosis following surgical treatment for Scheuermann kyphosis: Minimum five-year follow-up. *Spine (Phila Pa 1976)* 2009;34(20):E729-E734.

   An analysis of risk factors associated with proximal junctional kyphosis and distal junctional kyphosis revealed that failure to fuse the proximal end vertebra or disruption of the junctional ligamentum flavum led to proximal junctional kyphosis and that fusing short of the first lordotic disk led to distal junctional kyphosis.

9. Poolman RW, Been HD, Ubags LH: Clinical outcome and radiographic results after operative treatment of Scheuermann's disease. *Eur Spine J* 2002;11(6):561-569.

10. Reinhardt P, Bassett GS: Short segmental kyphosis following fusion for Scheuermann's disease. *J Spinal Disord* 1990;3(2):162-168.

11. Cho KJ, Lenke LG, Bridwell KH, Kamiya M, Sides B: Selection of the optimal distal fusion level in posterior instrumentation and fusion for thoracic hyperkyphosis: The sagittal stable vertebra concept. *Spine (Phila Pa 1976)* 2009;34(8):765-770.

    The distal end of a fusion for Scheuermann kyphosis should include the sagittal stable vertebra. The sagittal stable vertebra is the most proximal lumbar vertebra touched by a vertical line from the posterosuperior corner of the sacrum. Distal junction kyphosis was found to develop even if fusion included the first lordotic disk.

12. Lee SS, Lenke LG, Kuklo TR, et al: Comparison of Scheuermann kyphosis correction by posterior-only thoracic pedicle screw fixation versus combined anterior/posterior fusion. *Spine (Phila Pa 1976)* 2006;31(20):2316-2321.

    Retrospective comparison of posterior-only thoracic pedicle screw fusion and anterior-posterior fusion (in 18 or 21 patients with Scheuermann kyphosis, respectively) revealed shorter surgical times, less blood loss, better correction, and fewer complications with posterior-only fixation.

13. Arlet V, Schlenzka D: Scheuermann's kyphosis: Surgical management. *Eur Spine J* 2005;14(9):817-827.

14. Hosman AJ, Langeloo DD, de Kleuver M, Anderson PG, Veth RP, Slot GH: Analysis of the sagittal plane after surgical management for Scheuermann's disease: A view on overcorrection and the use of an anterior release. *Spine (Phila Pa 1976)* 2002;27(2):167-175.

15. Putz C, Stierle I, Grieser T, et al: Progressive spastic paraplegia: The combination of Scheuermann's disease, a short-segmented kyphosis and dysplastic thoracic spinous processes. *Spinal Cord* 2009;47(7):570-572.

   Progressive incomplete spastic paraplegia is described in a patient with localized Scheuermann disease and segmental dysplastic spinous processes. Significant neurologic improvement followed a posterior spine fusion.

16. Lenke LG, O'Leary PT, Bridwell KH, Sides BA, Koester LA, Blanke KM: Posterior vertebral column resection for severe pediatric deformity: Minimum two-year follow-up of thirty-five consecutive patients. *Spine (Phila Pa 1976)* 2009;34(20):2213-2221.

   Retrospective review of 35 consecutive patients with a severe pediatric spine deformity found posterior-based vertebral column resection to be safe but challenging. Intraoperative neurologic monitoring is essential.

17. Cheh G, Lenke LG, Padberg AM, et al: Loss of spinal cord monitoring signals in children during thoracic kyphosis correction with spinal osteotomy: Why does it occur and what should you do? *Spine (Phila Pa 1976)* 2008;33(10):1093-1099.

   With loss of spinal cord monitoring signals during correction of a kyphotic deformity, preserving spinal cord function requires awareness of the causes and mechanisms, including blood pressure elevation, malalignment adjustments, and further bony decompression.

18. Daniels AH, Jurgensmeier D, McKee J, Harrison MW, d'Amato CR: Acute celiac artery compression syndrome after surgical correction of Scheuermann kyphosis. *Spine (Phila Pa 1976)* 2009;34(4):E149-E152.

   A patient developed acute celiac artery compression syndrome after surgical correction of Scheuermann kyphosis, leading to necrosis of the intestine and a complicated postoperative course.

Chapter 40

Traumatic Pediatric Spine Injuries

Ying Li, MD   Daniel Hedequist, MD

Introduction

Five percent of all pediatric fractures are in the spine, and 60% to 80% of all traumatic pediatric spine injuries are in the cervical spine.[1] These cervical spine injuries carry a high rate of morbidity and mortality, with the accompanying head injuries contributing to the high mortality rate. The unique anatomic and biomechanical features of the immature cervical spine make it susceptible to injury.

Children age 8 years or younger are most likely to sustain an upper cervical spine injury, and children older than 8 years are most likely to sustain a lower cervical spine injury.[1,2] A recent review of the National Trauma Data Bank found an almost even distribution of upper and lower cervical spine injuries in children younger than 3 years,[3] suggesting that the frequency of lower cervical spine injuries in young children may be higher than previously believed. Young children are most commonly injured in a motor vehicle crash or a pedestrian-vehicle collision. Older children are most commonly injured during a sports activity. The use of an inappropriate or inadequate vehicular restraint can lead to a cervical spine injury in a young child; a small child placed in an adult three-point seatbelt may sustain a cervical spine injury during sudden deceleration, when the torso is restrained but the neck hyperflexes.[4] Child abuse always should be considered as the cause of a spine injury in an infant or young child.

Anatomy

Young children are particularly at risk of cervical spine injury because of their high head-to-body ratio, underdeveloped neck musculature, ligamentous laxity, and horizontal facet joints. In children older than 8 years, the anatomic and biomechanical features of the cervical spine more closely resemble those of adults. The normal radiographic parameters of the cervical spine in

children age 8 years or younger are listed in Table 1. Some normal pediatric radiographic findings may be misinterpreted as indicating an injury; these include an absence of cervical lordosis, a large atlantodens interval, pseudosubluxation of C2 on C3, a wide retropharyngeal space, anterior wedging of the cervical vertebral bodies, and incomplete ossification and open synchondroses.[5]

Initial Management

Any child with a traumatic injury should be assumed to have a spine injury for purposes of emergency transport and initial evaluation. A young child's disproportionately large head leads to excessive neck flexion during transport on a standard backboard. The child should be transported on a backboard with a cutout for the occiput or a pad that raises the body to allow safe supine cervical positioning[6] (Figure 1). A standard history and physical examination should be performed in the hospital. The child may be unable to cooperate with a detailed neurologic examination because of young age, anxiety, or altered mental status, and repeat examinations are important.

Table 1

Radiographic Parameters of the Pediatric Cervical Spine

Characteristic*	Normal Parameter
Larger atlantodens interval	Less than 5 mm
Pseudosubluxation of C2 on C3	Less than 4 mm
No cervical lordosis	
Larger retropharyngeal space	More than 6 mm at C2 More than 22 mm at C6
Wedging of cervical vertebral bodies	
Neurocentral synchondroses	Closure by age 7 years

*Compared with the adult cervical spine.

Adapted from Hedequist D: Pediatric spine trauma, in Abel MF, ed: *Orthopaedic Knowledge Update: Pediatrics*, ed 3. Rosemont, IL, American Academy of Orthopaedic Surgeons, 2006, p 324.

Dr. Hedequist or an immediate family member serves as a paid consultant to or is an employee of Medtronic Sofamor Danek. Neither Dr. Li nor any immediate family member has received anything of value from or owns stock in a commercial company or institution related directly or indirectly to the subject of this chapter.

5: The Pediatric Spine

Radiographic Evaluation

The initial imaging should include AP and lateral plain radiographs. Because multilevel fractures are common, a child with a documented spine fracture should undergo imaging of the entire spine to detect any noncontiguous fractures.[7] CT or MRI should be considered for further evaluation of fractures seen on plain radiographs or in the presence of a significant mechanism of injury, a high clinical suspicion of a spine injury, a head or facial injury, a suspected ligamentous injury, altered mental status, or an inability to cooperate with the physical examination. CT is more sensitive than plain radiographs for detecting a cervical spine fracture.[8] A pediatric CT protocol should be used to limit the patient's radiation exposure. MRI is the study of choice for assessing soft-tissue abnormalities such as disk herniation, ligamentous disruption, and injury to the spinal cord. MRI also can be helpful in spine clearance of an obtunded or intubated patient in the intensive care setting, although its use for this purpose is controversial.[4,9,10] MRI was used for adjunct imaging of the cervical spine in children who were obtunded or intubated, had equivocal plain radiographic or CT findings, had neurologic symptoms, or could not be cleared within 3 days after injury based on clinical or radiographic evidence.[10] MRI allowed cervical spine clearance in 88% of the patients; in the remaining 12%, MRI was used to detect significant injuries requiring treatment.

Cervical Spine Injuries

Occipital Condyle Fracture
Most occipital condyle fractures are associated with a head injury. A high index of suspicion is necessary because plain radiographs do not clearly show these fractures. Patients who have a lower cranial nerve deficit, a basilar skull fracture, another head injury, or neck pain with normal radiographs should undergo CT.[11] An impaction fracture or basilar skull fracture extending into the condyle is stable and can be treated with the use of a cervical collar. Avulsion of the alar ligament off the inferomedial portion of the condyle can lead to instability, especially if the contralateral alar ligament and tectorial membrane also are disrupted.[12] Halo immobilization or occipitocervical arthrodesis is recommended for an unstable fracture.[11,13]

Atlanto-occipital Dislocation
Atlanto-occipital dislocation is an unstable injury that can be difficult to diagnose. These injuries previously were considered rare and usually fatal. Survival now is more likely, probably because of improved emergency care, better initial cervical immobilization, and earlier diagnosis.[14,15] The mechanism of injury is a sudden deceleration that causes the head to be thrown forward.

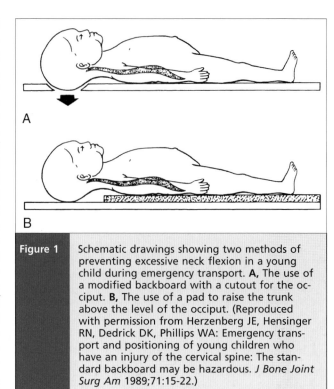

Figure 1 Schematic drawings showing two methods of preventing excessive neck flexion in a young child during emergency transport. **A,** The use of a modified backboard with a cutout for the occiput. **B,** The use of a pad to raise the trunk above the level of the occiput. (Reproduced with permission from Herzenberg JE, Hensinger RN, Dedrick DK, Phillips WA: Emergency transport and positioning of young children who have an injury of the cervical spine: The standard backboard may be hazardous. *J Bone Joint Surg Am* 1989;71:15-22.)

The atlanto-occipital joint has little inherent bony stability and is primarily stabilized by the ligaments around the joint. A high index of suspicion is required if a child has a closed head injury or significant facial trauma. Possible signs of this injury include unexplained headaches, ataxia, motor or sensory deficits, and difficulty in breathing after a significant trauma. Plain radiographs and MRI are used to diagnose the injury. Because atlanto-occipital dislocation is a ligamentous injury, the treatment of choice is surgical stabilization with an occiput-to-C2 fusion, followed by immobilization with a halo device.[15]

Atlas Fracture
The atlas has three primary ossification centers. The two neural arch ossification centers appear at approximately the seventh week of gestation; the anterior arch ossification center is visible at birth in 20% of individuals and appears by age 9 to 12 months in the remaining 80%. Fusion of the posterior synchondrosis occurs at approximately age 3 years, and the neurocentral synchondrosis fuses by age 7 years.[5,16,17] A fracture of the ring of C1 (Jefferson fracture) can occur through the synchondroses in the immature spine. A synchondrosis fracture can be difficult to appreciate on radiographs and may be more common than usually is recognized.[17] The mechanism of injury is an axial load applied to the head, resulting in force transmission from the occipital condyles to the lateral masses of C1. Separation of the lateral masses can lead to rupture or avulsion of the transverse ligament, which can cause C1-C2 instability. Diagnosis can be made if an AP radiograph reveals

more than 6.9 mm of combined lateral overhang of the lateral masses of C1 on C2. As much as 6 mm of pseudospread of the lateral masses relative to the dens is common in children younger than 4 years because the atlas grows more rapidly than the axis, and sometimes pseudospread is seen in children as old as 7 years.[16,17] CT may facilitate the diagnosis if the plain radiographic findings are inconclusive. The treatment consists of immobilization in a cervical collar or halo device. The use of halo traction followed by a halo device is recommended if there is more than 6.9 mm of widening of the lateral masses.

Atlantoaxial Injury

The transverse ligament is the primary stabilizer of the atlantoaxial joint, and the apical and alar ligaments are secondary stabilizers. Traumatic disruption of the transverse ligament leads to atlantoaxial instability. Avulsion of the transverse ligament off the lateral mass of C1 is the most common adult atlantoaxial injury. Midsubstance rupture of the transverse ligament is more common in young children, possibly secondary to ligamentous laxity, incomplete ossification of the vertebrae, and shallow, horizontally oriented facet joints.[18,19] A patient with this injury has neck pain and muscle spasms after a trauma. An atlantodens interval greater than 5 mm on lateral radiographs indicates disruption of the transverse ligament and instability. CT may reveal a bony avulsion off the lateral mass of C1. Surgical stabilization, consisting of posterior atlantoaxial arthrodesis with instrumentation, is recommended for ligamentous disruption. A bony avulsion can be treated with immobilization in a cervical collar or halo device,[20,21] but surgical stabilization is necessary if nonunion with persistent instability develops.[20]

Atlantoaxial Rotatory Subluxation

The atlantoaxial joint is responsible for 50% of cervical rotation. Atlantoaxial subluxation can occur with attenuation of the synovial capsule, the transverse ligament, or both. Rotatory subluxation most commonly occurs after trauma or an upper respiratory infection (known as Grisel syndrome). The patient typically has neck pain, limited rotation, torticollis, and a cock-robin position in which the head is rotated to one side and tilted laterally to the opposite side. Plain radiographs can be difficult to interpret because of the abnormal position of the head and neck. Dynamic CT obtained with the head in neutral position and rotated in each direction is useful for establishing the diagnosis because it allows evaluation of the dynamic relationship between C1 and C2 and the presence of fixed malalignment.[22] Treatment is based on the duration of symptoms.[23,24] Rotatory subluxation that has been present for less than 1 week can be treated using a soft collar, anti-inflammatory medications, and physical therapy. If rotatory subluxation persists, head-halter traction and muscle relaxants are used. Rotatory subluxation that continues for more than 3 to 4 weeks is significantly

more likely to lead to persistent or recurrent subluxation.[23,24]

Reduction can be attempted with halo traction. If the reduction is successful, immobilization with a halo device is used. If the reduction is unsuccessful or is not maintained, posterior atlantoaxial arthrodesis is recommended.[23-26] Reduction of rotatory subluxation before arthrodesis is controversial. Both in situ fusion and preoperative traction have been recommended for achieving as much correction of the clinical deformity as possible.[23,25] Preoperative traction has been used in an attempt to reduce the rotatory subluxation before fusion or open reduction.[24,26]

Odontoid Fracture

Odontoid fracture is one of the most common cervical spine fractures in children. In young children, an odontoid fracture usually occurs through the synchondrosis at the base of the odontoid, which fuses at approximately age 6 years.[5,27-30] The mechanism of injury in adults is a combination of hyperextension, axial rotation, shear, and compression.[31] More than 50% of pediatric odontoid fractures result from a motor vehicle crash in which the child was fastened in a forward-facing car seat; this factor suggests that sudden deceleration with forced flexion of the head is the mechanism of injury.[32] Neck pain and resistance to neck extension are common symptoms of a traumatic odontoid fracture. Fractures at the level of the synchondrosis frequently are missed during the initial assessment and are diagnosed later as neck pain and stiffness persist.[2,30,32] The diagnosis can be made with lateral radiographs, on which anterior displacement of the odontoid can be seen. CT with sagittal and coronal reconstruction can further delineate the fracture if the plain radiographic findings are equivocal.[2,30]

Odontoid fractures in children usually heal uneventfully because of the stability provided by an intact anterior periosteal sleeve. The treatment usually consists of closed reduction in extension followed by 8 weeks of immobilization in a Minerva orthosis or halo device.[2,30,32] Eleven of 15 children younger than 6 years were treated nonsurgically after an odontoid fracture: 4 had Minerva cast immobilization without reduction, 3 had acute closed reduction in hyperextension followed by immobilization in a halo device, and 4 had gradual reduction with traction followed by immobilization in a Minerva cast.[32] Three children were treated surgically with posterior spine fusion and C1-C2 wiring. One child had a delayed diagnosis, and the fracture had healed when it was discovered 6 months after injury. All of the odontoid fractures healed, and none of the nonsurgically treated patients had a complication. All three surgically treated patients had at least one complication, including delayed union, deep wound infection, loss of reduction, and fusion at C2-C3.[32]

Odontoid fractures in patients with an open basilar synchondrosis were classified based on the amount of fracture displacement and the location of the fracture

5: The Pediatric Spine

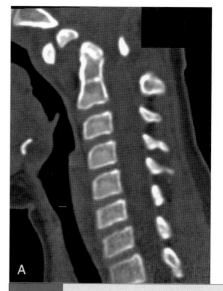
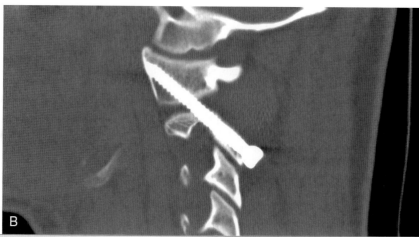

| Figure 2 | A child with Down syndrome had progressive gait changes and increased frequency of falling. **A,** Preoperative CT showing an os odontoideum and C1-C2 instability. **B,** Postoperative CT showing posterior C1-C2 fusion with transarticular screws and Brooks-type wiring. |

in relation to the synchondrosis. All patients with a fracture proximal to the synchondrosis, as well as 92% of patients with a fracture at the level of the synchondrosis and less than 100% displacement, healed with nonsurgical management using a Minerva orthosis or halo device.[30] Two patients had a fracture at the level of the synchondrosis with more than 100% displacement. One of these patients died, and the second patient underwent posterior C1-C2 fusion after a nonunion developed during halo immobilization.

Os Odontoideum

Os odontoideum is believed to result from an unrecognized odontoid fracture in which the alar ligaments pull the tip of the fractured odontoid away from the base, leading to a nonunion.[33] The condition is asymptomatic in many individuals and may be diagnosed incidentally on radiographs obtained after a motor vehicle crash. The symptoms vary; the patient may have neck pain with a normal neurologic examination, transient neurologic findings, or myelopathy secondary to instability. On plain radiographs, the os odontoideum appears as a round ossicle with sclerotic borders, separated from the base of the odontoid by a wide space. Instability can be determined on lateral flexion-extension radiographs. The free ossicle moves as a unit with the anterior arch of C1. Movement of the ossicle by 8 mm or more with respect to the body of C2 is evidence of instability (Figure 2).

The recommended treatment is surgical stabilization with posterior atlantoaxial arthrodesis. Posterior wiring leads to high rates of nonunion in both pediatric and adult patients. An 84% fusion rate was found in 25 children who underwent posterior upper cervical spine fusion using the Brooks or Gallie technique.[34] Un-

successful internal fixation or postoperative immobilization was identified as leading to nonunion. Screw fixation is reported to be safe for posterior C1-C2 fusion even in very young children, with union rates of 100%.[35-38] The fixation options include the use of C1-C2 transarticular screws and C1 lateral mass screws with C2 pedicle or translaminar screws. Postoperative immobilization in a cervical orthosis often is sufficient.[36,37]

Hangman's Fracture

Traumatic C2 spondylolisthesis (hangman's fracture) is rare in children and usually occurs in children younger than 2 years.[39-42] The mechanism of injury is hyperextension with axial loading. The possibility of child abuse must be considered in a child with this injury. Lateral radiographs reveal a fracture in the region of the pars of C2 with anterolisthesis of C2 on C3. A persistent synchondrosis can mimic a fracture. CT or MRI is useful for differentiating a fracture from a persistent synchondrosis, which is characterized by smooth cortical margins, lack of instability, and absence of soft-tissue swelling.[43] The treatment consists of closed reduction with extension of the neck, followed by 8 weeks of immobilization in a Minerva cast or halo device.[39,40,42] Posterior C1-C3 arthrodesis or anterior C2-C3 arthrodesis is recommended if there is nonunion or instability.

Lower Cervical Spine Injury

Injury to the lower cervical spine (C3-C7) is more common in older children and adolescents than in young children. The fracture can occur through the cartilaginous end plate, with the inferior end plate most commonly involved.[2,44] End plate fractures are associated with significant risk of neurologic injury. The fracture can be difficult to visualize on plain radiographs and is more clearly defined on CT or MRI. The treatment consists of closed reduction followed by immobilization in a halo device.[2]

Other injury patterns in the lower cervical spine are similar to those of adults, including posterior ligamentous disruption, compression fracture, burst fracture, facet dislocation, and spondylolysis and spondylolisthesis. The patient has neck pain and point tenderness. Radiographs may be normal or show a loss of cervical lordosis or a widening of the interspinous process space posteriorly. MRI is useful for diagnosing a ligamentous injury. The treatment consists of immobilization in a cervical collar until the patient is able to undergo voluntary flexion-extension lateral radiographs. Posterior arthrodesis is recommended if there is evidence of instability. In a child, instability is defined as more than 7° of sagittal angulation between adjacent vertebrae or more than 3.5 mm of translation.[45]

A compression fracture is the most common injury to the lower cervical spine in children. The mechanism of injury is flexion and axial loading. Lateral radiographs show a loss of anterior vertebral height and localized kyphosis. A compression fracture is stable and can be treated with 3 to 6 weeks of immobilization in a cervical collar. Flexion-extension lateral radiographs should be obtained after the collar is removed to confirm stability. A burst fracture is rare in children and results from axial loading. CT is useful for detecting spinal canal compromise from retropulsed fragments. A patient who is neurologically intact and has no significant canal compromise can be treated with 6 to 8 weeks of immobilization in a halo device. Arthrodesis and possibly spinal cord decompression are required if a neurologic deficit or significant canal compromise is present.

Unilateral or bilateral facet dislocation usually occurs in adolescents. Lateral radiographs are diagnostic. Reduction can be obtained with traction if the patient is awake and cooperative. Open reduction is necessary if the patient is obtunded or closed reduction is unsuccessful. After closed or open reduction is achieved, surgical stabilization with arthrodesis is performed.

Acute spondylolysis and spondylolisthesis of the lower cervical spine have been reported in children.[46,47] These fractures result from hyperextension or flexion and axial loading. Lateral radiographs show lucency through the pars. CT can be useful for distinguishing between a fracture and a synchondrosis. Immobilization in a cervical collar or halo device is the recommended treatment. An unstable fracture or nonunion requires posterior arthrodesis.

Spinal Cord Injury Without Radiographic Abnormality (SCIWORA)

The term SCIWORA was developed before the availability of MRI for diagnosing soft-tissue injury to the spinal column or spinal cord. SCIWORA is defined as traumatic myelopathy without overt vertebral column disruption on radiographs and CT.[48] SCIWORA is diagnosed in 30% to 40% of all children who sustain a traumatic spinal cord injury.[48] The upper cervical spinal cord is most commonly affected. SCIWORA is believed to result from stretching of the spinal column, leading to stretching, tearing, or contusion of the spinal cord. The child's ligamentous laxity allows the spinal column to stretch as much as 5 cm before rupturing, but the spinal cord is tethered and able to stretch only 5 to 6 mm before rupturing. SCIWORA occurs with hyperextension, hyperflexion, a distraction injury, or spinal cord ischemia. Because of biomechanical maturation of the pediatric cervical spinal column, SCIWORA is less common in children older than 8 years; one study found SCIWORA only in children age 8 years or younger.[1,48] The cause of injury varies with age, and the possibility of child abuse must be considered in an infant or young child. Young children are most commonly injured in a pedestrian-vehicle collision or a fall. Older children and adolescents are more commonly injured in a motor vehicle crash or sports activity.

The neurologic injury can be severe in a young child, with a complete injury having a poor prognosis. Symptoms of SCIWORA may appear as late as 4 days after the injury. Therefore, it is important for a patient with transient neurologic symptoms after trauma to be closely monitored and undergo neck immobilization.[4] The findings of plain radiographs and CT are negative. MRI may show damage to the soft tissues, including ligament rupture, disk herniation, and muscle edema. The patterns of spinal cord injury on MRI include complete disruption, cord hemorrhage, and cord edema. The location of the spinal cord injury may be remote from that of the soft-tissue injury. Somatosensory-evoked potentials can help evaluate the patient for myelopathy if a neurologic examination is inconclusive. The treatment consists of immobilization in a brace to prevent further injury.

Pediatric Halo Placement

A halo device often is used in the management of an unstable cervical spine injury in a child older than 1 year. This method of treatment is an effective alternative if the child's small size and future growth potential limit the surgical treatment options. Skull development and skull thickness are important considerations in young children. Placing a halo device can be problematic for a child younger than 18 months because cranial suture interdigitation may be incomplete and the fontanels may still be open[49] (the posterior fontanels close by age 6 months and the anterior fontanels close by age 18 months). Skull thickness is variable in children, and skull penetration is a potential complication.[49,50] Preoperative CT in young children permits the bone structure and skull thickness to be evaluated.

In a young child, the halo device is placed under general anesthesia. A local anesthetic can be used for an older child or adolescent. Pin placement is safest

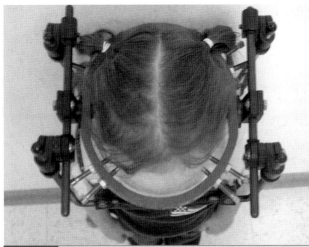

Figure 3   Clinical photograph showing a 6-year-old girl with a halo device. Eight pins are used, with each anterior pin placed diagonally and directly opposite a posterior pin. (Reproduced from Hedequist D: Pediatric spine trauma, in Abel MF, ed: *Orthopaedic Knowledge Update: Pediatrics 3.* Rosemont, IL, American Academy of Orthopaedic Surgeons, 2006, p 327.)

anterolaterally and posterolaterally, where the skull is thickest.[51] The pins are placed below the equator of the skull and 1 cm above the eyebrows and ears. The anterior pins are placed over the lateral two thirds of the orbit to avoid the frontal sinus and supratrochlear and supraorbital nerves. Placement of the anterior pins too laterally may lead to penetration of the temporalis muscle and interference with mastication. The posterior pins ideally are placed diagonally opposite the anterior pins. In children age 8 years or younger, multiple pins should be inserted at relatively low torque to decrease the risk of inadvertent skull penetration.[49] Eight to 12 pins are inserted to finger tightness (2 to 4 in-lb of torque) in these patients (Figure 3). The pins must not be retightened in a young child because of the risk of skull penetration. Some experts recommend limiting a toddler's ambulation during halo treatment to avoid injury from falling.[52]

Thoracic and Lumbar Spine Injuries

Thoracic and lumbar spine fractures result from axial loading, flexion, distraction, or shear forces. Incorrect placement of a vehicle lap belt can lead to an intra-abdominal or spine injury in a child. A correctly placed seat belt should lie across the pelvis; in a small child, however, a lap belt tends to ride up over the abdomen during deceleration, causing hyperflexion of the spine and leading to compression anteriorly and distraction posteriorly. This injury can be prevented by using a shoulder strap with the lap belt or placing the child in a child car seat with a frontal harness.

Compression Fracture

Compression fracture is the most common thoracolumbar spine injury in children and adolescents.[7] The mechanism of injury is axial compression with flexion. Lateral radiographs show an anterior loss of vertebral height. A compression fracture usually is stable, and neurologic injury is rare. An isolated fracture is treated with 6 weeks of brace immobilization. A contiguous fracture can lead to a kyphotic deformity, which requires posterior spine fusion if it becomes progressive.

Burst Fracture

Burst fracture occurs with axial loading and is most common around the thoracolumbar junction. Retropulsed bone and entrapped lamina fracture fragments can cause neurologic deficits. A study of thoracolumbar burst fractures in children and adolescents found that the level of injury is more important than the extent of spinal canal compromise in determining the risk of neurologic compromise; a thoracic-level fracture carries the greatest risk.[53] Loss of vertebral body height, kyphosis, and spinal canal compromise can be determined on plain radiographs and CT. MRI can be useful for distinguishing between a stable and an unstable burst fracture by showing injury to the posterior ligamentous structures. A stable burst fracture without a neurologic deficit is treated in a hyperextension cast or brace. An unstable burst fracture is treated with either posterior instrumentation and fusion or anterior corpectomy and strut grafting, followed by either anterior or posterior instrumentation and fusion.[53,54] Brace or cast treatment may be necessary after single-level stabilization.

Chance Fracture

A Chance fracture in a child is a flexion-distraction injury usually resulting from incorrect lap belt use in a motor vehicle crash. Almost 50% of children with a Chance fracture have intra-abdominal injury from compression of the intra-abdominal contents between the lap belt and the spine.[55] Abdominal ecchymosis warrants further evaluation to detect this life-threatening injury. Bony or ligamentous disruption of the posterior elements can occur. Plain radiographs, CT, and MRI are useful for evaluation. Patients with primarily bony involvement and no intra-abdominal injury can be treated using a hyperextension cast or brace. If MRI reveals disruption of the posterior ligamentous complex, surgical stabilization with posterior spine instrumentation and fusion is required (Figure 4).

Fracture-Dislocation

A fracture-dislocation typically is a highly unstable injury resulting from shearing or rotational displacement. Displacement can occur through the vertebral end plates in a young child; bone, ligamentous, or disk injury occurs in an older child. Neurologic injury is likely, and surgical stabilization with posterior spine instrumentation and fusion usually is required. Children are

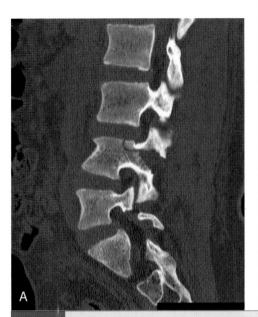
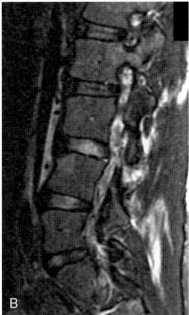
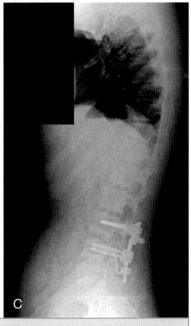

Figure 4 A pediatric lumbar Chance fracture. **A,** CT showing a Chance fracture at L4. **B,** MRI showing disruption of the posterior ligamentous complex. **C,** Postoperative lateral radiograph showing posterior instrumented fusion.

more capable than adults of significantly or completely recovering from a severe spinal cord injury. Age younger than 7 years, an incomplete neurologic deficit, and SCIWORA are associated with the best prognosis.[56] Paralytic scoliosis that is resistant to bracing is almost certain to develop in children younger than 10 years with a complete spinal cord injury.

Apophyseal Injury

Apophyseal avulsion fracture is unique to the pediatric population and typically occurs in adolescent boys. In this flexion injury, the posterior portion of the end plate (ring apophysis) fractures and displaces into the spinal canal. The lumbar spine is most commonly involved. Patients have back pain and often radicular symptoms similar to those of a disk herniation. The initial treatment consists of anti-inflammatory medications, physical therapy, and bracing. Patients with a large central fragment often have recalcitrant back pain and neurologic findings, and excision of the protruding disk and bone is required[57] (Figure 5). Fractures at the level of the spinal cord are treated with anterior decompression with instrumentation and fusion, and fractures in the lower lumbar spine are treated with posterior instrumentation and fusion.

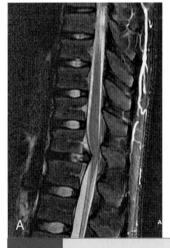
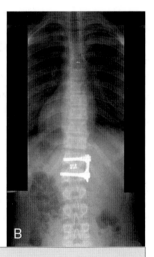

Figure 5 An adolescent boy had excruciating back and bilateral leg pain after a football tackle. **A,** MRI showing an apophyseal avulsion fracture at T12-L1 with significant posterior displacement into the spinal canal. **B,** AP radiograph showing excision of the disk and end plates and anterior instrumented fusion.

Summary

Pediatric spine fractures are rare. The anatomic and biomechanical features of the immature spine lead to injury patterns different from those of adults. Appropriate initial management is crucial, with cervical immobilization and transportation on a backboard de-

signed to accommodate a young child's large head. The evaluation should begin with a careful history, a physical examination, and plain radiographs. A fracture through the synchondrosis or cartilaginous end plate may be better seen on CT or MRI than plain radiographs. The treatment depends on the fracture pattern as well as the child's size and potential for healing and growth. A high index of suspicion and prompt evaluation and treatment of a pediatric spine injury can limit the associated morbidity and lead to the best outcome.

5: The Pediatric Spine

Annotated References

1. Platzer P, Jaindl M, Thalhammer G, et al: Cervical spine injuries in pediatric patients. *J Trauma* 2007;62(2):389-396.

   A retrospective review found significantly more upper cervical spine injuries in children age 8 years or younger and significantly more lower cervical spine injuries in children older than 8 years. SCIWORA was found only in children age 8 years or younger.

2. Reilly CW: Pediatric spine trauma. *J Bone Joint Surg Am* 2007;89(suppl 1):98-107.

   The diagnostic workup and treatment of spine injuries unique to the pediatric population are described.

3. Polk-Williams A, Carr BG, Blinman TA, Masiakos PT, Wiebe DJ, Nance ML: Cervical spine injury in young children: A National Trauma Data Bank review. *J Pediatr Surg* 2008;43(9):1718-1721.

   A review of cervical spine injury in 1,523 children younger than 3 years found an almost equal distribution of upper and lower cervical spine fractures. The frequency of lower cervical spine injuries in this age group may be higher than previously believed.

4. Hutchings L, Willett K: Cervical spine clearance in pediatric trauma: A review of current literature. *J Trauma* 2009;67(4):687-691.

   A review of current literature on cervical spine clearance in pediatric trauma patients noted that CT and MRI may aid in cervical spine clearance in unconscious and high-risk patients.

5. Khanna G, El-Khoury GY: Imaging of cervical spine injuries of childhood. *Skeletal Radiol* 2007;36(6):477-494.

   The unique anatomy of the pediatric cervical spine is reviewed, with normal developmental variants.

6. Herzenberg JE, Hensinger RN, Dedrick DK, Phillips WA: Emergency transport and positioning of young children who have an injury of the cervical spine: The standard backboard may be hazardous. *J Bone Joint Surg Am* 1989;71(1):15-22.

7. Carreon LY, Glassman SD, Campbell MJ: Pediatric spine fractures: A review of 137 hospital admissions. *J Spinal Disord Tech* 2004;17(6):477-482.

8. Silva CT, Doria AS, Traubici J, Moineddin R, Davila J, Shroff M: Do additional views improve the diagnostic performance of cervical spine radiography in pediatric trauma? *AJR Am J Roentgenol* 2010;194(2):500-508.

   A retrospective review of cervical spine imaging in 234 pediatric patients found that lateral radiographs were 73% sensitive and 92% specific for cervical spine injury compared with CT. The addition of other radiographic views did not improve sensitivity.

9. Anderson RC, Kan P, Vanaman M, et al: Utility of a cervical spine clearance protocol after trauma in children between 0 and 3 years of age. *J Neurosurg Pediatr* 2010;5(3):292-296.

   The protocol for cervical spine clearance at two level I pediatric trauma centers is presented. Clearance of the cervical spine in 575 children age 3 years or younger usually was possible without the use of CT or MRI.

10. Flynn JM, Closkey RF, Mahboubi S, Dormans JP: Role of magnetic resonance imaging in the assessment of pediatric cervical spine injuries. *J Pediatr Orthop* 2002;22(5):573-577.

11. Tuli S, Tator CH, Fehlings MG, Mackay M: Occipital condyle fractures. *Neurosurgery* 1997;41(2):368-377.

12. Sun PP, Poffenbarger GJ, Durham S, Zimmerman RA: Spectrum of occipitoatlantoaxial injury in young children. *J Neurosurg* 2000;93(1 suppl):28-39.

13. Anderson PA, Montesano PX: Morphology and treatment of occipital condyle fractures. *Spine (Phila Pa 1976)* 1988;13(7):731-736.

14. Kenter K, Worley G, Griffin T, Fitch RD: Pediatric traumatic atlanto-occipital dislocation: Five cases and a review. *J Pediatr Orthop* 2001;21(5):585-589.

15. Steinmetz MP, Lechner RM, Anderson JS: Atlantooccipital dislocation in children: Presentation, diagnosis, and management. *Neurosurg Focus* 2003;14(2):ecp1.

16. Lustrin ES, Karakas SP, Ortiz AO, et al: Pediatric cervical spine: Normal anatomy, variants, and trauma. *Radiographics* 2003;23(3):539-560.

17. AuYong N, Piatt J Jr: Jefferson fractures of the immature spine: Report of 3 cases. *J Neurosurg Pediatr* 2009;3(1):15-19.

   Jefferson fracture is described in three young children. In the immature spine, Jefferson fracture may be grossly underrecognized. Plain radiographs may appear normal despite a fracture through the synchondrosis.

18. McGrory BJ, Klassen RA, Chao EY, Staeheli JW, Weaver AL: Acute fractures and dislocations of the cervical spine in children and adolescents. *J Bone Joint Surg Am* 1993;75(7):988-995.

19. Lui TN, Lee ST, Wong CW, et al: C1-C2 fracture-dislocations in children and adolescents. *J Trauma* 1996;40(3):408-411.

20. Dickman CA, Greene KA, Sonntag VK: Injuries involving the transverse atlantal ligament: Classification and treatment guidelines based upon experience with 39 injuries. *Neurosurgery* 1996;38(1):44-50.

21. Lo PA, Drake JM, Hedden D, Narotam P, Dirks PB: Avulsion transverse ligament injuries in children: Successful treatment with nonoperative management. Report of three cases. *J Neurosurg* 2002;96(3, suppl):338-342.

22. McGuire KJ, Silber J, Flynn JM, Levine M, Dormans JP: Torticollis in children: Can dynamic computed tomography help determine severity and treatment? *J Pediatr Orthop* 2002;22(6):766-770.

23. Phillips WA, Hensinger RN: The management of rotatory atlanto-axial subluxation in children. *J Bone Joint Surg Am* 1989;71(5):664-668.

24. Subach BR, McLaughlin MR, Albright AL, Pollack IF: Current management of pediatric atlantoaxial rotatory subluxation. *Spine (Phila Pa 1976)* 1998;23(20):2174-2179.

25. Fielding JW, Hawkins RJ: Atlanto-axial rotatory fixation (fixed rotatory subluxation of the atlanto-axial joint). *J Bone Joint Surg Am* 1977;59(1):37-44.

26. Lee SC, Lui TN, Lee ST: Atlantoaxial rotatory subluxation in skeletally immature patients. *Br J Neurosurg* 2002;16(2):154-157.

27. Griffiths SC: Fracture of odontoid process in children. *J Pediatr Surg* 1972;7(6):680-683.

28. Seimon LP: Fracture of the odontoid process in young children. *J Bone Joint Surg Am* 1977;59(7):943-948.

29. Sherk HH, Nicholson JT, Chung SM: Fractures of the odontoid process in young children. *J Bone Joint Surg Am* 1978;60(7):921-924.

30. Hosalkar HS, Greenbaum JN, Flynn JM, Cameron DB, Dormans JP, Drummond DS: Fractures of the odontoid in children with an open basilar synchondrosis. *J Bone Joint Surg Br* 2009;91(6):789-796.

    Odontoid fractures in children with an open basilar synchondrosis are classified. Almost all fractures through the synchondrosis with less than 100% displacement and all fractures proximal to the synchondrosis healed with nonsurgical management.

31. Puttlitz CM, Goel VK, Clark CR, Traynelis VC: Pathomechanisms of failures of the odontoid. *Spine (Phila Pa 1976)* 2000;25(22):2868-2876.

32. Odent T, Langlais J, Glorion C, Kassis B, Bataille J, Pouliquen JC: Fractures of the odontoid process: A report of 15 cases in children younger than 6 years. *J Pediatr Orthop* 1999;19(1):51-54.

33. Fielding JW, Hensinger RN, Hawkins RJ: Os odontoideum. *J Bone Joint Surg Am* 1980;62(3):376-383.

34. Lowry DW, Pollack IF, Clyde B, Albright AL, Adelson PD: Upper cervical spine fusion in the pediatric population. *J Neurosurg* 1997;87(5):671-676.

35. Wang J, Vokshoor A, Kim S, Elton S, Kosnik E, Bartkowski H: Pediatric atlantoaxial instability: Management with screw fixation. *Pediatr Neurosurg* 1999;30(2):70-78.

36. Gluf WM, Brockmeyer DL: Atlantoaxial transarticular screw fixation: A review of surgical indications, fusion rate, complications, and lessons learned in 67 pediatric patients. *J Neurosurg Spine* 2005;2(2):164-169.

    Sixty-seven pediatric patients underwent transarticular screw fixation for trauma, os odontoideum, or congenital anomaly. The fusion rate was 100%. Seven patients had a complication, including two vertebral artery injuries. Careful patient selection and preoperative planning can minimize the risks of transarticular screw fixation in children.

37. Reilly CW, Choit RL: Transarticular screws in the management of C1-C2 instability in children. *J Pediatr Orthop* 2006;26(5):582-588.

    Twelve pediatric patients with C1-C2 instability were treated using transarticular screws. All patients had successful fusion, including three patients with an os odontoideum and an earlier nonunion. C1-C2 transarticular screws were found to be safe and effective in children.

38. Heuer GG, Hardesty DA, Bhowmick DA, Bailey R, Magge SN, Storm PB: Treatment of pediatric atlantoaxial instability with traditional and modified Goel-Harms fusion constructs. *Eur Spine J* 2009;18(6):884-892.

    Six pediatric patients with an os odontoideum and C1-C2 instability underwent fusion with C1 lateral mass screws and C2 pedicle or translaminar screws. All patients had a solid fusion. The Goel-Harms fusion construct was determined to be safe and effective in children.

39. Pizzutillo PD, Rocha EF, D'Astous J, Kling TF Jr, McCarthy RE: Bilateral fracture of the pedicle of the second cervical vertebra in the young child. *J Bone Joint Surg Am* 1986;68(6):892-896.

40. Ruff SJ, Taylor TK: Hangman's fracture in an infant. *J Bone Joint Surg Br* 1986;68(5):702-703.

41. Kleinman PK, Shelton YA: Hangman's fracture in an abused infant: Imaging features. *Pediatr Radiol* 1997;27(9):776-777.

42. Ranjith RK, Mullett JH, Burke TE: Hangman's fracture caused by suspected child abuse: A case report. *J Pediatr Orthop B* 2002;11(4):329-332.

43. Williams JP III, Baker DH, Miller WA: CT appearance of congenital defect resembling the hangman's fracture. *Pediatr Radiol* 1999;29(7):549-550.

44. Lawson JP, Ogden JA, Bucholz RW, Hughes SA: Physeal injuries of the cervical spine. *J Pediatr Orthop* 1987;7(4):428-435.

45. Lam FC, Irwin BJ, Poskitt KJ, Steinbok P: Cervical spine instability following cervical laminectomies for Chiari II malformation: A retrospective cohort study. *Childs Nerv Syst* 2009;25(1):71-76.

    Postlaminectomy cervical instability can occur after decompression for Chiari II malformation. Published radiographic criteria were used to determine instability in

5: The Pediatric Spine

pediatric patients who underwent this surgery. No patients showed clinical instability or required fusion.

46. Sasa T, Yoshizumi Y, Imada K, et al: Cervical spondylolysis in a judo player: A case report and biomechanical analysis. *Arch Orthop Trauma Surg* 2009;129(4): 559-567.

   A 12-year-old boy was diagnosed with a C6 grade I spondylolisthesis after he was thrown during a judo match. The treatment was nonsurgical. Biomechanical analysis showed increased disk stresses and hypermobility with cervical spondylolysis.

47. Legaye J, Horduna M: Cervical spondylolysis in a child: A case with hypermobility. *Spine J* 2009;9(1):e15-e19.

   A 7-year-old boy was found to have a C6 grade I spondylolisthesis after falling during gymnastics. MRI showed slight dehydration of the C6-7 disk, indicating mild degeneration. He was treated successfully using a cervical collar.

48. Pang D: Spinal cord injury without radiographic abnormality in children, 2 decades later. *Neurosurgery* 2004; 55(6):1325-1343.

49. Mubarak SJ, Camp JF, Vuletich W, Wenger DR, Garfin SR: Halo application in the infant. *J Pediatr Orthop* 1989;9(5):612-614.

50. Wong WB, Haynes RJ: Osteology of the pediatric skull: Considerations of halo pin placement. *Spine (Phila Pa 1976)* 1994;19(13):1451-1454.

51. Garfin SR, Roux R, Botte MJ, Centeno R, Woo SL: Skull osteology as it affects halo pin placement in children. *J Pediatr Orthop* 1986;6(4):434-436.

52. Caird MS, Hensinger RN, Weiss N, Farley FA: Complications and problems in halo treatment of toddlers: Limited ambulation is recommended. *J Pediatr Orthop* 2006;26(6):750-752.

   A review determined that halo fixation is safe in children age 3 years or younger. Falls are common in these children, and limited ambulation is recommended to prevent complications.

53. Vander Have KL, Caird MS, Gross S, et al: Burst fractures of the thoracic and lumbar spine in children and adolescents. *J Pediatr Orthop* 2009;29(7):713-719.

   In a review of 37 pediatric burst fractures, the risk of neurologic injury was more closely related to the level of injury than the extent of spinal canal compromise, with thoracic injuries at highest risk.

54. Lalonde F, Letts M, Yang JP, Thomas K: An analysis of burst fractures of the spine in adolescents. *Am J Orthop (Belle Mead NJ)* 2001;30(2):115-120.

55. Mulpuri K, Reilly CW, Perdios A, Tredwell SJ, Blair GK: The spectrum of abdominal injuries associated with Chance fractures in pediatric patients. *Eur J Pediatr Surg* 2007;17(5):322-327.

   A retrospective review found that almost 50% of children with a Chance fracture sustain associated intra-abdominal injury. It is important to evaluate for intra-abdominal injuries because they can be life threatening.

56. Wang MY, Hoh DJ, Leary SP, Griffith P, McComb JG: High rates of neurological improvement following severe traumatic pediatric spinal cord injury. *Spine (Phila Pa 1976)* 2004;29(13):1493-1497, discussion E266.

57. Chang CH, Lee ZL, Chen WJ, Tan CF, Chen LH: Clinical significance of ring apophysis fracture in adolescent lumbar disc herniation. *Spine (Phila Pa 1976)* 2008; 33(16):1750-1754.

   Adolescents with lumbar disk herniation had a high incidence of ring apophysis fractures and were likely to require surgery.

Chapter 41

Spondylolysis and Spondylolisthesis in Children and Adolescents

Martin J. Herman, MD   Peter D. Pizzutillo, MD

Introduction

Spondylolysis and spondylolisthesis are common causes of low back pain in children and adolescents. Although these clinical entities are familiar to clinicians, there is no consensus on the appropriate use of diagnostic imaging modalities, nonsurgical management, and surgical interventions. Imprecise, confusing terminology and a dearth of evidence-based published studies are responsible for marked variations in clinical practice. In recent years, the debate has focused on the best management of spondylolysis and spondylolisthesis in active children and adolescents with spondylolysis as well as surgical decision making for patients with high-grade spondylolisthesis and spondyloptosis. A framework is needed for patient evaluation, the use of imaging modalities, and nonsurgical and surgical treatment decision making.

Definitions

The term spondylolysis refers to a defect or structural abnormality of the vertebral pars interarticularis. Sclerosis within the pars or in its adjacent lamina or pedicle, in the absence of cortical disruption, is consistent with a stress reaction. The term stress fracture refers to a defect of the pars with cortical disruption but without resorption or sclerosis, as seen on CT. Isthmic or spondylolytic spondylolysis is a pars defect with a well-defined lucent gap bordered by mature cortical edges. Isthmic or spondylolytic spondylolysis may have a developmental etiology or may result from nonunion of a stress fracture of the pars.

Spondylolisthesis is the forward translation of a vertebral segment on its adjacent caudal vertebral seg-

ment. In children and adolescents, spondylolysis and spondylolisthesis most commonly occur at the lumbosacral junction secondary to an abnormality of the L5 pars. Pediatric spondylolysis and spondylolisthesis can occur at a more cephalad lumbar level, but simultaneous involvement of multiple lumbar levels is rare. Although spondylolysis and spondylolisthesis may be diagnosed using plain radiography, CT provides more discrete visualization of pars abnormalities and the bony anatomy of spondylolisthesis (Figure 1).

Some immature patients with spondylolisthesis do not have a pars defect but instead have intact posterior elements in association with dysplasia of the L5-S1 articulation. Congenital or dysplastic spondylolisthesis can take the form of maloriented or hypoplastic facets, an elongated pars, or a sacral end plate deficiency.

Low-grade spondylolisthesis is defined as a forward vertebral translation of less than 50% (Meyerding grade I or II). High-grade spondylolisthesis is a forward vertebral translation of more than 50% (Meyerding grade III or IV). Spondyloptosis is a more-than-100% forward translation of a vertebra onto its caudal neighbor.

Epidemiology

The reported prevalence of spondylolysis among adults is 6%.[1] However, lumbar spondylolysis was found in 21 of 188 adults (11.5%) who underwent CT in an ancillary project of the Framingham Heart Study.[2] Spondylolysis is rarely reported in infants, but children older than 6 years have a prevalence similar to that of adults.[3] Some patients have a hereditary predisposition to the condition; 22% to 26% of first-degree relatives of patients with isthmic spondylolysis and spondylolisthesis had similar radiographic findings, although most were asymptomatic.[4]

Anatomic variations may be significant in the development of spondylolysis. An anatomic evaluation of lumbar vertebrae from the Hamann-Todd Osteological Collection of the Cleveland Museum of Natural History suggests that inadequate spacing between the infe-

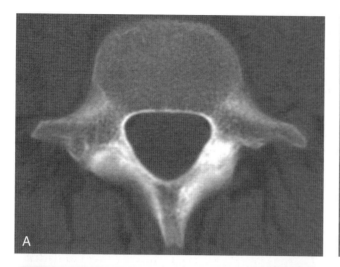

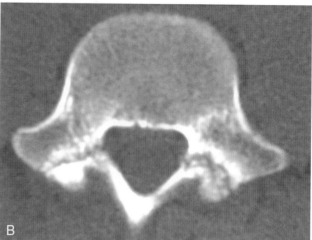

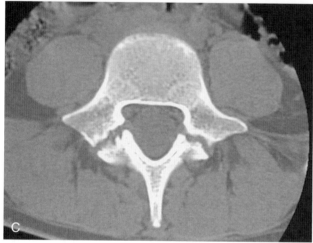

Figure 1 CT showing a traumatic spondylolytic stress reaction (**A**), a stress fracture (**B**), and a pars nonunion or spondylolytic defect (**C**).

rior articular processes of L4 and the superior articular facets of S1 causes abnormal contact pressures on both sides of the L5 pars and may result in spondylolysis.[5] A radiographic evaluation of 41 pediatric patients with spondylolytic defects concluded that narrow spacing between lumbar facets may contribute to the development of a pars defect.[6] The narrow spacing between lumbar facets may create a risk of spondylolysis because of abnormally high pars stresses during hyperextension activities.

Abnormalities of the spinopelvic parameters and pelvic balance have been identified in patients with pars abnormalities and spondylolisthesis. Patients with spondylolysis and low-grade spondylolisthesis were found to have a significantly increased pelvic incidence, an increased lumbar lordosis, and less segmental extension between L5 and S1 than normal individuals.[7] The observation that pelvic incidence, sacral slope, pelvic tilt, and lumbar lordosis are greater in those with spondylolisthesis suggests that alterations in pelvic anatomy may influence the development of spondylolisthesis.[8] Repetitive hyperextension and rotational loading of the lumbar spine result in increased forces at the pars interarticularis, causing stress reaction, stress fracture,

and nonunion of the pars that may be indistinguishable from those of isthmic spondylolysis.[9,10] Spondylolysis and spondylolisthesis are more likely to develop in high-level athletes in competitive sports such as gymnastics, football, diving, rowing, and tennis than in the general population.[11,12]

Classification

The well-known Wiltse-Newman classification describes five types of spondylolisthesis, of which types I and II are common in children and adolescents.[13] Type I, dysplastic spondylolisthesis, is the result of congenital abnormalities of the lumbosacral junction. Type II, isthmic spondylolisthesis, results from abnormalities of the pars interarticularis and has three subtypes. Type IIA is a disruption of the pars as the result of stress reaction or stress fracture and is the most common. Type IIB, an elongation of the pars, and type IIC, an acute pars fracture, are uncommon. In the Wiltse-Newman system, isthmic defects result from a repetitive loading of the pars, possibly with a hereditary predisposition to failure.

The Marchetti-Bartolozzi system broadly classifies spondylolisthesis as developmental or acquired. Developmental spondylolisthesis results from a combination of an inherited abnormality of the lumbosacral articulation and a pars failure.[14] Acquired spondylolisthesis can result from various factors; in children and adolescents, the most common type is traumatic, in which the cause is repetitive stress or acute injury. The Marchetti-Bartolozzi classification is comprehensive and useful for surgical planning, but it is complicated and difficult to apply.

The currently used classification systems do not allow isthmic defects to be clearly categorized as developmental or traumatic. The terms congenital and dysplastic are used interchangeably. In the Herman-Pizzutillo system, which is specific to children and adolescents, a uniform terminology is designed to clearly indicate etiology and interventions.[15] Three types of spondylolysis are described: dysplastic, developmental, and traumatic. Dysplastic spondylolisthesis mirrors the Wiltse-Newman dysplastic type. Developmental spondylolysis refers to a well-defined lytic pars defect that is either observed in a patient who is symptomatic or incidentally detected on radiographs. Developmental spondylolysis is frequently associated with spina bifida occulta of S1 and is hereditary.[4] Traumatic spondylolysis occurs in athletes and others with a history of repetitive activities that stress the lumbosacral spine, as well as patients with an acute spine injury. Traumatic spondylolysis caused by repetitive injury is further subdivided on the basis of CT as a stress reaction, stress fracture, or spondylolytic (nonunion) pars defect (Figure 1). It can be difficult to distinguish a developmental defect from a traumatic nonunion defect. Most traumatic spondylolytic nonunions have irregular cortical margins and a narrow space across the pars defect, but a developmental defect typically has sharply defined cortical margins and a uniform gap across the pars defect, sometimes in association with spina bifida occulta and sacral dysplasia.

The Mac-Thiong and Labelle classification is designed to guide the surgical treatment of L5-S1 spondylolisthesis.[16] This scheme allows low-dysplastic and high-dysplastic spondylolisthesis to be differentiated and incorporates the concept of sagittal spinopelvic balance. The spondylolisthesis is classified radiographically on the basis of degree of slip, dysplasia at the lumbosacral junction, and measurements of pelvic incidence, sacral slope, pelvic tilt, and pelvic balance. The unbalanced pelvis is retroverted, with a high sacral slope and low pelvic tilt in comparison with the pelvis of a normal adolescent.[17] On the basis of this classification, surgical reduction of the slip may be indicated for a patient with an unbalanced pelvis, but in situ surgical technique may be more appropriate for a patient with a normal spinopelvic balance.[17,18]

Clinical Evaluation

History

Children and adolescents with spondylolysis and spondylolisthesis commonly have low back pain, with or without radiating pain to the buttocks and posterior thigh. The pain usually has an insidious onset and may be activity related. Details of the patient's specific activity, such as sports type, intensity of participation, and training methods, as well as any acute injury, are helpful for establishing the diagnosis. For example, an athlete in a sport involving repetitive lumbar loading or rotation, such as American football or gymnastics, may be at increased risk for spondylolysis. A patient with high-grade spondylolisthesis or spondyloptosis may have back pain or a cosmetic concern related to flattening of the lumbar lordosis, sacral prominence, or scoliosis. Back pain may be associated with radicular symptoms, weakness of the lower extremity, or bowel and bladder dysfunction.

Examination

Patients with high-grade spondylolisthesis typically walk with a shortened stride and persistent hip and knee flexion as the result of altered spinopelvic mechanics and hamstring contracture. With the patient wearing a gown that opens in the back, the spine is examined for shoulder or trunk imbalance, limb-length discrepancy, and coronal spine deformity. Spine deformity in association with spondylolisthesis may be the result of concomitant idiopathic scoliosis, antalgic scoliosis caused by pain and spasm, or olisthetic scoliosis caused by asymmetric forward slippage of vertebrae. Patients with high-grade spondylolisthesis have sagittal plane deformity with flattening of lumbar lordosis, prominence of the sacrum, forward translation of the trunk on the pelvis with prominence of the buttocks, and a visible or palpable step-off at the lumbosacral junction.

The lumbosacral paraspinal muscles are palpated to detect local tenderness and spasm. The spine range of motion typically is limited in all planes in a patient with acute symptoms but may be relatively well preserved in a patient with chronic symptoms. Passive hyperextension of the lumbar spine frequently produces pain in a patient with spondylolysis and spondylolisthesis. Measurement of popliteal angle is important; severe hamstring contracture usually occurs only in a patient with symptoms, and it may be the only positive physical finding other than limited or painful spine motion.

The neurologic evaluation includes a complete assessment of lumbosacral nerve root function. An assessment of rectal tone is indicated if the patient reports bowel or bladder dysfunction. The straight leg raise test is useful for diagnosing nerve root irritation from a herniated disk, which is a relatively common etiology of low back pain in pediatric patients but may be difficult to detect if the patient has severe hamstring contrac-

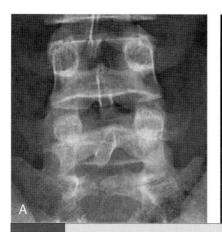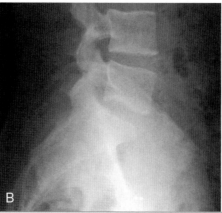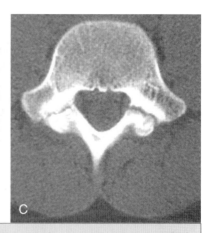

Figure 2 A 14-year-old boy who participates in wrestling had 5 months of low back pain and stiffness after activity, but he described no single injury and had no leg pain. Examination revealed pain with spine hyperextension and popliteal angles of 30°. Standing PA (**A**) and lateral (**B**) radiographs appeared normal. **C,** CT better defined the morphology as an established nonunion of the pars. The patient was treated with activity restriction and rehabilitation, and he returned to sports 3 months after he became pain free and had no hamstring tightness.

ture. Most patients with symptomatic spondylolysis or spondylolisthesis have a normal neurologic assessment.

Imaging

Standing PA radiographs of the thoracolumbosacral spine, including the hips and pelvis, allow spina bifida occulta of S1 to be determined and the Cobb angle to be measured in a patient with scoliosis. A standing lateral radiograph of the thoracolumbosacral spine and a coned-down or spot-lateral radiograph of the lumbosacral junction allow measurement of the anterior slippage for determining the Meyerding classification, the slip angle, and the overall sagittal balance (the relationship of the body of S1 to a vertical line from the C7 midbody). Radiographic documentation of pelvic incidence, sacral slope, and pelvic tilt, among other parameters, defines the patient's spinopelvic balance and can be used to assess the severity of the patient's overall lumbosacral deformity.[8] A supine oblique radiograph of the lumbosacral spine and a Ferguson-view (20° caudal-cephalad) PA radiograph of the lumbosacral junction are helpful for defining the morphology of the pars and lumbosacral segment. Lateral flexion-extension views of the lumbosacral junction can be used to assess mobility and the potential for reduction of the spondylolisthesis.

If the patient's radiographic findings are normal but the history and physical examination suggest a diagnosis of spondylolysis, single-photon emission computed tomography (SPECT) is sensitive and specific for determining the presence and location of increased bone activity. In a patient with painful spondylolysis and normal radiographs, SPECT usually shows increased uptake in the area of the pars or its adjacent structures.[19] Some patients whose radiographs reveal spondylolysis with established nonunion or spondylolisthesis have normal SPECT results, however.[20] In a patient with an obvious pars defect on radiographs but normal

SPECT, sources of back pain other than the pars defect must be considered, including segmental instability, disk degeneration, nerve root irritation, and facet joint pathology. CT of the identified level can more precisely define the bony morphology (Figure 2).

MRI can approach the sensitivity of SPECT for identifying spondylolysis.[21] The extent of osseous edema, as seen on MRI, may be correlated with the potential for a stress reaction or stress fracture to heal with nonsurgical intervention. In patients with high signal changes within the ipsilateral pedicles, as seen on axial T2-weighted MRI, 79% of pars defects healed with nonsurgical treatment.[22] MRI allows concurrent evaluation of disk health, any nerve root compression, and the integrity of the spinal cord and spinal column.

Nonsurgical Treatment

Stress Reactions and Stress Fractures

Stress reactions and stress fractures of the pars interarticularis are most common in athletes and others whose activities involve repetitive loading of the lumbar spine. These defects can be unilateral or bilateral and may involve the pars and the adjacent lamina and pedicle. The goals of treatment are to achieve bone healing and prevent nonunion of the pars defect. The use of a thoracolumbosacral orthosis or body cast is recommended to limit lumbar motion. The patient should be instructed to avoid the offending activity. A thigh extension of the thoracolumbosacral orthosis can be used to further restrict mobility but usually is not necessary. After 8 to 12 weeks of immobilization, CT evidence of either pars defect healing or an established nonunion is an indication for discontinuing bracing or casting. Physical therapy, consisting of core strengthening and hamstring stretching, is initiated. When hamstring contracture is resolved and normal core strength is restored, the patient is guided through a gradual return to sports. Rehabilitation and a gradual return to full activity without restriction are encouraged as long as the pain does not recur.

Isthmic Spondylolysis

Bony healing of the pars cannot be achieved nonsurgically in a child or adolescent with a well-defined isthmic pars defect, whether the defect is developmental or the result of nonunion. Instead, the primary treatment objectives are to relieve back and leg pain, improve low back motion and strength, and allow a return to full activity. The nonsurgical treatment consists of 6 to 8 weeks of activity restriction coupled with a focused rehabilitation program. A gradual return to activities is permitted when the patient is pain free, has improved spine mobility, and has no residual hamstring contracture. Nonsteroidal anti-inflammatory drugs are prescribed at the time of initial diagnosis for use whenever the symptoms worsen. Steroids, muscle relaxants, and narcotic pain medication are not routinely prescribed. For some patients with moderate or more severe discomfort, an antilordotic thoracolumbosacral orthosis can be used for a short period of time to alleviate pain and to allow rehabilitation to be initiated.[23] The patient is rapidly weaned from the brace when the symptoms improve.

The Results of Nonsurgical Treatment

Radiographic healing of stress reactions and stress fractures can be achieved by nonsurgical means.[24] A CT study of 239 pars defects in 134 patients younger than 18 years found that 62.9% of L4 defects and 8.8% of L5 defects healed with use of a spine corset, activity restriction, and rehabilitation.[25] Early-stage defects and defects at L4 were most likely to heal with nonsurgical treatment. Healing also is more likely to occur if there is pedicle edema adjacent to the pars defect, as seen on MRI.[22]

Clinical outcomes and radiographic evidence of union of the pars abnormality were pooled in a recent meta-analysis of observational studies of the nonsurgical treatment of spondylolysis and grade I spondylolisthesis.[26] In 15 studies, 665 patients were followed at least 1 year after treatment; 83.9% had a satisfactory outcome. No difference in outcome was noted based on whether patients were treated with a brace. In 10 studies, radiographic healing was documented in 28% of pars defects. Unilateral defects healed significantly more frequently than bilateral defects, and defects designated as acute were more likely to heal than so-called progressive or terminal defects. Despite a relatively low rate of healing in pars defects, the meta-analysis concluded that successful clinical outcomes can be expected in most nonsurgically treated patients with spondylolysis and grade I spondylolisthesis. This finding suggests that complete bone healing of the pars defects may not be necessary to obtain a satisfactory result.

Low-Grade Spondylolytic or Isthmic Spondylolisthesis

More than 67% of patients with symptomatic low-grade spondylolisthesis responded favorably to nonsurgical treatment[27] (Figure 3). Children and adolescents who are asymptomatic may be incidentally diagnosed with low-grade developmental spondylolisthesis and require no treatment. Follow-up clinical examination and radiographs are not routinely prescribed for a patient who is asymptomatic, but serial evaluations are indicated if pain, deformity, or hamstring tightness develop. Progressive slippage develops in fewer than 4% of pediatric patients with spondylolysis or low-grade spondylolytic spondylolisthesis.[28]

Low-Grade Dysplastic Spondylolisthesis

Patients with low-grade spondylolisthesis secondary to a lumbosacral anomaly or facet hypoplasia are at risk for progressive slippage and the development of neurologic symptoms. Careful clinical and radiographic follow-up at 4- to 6-month intervals is recommended for these patients. Nonsurgical treatment may be helpful for a child or adolescent with mild to moderate pain, normal neurologic status, and stable spine alignment. Progression of deformity occurs in most patients with dysplastic spondylolisthesis and can result in radicular symptoms including pain, weakness, and sphincter dysfunction. Surgical intervention is indicated to halt the progression of deformity, relieve symptoms, and improve the neurologic impairment.

Surgical Treatment

Spondylolysis and Low-Grade Spondylolisthesis

Few children or adolescents require surgery for the treatment of spondylolysis or low-grade spondylolytic spondylolisthesis. Most patients with symptoms respond well to nonsurgical treatment and are able to return to competitive sports without limitation. A patient whose condition does not respond to a minimum of 6 months of nonsurgical therapy or who has recurrent, intractable symptoms is a candidate for surgical intervention.

Pars Repair

Pars repair at the L5 level has been successful in patients whose L5-S1 disk is normal on preoperative MRI.[29] Pars repair primarily is indicated for a patient with symptomatic spondylolysis and reducible low-grade spondylolisthesis cephalad to L5, after at least 6 months of unsuccessful nonsurgical treatment; or a patient with pars defects at multiple vertebral levels. No significant difference was found in the clinical outcome of direct spondylolysis repair or fusion at a mean 14-year follow-up.[30] Although a lesion at the L5 level may be amenable to repair, L5-S1 fusion is preferable.

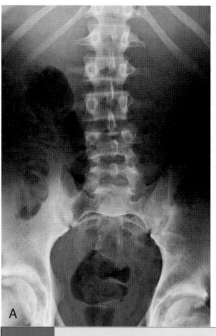
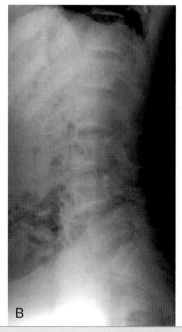
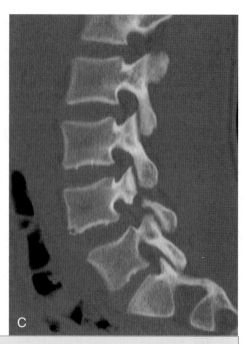

Figure 3 A 15-year-old boy was referred for treatment of scoliosis after 3 months of low back pain. Mild lumbar scoliosis and a grade I spondylolisthesis at L4 were revealed by standing PA (**A**) and lateral radiographs (**B**), and CT (**C**) confirmed a pars defect. The patient was treated in a lumbosacral orthosis for 6 weeks and progressed to rehabilitation. He was pain free and had no change in the deformity at 1-year follow-up.

Several techniques for repair of a pars defect have been described, including wiring, bone grafting, and direct screw repair.[31,32] Internal fixation with pedicle screws and sublaminar hooks compressed across the grafted pars defect is frequently used.[33] Similar minimally invasive procedures using advanced osteobiologics hold promise.[34] The current recommendation is direct pars repair by compression across the pars defect with a pedicle screw and sublaminar hook.

Fusion

In situ posterolateral fusion of L5-S1 without instrumentation is the gold standard for treating pediatric patients with persistently symptomatic spondylolysis and low-grade spondylolisthesis at the lumbosacral junction[35-37] (Figure 4). A mean 15.9-year follow-up of young patients treated with in situ fusion for spondylolysis and low-grade spondylolisthesis found that pseudarthrosis had developed in 13% of patients with posterolateral fusion and 34% of patients with posterior fusion only.[38] The clinical outcomes were generally satisfactory, with an average Oswestry Disability Index score of 8.2. Fourteen percent of the patients reported pain at rest. Persistent back pain was reported after fusion surgery for spondylolisthesis in older adolescents and young adults.[36] In these patients, posterior fusion with interbody support or pedicle screw instrumentation may increase the reliability of the fusion and eliminate the need for postoperative immobilization.

High-Grade Spondylolisthesis

The surgical treatment of children and adolescents with high-grade spondylolisthesis is a controversial topic. Specific procedural recommendations often are based on surgeon preference. All of the techniques include fusion, but serious differences of opinion exist concerning the advantages of posterolateral fusion alone compared with circumferential fusion and the advantages of in situ fusion with postural reduction of deformity compared with instrumented surgical reduction of deformity.

In Situ Posterolateral Fusion

Noninstrumented posterolateral fusion from L4 to S1 with postural reduction of deformity is the traditional treatment of high-grade spondylolisthesis in pediatric patients. The efficacy of this technique for achieving fusion and relieving pain is well documented.[35,37] Postural reduction of deformity is achieved after surgery with application of a pantaloon body cast. The patient is awake during the reduction and casting and is able to immediately communicate the development of pain or paresthesias. The incidence of postoperative progression and nonunion is low when posterolateral fusion is combined with pantaloon cast immobilization.[35,37] Relief of pain, nerve root symptoms, and hamstring contracture was maintained more than 15 years after surgery, without evidence of deformity progression or disk or facet degeneration.[39] To decrease the incidence of pseudarthrosis, the standard technique has been modi-

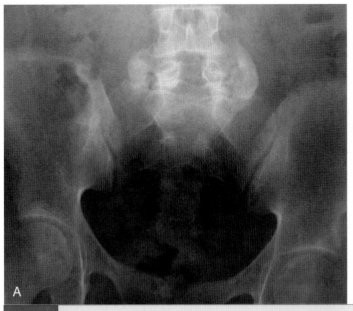
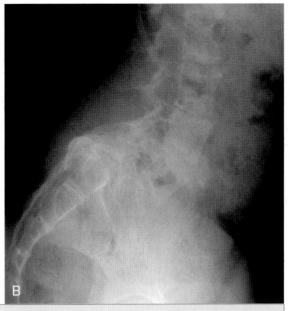

Figure 4 A 13-year-old girl had in situ fusion for high-grade spondylolytic (isthmic) spondylolisthesis, as seen on standing PA (**A**) and lateral (**B**) radiographs 1 year after surgery. The patient was pain free and had resumed all of her activities.

fied by insertion of a fibular strut graft through a hole drilled from the posterior body of S1 into the body of L5[40] (Figure 5). Partial reduction of high-grade spondylolisthesis combined with this transsacral grafting technique yielded satisfactory results in the primary treatment of high-grade spondylolisthesis and revision of unsuccessful posterolateral fusion in young adults.[41]

The largest study of adolescents with spondylolysis and spondylolisthesis who underwent in situ fusion and postural reduction with pantaloon immobilization reported that pain and neurologic symptoms were uniformly relieved and that the rate of pseudarthrosis with progressive slip was 5%.[35] Other studies found a pseudarthrosis rate as high as 45% if posterolateral fusion was not followed by immobilization.[42] The incidence of neurologic complications was much lower in patients treated with in situ fusion and postural reduction than in those treated with surgical fusion and reduction. Nerve root impingement and cauda equina syndrome were reported in patients who underwent either treatment.[43] The in situ technique also is limited in its ability to restore normal sagittal spine balance in patients with high-grade spondylolisthesis, and it may contribute to an unacceptable cosmetic result or a future complication such as back pain or worsening deformity.[18,44] Postural reduction typically improves translation by a maximum of one grade, with a moderate degree of sagittal deformity correction as determined by a decreased slip angle and increased lumbar lordosis.

Reduction and Fusion
Surgical reduction in association with fusion and spine instrumentation can be used to treat high-grade spon-

dylolisthesis. In one study, instrumented fusion from L4 to the sacrum (including S1 and S2 segments) was used to maintain partial reduction; the fusion rate was 100%.[17] Wide nerve root decompression of the L4, L5, and sacral nerve roots has been recommended before surgical reduction to reduce the likelihood of neurologic injury from stretch or impingement.[45] Excision of the L5-S1 disk with a portion of the superior sacral end plate facilitates insertion of an interbody support from the posterior approach and may increase the success of both the reduction and fusion. Pedicle screws at L4 and L5 are linked to pelvic fixation to maintain reduction and facilitate fusion. Although anatomic reduction may not be achieved, the extent of reduction must be sufficient to allow insertion of an anterior interbody graft (Figure 6). Excellent results were achieved with L5-S1 fusion using posterior instrumentation, reduction of the forward translation to a grade I spondylolisthesis, and placement of an anterior interbody cage with autogenous bone graft.[46] Anterior column support and posterior compressive instrumentation were found to restore the biomechanics necessary to facilitate fusion and maintain reduction.

Intraoperative monitoring by a neurophysiologist is important during the reduction maneuver for detecting early neurologic compromise, particularly an L4 or L5 nerve root injury. Total intravenous anesthesia without neuromuscular blockade can be used to monitor transcranial motor-evoked potentials in the cauda equina roots, as reflected by L2-S4 myotomes. Baseline somatosensory-evoked potentials are recorded to assess the sensory components of the L4 and L5 nerve roots. Normal mean arterial pressures are maintained during the procedure.[47] Baseline measurements are obtained

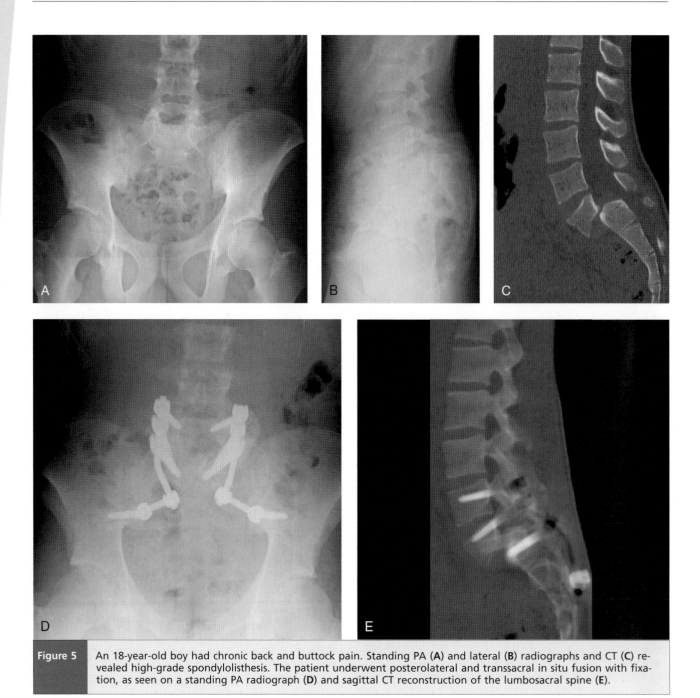

Figure 5 An 18-year-old boy had chronic back and buttock pain. Standing PA (**A**) and lateral (**B**) radiographs and CT (**C**) revealed high-grade spondylolisthesis. The patient underwent posterolateral and transsacral in situ fusion with fixation, as seen on a standing PA radiograph (**D**) and sagittal CT reconstruction of the lumbosacral spine (**E**).

both before and after prone positioning for surgery, and motor- and somatosensory-evoked potentials are monitored frequently throughout the procedure to allow early detection of nerve injury, especially during a slow reduction of deformity. The L5 nerve root is particularly at risk for stretch injury or impingement during reduction. Pedicle screws are tested with stimulated electromyography after their placement. Early identification of changes in root function allows the surgeon to make immediate adjustments to reduce the risk of permanent injury.

Reduction of high-grade spondylolisthesis and fusion generally yields radiographic fusion and a satisfac-

tory clinical outcome, as determined by diminished pain and neurologic symptoms as well as improved sagittal alignment.[17,42,48,49] Fusion and surgical reduction techniques were found to restore spinopelvic balance in most of the 73 patients (age 10 to 30 years) in a multicenter radiographic study.[18]

Pseudarthrosis can occur despite the use of internal fixation and circumferential fusion techniques.[42,48,49] From 1996 to 2002, the overall rate of neurologic complications was reported to increase from 1.3% to 3.1% in patients undergoing spondylolisthesis surgery.[44] The increase in complications corresponded to a twofold increase in the number of patients who had reduction.

Nerve root and cauda equina injuries are the most common serious complications of reduction and fixation of high-grade spondylolisthesis; they are less common with in situ techniques.[42] A review of neurologic outcomes from several published studies found that 12.5% of patients had a neurologic deficit after reduction and fusion of high-grade spondylolisthesis.[50] Most neurologic deficits are temporary, but permanent injuries that result in foot drop, sphincter dysfunction, or chronic nerve pain can occur and can dramatically influence the patient's outcome. Other long-term complications include degenerative changes in adjacent segments cephalad to the fusion and sacral deformities caudal to the fusion.[44]

In Situ Fusion Versus Reduction and Fusion

A meta-analysis compared in situ fusion with surgical reduction for the treatment of high-grade spondylolisthesis and found that fusion rates were generally higher in patients who had surgical reduction, but clinical outcomes did not significantly differ.[51] Relief of back pain, improvement in nerve root symptoms, and risk of complications also did not depend on treatment. Patients who had in situ fusion were found to have better outcomes at a mean 15-year follow-up, however.[52] The paucity of high-level published evidence precluded the development of definitive guidelines for treating high-grade spondylolisthesis.[51] Radiographically improved pelvic balance after surgical reduction has yet to be correlated with improved clinical outcomes, compared with in situ techniques.[17,18]

Summary

Spondylolysis and spondylolisthesis are common causes of low back pain in children and adolescents. A child or adolescent with spondylolysis and low-grade spondylolisthesis frequently has symptom relief and is able to return to full activity after nonsurgical treatment. A patient with symptomatic high-grade spondylolisthesis is unlikely to respond favorably to nonsurgical treatment and often requires surgical intervention. The surgical treatments include in situ fusion, with or without pantaloon postural reduction and immobilization; in situ fusion with internal fixation; and surgical reduction with internal fixation and circumferential fusion.

In situ fusion with postural reduction and pantaloon casting is the current standard of treatment. The patient usually has relief of symptoms, and the incidence of progressive deformity, pseudarthrosis, or neurologic injury is low. The disadvantages of in situ fusion, postural reduction, and pantaloon casting include inability to achieve complete reduction of spondylolisthesis, inability to recreate a normal spinopelvic alignment appearance, and prolonged immobilization.

Surgical reduction of high-grade spondylolisthesis in an adolescent may result in a significantly improved appearance, a successful fusion, and a reduced need for

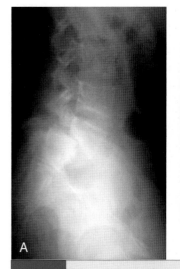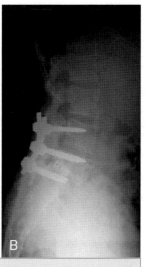

Figure 6 A 14-year-old boy had back and leg pain. **A,** Standing lateral radiograph showing high-grade (dysplastic) spondylolisthesis with severe deformity of the sacral dome and L5 vertebra. **B,** Standing lateral radiograph after decompression, reduction of the spondylolisthesis from grade IV to grade I, and posterolateral and transforaminal interbody fusion with fixation.

postoperative immobilization. The disadvantages include an inability to obtain complete reduction, as well as possible hardware failure, pseudarthrosis, progressive deformity, or neurologic injury.

Effective treatment of a child or adolescent requires diagnosis of the specific type of spondylolysis or spondylolisthesis. Children and adolescents are not at risk for the severe disk degeneration and facet joint arthritis that develop in adults with spondylolisthesis. The clinician should use a classification system that is specific to pediatric patients and should avoid associating the adult and pediatric clinical manifestations.

Annotated References

1. Fredrickson BE, Baker D, McHolick WJ, Yuan HA, Lubicky JP: The natural history of spondylolysis and spondylolisthesis. *J Bone Joint Surg Am* 1984;66(5):699-707.

2. Kalichman L, Kim DH, Li L, Guermazi A, Berkin V, Hunter DJ: Spondylolysis and spondylolisthesis: Prevalence and association with low back pain in the adult community-based population. *Spine (Phila Pa 1976)* 2009;34(2):199-205.

   An 11.5% prevalence of lumbar spondylolysis was found in a CT review of an unselected community-based population from the Framingham Heart Study. This was a higher number than reported in radiographic studies.

3. Turner RH, Bianco AJ Jr: Spondylolysis and spondylolisthesis in children and teen-agers. *J Bone Joint Surg Am* 1971;53(7):1298-1306.

5: The Pediatric Spine

4. Albanese M, Pizzutillo PD: Family study of spondylolysis and spondylolisthesis. *J Pediatr Orthop* 1982;2(5): 496-499.

5. Ward CV, Latimer B: Human evolution and the development of spondylolysis. *Spine (Phila Pa 1976)* 2005; 30(16):1808-1814.

Evaluation of lumbar vertebrae from the Hamann-Todd Osteological Collection revealed that individuals with L5 spondylolysis had a smaller separation between the inferior facet of L4 and the superior facet of S1, compared with control subjects.

6. Zehnder SW, Ward CV, Crow AJ, Alander D, Latimer B: Radiographic assessment of lumbar facet distance spacing and pediatric spondylolysis. *Spine (Phila Pa 1976)* 2009;34(3):285-290.

Radiographs of 41 pediatric patients with spondylolytic defects were evaluated. Insufficient caudal increase in lumbar interfacet spacing was found to be a possible anatomic explanation for the condition, compared with control subjects.

7. Roussouly P, Gollogly S, Berthonnaud E, Labelle H, Weidenbaum M: Sagittal alignment of the spine and pelvis in the presence of L5-s1 isthmic lysis and low-grade spondylolisthesis. *Spine (Phila Pa 1976)* 2006;31(21): 2484-2490.

Several sagittal alignment parameters were measured on the radiographs of 82 patients with L5-S1 spondylolysis and low-grade spondylolisthesis. The conclusion was that sagittal alignment may influence the biomechanical environment and influence the condition.

8. Labelle H, Roussouly P, Berthonnaud E, Dimnet J, O'Brien M: The importance of spino-pelvic balance in L5-S1 developmental spondylolisthesis: A review of pertinent radiologic measurements. *Spine (Phila Pa 1976)* 2005;30(6, suppl):S27-S34.

Radiographic analysis of L5-S1 developmental spondylolisthesis revealed that pelvic morphology and spinopelvic balance were abnormal in these patients, compared with control subjects. Pelvic incidence, sacral slope, pelvic tilt, and lumbar lordosis were the most different characteristics.

9. Troup JD: The etiology of spondylolysis. *Orthop Clin North Am* 1977;8(1):57-64.

10. Dietrich M, Kurowski P: The importance of mechanical factors in the etiology of spondylolysis: A model analysis of loads and stresses in human lumbar spine. *Spine (Phila Pa 1976)* 1985;10(6):532-542.

11. Ciullo JV, Jackson DW: Pars interarticularis stress reaction, spondylolysis, and spondylolisthesis in gymnasts. *Clin Sports Med* 1985;4(1):95-110.

12. Micheli LJ, Wood R: Back pain in young athletes: Significant differences from adults in causes and patterns. *Arch Pediatr Adolesc Med* 1995;149(1):15-18.

13. Wiltse LL, Newman PH, Macnab I: Classification of spondylolisis and spondylolisthesis. *Clin Orthop Relat Res* 1976;117:23-29.

14. Marchetti PG, Bartolozzi P: Classification of spondylolisthesis as a guideline for treatment, in Bridwell KH, DeWald RL, eds: *The Textbook for Spinal Surgery*, ed 2. Philadelphia, PA, Lippincott-Raven, 1997, pp 1211-1254.

15. Herman MJ, Pizzutillo PD: Spondylolysis and spondylolisthesis in the child and adolescent: A new classification. *Clin Orthop Relat Res* 2005;434:46-54.

A classification of spondylolysis and spondylolisthesis specific to children and adolescents considers clinical factors and CT morphology of the spondylolytic defects to guide treatment.

16. Mac-Thiong JM, Labelle H: A proposal for a surgical classification of pediatric lumbosacral spondylolisthesis based on current literature. *Eur Spine J* 2006;15(10): 1425-1435.

A surgical classification of L5-S1 spondylolisthesis is based on the degree of slip, the degree of dysplasia, and the sagittal spinopelvic balance. A tentative algorithm for surgical treatment is provided.

17. Hresko MT, Hirschfeld R, Buerk AA, Zurakowski D: The effect of reduction and instrumentation of spondylolisthesis on spinopelvic sagittal alignment. *J Pediatr Orthop* 2009;29(2):157-162.

A retrospective study of 26 adolescents who had partial reduction and L4-sacrum fusion concluded that achieving solid fusion may be more important than reducing the deformity in determining spinopelvic sagittal balance. Level of evidence: IV.

18. Labelle H, Roussouly P, Chopin D, Berthonnaud E, Hresko T, O'Brien M: Spino-pelvic alignment after surgical correction for developmental spondylolisthesis. *Eur Spine J* 2008;17(9):1170-1176.

A retrospective multicenter analysis concluded that classifying high-grade spondylolisthesis into the unbalanced or balanced pelvis group may be useful for guiding surgical technique. Reduction should be considered for an unbalanced retroverted pelvis.

19. Bellah RD, Summerville DA, Treves ST, Micheli LJ: Low-back pain in adolescent athletes: Detection of stress injury to the pars interarticularis with SPECT. *Radiology* 1991;180(2):509-512.

20. Lusins JO, Elting JJ, Cicoria AD, Goldsmith SJ: SPECT evaluation of lumbar spondylolysis and spondylolisthesis. *Spine (Phila Pa 1976)* 1994;19(5):608-612.

21. Hollenberg GM, Beattie PF, Meyers SP, Weinberg EP, Adams MJ: Stress reactions of the lumbar pars interarticularis: The development of a new MRI classification system. *Spine (Phila Pa 1976)* 2002;27(2):181-186.

22. Sairyo K, Katoh S, Takata Y, et al: MRI signal changes of the pedicle as an indicator for early diagnosis of

spondylolysis in children and adolescents: A clinical and biomechanical study. *Spine (Phila Pa 1976)* 2006;31(2): 206-211.

The authors compared CT and MRI of patients with spondylolysis and concluded that high-signal changes on MRI allow an early diagnosis of spondylolysis and may predict healing potential.

23. Steiner ME, Micheli LJ: Treatment of symptomatic spondylolysis and spondylolisthesis with the modified Boston brace. *Spine (Phila Pa 1976)* 1985;10(10):937-943.

24. Sys J, Michielsen J, Bracke P, Martens M, Verstreken J: Nonoperative treatment of active spondylolysis in elite athletes with normal X-ray findings: Literature review and results of conservative treatment. *Eur Spine J* 2001; 10(6):498-504.

25. Fujii K, Katoh S, Sairyo K, Ikata T, Yasui N: Union of defects in the pars interarticularis of the lumbar spine in children and adolescents: The radiological outcome after conservative treatment. *J Bone Joint Surg Br* 2004; 86(2):225-231.

26. Klein G, Mehlman CT, McCarty M: Nonoperative treatment of spondylolysis and grade I spondylolisthesis in children and young adults: A meta-analysis of observational studies. *J Pediatr Orthop* 2009;29(2):146-156.

Extensive meta-analysis of the literature on spondylolysis and grade I spondylolisthesis concluded that after 1 year, 83.9% of patients are clinically improved with nonsurgical treatment, bracing does not influence the outcome, and most defects do not heal. Level of evidence: IV.

27. Pizzutillo PD, Hummer CD III: Nonoperative treatment for painful adolescent spondylolysis or spondylolisthesis. *J Pediatr Orthop* 1989;9(5):538-540.

28. Seitsalo S, Osterman K, Hyvärinen H, Tallroth K, Schlenzka D, Poussa M: Progression of spondylolisthesis in children and adolescents: A long-term follow-up of 272 patients. *Spine (Phila Pa 1976)* 1991;16(4):417-421.

29. Roca J, Iborra M, Cavanilles-Walker JM, Albertí G: Direct repair of spondylolysis using a new pedicle screw hook fixation: Clinical and CT-assessed study. An analysis of 19 patients. *J Spinal Disord Tech* 2005;18(suppl): S82-S89.

A review of 19 patients treated with segmental pedicle screw hook fixation concluded that this technique achieves reliable union of a pars defect, but only if the patient is younger than 20 years.

30. Schlenzka D, Remes V, Helenius I, et al: Direct repair for treatment of symptomatic spondylolysis and low-grade isthmic spondylolisthesis in young patients: No benefit in comparison to segmental fusion after a mean follow-up of 14.8 years. *Eur Spine J* 2006;15(10):1437-1447.

At an average 14.8-year follow-up, the outcomes of pars repair with a cerclage wire and in situ segmental fusion were the same for adolescents with symptomatic spondylolysis or low-grade spondylolisthesis.

31. Askar Z, Wardlaw D, Koti M: Scott wiring for direct repair of lumbar spondylolysis. *Spine (Phila Pa 1976)* 2003;28(4):354-357.

32. Buck JE: Direct repair of the defect in spondylolisthesis: Preliminary report. *J Bone Joint Surg Br* 1970;52(3): 432-437.

33. Kakiuchi M: Repair of the defect in spondylolysis: Durable fixation with pedicle screws and laminar hooks. *J Bone Joint Surg Am* 1997;79(6):818-825.

34. Noggle JC, Sciubba DM, Samdani AF, Anderson DG, Betz RR, Asghar J: Minimally invasive direct repair of lumbar spondylolysis with a pedicle screw and hook construct. *Neurosurg Focus* 2008;25(2):E15.

In a review of five patients, the authors found that minimally invasive L5 pars repairs with a pedicle screw hook construct can be done safely, with decreased collateral soft-tissue injury, and has a reliable clinical result.

35. Pizzutillo PD, Mirenda W, MacEwen GD: Posterolateral fusion for spondylolisthesis in adolescence. *J Pediatr Orthop* 1986;6(3):311-316.

36. Frennered AK, Danielson BI, Nachemson AL, Nordwall AB: Midterm follow-up of young patients fused in situ for spondylolisthesis. *Spine (Phila Pa 1976)* 1991;16(4): 409-416.

37. Burkus JK, Lonstein JE, Winter RB, Denis F: Long-term evaluation of adolescents treated operatively for spondylolisthesis: A comparison of in situ arthrodesis only with in situ arthrodesis and reduction followed by immobilization in a cast. *J Bone Joint Surg Am* 1992; 74(5):693-704.

38. Helenius I, Lamberg T, Osterman K, et al: Scoliosis research society outcome instrument in evaluation of long-term surgical results in spondylolysis and low-grade isthmic spondylolisthesis in young patients. *Spine (Phila Pa 1976)* 2005;30(3):336-341.

In a long-term outcome study of posterolateral fusion for low-grade spondylolisthesis, the Scoliosis Research Society questionnaires and Oswestry Disability Index were found to be correlated and satisfactory. The Scoliosis Research Society tool could be used for young patients.

39. Lamberg T, Remes V, Helenius I, Schlenzka D, Seitsalo S, Poussa M: Uninstrumented in situ fusion for high-grade childhood and adolescent isthmic spondylolisthesis: Long-term outcome. *J Bone Joint Surg Am* 2007; 89(3):512-518.

This long-term study of 69 patients who had uninstrumented in situ fusion for high-grade childhood or adolescent spondylolisthesis found only minimal advantages

5: The Pediatric Spine

to circumferential fusion over posterolateral and anterior fusion. Patients in all groups had satisfactory results.

40. Smith MD, Bohlman HH: Spondylolisthesis treated by a single-stage operation combining decompression with in situ posterolateral and anterior fusion: An analysis of eleven patients who had long-term follow-up. *J Bone Joint Surg Am* 1990;72(3):415-421.

41. Hanson DS, Bridwell KH, Rhee JM, Lenke LG: Dowel fibular strut grafts for high-grade dysplastic isthmic spondylolisthesis. *Spine (Phila Pa 1976)* 2002;27(18):1982-1988.

42. Molinari RW, Bridwell KH, Lenke LG, Ungacta FF, Riew KD: Complications in the surgical treatment of pediatric high-grade, isthmic dysplastic spondylolisthesis: A comparison of three surgical approaches. *Spine (Phila Pa 1976)* 1999;24(16):1701-1711.

43. Schoenecker PL, Cole HO, Herring JA, Capelli AM, Bradford DS: Cauda equina syndrome after in situ arthrodesis for severe spondylolisthesis at the lumbosacral junction. *J Bone Joint Surg Am* 1990;72(3):369-377.

44. Ogilvie JW: Complications in spondylolisthesis surgery. *Spine (Phila Pa 1976)* 2005;30(6, suppl):S97-S101.

    A review of the literature on surgical complications of isthmic spondylolisthesis treatment revealed that neurologic complications increased from 1996 to 2002. Pseudarthrosis was the most common complication.

45. Lenke LG, Bridwell KH: Evaluation and surgical treatment of high-grade isthmic dysplastic spondylolisthesis. *Instr Course Lect* 2003;52:525-532.

46. Shufflebarger HL, Geck MJ: High-grade isthmic dysplastic spondylolisthesis: Monosegmental surgical treatment. *Spine (Phila Pa 1976)* 2005;30(6, suppl):S42-S48.

    Eighteen patients had a good outcome at 2-year follow-up after monosegmental fusion and near-anatomic correction of high-grade spondylolisthesis. Anterior column support and posterior compressive instrumentation enhanced the outcome.

47. Schwartz DM, Auerbach JD, Dormans JP, et al: Neurophysiological detection of impending spinal cord injury during scoliosis surgery. *J Bone Joint Surg Am* 2007; 89(11):2440-2449.

    A large multicenter study of intraoperative neuromonitoring for adolescent idiopathic scoliosis found that monitoring both somatosensory and transcranial electric motor-evoked potentials was advantageous for detecting early changes in spinal cord function.

48. Muschik M, Zippel H, Perka C: Surgical management of severe spondylolisthesis in children and adolescents: Anterior fusion in situ versus anterior spondylodesis with posterior transpedicular instrumentation and reduction. *Spine (Phila Pa 1976)* 1997;22(17):2036-2043.

49. Poussa M, Schlenzka D, Seitsalo S, Ylikoski M, Hurri H, Osterman K: Surgical treatment of severe isthmic spondylolisthesis in adolescents: Reduction or fusion in situ. *Spine (Phila Pa 1976)* 1993;18(7):894-901.

50. Lamartina C, Zavatsky JM, Petruzzi M, Specchia N: Novel concepts in the evaluation and treatment of high-dysplastic spondylolisthesis. *Eur Spine J* 2009;18(suppl 1):133-142.

    A retrospective case study reviewed the outcomes of reduction and fusion for high-dysplastic developmental spondylolisthesis. Restoration of sagittal balance and fusion can be achieved safely, but care must be taken to avoid L5 neurologic injury.

51. Transfeldt EE, Mehbod AA: Evidence-based medicine analysis of isthmic spondylolisthesis treatment including reduction versus fusion in situ for high-grade slips. *Spine (Phila Pa 1976)* 2007;32(19, suppl):S126-S129.

    A literature review of treatments for high-grade spondylolisthesis concluded that clear guidelines for treatment cannot be formulated because of insufficient levels of evidence.

52. Poussa M, Remes V, Lamberg T, et al: Treatment of severe spondylolisthesis in adolescence with reduction or fusion in situ: Long-term clinical, radiologic, and functional outcome. *Spine (Phila Pa 1976)* 2006;31(5):583-592.

    At 14.8-year follow-up of 22 adolescents who were surgically treated for high-grade spondylolisthesis, those with in situ fusion had a better outcome than those who had reduction and fusion.

Section 6

Spine Disorders

SECTION EDITOR
CHRISTOPHER M. BONO, MD

Chapter 42
Primary and Metastatic Spine Tumors

Kenny S. David, MS (Orth)   Moshe Yanko, MD   Alan M. Levine, MD

Introduction

Tumors involving the spinal column are challenging to treat. The biomechanical requirements of the spine, the neurologic structures incorporated into each segment, and the close proximity of major vascular structures often dictate treatment strategies different from those used for tumors in other parts of the skeleton. Advances in technology have led to the development of powerful diagnostic modalities and increasingly sophisticated methods of treatment. As a result, patients' quality of life and life expectancy have improved. This trend is likely to accelerate in the future.

The early symptoms of neoplastic spinal column involvement frequently are nonspecific, and a delay in diagnosis can result. Paying careful attention to the patient's history and obtaining relevant laboratory studies and imaging can save precious time and improve the prognosis. A multidisciplinary approach including oncologists, radiologists, internists, orthopaedic surgeons, and paramedical personnel can improve outcomes. Close interaction with family members and caregivers as well as the patient is required at every step of treatment for a patient with an oncologic diagnosis.

Prevalence and Characteristics

Approximately 2,000 new skeletal malignancies are detected every year in the United States, 5% of which involve the spine. The estimated prevalence of primary spine tumors is 3.6 per 100,000 people.[1] Benign primary tumors most commonly occur during the first

Dr. Levine is deceased. At the time this chapter was written he or an immediate family member had received royalties from Elsevier and US Spine; was a member of a speakers' bureau or had made paid presentations on behalf of Accuray; served as a paid consultant to or was an employee of US Spine; and had received research or institutional support from Accuray, Amgen, and Medtronic Sofamor Danek. Neither of the following authors nor any immediate family member has received anything of value from or owns stock in a commercial company or institution related directly or indirectly to the subject of this chapter: Dr. David, Dr. Yanko.

three decades of life. With the exception of osteosarcoma and Ewing sarcoma, malignant primary tumors usually affect patients older than 21 years. Spine metastases most often occur in patients older than 40 years.

Benign tumors most frequently involve the posterior elements of the spinal column. In contrast, malignant tumors have a predilection for the vertebral bodies. Hemangioma is the most commonly encountered benign tumor of the spine. Multiple myeloma and lymphoma are the two most common malignant tumors.[2] Chordoma is the most common tumor in the sacral and cervical regions of the spine.[1] The most common symptom of a spine tumor is pain, which occurs in 76% of patients with a benign tumor and 95% of patients with a malignant tumor. Neurologic involvement was found in 5 of 29 patients (17%) with a benign tumor and 51 of 98 patients (52%) with a primary spine malignancy.[1]

Metastatic spine tumors are 25 to 40 times more common than primary spine tumors and are the most common type of tumor involving the vertebral column. Improvements in diagnostic and therapeutic capabilities in oncology have led to increased long-term survival, with the resultant effect of increasing the prevalence of metastatic spine involvement. The rate of spine complications of metastatic disease has simultaneously decreased as a result of the use of bisphosphonates for many types of tumors. Carcinomas of the breast, prostate gland, kidney, and thyroid gland account for 80% of all skeletal metastases, with the spine as the most common site.[3] Of approximately 8,000 sarcomas diagnosed annually in the United States, only 10% are primary malignancies of the spine. Malignant cells tend to invade the basal membrane of the nutrient artery in the posterior aspect of the vertebral body. The later involvement of the vertebral cortex creates the potential for pathologic fracture, instability, and tumor spread beyond the anatomic boundaries of the vertebral body.

Evaluation

History and Physical Examination
Nonspecific neck and back pain is one of the most frequent reasons patients consult a physician. Back pain

that is prolonged, has a slow and insidious onset (with or without trauma), does not improve with rest, and wakes the patient from sleep should be considered suspicious. The presence of a vertebral fracture after a relatively minor trauma or without a precipitating incident also can offer a clue to underlying pathology. Recent-onset back pain in a patient with a previous malignancy should be considered a recurrence or metastasis until proved otherwise. The interval between primary tumor occurrence and the appearance of a metastasis can be more than 10 years in some types of tumor. Radioisotope scintigraphy detected spine metastatic lesions an average of 3.6 months after the primary tumor diagnosis in pulmonary cancers; the corresponding intervals for prostate, cervical, and breast malignancies were 12.8, 21.4, and 29.4 months, respectively.[4]

It is important to obtain an accurate social and occupational history from the patient, with careful questioning about exposure to potential carcinogenic agents. Asbestos exposure has been implicated in tumors of the lung and gastrointestinal tract. Exposure to arsenic, benzene, or cadmium has been associated with tumors of the lung, blood (leukemias and non-Hodgkin lymphoma), and prostate gland, respectively. Liver malignancies have been linked to vinyl chloride, a chemical used as a refrigerant. Familial predisposition has been reported to carcinomas of the breast, colon, ovary, and brain. A familial cancer may be characterized by an early age at onset and the presence of multiple or bilateral tumors. A review of systems is important and should focus on constitutional symptoms such as unintentional weight loss, with or without loss of appetite; mood changes; and chronic fatigue. A history of dyspepsia, hematochezia, cough, shortness of breath, bowel or bladder habit changes, skin lesions, petechiae, or hematomas can suggest the presence of a malignancy.

The physical examination should include an inspection of the patient's general posture, gait, and balance. The spinal column should be inspected for asymmetry, especially if there is no history of scoliosis, as well as for swellings or muscle wasting. The entire spine should be palpated, including the paraspinal areas, shoulder blades, rib cage, waists, sacrococcygeal regions, and pelvis. Percussion of the affected areas may elicit focal tenderness. The range of motion of the spine should be assessed. A careful neurologic examination of motor strength, sensation, and deep tendon reflexes should be performed, and any pathologic finding such as a Hoffman sign, clonus, or Babinski reflex should be noted.

Laboratory Studies

Laboratory testing is among the first steps in the evaluation of a patient with a suspected spine tumor. Anemia can be detected through a complete blood cell count. The white blood cell count may be abnormally elevated with a tumor that involves the myeloprolifera-

tive system, such as lymphoma, multiple myeloma, or plasmocytoma. The erythrocyte sedimentation rate is nonspecific but is elevated in a variety of diseases, including malignancies. Abnormalities in routine urine analysis, blood urea nitrogen, and serum creatinine can be present with renal cell carcinoma. A tumor that involves bone, whether it is osteoblastic or osteolytic, can cause changes in serum calcium, phosphate, parathyroid hormone, and alkaline phosphate levels. The hypercalcemia that often occurs with metastatic disease is believed to be partly the result of bone resorption at the site of the osteolytic lesions. Elevated alkaline phosphatase levels are associated with osteosarcoma. Over time, the monitored serum levels are correlated with disease activity. Multiple myeloma and solitary plasmacytoma produce monoclonal gammopathy, which can be detected by serum and urine protein electrophoresis. Thyroid malignancy can cause alterations in the levels of triiodothyronine, thyroxine, and thyroid-stimulating hormone. Prostate cancer should be considered as a possible diagnosis if the patient has a prostate-specific antigen level above 4 ng/mL or an increased serum acid phosphate level. A malignancy of the gastrointestinal system is suggested by an elevated serum carcinoembryonic antigen marker and altered liver function tests.

Imaging

Plain radiography of the vertebral column often is the first step in an evaluation for a possible spine tumor and should be done for any patient with back pain of more than 6 weeks' duration. However, a tumor is detectable on plain radiographs only if at least 30% to 40% of the vertebral body is involved. Extension of tumor into the surrounding soft tissues may appear as increased paraspinal soft-tissue width. Metastatic and primary malignant tumors can have a blastic or lytic radiographic pattern. On an AP radiograph, unilateral pedicle destruction (the so-called winking owl sign) strongly suggests neoplastic involvement. The intervertebral disk is avascular and therefore usually is a barrier to tumor growth. A process that crosses the disk space is more likely to be an infection than a tumor. The development of symptoms is not directly correlated with radiographic findings. In a study of patients with known metastatic involvement of the spinal column, tumor was detectable on radiographs in 94% of patients with primary breast carcinoma, 74% of those with lung carcinoma, and 40% of those with lymphoma.

A bone scan uses technetium 99m–methylene diphosphonate to detect changes in metabolic bone turnover. An intravenous injection of radioactive tracer is followed by a skeletal scan using a gamma camera. Areas of high bone turnover are seen as increased tracer uptake, and areas of low turnover are seen as photopenic. Bone marrow tumors, such as plasmacytoma and multiple myeloma, may be undetectable on a bone scan until the later phases of involvement. The most important uses of bone scans in a neoplastic evaluation are to detect possible distant skeletal lesions and to evaluate the metabolic characteristics of a known tumor. Bone scans have high sensitivity (90% to 100%) but low specificity for the detection of tumor involvement; a negative predictive value for metastasis as high as 100% was found.[5] The drawbacks to using bone scans include the low rate of specificity as well as the difficulty of reliably distinguishing among infections, fractures, degenerative conditions, and tumors.

Single photon emission computed tomography is similar to conventional nuclear scanning using a gamma camera and requires a similar radiation exposure. Three-dimensional data that can be freely reformatted or manipulated are obtained. Positive findings can be accurately located, with greater specificity, sensitivity, and positive and negative predictive values than conventional bone scanning.[6] This modality is not superior to MRI for the early detection of metastatic vertebra-pedicle involvement.

Positron emission tomography (PET) produces a three-dimensional image of functional processes in the body. The system detects pairs of gamma rays emitted indirectly by a positron-emitting radionuclide tracer that is introduced into the body on fluorodeoxyglucose, a biologically active molecule. Areas of increased glucose uptake can be detected and monitored. The three-dimensional PET reconstruction often is produced with CT done during the same session in the same machine. The role of PET in spine tumor evaluation and follow-up has become more important in recent years. In prostate cancer, PET is recommended for staging newly diagnosed tumors and assessing the response to therapy.[6] A recent study of 82 patients with spine metastatic disease examined the accuracy of PET as a screening test. All patients underwent biopsy, MRI, and CT as well as PET. The authors concluded that PET is an accurate screening test for all vertebral metastases in cancer patients, and it is particularly accurate for patients with a nonsclerotic vertebral lesion or a history of solid malignancy.[7]

MRI can be useful in distinguishing a pathologic fracture from a benign compression fracture or an infection. Pathologic fractures usually are isointense on T1-weighted studies and hyperintense on T2-weighted studies. Chronic, benign fractures differ from pathologic fractures in having a normal bone marrow appearance and an absence of soft-tissue involvement. Recent research has found that diffusion-weighted imaging is more specific than conventional MRI for differentiating between metastatic and benign vertebral fracture edema.[8] On diffusion-weighted MRI, metastases usually are hypointense on T1-weighted studies, but the surrounding bone marrow is hyperintense. Vertebral osteomyelitis or diskitis usually involves contiguous segments, with the involvement of intervertebral disk and adjacent end plates; in contrast, vertebral body involvement and sparing of the disk characterize neoplastic processes.

Biopsy

The diagnosis of a tumor is not considered definitive until a tissue sample has been obtained and histologically evaluated. The histologic type and grade of tumor can influence treatment decision making. Biopsy sometimes is not warranted or feasible, however. The findings of the clinical examination, laboratory studies, and imaging should be carefully considered before deciding whether to subject the patient to an invasive bone biopsy. A biopsy should be done in accordance with the strict rules of surgical oncology. A needle biopsy can be performed if the cellular architecture of the tissue is not important. A core needle biopsy under CT guidance or an open incisional biopsy provides structurally preserved tissue. A laminectomy for an open biopsy carries the risk of contaminating the epidural space. An excisional biopsy aims to remove tumor tissue and, if a malignancy is suspected, a clean oncologic margin of normal tissue. Every biopsy should be done as safely as possible, with consideration of the need to avoid spreading malignant cells to the bloodstream or along the incisional tract.

CT-guided biopsy is a popular method of obtaining tissue for diagnosis. Using this technique, a positive diagnosis can be obtained in as many as 90% of patients.[9] CT fluoroscopy, which combines the capabilities of conventional CT with real-time imaging, significantly reduces the time required for needle placement and reduces the overall procedure time by as much as 50%, compared with conventional CT.[10]

Oncologic and Surgical Staging

Staging systems are used to help define the full extent of the disease, plan therapeutic interventions, and compare treatment protocols. Tumor staging is based on the histologic grade, size, and local extent of the primary mass as well as the presence of metastasis. Oncologic staging attempts to predict an outcome based on variables such as histologic differentiation, local extension, and systemic spread. Although not specific to the spine, the Enneking system is useful in differentiating among the stages of benign and malignant lesions (Table 1).

In many primary spine tumors, proximity of the spinal cord and the great vessels to the vertebrae means that wide margins cannot be achieved. Some researchers have used an artificial division of the vertebrae into axial sections for planning en bloc resection. The Weinstein-Boriani-Biagini classification delineates 12 radiating clockface zones and five concentric layers in the axial plane, from the outer aspect of the vertebra to the dural surface.[11] The Tomita surgical classification system differentiates between tumor within the vertebral body (intracompartmental), extension outside the vertebral body (extracompartmental), and contiguous vertebral segment involvement; the purpose is to help in choosing between curative and palliative resection.

Treatment of a spine tumor is initiated after the diagnosis is established and staging is complete for a

6: Spine Disorders

Table 1

The Enneking Surgical Staging of Benign and Malignant Tumors

Benign Tumor

Stage	Description	Grade	Site	Metastasis
S1	Latent or inactive	G0	T0	M0
S2	Active	G0	T0	M0
S3	Aggressive	G0	T1 or T2	M0 or M1

Malignant Tumor

Stage	Description	Grade	Site	Metastasis
IA	Low-grade intracompartmental	G1	T1	M0
IB	Low-grade extracompartmental	G1	T2	M0
IIA	High-grade intracompartmental	G2	T1	M0
IIB	High-grade extracompartmental	G2	T2	M0
III	Metastatic	G1 or G2	T1 or T2	M1

M0 = no metastasis, M1 = metastasis present, T0 = intracapsular, T1 = extracapsular but intracompartmental, T2 = extracompartmental.

Adapted with permission from Enneking WF, Spanier SS, Goodman MA: A system for the surgical staging of musculoskeletal sarcoma. *Clin Orthop Relat Res* 1980;153: 106-120; and Enneking WF: A system of staging musculoskeletal neoplasms. *Clin Orthop Relat Res* 1986;204:9-24.

malignant tumor. If the patient is at risk for deteriorating function related to the spinal cord or cauda equina, treatment may be initiated before the tissue diagnosis and staging are complete. Surgical decompression and stabilization, radiation therapy, and chemotherapy are the primary treatment options. Arteriographic embolization can be used as an adjunct before surgery to decrease the intraoperative blood loss from a highly vascular tumor such as a renal cell tumor or thyroid carcinoma.

Treatments and Outcomes

Benign Tumors
Osteoid Osteoma
Osteoid osteoma is among the most common skeletal tumors, accounting for 11% of all benign bone tumors. It originates from osteoblast cells and is believed to be a small osteoblastoma. By definition, the lesion is less than 15 mm in diameter. Osteoid osteoma most frequently occurs during the first three decades of life. Malignant transformation of osteoid osteoma has not been reported.

As many as 25% of all osteoid osteomas are found in the spine; 60% of these are in the lumbar spine, 25% in the cervical spine, 13% in the thoracic spine, and 2% in the sacrum.[12] Osteoid osteoma of the spine most often is located in the posterior elements, and it may lead to painful scoliosis. Severe pain typically occurs at night and is relieved by prostaglandin inhibitors such as aspirin and nonsteroidal anti-inflammatory drugs. Because osteoid osteoma is vascular, substances that cause vasodilatation, such as alcohol, can precipitate an acute pain crisis.

An osteoid osteoma typically appears radiographically as a round lucency surrounded by sclerotic bone. CT is the best imaging modality for detecting and assessing an osteoid osteoma. Histologically, an osteoid osteoma is a nidus composed of thick vascular bars of osteoblastic tissue that is surrounded by vascular fibrous tissue and ultimately surrounded by mature reactive cortical bone.

An osteoid osteoma can resolve spontaneously within 2 to 4 years. The treatment is determined by the intensity of symptoms. Unremitting pain is the most common surgical indication, but persistent secondary scoliosis lasting more than 1 year also is considered an indication for surgical intervention. Some spine osteoid osteomas can be treated with radiofrequency ablation, which involves CT-guided percutaneous insertion of a radiofrequency electrode with a tip that reaches a temperature as high as 90°C. This treatment of extraspinal lesions has had results comparable to those of standard open surgical excision, and several small studies have documented its success in the spine.[13-15] Incorrect placement of the probe has the potential to cause neurologic injury, however. Full-thickness skin necrosis is uncommon but can occur. The open surgical treatment of an osteoid osteoma is excision by intralesional curettage, which includes resecting the overlying margin of reactive bone until the nidus can be extirpated with a curette. Persistent pain after surgery usually implies that the excision was incomplete.

Osteoblastoma
Osteoblastoma is a rare benign primary neoplasm, accounting for approximately 1% of all primary bone tumors. The spine is the most common site of osteoblas-

toma. The posterior elements are the favored location within the spine, with only 3% of osteoblastomas involving the vertebral body. This lesion most commonly appears in patients younger than 30 years, and it is twice as common in men as in women. Osteoblastoma is histologically similar to osteoid osteoma but is differentiated by having a gross diameter of more than 15 to 20 mm.[16]

Microscopically, an osteoblastoma consists of vascular spindle cell stroma with abundant irregular spicules of osteoid and mineralized bone. Areas of cystic degeneration and hemorrhage can create the appearance of an aneurysmal bone cyst, sometimes leading to diagnostic confusion. Penetration of the cortex and extension into the soft tissue may be signs of aggressive behavior. The presence of cartilage within the tumor is unusual and should raise suspicion of an osteosarcoma. Most osteoblastomas have benign cytologic characteristics, remain intracapsular, and do not metastasize. Some are much more aggressive, however, and extend into the epidural space despite their benign histologic appearance.

The primary symptom of osteoblastoma is pain, often characterized as a dull ache. In comparison with osteoid osteoma, osteoblastoma produces a more general pain that is less likely to be relieved by aspirin or nonsteroidal anti-inflammatory drugs. A patient with osteoblastoma of the spine may have neurologic symptoms as a result of spinal cord or nerve root compression. Scoliosis or torticollis also may be present. In one report, 6 of 30 patients with spine osteoblastoma had neurologic symptoms before treatment; the highest incidence of neurologic involvement was in patients with a thoracic lesion.[17]

An osteoblastoma appears on plain radiographs as a bone-forming lesion located in the cortex, medullary canal, or periosteal region. In the spine, an osteoblastoma usually arises in the posterior elements, producing a destructive expansile lesion with a central hyperdense nidus that can be seen on CT (Figure 1). MRI shows enhancement of the reactive bone within the lesion as well as any thecal or nerve root impingement. Nuclear scanning is a useful screening tool for both osteoblastoma and osteoid osteoma.

The preferred surgical treatment of osteoblastoma is complete excision. Only limited information is available on the outcomes of surgically treated osteoblastoma. The single largest study of surgically treated spine osteoblastomas found that radical excision can lead to an extended tumor-free period but that intralesional excision is associated with local recurrence.[18] A recent systematic review concluded that the likelihood of recurrence also may be related to tumor grade. After incomplete resection, the aggressive type of osteoblastoma reappeared more often than the less aggressive type (50% or 10% to 15% recurrence, respectively).[19] Postoperative radiation is the most commonly used adjunct therapy if complete excision was not achieved. There is, however, no evidence to show that radiation

therapy controls residual disease after incomplete resection or reduces the local recurrence rate.

Aneurysmal Bone Cyst

An aneurysmal bone cyst is a benign, expansile osteolytic bone tumor of unknown origin that creates a thin-walled, blood-filled cyst. The prevalence of aneurysmal bone cyst is 0.14 per 100,000 people, accounting for 1.4% of all primary bone tumors.[20] Most patients are adolescents, and these tumors are extremely rare after age 30 years. An aneurysmal bone cyst is either primary (with no underlying lesion) or secondary (associated with another type of lesion, such as giant cell tumor or osteoblastoma). In the spine, 60% of aneurysmal bone cysts originate in the posterior elements of the cervical or thoracic spine, but they can extend anteriorly into the vertebral bodies. Although aneurysmal bone cysts are histologically benign, they often enlarge rapidly and cause bone destruction. The patient may have local pain or neurologic symptoms secondary to compression by the expansile tumor tissue.

An aneurysmal bone cyst has an initial growth phase characterized by rapid destruction of bone and a subperiosteal blowout pattern. A stabilization phase follows, with formation of a distinct peripheral bony shell and internal bony septae and trabeculae that produce the classic soap-bubble radiographic appearance. The mature stage is marked by bone healing, in which progressive calcification and ossification of the cyst eventually leads to its transformation into a dense bony mass with an irregular structure.

The treatment options for a spine aneurysmal bone cyst include radiation, arterial embolization, injection of sclerosing agents, and surgical resection with bone grafting or cement augmentation. External beam radiation has been used for lesions considered inoperable, although it carries a risk of sarcomatous transformation, growth plate damage before skeletal maturity, and radiation myelopathy. Recurrence rates as high as 25% have been reported after the use of radiation alone.[21] Relatively new techniques using megavoltage radiation may be more effective for tumor control and have fewer adverse effects.

Selective arterial embolization has been promoted as the preferred primary treatment for a spine aneurysmal bone cyst or as a preliminary step before surgical resection.[19,22] The success of selective arterial embolization depends on the presence of a major feeder vessel, and sometimes more than one treatment is required to achieve the desired effect. The potential for iatrogenic spinal cord ischemia should always be kept in mind when considering selective arterial embolization. Percutaneous intralesional injections using calcitonin also are reported to be an effective primary treatment modality.[23] Calcitonin is believed to act by suppressing osteoclastic activity and stimulating the formation of trabecular bone within the fibrous septae of the aneurysmal bone cyst.[24]

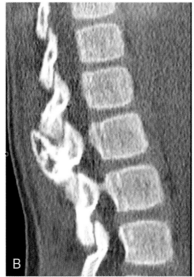

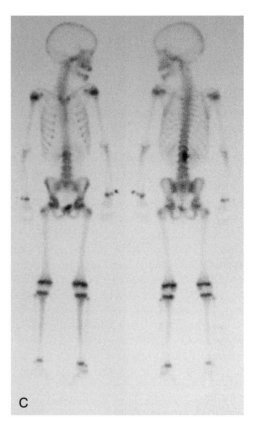

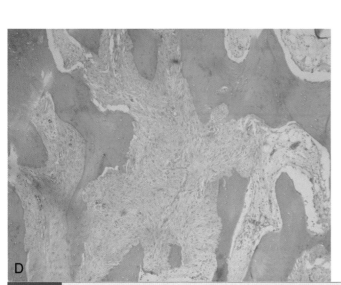

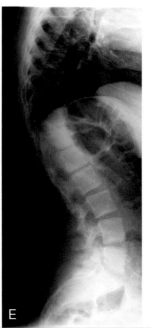

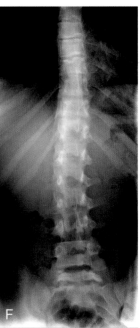

Figure 1   An 8-year-old girl had axial low back pain of 3 months' duration. Plain radiographic findings were inconclusive. **A** and **B,** CT showing an expansile lesion originating in the left L2 lamina. **C,** Bone scan showing intense uptake at L2, with no other skeletal lesions. En bloc excision confirmed the clinical diagnosis of osteoblastoma. **D,** Histologic section showing the typical appearance of abundant osteoblasts with interspersed woven bone trabeculae. Standing lateral (**E**) and PA (**F**) radiographs taken at 2-year follow-up. The patient was actively involved in gymnastics and cheerleading. (Courtesy of Raj Rao, MD, Milwaukee, WI.)

Surgical intervention usually is considered necessary if the patient has neurologic involvement. Impending or frank pathologic fracture also is an indication for spine reconstruction. Curettage and implantation of morcellized allograft or polymethylmethacrylate (PMMA) can lead to recurrence. An en bloc resection (spondylectomy) carries the lowest risk of tumor recurrence.[22] However, this procedure is technically demanding, and it is not universally considered to be justified in view of the benign nature of the disease. Wide laminectomy may be adequate for complete resection of a lesion that is restricted to the posterior arch. Intralesional or incomplete procedures followed by bone grafting have been effective in a large percentage of patients, with an overall recurrence rate of 10% reported at 10-year follow-up.[25] Preoperative arterial embolization may reduce blood loss during an intralesional procedure.

Langerhans Cell Histiocytosis

Langerhans cell histiocytosis (formerly known as histiocytosis X) is a generic term for neoplasms of the Langerhans cells. The Langerhans cells are dendritic mononuclear cells (histiocytes) of the skin and lymph nodes. The three clinical forms of Langerhans cell histiocytosis are eosinophilic granuloma, a benign, self-limiting solitary form that occurs during the first two decades of life; Hand-Schüller-Christian disease, a polyostotic form with limited involvement of other systems; and Letterer-Siwe disease, an aggressive variant often associated with multiorgan involvement.

Eosinophilic granuloma is the most common form of Langerhans cell histiocytosis. The spine is involved in 10% to 15% of patients.[26] Most patients are in the first two decades of life. A thoracic vertebral body is the most common location in children, and the cervical spine is slightly more commonly affected in adults. The destruction of a solitary vertebra, resulting in a so-called coin-on-end or vertebra plana appearance with no soft-tissue mass, is pathognomonic. The histologic appearance is of a combination of histiocytes with coffee bean–shaped nuclei and eosinophils. The clinical symptoms include localized pain and decreased range of motion. Neurologic symptoms are unusual but may occur with a cervical lesion. In addition to the flattening of the vertebral body, the typical radiographic findings include sparing of the posterior elements, absence of kyphosis, and preservation of adjacent disk spaces. Bone scans may be negative. MRI usually is not diagnostic but is useful in excluding other possible pathologies, such as infection, aneurysmal bone cyst, or osteoblastoma.

Eosinophilic granuloma generally has a self-limiting natural history. The lesion may require only close observation. The vertebral body is reconstituted to a near-normal height in most children, without active treatment,[27] although a spine brace can be used to control pain and maintain spine alignment during the phase of acute symptoms. A core or percutaneous fine-needle aspiration biopsy followed by an intralesional corticosteroidal injection can serve as both a diagnostic and a therapeutic measure. Radiation or surgical intervention is rarely indicated unless there is neurologic compression, instability, or structural deformity.

Hemangioma

Hemangioma is the most common benign tumor of the spine and probably is a vascular malformation rather than a true neoplasm. An autopsy study of the spine found a prevalence of 10% to 12%.[28] Three clinical varieties have been described: asymptomatic, symptomatic, and aggressive. Most hemangiomas are asymptomatic, and aggressive hemangiomas are rare. The patient may have pain and local tenderness caused by bony erosion, vertebral microfracture, or collapse of the vertebral body. Rarely, epidural extension of the lesion can cause neurologic manifestations. An aggressive hemangioma generally exhibits at least one distinct radiologic sign: location between T3 and T9; total involvement of the vertebral body; extension into the posterior elements; irregular trabeculations; a soft-tissue component; or an expanded, poorly defined cortex.

Plain radiographs of a large hemangioma may show a coarse vertical striation, often referred to as a jailhouse appearance, which is caused by linear reactive calcification around the radiolucent vascular tissue. This trabecular thickening and reinforcement is believed to be a response to stress, and it could explain the rarity of vertebral fractures in these lesions. An axial CT section shows a stippled appearance and may show a soft-tissue mass with variable enhancement. A phlebolith occasionally appears within a large, cavernous hemangioma in the calvaria. MRI is the modality of choice for revealing the relationship between a hemangioma and the adjacent anatomic structures. A hemangioma appears as an ill-defined, hyperintense mass on T1- and T2-weighted MRI.

Treatment can be considered for a large, symptomatic hemangioma or a hemangioma with an impending pathologic fracture. Radiation therapy was found to be useful in providing pain relief, possibly through its anti-inflammatory action. A study of fractionated external beam radiation using a total dose of 20 to 30 Gy found that two thirds of the patients reported complete pain relief and the remaining patients reported partial relief after 5 months of treatment. No dose-response relationship was found. The authors concluded that radiation is an effective treatment for painful vertebral hemangiomas.[29] The drawbacks to radiation therapy include the delayed onset of analgesic effect and the possibility of radionecrosis. The injection of ethanol into the lesion was found to be effective, although a preliminary contrast injection is necessary to ensure that the dye is contained within the vertebral body.[30] Transarterial embolization was successfully used to treat a spinal vascular bony lesion, with 17 of 19 patients reporting complete pain relief.[31]

The long-term radiologic outcome of an untreated hemangioma usually is ossification of the involved vertebra. Vertebroplasty using PMMA helps consolidate the weakened vertebral body and thus allows any further surgery to be limited to a posterior approach. The use of cement also may have a hemostatic effect, reducing blood loss in later surgery.[32] Surgical intervention should be reserved for patients with spinal canal compromise causing neurologic deficits, significant deformity from vertebral collapse, or pain not responsive to nonsurgical measures. Presurgical embolization should be considered for these patients. The surgical approach is dictated by the anatomic location of the lesion. En bloc excision should be done if possible and is curative.

Giant Cell Tumor

Giant cell tumors of the vertebrae are rare, accounting for 3% to 5% of all primary bone tumors in the United States.[33] Only 2.7% of all giant cell tumors are in the spine.[34] Although the tumor is histologically benign, recurrence rates are as high as 49%,[35] and giant cell tumor therefore is categorized as a benign aggressive tumor. Distant metastasis to the lungs has been reported in as many as 9% of patients.[36] Malignant transformation after local radiation was reported to occur in 11% of pelvic and sacral giant cell tumors.[35] Histologically, the tumor is characterized by mononuclear stromal cells, mononuclear monocytes, and multinucleated giant cells. The tumor usually develops in the vertebral body and may spread to the posterior elements in the advanced stages. The sacrum is the most commonly affected spine location, followed by the thoracic, cervical, and lumbar regions. Giant cell tumor is more common in women than in men; it affects patients in the second through fourth decades of life. Plain radiographs reveal an expansile lytic cavity, without septation or mineralized matrix, surrounded by reactive bone. CT is ideal for identifying cortical destruction. The MRI appearance is of heterogeneous signal intensity.

The surgical treatment of a spine giant cell tumor can be challenging because of its axial location and often its advanced stage at diagnosis. Oncologic staging is useful in formulating a surgical strategy after the diagnosis is confirmed. Complete surgical excision, if feasible, is curative. Although en bloc resection is technically demanding, the subsequent recurrence rate is lower than 25%. In contrast, the recurrence rate after intralesional surgery is as high as 47%.[35] Before an intralesional procedure is attempted, arterial embolization should be considered to minimize intraoperative blood loss. Intralesional curettage followed by radiation therapy may provide a disease-free interval, although recurrence is common, and multiple procedures may be needed. Therapeutic embolization may be indicated for a large, unresectable tumor, particularly in the sacrum.[37] Radiation therapy has been used as an adjunct to incomplete surgical excision, and it may be indicated alone for some unresectable tumors, despite the 5% to 15% risk of malignant transformation.[38] Recent breakthroughs in understanding the molecular and cellular biology of giant cell tumors has led to the identification of receptor activator for nuclear factor κ-B ligand (RANKL), a factor required for osteoclast formation and expressed by a variety of cells within giant cell tumors.[39-41] Denosumab has been developed as a human monoclonal antibody to RANKL, and it has had promising early results in treating giant cell tumor.[33]

Malignant Tumors

Chordoma

Chordoma is a slow-growing but locally invasive primary malignant bone tumor. It arises from the embryonic notochordal remnants in the midline of the neuraxis, from the base of the skull to the sacrum. Chordoma accounts for 1% to 4% of all primary bone tumors and is the most common primary bone tumor in the spine.[42] The age-adjusted prevalence is 0.8 per 1 million people in the United States.[43] Men are affected twice as often as women. Approximately 50% of chordomas occur in the sacrococcygeal region, 35% in the spheno-occipital region, and 15% in the mobile spine.[44] Chordomas typically are diagnosed at a late stage because of their indolent growth rate and nonspecific symptoms, which often are ignored during the initial stages of the disease. Although a chordoma can metastasize to the lung, bone, and brain, the patient's long-term survival appears to be more closely related to local disease progression than to metastatic activity. Bone destruction and neurologic involvement are common.

En bloc excision of the tumor, if feasible, is the mainstay of treatment. En bloc procedures were found to lead to longer disease-free survival than other procedures.[45] There is a strong correlation between tumor-free margins and long-term survival.[46-48] However, clear margins could be obtained in only half of sacrococcygeal lesions and in even fewer lesions located in the mobile spine or skull base.[43,46,47,49,50] The risk of local recurrence or distant spread is related to tumor histology as well as the extent of resection. The overall 10-year survival rate after sacral chordoma resection is approximately 50%.[43]

Bowel and bladder function appears to be unaffected after surgery if both S3 roots or all of the S1-5 roots on one side were spared. Significant bowel and bladder dysfunction almost always occurs if both S2 roots were removed. Loss of one or both S1 roots may produce some lower limb weakness, but an intact L5 root generally permits the patient to ambulate without assistance.

Chemotherapy is not effective for treating chordoma.[43] The ability to achieve curative radiation dosages is limited by proximity of a chordoma to the spinal cord and roots, brainstem, optic pathways, or rectum.[51] Proton beam therapy has the advantage over conventional radiation therapy of allowing the radiation to be precisely directed, and it has had encouraging results when combined with surgery.[52] Stereotactic radiosurgery has been used with favorable short-term results and minimal toxicity.[53]

Osteosarcoma
Osteosarcoma is the most common malignant bone tumor in children, with a reported incidence of 5.6 per 1 million children younger than 15 years. Fewer than 5% of osteosarcomas involve the spine, and these account for only 5% of all of the primary malignancies of the spine. Exposure to ionizing radiation and a history of hereditary retinoblastoma increase the risk of osteosarcoma. Secondary osteosarcoma can occur in a patient with Paget disease, fibrous dysplasia, or enchondromatosis.

A patient with spine osteosarcoma most commonly has pain and neurologic symptoms. Radiography during the initial stages of osteosarcoma may reveal negative findings or may show a combination of sclerosis and lysis, usually involving the anterior column. CT is the best modality for assessing bony involvement and showing the mineralized osteoid. MRI is best for defining the surrounding soft tissue and any neural element involvement. PET is useful in staging the disease and monitoring the response to therapy. Nuclear isotope scans can identify skip lesions or diffuse skeletal involvement. Because of the strong metastatic potential of spine osteosarcomas, chest and abdominal CT always should be obtained to detect any visceral disease spread. A needle biopsy is used for confirmatory diagnosis.

Treatment is initiated after the diagnosis and staging are complete. The only treatment that offers the possibility of tumor eradication is preoperative neoadjuvant chemotherapy followed by wide local excision or total spondylectomy. These tumors are highly resistant to conventional doses of external beam radiation, and therefore radiation should not be offered except as a palliative measure. Overall survival times may be longer after wide marginal surgery than after intralesional surgery. Postsurgical chemotherapy may have a role, as determined by the extent of tumor necrosis found in the excised specimen.

Chondrosarcoma
A chondrosarcoma is a malignant hyaline cartilage–forming tumor. Chondrosarcomas account for 7% to 12% of all spine tumors.[54] Although spine chondrosarcoma most commonly occurs de novo in normal bone, a small subset arises as a malignant transformation of a preexisting osteochondroma or enchondroma. Men are more often affected than women, and most patients are in the fifth or sixth decade of life. The patient is likely to have pain associated with a neurologic deficit. The radiographic appearance of chondrosarcoma ranges from lobular with varying calcifications to pleomorphic with spotty calcification and destruction of the vertebral body.

The preferred treatment of spine chondrosarcoma is complete surgical excision of the tumor. If clean margins cannot be achieved, cryosurgery using liquid nitrogen may decrease the likelihood of local recurrence.[55] Chemotherapy has minimal benefit for treating chon-

drosarcoma. Chondrosarcoma also is resistant to conventional radiation therapy, but the use of proton beam radiation has increased disease-free intervals and survival rates.[56]

Ewing Sarcoma
Ewing sarcoma is the most common primary malignant spine tumor in children. Primary Ewing sarcoma accounts for fewer than 10% of all spine tumors in children and adults. Sacrococcygeal involvement is more common than thoracic or lumbar involvement, and the cervical spine is least commonly affected. The tumor is likely to be in the vertebral body, possibly extending to the posterior elements. As many as 20% of patients have metastatic disease when they are first seen, but this factor does not appear to affect the long-term prognosis. Patients typically are in the first to fourth decades of life; the average patient age is 16.5 years. The patient may have pain, fever, a palpable mass, and neurologic involvement. If there is neural compression, emergency decompression usually is performed before Ewing sarcoma is diagnosed. A hemogram may reveal anemia, leukocytosis, and an elevated erythrocyte sedimentation rate. An elevated lactic dehydrogenase level is a reliable blood marker that can be used as an indicator of tumor load during follow-up.

Radiographs show a lytic lesion of the vertebral body, often surrounded by a sclerotic margin. CT and MRI show the soft-tissue component; the tumor displays an intermediate signal on T1-weighted MRI and a high signal on T2-weighted MRI. Most vertebral Ewing sarcomas are the result of secondary spread to the spine, and nuclear scans are essential for detecting or ruling out the presence of other lesions. A tissue biopsy is confirmatory. Cytogenetic studies typically reveal a translocation of chromosomes 11 and 22.

Systemic chemotherapy is the recommended initial treatment. Ewing sarcoma is both radiosensitive and chemosensitive, and surgery therefore is indicated only in specific situations. Newer chemotherapeutic regimens have led to 3-year survival in 80% of patients with local disease.[57] The negative prognostic signs include metastases at presentation and large tumor size.

Local recurrence rates as high as 25% have been reported in patients who underwent intensive chemotherapy and local radiation.[58] En bloc resection is recommended whenever possible because it can improve the local control of disease and length of patient survival.

Soft-Tissue Sarcomas
Paraspinal soft-tissue sarcomas such as liposarcoma, malignant histiocytoma, leiomyosarcoma, synovial sarcoma, angiosarcoma, and neurofibrosarcoma rarely arise in the spine as a primary tumor. These tumors originate in the paraspinous regions, and often they are aggressive and metastasize early. The radiographic appearance varies with the tumor type. One classification system divides these tumors into three groups based on their anatomic location: paraspinal musculature only;

extension to or erosion of the posterior lamina, without spread to the epidural space; and extension into the epidural space.[59]

The treatment usually consists of neoadjuvant chemotherapy followed by a wide resection of the tumor. Postoperative radiation therapy also can be used. The proximity of the spinal cord can be a limiting factor for radiation, however, particularly if the tumor extends to the dural margins.

Solitary Plasmacytoma

Plasmacytoma is a malignant neoplasm that originates in abnormal plasma cells. The various tissues that contain plasma cells can be affected, including the bone marrow, lymph nodes, spleen, gastrointestinal tract, and respiratory tract. The spine is the most commonly involved part of the skeleton, followed by the ribs, skull, and pelvis. Within the spine, the thoracic region is most commonly affected. Patients typically are older than 50 years, and men are affected two to three times more often than women. Back pain with or without radicular symptoms usually is the first symptom. Paraproteins produced by the tumor sometimes lead to coagulopathy, hyperviscosity, amyloidosis, and renal failure.

Plain radiographs may show a destructive lytic lesion, often with collapse of the affected vertebral body. Bone scans may not show increased uptake unless a fracture has occurred. A skeletal survey is helpful for ruling out the presence of other lesions and distinguishing plasmacytoma from multiple myeloma. CT and MRI are particularly useful for detecting lesions in the sacrum or pelvis. Even in the absence of other skeletal lesions, bone marrow biopsy should be done to rule out a progression to multiple myeloma, which occurs in half of patients. A monoclonal serum immunoglobulin can be detected in as many as 7% of patients.[60] A sudden increase may indicate transformation of a solitary lesion into a multiple myeloma. A few patients have normal electrophoretic patterns in urine and blood samples, and bone marrow biopsy therefore remains the definitive method of diagnosis. Histopathologically, the bone typically is infiltrated by monoclonal plasma cells.

Plasmacytoma is highly radiosensitive, so the first-line treatment is radiation therapy. The medical treatment options include bisphosphonates and thalidomide-dexamethasone combinations. Surgical intervention is reserved for patients with spinal cord compression or instability. Paraprotein levels can be monitored to measure the treatment response and prognosis. The persistence or reappearance of paraproteins should be considered a possible indicator of transformation into myeloma.

Multiple Myeloma

Multiple myeloma is the most common primary malignant tumor of bone. It is the second most common hematologic malignancy (after non-Hodgkin lymphoma) and is clinically characterized by malignant plasma cells in the bone marrow and monoclonal immunoglobulins in the serum and/or urine. Lytic bone lesions can be identified in at least 70% of patients with multiple myeloma.[61] Patients usually are 50 to 75 years old, with an equal sex distribution. The initial symptoms may result from renal and hematopoietic involvement or bone involvement. The patient sometimes has symptoms of neurologic compression. It is therefore imperative that serum protein electrophoresis be requested for all older adult patients with a pathologic vertebral compression fracture but no obvious primary malignancy.

Because of the systemic nature of multiple myeloma, the radiographic workup should include a skeletal survey. Lytic lesions become visible on plain radiographs only after destruction of approximately 30% of the trabecular bone in the vertebral body. Bone scans are classically negative because of osteoblastic suppression by the disease. PET is increasingly popular as a more sensitive method than plain radiography for skeletal survey and disease monitoring.[62] CT and MRI can be used to improve the characterization of involved areas. Serum protein electrophoresis is routinely used to detect the presence of a monoclonal protein (immunoglobulin G or A) producing the characteristic M spike, but the diagnosis should be confirmed by bone marrow biopsy.

A combination of chemotherapy and radiation therapy is the mainstay of treatment. The use of bisphosphonates, thalidomide, and proteosome inhibitors such as bortezomib has improved the medical management of patients with multiple myeloma. Nonetheless, some patients develop painful compression fractures with segmental instability and kyphosis. Percutaneous cement augmentation techniques such as vertebroplasty and kyphoplasty may provide pain relief for these patients. Neurologic impairment may necessitate decompression and stabilization of the affected motion segments. The widespread osteopenia in these patients makes instrumentation procedures challenging.

Metastatic Tumors

The spine is the most common site of metastatic skeletal involvement. The primary tumor most often originates in the breast, prostate gland, lung, thyroid gland, or kidney. The average age of a patient with spine metastasis is 50 to 60 years. The prevalence of spine metastasis is related to location and increases from the cranial to the caudal spine. The anterior elements are involved 20 times more often than the posterior elements.[63] The Batson plexus (a low-pressure, valveless venous system that communicates with the intraosseous venous channels of the thoracic and lumbar vertebral bodies) may be a mode of metastatic seeding of the spine. Metastatic tumors, unlike most spine infections, spare the disk space. The most common symptom is pain, which often is relieved by activity and most intense when the patient is resting. Neurologic symptoms are more common if the patient has thoracolumbar rather than cervical spine involvement. Symptomatic vertebral metastatic lesions are most common in the thoracic spine (70%), followed by the lumbar spine (20%) and cervical spine (10%).[64]

The plain radiographic appearance of tumors varies by primary tumor type. Prostate metastases typically are osteoblastic, those from the lung typically are osteolytic, and those from the breast often are a combination of osteoblastic and osteolytic. The winking owl sign on an AP spine radiograph indicates unilateral pedicle destruction. Bone scans and PET are used to detect the other sites of involvement, the nature of which can influence treatment decision making. MRI of the entire spine is useful for screening if spine metastatic involvement is suspected.[65-67] CT is more useful than MRI for revealing the extent of osseous destruction.

The treatment decisions in spine metastatic disease depend on the primary tumor type, the extent of spine involvement, the extent of systemic spread, the presence or absence of mechanical pain or neurologic symptoms, and the patient's general condition and life expectancy. A multidisciplinary approach is essential for achieving the best possible clinical result and optimizing the patient's quality of life. The treatment options for systemic disease include chemotherapy and hormonal therapy. More locally directed measures include radiation therapy, bracing, surgery, and vertebroplasty.

The accepted indications for surgical intervention in spine metastatic disease include instability, as evidenced by mechanical pain, significant deformity, or neurologic signs or symptoms; neural compression from a retropulsed bony fragment, as opposed to compression from tumoral soft tissue; a maximally radiated lesion that continues to be symptomatic; a radioresistant tumor; or a tumor of unknown origin from which tissue is needed for diagnosis. The goals of surgery in metastatic disease are to control pain, preserve or improve neurologic function, achieve local tumor control, and preserve or improve the ambulatory status of the patient. In patients with a single spine lesion and a life expectancy of more than 6 months, surgical intervention may be undertaken to achieve long-term local control. A randomized controlled study comparing radiation alone to surgery with radiation for treating spine metastatic disease found significant benefits to surgery with respect to walking ability and the need for opioid analgesia.[68]

The development of scoring systems has helped guide surgical decision making in spine metastatic disease. The Tokuhashi system is intended to guide the choice of nonsurgical treatment, palliative surgery, or excisional surgery by scoring six clinical categories that reflect the patient's general condition, the primary tumor, and the number of extraspinal bone metastases[69] (Table 2). A higher numeric score predicts a relatively long life expectancy and supports more aggressive excisional intervention; a lower score indicates a poorer prognosis and supports more limited palliative intervention. In the Tomita surgical classification system, three variables (tumor grade, visceral metastases, and bony metastases) are used to recommend palliative resection, marginal-intralesional resection, or wide resection.[70]

Local and systemic factors such as life expectancy, tumor histology and grade, spine stability, and neurologic symptoms must be considered in deciding on surgical intervention for spine metastases. For a patient who has mechanical pain caused by instability and a life expectancy of more than 6 months, posterior instrumented fusion offers rapid pain relief and improved quality of life. If the patient has neurologic deficits, an additional decompressive procedure is required. Because the bulk of the metastatic disease is in the anterior vertebral body, the proposed surgical procedure should treat the compression ventral to the thecal sac (Figure 2). Preoperative arterial embolization can be valuable in minimizing intraoperative blood loss in highly vascular tumors, such as those arising from the kidney or thyroid gland. Embolization also has been used as a stand-alone nonsurgical treatment to achieve tumor necrosis by embolizing feeder vessels.[71] As a preoperative intervention, embolization was found to reduce blood loss significantly in more than 80% of patients.[72]

In the cervical spine, the presence of bilateral vertebral arteries extending down to the C6 level precludes a posterior-only approach to the vertebral bodies. Anterior decompression therefore is favored for the cervical spine, followed by anterior column reconstruction using cages or cement spacers. Anterior plate augmentation of the reconstruction may suffice for disease at one or two vertebral levels. Involvement of more than two vertebral segments, the presence of a kyphotic deformity, or the presence of a lesion at the cervicothoracic junction may require additional posterior instrumentation to prevent construct failure.

For thoracic-level metastases, the traditional approach has been a thoracotomy followed by anterior decompression and reconstruction of the diseased segments. In recent years, however, there has been a trend toward posterior-only procedures using transpedicular and costotransversectomy or extrapleural techniques. Sacrificing one thoracic root unilaterally (with the exception of T1) may significantly improve access to the vertebral body. Anterior column reconstruction can then be done using PMMA or expandable titanium cages. For single-level disease, carefully controlled three-column shortening is an alternative procedure. The advantage of these posterior-based approaches is the ability to achieve circumferential decompression and posterior stabilization in a single stage, using one incision, and to avoid the morbidity associated with a thoracotomy in this population. A similar technique is useful in the lumbar spine, except that a lumbar nerve root cannot be sacrificed without consequence.

Radiation therapy is used as a palliative measure in most patients with spine metastases. The goals of radiation are pain relief and control of local tumor progression, which could eventually lead to pathologic fracture

Table 2

The Revised Tokuhashi Prognostic Scoring System for Spine Metastatic Tumors

Patient Criterion	Category	Score
1. General condition (performance status)	Poor (performance status, 10% to 40%)	0
	Moderate (performance status, 50% to 70%)	1
	Good (performance status, 80% to 100%)	2
2. Number of extraspinal foci of bone metastasis	≥ 3	0
	1-2	1
	0	2
3. Number of metastases in the vertebral body	≥ 3	0
	1-2	1
	0	2
4. Metastasis to major internal organs	Unremovable	0
	Removable	1
	None	2
5. Primary site of the cancer	Lungs, osteosarcoma, stomach, bladder, esophagus, pancreas	0
	Liver, gall bladder, unidentified	1
	Other	2
	Kidney, uterus	3
	Rectum	4
	Thyroid, breast, prostate gland; carcinoid tumor	5
6. Palsy	Complete (Frankel A or B)	0
	Incomplete (Frankel C or D)	1
	None (Frankel E)	2

Total Score	Life Expectancy
0-8	≤ 6 months
9-11	6-12 months
12-15	>12 months

Adapted with permission from Tokuhashi Y, Matsuzaki H, Oda H, Oshima M, Ryu J: A revised scoring system for preoperative evaluation of metastatic spine tumor prognosis. *Spine (Phila Pa 1976)* 2005;30(19):2186-2191.

and neural compression. The effectiveness of radiation therapy depends on the radiosensitivity of the tumor, the size and extent of the tumor, and its pathologic grading. Radiosensitive tumors typically include breast and prostate carcinomas, lymphomas, leukemias, myelomas, and Ewing sarcoma. There is level I evidence that as many as 74% of patients with metastatic epidural compression remain ambulatory after standard external beam radiation alone; however, fewer than 34% of nonambulatory patients regain ambulation after radiation alone.[73]

The most important constraint in radiation therapy to the spinal column is its collateral effect on the neural elements, which often dictates a limited dosage far below the therapeutic level and leads to a suboptimal clinical response. The advent of stereotactic radiation therapy is encouraging because a higher dose of radiation can be delivered to the target tissue using multiplanar radiation beams in a focused manner, thus minimizing the deleterious effects of radiation spillover to neighboring tissues.

Surgery in a previously irradiated field carries a significantly increased risk of infection and wound-healing complications. If both radiation therapy and surgery are planned, performing surgery before radiation and delaying radiation at least 3 weeks after surgery may prevent wound-healing complications. This limitation may not apply to stereotactic radiation because of the steep fall-off gradient of the target dosage and the negligible skin exposure.

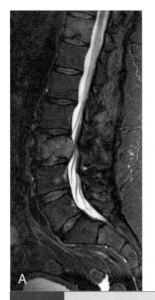
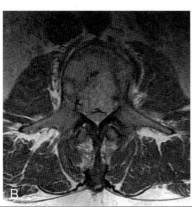
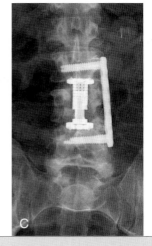
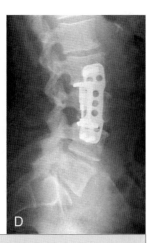

Figure 2 A 49-year-old man with an earlier diagnosis of papillary thyroid carcinoma had cauda equina compression and intractable back pain secondary to a metastatic lesion of L3. **A,** Sagittal short tau inversion recovery MRI showing a partial collapse of the L3 body with spinal canal compromise. **B,** T2-weighted axial MRI at the level of the L1 pedicle showing retropulsion of bone-tumor tissue into the spinal canal. AP (**C**) and lateral (**D**) lumbar spine radiographs taken 2 years after anterior corpectomy of L3 and stabilization using an expandable titanium cage supplemented with anterolateral plate fixation at L2-L4. (Courtesy of Raj Rao, MD, Milwaukee, WI.)

There is little information on the benefits of chemotherapy in spine metastatic disease. It is generally agreed, however, that the decision whether to offer chemotherapy should be guided by the primary tumor type and grade. Chemotherapy has limited use as a stand-alone treatment in spine metastatic disease, but it is valuable in lengthening survival for patients with breast carcinoma and some other tumor types. Corticosteroids, such as dexamethasone, are indicated in patients with acute neurologic compromise with compression.

Vertebroplasty is a percutaneous technique in which PMMA is injected into a diseased vertebral body to augment its mechanical strength. Kyphoplasty involves inserting and inflating a balloon in the collapsed vertebral body and filling the resulting cavity with PMMA. In addition to its use in reinforcing weakened bone, PMMA may have local antitumor action because of its cytotoxic and thermal effects. Vertebroplasty and kyphoplasty are most commonly used in patients with axial pain caused by vertebral collapse. Biomechanical research found that stiffness can be restored to the affected vertebra by a cement fill of 30%, which corresponds to approximately 4 mL of cement in the thoracic vertebral body and 6 to 8 mL in the lumbar vertebral body.[71,74] A recent systematic review found that vertebroplasty and kyphoplasty are uniformly effective in improving pain and functional outcome in spine metastatic disease.[75] The most important stated advantage of kyphoplasty is its ability to improve the sagittal profile in patients with a kyphotic collapse. This beneficial effect was found in the short term, and it is unclear whether it continues into the long term. The complications of these techniques can include pulmonary embolism; extravasation of PMMA, leading to neurologic symptoms; and adjacent segment fracturing. Vertebroplasty was found to have an overall medical complication rate of 1.3%, a symptomatic cement extravasation rate as high as 13%, and an adjacent segment fracture rate of 1.9%. The corresponding figures for kyphoplasty were 0.3%, 0%, and 1.8%, respectively.[75]

Summary

Tumors of the spine are diverse and present many clinical challenges. Diagnosis and treatment strategies must adhere to sound oncologic principles to yield an optimal outcome. A high index of suspicion and early referral to an appropriate facility can ensure minimal delay between the onset of symptoms and the final diagnosis. Close interdisciplinary collaboration across subspecialists and clinical support staff is necessary for formulating an individualized management plan that will minimize morbidity while striving for tumor eradication. Oncologic staging and a careful assessment of impairment and comorbidity should guide the choice of therapeutic options, in particular the choice between curative and palliative surgical intervention. Although curative resections are technically feasible in carefully selected situations, they are not without morbidity. Oncologic goals and surgical morbidity must be balanced to achieve acceptable outcomes.

Acknowlegment

Dr. David and Dr. Yanko acknowledge the significant contribution of Raj D. Rao, MD, to the preparation of this chapter, particularly after the untimely death of Dr. Alan Levine.

Annotated References

1. Kelley SP, Ashford RU, Rao AS, Dickson RA: Primary bone tumours of the spine: A 42-year survey from the Leeds Regional Bone Tumour Registry. *Eur Spine J* 2007;16(3):405-409.

   A 42-year survey of a single population district identified 2,750 bone tumors, of which 126 (4.6%) were primary spine tumors.

2. Rodallec MH, Feydy A, Larousserie F, et al: Diagnostic imaging of solitary tumors of the spine: What to do and say. *Radiographics* 2008;28(4):1019-1041.

   The radiographic features and differential diagnosis of common benign and malignant spine tumors are reviewed.

3. Guillevin R, Vallee JN, Lafitte F, Menuel C, Duverneuil NM, Chiras J: Spine metastasis imaging: Review of the literature. *J Neuroradiol* 2007;34(5):311-321.

   The pertinent radiologic findings encountered in metastatic spine disease are reviewed, with the usefulness and limitations of different radiologic modalities.

4. Tatsui H, Onomura T, Morishita S, Oketa M, Inoue T: Survival rates of patients with metastatic spinal cancer after scintigraphic detection of abnormal radioactive accumulation. *Spine (Phila Pa 1976)* 1996;21(18):2143-2148.

5. Kim CK, Park KW: Characteristic appearance of facet osteoarthritis of the lower lumbar spine on planar bone scintigraphy with a high negative predictive value for metastasis. *Clin Nucl Med* 2008;33(4):251-254.

   In patients with metastatic disease, tracer uptake in lower lumbar facet arthritis was reliably differentiated from uptake caused by metastatic deposits. More extensive imaging was not required.

6. Beheshti M, Langsteger W, Fogelman I: Prostate cancer: Role of SPECT and PET in imaging bone metastases. *Semin Nucl Med* 2009;39(6):396-407.

   The scope of radioisotope studies for detecting metastatic deposits from prostatic malignancy is reviewed.

7. Laufer I, Lis E, Pisinski L, Akhurst T, Bilsky MH: The accuracy of [(18)F]fluorodeoxyglucose positron emission tomography as confirmed by biopsy in the diagnosis of spine metastases in a cancer population. *Neurosurgery* 2009;64(1):107-114.

   In a retrospective study of 82 patients, fluorodeoxyglucose(18F)-PET tracer uptake was greatest in metastatic disease, followed by active malignant disease, and was least in benign tumors.

8. Oztekin O, Ozan E, Hilal Adibelli Z, Unal G, Abali Y: SSH-EPI diffusion-weighted MR imaging of the spine with low b values: Is it useful in differentiating malignant metastatic tumor infiltration from benign fracture edema? *Skeletal Radiol* 2009;38(7):651-658.

   In a prospective study, 47 patients (20 with benign fractures and 27 with metastatic deposits) underwent both conventional and diffusion-weighted MRI. The diffusion-weighted images were excellent for distinguishing between metastatic tumor infiltration and benign vertebral fracture edema and were highly specific for metastatic lesions.

9. Babu NV, Titus VT, Chittaranjan S, Abraham G, Prem H, Korula RJ: Computed tomographically guided biopsy of the spine. *Spine (Phila Pa 1976)* 1994;19(21): 2436-2442.

10. Obray R, Murphy KJ: Percutaneous diagnostic biopsy techniques for tumors of the spine and peripheral nerves, in Dickman CA, Fehlings MG, Gokaslan ZL, eds: *Spinal Cord and Spinal Column Tumors: Principles and Practice.* New York, NY, Thieme Medical Publishers, 2006, pp 279-285.

11. Boriani S, Bandiera S, Biagini R: Staging and treatment of primary tumors of the spine. *Curr Opin Orthop* 1999;10:193-200.

12. Janin Y, Epstein JA, Carras R, Khan A: Osteoid osteomas and osteoblastomas of the spine. *Neurosurgery* 1981;8(1):31-38.

13. Barsa P, Suchomel P, Lukás R, Taller S, Endrych L: Percutaneous CT-guided radiofrequency ablation in spinal osteoid osteoma treatment. *Acta Chir Orthop Traumatol Cech* 2007;74(6):401-405.

    Four patients with osteoid osteoma of the lumbar or sacral spine were prospectively studied. All reported pain relief immediately after CT-guided radiofrequency ablation, with no symptom recurrence at 2-year follow-up.

14. Hadjipavlou AG, Lander PH, Marchesi D, Katonis PG, Gaitanis IN: Minimally invasive surgery for ablation of osteoid osteoma of the spine. *Spine (Phila Pa 1976)* 2003;28(22):E472-E477.

15. Hoffmann RT, Jakobs TF, Kubisch CH, et al: Radiofrequency ablation in the treatment of osteoid osteoma: 5-year experience. *Eur J Radiol* 2010;73(2):374-379.

    CT-guided radiofrequency ablation was effective for treating spine osteoid osteomas in two patients. This method is recommended for lesions not immediately adjacent to the neural elements.

16. Nemoto O, Moser RP Jr, Van Dam BE, Aoki J, Gilkey FW: Osteoblastoma of the spine: A review of 75 cases. *Spine (Phila Pa 1976)* 1990;15(12):1272-1280.

17. Boriani S, Capanna R, Donati D, Levine A, Picci P, Savini R: Osteoblastoma of the spine. *Clin Orthop Relat Res* 1992;278:37-45.

18. Lucas DR, Unni KK, McLeod RA, O'Connor MI, Sim FH: Osteoblastoma: Clinicopathologic study of 306 cases. *Hum Pathol* 1994;25(2):117-134.

19. Harrop JS, Schmidt MH, Boriani S, Shaffrey CI: Aggressive "benign" primary spine neoplasms: Osteoblastoma, aneurysmal bone cyst, and giant cell tumor. *Spine (Phila Pa 1976)* 2009;34(22, suppl):S39-S47.

    This systematic review examined the results of treating osteoblastoma, aneurysmal bone cyst, and giant cell tumor. En bloc resection is recommended wherever possible, although anatomic location and potential morbidity often preclude radical surgery.

20. Wang VY, Deviren V, Ames CP: Reconstruction of C-1 lateral mass with titanium mesh cage after resection of an aneurysmal bone cyst of the atlas. *J Neurosurg Spine* 2009;10(2):117-121.

    The authors describe their technique for reconstructing the C1 lateral mass in a child after resection of an aneurysmal bone cyst.

21. Capanna R, Albisinni U, Picci P, Calderoni P, Campanacci M, Springfield DS: Aneurysmal bone cyst of the spine. *J Bone Joint Surg Am* 1985;67(4):527-531.

22. Boriani S, De Iure F, Campanacci L, et al: Aneurysmal bone cyst of the mobile spine: Report on 41 cases. *Spine (Phila Pa 1976)* 2001;26(1):27-35.

23. Gladden ML Jr, Gillingham BL, Hennrikus W, Vaughan LM: Aneurysmal bone cyst of the first cervical vertebrae in a child treated with percutaneous intralesional injection of calcitonin and methylprednisolone: A case report. *Spine (Phila Pa 1976)* 2000;25(4):527-530, discussion 531.

24. Szendröi M, Antal I, Liszka G, Kónya A: Calcitonin therapy of aneurysmal bone cysts. *J Cancer Res Clin Oncol* 1992;119(1):61-65.

25. Papagelopoulos PJ, Currier BL, Shaughnessy WJ, et al: Aneurysmal bone cyst of the spine: Management and outcome. *Spine (Phila Pa 1976)* 1998;23(5):621-628.

26. Weinstein JN, McLain RF: Primary tumors of the spine. *Spine (Phila Pa 1976)* 1987;12(9):843-851.

27. Yasko AW, Fanning CV, Ayala AG, Carrasco CH, Murray JA: Percutaneous techniques for the diagnosis and treatment of localized Langerhans-cell histiocytosis (eosinophilic granuloma of bone). *J Bone Joint Surg Am* 1998;80(2):219-228.

28. Fox MW, Onofrio BM: The natural history and management of symptomatic and asymptomatic vertebral hemangiomas. *J Neurosurg* 1993;78(1):36-45.

29. Miszczyk L, Ficek K, Trela K, Spindel J: The efficacy of radiotherapy for vertebral hemangiomas. *Neoplasma* 2001;48(1):82-84.

30. Bas T, Aparisi F, Bas JL: Efficacy and safety of ethanol injections in 18 cases of vertebral hemangioma: A mean follow-up of 2 years. *Spine (Phila Pa 1976)* 2001; 26(14):1577-1582.

31. De Cristofaro R, Biagini R, Boriani S, et al: Selective arterial embolization in the treatment of aneurysmal bone cyst and angioma of bone. *Skeletal Radiol* 1992;21(8): 523-527.

32. Ide C, Gangi A, Rimmelin A, et al: Vertebral haemangiomas with spinal cord compression: The place of preoperative percutaneous vertebroplasty with methyl methacrylate. *Neuroradiology* 1996;38(6):585-589.

33. Thomas DM, Skubitz KM: Giant cell tumour of bone. *Curr Opin Oncol* 2009;21(4):338-344.

    This is a review of the current understanding of the pathogenesis of giant cell tumor and the efficacy of human monoclonal antibody in the treatment of surgically unresectable lesions.

34. Kwon JW, Chung HW, Cho EY, et al: MRI findings of giant cell tumors of the spine. *AJR Am J Roentgenol* 2007;189(1):246-250.

    The salient MRI characteristics of spine giant cell tumors are described. The most consistent findings were a heterogenous expansile lesion with low-intermediate intensity on T2-weighted images and a curvilinear signal void on both T1- and T2-weighted images.

35. Leggon RE, Zlotecki R, Reith J, Scarborough MT: Giant cell tumor of the pelvis and sacrum: 17 cases and analysis of the literature. *Clin Orthop Relat Res* 2004; 423:196-207.

36. Fidler MW: Surgical treatment of giant cell tumours of the thoracic and lumbar spine: Report of nine patients. *Eur Spine J* 2001;10(1):69-77.

37. Hosalkar HS, Jones KJ, King JJ, Lackman RD: Serial arterial embolization for large sacral giant-cell tumors: Mid- to long-term results. *Spine (Phila Pa 1976)* 2007; 32(10):1107-1115.

    Nine sacral giant cell tumors were treated with serial arterial embolization as the primary modality. Seven of the nine patients had disease control at an average 8.9-year follow-up. Level of evidence: III.

38. Feigenberg SJ, Marcus RB Jr, Zlotecki RA, Scarborough MT, Berrey BH, Enneking WF: Radiation therapy for giant cell tumors of bone. *Clin Orthop Relat Res* 2003; 411:207-216.

39. Dougall WC, Glaccum M, Charrier K, et al: RANK is essential for osteoclast and lymph node development. *Genes Dev* 1999;13(18):2412-2424.

40. Kim N, Odgren PR, Kim DK, Marks SC Jr, Choi Y: Diverse roles of the tumor necrosis factor family member TRANCE in skeletal physiology revealed by TRANCE deficiency and partial rescue by a lymphocyte-expressed TRANCE transgene. *Proc Natl Acad Sci U S A* 2000; 97(20):10905-10910.

6: Spine Disorders

41. Simonet WS, Lacey DL, Dunstan CR, et al: Osteoprotegerin: A novel secreted protein involved in the regulation of bone density. *Cell* 1997;89(2):309-319.

42. Sciubba DM, Cheng JJ, Petteys RJ, Weber KL, Frassica DA, Gokaslan ZL: Chordoma of the sacrum and vertebral bodies. *J Am Acad Orthop Surg* 2009;17(11):708-717.

    The epidemiology, pathology, clinical presentation, and treatment of chordomas of the axial skeleton are reviewed.

43. Casali PG, Stacchiotti S, Sangalli C, Olmi P, Gronchi A: Chordoma. *Curr Opin Oncol* 2007;19(4):367-370.

    Recent developments in the nonsurgical treatment of spine chordomas are reviewed, including proton beam and intensity-modulated radiation.

44. Park L, Delaney TF, Liebsch NJ, et al: Sacral chordomas: Impact of high-dose proton/photon-beam radiation therapy combined with or without surgery for primary versus recurrent tumor. *Int J Radiat Oncol Biol Phys* 2006;65(5):1514-1521.

    Surgery and proton beam radiation were found to achieve local control more commonly in primary tumors (12 of 14 patients) than in recurrent tumors (1 of 7 patients). When proton beam radiation was used alone, local control lasted up to 7.6 years.

45. Boriani S, Saravanja D, Yamada Y, Varga PP, Biagini R, Fisher CG: Challenges of local recurrence and cure in low grade malignant tumors of the spine. *Spine (Phila Pa 1976)* 2009;34(22, suppl):S48-S57.

    A systematic review and multicenter study concluded that en bloc resection should be undertaken for spine chordoma or chondrosarcoma and that radiation therapy is indicated if the resection is incomplete.

46. Fuchs B, Dickey ID, Yaszemski MJ, Inwards CY, Sim FH: Operative management of sacral chordoma. *J Bone Joint Surg Am* 2005;87(10):2211-2216.

    This large study of 52 surgically treated sacrococcygeal chordomas confirmed that tumor-free margins are the most important predictors of survival. A combined anterior-posterior approach offers the greatest likelihood of achieving clear margins. Level of evidence: IV.

47. Osaka S, Kodoh O, Sugita H, Osaka E, Yoshida Y, Ryu J: Clinical significance of a wide excision policy for sacrococcygeal chordoma. *J Cancer Res Clin Oncol* 2006;132(4):213-218.

    In 12 patients with sacrococcygeal chordoma who underwent wide surgical excision, the 20-year survival rate was 55%, but the 20-year recurrence rate was 67%. The use of a threadwire saw is recommended to minimize intraoperative contamination of the surrounding tissue.

48. Boriani S, Bandiera S, Biagini R, et al: Chordoma of the mobile spine: Fifty years of experience. *Spine (Phila Pa 1976)* 2006;31(4):493-503.

    This is one of the largest studies of spine chordoma. The epidemiology and clinical presentation of 52 chordomas of the mobile spine are reviewed. En bloc resection with tumor-free margins was the only treatment method that led to long-term (more than 5 years) disease-free survival.

49. Baratti D, Gronchi A, Pennacchioli E, et al: Chordoma: Natural history and results in 28 patients treated at a single institution. *Ann Surg Oncol* 2003;10(3):291-296.

50. York JE, Kaczaraj A, Abi-Said D, et al: Sacral chordoma: 40-year experience at a major cancer center. *Neurosurgery* 1999;44(1):74-80.

51. Tai PT, Craighead P, Bagdon F: Optimization of radiotherapy for patients with cranial chordoma: A review of dose-response ratios for photon techniques. *Cancer* 1995;75(3):749-756.

52. Brada M, Pijls-Johannesma M, De Ruysscher D: Proton therapy in clinical practice: Current clinical evidence. *J Clin Oncol* 2007;25(8):965-970.

53. Henderson FC, McCool K, Seigle J, Jean W, Harter W, Gagnon GJ: Treatment of chordomas with CyberKnife: Georgetown University experience and treatment recommendations. *Neurosurgery* 2009;64(2, suppl):A44-A53.

    CyberKnife (Accuray, Sunnyvale, CA) was used to treat 24 spine chordomas. The local control rate at 65-month follow-up was 59.1%, with overall patient survival of 74.3%. The authors concluded that CyberKnife is effective in achieving local tumor control.

54. Shives TC, McLeod RA, Unni KK, Schray MF: Chondrosarcoma of the spine. *J Bone Joint Surg Am* 1989;71(8):1158-1165.

55. Kollender Y, Meller I, Bickels J, et al: Role of adjuvant cryosurgery in intralesional treatment of sacral tumors. *Cancer* 2003;97(11):2830-2838.

56. Rutz HP, Weber DC, Goitein G, et al: Postoperative spot-scanning proton radiation therapy for chordoma and chondrosarcoma in children and adolescents: Initial experience at Paul Scherrer Institute. *Int J Radiat Oncol Biol Phys* 2008;71(1):220-225.

    At a mean 36-month follow-up after radiation therapy, 10 patients with chordoma or chondrosarcoma had a successful outcome. Three patients had a mild or moderate adverse effect.

57. Grier HE, Krailo MD, Tarbell NJ, et al: Addition of ifosfamide and etoposide to standard chemotherapy for Ewing's sarcoma and primitive neuroectodermal tumor of bone. *N Engl J Med* 2003;348(8):694-701.

58. Sundaresan N, Rosen G, Boriani S: Primary malignant tumors of the spine. *Orthop Clin North Am* 2009;40(1):21-36, v.

    Philosophical changes of the past 20 years related to the surgical treatment of malignant spine tumors are discussed.

59. Guest C, Wang EH, Davis A, et al: Paraspinal soft-tissue sarcoma: Classification of 14 cases. *Spine (Phila Pa 1976)* 1993;18(10):1292-1297.

60. McCarthy EF: Hematopoietic tumors, in Folpe AL, Inwards CY, eds: *Bone and Soft Tissue Pathology.* Philadelphia, PA, Saunders, 2010, pp 379-387.

61. Hussein M: Multiple myeloma and plasmacytoma, in McLain R, ed: *Cancer of the Spine: Comprehensive Care.* Totowa, NJ, Humana Press, 2006, pp 101-111.

62. Roodman GD: Skeletal imaging and management of bone disease. *Hematology Am Soc Hematol Educ Program* 2008;313-319.

   The imaging and treatment of osteolytic bone lesions in patients with multiple myeloma are discussed.

63. Asdourian PL, Weidenbaum M, DeWald RL, Hammerberg KW, Ramsey RG: The pattern of vertebral involvement in metastatic vertebral breast cancer. *Clin Orthop Relat Res* 1990;250 :164-170.

64. Klimo P Jr, Kestle JR, Schmidt MH: Treatment of metastatic spinal epidural disease: A review of the literature. *Neurosurg Focus* 2003;15(5):E1.

65. Algra PR, Bloem JL, Tissing H, Falke TH, Arndt JW, Verboom LJ: Detection of vertebral metastases: Comparison between MR imaging and bone scintigraphy. *Radiographics* 1991;11(2):219-232.

66. Avrahami E, Tadmor R, Dally O, Hadar H: Early MR demonstration of spinal metastases in patients with normal radiographs and CT and radionuclide bone scans. *J Comput Assist Tomogr* 1989;13(4):598-602.

67. Li KC, Poon PY: Sensitivity and specificity of MRI in detecting malignant spinal cord compression and in distinguishing malignant from benign compression fractures of vertebrae. *Magn Reson Imaging* 1988;6(5):547-556.

68. Patchell RA, Tibbs PA, Regine WF, et al: Direct decompressive surgical resection in the treatment of spinal cord compression caused by metastatic cancer: A randomised trial. *Lancet* 2005;366(9486):643-648.

   This landmark multicenter randomized study found that the results of surgery followed by radiation were superior to those of radiation alone in patients with metastatic spinal cord compression and neurologic symptoms.

69. Tokuhashi Y, Matsuzaki H, Oda H, Oshima M, Ryu J: A revised scoring system for preoperative evaluation of metastatic spine tumor prognosis. *Spine (Phila Pa 1976)* 2005;30(19):2186-2191.

   The revision of the scoring system originally put forward by the authors in 1989 was found to offer at least 75% consistency between predicted prognosis and actual survival period in each metastatic spine disease subgroup.

70. Tomita KN, Kawahara N, Baba H, Tsuchiya H, Fujita T, Toribatake Y: Total en bloc spondylectomy: A new surgical technique for primary malignant vertebral tumors. *Spine (Phila Pa 1976)* 1997;22(3):324-333.

71. Singh K, Samartzis D, Vaccaro AR, Andersson GB, An HS, Heller JG: Current concepts in the management of metastatic spinal disease: The role of minimally-invasive approaches. *J Bone Joint Surg Br* 2006;88(4):434-442.

   The results of minimal-access approaches such as endoscopic surgery, cement augmentation, radiofrequency ablation, stereotactic radiosurgery, and intensity-modulated radiotherapy are reviewed.

72. Prabhu VC, Bilsky MH, Jambhekar K, et al: Results of preoperative embolization for metastatic spinal neoplasms. *J Neurosurg* 2003;98(2, suppl):156-164.

73. Gerszten PC, Mendel E, Yamada Y: Radiotherapy and radiosurgery for metastatic spine disease: What are the options, indications, and outcomes? *Spine (Phila Pa 1976)* 2009;34(22, suppl:)S78-S92.

   A systematic literature review concluded that conventional radiation therapy is safe and effective for local disease and symptom control. Radiosurgery should be considered instead for treating solid spine metastases in oligometastatic or radioresistant disease.

74. Molloy S, Mathis JM, Belkoff SM: The effect of vertebral body percentage fill on mechanical behavior during percutaneous vertebroplasty. *Spine (Phila Pa 1976)* 2003;28(14):1549-1554.

75. Mendel E, Bourekas E, Gerszten P, Golan JD: Percutaneous techniques in the treatment of spine tumors: What are the diagnostic and therapeutic indications and outcomes? *Spine (Phila Pa 1976)* 2009;34(22, suppl): S93-S100.

   The literature on the scope and results of vertebroplasty and kyphoplasty for painful metastatic vertebral fractures is reviewed. Significant pain relief was reported when either technique was used, with a very low complication rate.

6: Spine Disorders

Chapter 43

Spinal Tumors, Syringomyelia, Vascular Malformations, and Intradural Infections

Patrick Shih, MD   Richard G. Fessler, MD, PhD

Introduction

The advent of MRI has led to widespread recognition of an array of intradural lesions that can be safely and effectively treated. Many such lesions have similar clinical and imaging characteristics. It can be difficult to distinguish an intradural lesion from transverse myelitis, a demyelinating condition, or another lesion not suitable for surgery.

A careful history and physical examination can assist in the diagnosis. Establishing a timeline of the appearance of symptoms can be important in differentiating lesions that appear acutely from those that progress slowly. A careful physical examination can isolate the level of involvement along the spinal cord as well as the axial plane location of the lesion. These factors can affect both the nonsurgical and surgical management of the lesion. The risk of surgical damage to critically important regions surrounding a lesion must be weighed against risks associated with nonsurgical management, and clinicians should carefully study the imaging results to weigh the risks of a planned surgical intervention. It is important to understand the natural history of the disease, which can dictate the aggressiveness of a surgical resection.

Tumors

Although primary central nervous system (CNS) tumors are more common intracranially, 2% to 4% of such tumors occur in the spine; 850 to 1,700 such tu-

mors are diagnosed annually in the United States.[1] A primary CNS tumor of the spine is classified as extradural, intradural extramedullary, or intradural intramedullary. An extradural tumor typically represents a metastasis or lymphoma, as discussed elsewhere in this section.

Intradural Extramedullary Tumors

Intradural extramedullary tumors account for 60% to 70% of all primary spinal cord tumors.[1] Most of these tumors are nerve sheath tumors or meningiomas. Patients usually have symptoms related to cord compression, including local or radicular pain. The patient often reports a deep-seated pain in the back. The pain is most intense at night, and obtaining some relief may require the patient to get out of bed and walk. Sphincter dysfunction may be the initial symptom of a cauda equina lesion. Less common initial symptoms include gait ataxia, torticollis, spine deformity, or a symptom associated with a hereditary disorder such as neurofibromatosis.

Schwannoma

Schwannoma is a type of nerve sheath tumor (World Health Organization [WHO] grade I) that usually is benign, although malignant subtypes exist. A schwannoma commonly originates from the dorsal nerve root. The peak incidence of these tumors is during the fourth and fifth decades of life, and they occur equally among men and women. The tumor may be associated with neurofibromatosis type II. Patients with neurofibromatosis type II have multiple lesions, with a relatively high risk of malignant transformation. A schwannoma can be discovered incidentally, or the patient may report mild paresthesias or shooting pain when the nerve is palpated. Patients rarely have spontaneous pain.

On MRI, a schwannoma appears as a lesion arising from the dorsal root (Figure 1) and sometimes as a dumbbell lesion with both intradural and extradural components. T1-weighted MRI images show isointensity, and T2-weighted images show marked

Dr. Fessler or an immediate family member has received royalties from Medtronic and DePuy, a Johnson & Johnson company; serves as a paid consultant to or is an employee of Medtronic Sofamor Danek and Stryker; and has received research or institutional support from Medtronic Sofamor Danek. Neither Dr. Shih nor any immediate family member has received anything of value from or owns stock in a commercial company or institution related directly or indirectly to the subject of this chapter.

6: Spine Disorders

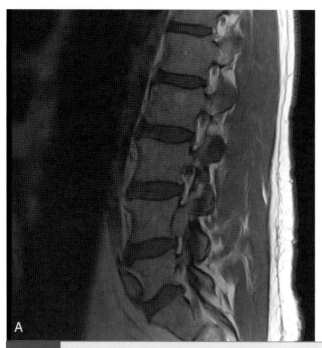
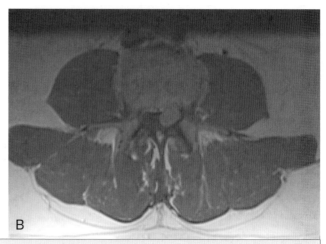

| Figure 1 | Spinal schwannoma. Sagittal (**A**) and axial (**B**) T1-weighted MRIs show a contrast-enhanced lesion entering the right L4 foramen. |

hyperintensity; the contrast enhancement is variable. Tumors that have existed for a long period of time can erode the neural foramina or cause scalloping of the posterior vertebral body. Schwannomas occur in the cervical spine (31%), cauda equina (24%), thoracic spine (22%), upper cervical spine (16%), or conus medullaris (7%).[2] Calcification and hemorrhage are unusual. It can be difficult to distinguish a schwannoma from a neurofibroma. Enlarging or symptomatic lesions should be surgically resected; typically, they can be peeled away from the nerve root. After a subtotal resection, the tumor should be monitored. Postoperative radiation is needed for a malignant tumor.

Neurofibroma

Neurofibromas originate in the peripheral nerve and tend to favor the ventral root. They are classified as general or plexiform. A solitary general neurofibroma is a discrete, well-circumscribed lesion with a fusiform or globular appearance. The peak incidence is during the fourth and fifth decades of life, with equal distribution among men and women. The lesion is located in the cutaneous or subcutaneous tissue and often appears as a painless nodule that creates a cosmetic disfigurement. In plexiform neurofibroma, a disorganized array of nerves is intermingled with tumor. Spontaneous pain (not originating with palpation) is typical. The presence of multiple neurofibromas can suggest neurofibromatosis type I. Although 50% of patients with neurofibromatosis type I have a malignant peripheral nerve sheath tumor,[3] only a few of the patients in whom a malignant peripheral nerve sheath tumor is diagnosed have neurofibromatosis type I.

Like a schwannoma, a neurofibroma appears as a well-circumscribed, rounded, or fusiform lesion that may be dumbbell shaped. The imaging characteristics also are similar, including isointensity on T1-weighted MRI and marked hyperintensity on T2-weighted MRI with intense contrast enhancement. A long-standing tumor can cause erosion through the posterior vertebral body. A solitary symptomatic lesion should be surgically resected. Because neurofibromas encase nerve roots, the ability to separate the lesion from the nerve root is limited.

Meningioma

Meningioma is a dura-based benign tumor that accounts for 25% of all primary spinal cord tumors.[1] More than 80% of spinal meningiomas are diagnosed in women, most often in the thoracic spine. In men, meningiomas occur with equal frequency in the cervical and thoracic spine. The peak incidence of these tumors is during the fifth and sixth decades of life. Most meningiomas are classified as WHO grade I. The risk factors associated with meningioma are neurofibromatosis type II and a history of radiation exposure. Ninety-four percent of spine meningiomas are intradural, and 6% are extradural.[1]

On MRI, a meningioma appears as a well-circumscribed, dura-based lesion. The tumor is isointense or hypointense on T1-weighted studies and slightly hyperintense on T2-weighted studies, with homogenous intense contrast enhancement. Calcifications sometimes are present. In contrast with neurofibromas, meningiomas usually are entirely intradural or extradural. Multiple meningiomas are particularly associated with neurofibromatosis type II.

Surgery should be performed if the patient is symptomatic. A complete resection can be curative; the rates of recurrence 5 and 10 years after resection are 3% and 6%, respectively.[4-6] An anaplastic or atypical phenotype is associated with a greater likelihood of recurrence. Radiotherapy should be considered for recurrent lesions. There is no standard chemotherapy protocol.

Meningeal Hemangiopericytoma

Meningeal hemangiopericytoma is an extremely rare tumor, with only a few incidences reported in the literature. Malignant features are more common than in other types of intradural extramedullary tumors. The malignant subtypes of hemangiopericytoma are suggested by increased mitotic activity, dense cellularity, the presence of pleomorphic cells, and regions of necrosis or hemorrhage. The lesion has a lobular appearance on MRI, with heterogeneity on T1- and T2-weighted studies. An angiogram reveals corkscrew vessels with an associated tumor blush.[7] Embolization should be considered before surgery because of the vascularity of these lesions. A complete resection should be attempted. Limited data suggest that postoperative radiotherapy is useful for local control of spine lesions,[8] and it is frequently used for intracranial hemangiopericytoma.

Dermoid and Epidermoid Cysts

Dermoid and epidermoid cysts arise from an abnormal heterotopic presence of ectodermal cells in the neural tube during embryonic development. Approximately 40% of epidermoid cysts in the spine are a late complication of lumbar puncture in which epidermal tissue was implanted in the thecal sac.[9] These lesions usually are found in the lumbosacral spine, although they also can appear in the thoracic region. Epidermoid cysts typically appear during the the fourth decade of life; dermoid cysts appear during the third decade.[10] If the lesion ruptures, chemical meningitis can ensue.

An epidermoid cyst can be difficult to see on MRI because its consistency is similar to that of cerebrospinal fluid (CSF). Diffusion-weighted MRI can be useful for distinguishing an epidermoid cyst from an arachnoid cyst. Dermoid cysts contain solid cholesterol, and their signal intensities can be similar to those of fat. The surgical goal for an epidermoid or dermoid cyst is total resection, but this goal may not be achievable if the lesion is adhering to surrounding structures. Removal of the cystic contents may improve the patient's symptoms. The contents of these lesions can produce a granulomatous reaction that is treatable using corticosteroids. Radiotherapy or chemotherapy is not used.

Lipoma

Intradural extramedullary lipomas are congenital, linked to spinal dysraphism, and usually found in children (from infants to age 19 years).[11] The typical regions of involvement are the lower thoracic and lumbosacral spine. A lipoma in the region of the cauda equina can cause tethered cord syndrome, leading to pain, bladder dysfunction, sensorimotor changes, and spine deformity. On MRI, the appearance of lipoma is characteristic of adipose tissue (hyperintense on T1-weighted and hypointense on T2-weighted studies). Surgical decompression and untethering of neural elements is performed with the use of spontaneous and triggered electromyography. Occasionally a fatty filum terminale is incidentally discovered in a pediatric patient, and a surgical resection can prevent tethered cord syndrome from developing later in the patient's life.

Paraganglioma

A paraganglioma is a nonsecreting tumor derived from paraganglion cells of the autonomic nervous system. These tumors are considered benign, though aggressive metastatic tumors have been reported.[12] The mean age of patients is 48 years, and more men than women are affected. A paraganglioma typically involves the conus medullaris, cauda equina, or filum terminale. The signal is hypointense or isointense on T1-weighted MRI and heterogeneous on T2-weighted MRI. Hemosiderin deposits on the periphery of the tumor can appear as a rim of T2-weighted or gradient echo hypointensity. An infusion of contrast can produce the classic salt-and-pepper appearance. A hypervascular element is suggested by the presence of flow voids corresponding to dilated serpentine vessels around and within the tumor. Extratumoral cysts can exist. Gross total resection can provide a cure, and postoperative radiation provides no additional benefit.

Extramedullary Metastasis

The metastatic spread of a malignant tumor to the CNS usually indicates an advanced progression of systemic disease. Drop metastasis may occur from an intracranial metastatic lesion or a primary tumor of the CNS, particularly a medulloblastoma or glioma. Dissemination of cells through the CSF can lead to multiple lesions. Drop metastases predominantly appear in the thoracic and thoracolumbar spine. The typical prognosis for a patient with extramedullary metastasis is dismal. Surgery has only a limited role. Radiotherapy can be used to limit tumor progression, and steroids may provide some short-term symptomatic relief. Intrathecal chemotherapy agents have been used to control tumor burden.

Intradural Intramedullary Tumors

Intramedullary tumors represent 20% to 30% of all intradural tumors in adults and 50% of intradural tumors in children.[13,14] More than 80% of intramedullary tumors are classified as gliomas.[3] Thirty percent to 40% of intramedullary tumors are classified as astrocytomas, and 60% to 70% are classified as ependymomas.[1] Astrocytomas are more common in children, and ependymomas are more common in adults. Hemangioblastoma accounts for 3% to 8% of primary intramedullary tumors; it is associated with von Hippel–Lindau

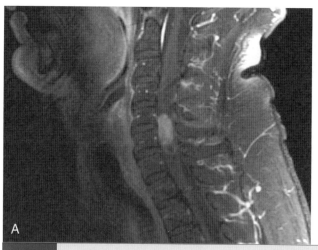
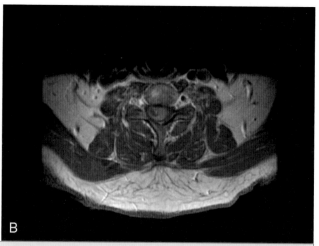

Figure 2   Cellular ependymoma. Sagittal (**A**) and axial (**B**) T1-weighted MRIs show contrast-enhanced lesions associated with an inferior polar cyst at C5-C6.

disease in 15% to 20% of patients.[1] Only 2% of intramedullary tumors are of metastatic origin.[1] Other rare tumors located within the spinal cord include subependymoma, oligodendroglioma, ganglioglioma, lipoma, teratoma, and lymphoma.

The symptoms of a tumor vary with its location. Local or radicular pain is common. Motor deficits occur in 50% to 69% of patients, and sensory deficits occur in 64% to 65%.[15,16] Sphincter dysfunction is the initial symptom in 14% to 38% of patients.[15,16] Gait disturbance, torticollis, or kyphoscoliosis also can be the initial symptom. Patients may have symptoms related to a syrinx.

Treatment should be considered for any symptomatic lesion. The natural history of these tumors is a progressive decline in neurologic function, and acute hemorrhage can lead to a stepwise decline. To maintain neurologic function, decompression should be performed shortly after the onset of symptoms. The patient's preoperative neurologic status may be the most important indicator of the neurologic and functional outcome of treatment.[17] The use of motor-evoked potentials during surgery can help prevent acute neurologic decline. Gross total resection was found to be correlated with a favorable prognosis for hemangioblastoma or ependymoma. Identification of a tumor plane can help accomplish the difficult task of gross total resection. The tumor plane is dependent on the underlying microscopic anatomy. Progression-free survival can depend on the tumor anatomy as well as the presence of a tumor plane.[16]

Ependymoma

Ependymoma is the most common intramedullary tumor. An ependymoma typically is classified as cellular (WHO grade II) or myxopapillary (WHO grade I). Myxopapillary ependymoma accounts for approximately 40% to 50% of spine ependymomas.[9,18,19] Clear-cell, papillary, anaplastic, and mixed variant sub-

types also exist. The incidence of cellular ependymoma peaks during the fourth and fifth decades of life. Cellular ependymoma represents 40% to 60% of all intramedullary tumors in adults and 16% to 35% in children.[19,20] Myxopapillary and cellular ependymoma are histologically distinct, but both are considered benign. The malignant variants are classified as anaplastic ependymomas (WHO grade III).

Cellular ependymoma appears as a focal enlargement of the spinal cord. The cervical spinal cord is affected in 42% of patients, although cellular ependymoma can occur anywhere in the neuroaxis.[1] The characteristic appearance on MRI is diffuse heterogeneous contrast enhancement, with isointensity or hypointensity on T1-weighted studies and hyperintensity on T2-weighted studies. Polar cyst formation and hemorrhage are common (Figure 2). Syringomyelia is associated with cervical ependymoma.

The initial treatment is an attempt at gross total resection, which offers control in 90% to 100% of patients.[21-23] Although a distinct plane can be identified between the spinal cord and a cellular ependymoma, a gross total resection usually is not achieved. The likelihood of tumor recurrence corresponds to the amount of residual tumor. After a gross total resection, the rate of tumor recurrence is less than 10%, but after a subtotal resection, the rate is 50% to 70%.[15,24] The 5-year survival rate after resection of a low-grade intramedullary ependymoma is 83% to 100%.[15,22,25] Radiation is used as an adjuvant therapy after a subtotal resection or for a malignant phenotype.

Myxopapillary ependymoma is an encapsulated lesion in the filum terminale. T1-weighted MRI typically is isointense or hypointense, but dense mucin or hemorrhage can cause hyperintensity. T2-weighted MRI has a hyperintense signal. Contrast enhancement is heterogeneous. Cyst formation and hemorrhage contribute to a heterogeneous radiographic appearance. Vertebral body scalloping, neural foraminal enlargement, scoliosis, and tumor seeding in the sacrum can be seen on MRI (Figure 3).

A myxopapillary ependymoma should be resected, with the capsule left intact to prevent seeding of the tumor in the CNS. If the spinal roots are involved, en bloc resection may not be possible. Focal fractionated radiotherapy can be of benefit for controlling tumor progression or improving the neurologic outcome after a subtotal resection. However, broader field radiation is warranted if there is tumor seeding in the subarachnoid space.

Astrocytoma

Seventy-five percent of astrocytomas are benign (WHO grade II). They typically occur during the third decade of life, with no preference for men or women. In children, astrocytoma represents as many as 80% to 90% of intramedullary tumors, compared with 25% in adults.[13,15,19,20,26-30] Histologic evidence of WHO grade III or IV is found in 25% of these tumors, leading to a grim prognosis.[1]

Astrocytomas have a fusiform appearance on MRI, with irregular margins and intratumoral, caudal, or rostral cysts that can evolve into syringomyelia extending over multiple vertebral levels. The appearance is hypointense to isointense on T1-weighted MRI and hyperintense on T2-weighted MRI, with variable contrast enhancement. With a low-grade lesion, there is no surrounding edema or hemorrhage. However, with a high-grade lesion, there is more prominent enhancement; intratumoral cysts can appear, and the surrounding edema and necrosis become more obvious. An astrocytoma typically is located in the cervicothoracic or thoracic spine in children. The tumor is more common in the cervical spine of adults. Usually the tumor does not extend over more than four vertebral segments.

Surgery is performed to establish a diagnosis and attempt a cure. Because of the infiltrative nature of astrocytoma, gross total resection is difficult to achieve without significant postsurgical morbidity. Radiation therapy is used only if a substantial resection cannot be achieved, there is clinical or radiographic progression of disease, or the subtype is malignant. Chemotherapy can offer some marginal benefit in treating spine as well as cranial astrocytoma, although the relevant data are limited.[31-34]

Juvenile pilocytic astrocytoma (WHO grade I) is a rare and relatively unaggressive glioma. This tumor tends to be well circumscribed and homogenously enhancing on MRI, and it also may appear as a solid mural nodule attached to a cyst. Complete resection is achievable in 80% of tumors.[15]

Hemangioblastoma

A hemangioblastoma is a benign vascular tumor. Although 10% to 25% are associated with von Hippel–Lindau disease,[1] the clinical sequelae are unaffected by the association. Sporadic tumors occur predominantly in men and typically appear during the fourth decade

| Figure 3 | Myxopapillary ependymoma. Sagittal T1-weighted MRI shows a contrast-enhanced lesion arising from the conus medullaris with associated seeding of sacral roots. |

of life, although the age of onset is earlier in patients with von Hippel–Lindau disease. The tumor favors a dorsal location and thus tends to affect sensation. Subarachnoid or intramedullary hemorrhage is rare. Most of these lesions are solitary and are found in the cervical or thoracic spine.

MRI reveals a homogeneously enhancing nodule accompanied by a cyst and sometimes by peritumoral edema or syringomyelia. A relatively small lesion appears isointense on T1-weighted MRI and hyperintense on T2-weighted studies. A larger lesion appears isointense to hypointense with T1 weighting and heterogeneous with T2 weighting. Heterogeneous contrast enhancement is seen within the nodule. The presence of a syrinx favors a diagnosis of hemangioblastoma over a vascular malformation. Spine angiography can reveal prominent feeding arteries and draining vessels, which translate into flow voids on MRI.

Gross total resection can provide a cure for a solitary lesion. If the patient has multiple lesions, the goal should be to resect the symptomatic lesions. Preoperative embolization should be considered to lessen the amount of bleeding during resection. Radiation therapy and chemotherapy are not routinely used.

Subependymoma

Fewer than 50 incidences of subependymoma have been reported, predominantly in men in their fourth or fifth decade of life.[35] A subependymoma is located in the cervical spine or, less commonly, in the thoracic spine. A subependymoma mimics a spine ependymoma on MRI, with hypointensity on a T1-weighted image,

6: Spine Disorders

hyperintensity on a T2-weighted image, and heterogeneous enhancement. A subependymoma can be differentiated from an ependymoma by its eccentric location, compared with the central location of an ependymoma. These tumors are well demarcated, and a gross total resection should be achievable. Postoperative radiation and chemotherapy have proved useful.

Oligodendroglioma

Most oligodendrogliomas are intracranial, and only 2% are located in the spine.[36,37] On average, patients are in the second or third decade of life. This tumor tends to favor the thoracic spine, and it may be associated with a spine deformity. The tumor appears isointense on T1-weighted MRI and hyperintense on T2-weighted MRI and is heterogeneously enhanced. Gross total resection is difficult because the tumor is infiltrative. There may be leptomeningeal spread. Postoperative radiation treatment was found beneficial in a recent case report.[36]

Ganglioglioma

A ganglioglioma consists of neuronal and glial cells. These tumors are benign (WHO grade I or II), although malignant anaplastic ganglioglioma occurs rarely. Gangliogliomas appear during the fourth decade of life, slightly more often among men than women. Typically the cervicothoracic or thoracic region is involved. The MRI appearance is inconsistent, with variable intensity on T1-weighted studies and hyperintensity on T2-weighted studies. Contrast enhancement is variable and may extend to the surface of the cord. Cysts, scalloping of the bone, or scoliosis may be seen. Edema and hemosiderin usually are absent. The goal of surgery is gross total resection, which is achievable in 80% to 90% of tumors.[38,39] Recurrence occurs in 30% to 47% of patients, and the 5-year survival rate is 88% to 89%.[38,40] Radiation can be considered if progression occurs. There are no data on the role of chemotherapy.

Lymphoma

Lymphoma as an isolated lesion in the spine is rare. Therefore, a suggested diagnosis of lymphoma requires a screening of the CNS to detect any additional lesions. On T2-weighted MRI, lymphoma appears as an ill-defined hyperintense lesion, with marked homogenous contrast enhancement. There is less cord enlargement than with other intramedullary tumors. The lesion most commonly appears in the cervical spine, followed by the thoracic and lumbar spine. The typical treatment is a methotrexate-based chemotherapy regimen.

Germinoma

Several incidences of germinoma of the spine have been reported.[41-43] Because of the rarity of this tumor in the spine, the entire neuroaxis should be evaluated for disease. CSF cytology studies can be used to confirm a diagnosis; if the cytology findings are negative, the diagnosis also can be confirmed by biopsy before treatment is initiated. Germinomas are radiosensitive; they can be treated with radiotherapy alone or in conjunction with chemotherapy.

Melanoma

Melanoma can arise in the spine. However, when intramedullary melanoma of the spine is found, an extensive workup should be performed to rule out metastasis from another site of origin. Primary lesions of the spine usually are more indolent than metastatic lesions. Gross total resection can achieve a clinical cure of primary melanoma of the spine. If gross total resection is not possible, postoperative radiation and adjuvant chemotherapy can be used to control the tumor. Hemorrhage is typical of this tumor, and therefore it may be mistaken for a vascular malformation.

Lipoma

A spine lipoma is a congenital lesion that appears in early adulthood and thus may be associated with spinal dysraphism. The lesion typically is located in the cervical or thoracic spine, and it is rare for it to occupy the entire cord. MRI suggests a fatty constituent; T1-weighted studies are hyperintense, and T2-weighted studies are hypointense. The goal of surgery is to debulk the tumor rather than achieve gross total resection. These lesions impede maturation of the surrounding neural tissue, and usually the symptoms do not improve after surgical debulking for detethering of the spinal cord.

Teratoma

Case reports of intramedullary teratoma have been published.[44,45] This lesion usually is found in the conus medullaris, typically with the mature phenotype, and it is considered benign. Surgical resection is associated with a good outcome. Recurrence is uncommon.

Intramedullary Metastasis

Intramedullary metastasis is rare, occurring in fewer than 1% of all patients with a systemic malignancy.[46] Most patients have lung cancer, particularly small cell carcinoma, and some have breast cancer; other primary sources include renal cell carcinoma and melanoma. The common locations of metastasis include the cervical region and conus medullaris. Patients with intramedullary metastasis may have a Brown-Séquard syndrome. A single lesion usually is identified. MRI findings are nonspecific. The edema appears to be out of proportion to the size of the tumor.

Patients found to have intramedullary metastasis usually also have metastasis elsewhere, and the average length of survival after diagnosis is 3 months.[3] If the diagnosis is otherwise uncertain, surgery can be performed to obtain a tissue diagnosis. The treatment is palliative. Radiotherapy, in conjunction with corticosteroids, can reduce pain and preserve neurologic function.

Syringomyelia

The term syringomyelia describes a nonspecific cystic fluid collection in the spinal cord, the clinical manifestations of which vary with the extent of the fluid collection. The cystic cavitation typically impairs the anterior white commissure (the crossing fibers of the spinothalamic tract) leading to impaired pain and temperature sensation. The dorsal columns are normal and preserve two-point discrimination and proprioception. Involvement of the anterior horn cells can lead to weakness at the affected levels. Atrophy of the hands may occur. Compression on the lateral corticospinal tracts can contribute to weakness distally. Disruption of the sympathetic tracts can lead to a Horner syndrome. The treatment of syringomyelia is based on the underlying cause.

Posttraumatic Syringomyelia

Syringomyelia occurs in 21% to 28% of patients with a spinal cord injury, with cystic changes noted in 30% to 50%.[47-51] Only 3% to 4% of patients with a spinal cord injury have symptoms related to syringomyelia, however.[52] There is some ambiguity as to how syringomyelia develops after a spinal cord injury. Inflammation, ischemia of the cord with surrounding edema, arachnoiditis, and persistent deformity and stenosis are all believed to contribute. Patients develop a dissociated sensory loss 3 to 34 months after their injury. In addition, pain or a dull burning sensation may develop proximal to the level of the injury.[47,53-55] The pain can be intense. MRI may be useful in determining the extent of the syringomyelia, levels of stenosis, regions of tethering, and presence of arachnoiditis.

Although posttraumatic syringomyelia is easily diagnosed, it is difficult to treat. The only available surgical procedures involve shunting, lysis of adhesions, correction of deformity, decompression, or cord transection. Medical treatment is intended to alleviate the symptoms. Neuropathic pain can be reduced with the use of tricyclic antidepressants such as amitriptyline or anticonvulsants such as gabapentin. Anticholinergic agents can limit secretions and sweating. Antispasmodic agents can improve function and limit the pain associated with spasticity.

Syringomyelia and Chiari Malformation

Chiari malformation is described as cerebellar tonsillar ectopia below the foramen magnum. Symptomatic Chiari malformation can lead to exertional occipital headaches. The diagnostic workup includes imaging studies of the neuroaxis to evaluate for syringomyelia. Many theories have been proposed as to why syringomyelia develops in patients with Chiari malformation. The Gardner hydrodynamic theory proposes that syringomyelia forms as a result of a caudally directed pulse wave that forces CSF into the central canal through the obex while the foramen of Magendie is obstructed.[56] The Williams theory focuses on the subarachnoid pressure differential between the cranium and spine at the foramen of Monroe; an obstruction in the hindbrain prevents increased intracranial CSF pressure from migrating inferiorly, and thus it dissipates through the cord.[57] The Oldfield hypothesis is based on the downward displacement of cerebellar tonsils during systole on a dynamic MRI. This piston effect forces CSF into the perivascular and interstitial spaces, creating a syrinx.[58]

The optimal treatment of syringomyelia associated with Chiari malformation is a subject of debate. There is evidence that a suboccipital craniectomy with duraplasty can reduce the size of the syrinx, but a shunt is needed as the syrinx progresses.[59]

Syringomyelia and Intramedullary Tumors

Syringomyelia is found in 45% of patients with an intramedullary tumor, commonly in the lower cervical to upper thoracic region.[60] Syringomyelia is commonly associated with hemangioblastomas and glial tumors and is more common in ependymomas than in astrocytomas.[60]

The etiology of syringomyelia is not well understood, although many theories have been proposed. Some theories suggest that syrinxes are inherent to the neoplasm, and one theory focuses on the tumor and syrinx arising from a single developmental abnormality. The diminution of the syrinx seen with tumor resection argues against these two hypotheses. Another possible mechanism of syrinx development relates to the effect of the tumor on the surrounding tissues. It has also been proposed that the tumor can cause an obstruction in CSF flow.[60] Regardless of etiology, it is known that syrinxes improve with tumor resection. In addition, the presence of syringomyelia can make surgical tumor resection easier and lead to better recovery.

Syringomyelia and Spinal Dysraphism

Syringomyelia is common in patients with spina bifida. The incidence is higher among patients with myelomeningocele than patients with spina bifida occulta. In spina bifida occulta from a lipoma, it is believed that the syrinx is an enlarged central canal, usually identified rostral to the lipoma. In myelomeningocele, a link probably exists between the formation of syringomyelia, the presence of hydrocephalus, and Chiari II malformation. A symptomatic syringomyelia is rare in a patient with spinal dysraphism. It can be difficult to ascertain whether the patient's motor or sensory deficits are related to tethered cord syndrome or syringomyelia. The presence of scoliosis can suggest syringomyelia. The role of suboccipital craniectomy in the treatment of syringomyelia in a Chiari II malformation is not clear. A syringosubarachnoid or syringoperitoneal shunt can be considered if the syrinx is large and the progressive motor weakness and pain are not attributable to tethered cord syndrome.

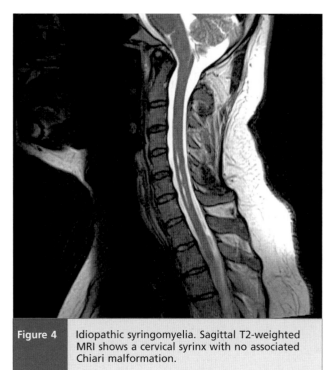

Figure 4 Idiopathic syringomyelia. Sagittal T2-weighted MRI shows a cervical syrinx with no associated Chiari malformation.

Syringomyelia and Arachnoiditis

Arachnoiditis can develop as a result of spine surgery, meningitis, or myelography. Over time, arachnoiditis can lead to disturbance in CSF flow and then to the formation of an intramedullary cyst. It has been hypothesized that the blocked subarachnoid space creates transmural avenues for CSF diversion.[61] The surgical options are limited and do not yield satisfactory results. Lysis of adhesions may provide some benefit, although this surgical intervention carries some risk. Syringoperitoneal, syringopleural, or syringosubarachnoid shunting has not had long-term success and is associated with high rates of malfunction and recurrence.[62,63] Shunting can contribute to future arachnoiditis.

Idiopathic Syringomyelia

Several reported instances of syringomyelia have had no discernable cause (Figure 4), and the treatment of such patients is a subject of debate. It is possible that, despite the absence of visible tonsillar ectopia on MRI, an abnormal configuration in the posterior fossa leads to disruptions in CSF flow. Some authors believe a small posterior fossa and narrow CSF space can alter the dynamics of CSF, thus creating a syrinx.[64] It has been suggested that the syringomyelia can be improved by performing a suboccipital craniectomy similar to the procedure for symptomatic Chiari malformation. Some instances of idiopathic syringomyelia have been attributed to arachnoid webs. For these patients, there may be some benefit to arachnoid web resection.[65,66] CT myelography and cine MRI are used to predict whether surgery will improve the patient's condition. An MRI-monitored asymptomatic idiopathic syrinx was found to resolve spontaneously, without treatment.[66]

Vascular Malformations

Spinal vascular malformations have the potential to inflict devastating damage on the CNS. Only approximately 300 such lesions are diagnosed each year.[67] The symptoms arise through mass effect, vascular steal, or hemorrhage leading to neurologic compromise. Treatment requires an understanding of the relevant natural history and complex anatomy. These lesions can be most safely and effectively treated with combined surgical and endovascular techniques.

Since the development of angiography, spine vascular malformations have been classified into multiple systems based on anatomic location as well as hematologic and morphologic properties. The most widely accepted classification system identifies four types of spine vascular malformations: I, dural arteriovenous fistula; II, glomus arteriovenous malformation; III, juvenile arteriovenous malformation; and IV, perimedullary arteriovenous fistula.[68]

Dural Arteriovenous Fistula (Type I)

Dural arteriovenous fistula accounts for approximately 70% of all spine vascular malformations.[69,70] Men are affected four times as often as women, and the average patient age at diagnosis is 55 to 60 years.[71,72] Most of the lesions are located between T6 and L2.[73]

These lesions are believed to be acquired. They are the result of aberrant connections between the radicular artery and the radicular vein, located within the dorsal surface of the dural sleeve of the nerve root in the intervertebral foramen. Thus, the connection is located beneath the pedicle. In these hemodynamically low-flow lesions, retrograde flow to the venous plexuses surrounding the spinal cord leads to perimedullary venous plexus congestion and cord ischemia. The coronal system, which drains the posterior two thirds of the cord, is predominantly affected. The anterior spine veins do not become arterialized until later in the disease. The measured pressure of the arterialized veins is as high as 74% of the systemic arterial pressure.[74]

Patients typically develop progressive myelopathy with varying symptoms that may include back pain, radicular pain, or gait instability. Paresis, paralysis, or bowel or bladder dysfunction may develop in severe disease. The clinical symptoms can become worse with an exertion-associated rise in blood pressure. The average length of time between the onset of symptoms and the diagnosis is 18.7 months.[71] A delay in diagnosis can lead to incontinence and loss of the ability to walk.

The diagnosis can be difficult. Noninvasive imaging may have nonspecific findings. A finding of filling defects on myelography suggests the presence of engorged veins, and myelography coupled with CT is even more sensitive for diagnosing dural arteriovenous fistula. T2-weighted MRI can show increased intensity within the spinal cord, surrounded by a small rim of hypointensity, as seen on T1-weighted MRI. The hyperintensity seen on T2-weighted studies usually is not well defined and may extend to multiple segments within the spinal cord. Flow voids can be enhanced by contrast dye and may suggest the presence of perimedullary vessels. Also on MRI, chronic venous congestion may appear as diffuse enhancement of the cord resulting from breakdown of the blood-brain barrier. Contrast enhancement, coupled with enlargement of the spinal cord, sometimes leads to a false diagnosis of spinal cord tumor. Newer techniques including CT angiography and magnetic resonance angiography may be helpful in locating the fistula. A fistula can be indirectly revealed if delayed venous return is seen when contrast is injected into the anterior spinal artery on two-dimensional angiography (Figure 5). Retrograde flow of contrast through the radiculomedullary veins is seen with direct injection of a segmental artery supplying the arteriovenous fistula.

Surgical intervention is intended to halt progression of the disease. After treatment, two thirds of patients have improved motor symptoms (including gait), and one third have improved sensory function. Impotence and sphincter dysfunction are more resistant to reversal, and pain syndromes may persist after surgery.[75] The shunting vein is disconnected from the perimedullary venous plexus, thus preventing high-pressure arterialized blood from causing venous congestion. A laminectomy typically is done to provide exposure to the dilated tortuous vein; after the enlarged vein is identified, a clip is placed on it in close proximity to the dura. This strategy leads to a 98% obliteration rate, with significant morbidity in fewer than 2% of patients.[76,77] Endovascular treatment with polyvinyl chloride has been criticized because of the associated high risk and high recurrence rate.[78] Advancements in the use of liquid adhesive embolic agents may alter the future management of dural arteriovenous fistula.

Glomus Arteriovenous Malformation (Type II)
In a glomus arteriovenous malformation, a nidus is present within the spinal cord. In these high-flow, low-resistance lesions, the arterial supply characteristically arises from the anterior or posterior spinal artery, with drainage into the medullary veins. The most common location is at the cervicomedullary junction. Glomus arteriovenous malformation usually is diagnosed in a child or young adult, and both sexes are equally affected.

A type II lesion typically appears as a subarachnoid hemorrhage or a hemorrhage within the spinal cord, leading to new, acute neurologic deficits or a worsening of preexisting deficits. The rate of rehemorrhage was found to be 10% within the first 30 days after the initial hemorrhage and as high as 40% within the next year.[79] Progressive myelopathy occurs as the lesion causes chronic compression of the spinal cord.

MRI and angiography are used to understand the architectural makeup of these lesions. MRI is helpful for determining the location of the lesion in the spinal cord, and it may reveal hemorrhage or thrombosis of

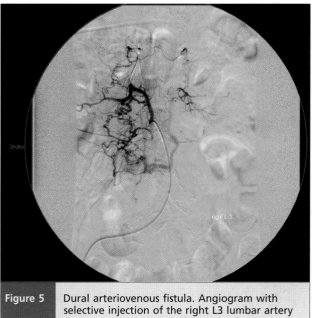

Figure 5 Dural arteriovenous fistula. Angiogram with selective injection of the right L3 lumbar artery shows anastomosis into the epidural venous system.

the lesion. Angiography allows a detailed analysis of the spatial consistency of the vascular makeup as well as identification of an intranidal aneurysm. Temporal resolution allows separation of the venous, arterial, and nidal components of the lesion. Angiography also is helpful in determining the risk of an infarct from embolization in the vessels that jointly supply the arteriovenous malformation and the spinal cord.

An intramedullary arteriovenous malformation is challenging to treat. Urgent surgery usually is not necessary after acute bleeding because of the low risk of immediate further bleeding. Although the cure is complete excision of the nidus, partial excision of the nidus has been found to improve symptoms.[80] The risk associated with the treatment is secondary to direct injury to the surrounding eloquent tissue and disruption of vascular supply to the spinal cord. Microsurgery is the traditional first treatment. Spinal arteriovenous malformations are easily accessible if they are located on the dorsal surface of the spinal cord and have a tight nidus. Sometimes endovascular treatment is performed first, although it can be associated with high rates of recanalization and complications. Embolization was reported to offer an angiographic cure in 37.5% of patients.[81] Even if embolization does not provide an angiographic cure, it can stabilize or improve the patient's signs and symptoms, possibly by reducing pressure and attenuation of the draining vein. Preoperative embolization may assist with microsurgical resection. Although radiosurgery is used for intracranial arteriovenous malformations, it is not considered an option for treating spinal arteriovenous malformations.

6: Spine Disorders

Juvenile Arteriovenous Malformation (Type III)

A juvenile arteriovenous malformation is found in children and young adults; it is the least common of the spinal vascular abnormalities. This large lesion consists of an intramedullary component and an extensive extramedullary component that may extend into the spinal column and paraspinal tissues. A juvenile arteriovenous malformation is supplied by multiple feeders over several vertebral levels and is associated with high flow. The symptoms may result from cord compression, venous congestion, subarachnoid hemorrhage, or vascular steal. The most common findings are pain and progressive myelopathy, although there may be acute neurologic deficits. A high cardiac output sometimes occurs. Bruits may be heard on physical examination. An untreated juvenile arteriovenous malformation has a poor prognosis, with most patients becoming severely disabled over time.

Curing juvenile arteriovenous malformation requires multiple-stage treatment using a combined surgical and endovascular approach, and a cure has been reported in a few patients.[82] The treatment usually is palliative or targeted toward reducing venous hypertension. The goal of endovascular treatment is partial embolization of the arterial feeders to reduce the risk of bleeding. Because of the typical size of the lesion, endovascular treatment may be the only option. After microsurgical resection, angiography should be used to identify residual arteriovenous malformation so it can be treated before scarring develops.

Perimedullary Dural Arteriovenous Fistula (Type IV)

A perimedullary arteriovenous fistula is a direct arteriovenous shunt fed by the anterior and/or posterior spinal arteries. The lesion typically is located near the conus medullaris on the surface of the spinal cord or underneath the pia mater. As in a type I lesion, there is no nidal vascular abnormality between the feeding artery and the draining vessel. Perimedullary arteriovenous fistula represents approximately 15% to 40% of all spinal cord vascular malformations.[83] The presence of an intranidal aneurysm or ecstatic venous anomaly is a reflection of the high-flow nature of these lesions. Patients with a perimedullary arteriovenous fistula typically are younger than those with dural arteriovenous fistula. The average time between the onset of symptoms and the diagnosis is 9 years.[84] The clinical appearance of perimedullary arteriovenous fistula may be consistent with conus medullaris or cauda equina syndrome. Venous hypertension leads to progressive myelopathy. Spontaneous hemorrhage can occur with aneurysm rupture. The treatment options are based on the angiographic makeup of the lesion; injection should be done through all the pedicles.

Two similar classification systems have been developed for perimedullary arteriovenous fistula, based on the size of the lesion, the number of feeding and drain-ing vessels, and the amount of venous congestion. In the Merland classification, a type I lesion is a small, low-flow lesion with moderate venous hypertension, usually from the anterior spinal artery; a type II lesion is a large, fistulous connection composed of several distinct shunts fed by the swollen anterior or posterior spinal artery; and a type III lesion is a giant lesion arising from a single fistula between multiple dilated arteries supplying the draining vessels. The Spetzler classification is analogous to the Merland classification: a type A lesion is a simple, low-flow perimedullary arteriovenous fistula from a single arterial supply; a type B lesion has multiple feeders that translate into increased flow and dilatation of the draining veins; and a type C lesion is a giant lesion with large shunt volumes from multiple feeding arteries leading to dilated, tortuous veins. Type C lesions are considered high-flow, high-pressure systems.

The treatment is aimed at complete obliteration of the fistula. Additional vessel recruitment can occur if the fistula persists after treatment. The treatment varies with the type of lesion. In a type I or type A lesion, the small feeders from the anterior spinal artery may be difficult to embolize and may be associated with a high recanalization rate. Embolization offers an angiographic cure in as many as 33% of patients.[83] Thus, surgical treatment of these lesions is preferred. If dorsal feeders arising from the posterior spinal artery are supplying the fistula, a posterior approach is favored, using a laminectomy. An anterior approach using a retroperitoneal dissection or a thoracotomy with corpectomy may be needed to gain access to anteriorly located lesions. A type II or type B lesion is difficult to treat because of the presence of multiple feeders. A cure usually is not possible with endovascular treatment alone, especially if a long, tortuous feeding vessel from the anterior spinal artery is supplying the fistula. Some form of combined treatment is needed, using microsurgical and endovascular techniques. Microsurgical treatment with preoperative embolization can yield satisfactory results.[83-85] A type III or type C lesion usually is considered to be difficult to treat surgically but can be cured with embolization.

Spinal Cord Cavernous Malformation

A cavernous malformation is composed of a conglomerate of sinusoidal channels filled with blood. The vessel walls are composed of endothelial cells, with a thin layer of adventitia lacking any elastin or smooth muscle. A cavernous malformation is able to enlarge or reduce in size over time. Although a cavernous malformation is a low-pressure lesion, it can bleed and damage surrounding neurologic structures. Some cavernous malformations grow to cause a local mass effect on the surrounding structures, although the natural history of hemorrhage from a spinal cord cavernous malformation is not well known. The annual hemorrhage risk associated with each lesion is believed to be 1.4% to 4.5%.[86,87]

The average patient age at clinical presentation is 40 years.[88] The clinical appearance of spinal cord cavernous malformation is similar to that of multiple sclerosis. The four clinical types of spinal cord cavernous malformation are episodic neurologic decline with variable improvement between episodes; gradual progression of neurologic deterioration; acute onset of symptoms, usually with swift decline; and gradual progression of neurologic deterioration after acute, mild symptoms.[89] The diagnosis is made in 38% of patients after acute symptoms occur and in 60% of patients after progressive symptoms occur; only 2% of patients are asymptomatic at initial diagnosis.[88] A spinal cord cavernous malformation tends to be most prominent in the thoracic region, followed by the cervical region, and is more likely to occur in a central or posterior location rather than a lateral or anterior position. Although sensory and motor deficits commonly coexist, sensory deficits are likely to be more prominent. The findings of T1- and T2-weighted MRI may vary centrally, depending on the elapsed time since the bleeding episode. Gradient echo sequences are sensitive for detecting the hemosiderin present in spinal cord cavernous malformations. A normal angiogram can support the diagnosis and argue against the presence of a vascular malformation.

Surgery is an option if the patient has a history of multiple bleeding episodes in a readily accessible location. Surgery improves the symptoms in approximately half of patients. In general, the outcome is more favorable if the lesion has a posterior location rather than an anterior location. These lesions typically can be reached with a posterior laminectomy. The average spinal cord cavernous malformation is 16.3 mm high and 7 mm wide, and a limited hemilaminectomy or laminectomy over two or three vertebral segments is sufficient for resection.[88] Reaching an anteriorly positioned lesion in the thoracic or cervical spine requires a thoracotomy or a ventral neck dissection, respectively.

Intradural Infections

Epidural abscess and vertebral osteomyelitis or diskitis account for most infections associated with the spine. Intradural infections are extremely rare. Patients with a medical comorbidity such as diabetes or immunocompromise are especially at risk for infection of the spine. The treatment and prognosis of these lesions differ, and a timely diagnosis is needed for a satisfactory outcome.

Subdural Abscess

A spinal subdural abscess is a rare entity that usually is associated with an underlying source of infection, most commonly a neighboring infection, meningitis, or an iatrogenic infection. The most common bacterial agent is *Staphylococcus aureus*. Back pain, fever, and neurologic deficits are common. Neurologic symptoms develop in three stages: I, fever without accompanying neurologic findings; II, mild neurologic symptoms; and III, complete paralysis or sensory loss below the level of

the lesion. Gadolinium-enhanced and diffusion-restricted MRI is used for diagnosis. An abscess is suggested by hypointensity on T1-weighted images and hyperintensity on T2-weighted images, with capsular enhancement and restricted diffusion. The white blood cell count, erythrocyte sedimentation rate, and C-reactive protein level are elevated. A subdural abscess is considered a neurosurgical emergency. In the absence of treatment, stage III infection will ensue, with significant morbidity and mortality. Broad-spectrum antibiotics should be promptly initiated and tailored when cultures and sensitivities are obtained.

Intramedullary Pyogenic Abscess

An intradural infection may mimic an intradural neoplasm, with a similar clinical appearance and imaging characteristics. In adults, the infection is derived from a source elsewhere in the body and spreads hematogenously. In children, half of these infections arise from a congenital dermal sinus tract (an epithelialized tract connecting the contents of the thecal sac to the surface of the skin, caused by a developmental error in the separation of the cutaneous and neural ectoderm). Most dermal sinus tracts are discovered in children with meningitis, although direct contact of the tract with the spinal cord also can lead to abscess formation. In children, the organism typically is *S aureus*, and the mean age at presentation is 15.5 months.[90] The infection may mimic an epidural abscess. Because the clinical findings are nonspecific, the diagnosis is difficult. Sixty percent of adult and juvenile patients have pain, 68% have motor and sensory deficits, 56% have urinary dysfunction, and 12% have meningismus.[91] Fever is present only in 40%.[91] A rapidly progressing abscess has a poor prognosis. The mortality rate is 90% for patients whose symptoms appeared fewer than 4 days before clinical presentation. The mortality rate is only 67% for those who had gradually progressing symptoms for longer than 7 days.[92-94]

The standard imaging includes MRI with gadolinium contrast. The MRI findings vary as the infection evolves from myelitis into an abscess. The entire neuroaxis should be reviewed for the presence of additional abscesses. Diffusion-weighted imaging can be helpful in differentiating a tumor from an abscess, as purulent fluid has decreased diffusion properties on diffusion-weighted imaging. Abscesses appear hyperintense on diffusion-weighted imaging and hypointense on the apparent diffusion coefficient. Careful screening by pediatricians to detect dermal sinus tracts can prevent a catastrophic infection from developing. When a dermal sinus tract is found, it should be surgically resected. Dermal sinus tracts are most common in the distal thoracic spine and conus medullaris.

The rates of morbidity and mortality are significant for patients whose infection is not diagnosed in a timely fashion. Surgery, in conjunction with intravenous antibiotics, offers the best chance of recovery. A laminectomy and myelotomy are performed to gain

6: Spine Disorders

access to the abscess. If the abscess extends to multiple levels, a catheter can be used to drain the purulent collection from the septated regions. Broad-spectrum antibiotics should be initiated and tailored when cultures and sensitivities are available. An 8% mortality rate and a 70% rate of permanent neurologic deficit were reported when current treatments were used.[91]

Intramedullary Tuberculosis

Tuberculosis is a common endemic disease in some countries. In the United States, tuberculosis predominantly occurs among immunocompromised individuals. Tuberculosis affects the CNS in 10% to 15% of patients.[95] Intramedullary tuberculosis is a rare entity that appears in the thoracic spine more often than the cervical spine.[96] Ninety-three percent of patients initially have subacute tuberculosis with motor and sensory abnormalities.[96] Bowel and bladder dysfunction develops later in the course of the disease. Intramedullary tuberculosis can occur in isolation, with no apparent pulmonary involvement. The infection, including Pott disease, can occur at other CNS sites, and therefore the entire neuroaxis should be evaluated. The lesions appear hypointense on T1-weighted MRI and hyperintense on T2-weighted MRI. Cord expansion also may be seen. Enhancement may be heterogeneous but is seen along the periphery of the lesion if caseation necrosis is present. The nonsurgical management includes a regimen of four antituberculosis medications administered for 18 to 24 months. It can be difficult to obtain a nonsurgical diagnosis for initiating treatment, and a surgical biopsy can be especially useful if systemic lesions have not otherwise been found. Surgery should be considered for patients with acute deterioration and is required for patients whose disease progresses despite ongoing antituberculosis treatment.

Spinal Schistosomiasis

Schistosomiasis is a tropical disease caused by the trematode *Schistosoma*. Schistosomiasis affects 200 to 300 million people worldwide, and travelers to endemic regions may be vulnerable to it.[97] *Schistosoma mansoni* is most commonly responsible for spinal schistosomiasis, but *Schistosoma hematobium* and *Schistosoma japonicum* also can damage the spinal cord. Adult schistosome worms deposit their eggs into vessels of the digestive tract and sometimes into the perimedullary vessels of the spinal cord. Eggs deposited in the spinal cord may not cause symptoms but can lead to granulomatous inflammation in the conus medullaris, the cauda equina, or an extramedullary location. Granulomatous changes may cause an acute transverse myelitis. Anterior spinal artery occlusion leading to spinal cord infarction has been reported.[98] The disease usually occurs in men, who describe lumbar pain of radicular nature with rapidly developing weakness in association with autonomic dysfunction (in particular, bladder dysfunction).

The MRI findings are nonspecific but consistent with an inflammatory or neoplastic process. T1-weighted images are hypointense, and T2-weighted images are markedly hyperintense. Contrast enhancement has variable results, but a diffuse granular pattern may appear. The cauda equina nerve roots may appear thickened on contrast-enhanced images. The cord is somewhat widened or enlarged. In 87.5% of patients with spinal schistosomiasis, there is no visceral involvement.[99] The disease usually is in the conus medullaris and lower thoracic cord. Lumbar puncture reveals a mild elevation in total protein. CSF pleocytosis is common. Eosinophils are found in the CSF in 46.9% of patients.[99] Eosinophils should be tested in the peripheral blood count, and stool should be tested for the presence of ova and parasites. To confirm the diagnosis, enzyme-linked immunosorbent assay can be used for serologic testing to reveal positive antibodies.

Nonsurgical therapy using praziquantel alone is the most conservative treatment. However, early surgery, before any permanent neurologic damage occurs, is correlated with a favorable outcome. Corticosteroid use is associated with an improvement in neurologic symptoms.

Summary

It can be difficult to differentiate the intradural pathologies. A detailed history, physical examination, and timeline of symptoms, in conjunction with specific MRI findings, can help in determining an appropriate differential diagnosis. Some spinal cord tumors can be safely resected to provide a cure. Newer modalities such as endovascular treatments have allowed difficult vascular lesions to be successfully treated. Nonetheless, some lesions such as syringomyelia can be difficult to treat. Although intradural infections are rare, they should be considered in the differential diagnosis and often can be treated medically. After the diagnosis is made, knowledge of the natural history of the disease can lead to appropriate treatment.

Annotated References

1. Grimm S, Chamberlain MC: Adult primary spinal cord tumors. *Expert Rev Neurother* 2009;9(10):1487-1495.

   The incidence, presentation, radiographic appearance, treatment, and outcome of intradural tumors are reviewed.

2. Jinnai T, Koyama T: Clinical characteristics of spinal nerve sheath tumors: Analysis of 149 cases. *Neurosurgery* 2005;56(3):510-515.

   This retrospective analysis evaluates the relationship of nerve sheath tumors to the dura mater and the intervertebral foramen.

3. Traul DE, Shaffrey ME, Schiff D: Part I: Spinal-cord neoplasms: Intradural neoplasms. *Lancet Oncol* 2007; 8(1):35-45.

This is a comprehensive review of intradural tumors and their evaluation and treatment.

4. Gezen F, Kahraman S, Canakci Z, Bedük A: Review of 36 cases of spinal cord meningioma. *Spine (Phila Pa 1976)* 2000;25(6):727-731.

5. Peker S, Cerçi A, Ozgen S, Isik N, Kalelioglu M, Pamir MN: Spinal meningiomas: Evaluation of 41 patients. *J Neurosurg Sci* 2005;49(1):7-11.

The outcome of spinal meningioma resection is retrospectively analyzed.

6. Solero CL, Fornari M, Giombini S, et al: Spinal meningiomas: Review of 174 operated cases. *Neurosurgery* 1989;25(2):153-160.

7. Fitzpatrick D, Mahajan J, Lewkowitz M, Black K, Setton A, Woldenberg R: Intradural hemangiopericytoma of the lumbar spine: A rare entity. *AJNR Am J Neuroradiol* 2009;30(1):152-154.

Angiographic findings of intradural hemangiopericytoma are reviewed.

8. Schiariti M, Goetz P, El-Maghraby H, Tailor J, Kitchen N: Hemangiopericytoma: Long-term outcome revisited. *J Neurosurg* 2011;114(3):747-755.

At a mean 123-month follow-up, a significant number of patients with hemangiopericytoma had extended survival after gross total resection and external beam radiation therapy.

9. Per H, Kumandaş S, Gümüş H, Yikilmaz A, Kurtsoy A: Iatrogenic epidermoid tumor: Late complication of lumbar puncture. *J Child Neurol* 2007;22(3):332-336.

The incidence of epidermoid tumor resulting from lumbar punctures is evaluated.

10. Lunardi P, Missori P, Gagliardi FM, Fortuna A: Long-term results of the surgical treatment of spinal dermoid and epidermoid tumors. *Neurosurgery* 1989;25(6):860-864.

11. Muthukumar N: Congenital spinal lipomatous malformations: Part II. Clinical presentation, operative findings, and outcome. *Acta Neurochir (Wien)* 2009;151(3):189-197.

Congenital spinal lipomatous malformations can be classified into two groups based on the presence of a dural defect.

12. Sundgren P, Annertz M, Englund E, Strömblad LG, Holtås S: Paragangliomas of the spinal canal. *Neuroradiology* 1999;41(10):788-794.

13. Constantini S, Houten J, Miller DC, et al: Intramedullary spinal cord tumors in children under the age of 3 years. *J Neurosurg* 1996;85(6):1036-1043.

14. Stein BM, McCormick PC: Intramedullary neoplasms and vascular malformations. *Clin Neurosurg* 1992;39:361-387.

15. Raco A, Esposito V, Lenzi J, Piccirilli M, Delfini R, Cantore G: Long-term follow-up of intramedullary spinal cord tumors: A series of 202 cases. *Neurosurgery* 2005;56(5):972-981.

This retrospective analysis evaluates the long-term outcome of intramedullary tumors and the predictors of a good outcome.

16. Garcés-Ambrossi GL, McGirt MJ, Mehta VA, et al: Factors associated with progression-free survival and long-term neurological outcome after resection of intramedullary spinal cord tumors: Analysis of 101 consecutive cases. *J Neurosurg Spine* 2009;11(5):591-599.

A retrospective analysis evaluates the factors associated with progression-free survival and long-term neurologic outcome after resection of intramedullary tumor.

17. Harrop JS, Ganju A, Groff M, Bilsky M: Primary intramedullary tumors of the spinal cord. *Spine (Phila Pa 1976)* 2009;34(22, suppl):S69-S77.

The literature on treating intramedullary tumors is reviewed, and useful predictors of good outcomes are evaluated.

18. Kane PJ, el-Mahdy W, Singh A, Powell MP, Crockard HA: Spinal intradural tumours: Part II. Intramedullary. *Br J Neurosurg* 1999;13(6):558-563.

19. Miller DC: Surgical pathology of intramedullary spinal cord neoplasms. *J Neurooncol* 2000;47(3):189-194.

20. Innocenzi G, Raco A, Cantore G, Raimondi AJ: Intramedullary astrocytomas and ependymomas in the pediatric age group: A retrospective study. *Childs Nerv Syst* 1996;12(12):776-780.

21. Cooper PR, Epstein F: Radical resection of intramedullary spinal cord tumors in adults: Recent experience in 29 patients. *J Neurosurg* 1985;63(4):492-499.

22. McCormick PC, Torres R, Post KD, Stein BM: Intramedullary ependymoma of the spinal cord. *J Neurosurg* 1990;72(4):523-532.

23. Volpp PB, Han K, Kagan AR, Tome M: Outcomes in treatment for intradural spinal cord ependymomas. *Int J Radiat Oncol Biol Phys* 2007;69(4):1199-1204.

The treatment outcome of ependymoma is reviewed after surgery with or without external beam radiotherapy.

24. Chang UK, Choe WJ, Chung SK, Chung CK, Kim HJ: Surgical outcome and prognostic factors of spinal intramedullary ependymomas in adults. *J Neurooncol* 2002;57(2):133-139.

25. Lee TT, Gromelski EB, Green BA: Surgical treatment of spinal ependymoma and post-operative radiotherapy. *Acta Neurochir (Wien)* 1998;140(4):309-313.

6: Spine Disorders

26. Helseth A, Mørk SJ: Primary intraspinal neoplasms in Norway, 1955 to 1986: A population-based survey of 467 patients. *J Neurosurg* 1989;71(6):842-845.

27. Rodrigues GB, Waldron JN, Wong CS, Laperriere NJ: A retrospective analysis of 52 cases of spinal cord glioma managed with radiation therapy. *Int J Radiat Oncol Biol Phys* 2000;48(3):837-842.

28. Rossitch E Jr, Zeidman SM, Burger PC, et al: Clinical and pathological analysis of spinal cord astrocytomas in children. *Neurosurgery* 1990;27(2):193-196.

29. Nadkarni TD, Rekate HL: Management of intractable intracranial hypertension in severely head-injured patients: Second-tier therapy. *Crit Rev Neurosurg* 1998; 8(6):323-332.

30. Innocenzi G, Salvati M, Cervoni L, Delfini R, Cantore G: Prognostic factors in intramedullary astrocytomas. *Clin Neurol Neurosurg* 1997;99(1):1-5.

31. Chamberlain MC: Temozolomide for recurrent low-grade spinal cord gliomas in adults. *Cancer* 2008; 113(5):1019-1024.

    A retrospective review found modest efficacy when temozolomide was used to treat 22 patients with a recurrent low-grade spinal cord glioma.

32. Allen JC, Aviner S, Yates AJ, et al: Treatment of high-grade spinal cord astrocytoma of childhood with "8-in-1" chemotherapy and radiotherapy: A pilot study of CCG-945. *J Neurosurg* 1998;88(2):215-220.

33. Lefkowitz IB, Packer RJ, Sutton LN, et al: Results of the treatment of children with recurrent gliomas with lomustine and vincristine. *Cancer* 1988;61(5):896-902.

34. Lowis SP, Pizer BL, Coakham H, Nelson RJ, Bouffet E: Chemotherapy for spinal cord astrocytoma: Can natural history be modified? *Childs Nerv Syst* 1998;14(7):317-321.

35. Sarkar C, Mukhopadhyay S, Ralte AM, et al: Intramedullary subependymoma of the spinal cord: A case report and review of literature. *Clin Neurol Neurosurg* 2003; 106(1):63-68.

36. Kim SK, Cho BK, Paek SH, et al: The detection of p53 gene mutation using a microdissection technique in primary intracranial germ cell tumors. *Int J Oncol* 2001; 18(1):111-116.

37. Fountas KN, Karampelas I, Nikolakakos LG, Troup EC, Robinson JS: Primary spinal cord oligodendroglioma: Case report and review of the literature. *Childs Nerv Syst* 2005;21(2):171-175.

    This is a case report of spinal oligodendroglioma and a review of the literature on its clinical, pathologic, and radiographic features.

38. Jallo GI, Freed D, Epstein F: Intramedullary spinal cord tumors in children. *Childs Nerv Syst* 2003;19(9):641-649.

39. Park CK, Chung CK, Choe GY, Wang KC, Cho BK, Kim HJ: Intramedullary spinal cord ganglioglioma: A report of five cases. *Acta Neurochir (Wien)* 2000; 142(5):547-552.

40. Lang FF, Epstein FJ, Ransohoff J, et al: Central nervous system gangliogliomas: Part 2. Clinical outcome. *J Neurosurg* 1993;79(6):867-873.

41. Aoyama T, Hida K, Ishii N, Seki T, Ikeda J, Iwasaki Y: Intramedullary spinal cord germinoma: 2 case reports. *Surg Neurol* 2007;67(2):177-183.

    The successful treatment of two patients with primary intramedullary spinal cord germinoma is described, with a review of the literature.

42. Kinoshita Y, Akatsuka K, Ohtake M, Kamitani H, Watanabe T: Primary intramedullary spinal cord germinoma. *Neurol Med Chir (Tokyo)* 2010;50(7):592-594.

    A 21-year-old woman with intramedullary spinal cord germinoma had no tumor recurrence 3 years after surgery, chemotherapy, and radiation.

43. Chute DJ, Burton EC, Klement IA, Frazee JG, Vinters HV: Primary intramedullary spinal cord germinoma: Case report. *J Neurooncol* 2003;63(1):69-73.

44. Sharma MC, Jain D, Sarkar C, et al: Spinal teratomas: A clinico-pathological study of 27 patients. *Acta Neurochir (Wien)* 2009;151(3):245-252.

    A retrospective review determined patient characteristics and diagnostic tools in spinal teratomas.

45. Işik N, Balak N, Silav G, Elmaci I: Pediatric intramedullary teratomas. *Neuropediatrics* 2008;39(4):196-199.

    Intramedullary teratomas are described in children.

46. Connolly ES Jr, Winfree CJ, McCormick PC, Cruz M, Stein BM: Intramedullary spinal cord metastasis: Report of three cases and review of the literature. *Surg Neurol* 1996;46(4):329-338.

47. Backe HA, Betz RR, Mesgarzadeh M, Beck T, Clancy M: Post-traumatic spinal cord cysts evaluated by magnetic resonance imaging. *Paraplegia* 1991;29(9):607-612.

48. Williams B: Pathogenesis of post-traumatic syringomyelia. *Br J Neurosurg* 1992;6(6):517-520.

49. Wang D, Bodley R, Sett P, Gardner B, Frankel H: A clinical magnetic resonance imaging study of the traumatised spinal cord more than 20 years following injury. *Paraplegia* 1996;34(2):65-81.

50. Perrouin-Verbe B, Lenne-Aurier K, Robert R, et al: Post-traumatic syringomyelia and post-traumatic spinal canal stenosis: A direct relationship. Review of 75 patients with a spinal cord injury. *Spinal Cord* 1998;36(2):137-143.

51. Abel R, Gerner HJ, Smit C, Meiners T: Residual deformity of the spinal canal in patients with traumatic paraplegia and secondary changes of the spinal cord. *Spinal Cord* 1999;37(1):14-19.

6: Spine Disorders

52. Goetz L, Priebe M: Posttraumatic Syringomyelia. http://emedicine.medscape.com/article/322348-overview. October 22, 2009. Accessed March 15, 2010.

This is an overview of posttraumatic syringomyelia.

53. Rossier AB, Foo D, Shillito J, Dyro FM: Posttraumatic cervical syringomyelia: Incidence, clinical presentation, electrophysiological studies, syrinx protein and results of conservative and operative treatment. *Brain* 1985; 108(pt 2):439-461.

54. Schurch B, Wichmann W, Rossier AB: Post-traumatic syringomyelia (cystic myelopathy): A prospective study of 449 patients with spinal cord injury. *J Neurol Neurosurg Psychiatry* 1996;60(1):61-67.

55. Milhorat TH: Classification of syringomyelia. *Neurosurg Focus* 2000;8(3):E1.

56. Newman PK, Terenty TR, Foster JB: Some observations on the pathogenesis of syringomyelia. *J Neurol Neurosurg Psychiatry* 1981;44(11):964-969.

57. Williams B: Pathogenesis of syringomyelia. *Acta Neurochir (Wien)* 1993;123(3-4):159-165.

58. Oldfield EH, Muraszko K, Shawker TH, Patronas NJ: Pathophysiology of syringomyelia associated with Chiari I malformation of the cerebellar tonsils: Implications for diagnosis and treatment. *J Neurosurg* 1994; 80(1):3-15.

59. Munshi I, Frim D, Stine-Reyes R, Weir BK, Hekmatpanah J, Brown F: Effects of posterior fossa decompression with and without duraplasty on Chiari malformation-associated hydromyelia. *Neurosurgery* 2000;46(6):1384-1390.

60. Samii M, Klekamp J: Surgical results of 100 intramedullary tumors in relation to accompanying syringomyelia. *Neurosurgery* 1994;35(5):865-873.

61. Koyanagi I, Iwasaki Y, Hida K, Houkin K: Clinical features and pathomechanisms of syringomyelia associated with spinal arachnoiditis. *Surg Neurol* 2005;63(4):350-356.

The clinical findings, radiographic findings, and treatment of syringomyelia associated with spinal arachnoiditis are described.

62. Klekamp J, Batzdorf U, Samii M, Bothe HW: Treatment of syringomyelia associated with arachnoid scarring caused by arachnoiditis or trauma. *J Neurosurg* 1997; 86(2):233-240.

63. Sgouros S, Williams B: A critical appraisal of drainage in syringomyelia. *J Neurosurg* 1995;82(1):1-10.

64. Brodbelt AR, Stoodley MA: Post-traumatic syringomyelia: A review. *J Clin Neurosci* 2003;10(4):401-408.

65. Mallucci CL, Stacey RJ, Miles JB, Williams B: Idiopathic syringomyelia and the importance of occult arachnoid webs, pouches and cysts. *Br J Neurosurg* 1997;11(4):306-309.

66. Ozisik PA, Hazer B, Ziyal IM, Ozcan OE: Spontaneous resolution of syringomyelia without Chiari malformation. *Neurol Med Chir (Tokyo)* 2006;46(10):512-517.

This is a case report of a patient with a spontaneously resolving idiopathic syringomyelia.

67. Lad SP, Santarelli JG, Patil CG, Steinberg GK, Boakye M: National trends in spinal arteriovenous malformations. *Neurosurg Focus* 2009;26(1):1-5.

The incidence of spinal vascular malformations in the community is described.

68. Oldfield EH, Doppman JL: Spinal arteriovenous malformations. *Clin Neurosurg* 1988;34:161-183.

69. Kendall BE, Logue V: Spinal epidural angiomatous malformations draining into intrathecal veins. *Neuroradiology* 1977;13(4):181-189.

70. Merland JJ, Riche MC, Chiras J: Intraspinal extramedullary arteriovenous fistulae draining into the medullary veins. *J Neuroradiol* 1980;7(4):271-320.

71. Narvid J, Hetts SW, Larsen D, et al: Spinal dural arteriovenous fistulae: Clinical features and long-term results. *Neurosurgery* 2008;62(1):159-167.

A 20-year retrospective study examined a single institution's experience in treating spinal dural arteriovenous fistula.

72. Jellema K, Tijssen CC, Sluzewski M, van Asbeck FW, Koudstaal PJ, van Gijn J: Spinal dural arteriovenous fistulas: An underdiagnosed disease. A review of patients admitted to the spinal unit of a rehabilitation center. *J Neurol* 2006;253(2):159-162.

The incidence of undiagnosed spinal dural arteriovenous fistula is retrospectively reviewed.

73. Krings T, Geibprasert S: Spinal dural arteriovenous fistulas. *AJNR Am J Neuroradiol* 2009;30(4):639-648.

This is an overview of the clinical manifestations, radiographic findings, and treatment options for dural arteriovenous fistulas.

74. Hassler W, Thron A, Grote EH: Hemodynamics of spinal dural arteriovenous fistulas: An intraoperative study. *J Neurosurg* 1989;70(3):360-370.

75. Aghakhani N, Parker F, David P, Lasjaunias P, Tadie M: Curable cause of paraplegia: Spinal dural arteriovenous fistulae. *Stroke* 2008;39(10):2756-2759.

The treatment outcomes of patients with neurologic deficit and dural arteriovenous malformation are described.

76. Steinmetz MP, Chow MM, Krishnaney AA, et al: Outcome after the treatment of spinal dural arteriovenous fistulae: A contemporary single-institution series and meta-analysis. *Neurosurgery* 2004;55(1):77-88.

6: Spine Disorders

77. Martin NA, Khanna RK, Batzdorf U: Posterolateral cervical or thoracic approach with spinal cord rotation for vascular malformations or tumors of the ventrolateral spinal cord. *J Neurosurg* 1995;83(2):254-261.

78. Hall WA, Oldfield EH, Doppman JL: Recanalization of spinal arteriovenous malformations following embolization. *J Neurosurg* 1989;70(5):714-720.

79. Veznedaroglu E, Nelson PK, Jabbour PM, Rosenwasser RH: Endovascular treatment of spinal cord arteriovenous malformations. *Neurosurgery* 2006;59 (5, suppl 3):S202-S209, discussion S3-S13.

    This review evaluates the endovascular treatment options for spinal vascular malformations.

80. Boström A, Krings T, Hans FJ, Schramm J, Thron AK, Gilsbach JM: Spinal glomus-type arteriovenous malformations: Microsurgical treatment in 20 cases. *J Neurosurg Spine* 2009;10(5):423-429.

81. Corkill RA, Mitsos AP, Molyneux AJ: Embolization of spinal intramedullary arteriovenous malformations using the liquid embolic agent, Onyx: A single-center experience in a series of 17 patients. *J Neurosurg Spine* 2007;7(5):478-485.

    A retrospective analysis evaluates the treatment of liquid embolic agents used for spinal intramedullary arteriovenous malformations.

82. Spetzler RF, Zabramski JM, Flom RA: Management of juvenile spinal AVM's by embolization and operative excision: Case report. *J Neurosurg* 1989;70(4):628-632.

83. Cho KT, Lee DY, Chung CK, Han MH, Kim HJ: Treatment of spinal cord perimedullary arteriovenous fistula: Embolization versus surgery. *Neurosurgery* 2005;56(2):232-241.

    A retrospective analysis evaluates the suitability of treatment options for the types of perimedullary arteriovenous fistulas.

84. Mourier KL, Gobin YP, George B, Lot G, Merland JJ: Intradural perimedullary arteriovenous fistulae: Results of surgical and endovascular treatment in a series of 35 cases. *Neurosurgery* 1993;32(6):885-891.

85. Hida K, Iwasaki Y, Goto K, Miyasaka K, Abe H: Results of the surgical treatment of perimedullary arteriovenous fistulas with special reference to embolization. *J Neurosurg* 1999;90(2, suppl):198-205.

86. Zevgaridis D, Büttner A, Weis S, Hamburger C, Reulen HJ: Spinal epidural cavernous hemangiomas: Report of three cases and review of the literature. *J Neurosurg* 1998;88(5):903-908.

87. Sandalcioglu IE, Wiedemayer H, Gasser T, Asgari S, Engelhorn T, Stolke D: Intramedullary spinal cord cavernous malformations: Clinical features and risk of hemorrhage. *Neurosurg Rev* 2003;26(4):253-256.

88. Labauge P, Bouly S, Parker F, et al: Outcome in 53 patients with spinal cord cavernomas. *Surg Neurol* 2008; 70(2):176-181.

    A retrospective analysis evaluates the surgical outcome of patients with spinal cavernous malformation.

89. Ogilvy CS, Louis DN, Ojemann RG: Intramedullary cavernous angiomas of the spinal cord: Clinical presentation, pathological features, and surgical management. *Neurosurgery* 1992;31(2):219-230.

90. Simon JK, Lazareff JA, Diament MJ, Kennedy WA: Intramedullary abscess of the spinal cord in children: A case report and review of the literature. *Pediatr Infect Dis J* 2003;22(2):186-192.

91. Chan CT, Gold WL: Intramedullary abscess of the spinal cord in the antibiotic era: Clinical features, microbial etiologies, trends in pathogenesis, and outcomes. *Clin Infect Dis* 1998;27(3):619-626.

92. Blacklock JB, Hood TW, Maxwell RE: Intramedullary cervical spinal cord abscess: Case report. *J Neurosurg* 1982;57(2):270-273.

93. Menezes AH, Graf CJ, Perret GE: Spinal cord abscess: A review. *Surg Neurol* 1977;8(6):461-467.

94. Maurice-Williams RS, Pamphilon D, Coakham HB: Intramedullary abscess: A rare complication of spinal dysraphism. *J Neurol Neurosurg Psychiatry* 1980;43(11): 1045-1048.

95. Prabhakar S, Thuss UA: Central nervous system tuberculosis. *Neurol India* 1997;45(3):132-140.

96. Ramdurg SR, Gupta DK, Suri A, Sharma BS, Mahapatra AK: Spinal intramedullary tuberculosis: A series of 15 cases. *Clin Neurol Neurosurg* 2009;111(2):115-118.

    This retrospective analysis evaluates the clinicoradiologic presentation of intramedullary tuberculosis and treatment-associated surgical outcomes.

97. Lighter J, Kim M, Krasinski K: Intramedullary schistosomiasis presenting in an adolescent with prolonged intermittent back pain. *Pediatr Neurol* 2008;39(1):44-47.

    The workup required to diagnose intramedullary schistosomiasis is described.

98. Siddorn JA: Schistosomiasis and anterior spinal artery occlusion. *Am J Trop Med Hyg* 1978;27(3):532-534.

99. Saleem S, Belal AI, el-Ghandour NM: Spinal cord schistosomiasis: MR imaging appearance with surgical and pathologic correlation. *AJNR Am J Neuroradiol* 2005; 26(7):1646-1654.

    The MRI appearance of intramedullary schistosomiasis is described.

Chapter 44

Spine Infections

Kasra Rowshan, MD   Frank J. Eismont, MD

Introduction

Spine infections are difficult to diagnose and treat, regardless of whether they are primary or secondary. People who are obese, malnourished, immunocompromised, or diabetic, as well as those who use tobacco or illicit intravenous drugs, are at high risk.[1,2] A spine infection may be indolent with vague symptoms, or appear as nontraumatic back pain. A delay in diagnosis and treatment is common if the clinical appearance is subtle and without systemic signs such as fever or weight loss. Failure to diagnosis and treat a spine infection can lead to structural instability, spine deformity, sepsis, paralysis, and even death.

A spine infection is evaluated and managed based on its location, the organism, and the age and immune status of the patient. The most common location is the lumbar spine, followed by the thoracic spine and, least commonly, the cervical spine. Neurologic deficits are most common if the infection affects the thoracic or cervical region because the spinal cord is more susceptible to compression than the lumbar rootlets.

The pathogen in a spine infection usually is a bacterium, but a fungus also may be responsible. Some spine infections result from tuberculosis. *Staphylococcus aureus* is the cause of more than half of all spine infections.[3,4] A gram-negative organism frequently is found in association with a genitourinary tract infection.[5] *Salmonella,* although uncommon, generally is found in a patient with an acute intestinal infection or sickle cell disease.[6] Mycobacteria and fungi are more likely to cause infection in individuals who are immunocompromised, abuse intravenous drugs, or are incarcerated.

Dr. Eismont or an immediate family member serves as a board member, owner, officer, or committee member of the American Orthopaedic Association; serves as a paid consultant to or is an employee of Alphatec Spine and Elsevier; has received research or institutional support from Biomet, Pfizer, Smith & Nephew, Spinevision, Stryker, and Synthes; and owns stock or stock options in Alphatec Spine. Neither Dr. Rowshan nor any immediate family member has received anything of value from or owns stock in a commercial company or institution related directly or indirectly to the subject of this chapter.

Pyogenic Vertebral Osteomyelitis

Pyogenic (pus-forming) vertebral osteomyelitis accounts for 2% to 7% of all incidences of osteomyelitis.[7] The mortality from sepsis and infection spread is reported to be 2% to 12%.[7] The reported incidence of infectious endocarditis is as high as 30.8% in the presence of vertebral osteomyelitis, with a 7.1% mortality rate.[8] The presence of bacteriuria suggests a focus of infection in the vertebral column. Vertebral osteomyelitis and diskitis have a bimodal age distribution. The mean age of patients with childhood diskitis is 7 years; the incidence decreases until middle age, with a second peak at approximately age 50 years.[3,9] Pyogenic vertebral osteomyelitis is found in the lumbar spine in 55% of patients, in the thoracic spine in 37%, and in the cervical spine in 7%.[10,11] The infection is in two noncontiguous areas of the spine in 5% of patients.[9]

Pathogenesis

Diskitis and pyogenic vertebral osteomyelitis generally result from arterial or venous hematogenous seeding.[12] Spine seeding can occur from infection in the urinary tract, respiratory tract, soft tissue, or elsewhere. The spine also can be seeded from infection related to an intravenous catheter or intravenous drug abuse. The source cannot be identified in approximately 37% of infections.[10]

In adults, the nucleus pulposus is avascular tissue that receives nutrients through diffusion across the end plates.[12] The terminal blood vessels in the end plates are composed of small, low-flow, vascular channels adjacent to the nucleus pulposus; they provide an ideal environment for bacterial growth. Infection is generally believed to start in one end plate, spread to the avascular disk, and then spread to the adjacent vertebral body.[10,11]

The spine venous system forms an anastomotic plexus around the periphery of the spine and within the epidural space (the Batson plexus) that can be a route of infection.[13] Retrograde flow into the valveless vertebral venous plexus is possible when pressure is applied to the lower abdominal wall, as in the Valsalva maneuver. Venous seeding through the Batson plexus probably is the mechanism by which an intrapelvic infection, such as a urinary tract infection, is spread to the spine.

Infection in the spine has a predilection for abscess formation. Psoas abscess is common in the lumbar spine, paraspinous abscess is common in the thoracic spine, and retropharyngeal abscess is common in the cervical spine. An abscess may spread into the epidural space, greatly increasing the risk of paralysis.

Clinical Evaluation

The clinical appearance of a spine infection is determined by the virulence of the organism, the location of the infection, and the immune status of the host. Only 52% of patients have fever, but more than 90% have pain.[10,11] Pain is frequently present at night and is unrelated to activity. Weight loss is gradual and may take months to become noticeable. A positive straight leg raise test may indicate lumbar spine involvement, with hip flexion contracture caused by psoas abscess formation.

The history of a chronic or subacute infection is relatively vague, and pain may be the only symptom. Chest pain, abdominal pain, hip pain, or radicular symptoms are present in 15% of patients.[10] Approximately 17% of patients have a neurologic deficit secondary to nerve root or spinal cord compression.[10] The risk factors for neurologic symptoms include diabetes, rheumatoid arthritis, advancing age, a relatively cephalad level of infection, and the use of systemic corticosteroids.[14] Myelopathy is more common with a cervical or thoracic infection, and radicular symptoms are more common with a lumbar infection.[14]

Laboratory Studies

The commonly ordered laboratory studies include a white blood cell (WBC) count with differential, C-reactive protein (CRP) level, and erythrocyte sedimentation rate (ESR), as well as a Gram stain and culture. Microbiology specimens are obtained from the blood or directly from the spine. The WBC count is elevated in only 42% of patients and usually is normal in patients with a chronic infection.[9,10] The CRP level and ESR are elevated in almost all patients with a pyogenic vertebral infection. The CRP level increases within 4 hours of infection onset, doubles every 8 hours to a peak at 36 to 50 hours after infection onset, and returns to normal within 10 days. The ESR gradually increases to a peak at 7 days after infection onset, and at least 3 additional weeks are required for a return to the baseline level.

A diagnosis of vertebral osteomyelitis requires identification of the organism through a positive blood culture or tissue biopsy, both of which are necessary for treatment decision making.[9] Blood cultures are positive only in 20% of patients, usually with an accurate identification of the organism. A closed needle biopsy successfully identifies the organism in 68% to 86% of patients.[3,10,14] If a closed biopsy is nondiagnostic, the patient can be observed without antibiotic administration and a repeat biopsy can be performed. The indications for open biopsy include unsuccessful needle biopsy, significant structural damage with unacceptable

deformity, or neurologic compromise. Open biopsy has an accuracy rate of 92%.[15]

Blood samples should be sent for Gram staining, acid-fast staining, polymerase chain reaction, and culturing for aerobic, anaerobic, fungal, and tuberculosis organisms. Histologic studies should always be done to detect metabolic or neoplastic processes. All cultures should be kept for 10 days to detect fastidious organisms and minimize the possibility of a false-negative result.

Imaging

Pyogenic vertebral osteomyelitis may not be visible on plain radiographs until 2 to 4 weeks after the onset of symptoms (Figure 1). Structural changes are seen on CT as early as 10 days after infection onset, but changes appear on CT only in 74% of patients with infection.[10] MRI, the imaging modality of choice, is accurate for more than 94% of patients.[16] MRI has the ability to anatomically localize the infection, reveal paravertebral or intraspinal abscesses, and differentiate between infection and degenerative or neoplastic lesions. Decreased signal intensity is seen at the site of infection on T1-weighted MRI. The signal intensity is higher than normal on T2-weighted MRI. The disk and the involved area of the bone and granulation tissue are enhanced on MRI by administration of gadolinium.

Nonsurgical Treatment

The treatment of a spine infection focuses on eradicating the infection, preventing instability or deformity, relieving pain, minimizing neurologic loss, and providing nutritional support. When the organism and its sensitivity have been determined, a 6-week course of the appropriate intravenous antibiotics should be administered, followed, if necessary, by a course of oral antibiotics.

Laboratory markers are useful for determining whether the infection has resolved (Figure 2). The ESR is a reasonable guide to treatment response; it can be expected to drop to one half to two thirds of the pretreatment level at the completion of a successful course of treatment. If the ESR does not decline, an additional biopsy should be considered. Although the CRP level is a sensitive marker for infection, little information is available on its use in treatment decisions.[17]

The penetration of an antibiotic of any class into osteomyelitic bone is known to be similar to its concentration in serum.[18] However, penetration into the disk varies and is greatly influenced by the charge of the antibiotic relative to the negatively charged nucleus pulposus. Cephalosporins and other penicillins are negatively charged and have a poor ability to penetrate the nucleus pulposus. Vancomycin, gentamicin, tobramycin, clindamycin, and teicoplanin are positively charged and penetrate the nucleus pulposus well.[18] Linezolid was found to be less effective against a methicillin-resistant *S aureus* disk space infection than intravenous vancomycin.[19]

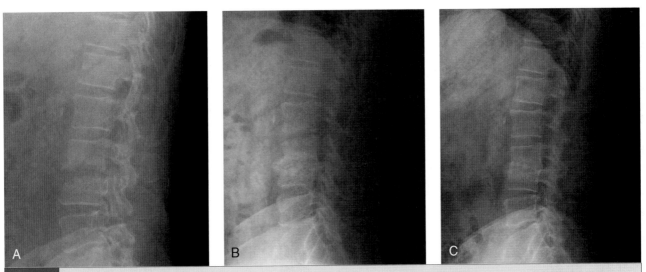

Figure 1 Lateral radiographs of the spine showing pyogenic vertebral osteomyelitis in a 52-year-old man with a history of human immunodeficiency virus (HIV) infection. The patient had back pain for 2 months before treatment. **A,** Disk infiltration and alteration in the end plate at L3-4. **B,** A 6-week course of intravenous vancomycin led to some resolution of infection. **C,** After 6 weeks of a subsequent 6-month course of oral ciprofloxacin, the patient had complete resolution of pain. Lysis of the end plates is no longer seen, and there is possible fusion of the disk space.

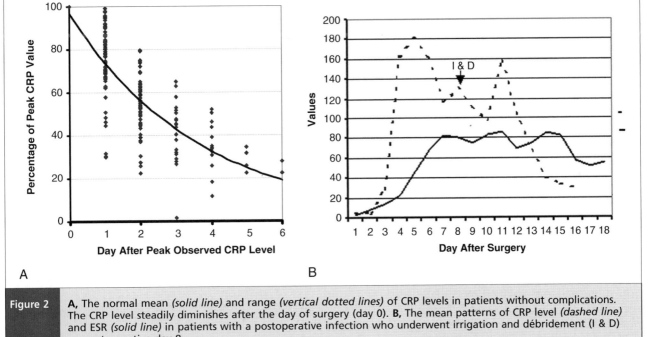

Figure 2 **A,** The normal mean *(solid line)* and range *(vertical dotted lines)* of CRP levels in patients without complications. The CRP level steadily diminishes after the day of surgery (day 0). **B,** The mean patterns of CRP level *(dashed line)* and ESR *(solid line)* in patients with a postoperative infection who underwent irrigation and débridement (I & D) on postoperative day 8.

External immobilization for 8 to 12 weeks generally is recommended to reduce pain and prevent deformity. A thoracolumbosacral orthosis is ideal for use with thoracic and lumbar lesions, and a halo vest is effective for cervical and cervicothoracic lesions.

Surgical Treatment

Surgery is indicated in several situations: to obtain a biopsy sample after two unsuccessful closed biopsies, if the infection has not responded to nonsurgical treatment; to drain an abscess causing neurologic deficit or sepsis; to resolve clinical symptoms after unsuccessful nonsurgical treatment; to manage neurologic deficits secondary to a mass effect from abscess or deformity caused by bone destruction, especially at the level of the spinal cord; or to prevent structural destruction resulting in significant deformity[14] (Figure 3). An infection of the cervical spinal column often requires surgery secondary to instability.

The location of the infection determines the surgical

6: Spine Disorders

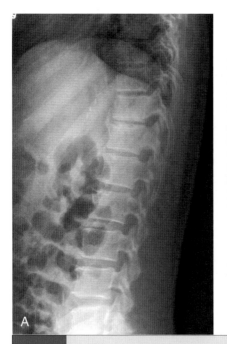
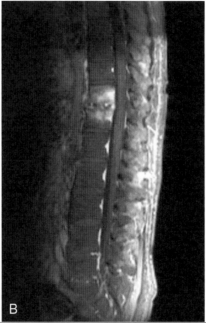
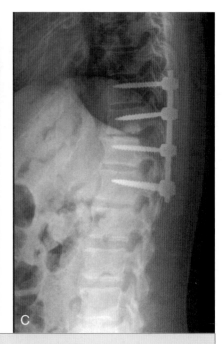

Figure 3   A 50-year-old man with a transplanted liver was being treated with immunosuppressive drugs and had back pain of 1 month's duration. Pyogenic vertebral osteomyelitis was diagnosed. Meropenem was administered for 6 weeks without resolution of symptoms or objective findings. **A,** Lateral radiograph showing end plate changes and decreased disk height suggestive of infection. **B,** T2-weighted MRI showing disk hyperintensity suggestive of infection. **C,** Lateral radiograph after surgical débridement with posterior instrumentation and removal of infectious material; *Escherichia coli* was cultured despite the earlier antibiotic course.

approach. An anterior approach is common because most infections involve the anterior elements.[14,20] The anterior approach allows direct access to the infected body and disk. Laminectomy is contraindicated because it leads to further instability and can increase neurologic deficits in the presence of anterior column destruction.[14] Autogenous structural graft is used for reconstructing the anterior column after débridement. Titanium mesh cages filled with autograft also can be used and may be resistant to bacterial biofilm formation. The use of recombinant human bone morphogenetic protein–2 was found to improve fusion rates in thoracic and lumbar spine reconstructions for patients with pyogenic vertebral osteomyelitis.[21] Posterior instrumentation can be added to improve deformity correction and fusion speed. Posterior instrumentation is safe and effective after anterior débridement and fusion in a patient with infection.[22] The risk of persistent infection is not increased when posterior instrumentation is used.[3]

Prognosis

Pyogenic vertebral osteomyelitis has a generally favorable prognosis if appropriate treatment is initiated early. The rate of infection relapse ranged from less than 2% to 5% after a 6-week or longer course of antibiotics.[14] The relapse rate was 25% after parenteral antibiotics were used for a maximum of 4 weeks.[14] The mortality rate is lower than 5% among otherwise healthy adult patients but is as high as 16% in patients with multiple comorbidities.[14] There is an association between mortality rate and patient age, immune status, and *S aureus* infection. Patients with a lumbar nerve root deficit had a satisfactory outcome after surgical or nonsurgical treatment.[14] Spinal cord compression with neurologic deficit has a much better outcome if it is treated surgically rather than nonsurgically.[14]

Patients who abuse intravenous drugs typically have a favorable outcome, possibly because they have a low pain threshold and therefore seek early treatment.[23] In one study, 92% of such patients responded to a regimen of intravenous antibiotics, with no deaths or permanent neurologic sequelae.[23]

Epidural Abscess

An epidural abscess is located within the spinal canal and around the dura. Early diagnosis is important because this condition progresses rapidly, and a delay in treatment has significant neurologic consequences. Seventy-five percent of patients initially report localized back pain, 50% have fever, and 33% have neurologic deficits.[24] Spine pain at the level of the infection advances to nerve root irritation, sensory deficits, motor weakness, and bladder and bowel dysfunction. Paralysis eventually develops over hours or days in 4% to 22% of patients.[25]

The diagnosis is made by clinical evaluation, supported by laboratory studies and imaging. The CRP

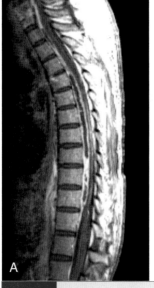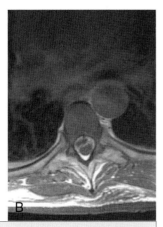

Figure 4 Sagittal (**A**) and axial (**B**) T1-weighted MRI with gadolinium contrast showing an epidural abscess in a 64-year-old man.

level and ESR are universally elevated. Leukocytosis is detected in 67% of patients.[26] Bacteremia is present in 60% of patients, with *S aureus* the most common organism.[27] Cerebrospinal fluid analysis is not specific for epidural infection, and cultures are positive in fewer than 25% of patients.[28] Lumbar puncture is not indicated because it provides little information and carries a risk of inoculating the spinal fluid. MRI with gadolinium enhancement is more than 90% sensitive for the diagnosis[24] (**Figure 4**).

The traditional treatment is surgical decompression followed by systemic antibiotics. Patients who are neurologically intact can be treated nonsurgically with intravenous antibiotics, but the microorganism must be identified and neurologic status must be closely monitored. The rate of neurologic deterioration varies and may be rapid. Surgical decompression and débridement should be done on an emergency basis if the patient has a neurologic deficit, especially if the deficit has progressed. The exception is a patient who is at high risk for surgical complications or has complete paralysis of more than 24 to 36 hours' duration. Preoperative neurologic status is the most important predictor of the final neurologic outcome; after adequate decompression, the final outcome usually is the same or better than the patient's preoperative condition. Mortality is reported in fewer than 5% of patients and is attributable to uncontrolled sepsis, worsening meningitis, or another underlying medical condition.[29]

Postoperative Spine Infection

Postoperative spine infections range from a superficial wound infection to a deep, complex infection. The

Table 1

Risk Factors for Postoperative Spine Infection

Immunocompromise-Related Factors
Cancer
Corticosteroid use
Diabetes
HIV-positive status
Malnutrition
Rheumatoid arthritis

Other Patient-Related Factors
Adrenocortical insufficiency
Comorbidity
Obesity
Radiation therapy
Tobacco use
Traumatic open injury

Postoperative Care–Related Factors
Concomitant infection
Early radiation[a]
Long intensive care stay
Wound seroma

Procedure-Related Factors
Extensive blood loss
Lengthy surgery
Fusion
Instrumentation
Posterior approach

[a]A 2- to 3-week delay is advisable between surgery and radiation therapy; a 6- to 12-week delay is advisable between radiation therapy and elective surgery.

most common organisms are *S aureus*, *Staphylococcus epidermidis*, and *Enterococcus*.[4] The incidence of spine infection after routine spine surgery varies with the type of surgery. The rate of infection is 1% after lumbar decompression with or without diskectomy but is approximately 4% if instrumentation was used.[2,22] Some studies have reported an incidence as high as 20%, however.[2,22] The risk factors are related to surgical time, dead space, blood loss, and the soft-tissue dissection that accompanies instrumentation. Anterior cervical spine infection is reported after 0.1% to 0.25% of procedures.[30]

Risk Factors

The risk factors include patient variables, the type of procedure, and postoperative factors.[1,9,31,32] A patient who is immunocompromised because of malnutrition, corticosteroid use, rheumatoid arthritis, diabetes, cancer, or HIV infection is at increased risk (**Table 1**).[33] Malnutrition is particularly associated with wound complications; as many as 25% of patients undergoing elective lumbar fusion were found to be malnourished.[30] The parameters that define malnutrition are serum albumin of less than 3.5 g per dL, a recent weight loss of more than 10 lb, skin test anergy, a total lymphocyte count lower than 1,500/mm³, and an arm muscle circumference less than 80% of normal.[34] Routine screening is recommended, with appropriate intervention.

6: Spine Disorders

Clinical Evaluation

A superficial wound infection (in the dermis and subcutaneous layers above the fascia) usually occurs within 2 weeks after surgery. Edema, erythema, and/or fluctuance are visible. Fever may be present, though the WBC count usually is normal. The CRP level and ESR are moderately elevated but are difficult to interpret because postoperative elevation is normal.[17] A deep wound infection (below the fascia) is more difficult to diagnose. The overlying skin may have a normal appearance. The patient has more pain than expected, malaise, fever, and possibly anorexia. The CRP level and ESR usually are much higher than expected, but the WBC count may be normal or slightly above normal.[17]

Radiographs provide little information about an early postoperative infection.[9] MRI, with or without gadolinium enhancement, is the best imaging modality for diagnosing infection after a lumbar diskectomy. Typical MRI findings include confluent areas of hypointensity in the involved body and disk spaces on T1-weighted images, hyperintensity in the involved bone and disk on T2-weighted images, loss of the distinction between adjacent involved bodies and the disk, and an abnormal disk appearance. MRI is much less helpful for detecting a postoperative infection after a spine surgical procedure other than a diskectomy, except to confirm the presence of a fluid collection. In a chronic infection, rim enhancement with gadolinium may confirm the presence of an abscess.

Treatment

A superficial wound should be treated early with oral antibiotics. An unresolved superficial infection or an infection suspected of being deep requires surgical treatment. Débridement should be done in a stepwise manner in which removal of the dermal margins is followed by subcutaneous débridement and opening of the fascial layer. All devitalized tissue, loose bone fragments, absorbable gelatin sponge, and fat grafts should be removed. Noninfected bone graft material and well-fixed instrumentation should not be removed. Primary closure in layers should be done over a deep drain. A second-look débridement may be needed 48 to 72 hours later if there has been no clinical improvement.

Intraoperative culturing for aerobic, anaerobic, or fungal organisms is mandatory. Antibiotics should be withheld until the culturing, and broad-spectrum antibiotics should be used until the culture results are available.

Well-fixed instrumentation should be left in place because removal can result in spine instability and deformity.[35] There is no clinical evidence to support the belief that an infection cannot be eradicated in the presence of hardware. Titanium implants are more bacteria resistant than cobalt or steel implants. Early débridement without implant removal was found to lead to a successful fusion; patients had function and pain equivalent to that of patients who had not had an infection.[35]

Spine Tuberculosis and Other Nonpyogenic Vertebral Osteomyelitis

Unlike a pyogenic infection, a nonpyogenic infection causes a granulomatous immune response. A nonpyogenic infection is histologically described as a multinucleated giant cell reaction enveloping a central region of caseating necrosis. The outer layer is composed of fibroblasts that are attempting to close the area of inflammation and infection with a layer of fibrous connective tissue. Tuberculosis, caused by *Mycobacterium tuberculosis*, is the most common granulomatous infection of the spine.[36] Other possible organisms include fungi, such as *Coccidioides immitis*, *Aspergillus*, *Cryptococcus neoformans*, and *Blastomyces dermatitidis*, and a few bacteria, such as *Brucella* and *Actinomyces israelii*. Most patients with nonpyogenic vertebral osteomyelitis are immunocompromised, and many are HIV positive (with a CD4 cell count lower than 200/mm^3).[33]

Most patients with tuberculosis live or have lived in economically developing countries.[9] Spine tuberculosis (Pott disease) typically results from hematogenous spread of infection from a pulmonary or genitourinary lesion. Occasionally the infection spreads through the lymphatic system.[9,37] Patients at particular risk for spine tuberculosis include those who are older, immunocompromised, intravenous drug abusers, or HIV positive; have a chronic debilitating condition; or have a history of incarceration.[37] Spine tuberculosis is the most dangerous form of skeletal tuberculosis because of its ability to cause significant bone destruction, spine deformity, and paraplegia. A neurologic deficit develops in 10% to 47% of patients, often because of late diagnosis. Many of the data have been collected in economically developing countries with limited medical care, however.[38]

Pathophysiology

In contrast with a pyogenic infection, spine tuberculosis usually preserves the intervertebral disk, even when there is extensive bone loss. The lesion usually begins in the peridiskal area, but in approximately 10% of patients it begins in the vertebral body, causing significant body destruction and severe deformity.[36] The infection has the ability to extend to multiple segments through the undersurface of the anterior longitudinal ligament.

Clinical Evaluation

Patients often have an indolent disease course with back pain as the major symptom. Other common systemic signs include weight loss, malaise, and intermittent fever. Spine deformity and neurologic deficits may occur over time. The thoracic spine is the most common site of infection, followed by the lumbar spine and, rarely, the cervical spine. A persistent, productive cough may suggest that the patient has pulmonary tuberculosis.

Laboratory markers such as the CRP level and ESR usually are elevated but nonspecific. A positive tuberculin-purified protein derivative skin test indicates exposure to the organism but cannot differentiate between current and past exposure.[36] Urine cultures may be helpful if the infection has a genitourinary origin, and sputum can be evaluated to detect a pulmonary infection. An absolute diagnosis can be obtained only through biopsy. Culturing may require weeks and have limited sensitivity. Acid-fast bacillus staining and smear studies are successful but require a large bacterial load. Recently, polymerase chain reaction has been used to rapidly identify *Mycobacterium* DNA or RNA. Molecular tests are able to evaluate genes for resistance to drugs such as rifampin, isoniazid, pyrazinamide, ethambutol, and streptomycin.[9]

Radiographs may show bone rarefaction and destruction with a relatively well-preserved disk space. If multiple segments are involved, the adjacent vertebrae may be eroded in a scalloped fashion. The appearance of an involved central body may resemble that of a tumor or compression fracture. MRI is the imaging modality of choice for revealing subligamentous abscesses, disk space preservation, and abnormal signal in multiple segments. Involved vertebrae have low signal on T1-weighted images and high signal on T2-weighted images. Paraspinal and occasionally epidural abscesses can be seen.

Treatment

The nonsurgical treatment of spine tuberculosis includes multiple drug therapy for as long as 12 months, depending on the patient's antibiotic sensitivities.[36,39,40] The infection can be eliminated by a combination of bactericidal drugs (isoniazid, rifampin, streptomycin, and pyrazinamide) and bacteriostatic drugs (ethambutol and thiacetazone). The US Food and Drug Administration recommends a 2-month course of isoniazid, rifampin, ethambutol, and pyrazinamide, followed by a 7-month course of isoniazid and rifampin.[36,39,40] However, randomized controlled studies found that the effectiveness of a 6-month regimen is equivalent to that of a 9-month regimen, unless the patient is younger than 15 years.[36,39,40] Multidrug resistance should be considered if there is no clinical improvement after 4 weeks of treatment. Streptomycin and ciprofloxacin can be used if the infection is caused by a multidrug-resistant organism. More than 90% of patients respond to nonsurgical treatment.

Surgery is recommended if the patient has paralysis or unacceptable deformity or has not responded to nonsurgical treatment. Radical débridement and anterior fusion with autogenous bone graft and posterior instrumentation are recommended, in combination with long-term chemotherapy.[41] Five years after surgery, the success rate of fusion and eradication of infection is 94%.[40] Laminectomy generally is contraindicated because it can further destabilize the spinal column and lead to neurologic deficit. The only indication for laminectomy is in atypical disease involving the neural arch and causing posterior spinal cord compression.

Fungal Infection

Fungal spine infections are uncommon and usually occur in patients who are immunocompromised.[14] The clinical course often is indolent. The radiographic features are difficult to distinguish from those of other infections, and the diagnosis relies on tissue biopsy. Closed biopsy is reported to be positive only in 50% of affected patients, but open biopsy is positive in most patients.[14,37]

The primary treatment of a fungal infection is with antifungal drugs. In the past, amphotericin B was administered empirically. Amphotericin B has poor penetrance into the disk, however.[42] A large number of patients treated with amphotericin B did not show clinical improvement and required subsequent surgical treatment. Fluconazole has excellent nucleus pulposus penetration and probably should be the first-line empiric treatment of fungal spine infections.[37]

Spine Infection and HIV

Patients who are HIV positive are more susceptible to spine infection than the general population.[33] The most common symptom is pain. *S aureus*, the most common organism, responds to conventional antibiotic treatments provided the patient's CD4 cell count is higher than 200/mm³. In patients with a CD4 cell count of 50 to 200/mm³, *M tuberculosis* is the most common infectious organism. A CD4 cell count lower than 50/mm³ usually is associated with a fungal infection, an epidural abscess, or an uncommon species of bacteria such as *Nocardia*. Mortality is highest among patients with a CD4 cell count lower than 50/mm³. The CBC count, ESR, CRP level, and CD4 cell count should be monitored in all patients who are HIV positive and may have vertebral osteomyelitis.

Pediatric Diskitis

Pediatric diskitis is a bacterial infection involving the disk space and often the adjacent vertebral end plates.[43] It is commonly caused by hematogenous spread of infection from a source such as otitis media, urinary tract infection, or respiratory infection.[44] In children, multiple small vessels traverse the cartilaginous end plates of the vertebral body and end within the disk space. These vascular channels allow hematogenous bacteria access to an avascular, immune-free disk environment. As the infection progresses, the end plates begin to erode, and a sawtooth appearance can be seen on radiographs.

Patients have local back pain and often are unwilling to ambulate. Fever and local spine tenderness may be

6: Spine Disorders

present. The WBC count may be normal, although the CRP level and ESR usually are elevated. *S aureus* is the most common organism, but blood cultures are positive in only 50% of patients.[43,45] MRI usually is diagnostic and is the study of choice despite the need for sedation or anesthesia in children.[43]

A bacterium was isolated in 22 of 35 pediatric patients (63%) after needle aspiration of the disk.[45] *S aureus* was found in 55%, and *Kingella kingae*, a fastidious gram-negative coccobacillus found in the normal throat flora of young children, was found in 27%. This finding emphasizes the importance of keeping all cultures for 10 days, especially in pediatric patients.

An intravenous antistaphylococcal antibiotic generally is recommended for initial treatment.[43] There are no strict guidelines as to the duration of intravenous or oral antibiotic treatment. It is acceptable to administer a 2-week course of intravenous antibiotics followed by a 4- to 6-week course of oral antibiotics, with strict monitoring of laboratory markers to assess the response. Controversy exists as to the need for a tissue biopsy to identify the microorganism. Biopsy is indicated if the child does not respond to empiric treatment or has negative blood cultures.[45,46] Surgical débridement is indicated if the patient has an abscess or a progressive neurologic deficit.

Summary

A spine infection can be destructive and life threatening. The systemic signs may be vague, and the clinician should maintain a high index of suspicion when evaluating a patient with intractable and unexpectedly severe spine pain. A thorough history, a physical examination, laboratory studies, and a radiologic examination should be performed. The CRP level and ESR are useful markers for infection and resolution of infection, and MRI is the imaging modality of choice. Definitive identification of the organism is critical to achieving a successful long-term outcome. *S aureus* is the most commonly isolated organism. Prompt and appropriate medical management has a favorable outcome, with a minimal risk of significant deformity or neurologic deterioration. Surgery usually is unnecessary. Additional care must be taken with a patient who is immunocompromised or malnourished.

Annotated References

1. Capen DA, Calderone RR, Green A: Perioperative risk factors for wound infections after lower back fusions. *Orthop Clin North Am* 1996;27(1):83-86.

2. Rechtine GR, Bono PL, Cahill D, Bolesta MJ, Chrin AM: Postoperative wound infection after instrumentation of thoracic and lumbar fractures. *J Orthop Trauma* 2001;15(8):566-569.

3. Carragee EJ: Pyogenic vertebral osteomyelitis. *J Bone Joint Surg Am* 1997;79(6):874-880.

4. Massie JB, Heller JG, Abitbol JJ, McPherson D, Garfin SR: Postoperative posterior spinal wound infections. *Clin Orthop Relat Res* 1992;284:99-108.

5. Labbé AC, Demers AM, Rodrigues R, Arlet V, Tanguay K, Moore DL: Surgical-site infection following spinal fusion: A case-control study in a children's hospital. *Infect Control Hosp Epidemiol* 2003;24(8):591-595.

6. Carvell JE, Maclarnon JC: Chronic osteomyelitis of the thoracic spine due to Salmonella typhi: A case report. *Spine (Phila Pa 1976)* 1981;6(5):527-530.

7. Waldvogel FA, Medoff G, Swartz MN: Osteomyelitis: A review of clinical features, therapeutic considerations and unusual aspects. *N Engl J Med* 1970;282(4):198-206.

8. Pigrau C, Almirante B, Flores X, et al: Spontaneous pyogenic vertebral osteomyelitis and endocarditis: Incidence, risk factors, and outcome. *Am J Med* 2005; 118(11):1287.

   The risk factors, incidence, and outcomes of infectious endocarditis in patients with pyogenic vertebral osteomyelitis were retrospectively evaluated. A high incidence was found. Relatively short treatment protocols had a favorable outcome unless a difficult-to-treat microorganism was present.

9. Tay BK, Deckey J, Hu SS: Spinal infections. *J Am Acad Orthop Surg* 2002;10(3):188-197.

10. Sapico FL, Montgomerie JZ: Pyogenic vertebral osteomyelitis: Report of nine cases and review of the literature. *Rev Infect Dis* 1979;1(5):754-776.

11. Sapico FL, Montgomerie JZ: Vertebral osteomyelitis. *Infect Dis Clin North Am* 1990;4(3):539-550.

12. Wiley AM, Trueta J: The vascular anatomy of the spine and its relationship to pyogenic vertebral osteomyelitis. *J Bone Joint Surg Br* 1959;41-B:796-809.

13. Batson OV: The function of the vertebral veins and their role in the spread of metastases. *Ann Surg* 1940; 112(1):138-149.

14. Eismont FJ, Bohlman HH, Soni PL, Goldberg VM, Freehafer AA: Pyogenic and fungal vertebral osteomyelitis with paralysis. *J Bone Joint Surg Am* 1983;65(1): 19-29.

15. Stringham DR, Hadjipavlou A, Dzioba RB, Lander P: Percutaneous transpedicular biopsy of the spine. *Spine (Phila Pa 1976)* 1994;19(17):1985-1991.

16. Modic MT, Feiglin DH, Piraino DW, et al: Vertebral osteomyelitis: Assessment using MR. *Radiology* 1985; 157(1):157-166.

17. Mok JM, Pekmezci M, Piper SL, et al: Use of C-reactive protein after spinal surgery: Comparison with erythrocyte sedimentation rate as predictor of early postoperative infectious complications. *Spine (Phila Pa 1976)* 2008;33(4):415-421.

    A prospective observational study of patients undergoing spine surgery found that preoperative CRP level, lumbar region involvement, and number of involved spine levels were significant predictors of peak postoperative CRP level. The CRP level exponentially decreased after the peak, with a 2.6-day half-life. A second rise in CRP level or a failure to decrease as expected had a sensitivity, specificity, positive predictive value, and negative predictive value of 82%, 48%, 41%, and 86%, respectively, for an infectious complication. Level of evidence: II.

18. Riley LH III, Banovac K, Martinez OV, Eismont FJ: Tissue distribution of antibiotics in the intervertebral disc. *Spine (Phila Pa 1976)* 1994;19(23):2619-2625.

19. Conaughty JM, Chen J, Martinez OV, Chiappetta G, Brookfield KF, Eismont FJ: Efficacy of linezolid versus vancomycin in the treatment of methicillin-resistant Staphylococcus aureus discitis: A controlled animal model. *Spine (Phila Pa 1976)* 2006;31(22):E830-E832.

    Linezolid and vancomycin were compared for the treatment of methicillin-resistant *S aureus* diskitis in rabbits. Vancomycin treatment led to less bacterial growth, although linezolid is a clinically attractive alternative because of its milder adverse effects.

20. Bohlman HH, Eismont FJ: Surgical techniques of anterior decompression and fusion for spinal cord injuries. *Clin Orthop Relat Res* 1981;154:57-67.

21. Allen RT, Lee YP, Stimson E, Garfin SR: Bone morphogenetic protein-2 (BMP-2) in the treatment of pyogenic vertebral osteomyelitis. *Spine (Phila Pa 1976)* 2007;32(26):2996-3006.

    A retrospective case study found that in patients with medically nonresponsive pyogenic vertebral osteomyelitis, the use of recombinant human bone morphogenetic protein–2 in combination with surgery resulted in eradication of infection, solid fusion, and good clinical results without complications.

22. Mok JM, Guillaume TJ, Talu U, et al: Clinical outcome of deep wound infection after instrumented posterior spinal fusion: A matched cohort analysis. *Spine (Phila Pa 1976)* 2009;34(6):578-583.

    A retrospective case control study determined the impact of infection on clinical outcome after spine surgery. The most commonly isolated organisms were *S epidermidis, Enterococcus,* and *S aureus*. Multiple débridements were significantly associated with polymicrobial infection and pseudarthrosis requiring reoperation. No significant difference in outcomes was detected. Level of evidence: III.

23. Sapico FL, Montgomerie JZ: Vertebral osteomyelitis in intravenous drug abusers: Report of three cases and review of the literature. *Rev Infect Dis* 1980;2(2):196-206.

24. Rigamonti D, Liem L, Sampath P, et al: Spinal epidural abscess: Contemporary trends in etiology, evaluation, and management. *Surg Neurol* 1999;52(2):189-197.

25. Lu CH, Chang WN, Lui CC, Lee PY, Chang HW: Adult spinal epidural abscess: Clinical features and prognostic factors. *Clin Neurol Neurosurg* 2002;104(4):306-310.

26. Soehle M, Wallenfang T: Spinal epidural abscesses: Clinical manifestations, prognostic factors, and outcomes. *Neurosurgery* 2002;51(1):79-87.

27. Curry WT Jr, Hoh BL, Amin-Hanjani S, Eskandar EN: Spinal epidural abscess: Clinical presentation, management, and outcome. *Surg Neurol* 2005;63(4):364-371.

    The clinical characteristics, treatment, and outcomes of patients with spinal epidural abscess were retrospectively reviewed. Delay in surgery was correlated with poor outcomes, and urgent surgery therefore is recommended.

28. Darouiche RO, Hamill RJ, Greenberg SB, Weathers SW, Musher DM: Bacterial spinal epidural abscess: Review of 43 cases and literature survey. *Medicine (Baltimore)* 1992;71(6):369-385.

29. Darouiche RO: Spinal epidural abscess. *N Engl J Med* 2006;355(19):2012-2020.

    The pathogenesis, clinical features, and diagnosis of spinal epidural abscesses are described, with treatment options.

30. Cruse PJ, Foord R: The epidemiology of wound infection: A 10-year prospective study of 62,939 wounds. *Surg Clin North Am* 1980;60(1):27-40.

31. Olsen MA, Mayfield J, Lauryssen C, et al: Risk factors for surgical site infection in spinal surgery. *J Neurosurg* 2003;98(2, suppl):149-155.

32. Veeravagu A, Patil CG, Lad SP, Boakye M: Risk factors for postoperative spinal wound infections after spinal decompression and fusion surgeries. *Spine (Phila Pa 1976)* 2009;34(17):1869-1872.

    The risk of postoperative spine wound infection was associated with length of hospital stay, 30-day mortality rate, other complications, and rate of return to the operating room. Diabetes, smoking, disseminated cancer, fusion, and surgical duration of more than 6 hours are statistically significant predictors of postoperative infection. Level of evidence: III.

33. Weinstein MA, Eismont FJ: Infections of the spine in patients with human immunodeficiency virus. *J Bone Joint Surg Am* 2005;87(3):604-609.

    Diskitis or osteomyelitis was found in patients who were HIV positive, had a CD4 cell count of at least 200/mm^3, and responded to antibiotics. Spine tuberculosis may develop in patients with a CD4 cell count of 50/mm^3 to 200/mm^3. Patients with a low CD4 cell count are more likely to have an epidural abscess with uncommon species such as *Nocardia*; these patients have a higher mortality than others. CD4 cell count can be

6: Spine Disorders

used to predict clinical course. Identification of the organism remains paramount for treatment. Level of evidence: III.

34. Jensen JE, Jensen TG, Smith TK, Johnston DA, Dudrick SJ: Nutrition in orthopaedic surgery. *J Bone Joint Surg Am* 1982;64(9):1263-1272.

35. Bose B: Delayed infection after instrumented spine surgery: Case reports and review of the literature. *Spine J* 2003;3(5):394-399.

36. Lifeso RM, Weaver P, Harder EH: Tuberculous spondylitis in adults. *J Bone Joint Surg Am* 1985;67(9):1405-1413.

37. Frazier DD, Campbell DR, Garvey TA, Wiesel S, Bohlman HH, Eismont FJ: Fungal infections of the spine: Report of eleven patients with long-term follow-up. *J Bone Joint Surg Am* 2001;83-A(4):560-565.

38. Hodgson AR, Stock FE, Fang HS, Ong GB: Anterior spinal fusion: The operative approach and pathological findings in 412 patients with Pott's disease of the spine. *Br J Surg* 1960;48:172-178.

39. Medical Research Council Working Party on Tuberculosis of the Spine: A 10-year assessment of controlled trials of inpatient and outpatient treatment and of plaster of Paris jackets for tuberculosis of the spine in children on standard chemotherapy: Studies in Masan and Pusan, Korea. Ninth report. *J Bone Joint Surg Br* 1985; 67(1):103-110.

40. Medical Research Council Working Party on Tuberculosis of the Spine: Five-year assessment of controlled trials of short-course chemotherapy regimens of 6, 9 or 18 months' duration for spinal tuberculosis in patients ambulatory from the start or undergoing radical surgery: Fourteenth report. *Int Orthop* 1999;23(2):73-81.

41. Ozdemir HM, Us AK, Oğün T: The role of anterior spinal instrumentation and allograft fibula for the treatment of Pott disease. *Spine (Phila Pa 1976)* 2003;28(5): 474-479.

42. Conaughty JM, Khurana S, Banovac K, Martinez OV, Eismont FJ: Antifungal penetration into normal rabbit nucleus pulposus. *Spine (Phila Pa 1976)* 2004;29(14): E289-E293.

43. Eismont FJ, Bohlman HH, Soni PL, Goldberg VM, Freehafer AA: Vertebral osteomyelitis in infants. *J Bone Joint Surg Br* 1982;64(1):32-35.

44. Ring D, Johnston CE II, Wenger DR: Pyogenic infectious spondylitis in children: The convergence of discitis and vertebral osteomyelitis. *J Pediatr Orthop* 1995; 15(5):652-660.

45. Garron E, Viehweger E, Launay F, Guillaume JM, Jouve JL, Bollini G: Nontuberculous spondylodiscitis in children. *J Pediatr Orthop* 2002;22(3):321-328.

46. Hoffer FA, Strand RD, Gebhardt MC: Percutaneous biopsy of pyogenic infection of the spine in children. *J Pediatr Orthop* 1988;8(4):442-444.

Chapter 45

Spine Osteoporosis and Osteoporotic Fractures

Tom Faciszewski, MD   Fergus E. McKiernan, MD

Assessing Osteoporosis and Fracture Risk

Osteoporosis is clinically defined by low bone mineral density (BMD) or the presence of a fragility fracture (a fracture resulting from the energy of a fall from standing height). The spine is predominantly composed of trabecular bone and therefore is an important site of osteoporosis and osteoporotic fracture. Dual x-ray absorptiometry (DXA) is the most commonly used method of measuring BMD.[1] The BMD T-scores indicate the number of standard deviations the measured result differs from a normative mean in healthy 20- to 30-year-old, sex-matched Caucasians. In 1995 a World Health Organization (WHO) Working Group defined osteoporosis in postmenopausal Caucasian women as a T-score of −2.5 or lower at the lumbar spine, proximal femur, or nondominant radius (Table 1). Modifications of the WHO diagnostic criteria have been proposed for application to other populations affected by osteoporosis, including premenopausal women, non-Caucasians, men, and children.[1] An individual's risk of fracture varies inversely with the T-score, although this correlation is substantially conditioned by age, race, sex, family history, previous fracture, lifestyle, drug use, exposure to toxins such as alcohol and cigarette smoke, and various medical conditions. Despite the tight correlation between T-score and fracture risk, any analogous correlation between T-score and the surgical, clinical, or radiographic outcomes of spine surgery is conjectural.

A DXA report also routinely includes Z-scores, which represent the number of standard deviations the patient's BMD differs from a normative mean database matched for sex, age, race, and, sometimes, body mass index. A very low Z-score (−2.0 or lower) suggests an unusual degree of skeletal demineralization and may indicate the presence of a secondary cause of osteoporosis.[2]

The WHO recently developed the Fracture Risk Assessment Tool (FRAX) in recognition that T-scores alone are insufficient to adequately estimate fracture risk.[3] This Internet-based algorithm uses femoral neck BMD and 11 clinical variables to estimate an individual's 10-year probability of an osteoporotic fracture. The FRAX output consists of two numeric estimates: the 10-year risk of any of four major clinical fractures (spine, hip, humerus, or wrist) and the 10-year risk of a hip fracture. Individual national health care systems are expected to determine consensus treatment intervention thresholds for osteoporosis based on the local economy and health care preferences. In the United States, the National Osteoporosis Foundation has recommended that drug treatment should be considered if an individual's 10-year FRAX risk estimate exceeds 20% for any of the four major fractures or 3% for hip fracture. However, the use of these thresholds may lead to drug intervention recommendations in situations for which fracture prevention efficacy is not yet proved. Table 2 illustrates how FRAX risk estimates can alter treatment recommendations for women with either osteoporotic or nonosteoporotic T-scores.

Vertebral fracture analysis is a low-radiation image of the lateral spine, obtained at the DXA point of service and intended to identify the presence of existing or prevalent vertebral fractures between approximately T6 and L4. Prevalent vertebral fractures, whether symptomatic or not, substantially increase the risk of future vertebral and nonvertebral fracture independent of

Dr. McKiernan or an immediate family member serves as an unpaid consultant to Amgen Co. Neither Dr. Faciszewski nor any immediate family member has received anything of value from or owns stock in a commercial company or institution related directly or indirectly to the subject of this chapter.

Table 1	
WHO Diagnostic Categories Based on Bone Mineral Density T-Scores of the Lumbar Spine, Proximal Femur, or Nondominant Radius in Postmenopausal Caucasian Women	
T-Score	**Diagnostic Category**
+1.0 to −1.0	Normal BMD
−1.1 to −2.4	Osteopenia (low bone mass)
≤ −2.5	Osteoporosis

6: Spine Disorders

BMD.[1] FRAX and vertebral fracture analysis software are increasingly being incorporated into clinical DXA units. BMD T-scores, FRAX estimates, and vertebral fracture analysis results guide clinical judgment in the decision to treat skeletal fragility with medications.

The Modulation of Bone Metabolism

There have been tremendous recent advances in understanding the cellular and molecular pathophysiology of osteoporosis. Familiarity with these advances is important because many patients with osteoporosis take drugs that affect bone metabolism and fracture healing. Figure 1 outlines key pathways in bone remodeling and fracture repair that are currently being elucidated. Among these are the emerging roles of receptor activator of nuclear factor κ-β (RANK), RANK ligand (RANKL), osteoprotegerin, the canonical β-catenin pathway, wingless (Wnt) signaling, prostaglandins, cathepsins, sclerostin, and gut-derived serotonin.[4] The skeleton is increasingly understood to actively interact with the brain, fat tissue, and the gastrointestinal, renal, and neuromuscular systems.

Nitrogen-containing bisphosphonates (nBPs) such as alendronate and risedronate are the most widely prescribed osteoporosis medications. By reducing bone remodeling rates to premenopausal levels, nBPs preserve skeletal microarchitecture and have been found to reduce the risk of a spine fracture by 50% to 70% in patients with osteoporosis.[5] The pharmacology of these nonhydrolysable agents is characterized by inefficient gastrointestinal absorption (less than 1%), marked avidity for bone hydroxyapatite, and prolonged skeletal retention (at least 10 years). The primary toxicity of oral nBPs is gastroesophageal. In patients who have received long-term nBP treatment, long bone fracture repair results in large, hypertrophic callus with delayed secondary mineralization but normal ultimate strength.[6,7] There is little compelling evidence that oral nBPs should be discontinued after a patient has an osteoporotic fracture or undergoes spine surgery. It has been suggested, however, that initiation of intravenous nBP therapy should be delayed several weeks after a major fracture or spine surgery to avoid disproportionate localization of the injected agent to the skeletal repair sites.[8] The effect of nBPs on implanted hardware continues to be studied, although the available data suggest that nBP-treated bone has increased resistance to screw pullout, reduced periprosthetic osteolysis, and

Table 2

Comparison of Intervention Thresholds Based on T-Score and FRAX Risk Estimate in Two Sample Patients

Patient 1. Postmenopausal Caucasian Woman, Age 74 Years, Maternal Hip Fracture

DXA	BMD (g/cm²)	T-Score	BMD Classification	Drug Treatment Recommendation
Lumbar spine	1.189	+0.1	Normal	*Not* indicated
Femoral neck	0.897	−1.0		

FRAX	10-Year Fracture Risk		Classification	Drug Treatment Recommendation
Four major fractures	15.0%		10-year hip fracture risk higher than 3.0%*	*Should be* considered
Hip fracture	5.1%			

Patient 2. Postmenopausal Caucasian Woman, Age 50 Years, No Clinical FRAX Risks

DXA	BMD (g/cm²)	T-Score	BMD Classification	Drug Treatment Recommendation
Lumbar spine	1.016	−1.4	Osteoporosis	*Should be* considered
Femoral neck	0.682	−2.6		

FRAX	10-Year Fracture Risk		Classification	Drug Treatment Recommendation
Four major fractures	11.0%		10-year hip fracture risk lower than 3.0%*	*Not* indicated
Hip fracture	2.3%			

*The National Osteoporosis Foundation treatment threshold is 3.0%.

reduced prosthesis migration. Bone grafts saturated with nBP may resist resorption and subsidence.

There is an association between nBP use and both osteonecrosis of the jaw and atypical subtrochanteric and diaphyseal femoral fractures.[9,10] Although these adverse events are uncommon, their potential is distressing for patients and health care providers and underscores the importance of reserving nBPs for patients at high risk for fracture, who are most likely to benefit from these medications.

Denosumab, a fully human immunoglobulin-G2 monoclonal antibody to RANKL, inhibits bone remodeling more potently than the nBPs. By targeting and neutralizing RANKL, denosumab inhibits osteoclast induction, maturation, and recruitment, thereby simulating the effect of osteoprotegerin.[11] The effect of denosumab on implant stability is unknown, but its effect on fracture healing appears to be similar to that of alendronate.[6] Other promising antiremodeling agents include odanacatib, a cathepsin-K inhibitor that prevents dissolution of organic bone matrix; and glucagon-like peptide 2, a central nervous system mediator of bone mass. Skeletal anabolics are of particular interest to spine surgeons. Bone morphogenetic proteins are members of the transforming growth factor–β family that regulate osteogenesis through nuclear transcription factor SMAD protein signaling. Recombinant human bone morphogenetic protein–2 (INFUSE, Medtronic, Minneapolis, MN) has been approved by the US Food and Drug Administration (FDA) for clinical use in the anterior lumbar spine and was found to increase fusion rates in this application.[12] Teriparatide (recombinant human PTH_{1-34}) is the only FDA-approved systemic skeletal anabolic agent for severe age-related and glucocorticoid-induced osteoporosis in women and men. Animal models suggest that teriparatide may accelerate fracture repair and increase final mechanical strength, but the results of human studies have been disappointing.[13] Fracture repair is not an FDA-approved indication for teriparatide, but its use might be considered in patients with severe osteoporosis at high risk for fracture when no contraindications exist and accelerated fracture repair is desired. Teriparatide is remarkably well tolerated, but it must be administered by daily subcutaneous injection, is expensive, and carries a black box warning because in Fisher-344 rats it causes proliferative skeletal lesions, including osteosarcoma. Other anabolic agents, such as those targeting the calcium-sensing receptor (calcilytics), sclerostin and other components of the canonical Wnt/β-catenin pathway, and activin receptor IIA, are not likely to be clinically available in the near future. Mesenchymal stem cell therapy is promising but remains investigational.[14]

Adequate intake of calcium, phosphorus, and vitamin D is essential for normal fracture repair and bone remodeling. The Institute of Medicine recently recommended a daily intake of 1,000 mg to 1,200 mg of calcium for adult men and women, preferably obtained

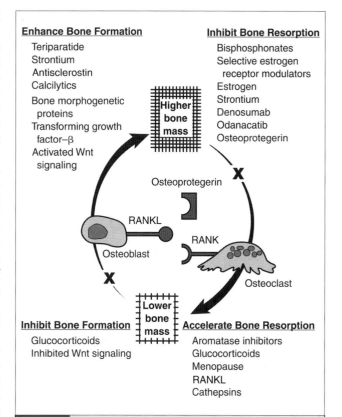

Enhance Bone Formation
Teriparatide
Strontium
Antisclerostin
Calcilytics
Bone morphogenetic proteins
Transforming growth factor–β
Activated Wnt signaling

Inhibit Bone Resorption
Bisphosphonates
Selective estrogen receptor modulators
Estrogen
Strontium
Denosumab
Odanacatib
Osteoprotegerin

Higher bone mass

Osteoprotegerin

RANKL

RANK

Osteoblast

Osteoclast

Lower bone mass

Inhibit Bone Formation
Glucocorticoids
Inhibited Wnt signaling

Accelerate Bone Resorption
Aromatase inhibitors
Glucocorticoids
Menopause
RANKL
Cathepsins

Figure 1 Schematic diagram showing the central role of osteoclasts and osteoblasts in regulating bone mass. Osteoclasts are of hemopoietic origin, and osteoblasts have a mesenchymal stem cell origin. The key cellular interactions are mediated by osteoprotegerin, RANK-L, and RANK and they are substantially conditioned by numerous pathways and molecular signals including Wnt and bone morphogenetic proteins. Antiresorptive osteoporosis drugs primarily target osteoclasts, and anabolic drugs primarily target osteoblasts. Bone-lining cells and osteocytes (terminally differentiated osteoblasts) play important roles in mechanosensing and fracture repair and are not shown.

through diet but supplemented as necessary.[15] The Institute of Medicine also recommended an adult daily intake of 600 IU to 800 IU of vitamin D, but this recommendation is controversial. More generous supplementation of vitamin D_2 or D_3 (up to 2,000 IU daily) is safe and widely practiced.[15]

Glucocorticoids and chemotherapeutic agents can impair fracture healing and graft incorporation. The effects of cyclooxygenase (COX) I and II inhibitors on fracture healing and bone graft incorporation remain somewhat controversial. Studies with animal models, including COX II knockout models, suggest that this enzyme has a dominant role in normal fracture, but available data on its use in humans are conflicting.[16] Well-designed prospective randomized placebo-controlled studies are necessary for resolving these questions. Until such study results are available, it may

6: Spine Disorders

be prudent to avoid using COX I and COX II inhibitors during the perioperative period until fracture union or graft incorporation is complete. The use of anti–tumor necrosis factor agents such as etanercept and adalimumab, which are commonly used to treat inflammatory arthritis, has not been implicated in impaired fracture healing or graft incorporation.[7]

Epidemiology of Osteoporotic Vertebral Fractures

Osteoporotic fractures lead to more than 432,000 hospitalizations, 2.5 million physician office visits, and 180,000 nursing home admissions every year in the United States.[17] Vertebral fracture accounts for as many as 70,000 of these hospitalizations, half of which are followed by admission to a skilled nursing facility. The cost of osteoporotic fractures to the US health care system was $17 billion in 2005. Although this cost burden is largely driven by hip fractures, vertebral fractures have a similar impact on quality of life and 2-year mortality rates. Physical functioning and health-related quality-of-life indices, as well as health care costs, are substantially affected by a vertebral fracture, regardless of whether the fracture is symptomatic (clinical) or asymptomatic (radiographic). Greater vertebral fracture severity and number are correlated with proportionately worse health state measures and a higher risk of future vertebral and nonvertebral fractures. Very low BMD and prevalent vertebral fractures are surrogates not only for skeletal fragility but also for medical frailty, postoperative complications, and increased mortality.

Vertebral Augmentation

Indications and Evaluation

The term vertebral augmentation generally refers to vertebroplasty and kyphoplasty, with percutaneous intravertebral injection of polymethylmethacrylate (PMMA) into a fracturing vertebra.[18] Vertebroplasty was first described in 1987 as a novel, minimally invasive intervention to treat an aggressive vertebral hemangioma. The technique was quickly adapted to treat painful vertebral fractures caused by osteoporosis, myeloma, or tumor. Kyphoplasty is a proprietary derivative of vertebroplasty in which an inflatable balloon is first introduced into the fracturing vertebral body in an attempt to restore vertebral height before injection of PMMA. The primary indication for vertebral augmentation worldwide is relief of pain from osteoporotic vertebral fracture. Sacroplasty and other derivative augmentation procedures have also been described.[19] Many of the technical principles of sacroplasty are similar to those of vertebroplasty.[18,19] Although vertebral augmentation can appear seductively straightforward, care is required to avoid poor outcomes. Research reporting standards for vertebral augmentation have been published.[20]

Most adults experience back pain at some point during their life. Older adults with osteoporosis frequently have multiple painful or potentially painful spine comorbidities including previous vertebral fracture, degenerative spondylosis, facet arthrosis, lumbar stenosis, and thoracolumbar kyphosis. The determination that back pain is specifically caused by vertebral fracture is, ultimately, a clinical judgment supported by characteristic elements of the patient's clinical history, physical examination, and diagnostic imaging. Patients with acute, painful osteoporotic vertebral fracture often can estimate the onset of pain, but fewer than half can ascribe the fracture to a specific event. Acute vertebral fracture pain is predominantly posterior and axial. Pain may radiate caudally or wrap around the trunk and mimic retroperitoneal or abdominal pathology. Typically, the pain surges in intensity with Valsalva maneuvers and large truncal movements such as getting in and out of bed. These maneuvers may be accompanied by painful muscle spasms. Nonetheless, most patients can find a position in which they are almost completely, if only briefly, free of pain. The position of maximal comfort often is in the quiet supine or semirecumbent position in bed or a recliner, but a substantial minority of patients report that they are most comfortable while standing. Pain from thoracolumbar fracture often radiates to the posterosuperior iliac spine, but pain radiating deep into the buttocks or lower extremities should suggest the possibility of an alternate or coexisting cause. On physical examination, a patient with an unhealed vertebral fracture may resist assuming the supine position or, having done so, dreads resuming a seated position. Focal spinous process tenderness is often present, but this sign discriminates poorly between the presence and absence of vertebral fracture and is an unreliable guide to fracture level.[21] Rib, sacral, or pelvic fractures can have a similar presentation and may accompany vertebral fracture.[22] Therefore, clinicians should be vigilant for synchronous, nonvertebral osteoporotic fractures in any at-risk person who has back, flank, sacral, hip, or abdominal pain. The intense surges of pain associated with transitioning maneuvers gradually diminish as the fracture union matures. When patients begin to increase weight-bearing physical activity, they may report limited endurance for unsupported standing because of crescendo backache, muscular fatigue, and general exhaustion. This postural-fatiguing pain must be carefully distinguished from acute vertebral fracture pain because it is unlikely to benefit from vertebral augmentation.

A comprehensive history and a physical examination are mandatory for a patient with an osteoporotic vertebral fracture. The surgeon must consider the possibility that the patient's fracture is the first clinical expression of a previously unrecognized medical condition, such as hypercortisolism, hyperparathyroidism, or multiple myeloma. Early consultation with a metabolic bone disease specialist, a geriatrician, or another physician

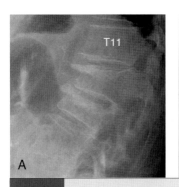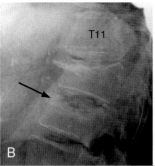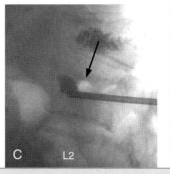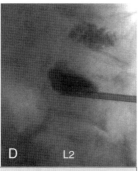

Figure 2 A through D, The nonfractured bodies of T11 and L2 are labeled for reference. A, Standing lateral radiograph showing a moderate T12 wedge and a severe L1 crush fracture. B, Cross-table lateral supine radiograph showing dynamic mobility of the L1 vertebral fracture and an intravertebral cleft elicited beneath the superior end plate *(arrow)*. T12 does not change fracture morphology. Air density is also seen in intravertebral disks. C, Intraoperative prone lateral radiograph showing the trabecular PMMA fill pattern at T12. Subatmospheric pressure within the clefted, dynamically mobile L1 fracture results in intravertebral air *(arrow)* with needle penetration (a vacuum cleft), which is followed by a confluent pool of injected PMMA. D, Intraoperative prone lateral radiograph showing the nearly completed cleft PMMA fill pattern at L1. Note the substantial height restoration of the L1 body, in comparison with A.

with expertise in osteoporosis is recommended in evaluating the patient's skeletal fragility, preparing the patient for vertebral augmentation, and managing the patient's osteoporosis postoperatively. Laboratory tests including a complete blood count, comprehensive metabolic panel, erythrocyte sedimentation rate, serum and urine protein electrophoresis, and serum 25-hydroxyvitamin D can suggest underlying infectious, metabolic, or malignant processes.

Vertebral augmentation should be considered when vertebral fracture pain is substantially disruptive to the patient's activities of daily living or threatens the patient's functional independence despite at least 1 or 2 weeks of appropriate analgesia, bracing, domestic or institutional rest, physical assistance, and nursing care. Any specific threshold for the magnitude or duration of pain, degree of functional impairment, or care paradigm is largely subjective, untested, and without expert consensus. In some circumstances, performing vertebral augmentation soon after fracture pain onset might be considered more conservative than continuing nonsurgical management. Vertebral augmentation may be performed in patients with osteoporosis, whether primary (postmenopausal or senescent) or secondary (glucocorticoid or endocrine), and it has been performed in patients with an unusual cause of skeletal fragility such as osteogenesis imperfecta.

Imaging Studies

Most radiographic vertebral fractures are not painful and should not be considered for augmentation. Conversely, painful fracturing vertebrae may not be evident until the vertebral shape has changed sufficiently to be appreciated radiographically. Failure to appreciate the dyssynchrony between the clinical and radiographic evolution of osteoporotic vertebral fracture can lead to diagnostic errors, prolonged suffering, and missed op-

portunities. A single standing lateral (axially loaded) radiograph centered on the spine region of interest may elicit subtle changes in vertebral shape sooner than conventional supine PA and lateral decubitus axially unloaded radiographs. Furthermore, a standing radiograph is likely to be better tolerated by a patient with vertebral fracture than conventional radiographs. Many osteoporotic vertebral fractures change their configuration under different loading conditions and with different body positions. This dynamic mobility has been identified in a substantial proportion of patients referred for vertebral augmentation.[23] On a preoperative supine cross-table lateral radiograph centered on the index vertebra, the height of the fractured vertebra may be greater than the height of the same vertebra on a preoperative standing lateral radiograph (Figure 2).

Care must be taken to exclude parallax and magnification effects before concluding that a vertebral fracture is dynamically mobile. Dynamic mobility most frequently occurs at the thoracolumbar junction, and it implies complete corticocancellous disruption. The radiographic correlate of this disruption is the intravertebral cleft.[24] Intravertebral clefts most frequently occur beneath the superior end plate, near the ventral margin of the vertebra. Cleft margins may appear increasingly sclerotic over time, and persistent fracture nonunion may result in intravertebral pseudarthrosis with hyalinization of the cleft margins. In some instances, fracture mobility can be seen only after the patient maintains the supine position overnight or longer. This latent mobility should be suspected in a relatively recent, severe thoracolumbar junction fracture if dynamic mobility was anticipated but not seen.[25] Dynamic and/or latent mobility should be identified preoperatively for several reasons: a severely compressed vertebra might wrongly be considered inoperable if dynamic

6: Spine Disorders

mobility is unrecognized; failure to fill the entire cleft could result in persistent postoperative dynamic mobility and fracture pain; and dynamic mobility can be harnessed intraoperatively to provide some vertebral height restoration.

Ironically, a collapsed osteoporotic vertebra may appear denser as the trabecular bone is compacted into a smaller space than normal. Needle penetration into a radiographically dense, nonmobile vertebral fracture can be surprisingly difficult; this finding should prompt reconsideration of the usefulness of augmentation. The possibility of a malignancy should always be considered in a patient who is elderly and has a nontraumatic vertebral fracture. Concern for malignancy should be heightened if an atraumatic vertebral fracture occurs in the absence of generalized osteoporosis, is located cephalad to T5, has atypical radiographic features (such as loss of cortical margins), or occurs in a patient with significant constitutional symptoms.

Nuclear scintigraphy (bone scanning) is a sensitive, accessible, and relatively inexpensive means of detecting vertebral fracture. Acute vertebral fracture typically appears as intense, linear radionuclide uptake spanning the width of the vertebra. A false-negative result can occur if the time since fracturing is less than 72 to 96 hours, which is insufficient time for radionuclide to localize to the fracture site; or if the bone is osteonecrotic, because adequate blood supply is necessary for radionuclide accumulation. Radionuclide uptake wanes slowly after an acute vertebral fracture and may persist as long as 2 years. Therefore, the ability of nuclear scintigraphy to discriminate between acute and subacute vertebral fractures is limited. Single-photon emission computed tomography enhances the sensitivity and specificity of nuclear scintigraphy by improving spatial localization of radionuclide uptake, allows radionuclide uptake in the posterior elements to be distinguished from uptake in the vertebral body, and provides good visualization of the posterior vertebral cortex. Nuclear scintigraphy has the added benefit of detecting synchronous fractures of the sacrum, pelvis, ribs, or spine. An acute sacral fracture typically results in intense vertical radionuclide uptake in both sacral ala and horizontal uptake across the sacral body, forming the Honda sign.[22] Multiple skeletal lesions on nuclear scintigraphy may suggest metastases. In a vertebral fracture older than 1 month, a standard uptake value greater than 2.5 on positron emission tomography suggests malignancy rather than osteoporosis. Position emission tomography has a low positive predictive value and is less useful in a vertebral fracture less than 1 month old.

MRI is the single most useful imaging modality for evaluating an osteoporotic vertebral fracture because it can identify vertebral trabecular injury within hours of fracture, identify all fracturing levels, detect intravertebral clefts, define the state of the posterior cortex, and help in excluding malignancy and infection. An osteoporotic vertebral fracture typically appears as low signal on a T1-weighted image and as high signal on a T2-weighted or short tau inversion recovery (STIR) sequence. Clefts may appear as air or water density, depending on the length of time the patient has been supine and the biomechanical forces acting on the fractured level.[24] Signal abnormalities in the pedicle or posterior elements, particularly in the presence of soft tissue in the epidural or paraspinal space, should alert the clinician to the possibility of an underlying malignancy or infection. STIR sequences also can reveal a previously unappreciated but synchronous vertebral or sacral fracture that could affect surgical planning and postoperative expectations. The time interval between MRI and augmentation is important because new vertebral fracture occurrence in that time interval is not uncommon.[26] CT with sagittal and coronal reconstruction can be helpful in assessing complex fracture patterns, defining the posterior vertebral cortex, and precisely visualizing the bony neuroforamen when radicular syndromes complicate fracture. Small sagittal and coronal intravertebral splits should alert the operator to potential pathways for undesirable PMMA flow, particularly into the adjacent disk. The size, shape, contours, and angular relationship of the pedicle to the vertebral body are best appreciated on MRI and CT. This anatomy must be appreciated because it serves as the basis for successful intraoperative needle trajectory.

Contraindications

The medical contraindications to vertebral augmentation include uncorrected coagulopathy, unresolved systemic or local infection, and insufficient medical stability to endure the procedure. The anticoagulant-antiplatelet effects of warfarin, enoxaparin, clopidogrel, prasugrel, and possibly aspirin should be allowed to wane before vertebral augmentation. The vertebral contraindications to augmentation include compression so severe that instrumentation is deemed unsafe in the absence of dynamic or latent mobility; complex cortical disruption that could lead to uncontrollable venous, foraminal, or intraspinal PMMA leakage; and myelopathy or neurologic deficit, with the possible exception of dynamic radicular syndromes resulting from a mobile vertebral fracture. Fracture age is a surrogate for fracture healing and by itself is not a contraindication to vertebral augmentation. A completely healed vertebral fracture should not be augmented, however.

Vertebral augmentation of a fracture from high-energy trauma, in healthy bone, or in a young patient should be performed only if the perceived benefit of rapid pain relief or vertebral stabilization outweighs the risk of permanently displacing normally repaired and remodeled bone by PMMA.[27,28] High-energy trauma, or trauma sufficient to fracture normal or younger bone, is likely to result in painful annular, musculoligamentous, and facet injury that will not benefit from vertebral augmentation. Accordingly, the outcome of vertebral augmentation in these situations cannot be expected to match those in low-energy, osteoporotic vertebral fracture. There is no evidence to justify vertebral augmentation solely for restoration of vertebral height or spinal alignment. So-called prophylactic or diagnostic vertebral augmentation is not recommended.

Surgical Considerations and Technique

Spine surgeons who are experienced in managing complex, high-energy spine fractures should be wary of directly transferring that experience to the percutaneous or open surgical management of spine conditions in patients with osteoporosis. Vertebral augmentation may be performed in an interventional radiology suite, ambulatory surgery center, or hospital operating room. Secure venous access, emergency resuscitation equipment, continuous pulse oximetry, and blood pressure and electrocardiographic monitoring are mandatory. The mode of anesthesia should be individually determined by the patient's health and preference, the specific characteristics of the vertebral fracture, the location and goals of the augmentation procedure, and the experience of the surgeon and the anesthesiologist. General anesthesia, monitored anesthesia with intravenous sedation, and local anesthesia are all acceptable. The use of general anesthesia is preferred to enhance muscle relaxation during vertebral height restoration. In a patient with tenuous cardiopulmonary function, the use of general anesthesia allows greater airway security and avoids any need for a difficult midprocedure conversion to general anesthesia. Preoperative intravenous antibiotic prophylaxis should be administered within 1 hour of the skin incision.

The patient is gently rolled into the prone position on a radiolucent Jackson table, and all bony and neural prominences are generously padded. Careful positioning in slight extension may result in vertebral height restoration, particularly in a clefted vertebral fracture with preoperative dynamic mobility. A well-informed, engaged, proactive radiology technician should be familiar with the anatomic landmarks necessary for capturing true PA and lateral views of the target vertebrae. Biplanar fluoroscopy allows almost instantaneous visualization of the needle placement and PMMA flow. The use of protective eyewear and attire (lead-lined glasses and lead gowns) is mandatory to avoid fluoroscopic exposure to high levels of ionizing radiation. To minimize operator radiation exposure from scatter, the C-arm gantries should be positioned so that radiation enters the patient from the floor (AP plane imaging) or from the side opposite the operator (lateral plane imaging). Continuous pulsed fluoroscopy with tight collimation can be used during PMMA injection, or intermittent controlled fluoroscopy can be used after injection of small aliquots of PMMA. Some surgeons prefer the use of intermittent spot images to identify and document PMMA leakage. Both the magnification function and high-level fluoroscopy should be avoided. No one who is pregnant should be present during imaging.

The pedicle margins as seen on the AP view represent the waist of the pedicle, which is its narrowest por-

tion. Although the pedicle waist generally is at the midpoint of the pedicle, its exact location varies and must be extrapolated from preoperative MRI and CT, then confirmed intraoperatively on the lateral view. The pedicle flares to become trumpet shaped as it joins the vertebral body. In general, a thoracic pedicle flares less than a lumbar pedicle. The location of the pedicle waist and the contour of its flare are important determinants of the needle trajectory. Successful needle placement is predicated on a thorough understanding of the relationship between the vertebral body and its pedicle, as gleaned in two dimensions from preoperative MRI and CT and three-dimensional projection and manipulation of this relationship intraoperatively.

To provide external reference points throughout the procedure, the patient's skin should be marked with indelible ink over the center of the spinous process and over the lateral and superior borders of both pedicles. The entry point for instrumentation is approximately 1 to 2 cm lateral to the intersection of lines drawn between the superior pedicle margins and the lateral margins of each pedicle of the target vertebra. The precise entry point varies depending on body habitus, spine level, and vertebral anatomy. Patient preparation and draping are completed after the anatomic landmarks and imaging orientation are confirmed.

Vertebral body instrumentation can be done through a transpedicular or an extrapedicular (transcostovertebral or posterolateral) approach. At T12 or a lumbar vertebral body, the transpedicular approach is facilitated by the larger pedicle size. However, satisfactory vertebral filling may require a larger volume of PMMA as well as bilateral instrumentation. In the axial plane, thoracic vertebral bodies usually are relatively conical or bullet shaped dorsal to ventral, and the pedicles are narrower and more cephalad than those of lumbar vertebral bodies. For these reasons, the parapedicular or transcostovertebral approach usually is preferred for the thoracic vertebrae. Above T12, a smaller volume of PMMA is required, and often it can be delivered to the center of the vertebral body by unilateral instrumentation. A complex fracture pattern requires an individualized instrumentation strategy based on careful evaluation of the preoperative and intraoperative imaging studies. For example, bipedicular instrumentation may be necessary if a severe biconcave deformity precludes navigation of the needle to the exact midline of the vertebral body.

All of the available vertebroplasty needle options are acceptable (for example, Precision Cement Delivery System, Stryker, Kalamazoo, MI). Proprietary instrumentation is available for kyphoplasty (Medtronic, Minneapolis, MN). Most of the needles are variations of the Jamshidi needle, and they are available with diamond-tipped or single- or multiple-beveled stylet options. Using a diamond-tipped stylet may reduce needle slippage on the cortical surface of the vertebra. After cortical penetration, some surgeons exchange the diamond-tipped stylet for a single-beveled stylet because the latter may allow better steering. The needle length (10 or 15 cm) and gauge (11, 13, or 15 G) are determined by vertebral and patient anatomic factors. Using a small needle may risk polymer clogging at the needle tip. Physician-operator training, experience, and preference are the primary factors in needle selection.

If general anesthesia is not used, the skin is infiltrated with a local anesthetic. Under AP-view fluoroscopic guidance, a 0.045-mm guidewire is passed through the skin and docked on the left and/or right pedicle at the 10 o'clock and/or 2 o'clock position, respectively. A 1-cm cephalocaudal skin incision encompassing the docked guidewire(s) is made using a number 10 scalpel blade. A vertebroplasty needle is then passed over the guidewire(s) and firmly docked into the vertebral cortex. It is critical to stabilize a guidewire or needle whenever it is being manipulated because it can slip off the bone, penetrate too deeply, and cause harm to soft tissues. The guidewire is removed, the needle trocar is replaced, and the needle is cautiously advanced with a hand mallet in the predetermined transpedicular or extrapedicular trajectory. The surgeon must be wary because the minimal resistance offered by osteoporotic bone can suddenly vanish when an intravertebral cleft is penetrated. Anticipatory restraint will prevent penetration of the anterior vertebral cortex or the more ventral soft-tissue structures. In the transpedicular approach, the desired needle trajectory should form a near tangent with the medial trumpeted wall of the pedicle as the needle aims for the center of the vertebral body.

The angle of needle trajectory is determined by the location of the waist of the pedicle, the slope of pedicle flare as it joins the vertebral body, the fracture pattern, and the vertebral shape. The lateral view ensures appropriate needle trajectory in the cephalocaudal plane and allows ventral needle penetration to be monitored. The needle tip should not breach the medial pedicle shadow (as seen in the AP view) until it has safely passed the posterior cortex of the vertebral body (as seen in the lateral view), unless permitted by broadly flaring pedicles. When the extrapedicular approach is used in thoracic vertebrae, the 0.045-mm guidewire initially should be docked slightly cephalad and lateral to the 2 o'clock or 10 o'clock position. The desired final needle depth is in the anterior 20% of the vertebral body. In contrast with pedicle screw instrumentation, the final needle position in the cephalocaudal plane varies, as determined by the distorted configuration of the fractured vertebral body. In bipedicular instrumentation, both needles should be placed before PMMA injection. Venography was formerly recommended for predicting PMMA flow and leak direction; however, it has generally lost support because the rheologic properties of the contrast material do not necessarily predict the properties of PMMA, and retained contrast material may obscure subsequent PMMA visualization.

The FDA has approved several cements for use in vertebral augmentation (for example, Spineplex,

Stryker, Kalamazoo, MI; KyphX HV-R, Medtronic, Minneapolis, MN). These cements consist of a PMMA–barium sulfate mixture in a fixed ratio of approximately 70:30 that has favorable handling and visualization characteristics. Individual PMMA products have unique mixing ratios, polymerization times, and performance characteristics, and operators should thoroughly familiarize themselves with the manufacturer's instructions. Modification of any PMMA product, such as by adding opacifying agents or antibiotics, alters its performance characteristics and creates a new, non–FDA-approved medical device. Using an FDA-approved PMMA product avoids the potential medicolegal consequences of off-label use. FDA-approved calcium phosphate cements are less commonly used than PMMA cements; there are concerns regarding fatigue failure during repeated cyclic loading, and the material's high viscosity necessitates insertion through a larger bore needle, as is used in kyphoplasty.

Manual injection of PMMA can be performed directly or remotely. Direct syringe-to-needle PMMA injection using 1- to 3-mL preloaded plastic syringes gives the operator direct tactile feedback as to cement flow but requires increased radiation exposure. Several proprietary devices (for example, Precision Cement Delivery System) permit remote PMMA injection by interposing a delivery system between the operator and the needle. Remote injection reduces the radiation exposure at the cost of decreased tactile feedback and increased resistance to flow within the delivery system.

Although the use of relatively viscous cement may reduce the risk of cement leakage, the optimal cement viscosity is unknown and may vary.[29] Viscosity must be considered in view of the length and diameter of the delivery device, the rate of delivery, the ambient temperature, the intravertebral pressure, the configuration of the fracture, and the presence or absence of intravertebral clefts. Some of these variables are under operator control; others can be anticipated but not directly controlled. Resistance to injection at the syringe level can be reduced, working times can be prolonged, and the risk of cement leakage can be minimized by injecting relatively less viscous PMMA at a slower rate. Keeping PMMA monomer and polymer on ice before mixing will retard polymerization. A temperature difference between the delivery tubing and the delivery needle can lead to rapid cement setting within the needle and cause needle clogging.

A planned vertebral body biopsy should be performed before full needle penetration. Vertebral biopsy before cement injection discloses an unsuspected malignancy in as many as 3.8% of patients.[30] Although an ex vivo study found that small cement volumes were required to normalize stress distributions on the vertebral bodies, the final in vivo cement fill volume varies with the vertebral level, fracture morphology, fracture severity, presence or absence of clefts, and fill pattern.[31] In general, the recommendation is to use the smallest PMMA volume sufficient to stabilize the fracture or cleft (2 to 4 mL in the thoracic vertebrae, 4 to 8 mL in the lumbar vertebrae). The surgeon must be vigilant to detect small intravertebral splits that fill preferentially and wick PMMA quickly into the disk, vascular space, or extravertebral space. A small PMMA leak should be allowed to set, and the surgeon should reposition the needle before cautiously resuming the injection ipsilaterally or completing the augmentation contralaterally. Vertebral filling should cease when the operator believes the biomechanically vulnerable segment (as determined on preoperative imaging) has been filled, PMMA has entered the dorsal third of the vertebra, or a leak cannot be controlled. Spinning the needle before withdrawing it should amputate the cement pillar and prevent a cement tail from forming. At the completion of the procedure, the subcutaneous tissue and skin are closed with absorbable suture, and the skin is dressed. The patient should remain supine for at least 1 hour after vertebroplasty and should be actively monitored before dismissal for adverse anesthetic, cardiopulmonary, or neurologic effects. A patient who is medically frail or has undergone a high-risk augmentation, such as for multiple levels or a large vertebral fracture, should be observed overnight or until a thoracolumbosacral orthosis is constructed and fitted. In the absence of an access cannula, a clogged needle must be removed, and the vertebra must be reinstrumented. Transpedicular instrumentation through a very narrow pedicle may result in an undesirable lateralized needle tip position within the vertebral body; in this case, an extrapedicular approach should be chosen.

Complications

Clinical complications of vertebroplasty are infrequent, often avoidable, and usually the result of inaccurate needle placement or inattention to PMMA flow during injection. The reported rates of PMMA leakage have varied widely and reflect the underlying skeletal diagnosis, anatomic integrity of the fractured vertebra, technical proficiency of the operator, method of radiographic ascertainment, and, possibly, biases in reporting. A PMMA leak is more likely in the presence of an extensive vertebral disruption or a malignancy. Often a risk of leakage can be anticipated by careful review of the preoperative images. Radiographic leakage rates in osteoporotic vertebrae are commonly reported to be approximately 10%, with symptomatic leakage reported in considerably fewer than 1%. Clinical pulmonary PMMA embolism is rare, but two recent studies reported that small, asymptomatic pulmonary PMMA emboli were detected by thin-section CT after one quarter of vertebroplasty procedures.[29,32] Although a small, asymptomatic disk or paravertebral PMMA leak is undesirable, the resulting deposit appears harmless. Vigilance during injection using biplanar imaging is usually sufficient to recognize and abort azygos or caval propagation. Epidural venous leakage can be avoided by terminating the injection as soon as PMMA reaches the junction of the middle and posterior thirds

of the vertebral body. Lower rates of PMMA leakage have been reported following kyphoplasty and appear to be explained by trabeculae damming on the surface of the expanding balloon. Whether a lower leakage rate justifies sacrificing viable vertebral trabeculae and microarchitecture is unknown. Altering PMMA viscosity and delivery rate may result in lower leakage rates during vertebroplasty.[33]

In the VERTOS II study, the incidence of subsequent vertebral fracture was no greater after vertebral augmentation than was observed with nonsurgical care.[34] The risk of a subsequent vertebral fracture may be higher after augmentation of large clefts, but it is unknown whether the cause is that these fractures are surrogates for greater skeletal fragility or that the augmentation results in greater focal stress.[35-40] Persistent MRI fluid signal surrounding the confluent PMMA filling of a large cleft may be a harbinger of a poorer functional outcome and a higher incidence of subsequent vertebral fracture.[35,38] Vertebral subsidence can occur above a PMMA mantle, and successful repeat augmentation has been described.[41,42] Serious harm including spinal cord and nerve root injury, hemothorax, systemic and cerebral PMMA embolism, cardiac penetration, vertebral infection, and even death have been reported to complicate augmentation.[43,44] PMMA monomer cardiac toxicity during vertebral augmentation has not been reported. The biomechanical implications of leaving an unfractured vertebra between two augmented vertebrae or between an augmented vertebra and a rigid construct (as in ankylosing spondylitis, diffuse idiopathic skeletal hyperostosis, or a previously instrumented spine) present an unresolved conundrum.

Outcomes

Two small prospective randomized controlled studies published in 2009 (known as the INVEST and Buchbinder studies) concluded that vertebroplasty is not superior to a sham procedure.[45,46] Nearly simultaneously, a meta-analysis of voluminous lower level data concluded that vertebroplasty and kyphoplasty both result in rapid, substantial, and durable relief of pain and improved quality of life.[43,44] Passionate debate followed publication of the INVEST and Buchbinder studies.[47] Vertebroplasty continues to be performed, although perhaps less frequently, even by the authors of the INVEST study.[48] The American Academy of Orthopaedic Surgeons (AAOS) recently published a guideline on the treatment of osteoporotic spinal compression fractures.[49] The AAOS guideline consists of one "strong," one "moderate," and nine "weak" and "inconclusive" recommendations for the clinical management of patients with osteoporotic spinal compression fracture. The "strong" recommendation is against performing vertebroplasty. The AAOS guideline recommends that kyphoplasty remain an option for neurologically intact patients who have an osteoporotic spinal compression fracture on imaging, with correlating clinical signs and symptoms.[49] The primary basis for this endorsement appears to be the favorable results of a prospective randomized controlled comparison of kyphoplasty and continued nonsurgical care, known as the FREE study,[50] as well as the absence of noninferiority data from comparison studies such as the INVEST and Buchbinder studies. The AAOS guideline does not appear to have taken into consideration the results of a prospective randomized controlled comparison of vertebroplasty and continued nonsurgical care (known as the VERTOS II study[34]), which showed favorable efficacy in vertebroplasty. The single "moderate" recommendation in the AAOS guideline is to use calcitonin for 4 weeks in the acute vertebral fracture setting. This recommendation is not consistent with calcitonin prescribing information.

The outcomes of vertebral augmentation reflect accurate patient selection, the technical proficiency of the surgeon, and the postsurgical care of the patient's osteoporosis. In both the FREE and VERTOS II studies, pain (measured on the visual analog scale), quality of life (measured with appropriate health-related quality-of-life instruments), and physical function improved rapidly after augmentation, and these results were durable for 1 year. The pain, function, and health-related quality of life outcome metrics used in the FREE and VERTOS II studies were the same as the metrics used in the INVEST and Buchbinder studies. Substantial numeric improvements in these metrics were reported in the FREE and VERTOS II studies, compared with those reported in the sham studies. The rates of subsequent vertebral fracture were not increased in either the FREE or VERTOS II study, and the complication rates were low.

Vertebral height restoration commonly occurs during vertebral augmentation, with little or no difference between vertebroplasty and kyphoplasty.[23,51] The small vertebral height restorations reported thus far have had no measurable clinical significance.[52] In light of the complexities and controversies surrounding vertebroplasty, the similarly promising results of the less extensively studied sacroplasty must be viewed with caution.[19,53]

Open Surgical Treatment of the Osteoporotic Spine

Open surgical treatment of the osteoporotic spine can be perilous. The potential indications for open surgical treatment are substantial neurologic deficit, incapacitating fracture pain, and severe deformity. The defining surgical challenge of open treatment is the biomechanically deficient interface between the bone and the instrumentation. Osteoporosis can cause spinal curve progression through asymmetric compression fracturing. Surgical correction of the deformity is complicated by loss of fixation points during correction maneuvers. After a successful deformity correction, osteoporosis can cause junctional kyphosis with compression fractures.

When osteoporosis is suspected in a patient with a spine deformity, DXA should be used for preoperative evaluation, surgical planning, and surgical preparation. The presence of osteoporosis greatly reduces the pullout strength, cutout strength, and maximal insertional torque of all implant devices. Failure to address these biomechanical realities risks premature instrumentation failure, progressive deformity, and a worsening neurologic deficit. Several biomechanical principles must be considered to improve the likelihood of successful instrumentation. The most important principle is to minimize load bearing at individual fixation points and maximize fixation strength at individual implant anchor points. Load bearing can be minimized by ensuring adequate sagittal balance, using multiple fixation points, and increasing the construct length.[54] Although osteoporosis substantially degrades the performance of all implant devices, it particularly affects the fixation strength of pedicle screws.[55]

Various compensatory strategies have been developed. Fixation strength can be increased by augmenting pedicle screws with PMMA using standard Jamshidi needles or specialized pedicle tap instruments. The primary risk of PMMA augmentation is an extravertebral cement leak, with its potential for soft-tissue or neurologic injury. The use of conical screws tailored to fit the pedicle improves pullout strength but is technically demanding, and maintenance of the bone-implant interface can be tenuous. Expandable pedicle screws also improve pullout strength, but pedicle burst fractures occur when the outside screw diameter exceeds the inner diameter of the pedicle. Screw triangulation increases the total implant-bone interface and more firmly anchors the implant in the bone. Reinforcing pedicle screws with sublaminar wires and/or offset sublaminar hooks harnesses intact cortical bone, thereby dissipating stress at the implant-bone fixation point. Thoracic hyperkyphosis and loss of lumbar lordosis are common in the osteoporotic spine, and they increase instrumentation strain. Postinstrumentation restoration of normal sagittal balance is desirable, but excessive instrumentation force increases the strain at both ends of the construct and further risks bone-implant interface failure. Lumbar osteotomy, aggressive facet excision, and even Smith-Peterson or pedicle subtraction osteotomy may be required to restore lumbar lordosis. Anterior interbody bone grafts may be necessary to maintain lumbar lordosis, but care should be taken not to violate bony end plates, so that vertebral body strength is maintained and graft subsidence is limited.

Anterior reconstruction followed by posterior instrumented fusion historically has been recommended if direct open anterior decompression of the osteoporotic spine is required for neurologic indications. More recently, stand-alone posterior instrumented fusion has led to durable surgical outcomes and reduced surgical morbidity.[56] Other surgical options include combined posterior instrumented fusion and open vertebral augmentation to augment the anterior column.[57-59] The length of the posterior instrumentation should be individually tailored and determined by the patient's bone quality, extent of deformity, implant choice, and extent of implant augmentation.[60]

Recurrent or persistent back pain after vertebral augmentation most likely indicates a new vertebral fracture but occasionally indicates a residual vacuum cleft, inadequate surgical augmentation, pyogenic spondylitis, cement migration, or cement fragmentation.[54] Repeat vertebral augmentation should be needed only rarely. Anterior débridement and reconstruction followed by posterior instrumentation and fusion and prolonged antibiotic therapy are the treatments of choice for pyogenic spondylitis. Anterior and posterior reconstruction may be appropriate if cement migration or fragmentation has caused substantial neurologic deficit, incapacitating pain, or deformity.

Postsurgical Osteoporosis Management

Vertebral augmentation can repair a fractured vertebra but cannot reverse osteoporosis. After the occurrence of a vertebral fracture, the risk of a future fracture is multiplied nonlinearly and independently of BMD. Therefore, fracture risk is higher in patients who have undergone vertebral augmentation. The fracture risk is further increased by more numerous and more severe vertebral fractures, increasing age, medical frailty, and a history of falling. Vertebral augmentation should be viewed as part of a comprehensive osteoporosis management program, not as a stand-alone procedure. In addition to explicit instruction regarding wound care, the patient should receive basic instruction in safe movement, transfers, and essential activities of daily living. This instruction should be provided preferably before vertebral augmentation and certainly before the postoperative return home. One to 2 weeks after surgery, the surgeon should examine standing AP and lateral radiographs centered on the index vertebra, inspect the surgical site, advance the comprehensive rehabilitation program, and consider best options for the medical management of skeletal fragility. Physical therapy should emphasize fall risk reduction, safe body movements, and a graduated, extension-based core-strengthening program. Although the value of bracing a high-energy thoracolumbar fracture recently has been challenged,[61] perioperative bracing with a prefabricated or custom-made thoracolumbosacral orthosis is recommended for a biomechanically high-risk thoracolumbar fracture or augmentation. These fractures include dynamically mobile thoracolumbar fractures with large clefts, multilevel vertebral fractures, and vertebral fractures that occur at the end of a long rigid construct, as in diffuse idiopathic skeletal hyperostosis or ankylosing spondylitis.

Identifying and correcting hypovitaminosis D and dietary calcium insufficiency, which are highly prevalent in patients with osteoporosis, can decrease the risk of falling and optimize skeletal responsiveness to drug therapy. All currently available antiosteoporosis drugs can be considered anabolic (teriparatide) or antiresorptive (bisphosphonates, raloxifene, estrogens, calcitonin, denosumab). These agents have been found to reduce the risk of vertebral fracture by 50% to 70%. Only bisphosphonates, denosumab, and estrogens have been found to reduce the risk of hip fracture risk by as much as 50%.[5,8,11] No definitive head-to-head comparison of the effect of these agents on fracture outcomes is available. Greater increases in BMD occur in treatment-naïve patients with the use of teriparatide than with any other single antiosteoporosis agent. Denosumab and zoledronic acid are the most potent available anti-remodeling agents. With the possible exception of the combination of teriparatide and zoledronic acid, the use of combination drug therapies should be discouraged because fracture data are absent, the cost is substantial, and some combinations may be counterproductive or harmful.[62]

Summary

The spine is predominantly composed of trabecular bone and therefore is an important site of osteoporosis and osteoporotic fracture. Pharmacotherapy for osteoporosis is becoming increasingly complex. Nonsurgical and surgical management of osteoporosis and osteoporotic spine fracture should be multidisciplinary and collaborative. Surgical intervention in osteoporotic bone presents challenging clinical, biomechanical, and technical issues. The future of vertebral augmentation in managing painful osteoporotic vertebral fractures is uncertain.

Annotated References

1. Lewiecki EM: Bone densitometry and vertebral fracture assessment. *Curr Osteoporos Rep* 2010;8(3):123-130.

2. McKiernan FE, Berg RL, Linneman JG: The utility of BMD Z-score diagnostic thresholds for secondary causes of osteoporosis. *Osteoporos Int* 2011;22(4):1069-1077.

3. World Health Organization: FRAX fracture risk assessment tool. http://www.shef.ac.uk/FRAX/tool.jsp?location Value=9. Accessed March 20, 2011.

4. Yadav VK, Ryu JH, Suda N, et al: Lrp5 controls bone formation by inhibiting serotonin synthesis in the duodenum. *Cell* 2008;135(5):825-837.

5. Boonen S, Body JJ, Boutsen Y, et al: Evidence-based guidelines for the treatment of postmenopausal osteoporosis: A consensus document of the Belgian Bone Club. *Osteoporos Int* 2005;16(3):239-254.

6: Spine Disorders

6. Gerstenfeld LC, Sacks DJ, Pelis M, et al: Comparison of effects of the bisphosphonate alendronate versus the RANKL inhibitor denosumab on murine fracture healing. *J Bone Miner Res* 2009;24(2):196-208.

7. Pountos I, Georgouli T, Blokhuis TJ, Pape HC, Giannoudis PV: Pharmacological agents and impairment of fracture healing: What is the evidence? *Injury* 2008; 39(4):384-394.

8. Eriksen EF, Lyles KW, Colón-Emeric CS, et al: Antifracture efficacy and reduction of mortality in relation to timing of the first dose of zoledronic acid after hip fracture. *J Bone Miner Res* 2009;24(7):1308-1313.

9. Khan AA, Sándor GK, Dore E, et al: Bisphosphonate associated osteonecrosis of the jaw. *J Rheumatol* 2009; 36(3):478-490.

10. Shane E, Burr D, Ebeling PR, et al: Atypical subtrochanteric and diaphyseal femoral fractures: Report of a task force of the American Society for Bone and Mineral Research. *J Bone Miner Res* 2010;25(11):2267-2294.

11. Lewiecki EM: Clinical use of denosumab for the treatment for postmenopausal osteoporosis. *Curr Med Res Opin* 2010;26(12):2807-2812.

12. Burkus JK, Transfeldt EE, Kitchel SH, Watkins RG, Balderston RA: Clinical and radiographic outcomes of anterior lumbar interbody fusion using recombinant human bone morphogenetic protein-2. *Spine (Phila Pa 1976)* 2002;27(21):2396-2408.

13. Aspenberg P, Genant HK, Johansson T, et al: Teriparatide for acceleration of fracture repair in humans: A prospective, randomized, double-blind study of 102 postmenopausal women with distal radial fractures. *J Bone Miner Res* 2010;25(2):404-414.

14. Undale AH, Westendorf JJ, Yaszemski MJ, Khosla S: Mesenchymal stem cells for bone repair and metabolic bone diseases. *Mayo Clin Proc* 2009;84(10):893-902.

15. Committee to Review Dietary Reference Intake for Vitamin D and Calcium: *Institute of Medicine: Dietary Reference Intakes for Vitamin D and Calcium.* Washington, DC, National Academies Press, 2011.

16. Gerstenfeld LC, Einhorn TA: COX inhibitors and their effects on bone healing. *Expert Opin Drug Saf* 2004; 3(2):131-136.

17. Burge R, Dawson-Hughes B, Solomon DH, Wong JB, King A, Tosteson A: Incidence and economic burden of osteoporosis-related fractures in the United States, 2005-2025. *J Bone Miner Res* 2007;22(3):465-475.

18. Peh WC, Munk PL, Rashid F, Gilula LA: Percutaneous vertebral augmentation: Vertebroplasty, kyphoplasty and skyphoplasty. *Radiol Clin North Am* 2008;46(3): 611-635.

19. Bayley E, Srinivas S, Boszczyk BM: Clinical outcomes of sacroplasty in sacral insufficiency fractures: A review of the literature. *Eur Spine J* 2009;18(9):1266-1271.

   A review of the literature on sacroplasty, including cement sacroplasty and augmented iliosacral (transsacral) screw fixation in patients with insufficiency fracture, found that sacroplasty with or without iliosacral screw fixation results in substantial improvement on the visual analog scale.

20. Radvany MG, Murphy KJ, Millward SF, et al: Research reporting standards for percutaneous vertebral augmentation. *J Vasc Interv Radiol* 2009;20(10):1279-1286.

21. Rad AE, Kallmes DF: Pain relief following vertebroplasty in patients with and without localizing tenderness on palpation. *AJNR Am J Neuroradiol* 2008;29(9): 1622-1626.

22. Schindler OS, Watura R, Cobby M: Sacral insufficiency fractures. *J Orthop Surg (Hong Kong)* 2007;15(3):339-346.

23. McKiernan FE, Jensen R, Faciszewski T: The dynamic mobility of vertebral compression fractures. *J Bone Miner Res* 2003;18(1):24-29.

   The frequency of dynamic mobility in patients referred for vertebroplasty and the magnitude and nature of dynamic mobility are described in one of the first reports documenting the existence of dynamic fracture mobility in patients with osteoporotic vertebral compression fractures.

24. McKiernan F, Faciszewski T: Intravertebral clefts in osteoporotic vertebral compression fractures. *Arthritis Rheum* 2003;48(5):1414-1419.

   This is a prospective study of 50 consecutive patients with 82 vertebral compression fractures who underwent vertebroplasty at a tertiary referral center. The characteristics, radiographic appearance, and significance of intravertebral clefts in vertebral compression fractures are described in patients with osteoporosis who are undergoing vertebroplasty.

25. McKiernan FE, Faciszewski T, Jensen R: Latent mobility of osteoporotic vertebral compression fractures. *J Vasc Interv Radiol* 2006;17(9):1479-1487.

   In this retrospective study of 14 patients with painful, severe osteoporotic vertebral compression fracture, vertebroplasty initially was deemed unsafe or technically impossible for some patients because of severe collapse. Overnight confinement to the supine position restored sufficient additional vertebral height to allow safe percutaneous vertebroplasty the following morning.

26. Benz BK, Gemery JM, McIntyre JJ, Eskey CJ: Value of immediate preprocedure magnetic resonance imaging in patients scheduled to undergo vertebroplasty or kyphoplasty. *Spine (Phila Pa 1976)* 2009;34(6):609-612.

27. Kim HS, Park SK, Joy H, Ryu JK, Kim SW, Ju CI: Bone cement augmentation of short segment fixation for unstable burst fracture in severe osteoporosis. *J Korean Neurosurg Soc* 2008;44(1):8-14.

28. Knavel EM, Thielen KR, Kallmes DF: Vertebroplasty for the treatment of traumatic nonosteoporotic compression fractures. *AJNR Am J Neuroradiol* 2009;30(2): 323-327.

29. Venmans A, Klazen CA, Lohle PN, et al: Percutaneous vertebroplasty and pulmonary cement embolism: Results from VERTOS II. *AJNR Am J Neuroradiol* 2010; 31(8):1451-1453.

    The incidence of PMMA embolization was carefully analyzed using postoperative thin-section CT in patients undergoing vertebroplasty.

30. Muijs SP, Akkermans PA, van Erkel AR, Dijkstra SD: The value of routinely performing a bone biopsy during percutaneous vertebroplasty in treatment of osteoporotic vertebral compression fractures. *Spine (Phila Pa 1976)* 2009;34(22):2395-2399.

31. Luo J, Daines L, Charalambous A, Adams MA, Annesley-Williams DJ, Dolan P: Vertebroplasty: Only small cement volumes are required to normalize stress distributions on the vertebral bodies. *Spine (Phila Pa 1976)* 2009;34(26):2865-2873.

32. Kim YJ, Lee JW, Park KW, et al: Pulmonary cement embolism after percutaneous vertebroplasty in osteoporotic vertebral compression fractures: Incidence, characteristics, and risk factors. *Radiology* 2009;251(1):250-259.

33. Georgy BA: Clinical experience with high-viscosity cements for percutaneous vertebral body augmentation: Occurrence, degree, and location of cement leakage compared with kyphoplasty. *AJNR Am J Neuroradiol* 2010;31(3):504-508.

34. Klazen CA, Lohle PN, de Vries J, et al: Vertebroplasty versus conservative treatment in acute osteoporotic vertebral compression fractures (Vertos II): An open-label randomised trial. *Lancet* 2010;376(9746):1085-1092.

    A prospective, randomized comparison of vertebroplasty and continued nonsurgical care in 202 patients with osteoporosis found that pain relief after vertebroplasty was immediate, sustained for at least 1 year, significantly greater than pain relief with nonsurgical treatment, and achieved at an acceptable cost.

35. Lin CC, Wen SH, Chiu CH, Chen IH, Yu TC: The clinical influence of fluid sign in treated vertebral bodies after percutaneous vertebroplasty. *Radiology* 2009; 251(3):866-872.

36. Trout AT, Kallmes DF, Lane JI, Layton KF, Marx WF: Subsequent vertebral fractures after vertebroplasty: Association with intraosseous clefts. *AJNR Am J Neuroradiol* 2006;27(7):1586-1591.

37. Tanigawa N, Komemushi A, Kariya S, et al: Relationship between cement distribution pattern and new compression fracture after percutaneous vertebroplasty. *AJR Am J Roentgenol* 2007;189(6):W348-W352.

38. Yu CW, Hsu CY, Shih TT, Chen BB, Fu CJ: Vertebral osteonecrosis: MR imaging findings and related changes on adjacent levels. *AJNR Am J Neuroradiol* 2007;28(1): 42-47.

39. Kim HW, Kwon A, Lee MC, Song JW, Kim SK, Kim IH: Analysis of results using percutaneous vertebroplasty for the treatment of avascular necrosis of the vertebral body. *J Korean Neurosurg Soc* 2009;45(4):209-212.

40. Wiggins MC, Sehizadeh M, Pilgram TK, Gilula LA: Importance of intravertebral fracture clefts in vertebroplasty outcome. *AJR Am J Roentgenol* 2007;188(3): 634-640.

41. Frey ME: Redo kyphoplasty with vertebroplasty technique: A case report and review of the literature. *Pain Physician* 2009;12(3):645-649.

42. Gaughen JR Jr, Jensen ME, Schweickert PA, Marx WF, Kallmes DF: The therapeutic benefit of repeat percutaneous vertebroplasty at previously treated vertebral levels. *AJNR Am J Neuroradiol* 2002;23(10):1657-1661.

43. Hurley MC, Kaakaji R, Dabus G, et al: Percutaneous vertebroplasty. *Neurosurg Clin N Am* 2009;20(3):341-359.

44. McGirt MJ, Parker SL, Wolinsky JP, Witham TF, Bydon A, Gokaslan ZL: Vertebroplasty and kyphoplasty for the treatment of vertebral compression fractures: An evidenced-based review of the literature. *Spine J* 2009; 9(6):501-508.

45. Kallmes DF, Comstock BA, Heagerty PJ, et al: A randomized trial of vertebroplasty for osteoporotic spinal fractures. *N Engl J Med* 2009;361(6):569-579.

    A prospective, randomized study of vertebroplasty and a control procedure in 131 patients found similar improvements in pain and pain-related disability associated with osteoporotic compression fracture in both groups of patients.

46. Buchbinder R, Osborne RH, Ebeling PR, et al: A randomized trial of vertebroplasty for painful osteoporotic vertebral fractures. *N Engl J Med* 2009;361(6):557-568.

    A prospective, randomized, double-blind, placebo-controlled study of vertebroplasty and a sham procedure in patients with painful osteoporotic vertebral fracture found no beneficial effect of vertebroplasty, as compared with a sham procedure, at 1 week or 1, 3, or 6 months after treatment.

47. Clark W, Goh AC: Vertebroplasty for acute osteoporotic spinal fractures-best evidence? *J Vasc Interv Radiol* 2010;21(9):1330-1333.

48. Luetmer MT, Kallmes DF: Have referral patterns for vertebroplasty changed since publication of the placebo-controlled trials? *AJNR Am J Neuroradiol* 2011;32(4): 647-648.

49. American Academy of Orthopaedic Surgeons: Guideline on the treatment of symptomatic osteoporotic spinal compression fractures. Rosemont, IL, American Academy of Orthopaedic Surgeons, 2010. http://www.aaos.org/Research/guidelines/SCFguideline.asp. Accessed March 20, 2011.

6: Spine Disorders

50. Wardlaw D, Cummings SR, Van Meirhaeghe J, et al: Efficacy and safety of balloon kyphoplasty compared with non-surgical care for vertebral compression fracture (FREE): A randomised controlled trial. *Lancet* 2009; 373(9668):1016-1024.

A prospective, randomized study of balloon kyphoplasty and continued nonsurgical care in patients with painful osteoporotic vertebral fracture found that balloon kyphoplasty is effective and safe for patients with acute vertebral fracture pain.

51. Hiwatashi A, Westesson PL, Yoshiura T, et al: Kyphoplasty and vertebroplasty produce the same degree of height restoration. *AJNR Am J Neuroradiol* 2009; 30(4):669-673.

52. McKiernan FE, Faciszewski T, Jensen R: Does vertebral height restoration achieved at vertebroplasty matter? *J Vasc Interv Radiol* 2005;16(7):973-979.

A prospective study of 46 consecutive patients with osteoporotic vertebral compression fracture found no difference in disease-specific heath-related quality-of-life outcomes in patients with vertebral height restoration, compared with those without vertebral height restoration.

53. Frey ME, Depalma MJ, Cifu DX, Bhagia SM, Carne W, Daitch JS: Percutaneous sacroplasty for osteoporotic sacral insufficiency fractures: A prospective, multicenter, observational pilot study. *Spine J* 2008;8(2):367-373.

54. Yang SC, Chen WJ, Yu SW, Tu YK, Kao YH, Chung KC: Revision strategies for complications and failure of vertebroplasties. *Eur Spine J* 2008;17(7):982-988.

Revision surgery after unsuccessful percutaneous vertebroplasty was studied in 22 patients. The revision strategies of repeat percutaneous vertebroplasty, posterior open surgery, and combined anterior and posterior open surgery are discussed.

55. Frankel BM, Jones T, Wang C: Segmental polymethylmethacrylate-augmented pedicle screw fixation in patients with bone softening caused by osteoporosis and metastatic tumor involvement: A clinical evaluation. *Neurosurgery* 2007;61(3):531-538.

56. Ataka H, Tanno T, Yamazaki M: Posterior instrumented fusion without neural decompression for incomplete neurological deficits following vertebral collapse in the osteoporotic thoracolumbar spine. *Eur Spine J* 2009;18(1):69-76.

57. Fuentes S, Blondel B, Metellus P, Adetchessi T, Gaudart J, Dufour H: Open kyphoplasty for management of severe osteoporotic spinal fractures. *Neurosurgery* 2009; 64(5, suppl 2):350-355.

58. Fuentes S, Métellus P, Pech-Gourg G, Adetchessi T, Dufour H, Grisoli F: Open kyphoplasty for management of metastatic and severe osteoporotic spinal fracture: Technical note. *J Neurosurg Spine* 2007;6(3):284-288.

59. Klineberg E, McHenry T, Bellabarba C, Wagner T, Chapman J: Sacral insufficiency fractures caudal to instrumented posterior lumbosacral arthrodesis. *Spine (Phila Pa 1976)* 2008;33(16):1806-1811.

60. Aydogan M, Ozturk C, Karatoprak O, Tezer M, Aksu N, Hamzaoglu A: The pedicle screw fixation with vertebroplasty augmentation in the surgical treatment of the severe osteoporotic spines. *J Spinal Disord Tech* 2009; 22(6):444-447.

61. Giele BM, Wiertsema SH, Beelen A, et al: No evidence for the effectiveness of bracing in patients with thoracolumbar fractures. *Acta Orthop* 2009;80(2):226-232.

62. Cosman F, Eriksen EF, Recknor C, et al: Effects of intravenous zoledronic acid plus subcutaneous teriparatide [rhPTH(1-34)] in postmenopausal osteoporosis. *J Bone Miner Res* 2011;26(3):503-511.

6: Spine Disorders

Chapter 46

Inflammatory Arthritides of the Spine

R. Todd Allen, MD, PhD   Vidyadhar V. Upasani, MD

Introduction

The inflammatory spine arthritides are rheumatoid arthritis (RA) and the seronegative spondyloarthropathies, which include ankylosing spondylitis (AS) and psoriatic, reactive, enteropathic, and diffuse idiopathic skeletal hyperostosis (DISH). These disorders affect the joints, bones, ligaments, tendons, and synovial tissues throughout the axial and appendicular skeleton. Some of the inflammatory spine arthritides have a predilection for a specific anatomic location (for example, upper cervical spine disease in RA). Recognizing the features that differentiate these arthritic conditions is essential for developing an appropriate treatment plan. Recent medical advances, primarily aimed at limiting inflammation and overall disease severity, have increased the effectiveness of nonsurgical treatments. Surgical intervention may be required to treat a neurologic deficit, instability, or spine deformity. A thorough understanding of disease pathology and surgical indications is required for surgical planning and decision making leading to a satisfactory outcome.

Rheumatoid Arthritis

Epidemiology

RA is a chronic, systemic, and progressive autoimmune inflammatory disease that causes pain, inflammation, and destruction in synovial joints and connective tissues. RA is present in 1% to 3% of the US population and is two to three times more common in women than in men.[1,2] The condition can occur at any age; most commonly, it begins during the fourth or fifth decade of life and is diagnosed at age 40 to 70 years.

Dr. Allen or an immediate family member serves as a paid consultant to or is an employee of Stryker; and has received research or institutional support from Biomet, Nuvasive, Synthes, and DePuy, a Johnson & Johnson company. Neither Dr. Upasani nor any immediate family member has received anything of value from or owns stock in a commercial company or institution related directly or indirectly to the subject of this chapter.

Aside from the metacarpophalangeal and metatarsophalangeal joints, the cervical spine is the site most commonly affected by RA; 60% to 80% of patients with RA have symptomatic cervical spine disease.[3-11] The lumbar spine is rarely involved. Synovitis induced by cervical spine RA and subsequent erosive changes typically occur in a patient with active peripheral RA. Although as many as 86% of patients with RA have radiographic evidence of cervical spine involvement, only approximately 10% of those patients have neurologic symptoms such as weakness or myelopathy.[10]

Pathogenesis

The characteristic pathology in RA is an erosive and hypertrophic synovitis, often described as a pannus. The synovitis is a chronic immune-mediated process in which initiation and perpetuation of the inflammation is dependent on a T-lymphocyte response to unknown antigens expressed on synovial cells. The synovium of patients with RA has an increased number of CD4+ T lymphocytes, which activate B lymphocytes to produce antibodies that interact with the synovial cell–expressed antigens. Concomitantly, the activation of macrophages results in the production of monokines, including tumor necrosis factor (TNF)–α and interleukin-1 (IL-1), which attract more lymphocytes and neutrophils and expand the inflammatory cascade. Angiogenic factors stimulate the ingrowth of new capillaries, thus expanding the pannus, vascularity, and inflammatory cycle. Arachidonic acid metabolites also contribute to the inflammatory response. Synovial cells are induced to release activated metalloproteinases such as procollagenase and progelatinase, which promote wide-scale destruction of the joint, bone, and surrounding tissues.

The main patterns of cervical instability that develop as a result of RA are atlantoaxial subluxation, subaxial subluxation, and atlantoaxial impaction. Rheumatoid synovitis at the C1-C2 joints and around the stabilizing transverse, alar, and apical ligaments between C1 and C2 leads to atlantoaxial instability. Atlantoaxial subluxation (an abnormal motion of C1 on C2) is the most common cervical instability pattern, and often it is associated with periodontoid pannus and progressive, systemic inflammation. Pannus forms at the synovial joint between the transverse ligament, the posterior surface of the anterior arch of the atlas, and the base of the odontoid, compressing the spinal cord or causing atlantoaxial subluxation by eroding the dens, the periodontoid ligamentous structures (the transverse, alar, and apical ligaments), and occasionally the lateral C1-C2 articular masses.

Atlantoaxial subluxation and/or frank instability (most commonly anterior) occurs in 50% to 70% of patients with RA cervical spine disease. Subluxation may occur posteriorly, rotationally, or laterally (more than 2 mm of C1-C2 lateral mass displacement).[3,4] Atlantoaxial subluxation of less than 3 mm usually is considered normal in an adult; 3 to 6 mm of subluxation suggests instability from disruption of the transverse ligament, and 9 mm or more suggests gross instability with disruption of the periodontoid-ligamentous and capsular structures.[5-7] Periodontoid pannus can result in myeloradiculopathy and sometimes in sudden death from mechanical compression or vascular impairment.[8] Continued instability may worsen periodontoid pannus and spinal cord compression. Decompression and stabilization have been shown to reverse the pannus buildup.[9]

Subaxial subluxation (between C3 and C7) is the second most common instability pattern, occurring in 7% to 29% of patients with RA.[10] Subaxial subluxation results from RA-induced laxity and inflammatory destruction of the facet and uncovertebral joints and the interspinous ligaments. Sagittal plane instability can occur with subaxial subluxation, commonly as a stairstep- or stepladder-type deformity at C3-C4 and C4-C5.[12,13] Painful rheumatoid-induced inflammation of the uncovertebral joints and disk (spondylodiskitis) can lead to instability and neural compression.

Atlantoaxial impaction (also called cranial settling or basilar invagination) occurs from RA-induced destruction of bone at the occipital condyles, C1 lateral masses, or C1-C2 articulation or from RA-induced destruction of cartilage at the atlantoaxial and occipitoatlantal joints. The relative upward (cranial) odontoid migration carries a risk of sudden death as the result of static or dynamic foramen magnum stenosis and compression of the medulla oblongata (the brainstem). Unilateral joint destruction can lead to head tilt and/or fixed rotational deformities. Obstructive hydrocephalus or syringomyelia also can occur.

Clinical Evaluation

Physical Examination
Systemically active RA is common among patients with cervical spine symptoms. On examination, the peripheral joints may be warm, swollen, and tender, with deformity and a decreased range of motion. Extensor surface nodules are present in approximately 20% of patients with systemically active RA. Most patients with rheumatoid involvement of the cervical spine do not have symptoms. Deep, aching neck pain is common among patients who are symptomatic. The pain generally is initiated or aggravated by neck movement. Patients with upper atlantoaxial pathology or cranial set-

tling may have suboccipital pain that can radiate into the occipital, temporal, and frontal regions. In patients with atlantoaxial subluxation, the C2 spinous process may become prominent with neck flexion. The head may be held asymmetrically, with a downward and lateral tilt believed to be caused by asymmetric destruction of the lateral atlantoaxial joints. Cervical instability may cause secondary impingement of the greater and lesser occipital nerves, often leading to occipital headaches. (The greater occipital nerve arises from the medial branch of the dorsal primary ramus of C2 and some fibers of C3. The lesser occipital nerve arises mainly from the lateral branch of the ventral ramus of C2.) Irritation of the C2 nerve roots may cause regional pain in the face, ear, or mastoid. A patient with C1-C2 subluxation may report a sensation of the head falling forward with neck flexion, as well as vertigo, loss of consciousness or syncope, nystagmus, dysarthria, or facial paresthesias.[14] The more profound symptoms include incontinence, dysphagia, convulsions, and hemiplegia. Patients with C1-C2 instability may report a clunking sensation in the neck with neck motion during spontaneous reduction of the subluxation with neck extension (the Sharp-Purser test).[15] C1-C2 subluxation has been associated with the presence of serum rheumatoid factor, hand and feet joint erosion, and subcutaneous nodules.

Subaxial cervical spine disease in a patient with RA may result in pain in the mid or lower cervical region, radiating to the clavicles at C3-C4, to the lateral aspects of the neck, or over the shoulders at C5-C6. Painful neck stiffness may evolve into a fixed deformity, called postinflammatory ankylosis. The extent of radiographically detected cervical spine destruction is not always correlated with the patient's symptoms.

Neurologic abnormality is present in approximately 10% of patients who have RA cervical spine involvement.[3-11] Myelopathy and vertebrobasilar dysfunction can result from mechanical or ischemic damage.[8] The patient's hands may feel numb and clumsy; tactile agnosia can occur with C6-C8 nerve compression.[16] Patients with isolated sensory deficits may attribute the symptoms to hand deformity or arthritis, and the result can be a potentially devastating delay in the diagnosis of cervical myelopathy.[17] Myelopathy may be manifested as a gradual deterioration in the patient's ambulatory status, eventually leading to wheelchair dependence. Deteriorating ambulatory status may be mistakenly attributed to large joint involvement rather than myelopathy. Other signs of neurologic dysfunction include paresthesias, spasticity, gait imbalance, incontinence, and quadriplegia. The Ranawat grading criteria can provide useful clinical information for the assessment of a patient with a neurologic deficit[18] (Table 1).

Laboratory Data and Diagnosis
The rheumatoid factor antibodies are directed against host antibodies and are present in approximately 80% of patients with RA. Antinuclear antibodies are present

6: Spine Disorders

Table 1

The Ranawat Criteria for Assessing Pain and Neurologic Status in the Rheumatoid Spine

Pain		Neurologic Status	
Grade	Description	Class	Description
0	None	I	No deficit
I	Mild, intermittent Relieved by aspirin analgesia	II	Subjective weakness with hyperreflexia and dysesthesias
II	Moderate Relieved by cervical collar	IIIA	Objective finding of paresis and long tract signs Ability to walk
III	Severe, not relieved by aspirin or collar	IIIB	Quadriparesis Inability to walk or feed self

in 30% of patients with RA.[14] Anemia and thrombocytosis are common in patients with active RA disease. Inflammatory markers including the erythrocyte sedimentation rate, C-reactive protein (CRP) level, and serum globulin level are abnormally elevated. Serial evaluation of the acute-phase CRP level can be useful for predicting an increased risk of joint deterioration or measuring the response to pharmacologic therapy. Patients with persistent elevation in CRP level are at risk for progressive cervical spine subluxations. The synovial fluid in patients with RA has a greater-than-normal number of white blood cells and protein levels, with a decreased level of glucose and poor viscosity. The anticyclic citrullinated protein antibodies (anti-CCP1 and anti-CCP2) may be as sensitive and more specific for RA than rheumatic factor antibodies.[19] Anti-CCP antibodies may be of greater diagnostic utility in early RA than rheumatoid factor antibodies. In early or established disease, patients who are seronegative for the rheumatoid factor but positive for anti-CCP antibodies have increased radiographic progression and poorer functional outcomes than other patients with RA.

Radiographic Evaluation

The common radiographic findings in RA cervical spine disease include narrow disk spaces with few or no osteophytes, erosive changes within the end plates and apophyseal joints, blurred facets, atlantoaxial subluxation of 12.5 mm or more, multiple subluxations at C2-C6, a pointed odontoid with erosions or cortical loss, basilar impression, and osteopenia. Initial lateral cervical spine radiographs are essential. Dynamic flexion-extension lateral radiographs help define subluxations as well as the anterior and posterior atlantodens intervals (ADIs). The anterior ADI is the distance between the anterior surface of the odontoid and the posteroinferior C1 tubercle; the normal ADI is 2.5 mm in adult women and 3.0 mm in men. An anterior ADI of 3 to 6 mm suggests instability in a patient who does not have RA. In a patient with RA, however, an anterior ADI of more than 5 mm marks true atlantoaxial instability, probably resulting from disruption of the

transverse ligament, rather than from laxity of ligamentous stabilizing structures such as the facet capsules, disk, or transverse and other ligamentous structures. In pediatric patients, an anterior ADI of more than 5 mm indicates instability. The posterior ADI, measured as the distance between the posterior odontoid process and anterior edge of the posterior ring of the atlas, most accurately represents the true space available for the spinal cord (SAC). The normal posterior ADI is greater than 14 mm. Neurologic recovery may occur after surgery in a patient with symptomatic RA and a posterior ADI of 10 to 14 mm. However, neurologic recovery is limited or nonexistent in a patient with RA, myelopathy, and a posterior ADI of less than 10 mm. The posterior ADI has more prognostic value than the anterior ADI during surgical planning for RA and spinal cord compression.[7]

The open-mouth radiographic view may show odontoid erosions and narrowed occipitoatlantal and atlantoaxial joints. Bony erosion is the most important factor in the development of severe lateral subluxation. Odontoid erosions and osteopenia may lead to an underestimation of the extent of vertical migration and cord or brainstem compression. The techniques for measuring cranial settling on lateral plain radiographs have varying sensitivity and specificity. The most accurate, reliable, and predictable definition of the extent of vertical migration is obtained by measuring the location of the atlas in relation to the odontoid process in the sagittal plane. This Clark station of the atlas should be used in combination with the Redlund-Johnell and Ranawat criteria, which were found to have a combined sensitivity of 94%, with a negative predictive value of 91% for diagnosing basilar invagination of the dens[20] (Figure 1). If one of the measurements is positive, the sensitivity is 94% for diagnosing superior migration of the odontoid; if all measurements are negative, there is only a 9% chance that the patient has superior migration of the odontoid.

Subaxial subluxation (translation of one vertebral body on another, from C3 to C7) of more than 3.5 mm may be visible on lateral radiographs. A segmental ky-

6: Spine Disorders

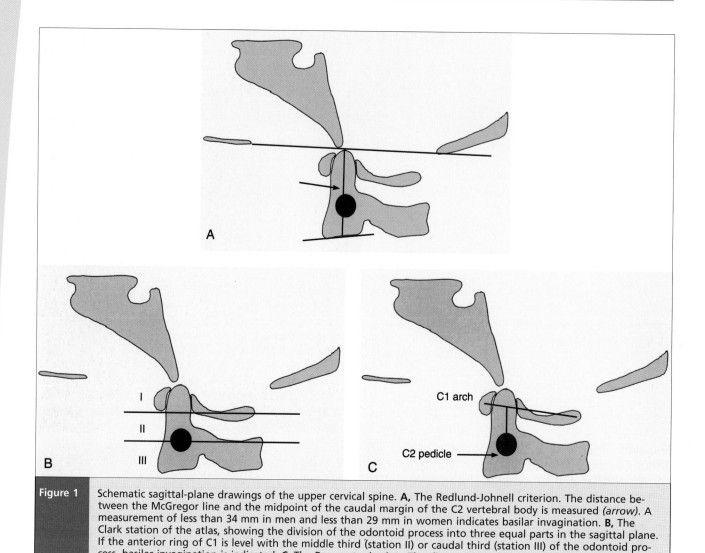

Figure 1   Schematic sagittal-plane drawings of the upper cervical spine. **A,** The Redlund-Johnell criterion. The distance between the McGregor line and the midpoint of the caudal margin of the C2 vertebral body is measured *(arrow)*. A measurement of less than 34 mm in men and less than 29 mm in women indicates basilar invagination. **B,** The Clark station of the atlas, showing the division of the odontoid process into three equal parts in the sagittal plane. If the anterior ring of C1 is level with the middle third (station II) or caudal third (station III) of the odontoid process, basilar invagination is indicated. **C,** The Ranawat criterion. The distance between the center of C2 and the transverse axis of C1 is measured along the axis of the odontoid process. A measurement of less than 15 mm in men or 13 mm in women indicates basilar invagination. (Reproduced with permission from Riew KD, Hilibrand AS, Palumbo MA, Sethi N, Bohlman HH: Diagnosing basilar invagination in the rheumatoid patient: The reliability of radiographic criteria. *J Bone Joint Surg Am* 2001;83:194-200.)

phosis of more than 10° also may indicate instability, although this finding is not specific to RA. In the later stages of RA cervical disease, multiple subaxial subluxations may appear in a staircase pattern on lateral radiographs (Figure 2).

In patients with neurologic findings, MRI is valuable in assessing soft-tissue abnormalities, pannus, the extent of neural compression, and signal changes suggestive of myelomalacia or cord edema. CT is preferred for evaluating the extent of bony destruction and ruling out anatomic variations that may preclude the use of certain bone fixation techniques. Magnetic resonance angiography should be considered. In a recent study, magnetic resonance angiography revealed a vertebral artery abnormality (occlusion, stenosis, or another anomaly) in 34% of patients with RA who had upper cervical lesions, compared with 2% of healthy subjects.[21] The severity of vertical subluxation was corre-

lated with the presence of a vertebral artery abnormality in the patients with RA. MRI can be used to assess the cervicomedullary angle; an angle of less than 135° is consistent with superior migration of the odontoid and may be correlated with signs of neurologic compression.[11]

Natural History and Prognosis

Because of the wide variance in the severity and age of onset of RA, it is difficult to predict the course and outcome of the disease. Patients who are resistant to multidrug therapies may have a progressive, disabling disease course with peripheral and axial joint destruction. Some patients respond favorably to medications even if their disease was diagnosed at a relatively late stage. Patients who are older than 70 years, have nodules, have a relatively long disease duration, and/or are seropositive are at increased risk for cervical spine disease.

Subluxations do not develop in all patients with RA who have cervical spine disease. In the RA-affected subaxial spine, myelopathy is associated with narrowing of the canal, relatively long disease duration, axial shortening, destruction of spinous processes, relatively young patient age, high-dosage corticosteroid use, and a late stage of disease. Sudden death is possible in RA cervical spine disease, particularly in patients with vertical subluxation, because the odontoid pannus can lead to devastating brainstem compression. Patients with RA vertical subluxation have eight times the mortality of other patients with RA.[3-14,22-25]

Early, aggressive medical therapies may alter the natural history of RA. In most patients, atlantoaxial instability is detected 2 to 10 years after disease onset. There is a strong correlation between cervical spine subluxation and peripheral erosions of the hands and feet. Approximately 10% of patients with cervical spine involvement eventually require surgery for instability and/or neurologic impairment. Traditionally, the natural history of RA spine disease not surgically treated has been progressive disability and a risk of sudden death, particularly in patients with myelopathy or vertical migration of the odontoid.[22] At an average 6-year follow-up, 16 of 21 medically treated patients with RA-associated upper cervical lesions (76%) had deteriorated neurologically.[23] All 16 patients became bedridden within 3 years of developing myelopathy and died within 7 years. The risk factors for progression of RA include mutilating articular disease, a history of high-dosage corticosteroid use, high seropositivity, rheumatoid subcutaneous nodules, vasculitis, and male sex. Other possible risk factors for RA cervical involvement include high CRP levels and human leukocyte antigen (HLA)–Dw2 or HLA-B27 positivity.

Treatment

Nonsurgical Management

The mainstay nonsurgical treatments for RA are physical therapy, patient education, and medications. Nonsteroidal anti-inflammatory drugs often are used to treat the symptoms for a few weeks while the diagnosis, workup, and treatment plan are formulated. Close serial rheumatologic follow-up is essential. The use of soft and rigid cervical collars can be helpful, particularly when flares arise in the early or intermediate disease stages or when late-stage instability occurs. A soft collar may be used for comfort but is not protective against subluxations. It is important to note that although rigid collars can help limit anterior subluxations and symptomatic instability, they do not allow spontaneous reduction of anterior atlantoaxial subluxations in extension. Patients with temporomandibular disease, a dental condition, or skin sensitivity often are unable to tolerate a rigid collar.

The number of patients who progress to advanced disease, the extent of their disability, and their overall level of bone destruction have been reduced by the early initiation of relatively new immune-modulating

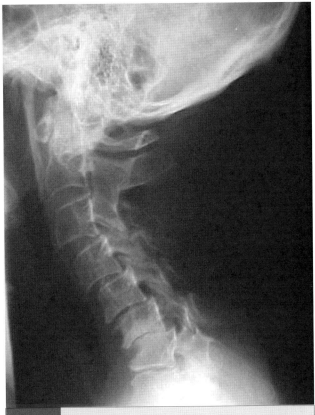

Figure 2 Lateral radiograph showing a staircase pattern created by multiple subaxial subluxations in a patient with rheumatoid arthritis.

biologic medications and other multidrug therapies, including those with significant adverse effects. An American College of Rheumatology treatment algorithm recommends the use of disease-modifying antirheumatic agents such as gold salts, penicillamine, and hydrochloroquine; corticosteroids; immunosuppressive agents such as methotrexate; and TNF-α and IL-1.

The initial pharmacologic therapy often includes methotrexate (7.5 to 15 mg per week), with or without the pyrimidine inhibitor leflunomide. The adverse effects include diarrhea, abnormal liver function tests, and hepatotoxicity. The use of methotrexate and leflunomide in combination limits medication tolerability and requires monitoring of liver function tests. Systemic corticosteroids are the most powerful agents for immediate relief of symptoms; they act by potently controlling RA-induced inflammation. However, toxicities and comorbidities associated with corticosteroid use, such as hypertension, obesity, diabetes, and cataract formation, limit their tolerability.

The anti–TNF-α therapies include etanercept as well as infliximab and adalimumab, which are monoclonal antibodies to TNF-α. These therapies are strong inhibitors of inflammation and are efficacious for treating RA disease. The main concern when using anti–TNF-α therapies is the risk of serious infection; in particular, inhibition of TNF-α has been associated with a reacti-

6: Spine Disorders

vation of tuberculosis. Immunosuppressive agents such as azathioprine, chlorambucil, cyclophosphamide, and cyclosporine may be used for RA that is severe or refractory to other medical therapies. Immunosuppressive agents are associated with severe adverse effects including cancer and anaplastic anemia, and therefore they are used only for a small number of RA patients.

Surgical Management

Surgery is indicated if a patient with RA cervical disease has intractable axial or radicular pain or progressive neurologic deficit or myelopathy. The radiographic indicators include an anterior ADI of 9 mm or more, a posterior ADI or SAC of less than 14 mm,[24] a mobile subaxial subluxation of more than 3.5 mm, a proximal odontoid migration (basilar invagination) rostral to the McGregor line of at least 5 mm, and cranial settling (most accurately assessed by the Clark station, Redlund-Johnell, and Ranawat criteria).[20] Stabilization and decompression should be considered if these indicators are present, even if the patient is asymptomatic. It is preferable to surgically correct myelopathy before it progresses to Ranawat grade III, because at this stage the neurologic improvement after surgery is limited at best.[25]

The goals of surgery include relief of pain, neurologic decompression and prevention of further neurologic decline, stabilization of all involved segments, and optimization of spine alignment. Thorough preoperative planning and imaging are essential for surgical success and a good patient outcome. Often the patient is medically fragile, with poor-quality bone, irreducible subluxations, deformity, and multiple medical comorbidities. Many patients require awake fiberoptic nasal or endotracheal intubation. In a patient who has myelopathy or instability or who requires reduction maneuvers, somatosensory-evoked and motor-evoked potentials are important for monitoring spinal cord function during positioning and surgery.

Preoperative skeletal traction with a halo ring or Gardner-Wells tongs should be considered for patients with severe basilar invagination.[26] The halo ring may be incorporated into the halo vest after surgery. Several studies found that pain, neurologic symptoms, and spine alignment can be improved by constant, carefully monitored preoperative traction for 3 days to 3 weeks. Midline longitudinal traction of 7 to 12 lb can be effective, but hyperflexion or hyperextension must be avoided. Neurologic monitoring is essential.

The choice of surgical procedure depends on the underlying pathologic process, anatomic limitations, and surgical goals. For atlantoaxial instability, the standard approach is posterior, using one of several techniques. Sublaminar or interspinous wiring with structural corticocancellous iliac crest bone grafts and external immobilization is the traditional fixation and has acceptable results. This construct has limited stability in rotation and axial loading but can augment newer fixation techniques. Fixation using a biomechanically su-

perior construct is preferable for a patient with poor bone quality or a patient with spine compression and irreducible C1-C2 subluxations requiring a C1 decompressive laminectomy. These constructs include transarticular C1-C2 screws and C1 lateral mass screws with C2 pars, pedicle, or interlaminar screws.[27] Rigid transarticular C1-C2 screw fixation leads to unilateral or bilateral fusion in as many as 95% or 100% of patients, respectively, and may obviate the need for postoperative immobilization. Transarticular screws carry a relatively high risk of vertebral artery injury, particularly if there is a large or aberrant foramen transversarium or vertebral artery anomaly.[28] Rigid fixation can be achieved with a theoretically lower risk to the vertebral artery through the Harms-Melcher technique of fixation with C1 lateral mass screws and C2 pars screws.[29] This technique has the disadvantage of possible bleeding from the venous lakes when the C1 lateral mass is exposed. C1-C2 screw-rod constructs and transarticular screws typically do not require postoperative halo traction, even after fixation to the occiput. Occipitocervical fixation using C2 translaminar screws may be less stable, however, and postoperative halo traction should be considered.

The surgical risk factors for future subluxations in the subaxial spine are excessive correction of the atlantoaxial angle, which is likely to cause loss of cervical lordosis, and an extension of fusion to C2-C3 after C1-C2 arthrodesis.[30] A stable C1-C2 fusion can relieve the neurologic symptoms of atlantoaxial subluxation associated with mild to moderate compression and pannus, cause some regression of the C2 pannus, and slow the cranial settling. In general, a posterior C1 laminectomy is added to the procedure if there is mild or moderate spinal cord compression and fixed atlantoaxial subluxation causing posterior cord compression from the ring of C1. If cranial settling has occurred, fixation to the occiput often is needed to prevent further settling and neurologic dysfunction. Several occipital fusion constructs are available. The relatively rigid modern screw, plate, or rod construct designs are biomechanically superior, easier to use than contoured plates or sublaminar wires, and less likely to collapse after surgery than loop-wire constructs.

The use of traction with close neurologic monitoring may be helpful. If reduction is achieved, it may be possible to proceed with fixation without decompression. If there is nonreducible settling or severe compression anterior to the cord, decompression often is required. An anterior C2 odontoid resection may be the best method for moderate or severe compression at the cervicomedullary junction, particularly if the compression is anterior and caused by pannus or a severely migrated odontoid. Transoral resections are associated with a risk of infection from mouth flora, and an extrapharyngeal approach therefore may be preferred. Unless there was an earlier posterior fusion, an anterior strut graft with iliac crest or fibula can be used between the clivus and C2 or C3 and followed by a posterior occipitocervical fusion. A mobile temporomandibular joint with a 2.5- to 3-cm opening is required for an anterior resection procedure. Head positioning is crucial; fixed extension with a relatively long occipitocervical construct can be debilitating, as can excessive kyphosis. Creating an occiput-C2 angle greater than 30° is associated with earlier subaxial subluxations, and intraoperative assessment during fusion is important for confirming that the angle is less than 30°[31] (Figure 3). The preoperative use of halo traction for physiologic head positioning may minimize the risk of swallowing-related complications after occipitocervical fusion. Occipitocervical fusion in patients with RA and upper cervical lesions may lead to an improvement in sleep apnea, particularly if the occipitant-C2 angle is positively changed.[32] A negative occipitant-C2 angle can result in upper airway narrowing, and therefore improving this angle and correcting kyphosis at the craniovertebral junction may relieve sleep apnea in a patient with RA.

Patients may require surgery for fixed or mobile subaxial subluxations greater than 3.5 mm. Mobile single or multilevel subluxations typically can be successfully treated with a posterior arthrodesis using lateral mass fixation with plate or screw-rod constructs. Some surgeons use traction to align mobile subluxations, followed by posterior arthrodesis. Fixed subluxations may be best treated by anterior cervical decompression and fusion. Supplemental posterior fixation should be strongly considered if the patient has multilevel subluxations or osteoporosis because anterior graft resorption can lead to anterior column collapse. Inclusion of all unstable levels in the initial fusion may reduce the risk of subsequent adjacent-level subluxations.

During C1-C2 or occipitocervical fixation, the surgical exposure should stay 1 to 1.5 cm midline on the C1 posterior ring to avoid the vertebral artery. Meticulous subperiosteal dissection at C1-C2 and packing with thrombin-Gelfoam (Pfizer, New York, NY) can minimize bleeding from the extensive venous plexus. The isthmus at C2 must be able to accommodate a 3.5-mm screw. C1-C2 transarticular screw placement is strongly discouraged if the C1 lateral mass is not reduced and aligned with the C2 facet or there is significant cranial settling with collapsed lateral masses or a comminuted fracture of C1 or C2. Intraoperative fluoroscopy and preoperative axial imaging are required to determine the feasibility of screw placement. The use of navigation techniques may increase safety.[33]

Ankylosing Spondylitis

AS is a spondyloarthropathy that is seronegative for the rheumatoid factor. This condition affects 1% to 2% of the Caucasian population. Although almost 90% of patients with AS are positive for the histocompatibility complex antigen HLA-B27, fewer than 10% of patients with this antigen have signs and symptoms of AS.[34,35] AS most likely is caused by an autoimmune host re-

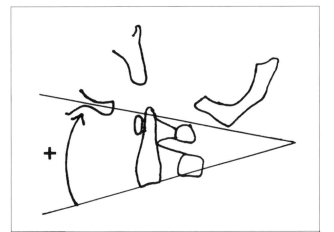

Figure 3 Schematic representation of the association between the occipital bone and the axis, as determined by the angle (curved arrow) made by the McGregor line and the inferior surface of the axis. (Reproduced with permission from Matsunaga S, Onishi T, Sakou T: Significance of occipitoaxial angle in subaxial lesion after occipitocervical fusion. *Spine (Phila Pa 1976)* 2001;26: 161-165.)

sponse to an environmental pathogen in a genetically susceptible individual.

Unlike RA, which primarily causes synovitis, AS is characterized by enthesitis. The inflammation occurs at an enthesis, which is the insertion of a tendon, ligament, or muscle into bone. The condition most commonly begins in the axial skeleton, affecting the sacroiliac joints, spine apophyseal joints, and symphysis pubis. Ossification of the surrounding soft-tissue structures eventually results in joint ankylosis. The hip, knee, shoulder, or elbow is involved in approximately 30% of patients with AS.

Clinical Evaluation
Four times as many men as women are affected by AS, most commonly in the third decade of life.[36] Back pain and stiffness, usually beginning in the lumbosacral spine, are present in almost all patients. Patients occasionally report sciatica, which probably originates as sacroiliitis or piriformis muscle spasms. Involvement of the thoracic and cervical spine occurs later in the disease. Thoracic spine disease can limit motion at the costovertebral joints, resulting in reduced chest expansion and impaired pulmonary function. The symptoms of cervical spine involvement may include neck pain and stiffness as well as intermittent episodes of torticollis.

Physical Examination
Both ankylosis of the spine in kyphosis and flexion deformity of the hips contribute to a loss of sagittal balance in patients with AS. Examination of the patient in the standing, sitting, and supine positions allows the surgeon to determine whether the major component of the deformity is in the hips, the thoracolumbar or lum-

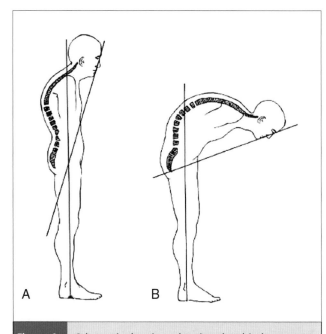

Figure 4   Schematic drawings showing the chin-brow–to-vertical angle, as used to measure the extent of kyphosis in a patient with a neutral or fixed neck (**A**) and full hip and knee extension (**B**). (Reproduced with permission from Kostuik JP: Ankylosing spondylitis: Surgical treatment, in Frymoyer JW, ed: *The Adult Spine: Principles and Practice.* New York, NY, Raven Press, 1991, p 724.)

bar spine, or the cervicothoracic spine. The chin-brow–to-vertical angle, measured clinically or from a standing full-spine lateral radiograph, is helpful in preoperative planning (Figure 4). The ideal chin-brow–to-vertical angle is 0°; there is a significant relationship between correction of this angle and subjective measures of clinical success.

The Schober test is used to evaluate lumbar stiffness. With the patient standing upright, points are drawn in the midline of the lower back 10 cm above and 5 cm below the lumbosacral junction. Less than 5 cm of excursion between the two points with full forward flexion is believed to indicate reduced spine mobility. Ankylosis of the costovertebral joints is indicated by chest expansion of less than 2.5 cm, as measured at the fourth intercostal space.[37]

Several provocative tests are used to assess pain at the sacroiliac joint. Pain can be elicited with flexion-abduction and external rotation of the ipsilateral hip joint (the FABER test). The Yoeman test elicits pain during hyperextension of the thigh when the patient is prone. The Gaenslen test places pressure on a hyperextended thigh with a contralateral flexed hip. A local anesthetic injection into the sacroiliac joint under fluoroscopic guidance often is the most sensitive diagnostic test.

A fracture should be suspected if a patient with AS has acute neck or back pain. The most common site

of fracture is the cervicothoracic or thoracolumbar junction, and such a fracture often involves all three columns of the spine. CT often is required to clearly delineate the fracture, particularly if it is at the cervicothoracic junction. MRI is used to rule out epidural hematoma in a patient with neurologic findings.

Laboratory and Radiographic Diagnosis
The sacroiliac joint usually is involved early in the disease process. The radiographic criteria for diagnosing AS include abnormalities of the sacroiliac joint such as erosions, sclerosis, narrowing, osteophyte formation, and partial or complete ankylosis. The Ferguson pelvic view, in which the x-ray beam is directed 15° to 30° cephalad, allows evaluation of the anterior portion of the sacroiliac joint. Other characteristic radiographic findings include squared anterior vertebral bodies secondary to periostosis, fusion of the apophyseal joints, and vertical calcifications of the anulus fibrosus and anteroposterior longitudinal ligaments (resulting in a so-called bamboo spine). Laboratory tests reveal nonspecific elevations in the erythrocyte sedimentation rate and CRP level and usually have little diagnostic value.

Treatment
Medical Management
The consensus recommendations on the medical management of AS include the use of nonsteroidal anti-inflammatory drugs or selective cyclooxygenase-2 inhibitors as the first choice for treating pain and stiffness.[38] Nonpharmacologic treatments such as physical therapy, exercise, and patient education can also be beneficial in maintaining function.[39,40] The use of oral steroids is not recommended, but local injections of a steroid at sites of inflammation can be considered. If these treatments do not sufficiently control disease activity, the use of anti-TNF drugs such as infliximab, etanercept, and adalimumab can be considered. Several studies found that the use of TNF blockers led to significant clinical improvement in patients with AS. The severity of symptoms was reduced in 54.5% of patients who received 40 mg of adalimumab every 2 weeks, compared with 12.5% of control subjects, with efficacy sustained over 52 weeks in all patients who completed the study.[41] Switching TNF inhibitors was successful in patients who had a temporary positive response to an earlier TNF inhibitor. At 2- and 5-year follow-up, disease activity was slowed in most patients with AS.[42-44]

Fracture Management
In a patient with an acute fracture, low-weight traction can be used to facilitate fracture reduction and prevent further injury to neurovascular structures. Definitive management with an external brace or halo vest may be indicated if the fracture appears to be relatively stable, the patient has no neurologic deficits, and fracture reduction can be easily obtained. If fracture reduction is not possible, internal fixation should be performed with or without decompression, depending on the pa-

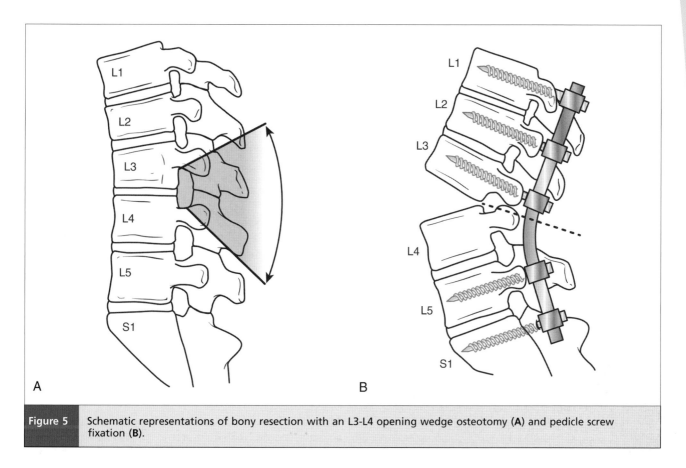

Figure 5 Schematic representations of bony resection with an L3-L4 opening wedge osteotomy (**A**) and pedicle screw fixation (**B**).

tient's neurologic status. Most fractures can be fixed from a posterior approach using screws or interspinous wiring. Additional anterior stabilization may be required if the anterior column is compromised secondary to a pseudarthrosis or osteopenia. A high incidence of complications, including deformity progression, neurologic compromise, nonunion, hardware failure, and infection, has been reported in patients with AS who sustain a traumatic spine fracture.[45]

Spine Deformity Management

The goals of surgical correction in patients with progressive AS deformity include restoration of sagittal balance and horizontal gaze. Primary thoracic and lumbar deformity is treated using osteotomy in the lumbar spine. Lumbar osteotomies avoid the thoracic cage, reduce the risk of injury to the spinal cord, and are believed to achieve greater sagittal plane correction because of the long lever arm. As the osteotomy site progresses caudally, a greater correction in sagittal balance is obtained without changing the angle of correction. However, an iatrogenically created abnormal gaze angle can be created (See chapter 31, Figure 17).

Three types of osteotomy are commonly used. One technique is an opening wedge osteotomy that hinges on the posterior edge of the vertebral body and often ruptures the anterior longitudinal ligament[46] (Figure 5). The second technique is a multisegment opening osteotomy that involves removal of less bone over more levels

to gradually decrease the kyphosis and prevent rupture of the anterior longitudinal ligament.[47] The third technique is a closing wedge osteotomy that can be performed by using an anterior cortical hinge with a transpedicular decancelization procedure and resection of the posterior elements[48] (Figure 6). This type of osteotomy is preferred for patients with AS because it results in a greater deformity correction (30° to 40° per level) and possibly in more rapid consolidation secondary to direct bony apposition.[49]

Deformity in the cervicothoracic spine cannot be adequately treated with lumbar osteotomies. A spinal osteotomy for the treatment of cervicothoracic deformity can be done at C7-T1,[50] where the vertebral arteries are extraosseous, the canal diameter is relatively large, and the nerve root mobility (at C8) is greater than at the upper cervical levels. Undercorrection of the chin-brow–to-vertical angle to approximately 10° usually is recommended to avoid an upward gaze and allow the patient to see the floor while walking. A wide decompression at C7 and T1, including dorsal unroofing of both C8 nerve roots, resection of C7 lateral masses, and resection of portions of the C7 and T1 pedicles, is important for avoiding iatrogenic injury to the spinal cord (Figure 7). Sublaminar hooks, lateral mass screws, or pedicle screws are used to provide rigid stabilization and prevent translation. Postoperative immobilization in a halo vest should be considered, especially if the patient has osteoporosis.

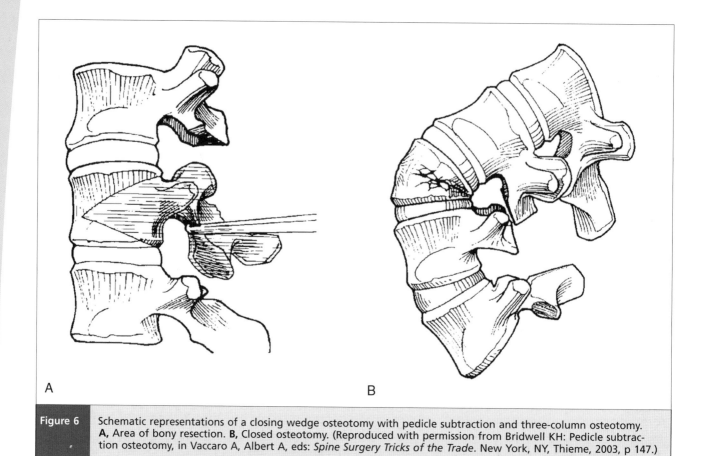

A   B

Figure 6	Schematic representations of a closing wedge osteotomy with pedicle subtraction and three-column osteotomy. **A,** Area of bony resection. **B,** Closed osteotomy. (Reproduced with permission from Bridwell KH: Pedicle subtraction osteotomy, in Vaccaro A, Albert A, eds: *Spine Surgery Tricks of the Trade*. New York, NY, Thieme, 2003, p 147.)

Diffuse Idiopathic Skeletal Hyperostosis

DISH is characterized by calcification and ossification of soft tissues, primarily the ligaments and entheses. Spine involvement results in flowing mantles of ossification of the anterior longitudinal ligament and, to a lesser extent, the paravertebral connective tissue and the peripheral part of the anulus fibrosus. Four contiguous vertebral bodies must be involved for a diagnosis of DISH. AS and DISH can be readily differentiated using certain clinical and radiographic factors (Table 2). CT of the sacroiliac joints differentiates hyperostotic joint changes from those associated with joint erosion and fusion. Occasionally, a patient has both AS and DISH.

Psoriatic Arthritis

As many as 23% of patients with psoriatic arthritis have associated spine disease. Most patients with psoriatic spondyloarthropathy are men. Typically, patients with axial disease have a later onset of symptoms; at least 25% have unilateral or bilateral sacroiliac joint inflammation (sacroiliitis).[51] Psoriatic arthritis typically affects only one side of the body. This characteristic can be useful in making the diagnosis. Axial disease may ascend the spine in a pattern similar to that of AS, and

patients with axial psoriatic arthritis are likely to be HLA-B27 positive.

The features of psoriatic arthritis on standard radiographs include asymmetric vertebral body involvement, facet joint arthrosis, and anterior nonmarginal osteophytes. The treatment is aimed at controlling joint inflammation and the associated pain and bony destruction. Early, aggressive physical therapy and medical management are the mainstay of treatment algorithms, particularly for axial skeleton disease. Medications used to treat peripheral arthritis, including anti-inflammatory and immunosuppressive drugs and TNF-α inhibitors, are being studied for the treatment of axial disease.

Reactive Arthritis

Reactive arthritis is an aseptic inflammatory condition leading to peripheral joint and axial skeleton inflammation, pain, and stiffness. The etiology of reactive arthritis probably is an immunologic reaction to a systemic infection or another environmental factor in a genetically predisposed host. In 60% to 80% of affected individuals, reactive arthritis is associated with HLA-B27. Reactive arthritis primarily affects the lower extremity joints and low back. Cervical spine involvement is rare.

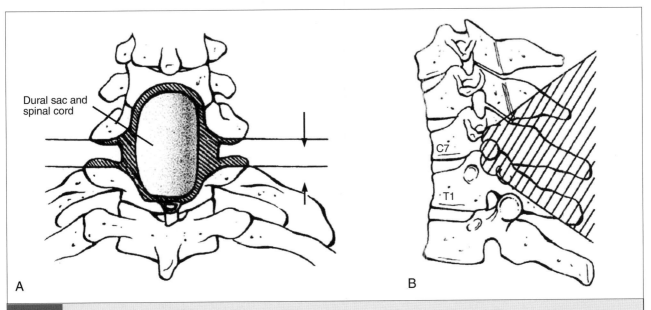

Figure 7 Posterior **(A)** and lateral **(B)** schematic drawings showing the bony resection required for cervicothoracic osteotomy. The pedicles are undercut to avoid impingement of the C8 root; the cut surface is beveled on its deep surface to avoid dural impingement. The upper and lower limits of the osteotomy are shown *(lines, arrows)*. (Adapted with permission from Simmons EH: The cervical spine in ankylosing spondylitis, in Bridwell KH, DeWald RL, eds: *The Textbook of Spinal Surgery*, ed 3. Philadelphia, PA, Lippincott-Raven, 1997, p 1143.)

Table 2

The Clinical and Radiographic Features of AS and DISH

Feature	AS	DISH
Age at onset	< 40 years	> 50 years
Pain	Common	Unusual
Sacroiliac joint erosion	Common	Absent
Synovial sacroiliac joint obliteration	Common	Unusual
Apophyseal joint obliteration	Common	Absent
Anterior longitudinal ligament ossification	Unusual	Common

Sulfasalazine can be used to substantially decrease spine pain, joint pain, and swelling in patients with reactive arthritis. Oral corticosteroids can be helpful but are less effective than for patients with RA. Immunosuppressive drugs such as methotrexate typically are used to treat otherwise uncontrollable progressive joint disease and its extensive skin manifestations. Controversy remains concerning the role of antibiotic therapy in treating acute reactive arthritis.

bowel disease and generally is nondeforming. Axial enteropathic arthritis usually is independent of bowel inflammatory activity, however, and may have a hereditary component; approximately 70% of patients are HLA-B27 positive. The nonsurgical treatment of enteropathic spondylitis is similar to that of AS. The use of TNF-α inhibitors may modify the course of the disease, but the prognosis primarily depends on the severity of the bowel disease.

Enteropathic Arthritis

The term enteropathic arthritis refers to inflammatory axial and peripheral arthritis occurring in association with an inflammatory bowel disease such as Crohn disease or ulcerative colitis. The course of peripheral arthritis typically follows the activity of the underlying

Summary

The inflammatory spine arthritides are RA and the seronegative spondyloarthropathies including AS, DISH, and psoriatic, reactive, and enteropathic arthritis. The resulting inflammation in the synovial tissue, joints, and ligaments produces disorder-specific pathologic

6: Spine Disorders

patterns in the axial and appendicular skeleton. Recognizing the features that differentiate these conditions is essential to developing an algorithm for workup and treatment. RA is characterized by upper cervical instability, pannus, neural element compression, and axial and peripheral deformities. AS is characterized by enthesitis, early sacroiliitis, a flowing bamboo spine, and kyphosis-inducing features producing rigid deformities of the spine and hips. Psoriatic arthritis is characterized by one-sidedness and an ability to ascend the spine like AS, but with peripheral manifestations and nonmarginal osteophytes that differ from AS radiographically.

Recent advances in pharmacologic management have improved the ability to limit inflammation and overall disease severity. Disease-modifying antirheumatic agents such as gold salts, penicillamine, and hydrochloroquine; corticosteroids; immunosuppressive agents such as methotrexate; and immune modulators such as TNF-α and IL-1 are being used in combination early in treatment.

Surgical intervention may be required for a patient with a neurologic deficit, instability, pain, or spine deformity. A thorough understanding of the disease pathology and surgical indications is essential for preoperative planning, surgical decision making, and satisfactory patient outcomes.

Annotated References

1. Helmick CG, Felson DT, Lawrence RC, et al: Estimates of the prevalence of arthritis and other rheumatic conditions in the United States: Part I. *Arthritis Rheum* 2008;58(1):15-25.

   Published analyses were reviewed to derive estimates of the prevalence of arthritis and other rheumatic conditions.

2. Silman A: Rheumatoid arthritis, in Silman A, Hochberg MC, eds: *Epidemiology of the Rheumatic Diseases.* New York, NY, Oxford University Press, 2001, pp 31-71.

3. Bogduk N, Major GA, Carter J: Lateral subluxation of the atlas in rheumatoid arthritis: A case report and postmortem study. *Ann Rheum Dis* 1984;43(2):341-346.

4. Rana NA: Natural history of atlanto-axial subluxation in rheumatoid arthritis. *Spine (Phila Pa 1976)* 1989; 14(10):1054-1056.

5. Papadopoulos SM, Dickman CA, Sonntag VK: Atlantoaxial stabilization in rheumatoid arthritis. *J Neurosurg* 1991;74(1):1-7.

6. Rana NA, Hancock DO, Taylor AR, Hill AG: Atlantoaxial subluxation in rheumatoid arthritis. *J Bone Joint Surg Br* 1973;55(3):458-470.

7. Weissman BN, Aliabadi P, Weinfeld MS, Thomas WH, Sosman JL: Prognostic features of atlantoaxial sublux-

ation in rheumatoid arthritis patients. *Radiology* 1982; 144(4):745-751.

8. Delamarter RB, Bohlman HH: Postmortem osseous and neuropathologic analysis of the rheumatoid cervical spine. *Spine (Phila Pa 1976)* 1994;19(20):2267-2274.

9. Larsson EM, Holtås S, Zygmunt S: Pre- and postoperative MR imaging of the craniocervical junction in rheumatoid arthritis. *AJR Am J Roentgenol* 1989;152(3): 561-566.

10. Halla JT, Hardin JG, Vitek J, Alarcón GS: Involvement of the cervical spine in rheumatoid arthritis. *Arthritis Rheum* 1989;32(5):652-659.

11. Narváez JA, Narváez J, Serrallonga M, et al: Cervical spine involvement in rheumatoid arthritis: Correlation between neurological manifestations and magnetic resonance imaging findings. *Rheumatology (Oxford)* 2008; 47(12):1814-1819.

    A retrospective review of 41 consecutive patients found a strong correlation between the development of neurologic dysfunction and MRI identification of atlantoaxial spinal canal stenosis, especially in patients with evidence of upper cervical cord or brainstem compression and subaxial myelopathy changes.

12. Braun J, Bollow M, Sieper J: Radiologic diagnosis and pathology of the spondyloarthropathies. *Rheum Dis Clin North Am* 1998;24(4):697-735.

13. Smith PH, Sharp J, Kellgren JH: Natural history of rheumatoid cervical subluxations. *Ann Rheum Dis* 1972;31(3):222-223.

14. Gordon DA, Hastings DR: Clinical features of rheumatoid arthritis, in Hochberg MC, Silman AJ, Smolen JS, eds: *Rheumatology*, ed 3. Edinburgh, Scotland, Mosby, 2003, pp 765-780.

15. Sharp J, Purser DW: Spontaneous atlanto-axial dislocation in ankylosing spondylitis and rheumatoid arthritis. *Ann Rheum Dis* 1961;20(1):47-77.

16. Chang MH, Liao KK, Cheung SC, Kong KW, Chang SP: "Numb, clumsy hands" and tactile agnosia secondary to high cervical spondylotic myelopathy: A clinical and electrophysiological correlation. *Acta Neurol Scand* 1992;86(6):622-625.

17. Zeidman SM, Ducker TB: Rheumatoid arthritis: Neuroanatomy, compression, and grading of deficits. *Spine (Phila Pa 1976)* 1994;19(20):2259-2266.

18. Ranawat CS, O'Leary P, Pellicci P, Tsairis P, Marchisello P, Dorr L: Cervical spine fusion in rheumatoid arthritis. *J Bone Joint Surg Am* 1979;61(7):1003-1010.

19. Avouac J, Gossec L, Dougados M: Diagnostic and predictive value of anti-cyclic citrullinated protein antibodies in rheumatoid arthritis: A systematic literature review. *Ann Rheum Dis* 2006;65(7):845-851.

A systematic literature analysis evaluated the use of anti-CCP1 and anti-CCP2 as diagnostic markers for RA. Second-generation anti-CCP was found to have sensitivity close to that of rheumatoid factor, with higher specificity, for distinguishing RA from other rheumatic diseases. Anti-CCP antibodies were highly predictive of the future development of RA in healthy subjects and patients with undifferentiated arthritis.

20. Riew KD, Hilibrand AS, Palumbo MA, Sethi N, Bohlman HH: Diagnosing basilar invagination in the rheumatoid patient: The reliability of radiographic criteria. *J Bone Joint Surg Am* 2001;83(2):194-200.

21. Zenmyo M, Ijiri K, Sasaki H, et al: Magnetic resonance angiography for vertebral artery evaluation in rheumatoid arthritis patients. *Neurosurgery* 2010;66(6):1174-1180.

    The radiologic features of vertebral artery displacement and occlusion associated with RA were examined using magnetic resonance angiography. The incidence of vertebral artery abnormality was 34%, with occlusion in 8.5%, stenosis in 19.1%, and another anomaly in 6.4% of patients.

22. Sunahara N, Matsunaga S, Mori T, Ijiri K, Sakou T: Clinical course of conservatively managed rheumatoid arthritis patients with myelopathy. *Spine (Phila Pa 1976)* 1997;22(22):2603-2608.

23. Matsunaga S, Sakou T, Onishi T, et al: Prognosis of patients with upper cervical lesions caused by rheumatoid arthritis: Comparison of occipitocervical fusion between c1 laminectomy and nonsurgical management. *Spine (Phila Pa 1976)* 2003;28(14):1581-1587.

24. Oda T, Yonenobu K, Fujimura Y, et al: Diagnostic validity of space available for the spinal cord at C1 level for cervical myelopathy in patients with rheumatoid arthritis. *Spine (Phila Pa 1976)* 2009;34(13):1395-1398.

    The diagnostic validity of the SAC at C1 for myelopathy was retrospectively evaluated in 140 patients with upper cervical RA and myelopathy as well as 99 patients with upper cervical RA but no associated myelopathy. SAC was a reliable parameter for relating myelopathy in patients with upper cervical subluxations in RA. For screening purposes in patients at high risk for myelopathy, a SAC of 14 mm or less was recommended as a cutoff point.

25. Wolfs JF, Kloppenburg M, Fehlings MG, van Tulder MW, Boers M, Peul WC: Neurologic outcome of surgical and conservative treatment of rheumatoid cervical spine subluxation: A systematic review. *Arthritis Rheum* 2009;61(12):1743-1752.

    A systematic literature review was performed to determine Ranawat neurologic outcome and survival time after treatment for RA. Twenty-five observational studies but no randomized clinical studies were found. Neurologic outcomes were better after surgical than nonsurgical treatment in all patients with cervical spine involvement. In asymptomatic patients with no neurologic impairment, the outcomes were similar.

26. Bagley CA, Witham TF, Pindrik JA, et al: Assuring optimal physiologic craniocervical alignment and avoidance of swallowing-related complications after occipitocervical fusion by preoperative halo vest placement. *J Spinal Disord Tech* 2009;22(3):170-176.

    A retrospective review evaluated postoperative complications after occipitocervical fusion in 12 patients with preoperative halo immobilization. All patients achieved satisfactory head position, and there were no halo complications. One patient had transient dysphagia not requiring intervention.

27. Nagaria J, Kelleher MO, McEvoy L, Edwards R, Kamel MH, Bolger C: C1-C2 transarticular screw fixation for atlantoaxial instability due to rheumatoid arthritis: A seven-year analysis of outcome. *Spine (Phila Pa 1976)* 2009;34(26):2880-2885.

    An observational study reported the surgical and radiographic outcomes of 37 patients with RA atlantoaxial instability after transarticular screw fixation. At a minimum 7-year follow-up, 90% of patients with neck and suboccipital pain had a more than 50% improvement in visual analog score. There was bony fusion in 97%. Transarticular screws were bilateral in 33 patients and unilateral in 4 patients. Ranawat grades and Myelopathy Disability Index scores were significantly improved.

28. Hirano K, Matsuyama Y, Sakai Y, et al: Surgical complications and management of occipitothoracic fusion for cervical destructive lesions in RA patients. *J Spinal Disord Tech* 2010;23(2):121-126.

    A retrospective review of patients with myelopathy and/or occipitocervical pain caused by destructive cervical lesions compared the use of unit rods (38 patients) to cervical pedicle screws (18 patients). At a mean 36.2-month follow-up, 82% of patients had neurologic improvement of at least one grade on the modified Ranawat scale. Perioperative complications occurred in 28.6%, thoracic spine lesions in 19.6%, implant failure in 23.2%, and surgical site infection in 14.3%. There was a tendency for fracture or pedicle screw pullout to occur at the lowest level of the fusion area.

29. Harms J, Melcher RP: Posterior C1-C2 fusion with polyaxial screw and rod fixation. *Spine (Phila Pa 1976)* 2001;26(22):2467-2471.

30. Ishii K, Matsumoto M, Takahashi Y, et al: Risk factors for development of subaxial subluxations following atlantoaxial arthrodesis for atlantoaxial subluxations in rheumatoid arthritis. *Spine (Phila Pa 1976)* 2010;35(16):1551-1555.

    Fifty-eight patients with RA were retrospectively reviewed an average of 137 months after C1-C2 fusion for atlantoaxial subluxation. Excessive correction of the atlantoaxial angle was likely to cause loss of cervical lordosis and result in the development of subaxial subluxations. C3-C4 subluxation was likely to occur after excessive fusion at C2-C3.

31. Matsunaga S, Onishi T, Sakou T: Significance of occipitoaxial angle in subaxial lesion after occipitocervical fusion. *Spine (Phila Pa 1976)* 2001;26(2):161-165.

6: Spine Disorders

32. Ataka H, Tanno T, Miyashita T, Isono S, Yamazaki M: Occipitocervical fusion has potential to improve sleep apnea in patients with rheumatoid arthritis and upper cervical lesions. *Spine (Phila Pa 1976)* 2010;35(19): E971-E975.

Eight consecutive patients with RA upper cervical lesions were retrospectively studied to analyze the factors contributing to the development of sleep apnea. All patients with postoperative improvement in sleep apnea had a positive change of more than 5° in the occiput-C2 angle. The authors concluded that a negative occiput-C2 angle may cause upper airway narrowing, increasing the severity of sleep apnea. Occipitocervical fusion with correction of kyphosis at the craniovertebral junction has the potential to improve sleep apnea in patients with RA.

33. Krauss WE, Bledsoe JM, Clarke MJ, Nottmeier EW, Pichelmann MA: Rheumatoid arthritis of the craniovertebral junction. *Neurosurgery* 2010;66(3, suppl):83-95.

An exhaustive literature review was conducted on the modern surgical management of the three major manifestations of cervical spine RA: basilar invagination, atlantoaxial instability, and subaxial subluxations. Transoral odontoidectomy, occipital cervical fusion, and atlantoaxial fusion are described in detail, with navigation during these procedures.

34. West HF: The aetiology of ankylosing spondylitis. *Ann Rheum Dis* 1949;8(2):143-148.

35. Lawrence JS: The prevalence of arthritis. *Br J Clin Pract* 1963;17:699-705.

36. Gran JT, Husby G, Hordvik M: Prevalence of ankylosing spondylitis in males and females in a young middle-aged population of Tromsø, northern Norway. *Ann Rheum Dis* 1985;44(6):359-367.

37. Thomas E, Silman AJ, Papageorgiou AC, Macfarlane GJ, Croft PR: Association between measures of spinal mobility and low back pain: An analysis of new attenders in primary care. *Spine (Phila Pa 1976)* 1998; 23(3):343-347.

38. Zochling J, van der Heijde D, Dougados M, Braun J: Current evidence for the management of ankylosing spondylitis: A systematic literature review for the ASAS/EULAR management recommendations in ankylosing spondylitis. *Ann Rheum Dis* 2006;65(4):423-432.

A systematic review formed the evidence base for the Assessment of Spondyloarthritis International Society–European League Against Rheumatism (ASAS/EULAR) recommendations for managing AS. Level IB evidence supported the use of nonsteroidal anti-inflammatory drugs and cyclooxygenase-2 inhibitors for symptomatic treatment. Nonpharmacologic treatments such as physical therapy were supported for maintaining function. Level IB evidence supported the use of TNF inhibitors for spine pain and function in the short term. Level IV evidence supported surgical interventions in specific patients.

39. Dagfinrud H, Kvien TK, Hagen KB: Physiotherapy interventions for ankylosing spondylitis. *Cochrane Database Syst Rev* 2004;4:CD002822.

40. Braun J: Therapy of spondyloarthritides. *Adv Exp Med Biol* 2009;649:133-147.

The clinical and genetic features of spondyloarthropathies affecting the spine and peripheral joints are discussed, with diagnostic and prognostic factors. Medical management of AS is emphasized, including the importance of physical therapy.

41. van der Heijde D, Pangan AL, Schiff MH, et al: Adalimumab effectively reduces the signs and symptoms of active ankylosing spondylitis in patients with total spinal ankylosis. *Ann Rheum Dis* 2008;67(9):1218-1221.

In a prospective randomized study, 315 patients with active AS received 40 mg of adalimumab or a placebo every 2 weeks, followed by open-label use of adalimumab for as long as 5 years. Two-year efficacy and safety data revealed rapid and clinically significant improvement in the signs and symptoms of active disease.

42. Braun J, Brandt J, Listing J, et al: Treatment of active ankylosing spondylitis with infliximab: A randomised controlled multicentre trial. *Lancet* 2002;359(9313): 1187-1193.

43. Calin A, Dijkmans BA, Emery P, et al: Outcomes of a multicentre randomised clinical trial of etanercept to treat ankylosing spondylitis. *Ann Rheum Dis* 2004; 63(12):1594-1600.

44. van der Heijde D, Dijkmans B, Geusens P, et al: Efficacy and safety of infliximab in patients with ankylosing spondylitis: Results of a randomized, placebo-controlled trial (ASSERT). *Arthritis Rheum* 2005;52(2):582-591.

In a randomized study, 201 patients received 5 mg/kg infliximab, and 78 received a placebo. After 24 weeks, infliximab was well tolerated and clinically effective in improving subjective, chest expansion, and physical component summary scores on the Medical Outcomes Study Short Form-36 Health Survey.

45. Olerud C, Frost A, Bring J: Spinal fractures in patients with ankylosing spondylitis. *Eur Spine J* 1996;5(1):51-55.

46. Smith-Petersen MN, Larson CB, Aufranc OE: Osteotomy of the spine for correction of flexion deformity in rheumatoid arthritis. *Clin Orthop Relat Res* 1969;66: 6-9.

47. Wilson MJ, Turkell JH: Multiple spinal wedge osteotomy: Its use in a case of Marie-Strumpell spondylitis. *Am J Surg* 1949;77(6):777-782.

48. Thomasen E: Vertebral osteotomy for correction of kyphosis in ankylosing spondylitis. *Clin Orthop Relat Res* 1985;194:142-152.

49. Gill JB, Levin A, Burd T, Longley M: Corrective osteotomies in spine surgery. *J Bone Joint Surg Am* 2008; 90(11):2509-2520.

A review of the Smith-Peterson, pedicle subtraction, and cervical extension osteotomies and vertebral column resectioning found that spine osteotomies to treat a variety of disorders had a high patient satisfaction rate and good functional outcomes.

50. Urist MR: Osteotomy of the cervical spine: Report of a case of ankylosing rheumatoid spondylitis. *J Bone Joint Surg Am* 1958;40(4):833-843.

51. Gladman DD, Antoni C, Mease P, Clegg DO, Nash P: Psoriatic arthritis: Epidemiology, clinical features, course, and outcome. *Ann Rheum Dis* 2005;64(suppl 2): ii14-ii17.

This is an overview of psoriatic arthritis, an unusual inflammatory condition associated with psoriasis.

6: Spine Disorders

Spine Care and US Health Policy

SECTION EDITOR
RAJ D. RAO, MD

Chapter 47

Spine Care and Health Policy in the United States

Alok D. Sharan, MD   Raj D. Rao, MD

Introduction

The US health care system is undergoing a process of transformation. The excellent health care traditionally provided in the United States has resulted from exemplary training of medical professionals as well as the use of leading technologies, but the cost of providing this care is increasing at an unsustainable rate. The estimated $2.26 trillion spent on health care in 2007 amounted to approximately 16% of the US gross domestic product.[1] Despite spending at this level, 50.7 million individuals were uninsured in 2009, representing approximately 16.7% of the US population.[2] Medicare enrollment in the United States is anticipated to increase as the population grows older. The first of the baby boom generation reached age 65 years in 2011, and an increase in age-related diseases is anticipated to add to the strain on current health care resources.[3]

Diseases of the spine are becoming more prevalent as the population ages. Low back pain currently accounts for an estimated 2% of all physician visits, exceeded in number only by visits for routine physical examination, hypertension, and diabetes.[4] In a 2002 survey, 26% of adults reported back pain and 14% reported neck pain within the preceding 3 months.[5] In 2005 the total expenditure for the treatment of back and neck disorders was approximately $86 billion.[5] This economic burden is comparable to that of treating other disabling conditions, including arthritis ($80.3 billion), cancer ($89 billion), diabetes ($98.1 billion), and heart disease and stroke ($257.6 billion).[6-9]

A World Health Organization comparison of the health care systems of 191 member nations ranked the US system in 37th place.[10] This analysis examined three main aspects of a nation's heath care system: respon-

siveness, fairness, and goodness. Responsiveness was measured by analyzing factors such as waiting times to see a specialist and the ability to choose a doctor or hospital. The US ranked first among all nations in this area. Fairness measured factors such as equality of treatment for rich and poor individuals. The United States ranked 32nd because many low-income individuals are uninsured or required to pay significant sums for health care. The fairness area also assessed the overall financing of the health care system by rich or poor individuals. The United States ranked 54th on fairness of financial contributions. Goodness was measured based on both healthy life expectancy (the number of years an individual can expect to live a life of full health, without disabling diseases or morbidities) and overall life expectancy. The US ranked 24th on healthy life expectancy and 47th on overall life expectancy. In 2011 the Organisation of Economic Co-operation and Development reported that US life expectancy is 78.2 years, compared with an average of 79.4 years for other member nations.[11] The infant mortality rate in the United States was 6.5 per 1,000 births, compared with an average of 4.6 per 1,000 births in other member nations.

Health care in the United States is delivered through a complex system with many distinct components. Within the context of rising costs and less-than-optimal health quality outcomes, US policy makers are questioning the current allocation of health care resources and searching for ways to improve health care quality, access, and delivery mechanisms.

Health Insurance in the United States

Private medical insurance was introduced to the United States in 1929 when a group of Dallas teachers contracted with Baylor Hospital to provide 21 days of hospitalization for a fixed payment of $6 per person.[12] Several insurance plans subsequently were developed to defray the rising cost of hospital services only, and the American Hospital Association developed the Blue Cross program to oversee these insurance plans. In 1939 a group of California physicians developed California Physicians' Services to provide physician services

Dr. Sharan or an immediate family member is a member of a speakers' bureau or has made paid presentations on behalf of Synthes; and serves as a paid consultant to or is an employee of Paradigm Spine. Dr. Rao or an immediate family member serves as a board member, owner, officer, or committee member of the North American Spine Society, the Lumbar Spine Research Society, and US Food and Drug Administration Orthopaedic and Rehabilitation Devices Scientific Advisory Panel.

in return for a prepaid fee ($1.70 per month for an employee earning less than $3,000 per year). Blue Shield was later established as the governing body for various insurance programs covering physician services.[12]

The US government imposed wage restrictions to control competition for employees during the labor shortage after World War II. In response, employers began to offer generous employee and family health care benefits as a means of attracting workers. In 1954 employer-provided health insurance benefits became exempt from taxation as income to workers, and this change in Internal Revenue Service regulation led to a great expansion in employer-sponsored health insurance.[13] The employer-sponsored health insurance system covered most of the US working population in the 1950s and 1960s. During the same period, many other developed nations established a universal health care program. Realizing the legislative difficulty of enacting a universal health care program in the United States, President Kennedy instead promoted government-sponsored health insurance for individuals who were age 65 years or older or had a poverty-level income. The Medicare and Medicaid programs were established in 1965 during President Johnson's administration. These programs subsequently were expanded to include coverage for certain individuals with disabilities. The federal Children's Health Insurance Program was created in 1997 to provide health care coverage for uninsured children.

An estimated 83.3% of Americans had health insurance in 2009: government-sponsored programs, including those for military personnel, insured 30.6%; 55.8% received health care benefits through an employer; and 8.9% purchased insurance independently.[2]

Medicare

Medicare is a federally funded health insurance program for US citizens and legal residents (of at least 5 years' duration) who are 65 years or older, have end-stage renal disease, or have certain other types of disabilities. The program is administered by the Centers for Medicare and Medicaid Services (CMS), an agency of the US Department of Health and Human Services. The Medicare program has four distinct components. Medicare Part A applies to inpatient hospital care, some inpatient extended care, and hospice care for a terminally ill participant. Part B applies to physician fees, outpatient services, laboratory and diagnostic tests, physician-administered drugs, and some home health care services. Part D provides subsidized access to prescription drugs. Part C, also known as Medicare Advantage, comprises a variety of privately administered insurance plans that offer optional insurance under CMS oversight against costs not covered by Medicare parts A, B, and D. The Medicare program is financed through a combination of payroll tax revenue, premiums paid by individual enrollees, and general

government revenue. Medicare Part A is financed through a payroll tax jointly paid by an employer and employee. Part B is financed through both individual premiums and general government revenue.

Medicaid

The Medicaid program provides basic health services to individuals with a low income and limited assets and to their children, pregnant women, older adults needing nursing home care, and others with disabilities. Each state can independently decide who qualifies for Medicaid benefits, as long as the state criteria comply with federal standards. The Medicaid program is administered by state health departments under guidelines issued by CMS. The program is jointly financed by the state and federal governments, with the federal government often providing block grants to states. In 2008 the federal government spent $204 billion on the Medicaid program, representing 57% of the total expenses of this program.[14] Medicaid benefits include inpatient and outpatient hospital care, physician services, family planning services and supplies, prenatal and nurse-midwife services, childhood vaccinations, skilled nursing home or home health care services for adults, and laboratory and radiographic studies.

Private Insurance

Private health insurance companies are able to provide benefits to individuals through distribution of risk. An insurance plan enrollee typically pays a monthly premium for services, with an employer often contributing a portion of the premium. Relatively healthy enrollees typically use few health care resources, and the insurance company uses a portion of their premium payments to cover the cost of resources provided to relatively unhealthy, higher risk enrollees. If healthy enrollees begin to drop their health insurance, the insurance company typically raises the premium charged to the remaining enrollees. In addition, higher premiums can be charged to cover the increasing cost of health care services. An employer may require employees to contribute an increased portion of the premium, especially during periods of low profitability, thus further increasing an individual's incentive to drop health care insurance coverage.

Physician Reimbursement Under the Medicare System

Payment for physician services under the Medicare system has undergone a significant evolution. When the Medicare program was initiated, physicians were paid under a fee system related to the "usual and customary" charge for a particular service. As the expense of covered physician services grew, Congress enacted the Resource-Based Relative Value Scale, implemented in 1992.[15] This scale assigns a value to each service based on the physician work involved, the expense of providing the service, and the cost of malpractice insurance. Many third-party payers use the scale as a benchmark for their provider reimbursement rates.

The Resource-Based Relative Value Scale is based on a current procedural terminology (CPT) code assigned to each service. In the first CPT manual, published by the American Medical Association in 1966, many of the listed codes identified surgical procedures.[16] Internal medicine and other specialties were gradually added beginning in 1970. The fifth edition of the CPT manual was accepted for use in 1983 as part of the Healthcare Common Procedure Coding System of the Health Care Financing Administration (later renamed CMS). CMS subsequently mandated the use of the Healthcare Common Procedure Coding System for reporting services provided under Part B of the Medicare program.

The Code Creation Process

CPT codes are created by the CPT Editorial Panel, which is an American Medical Association committee composed of 17 members, each of whom is from a different organization: 11 physicians are nominated by a national medical specialty society (one of these physicians must have experience with performance measurement); 5 physicians are nominated from the Blue Cross and Blue Shield Association, the America's Health Insurance Plans, the American Hospital Association, and CMS; and 2 members are from the CPT Health Care Professionals Advisory Committee. The code creation process begins with a request from an individual, vendor, physician, or medical society.[17] The editorial panel typically seeks and reviews comments on the proposed code, after which it is brought up for discussion or delegated to a work group for later review. A secret ballot of the editorial panel assigns an accepted code to one of three categories. Category I represents frequently used CPT codes. A code assigned to category I is sent to the Relative Value Update Commission (RUC), where it is assigned the value that will be used to calculate reimbursement. Category II typically represents performance measure codes not subject to reimbursement. Category III codes apply to a new technology. No value is assigned, but the code is used to track procedures. When enough data are collected, a category III code can be converted to a category I code.

The RUC, also administered by the American Medical Association, is composed of 29 physicians: 23 are selected from medical societies, and the remaining 6 seats are filled by the RUC chair, the cochair of the RUC Health Care Professionals Advisory Committee Review Board, the chair of the Practice Expense Review Committee, and representatives from the American Medical Association, American Osteopathic Association, and CPT Editorial Panel. Medical societies that are recognized by the American Board of Medical Specialties, have a high percentage of physician members

in patient care, and account for a high percentage of Medicare expenditures nominate a representative to the RUC committee. Three of the 23 seats rotate on a 2-year basis, with 2 of these seats coming from an internal medicine subspecialty and 1 from any other specialty.[18] The RUC assigns each category I CPT code a relative value unit (RVU) that reflects the resources required to provide that service. The RVU of a service is based on the physician work required (52%), the expenses of the practice (44%), and the cost of professional liability insurance (4%). The amount of work required to provide a service often is calculated by members of the relevant medical specialty society, which may survey its members to determine the work required for a particular service. The RUC submits its RVU recommendations to CMS, which has accepted more than 90% of all RUC recommendations without change.[15] CMS calculates the final code-related reimbursement by multiplying each of the three components of CPT valuation by a geographic index factor that takes into account regional variations in the cost of providing the service. This value is multiplied by the annual conversion factor, a complex formula that includes the sustainable growth rate. These calculations provide a reimbursement amount for each CPT code under Medicare Part B.

The process of valuing a code can be lengthy. Because the value of services changes over time, Congress mandated the RUC to review RVU valuations every 5 years. Not all codes are evaluated during this review, and specialty societies often initiate a code review.

The Sustainable Growth Rate Formula

The sustainable growth rate formula was implemented in 1998 as a means of slowing growth in spending for physician services.[19] The sustainable growth rate essentially applies an annual target for overall Medicare spending. The spending target includes payments to physicians under Medicare Part B, laboratory and radiography services, and physician-administered drugs.[20] If actual spending for the year exceeds the target, physician reimbursement is decreased to meet the target for the following year. If spending does not exceed the target, physician reimbursement is increased.

When the sustainable growth rate was first implemented, the estimated target expenditure exceeded the actual annual expenditure, leading to an increase in physician reimbursements. Since 2001 actual spending has exceeded the estimates, resulting in subsequent-years cuts in physician reimbursement. Congress has prevented some mandated cuts from taking effect; without such legislative action, physician reimbursements would have been reduced 5% to 25% for each subsequent year. Many proposals have been submitted to Congress to replace the sustainable growth rate formula with a system that better reflects the costs of providing medical care.

Government Subsidies for Graduate Medical Education

The federal government had no role in the training of physicians until the 1960s. Hospitals paid a modest salary to a physician in training, who often lived in the hospital. During the debate that preceded passage of the Medicare and Medicaid legislation, the American Medical Association strongly promoted government funding for graduate medical education funding. The reasoning was that the expansion of health care insurance coverage under Medicare and Medicaid would burden hospitals, many of which were not equipped to handle the influx of patients. Under Medicare Part A, the federal government took some responsibility for funding the education of medical interns and residents. Funding of graduate medical education has allowed the United States to achieve an adequate supply of physicians. Since the 1960s, the approximate number of physicians per 1,000 people in the United States has risen from 1.1 to 1.8.

Funding for graduate medical education is primarily allocated from two Medicare Part A sources as direct and indirect subsidies. Direct medical education subsidies cover a teaching hospital's direct costs of training residents, including stipends and benefits, teacher salaries, and general program expenses. Several variables are used in calculating a teaching hospital's direct medical education subsidy, including the number of residents in training, the cost of training a resident (based on the cost in 1984 as adjusted for inflation), and the number of Medicare patients treated at the hospital. Direct medical education payments from Medicare were approximately $3.0 billion in 2007.[21]

The indirect medical education subsidy covers indirect hospital expenses related to resident training, such as the larger number of tests ordered by residents, inefficiencies resulting from residents' lack of experience, the burden of uncompensated care, and the need to be at the forefront of research and technology. Indirect medical education subsidies from Medicare to hospitals amounted to approximately $5.8 billion in 2007.[21]

An estimated 2.5% to 7% of a teaching hospital's budget comes from graduate medical education funding, and many teaching hospitals depend heavily on this federal government subsidy. Part of the formula for calculating indirect medical education funding depends on a ratio that includes the severity of patient conditions treated under Medicare, and many teaching hospitals rigorously identify such severe conditions to capture the appropriate subsidy.

Medical Malpractice and Health Care Reform

Medical malpractice is defined as a health care professional's failure to provide a service in a manner expected of a skillful and conscientious practitioner of the profession. Malpractice is considered to occur when a professional's failure leads to injury, loss, or damage to the recipient of the service. Medical malpractice litigation most commonly arises from a charge of negligence by the treating physician.[22] The current system of medical malpractice liability in the United States has two primary goals: to compensate patients who have been harmed by negligent medical care and to discourage health care providers from providing negligent or substandard care. A patient who has been injured can make a claim of malpractice against the treating physician, and a provider who is found guilty is responsible for compensating the injured patient. Under common law, the compensation amount takes into account both economic damages, such as loss of income and direct medical expenses, and noneconomic damages, such as pain and suffering resulting from the injury.

Malpractice insurance is regulated by state governments, and most states require physicians to carry malpractice insurance. The insurance commissioner of the state has the ability to limit the premiums insurance companies can charge. A hospital typically requires physicians who treat its patients to carry insurance. Some hospitals create their own insurance company or enter a multihospital self-insurance pool. Often physicians who work for a federal or state hospital do not need to carry malpractice insurance because of their government employee status.

In recent years the cost of malpractice insurance in the United States has increased significantly as a result of intersecting insurance company and physician factors. Many insurance companies lost investment income during the past decade's recessions, and premiums have increased as a result. In addition, many insurance companies have chosen not to underwrite physician clients in specialties or geographic markets considered to be high risk.

The growth in the size of malpractice damage awards also has contributed to insurance premium increases. The Physician Insurers Association of America (PIAA) is a trade association of more than 50 professional-liability insurance companies owned and operated by physicians and dentists. These companies collect and report information on their indemnity claims through the PIAA Data Sharing Project and *Claim Trend Analysis*.[23] The average indemnity payment for a paid claim was $324,969 in 2009; this figure represents an increase of 13.9% from the average $285,246 payment reported in 2000. In 2009 the average cost of legal defense against a claim that was settled was $69,244. For a claim that went to trial, the cost was $140,684 if the defendant prevailed and $170,837 if the plaintiff prevailed. The average cost of defense for a claim that was dropped was $26,245.[23] The high level of damage awards as well as the cost of defending against a malpractice lawsuit has helped drive increases in malpractice insurance premiums. In 2008 61% of medical malpractice claims were dismissed as having insufficient merit to be pursued further, and another 32% were settled out of court. Only 7% reached trial, and in 86% of these cases the ruling was in favor of the physician defendant. It is estimated that only 1% of all malpractice lawsuits lead to a ruling in favor of the plaintiff.[24]

The practice of defensive medicine is a factor in cost increases related to medical malpractice liability. A physician might order a diagnostic test not because of its medical usefulness but because of its possible usefulness in a malpractice lawsuit. In 2009 a report by the Congressional Budget Office estimated the annual cost of defensive medicine to be $6.6 billion and estimated that medical liability reform would save $54 billion over 10 years.[25] A recent nongovernment study estimated the cost of defensive medicine to be as high as $210 billion per year.[26] The difficulty of estimating the total direct and indirect costs of defensive medicine is exemplified by the gap between these two estimates.

Many current proposals for reforming the medical liability system are based on events that occurred in California. Between 1968 and 1974 the number of medical lawsuits settled for more than $300,000 increased 11-fold in California. As a result, in 1975 two medical insurance companies notified 2,000 physicians in southern California that their malpractice insurance coverage would not be renewed. One insurance company notified 4,000 physicians in northern California that their premiums would increase an average of 380%. The state government concluded that the practice of medicine would become uninsurable and feared that many physicians would leave the practice of medicine or move to another state.[27] In 1975 the California Medical Injury Compensation Reform Act established a $250,000 cap on noneconomic damages such as pain and suffering, but no limit was placed on economic damages. The overall results have been a reduction in medical malpractice liability costs in California, a reduction in the number of claims filed, and no reduction in patients' access to the courts. The law has had the effect of limiting the rate of increase in California malpractice premiums to approximately one fourth of the average rate of increase in the other states. In addition, the time required to settle malpractice claims has declined by one third. The overall costs of litigation have been lowered, and patients who are injured are more quickly indemnified. The total amount of insurance payouts has been reduced, and a larger portion of awards has been directed to plaintiff patients rather than to trial lawyers.[28]

Several other states have followed California's lead and established a cap on noneconomic damages. In states with medical malpractice liability reform, it is estimated that all hospital expenditures have decreased 5% to 9%.[29] It is estimated that if these savings were available to hospitals nationwide, annual health care spending would be reduced $83 to $151 billion.[29] The Congressional Budget Office in 1998 stated that caps "have been found to be extremely effective in reducing the amount of claims paid and medical liability premiums."[30]

Health Care Value as a New Model

The Medicare program originally was enacted as a fee-for-service program. Policy makers intended to establish a health insurance program that would not be overly disruptive to the health care system. As a result, Medicare is a passive payment system in which providers are reimbursed for their services regardless of the outcome. The concept of health care value, loosely defined as the relationship of quality to cost, is being used by the federal government in an attempt to maximize the value of its health care expenditure, in terms of patient outcomes and satisfaction. The intent is for Medicare to become a more active purchaser of health care by reimbursing providers for higher quality and more efficient care. The concept of the government paying for higher quality care also is known as value-based purchasing.

The care of patients with diabetes often is cited as exemplifying the need for changes in the reimbursement system: under the current system, a physician is reimbursed for treating a patient who is hospitalized because of a diabetes complication; the physician has no financial incentive to prevent the complication from occurring and thereby to avoid the hospital admission.

CMS has established demonstration programs to determine whether linking outcomes to reimbursement can improve the quality of care. In the Premier Hospital Quality Incentive Demonstration Project established by CMS in 2003, 270 hospitals across the nation were rewarded for achieving specific outcome measures in patients with pneumonia, heart attack, heart failure, coronary artery bypass graft surgery, or hip or knee replacement surgery. A hospital's reward for achieving a quality outcome measure was an increased reimbursement for the specific diagnosis-related group (DRG). Hospitals that did not achieve an outcome measure were penalized with a decrease in DRG reimbursement. Seventeen percent of the participating hospitals had improvement in the overall quality composite score, and DRG incentives of $36.6 million were distributed.[31] The Premier program was the first demonstration that a realignment of incentives can lead to improved health care quality.

CMS also has conducted demonstration programs involving physician groups, nursing homes, and health information technology or electronic prescribing programs. The Physician Quality Reporting System was established by CMS in 2007 as an initial effort to realign physician reimbursements toward a quality focus. Individual physicians can be reimbursed for providing and reporting on quality measures selected by CMS with advice from medical societies. As the program evolves, CMS intends to penalize physicians who do not reach appropriate quality outcomes.

The meaning of the terms value and quality, as used in health care, is evolving through a vigorous national attempt to develop fair and universally applicable definitions. Value needs to be defined in relation to the use

7: Spine Care and US Health Policy

Table 1

Topics Proposed by the Institute of Medicine for Comparative Effectiveness Research in Spine Disorders

Establish a prospective registry to compare the effectiveness of treatment strategies for low back pain without neurologic deficit or spinal deformity.

Compare the effectiveness of treatment strategies (eg, artificial cervical disks, spine fusion, pharmacologic treatment with physical therapy) for cervical disk and neck pain.

Compare the long-term effectiveness of weight-bearing exercise and bisphosphonates in preventing hip and vertebral fractures in older women with osteopenia and/or osteoporosis.

Establish a prospective registry to compare the effectiveness of surgical and nonsurgical strategies for treating cervical spondylotic myelopathy in patients with different characteristics to delineate predictors of improved outcomes.

Compare the effectiveness of traditional and newer imaging modalities (eg, routine imaging, MRI, CT, positron emission tomography) when ordered for neurologic and orthopaedic indications by primary care practitioners, emergency department physicians, or specialists.

Compare the effectiveness (eg, pain relief, functional outcomes) of different surgical strategies for symptomatic cervical disk herniation in patients for whom appropriate nonsurgical care has failed.

Adapted from Institute of Medicine: Initial National Priorities for Comparative Effectiveness Research. June 30, 2009. http://www.iom.edu/Reports/2009/ComparativeEffectivenessResearchPriorities.aspx. Accessed May 2, 2011.

of expensive technology, the appropriate use of diagnostic tests, and specific physician services. CMS strongly encourages the use of health care information technology because ease of access to health care records is seen as critical to improving outcomes. Private payers also are endeavoring to determine standards and reimbursement for value-oriented care. The concept of value-based purchasing is gaining increased attention and most likely will be incorporated into future health care reform efforts.

Comparative Effectiveness Research

Comparative effectiveness research is a rigorous method of comparing the drugs, devices, and procedures available for treating a specific medical condition and determining which are most effective. Policy makers are investigating the use of comparative effectiveness research for obtaining value in the US health care system. An analysis may be restricted to the relative medical benefits and risks of each treatment option, or it may weigh the costs and benefits of each option. The American Recovery and Reinvestment Act of 2009 al-

located $1.1 billion for study of comparative effectiveness research by the National Institutes of Health, Agency for Healthcare Research and Quality, and Department of Health and Human Services.[32] The Institute of Medicine in 2009 released *Initial National Priorities for Comparative Effectiveness Research*, which defined comparative effectiveness research as "the generation and synthesis of evidence that compares the benefits and harms of alternative methods to prevent, diagnose, treat, and monitor a clinical condition or to improve the delivery of care. The purpose of comparative effectiveness research is to assist consumers, clinicians, purchasers, and policy makers to make informed decisions that will improve health care at both the individual and population levels."[33] The report established 100 medical priorities for comparative effectiveness research (Table 1).

Comparative effectiveness research programs have been established in many nations to study new technologies and determine their effectiveness. In Britain, the National Institute for Health and Clinical Effectiveness was established as an independent agency for the study of new technologies. Any new drug or medical device is rigorously studied before being released to the public. A pharmaceutical company or device maker must submit data on the safety of its product and effectiveness compared with other products. A new drug or device is not approved unless is shown to be more effective than other products. Similar programs to weigh costs and benefits also exist within many private insurance companies.

Comparative effectiveness research has been criticized based on the method of analysis. Physician groups have requested that comparative effectiveness research on a specific medical condition be performed by a federal agency, with substantial advice solicited from specialists who care for patients with the condition. There is concern that comparative effectiveness research could be used as a tool to limit the use of new devices or drugs based solely on their cost or that the analysis might fail to take individual patient variations into account. Some groups believe that comparative effectiveness research could be used as a mechanism for rationing care and lead to increased government intrusion into the physician-patient relationship.

Summary

Many economic, political, and social forces influence the practice of medicine, including spine care. Many of these forces will shape the future of medical care in the United States. Physicians who understand these issues will be better able to navigate the complexities of health care reform and help to determine the future of the relationship between the physician and the patient.

Annotated References

1. National Health Expenditure Data: *Forecast Summary and Selected Tables*. Baltimore, MD, Office of the Actuary in the Centers for Medicare and Medicaid Services. 2008. http://www.cms.gov/NationalHealthExpendData/02_NationalHealthAccountsHistorical.asp. Accessed July 29, 2011.

    The National Health Expenditure Data webpage provides official estimates of total health care spending in the United States, including annual expenditures for health care–related goods and services, public health activities, government administration, and the net cost of health insurance.

2. DeNavas-Walt C, Proctor BD, Smith JC: *Income, Poverty, and Health Insurance Coverage in the United States: 2009*. Current Population Reports, P60-238. Washington, DC, US Census Bureau, September 2010. http://www.census.gov/prod/2010pubs/p60-238.pdf. Accessed July 29, 2011.

    The US Census Bureau provides data on the income, poverty, and health insurance status of the civilian noninstitution-dwelling population of the United States.

3. He W, Sengupta M, Velkoff VA, DeBarros KA: *65+ in the United States: 2005*. Current Population Reports, P23-209. Washington, DC, National Institute on Aging, US Census Bureau, December 2005. http://www.census.gov/prod/2006pubs/p23-209.pdf. Accessed May 2, 2011.

    The US Census Bureau, in conjunction with the National Institute on Aging, provides a profile of the US population older than 65 years.

4. Deyo RA, Mirza SK, Martin BI: Back pain prevalence and visit rates: Estimates from U.S. national surveys, 2002. *Spine (Phila Pa 1976)* 2006;31(23):2724-2727.

5. Martin BI, Deyo RA, Mirza SK, et al: Expenditures and health status among adults with back and neck problems. *JAMA* 2008;299(6):656-664.

    Expenses related to back and neck difficulties were studied using data from the Medical Expenditure Panel Survey. Both the percentage of individuals reporting back or neck pain and related expenses increased from 1997 to 2005.

6. Yelin E, Murphy L, Cisternas MG, Foreman AJ, Pasta DJ, Helmick CG: Medical care expenditures and earnings losses among persons with arthritis and other rheumatic conditions in 2003, and comparisons with 1997. *Arthritis Rheum* 2007;56(5):1397-1407.

    The costs associated with arthritis care were examined based on the Medical Expenditure Panel Survey. Medical care expenditures increased between 1997 and 2003 because the number of individuals with arthritis increased.

7. U.S. Department of Health and Human Services: *Direct and Indirect Costs of Illness by Major Diagnosis, U.S. 2006*. Bethesda, MD, National Heart, Lung and Blood Institute, 2006. http://www.nhlbi.nih.gov/about/factbook/toc.htm. Accessed May 2, 2011.

    The National Heart, Lung, and Blood Institute reports the costs associated with different diseases and their impact on the US population.

8. Hogan P, Dall T, Nikolov P, American Diabetes Association: Economic costs of diabetes in the US in 2002. *Diabetes Care* 2003;26(3):917-932.

9. American Heart Association: *Heart Disease and Stroke Statistics: 2005 Update*. Dallas, TX, American Heart Association, 2005.

    The American Heart Association reports that cardiovascular disease was the leading cause of death in the United States in 2005.

10. World Health Organization: *The World Health Report 2000: Health Systems. Improving Performance*. Geneva, Switzerland, World Health Organization, 2001.

11. Organisation of Economic Co-operation and Development: *OECD Health Data 2011*. http://www.oecd.org/document/16/0,3746,en_2649_37407_2085200_1_1_1_37407,00.html. Accessed July 29, 2011.

    This website provides a link to the Organisation of Economic Co-operation and Development Frequently Requested Data file.

12. Starr P: *The Social Transformation of American Medicine*. New York, NY, Basic Books, 1984.

13. Blumenthal D: Primum non nocere: The McCain plan for health insecurity. *N Engl J Med* 2008;359(16):1645-1647.

    A health care proposal by Sen. John McCain centered on ending the tax exemption for employer-sponsored health insurance.

14. Office of Management and Budget: *Budget of the United States Government: Fiscal Year 2008*. http://www.gpoaccess.gov/usbudget/fy08. Accessed July 29, 2011.

    The US President's budget proposal for 2008 included $204 billion funding for the Medicaid program, which represented 57% of all Medicaid expenses.

15. Przybylski GJ: Understanding and applying a resource-based relative value system to your neurosurgical practice. *Neurosurg Focus* 2002;12(4):e3.

16. Bean JR: Valuing neurosurgery services: Part I. The historical development and interrelationships of current procedural terminology and the medicare fee schedule. *Neurosurg Focus* 2002;12(4):e1.

17. Department of CPT Editorial Research and Development: *CPT Process*. Chicago, IL, American Medical Association, 2001, pp 1-15.

18. American Medical Association: *The Resource Based Relative Value Scale: The RVS Update Committee*. http://www.ama-assn.org/ama/pub/physician-resources/solutions-managing-your-practice/coding-billing-insurance/medicare/the-resource-based-relative-value-

scale/the-rvs-update-committee.page. Accessed July 29, 2011.

The composition of the RUC is outlined.

19. Laugesen MJ: Siren song: physicians, congress, and medicare fees. *J Health Polit Policy Law* 2009;34(2): 157-179.

A history of the sustainable growth rate formula is outlined. The Medicare program originally was supported by physician groups, with the understanding that the government would not be involved in regulating payment.

20. Congressional Budget Office: The sustainable growth rate formula for setting Medicare's physician payment rates. *CBO Economic and Budget Issue Brief*. September 6, 2006.

The sustainable growth rate is described in detail, with options for replacing the formula.

21. Iglehart JK: Medicare, graduate medical education, and new policy directions. *N Engl J Med* 2008;359(6):643-650.

A brief history of graduate medical education funding is provided, with a discussion of options for reform.

22. Hoffman PJ, Plump JD, Courtney MA: The defense counsel's perspective. *Clin Orthop Relat Res* 2005;433: 15-25.

Information is provided to help physicians prepare for a medical malpractice lawsuit.

23. Guardado JR: Professional liability insurance indemnity and expenses, claim adjudication, and policy limits, 2000-2009. *Policy Research Perspectives No. 2010-2*. Chicago, IL, American Medical Association, 2010. http://www.ama-assn.org/resources/doc/health-policy/x-ama/prp201002-piaa-data.pdf.

Information from the PIAA Data Sharing Project is provided to members of the American Medical Association.

24. *Patient Access Crisis: The Role of Medical Litigation: Joint Hearing Before the Committee on the Judiciary and the Committee on Health, Education, Labor, and Pensions, United States Senate*, 108th Cong, 1st Sess (2003) (testimony of Lawrence E. Smarr, Physician Insurers Association of America).

25. Elmendorf DW: *Letter to Honorable Bruce L. Braley*. http://www.cbo.gov/ftpdocs/108xx/doc10872/12-29-Tort_Reform-Braley.pdf. December 29, 2009. Accessed July 29, 2011.

The director of the Congressional Budget Office analyzed budgetary factors related to proposals for tort reform.

26. PricewaterhouseCoopers Health Research Institute: *The Price of Excess: Identifying Waste in Health Care Spending*. New York, NY, PricewaterhouseCoopers LLP, 2008. http://www.pwc.com/us/en/healthcare/publications/the-price-of-excess.jhtml. Accessed May 2, 2011.

Research from PricewaterhouseCoopers estimated that wasteful health care spending amounts to $1.2 trillion of the $2.2 trillion annual US health care expenditure.

27. Anderson RE: Defending the practice of medicine. *Arch Intern Med* 2004;164(11):1173-1178.

28. Pace NM, Golinelli D, Zakaras L: *Capping Non-Economic Awards in Medical Malpractice Trials: California Jury Verdicts Under MICRA*. Santa Monica, CA, RAND Corporation, 2004.

29. Kessler D, McClellan M: Do doctors practice defensive medicine? *Q J Econ* 1996;111:353-390.

30. Congressional Budget Office: *Preliminary Cost Estimate: H.R. 4250. Patient Protection Act of 1998 With Proposed Amendment*. Washington, DC, Congressional Budget Office, 1998.

31. Centers for Medicare and Medicaid Services: *Premier Hospital Quality Incentive Demonstration Project: Project Overview and Findings from Year One*. http://www.premierinc.com/p4p/hqi/hqi-whitepaper041306.pdf. Accessed July 29, 2011.

The outcomes of the CMS Premier Demonstration Project were reported.

32. Department of Health and Human Services: *Comparative Effectiveness Research Funding*. http://www.hhs.gov/recovery/programs/cer/index.html. Accessed July 29, 2011.

The American Recovery and Reinvestment Act of 2009 created the Federal Coordinating Council for Comparative Effectiveness Research to coordinate research and recommend allocations.

33. Institute of Medicine: *Initial National Priorities for Comparative Effectiveness Research*. June 30, 2009. http://www.iom.edu/Reports/2009/Comparative EffectivenessResearchPriorities.aspx. Accessed May 2, 2011.

The US Congress directed the Institute of Medicine to develop this report, which includes a working definition of comparative effectiveness research, topics for research, and identification of the necessary requirements to support a robust and sustainable comparative effectiveness research enterprise.

Chapter 48

The Role of the US Food and Drug Administration in Spine Care

Ronald P. Jean, PhD   Sergio M. de del Castillo, BS   Barbara Buch, MD   Raj D. Rao, MD

Introduction

The US Food and Drug Administration (FDA) is charged with protecting public health in the United States through the regulation of food, cosmetic, and medical products. Orthopaedic spine surgeons use an array of FDA-regulated products, most of which are medical tools and implants. Thus, it is important to have an understanding of the FDA process by which these products reach the marketplace.

Legislative History

The FDA is an agency of the US Department of Health and Human Services. The legislative branch of government (the US Congress) is responsible for writing and enacting laws related to medical products, and the FDA is responsible for implementing those laws. The regulatory authority of the FDA dates to the 1906 passage of the Federal Food and Drugs Act, which granted the newly minted agency the authority to regulate meat products and to prohibit adulterated food and drug products from being sold or distributed in the United States.[1] Medical devices were not regulated until 1976, when the Medical Device Amendments to the Federal Food, Drug and Cosmetics Act expanded the authority of the FDA to cover these products.[2] Under the Medical Device Amendments, the FDA established panels of experts in individual specialties to create definitions and classifications that would apply to every commercially available medical device. In 1990 the Safe Medical Device Act required institutions to report any adverse event involving a medical device to the manufacturer

Dr. Rao or an immediate family member serves as a board member, owner, officer, or committee member of the North American Spine Society, the Lumbar Spine Research Society, and the United States Food and Drug Administration Orthopaedic and Rehabilitation Devices Scientific Advisory Panel. None of the following authors or an immediate family member has received anything of value from or owns stock in a commercial company or institution related directly or indirectly to the subject of this chapter: Dr. Jean, Mr. de del Castillo, Dr. Buch.

and, under certain circumstances, to the FDA.[3] The Medical Device User Fee and Modernization Act of 2002 granted the FDA authority to collect user fees from sponsors to help cover the cost of premarket review of devices; in return, timelines were established for the review of different types of premarket device applications.[4] The Food and Drug Administration Amendments Act of 2007 focused on pediatric safeguards, research, and innovation, and it strengthened the transparency of clinical study results.[5]

Organization

The FDA has regulatory purview over numerous food products, cosmetics, biologically derived therapeutic products, human therapeutic drugs, animal drugs and feed products, and medical devices. The FDA is partitioned into multiple centers and offices (Figure 1). The Center for Devices and Radiological Health (CDRH) is in charge of reviewing medical devices through its eight offices. Under the CDRH, the Office of Device Evaluation handles premarket device regulation. The Office of Device Evaluation has five divisions, each of which focuses on a different medical specialty, and each division has multiple branches. Most devices used in the diagnosis and treatment of musculoskeletal disorders are under the authority of the Division of Surgical, Orthopedic and Restorative Devices. The Orthopedic Spine Devices Branch is responsible for the premarket review of spine implants including pedicle screw systems, fusion cages, intervertebral body replacements, and total disk replacements. Other products used in the spine, such as bone morphogenetic protein combination products, bone void fillers, and bone cements, are reviewed by the Restorative Devices Branch. Several offices of the CDRH other than the Office of Device Evaluation also are involved in the regulation of orthopaedic medical devices. For example, the Office of Surveillance and Biometrics monitors adverse events and has the authority to require postmarket studies; the Office of Compliance conducts inspections and audits to ensure that quality systems regulations and good manufacturing practices are followed.

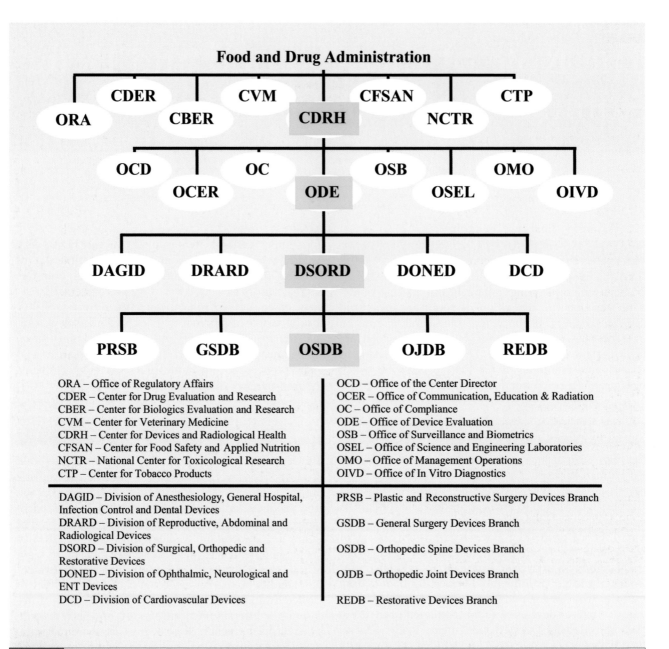

Food and Drug Administration

ORA   CDER   CBER   CVM   CDRH   CFSAN   NCTR   CTP

OCD   OCER   OC   ODE   OSB   OSEL   OMO   OIVD

DAGID   DRARD   DSORD   DONED   DCD

PRSB   GSDB   OSDB   OJDB   REDB

ORA – Office of Regulatory Affairs
CDER – Center for Drug Evaluation and Research
CBER – Center for Biologics Evaluation and Research
CVM – Center for Veterinary Medicine
CDRH – Center for Devices and Radiological Health
CFSAN – Center for Food Safety and Applied Nutrition
NCTR – National Center for Toxicological Research
CTP – Center for Tobacco Products

OCD – Office of the Center Director
OCER – Office of Communication, Education & Radiation
OC – Office of Compliance
ODE – Office of Device Evaluation
OSB – Office of Surveillance and Biometrics
OSEL – Office of Science and Engineering Laboratories
OMO – Office of Management Operations
OIVD – Office of In Vitro Diagnostics

DAGID – Division of Anesthesiology, General Hospital, Infection Control and Dental Devices
DRARD – Division of Reproductive, Abdominal and Radiological Devices
DSORD – Division of Surgical, Orthopedic and Restorative Devices
DONED – Division of Ophthalmic, Neurological and ENT Devices
DCD – Division of Cardiovascular Devices

PRSB – Plastic and Reconstructive Surgery Devices Branch

GSDB – General Surgery Devices Branch

OSDB – Orthopedic Spine Devices Branch

OJDB – Orthopedic Joint Devices Branch

REDB – Restorative Devices Branch

Figure 1   The organizational structure of the FDA. The offices most involved in regulating orthopaedic devices are highlighted. (Courtesy of the US Food and Drug Administration, Silver Spring, MD.)

Medical Device Classifications

Medical devices are classified by the FDA based on the level of risk to a patient and the ability to mitigate the risk. The three classes of risk control are based on the level of evidence necessary to demonstrate a product's safety and effectiveness.[6]

Class I: General Controls

Class I, general controls, applies to all medical devices. These basic standards for ensuring consistent safety and effectiveness include requirements for annual regis- tration of companies such as manufacturers, distribu- tors, repackagers, and relabelers; annual listing of de- vices to be marketed and activities to be performed using the devices; and device labeling or premarketing notification. The general controls also include quality systems regulations related to good design, manufactur- ing practices, record keeping, and reporting. A class I device is one for which these general controls are suffi- cient for providing a reasonable assurance of safety and effectiveness. For example, a manual orthopaedic surgi- cal instrument that is not system specific, such as a drill, scalpel, or retractor, is a class I device.

7: Spine Care and US Health Policy

Table 1				

FDA Classification and Jurisdiction for Orthopaedic Spine Devices

Device Type	Classification	Code of Federal Regulations (CFR) Section	Regulatory Submission Type	FDA Review Jurisdiction
Lumbar posterior pedicle screw system	Class II Class III (for treating degenerative disk disease and lower grade spondylolisthesis)	21 CFR 888.3070	510(k)	OSDB
Cervical pedicle screw system	Unclassified[a]	Unclassified[a]	PMA	OSDB
Lumbar posterior hook system	Class II	21 CFR 888.3050	510(k)	OSDB
Cervical posterior hook system	Class II	21 CFR 888.3050	510(k)	OSDB
Anterior or anterolateral spine plate	Class II	21 CFR 888.3060	510(k)	OSDB
Lumbar vertebral body replacements	Class II	21 CFR 888.3060	510(k)	OSDB
Lumbar cage	Class II	21 CFR 888.3080	510(k)	OSDB
Cervical cage	Class II	21 CFR 888.3080	510(k)	OSDB
Total disk replacement Disk nucleus replacement Dynamic stabilization system for nonfusion Facet replacement	Class III	No classification regulation[b]	PMA	OSDB
Interspinous process spacer	Class III	No classification regulation[b]	PMA	OSDB
Bone void filler	Class II	21 CFR 888.3045	510(k)	REDB
Filler with bone morphogenetic protein	Class III	No classification regulation[b]	PMA	REDB

OSDB = Orthopaedic Spine Devices Branch, PMA = Premarket approval, REDB = Restorative Devices Branch
[a]A preamendment device category for which a classification regulation has not yet been written.
[b]A device (such as a new technology) for which the FDA has not received a marketing application or rendered a final regulatory decision. If the device is found "not substantially equivalent" through the 510(k) regulatory pathway to a preamendment or postamendment predicate device, it is automatically assigned class III status.

Class II: Special Controls

Class II applies to types of devices for which the general controls are not sufficient. Additional, special controls are required to adequately mitigate the risks posed by the device type.[6] The special controls for devices in a particular classification may include specific labeling requirements, preclinical performance testing based on FDA guidance documents or recognized standards, patient registries, clinical data, or postmarket surveillance. Most orthopaedic spine devices are designated as class II devices (Table 1).

Class III: Premarket Approval

The highest risk devices are designated as class III. For these products, the general controls are not adequate for mitigating the risk, and the available data are insufficient for creating special controls. A class III device usually is intended to sustain life or prevent significant health impairment, but with substantial risk of causing

harm to the patient. Such a device typically requires the highest level of scrutiny including a complete preclinical and clinical review. Most such devices require premarket clinical studies, and some also require post-approval clinical studies. Total disk replacement prostheses, disk nucleus replacements, dynamic stabilization systems for nonfusion, and facet replacement devices are class III devices.

Major Device Regulatory Pathways

The general regulatory pathways for premarketing approval of a product are outlined here. However, not all classifications are straightforward, and a manufacturer must confirm a product's status as well as the applicable limitations. A company also may request specific classification information.[7] Most class I devices are exempt from premarket review and FDA clearance, although the general controls apply to these products. The manufacturer is required on an annual basis to register and list the generic category or classification of the device with the FDA.

Most class II devices require submission of a premarketing notification application (known as a 510[k] application). Under the 510(k) pathway, the FDA reviews the device by comparing it to a legally marketed predicate device. A predicate device meets one of three conditions: it was legally commercially marketed before 1976, it is a device for which the regulatory panel decided that special controls should be established, or it was found to be substantially equivalent to a preamendment device (a device that was legally marketed before 1976). Typically, a company submitting a marketing application for a new device identifies any relevant predicate devices, but the FDA can identify additional predicate devices to determine substantial equivalence during its internal review. For example, a company may submit a 510(k) application for a cobalt-chromium alloy rod as part of a pedicle screw system, identifying earlier 510(k) clearance for a larger diameter cobalt-chromium alloy spinal fusion rod. If the FDA is aware of an already cleared cobalt-chromium rod of a more similar diameter, both predicate devices can be used for determining the new product's substantial equivalence. The FDA grants clearance for the new device if it meets all criteria for substantial equivalence to a legally marketed predicate device. If the FDA finds the device not to be substantially equivalent, usually it is designated a class III device.

It is important to note the distinction between clearance and approval. For a clearance, the FDA determines that a device is substantially equivalent to a legally marketed predicate device. For an approval, a clinical data set must demonstrate reasonable assurance of safety and effectiveness. Most new class III devices require FDA review through the Premarket Approval (PMA) pathway. The general controls are not sufficient for these devices, and there is not enough information to establish special controls for the device. To gain approval, the company must demonstrate a reasonable assurance of safety and effectiveness using valid scientific evidence, such as well-controlled clinical studies or significant, detailed data on long-term clinical experience with the device.[8]

The Humanitarian Device Exemption (HDE) is an alternative regulatory pathway. Before the application is considered, the Office of Orphan Product Development in the Office of Special Medical Programs under the Office of the FDA Commissioner must designate the product for humanitarian use. A humanitarian use device is intended for a particular small, targeted population, usually to treat a rare disease or condition that affects fewer than 4,000 patients a year and for which no other treatment is available. The HDE regulatory pathway may provide patients with access to a medical device intended to treat a rare congenital malformation or syndrome. To obtain approval of its HDE applica-

tion, the company must demonstrate that the device has a reasonable assurance of safety and a probable benefit for the intended patient population. In contrast to a PMA application, the HDE effectiveness requirement only requires the probable benefit from use of the device to outweigh the risks.

The Investigational Device Exemption (IDE) program does not involve a marketing application. Instead, an IDE allows a company or academic investigator to conduct a clinical study using an investigational or experimental device that does not have marketing clearance or approval or to use a marketed device for a new, investigational use. The FDA reviews an IDE application to ensure that patients enrolled in the clinical study will be adequately protected. Implants are considered to be significant-risk devices, and an IDE is required before a US clinical study can be conducted. However, a device with marketing clearance or approval can be studied in a manner that conforms to the device labeling.

Device Evaluation After Approval or Clearance

The FDA continues to evaluate the safety and effectiveness of a product after it is commercially distributed. In addition to the traditional evaluation of peer-reviewed literature and clinical case studies, the FDA obtains safety and effectiveness data through several mechanisms. A postapproval study is commonly requested to collect long-term safety and effectiveness information, particularly if the product was approved through a PMA. These studies typically are determined at the time of PMA approval for a device of a relatively new type, for which longer term safety and effectiveness data are limited. A postapproval study also may be required to answer specific longer term safety and effectiveness questions outside the scope of a traditional IDE clinical study.

The FDA MedWatch program collects safety information and reports of adverse events related to the use of medical devices. Anyone who is aware of a device-related failure, breakage, or other adverse event related to the device's clinical use may submit this information to the FDA through a medical device report. Orthopaedic surgeons are vital to the success of this program because of their direct clinical experience with medical devices. Medical device reports are analyzed by the FDA to detect any trends or serious risks to public health.

Section 522 of the Food and Drug Administration Modernization Act authorizes the FDA to order a postmarket evaluation of a class II or class III device, "the failure of which would be reasonably likely to have serious adverse health consequences or which is intended to be (1) implanted in the human body for more than one year, or (2) a life sustaining or life supporting device used outside a device user facility."[9] Specifically, the FDA may order postmarket surveillance if there is a specific postmarket question about the safety and effectiveness of a device. Questions may be raised as a result of a new or expanded use (for example, expansion from hospital to home use); an expanded indication for use; a significant change in the device technology (for example, a developmental change in the design); an increase in the severity or frequency of serious adverse events; or a rare adverse event for which preclinical testing provided little to no useful information.

The data from postmarket evaluation and other sources are used in a variety of activities including the development or improvement of preclinical testing, testing standards, guidance documents, clinical study designs, device design alterations, and product recalls, all of which are intended to improve and protect the public health.

Spine Surgeons and the FDA

Many surgical products are available to an orthopaedic surgeon for the treatment of musculoskeletal disease, deformity, and trauma. Orthopaedic surgeons assist product manufacturers in designing new technologies or providing feedback to improve existing products. Surgeons also help companies by participating in clinical studies to assess the safety and effectiveness of new products. Orthopaedic organizations as well as individual surgeons have significant interactions with the FDA. For example, the FDA cooperates with the American Academy of Orthopaedic Surgeons (AAOS) every year to ensure that the FDA status of commercial products displayed at the AAOS annual meeting is accurately described. The AAOS requests that scientific presentations at the annual meeting include the FDA status of relevant products, so that the audience is informed whether the product use has been cleared or approved.

Board-certified orthopaedic surgeons employed by the FDA typically are involved in the premarket review of medical devices. These physicians analyze clinical study designs and data, review product labeling, and educate regulatory staff on the product use in different clinical scenarios. Under the FDA's Medical Devices Fellowship Program, a few senior orthopaedic surgery residents are able to work in the FDA for part of their residency.[10] The FDA benefits from the program through the resident's clinical perspectives, and the resident gains an appreciation for the FDA contribution to development of a product throughout its life cycle.

Orthopaedic surgeons have served on the Orthopaedic and Rehabilitation Devices Advisory Panel of the FDA Medical Devices Advisory Committee since its inception in the 1970s. This panel makes recommendations regarding FDA approval or clearance for products that use new technology, have a new indication for use, or involve a complex clinical issue. The panel also advises the FDA on urgent matters, matters having a broad impact on orthopaedic surgeons, and petitions to reclassify a device category. Orthopaedic surgeons are chosen to serve on the panel on the basis of their clini-

cal expertise, but to maintain scientific equipoise they undergo rigorous screening for conflicts of interest. The FDA is indebted to these physicians for their commitment to public service.

Every orthopaedic surgeon can interact with the FDA in several simple ways. The FDA tracks selected products after clearance or approval through formal, hypothesis-driven studies or reports of problematic incidents. By understanding good clinical study design, a surgeon is able to provide accurate scientific data for the FDA to use in evaluating a medical product. The FDA and manufacturers depend on communications from clinicians for assembling an accurate assessment of the scope and nature of incidents associated with product use. Severe or frequent incidents associated with the use of a particular device can lead to a mandatory recall if there is an imminent risk to public safety. Therefore, orthopaedic surgeons collectively can make a tremendous contribution to the public health by providing timely and detailed adverse event reports to the FDA and manufacturers.

Orthopaedic surgeons also can assist the FDA by understanding a product's approval or clearance status, the FDA process before a new device is marketed, and the basic processes and laws that guide the FDA's operations. A thorough understanding of the physician's responsibilities related to physician-directed (off-label) use of a product is important to patient care. The FDA does not have authority over physicians or the practice of medicine. If a physician believes the best interest of a patient can be served by the use of an unapproved device or the use of a legally marketed device in a manner other than intended or labeled, the physician must assume responsibility and liability for the use. The true safety profile and performance of a product used in such circumstances may be unknown because there has been no FDA review. Therefore, the physician has a responsibility to be well informed about the product's function and safety profile, to base its use on a firm scientific rationale and sound medical evidence, and to maintain records of the product's use, including both positive and adverse effects. By law, manufacturers are not allowed to promote the off-label use of their products. An IDE or Investigational New Drug application must be submitted and approved before a physician is authorized to study the use of a product for an indication that has not been approved or cleared and to submit the resulting data in support of a marketing application.

The FDA is legally bound to protect confidentiality and trade secrets related to any application submitted for review. Although FDA personnel interact with professional societies such as the AAOS through educational programs and meetings, they cannot discuss applications or products under review with anyone outside the FDA. The only public acknowledgements relate to device clearances, approvals, and applications presented to an advisory panel. These events are posted on the FDA website as they occur.[11] The FDA cannot

7: Spine Care and US Health Policy

respond to inquiries concerning the existence or status of an application unless the application submitter has granted express permission for the application to be discussed with the physician, patient, or other interested party making the inquiry.

Summary

The FDA's role in regulating medical products used by orthopaedic spine surgeons is diverse and far reaching. A product's FDA classification and regulatory pathway are based on the ability of the manufacturer to provide data to ensure the product is safe and effective for its intended use as well as evidence that the risks of using the product can be mitigated by predictable controls. Orthopaedic surgeons can make important contributions during all phases of a medical product's life cycle and thereby assist the FDA in its mission to protect public health. Orthopaedic surgeons can advance the FDA's goals through good clinical study design, responsible physician-directed use, and accurate, timely reporting of adverse events. The FDA strives to adapt its policies and procedures to accommodate changes in orthopaedic spine science and technology and to understand devices incorporating new technology.

Acknowledgement

Mr. Mark Melkerson is thanked for his assistance during the preparation of this chapter.

Annotated References

1. Federal Food and Drugs Act of 1906, Pub. L. No. 59-384 (1906).

2. Medical Device Amendments to the Federal Food, Drug and Cosmetics Act of 1976, Pub. L. No. 94-295.

3. Safe Medical Devices Act of 1990, Pub. L. No. 101-629.

4. Medical Device User Fee and Modernization Act of 2002, Pub. L. No. 107-250.

5. Food and Drug Administration Amendments Act of 2007, Pub. L. No. 110-85.

   The Federal Food, Drug and Cosmetics Act was amended to revise and extend FDA programs and authority including those pertaining to user fees, postmarket studies, the Pediatric Research Equity Act, and transparency of clinical study information.

6. Food and Drug Administration: Medical Devices: General and Special Controls. http://www.fda.gov/Medical Devices/DeviceRegulationandGuidance/Overview/GeneralandSpecialControls/default.htm. Accessed July 12, 2011.

The Device Advice website is designed to help the public understand CDRH regulation of medical devices. The section on general and special controls discusses device classification by risk and the requirement that medical devices in each classification conform to controls or strategies to mitigate known risks.

7. Food and Drug Administration: Medical Devices: Overview of Device Regulation. http://www.fda.gov/MedicalDevices/DeviceRegulationandGuidance/Overview/default.htm. Accessed May 25, 2011.

   This Device Advice webpage discusses device classification and provides links to other topics related to the risk-based paradigm for classifying and reviewing medical product marketing applications.

8. Code of Federal Regulations, Title 21, Section 860.7. http://www.accessdata.fda.gov/scripts/cdrh/cfdocs/cfcfr/CFRSearch.cfm?FR=860.7. Accessed Jan 21, 2009.

   This section of the Code of Federal Regulations outlines the criteria for determining the safety and effectiveness of medical devices, including the FDA's reliance on valid scientific evidence (in part [c]).

9. Food and Drug Administration Modernization Act of 1997, Pub. L. No. 110-85.

   This amendment to the Federal Food, Drug and Cosmetics Act expanded the focus on medical devices presenting great patient risk by directing the FDA to focus its postmarket surveillance on higher risk devices and expanding FDA accreditation of outside (third-party) initial reviewers of class I and low- to intermediate-risk class II devices. The FDA was authorized to keep off of the market any product with manufacturing processes so deficient as to present a serious health hazard and to take appropriate action if a device is likely to be used for a harmful unlabeled use.

10. Food and Drug Administration: About FDA: Medical Device Fellowship Program. http://www.fda.gov/AboutFDA/WorkingatFDA/FellowshipInternship GraduateFacultyPrograms/MedicalDeviceFellowship ProgramCDRH/default.htm. Accessed May 25, 2011.

    The Medical Device Fellowship Program was established to increase the range and depth of collaboration between the CDRH and the outside scientific community. This program offers short- and long-term fellowship opportunities for individuals interested in learning about the regulatory process and sharing their knowledge and experience with simple to complex medical devices. Participants have included physicians with clinical or surgical expertise; engineers in biomedical, mechanical, electrical, and software areas; and others including students from many scientific disciplines.

11. Food and Drug Administration: Medical Devices: Recently-Approved Devices. http://www.fda.gov/MedicalDevices/ProductsandMedicalProcedures/DeviceApprovalsandClearances/Recently-ApprovedDevices/default.htm. Accessed May 25, 2011.

    Device events including clearances, approvals, and applications to an advisory panel are posted on the FDA website as they occur.

Chapter 49

Spine Care and the US Workers' Compensation System

Edward Radcliffe Anderson III, MD   Garrick W. Cason, MD   Chetan K. Patel, MD

Introduction

The workers' compensation system in the United States represents a constellation of interwoven medical, legal, and social insurance elements regulated at both the federal and state levels. The current system evolved over the 20th century in response to the incidence of job-related injury during the course of the Industrial Revolution.[1,2]

History

The first social insurance program to provide care for injured laborers was adopted in Germany in 1884 under Chancellor Otto von Bismarck. The United Kingdom adopted a program in 1897, and most other Western European countries followed suit before the United States enacted the Federal Employees' Compensation Act in 1908.[3] The US law was weaker than the European laws but represented the nation's first attempt to provide a social safety net for injured laborers. The first state workers' compensation law was passed in New York in 1910 but was overturned by a state court.[4,5] Wisconsin was the first state to both pass (in 1911) and sustain a viable workers' compensation reform package. By 1920 all except eight US states had passed constitutionally valid workers' compensation reform laws.

The impetus for reform stemmed from several factors: a societal revolt against the unpalatable human consequences of industrial accidents; the failure of the legal system to provide timely, adequate aid to injured laborers; the need for a social insurance system to provide such aid; and employers' concern about the growing costs of litigation and jury awards to plaintiff workers. The push for workers' compensation reform began on two normally opposing fronts, as both employers and the burgeoning labor movement sought a remedy under US common law. Employers had become increasingly interested in legal reform to eliminate the burden of legal fees, the threat of large jury awards, and the societal repercussions of causing an industrial injury. Employees favored legal reform as a means of providing financial and medical relief after a work-related injury.

The only available remedy for an injured worker at the turn of the 20th century was through litigation, which was lengthy, expensive, and likely to result in loss of employment. Under US common or tort law, an injured worker often faced an insurmountable evidential and financial burden. In contrast, an employer was protected against liability for a work-related injury by three strong common law defenses: the fellow servant doctrine protected the employer if an on-the-job injury could be attributed to the negligence of another employee, the assumption of risk doctrine protected the employer if the injured employee had performed the job despite knowledge of the associated risk, and the contributory negligence doctrine protected the employer against any liability if the employee was even partly responsible for the injury. Fellow employees typically were reluctant to testify on behalf of an injured colleague for fear of retribution in the form of employment termination. The three strong employer defenses, combined with the worker's evidential burden, a lack of witnesses, and the expense of a protracted legal battle against a deep-pocketed employer, dissuaded many injured workers from filing a lawsuit.

Although jurisdiction over workers' compensation generally is at the state level, the first (1908) legislation provided protection for federal employees. Federal workers' compensation later was expanded by the Longshore and Harbor Workers' Compensation Act, Black Lung Benefits Act, Federal Employers Liability Act, and US Veterans Compensation Program. The National Commission on State Workmen's Compensation was established by the Occupational Safety and Health Act of 1970 to set a national benchmark for state and federal workers' compensation policies.

Dr. Anderson or an immediate family member has received research or institutional support from DePuy, a Johnson & Johnson company. Dr. Patel or an immediate family member has received royalties from Globus Medical; is a member of a speakers' bureau or has made paid presentations on behalf of Medtronic and Stryker; serves as a paid consultant to or is an employee of Stryker; and owns stock or stock options in Medtronic. Neither Dr. Cason nor any immediate family member has received anything of value from or owns stock in a commercial company or institution related directly or indirectly to the subject of this chapter.

Table 1

The Six Principles of the Workers' Compensation System

Principle	Description
No-fault compensation	A claimant is eligible for compensation after a work-related injury, regardless of fault.
Just compensation	Compensation is prescribed by statute based on the claimant's average wage or salary and the effect of the injury on the claimant's ability to work.
Collective liability	Risk is distributed among employers in each industrial sector, who collectively fund and share the liability for workers' compensation.
Mandatory coverage	Employer participation is mandatory. In some states, an employer may self-insure by fulfilling workers' compensation obligations directly.
Protection from litigation	The workers' compensation system generally is the sole venue for resolving a work-related injury claim. The civil tort-based legal system is available only for adjudication of a claim involving an egregious wrong.
Right of appeal	An employer or claimant can appeal a benefit coverage decision of the workers' compensation insurance provider.

Adapted with permission from Plumb JM, Cowell JWF: An overview of workers' compensation. *Occup Med* 1998;13(2):241-272.

Principles of Workers' Compensation

Workers' compensation benefits for most workers are regulated by a state workers' compensation commission. The recommendations of the National Commission on State Workmen's Compensation have led to similarities among the state systems, however. Six principles underlie these systems[4] (Table 1). These principles represent concessions by both the employer and the employee to achieve a common purpose: providing an injured worker with access to medical care during the immediate postinjury period and defraying the effects of income lost because of an inability to work. Employers agree to guarantee a standard, fair-value level of benefits to an injured worker, regardless of negligence by either party. In exchange, employees agree that the workers' compensation system is the exclusive remedy for an injured worker, thereby relinquishing the use of the common law tort system as a means of achieving compensation.

An injured employee must meet several criteria to qualify to file a workers' compensation claim: the claimant must demonstrably be an employee, not an independent contractor, at the time of injury; the injury must be sustained "arising out of" or "in the course of" the claimant's employment and within the scope of the job description; a causal relationship must exist between the injury or illness and the claimant's employment duties; the injury or illness must lead to an assignable functional or occupational impairment causing an occupational disability, such as diminished earning potential; the claimant must follow competent medical advice; and the claim must be filed in a timely manner and through appropriate channels.[3] The final criterion protects both the claimant and the employer because a delay in filing a claim leads to a delay in initiating benefits and may lead to a less than optimal medical outcome (Figure 1). Workers' compensation benefits are not available if the injury resulted from willful employee negligence, such as from workplace horseplay, intoxication, or a violent act between employees.

Health Care Providers and Workers' Compensation

Coverage and Benefits

The central tenet of the workers' compensation system is that an employee injured on the job is entitled to both medical and disability benefits, regardless of fault.[5-7] The injured employee can be treated by the physician of his or her choice, with the understanding that the employer or insurance provider may request a provider change if the physician or hospital does meet the standard of care or the employee has not demonstrably benefited from treatment. To control escalating health care costs, many state workers' compensation commissions have retained managed care organizations to analyze and process claims and have implemented standardized fee schedules for provider compensation.[5,6] A few states also have stipulated that physicians wishing to participate in the care of patients under the workers' compensation system must undergo training in workers' compensation evaluation and become certified.

Disability benefits defray the effects of lost income resulting from a work-related injury. The type of disability benefit awarded (temporary or permanent, total or partial) is primarily based on the time required for recovery, as related to the type of injury and the patient's reaching maximal medical improvement.[8-10] Maximal medical improvement is defined as the "date from which further recovery or deterioration is not anticipated."[10] Maximal medical improvement generally is reached after a period of treatment and convales-

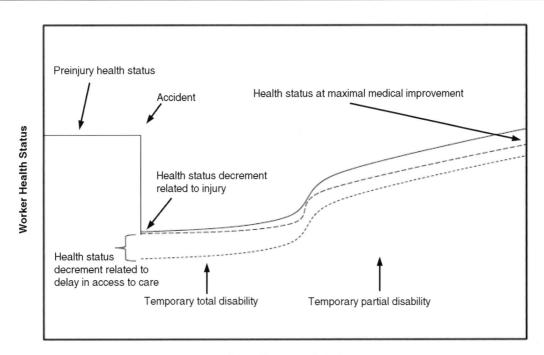

Figure 1 Schematic diagram showing worker health status from injury to maximal medical improvement. Solid line = return to preinjury level of health, long-dashed line = permanent impairment resulting from the injury, short-dashed line = permanent impairment resulting from delayed access to health care or failure to follow competent medical advice. (Adapted with permission from Plumb JM, Cowell JWF: An overview of workers' compensation. *Occup Med* 1998;13[2]:241-272.)

cence, but a patient is not required to undergo any form of treatment to reach maximal medical improvement. If the patient declines treatment, the physician must decide whether an impairment exists and whether treatment could be expected to improve the impairment.

A worker who is unable to work because of a work-related injury is eligible for temporary total disability payments immediately after the injury[4] (Figure 1). The benefit continues as long as the patient remains unable to work because of injury-associated impairment, and it ends when the patient recovers sufficiently for limited duty or reaches maximal medical improvement. The temporary total disability benefit is equivalent to an administratively prescribed percentage of the worker's average wage or salary, subject to statutory limitations. A temporary partial disability benefit may be payable if the injured worker is able to return to work in a limited capacity and the employer can make suitable accommodations.

A determination of the presence or absence of a permanent impairment is of utmost importance when the workers' compensation physician determines that the patient has reached maximal medical improvement. If a permanent impairment exists, an impairment rating is assigned, and the temporary disability benefit is replaced by a permanent disability benefit. The adminis-

tratively prescribed payment schedule for the permanent disability benefit is based on a functional impairment rating, and/or the patient's occupational impairment percentage. The functional or occupational impairment rating is independent of the injured worker's physical limitations for job performance. Permanent total or partial disability is determined based on an assigned functional or occupational impairment rating. In most jurisdictions, the impairment rating is based on one or more editions of the American Medical Association *Guides to the Evaluation of Permanent Impairment*, but some states use their own criteria (Table 2).

The Role of the Spine Physician

The physician's primary role in the workers' compensation system is to promote healing and rehabilitation, with the goal of attaining the best possible outcome. A spine care provider may become involved in the care of an injured worker at multiple points during the postinjury and recovery periods. As a workers' compensation health care provider, provider of a second opinion, or independent medical examiner, the physician should communicate to the patient, employer, and case worker (if any) on the patient's progress and ability to return to work at full or limited capacity. Although the workers'

Table 2

Reference Used for Rating Workers' Compensation Impairment, by Jurisdiction or Worker Classification

American Medical Association: *Guides to the Evaluation of Permanent Impairment* (AMA *Guides*), 3rd edition: Colorado, Oregon.

AMA *Guides,* 4th edition: Alabama, Arkansas, Kansas, Maine, Maryland, South Dakota, Texas, West Virginia.

AMA *Guides,* 5th edition: California, Delaware, Georgia, Hawaii, Idaho, Indiana, Iowa, Kentucky, Massachusetts, Nevada, New Hampshire, North Dakota, Ohio, Rhode Island, Vermont, Washington.

AMA *Guides,* 6th edition: Alaska, Arizona, Louisiana, Mississippi, Montana, New Mexico, Oklahoma, Pennsylvania, Tennessee, Wyoming.

AMA *Guides,* no edition specified: Connecticut.

Jurisdiction-specific regulations: Florida, Illinois, New York, North Carolina, Utah, Wisconsin, US Department of Veterans Affairs.

No specified reference: Michigan, Missouri, Nebraska, New Jersey, South Carolina, Virginia.

US Federal Employees' Compensation Act: All civilian employees of the US government.

US Longshore and Harbor Workers' Compensation Act: All longshore, harbor, and maritime employees.

compensation system is based on a no-fault principle, an adversarial relationship often develops among the injured employee, employer, and insurance provider. The physician may be thrust into this conflict but must remember that the fiduciary responsibility is to the patient. Duty to the patient requires the physician to remain impartial, provide an honest evaluation and treatment that meets care standards, and effectively communicate with all involved parties throughout the process.

Evaluation and Documentation

Patient History and Examination
The history is critical in the evaluation of a patient with a work-related spine injury, whether the injury is acute or repetitive. The reported lifetime incidence of low back pain is 70% to 85% of the population, and the annual incidence is 15% to 45%. Approximately 2% of the US workforce receive workers' compensation medical benefits every year for a work-related back injury. Because of the near-pandemic but transient nature of low back pain, it is difficult to assign a causal relationship between a patient's work and pain. Establishing the compensable nature of a patient's injury requires demonstrating that the causal factors are work related ("arising out of" or "in the course of" employ-

ment). For this purpose, the physician must thoroughly understand the patient's working conditions and the job duties that link the patient's injury to her or his employment.[11] A professional who evaluates, diagnoses, and treats a patient who is work injured should make every effort to obtain and document details of the injury, the patient's condition after any treatment, any earlier similar pain, and any other medical conditions.[12] A preexisting condition may be exacerbated by a work-related injury. It is critical to document such a preexisting condition as well as any earlier symptoms and treatment. The physician's opinion as to the cause of the condition must be documented.

The physical examination includes the typical inspection, palpation, assessment of range of motion, graded motor examination, sensory examination, reflex examination, gait evaluation, and evaluation for long tract signs. Because of the potential for an inorganic etiology of the back pain or a secondary gain issue, the provider also must look for physical examination signs that suggest malingering or a psychologic etiology[13] (Table 3). The presence of one or two such signs generally is insignificant, but the presence of multiple signs should alert the examiner to assess the possibility of a behavioral etiology. A provider who evaluates and treats patients with occupational back injury should routinely consider involving a behavioral health specialist. Physical injury leading to impairment, disability, and chronic pain can lead to or exacerbate a behavioral or psychologic disorder.

Preexisting Conditions
A preexisting medical condition typically is not covered under workers' compensation insurance, but a new injury or illness as well as an exacerbation or aggravation of an existing condition is covered and compensable if it resulted from job performance. In general, the preexisting condition must be documented, and impairment resulting from a preexisting condition or a work-related secondary injury must be separated. A percentage of the liability is apportioned to the work-related injury and is assigned to the workers' compensation insurance provider. Unfortunately, assigning causal relationships in back injury can be difficult because of the ubiquitous nature of back pain and degenerative disk disease. A proclivity for repetitive use injury may arise from many nonoccupational activities of daily living, such as lifting, bending, and twisting related to housework, sports, or driving as well as degenerative or inflammatory arthritic processes, age, and sex. Employers and workers' compensation insurance providers rightly argue that they should not be held responsible for bearing the percentage of causation apportioned to nonemployment activities or a preexisting condition. To protect employers from being burdened with such liability, most state workers' compensation commissions have instituted a state-sponsored secondary injury fund that is collectively supported by employer and insurer contributions. The purpose is to dilute employer liability

Table 3

Physical Examination Signs Suggesting an Organic or a Nonorganic Source of Back Pain

Test	Normal Sign[a]	Waddell Sign[b]
Tenderness to light palpation	Anatomic distribution	Nonanatomic distribution
Axial loading	No pain	Lumbar pain
Simulated rotation	No pain	Lumbar pain
Straight leg raise (sitting, supine, contralateral)	Similar results	Nonconcordant results
Sensory examination	Dermatomal distribution	Nondermatomal distribution
Motor examination	Myotomal distribution	Pseudoweakness, jerkiness, nonmyotomal distribution

[a]Suggesting an anatomic or physiologic pain etiology.
[b]Suggesting a nonorganic or psychologic pain etiology.

Adapted with permission from Waddell G, Bircher M, Finlayson D, et al: Symptoms and signs: Physical disease or illness behavior? *BMJ* 1984;289:739.

Table 4

Criteria for Establishing a Causal Relationship Between Injury and Employment

Criterion	Description
Temporality	The cause must precede the effect.
Mechanism	The mechanism of injury must be anatomically and physically plausible and consistent with the history, physical examination, radiography, and ancillary testing.
Contiguity	A clear cause-and-effect relationship must be established. Greater exposure must increase the effect in a repetitive use injury.
Consistency	The injury pattern must consistently lead to the specific impairment, as established in the literature, legislation, or case law.
Specificity	The injury cannot be the result of factors unrelated to the claimant's job; the cause must be specific for the effect.
Coherence	The presumption of work relatedness in an individual claim should be consistent with the medical literature.

Adapted with permission from Genovese E: Causality, in Demeter SL, Andersson GB, eds: *Disability Evaluation*, ed 2. St, Louis, MO, Mosby, 2003, p 95.

for preexisting injuries and to encourage employers to hire workers who have recovered from an earlier injury.

Establishing Causation

Establishing a causal relationship between a claimant's duties and injury, based on a thoroughly documented history and physical examination, is important for assigning liability. For most orthopaedic injuries, causation is accepted by the employer or insurer based on the traumatic nature of the injury or the presumption of the medical literature, case law, or legislation. The ubiquitous nature of adult axial back pain and the prevalence of earlier injury mean that establishing causation in a workers' compensation back injury claim can be difficult. The patient's health care provider often accepts the patient-provided medical history as fact. The murky nature of assignment of causation often requires an independent medical examiner to become involved. The independent medical examiner has no

doctor-patient relationship and is better able to objectively evaluate the patient for a causal relationship between injury and employment, using six criteria (Table 4). The independent medical examiner serves as the medical arbiter of causation in workers' compensation claims.

Return to Work and Work Restrictions

A physician caring for a patient with a work-related back injury must be extremely careful when clearing the patient for a return to work and setting work restrictions. When medically indicated, an early return to work can prevent the patient from developing a so-called disability attitude.[14] Thorough knowledge of the patient's work conditions and job duties as well as the availability of light duties is crucial to defining the timing of return to work. For setting work restrictions, the physician should be well versed in the terms used to describe physical work activities[8] (Table 5).

Impairment Rating

When the patient has achieved maximal medical improvement of a residual impairment, the claimant, case worker, employer, claimant's attorney, and insurer request an impairment rating. In most jurisdictions, the American Medical Association *Guides to the Evaluation of Permanent Impairment* is used for this purpose.[10] The impairment is analyzed first on the basis of injured organ systems and then as it affects the whole person. The impairment rating and any future job restrictions form the foundation for determining a disability benefit. The formula for a permanent partial or total disability rating varies by state or federal agency.

Americans With Disability Act and the Family Medical Leave Act

The workers' compensation system in the United States is standardized but not completely uniform from state to state or within the federal government. Federal laws have attempted to eliminate abuse by working through the state systems. In addition, the Americans With Disability Act and Family Medical Leave Act (FMLA) affect the state workers' compensation systems; 80% of all claims under the Americans with Disability Act have been filed by injured workers, and only 13% have been filed by new job applicants. Physicians must be prepared to stipulate the accommodations required for a worker with an impairment rating to return to the workplace. The FMLA interacts with state workers' compensation systems by establishing minimal leave requirements. The FLMA is used in determining whether leave requested by a worker with a disability is a "reasonable accommodation" or an "undue hardship" for the employer under the Americans With Disability Act. If an employee is placed on leave under the FMLA, the employer cannot require light duty work even if a prescription for light duty is appropriate.

Summary

The workers' compensation system in the United States, although complicated and under many jurisdictions, is based on six common principles. A physician treating a patient with a back injury under the workers' compensation system must remember that first and foremost she or he is an advocate for the patient; the exception is a physician serving as an independent medical examiner. Meticulous, thorough record keeping is essential because the medical record serves as the basis for the worker's claim and ultimately the impairment rating at maximal medical improvement. The process can be rewarding if the physician endeavors to understand the intricacies of the system as well as the needs of the patient, case worker, employer, and insurer.

Table 5

Types of Work Activity

Type of Work	Maximum Daily Requirements
Sedentary	Lifting: 10 lb Carrying: little or none Walking: 2 hours Standing: 2 hours Sitting: 6 to 8 hours
Light	Lifting: 20 lb Carrying: 10 lb Walking: 4 hours Standing: 4 to 8 hours Sitting: pushing or pulling using leg controls
Light Medium	Lifting: 30 lb Carrying: 20 lb Walking: 4 hours Standing: 4 to 8 hours Sitting: pushing or pulling using leg controls
Medium	Lifting: 50 lb Carrying: 25 lb Standing: 8 hours Walking: 8 hours
Light Heavy	Lifting: 75 lb Carrying 40 lb Standing: 8 hours Walking: 8 hours
Heavy	Lifting: 100 lb Carrying: 50 lb Standing: 8 hours Walking: 8 hours
Very Heavy	Lifting: more than 100 lb Carrying: more than 50 lb Standing: 8 hours Walking: 8 hours

Adapted with permission from Demeter SL: How to fill out disability and return to work forms, in Demeter SL, Andersson GB, eds: *Disability Evaluation*, ed 2. St Louis, MO, Mosby, 2003, pp 871-891.

Annotated References

1. Norris CR: Understanding workers' compensation law. *Hand Clin* 1993;9(2):231-239.

2. Yorker B: Workers' compensation law: An overview. *AAOHN J* 1994;42(9):420-424.

3. Kiselica D, Sibson B, Green-McKenzie J: Workers' compensation: A historical review and description of a legal and social insurance system. *Clin Occup Environ Med* 2004;4(2):237-247.

4. Plumb JM, Cowell JW: An overview of workers' compensation. *Occup Med* 1998;13(2):241-272.

5. D'Andrea DC, Meyer JD: Workers' compensation reform. *Clin Occup Environ Med* 2004;4(2):259-271.

6. Boden LI: Workers' compensation in the United States: High costs, low benefits. *Annu Rev Public Health* 1995; 16:189-218.

7. Boden LI: Workers' compensation, in Levy BS, Wegman DS, eds: *Occupational Health: Recognizing and Preventing Work Related Disease and Injury*. Philadelphia, PA, Lippincott, Williams, and Wilkins, 2000, pp 237-256.

8. Demeter SL: How to fill out disability and return to work forms, in Demeter SL, Andersson GB, eds: *Disability Evaluation*, ed 2. St Louis, MO, Mosby, 2003, pp 871-891.

9. Genovese E: Causality, in Demeter SL, Andersson GB, eds: *Disability Evaluation*, ed 2. St Louis, MO, Mosby, 2003, p 95.

10. American Medical Association: *Guides to the Evaluation of Permanent Impairment*, ed 6. Chicago, IL, American Medical Association, 2007.

    A diagnosis-based chart for each organ system is useful in classifying impairments by their severity.

11. Dunning KK, Davis KG, Cook C, et al: Costs by industry and diagnosis among musculoskeletal claims in a state workers compensation system: 1999-2004. *Am J Ind Med* 2010;53(3):276-284.

    The costs associated with workers' compensation claims are analyzed based on the anatomic location of injury and the type of industry in which the injury occurred.

12. DeBerard MS, Wheeler AJ, Gundy JM, Stein DM, Colledge AL: Presurgical biopsychological variables predict medical, compensation, and aggregate costs of lumbar discectomy in Utah workers' compensation patients. *Spine J* 2011;11(5):395-401.

    Medical comorbidities, psychologic factors, and social circumstances are identified as affecting the outcome of surgery in patients with a workers' compensation claim.

13. Waddell G, Bircher M, Finlayson D, Main CJ: Symptoms and signs: Physical disease or illness behaviour? *Br Med J (Clin Res Ed)* 1984;289(6447):739-741.

14. Nguyen TH, Randolph DC, Talmage J, Succop P, Travis R: Long-term outcomes of lumbar fusion among worker's compensation subjects: A historical cohort study. *Spine (Phila Pa 1976)* 2011;36(4):320-331.

    Lumbar fusion for disk degeneration or herniation is associated with a poor outcome in patients with a workers' compensation claim. Total number of days away from work is a highly significant negative predictor of return to work after nonsurgical or surgical treatment.

7: Spine Care and US Health Policy

Chapter 50
Safety and Functional Outcome Assessment in Spine Surgery

Sohail K. Mirza, MD, MPH   Mark A. Konodi, MS   Brook I. Martin, PhD, MPH

Kevin F. Spratt, PhD

Introduction

Orthopaedic surgeon Ernest Amory Codman, MD began his passionate advocacy for the systematic assessment of surgical outcomes approximately 100 years ago.[1] Codman rigorously and candidly recorded the outcome for each of his own patients, and he established the End Result Hospital in Boston based on "the duty of every hospital to establish a follow-up system, so that as far as possible the result of every case will be available at all times for investigation by members of the staff, the trustees, or administration, or by other authorized investigators or statisticians."[2] Between 1911 and 1917, the short-lived hospital published outcomes including 130 errors that affected 337 patients. A century later, the medical profession is still struggling to develop the commitment and tools required for attaining Codman's vision.

Spine surgery is second only to cardiac procedures as a cause of health care expenditure in the United States.[3] Although patients, surgeons, hospital, insurers, regulators, and policy makers agree that measuring outcomes is essential to informed decision making, there is only a weak evidence base for many common spine and other procedures.[4-8] The available tools for measuring spine surgery outcomes are limited in their ability to distinguish among surgical techniques, implanted devices, hospitals, and surgeons. Research designs, definitions related to benefit and harm, ascertainment methods, and analytic approaches are not sufficiently standardized to allow meaningful comparisons.[9] New spine surgery devices frequently are approved by the US Food and Drug Administration (FDA) on the basis of premarket approval studies using a noninferiority research design, which in some areas of spine surgery

may not be consistent with clinical practice or the state of knowledge.[10-26]

Many stakeholders consider both safety and effectiveness data to be crucial for evaluating procedures, settings, and devices.[27] Patients must weigh their specific risk factors to make an informed choice as to the risk-benefit trade-offs associated with surgery.[28] Hospitals are committed to improving safety and quality, but achieving their objectives remains problematic.[29] In the absence of consistent definitions of effectiveness and safety, it is not possible to compare treatments, hospitals, surgeons, or improvements over time. Even if standard definitions were available, differences in ascertainment methods would yield different complication rates; the more diligently adverse events are sought, the more likely they are to be found.[30-33]

Nuances in the analysis of results can profoundly influence interpretation. In contrast to the lack of tools for safety measurement, reliable instruments are available for measuring general health status, physical function, and disease-specific outcomes as a result of two decades of research on the development and scoring of patient-reported outcomes questionnaires. These methods for the most part focus on measurements at the group level, and inaccuracies can result when the results are extrapolated to the individual level. The limitations are related to four fundamental factors in spine surgery outcomes assessment: research design, definitions related to safety measurement, ascertainment methods for safety evaluation, and individual patient–level interpretation of outcomes.

Noninferiority Studies of Spine Surgery

The superiority study is the optimal research design for evaluating the efficacy of an investigational treatment or device. This type of randomized controlled study is designed to determine whether at a specified end point the investigational treatment is more effective than another treatment or placebo (the standard medication or procedure, an ineffective medication, or a sham surgical procedure). A superiority study requires no assump-

None of the following authors nor any immediate family member has received anything of value from or owns stock in a commercial company or institution related directly or indirectly to the subject of this chapter: Dr. Mirza, Mr. Konodi, Dr. Martin, Dr. Spratt.

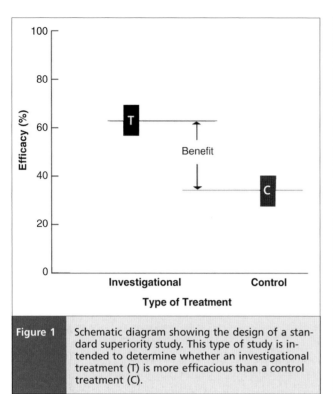

Figure 1   Schematic diagram showing the design of a standard superiority study. This type of study is intended to determine whether an investigational treatment (T) is more efficacious than a control treatment (C).

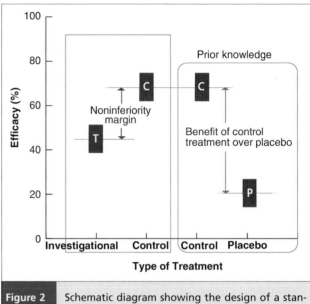

Figure 2   Schematic diagram showing the design of a standard noninferiority study, which is intended to determine whether the efficacy of an investigational treatment (T) is within a specified margin of the efficacy of a control treatment (C). This study design assumes that the control intervention has been proved more efficacious than placebo (P), and it assumes that the extent of the benefit of the control intervention over placebo is known.

Table 1

The Preconditions for Conducting a Noninferiority Study

1. It would be unethical to conduct a superiority study comparing the investigational treatment to a placebo treatment.

2. A treatment exists that has accepted efficacy and can be administered to patients in the control group.

3. The margin chosen to establish the noninferiority of the investigational treatment is clinically meaningful and statistically sound.

4. The investigational treatment is being compared to the most efficacious control intervention.

tions concerning the efficacy of the investigational treatment or the control intervention, and a head-to-head comparison can reveal which treatment is more effective (Figure 1). A superiority study tests the hypothesis that one treatment is superior to other treatments. If the standard treatment is found to be superior to the investigational treatment, the study is still a superiority study. The null hypothesis is no difference, against the alternative hypothesis that the treatment groups are different. If one treatment is specified to be better than the other, a directional hypothesis might be used, in which type I error is relaxed. A directional hypothesis test therefore is less rigorous than a two-tailed hypothesis test.

Regulatory agencies such as the FDA frequently allow sponsors to evaluate their new devices using a noninferiority research paradigm. A noninferiority study is designed to allow approval of devices substantially similar in efficacy. This research methodology formed the basis of the FDA assessment of artificial disks.[23,24] In comparison with a case study, any randomized study can provide strong evidence of device efficacy, but the design of a noninferiority study requires that the results be interpreted more cautiously.

A noninferiority study is designed to test the hypothesis that the investigational treatment is as efficacious or almost as efficacious as the control treatment (Figure 2). The bar for efficacy is lower in a noninferiority study than in a superiority study. The investigators may believe the investigational treatment has advantages (such as in safety, cost, or administration) that make it preferable to the control treatment, even if it is slightly less efficacious. The allowable difference in efficacy is specified at study inception as the noninferiority margin.[34] The investigators are able to claim superiority if the investigational treatment is found to be more efficacious than the control treatment.[35] If the investigational treatment is not found to be more efficacious, the investigators can make an "at least as good as control" claim if the preconditions for a noninferiority study were satisfied[34-36] (Table 1).

A noninferiority research study may be the only option if the study involves a treatable fatal or progressive disease, such as a cancer or infection, for which a highly effective standard treatment is known to exist. It would be unethical to withhold the benefits of standard treatment from patients in the control or experimental arm of the study. A new drug and an established drug may be compared in a noninferiority study if the new drug is believed to be no more efficacious than the established drug but to have advantages such as lower cost or fewer adverse effects.[37]

In addition to the established efficacy of the intervention administered to patients in the control group, the noninferiority study design requires that the extent of the benefit offered by the control intervention, compared with placebo, be known and consistently measurable.[34,35] Furthermore, there should be reasonable assurance that the conditions of the study preserves the benefit of the control intervention over placebo.[34] In practice, this constancy assumption requires that the research methods and settings under which the control intervention was proved more effective than placebo must be replicated in the current noninferiority study.

Because a noninferiority study assumes that the control intervention has proven efficacy (Figure 2 and Figure 3), at least one previous randomized study should be available to establish the control intervention as preferable to placebo.[34,36-38] For example, this condition is satisfied for a study of fusion to treat back pain if the 2001 study by the Swedish Lumbar Spine Study Group is considered to provide acceptable evidence.[39] If multiple studies have been performed, the results should consistently favor the control intervention over placebo. At the beginning of the most recent FDA studies of disk replacement, such study data were not available to support the surgical treatment of chronic discogenic back pain. More recently, several randomized studies have compared fusion to nonsurgical treatment.[39-41] Data from these studies most closely approximate data on the efficacy of fusion surgery. Unfortunately, they do not allow consistent generalization. Fusion is more effective than unstructured nonsurgical care but has equivalent efficacy to cognitive-behavioral therapy for improvement of back-specific function.[39-41]

The Noninferiority Margin

Before a noninferiority study begins, a crucial decision is made as to the acceptable difference in the efficacy of the investigational and control treatments.[34-36] If previous randomized studies compared the control intervention with placebo, statistical analysis can be used to estimate the benefit of each.[38] Nonetheless, clinical judgment is necessary for determining how much of this benefit the investigational treatment must retain to be considered not inferior to the control treatment.[34,37] Specifying a very narrow margin increases the number of patients needed for the study, prolongs the investigational phase of a new treatment, and increases the eventual cost of the new treatment, if it becomes established. Specifying a wide margin may allow the investigational treatment to be considered not inferior even if it is no better than placebo. The lack of a clearly effica-

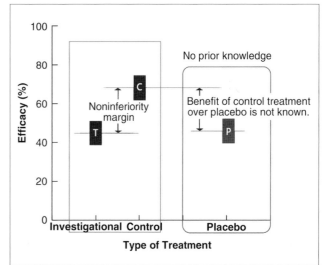

Figure 3 Schematic diagram showing that a noninferiority study cannot establish scientific proof of the efficacy of an investigational treatment (T) if the control intervention (C) is not a widely accepted standard treatment, the efficacy of the control intervention is in doubt, or the margin of benefit of the control treatment over placebo (P) is not well established. Under these conditions, the efficacy of the investigational treatment can be equivalent to that of the control treatment within a specified noninferiority margin but still be no better than the efficacy of placebo or no treatment.

cious treatment for nonspecific discogenic axial back pain prevents investigators from specifying a noninferiority margin (Figure 3).

A new treatment established on the basis of a noninferiority study can serve as the control intervention in a future noninferiority study. The gradual lowering of the efficacy bar in this fashion has been called biocreep.[34] Even after a valid initial noninferiority study, the progressive stepwise degradation of efficacy may eventually lead to a new treatment being found simultaneously not inferior to its immediate control treatment and no better than placebo. This difficulty can be avoided if noninferiority studies always are designed using the most efficacious treatment as the comparison control intervention.[34]

The Role of Noninferiority Studies and Sham Surgery in Spine Surgery

The noninferiority framework has a useful role in clinical research. As a regulatory tool, it allows development of "me too" products; a developer can enter the competition by providing an alternative that is "at least as good as" a standard therapy for achieving the specified benefit with an acceptable safety profile.[36] Market forces then can determine the success or failure of the new product, based on its effectiveness, cost, safety, ease of administration, and other factors. Randomized studies comparing surgical to nonsurgical care are dif-

7: Spine Care and US Health Policy

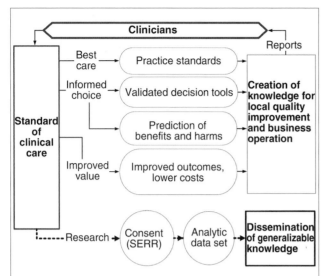

Figure 4	Schematic diagram showing a conceptual framework for integration of the Spine End Results Registry with routine clinical care and medical record documentation. All patients contributed to internal hospital-specific analyses and provided feedback for improving the local standard of care. The patients who prospectively provided informed consent were eligible for inclusion in a research data set that can be analyzed to generate generalizable knowledge.

ficult to design and execute, and the ethics of sham surgery are controversial. Such considerations may have been important in the FDA's acceptance of noninferiority studies for evaluating new spine technologies. However, a superiority research design is preferable if a noninferiority margin cannot be reasonably estimated from data available at the inception of a study.

The use of placebo sham procedures often is impractical in surgical studies, and the ethics of sham surgery are intensely debated.[42-45] The alternatives to sham surgical treatment are nonsurgical treatment or a surgical procedure known to be efficacious. If providing some patients with sham surgery or no treatment would be unethical or if an available treatment is uniformly accepted as standard treatment for a progressive or fatal condition, a noninferiority randomized controlled study is appropriate.[34] These are not the circumstances for chronic axial back pain attributed to degenerative disk disease, however. A standard treatment does not exist; fusion and other surgical treatments appear to have efficacy similar to that of a structured rehabilitation program. Delaying treatment can prolong disability but does not create a risk of death or other irreversible harm. Despite the high cost, a randomized controlled study designed to determine whether the investigational treatment for chronic back pain is superior to sham surgery or nonsurgical treatment remains the best research design for scientifically establishing the efficacy of an investigational treatment.[34]

Defining and Ascertaining Harms in Spine Surgery: The Spine End Results Registry

Defining Harms

Patient safety is a focus of current medical literature and general news reports as well as noninferiority studies of new technologies. Despite this emphasis, the actual measurement of complications in spine care remains problematic. The fundamental difficulties include a lack of agreement regarding the complications that warrant routine measurement, a lack of consistent definitions for common complications, and inattention to ascertainment methods in the published literature.

The challenges are illustrated by the history of a novel quality improvement program, the Spine End Results Registry (SERR).[9] This federally funded research project was designed to provide prospective active surveillance of adverse occurrences and patient-reported outcomes associated with spine surgery. SERR was intended to provide a sustainable, enhanced method for quality improvement at two participating hospitals, in which research and clinical care would be integrated using a conceptual framework (Figure 4). Modified Delphi interviews were conducted before the program was launched to evaluate surgeons' beliefs and attitudes (Figure 5). More than 60% of the participating spine surgeons agreed that the highest quality evaluation priority should be to measure the rates of five types of adverse occurrences (neurologic injury, infection, reoperation, medical complications, and cerebrospinal fluid [CSF] leakage) (Table 2). The surgeons differed on how these events should be defined and measured, however (Table 3). During the 2-year study period, infection rates ranging from 0.3% to 5.9% were measured, depending on the definition of infection (Table 3). The rates of CSF leakage ranged from 0.4% to 8.6%, depending on the definition of this event.

The use of standardized definitions is necessary for safety surveillance of patients with spine disorders. The term complication is problematic because it can imply failure, with resulting damage to a professional reputation as well as credentialing and legal consequences.[46] In the SERR program, unwanted events were called adverse occurrences.[9] The term adverse event was reserved for an adverse occurrence associated with a change in patient monitoring, an intervention, or an outcome. Consensus-based definitions were developed for the 175 adverse occurrences monitored in SERR.[9]

To be broadly useful, definitions must be refined, standardized, and adopted by a large multispecialty spine registry, a professional society, or a regulatory agency. Such a broad consensus simplifies safety reporting in spine care and allows patients to become more informed participants in their own care. The World Health Organization has proposed a conceptual framework, the International Classification for Patient Safety,[47] which was implemented for spine surgery in the SERR program (Figure 6). The World Health Orga-

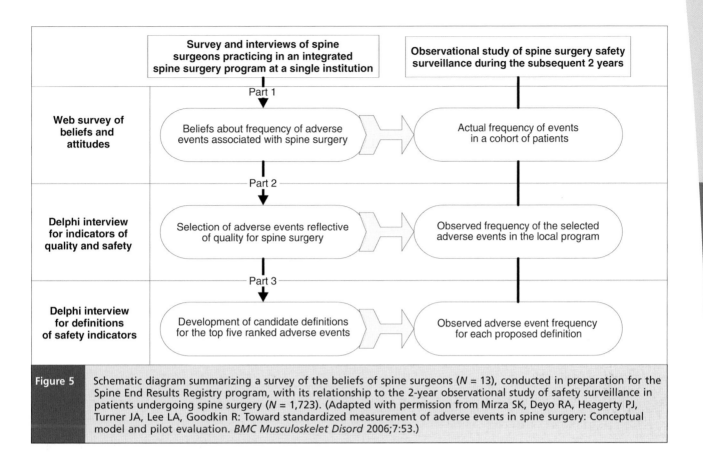

	Survey and interviews of spine surgeons practicing in an integrated spine surgery program at a single institution	Observational study of spine surgery safety surveillance during the subsequent 2 years
	Part 1	
Web survey of beliefs and attitudes	Beliefs about frequency of adverse events associated with spine surgery	Actual frequency of events in a cohort of patients
	Part 2	
Delphi interview for indicators of quality and safety	Selection of adverse events reflective of quality for spine surgery	Observed frequency of the selected adverse events in the local program
	Part 3	
Delphi interview for definitions of safety indicators	Development of candidate definitions for the top five ranked adverse events	Observed adverse event frequency for each proposed definition

Figure 5 Schematic diagram summarizing a survey of the beliefs of spine surgeons (*N* = 13), conducted in preparation for the Spine End Results Registry program, with its relationship to the 2-year observational study of safety surveillance in patients undergoing spine surgery (*N* = 1,723). (Adapted with permission from Mirza SK, Deyo RA, Heagerty PJ, Turner JA, Lee LA, Goodkin R: Toward standardized measurement of adverse events in spine surgery: Conceptual model and pilot evaluation. *BMC Musculoskelet Disord* 2006;7:53.)

nization effort still is in its early stages. Its focus is to incorporate key concepts in patient safety (risk identification, prevention, detection, reduction of risk, incident recovery, and system resilience) into a continuous learning and improvement cycle.

Ascertaining Harms

Patients who are selecting a surgical procedure, surgeon, or hospital need specific comparative safety information, but in practice this information is extremely difficult to provide. In addition to prospectively agreed-upon event definitions, consistent methods of ascertainment are needed. The data extracted from standard medical record templates for the SERR program were incomplete and inaccurate.[9] During the first year of the project, even the most enthusiastic, committed, and best performing surgeons were able to complete the standardized surgical note template for only 50% of their patients (Figure 7). Surgeons accurately noted the duration of surgery, the patient's blood loss, and the involved spine levels for only 30% of spine surgeries. Only one of the four participating clinical care teams (residents, fellows, and nurses) achieved the goal of recording neurologic status information consistently at admission and discharge. These low rates of reporting occurred despite 12 months of training and persistent reminders to the attending surgeons and their teams to explicitly document neurologic status in the medical record, using a structured format (Figure 8). (The medical record was marked using a stamp with blanks to in-

dicate the pattern of neurologic deficit [none, radiculopathy, myelopathy, cord injury], neurologic level, and motor score.) The reason for the low rates of SERR reporting was determined to be that clinicians were too busy to gather structured data that could be used for research, even though the research and clinical documentation overlapped.

The cost of adverse occurrence surveillance by nurses and research coordinators was estimated at $349 per patient in the SERR program.[9] This estimate did not include the time required from surgeons, investigators, researchers, and analysts, or the cost of the informatics system. It is difficult to estimate the return on this investment in terms of creating a learning organization that could lead to improvements in adverse event prevention. The only direct benefit of such a surveillance system is greater recognition of adverse occurrences, which may not reflect well on participating surgeons and hospitals. During the SERR program, it was observed that surgeons sometimes excluded research personnel from team clinics and rounds because they were perceived to slow the work flow or to gather data with the potential for embarrassing the surgeon or hospital. The SERR experiment revealed that an adverse occurrence surveillance system still is not financially or culturally feasible almost 100 years after the failure of Codman's End Result Hospital.

The largest National Institutes of Health–funded spine surgery study to date, the Spine Patient Outcomes Research Trial, expended $30 million to evaluate the

7: Spine Care and US Health Policy

Table 2

Comparison of Quality Indicators Identified in Pre-SERR Interviews With Spine Surgeons and Actual Observed Rates

Quality Indicator	Indicator Rank[a]	Number (Percentage) of Surgeons Identifying the Indicator (N = 12)[b]	Average Rank[c]	Actual Observed Rate
Neurologic injury	1	11 (91%)	2.5	3.9%
Infection	2	11 (91%)	2.8	3.4%
Reoperation	3	11 (91%)	3.9	8.1%
Medical complications	4	8 (66%)	4.9	27.0%
CSF leakage	5	7 (58%)	3.1	8.6%
Length of stay	6	4 (33%)	3.8	NA
Death	7	3 (25%)	3.3	1.9%
Blood loss	8	3 (25%)	3.7	NA
Duration of surgery	9	2 (16%)	3.5	NA
Instrumentation complications	10	2 (16%)	5.0	3.4%
Technical complications	11	2 (16%)	5.0	9.6%
Wrong-level surgery	12	2 (16%)	6.5	0.1%
Administration of excessive intravenous fluid	13	1 (8%)	2.0	0.0%
Delayed diagnosis	14	1 (8%)	4.0	1.0%
Disposition at discharge	15	1 (8%)	5.0	NA
Loss of surgical correction	16	1 (8%)	5.0	2.6%
Persistent pain	17	1 (8%)	5.0	NA
Perception of care	18	1 (8%)	6.0	NA
Positioning complication	19	1 (8%)	9.0	1.1%
Spinal cord monitoring alert	20	1 (8%)	10.0	1.7%
Deep vein thrombosis/ pulmonary embolism	21	1 (8%)	11.0	4.1%
Cardiac event	22	1 (8%)	12.0	6.0%
Urologic complication	23	1 (8%)	13.0	7.6%
Pulmonary complication	24	1 (8%)	14.0	7.8%

NA = not applicable (the indicator cannot be measured as a simple rate).

[a]Ranking by the number of surgeons identifying the indicator as among the five most important.
[b]Data reflect that five surgeons (41%) selected one or more additional quality indicators, two (16%) changed their ranking of quality indicators, and two (16%) deleted one or more quality indicators after reviewing the collated interview data.
[c]Average across-surgeons ranking.

outcomes of approximately 2,500 patients; the average per-patient cost was $12,000.[48-53] In the current climate of health care economics, the high cost of gathering reliable data for comparative effectiveness research will be prohibitive unless research-grade data can be derived from electronic health records.

Lessons Learned From a Failed Attempt to Integrate Research and Clinical Care

Although the SERR program was not sustained after the expiration of grant funding, the project was instruc-

tive for the investigators. The institutional review board approval process clarified areas in which research and clinical activities overlapped or were separated. Quality goals were evaluated from patient, surgeon, hospital, and payer perspectives; this focus allowed collaboration among participants in otherwise potentially competing programs. Consensus recommendations from surgeons and anesthesiologists were useful in developing definitions and explicit criteria for tracking 175 spine surgery–specific adverse occurrences. All team members, including surgeons, nurses,

Table 3			

The Effect of SERR Quality Indicator Definitions on Observed Adverse Event Rates

Category	Number of Surgeons Identifying the Indicator (N = 12)[a]	Definition	Actual Observed Rate
Neurologic injury	3	Any new or worsening motor weakness or sensory loss	3.9%
	3	Only motor weakness of two or more grades	1.3%
	1	Only motor weakness, of any grade	1.9%
	1	Any new sensory or motor symptoms lasting more than 90 days after surgery, including sensory symptoms, pain, numbness, motor loss, sympathetic and parasympathetic effect, retrograde ejaculation	0% (retrograde ejaculation)
	1	Bladder or bowel disturbance, cauda equina syndrome, motor loss of one grade or more	0.6%
	1	Intraoperative change in electromyogram or somatosensory-evoked potentials, regardless of subsequent clinical manifestations	1.7%
	1	Known direct cut or injury to nerve tissue, even if no overt deficit is later observed; or new pain, numbness, or weakness not present preoperatively or worse postoperatively (includes blindness and stroke)	0.0%
Infection	9	Any treatment, such as oral or intravenous antibiotics (superficial) or débridement (deep)	5.9% superficial 3.4% deep
	2	Any infection requiring treatment (such as antibiotics or surgery). Infection is classified as superficial, deep, epidural, or meningeal.	0.3% epidural 0.6% meningeal
	1	Any infection requiring treatment (such as antibiotics or surgery). Infection is classified as superficial, deep, or stitch abscess.	Not measured
	1	Infection requiring a return to the operating room, with irrigation and débridement or long-term antibiotics. Excludes wound complications requiring oral antibiotics for 1 week	3.5%
Reoperation	6	Any reoperation within 30 days of surgery	5.0%
	3	Reoperation within 6 months	
	1	Reoperation within 1 year	7.4% (8.1% at 2 years)
	1	Definition based on underlying condition: after diskectomy, reoperation within 1 year at the same level; after fusion, reoperation at any time at an adjacent level	2.0% after decompression 5.5% after fusion 0.6% after other surgery
Medical complications	11	Any medical event requiring diagnostic or treatment intervention	27%
	1	Only an event with major, permanent consequences such as blindness, stroke, or heart attack	0.1% to 6.0%
	11	List of 21 different medical conditions	0% to 4.9%
CSF leakage	9	Arachnoid is violated, and CSF is expressed	8.6%
	1	Only with associated nerve root injury	0.4%
	1	Only if CSF leakage leads to complications such as pseudomeningocele; satisfactorily repaired CSF leakage is not included	0.8% (pseudomeningocele)
	1	Excludes CSF leakage in revision surgery	3.5%

[a]Data reflect that some surgeons provided more than one definition for an event type and some surgeons did not provide a definition for every event type.

7: Spine Care and US Health Policy

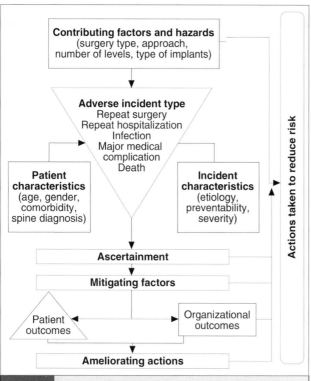

Figure 6 Schematic diagram showing the conceptual framework of the World Health Organization International Classification for Patient Safety, as applied in the Spine End Results Registry. (Adapted with permission from Mirza SK, Deyo RA, Heagerty PJ, Turner JA, Lee LA, Goodkin R: Toward standardized measurement of adverse events in spine surgery: Conceptual model and pilot evaluation. *BMC Musculoskelet Disord* 2006;7:53.)

dures,[54] but case-mix adjustments were limited by a lack of quantitative methods for classifying disease severity using such criteria as severity of degeneration, deformity, and neural compromise.

To be sustainable, a program such as SERR would require an adequate infrastructure for patient follow-up as well as simple methods for providing feedback to surgeons and patients. Systems of care need to be restructured to create an environment in which the conditions that lead to adverse occurrences are eliminated. Reducing the number and severity of adverse occurrences associated with medical and surgical care requires a health care culture that values error-free care, efficient registries and surveillance systems that monitor the magnitude of the difficulties and identify contributing factors, the linking of errors to outcomes and costs, and legal safeguards to facilitate learning and reduce risk (Figure 6). The first step must be to create a culture of safety, in which every member of the health care organization is valued for contributing to safety improvement.

Issues Related to Individual-Level Patient Outcomes

Evaluating Patient Outcome in Research Studies

In a clinical study, a primary treatment outcome is evaluated by assessing the patient's condition before and after treatment for the purpose of determining treatment efficacy. In orthopaedic research during the past 20 years, the primary outcomes in randomized controlled studies generally have been related to health-related quality of life (HRQOL) measures. Patient data are collected on demographic factors (age, sex, education, marital status), work (type of work, workers' compensation status), and health (comorbidities, duration of symptoms, expected outcome, treatment preference). The current statistical practice is to evaluate change across time using longitudinal mixed-model regression methods. Change is evaluated from the baseline for each outcome relative to the research factors. These factors typically include the fixed and random effects of treatment, the assessment interval, the intercept, and the delta time (the number of days the scores were observed, measured from the center point of the time interval). The basic model is adjusted for patient factors including baseline score (the starting point), which is necessary for interpreting change; selected patient covariates, such as age, sex, ethnicity, and comorbidities; and study factors, such as study site. The covariates typically are selected based on their association with crossover and patient loss to follow-up, as a means of statistically controlling potential data interpretation bias. Finally, the model is adjusted to account for the deviation of observed scores from the midpoint of the assessment interval by specifying that mean estimates must be based on a delta time of 0 to reflect a patient's

fellows, residents, and support staff, were intensively trained before program implementation, but the training proved insufficient. Changing team members' beliefs, attitudes, and culture required an intense focus on quality, with continual emphasis during routine care on team activities such as daily team rounds, weekly team meetings to review the indications for upcoming surgeries, and monthly team morbidity and mortality conferences to discuss adverse occurrences, their possible causes, and prevention strategies. It was essential to have the active cooperation of the hospital administration, anesthesia department, operating room managers, medical records committee, and risk managers, as well as an information system designed specifically for tracking adverse occurrences in patients undergoing spine surgery.

The SERR program gathered pilot data to establish benchmarks and define acceptable ranges, but larger patient groups are required for discerning changes in quality. The analysis was complicated by variability in coding etiology as well the severity and preventability of adverse occurrences. A valid method has been developed for classifying the invasiveness of surgical proce-

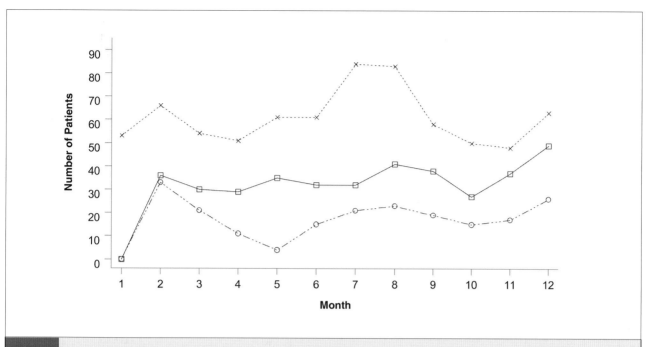

Figure 7 Schematic diagram comparing the number of patients undergoing spine surgery *(dotted line)*, the number of surgical data forms submitted *(solid line)*, and the number of surgical data forms containing accurate information *(dashed line)* during the first 12 months of the Spine End Results Registry program. (Adapted with permission from Mirza SK, Deyo RA, Heagerty PJ, Turner JA, Lee LA, Goodkin R: Toward standardized measurement of adverse events in spine surgery: Conceptual model and pilot evaluation. *BMC Musculoskelet Disord* 2006;7:53.)

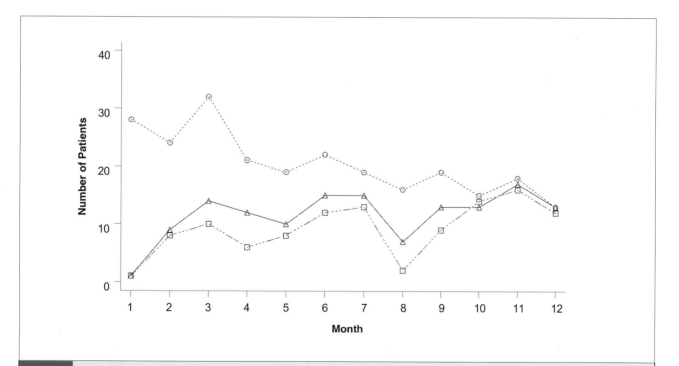

Figure 8 Schematic diagram comparing the number of patients admitted for spine surgery *(dotted line)*, the number for whom neurologic status information (a motor score) was completed at admission *(solid line)*, and the number for whom neurologic status information (a motor score) was completed at discharge *(dashed line)* during the first 12 months of the Spine End Results Registry program. (Adapted with permission from Mirza SK, Deyo RA, Heagerty PJ, Turner JA, Lee LA, Goodkin R: Toward standardized measurement of adverse events in spine surgery: Conceptual model and pilot evaluation. *BMC Musculoskelet Disord* 2006;7:53.)

7: Spine Care and US Health Policy

score at the midpoint. These analyses produce a point estimate (a mean change in outcome) for patients in each treatment group. Thus, the adjusted change in the Medical Outcomes Study Short Form-36 Health Survey physical function (SF-36 PF) outcome score from baseline to 1-year follow-up might be 20 points for patients in treatment group A and 10 points for patients in treatment group B. The adjusted change from baseline is determined to be statistically significantly different based on type I error tolerance. For example, a type I error tolerance set at 0.05 means that the investigators are willing to interpret a between-group observed difference as real or reliable even though the observed difference reflects a between-group sampling variation only 5% of the time (5 of 100 times).

Evaluating Patient Outcome in Clinical Practice

The controlled conditions of a scientific experiment may not be replicated in actual clinical practice. In a clinical study of a surgical procedure, the patients may be carefully selected and the surgery performed by elite surgeons in a specialized hospital. In clinical practice, however, the patients may be more heterogeneous and the surgeons may be less elite. The study may demonstrate the efficacy of the surgical procedure, but the procedure may be ineffective in actual practice.

The term efficacy refers to success of a treatment under ideal conditions. The term effectiveness refers to success measured in actual practice. Efficacy usually is evaluated through clinical studies, and effectiveness is evaluated through observational data and patient registries. Clinicians have at least as much information available as researchers about individual patients participating in a comprehensive clinical study, but clinicians in most areas of medicine do not have the tools or time to consider the large quantity of information available for a given patient or to use this information for evaluating treatment outcomes or estimating the likelihood of a particular outcome. Randomized controlled studies are expensive to conduct and require additional time from both the clinician and the patient. Such studies should include a means of translating the study findings into information to guide treatment decision making. The development of clinical practice guidelines is one mechanism for integrating and disseminating the results of clinical studies as clinically useful information. Clinical practice guidelines typically are based on the results of meta-analyses, which are a hallmark of evidence-based medicine.

Defining Success

The results of randomized controlled studies usually are summarized as the nature of treatment difference based on mean differences. Thus, a result might be reported as an average improvement in outcome of 20 points for patients who underwent treatment A, compared with an average improvement in outcome of 10 points for patients who underwent treatment B (*P* <

0.027). These are the study results available for meta-analysis or guideline development. These data also allow the following interpretation: 40% of the patients in treatment group A had substantial improvement, compared with 60% of the patients in treatment group B (*P* < 0.016). Although the second interpretation of the data provides more useful information for a clinician and a patient who are evaluating treatment options, it requires a clear definition of "substantial improvement."

Some researchers believe the concept of minimal clinically important difference (MCID) is useful for establishing substantial improvement, but others have suggested that "minimally important" and "substantial" improvement do not have the same meaning for all clinicians or patients. A 30% change has been suggested as a definition of MCID.[54] The FDA has used a standard of absolute change, such as a 15-point improvement on the Oswestry Disability Index (ODI). When 30% change from the baseline score was defined as 30% of the smaller distance from the observed score and the two possible extreme scores, the 30% rule was found to provide results similar to those of a patient-level MCID computed on the basis of person-level standard errors of measurement combined with cut scores.[55] For example, the SF-36 PF scale is scored from 0 to 100, with 100 reflecting the best possible physical function (all 10 questions answered "No limitations").[56-61] If the baseline score is 25, the shortest distance to an extreme score is 25 points (25 to 0 = 25, as opposed to 25 to 100 = 75), so the 30% change required to achieve a minimal clinically important change is 0.3 × 25 = 7.5 points. Because the granularity of the SF-36 PF scale is 5 (the possible scores progress from 0, 5, 10 to 85, 90, 95, 100) the effective minimal important change would be 10 points. If a 30% change is accepted as a reasonable threshold for defining a MCID, a 50% change might reasonably be defined as a substantial change. In this example, a 50% change would be calculated as 0.5 × 25 = 12.5, which would translate into an effective change of 15 points. Table 4 summarizes the use of these rules to calculate minimal and substantial change.

This approach is a simple and transparent means of classifying change into one of five categories: C1, substantial improvement (at least 50% of the potential improvement); C2, real improvement (30% of potential improvement, which is outside a reasonable range of measurement error); C3, no change (any observed differences are within the margin of measurement error); C4, real worsening (at least 30% of the potential worsening); and C5, substantial worsening (at least 50% of potential worsening). Determining the percentage of patients in each treatment group whose change is in each of these five categories provides a better clinical understanding of treatment efficacy than determining a mean and the standard error of estimate associated with the mean. Furthermore, combining some of these categories may represent a clinically understandable

Table 4

Change Interpretation Using 50% and 30% Change Rules[a]

Baseline Score	50% Change	30% Change	Effective Cut Points		Postscore	Change	Interpretation (Classification)
			50%	30%			
0	2.5	1.5	5	-	5	5	Substantial improvement (C1)
0	2.5	1.5	5	-	0	0	No change (C3)
5	2.5	1.5	10	5	15	10	Substantial improvement (C1)
5	2.5	1.5	10	5	10	5	Real improvement (C2)
5	2.5	1.5	10	5	5	0	No change (C3)
5	2.5	1.5	10	5	0	-5	Substantial worsening (C5)
20	10	6	15	10	35	15	Substantial improvement (C1)
20	10	6	15	10	30	10	Real improvement (C2)
20	10	6	15	10	25	5	No change (C3)
20	10	6	15	10	20	0	No change (C3)
20	10	6	15	10	15	-5	No change (C3)
20	10	6	15	10	10	-10	Real worsening (C4)
20	10	6	15	10	5	-15	Substantial worsening (C5)
40	20	12	20	15	60	20	Substantial improvement (C1)
40	20	12	20	15	55	15	Real improvement (C2)
40	20	12	20	15	50	10	No change (C3)
40	20	12	20	15	45	5	No change (C3)
40	20	12	20	15	40	0	No change (C3)
40	20	12	20	15	35	-5	No change (C3)
40	20	12	20	15	30	-10	No change (C3)
40	20	12	20	15	25	-15	Real worsening (C4)
40	20	12	20	15	20	-20	Substantial worsening (C5)
55	22.5	13.5	25	15	80	25	Substantial improvement (C1)
55	22.5	13.5	25	15	75	20	Real improvement (C2)
55	22.5	13.5	25	15	70	15	Real improvement (C2)
55	22.5	13.5	25	15	65	10	No change (C3)
55	22.5	13.5	25	15	60	5	No change (C3)
55	22.5	13.5	25	15	55	0	No change (C3)
55	22.5	13.5	25	15	50	-5	No change (C3)
55	22.5	13.5	25	15	45	-10	No change (C3)
55	22.5	13.5	25	15	40	-15	Real worsening (C4)
55	22.5	13.5	25	15	35	-20	Real worsening (C4)
55	22.5	13.5	25	15	30	-25	Substantial worsening (C5)
90	5	3	10	5	100	10	Substantial improvement (C1)
90	5	3	10	5	95	5	Real improvement (C2)
90	5	3	10	5	90	0	No change (C3)
90	5	3	10	5	85	-5	Real worsening (C4)
90	5	3	10	5	80	-10	Substantial worsening (C5)

[a]The scale ranges from 0 to 100, with a 5-point unit of change (granularity). A higher value reflects a better outcome.

(continued on page 600.)

7: Spine Care and US Health Policy

| Table 4 | (continued) |

Baseline Score	50% Change	30% Change	Effective Cut Points		Postscore	Change	Interpretation (Classification)
			50%	30%			
95	2.5	1.5	10	5	100	5	Real improvement (C2)
95	2.5	1.5	10	5	95	0	No change (C3)
95	2.5	1.5	10	5	90	-5	Real worsening (C4)
95	2.5	1.5	10	5	85	-10	Substantial worsening (C5)
100	2.5	1.5	5	-	100	0	No change (C3)
100	2.5	1.5	5	-	95	-5	Substantial worsening (C5)

and relevant definition of success. For example, success might be defined as a gain of at least 30% (categories C1 and C2); this result could be compared to that of the combined C3, C4, and C5 categories using logistic regression, Poisson regression, or recursive partitioning modeling such as chi-square automatic interaction detection[62] to predict the likelihood of patient-level success (defined as a score in the C1 or C2 category).

What Outcome for Which Patient?

In the clinical setting, the most appropriate outcome can be determined at baseline as part of a shared decision-making process. The most appropriate outcome probably is the outcome that most interests or concerns the patient and is most likely to be attained. It is important to consider the quality of the information being used in this situation to select the best outcome or determine posttreatment success. The most reasonable approach to retrospective outcomes evaluation may be to consider the baseline magnitude of the available HRQOL measures and their accuracy.

Outcome Magnitude

Clinical studies frequently specify multiple outcomes. Studies of lumbar surgery often report results using a general health measure such as the SF-36 PF scale, a disease-specific measure such as the ODI,[63-66] and a measure of pain such as the Medical Outcomes Study Short Form-36 Health Survey bodily pain (SF-36 BP) scale. A common pattern is a rapid recovery in patients in both treatment groups during the first 6 months after surgery. After 6-month follow-up, the average change from baseline on the SF-36 PF, SF-36 BP, and ODI measures often becomes stable. It might be concluded from these results that any of the three measures would be suitable for evaluating the primary outcome. However, close analysis of the data reveals that although all three measures show positive correlations, the magnitude of these correlations is not high enough to suggest that they are exchangeable. This distinction is consistent with the common finding in the orthopae-

dic literature that patient-reported pain and disability magnitudes are not always consistent.

It is important to ensure an "apples to apples" comparison across treatment groups, usually relative to a specified outcome. At the individual patient level, this type of comparison is between baseline and follow-up scores on the same measure. It is unnecessary to use the same measure for comparing all patients with the same condition, however. Recent musculoskeletal functional rehabilitation research has begun evaluating patient outcomes using patient-determined goals set at baseline. The results of preliminary studies suggest that goal attainment is at least as good a predictor of patient satisfaction as improvement in self-reported SF-36 PF and SF-36 BP scores.[67]

Clinicians might consider prospectively evaluating HRQOL outcomes that are of particular interest to the patient, as inferred from the patient's expectations and stated goals. Researchers may not be able to retrospectively match a particular outcome to the patient, however. It may be useful for a researcher to assume that the outcome of greatest importance to the patient is related to the poorest baseline score on an outcome measure; that is, the patient is likely to be most interested in improving the most severe impairment resulting from his or her condition. Presumably the researcher could determine the patient's worst health state (function, bodily pain, disability) by comparing scores on the SF-36 PF, SF-36 BP, or ODI (rescaled so that a higher score reflects a better outcome). The lowest score should be associated with the worst health state.

This assumption may not be accurate, however, as shown by two examples from sports. A baseball player's batting average and a basketball player's free-throw percentage measure success as the number of hits or free throws, respectively, compared with the number of opportunities. The batting average is reported in three digits; for example, 0.300 or 300 is a 30% success rate. The reasoning for ordering the SF-36 PF, SF-36 BP, and ODI scores is based on the fact that all three measures can easily be converted to a 0 to 100 scale, with 100 the best health state and 0 the worst health state. If this reasoning is applied to batting and free-throw success, the worst score almost always is associated with batting average. In major league baseball, a batting average above 0.300 is good and above 0.400 is almost unattainable. In professional basketball, a free-throw percentage of 0.418 would be one of the worst in the history of the game. Thus, a linear transformation of scores onto a common scale does not necessarily allow accurate across-instrument comparisons. The scales must be equated by an area transformation. The most common such method is equal percentile equating, which essentially links scores on a 0 to 100 linearly transformed score to percentile ranks in which a patient's score is interpreted in comparison with the number of patients who scored at that level or lower. In this way, the lowest percentile rank reflects the worst performance on all scales.

Outcome Accuracy

If two scales have an equal or almost-equal percentile rank value, it is preferable to use the more consistent scale. Most of the psychometric literature regarding response pattern error has its origin in the work of Louis Guttman.[68] In the achievement-testing domain, Guttman's approach was to order items from lowest to highest difficulty, then to examine each respondent's item pattern (using 0 to indicate an incorrect answer and 1 to indicate a correct answer). The Guttman error is based on the number and magnitude of disordinal responses across a set of items thought to reflect a unidimensional construct such as pain or function. For example, in achievement testing a correct answer to a relatively difficult question and an incorrect answer to an easier question represent a disordinal response; the magnitude of this disordinality is based on the difference in the item difficulty. Table 5 illustrates one approach for estimating the Guttman error in a three-item test and scaling the Guttman error as a percentage of maximum possible error. In Table 5, there are eight possible response patterns, of which four have no Guttman error (the responses are perfectly ordered). Two of the response patterns (1 0 1 and 0 1 0) demonstrate a single response variance. Two other response patterns (0 0 1 and 0 1 1) demonstrate two response variations generating a Guttman error greater than 50% of the possible error. As the Guttman error increases, the interpretation of the score becomes less certain. If the Guttman error is greater than 50% of the possible error, it may be inappropriate to make a decision based on the score. This consideration becomes more important as the number of items being compared increases. In measurement theory, interpretation of the Guttman error is relevant to the difficulty of realizing both reliability and validity when constructs are assessed with only a few items, especially if the construct is relatively complex. Guttman error estimation is not limited to binary (0/1) responses, but it is limited to unidimensional scales. Factor analysis of multidimensional scales can

be used to identify the dimensions in the scale, and the Guttman error can be computed for items within each dimension. The errors within each domain are summed across domains to provide guidance regarding the usefulness of the scores.

In Table 5, a patient whose response pattern is 0 0 1 has indicated an inability to breath without assistance, an inability to walk to the bathroom without aid, and an ability to run 1 mile. The Guttman error of 0.7 for this response pattern represents 87.5% of the maximum possible Guttman error for these items and indicates that the total score (0 + 0 + 1 = 1) is based on a pattern of response that cannot be trusted. It would not be advisable for a clinician to use this score to make a decision based on the patient's health status, to use this score as a basis for defining necessary change, or to classify the patient's outcome as C1 to C5.

To determine which of the HRQOL scores is most appropriate for use in interpreting treatment results, it is necessary to consider both the severity of the patient's baseline health status and the accuracy of the score based on the patient's response pattern (using the Guttman error and the percentage of maximum possible Guttman error). For outcomes related to safety, this process is simple: success is defined as the absence of a safety issue (0), and failure is defined as the presence of a safety issue (1). However, the results can be greatly influenced by the definition and ascertainment method used for the safety outcome.

Summary

The state of knowledge in the field must be considered during the process of designing a clinical study to evaluate patient outcomes. Noninferiority studies have a limited role in studies related to many established spine treatments because of their limited evidence base. Before comparing adverse event rates, precise and practical definitions must be constructed and ascertainment methods must be specified. The ultimate goal of all clinical research is extrapolation of the results to the treatment of individual patients, but inconsistent patient responses and the limitations of measurement scales are limiting factors.

Clinicians and patients must determine which treatment has the greatest likelihood of success for the individual patient based on the patient's personal and health factors, goals, and expectations. To provide such information, the accuracy and precision of reported outcomes must be improved. Careful documentation of clinical assessments, diagnoses, treatments, and patient-relevant efficacy and safety outcomes must become standard. Electronic medical record keeping is essential for providing the extensive high-quality data necessary for improving patient-level predictive models to show the efficacy and safety of specific treatments for specific patients.

Table 5

Sample Computation of Guttman Error

1. Three-Item Questionnaire With Difficulty Index

Item	Content[a]	Difficulty Index[b]
1	Are you able to breathe on your own?	0.9
2	Are you able to walk to the bathroom in your home without aid?	0.6
3	Are you able to run a mile?	0.4

[a]Possible responses: 0 = No, 1 = Yes.
[b]The proportion of respondents who answered "Yes." As in classical test theory, a higher difficulty index reflects a relatively easy achievement. In this questionnaire, a higher difficulty index reflects higher health status.

2. Computation of Guttman Error

Item 1	Item 2	Item 3	Score	Guttman Error	Percentage Guttman Error	2-1	3-1	3-2	1-2	1-3	2-3	1 × 2	1 × 3	2 × 3	Sum
0	0	0	0	0	0.0%	0	0	0	0.3	0.5	0.2	0	0	0	0
1	0	0	1	0	0.0%	1	1	0	0.3	0.5	0.2	0	0	0	0
0	1	0	1	−0.3	37.5%	−1	0	1	0.3	0.5	0.2	−0.3	0	0	−0.3
0	0	1	1	−0.7	87.5%	0	−1	−1	0.3	0.5	0.2	0	−0.5	−0.2	−0.7
1	0	1	2	−0.2	25.0%	1	0	−1	0.3	0.5	0.2	0	0	−0.2	−0.2
0	1	1	2	−0.8	100.0%	−1	−1	0	0.3	0.5	0.2	−0.3	−0.5	0	−0.8
1	1	0	2	0	0.0%	0	1	1	0.3	0.5	0.2	0	0	0	0
1	1	1	3	0	0.0%	0	0	0	0.3	0.5	0.2	0	0	0	0

Column groups: Response Pattern (Item 1, Item 2, Item 3); Difference Direction (2-1, 3-1, 3-2); Distance[a] (1-2, 1-3, 2-3); Difference Direction × Distance[b] (1 × 2, 1 × 3, 2 × 3, Sum)

[a]Based on estimated item-difficulty values for the test population.
[b]Computed only if the difference direction is less than 0.

Annotated References

1. Codman EA: *The Shoulder*. Boston, MA, Thomas Todd, 1934.

2. Codman EA: A *Study in Hospital Efficiency as Demonstrated by the Case Report of the First Five Years of a Private Hospital*. Boston, MA, Thomas Todd, 1917. Oakbrook Terrace, IL, Joint Commission on Accreditation of Healthcare Organizations, 1996.

3. Healthcare Utilization Project: *HCUP Facts and Figures: Statistics on Hospital-Based Care in the United States, 2008*. Rockville, MD, Agency for Healthcare Research and Quality, 2010. http://www.hcup-us.ahrq.gov/reports/factsandfigures/2008/TOC_2008.jsp.

This online query system is the largest provider of publicly available all-payer health care utilization data. Graphs and tables of statistics and trends can be created from data in the Nationwide Inpatient Sample, Kids' Inpatient Database, State Inpatient Databases, and State Emergency Department Databases.

4. Chou R: Critiquing the critiques: The American Pain Society guideline and the American Society of Interventional Pain Physicians' response to it. *Pain Physician* 2011;14(1):E69-E73; author reply E73-E82.

The American Pain Society guideline for low back pain is critiqued, with discussion of issues related to many special interest–driven guidelines

5. Chou R: Letter to the editor. *Spine (Phila Pa 1976)* 2011;36(7):590.

The steps in an evidence synthesis are described.

6. Chou R, Loeser JD, Owens DK, et al: Interventional therapies, surgery, and interdisciplinary rehabilitation for low back pain: An evidence-based clinical practice guideline from the American Pain Society. *Spine (Phila Pa 1976)* 2009;34(10):1066-1077.

The American Pain Society guideline does not recommend diskography, facet joint corticosteroid injection, prolotherapy, or intradiskal corticosteroid injection. Interdisciplinary rehabilitation and cognitive-behavioral therapy are recommended. The risks and benefits of surgery are discussed.

7. Chou R, Atlas SJ, Stanos SP, Rosenquist RW: Nonsurgical interventional therapies for low back pain: A review of the evidence for an American Pain Society clinical practice guideline. *Spine (Phila Pa 1976)* 2009;34(10):1078-1093.

   The therapies with moderate evidence of efficacy for chronic or subacute low back pain are cognitive-behavioral therapy, exercise, spinal manipulation, and interdisciplinary rehabilitation. The only therapy with good evidence of efficacy for acute low back pain is superficial heat.

8. Chou R, Baisden J, Carragee EJ, Resnick DK, Shaffer WO, Loeser JD: Surgery for low back pain: A review of the evidence for an American Pain Society Clinical Practice Guideline. *Spine (Phila Pa 1976)* 2009;34(10):1094-1109.

   Surgery for radiculopathy with a herniated lumbar disk or symptomatic spinal stenosis was determined to have short-term benefits over nonsurgical therapy. Fusion for nonradicular back pain with common degenerative changes was no more effective than intensive rehabilitation but had some benefit compared with standard nonsurgical therapy.

9. Mirza SK, Deyo RA, Heagerty PJ, Turner JA, Lee LA, Goodkin R: Towards standardized measurement of adverse events in spine surgery: Conceptual model and pilot evaluation. *BMC Musculoskelet Disord* 2006;7:53.

   The conceptual framework and initial experience of the Spine End Results Registry are presented. Included are operational definitions of 176 adverse occurrences; adverse occurrence reporting; methods of quantifying adverse occurrence severity, lumbar spine degeneration, and procedure invasiveness; and agreement assessment for reviewers independently coding etiology, preventability, and severity of adverse occurrences, lumbar spine degenerative changes, and surgical invasiveness.

10. Baskin DS, Ryan P, Sonntag V, Westmark R, Widmayer MA: A prospective, randomized, controlled cervical fusion study using recombinant human bone morphogenetic protein-2 with the CORNERSTONE-SR allograft ring and the ATLANTIS anterior cervical plate. *Spine (Phila Pa 1976)* 2003;28(12):1219-1225.

11. Boakye M, Mummaneni PV, Garrett M, Rodts G, Haid R: Anterior cervical discectomy and fusion involving a polyetheretherketone spacer and bone morphogenetic protein. *J Neurosurg Spine* 2005;2(5):521-525.

    The FDA approval study used a noninferiority design to compare cervical disk replacement with anterior fusion, but the results were interpreted as for a superiority study.

12. Boden SD, Kang J, Sandhu H, Heller JG: Use of recombinant human bone morphogenetic protein-2 to achieve posterolateral lumbar spine fusion in humans: A prospective, randomized clinical pilot trial. *Spine (Phila Pa 1976)* 2002;27(23):2662-2673.

13. Boden SD, Zdeblick TA, Sandhu HS, Heim SE: The use of rhBMP-2 in interbody fusion cages: Definitive evidence of osteoinduction in humans. A preliminary report. *Spine (Phila Pa 1976)* 2000;25(3):376-381.

14. Burkus JK, Gornet MF, Dickman CA, Zdeblick TA: Anterior lumbar interbody fusion using rhBMP-2 with tapered interbody cages. *J Spinal Disord Tech* 2002;15(5):337-349.

15. Burkus JK, Heim SE, Gornet MF, Zdeblick TA: Is INFUSE bone graft superior to autograft bone? An integrated analysis of clinical trials using the LT-CAGE lumbar tapered fusion device. *J Spinal Disord Tech* 2003;16(2):113-122.

16. Burkus JK, Sandhu HS, Gornet MF, Longley MC: Use of rhBMP-2 in combination with structural cortical allografts: Clinical and radiographic outcomes in anterior lumbar spinal surgery. *J Bone Joint Surg Am* 2005;87(6):1205-1212.

    Data from a pilot study and a pivotal study were combined to compare anterior lumbar interbody fusion using bone morphogenetic protein (BMP) allograft or iliac crest autograft. The mixed analysis illustrates the issues in selectively combining data to draw conclusions unsupported by the original study designs.

17. Burkus JK, Transfeldt EE, Kitchel SH, Watkins RG, Balderston RA: Clinical and radiographic outcomes of anterior lumbar interbody fusion using recombinant human bone morphogenetic protein-2. *Spine (Phila Pa 1976)* 2002;27(21):2396-2408.

18. Dawson E, Bae HW, Burkus JK, Stambough JL, Glassman SD: Recombinant human bone morphogenetic protein-2 on an absorbable collagen sponge with an osteoconductive bulking agent in posterolateral arthrodesis with instrumentation: A prospective randomized trial. *J Bone Joint Surg Am* 2009;91(7):1604-1613.

    All measured end results favored the use of BMP in this noninferiority study. The limitations of the noninferiority design were ignored in reporting the methods and results.

19. Dimar JR II, Glassman SD, Burkus JK, Pryor PW, Hardacker JW, Carreon LY: Clinical and radiographic analysis of an optimized rhBMP-2 formulation as an autograft replacement in posterolateral lumbar spine arthrodesis. *J Bone Joint Surg Am* 2009;91(6):1377-1386.

    All outcomes of this study favored the use of BMP, but the report did not mention that a noninferiority design was used.

20. Dimar JR, Glassman SD, Burkus KJ, Carreon LY: Clinical outcomes and fusion success at 2 years of single-level instrumented posterolateral fusions with recombinant human bone morphogenetic protein-2/compression resistant matrix versus iliac crest bone graft. *Spine (Phila Pa 1976)* 2006;31(22):2534-2540.

    A P value of 0.0512 was interpreted as showing superiority in a noninferiority study.

21. Glassman SD, Dimar JR III, Burkus K, et al: The efficacy of rhBMP-2 for posterolateral lumbar fusion in smokers. *Spine (Phila Pa 1976)* 2007;32(15):1693-1698.

In a subgroup analysis with limited power, there was no discussion of the noninferiority design of the parent study.

22. Haid RW Jr, Branch CL Jr, Alexander JT, Burkus JK: Posterior lumbar interbody fusion using recombinant human bone morphogenetic protein type 2 with cylindrical interbody cages. *Spine J* 2004;4(5):527-539.

23. Blumenthal S, McAfee PC, Guyer RD, et al: A prospective, randomized, multicenter Food and Drug Administration investigational device exemptions study of lumbar total disc replacement with the CHARITE artificial disc versus lumbar fusion: Part I. Evaluation of clinical outcomes. *Spine (Phila Pa 1976)* 2005;30(14):1565-1575, discussion E387-E391.

In a noninferiority study comparing artificial disk to anterior cage fusion, the efficacy of anterior fusion compared with placebo was not established.

24. McAfee PC, Cunningham B, Holsapple G, et al: A prospective, randomized, multicenter Food and Drug Administration investigational device exemption study of lumbar total disc replacement with the CHARITE artificial disc versus lumbar fusion: Part II. Evaluation of radiographic outcomes and correlation of surgical technique accuracy with clinical outcomes. *Spine (Phila Pa 1976)* 2005;30(14):1576-1583, discussion E388-E390.

Secondary outcomes from a noninferiority study comparing artificial disk to anterior cage fusion found advantages to the use of an artificial disk. The control treatment had not been established as more efficacious than placebo or nonsurgical treatment, however.

25. Murrey D, Janssen M, Delamarter R, et al: Results of the prospective, randomized, controlled multicenter Food and Drug Administration investigational device exemption study of the ProDisc-C total disc replacement versus anterior discectomy and fusion for the treatment of 1-level symptomatic cervical disc disease. *Spine J* 2009;9(4):275-286.

A noninferiority study compared cervical disk replacement to anterior diskectomy and fusion. The results were reported as if a superiority study had been performed.

26. Zigler J, Delamarter R, Spivak JM, et al: Results of the prospective, randomized, multicenter Food and Drug Administration investigational device exemption study of the ProDisc-L total disc replacement versus circumferential fusion for the treatment of 1-level degenerative disc disease. *Spine (Phila Pa 1976)* 2007;32(11):1155-1163.

A noninferiority study compared artificial disk to 360° lumbar cage fusion, although the efficacy of 360° compared with placebo had not been established.

27. US Department of Health and Human Services, Food and Drug Administration: What We Do: 2010. http://www.fda.gov/aboutfda/whatwedo/default.htm.

28. *The CAHPS Improvement Guide: Practical Strategies for Improving the Patient Care Experience. Shared Decision Making.* Rockville, MD, Agency for Healthcare Research and Quality, 2011. https://www.cahps.ahrq.gov/qiguide/content/interventions/SharedDecisionMaking.aspx.

A national, standardized, publicly reported survey of patient perspectives on hospital care is designed to allow objective comparison of hospitals on topics important to consumers, create incentives for hospitals to improve quality of care, and enhance public accountability by increasing the transparency of hospital care in return for the public investment.

29. Joint Commission: 2011 National Patient Safety Goals Now Available. http://www.jointcommission.org/standards_information/npsgs.aspx.

The Joint Commission's annual National Patient Safety Goals are designed to focus the attention of accredited organizations on straightforward, inexpensive patient safety solutions. Compliance with the specific requirements is evaluated during on-site accreditation surveys, and performance is publicly reported.

30. Reynolds MW, Shibata A, Zhao S, Jones N, Fahrbach K, Goodnough LT: Impact of clinical trial design and execution-related factors on incidence of thromboembolic events in cancer patients: A systematic review and meta-analysis. *Curr Med Res Opin* 2008;24(2):497-505.

Study design was found to influence reported results.

31. Lassere MN, Johnson KR, Boers M, et al: Standardized assessment of adverse events in rheumatology clinical trials: Summary of the OMERACT 7 drug safety module update. *J Rheumatol* 2005;32(10):2037-2041.

Standard definitions are an essential prerequisite for a comparative study.

32. Lassere MN, Johnson KR, Woodworth TG, et al: Challenges and progress in adverse event ascertainment and reporting in clinical trials. *J Rheumatol* 2005;32(10):2030-2032.

An expert consensus-based approach can help established standards for comparing adverse events.

33. Bruce J, Russell EM, Mollison J, Krukowski ZH: The measurement and monitoring of surgical adverse events. *Health Technol Assess* 2001;5(22):1-194.

34. D'Agostino RB Sr, Massaro JM, Sullivan LM: Noninferiority trials: Design concepts and issues. The encounters of academic consultants in statistics. *Stat Med* 2003;22(2):169-186.

35. Committee for Proprietary Medicinal Products: *Points to Consider on Switching Between Superiority and Non-Inferiority.* London, England, European Medicines Agency, 2006.

Although the objective of a noninferiority study may be to demonstrate that a product is not inferior to a comparator, only a superiority study can achieve this objective. A noninferiority study can only demonstrate that the test product is not worse than the comparator by more than a small prespecified amount.

36. Laster LL, Johnson MF: Non-inferiority trials: The 'at least as good as' criterion. *Stat Med* 2003;22(2):187-200.

37. Pater C: Equivalence and noninferiority trials: Are they viable alternatives for registration of new drugs? *Curr Control Trials Cardiovasc Med* 2004;5(1):8.

38. Committee for Proprietary Medicinal Products: *Guideline on the Choice of Non-Inferiority Margin.* London, England, European Medicines Agency, 2005.

    The choice of margin always must be justified on clinical and statistical grounds and tailored to the particular clinical context. No rule can cover all clinical situations. The study protocol should prespecify a noninferiority margin. At completion, a two-sided 95% confidence interval (or a one-sided 97.5% interval) should be constructed for the true difference between the two agents. The 95% confidence interval should lie entirely on the positive side of the noninferiority margin.

39. Fritzell P, Hägg O, Wessberg P, Nordwall A, Swedish Lumbar Spine Study Group: Lumbar fusion versus nonsurgical treatment for chronic low back pain: A multicenter randomized controlled trial from the Swedish Lumbar Spine Study Group. *Spine (Phila Pa 1976)* 2001;26(23):2521-2534.

40. Brox JI, Sørensen R, Friis A, et al: Randomized clinical trial of lumbar instrumented fusion and cognitive intervention and exercises in patients with chronic low back pain and disc degeneration. *Spine (Phila Pa 1976)* 2003; 28(17):1913-1921.

41. Fairbank J, Frost H, Wilson-MacDonald J, et al: Randomised controlled trial to compare surgical stabilisation of the lumbar spine with an intensive rehabilitation programme for patients with chronic low back pain: The MRC spine stabilisation trial. *BMJ* 2005; 330(7502):1233.

    Outcomes were similar for patients who underwent lumbar fusion or structured rehabilitation for nonspecific low back pain.

42. Miller FG: Sham surgery: An ethical analysis. *Sci Eng Ethics* 2004;10(1):157-166.

43. Kim SY: The sham surgery debate and the moral complexity of risk-benefit analysis. *Am J Bioeth* 2003;3(4): 68-70.

44. Clark PA: Sham surgery: To cut or not to cut, that is the ethical dilemma. *Am J Bioeth* 2003;3(4):66-68.

45. Angelos P: Sham surgery in research: A surgeon's view. *Am J Bioeth* 2003;3(4):65-66.

46. Krizek TJ: Surgical error: Ethical issues of adverse events. *Arch Surg* 2000;135(11):1359-1366.

47. World Health Organization: International Classification for Patient Safety (ICPS). http://www.who.int/patientsafety/implementation/taxonomy/en/index.html. Accessed September 23, 2011.

    The World Health Organization established a work group to develop a standard nomenclature for patient safety concepts.

48. Desai A, Ball PA, Bekelis K, et al: SPORT: Does incidental durotomy affect long-term outcomes in cases of spinal stenosis? *Neurosurgery* 2011;69(1):38-44.

    Patient-reported outcomes were similar regardless of incidental durotomy, although the comparison was underpowered. Patients with CSF leakage had more blood loss, longer hospital stay, and more repeat surgery than patients without CSF leakage.

49. Weinstein JN, Lurie JD, Tosteson TD, et al: Surgical compared with nonoperative treatment for lumbar degenerative spondylolisthesis: Four-year results in the Spine Patient Outcomes Research Trial (SPORT) randomized and observational cohorts. *J Bone Joint Surg Am* 2009;91(6):1295-1304.

    This comparison of surgical and nonsurgical treatment of lumbar degenerative spondylolisthesis found that the surgical advantage decreased at 4-year follow-up.

50. Weinstein JN, Lurie JD, Tosteson TD, et al: Surgical versus nonoperative treatment for lumbar disc herniation: Four-year results for the Spine Patient Outcomes Research Trial (SPORT). *Spine (Phila Pa 1976)* 2008; 33(25):2789-2800.

    This comparison of surgical and nonsurgical treatment of lumbar disk herniation found that the surgical advantage decreased at 4-year follow-up.

51. Weinstein JN, Lurie JD, Tosteson TD, et al: Surgical vs nonoperative treatment for lumbar disk herniation: The Spine Patient Outcomes Research Trial (SPORT) observational cohort. *JAMA* 2006;296(20):2451-2459.

    Observational data showed surgery to be more effective than nonsurgical treatment for lumbar disk herniation.

52. Weinstein JN, Tosteson TD, Lurie JD, et al: Surgical vs nonoperative treatment for lumbar disk herniation: The Spine Patient Outcomes Research Trial (SPORT). A randomized trial. *JAMA* 2006;296(20):2441-2450.

    A randomized controlled comparison of surgical and nonsurgical treatment for lumbar disk herniation did not reach a conclusion based on the intent-to-treat analysis.

53. Birkmeyer NJ, Weinstein JN, Tosteson AN, et al: Design of the Spine Patient outcomes Research Trial (SPORT). *Spine (Phila Pa 1976)* 2002;27(12):1361-1372.

54. Ostelo RW, Deyo RA, Stratford P, et al: Interpreting change scores for pain and functional status in low back pain: Towards international consensus regarding minimal important change. *Spine (Phila Pa 1976)* 2008; 33(1):90-94.

    A 30% improvement from baseline score was recommended as the threshold for defining success.

55. Spratt KF: Patient-level minimal clinically important difference based on clinical judgment and minimally detectable measurement difference: A rationale for the

7: Spine Care and US Health Policy

SF-36 physical function scale in the SPORT intervertebral disc herniation cohort. *Spine (Phila Pa 1976)* 2009; 34(16):1722-1731.

MCID values for 30% gain had substantially lower sensitivity to change for baseline SF-36 PF scores in the 0 to 50 range but were similar to the level of classic test theory score-based MCIDs when baseline scores were above 50.

56. Ware JE, Kosinski M: Interpreting SF-36 summary health measures: A response. *Qual Life Res* 2001;10(5): 405-413, discussion 415-420.

57. Ware JE Jr: SF-36 health survey update. *Spine (Phila Pa 1976)* 2000;25(24):3130-3139.

58. Ware JE Jr, Gandek B: Overview of the SF-36 Health Survey and the International Quality of Life Assessment (IQOLA) Project. *J Clin Epidemiol* 1998;51(11):903-912.

59. McHorney CA, Ware JE Jr, Lu JF, Sherbourne CD: The MOS 36-item Short-Form Health Survey (SF-36): III. Tests of data quality, scaling assumptions, and reliability across diverse patient groups. *Med Care* 1994;32(1): 40-66.

60. McHorney CA, Ware JE Jr, Raczek AE: The MOS 36-Item Short-Form Health Survey (SF-36): II. Psychometric and clinical tests of validity in measuring physical and mental health constructs. *Med Care* 1993;31(3): 247-263.

61. Ware JE Jr , Sherbourne CD: The MOS 36-item short-form health survey (SF-36). I. Conceptual framework and item selection. *Med Care* 1992;30(6):473-483.

62. Kass GV: An exploratory technique for investigating large quantities of categorical data. *Appl Stat* 1980;29: 119-127.

63. Fairbank JC: Use and abuse of Oswestry Disability Index. *Spine (Phila Pa 1976)* 2007;32(25):2787-2789.

An ODI score change of no more than 4 is considered noise. A change of more than 10 is clinically meaningful. The FDA requires at least one 15-point change to establish success in a back pain study.

64. Fairbank JC, Pynsent PB: The Oswestry Disability Index. *Spine (Phila Pa 1976)* 2000;25(22):2940-2952.

65. Fairbank JC: The use of revised Oswestry Disability Questionnaire. *Spine (Phila Pa 1976)* 2000;25(21): 2846-2847.

66. Fairbank J: Revised Oswestry Disability questionnaire. *Spine (Phila Pa 1976)* 2000;25(19):2552.

67. Hazard RG, Spratt KF, McDonough CM, et al: The impact of personal functional goal achievement on patient satisfaction with progress one year following completion of a functional restoration program for chronic disabling spinal disorders. *Spine (Phila Pa 1976)* 2009; 34(25):2797-2802.

Patient satisfaction scores were correlated with personal goals rather than with patient-reported outcome measures such as SF-36 or ODI.

68. Guttman L, ed: *The Basis for Scalogram Analysis.* Princeton, NJ, Princeton University Press, 1950.

Index

Index

intervertebral disk degenerative
changes, 22, 23*f*
load-controlled testing, 23
long segment testing with follower
load, 24
mechanical behaviors of biologic
structures, 19–20
viscoelastic behaviors, 20
of whiplash-associated disorders, 273,
274*f*, 274*t*
Biopsychosocial model of spine
disorders, 163–165
Bone graft
autogenous, 395–399
iliac crest, 14–16, 15*f*
materials, alternative, 395–399, 396*t*,
399*t*
allograft bone, 397
bone marrow aspirate, 397
bone morphogenetic proteins,
395–397
ceramics, 398
demineralized bone matrix, 397–
398
gene therapy, 398–399
Bone marrow aspirate, 397
Bone metabolism, modulation, 536–
538, 537*f*
Bone morphogenetic proteins, 395–397
Bryan disk (Medtronic Sofamor Danek),
374, 378, 27*t*
Buprenorphine, 176
Bupropion, 177
Burners, sports spine injuries and,
266–267
Burst fractures
lumbar, 239–241, 240*f*
pediatric, 472
subaxial cervical spine, 224
thoracic, 239–241, 240*f*

C

Calcitonin, intranasal, 95
Carbamazepine, 98
Cardiopulmonary symptoms in spine
deformity, 352
Carisoprodol, 97, 98, 177
Carpal tunnel syndrome diagnosis,
electrodiagnostic studies, 151–152
Caudal regression syndrome, 411
Celecoxib, 95
Cellular therapies, 71–72
Ceramics as bone graft material, 398
Cervical collar, 181–182, 181*f*
Cervical disk replacement, 300, 371–
380
complications, 378–379
contraindications, 374–376, 376*f*
design goals, 371–374, 373*f*
indications, 374, 375*f*
outcomes, 377–378

rationale, 371–374, 372*f*
technical considerations, 376–377,
377*f*
Cervical instability, 222, 407–409, 408*f*
Cervical myelopathy, total disk
replacement for, 299–300
Cervical neuroforamen, 10–11, 10*f*
Cervical orthoses
cervical collar, 181–182, 181*f*
choosing a brace, 183
halo brace, 182–183
human motion studies and, 184–185,
184*t*
Minerva brace, 182, 182*f*
SOMI brace, 182
Cervical pain. *See also* Axial neck pain
discogenic, 137, 138*f*
facet joint, 135–136, 136*f*
radicular, treatment
interlaminar injections, 137
percutaneous diskectomy, 138–139
transforaminal injections, 137–138,
138*f*
Cervical radiculopathy
clinical evaluation, 293–296
clinical implications, 46
epidemiology, 293
natural history, 293
nerve root injury and, 44–46, 46*t*
pathophysiology, 43–46
prevalence, 43
radicular pain and, 44–46
radiographic evaluation, 293–294,
294*t*
total disk replacement, 299–300
treatment, 46
anterior cervical diskectomy, 294–
295, 295*f*
corpectomy, 294–295
posterior laminoforaminotomy,
295–296
Cervical spinal column, 51–53
sagittal alignment, 54
Cervical spinal cord, 51–53, 52*f*
compression, 53
histopathology, 55
vascular supply, 53
Cervical spine
anatomy, 8–9
cervical spondylotic myelopathy,
51–53, 51*f*
upper cervical spine, 209
congenital anomalies
congenital muscular torticollis,
406–407
instability, 407–409, 408*f*
Klippel-Feil syndrome, 405–406,
406*f*
human motion studies, 184–185, 184*t*
neuroanatomy, 33, 34*f*
posterior, 9, 9*f*
spinal canal stenosis, 11

trauma, instability after, 222
Cervical spine disorders, interventional
spine care
axial cervical pain, 135
cervical discogenic pain, 137, 138*f*
cervical facet joint pain, 135–136
cervical radicular pain, 137–139
complications, 139
Cervical spine injuries
atlantoaxial instability, 214–215
craniocervical instability, 211–212,
212*f*, 212*t*
complications, 218
diagnosis
physical examination, 209–210
radiographic examination, 210,
210*f*
occipital condyle fractures, 210, 211*f*,
211*t*
pediatric, 470–471, 470*f*, 472*f*
atlantoaxial injury, 469
atlantoaxial rotatory subluxation,
469
atlanto-occipital dislocation, 468
atlas fracture, 468–469
halo device placement, 471–472,
472*f*
hangman's fracture, 470
occipital condyle fracture, 468
odontoid fracture, 469–470
os odontoideum, 470, 470*f*
SCIWORA, 471
sports-related, return-to-play
guidelines, 269–270
subaxial, 221–229
upper, 209–218
Cervical spondylotic myelopathy
cervical spine anatomy, 51–53, 51*f*
clinical findings, 296–297
cord signal, 55–56
epidemiology, 296
etiologies, 51
imaging, 55–56, 56*f*
pathomechanisms
dynamic factors, 54
ossification of ligamentum flavum,
54
ossification of posterior longitudinal
ligament, 54
sagittal alignment of cervical spinal
column, 54
spinal cord compression, 53
vascular factors, 54–55
pathophysiology, 56
radiographic evaluation, 297
treatment, 297–299
combined anterior-posterior
procedures, 299, 299*f*
laminoplasty, 298–299, 298*f*
posterior cervical laminectomy,
298, 298*f*
Cervicothoracic junction, 11

Index

Degenerative spondylolisthesis, lumbar, 329–335

Delayed gadolinium-enhanced magnetic resonance imaging of cartilage (dGEMRIC), 387

Demineralized bone matrix, 395
  as alternative bone graft material, 397–398

Denis classification
  sacral fractures, 252, 254f
  thoracolumbar injury, 237–238, 237f

Dermatomes, radiculopathy and pain distribution, 43, 44f

Dermoid cysts, 511

Desipramine, 176

Desmethylvenlafaxine, 176

Diagnostic and Statistical Manual of Mental Disorders, 174

Diazepam, 97–98

Diffuse idiopathic skeletal hyperostosis (DISH), 226–227, 558, 559t

Directional preference exercises, 110–111

Disability assessment, 174

Discogenic low back pain. *See also* Low back pain
  analgesic diskography, 124–125, 124f
  diagnosis, 121–123
  interventional spine care, 121–126
  provocation lumbar diskography, 123–124, 123f
  treatment
    intradiskal biologic repair, 126, 126f
    intradiskal heating, 125, 125f
    intradiskal neurolytic procedures, 125–126

Discogenic pain, cervical, 137, 138f

Disk degeneration, 22, 38, 23f

Diskectomy
  anterior cervical, 294–295, 295f
  microendoscopic, thoracic disk herniation, 325
  open, lumbar disk herniation, 310
  percutaneous
    cervical radicular pain, 138–139
    lumbosacral radiculopathy, 133, 134f
  percutaneous laser, thoracic disk herniation, 325

Disk herniation
  lumbar, 305–311
    clinical evaluation/imaging, 305–308, 306t, 307t, 308t
    nonsurgical treatment, 308–309
    special considerations, 306
    surgical treatment, 310–311
  sports and, 265–266, 266t
  thoracic, 317–327
    clinical evaluation, 318–319, 319t, 320f, 321f
    etiology, 317–318

natural history, 317–318
  nonsurgical treatment, 319–320
  surgical treatment, 320–326, 322f, 322t, 323f, 533

Diskitis, pediatric, 531–532

Diskography
  analgesic, discogenic low back pain, 124–125, 124f
  for lumbar disk herniation, 309

Diskoligamentous complex, 222, 223f

Diskoscopy, lumbar disk herniation, 311

Disk replacement. *See* Cervical disk replacement, Lumbar disk replacement, Total disk replacement

Disk tissue neovascularization, spine pain and, 38–39, 38f

Dislocation
  atlanto-occipital, pediatric, 468
  fracture-dislocation, pediatric, 472–473
  sports and, 266

Displacement-controlled testing, 23

Distraction injuries, 244f, 245

Dorsal root ganglion, low back pain and, 36

Doxepin, 177

Duloxetine, 157–158, 176

Dural arteriovenous fistula, 516–517, 517f

Dynamic stabilization
  in lumbar spine, 385–390
  nonfusion implant disadvantages, 390
  posterior devices
    facet replacement technology, 389–390
    interspinous process, 388–389
    pedicle-based systems, 386–387, 386f
  spine kinetics and effects of, 385–386

Dynesys device (Zimmer), 28, 386–387, 386f

Dysmenorrhea, back pain and, 118

Dysplastic spondylolisthesis, low-grade, 481

E

Early-onset scoliosis
  idiopathic and congenital, 415–425
  lungs, spine development and, 415–416
  treatment outcomes and complications, 425

Early-onset spine deformity, management principles, 416

Elastic behaviors, 19–20, 20f

Electrodiagnostic studies
  in diagnosis of selected disorders, 151–152
  F-wave, 148–149
  H-reflex, 148–149

interpretation, 150
  ordering, 150–151
  performance, 149–150
  reporting, 150
  somatosensory-evoked potential studies, 149
  for suspected spine disorders, 147–152
  timing, 149
  types, 147–149
    needle electromyography, 148
    nerve conduction studies, 147–148, 148f
  uses, 147–149, 147t

Electromyography, 147
  needle, 148

Endogenous inflammatory cell response, 66–67

Endogenous reparative processes, spinal cord injury, 67–68

Endoscopy
  foraminal, lumbar disk herniation, 311
  interlaminar, lumbar disk herniation, 310–311

Enterococcus, postoperative spine infection, 529

Enteropathic arthritis, 559

Ependymoma, 512–513, 512f, 513f

Epidermoid cysts, 511

Epidural abscess, 528–529, 529f

Epidural injections
  for lumbar disk herniation, 308–309
  steroid, lumbosacral radiculopathy, 132–133, 132f
  transforaminal epidural steroid injection, 132–133, 138–139

Escitalopram, 177

Etanercept, 553, 556

Ewing sarcoma, 499

Exercises. *See also* Therapeutic exercise
  aerobic, 111
  axial low back/neck pain, 286
  directional preference, 110–111

Extension injuries, subaxial cervical spine, 226–229, 227f, 228f, 229f

Extramedullary tumors, intradural, 509–511
  dermoid cysts, 511
  epidermoid cysts, 511
  extramedullary metastasis, 511
  lipoma, 511
  meningeal hemangiopericytoma, 511
  meningioma, 510–511
  neurofibroma, 510
  paraganglioma, 511
  schwannoma, 509–510, 510f

F

Facet joint cyst rupture, lumbosacral radiculopathy, 133

Facet joint pain
  cervical, 135–136, 136f

Index